Microcontrollers: From Assembly Language to C Using the PIC24 Family

Robert Reese

J.W. Bruce

Bryan A. Jones

COURSE TECHNOLOGY
CENGAGE Learning

Australia • Brazil • Japan • Korea • Mexico • Singapore • Spain • United Kingdom • United States

COURSE TECHNOLOGY
CENGAGE Learning

Microcontrollers: From Assembly Language to C Using the PIC24 Family

Robert Reese

J. W. Bruce

Bryan A. Jones

Publisher and General Manager,
Course Technology PTR:
Stacy L. Hiquet

Associate Director of Marketing:
Sarah Panella

Content Project Manager: Jessica McNavich

Marketing Manager: Mark Hughes

Acquisitions Editor: Mitzi Koontz

Copy Editor:

Technical Reviewer: Dr. Sam Russ

CRM Editorial Services Coordinator:
Jennifer Blaney

Cover Designer: Mike Tanamachi

CD-Rom Producer: Brandon Penticuff

Indexer:

Proofreader:

Compositor: S4Carlisle Publishing Services

Printed in Canada
1 2 3 4 5 6 7 12 11 10 09 08

For product information and technology assistance, contact us at
Cengage Learning Customer & Sales Support, 1-800-354-9706
For permission to use material from this text or product, submit all requests online at **cengage.com/permissions.**
Further permissions questions can be e-mailed to
permissionrequest@cengage.com

Library of Congress Control Number: 2008938144

ISBN-13: 978-1-5845-0583-9

ISBN-10: 1-5845-0583-4

Course Technology
25 Thomson Place
Boston, MA 02210
USA

Cengage Learning is a leading provider of customized learning solutions with office locations around the globe, including Singapore, the United Kingdom, Australia, Mexico, Brazil, and Japan. Locate your local office at: international.cengage.com/region

Cengage Learning products are represented in Canada by Nelson Education, Ltd.

For your lifelong learning solutions, visit **courseptr.com**

Visit our corporate website at **cengage.com**

Certain materials contained herein are reprinted with permission of Microchip TechnologyIncorporated. No further reprints or reproductions may be made of said materials withoutMicrochip Technology Inc.'s prior written consent.

Acknowledgments

The authors would like to thank the following individuals for their assistance in preparing this book:

- ECE3724 students for their patience during the development of this text and the accompanying software libraries.
- Lee Hathcock and the students in ECE4723 who provided so many constructive comments on the organization of ESOS.
- Samuel Russ for his many insights on code and text improvements in his role as a technical reviewer for the manuscript.
- David Weaver, previously of Bell Laboratories, for serving as an ad-hoc technical reviewer and who provided many excellent suggestions for code and text improvements.
- Nathan Seidle of SparkFun Electronics for his collaboration and support on the mini-Bully PIC24 µC platform.
- Carol Popovich and the other members of the Microchip Academic Program team at Microchip Technology Inc. for their support in using Microchip products in a higher education environment.

About the Authors

Robert B. Reese received the B.S. degree from Louisiana Tech University, Ruston, in 1979 and the M.S. and Ph.D. degrees from Texas A&M University, College Station, in 1982 and 1985, respectively, all in electrical engineering. He served as a member of the technical staff of the Microelectronics and Computer Technology Corporation (MCC), Austin, TX, from 1985 to 1988. Since 1988, he has been with the Department of Electrical and Computer Engineering at Mississippi State University, where he is an Associate Professor. Courses that he teaches include Microprocessors, VLSI systems, Digital System design, and senior design. His research interests include self-timed digital systems and computer architecture.

J.W. Bruce received the B.S.E. from the University of Alabama in Huntsville in 1991, the M.S.E.E. from the Georgia Institute of Technology in 1993, and the Ph.D. from the University of Nevada Las Vegas in 2000, all in electrical engineering. Dr. Bruce has served as a member of the technical staff at the Mevatec Corporation providing engineering support to the Marshall Space Flight Center Microgravity Research Program. He also worked in the 3D Workstation Graphics Group at the Integraph Corporation designing the world's first OpenGL graphics accelerator for the Windows operating system. Since 2000, Dr. Bruce has served in the Department of Electrical and Computer Engineering at Mississippi State University. Dr. Bruce has contributed to the research areas of data converter architecture design and embedded systems design. His research has resulted in more than 30 technical publications and one book chapter.

Bryan A. Jones received the B.S.E.E. and M.S. degrees in electrical engineering from Rice University, Houston, TX, in 1995 and 2002, respectively, and the Ph.D. degree in electrical engineering from Clemson University, Clemson, SC, in 2005. From 1996 to 2000, he was a Hardware Design Engineer for Compaq, specializing in board layout for high-availability RAID controllers. He is currently an Assistant Professor at Mississippi State University. His research interests include robotics, real-time control-system implementation, rapid prototyping for real-time systems, and modeling and analysis of mechatronic systems.

Contents

Introduction

This book and its accompanying website *www.reesemicro.com* is intended as an introduction to microprocessors (μPs) and microcontrollers (μCs) for either the student or hobbyist. The book structure is:

■ Chapter 1: Review of digital logic concepts.

■ Chapter 2: Computer architecture fundamentals.

■ Chapters 3 through 6: Coverage of assembly language programming in a *C* language context using the PIC24 family.

■ Chapter 7: Advanced assembly language programming structured around computer arithmetic topics.

■ Chapters 8 through 12: Fundamental microcontroller interfacing topics such as parallel IO, asynchronous serial IO, synchronous serial IO (I^2C and SPI), interrupt-driven IO, timers, analog-to-digital conversion, and digital-to-analog conversion.

■ Chapter 13: Some advanced interfacing topics such as DMA, the USB and ECAN standards, slave I^2C operations, and the comparator module.

■ Chapter 14: An advanced chapter that covers the basics of real-time operating systems using a cooperative multitasking OS written by the authors. Topics include tasks, schedulers, scheduling algorithms, task synchronization and communication, semaphores, and queues.

■ Chapter 15: Presents three capstone projects involving topics from Chapters 8 through 13 and a brief survey of other microprocessor families.

THIS BOOK'S DEVELOPMENT

At Mississippi State University, majors in Electrical Engineering (EE), Computer Engineering (CPE), Computer Science (CS), and Software Engineering (SE) take our first course in microprocessors. Previous to spring 2002, this course emphasized

X86 assembly language programming with the lab experience being 100 percent assembly language based and containing no hardware component. We found that students entering our senior design course, which has the expectation of something "real" being built, were unprepared for doing prototyping activities or for incorporating a microcontroller component into their designs. We did offer a course in microcontrollers, but it was an elective senior-level course and many students had not taken that course previous to senior design. In spring 2002, the Computer Engineering Steering Committee reexamined our goals for the first course in microprocessors, and the approach for this book's predecessor (*From Assembly Language to C Using the PIC18Fxx2*) was developed. From fall 2003 through spring 2004, we used the Microchip PIC16 family, then used the PIC18 family from summer 2004 through spring 2008. In late fall 2007, the authors reexamined the course once again and decided to switch to the PIC24 family because of its rich instruction set architecture, 16-bit organization, and advanced on-chip peripherals.

USING THIS BOOK IN AN ACADEMIC ENVIRONMENT

This book is intended for use as a first course in microcontrollers/microprocessors (µC/µP) using the PIC24 family, with prerequisites of basic digital design and exposure to either *C* or *C++* programming. The book begins with simple microprocessor architecture concepts, moves to assembly language programming in a *C* language context, then covers fundamental hardware interfacing topics such as parallel IO, asynchronous serial IO, synchronous serial I/O (I^2C and SPI), interrupt-driven IO, timers, analog-to-digital conversion, and digital-to-analog conversion. Programming topics are discussed using both assembly language and *C*, while hardware interfacing examples use *C* to keep code complexity low and improve clarity. The assembly language programming chapters emphasize the linkage between *C* language constructs and their assembly language equivalent so that students clearly understand the impact of *C* coding choices in terms of execution time and memory requirements. A textbook with an assembly-only focus creates students who are experts only in assembly language programming, with no understanding of high-level language programming techniques and limited hardware exposure. Most embedded software is written in *C* for portability and complexity reasons, which argues favorably for reduced emphasis on assembly language and increased emphasis on *C*. Embedded system hardware complexity is steadily increasing, which means a first course in µC/µP that reduces assembly language coverage (but does not eliminate it) in favor of hands-on experience with fundamental interfacing allows students to begin at a higher level in an advanced course in embedded systems, the approach chosen for this textbook. Hardware interface topics included in this book cover the fundamentals (parallel IO, serial IO, interrupts, timers, analog-to-digital conversion, digital-to-analog conversion) using devices that do not require extensive circuits knowledge because of the lack of a circuits course prerequisite. The microcontroller interfacing topics presented in this textbook are sufficient for providing a skill set that is extremely useful to a student in a senior design capstone course or in an advanced embedded system course.

Thus, a principal motivation for this book is that microcontroller knowledge has become essential for successful completion of senior capstone design courses. These capstone courses are receiving increased emphasis under ABET 2000 guidelines. This places increased pressure on Computer Engineering and Electrical Engineering programs to include significant exposure to embedded systems topics as early in the curriculum as possible. A second motivation for this book is that the ACM/IEEE Computer Engineering model curriculum recommends 17 hours of embedded system topics as part of the Computer Engineering curriculum core, which is easily satisfied by a course containing the topics in this book. A third motivating factor is the increased pressure on colleges and universities to reduce hours in engineering curriculums; this book shows how a single course can replace separate courses in assembly language programming and basic microprocessor interfacing.

The course sequence used at Mississippi State University that this book fits into is:

■ Basic digital design (Boolean algebra, combinational, and sequential logic), which is required by EE, CPE, CS, and SE majors.
■ Introduction to microprocessors (this book), which is required for EE, CPE, CS, and SE majors.
■ Computer architecture as represented by the topic coverage of the Hennessy and Patterson textbook *Computer Organization & Design: The Hardware/ Software Interface.* This includes reinforcement of the assembly language programming taught in the microprocessor course via a general-purpose instruction set architecture (e.g., the MIPS) along with coverage of traditional high-performance computer architecture topics (pipelined CPU design, cache strategies, parallel bus I/O). Required for CPE, CS, and SE majors.
■ Advanced embedded systems covering topics such as (a) real-time operating systems, (b) Internet appliances, and (c) advanced interfaces such as USB, CAN, Ethernet, FireWire. Required for CPE majors.

Chapter 1 provides a broad review of digital logic fundamentals. Chapters 2 through 6 and 8 through 13 cover the core topics of assembly language programming and microcontroller interfacing. Chapter 15 contains three capstone projects that integrate the material of the previous chapters. Chapters 7 and 14 have optional topics on advanced assembly language programming and the basics of real-time operating systems, which can be used to supplement the core material. Appendix C contains a sequence of 11 laboratory experiments that comprise an off-the-shelf lab experience: one experiment on fundamental computer architecture topics, four experiments on PIC24 assembly language, and six hardware experiments. The hardware labs cover all major subsystems on the PIC24 µC: A/D, timers, asynchronous serial interface, SPI, and the I²C interface. The hardware experiments are based on a breadboard/parts kit approach where the students incrementally build a PIC24 system that includes a serial EEPROM, an external 8-bit DAC, and an asynchronous serial port via a USB-to-serial cable. A breadboard/part kits approach is used instead of a preassembled printed circuit board (PCB) for several important reasons:

- When handed a preassembled PCB, a student tends to view it as a monolithic element. A breadboard/parts kit approach forces a student to view each part individually and read datasheets to understand how parts connect to each other.
- Hardware debugging and prototyping skills are developed during the painful process of bringing the system to life. These hard-won lessons prove useful later when the student must do the same thing in a senior design context. This also provides students with the confidence that having done it one time they can do it again, this time outside of a fixed laboratory environment with guided instruction.
- A breadboard/parts kit approach gives the ultimate flexibility to modify experiments from semester to semester by simply changing a part or two; also, when the inevitable part failures occur, individual components are easily replaced.

In using this laboratory approach at Mississippi State University, the authors have seen a "Culture of Competence" develop in regard to microcontrollers and prototyping in general. All senior design projects now routinely include a microcontroller component (not necessarily Microchip-based). Students concentrate their efforts on design definition, development, and refinement instead of spending most of their time climbing the learning curve on prototyping and microcontroller usage.

There are more topics in this book than can be covered in a 16-week semester. In our introductory microprocessor course, we cover Chapters 1 through 6 for the assembly language coverage (about 6 weeks) and selected topics from Chapters 8 through 12 for the interfacing component. A course with more emphasis on assembly language may include Chapter 7 and fewer interfacing topics. Our follow-on embedded systems course uses Chapters 8 through 14 with an emphasis on writing applications using the embedded operating system approach described in Chapter 14 and a more in-depth coverage of all interfacing topics. A first course in microcontrollers that contains no assembly language component may want to assign Chapters 1 through 7 as background reading and use Chapters 8 through 15 as the primary course material.

This book's *C* examples on hardware interfacing strive for code clarity first and optimization second. A prefix naming convention (u8_, u16_, i32_, pu8_ etc.) is used for all variables, and a robust set of macros and library functions have been developed to make access to the on-chip resources easier for those encountering microcontrollers for the first time. The library functions emphasize runtime error trapping and reporting as a way of shedding more light on malfunctioning applications. Please check the *www.reesemicro.com* website for updates to the library functions.

FOR THE HOBBYIST

This book assumes very little background, and thus is appropriate for readers with widely varying experience levels. First, read chapter 8 and visit the companion website at *www.reesemicro.com* to build and install the hardware and software PIC24 development environment. Next, examine the experiments in Appendix C and find the ones that interest you. Then, read the chapter that is referenced by the experiment for the necessary background. This textbook includes numerous examples complete with schematics and working code to operate a number of useful peripherals, including temperature sensors, LCD displays, a robot, and a reflow oven, providing a good starting point for your designs.

FINAL THOUGHTS

We hope readers have as much fun exploring the world of μCs/μPs and the PIC24 family as the authors had in creating this text. And because we know that μC/μP development does not sit still, let us all look forward to new learning experiences beyond this text.

Bob Reese, Bryan A. Jones, J. W. Bruce
Mississippi State University
Starkville, Mississippi

PART I

Digital Logic Review and Computer Architecture Fundamentals

1 Number System and Digital Logic Review

This chapter reviews number systems, Boolean algebra, logic gates, combinational building blocks, sequential storage elements, and sequential building blocks.

Learning Objectives

After reading this chapter, you will be able to:

- Create a binary encoding for object classification.
- Convert unsigned decimal numbers to binary and hex representations and vice versa.
- Perform addition and subtraction on numbers in binary and hex representations.
- Identify NOT, OR, AND, NOR, NAND, and XOR logic functions and their symbols.
- Evaluate simple Boolean functions.
- Describe the operation of CMOS P and N transistors.
- Identify the CMOS transistor level implementations of simple logic gates.
- Compute clock period, frequency, and duty cycle given appropriate parameters.
- Identify common combinational building blocks.
- Identify common sequential building blocks.
- Translate a character string into ASCII encoded data and vice versa.

Binary number system representation and arithmetic is fundamental to all computer system operations. Basic logic gates, CMOS transistor operation, and combinational/sequential building block knowledge will help your comprehension of the diagrams found in datasheets that describe microprocessor subsystem functionality. A solid grounding in these subjects ensures better understanding of the microprocessor topics that follow in later chapters.

BINARY DATA

Binary logic, or digital logic, is the basis for all computer systems built today. *Binary* means two, and many concepts can be represented by two values: true/false, hot/cold, on/off, 1/0, to name a few. A single binary datum whose value is "1" or "0" is referred to as a *bit*. Groups of bits are used to represent concepts that have more than two values. For example, to represent the concepts hot/warm/cool/cold, two or more bits can be used as shown in Table 1.1.

To encode n objects, the minimum number of bits required is $k = ceil(\log_2 n)$, where *ceil* is the ceiling function that takes the nearest integer greater than or equal to $\log_2 n$. For the four values in Table 1.1, the minimum number of bits required is $ceil(\log_2 (4)) = 2$. Both encoding A and encoding B use the minimum number of bits, but differ in how codes are assigned to the values. Encoding B uses a special encoding scheme known as Gray code, in which adjacent table entries only differ by at most one bit position. Encoding C uses more than the minimum number of bits; this encoding scheme is known as *one-hot encoding*, as each code only has a single bit that is a "1" value.

Encoding A uses *binary counting order*, which means that the code progresses in numerical counting order if the code is interpreted as a *binary number* (base 2). In an unsigned binary number, each bit is weighted by a power of two. The rightmost bit, or *least significant bit* (LSb), has a weight of 2^0, with each successive bit weight increasing by a power of two as one moves from right to left. The leftmost bit, the *most significant bit* (MSb), has a weight of $2^n - 1$ for an n-bit binary number. A lowercase "b" is purposefully used in the LSb and MSb acronyms since the reference is to a single bit; the use of an uppercase "B" in LSB and MSB acronyms is discussed later.

The formal term for a number's base is *radix*. If r is the radix, then a binary number has $r = 2$, a decimal number has $r = 10$, and a hexadecimal number has $r = 16$. In general, each digit of a number of radix r can take on the values 0 through $r - 1$. The least significant digit (LSD) has a weight of r^0, with each successive digit increasing by a power of r as one moves from right to left. The leftmost digit, the *most significant digit* (MSD), has weight of r^{n-1}, where n is the number of digits in the number. For hexadecimal (hex) numbers, letters A through F represent the digits 10 through 15, respectively. Decimal, binary, and hexadecimal numbers are used exclusively in this book. If the base of the

TABLE 1.1 Digital encoding examples.

Value	Encoding A	Encoding B	Encoding C
Cold	0 0	0 0	0 0 0 1
Cool	0 1	1 0	0 0 1 0
Warm	1 0	1 1	0 1 0 0
Hot	1 1	0 1	1 0 0 0

number cannot be determined by context, a "0x" is used as the radix identifier for hex numbers (i.e., 0x3A) and "0b" for binary numbers (i.e., 0b01101000). No radix identifier is used for decimal numbers. Table 1.2 lists the binary and hex values for the decimal values 0 through 15. Note that 4 bits are required to encode these 16 values since $2^4 = 16$. The binary and hex values in Table 1.2 are given without radix identifiers. The "*" symbol in Table 1.2 is a multiplication operation; other symbols used in this book for multiplication are "$\times$" $(a \times b)$ and "$\cdot$" $(a \cdot b)$ with the usage made clear by the context.

A binary number of n bits can represent the unsigned decimal values of 0 to $2^N - 1$. A common size for binary data is a group of 8 bits, referred to as a byte. A byte can represent the unsigned decimal range of 0 to 255 (0x00 to 0xFF in hex). Groups of bytes are often used to represent larger numbers; this topic is explored in Chapter 5. Common powers of two are given in Table 1.3. Powers of two that are evenly divisible by 2^{10} can be referred to by the suffixes Ki (kibi, kilobinary, 2^{10}), Mi (mebi, megabinary, 2^{20}), and Gi (gibi, gigabinary, 2^{30}). The notation of Ki, Mi, and Gi is adopted from IEEE Standard 1541-2002, which was created to avoid confusion with the suffixes k (kilo, 10^3), M (mega, 10^6) and G (giga, 10^9). Thus, the value of 4096 can be written in the abbreviated form of 4 Ki ($4 * 1$ Ki $= 2^2 * 2^{10} = 2^{12} = 4096 = 4.096$ k).

TABLE 1.2   Binary encoding for decimal numbers 0–15.

Decimal	Binary	Binary to Decimal	Hex	Hex to Decimal
0	0000	$0*2^3 + 0*2^2 + 0*2^1 + 0*2^0$	0	$0*16^0$
1	0001	$0*2^3 + 0*2^2 + 0*2^1 + 1*2^0$	1	$1*16^0$
2	0010	$0*2^3 + 0*2^2 + 1*2^1 + 0*2^0$	2	$2*16^0$
3	0011	$0*2^3 + 0*2^2 + 1*2^1 + 1*2^0$	3	$3*16^0$
4	0100	$0*2^3 + 1*2^2 + 0*2^1 + 0*2^0$	4	$4*16^0$
5	0101	$0*2^3 + 1*2^2 + 0*2^1 + 1*2^0$	5	$5*16^0$
6	0110	$0*2^3 + 1*2^2 + 1*2^1 + 0*2^0$	6	$6*16^0$
7	0111	$0*2^3 + 1*2^2 + 1*2^1 + 1*2^0$	7	$7*16^0$
8	1000	$1*2^3 + 0*2^2 + 0*2^1 + 0*2^0$	8	$8*16^0$
9	1001	$1*2^3 + 0*2^2 + 0*2^1 + 1*2^0$	9	$9*16^0$
10	1010	$1*2^3 + 0*2^2 + 1*2^1 + 0*2^0$	A	$10*16^0$
11	1011	$1*2^3 + 0*2^2 + 1*2^1 + 1*2^0$	B	$11*16^0$
12	1100	$1*2^3 + 1*2^2 + 0*2^1 + 0*2^0$	C	$12*16^0$
13	1101	$1*2^3 + 1*2^2 + 0*2^1 + 1*2^0$	D	$13*16^0$
14	1110	$1*2^3 + 1*2^2 + 1*2^1 + 0*2^0$	E	$14*16^0$
15	1111	$1*2^3 + 1*2^2 + 1*2^1 + 1*2^0$	F	$15*16^0$

TABLE 1.3   Common powers of two.

Power	Decimal	Hex	Power	Decimal	Hex
2^0	1	0x1	$(Ki),2^{10}$	1024	0x400
2^1	2	0x2	2^{11}	2048	0x800
2^2	4	0x4	2^{12}	4096	0x1000
2^3	8	0x8	2^{13}	8192	0x2000
2^4	16	0x10	2^{14}	16384	0x4000
2^5	32	0x20	2^{15}	32768	0x8000
2^6	64	0x40	2^{16}	65536	0x10000
2^7	128	0x80	$(Mi),2^{20}$	1048576	0x100000
2^8	256	0x100	$(Gi),2^{30}$	1073741824	0x40000000
2^9	512	0x200	2^{32}	4294967296	0x100000000

However, be aware that the terminology of this IEEE standard is not in widespread use yet. The terms kBytes and MBytes are commonly used when referring to memory sizes and these mean the same as KiBytes and MiBytes.

Sample Question: ***What is the largest unsigned decimal number that can be represented using a binary number with 16 bits?***

Answer: From Table 1.3, we see that $2^{16} = 65536$, so $2^{16} - 1 = 65535$.

UNSIGNED NUMBER CONVERSION

To convert a number of any radix to decimal, simply multiply each digit by its corresponding weight and sum the result. The example that follows shows binary-to-decimal and hex-to-decimal conversion:

(binary to decimal) $0b0101\ 0010 = 0*2^7 + 1*2^6 + 0*2^5 + 1*2^4 + 0*2^3 + 0*2^2 + 1*2^1 + 0*2^0$

$$= 0 + 64 + 0 + 16 + 0 + 0 + 2 + 1 = 82$$

(hex to decimal) 0x52 $\quad = 5*16^1 + 2*16^0 = 80 + 2 = 82.$

To convert a decimal number to a different radix, perform successive division of the decimal number by the radix; at each step the remainder is a digit in the converted number, and the quotient is the starting value for the next step. The successive division ends when the quotient becomes less than the radix. The digits of the converted number are determined rightmost to leftmost, with the last quotient being the leftmost digit of the converted number. The following sample problem illustrates the successive division algorithm.

Sample Question: ***Convert 435 to hex.***

Answer:
Step 1: 435/16 = 27, remainder = 3 (rightmost digit).
Step 2: 27/16 = 1, remainder = 11 = 0xB (next digit).
Step 3: 1 < 16, so leftmost digit = 1.
Final answer: 435 = 0x1B3.

To check your work, perform the reverse conversion:

$$0x1B3 = 1*16^2 + 11*16^1 + 3*16^0 = 1*256 + 11*16 + 3*1 = 256 + 176 + 3$$
$$= 435.$$

HEX TO BINARY, BINARY TO HEX

Hex can be viewed as a shorthand notation for binary. A quick method for performing binary-to-hex conversion is to convert each group of four binary digits (starting with the rightmost digit) to one hex digit. If the last (leftmost) group of binary digits does not contain 4 bits, then pad with leading zeros to reach four digits. Converting hex to binary is the reverse procedure of replacing each hex digit with four binary digits. The easiest way to perform decimal-to-binary conversion is to first convert to hex then convert the hex number to binary. This involves fewer division operations and hence fewer chances for careless error. Similarly, binary-to-decimal conversion is best done by converting the binary number to a hex value, and then converting the hex number to decimal. The following examples illustrate binary-to-hex, hex-to-binary, and decimal-to-binary conversion.

Sample Question: ***Convert 0b010110 to hex.***

Answer: Starting with the rightmost digit, form groups of four: 01 0110. The leftmost group has only two digits, so pad this group with zeros as: 0001 0110. Now convert each group of four digits to hex digits (see Table 1.2):

0b 0001 0110 = 0x16.

Sample Question: ***Convert 0xF3C to binary.***

Answer: Replace each hex digit with its binary equivalent:
    0xF3C = 0b 1111 0011 1100

Sample Question: ***Convert 243 to binary.***

Answer: First, convert 243 to hex:
    Step 1: 243/16 = 15, remainder 3 (rightmost digit)
    Step 2: 15 < 16, so leftmost digit is 0xF (15). Hex result is 0xF3
    243 = 0xF3 = 0b 1111 0011 (final answer, in binary).
    Check: 0xF3 = 15*16 + 3 = 240 + 3 = 243

BINARY AND HEX ARITHMETIC

Addition, subtraction, and shift operations are implemented in some form in most digital systems. The fundamentals of these operations are reviewed in this section and revisited in Chapters 3 and 4 when discussing basic computer operations.

BINARY AND HEX ADDITION

Addition of two numbers, $i + j$, in any base is accomplished by starting with the rightmost digit and adding each digit of i to each digit of j, moving right to left. If the digit sum is less than the radix, the result digit is the sum and a carry of 0 is used in the next digit addition. If the sum of the digits is greater than or equal to the radix, a carry of 1 is added to the next digit sum, and the result digit is computed by subtracting r from the digit sum. For binary addition, these rules can be stated as:

- $0 + 0 = 0$, carry = 0
- $0 + 1 = 1$, carry = 0
- $1 + 0 = 1$, carry = 0
- $1 + 1 = 0$, carry = 1

Figure 1.1 shows a digit-by-digit addition for the numbers 0b110 + 0b011. Note that the result is 0b001 with a carry out of the most significant digit of 1. A carry out of the most significant digit indicates that the sum produced *unsigned overflow;* the result could not fit in the number of available digits. A carry out of the most significant digit is an unsigned error indicator if the numbers represent unsigned integers. In this case, the sum 0b110 + 0b011 is 6 + 3 with the correct answer being 9. However, the largest unsigned integer that can be specified in 3 bits is $2^3 - 1$, or 7. The value of 9 is too large to be represented in 3 bits, and thus the result is incorrect from an arithmetic perspective, but is correct by the rules of

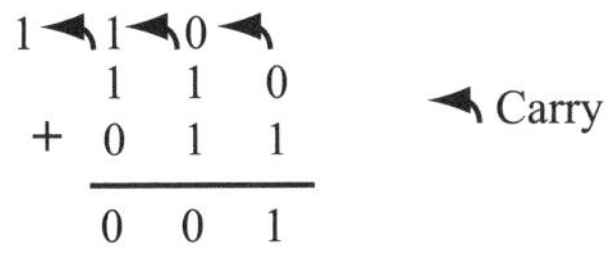

FIGURE 1.1   Binary addition example.

binary addition. This is known as the *limited precision* problem; only increasing the number of bits used for binary encoding can increase the number range. We study this problem and the consequences of using more or fewer bits for number representation in later chapters.

Sample Question: *Compute 0x1A3 + 0x36F.*

Answer: A digit-by-digit addition for the operation 0x1A3 + 0x36F is as follows. The rightmost result digit is formed by adding:

0x3 (3) + 0xF (15) = 18

Note the digit sum is greater than 16, so a carry of 1 is produced and the rightmost result digit is computed by subtracting the radix, or:

18 − 16 = 2 = 0x2

The middle digit sum is then:

0xA (10) + 0x6 (6) + 1 (carry) = 17

This digit sum is greater than 16, so this produces a carry of 1 with the middle digit computed as:

17 − 16 = 1 = 0x1

The leftmost digit sum is:

0x1 + 0x3 + 0x1 (carry) = 0x5

The result is then 0x1A3 + 0x36F = 0x512. Converting each number to decimal before summing, or 419 + 879 = 1298, checks this result. Verifying that 0x36F − 0x512 = 0x1A3 also checks this result, but this requires reading the next section on subtraction!

BINARY AND HEX SUBTRACTION

Subtraction of two numbers, $i − j$, in any base is accomplished by starting with the rightmost digit and subtracting each digit of j from each digit of i, moving right to left. If the i digit is greater or equal to the j digit, then the resulting digit is the subtraction $i − j$, with a borrow of 0 used in the next digit subtraction. If the i digit is less than the j digit, then a borrow of 1 is used in the next digit subtraction, and the resulting digit is formed by $i + r - j$ (the current i digit is increased by a weight of r). For binary subtraction, these rules can be stated as:

- $0 - 0 = 0$, borrow $= 0$
- $0 - 1 = 1$, borrow $= 1$
- $1 - 0 = 1$, borrow $= 0$
- $1 - 1 = 0$, borrow $= 0$

Figure 1.2 shows a digit-by-digit subtraction for the value 0b010 − 0b101. This operation produces a result of 0b101, and a borrow out of the most significant digit of 1. If interpreted as unsigned numbers, the operation is $2 - 5 = 5$, which is incorrect. A borrow out of the most significant digit of 1 indicates an *unsigned underflow;* the correct result is a number less than zero. But in unsigned numbers, there is no number less than zero, so the result is incorrect in an arithmetic sense (the operation is perfectly valid, however). A binary representation for *signed integers* is needed to interpret the binary result correctly; this topic is saved for Chapter 5.

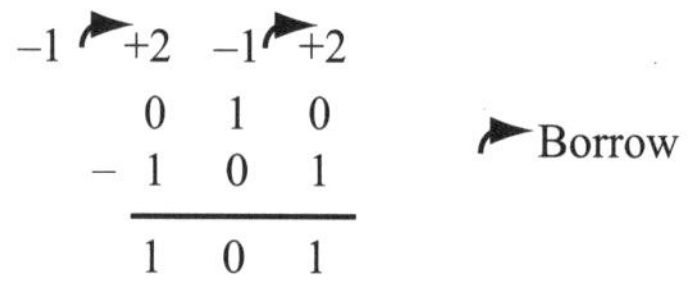

$$
\begin{array}{ccc}
-1 & +2 & -1 & +2 \\
0 & 1 & 0 \\
- \ \ 1 & 0 & 1 \\
\hline
1 & 0 & 1
\end{array}
$$

Borrow

FIGURE 1.2   Binary subtraction example.

The subtraction A − B can also be performed by the operation A + ~B + 1, where the operation ~B is called the *one's complement* of B and is formed by taking the complement of each bit of B. In review, the complement of a bit is its logical inverse or opposite, so the complement of 0xAE50 = 0b 1010 1110 0101 0000 is 0b 0101 0001 1010 1111 = 0x51AF. As an example of binary subtraction, consider the previous operation of 0b010 − 0b101. The one's complement of 0b101 is 0b010. The subtraction can be rewritten as:

$$A + \sim B + 1 = 0b010 + (0b010 + 0b001) = 0b010 + 0b011 = 0b101$$

This is the same result obtained when binary subtraction rules were used. The value ~B + 1 is called the *two's complement* of B, and this is discussed in more detail in Chapter 5, when signed integer representation is covered.

Sample Question: *Compute 0xA02 − 0x5C4.*

Answer: A digit-by-digit hex subtraction for the operation 0xA02 − 0x5C4 is as follows. The rightmost subtraction of 0x2 − 0x4 requires a borrow from the next digit, so the rightmost digit calculation becomes:

$$2 + 16 - 4 = 14 = 0xE$$

The middle digit calculation becomes 0x0 − 0xC − 0x1 (borrow). This requires a borrow from the next (leftmost) digit, so this calculation becomes:

$16 + 0 - 12 - 1 = 3 = 0x3$

The leftmost digit calculation is:

$0xA - 0x5 - 0x1 \text{ (borrow)} = 10 - 5 - 1 = 4 = 0x4$

Thus, the final result is 0xA02 − 0x5C4 = 0x43E. As always, this result can be checked by verifying that 0x5C4 + 0x43E = 0xA02 (and yes, it is correct!).

SHIFT OPERATIONS

A *right shift* of a binary value moves all of the bits to the right by one position and shifts a new bit value into the MSb. Shifting in a value of "0" is equivalent to dividing the binary value by two if the binary value represents an unsigned number (the differences between unsigned and signed number representation are discussed in Chapter 5). For example, using a "0" value for the bit shifted into the MSb, the unsigned binary value 0b1100 (12) shifted to the right by one position is 0b0110 (6). If this value is shifted to the right once more, the new value is 0b0011 (3). In this book, operators from the *C* language are used for expressing numerical operations. The *C* language operator for a right shift is >>, where A >> 1 reads "A shifted to the right by one bit."

A *left shift* of an unsigned binary value moves all of the bits to the left by one position, and shifts a new bit value into the LSb. If the new bit shifted in is a "0", this is equivalent to multiplying the binary value by two. For example, using a "0" value for the bit shifted into the LSb, the binary value 0b0101 (5) shifted to the left by one position is 0b1010 (10). If this value is shifted to the left once more, the new value is 0b0100 (4). The value 4 is not 10 * 2; the correct result should be 20. However, the value 20 cannot fit in 4 bits; the largest unsigned value represented in 4 bits is $2^4 - 1 = 15$. In this case, the bit shifted out of the MSb is a "1"; when this happens, unsigned overflow occurs for the shift operation and the new value is incorrect in an arithmetic sense. The *C* language operator for a left shift is <<, where A << 1 reads "A shifted to the left by one bit." Figure 1.3 gives additional examples of left and right shift operations.

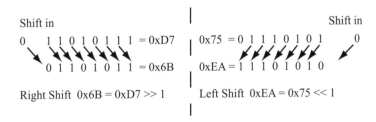

FIGURE 1.3   Shift operation examples.

If an *n*-bit value is shifted to the left or right *n* times, with "0" used as the shift-in value, the result is zero, as all bits become "0". When shifting a hex value, it is best to convert the hex number to binary, perform the shift, then convert the binary number back to hex.

> Sample Question: ***What is the new value of 0xA7 >> 2 assuming the MSb is filled with a "0"?***
>
> Answer: The value 0xA7 = 0b1010 0111, so 0xA7 >> 1 = 0b01010011. Shifting this value to the right by one more gives 0b01010011 >> 1 = 0b00101001 = 0x29. Therefore, 0xA7 >> 2 = 0x29.

COMBINATIONAL LOGIC FUNCTIONS

Boolean algebra defines properties and laws between variables that are binary valued. The basic operations of Boolean algebra are NOT, OR, and AND, whose definitions are:

- **NOT(A):** Is "1" if A = 0; NOT(A) is "0" if A = 1 (the output is said to be the complement or inverse of the input).
- **AND(A1, A2, ... An):** Is "1" only if all inputs A1 through An have value = 1.
- **OR(A1, A2, ... An):** Is "1" if any input A1 through An has value "1".

The *C* language operators for bitwise complement ("~"), AND ("&"), OR ("|") are used in this book for logic operations. Thus, NOT(A) = ~A, AND(A, B) = A & B, and OR(A, B) = A | B where the Boolean variables have values of either "0" or "1". Logic operations are also defined by *truth tables* and by distinctively shaped symbols. A truth table has all input combinations listed in binary counting order on the left side, with the output value given on the right side of the table. Figure 1.4 lists the two-input truth tables and shape distinctive symbols for the NOT, AND, OR, NAND, NOR, and XOR (exclusive-OR) logic functions.

A NAND function is an AND function whose output is complemented; similarly, a NOR function is an OR function whose output is complemented. An XOR function is defined by the truth table shown in Figure 1.4 or can be expressed using NOT, AND, OR operators as shown in Equation 1.1. The *C* language operator for XOR is ^, thus XOR(A,B) = A ^ B. Logically stated, XOR(A,B) is "1" if A is not equal to B, and "0" otherwise.

$$Y = (A \& (\sim B)) \mid ((\sim A) \& B) \quad \text{(Exclusive OR function)} \tag{1.1}$$

A	Y
0	1
1	0

A	B	Y
0	0	0
0	1	0
1	0	0
1	1	1

AND

A	B	Y
0	0	1
0	1	1
1	0	1
1	1	0

NAND

A	B	Y
0	0	0
0	1	1
1	0	1
1	1	0

XOR

A	B	Y
0	0	0
0	1	1
1	0	1
1	1	1

OR

A	B	Y
0	0	1
0	1	0
1	0	0
1	1	0

NOR

FIGURE 1.4   Truth table, logic symbols for basic two-input logic gates.

The distinctively shaped symbol for a Boolean logic function is also referred to as the logic gate for the Boolean operation. A network of logic gates is an alternative representation of a Boolean equation. Figure 1.5 shows the Boolean equation of the XOR function drawn as a logic network using 2-input gates.

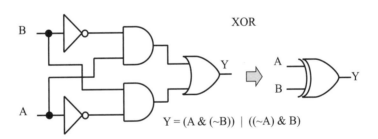

$$Y = (A \ \& \ (\sim B)) \ | \ ((\sim A) \ \& \ B)$$

FIGURE 1.5   AND/OR logic network for XOR function.

Figure 1.6 gives the AND/OR network, Boolean equation, and truth table for a three-input majority function, so named because the output is a "1" only when a majority of the inputs are a "1".

An important law relating AND/OR/NOT relationships is known as *DeMorgan's Law,* with its forms shown in Figure 1.7. A "circle" or "bubble" on a gate input means that input is complemented. Note that a NAND function can be replaced by an OR function with complemented inputs (Form 1), while a NOR function can be replaced by an AND function with complemented inputs (Form 2). Forms 1 and 2 of DeMorgan's Law can be validated by comparing the truth tables

Majority   Y = (A & B) | (B & C) | (A & C)

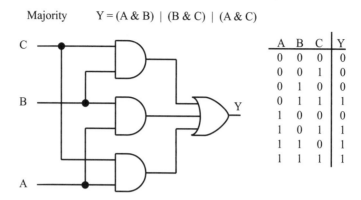

A	B	C	Y
0	0	0	0
0	0	1	0
0	1	0	0
0	1	1	1
1	0	0	0
1	0	1	1
1	1	0	1
1	1	1	1

FIGURE 1.6 AND/OR logic network for the three-input majority function.

(1) ~(A & B) = (~A) | (~B)

(2) ~(A | B) = (~A) & (~B)

(3) A & B = ~((~A) | (~B))

(4) A | B = ~((~A) & (~B))

FIGURE 1.7 DeMorgan's Law.

of the left- and right-hand sides, while forms 3 and 4 follow from substitution of forms 1 and 2. Complemented inputs/outputs are also known as *low-true* inputs/outputs, and uncomplemented inputs/outputs are called *high-true* inputs/outputs. Through DeMorgan's Law and the high-true, low-true terminology, the NAND gate of Figure 1.7 can be viewed as either an AND gate with high-true inputs and a low-true output, or as an OR gate with low-true inputs and a high-true output.

DeMorgan's law can be used to replace all of the AND/OR gates of Figure 1.6 with NAND gates as shown as in Figure 1.8. This is important as the physical implementation of a NAND gate using Complementary Metal Oxide Semiconductor (CMOS) transistors is faster and has fewer transistors than either an AND gate or an OR gate.

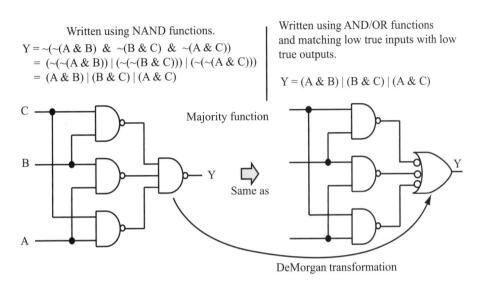

Written using NAND functions.

$Y = \sim(\sim(A \,\&\, B) \,\&\, \sim(B \,\&\, C) \,\&\, \sim(A \,\&\, C))$
$\quad = (\sim(\sim(A \,\&\, B))) \,|\, (\sim(\sim(B \,\&\, C))) \,|\, (\sim(\sim(A \,\&\, C)))$
$\quad = (A \,\&\, B) \,|\, (B \,\&\, C) \,|\, (A \,\&\, C)$

Written using AND/OR functions and matching low true inputs with low true outputs.

$Y = (A \,\&\, B) \,|\, (B \,\&\, C) \,|\, (A \,\&\, C)$

Majority function

Same as

DeMorgan transformation

FIGURE 1.8   NAND/NAND logic network for a three-input majority function.

LOGIC GATE CMOS IMPLEMENTATIONS

CMOS (pronounced as "see-moss") transistors are the most common implementation method used today for logic gates, which form the building blocks for all digital computation methods. We review the basics of CMOS transistor operation here and revisit the topic in Chapter 8 when discussing computer input/output. The "C" in CMOS stands for *complementary,* which refers to the fact that there are two types of MOS ("moss") transistors, N and P, whose operation is complementary to each other. Each MOS transistor type has four terminals, of which three of them are: *Gate* (g), *Source* (s), and *Drain* (d). The fourth terminal is the *substrate* or *bulk* terminal, which can be ignored in this discussion. For our purposes, we will view a MOS transistor as an ideal switch whose operation is controlled by the gate terminal. The switch is either closed (connection exists between source and drain, so current flows between source and drain) or open (no connection between source and drain, no current flow between source and drain). An N-type transistor is open when the gate has a logic "0" and closed when the gate has a logic "1". A P-type transistor has complementary operation; a "1" on the gate opens the switch, a "0" closes the switch. A logic "1" is physically represented by the power supply voltage of the logic gate, or *VDD*. The power supply voltage used for a CMOS logic gate can vary widely, from 5 V (Volts) down to approximately 1.0 V. A logic "0" is physically represented by the system ground, or *GND*, which has a voltage value of 0 V (VSS is also a common designation for ground). Figure 1.9 illustrates P and N transistor operation.

Multiple CMOS transistors can be connected to form logic gates. Figure 1.10 shows the simplest CMOS logic gate, which is the NOT function, or *inverter.* When

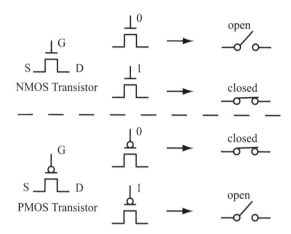

FIGURE 1.9   CMOS transistor operation.

the input value is "0", the upper switch (the P transistor) is closed, while the lower switch (the N transistor) is open. This connects the output to VDD, forcing the output to a "1". When the input value is "1", the upper switch is open, while the lower switch is closed. This connects the output to GND, forcing the output to a "0". Thus, for an input of "0" the output is "1"; for an input of "1" the output is a "0", which implements the NOT function.

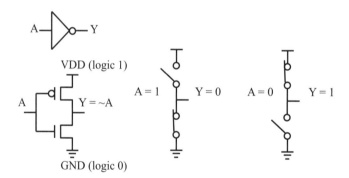

FIGURE 1.10   CMOS inverter operation.

Note that a buffer function Y = A is formed if two inverters are tied back to back as shown in Figure 1.11. It would seem that a better way to build a buffer is to switch the positions of the N and P transistors of the inverter, thus implementing the buffer with only two transistors instead of four. However, for physical reasons best left to an electronics book, a P transistor is always used to pass a "1" value, while an N transistor is always used to pass a "0" value. Thus, in digital logic, a P transistor is never tied to ground, and an N transistor is never tied to VDD, so the

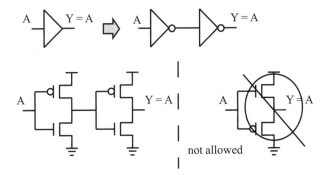

FIGURE 1.11   CMOS buffer.

two-transistor buffer shown in Figure 1.11 is illegal. Because of the rule given in the previous sentence, a non-inverting CMOS logic function always takes two stages of inverting logic.

Figure 1.12 shows the transistor configuration and operation of a two-input CMOS NAND gate. Note that the output is connected to ground (both bottom transistors are closed) only when both inputs are a "1" value. Also observe that no combination of inputs provides a direct path between VDD and GND; this would cause a *short* (low resistance path) between VDD and GND resulting in excessive current flow. The lack of a direct path from VDD to GND means that CMOS gates have a very low power consumption when they are not switching, which is

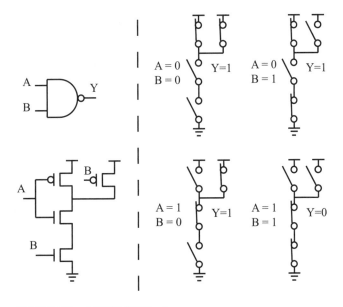

FIGURE 1.12   A CMOS NAND gate.

an important advantage of this technology. The four-transistor configuration for a CMOS NOR gate is left as an exercise for the review problems.

Figure 1.13 shows that a CMOS AND gate is actually built from a NAND gate followed by an inverter. Similarly, a CMOS OR gate is built from a NOR gate followed by an inverter. This clearly shows why replacing AND/OR logic with NAND gates via DeMorgan's Law is a good idea. The resulting circuit requires fewer transistors, meaning it is faster, consumes less power, and is cheaper to manufacture!

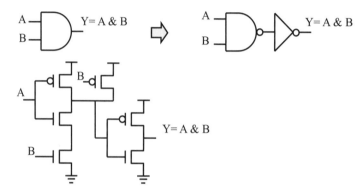

FIGURE 1.13   A CMOS AND gate.

COMBINATIONAL BUILDING BLOCKS

Building logic circuits on a gate-by-gate basis is an exercise that can be quite fun, once. After that, one should look for shortcuts that reduce design time for complex circuits. One method for building complex combinational circuits quickly is to use combinational *building blocks*. The following sections describe some commonly used combinational building blocks; this list is by no means exhaustive. It should not be surprising that some of these building blocks (the adder and shifter) implement the arithmetic operations discussed earlier.

THE MULTIPLEXER

A *K*-to-1 multiplexer (or mux) steers one of *K* inputs to the output. The most common mux type is a 2-to-1 mux (two inputs, one output). A select control input S chooses the input that is passed to the output. The operation of 2-to-1 mux is written in *C* code as:

```
if (S) Y = A; else Y = B;
```

This *C* code description of a mux reads as "if S is non-zero, output Y is equal to A, otherwise output Y is equal to B." The Boolean equation for a 1-bit 2-to-1 mux is given in Equation 1.2.

$$Y = (S \ \& \ I1) \mid (\sim S \ \& \ I0) \qquad (1.2)$$

Figure 1.14 shows the gate equivalent for a 1-bit 2-to-1 mux and how a 4-bit 2-to-1 mux is built from four of these 1-bit building blocks. The 4-bit mux symbol in Figure 1.14 uses a *bus* labeling notation for the A and B inputs. In this context, a *bus* is simply a collection of parallel wires; a bus named A with N wires is designated as $A[N-1:0]$. The LSb and MSb of bus A are $A[0]$ and $A[N-1]$, respectively. If $N = 8$, the entire bus A is labeled as $A[7:0]$, the LSb is $A[0]$, and the MSb is $A[7]$.

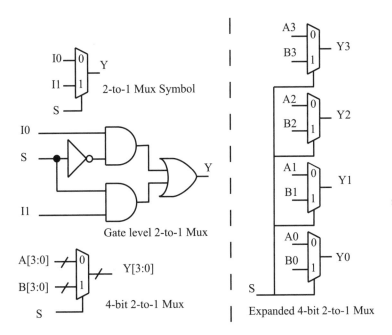

FIGURE 1.14   One-bit 2-to-1 mux, 4-bit 2-to-1 mux.

THE ADDER

The adder takes two *n*-bit inputs (A, B) and computes the *n*-bit sum (A + B). Most adders have a carry-in bit input for the LSb addition and a carry-out bit output from the MSb addition. A *full adder* logic circuit that adds A + B + Ci (carry-in) and produces the sum (S) and carry-out (Co) is a 1-bit building block of most adder circuits. Figure 1.15 shows the truth table, Boolean equations, and logic network for a full adder. The same figure shows how to build a 4-bit *ripple-carry* adder

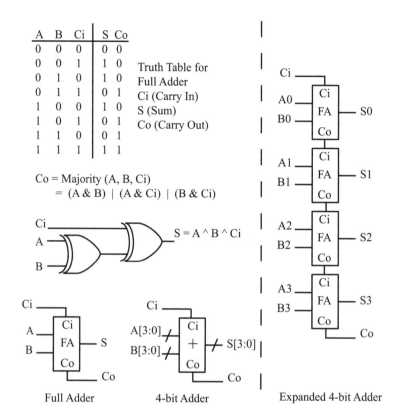

FIGURE 1.15   One-bit adder, 4-bit ripple adder.

from four 1-bit full adders; the term *ripple-carry* is used because the carry ripples from the least significant bit to the most significant bit. There are many other ways to build an adder; this is the simplest form of a binary adder.

THE INCREMENTER

The operation of an *incrementer* is described by the following *C* code:

```
if (INC) Y = A + 1; else Y = A;
```

The INC (increment) input is a single bit input that determines if the *n*-bit output is A + 1 or just A. An incrementer can be built from an adder by connecting all bits of one *n*-bit input to zero and using the carry-in input as the INC input. This computes the sum Y = A + 0 + 1 when INC = 1 or the value Y = A + 0 + 0 when INC = 0. There are more efficient methods in terms of logic gate count to implement an incrementer, but this illustrates the flexibility of combinational building blocks in implementing different functions.

THE SHIFTER

There are many varieties of shifter combinational building blocks. The simplest type shifts by only one position and in a fixed direction (either left or right). More complex types can shift multiple positions (a *barrel shifter*) in either direction. Figure 1.16 shows the logic symbol for an n-bit right shifter and the internal details of a 4-bit right shifter. When EN = 1, then Y = A >> 1 with the SI input providing the input bit for the MSb. When EN = 0, then Y = A, and the SI input has no effect. This is another example of simple combinational building blocks (2-to-1 muxes) being used to build a more complex combinational building block.

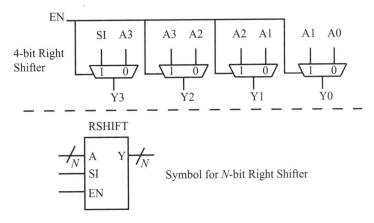

FIGURE 1.16   *N-bit right shift symbol and 4-bit right shift details.*

MEMORY

A K x N memory device has K locations, with each location containing n bits. Thus, a 16 x 1 memory has 16 locations, with each location containing 1 bit. The *address* inputs specify the location whose contents appear on the data output. Because the address bits uniquely specify 1 of K locations, the minimum width of the address bus is ceil($\log_2 K$). The output data bus has n bits as it is used to output a memory location's content. Following these rules, a 16 x 1 memory has ceil($\log_2 16$) = 4 address inputs and one data output. The idealistic view of memory presented here assumes a memory type with only these inputs and outputs, with memory contents loaded by some external means not discussed here. The most common usage of memory is to store data, and thus is actually a *sequential logic element* which is defined in the next section. However, a memory device can also be used to implement combinational logic functions, and so we discuss that usage scenario here. Figure 1.17 shows an 8 x 2 memory used to implement the sum and carry-out equations of the full adder. The full adder inputs are connected to the 3-bit address bus as A = ADDR2, B = ADDR1, and Ci = ADDR0. The 2-bit data output bus

Truth table for 8 x 2 Memory Contents

Location	A[2:0]	Data Out Q[1:0]
0	000	00
1	001	10
2	010	10
3	011	01
4	100	10
5	101	01
6	110	01
7	111	11

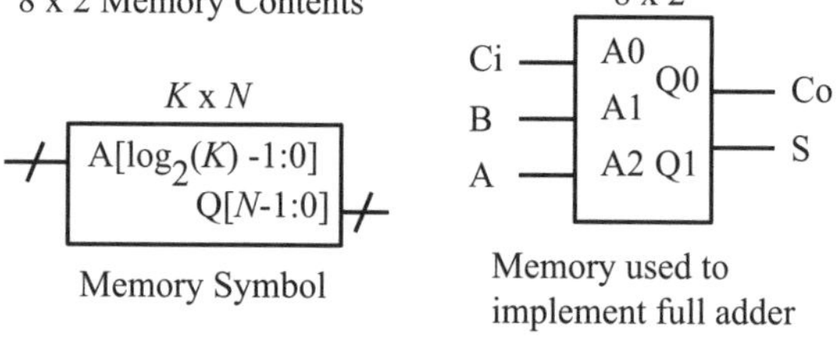

FIGURE 1.17 Full adder implemented by an 8 x 2 memory.

provides the outputs as Co = Q0 and S = Q1. When a memory is used in this way, it known as a *lookup table* (LUT). Changing the memory contents changes the logic function(s) implemented by the memory. Thus, a memory can be thought of as a *programmable* logic gate. *Field programmable gate arrays* (FPGAs) from Xilinx Inc. and Altera Corp. have thousands of small memories in one integrated circuit that can be programmed by the user for implementing logic functions.

Sample Question: ***How many address and data lines does a 4 Ki x 16 memory have?***

Answer: The number of address inputs is ceil($\log_2$ 4Ki) = ceil($\log_2 2^2 * 2^{10}$) = ceil($\log_2 2^{12}$) = 12. The number of data outputs is 16.

SEQUENTIAL LOGIC

The output of a combinational logic block is always uniquely defined by its current inputs. In contrast, the output of a *sequential* logic element is defined by its current inputs and also its *current state,* a value that is internal to the sequential logic element. A sequential logic element is a form of a memory device in that it retains internal state information between operations. In discussing sequential logic, the terms *asserted* and *negated* are used in reference to inputs, in addition to the previously defined terms of high-true and low-true. A high-true input has a high voltage level for TRUE and a low voltage level for FALSE. A low-true input has a low voltage level for TRUE and a high voltage level for FALSE. When an input is *asserted,* it is said to contain a TRUE value; a *negated* input contains a FALSE value. The symbol for a sequential logic element uses a bubble on an input to indicate low-true input or output.

THE CLOCK SIGNAL

An important signal in a sequential logic circuit is the *clock* signal, whose waveform and associated definitions are shown in Figure 1.18. The following definitions are used in reference to clock waveforms:

- A *rising edge* is a transition from low to high; a *falling edge* is a transition from high to low.
- The *period* of a clock is the time in seconds (s) between two edges of the same type. A clock waveform typically has a fixed period; in other words, the period does not vary over time.
- The *frequency* of a clock is defined as 1/(period) measured in Hertz (Hz), where 1 Hz = 1/(1 s) (a 1 Hz clock has a period of 1 second).
- The *high pulse width* (PW_H) is the amount of time the clock is high between a rising and falling edge; the *low pulse width* (PW_L) is the amount of time the clock remains low between a falling and rising edge. The *duty cycle* is the percentage of time that the clock remains high.

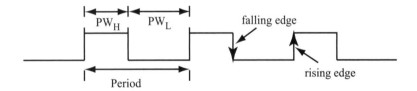

FIGURE 1.18   Clock signal definitions.

Clock signal equations are summarized in Equations 1.3 through 1.7 as:

$$\text{Frequency} = 1/\text{Period} \tag{1.3}$$

$$\text{Period} = 1/\text{Frequency} \tag{1.4}$$

$$\text{Duty\_cycle} = PW_H/\text{Period} \times 100\% \tag{1.5}$$

$$PW_H = \text{Duty\_cycle} \times \text{Period}/100 \tag{1.6}$$

$$PW_L = (100 - \text{Duty\_cycle}) \times \text{Period}/100 \tag{1.7}$$

Figure 1.18, the clock waveform, is an example of a *timing diagram,* which is a method for describing time-dependent behavior of digital systems. In a timing diagram, one or more waveforms can be displayed, and time is assumed to increase from left to right. A *waveform event* is a change in waveform value. If waveform event A occurs to the right of waveform event B, then A occurs after B in time.

Thus, there is an implied time ordering of events that flows left to right. The clock waveform shown in Figure 1.18 is an idealized view of a clock signal; an oscilloscope trace of an actual clock signal would reveal visible rise and fall times for clock edges, and perhaps ringing (small oscillations) on the end of rising and falling edges.

Table 1.4 lists commonly used units for time and frequency. A 1 kHz clock has a period of 1 ms, a 1 MHz clock has a period of 1 µs, and so forth. Timing and frequency specifications of digital circuits are contained in datasheets provided by the manufacturer. Time and frequency values are always specified using one of these units; in other words, a time is never specified as 1.05e–4 (shorthand for 1.05×10^{-4}); instead, it is specified as 105 µs.

TABLE 1.4   Common units for time and frequency.

Time	Frequency
milliseconds = ms = 10^{-3} s	kilohertz = kHz = 10^3 Hz
microseconds = µs = 10^{-6} s	megahertz = MHz = 10^6 Hz
nanoseconds = ns = 10^{-9} s	gigahertz = GHz = 10^9 Hz
picoseconds = ps = 10^{-12} s	terahertz = THz = 10^{12} Hz

Sample Question: *A clock has a duty cycle of 40 percent and a frequency of 19.2 kHz. What is the period and low pulse width, in microseconds?*

Answer: The period is $1/(19.2 \text{ kHz}) = 1/(19.2 \times 10^3) = 5.21 \times 10^{-5}$ s. To convert this value to microseconds, do a unit conversion via: $(5.21 \times 10^{-5} \text{ s}) \times (1 \text{ µs}/1 \times 10^{-6} \text{ s}) = 52.1$ µs.

$PW_L = ((100 - \text{Duty\_cycle}) \times \text{Period})/100 = ((100 - 40) \times 52.1 \text{ µs})/100 = 31.3$ µs.

THE D FLIP-FLOP

There are many varieties of sequential logic elements. In this section, we review only the dominant type used in digital logic design, the *D Flip-Flop* (DFF). A DFF, as seen in Figure 1.19, can have the following input signals:

■ **CK (input):** The clock input; the arrival of the clock active edge sets the internal state of the DFF equal to the data input if the asynchronous inputs R, S are negated. The rising clock edge is the active clock edge for the DFF in

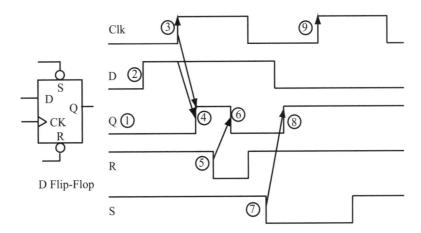

FIGURE 1.19 D flip-flop symbol and operation.

Figure 1.19; it is said to be rising-edge triggered. A falling-edge triggered DFF has a bubble on its clock input.

- **D (input):** The data input; the internal state of the DFF is set to this value on the arrival of an active clock edge if the asynchronous inputs R, S are negated. The D input is said to be a synchronous input as it can only affect the DFF on arrival of an active clock edge.
- **S (input):** The set input; the internal state of the DFF becomes a "1" when this input is asserted. In Figure 1.19 this is a low-true input, so a low voltage on this input asserts set. This input is said to be asynchronous as its operation is independent of the clock input.
- **R (input):** The reset input; the internal state of the DFF becomes a "0" when this input is asserted. In Figure 1.19 this is a low-true input, so a low voltage on this input asserts reset. This input is also an asynchronous input.
- **Q (output):** The Q output is the value of the internal state bit.

Not all DFFs have S and R inputs; all DFFs have at least CK, D, and Q. The timing diagram in Figure 1.19 contains the following sequence of events:

1. The initial value of the DFF state bit is "0" as reflected by the Q output.
2. The D input becomes a "1", but this has no effect on the Q output, as a rising clock edge has not occurred.
3. A rising clock edge arrives.
4. The Q output changes to a "1" as the D value of "1" is clocked into the DFF by the rising clock edge. The time delay between the rising clock edge and the Q output becoming a "1" is known as a propagation delay; changes cannot occur instantaneously in physical logic circuits. Propagation delay

values are dependent upon the transistor topology of a logic gate and have different values for different inputs and gate types. A propagation delay given in a datasheet is specified as a maximum time for a given operating condition (supply voltage, ambient temperature). Timing diagrams in this book show propagation delay where appropriate.

5. The R input becomes a "0", asserting this input.
6. The Q output becomes a "0" after a propagation delay; note that this occurs independently of the clock edge, as the R input is an asynchronous input.
7. The S input becomes a "0", asserting this input.
8. The Q output becomes a "1" after a propagation delay; again, this occurs independent of the clock edge, as the S input is an asynchronous input.
9. A rising clock edge arrives. The D input is a "0", but this value is not clocked into the DFF, as the S input is still asserted, which keeps the internal state at a "1".

The DFF is the most commonly used edge-triggered sequential logic element in digital logic, as it takes the fewest transistors to build. Other types of sequential logic elements that you may be familiar with are the JK Flip-Flop (JKFF) and T Flip-Flop (TFF); both of these can be built by placing logic gates around a DFF.

SEQUENTIAL BUILDING BLOCKS

Sequential building blocks are built using combinational building blocks and sequential logic elements. The following sections review some common sequential building blocks.

THE REGISTER

A *register* is used to store an *n*-bit value over successive clock periods. One may think that paralleling *n* DFFs would suffice, but the problem with a DFF is that it samples its D input on every active clock edge, potentially changing its value every active clock edge. Figure 1.20 shows an *n*-bit register built from an *n*-bit DFF and an *n*-bit 2-to-1 mux. When the load input (LD) is "1", the DFF D input receives the value of the external D input by way of the mux, and thus the register is loaded with a new value on the next active clock edge. When LD is "0", the DFF D input is connected to the DFF Q output; thus each active clock edge reloads the DFFs with their current output values. In this way, the register retains its current value over multiple clock cycles when the load input is negated (LD = 0). Registers are key components of all computers, and Figure 1.20 should be the physical element envisioned when the term register is used in future chapters on microprocessor operation.

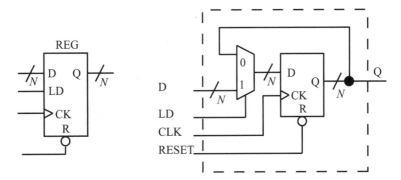

FIGURE 1.20 *n*-bit register.

THE COUNTER

A counter is a register that has the additional capability of being able to increment (count up) or decrement (count down), or both. Figure 1.21 shows an *n*-bit counter that can count up. An *n*-bit incrementer has been added to the register design of Figure 1.20 to provide the counter functionality. The counter counts up by one when INC = 1 and LD = 0 on a rising clock edge as the DFF D input sees the value Q + 1. When INC = 0 and LD = 1, the counter loads the external D input value on the active clock edge. This allows the counter to be initialized to a value other than zero. When INC = 0 and LD = 0, the counter holds its current value. Counters are useful for producing addresses used to access memories, as sequential access of memory content is a commonly needed operation in computer systems.

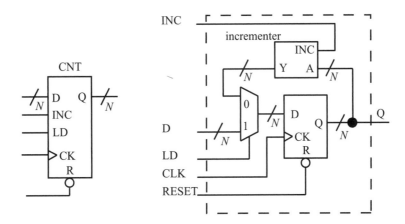

FIGURE 1.21 *n*-bit up counter.

THE SHIFT REGISTER

A shift register is a register that has the additional capability of being able to shift left, right, or both directions. Figure 1.22 shows a shift register that can shift right by 1 when SHIFT = 1 and LD = 0. It uses the same design as the counter, except that a shift-right block has replaced the incrementer block. Shift registers are useful in computer input/output where an *n*-bit value must be communicated serially, in other words, bit by bit, to another device. The concept of serial input/output is covered in much detail in Chapter 10.

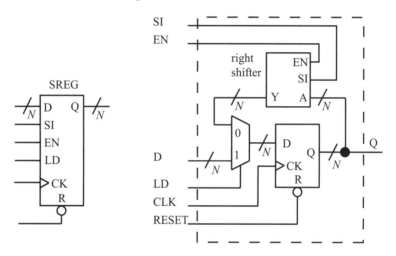

FIGURE 1.22   *n*-bit shift register.

At this point, the usefulness of the concept of combinational and sequential building blocks should be apparent. One can easily envision other useful combinational building blocks such as a subtractor, decrementer, adder/subtractor, and other sequential building blocks such as up/down counters, or combined counter/shift registers. These components form the basis for the logic circuits used within modern computers.

ENCODING CHARACTER DATA

Up to this point, the data encodings discussed have been for numerical representation of unsigned integers. Another common data type manipulated by computer systems is text, such as that printed on this page. The American Standard Code for Information Interchange (ASCII) is a 7-bit code used for encoding the English alphabet (the written form of the English language). The ASCII code contains uppercase letters, lowercase letters, punctuation marks, numerals, printer control codes, and special symbols. Table 1.5 shows the ASCII code; the top row specifies the most significant hex digit and the leftmost row the least significant hex digit of the 7-bit hex code. Thus, an "A" has the code 0x41, a "4" is 0x34, a "z" is 0x7A, and so on. The codes that are less than 0x20 are nonprintable characters that have various uses; some are printer control codes such as 0x0D (carriage return) and 0x0A (line feed). Eight bits are normally used to encode an ASCII character, with the eighth bit cleared to zero.

TABLE 1.5 ASCII table.

	Most Significant Digit							
	0x0	**0x1**	**0x2**	**0x3**	**0x4**	**0x5**	**0x6**	**0x7**
0x0	NUL	DLE	SPC	0	@	P	`	p
0x1	SOH	DC1	!	1	A	Q	a	q
0x2	STX	DC2	"	2	B	R	b	r
0x3	ETX	DC3	#	3	C	S	c	s
0x4	EOT	DC4	$	4	D	T	d	t
0x5	ENQ	NAK	%	5	E	U	e	u
0x6	ACK	SYN	&	6	F	V	f	v
0x7	BEL	ETB	'	7	G	W	g	w
0x8	BS	CAN	(	8	H	X	h	x
0x9	TAB	EM	)	9	I	Y	i	y
0xA	LF	SUB	*	:	J	Z	j	z
0xB	VT	ESC	+	;	K	[	k	{
0xC	FF	FS	,	<	L	\	l		
0xD	CR	GS	-	=	M	]	m	}
0xE	SO	RS	.	>	N	^	n	~
0xF	SI	US	/	?	O	_	o	DEL

With the advent of the World Wide Web and the necessity to exchange binary-encoded text in other languages, the universal character-encoding standard, *Unicode*, was created (see *www.unicode.org* for more information). The Unicode goal is to provide a unique encoding for every character, numeral, punctuation mark, and so forth, contained within every known language. The Unicode standard allows 8-bit (1 byte), 16-bit (2 byte), and 32-bit (4 byte) encodings. The 8-bit and 16-bit encodings are subsets of the 32-bit encodings; the first 128 codes (0x00 to 0x7F) are the same as the ASCII code for compatibility. Using 32 bits for each character allows for 4294967296 unique characters, which is sufficient for the known character sets of the world. Individual character sets (Latin, Greek, Chinese, etc.) are assigned ranges within Unicode. Portions of the code are also reserved for use by private applications, so these codes are not assigned to any language. This book uses ASCII exclusively for character data encoding, but be aware that more sophisticated methods for text encoding exist. The number of different items in the computer world that have binary encodings is large, and thus you must be told what is being encoded in order to decipher a binary code. For example, the binary value 0b01000001 (0x41) can represent either the ASCII code for an 'A' (uppercase A), or the number 65 (4 * 16 + 1 = 65), or something else entirely. Throughout this book's remaining chapters, you learn about other types of binary codes and the items that they encode.

> Sample Question: *What character string is represented by "0x48 0x65 0x6c 0x6c 0x6F 0x20 0x57 0x6F 0x72 0x6c 0x64 0x21"?*
>
> Answer: Translating character by character yields the popular test message: "Hello World!" Note that the string contains a space character (0x20) and an exclamation mark "!" (0x21).

SUMMARY

In this chapter, we hope to have refreshed some topics you have encountered previously concerning number systems, binary encoding, Boolean algebra, logic gates, combinational building blocks, and sequential building blocks. In the next chapter, we use these building blocks to introduce the concept of a stored program machine as a means of implementing a digital system.

REVIEW PROBLEMS

1. How many bits does it take to represent 40 items?
2. What is the largest unsigned integer that can be represented in 7 bits?
3. Convert the value 120 to binary using 8 bits.
4. Convert 89 to hex using 8 bits.
5. Convert 0xF4 to binary.
6. Convert 0xF4 to decimal.
7. Convert the value 0b10110111 to decimal.

8. Compute 0xB2 + 0x9F and give the result in hex.
9. Compute 0xB2 − 0x9F and give the result in hex. Check your work by verifying that 0xB2 + ~(0x9F) + 0x1 produces the same result. To compute ~(0x9F), complement each bit.
10. Draw the logic network and derive the truth table for the logic function F = (A&B) | C.
11. Derive the CMOS transistor network that implements the NOR function.
12. Compute 0xC3 >> 2; give the value in hex (this is a right shift by two).
13. Compute 0x2A << 1; give the value in hex (this is a left shift by one).
14. What is the period of a 400 kHz clock in microseconds?
15. Given a 30 percent duty cycle clock with a high pulse width of 20 µs, what is the clock frequency in kHz?
16. Design an n-bit subtractor using an adder with a carry-in input and the fact that A − B = A + ~B + 1.
17. Design an n-bit adder/subtractor that has an external input called SUB that when "1", performs a subtraction, when "0", performs an addition. (Hint: use an adder with a carry-in input and a mux.)
18. Design a left-shift by one combinational building block.
19. Design a counter that can count either up or down. Assume that you have incrementer and decrementer building blocks available.
20. Write your first name as 8-bit hex values using ASCII encoding.

2 The Stored Program Machine

This chapter introduces the fundamental concepts of computer operation by implementing a controller both as a finite state machine and as a stored program machine.

Learning Objectives

After reading this chapter, you will be able to:

- Compare and contrast controller designs using finite state machine and stored program machine approaches.
- Describe the operation of a finite state machine via an algorithmic state machine chart.
- Implement a finite state machine using a one-hot state encoding method.
- Discuss the basic elements of a stored program machine.
- Describe the meaning of the terms opcode, machine word, instruction mnemonic, address bus, data bus, instruction pointer, assembly, and disassembly.
- Describe the fetch and execute sequence of a stored program machine.
- Convert a simple assembly language program to machine code and vice versa.
- Follow the execution of a simple assembly language program.
- Write a simple assembly language program to solve a specified problem.

The preceding tasks introduce you to the concept of stored program machines, of which the PIC24HJ32GP202 microcontroller is a prime example, and is the principal focus of the rest of this book. The PIC24HJ32GP202 microcontroller is simply a more complex version of the stored program machine discussed in the following sections. This chapter provides you with the first chance to dip your toes into the vast ocean of microprocessor operation, programming, and application.

PROBLEM SOLVING THE DIGITAL WAY

Digital systems provide solutions for problems in which real-world inputs can be converted to a digital representation, which is then processed by a clever use of combinational and sequential building blocks to produce a digital output that is converted back to a useful quantity in the real world. As an example, consider a digital voice recorder:

- Pushbutton inputs on the recorder determine if the recorder is in record mode or playback mode. A microphone input with a biasing circuit converts voice that varies in amplitude over time to a continuously varying voltage between 0 V and the power supply voltage, where the voltage fluctuations are the sound wave variations of human speech.
- A building block called an analog-to-digital converter (ADC) produces a digital (binary) representation of the microphone output voltage at regular time intervals. Each converted digital value is called a voice sample.
- A digital building block called a controller monitors the button inputs on the recorder.
- In record mode, the controller reads the voice samples from the ADC and stores them in a memory device.
- In playback mode, the controller reads the memory contents sequentially and sends each voice sample to a building block called a digital-to-analog converter (DAC) that converts a digital input value to a voltage value between 0 V and a reference voltage VREF (which can be the power supply voltage). This voltage signal drives a speaker, allowing the recorded voice to be heard.

Analog-to-digital converters and digital-to-analog converters are essential parts of digital systems and are covered in Chapter 11. In this chapter, we are concerned with the design of the controller that sequences the events within a digital system.

Two basic choices exist for building a controller: a *finite state machine* (FSM) or a *stored program machine* (also known as a Von Neumann machine after the scientist who first proposed this approach [1], [2]). In an FSM, dedicated logic implements the event sequence required for a task. In a stored program machine, data stored in a memory specifies the event sequence for a particular task. An advantage of an FSM is that it usually takes fewer clock cycles than a stored program machine to perform a particular task. The principal advantage of a stored program machine is flexibility; a different task can be implemented by simply changing memory contents. An FSM requires redesign of its internal logic to implement a different task, which is a much more difficult problem than memory modification.

To illustrate the differences between these approaches, consider a digital system that continuously outputs the digits of a phone number, $Y_1Y_2Y_3\text{-}Z_1Z_2Z_3Z_4$. In local mode, only digits $Z_1Z_2Z_3Z_4$ are output, while in non-local mode all digits are output. In our controller designs for this problem, a common set of inputs and outputs is used for comparison purposes:

- **LOC (input):** When "1", the system is in local mode; when "0", in non-local mode.
- **CLK (input):** This is obviously a sequential system, as the output cannot be solely determined by the LOC input, so the system requires DFFs, which implies that a clock input is needed.
- **RESET# (input):** All sequential digital systems need an input signal that initializes the internal DFFs to a known state after power is applied, because the internal state of DFFs are indeterminate on power up. This signal is usually called RESET#; the "#" in the name indicates that this input is low-true.
- **DOUT[3:0] (output):** This 4-bit output bus is used to sequentially output the digits of the phone number. A digit has a value between 0 and 9, so 4 bits are sufficient for encoding purposes. Binary encoding is used for encoding these digits.

The following sections detail controller designs using both FSM and stored program machine approaches. Contrasting the two controller designs emphasizes the strengths and weaknesses of each approach.

FINITE STATE MACHINE DESIGN

An FSM can be thought of as a sequential building block that is custom-designed to solve a particular problem. The problem solved by an FSM is described as a series of transitions between *states,* where a transition from the *present state* to the *next state* is determined by the present state and the current inputs. A state can be thought of as one of the steps within a sequence of steps that are required to accomplish some task. The steps that come before and after it uniquely identify a state. The outputs of the FSM are also determined either by only the present state or a combination of the present state and current inputs. In this example, we use an *algorithmic state machine* (ASM) chart to describe the state sequencing of an FSM. An ASM chart is similar to a software flowchart for those familiar with that notation. Symbols used in an ASM chart are:

- **Rectangle:** This indicates a state. Outputs asserted during this state are written within the rectangle; these outputs are called unconditional outputs, as the assertion is dependent only upon the state, not upon any external input. Any outputs that do not appear in a state are assumed negated.
- **Diamond:** A decision point, with the input that the decision is based upon written within the diamond.
- **Oval:** This can only appear after a decision point and is used for conditional outputs, which is an output dependent upon both a state and some set of inputs.
- **Circle:** This appears next to each state and contains the state name.

The ASM chart in Figure 2.1 shows an FSM that outputs the number 324-8561 according to our problem specification. The ASM contains seven states with the S^* state being the state entered upon reset (the reset state is designated by the $*$ symbol). The state following S^* is dependent upon the LOC input; if LOC = 1, then the next state is Z_2, otherwise the next state is Y_2. The state progression for LOC = 0 is S^*, $Y_2, Y_3, Z_1, Z_2, Z_3, Z_4$, which then loops back to S^*. Each state requires one clock cycle, so this state progression requires seven clock cycles. If LOC = 1, the state progression is S^*, Z_2, Z_3, Z_4, again looping back to state S^*. The LOC input is only checked in the S^* state, so the sequence cannot be altered once state S^* has been exited. The DOUT output of the S^* state is conditional upon the LOC input; DOUT = 8 if LOC = 1, otherwise DOUT = 3. The DOUT output in all other states is unconditional.

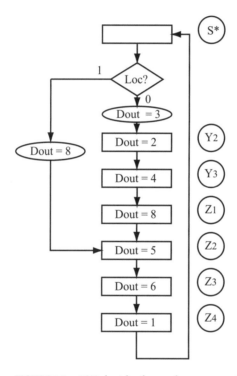

FIGURE 2.1   ASM chart for the number sequence 324-8561.

FINITE STATE MACHINE IMPLEMENTATION

A generic block diagram of an FSM implementation is shown in Figure 2.2. The state DFFs contain the present state of the FSM. The CLOGIC block is the combinational logic that produces the next state inputs to the state DFFs based upon the present state and external inputs. State changes occur on the active clock edge.

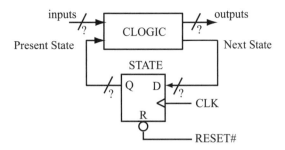

FIGURE 2.2   Finite state machine block diagram.

The first task in implementing this FSM is *state assignment*, which means assigning binary encodings for each state. The state assignment affects the number of state DFFs required and the combinational logic within the CLOGIC block. Table 2.1 lists two choices for state encoding; there are many others. Using binary encoding requires only three DFFs but more complex combinational logic; one-hot encoding requires one DFF per state (seven total) but simplifies the task of determining the required combinational logic equations. This is meant as an illustrative exercise, and not an exhaustive treatise on FSM design, so we will use one-hot encoding.

TABLE 2.1   Two possibilities for state assignment.

State	Binary Encoding	One-Hot Encoding
S*	000	0000001
Y2	001	0000010
Y3	010	0000100
Z1	011	0001000
Z2	100	0010000
Z3	101	0100000
Z4	110	1000000

Two sets of Boolean equations are required for the CLOGIC block: the set that controls the state sequencing, and the set that produces the required output values. The set of Boolean equations that controls the state sequencing consists of seven equations, one for each D input of a DFF. An advantage of one-hot encoding is that these equations can be easily determined by inspection of the ASM chart. As an example, consider the equation for the D input of state S*, designated by D_S*. This state is entered on the next clock cycle from state Z_4, and we know that the Q output of the state Z_4 DFF, denoted by Q_Z_4, will only be a "1" when the FSM is in state Z_4. Thus, the D_S^* Boolean equation has only one term as shown in Equation 2.1.

$$D\_S^* = Q\_Z_4; \qquad (2.1)$$

The equation for the D input of the Y_2 state is a bit more interesting, as this state is entered only if the current state is S^* and LOC is "0" as stated in Equation 2.2.

$$D\_Y_2 = (Q\_S^*) \,\&\, (\sim LOC); \qquad (2.2)$$

The Boolean equations for the remaining DFF inputs are derived through similar reasoning as shown in Equations 2.3 through 2.7.

$$D\_Y_3 = Q\_Y_2; \qquad (2.3)$$

$$D\_Z_1 = Q\_Y_3; \qquad (2.4)$$

$$D\_Z_2 = ((Q\_S^*) \,\&\, (LOC)) \,|\, (Q\_Z_1); \qquad (2.5)$$

$$D\_Z_3 = Q\_Z_2; \qquad (2.6)$$

$$D\_Z_4 = Q\_Z_3; \qquad (2.7)$$

The previous Boolean equations for state sequencing do not include the reset behavior. The reset signal input is tied to the set (S) input of the DFF for state S^* and to the reset (R) input of the remaining state DFFs. In this way, reset assertion forces the FSM to enter state S^* while reset negation allows normal state sequencing.

The Boolean equations for the DOUT outputs depend upon the current state and LOC input values. Table 2.2 lists the binary output values for DOUT given the current state and LOC values.

TABLE 2.2 Output values for DOUT referenced to states.

State	One-Hot Encoding	DOUT (LOC = 0)	DOUT (LOC = 1)
S^*	0000001	0011 (3)	1000 (8)
Y_2	0000010	0010 (2)	0010 (2)
Y_3	0000100	0100 (4)	0100 (4)
Z_1	0001000	1000 (8)	1000 (8)
Z_2	0010000	0101 (5)	0101 (5)
Z_3	0100000	0110 (6)	0110 (6)
Z_4	1000000	0001 (1)	0001 (1)

A Boolean logic equation is needed for each of the 4 bits of DOUT. We will write these equations by inspection and make no attempt at minimizing the amount of logic required for implementation. From Table 2.2, we see that the DOUT[0] output is a "1" for the following conditions: in state S* and LOC = 0, or in states Z_2 or Z_4. This is expressed as a Boolean equation for the DOUT[0] output as shown in Equation 2.8.

$$DOUT[0] = ((Q\_S^*) \& (\sim LOC)) \mid (Q\_Z_2) \mid (Q\_Z_4); \qquad (2.8)$$

The equations for the other DOUT bits are derived similarly as shown in Equations 2.9 through 2.11.

$$DOUT[1] = ((Q\_S^*) \& (\sim LOC)) \mid (Q\_Y_2) \mid (Q\_Z_3); \qquad (2.9)$$

$$DOUT[2] = (Q\_Y_3) \mid (Q\_Z_2) \mid (Q\_Z_3); \qquad (2.10)$$

$$DOUT[3] = ((Q\_S^*) \& (LOC)) \mid (Q\_Z_1); \qquad (2.11)$$

These Boolean equations can be mapped to logic gates for implementation; a simulation of the resulting gate level system is shown in Figure 2.3. Note that in clock cycle #1, the system is in state S* with DOUT = 3, but when state S* is reentered in clock cycle #8 the output is DOUT = 8, because now LOC = 1 (the changing of the LOC input value is arbitrary as it is an external input; it is changed in clock cycle #5 to illustrate that the LOC input affects only the FSM behavior in state S*).

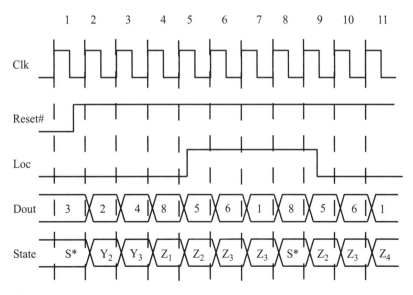

FIGURE 2.3   Simulation of the FSM implementation.

Note that if the phone number is changed, only the Boolean equations for DOUT must be changed; the Boolean equations for the state sequencing remain the same. However, if the number of phone digits is changed, say to $X_1X_2X_3$-$Y_1Y_2Y_3$-$Z_1Z_2Z_3Z_4$, this requires a new state sequence and hence different logic for state sequencing. This highlights the disadvantage of the FSM approach–changes to the function of the circuit require a logic redesign.

A STORED PROGRAM MACHINE

A stored program machine is the formal term for a computer. Three components of every stored program machine are:

- **Input/Output (I/O) signals** that are used for interfacing with the external world.
- **Memory** that stores the instructions that determine the sequence of events performed by the computer. An instruction is a binary datum that is usually a fixed width. Memory also stores data that instructions manipulate.
- **Control logic** that decodes the instructions and executes the actions specified by an instruction.

The common elements between a finite state machine and stored program machine are I/O and control; the memory component is the differentiating factor. Memory provides flexibility for a stored program machine; a stored program machine can be programmed to perform a different task by changing the instructions stored in memory. A *program* is a sequence of instructions that implement a particular task. A stored program machine continuously performs a *fetch/execute* action, in which an instruction is fetched from memory then executed. Instruction fetches typically progress through memory in a sequential manner. Instructions are divided into different classes; some instructions perform arithmetic operations, some perform input/output, and some perform control. An example of arithmetic instruction execution is binary addition. An example of an input/output instruction execution is placing a data value on an output bus. An example of a control instruction execution is a `goto X` (jump) that fetches the next instruction from location X instead of the next sequential memory location.

INSTRUCTION SET DESIGN AND ASSEMBLY LANGUAGE

The design of our stored program machine begins with determining what type of instructions it should execute and the format or binary encoding of these instructions. To determine this, we will describe the task as a sequence of statements in the *C* programming language, as seen in Listing 2.1.

LISTING 2.1 *C* language program of the number sequencing task.

```
START:
    if (loc) goto LOCAL;
    dout = 3;
    dout = 2;
    dout = 4;
LOCAL:
    dout = 8;
    dout = 5;
    dout = 6;
    dout = 1;
    goto START;
```

These statements represent three distinct operations:

- An **output operation** as specified by the statement dout = 2, which places the value 0b0010 on the DOUT data bus.
- An **unconditional transfer of control**, also known as a *goto* or *jump*, as specified by the statement goto START, which says to fetch the next instruction from the memory location represented by the label START.
- A **conditional transfer of control**, also known as a *branch* or a *conditional jump*, as specified by the statement if (loc) goto LOCAL. If loc is nonzero (i.e., true), the next instruction fetched is the one at label LOCAL. If loc is zero (i.e., false), the next sequential instruction in memory is fetched, which in this case is dout = 3.

These instruction types must be assigned a binary encoding so that they can be stored in memory. The encoding of an instruction must specify the type of instruction and the data required by the instruction (if the instruction requires data). The instruction bits that specify the instruction type form a bit field that is called the *opcode*. The data required by the instruction is more formally known as the *operand*. Figure 2.4 illustrates how instruction encoding is divided into opcode and operand fields.

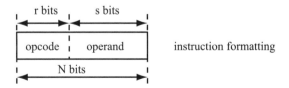

FIGURE 2.4 Instruction encoding split into opcode and operand fields.

Two bits are needed for the opcode to encode the three types of instructions in our computer. Table 2.3 lists the *instruction set* for our number sequencing

TABLE 2.3   Instruction encodings for the number sequencing computer.

Mnemonic	Opcode	Operand
JMP	00	instruction address
JC	01	instruction address
OUT	10	4-bit data

computer (NSC). The leftmost column contains the instruction *mnemonic*, which is the human-readable form of an instruction. The middle column gives the opcode encoding and the rightmost column the instruction operand.

Opcode encoding is usually chosen so that classes of instructions can be easily distinguished. In this case, the two control instructions JC and JMP are distinguished from the I/O instruction OUT by the most significant bit of the opcode. The OUT instruction operand is the 4-bit digit that appears on the DOUT data bus after the instruction is executed. The JMP and JC instructions have the same type of operand, which is the memory address of the target instruction of the jump. The number of bits required for this memory address depends on the maximum number of memory locations allowed in our number sequencing computer. For now, a total of 4 bits is used, which limits the total number of memory locations to $2^4 = 16$. Each memory location contains one instruction, so the maximum number of instructions in any program written for our computer is 16 instructions. Each of our instructions is 6 bits wide (2 bits of opcode, 4 bits of data), so a 16x6 memory device is required for storing the instructions of our program.

Listing 2.2 gives the C program of the number sequencing task translated into the instructions used by our computer. The translation of a high-level language to the native instructions of a computer is called *compilation*. A program specified using the instruction mnemonics of an instruction set is called an *assembly language* program. A computer program called a *compiler* is normally used to translate a high-level language program to assembly language, but in this book the process is done manually in many cases to illustrate the linkage between C statements and assembly language statements. The lines START: and LOCAL: are called *labels* and are not instructions. They are used as identifiers for particular program lines, and the reasoning for including them will soon become clear.

LISTING 2.2   Assembly language program for the number sequencing task.

```
START:
   JC LOCAL
   OUT 3
   OUT 2
   OUT 4
```

```
LOCAL:
   OUT  8
   OUT  5
   OUT  6
   OUT  1
   JMP  START
```

The next step is to translate our program into binary so that it can be stored in memory. This process is called *assembly* and is performed by a computer program called an *assembler*. The resulting binary codes are called the *machine code* of the assembly language program. The reverse process of converting machine code to assembly language mnemonics is called *disassembly*. The assembly process is done in two passes by the assembler; the first pass assembly does not assemble any JMP/JC instructions whose jump destination is ahead of the current instruction as the memory location of the jump destination is unknown. After the first pass assembly, the locations of all instructions are known so the second pass completes the assembly of any JMP/JC instructions that were not completed in the first pass. Table 2.4 gives the first pass result of this assembly process. The leftmost column contains the memory location where the machine code for the instruction is placed. We will place our instructions starting at location 0x0 in memory for reasons that are explained later. Each assembly language statement is translated individually to its machine code representation. Observe that the operand field of the first instruction is left as "????" because the location of the instruction represented by the label LOCAL is unknown by the assembler when this instruction is assembled during the first pass. The last instruction, JMP START, can be completely translated by the assembler because the label START

TABLE 2.4   First pass assembly of the number sequencing program.

Memory Location	Machine Code	Instruction
0x0	01 ????	START: JC LOCAL
0x1	10 0011	OUT 3
0x2	10 0010	OUT 2
0x3	10 0100	OUT 4
0x4	10 1000	LOCAL: OUT 8
0x5	10 0101	OUT 5
0x6	10 0110	OUT 6
0x7	10 0001	OUT 1
0x8	00 0000	JMP START

stands for the first instruction, which has already been translated and is located at location 0x0.

Once the first pass assembly is complete, we see that the value for label LOCAL is the memory address 0x4. Table 2.5 gives the second pass assembly of the number sequencing program; the values of all labels are now known so the machine code translation is complete.

TABLE 2.5   Second pass assembly of the number sequencing program.

Memory Location	Machine Code	Instruction
0x0	01 0100	START: JC LOCAL
0x1	10 0011	OUT 3
0x2	10 0010	OUT 2
0x3	10 0100	OUT 4
0x4	10 1000	LOCAL: OUT 8
0x5	10 0101	OUT 5
0x6	10 0110	OUT 6
0x7	10 0001	OUT 1
0x8	00 0000	JMP START

Our program consists of nine assembly language instructions; the remaining seven locations of our 16x6 memory are not needed for this program.

HARDWARE DESIGN

We must now design hardware that executes the machine code program of our number sequencing task. We will use the sequential blocks covered in the first chapter to make our job easier. Figure 2.5 shows what is currently known about the hardware components of our computer; it has a 16x6 memory, a 1-bit input called LOC, and a 4-bit output called DOUT.

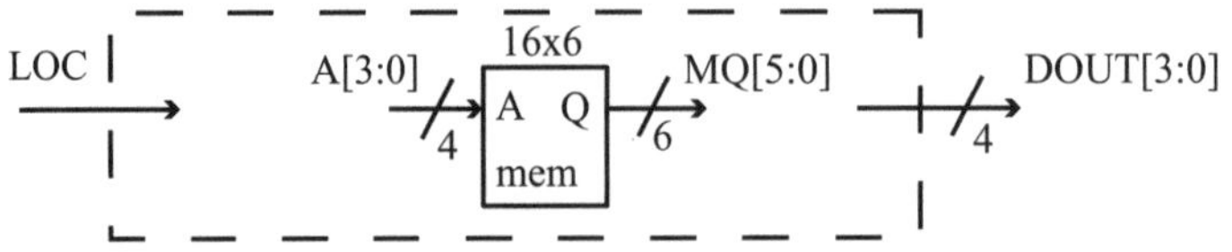

FIGURE 2.5   Number sequencing computer initial components.

In looking at Figure 2.5, we see several busses (DOUT, memory address bus, memory data bus) that connect to nothing, so this provides a logical place to begin adding components. Recall that a register is a sequential building block used to hold a value over one or more clock cycles. A 4-bit register is needed to drive the DOUT data bus; the register contents are modified by execution of the OUT instruction. Recall that a counter is a register that has the capability of counting up or down, or both. Instructions are usually fetched sequentially from memory, which means that the addresses provided to memory generally proceed in binary counting order. Thus, a 4-bit counter is the natural choice for providing the address to memory. This counter is an integral part of any computer and is known as the *program counter* (PC) or *instruction pointer* (IP). The PC register contains the address of the instruction currently being fetched from memory. Figure 2.6 shows the number sequencing computer hardware modified to contain the PC and output registers and supplemented with logic which controls these registers' operation.

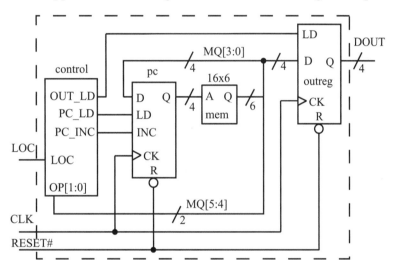

FIGURE 2.6   Number sequencing computer with program counter, output register, and control logic added.

The reset inputs of the PC and output register are tied to the external reset input. When reset is asserted, the PC register is cleared, which means the first instruction fetched from memory is at location 0, requiring the instructions in Table 2.5 to begin at location 0. Observe that the LD and INC control inputs of the PC and the LD input of the output register now connect to a general block named *control*. Modification of the PC and output registers is controlled by the current instruction. Table 2.6 lists the PC and output register control input values for each instruction. The output register is loaded when the OUT instruction is executed. The PC register is incremented if an OUT instruction is executed or when a JC instruction is executed and LOC = 0. The PC register is loaded when a JMP instruction is executed or when a JC instruction is executed and LOC = 1.

TABLE 2.6 PC, output register inputs for instruction execution.

Instruction	PC Register	Output Register
JC	LD = LOC, INC = ~LOC	LD = 0
JMP	LD = 1, INC = 0	LD = 0
OUT	LD = 0, INC = 1	LD = 1

The Boolean equations for the PC and output register control lines are shown in Equations 2.12 through 2.14 as determined from Table 2.6.

$$PC\_LD = (\sim MQ5\ \&\ \sim MQ4)\ |\ (\sim MQ5\ \&\ MQ4\ \&\ LOC) \qquad (2.12)$$

$$PC\_INC = \sim PC\_LD \qquad (2.13)$$

$$OUT\_LD = MQ5 \qquad (2.14)$$

The values MQ5 and MQ4 are the two most significant bits of the instruction word fetched from memory; these are the opcode bits of the instruction. The Boolean equation for the PC_INC signal is simply the complement of PC_LD, as the PC is incremented if it is not being loaded. The logic gates that implement the Boolean equations for PC_LD, PC_INC, and OUT_LD are placed in the control logic block as shown in Figure 2.7, which completes our design.

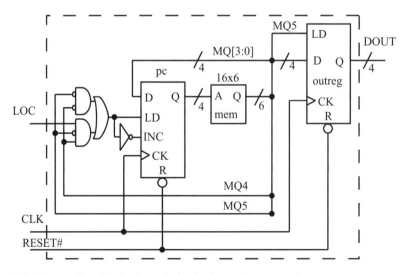

FIGURE 2.7 Complete hardware design for the number sequencing computer.

Figure 2.8 shows a simulation of the number sequencing computer. The PC waveform is the program counter value and is useful for tracking the instruction execution progress.

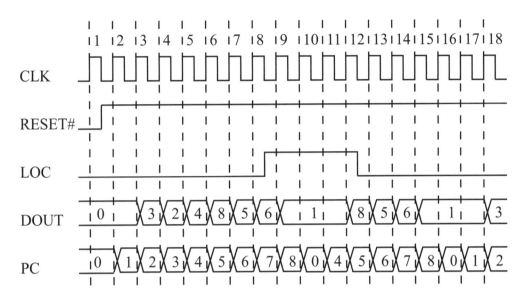

FIGURE 2.8   Simulation of the number sequencing computer.

Table 2.7 compares the number of clock cycles required for each number sequence in the finite state machine and stored program machine implementations. The stored program machine requires two more clock cycles for each sequence because of the JC instruction at the beginning of the sequence and the JMP at the end of the sequence. In general, a stored program machine will take more clock cycles to accomplish a task than a finite state machine, which is the penalty for increased flexibility and is a typical tradeoff when evaluating whether to use a general-purpose computer versus dedicated logic as a problem solution.

TABLE 2.7   FSM versus SPM clock cycles.

Condition	FSM Clock Cycles	SPM Clock Cycles
LOC = 0	7	9
LOC = 1	4	6

MODERN COMPUTERS

How does our number sequencing computer (NSC) compare against modern computers?

- Programs for the NSC reside in memory that has a maximum of 16 locations; modern computers have memory that contains billions of locations.
- The data register in the NSC is 4 bits wide; modern computers have data registers that are typically 32 or 64 bits wide, and even larger in some cases.
- The NSC has three different instructions; modern computers have tens to hundreds of different instructions.
- The NSC can be implemented in less than 100 logic gates; modern computers can require millions of logic gates.

Despite these differences, the NSC and modern computers share the basic components of all computers: input/output, memory, and control. These three components work together to fetch and execute instructions that are stored in memory.

SUMMARY

In this chapter, we introduced the basic concepts of stored program machines. Stored program machines offer more flexibility than finite state machines at the cost of lower performance. The next chapter introduces the stored program machine that is the main topic of this book, the PIC24HJ32GP202 microcontroller.

REVIEW PROBLEMS

1. Write an assembly language program for the number sequencing computer that outputs the four digit sequence 0, 2, 5, 7 if LOC = 0, otherwise output the sequence 1, 3, 6, 8. After a sequence is finished, loop back to program start. Convert your assembly language program to machine code starting at location 0.
2. Write the assembly language program corresponding to the NSC machine code program seen in Table 2.8.
3. For the NSC, assume that the LOC input is tied to the least significant bit of the DOUT bus. For the program in Table 2.9, give the location executed and the DOUT value for the first 10 clock cycles.
4. Repeat problem #3, except change the instruction at location #1 to OUT 4.

TABLE 2.8   NSC machine code program.

Memory Location	Machine Code
0	100000
1	010000
2	100001
3	010000
4	100010
5	010000
6	101001
7	000000

TABLE 2.9   NSC assembly language program.

Memory Location	Instruction
0	OUT 2
1	OUT 5
2	JC 5
3	OUT 4
4	JC 0
5	OUT 9
6	JC 2
7	JC 5
8	OUT 4
9	JC 0

5. Assume the number definition is changed to $1\text{-}X_1X_2X_3\text{-}Y_1Y_2Y_3\text{-}Z_1Z_2Z_3Z_4$, with the local number as $Y_1Y_2Y_3\text{-}Z_1Z_2Z_3Z_4$. How many instructions are required for the NSC to implement this program?

6. Modify the schematic of the NSC (Figure 2.7) to add support for a new instruction called INC that increments the current contents of the output register. Assign this new instruction the binary opcode "11"; the data field is unused. (Hint: Try replacing the output register with an up counter.)

TABLE 2.10 NSC assembly language program.

Memory Location	Instruction
0	OUT 0
1	INC
2	JC 1
3	JMP 3

7. Modify the schematic of the NSC (Figure 2.7) so that it can access a memory with 32 instructions. (Hint: Begin by extending the memory to 32 locations, then trace all of the changes required in the various components—you may be surprised at the number of modifications caused by this seemingly minor extension.)

8. Assume the NSC has a new instruction called INC (opcode = "11") that increments the contents of the OUT register; the INC instruction data field is unused. Also assume that the LOC input is tied to the complement of the DOUT[3] bit (LOC = ~DOUT3). For the program in Table 2.10, how many clock cycles does it take to reach location 3?

9. What changes have to be made to the NSC (Figure 2.7) to accommodate a maximum of eight instructions instead of four?

10. Assume the number definition is changed to $1\text{-}X_1X_2X_3\text{-}Y_1Y_2Y_3\text{-}Z_1Z_2Z_3Z_4$, with the local number as $Y_1Y_2Y_3\text{-}Z_1Z_2Z_3Z_4$. Draw the new ASM chart required to implement this number sequence. How many states are required? If binary encoding is used for the states, how many DFFs are required?

PART II

PIC24 μC Assembly Language Programming

3 Introduction to the PIC24 Microcontroller Family

This chapter introduces the PIC24 instruction set architecture by exploring the data memory structure and data transfer instructions of the PIC24 microcontroller (μC). The use of the MPLAB® Integrated Design Environment for assembly and simulation of PIC24 programs is also discussed.

Learning Objectives

After reading this chapter, you will be able to:

- Describe the data and program memory architecture of the PIC24 μC.
- Convert PIC24 instruction mnemonics to machine code and vice versa.
- Describe the operation of the register direct, register indirect, immediate, file register, and default working register addressing modes.
- Describe the operation of the `mov`, `add`, `sub`, `inc`, `inc2`, `dec`, `dec2`, and `goto` instructions.
- Translate (manually compile) a simple *C* program into PIC24 assembly language.
- Compute the number of clock cycles and the amount of time required to execute simple instruction sequences for the PIC24 μC.

INTRODUCTION TO MICROPROCESSORS AND MICROCONTROLLERS

In the previous chapter, a computer was defined as a digital system composed of control, input/output, and memory components whose operation is controlled by instructions stored in memory. The first computers were designed in the early 1940s and filled entire rooms, with total processing capability that was less than a modern digital watch. Early computers used *vacuum tubes* (grossly, a current amplifier within a glass tube) to implement logic, and a single logic gate could take up an entire board. Transistors were invented by Bell Labs in 1947 [1], allowing an order of magnitude reduction in the size of a logic gate implementation. However, transistors were packaged individually, and computers still required a large number of circuit boards to implement. In 1958, Jack Kilby, a researcher at Texas Instruments Inc. created the first integrated circuit [1], which is a silicon substrate upon which circuits with multiple transistors can be fabricated (the slang term *chip* is now commonly applied to integrated circuits). As integrated circuit fabrication techniques evolved, the size of integrated circuit transistors steadily decreased, allowing increasing numbers of transistors to be placed on the same silicon substrate. In 1971, Intel® developed a set of four integrated circuits that implemented a 4-bit computer [1]. The data paths were 4 bits, much like the number sequencing computer of Chapter 2. One chip, the 4004, implemented the instruction decode and execution (the *central processing unit*, or CPU), while the other chips implemented the memory and input/output. The term *microprocessor* (μP) was applied to this chipset, as it was a very small (micro) processing engine. The 4004 chip is generally regarded as the world's first microprocessor. Integrated circuit technology has continually improved since the 4004, producing two distinct paths of microprocessor evolution. One evolution path has stressed high performance, using the increasing number of transistors to build larger internal data paths (up to 64 bits) and registers, advanced numerical processing, and support for very large memory spaces. These microprocessors are referred to as *general purpose microprocessors* and expect programs and data to be stored in memory external to the microprocessor. General-purpose microprocessors require external support chips, known as a *chipset*, that allow them to interface with memory and input/output devices. Examples of general purpose microprocessors are the Intel Itanium®, the Advanced Micro Devices Athlon®, and the IBM PowerPC® families. Because of shrinking transistor size, it is now possible to integrate multiple high performance CPUs on the same chip, as evidenced by the Intel Core™2 and AMD Phenom™ processors that each have four cores.

The other microprocessor evolution path has stressed higher integration and lower cost, with the goal of producing a single-chip solution to problems requiring a stored program machine approach. The term microcontroller (μC) is generally applied to these devices. A microcontroller typically expects its program and data to be stored on-chip, with any logic required for external input/output devices also integrated into the same device. Thus, a microcontroller implements all of the components of a computer—control, memory, and input/output—in one chip. Microcontroller solutions are usually very cost sensitive, so applying exactly the right amount of processing power to a problem to minimize cost is important. As such, a large number of microcontroller families are available from 8 bits to 32 bits, with widely varying amounts of on-chip memory and different combinations of input/output interface options (whose number and variety grow each year).

Microcontroller versions of general purpose microprocessors have also been introduced over the years, so the distinction between a microcontroller and a microprocessor has become somewhat blurred and in some cases is an arbitrary labeling. In this book, the term *microcontroller* is applied to devices in the PIC24 family, but the term microprocessor is used any time a more general labeling is desired.

THE PIC24 MICROCONTROLLER FAMILY

The PIC24 microcontroller family, created by Microchip Technology Inc., is the focus of this book for discussing microprocessor programming, architecture, and interfacing topics. At the time of this writing, the two branches of the PIC24 family tree are the PIC24H and the PIC24F. The PIC24H is the high-speed branch, featuring a 3.0 V to 3.6 V external supply voltage and a maximum execution speed of 40 million instructions per second (MIPS). The PIC24F family is a lower-speed variant that uses an external supply voltage in the range of 2.0 V to 3.6 V and has a maximum execution speed of 16 MIPS. There are many versions of PIC24H/PIC24F microcontrollers available that differ in on-chip memory size, number of I/O pins, and on-chip peripheral features. However, all of the PIC24 family members use the same *instruction set architecture* (ISA). In fact, the PIC24 instruction set architecture is a subset of the dsPIC30/dsPIC33 ISA, another 16-bit microcontroller family from Microchip. In the hardware chapters of this book, the particular PIC24 microcontroller used for example purposes is the PIC24HJ32GP202 (the GP stands for *general purpose*, the 32 indicates the program memory size in kilobinary bytes). The reader's introduction to the PIC24 family begins with the instruction set architecture, and a good place to start is with a simplified block diagram of the processor core as shown in Figure 3.1 (a more complete architectural diagram is found in Appendix A).

The size of the internal data paths of the PIC24 CPU is 16 bits, so it is referred to as a 16-bit microcontroller. This means that the natural size for computations is 16 bits; arithmetic operations such as additions and subtractions that operate on 16-bit data or 8-bit data can be specified with one instruction. Operations on data larger than 16 bits can be performed but require multiple instructions to accomplish. The PIC24 instruction set defines 71 distinct instructions, of which the majority require 24 bits (3 bytes) to encode. The term *instruction word* is used to refer to a 24-bit machine code value. Two instruction types require two instruction words (6 bytes) to encode. The instruction register in Figure 3.1 contains the instruction word that is currently being executed. The arithmetic/logic unit (ALU) in Figure 3.1 is the combinational logic that performs operations such as addition, subtraction, bitwise AND/OR/XOR, and so forth. The left-hand ALU input is from a register bank of 16 *working registers* named W0-W15, each of which is 16 bits wide. The right-hand ALU input is connected to the *X-data bus,* which means that this operand can be from many different sources, with the most common sources being data memory or a working register. The ALU output is tied to the X-data bus, with the most common destination being data memory or a working register.

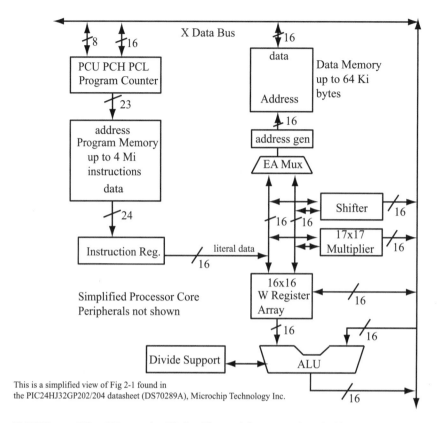

FIGURE 3.1 PIC24 CPU core simplified architectural diagram. (Adapted with permission of the copyright owner, Microchip Technology, Incorporated. All rights reserved. No further reprints or reproduction may be made without Microchip Inc.'s prior written consent.)

PROGRAM MEMORY ORGANIZATION

Figure 3.1 shows that the PIC24 µC has separate memories for program instructions and data. This type of arrangement is known as a *Harvard* architecture, as early electromechanical calculators such as the Harvard Mark I [1] read instructions from punched tape, with memory used only for storing data. Most microprocessors store programs and data in the same memory, which means that instructions can access memory that contains instructions as easily as locations that contain data. The majority of PIC24 instructions can only access data memory; a few special mechanisms are provided enabling instructions to access program memory. The *program counter* (PC) is a 23-bit register that provides the address for accessing program memory for instruction fetch. Figure 3.2 illustrates how the PC value is used to access an instruction word in program memory. Even though an instruction word is 24 bits (3 bytes), it is actually more convenient to think of an instruction word as being 32 bits that consists of a least significant word (LSW) and most significant

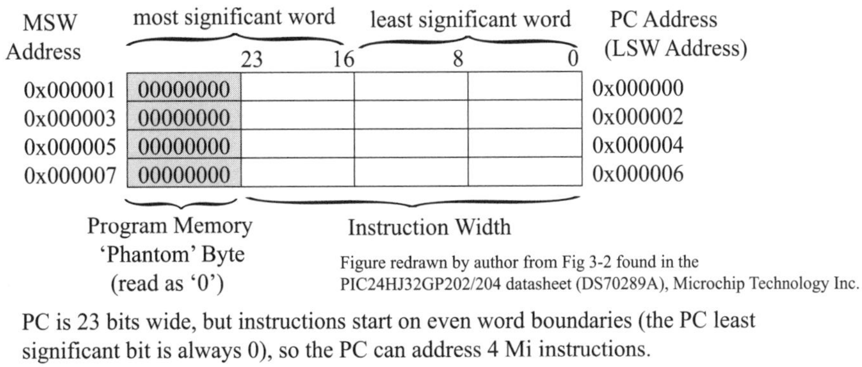

FIGURE 3.2 Program memory addressing. (Adapted with permission of the copyright owner, Microchip Technology, Incorporated. All rights reserved. No further reprints or reproduction may be made without Microchip Inc.'s prior written consent.)

word (MSW), each 16 bits wide. The upper 8 bits of the most significant word are unimplemented and read as zeros; this is the *phantom byte* shown in Figure 3.2. In this model, program memory is addressable in 16-bit words, and the PC always points to the beginning of an instruction word, or the least significant word. This means that the least significant bit of the PC is always 0, and that the upper 22 bits of the PC contain the address of one instruction word out of a possible $2^{22} = 4$ Mi instruction locations. At the time of the writing of this text, no PIC24 microcontroller physically implemented the full 4 Mi instruction space supported by the architecture definition. Circa 2008, PIC24 family members offer a wide range of physical memory sizes ranging from 6 Ki instructions up to approximately 85.5 Ki instructions, with new variants being regularly introduced.

Program memory is *nonvolatile,* meaning the memory contents are retained when power is removed. Some form of nonvolatile memory is required for any practical computer system, as this provides the instructions that are executed when power is applied. The PIC24 program memory is flash programmable, meaning that it can be electrically erased and programmed. Other types of nonvolatile memory are one-time-programmable (OTP), meaning it cannot be erased once programmed, and mask-programmed read-only memory (ROM), which means the memory contents are determined at memory manufacture time and cannot be changed. Read operations on flash memory are fast, in the tens of nanoseconds, but write operations require more time with a minimum of 20 µs required to write one program word.

DATA MEMORY ORGANIZATION

Figure 3.3 shows that the data memory address space is 64 KiB total and is organized as 16-bit words, with the lower 8 bits referred to as the *least significant byte* (LSB) and the upper 8 bits as the *most significant byte* (MSB). Observe that the LSB and

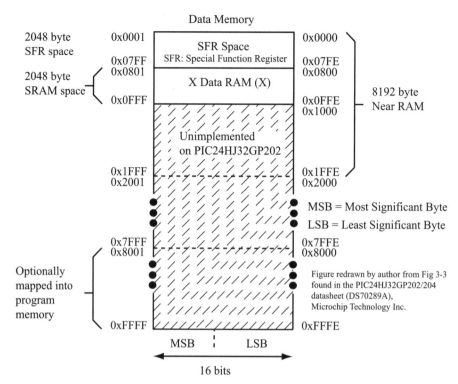

FIGURE 3.3 Data memory organization for the PIC24HJ32GP202. (Adapted with permission of the copyright owner, Microchip Technology, Incorporated. All rights reserved. No further reprints or reproduction may be made without Microchip Inc.'s prior written consent.)

MSB acronyms use a capital *B* in reference to *byte;* the acronyms LSb and MSb are reserved for least significant bit and most significant bit, respectively. Data memory is *byte addressable,* which means that the MSB and LSB portions of a 16-bit word can be modified individually. LSB addresses are at even locations, while MSB addresses are at odd locations. Data memory is *volatile,* meaning that its contents are lost if power is removed. Data memory is divided into the following sections:

■ **Special Function Registers.** The first 2048 locations of data memory (0x0000 to 0x07FF) are reserved for special function registers (SFR). An SFR is associated with some specific functionality implemented in the PIC24 µC. From an assembly language viewpoint, SFRs are treated in the same manner as a non-SFR data memory location, but their actual physical implementation is much different and depends upon the particular SFR. Most SFRs serve as data and control registers for on-chip peripherals such as the timers, the analog-to-digital converter, various serial interfaces, etc. The W0-W15 working registers are SFRs, as well as the Program Counter. Even though each SFR is assigned a specific address, it is more common to refer to an SFR by its name rather than its location.

■ **Data RAM.** Data memory locations that are not SFRs are referred to by various names such as *file registers, data RAM,* and *X data.* Data RAM is used for variable storage by user programs, but is also used as a side effect of instruction execution in some cases (i.e., the storage of a return address by a subroutine call, covered in Chapter 6). As with program memory, the amount of data RAM physically implemented is dependent upon the particular PIC24 μC. However, all PIC24 μCs have some amount of data RAM, and this begins at location 0x0800.

■ **Near Data Memory.** The first 8192 locations in data memory are known as *near RAM,* and certain instruction forms can only access data memory locations in near RAM. Many PIC24 μC variants have physical data RAM that does not exceed the boundaries of near data space, and thus this distinction is not important in those devices. The assembly language examples in this text generally assume that all data RAM is located in near RAM. The PIC24HJ32GP202 μC used in the hardware chapters of this text implements 2048 bytes of data RAM, and thus all of its data RAM is in near RAM. While 2048 bytes of RAM seems tiny compared to the millions (and in many implementations, billions) of RAM bytes in a personal computer that contains a general purpose microprocessor, it is a typical data memory size for microcontrollers.

■ **Program Space Visibility Area.** The upper 32 Ki of data memory is also known as the *program space visibility* (PSV) area, which allows a user program to access non-volatile data stored in program memory. The PSV is discussed in more detail in Chapter 6.

■ **DMA RAM.** Some PIC24 μCs have a portion of data RAM implemented as *direct memory access* (DMA) RAM. The DMA RAM and associated DMA peripheral block allow some on-chip peripherals such as the analog-to-digital converter to transfer data to DMA RAM without intervention by the CPU core (i.e., without executing assembly language instruction for performing this data movement). Chapter 13 contains further discussion of DMA RAM and its usage.

The sizes of program, data memory, and DMA RAM memories for some PIC24H variants are listed in Table 3.1.

ARRANGEMENT OF MULTIBYTE VALUES IN DATA MEMORY

This book's assembly language and *C* programs use 8-bit, 16-bit, and 32-bit data sizes. Table 3.2 shows the unsigned ranges for these data sizes; Chapter 5 discusses signed data ranges for these same data sizes. As previously discussed,

TABLE 3.1 Some PIC24 microcontroller memory sizes.

Device	Program Memory (bytes)	Data Memory (bytes)	DMA RAM (bytes)
PIC24HJ12GP202	12 Ki	1024	0
PIC24HJ32GP202	32 Ki	2048	0
PIC24HJ64GP510	64 Ki	8192	2048
PIC24HJ128GP510	128 Ki	8192	2048
PIC24HJ256GP610	256 Ki	16384	2048

the lower byte of a 16-bit or 32-bit value is referred to as the least significant byte (LSB), while the upper byte is referred to as the most significant byte (MSB). Using a 16-bit or 32-bit variable instead of an 8-bit variable allows a larger number range to be represented, at the cost of requiring more data memory bytes.

TABLE 3.2 Unsigned data ranges.

Size	Unsigned Range
8 bits	0 to $2^8 - 1$ (0 to 255, 0 to 0xFF)
16 bits	0 to $2^{16} - 1$ (0 to 65535, 0 to 0xFFFF)
32 bits	0 to $2^{32} - 1$ (0 to 4294967295, 0 to 0xFFFFFFFF)

When a 16-bit or 32-bit value is stored in data memory in the PIC24 μC, the bytes are arranged in least significant byte to most significant byte in increasing memory locations. This arrangement is known as *little-endian* byte order, and it is in common use in many microprocessor implementations. Some microprocessor families use the reverse arrangement of most significant byte to least significant byte in increasing memory locations, which is referred to as *big-endian* byte order. There is no inherent advantage to little-endian or big-endian byte order (computer architects have adopted these terms in a tongue-in-cheek reference to the book *Gulliver's Travels* published by Jonathon Swift in 1726, in which Lilliputians and Blefuscans disagree over which end of the egg to crack first, the little end or the big end, when enjoying boiled eggs). The microprocessor architects determine the byte ordering choice during the microprocessor's design phase. Figure 3.4 illustrates the storage of a 16-bit number and a 32-bit number in memory, with the memory shown in both 8-bit and 16-bit widths for

Assume the 16-bit value 0x8B1A stored at location 0x1000

Assume the 32-bit value 0xF19025AC stored at location 0x1002

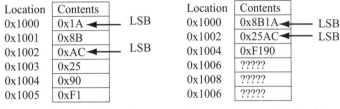

The LSB of a 16-bit or 32-bit value must begin at an even address (be *word aligned*).

FIGURE 3.4   Storage of multibyte data.

additional clarity. Memory diagrams in this book always show memory addresses increasing as one progresses down the page, and generally data memory is shown as 16 bits wide. The use of 32-bit data in assembly language programs is covered in Chapter 5.

A requirement of the PIC24 µC architecture is that 16-bit and 32-bit data must have the LSB start at an even location (i.e., be *word aligned*) if the data are to be accessed by PIC24 assembly language instructions in 16-bit chunks (also known as *word* mode). It is the responsibility of the assembly language programmer to ensure that 16-bit and 32-bit values are word-aligned in memory. A word access to an odd address is known as a *misaligned access,* which generates an *exception* that triggers execution of an *exception handler,* whose default action is to reset the processor (exceptions are covered in Chapter 9). A misaligned write operation does not alter data memory contents. The assembly language and C programs in this book assume that 16-bit and 32-bit values are correctly word-aligned in data memory. When writing assembly language programs by hand, it is often necessary to insert extra bytes in order to maintain this alignment.

DATA TRANSFER INSTRUCTIONS AND ADDRESSING MODES

One fundamental instruction class found within any microprocessor is the *data transfer* class. Data transfer instructions copy data between registers and locations in data memory, or write a value stored in the instruction word into data memory or registers. In most microprocessors, registers are separate from data memory, and instructions contain addresses for both registers and memory. However, special function registers on the PIC24 µC are simply data memory locations with addresses of 0x0000-0x07FF, making the terms *register* and *data memory location* interchangeable. This is why data memory locations are sometimes referred to as *file registers* in the Microchip PIC24 µC documentation.

The execution of data transfer instructions between data memory locations is described as:

$$(\text{src}) \rightarrow \text{dst} \quad \text{"copy the content of source location } \textit{src} \text{ to destination location } \textit{dst}\text{"}$$

The → symbol is a transfer symbol, and *(src) → dst* is called *register transfer notation,* which is used to symbolically describe instruction execution. The parenthesis "()" on the left-hand side is read as "content of," and indicates that we are transferring the content of a source memory location or register to a destination memory location or register. This is a common notation used to describe microprocessor instruction actions, and both register transfer notation and word descriptions are used in this book for discussing instruction execution.

REGISTER DIRECT ADDRESSING

For the PIC24 µC, instructions that copy data between data memory locations are called *move* instructions and the assembly language mnemonic is mov. This is somewhat unfortunate, as the word *move* implies removing data from one location and placing it in another location, but mov instructions do not affect the content of the source memory location. A mov instruction has two operands, source and destination, as noted earlier for data transfer operations. The two operands specify the addresses of the data to be moved. The method by which the address is specified is called the *addressing mode*. The simplest addressing mode is *register direct,* which specifies one of the 16 working registers. The following mov instruction copies the content of register W3 to W5:

```
mov      W3,W5        ;copy the content of W3 to W5
```

Observe that for the PIC24 mov instruction, the first register is the source and the second register is the destination; other microcontroller instruction sets may reverse this order. In this book, lowercase is generally used for assembly language mnemonics and uppercase for register names (instruction mnemonics and working register names are actually case insensitive, so upper/lower case is used for emphasis only). The mov instruction has other addressing modes that are available for both source and destination operands, namely *immediate, file register* and six types of *indirect* addressing. This chapter provides examples of register direct, immediate, and file register addressing. One form of indirect addressing is discussed as well, with detailed coverage of the various indirect addressing modes reserved for Chapter 6. Because a register placeholder in an instruction format can be one of several different addressing modes, the following register placeholder symbols are used when discussing instruction formats:

- **Wn:** register direct addressing; *Wn* specifies of one of W0, W1, ... W15.
- **Wns:** register direct addressing; *Wns* specifies of one of W0, W1, ... W15.
- **Wnd:** register direct addressing; *Wnd* specifies one of W0, W1, ... W15.
- **Wb:** register direct addressing; *Wb* specifies one of W0, W1, ... W15.
- **WREG:** the working register, specifies W0 in file register instructions.
- **Ws:** register direct (*Ws*) and indirect addressing modes ([*Ws*], [*Ws*++], [*Ws*−−], [++*Ws*], [−−*Ws*]); *Ws* specifies one of W0, W1, ... W15.
- **Wd:** register direct (*Wd*) and indirect addressing modes ([*Wd*], [*Wd*++], [*Wd*−−], [++*Wd*], [−−*Wd*]); *Wd* specifies one of W0, W1, ... W15.
- **Wso:** all of the addressing modes of **Ws**, with the additional mode of register offset indirect [*Wso* + *Wb*]; *Wso* specifies one of W0, W1, ... W15.
- **Wdo:** all of the addressing modes of **Wd**, with the additional mode of register offset indirect [*Wdo* + *Wb*]; *Wdo* specifies one of W0, W1, ... W15.

For example, the general form of the previous move instruction is mov *Wso, Wdo* with each operand able to use 7 different addressing modes. Examples are:

```
mov   W2, W3         ;both source and destination use reg. direct
mov   [W2], [W3+W7]  ;both source and destination use reg. indirect
mov   [--W4], W5     ;source uses reg. indirect, dest. uses reg. direct
```

As previously mentioned, only one indirect addressing mode is discussed in this chapter; the remaining are reserved for Chapter 6.

The previous mov instruction operates in word mode, that is, the 16 bits in W3 are copied to W5. Word mode operation is the default for instructions, and the mnemonic can be written with a .w extension if desired:

```
mov.w   W3,W5        ;copy the content of W3 to W5
```

A byte mode is also available, and must be specified with a .b extension as follows:

```
mov.b   W3,W5        ;copy the content of W3.LSB to W5.LSB
```

In this case, only the LSB of W3 is copied to the LSB of W5; the MSB of W5 is unaffected. This books use the notation *Wn*.LSB and *Wn*.MSB to refer to the least significant and most significant bytes of register *Wn*, respectively. Figure 3.5 shows another example of a mov using register direct addressing.

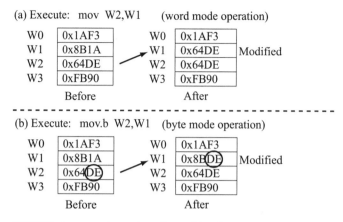

FIGURE 3.5   mov using register direct addressing.

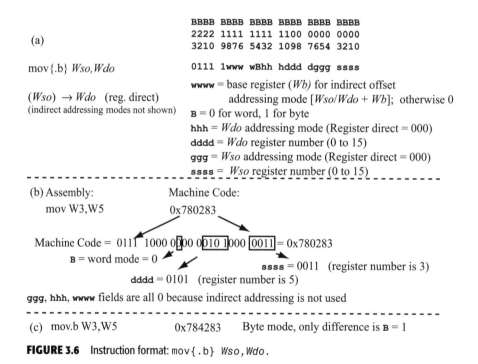

FIGURE 3.6   Instruction format: mov{.b} Wso,Wdo.

Figure 3.6a gives the instruction format for the mov.{b} Wso,Wdo instruction. Observe that the ssss bit field in the instruction format specifies the Wso register number, while the dddd bit field specifies the Wdo register number. The ggg and hhh fields specify the addressing modes of the source and destination operands, respectively. The www field is only used if a particular form of indirect addressing is used (register offset indirect). Figure 3.6b shows the conversion of the mov W3,W5 instruction to its machine code representation of 0x780283. The 3-bit code for register direct addressing is 0b000 (see Appendix A), which is used for the ggg, hhh fields since both the source and destination of the mov W3,W5 instruction uses register direct addressing. The www field is unused and can be set to 0b000 because register direct addressing, rather than indirect addressing, is used. The machine code for the mov.b W3,W5 instruction is given in Figure 3.6c with the B-field bit (byte versus word operation) being the only difference from Figure 3.6b.

This text does not attempt to discuss the instruction formats of every PIC24 instruction, but instead covers the formats of a few select instructions from the different classes of PIC24 instructions. A table of the machine code formats for all PIC24 instructions can be found in Appendix A.

FILE REGISTER ADDRESSING

File register addressing specifies a data RAM address encoded as part of the instruction machine code (in other microprocessor families, this type of addressing is called *memory direct* addressing, since the memory address is *directly* specified in the instruction word). Figure 3.7a shows the instruction format for a mov instruction whose source operand uses register direct addressing and whose destination operation uses file register addressing. This mov form only operates in word mode, so the file register address must be an even address to satisfy the word-alignment rules previously discussed. Because the file register address is word-aligned, its lower bit must be zero, so only the upper 15 bits of the 16-bit address are encoded in the instruction. The conversion of mov W3,0x1002 to machine code is given in Figure 3.7b.

(a)

mov Wn, f

```
BBBB BBBB BBBB BBBB BBBB BBBB
2222 1111 1111 1100 0000 0000
3210 9876 5432 1098 7654 3210
```

$(Wn) \rightarrow f$

```
1000 1fff ffff ffff ffff ssss
```

f ... f = upper 15 bits of 16-bit address (lower bit assumed = 0)
ssss = Wn register number (0 to 15)

- -

(b) Assembly: Machine Code:
    mov W3,0x1002   0x888013

Machine Code = 1000 1 000 1000 0000 0001 0011 = 0x888013

f ... f = 0001 0000 0000 001 0   ssss = 0011   (register number is 3)
(upper 15-bits of 0x1002)

FIGURE 3.7   Instruction format: mov Wn, f.

Figure 3.8 shows the operation of a mov W3,0x1002 instruction in word mode, causing the bytes in locations 0x1002 and 0x1003 to become copies of W3.LSB and W3.MSB, respectively.

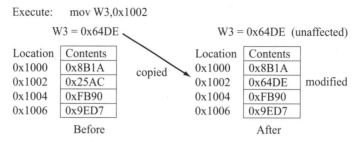

FIGURE 3.8   Example operation: mov Wn,f.

Given that there is a method for copying data from a working register to data RAM, it follows that the converse must be possible. Figure 3.9 shows the execution of the mov 0x1002,W3 instruction, which copies the content of data RAM location 0x1002 to W3. The general form of this mov form is mov f,Wn and it also can only function in word mode. See Appendix A for the machine code format of this mov type.

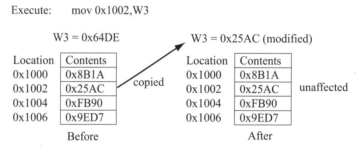

FIGURE 3.9   Example operation: mov f,Wn.

WREG—THE DEFAULT WORKING REGISTER

The astute reader may be wondering at this point how to transfer a byte between a working register and data RAM, since the mov Wn,f and mov f,Wn instructions only operate in word mode. Byte transfers between working registers and data memory are accomplished by either using the indirect addressing modes (Chapter 6) or by using a mov instruction form that uses the *default working register*. The mov{.b} WREG,f instruction format is shown in Figure 3.10. There are two important points about this instruction format. First, the default working register (WREG) is W0. Second, because only 13 bits are reserved for the data memory address, f has to be in the first 8192 locations ($2^{13} = 8192$) of data memory. As previously discussed, this area of data RAM is known as near RAM. Any PIC24 instruction that uses WREG and a file register address has this near RAM restriction.

mov{.b} WREG, *f*

(WREG) → *f*

```
BBBB BBBB BBBB BBBB BBBB BBBB
2222 1111 1111 1100 0000 0000
3210 9876 5432 1098 7654 3210

1011 0111 1B1f ffff ffff ffff
```

f … f = 13-bit address (first 8192 bytes of data memory)
B = 0 for word, 1 for byte

Assembly: Machine Code:

mov   WREG, 0x1000   0xB7B000   (**B** bit = 0 since word operation)
mov.b WREG, 0x1000   0xB7F000   (**B** bit = 1 since byte operation)
mov.b WREG, 0x1001   0xB7F001   (bytes can be written to odd addresses)

FIGURE 3.10   Instruction format: mov{.b} WREG,*f*.

Figure 3.11 illustrates a byte transfer from the LSB of W0 to memory location 0x1001 using the mov.b WREG,0x1001 instruction. While WREG is synonymous with W0 in terms of instruction execution, it is a syntax error to write this instruction form as mov.b W0,0x1001.

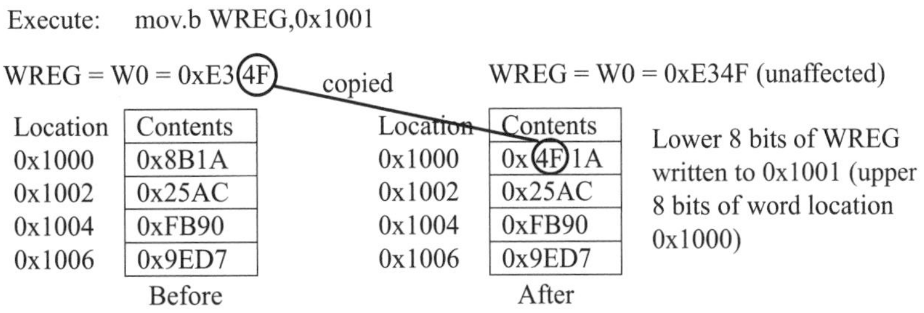

Execute: mov.b WREG,0x1001

WREG = W0 = 0xE3**4F** copied   WREG = W0 = 0xE34F (unaffected)

Location	Contents
0x1000	0x8B1A
0x1002	0x25AC
0x1004	0xFB90
0x1006	0x9ED7

Before

Location	Contents
0x1000	0x**4F**1A
0x1002	0x25AC
0x1004	0xFB90
0x1006	0x9ED7

After

Lower 8 bits of WREG written to 0x1001 (upper 8 bits of word location 0x1000)

FIGURE 3.11   Example operation: mov{.b} WREG,*f*.

To transfer the LSB of any other working register besides W0 to data RAM, execute a two-instruction sequence:

```
mov.b    Wn,W0      ;move the Wn.LSB to W0.LSB
mov.b    WREG,f     ;move W0.LSB to data memory
```

Figure 3.12 shows the format of the mov{.b} *f*{,WREG} instruction, which copies from a data memory location to either the WREG or back to itself. Observe that the D bit in the machine code selects between a destination of WREG (D bit = 0) or *f* (D bit = 1). At this point it may seem pointless to copy a data RAM value back to itself, but the usefulness of this operation is discussed in Chapter 4. Figure 3.13 shows an example operation of mov{.b} *f*{,WREG} for the case of mov.b 0x1000,WREG.

mov{.b} *f*, {WREG}

```
BBBB BBBB BBBB BBBB BBBB BBBB
2222 1111 1111 1100 0000 0000
3210 9876 5432 1098 7654 3210
```

(*f*) → *destination*

`1011 1111 1BDf ffff ffff ffff`

Destination is either *f* or WREG.

f ... **f** = 13-bit address (first 8192 bytes of data memory)
B = 0 for word, 1 for byte
D = destination = 0 for WREG, 1 for *f*

Assembly:
mov 0x1000,WREG

Machine Code:
0xBF9000

(**B** bit = 0 since word operation,
D bit = 0 since WREG destination)

mov.b 0x1000

0xBFF000

(**B** bit = 1 since byte operation,
D bit = 1 since *f* destination)

FIGURE 3.12 Instruction format: `mov{.b}` `f{,WREG}`.

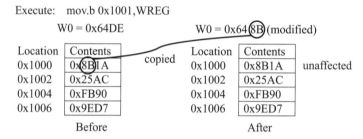

FIGURE 3.13 Example operation: `mov{.b}` `f{,WREG}`.

IMMEDIATE ADDRESSING

The *immediate addressing* mode encodes a *literal* (a constant) in the instruction word. Figure 3.14 shows the instruction format for immediate addressing used

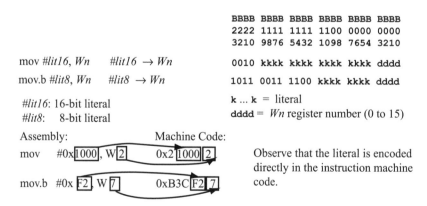

FIGURE 3.14 Instruction format: `mov #lit16 ,Wn`; `mov.b #lit8,Wn`.

in a mov instruction to load a working register with a constant. The constant is a 16-bit value if a word operation is performed and an 8-bit value if a byte operation is done. The instruction encoding is such that these are actually two different opcodes with the instruction encoding that is used dependent on the literal size.

It is common for a reader new to assembly language programming to confuse immediate addressing with file register addressing. The difference between these two addressing modes is illustrated in Figure 3.15. In Figure 3.15a, the mov #0x1000,W2 instruction (immediate addressing) copies the value 0x1000 into register W2. Contrast this with Figure 3.15b, where the mov 0x1000,W2 instruction copies the word located at data RAM location 0x01000 into W2, resulting in a modified W2 value of 0x8B1A. The # symbol used with 0x1000 differentiates immediate addressing from file register addressing. Figure 3.15c illustrates execution of a mov instruction that uses an 8-bit literal.

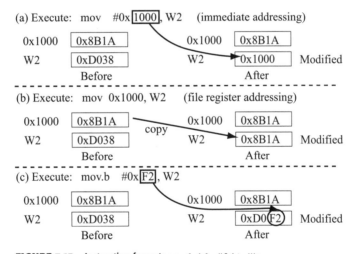

FIGURE 3.15   Instruction format: mov{.b} #lit,Wn.

INDIRECT ADDRESSING

A mov that uses one of the many forms of *indirect addressing* for both source and destination operands is:

```
mov     [Wns],[Wnd]   ;((Wns)) → (Wnd)
```

Compare this with a mov that uses register direct addressing for both operands:

```
mov      Wns,Wnd      ;(Wns) → Wnd
```

Note that the operands for the indirect addressing example use brackets [] around the Wns and Wnd operands, indicating an indirect addressing mode. The register transfer description for the indirect example has an extra set of parentheses () around both the Wns and Wnd operands. The *((Wns)) → (Wnd)* register transfer operation means the following:

■ The content of Wns, also written as *(Wns)*, is an address called the *source effective address*, abbreviated as EAs. The content of the source effective address, written as *(EAs)*, is the source operand. Thus, the source operand is fully specified as *((Wns))*.

■ The content of Wnd, also written as *(Wnd)*, is an address called the *destination effective address*, abbreviated as EAd. The mov copies the source operand to the memory location specified by the destination effective address, or in register transfer notation: *(EAs)→ EAd* or *((Wns))→(Wnd)*.

A mov instruction that uses indirect addressing for one or both of its operands has an instruction format much like the mov instructions that use immediate or direct addressing modes discussed earlier. The details of the instruction format for indirect addressing mov instruction are left as an exercise for the reader.

Figure 3.16 shows three mov instruction examples. Figure 3.16a shows a mov W0,W1 instruction; note that this uses register direct addressing for both source and destination operands. The end result of Figure 3.16a is that the content of W0 is copied to W1, modifying W1 to contain 0x1000. Figure 3.16b shows a mov [W0],[W1] instruction that uses register indirect addressing for both source and destination operands. The source operand's effective address is the content of W0, or 0x1000. The destination effective address is the content of W1, or 0x1002. Thus, the mov's execution copies the content of location 0x1000 to location 0x1002, modifying location 0x1002 to contain 0x8BFA. The final example in Figure 3.16c shows a mov W0,[W1] instruction, illustrating that different addressing modes can be used for the source (register direct) and destination (register indirect) operands. The mov instruction's execution copies the content of W0 to the destination effective address, which is the content of W1 (0x1002 as seen in the figure), thus modifying location 0x1002 to contain 0x1000.

There are other types of indirect addressing modes; these are reserved for Chapter 6 as indirect addressing is better appreciated when discussed in the context of pointer operations in the *C* language.

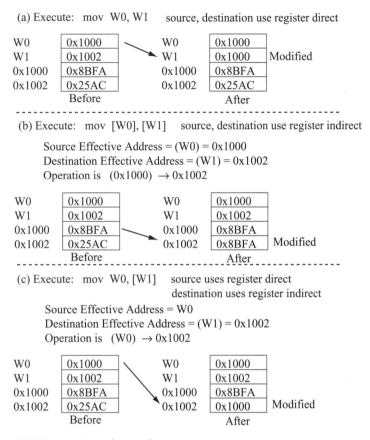

FIGURE 3.16   Example operation: mov.{b} *[Wns]*, *[Wnd]*.

INSTRUCTION SET REGULARITY

At this point the reader may be somewhat dizzy from the number of different mov types that have been covered and also fearful of the remaining 70 instructions yet to be discussed. In an attempt to put the reader's mind at ease, the authors assert that the reader will soon discover that there is a *regularity* to the PIC24 instruction set architecture. This means that once the rules are understood for one instruction class, the same rules apply to other instructions in the same class. The number of instruction classes is small, so there are not very many different rule sets that must be understood. Rest assured that the task is not as difficult as it may seem at this particular point!

Sample Question: *Assume that registers and memory contain the values of Table 3.3 at the START of EACH of the following instructions. Give the register or memory location that is modified by the instruction and its new value.*

TABLE 3.3   Register memory contents.

Location	Value	Location	Value
W0	0x1000	0x1000	0x382A
W1	0x1003	0x1002	0xFB80
W2	0x8345	0x1004	0xFFFF

1. mov W2, W0
2. mov 0x1000, W0
3. mov #0x1000, W0
4. mov W2, [W0]
5. mov.b W2, W0
6. mov W2, [W1]
7. mov 0x1000, WREG
8. mov 0x1000

Answers:
1. This performs (W2) → W0, or 0x8345 → W0, so W0 is modified to 0x8345.
2. This performs (0x1000) → W0, or 0x382A → W0, so W0 is modified to 0x382A.
3. This performs 0x1000 → W0, so W0 is modified to 0x1000.
4. This performs (W2) → (W0), or 0x8345 → 0x1000, so location 0x1000 is modified to 0x8345.
5. This performs (W2.LSB) → W0.LSB, so W0 is modified to 0x1045.
6. This performs (W2) → (W1), or 0x8345 → 0x1003, which is an illegal operation because a word operation is being done to an odd address. Location 0x1003 is not modified, and a misaligned address exception is generated (Chapter 9).
7. This performs (0x1000) → WREG, or 0x382A → W0, so W0 is modified to 0x382A.
8. This performs (0x1000) → 0x1000, or 0x382A → 0x1000, location 0x1000 is left unchanged as 0x382A.

BASIC ARITHMETIC AND CONTROL INSTRUCTIONS

Two other classes of microprocessor instructions are arithmetic and control classes. All microprocessors have arithmetic instructions such as addition, subtraction, increment (+1), and decrement (−1) instructions. Some microprocessors, such as the PIC24, also have instructions for multiplication and division; these can be implemented using addition, subtraction, and shifts if dedicated multiplication and division instructions are not present.

THREE-OPERAND ADDITION/SUBTRACTION

The PIC24 supports both a three-operand form and a two-operand form for addition and subtraction operations. The first three-operand forms to be discussed are:

```
add{.b} Wb,Ws,Wd          ;(Wb) + (Ws) → Wd
sub{.b} Wb,Ws,Wd          ;(Wb) − (Ws) → Wd
subr{.b} Wb,Ws,Wd         ;(Ws) − (Wb) → Wd
```

Please recall that the *Ws, Wd* symbols allow both register direct and register indirect addressing modes (with the exception of register offset indirect). The *Wb* operand is limited to register direct addressing. Examples of different addressing mode forms for these instructions are:

```
add W2,[W8],W3            ;reg. indirect for Ws, reg. direct for Wd
sub.b W3,W4,W5            ;reg. direct for Ws, Wd
subr W9,[W4++],[−−W8]     ;these indirect modes covered in Chapter 6
```

The advantage of a three-operand addition or subtraction is that the values of the two source operands can be preserved if desired. Figure 3.17 shows three addition examples using register direct addressing. Figure 3.17a illustrates execution of the add W0,W1,W2 instruction, while Figure 3.17b shows the same operation in byte mode. Figure 3.17c demonstrates that the three operands can be any of the working registers, including having all three operands from the same register.

Three subtraction examples are given in Figure 3.18. Because subtraction is not commutative, the instructions sub W0,W1,W2 and sub W1,W0,W2 are not mathematically equivalent. When using a subtraction instruction, one must remember that sub *Wb,Ws,Wd* implements (*Wb*) − (*Ws*) and not vice versa, as shown in Figures 3.18a and 3.18b. Byte mode operation for subtraction is shown in Figure 3.18c. The subr instruction forms perform the reverse subtraction operation, so subr *Wb,Ws,Wd* implements (*Ws*) − (*Wb*).

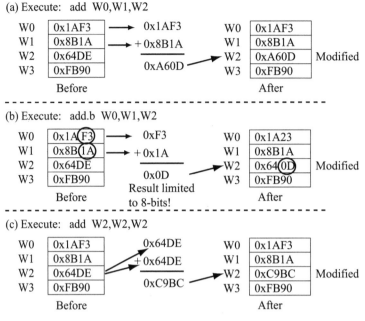

FIGURE 3.17   Instruction execution: add{.b} *Wb,Ws,Wd*.

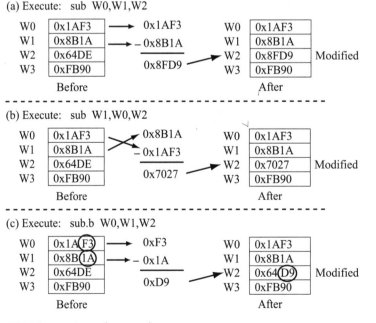

FIGURE 3.18   Instruction execution: sub{.b} *Wb,Ws,Wd*.

The three-operand forms for addition/subtraction using immediate addressing are:

```
add{.b} Wb,#lit5,Wd        ;(Wb) + #lit5 → Wd
sub{.b} Wb,#lit5,Wd        ;(Wb) − #lit5 → Wd
subr{.b} Wb,#lit5,Wd       ;#lit5 − (Wb) → Wd
```

The *#lit5* operand is a 5-bit unsigned literal, meaning the number range that can be encoded is 0 to 31. When this 5-bit unsigned literal is used in an operation with an 8-bit or 16-bit operand, its upper bits are filled with zeros to match the length of the other operand. This is known as *zero extension,* and this is discussed in more detail in Chapter 4. The previous addition and subtraction instructions are limited to a 5-bit literal because of the number of available bits in the 24-bit instruction word after the base register *Wb* and destination register *Wd* locations are encoded. Indirect addressing modes can be used with the *Wd* operand, while the *Wb* operand is limited to register direct addressing. These instructions form a convenient mechanism for adding or subtracting a small constant using a single instruction. A larger constant can be added or subtracted by the two-instruction sequence:

```
mov #lit16,Wx              ;#lit16 → Wx
add/sub Wb,Wx,Wd           ;Wb +/− Wx → Wd
```

TWO-OPERAND ADDITION/SUBTRACTION

The two-operand addition/subtraction forms use file register addressing and the default working registers as follows:

```
add{.b} f                  ;(f) + (WREG) → f
add{.b} f,WREG             ;(f) + (WREG) → WREG
sub{.b} f                  ;(f) − (WREG) → f
sub{.b} f,WREG             ;(f) − (WREG) → WREG
subr{.b} f                 ;(WREG) − (f) → f
subr{.b} f,WREG            ;(WREG) − (f) → WREG
```

As with the mov form that used these addressing modes, the data RAM address *f* must be in near RAM (the first 8192 locations). The advantage of the two-operand addition/subtraction forms is that a value can be added to a data memory location without first copying that location's value into a working register. The disadvantages of the two-operand addition/subtraction forms are that one of the source operands must be overwritten (destroyed) and the restriction to near memory for the data memory address.

Two-operand addition/subtraction using immediate addressing and register direct addressing are:

```
add{.b} #lit10,Wn     ;(Wn) + #lit10 → Wn
sub{.b} #lit10,Wn     ;(Wn) − #lit10 → Wn
```

The #*lit10* operand is a 10-bit unsigned literal whose range is 0 to 1023 for word operations and 0 to 255 for byte operations. These instructions forms are limited to register direct addressing for the *Wn* operand; there is not a subr form available.

INCREMENT, DECREMENT INSTRUCTIONS

Various increment and decrement instructions are provided; the first forms to be discussed are:

```
inc{.b} Ws,Wd        ;(Ws) + 1 → Wd
inc2{.b} Ws,Wd       ;(Ws) + 2 → Wd
dec{.b} Ws,Wd        ;(Ws) − 1 → Wd
dec2{.b} Ws,Wd       ;(Ws) − 2 → Wd
```

These increment/decrement instructions use register direct and register indirect addressing modes for the source and destination operands. The inc2/dec2 instructions provide increment/decrement by 2 instead of by 1, which is useful when incrementing a register containing a data memory address and one wishes the address to be incremented to the next 16-bit location. The reader may wonder why these instructions are included when it appears that the same functionality can be accomplished by use of the add/sub instructions using the short literal (#*lit5*). The answer is that the indirect modes available for the source operand (*Ws*) in the increment/decrement instructions provide more flexibility than add/sub instructions with a short literal. If the source operand uses register direct addressing, then there is no advantage either way in using the increment/decrement instructions versus using the add/sub instruction with a short literal.

Some additional forms of increment/decrement that use file register direct and the working register are:

```
inc{.b} f            ;(f) + 1 → f
inc{.b} f,WREG       ;(f) + 1 → WREG
inc2{.b} f           ;(f) + 2 → f
inc2{.b} f,WREG      ;(f) + 2 → WREG
dec{.b} f            ;(f) − 1 → f
dec{.b} f,WREG       ;(f) − 1 → WREG
dec2{.b} f           ;(f) − 2 → f
dec2{.b} f,WREG      ;(f) − 2 → WREG
```

As previously seen with the mov instruction using this addressing mode, *f* is limited to near RAM, the lowest 8192 locations in data memory.

PROGRAM CONTROL: *goto*

Control instructions affect the program counter content, with the simplest form being a goto, an unconditional transfer of control. Figure 3.19 shows the machine code format for the goto instruction.

```
                                              BBBB BBBB BBBB BBBB BBBB BBBB
                                              2222 1111 1111 1100 0000 0000
                                              3210 9876 5432 1098 7654 3210

goto    Expr      lit23 → PC                  0000 0100 nnnn nnnn nnnn nnn0

                                              0000 0000 0000 0000 0nnn nnnn
```

Expr is a label or expression that is resolved by the linker to a 23-bit program memory address known as the *target address* (this must be an even address).

nn ... nn0 = 23-bit value that is loaded into the program counter.

The GOTO instruction requires two instruction words:

Assembly:	Machine Code:	
goto 0x000800	0x04 0800	First word
	0x0000 00	Second word

FIGURE 3.19   Instruction format: `goto Expr`.

The `nnn ... nn` bits encoded in the `goto` machine code shown in Figure 3.19 specifies the program memory location that control is transferred to, which is known as the *target address*. The `nnn ... nn` bits form a 22-bit value that specifies one of the 4 Mi (2^{22}) possible instruction word locations; this 22-bit value is con-catenated with a "0" bit to form a 23-bit value that is loaded into the 23-bit pro-gram counter. The `goto` instruction requires two instruction words (6 bytes), with the second instruction word containing bits 22 through 16 of the target address and the first instruction word containing the remaining bits of the target address. There is only one other instruction in the PIC24 instruction set that requires two instruc-tion words to encode (a `call` instruction) and it also specifies a target address in the program address space. The `call` instruction is also in the control class, and its usage is covered in Chapter 6.

Sample Question: ***Assume that registers and memory contain the values of Table 3.4 at the START of EACH of the following instructions. Give the register or memory location that is modified by the instruction and its new value.***

TABLE 3.4   Register memory contents.

Location	Value	Location	Value
W0	0x1000	0x1000	0x382A
W1	0x1003	0x1002	0xFB80
W2	0x8345	0x1004	0xFFFF

```
1. add W2,W1,W0
2. add 0x1000,WREG
3. sub.b W0,#5,W1
4. inc [W0],W1
5. dec.b W0,[W1]
6. sub W2,[W0],[W0]
7. dec2.b W2,W1
8. inc 0x1004
```

Answers:

1. This performs (W2) + (W1) → W0, or 0x8345 + 0x1003 → W0, so W0 is modified to 0x9348.
2. This performs (0x1000) + W0 → W0, or 0x382A + 0x1000 → W0, so W0 is modified to 0x482A.
3. This performs (W0.LSB) − 5 → W1.LSB, or 0x00 − 5 → W1.LSB, so W1 is modified to 0x10FB.
4. This performs ((W0)) +1 → W1, or (0x1000)+1 → W1, or 0x382A + 1 → W1, so location W1 is modified to 0x382B.
5. This performs (W0.LSB) − 1 → (W1), or 0x00 − 1 → 0x1003, so 0x1003 is modified to 0xFF. The word at location 0x1002 now reads as 0xFF80.
6. This performs (W2) − ((W0)) → (W0), or 0x8345 − (0x1000) → 0x1000, or 0x8345 − 0x382A → 0x1000, so location 0x1000 is modified to 0x4B1B.
7. This performs (W2.LSB) −2 → W1.LSB, or 0x45−2 → W1.LSB, so W1 is modified to 0x1043.
8. This performs (0x1004) + 1 → 0x1004, or 0xFFFF + 1 → 0x1004, location 0x1004 is modified to 0x0000 (0xFFFF + 1 wraps back to 0x0000).

A PIC24 ASSEMBLY LANGUAGE PROGRAM

At this point, we have more than enough instructions to write a simple PIC24 assembly language program. In this book, programs are first written in *C* then translated (*compiled*) to assembly language. This is done for the instructional purpose of illustrating the linkage between high-level programming language statements and their implementation in assembly language. Furthermore, programs written in a high-level language such as *C* improves the clarity of the program's functionality, as assembly language can be obtuse, especially for readers new to assembly language programming. This also prepares you for the hardware interfacing chapters of this book, which uses the *C* language for all its example programs. If you are new to the *C* language, do not worry, as *C* language statements are introduced gradually and are fully explained. A previous exposure to any modern programming language is all that is necessary to understand the *C* program examples used in this book. Example *C* programs only use those *C* language statements necessary to demonstrate PIC24 µC capabilities and do not attempt to cover the entire *C* language. A program called a *compiler* is generally used to perform the translation from *C* to assembly language. This book uses the MPLAB PIC24 compiler for this task when *C* programs illustrating microcontroller hardware interfacing are covered beginning in Chapter 8.

Table 3.5 shows the standard *C* data types of char, short, int, long, and long long in their unsigned and signed varieties and how these types are referred to in this book. The standard *C* types represent different sized variables, with a char variable always requiring 8 bits (1 byte). A problem with the standard *C* data types is that the sizes of the int and long types are compiler-dependent. For example, in the *C* compiler used in this book for the PIC24 µC, the int and long types are 16 bits and 32 bits. However, these same types may be 32 bits and 64 bits for a different processor/compiler combination. It has become common practice for *C* programmers, especially when writing code for microcontrollers, to create user-defined types that expose the variable size because variable size affects both data and program storage requirements, along with program execution time. So, referring to Table 3.5 for an example, an unsigned int variable is declared as a uint16 variable in any *C* program used in this book.

TABLE 3.5 *C* data types.

Standard	This Book	PIC24 Size (in bits)
unsigned char	uint8	8
unsigned short	uint16	16
unsigned int	uint16	16
unsigned long	uint32	32
unsigned long long	uint64	64
signed char	int8	8
signed short	int16	16
signed int	int16	16
signed long	int32	32
signed long long	int64	64

The type definitions of Table 3.5 are declared in a header file that is included by the compiler during the compilation process for the *C* examples in this book; these type definitions are:

```
typedef unsigned char        uint8;      //8 bits
typedef unsigned short       uint16;     //16 bits
typedef unsigned long        uint32;     //32 bits
typedef unsigned long long   uint64;     //64 bits
typedef signed char          int8;       //8 bits
typedef signed short         int16;      //16 bits
typedef signed long          int32;      //32 bits
typedef signed long long     int64;      //64 bits
```

Be sure to include these type definitions when using any of the *C* examples found in this book.

C-TO-PIC24 ASSEMBLY LANGUAGE

A *C* program that uses the data transfer and arithmetic operations discussed so far is shown in Listing 3.1. Line numbers have been added for clarity, but would not be part of the actual *C* program source code.

LISTING 3.1   A "simple" *C* program.

```
(1) #define avalue 100
(2) uint8 i,j,k;
(3) main(void) {
(4)    i = avalue;        // avalue is 100 (0x64)
(5)    i = i + 1;         // i++, i = 101 (0x65)
(6)    j = i;             // j is 101 (0x65)
(7)    j = j - 1;         // j--, j is 100 (0x64)
(8)    k = j + i;         // k = 201 (0xC9)
(9) }
```

The *C* language is case sensitive, with all reserved key words, such as void, being low-ercase. Comments begin with two / / characters and can start anywhere on a line (this is actually a *C++* language comment but is accepted by modern *C* compilers). Comments can also be delimited by a starting /* and an ending */ with the delimiters spanning multiple lines. Simple *C* statements are terminated by a semicolon (";"). Compound statements, which are composed of multiple simple *C* statements, are bracketed by {}. Line 1 contains a define statement, which is a method for assigning a symbolic name to a value. Use of defines for constant values usually improves code clarity. Line 2 defines three variables of type uint8 (this code assumes that uint8 has been declared earlier, typically in an included header file), which from Table 3.5 means that each variable is 8 bits, or 1 byte, and represents unsigned data (unsigned char). The unsigned modifier tag combined with the 8-bit data size gives a value range of 0 to 255 for each variable. Chapter 5 discusses the difference between unsigned and signed data types and the effect this has on arithmetic operations. Line 3 defines the entry point for the *C* program, which must be named main. The (void) after the main label indicates that main receives no parameters, which will always be the case for *C* programs in this book. The body of the main code is a compound *C* statement, enclosed by {}. Line 4 assigns the constant value 100 to the variable i. Line 5 increments i by 1; i contains the value 101 after execution of this statement. The *C* statement i++, where ++ is the *C* increment operator, could be used instead of i=i+1. Line 6 copies the value of i to j. Line 7 decrements j, so j contains the value 100 after execution of this statement. The statement j-- could be used instead of j=j-1.

The first step in translating (i.e., *compiling*) the program in Listing 3.1 to PIC24 assembly language is to choose locations for the variables i, j, and k. This can be any data RAM location that is not assigned to a special function register. We could also simply use working registers to represent variables, and we do this when *C* functions are covered in Chapter 6. In this example, we will use data RAM, and for simplicity, we use the first available data RAM locations, which are 0x0800 for i, 0x0801 for j, and 0x0802 for k (recall that data RAM locations 0x0000 through 0x07FF are reserved for special function registers). Figure 3.20 shows the program of Listing 3.1 translated to PIC24 assembly language.

The compilation is straightforward when only one line is considered at a time. Optimizing *C* compilers (and expert assembly language programmers) consider multiple *C* language statements at a time during compilation in an effort to reduce the total number of instructions, and it may be difficult to correlate the final assembly code with the original *C* language statements. This book does not expect you to become an expert assembly language programmer; this only occurs

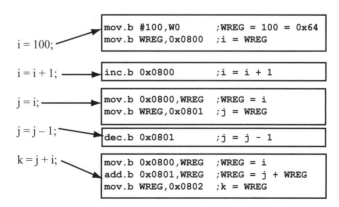

i is location 0x0800, *j* is location 0x0801, *k* is location 0x0802

FIGURE 3.20   The contents of main in the "simple" *C* program compiled to PIC24 assembly language.

after a considerable amount of time is spent crafting assembly language programs. Instead, this book strives for clarity and understanding, and will always perform C-to-PIC24 assembly language translation in the most straightforward manner possible. Some comments on the assembly code in Figure 3.20 are:

- Byte operations (.b) are used because i, j, k are uint8 (1 byte) variables.
- The reader may wonder why both W0 and WREG are used in the assembly language for the first C statement i = 100. Only WREG can be used in a mov instruction that is a byte operation and specifies a file register address, so the destination for the constant value 100 must be specified as WREG. However, the mov instruction with an immediate operand requires one of the working registers, W0 through W15, as its destination. It is a syntax error to write mov.b #100,WREG and also a syntax error to write mov.b W0,i even though W0 and WREG are physically the same register.
- The reader may wonder why the assembly statement mov.b 0x800,0x801 is not used for the j = i operation. The answer is simple—there is no PIC24 mov instruction that allows file register addresses to be specified for both the source and destination operands. Instead, i must be copied to a working register first, and then copied from the working register to j.

Of the C language statements in Figure 3.20, the statement k = j + i is the most difficult, and requires three PIC24 instructions to implement. In the resulting three-instruction sequence in Figure 3.20, observe that the destination of add.b 0x0801,WREG is WREG so that the value of 0x0801 (j) is left undisturbed. The mov.b WREG,0x0802 instruction copies the result of the addition into the k variable location (0x0802). This three-instruction sequence could be replaced by the instructions in Listing 3.2.

LISTING 3.2   Alternate implementation of k = j + i.

```
mov.b 0x0801,WREG          ;WREG = j
add.b 0x0800,WREG          ;WREG = i + WREG = i + j
mov.b 0x0802               ;k = WREG = i + j (result same as j + i)
```

This works because addition is a commutative operation; either i + j or j + i produces the same result. However, when performing subtraction one must be careful of the operand order because j − i is not equal to i − j. Listing 3.3 shows one way to implement the C language statement k = j − i.

LISTING 3.3   Implementation of k = j − i.

```
mov.b 0x0800,WREG          ;WREG = i
sub.b 0x0801,WREG          ;WREG = j − i
mov.b 0x0802               ;k = WREG = j − i
```

The code in Figure 3.20 makes heavy use of WREG because of the need for byte operations to data memory and the use of file register addressing. There are many other possible assembly language implementations using addressing modes such as indirect addressing, but we reserve that discussion for a later chapter.

The PIC24 assembly language of Figure 3.20 is somewhat obtuse because memory addresses (0x0800, 0x0801, 0x0802) are used instead of the variable names i, j, k. Also, there is still the problem of translating the PIC24 instruction mnemonics to machine code, a process that is interesting the first time, boring the second time, and painful thereafter. A program called an *assembler* automatically converts instruction mnemonics to machine code. Microchip Technology Inc. provides the MPLAB Integrated Design Environment (IDE), which contains an assembler and simulator for most Microchip microprocessors. Listing 3.4 gives the assembly language of Figure 3.20 written in a more readable form, and in a format compatible with the MPLAB PIC24 assembler (the line numbers are not part of the source file).

LISTING 3.4 MPLAB-compatible assembly source code for "simple" C example.

```
(1)    .include "p24Hxxxx.inc"
(2)    .global __reset          ;The label for the first line of code.
(3)       .bss                  ;uninitialized data section
(4)    ;;These start at location 0x0800 because 0-0x07FF are reserved for SFRs
(5)    i: .space 1              ;Allocating space (in bytes) to variable.
(6)    j: .space 1              ;Allocating space (in bytes) to variable.
(7)    k: .space 1              ;Allocating space (in bytes) to variable.
(8)    ;Code Section in Program Memory
(9)       .text                 ;Start of Code section
(10) __reset:                   ;first instruction located at __reset label
(11)    mov #__SP_init, W15      ;Initialize the Stack Pointer
(12)    mov #__SPLIM_init,W0
(13)    mov W0,SPLIM            ;Initialize the Stack Limit register
(14) ;User Code starts here.
(15)    .equ avalue, 100
(16) ;i = avalue; // avalue = 100
(17)    mov.b #avalue, W0       ;W0 = 100
(18)    mov.b WREG,i            ;i = 100
(19)
(20) ;i = i + 1;
(21)    inc.b i                 ;i = i + 1
(22)
(23) ;j = i
(24)    mov.b i,WREG            ;W0 = i
(25)    mov.b WREG,j            ;j = W0
(26)
```

```
(27)  ;j = j - 1;
(28)    dec.b j                  ;j = j - 1
(29)
(30)  ; k = j + i
(31)    mov.b i,WREG             ;W0 = i
(32)    add.b j,WREG             ;W0 = W0+j (WREG is W0)
(33)    mov.b WREG,k             ;k = W0
(34)
(35)  done:
(36)    goto done                ;Placeholder for last line of executed code
(37)
(38)  .end                       ;End of program code in this file
```

The .include statement in line 1 is called an *assembler directive,* which is an instruction to the assembler and not a PIC24 assembly language statement. Lines 1–3, 5–7, 9, 15, and 38 are all assembler directives. The .include statement causes the source file p24Hxxxx.inc to be included (read) during assembly. When assembling a PIC24 program, the assembler must be told the target device, in this case the 24HJ32GP202, by setting this device name within the MPLAB environment (see Appendix B). This device name is used by the generic p24Hxxxx.inc include file to select a device specific include file (i.e., the p24HJ32GP202.inc file) that defines symbolic names for all SFRs and named bits within SFRs.

The .global __reset assembler directive at line 2 declares the label __reset as a global label, that is, a label that is accessible outside of the scope of this file. Labels are used as symbolic names for the instruction addresses, generally to be used as the target of a change of control instruction, such as goto __reset. In this case, the label __reset is a special label required by the PIC24 assembler that must be used to label the first executable instruction in our program. Labels are case sensitive, while assembler directives and instruction mnemonics are case insensitive. Labels, assembler directives, and instruction mnemonics may start in any column that is desired. A semicolon is used to start a comment.

The .bss assembler directive at line 3 indicates the start of a section that contains uninitialized data to be placed in data RAM. The three .space assembler directives that follow allocate one byte of space for each of the i, j, and k variables. Observe that each .space directive is labeled with a variable name. The .space directives use the first available data memory location, and thus i is assigned the address 0x0800, j the address 0x0801, and k the address 0x0802. Using .space directives and labeling in this manner allow the i, j, k variables to be referenced by name within PIC24 instructions instead of using absolute memory locations, which greatly improves code clarity. The .space directive can also be used to insert bytes between declarations of different sized variables (8-bit, 16-bit, and 32-bit) to ensure that 16-bit and 32-bit variables start on a word boundary.

The .text assembler directive at line 9 indicates the start of a section that contains instructions to be placed in program memory. There must be separate assembler directives, .bss and .text, for data memory and program memory because these are two different physical memories in the PIC24 architecture. Locations 0x0 through 0x01FF of program memory are reserved for reset handling, and *trap* and *interrupt vectors* (discussed in Chapter 9), so the first instruction of our program is placed at 0x0200. At power up, the program counter is reset to 0x0. Thus, the first PIC24 instruction is fetched from program memory location 0x0, which is called the *reset* handler. The assembler automatically generates a `goto __reset` instruction that occupies the two words at program memory locations 0x0 and 0x2, which is the reason why the first executable instruction in our program must be labeled as `__reset`. In other words, the contents of locations 0x0 and 0x2 hold a `goto` statement to the start of the user program.

The `mov #__SP_init, W15` instruction loads the constant value `#__SP_init` into `W15`, where `__SP_init` is an automatically generated value that represents the first free location in data RAM after the variable declarations. This free space is reserved for *stack* space storage, which is discussed in detail in Chapter 6. Register `W15` is reserved for a special function known as the *stack pointer*. The two instruction sequence in lines 12 and 13 initialize the *stack limit register* to the value `__SPLIMIT_ init`, which is an automatically generated value that represents the maximum data memory address that is safely available for stack pointer usage. At this point, it is not necessary for the reader to understand stack operations to write simple assembly language programs. Lines 1 through 13 form a template that should be used for any assembly language program, modified with appropriate `.space` directives that match the variable needs of that program. Technically, this program does not need to initialize either the stack pointer or stack limit registers as no instructions that use the stack are executed, but it is a good idea to include this in your standard assembly language template since it will be needed in future examples.

The `.equ` assembler directive at line 15 assigns the value 100 to the label `avalue`. For those readers familiar with *C*, the assembler's `.equ` directive is very similar to *C*'s `#define` directive, which is discussed in more detail in Chapter 8. The instructions in lines 16–33 duplicate the instructions of Figure 3.20, except that the names `i`, `j`, and `k` are used instead of absolute addresses. Lines 35 and 36 contain the infinite loop `goto done`, where the target address `done` is the location of the `goto` instruction. A microcontroller program never really ends; it must always be doing something, as there is no place for the program to go when it finishes! When a program exits on a personal computer, control is returned to the operating system, which is in an infinite loop waiting for input from the keyboard, mouse, or some other input device. A microcontroller program is also typically an infinite loop that is waiting on input from some external device such as a car engine, sensor array, and so forth. In this simple example, the program execution is trapped when it falls into the `goto` done infinite loop. Another method to halt program execution is to stop the processor clock; this is discussed in Chapter 8. The .end assembler directive at line 38 is used to mark the end of the source code in this file; it is not strictly necessary and can be omitted if desired.

Listing 3.5 gives the machine code listing produced by the MPLAB assembler for the assembly language program of Listing 3.4. The *address* column gives the program memory location in hex and the *opcode* column the machine code for the mnemonic to the right. Not counting the reset vector, this program takes 13 PIC24 instructions to implement (locations 0x200 through 0x21A). The number of required instruction words is 14 (13+1), because the goto done instruction at location 0x218 requires two instruction words.

LISTING 3.5   Machine code listing for simple *C* program.

address	opcode	label	mnemonic
0000	040200		goto _reset
0002	000000		nop
0200	20804F	_reset	mov.w #0x804,W15
0202	20FF80		mov.w #0xff8,W0
0204	880100		mov.w #W0,0x0020
0206	B3C640		mov.b #0x64,W0
0208	B7E800		mov.b W0,i
020A	EC6800		inc.b i
020C	BFC800		mov.b i,W0
020E	B7E801		mov.b W0,j
0210	ED6801		dec.b j
0212	BFC800		mov.b i,W0
0214	B44801		add.b j,W0
0216	B7E802		mov.b W0,k
0218	040214	done	goto done
021A	000000		nop

THE nop INSTRUCTION

The second word of the goto instructions in Listing 3.5 displays as a nop instruction, which stands for "NO oPeration". A nop simply causes the instruction word to be fetched and the PC to be incremented to the next instruction word. One machine code encoding of a nop has the upper 8 bits as "0" and the remaining bits as don't-cares. All instructions that require two words have the second instruction word encoded such that the upper 8 bits are "0", as seen at locations 0x0002 and 0x021A in Listing 3.5. A second nop encoding has the upper 8 bits as "1", and the remaining bits as don't-cares. This second nop encoding was chosen because program memory contains all "1"s when the program memory is in a blank or erased

state. This means that the values of 0xFFFFFF and 0x000000 are both treated as
nop instructions. These nop encodings were selected because any erased location
contains 0xFFFFFF, and any memory location in the 4 Mi instruction word range
that is not physically implemented returns a 0x000000 when read. In this way, if a
program error causes a jump to a portion of program memory that is erased, continuous nop instructions (0xFFFFFF) are fetched until the program counter exceeds
physical memory. Then, 0x000000 values (nop instructions again) are read until the
PC wraps back to the reset location of 0x0, simulating a device reset. An internal
register of the PIC24 µC can be checked by the startup code to determine if a physical reset actually occurred; and if not, then an error indicator displayed indicating
that an anomalous reset condition occurred.

16-BIT (WORD) OPERATIONS

Assume the C program of Listing 3.1 is changed to use uint16 (16-bit) variables
for i, j, and k instead of uint8 variables. This means that all operations using these
variables now require 16-bit operations instead of 8-bit operations. Listing 3.6 gives
the new assembly language implementation assuming uint16 (16-bit) variables
(some lines that have not changed between Listing 3.4 and Listing 3.6 have been
deleted for reasons of brevity).

LISTING 3.6   Simple C program with 16-bit operations.

```
(1)   i: .space 2              ;Allocating space (in bytes) to variable.
(2)   j: .space 2              ;Allocating space (in bytes) to variable.
(3)   k: .space 2              ;Allocating space (in bytes) to variable.
(4)   ;Code Section in Program Memory
(5)      .text                 ;Start of Code section
(6)   __reset:                 ;first instruction located at __reset label
(7)      mov #__SP_init, W15    ;Initialize the Stack Pointer
(8)      mov #__SPLIM_init,W0
(9)      mov W0,SPLIM          ;Initialize the Stack Limit register
(10) ;User Code starts here.
(11)     .equ avalue, 2047
(12) ;i = avalue;              // avalue = 2047
(13)     mov #avalue, W0       ;W0 = 2047
(14)     mov WREG,i            ;i = 2047
(15)
(16) ;i = i + 1;
(17)     inc i                 ;i = i + 1
(18)
(19) ;j = i
(20)     mov i,WREG            ;W0 = i
```

```
(21)      mov WREG,j                      ;j = W0
(22)
(23)  ;j = j - 1;
(24)      dec j                           ;j = j - 1
(25)
(26)  ;k = j + i
(27)      mov i,WREG                      ;W0 = i
(28)      add j,WREG                      ;W0 = W0+j (WREG is W0)
(29)      mov WREG,k                      ;k = W0
(30)
(31)  done:
(32)      goto done                       ;Place holder for last line of executed code
```

The changes in Listing 3.6 to accommodate 16-bit operations are:

■ The .space directives in lines 1–3 now reserve two bytes (16 bits) instead of 1 byte for each variable. This means that the addresses of the i, j, k variables are now 0x0800, 0x0802, and 0x0804.

■ All of the byte (.b) operations in Listing 3.4 are removed so that 16-bit operations are performed.

■ The value of the constant avalue has also been changed from 100 to 2047 to illustrate that a larger number range is available with 16-bit variables.

Assembling the program of Listing 3.6 reveals that it has the same number of instruction words as Listing 3.4, and thus requires the same execution time. This is the advantage of a 16-bit CPU architecture in that 16-bit operations are as efficient as 8-bit operations in terms of program memory size and execution time. If the C data types of Listing 3.1 are changed to uint32 (32-bit) variables, then the assembly code of Listing 3.6 would change significantly, requiring approximately double the number of instructions and execution time. Operations on 32-bit data are examined in detail in Chapter 5.

Sample Question: ***Write a PIC24 assembly language fragment that implements the C statement*** "k = i + j + 20;" ***where*** k, i, j ***are all*** uint16 ***variables.***

Answer: One solution is:

```
          mov j,W0                  ;W0 = j
          add #20,W0                ;W0 = W0 + 20 = j + 20
          add i,WREG                ;W0 = i + W0 = i + j + 20
          mov W0,k                  ;k = W0 = i + j + 20
```

Observe that a single *C* statement may require several PIC24 assembly language statements, as several operations can be written in one *C* statement. Translating the *C* statement to PIC24 statements requires that you decompose the *C* statement into steps that the PIC24 can accomplish. The above solution also requires that the variables be in near RAM. If this assumption is not true, then the use of indexed addressing covered in Chapter 6 is required. This book assumes that all variables are in near RAM unless explicitly stated otherwise.

Sample Question: ***A neophyte assembly language programmer translated the C code fragment:***

```
uint16 k, j;
k = j + 1;
```

to the assembly language sequence of:

```
inc j
mov j,W1
mov W1,k
```

What is wrong with this?

Answer: The `inc j` instruction modifies the variable j. The *C* statement k = j + 1 only modifies k; the variable j is not modified. One correct solution is:

```
inc j,WREG
mov W0,k
```

The `inc j,WREG` instruction places j + 1 in WREG and leaves the memory location j unmodified.

THE CLOCK AND INSTRUCTION EXECUTION

The clock signal that controls instruction execution in the PIC24H µC supports a maximum frequency of 80 MHz for the devices available during the writing of this book. Methods for generating this clock signal and setting its frequency are discussed in Chapter 8. The symbol Fosc refers to the clock signal's frequency and Tosc refers to its period. A finite-state machine within the PIC24H µC controls the fetching, decoding, and execution of instructions. Most instructions require one instruction cycle to execute, with one instruction cycle equal to two clock cycles (two Tosc periods). Instruction execution frequency is referred to as Fcy and is equal to Fosc/2. A single instruction cycle requires a time of 1/Fcy. An 80 MHz clock has a 12.5 ns period, and one instruction cycle takes two clocks, so this is a time of 2 * 12.5 ns = 25 ns. This means that a PIC24H μC with an 80 MHz clock can execute instructions at a rate of approximately 40 million instructions per second (MIPS) as 1/25 ns = 40 x 10^6. The actual instruction execution rate will be somewhat lower than this, as any instruction that causes the program counter to change value, such as a goto instruction, requires two instruction cycles (4 Fosc clocks) to execute. There are other conditions, such as register dependencies in effective address calculations, that can require an extra instruction cycle—this is discussed in Chapter 6. The instruction table contained in Appendix A gives the number of instruction cycles required for each instruction.

> Sample Question: *How many clock cycles and instruction cycles are required to execute from location 0x200 through 0x0216 of Listing 3.5? Assuming Fosc = 80 MHz, how long do these instructions take to execute?*
>
> Answer: There are 12 instructions total, and each instruction takes 1 instruction cycle. So total instruction cycles = 12, and total clock cycles is 12 * 2 = 24.
> Total execution time = 1/Fosc * # of clock cycles
> = 1/(80 MHz) * 24 = 1/(80 x 10^6) * 24 = 12.5 ns * 24 = 300 ns

SUMMARY

In this chapter, we introduced the basic program and memory architecture of the PIC24 microcontroller and discussed a few PIC24 instructions from the data transfer, arithmetic, and control classes. Two versions of a simple C program were converted to PIC24 assembly language, one version that operated on 8-bit unsigned data and a second that used 16-bit unsigned data. This prepares you for the next chapter, in which additional arithmetic, shift, and logical operations on unsigned 8-bit and 16-bit data are covered, as well as conditional execution and loop structures.

REVIEW PROBLEMS

1. Convert the instruction mov 0x100A,WREG to machine code.
2. Convert the instruction mov W3,W5 to machine code.
3. Convert the instruction mov #0xA235,W3 to machine code.

4. Convert the instruction `mov.b #0xA2,W3` to machine code.
5. Convert the instruction `goto 0x02A0` to machine code.
6. Convert the instruction `add W0,W1,W2` to machine code.
7. Convert the machine code 0x780108 to a PIC24 instruction.
8. Convert the machine code 0xB3C228 to a PIC24 instruction. (Hint: This is a `mov` instruction.)
9. Convert the instruction word 0x809782 to a PIC24 instruction. (Hint: This is a `mov` instruction.)
10. Convert the instruction word 0x208507 to a PIC24 instruction. (Hint: This is a `mov` instruction.)
11. Given a 20 MHz Fosc, how long does it take the instruction `mov W2,W4` to execute in nanoseconds?
12. Write a PIC24 instruction sequence that accomplishes `k=i−j−32`, where `i`, `j`, and `k` are `uint16` variables.
13. Write a PIC24 instruction sequence that accomplishes `k=i−j−32`, where `i`, `j`, and `k` are `uint8` variables.
14. Write a PIC24 instruction sequence that copies data RAM locations 0x1000 through 0x1007 (8 bytes) to locations 0x1800 through 0x1807.
15. How many `add W0,W1,W2` instructions are executed in 1 second assuming a 25 MHz Fosc?

For the remaining problems, assume the memory/register contents of Table 3.6 at the start of EACH instruction and give the modified memory location or register and its content.

16. `mov W2,0x1008`
17. `mov.b 0x1001,WREG`
18. `mov #0x1001,W1`
19. `mov.b [W3],[W4]`
20. `mov [W0],W4`

TABLE 3.6 Register memory contents for sample problems.

Location	Value	Location	Value
W0	0x1006	0x1000	0x382A
W1	0x00BC	0x1002	0xFB80
W2	0x8345	0x1004	0x4D19
W3	0x1000	0x1006	0xE7C0
W4	0x1005	0x1008	0xFF00

21. `mov.b #0x20,W3`
22. `add W0,[W0],W1`
23. `dec 0x1004,WREG`
24. `add 0x1002`
25. `add.b 0x1000,WREG`
26. `sub W0,W1,[W0]`
27. `sub.b W4,#10,[W0]`
28. `dec2 0x1008`
29. `dec2.b 0x1008`
30. `inc W0,[W3]`
31. `inc2.b 0x1009`
32. `inc2 0x1008,WREG`

4

Unsigned 8/16-Bit Arithmetic, Logical, and Conditional Operations

This chapter examines additional features of the PIC24 instruction set architecture in the context of unsigned 8/16-bit arithmetic, bitwise logical, and conditional operations. These operations are used to implement equality, inequality, and comparison tests for conditional code execution and loop control.

Learning Objectives

After reading this chapter, you will be able to:

- Describe the operation of the bit manipulation instructions of the PIC24 instruction set.
- Translate *C* language statements that perform 8/16-bit addition, subtraction, bitwise logical, and shift operations into PIC24 instruction sequences.
- Translate *C* language statements that perform 8/16-bit zero, non-zero, equality, inequality, and unsigned comparison operations into PIC24 instruction sequences.
- Translate *C* conditional statements and loop structures such as if{}else{}, do{}while, while{}, and for{} into PIC24 instruction sequences.

BITWISE LOGICAL OPERATIONS, BIT OPERATIONS

Table 4.1 lists the *C* language arithmetic and logical operators discussed in this book. As seen in the previous chapter, the arithmetic/logic unit (ALU) implements these operations in the processor data path. The previous chapter covered some of the arithmetic capabilities of the ALU such as addition, subtraction, increment, and decrement. The *C* bitwise logical operations of & (AND), | (OR), ^ (XOR),

TABLE 4.1 C language arithmetic and logical operators.

Operator	Description
+, −	(+) addition, (−) subtraction
++, −−	(++) increment, (−−) decrement
*, /	(*) multiplication, (/) division
>>, <<	right shift (>>), left shift (<<)
&, |, ^	bitwise AND (&), OR (|), XOR (^)
~	bitwise complement

Name	Mnemonic	Operation

Bitwise AND	`and{.b} Wb, Ws, Wd`
	`and{.b} Wb, #lit5, Wd`
	`and{.b} #lit10, Wn`
	`and{.b} f`
	`and{.b} f, WREG`
		(Wb) & (Ws) → Wd
		(Wb) & #lit5 → Wd
		(Wn) & #lit10 → Wn
		(f) & (WREG) → f
		(f) & (WREG) → WREG

Bitwise Inclusive OR	`ior{.b} Wb, Ws, Wd`
	`ior{.b} Wb, #lit5, Wd`
	`ior{.b} #lit10, Wn`
	`ior{.b} f`
	`ior{.b} f, WREG`
		(Wb) | (Ws) → Wd
		(Wb) | #lit5 → Wd
		(Wn) | #lit10 → Wn
		(f) | (WREG) → f
		(f) | (WREG) → WREG

Bitwise Exclusive OR	`xor{.b} Wb, Ws, Wd`
	`xor{.b} Wb, #lit5, Wd`
	`xor{.b} #lit10, Wn`
	`xor{.b} f`
	`xor{.b} f, WREG`
		(Wb) ^ (Ws) → Wd
		(Wb) ^ #lit5 → Wd
		(Wn) ^ #lit10 → Wn
		(f) ^ (WREG) → f
		(f) ^ (WREG) → WREG

Bitwise Complement	`com{.b} Ws, Wd`
	`com{.b} f`
	`com{.b} f, WREG`
		~(Ws) → Wd
		~(f) → f
		~(f) → WREG

Clear	`clr{.b} Wd`
	`clr{.b} f`
	`clr{.b} f, WREG`
		00...00 → Wd
		00...00 → f
		00...00 → WREG

Set	`setm{.b} Wd`
	`setm{.b} f`
	`setm{.b} f, WREG`
		11...11 → Wd
		11...11 → f
		11...11 → WREG

FIGURE 4.1 Bitwise logical instructions.

and ~ (complement) as well as set (*bit* = 1) and clear (*bit* = 0) comprise the logical operations performed by the ALU.

Figure 4.1 shows the instructions for the bitwise logical operations implemented by the PIC24 µC family. The addressing mode forms for the bitwise *and, inclusive-or,* and *exclusive-or* operations are the same as for the addition and subtraction operations discussed in Chapter 3. Similarly, the addressing mode forms for the bitwise *complement* are the same as for the increment and decrement operations discussed in Chapter 3. The *clear* and *set* instructions only have one operand, but the *Wd* symbol indicates this destination register has the same addressing modes as the *Wd* operands of the other instructions in Figure 4.1. This is where the regularity of the PIC24 instruction becomes apparent. It is not necessary to discuss the addressing modes for these instructions since this has already been covered. Instead, we can focus on understanding the functionality of each operation.

The term bitwise is applied to the two-operand & (AND), | (OR), and ^ (XOR) operators because the logical operation is performed on a bit-by-bit basis on the operands. Bitwise logical operations are useful for clearing (AND), setting (OR), or complementing (XOR) groups of bits. The first row of Figure 4.2 shows a bitwise AND operation implementation of the *C* statement k = k & 0x0F where k is an uint8 variable. The constant 0x0F is called a *bit mask* (or simply "mask"). In the case of bitwise AND operations, any bit in the mask that is a "0" will clear the bit in the same position in the result, while a "1" in the mask leaves the result

Location 0x0800 is the `uint8` variable `k`, which contains the value 0x2C.

In *C*	In Assembly	Execution		
k = k & 0x0F; Bitwise AND	`mov.b #0x0F, W0` `and.b k`	`k`	`= 0x2C`	`= 0010 1100` `  &&&& &&&&`
		`mask = 0x0F`	`= 0000 1111` `---------`	
		`result`	`= 0000 1100 = 0x0C`	
k = k | 0x0F; Bitwise Inclusive OR	`mov.b #0x0F, W0` `ior.b k`	`k`	`= 0x2C`	`= 0010 1100` `  |||| ||||`
		`mask = 0x0F`	`= 0000 1111` `---------`	
		`result`	`= 0010 1111 = 0x2F`	
k = k ^ 0x0F; Bitwise Exclusive OR	`mov.b #0x0F, W0` `xor.b k`	`k`	`= 0x2C`	`= 0010 1100` `  ^^^^ ^^^^`
		`mask = 0x0F`	`= 0000 1111` `---------`	
		`result`	`= 0010 0011 = 0x23`	

k = ~k;
Bitwise
Complement
	`com.b k`	`k`	`= 0x2C`	`= 0010 1100`
				`  ~~~~ ~~~~`
				`---------`

		`result`	`= 1101 0011 = 0xD3`	
k = 0; Clear	`clr.b k`	`result`	`= 0000 0000 = 0x00`	
k = ~0; Set	`setm.b k`	`result`	`= 1111 1111 = 0xFF`	

FIGURE 4.2   Bitwise operation examples.

bit unchanged. Thus, the operation k = k & 0x0F leaves the lower 4 bits of k unchanged and clears the upper 4 bits. An easy way to remember this is the rule that "0 ANDed with anything is 0; 1 ANDed with anything is anything."

The OR bitwise logical operator is used to set groups of bits, as "1 ORed with anything is 1; 0 ORed with anything is anything." Thus, the operation k = k | 0x0F sets the lower 4 bits of k to "1"s, but leaves the upper 4 bits unchanged as shown in the second row of Figure 4.2. The XOR bitwise operation is used to complement groups of bits, as "1 XORed with anything is NOT(anything); 0 XORed with anything is anything." Thus, the operation k = k ^ 0x0F complements the lower 4 bits of k, but leaves the upper 4 bits unchanged. An example of an 8-bit bitwise XOR is shown in the third row of Figure 4.2. The com instruction implements the bitwise complement operation as represented by the *C* operation of k = ~k that complements (inverts) each bit in k. The clr instruction clears every bit of its target operand to 0, while the setm instruction sets each bit to a 1. The last three rows of Figure 4.2 give examples for the com, clr, and setm bitwise operations.

Why are bitwise operations useful? It will be seen in this book's hardware chapters that the special function registers used to control hardware peripherals such as the PIC24 timers have individual bits and bit fields whose values need to be set, cleared, or complemented to affect operation. For example, the most significant bit of the Timer1 control register (T1CON, a 16-bit register) is used to turn the timer off or on. The T1CON special function register is accessed in the same way as a data memory location. Using the bitwise logical operations to set or clear a particular bit takes two instructions, as seen in the following instruction sequence, which clears bit 15 of the special function register T1CON. Note that bits are numbered starting with 0 as the least significant bit and ending with 15, the most significant bit.

```
mov #0x7FFF,W0      ;W0 has the mask value of 0x7FFF
and T1CON           ;T1CON = (T1CON)&0x7FFF, clears bit 15
```

Clearing, setting, or complementing a single bit in a memory location is a commonly performed operation in much μC application software. To improve the efficiency of these operations, the instructions bset (bit set), bclr (bit clear), and btg (bit toggle) are included in the PIC24 instruction set as shown in Figure 4.3. In this figure, the literal *#bit4* specifies a bit number of the bit upon which the operation will be performed. The literal *#bit4* takes on the values 0 (the least significant bit) up to 7 (the most significant bit) for byte operations and 0 (the least significant bit) up to 15 (the most significant bit) for word operations.

Figure 4.4 gives examples of bclr, bset, and btg execution. The bit number for the most significant bit is 7 for a byte operation and 15 for a word operation. The bit number for the least significant bit is always 0. When affecting only 1 bit in a target memory location is required, the bclr/bset/btg instructions are more efficient than the bitwise logical instructions and/ior/xor. Of course, if you must set, clear, or

Name	Mnemonic	Operation
Bit Set	`bset{.b} Ws, #bit4`	1 → Ws<bit4>
	`bset{.b} f, #bit4`	1 → f<bit4>
Bit Clear	`bclr{.b} Ws, #bit4`	0 → Ws<bit4>
	`bclr{.b} f, #bit4`	0 → f<bit4>
Bit Toggle	`btg{.b} Ws, #bit4`	~Ws<bit4> → Ws<bit4>
	`btg{.b} f, #bit4`	~f<bit4> → f<bit4>

FIGURE 4.3 Single bit set, clear toggle.

Location 0x0800 is the `uint8` variable `k`, which contains the value 0x2C.

In *C*	In Assembly	Execution

k = k & 0xDF;	`bclr.b k,#5`	`k     = 0x2C  = 0010 1100`
		`bclr.b k,#5`
		`           result  = 0000 1100 = 0x0C`

k = k | 0x01;	`bset.b k,#0`	`k     = 0x2C  = 0010 1100`
		`bset.b k,#0`
		`           result  = 0010 1101 = 0x2D`

k = k ^ 0x08;	`btg.b k,#3`	`k     = 0x2C  = 0010 1100`
		`btg.b k,#3`
		`           result  = 0010 0100 = 0x24`

k = k ^ 0x80;	`btg.b k,#7`	`k     = 0x2C  = 0010 1100`
		`btg.b k,#7`
		`           result  = 1010 1100 = 0xAC`

FIGURE 4.4 Single bit set, clear toggle examples.

toggle (complement) multiple bits in the same location simultaneously, the bitwise logical operators and/ior/xor are your only option.

The previous code fragment that used a mask value and a bitwise AND operation to clear 15 of the T1CON special function register can be rewritten using a single `bclr` instruction as follows:

```
bclr T1CON,#15        ;clears bit 15 of the T1CON register
```

THE STATUS REGISTER

An important special function register that has been ignored to this point is the *status register* (SR), which is involved in the execution of most instructions. Some of the bits in the SR contain 1-bit flags (DC, N, OV, Z, C) that are set or cleared as a side effect of instruction execution. Figure 4.5 gives the names and positions of each of the bits within the SR.

The *zero* (Z) flag is set if the result of an instruction is zero, else it is cleared. The *carry* (C) flag is set equal to the carry out of the most significant bit. The *decimal*

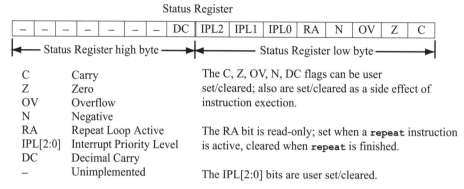

FIGURE 4.5 The status register (SR).

carry (DC), *overflow* (OV), and *negative* (N) flags are discussed in Chapter 5 (OV, N) and Chapter 7 (DC). The *interrupt priority level* (IPL[2:0]) bits are discussed in Chapter 9. The *repeat loop active* (RA) bit is read only; it is set when a repeat instruction is active and is cleared when a repeat instruction is finished. The repeat instruction is discussed in Chapter 6, as it is most commonly used with instructions that use indirect addressing.

Different instructions affect different flags in the status register (SR). The PIC24 instruction summary given in Appendix A, "PIC24 Architecture, Instruction Set, Register Summary," lists the flags affected by each instruction. For example:

- The add instruction affects the DC, N, OV, Z, C flags.
- The mov f instruction affects only the Z and N flags.
- The mov f, Wn instruction affects no flags.

If a flag is unaffected by an instruction, it retains its current value. Figure 4.6 shows how the Z and C flags are affected by different addition and subtraction byte operations.

Addition (byte mode)

```
   0x01              0x00              0xF0              0x80
 + 0xFF            + 0x00            + 0x20            + 0x7F
   0x00  C = 1       0x00  C = 0       0x10  C = 1       0xFF  C = 0
         Z = 1             Z = 1             Z = 0             Z = 0
```

Subtraction (byte mode)

```
   0x01              0x00              0xF0
 - 0xFF            - 0x00            - 0x20
   0x02  C = 0       0x00  C = 1       0xD0  C = 1
         Z = 0             Z = 1             Z = 0
```

FIGURE 4.6 C, Z flags for add/subtract operations.

A – B

$$A + {\sim}B + 1$$

```
   0xF0              0x20 = 0010 0000              0xF0
 - 0x20           ~(0x20)= 1101 1111            + 0xDF
   0xD0  C = 1          = 0xDF                  + 0x01
          Z = 0                                   0xD0  C = 1
                                                        Z = 0
```

FIGURE 4.7   Subtraction of A – B performed as A + (~B) + 1.

An addition operation sets the C flag for a carry out of the MSb, while a subtraction operation clears the C flag for a borrow into the MSb. Note that the flag combination of Z = 1 and C = 0 cannot occur after a subtraction, as zero is produced only if the numbers are equal, which cannot produce a borrow into the MSb. The reason behind the carry flag condition after a subtraction is explained in Figure 4.7. The subtraction operation A – B is actually performed in hardware as A + (~B) + 1, where the value ~B + 1 is called the *two's complement* of B. Two's complement representation and its uses are explored in the next chapter when discussing signed number encoding. Note that the carry flag produced by the addition operation A + (~B) + 1 in Figure 4.7 matches the behavior of carry = ~borrow; in other words, C = 0 if a borrow occurs, else C = 1.

Sample Question: ***What are the C, Z flag settings after the instruction*** sub W1,W1,W1 ***is executed? After*** mov k,W2? ***Use the instruction set table in Appendix A to determine the flags that are affected by instruction execution.***

Answer: The instruction sub W1,W1,W1 affects all flags; the result is 0 since the operation is W1 = W1 – W1. This produces no borrow, so the flag settings after execution are Z = 1, C = 1. The mov k,W2 instruction affects no flags, so the C, Z flag settings after mov k,W2 execution are left in the same state as before the instruction is executed.

SHIFT AND ROTATE OPERATIONS

Now that the status register has been discussed, we can move to the next class of arithmetic instructions, namely *shift* and *rotate* operations. Some of these instructions make use of the carry (C) flag during execution. Shift operations are useful for either multiplication (shift left) or division (shift right) by powers of two for unsigned numbers or for moving bits to new positions within a register. Figure 4.8a shows the various forms of the *logical shift right* (lsr) instruction. A logical

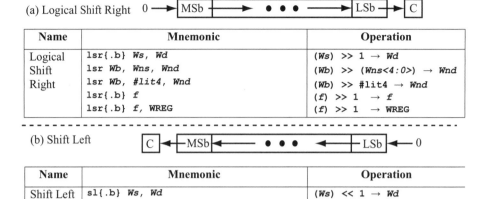

Note: The multiple-position shifts do NOT affect the C flag; all shifts affect the N, Z flags.

FIGURE 4.8 Logical shift right, shift left instructions.

shift right always shifts in a 0 for the MSb, with the carry flag set equal to the bit shifted out of the LSb. There is another form of right shift known as an *arithmetic shift right* that keeps the MSb unchanged; this form of right shift is discussed in Chapter 5. The "lsr{.b} Ws, Wd", "lsr{.b} f", and "lsr{.b} f, WREG" forms support byte operations but only shift by one position. The "lsr Wb,Wns,Wnd" and "lsr Wb, #lit4, Wnd" forms only support word operations, but allow a multiple-position shift that is executed in one instruction cycle. If the shift amount (taken from Wns<4:0>) for a multiple-position shift is greater than 15, then the result is 0. Note that the 4-bit literal #lit4 allows a maximum shift of 15 positions, so a multiple-position shift greater than 15 can only be done using the "lsr Wb,Wns,Wnd" form. Figure 4.8b shows the *shift left* instruction forms, which follow the same pattern as the logical shift right. The shift left operation shifts a "0" into the LSb, with the MSb shifted into the C flag. The shift left operation does not have the arithmetic/logical versions that the shift right operation possesses.

Two examples of *C* shift operations implemented in PIC24 assembly language are given in Figure 4.9. The *C* statement "u8_i = u8_i >> 2;" is implemented as two one-bit shifts because of the need for byte operations since the u8_i variable is a uint8 data type; recall that the multiple-position shifts allow only word operations. The *C* statement "u16_k = u16p << 10;" can make use of the multiple-position shift left instruction as shown in Figure 4.9 because the *C* statement uses 16-bit variables. Note that it was necessary to first move the u16_p variable into a working register before performing the shift left operation, and that the result is then moved into the

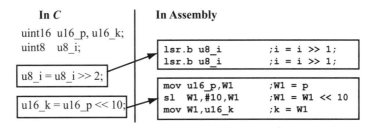

FIGURE 4.9   Shift operations: C to assembly.

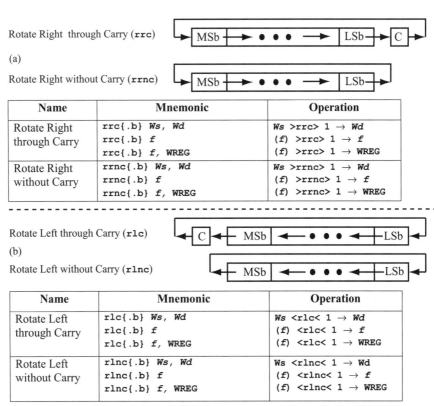

Note: All rotates affect the Z, N flags. Only the Rotates through Carry affect the C flag.

FIGURE 4.10   Rotate instructions.

u16_k variable after the shift is done. This is the first *C* code example that contains a mixture of 8-bit and 16-bit variables, and in these cases the variable names will generally have a prefix indicating the variable's data type as a reminder to the reader.

Figure 4.10 shows the four *rotate* instructions available in the PIC24 instruction set that can also be used for implementing shifts. The term *rotate* is applied to these instructions because instruction execution rotates the affected bits through a fixed set of positions; no bit is "lost" by the rotate operation. The rrnc (rotate right without carry) instruction rotates the bits one position to the right, with the most significant bit rotating to the least significant bit position. The rlnc (rotate left without carry) instruction rotates the bits one position to the left, with the least significant bit rotating to the most significant bit position. The rrc (rotate right through carry) and rlc (rotate left through carry) instructions include the C flag in this rotation. Each rotate instruction only shifts the bits by one position, unlike the shift right and shift left instructions that have forms that can perform multiple-position shifts. The rrc and rlc instructions can be used to implement the C shift operations if desired, but care must be taken to clear the C flag before execution to insure that the bit shifted in is a 0. This book uses the shift left and shift right instructions, not the rotate instructions, to implement C language shift operations for 8-bit and 16-bit data.

Sample Question: *Assume that registers and memory contain the values of Table 4.2 at the START of EACH of the following instructions. Give the register or memory location that is modified by the instruction and its new value, as well as the final Z and C flag values (assume that Z = 0 and C = 0 before instruction execution).*

TABLE 4.2   Register memory contents.

Location	Value	Location	Value
W0	0x1004	0x1000	0x382A
W1	0x1008	0x1002	0xFB80
W2	0x9335	0x1004	0xFFFF

1. lsr W2,W1,W0
2. sl W2,W0,W1
3. lsr W1,#15,W0
4. sl.b 0x1002
5. rlnc.b 0x1002

Answers:
1. A word operation; this performs (W2) >> (W1<4:0>) → W0, or 0x9335 >> 8 → W0, so W0 is modified to 0x0093. The result is non-zero, so Z = 0. The C flag is unaffected, so C = 0.
2. A word operation; this performs (W2) << (W0<4:0>) → W1, or 0x9335 << 4 → W1, so W1 is modified to 0x3550. The result is non-zero, so Z = 0. The C flag is unaffected, so C = 0.

3. A word operation; this performs (W1) >> 15 → W0, or 0x1008 >> 15 → W0, so W0 is modified to 0x0000. The result is zero, so Z = 1. The C flag is unaffected, so C = 0.

4. A byte operation; this performs (0x1002) << 1 → 0x1002, or 0x80 << 1 → 0x1002, so the byte in 0x1002 is modified to 0x00 (location 0x1002 contains 0xFB00 when viewed as a word). The result is zero, so Z = 1. The C flag is set to the value shifted out of the MSb, so C = 1.

5. A byte operation; this performs (0x1002) <rlnc< 1 → 0x1002, or 0x80 <rlnc< 1 → 0x1002, so the byte in 0x1002 is modified to 0x01 as the MSb is rotated into the LSb (location 0x1002 contains 0xFB01 when viewed as a word). The result is non-zero, so Z = 0. The C flag is left unaffected, so C = 0.

MIXED 8-BIT/16-BIT OPERATIONS, COMPOUND OPERATIONS

The *C*-to-assembly examples to this point have used operations that involved the same data types, either unsigned 8-bit (uint8) or unsigned 16-bit (uint16). Care must be taken with operations that mix the data types, as shown in Figure 4.11a that computes the sum of a uint8 variable and a uint16 variable. The assembly code in Figure 4.11a first uses a byte operation to load the 8-bit u8_i variable into the LSB of W0 then performs a word addition operation of W0.LSB and the 16-bit u16_p variable. This assembly solution may provide an incorrect result because the upper 8 bits of W0 are unknown when the addition is performed. Mixed 8-bit/16-bit operations require that 8-bit variables be *extended,* or *promoted,* to 16 bits before use in a 16-bit operation. For unsigned variables, extension to 16 bits means that the value is *zero-extended,* that is, the upper 8 bits are set to 0. The zero-extend (ze) instruction is provided for this purpose. Its general form is ze Ws,Wnd with register direct and indirect addressing modes allowed for Ws but only register direct allowed for Wnd. Figure 4.11b shows assembly code that uses the ze instruction to zero-extend the 8-bit u8_i variable before it is added to the 16-bit u16_p variable. In general, when a variable of one data type is converted to another data type, this is known as *type conversion.*

Extension of 8-bit variables to 16-bit variables is necessary if the result is being stored to a 16-bit variable. If the variable on the left-hand side of the assignment is an 8-bit variable, then the operations on the right side are done in 8-bit precision. Figure 4.12 shows an addition of a 16-bit variable and an 8-bit variable, with the sum assigned to an 8-bit variable. Observe that the sum is performed in 8-bit precision and thus the zero-extension of u8_i is not needed. In general, the variable

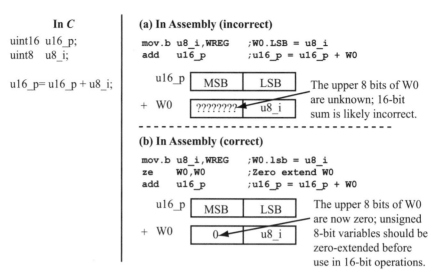

FIGURE 4.11   Mixed 8-bit/16-bit operation.

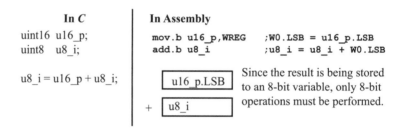

FIGURE 4.12   Mixed 8-bit/16-bit operation with assignment to an 8-bit variable.

size of the left-hand side of an assignment operation controls the precision of the operations performed on the right-hand side.

In practice, the *default* type conversion rules are compiler dependent, depending on whether the compiler follows "traditional *C*" conversion rules as originally specified by the inventors of the *C* language, or ANSI *C* conversion rules, where ANSI *C* is a standard approved in 1989 that extended traditional *C* syntax. Because of differences in default type conversions, the safe approach is to use explicit *typecasts* for type conversion as shown in the following *C* code fragment:

```
uint8 u8_i, u8_k;
uint16 u16_p;

u16_p = u16_p + (uint16) u8_i;    //typecast u8_i to uint16
u8_k = (uint8) u16_p + u8_i;      //typecast u16_p to uint8
```

The statement (uint16) u8_i explicitly instructs the compiler to convert the variable u8_i to a uint16 type. Typecast statements such as these may be redundant in some cases as they do not differ from the compiler's default behavior, but they serve as an explicit reminder that mixed precision operations are being done. Mixed precision operations are sometimes characterized as poor programming practice because of the possibility of an unforeseen result, but in microcontroller programming they are generally unavoidable. Using techniques such as explicit typecasts and variable names with type prefixes such as u8_ or u16_ serve as good documentation and can help avoid unintended results. The type prefixes used in this section greatly improve the ability of the programmer to convey the software's intent unambiguously. Writing code that can be understood by a third party reader is important, as many programs are maintained over a period of several years by parties other than the original authors. In software operations that involve type conversion or multiple data types, these type prefixes become invaluable. You will see as we progress through the chapters that variables of varying data types will be manipulated simultaneously much more often; therefore, we will eventually need to prefix all variables with their data type to aid the programmer and reduce errors. Software errors can be extremely costly in practice, so enforcing coding standards as a means of reducing errors is a common industry practice. In an infamous software reliability case that occurred on June 4, 1996, a 16-bit integer overflow caused by a conversion from a larger range type triggered a series of events that caused the French rocket, Ariane 5, to self destruct soon after launch [45].

Working Register Usage

A *C* statement can specify many different operations in a single line of code, as shown in Figure 4.13. The *C* statement k = n + (i<<3) − p contains addition, left shift, and subtraction operations. Converting this to assembly requires that the *C* statement be split into operations that the PIC24 μC supports, with working registers used to hold intermediate results. Figure 4.13b shows the *C* statement written as a series of steps that can be accomplished using PIC24 instructions, with Figure 4.13c implementing these steps in assembly language. Observe that both W0 and W1 are used to hold intermediate results.

At this point, you may wonder when our code examples will begin using registers other than W0, W1, and W2! Use of multiple registers requires *C*-to-assembly conversion using much larger *C* code fragments than what has been used to this point, and the pedagogical benefit of large, complex examples is doubtful. Be aware that *C* compilers do a good job in using working registers, so those registers are not wasted! The examples in Chapter 6 will have a reason to use a few more working registers during the coverage of pointers and subroutine parameter passing.

(a) In C

```
uint16 i,n,p;

k = n + (i<<3) - p;
```

- - - - - - - - - - - -

(b) Steps:

Copy *n, i* to working registers
Perform *i* << 3
Add to *n*
Subtract *p*
Write to *k*

(c) In Assembly

```
mov   n,W0        ;W0 = n
mov   i,W1        ;W1 = i
sl    W1,#3,W1    ;W1 = i << 3;
add   W0,W1,W0    ;W0 = n + (i<<3)
mov   p,W1        ;W1 = p
sub   W0,W1,W0    ;W0 = (n + (i<<3))-p
mov   W0,k        ;k  = (n + (i<<3))-p
```

FIGURE 4.13   A C statement with multiple operations converted to assembly.

LSB, MSB Operations

Sometimes it is desirable to manipulate the least significant and most significant bytes of a 16-bit variable independently. The following assembly code fragment performs a bitwise-AND of the LSB and MSB portions of a 16-bit variable named k.

```
(1)  k   .space 2        ;a 16-bit variable
(2)      mov.b  k,WREG    ;W0 has k.LSB
(3)      and.b  k+1,WREG  ;AND k.MSB with W0
```

Assuming that k is at location 0x0800, then k's LSB is at location 0x0800 and k's MSB is at location 0x0801 as discussed in Chapter 3. Line 2 in the previous code fragment moves the LSB of k into W0. The statement and.b k+1, WREG in line 3 AND k's MSB to the LSB of W0. The statement and.b k+1,WREG in line 3 may be confusing at first look, because it may appear that an attempt is being made to increment the value stored at variable k. Instead, what actually happens is that the assembler assigns a value of 0x0800 to the label k, and then translates the value k+1 to 0x800+1 or 0x801. Thus, the assembler interprets the statement and.b k+1,WREG as a and.b 0x0801, WREG instruction, which AND's the MSB of k with register W0. The assembler views the expression k+1 as an *address calculation* using the value of the label k, not as an operation being performed what is stored at location k.

Conditional Execution Using Bit Tests

Recall from Chapter 2 that *conditional execution* occurs when the program counter (PC) value is changed dependent on a condition that evaluates to *true* or *false*. If the condition is false, then the PC is loaded with the next sequential instruction address. If the condition is true, then the PC is loaded with a target address as specified in the conditional execution instruction. The goto instruction is an unconditional transfer of control, because the PC is always loaded with the target address. This section begins this chapter's extensive coverage of conditional execution by examining two bit-oriented conditional execution instructions named btsc f, #bit4 (bit test f, skip if clear) and btss f, #bit4 (bit test f, skip if set) instructions. The #bit4 value specifies the bit within location f that is to be tested for 0 (clear, in the case of btsc) or 1 (set, in the case of btss). If the test is true, then the next instruction is skipped. If the test is false, the next instruction is executed.

As an example of using the type of condition execution provided by the btsc and btss instructions, recall the program that was written for the number sequencing computer in Chapter 2. This program contained a conditional jump instruction (jc) that jumped to a target address if the LOC input was a "1". The jc instruction was used in a program that output the digit sequence "8,5,6,1" to the DOUT bus if LOC was "1"; otherwise the digit sequence "3,2,4,8,5,6,1" was output. Listing 4.1 shows a PIC24 program that implements the number sequencing program of Chapter 2 in PIC24 assembly language.

LISTING 4.1   PIC24 assembly program for number sequencing task.

```
(1)              .bss              ;unitialized data section
(2)   loc:       .space 1          ;byte variable
(3)   dout:      .space 1          ;byte variable
(4)              .text             ;Start of Code section
(5)   __reset:                     ;first instruction located at __reset label
(6)        mov #__SP_init, W15     ;Initialize the Stack Pointer
(7)        ;bclr   loc, #0         ;uncomment for loc<0>=0
(8)        bset    loc, #0         ;uncomment for loc<0>=1
(9)   loop_top:
(10)       btsc.b  loc,#0          ;skip next if loc<0> is 0
(11)       goto    loc_lsb_is_1
(12)  ;loc<0> is 0 if reached here
(13)       mov.b   #3,W0
(14)       mov.b   WREG,dout        ;dout = 3
(15)       mov.b   #2,W0
(16)       mov.b   WREG,dout        ;dout = 2
(17)       mov.b   #4,W0
(18)       mov.b   WREG,dout        ;dout = 4
(19)  loc_lsb_is_1:
(20)       mov.b   #8,W0
(21)       mov.b   WREG,dout        ;dout = 8
(22)       mov.b   #5,W0
(23)       mov.b   WREG,dout        ;dout = 5
(24)       mov.b   #6,W0
```

```
(25)      mov.b   WREG,dout        ;dout = 6
(26)      mov.b   #1,W0
(27)      mov.b   WREG,dout        ;dout = 1
(28)      goto    loop_top         ;loop forever
```

The single bit input LOC and output bus DOUT of the number sequencing computer are emulated in this program by the memory locations loc (0x0800) and dout (0x0801) using the .space assembler directive in lines 1–2. While this may seem like a poor replacement for external input/output pins, you will discover later that external pins on the PIC24 µC are actually accessed via data memory locations. Lines 7–8 initialize the least significant bit of loc to either "0" (line 7 uncommented) or "1" (line 8 uncommented). The btsc loc,#0 instruction in line 10 tests the least significant bit (i.e., bit 0) of loc; if this bit is "0", the goto loc_lsb_is_1 instruction at line 11 is skipped and the next instruction executed is at line 13. The dout memory location is then written in succession with the values "3,2,4,8,5,6,1". The goto loop_top instruction at line 28 causes a jump back to the btsc instruction at line 10. If the least significant bit of loc is given an initial value of "1", the btsc loc,0 instruction of line 10 will not skip the goto loc_lsb_is_1 instruction at line 11. This causes the program to jump to label loc_lsb_is_1 (the label for the instruction of line 20), skipping the instructions of lines 13 to 18. Thus, for loc<0> = 1, the number sequence "8,5,6,1" is written in succession into the dout memory location.

There are many other instructions that perform conditional tests as will be seen in the following sections. The bit test instructions btsc and btss can be somewhat confusing because their usage generally requires combining them with an unconditional jump (the bra instruction) as the potentially skipped instruction. Because of this, our usage of the btsc and btss instruction forms will be limited because other conditional execution forms offer better code clarity and are more efficient.

UNSIGNED CONDITIONAL TESTS

One use of the zero and carry flags is to implement conditional code execution. This requires an overview of conditional tests in *C*, which are used principally in if{} statements and loop structures.

CONDITIONAL TESTS IN C

Table 4.3 lists the conditional test operators for the *C* programming language. A conditional operator returns "1" if the test is true and "0" if the test is false.

Listing 4.2 shows examples of the conditional operators; after execution, a_lt_b is "1" (true), a_eq_b is "0" (false), a_gt_b is "0" (false), and a_ne_b is "1" (true).

TABLE 4.3   Conditional tests in C.

Operator	Description
==, !=	equal, not equal
>, >=	greater than, greater than or equal
<, <=	less than, less than or equal
&&, ||	logical AND, logical OR
!	logical negation

LISTING 4.2   Examples of *C* equality and inequality tests.

```
uint8 a, b, a_lt_b, a_eq_b, a_gt_b, a_ne_b;
a = 5; b = 10;
a_lt_b = (a < b);        // result is 1
a_eq_b = (a == b);       // result is 0
a_gt_b = (a > b);        // result is 0
a_ne_b = (a != b);       // result is 1
```

The logical AND (&&), OR (||), and negation (!) operators differ from the bit-wise logical operators of AND (&), OR (|), and complement (~) in the fact that the logical operators treat their operand(s) as either zero or non-zero, and always return a value of "0" or "1". Care must be taken to remember this important difference in order to avoid unexpected behavior from your *C* code. As a tip, remember that the logical operations are used for decision making, while the bitwise operations are primarily used for data extraction and insertion. Listing 4.3 compares results produced by logical versus bitwise operators. Observe that the logical operator && in line 3 gives the opposite result of the bitwise "&" operator. In line 3, a more verbose way to write the statement (a && b) is ((a != 0) && (b != 0)), which returns a "1" only if both a and b are non-zero. The second form clearly illustrates how the operands a, b are treated by the logical && operator. The statement (!b) in line 7 may be somewhat confusing at first, as it returns a "1" if b is zero. An alternate way to write (!b) is (b == 0). Thus, a statement such as (a && !b) is equivalent to ((a != 0) && (b == 0)), which returns a "1" only if a is non-zero and b is zero.

LISTING 4.3   Examples of *C* logical operators.

```
(1)    uint8 a, b, a_land_b, a_band_b;
       uint8 a_lor_b, a_bor_b, lneg_b, bcom_b;
(2)    a = 0xF0; b = 0x0F;
```

```
(3)    a_land_b = (a && b);    //logical and, result is 1
(4)    a_band_b = (a & b);     //bitwise and, result is 0
(5)    a_lor_b = (a || b);     //logical or, result is 1
(6)    a_bor_b = (a | b);      //bitwise or, result is 0xFF
(7)    lneg_b = (!b);          //logical negation, result is 0
(8)    bcom_b = (~b);          //bitwise negation, result is 0xF0
```

ZERO, NON-ZERO CONDITIONAL TESTS

The use of the conditional operators in Listings 4.2 and 4.3 is atypical, as they are most often used in conditional tests for if{}else{} statements or loop structures. The C if{}else{} statement structure is shown in Figure 4.14. Observe that the *if-body* is executed if the conditional test is true (returns 1), while the *else-body* is executed if the conditional test is false (returns 0). Use of an else{} clause in an if{} statement is optional.

```
if (condition_test) {
    if-body        ◄──── Executed when condition_test is non-zero (true)
} else {
    else-body    ◄──── Executed when condition_test is zero (false)
}
```

FIGURE 4.14   The if{}else{} statement in C.

Figure 4.15 shows a non-zero test used as the conditional for an *if{}* statement for a 16-bit variable k. The test if(k) is equivalent to if(k != 0); there is no advantage to either form. The non-zero test is accomplished by the mov k instruction, which copies the value of k back onto itself. While this leaves k unchanged, it does affect the Z, N flags in the status register (SR) which is the actual reason for executing this seemingly useless operation. The flag of interest in this case is the Z flag, which is "0" if k is non-zero. The btsc SR,#1 (bit test, skip if clear) skips the following instruction if Z = 0, causing the *if-body* to be executed. If Z = 1, the goto end_if instruction following the btsc instruction is executed, causing the *if-body* to be skipped.

```
      In C                           In Assembly
uint16 k;
                            mov    k          ; k = k, affects N,Z flags
                          ┌ btsc   SR,#1      ; skip if Z = 0 (Z is SR<1>)
if (k) {                  │ goto   end_if ──┐ ; Z = 1, k is 0
  if-body                 └►if-body stmt1    │
}                               ... stmtN    │
... rest of code          end_if: ◄──────────┘
                            ... rest of code
```

FIGURE 4.15   Non-zero test using mov/btsc/goto.

Since μC programs often check a variable for being non-zero, the PIC24 instruction set designers have provided another alternative. Another method for accomplishing the same nonzero test is shown in Figure 4.16, where the btsc/goto combination is replaced by the single instruction bra Z (branch if zero; e.g., branch if Z = 1). The bra z instruction branches (jumps) around the *if-body* when Z = 1, which is true if k is zero.

In *C*	In **Assembly**
uint16 k;	
	`    mov    k          ; k = k, affects N,Z flags`
if (k) {	`    bra    Z,end_if   ; skip if-body when Z = 1 (k is 0)`
if-body	`    if-body stmt1`
}	`        ... stmtN`
... *rest of code*	`  end_if:`
	`    ... rest of code`

FIGURE 4.16   Non-zero test using mov/bra Z.

Just like μC programs need to test a variable for being nonzero, μC programs often test a variable for being zero. A zero test is written as either if (!k) or as if (k == 0) and is implemented in the same manner as Figure 4.16, except a bra NZ instruction replaces the bra Z instruction.

The bra Z instruction and the bra NZ instruction are two of several branch instructions that perform a conditional jump based on the setting of a status register flag. PIC24 branch instructions include:

- **bra NZ,** <label>: (branch to <label> if not zero, Z = 0)
- **bra Z,** <label>: (branch to <label> if zero, Z = 1)
- **bra NC,** <label>: (branch to <label> if not carry, C = 0)
- **bra C,** <label>: (branch to <label> if carry, C = 1)
- **bra NN,** <label>: (branch to <label> if not negative, N = 0)
- **bra N,** <label>: (branch to <label> if negative, N = 1)
- **bra NOV,** <label>: (branch to <label> if no overflow, V = 0)
- **bra OV,** <label>: (branch to <label> if overflow, V = 1)
- **bra** <label>: (branch to <label> always, this is an unconditional branch)

Using branch instructions typically improves code clarity and generally results in fewer instruction words. The examples in this book use branch instructions wherever possible. The machine code format of branches is discussed in the next chapter, after signed number representation is covered.

Figure 4.17 shows the general method for converting an if{}else{} statement to assembly code. The branch instruction is chosen such that the branch is taken when the *condition_test* is *false*, causing the *if-body* to be skipped. The branch target is either the first instruction of the *else-body* if an *else-body* is present, or the first instruction

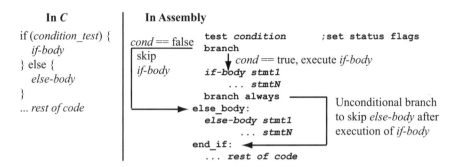

FIGURE 4.17   General `if{}else{}` form using branches.

following the *if-body* otherwise. If an *else-body* is present, the last instruction in the *if-body* must be an unconditional branch to the first instruction after the *else-body*.

BIT TESTS

Now that single flag branches have been introduced, it is instructive to revisit conditional execution using bit test instructions. Figure 4.18 shows the complete set of PIC24 bit test instructions; only the *bit test, skip if clear* (`btsc`) and the *bit test, skip if set* (`btsc`) have been previously discussed. The *bit test* (`btst`) instruction tests a bit in a source operand, and affects either the Z or C flags. When affecting the Z flag, the complemented bit value is copied to the Z flag. This sets the Z flag if the bit is 0, and clears it if the bit is non-zero. When affecting the C flag, the bit value is copied to the C flag. The bit to be tested is specified by either a 4-bit immediate (*#bit4*) or by a *Wb* register value (only the lower four bits of *Wb* are used). The bit test/set (`btsts`) instruction performs the same test as `btst`, with the additional action of setting the tested bit afterwards.

Name	Mnemonic	Operation
Bit Test, skip if clear	`btsc{.b} f, #bit4` `btsc{.b} Ws, #bit4`	Test *f<bit4>*, skip if clear Test *Ws<bit4>*, skip if clear
Bit Test, skip if set	`btss{.b} f, #bit4` `btss{.b} Ws, #bit4`	Test *f<bit4>*, skip if set Test *Ws<bit4>*, skip if set

Bit Test	`btst{.b} f, #bit4`
	`btst.Z{.b} Ws, #bit4`
	`btst.C{.b} Ws, #bit4`
	`btst.Z{.b} Ws, Wb`
	`btst.C{.b} Ws, Wb`
		$\sim f<bit4> \rightarrow Z$
		$\sim Ws<bit4> \rightarrow Z$
		$Ws<bit4> \rightarrow C$
		$\sim Ws<Wb> \rightarrow Z$
		$Ws<Wb> \rightarrow C$

Bit Test/Set	`btsts{.b} f, #bit4`
	`btsts.Z{.b} Ws, #bit4`
	`btsts.C{.b} Ws, #bit4`
		$\sim f<bit4> \rightarrow Z; 1 \rightarrow f<bit4>$
		$\sim Ws<bit4> \rightarrow Z; 1 \rightarrow Ws<bit4>$
		$Ws<bit4> \rightarrow C; 1 \rightarrow Ws<bit4>$

FIGURE 4.18   Bit test instructions.

Listing 4.4 shows the original instruction combination of `btsc.b/goto` that was used for testing the least significant bit of variable `loc` in the number sequencing program of Listing 4.1 replaced with an equivalent instruction combination using `btst.b/bra NZ`. The `bra NZ,loc_lsb_is_1` branch is taken if the least significant bit of variable `loc` is 1. The `btst` instruction forms are useful for branching on single bit conditions.

LISTING 4.4   Use of bit test for conditional execution.

```
;;;Original code from Listing 4.1
(9)   loop_top:
(10)     btsc.b   loc,#0              ;skip next if loc<0> is 0
(11)     goto     loc_lsb_is_1
(12)     ;loc<0> is 0 if reach here


;;;New code using btst
(9)   loop_top:
(10)     btst.b   loc,#0              ;test if loc<0> is 1
(11)     bra NZ,loc_lsb_is_1          ;take branch if loc<0> is 1
(12)     ;loc<0> is 0 if reached here
```

EQUALITY, INEQUALITY CONDITIONAL TESTS

Figure 4.19 shows the implementation in PIC24 assembly code of an `if{}` statement that has the equality test (`k == j`) as its condition, where j and k are 16-bit variables. The equality test is performed by the subtraction $k - j$, followed by a `bra NZ` that branches to the end of the `if{}` statement if Z = 0, indicating that k is not equal to j. The use of the subtraction operation to affect status flags for conditional test purposes is a common theme that is useful for all types of comparison operations. It does not matter if $k - j$ or $j - k$ is performed, as both affect the Z flag in the same way. An inequality test (`k != j`) is performed in a similar manner, with a `bra Z` replacing the `bra NZ` instruction.

```
In C                        In Assembly
uint16 k, j;                    mov    j,W0      ;W0 = j
                                sub    k,WREG    ;W0 = k - j
if (k == j) {                   bra    NZ,end_if ;skip if-body when Z=0 (k != j)
  if-body                       if-body stmt1
}                                      ... stmtN
... rest of code            end_if:
                                ... rest of code
```

FIGURE 4.19   Equality test using `sub/bra NZ`.

CONDITIONAL TESTS FOR >=, >, <, <=

Figure 4.20 illustrates how inequality tests such as >, >=, <, <= can be performed using subtraction and the C, Z flags. Two variables, k and j, are used as an example. Figure 4.20a shows the C, Z flag values after the subtraction k − j is performed for the cases of >, <, and ==. As an example of how the flags are derived in Figure 4.20a, consider the case of k > j. The C flag is "1" after k − j is performed because a smaller number (j) is subtracted from a larger number (k), resulting in no borrow (C = 1). Obviously, Z = 0 after (k − j) is performed because k is not equal to j if k > j.

To determine the flag tests for implementing > and >= comparisons in assembly language, one must consider the flag(s) that uniquely identifies the true conditions when considering the intersection of the > and == tests. For the >= comparison, C = 1 is true for both > and ==, so only the C flag must be tested to determine if k >= j is true after the subtraction k − j is performed. For the k > j comparison, C = 1 is true for both the > and == tests, so the Z = 0 flag condition must be included in the k > j test to distinguish the k > j condition from the k >= j condition. Thus, the true condition for the test k > j is "C = 1 and Z = 0", or written in a Boolean format is "C & ~Z". The <= test is the Boolean equivalent of "~(k > j)", so "~(C & ~Z)" is equal to "~C | Z" by DeMorgan's Law (Chapter 1), or <= is true when "C = 0 or Z = 1".

Figure 4.21 shows an if{} statement whose condition is k > j and the assembly language implementation using the test k − j. The false condition to branch around the *if-body* is k <= j, so the flag conditions from Figure 4.20a to accomplish this are "C = 0 or Z = 1", which is implemented using bra NC and bra Z instructions.

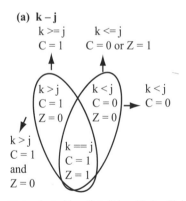

(a) k − j

Note: k <= j is ~(k > j) is ~(C & ~Z) is (~C | Z) by DeMorgan's law. Similarly, k < j is ~(k >= j) is ~(C) is ~C.

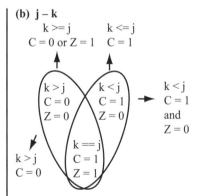

(b) j − k

Note: k < j is ~(k >= j) is ~(!C | Z) is (C & ~Z) by DeMorgan's law. Similarly, k <= j is ~(k > j) is ~(~C) is C.

FIGURE 4.20   Equality comparisons using C, Z flags and subtraction.

In *C*	In Assembly
uint16 k, j;	

```
               mov  j,W0        ;W0 = j
               sub  k,WREG      ;W0 = k - j
            ┌─ bra NC, end_if   ;skip if-body when C = 0 (k < j)
            │┌─ bra Z,  end_if  ;or skip if-body when Z = 1 (k == j)
            ││  if-body stmt1
            ││     ... stmtN
            └┴─end_if:
                   ... rest of code
```

In *C*:
```
if (k > j) {
    if-body
}
... rest of code
```

False condition of k > j is k <= j, so need branches that accomplish this.

FIGURE 4.21   Unsigned greater-than (k > j) test using k – j subtraction.

Figure 4.22 gives a more efficient manner for implementing the if{} of Figure 4.21 by using the subtraction j − k as the test, which allows the false condition of k <= j to be implemented using only the single flag test of C = 1 as derived in Figure 4.20b.

In *C*	In Assembly
uint16 k, j;	

```
               mov   k,W0       ;W0 = k
               sub   j,WREG     ;W0 = j - k
            ┌─ bra   C, end_if  ;skip if-body when C = 1 (k <= j)
            │  if-body stmt1
            │     ... stmtN
            └─end_if:
                  ... rest of code
```

In *C*:
```
if (k > j) {
    if-body
}
... rest of code
```

FIGURE 4.22   Unsigned greater-than (k > j) test using j – k subtraction.

COMPARISON AND UNSIGNED BRANCH INSTRUCTIONS

Using subtraction and simple flag tests can be confusing, as one must remember which subtraction to use, k − j or j − k, for implementing a particular unsigned branch in the most efficient manner. The PIC24 instruction set has a set of unsigned branches that can be used for unsigned comparisons as shown in Table 4.4. These flag conditions correspond to the k − j test in Figure 4.20a when comparing k to j where k and j are unsigned numbers. (Signed number comparison is covered in Chapter 5.)

As previously seen, the subtraction instruction can be used to affect the flags used by branch operations. However, a drawback of using the subtraction instruction is that a register or memory location value is destroyed by the subtraction result. Another way to affect flags for branch operations is to use a *compare* instruction, which performs subtraction with its two operands, but does not save the result, as shown in Figure 4.23. The cp{.b} *Wb*, *Ws* and cp{.b} *f* forms are useful for comparing two

TABLE 4.4 Unsigned branches.

Description	Syntax	Branch Taken When
Branch >, unsigned	bra GTU, <label>	C & ~Z
Branch >=, unsigned	bra GEU, <label>	C
Branch <, unsigned	bra LTU, <label>	~C
Branch <=, unsigned	bra LEU, <label>	~C | Z

Name	Mnemonic	Operation

Compare	`cp{.b} Wb, Ws`
	`cp{.b} Wb, #lit5`
	`cp{.b} f`
		(Wb) - (Ws)
		(Wb) - #lit5
		(f) - (WREG)

Compare with Zero	`cp0{.b} Ws` `cp0{.b} f`	(Ws) - 0 (f) - 0

Flags C, Z, DC, N, OV are affected by the compare instructions.

FIGURE 4.23 Compare instructions.

unsigned variables, while the cp{.b} Wb,#lit5 form is useful for comparing a variable against a constant. The cp0 (compare with zero) forms are a convenient method for comparing a variable against 0, whose addressing modes are more flexible than provided by the cp{.b} Wb, #lit5 instruction. Recall that Figure 4.16 used a mov instruction to accomplish a zero test by copying a memory location on top of itself to affect flags; the cp0 instruction can replace the mov instruction for the purposes of zero test.

Figure 4.24 shows the if{} code of Figure 4.21 implemented in assembly using a compare instruction and an unsigned branch. The false condition for k > j is k <= j, so a bra LEU (less than equal unsigned) is used to skip the *if-body*. Unsigned branches and compare instructions offer greater code clarity over simple branches, and thus will be used for inequality comparison from this point onward.

In *C*	In Assembly
| uint16 k, j;<br><br>if (k > j) {<br>  *if-body*<br>}<br>... *rest of code* | ```
     mov j,W0        ;W0 = j
     cp k            ;k - WREG
     bra LEU, end_if ;skip if-body when k <= j
     if-body stmt1
         ... stmtN
end_if:
     ... rest of code
``` |

FIGURE 4.24 Unsigned greater-than (k > j) test compare k – j and unsigned branch.
```

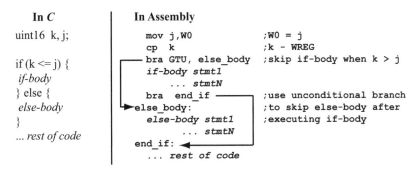

FIGURE 4.25   if{}else{} with <= test.

An example of an if{}else{} statement with a <= test is shown in Figure 4.25. The false condition of k <= j is k > j, so a bra GTU (greater than unsigned) instruction is used to target the first instruction of the *else-body,* thus skipping the *if-body.* Observe that the last instruction of the *if-body* is a bra to the first instruction following the *else-body.*

Figure 4.26 shows a couple of different ways for performing literal comparisons. Figure 4.26a compares k against 10 by first moving k into W0, then uses the cp W0,#10 instruction. This works because 10 is small enough to fit within the 5-bit literal field available to this compare form. Figure 4.26b cannot use this approach because 520 is greater than 31, the maximum value for a 5-bit literal compare. Thus, Figure 4.26b first moves the value 520 into W0, and then performs the comparison using the cp k instruction.

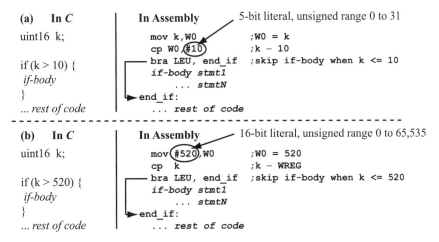

FIGURE 4.26   Unsigned literal comparisons.

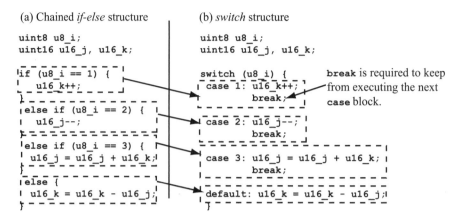

FIGURE 4.27 Switch statement.

The literal comparison method of Figure 4.26a is useful if the same variable is compared against multiple literal values. Figure 4.27a shows a chained `if{}else{}`structure that compares a variable against several constants, which can also be implemented using a `switch` statement as shown in Figure 4.27b. The `switch` *(variable)* statement compares *variable* against constants specified by the `case` *constant* statements. The compound statement following a `case` statement is executed if *variable* is equal to *constant*. The `break` statement at the end of each `case` compound statement causes an unconditional jump to the end of the `switch` statement. If the `break` statement is not included, then the next compound `case` statement is executed even if *variable* does not match the constant used in that `case` statement. Execution continues until a `break` is encountered or the end of the `switch` is reached. This behavior is generally not desirable, so one must be careful to include `break` statements at the end of each `case`. The `default` case is executed if *variable* does not match any of the `case` statement constants. In the later hardware chapters, you will discover that the `switch` statement is very useful for implementing input/output sequences written in a finite-state machine style.

Figure 4.28 shows an assembly language implementation of the `switch` statement of Figure 4.27. Observe that the switch variable u8_i is first loaded into W0 then multiple `cp` instructions are used to test u8_i against the `case` statement constants. This works because the `case` statement constants are all unsigned numbers less than 32, and thus can be encoded in 5 bits. An unconditional `bra` statement is used to implement each `break` statement.

Table 4.5 summarizes the preferred operations and flag tests for unsigned, zero, and equality comparison operations. The reader may find it useful to refer to Table 4.5 when trying to decide which branch to use for implementing a particular comparison.

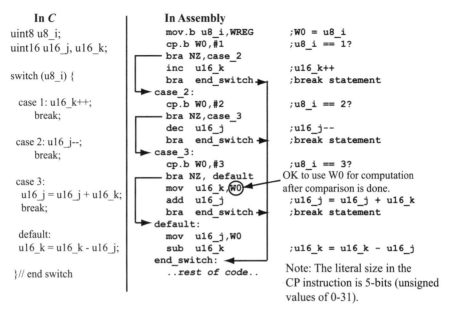

FIGURE 4.28   Switch statement implemented in assembly.

TABLE 4.5   Unsigned, zero, and equality comparison summary.

Comparison	Test	True Branch	False Branch
k == 0	k − 0	bra Z	bra NZ
k != 0	k − 0	bra NZ	bra Z
k == j	k − j	bra Z	bra NZ
k != j	k − j	bra NZ	bra Z
k > j	k − j	bra GTU	bra LEU
k >= j	k − j	bra GEU	bra LTU
k < j	k − j	bra LTU	bra GEU
k <= j	k − j	bra LEU	bra GTU

There are additional PIC24 instructions that combine a comparison with a skip operation, such as *Compare Wb with Wn, Skip if Equal*. This text will not discuss those comparisons, since their functionality can be implemented using other comparison/branch instruction combinations with the same efficiency in most cases.

COMPLEX CONDITIONAL EXPRESSIONS

Our conditional expressions to this point have used a single comparison, such as
k > j. Conditional expressions often use multiple comparisons that are connected
with && (logical AND) or || (logical OR) operators. Figure 4.29 shows the general
form of an if{}else{} statement that uses multiple comparisons, which are connected using && operators. During condition testing, the *else-body* is branched to
on the first condition that is *false*. This means that the *if-body* is executed only when
all conditions are *true*.

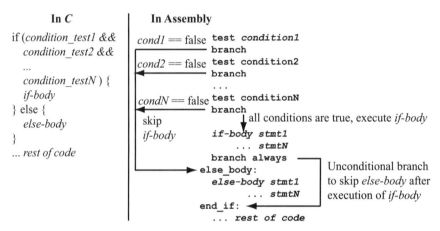

The *else-body* is branched to on the first condition that is false.
The *if-body* is executed if all conditions are true.

FIGURE 4.29 if{}else{} general form with complex conditional (&&).

An example of an if{}else{} statement using a complex conditional is shown
in Figure 4.30. The assembly language implementation uses a bra GEU as the branch
for the first comparison because the false condition for i < k is i >= k. The second
branch uses a bra Z instruction because the false condition for j != 20 is j == 20.

Figure 4.31 shows the general form of an if{}else{} statement that uses mul-
tiple comparisons which are connected using || operators. During the condition
testing, the *if-body* is branched to on the first condition that is *true*. The last condition branches to the *else-body* if it is *false*, causing the *else-body* to be executed only
when all conditions are *false*.

Figure 4.32 shows an if{}else{} example with multiple comparisons connected
by || operators. The first comparison uses a bra LTU to branch to the *if-body* because
this is the true condition for i < k. The second comparison uses a bra Z to branch
to the *if-body* because this is the true condition for j == p. The last comparison
uses a bra Z to branch to the *else-body* (skipping the *if-body*) because this is the false

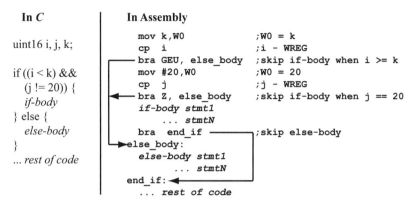

FIGURE 4.30   if{}else{} example using a complex conditional (&&).

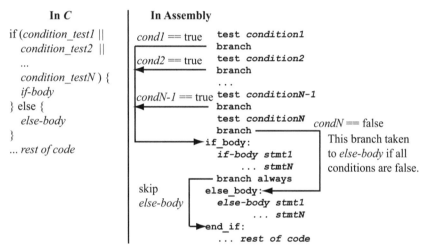

The *if-body* is branched to on the first condition that is true.
The *else-body* is executed if all conditions are false.

FIGURE 4.31   if{}else{} general form with complex conditional (||).

condition for q != 0. A common mistake for new assembly language programmers is to use the true condition for the last condition test since the true condition was used for all of the previous branches. If the true condition is used, then the branch target must be the *if-body*, with an unconditional jump to the *else-body* immediately following as shown in the circled code of Figure 4.32. This is not as efficient, but it may be easier to remember for new assembly language programmers.

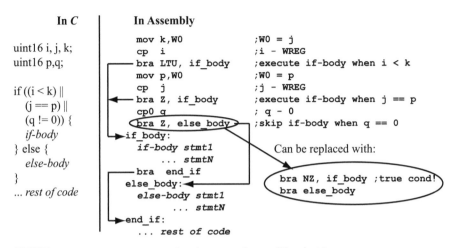

FIGURE 4.32   if{}else{} example using a complex conditional (||).

LOOPING

A while *(condition_test)* {*while-body*} loop structure has the same form as an if{} structure, except the *while-body* is executed as long as the *condition_test* is true. Figure 4.33 shows the general assembly language form for implementing a while{} loop. The condition test is done at the top of the loop, with the conditional branch skipping the *while-body* if the loop condition is false. The last statement in the *while-body* must be an unconditional jump back to the top of the loop, thus implementing the repeating behavior of a loop. A common mistake for new assembly programmers is for this unconditional jump to target the first instruction of the *while-body*, thus skipping the test and conditional branch and forming an infinite loop. Observe that the *while-body* is not executed if the conditional test is initially false.

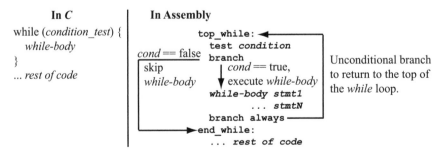

The *while-body* is not executed if the condition test is initially false.

FIGURE 4.33   General structure for while{} loop.

A `while{}` to assembly language example is given in Figure 4.34. The `bra LEU` instruction causes the *while-body* to be skipped if `k <= j`, which is the false condition for the `k > j` comparison.

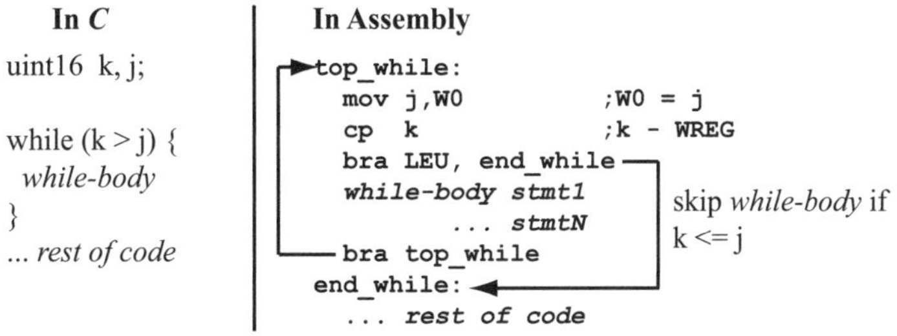

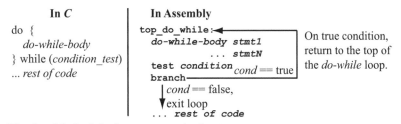

FIGURE 4.34 `while{}` loop to assembly language.

The general assembly language structure for a `do {do-while-body} while (condition_test)` loop is shown in Figure 4.35. The *do-while-body* is executed as long as the *condition_test* is true. Because the loop conditional test is located at the end of the loop body, the *do-while-body* executes at least one time. The branch instruction at the end of the loop body uses the true condition to return to the first instruction of the *do-while-body*. Execution falls out of the bottom of the loop when the condition test is false and the branch is not taken. A common mistake by new assembly language programmers is to use the general assembly language form for a `while{}` loop for a `do{}while` loop, or vice versa. This is incorrect as the two loop structures are not semantically the same because the *while-body* may not be executed if the initial test is false, while a *do-while-body* will always be executed at least once.

The *do-while-body* is always executed at least once.

FIGURE 4.35 General structure for `do{}while` loop.

An example `do{}while` to assembly language conversion is given in Figure 4.36. Observe that the condition test `k > j` is the same as used for the `while{}` example of

In *C*	In Assembly	
uint16 k, j;	`top_do_while:`	
	`  while-body stmt1`	
	`      ... stmtN`	return to top of
do {	`  mov j,W0      ;W0 = j`	*do{}while* loop if
while-body	`  cp  k          ;k - WREG`	k > j
}while (k > j);	`  bra GTU, top_do_while`	
... rest of code	`  ... rest of code`	

FIGURE 4.36   do{}while to assembly language example.

Figure 4.34, but that the assembly code uses a different branch after the loop condition test because the loop condition test is at the end of the loop rather than the top of the loop. In this case, a `bra GTU` instruction is used, which is the *true* condition for k > j, thus causing a return to the top of the loop.

Another commonly used loop structure in the *C* language is the for{} loop. Figure 4.37 shows that a for{} loop is simply a shorthand notation for a while{} loop. As such, the use of a for{} loop structure is optional, as it can always be written as a while{} loop.

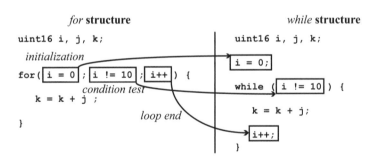

FIGURE 4.37   for{} loop structure.

SUMMARY

In this chapter, we explored 8/16-bit arithmetic, logical, shift, and unsigned comparison operations. The obvious limitations of 8/16-bit unsigned integer data will be removed in the next chapter when we discuss extended precision operations on signed integer data.

TABLE 4.6   Register memory contents.

Location	Value	Location	Value
W0	0x0804	0x0800	0x382A
W1	0x0806	0x0802	0xFB80
W2	0x8301	0x0804	0x80FF
W3	0xF0A2	0x0806	0x7B03
W4	0xFFFF	0x0808	0x0001

REVIEW PROBLEMS

For problems 1 through 34, give the Z and C flags and affected registers after execution of each instruction. Assume the register and memory contents of Table 4.6 at the beginning of EACH problem, with initial flag settings of Z = 0, C = 1.

1. `add.b W4, W2, W0`
2. `add W4, W2, W0`
3. `sub W1,W0,W2`
4. `sub.b W4,W2, W2`
5. `and.b W0, W1, W1`
6. `and W3, W2, W0`
7. `ior W3, W1, W0`
8. `ior.b W0, W1, W0`
9. `xor.b W3, W4, W4`
10. `xor W4, W3, W3`
11. `clr W4`
12. `clr.b W3`
13. `setm W1`
14. `setm.b W3`
15. `bset.b 0x0801,#6`
16. `bset 0x0804,#9`
17. `bclr 0x0804,#15`
18. `bclr.b 0x0805,#7`
19. `btg 0x0806,#3`
20. `btg.b 0x0808,#0`
21. `com.b 0x0803`
22. `com 0x0804`

```
23. lsr W3, #8, W3
24. lsr W2,#4, W0
25. sl W3,#12,W0
26. sl W1, #2, W0
27. rlnc.b 0x0800
28. rlnc 0x0800
29. rlc 0x802
30. rlc.b 0x803
31. rrnc 0x0800
32. rrnc.b 0x0800
33. rrc.b 0x802
34. rrc 0x806
```

Write PIC24 assembly language equivalents for the following *C* code fragments. Assume variables u16_i, u16_k, u16_j, u16_n are uint16 variables, while u8_p, u8_q, u8_r are uint8 variables.

35. Code fragment:

```
u16_k = u16_i + (u16_j << 1) − 0x30;
```

36. Code fragment:

```
u16_i = ((u16_k − u16_j) >> 4) & 0x0F;
```

37. Code fragment:

```
u16_k = (uint16) u8_p + (u16_j << 1) − 0x30;
```

38. Code fragment:

```
u16_i = ((u16_k − (uint8) u8_q) >> 4) & 0x0F;
```

39. Code fragment (use place holders for *if-body, else-body*):

```
if ((u16_k >= 0x0400) || (u8_r == 0)) {
    if-body statements
    } else {
      else-body statements
    }
```

40. Code fragment (use place holders for *if-body, else-body*):

```
if ((u16_k < u16_j) || (u8_r != u8_q)) {
    if-body statements
    } else {
      else-body statements
    }
```

41. Code fragment (use place holders for *if-body, else-body*):

```
if ((u16_k != 0x0400) && (u8_r > u8_p)) {
    if-body statements
    } else {
      else-body statements
    }
```

42. Code fragment (use place holders for *if-body, else-body*):

```
if ((u16_k != 0) && (u16_j >= u16_i)) {
    if-body statements
    } else {
      else-body statements
    }
```

43. Code fragment (use place holders for *loop-body*):

```
while (u16_i != u16_k) {
    loop-body statements
}
```

44. Code fragment (use place holders for *loop-body*):

```
while ((u8_r != 0) && (u8_p < u8_q)) {
    loop-body statements
}
```

45. Code fragment (use place holders for *loop-body*):

```
do {
    loop-body statements
    } while ((u8_r != 0) || (u8_p < u8_q))
```

46. Code fragment (use place holders for *loop-body*):

```
do {
    loop-body statements
} while ((u16_i != u16_k) && (u8_p > 0x50))
```

47. The following *C* code counts the number of "1" bits in j and returns the answer in k. Convert this to PIC24 assembly code. You may want to convert the for{} loop structure to a while{} loop structure.

```
uint8 u8_i,u8_j,u8_k;
u8_k = 0; // init bit count
for (u8_i = 0; u8_i != 8; u8_i++) { // do for 8 bits
    if ((u8_j & 0x01) == 1) {
    u8_k++; // LSb = 1, increment count
    }
 u8_j = u8_j >> 1; // look at the next bit
 }
```

48. The following *C* code shifts k to the left for each '0' bit present in j. Convert this to PIC24 assembly code. You may want to convert the for{} loop structure to a while{} loop structure.

```
uint16 u16_i,u16_j,u16_k;
u16_k = 1; // initialize k
for (u16_i = 0; u16_i != 16; u16_i++) { // do for 16 bits
    if ((u16_j & 0x0001) == 0) {
    u16_k = u16_k << 1;
    }
 u16_j = u16_j >> 1; // look at the next bit
 }
```

5 Extended Precision and Signed Data Operations

This chapter applies the arithmetic, logical, and shift operations discussed in the previous chapter to extended precision operands; that is, operands that are larger than 16 bits. Furthermore, signed number representation and its effect on shift and comparison operations are covered.

Learning Objectives

After reading this chapter, you will be able to:

- Translate *C* language statements that perform extended-precision addition, subtraction, bitwise logical, and shift operations into PIC24 instruction sequences.
- Compare and contrast signed magnitude, one's complement, and two's complement representations of signed integers.
- Translate *C* language statements that perform shift and comparison operations using signed operands into PIC24 instruction sequences.
- Translate PIC24 branch instructions into machine code and be able to discuss the meaning of relative addressing.

EXTENDED PRECISION OPERATIONS

Previous chapters have used unsigned 8-bit and 16-bit integers in *C* programs, which limits these variables to a 0 to 255 and 0 to 65,535 number range, respectively. Obviously, practical problems have a need to accommodate larger number ranges in *C* programs and PIC24 assembly language programs. The uint32 data type originally given in Table 3.4 of Chapter 3 is a 32-bit unsigned integer data type that provides a 0 to 4,294,967,295 ($2^{32}-1$) number range. The need for 32-bit data types depends upon the microcontroller application, but most often they are needed when manipulating high-precision timing intervals. The lower 16 bits of a 32-bit integer is referred to in this book as the *least significant word* (LSW) and the upper 16 bits as the *most significant word* (MSW). Because the PIC24 CPU is a 16-bit CPU, operations on 32-bit data require approximately twice the number of instructions as 16-bit operations, split between manipulation of the LSW and MSW portions of the 32-bit datum. Because of the doubled execution time, program space, and data RAM required for 32-bit integers, they should only be used when the extra precision is required by the application.

32-Bit Assignment Operations

To be consistent with PIC24 technical documentation, the term *double word* is also used in this text in reference to 32-bit data. Figure 5.1 shows the two forms of double word moves available in the PIC24 instruction set. The first form allows register indirect modes for the source operand and thus supports copies from data RAM into the working registers. The second form supports register indirect modes for the destination operand and thus supports working register to data RAM copies. When register direct addressing (*Wn*) is used for either *Ws*, *Wns*, *Wd*, or *Wnd* this specifies a double word value that resides in *Wn:Wn+1*, with *Wn* referring to the LSW and *Wn+1* to the MSW. Furthermore, register direct addressing is limited to even-numbered registers (i.e., W0, W2,...W14). When register indirect addressing is used for either *Ws* or *Wd*, any register (W0 through W15) may be used to specify the effective address of the LSW in data RAM, with the MSW address at address LSW + 2. The effective address of the LSW must be word-aligned.

Name	Mnemonic	Operation
double Word Move from Source to *Wnd*	`mov.d Ws, Wnd` (recall that `Ws` includes indirect modes)	`(Ws:Ws+1) → Wnd:Wnd+1`
double Word Move from *Wns* to Destination	`mov.d Wns, Wd` (recall that `Wd` includes indirect modes)	`(Wns:Wns+1) → Wd:Wd+1`

Note: When direct register addressing is used for either *Wns* or *Wnd*, then an even-numbered register (W0, W2, W4,...W14) must be used.

FIGURE 5.1   Double word (32-bit) `mov` instructions.

A double word move example that uses register direct addressing for both *Wns* and *Wnd* is shown in Figure 5.2a. Observe that `mov.d W0, W2` copies data from the `W0:W1` register pair to the `W2:W3` register pair. Figure 5.2b illustrates a double word move from data RAM to working registers, with register indirect addressing used for *Wns*. The data RAM effective address for the LSW of a double word move must be word-aligned (an even address), but the register used as the source register for an register indirect addressing mode can be any working register. Observe that the destination register W2 in Figure 5.2b is an even numbered register, fulfilling the requirement that a destination using register direct addressing for a double word move must be evenly numbered.

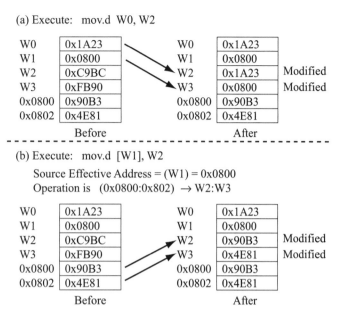

(a) Execute: mov.d W0, W2

(b) Execute: mov.d [W1], W2

Source Effective Address = (W1) = 0x0800

Operation is   (0x0800:0x802) → W2:W3

FIGURE 5.2   Double word (32-bit) mov examples.

Figure 5.3 illustrates PIC24 assembly language implementation of *C* language variable assignment operations involving uint32 data types. The PIC24 assembly language implementation for these particular assignments does not use any of the double word move forms, as it more efficient in this case to simply use individual 16-bit operations on the LSW and MSW portions of the uint32 data types. The double word move forms become more efficient for *C* pointer operations involving arrays of 32-bit data, which is covered in Chapter 6. In Figure 5.3, observe that the label k refers to the LSW of the uint32 k variable, while k+2 is used for the

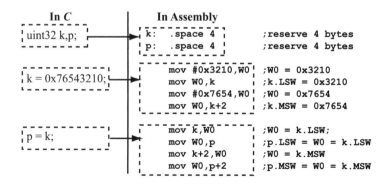

FIGURE 5.3   *C* Language 32-bit assignment operations.

MSW. For C language assignment of uint32 variables, the order in which the 16-bit assignments are made, LSW first or MSW first, does not matter as long as LSW is copied to LSW and MSW to MSW.

32-Bit Bitwise Logical Operations

Figure 5.4 shows a bitwise AND operation applied to uint32 operands. Note that the and instruction is applied to each word of the operands. It is immaterial as to the order in which a bitwise logical operation is applied to the words of a 32-bit operand, as each word operation is independent of each other, just as with the assignment operation.

In *C*	In Assembly	
uint32 k, j;	k: .space 4	;reserve 4 bytes
	j: .space 4	;reserve 4 bytes
k = k & j;	mov j,W0	;W0 = j.LSW
	and k	;k.LSW = k.LSW & W0 = k.LSW & j.LSW
	mov j+2,W0	;W0 = j.MSW
	and k+2	;k.MSW = k.MSW & W0 = k.MSW & j.MSW

FIGURE 5.4 *C* Language 32-bit bitwise logical operations.

32-Bit Addition/Subtraction

Figure 5.5 shows addition and subtraction using two 32-bit operands. For the addition operation, the two least significant words are added first, followed by the addition of the two most significant words, which includes the carry (C flag) produced by the least significant word addition. The subtraction is done similarly, except the subtraction of the most significant words includes the borrow produced by the least significant word subtraction. Note that unlike logical operations, the order of the operations for addition and subtraction matter in that the LSW operation is performed first, followed by the MSW operation.

To accommodate the needs of extended precision addition and subtraction, the PIC24 instruction set includes the instructions addc (add with carry) and subb

(a) Addition

C flag
1 ◀

```
    0x A734 F082
+   0x 13C0 4370
    ─────────────
    0x BAF5 33F2
```

(b) Subtraction

Borrow = ~C flag
−1 ◀

```
    0x A734 1082
−   0x 13C0 4370
    ─────────────
    0x 9373 CD12
```

FIGURE 5.5 Addition/subtraction with 32-bit operands.

(subtract with borrow) as shown in Figure 5.6. These instructions support the same addressing modes as add/sub instructions previously discussed. There is also a cpb (compare with borrow) instruction for use in comparing extended precision operands.

Name	Mnemonic	Operation
Add with Carry	addc{.b} Wb, Ws, Wd addc{.b} Wb, #lit5, Wd addc{.b} #lit10, Wn addc{.b} f addc{.b} f,WREG	(Wb)+(Ws)+(C) → Wd (Wb)+#lit5+(C) → Wd (Wn)+#lit10+(C) → Wn (f)+WREG+(C) → f (f)+WREG+(C) → WREG
Subtract with Borrow	subb{.b} Wb, Ws, Wd subb{.b} Wb, #lit5, Wd subb{.b} #lit10, Wn subb{.b} f subb{.b} f,WREG	(Wb)-(Ws)-(~C) → Wd (Wb)-#lit5-(~C) → Wd (Wn)-#lit10-(~C) → Wn (f)-WREG-(~C) → f (f)-WREG-(~C) → WREG
Subtract with Borrow Reverse	subbr{.b} Wb, Ws, Wd subbr{.b} Wb, #lit5, Wd subbr{.b} f subbr{.b} f,WREG	(Ws)-(Wb)-(~C) → Wd #lit5-(Wb)-(~C) → Wd WREG-(f)-(~C) → f WREG-(f)-(~C) → WREG
Compare with Borrow	cpb{.b} Wb, Ws cpb{.b} Wb, #lit5 cpb{.b} f	(Wb)-(Ws)-(~C) (Wb)-#lit5-(~C) (f)-WREG-(~C)

Note: These instructions affect the DC, N, OV, and C flags. The Z flag is sticky in that it can only be cleared by these instructions.

FIGURE 5.6   Addition/subtraction/compare instructions for extended precision operations.

Figure 5.7 illustrates the use of addc and subb instructions for performing k=k+j and p=p−q, where all of the variables are of type uint32. The add instruction is used for the LSW of k+j, followed by the addc instruction for the MSW. Similarly, the sub instruction is used for the LSW of p−q, followed by the subb instruction for the

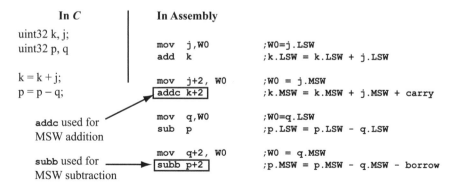

FIGURE 5.7   Addition/subtraction using addc/subb instructions.

MSW. The no carry version of addition (add) and the no borrow version of subtract (sub) is used on the LSW because there is no carry into or borrow from the LSW.

Another difference between the add/sub and addc/subb/cpb instructions, besides the inclusion of carry/borrow, is in the manner that the addc/subb instructions affect the Z flag. The Z flag is said to be *sticky* in that the addc/subb instructions can only clear the Z flag, not set it. This behavior means that in a 32-bit add/addc sequence or a sub/subb sequence, the Z flag represents the zero status of the entire 32-bit result and not just the zero status of the MSW. Figure 5.8 clarifies this by giving three 32-bit subtraction examples using sub/subb. Figure 5.8a shows a subtraction result whose 32-bit result is 0x0000F000, a non-zero result. After the LSW subtraction, the Z flag is 0 because the sub instruction produces a value of 0xF000. After the MSW subtraction using the subb instruction, the Z flag is still 0 even though the MSW is 0x0000 because the Z flag cannot be set by subb. Thus, the final Z flag value of 0 indicates that the 32-bit result of 0x0000F000 is non-zero. Figure 5.8b shows another 32-bit subtraction with a non-zero result of 0x00010000, except this time the MSW is non-zero and the LSW is zero. The Z flag is set after the LSW subtraction, but the MSW subtraction using subb produces a non-zero result,

(a) Subtraction, LSW result is non-zero, MSW result is zero.

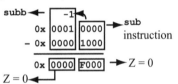

MSW is 0, but **subb** can only clear the Z flag, it cannot set the Z flag!
This means that the Z flag reflects the zero status of the 32-bit operation, which is non-zero.

(b) Subtraction, LSW result is zero, MSW result is non-zero.

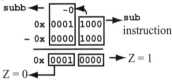

MSW is non-zero, so Z flag is cleared; 32-bit result is non-zero.

(c) Subtraction, LSW result is zero, MSW result is zero.

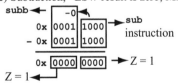

MSW is zero, so Z flag remains set from previous instruction; 32-bit result is zero.

FIGURE 5.8   Z flag behavior in addc/subb instructions.

so the subb instruction clears the Z flag. The final subtraction shown in Figure 5.8c produces a result of 0x00000000 and a final Z flag value of 1. The Z flag is set to a 1 by the sub instruction in the LSW operation. The Z flag remains a 1 after the MSW operation using the subb instruction because a zero result is produced, so subb leaves the Z flag at its previous value, which is a 1. This Z flag behavior means that the 32-bit equal (==) and (!=) testing can be performed using a cp/cpb instruction sequence followed by a branch on the Z flag.

Figure 5.9 shows increment/decrement operations on 32-bit variables. Because there is no increment with carry instruction, an inc/addc sequence is used as shown in Figure 5.9a where addc performs k.MSW+0+Carry after the inc instruction increments k.LSW. The W0 register is cleared first to ensure that addc k+2 adds a zero to k.MSW. The assembly code for decrementing a 32-bit variable in Figure 5.9b uses a similar approach via the dec/subb instruction sequence.

(a) Increment	(b) Decrement
uint32 k;	uint32 k;
k++;	k--;
`clr  W0    ;W0 = 0`	`clr  W0    ;W0 = 0`
`inc  k     ;inc k.LSW`	`dec  k     ;dec k.LSW`
`addc k+2   ;k.MSW = k.MSW + 0 + C`	`subb k+2   ;k.MSW = k.MSW - 0 - ~C`
Clear W0 so it is zero for **addc** to MSW.	Clear W0 so it is zero for **subb** from MSW.

FIGURE 5.9 32-bit increment/decrement operations.

32-Bit Logical Shift Right/Shift Left Operations

Figure 5.10a shows a 32-bit logical shift right operation. The MSW of k is shifted first using the lsr (logical shift right) instruction, followed by the rrc (rotate right with carry) instruction on the LSW. Recall that the rrc instruction shifts the C flag into the most significant bit. Thus, the C flag is used as a 1-bit storage register for transporting the bit shifted out of the MSW into the LSW. A shift left on a 32-bit variable is shown in Figure 5.10b. The LSW is shifted first using a sl (shift left) instruction, followed by a rlc (rotate left with carry) on the MSW with the C flag used to transport the bit shifted out of the LSW into the MSW.

Zero, Non-Zero Conditional Tests

A 32-bit non-zero test is shown in Figure 5.11. This is the same example used in Chapter 4 with the exception that the data type has been changed from uint16 to uint32. The most straightforward method of testing a 32-bit operand for zero/non-zero is to compare the least and most significant words against 0 using cp (compare) and cpb (compare with borrow), respectively. This works because the Z flag

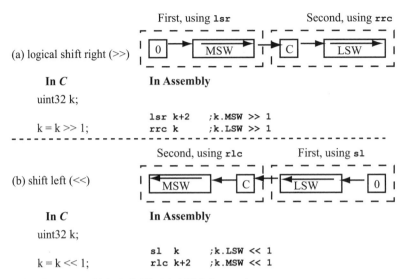

FIGURE 5.10 32-bit logical shift right/shift left operations.

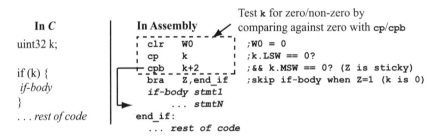

FIGURE 5.11 Assembly language for 32-bit non-zero test.

is sticky for cpb instruction, as previously mentioned. If the *C* code of Figure 5.11 is changed to the zero test if (!k) {}, the bra z instruction is replaced with a bra NZ instruction to skip the *if-body* when k is non-zero.

A slightly more efficient zero/non-zero test is performed on a 32-bit operand by bitwise-OR'ing the operand least significant and most significant words with each other as shown in Figure 5.12. After the bitwise-OR, a Z = 1 condition indicates an operand value of zero, as the final 32-bit result can only be zero if all bits in the least significant and most significant words are zero.

A more complex zero/non-zero test is shown in Figure 5.13, in which the *if-body* is executed if k is non-zero or j is zero (k || !j). Since both the k and j variables are being checked for their status with respect to zero, both variables are tested by the bitwise-OR of their most significant word with their least significant word. The *if-body* is skipped if k is zero and j is non-zero.

Test **k** for zero/non-zero by bitwise
OR'ing of MSW and LSW.

```
        In C                 In Assembly
uint32 k;                    mov    k,W0       ;W0 = k.LSW
                             ior    k+2,WREG   ;W0 = k.LSW | k.MSW
if (k) {                     bra    Z,end_if   ;skip if-body when Z=1 (k is 0)
  if-body                      if-body stmt1
}                                   ... stmtN
...rest of code              end_if:
                                   ... rest of code
```

FIGURE 5.12   Assembly language for 32-bit non-zero test.

```
       In C                 In Assembly
uint32 k, j;                mov    k,W0       ;W0 = k.LSW
                            ior    k+2,WREG   ;W0 = k.LSW | k.MSW
if (k || !j) {              bra    NZ,if_body ;execute if-body when k != 0
  if-body                   mov    j,W0       ;W0 = j.LSW
}                           ior    j+2,WREG   ;W0 = j.LSW | j.MSW
...rest of code             bra    NZ,end_if  ;skip if-body when j!=0
                            if_body:
                              if-body stmt1
                                   ... stmtN
                            end_if:
                              ... rest of code
```

FIGURE 5.13   Assembly language for 32-bit zero/non-zero test with two operands.

Please note that the logical OR condition || in the *C* code in Figure 5.13 is unrelated to the bitwise-OR used in testing each variable for zero/non-zero. If the condition in the *C* code in Figure 5.13 is changed to (k && !j), in which the *if-body* is executed only if k is non-zero and j is zero, a bitwise-OR operation is still used to test the k and j variables for zero/non-zero. Figure 5.14 shows the *C* and assembly language for this test of 32-bit variables.

```
       In C                 In Assembly
uint32 k, j;                mov    k,W0       ;W0 = k.LSW
                            ior    k+2,WREG   ;W0 = k.LSW | k.MSW
if (k && !j) {              bra    Z,end_if   ;skip if-body when k == 0
  if-body                   mov    j,W0       ;W0 = j.LSW
}                           ior    j+2,WREG   ;W0 = j.LSW | j.MSW
...rest of code             bra    NZ,end_if  ;skip if-body when j!=0
                            if_body:
                              if-body stmt1
                                   ... stmtN
                            end_if:
                              ... rest of code
```

FIGURE 5.14   Another assembly language for 32-bit zero/non-zero test with two operands.

A common mistake for new assembly language programmers is to test a 32-bit value for zero/non-zero as shown in Listing 5.1. Here, the zero/non-zero test is patterned after the method used for 16-bit operands in which the operand is copied to itself to affect the Z flag. However, this is an incorrect test, as the Z flag setting is only based on the value of the *most recent* mov instruction; i.e., the MSW of the variable k, and not the 32-bit value k (the combined MSW:LSW value).

LISTING 5.1   A common mistake for zero/non-zero test.

```
mov k            ;test k LSW
mov k+2          ;test k MSW
bra Z,k_is_zero  ;branches to k_is_zero if the MSW of k is equal to zero
                 ;which is incorrect if the LSW of k is non-zero
```

EQUALITY, INEQUALITY

Figure 5.15 shows assembly code for a 32-bit equality test. The *if-body* is executed if the test k==j is true. The test is performed by performing a 32-bit comparison of the operands and skipping the *if-body* if the Z flag is cleared after the comparison, indicating that the operands are not equal. The 32-bit comparison is performed by using the cp instruction for the LSW comparison and the cpb for the MSW comparison. As previously discussed, the sticky behavior of the Z flag for the cpb instructions allows the Z flag to indicate the zero status of the entire 32-bit subtraction performed by the comparison, not just the zero status of the MSW comparison. An inequality test of k!=j in the if condition only requires replacing bra NZ with a bra Z instruction (skip the *if-body* if k−j yields a zero result, indicating that k is equal to j).

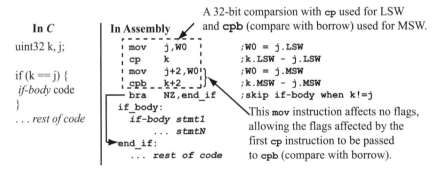

FIGURE 5.15   Assembly language for 32-bit equality test.

COMPARISONS OF >, >=, <, <= ON UNSIGNED 32-BIT OPERANDS

Figure 5.16 shows assembly code for a k>j comparison used in an if{} statement, where k, j are unsigned 32-bit operands. The only difference between this

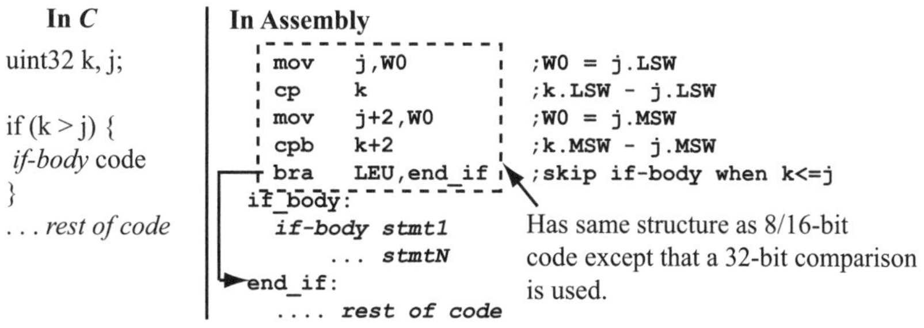

FIGURE 5.16   Assembly language for 32-bit greater-than test.

code and the 8/16-bit comparison code given in the previous chapter is that a 32-bit comparison (cp/cpb sequence) is used instead of a 16-bit comparison. It is easy to adapt any of the code examples from Chapter 4 for >, >=, <, <= comparisons for 32-bit operands by simply using 32-bit comparisons instead of 16-bit comparisons.

Sample Question: ***Implement the C code fragment shown here in PIC24 assembly.***

```
uint32 j, k;
do {
   j = j >> 1;
} while(k >= j);
```

Answer: One possible solution is given in Listing 5.2. The shift right of j is done by using a lsr instruction for the MSW, followed by a rrc on the LSW. The comparison k>=j is done by a 32-bit comparison of k, j using cp for the LSW comparison and cpb for the MSW comparison. Finally, a bra GEU is used to return to the top of the loop as the branch is taken if k>=j.

LISTING 5.2   Sample question solution.

```
top_loop:
   lsr j+2            ;logical shift right j.MSW
   rrc j             ;right shift j.LSW
   mov j,W0
   cp  k             ;k.LSW − j.LSW
   mov j+2,W0
   cpb k+2           ;k.MSW − j.MSW
   bra GEU, top_loop ;loop if k >= j
   ... rest of code
```

64-Bit Operations

A 64-bit unsigned integer is declared as `unsigned long long` in the *C* compiler used for this book, with `uint64` used as our shorthand notation that exposes the data size. Figure 5.17 shows the assembly code for a 64-bit addition of two `uint64` operands. A 64-bit variable consists of 8 bytes or four 16-bit words. Thus, four 16-bit additions are required, with the `addc` instruction used for all 16-bit additions after the first 16-bit addition. Because it is straightforward to extend the previously covered 32-bit operations to 64-bit operands, and because usage of 64-bit variables in 16-bit microcontroller code is rare, no further examples of 64-bit operations are given in this book.

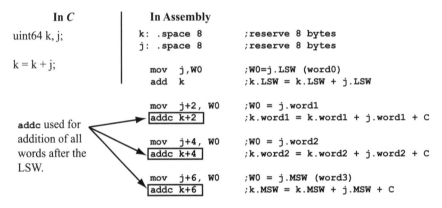

FIGURE 5.17   Assembly language for 64-bit addition.

Signed Number Representation

All examples up to this point have used unsigned data types. Obviously, we are also interested in performing operations on signed integers such as −100 or +27, but to do this, we must have a binary encoding method that includes the sign (+/−) of a number and its magnitude. Three binary encoding methods for signed integers are *signed magnitude, one's complement,* and *two's complement.* These encodings share two common features, one of which is that a positive number in any of these encodings is the same and is simply the binary representation of the number. The second common feature is that the most significant bit of a negative number is "1."

Signed Magnitude

Signed magnitude encoding is so named because the encoding is split into sign and magnitude, with the most significant bit used for the sign and the remaining bits for the magnitude. Figure 5.18 shows examples of signed magnitude encoding. With n bits, the number range is $-2^{(n-1)} - 1$ to $+2^{(n-1)} - 1$, or -127 to $+127$ for $n = 8$. Two encodings exist for zero, a positive zero and a negative zero. The advantage of signed magnitude is that the sign and magnitude are immediately accessible for manipulation by hardware, and it is inexpensive from a logic gate viewpoint to produce the negative of a number: simply complement the sign bit. However, one disadvantage of signed magnitude numbers is that the same binary adder logic used for unsigned numbers cannot be used for signed magnitude numbers. Signed magnitude arithmetic requires custom logic specifically designed for that encoding method. In a microprocessor, this would require special addition/subtraction instructions for use with signed magnitude integers and instructions for converting between unsigned and signed integer representations. Fortunately, as will be seen shortly, two's complement encoding allows the same binary adder logic to be used for both unsigned and signed representations, thus no separate instructions are needed for signed and unsigned addition/subtraction. However, there is one class of numbers, floating point numbers (i.e., -10.235), which do require their own dedicated arithmetic/logic units and instructions. Interestingly, a form of signed magnitude representation is used for floating point number encoding, which is discussed further in Chapter 7.

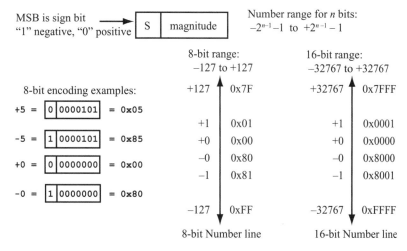

FIGURE 5.18   Signed magnitude encoding.

ONE'S COMPLEMENT

One's complement is so named because a $-k$ is found by complementing each bit in the $+k$ representation (i.e., $-k = \sim(+k)$). With n bits, the number range is

$-2^{(n-1)} - 1$ to $+2^{(n-1)} - 1$, or -127 to $+127$ for $n = 8$, the same as signed magnitude. Examples of one's complement encodings are given in Figure 5.19. Two encodings exist for zero, positive zero (all "0"s) and negative zero (all "1"s). The binary adder logic used for unsigned numbers can be used for one's complement numbers as long as an error of $+1$ is acceptable in the result, which occurs if adding two negative numbers or a positive and a negative number. For example, the correct result for the sum $+5 + (-2)$ is $+3$. Written as 8-bit numbers in one's complement, the sum is $0x05 + 0xFD = 0x02$ ($+2$), which is in error by $+1$. The advantage of one's complement is that the negative value of a number is "cheap and fast"—cheap in terms of logic gates and fast in terms of delay; all that is needed is an inverter for each bit, producing one gate delay for the negation operation. One's complement has been used within some graphics hardware accelerators for color operations on pixels, where speed is all-important and an error of 1 LSb is acceptable.

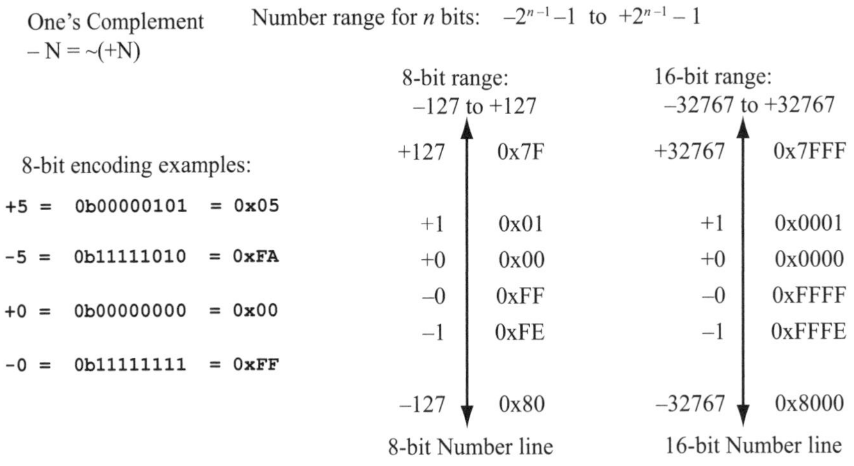

One's Complement
$-N = \sim(+N)$

Number range for n bits: $-2^{n-1} - 1$ to $+2^{n-1} - 1$

8-bit range:
-127 to $+127$

16-bit range:
-32767 to $+32767$

8-bit encoding examples:

$+5 = $ 0b00000101 $ = 0x05$

$-5 = $ 0b11111010 $ = 0xFA$

$+0 = $ 0b00000000 $ = 0x00$

$-0 = $ 0b11111111 $ = 0xFF$

	8-bit		16-bit	
	$+127$	0x7F	$+32767$	0x7FFF
	$+1$	0x01	$+1$	0x0001
	$+0$	0x00	$+0$	0x0000
	-0	0xFF	-0	0xFFFF
	-1	0xFE	-1	0xFFFE
	-127	0x80	-32767	0x8000

8-bit Number line

16-bit Number line

FIGURE 5.19 One's complement encoding.

TWO'S COMPLEMENT

The $+1$ error in one's complement addition using binary adder logic is corrected by encoding a $-k$ as $\sim(+k) + 1$, the one's complement plus one. This is called two's complement representation and is the standard method for encoding signed integers in microprocessors. With n bits, the number range is $-2^{(n-1)}$ to $+2^{(n-1)} - 1$, or -128 to $+127$ for $n = 8$. There is only one representation for zero (digits are all 0s), with the negative zero (digits are all 1s) of one's complement now representing a negative one (−1). The negative number range contains one more member than the positive range. Figure 5.20 gives examples of two's complement encodings.

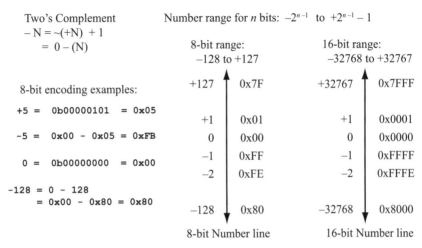

Two's Complement
$-N = \sim(+N) + 1$
$\qquad = 0 - (N)$

8-bit encoding examples:

+5 =   0b00000101   = 0x05

−5 =   0x00 - 0x05 = 0xFB

0 =   0b00000000   = 0x00

−128 = 0 - 128
      = 0x00 - 0x80 = 0x80

Number range for n bits: -2^{n-1} to $+2^{n-1} - 1$

8-bit range:
−128 to +127

16-bit range:
−32768 to +32767

8-bit		16-bit	
+127	0x7F	+32767	0x7FFF
+1	0x01	+1	0x0001
0	0x00	0	0x0000
−1	0xFF	−1	0xFFFF
−2	0xFE	−2	0xFFFE
−128	0x80	−32768	0x8000

8-bit Number line   16-bit Number line

FIGURE 5.20   Two's complement encoding.

As stated earlier, conversion of a positive decimal number $+k$ to two's complement is easy, as it is simply the binary (hex) representation. The conversion of a negative decimal number to two's complement using the formula $-k = \sim(+k) + 1$ is error prone, as it requires the number to be converted to binary then each bit to be complemented. An easier method is to use the fact that $-k = 0 - (+k)$, which computes $-k$ by converting $+k$ to hex, then subtracts that number from zero. Figure 5.21a summarizes these rules for signed decimal to two's complement conversion and contains two sample conversions.

An n-bit two's complement number can be converted to signed decimal by multiplying each binary digit by its appropriate weight, with the most significant digit having a negative weight. Thus, an 8-bit two's complement number of the form $b_7b_6b_5b_4b_3b_2b_1b_0$ is converted to decimal by the sum $-b_7{*}2^7 + b_6{*}2^6 + b_5{*}2^5 + b_4{*}2^4 + b_3{*}2^3 + b_2{*}2^2 + b_1{*}2^1 + b_0{*}2^0$. An easier and less error-prone method is to first write the binary number as a hex number. Converting the hexadecimal two's complement number to signed decimal requires determination of the sign and the magnitude. If the most significant bit is one (most significant hex digit is 8 or greater), the number is negative. To find the magnitude of this negative number, subtract the number from zero, as $+k = 0 - (-k)$, and convert the result to decimal. If the most significant bit is zero (hex digit is 7 or less), the number

a) Signed decimal to two's complement

If *n* is positive	Convert *n* to hex	+60 = 0x3C
If *n* is negative	Ignore sign, convert *n* to hex.	−60 = ?? 60 = 0x3C
	Then subtract from zero.	−60 = 0x00 − 0x3C = 0xC4

- -

b) Two's complement to signed decimal

If MSb is 0 (hex digit < 8)	Number is positive, convert to decimal	0x4D = +77
If MSb is 1 (hex digit > 7)	Number is negative, subtract from zero, convert to decimal to find magnitude.	0xB3= ?? 0x00 − 0xB3 = 0x4D 0x4D = 77
	Combine sign and magnitude	0xB3 = −77

FIGURE 5.21   Signed decimal to two's complement and vice versa.

is positive, and converting it to decimal provides +*k*. Figure 5.21b summarizes these rules and shows two examples of two's complement hex to signed decimal conversion.

SIGN EXTENSION

To convert, or promote, an 8-bit unsigned number to a 16-bit unsigned value, one simply adds extra zeros to the leftmost digits. As an example, the unsigned decimal number 128 in 8 bits is 0b10000000, or 0x80. In 16 bits, the same number is 0b0000000010000000, or 0x0080. For two's complement numbers, extra precision is gained by *sign extension,* which means the sign bit is replicated to produce the additional bits. Using the same example, the signed decimal number of −128 in 8 bits, two's complement is 0b10000000, or 0x80. In 16 bits, the same number is 0b1111111110000000, or 0xFF80. Note that if zeros are used for padding instead of the sign bit, a negative number is changed to a positive number, an obviously incorrect result. For hex representation, extending the sign bit means padding with "F" digits for negative numbers, and "0" digits for positive numbers. The ze (zero extension) PIC24 instruction performs zero extension, while the se (sign extension) instruction performs sign extension. Code examples using the ze and se instructions are provided later in this chapter.

Sample Question: *Give the value of −3 as a 16-bit two's complement number.*

Answer: The easiest way to accomplish this is to first write −3 as an 8-bit two's complement number then sign extend. You know that +3 = 0x03, so −3 = 0 − (+3) = 0x00 − 0x03 = 0xFD. Sign extending (adding "1"s in binary or 0xF digits in hex to the left) the 8-bit value 0xFD to a 16-bit value produces 0xFFFD. You can verify that this is correct by computing 0 − (−3) = +3, so 0x0000 − 0xFFFD = 0x0003 = +3.

Sample Question: *The 8-bit value 0xA0 is a two's complement number; give its decimal value.*

Answer: The MSb of 0xA0 is a "1", so this number is negative. We know that 0 − (−N) = +N, so 0x00 − 0xA0 = 0x60 = +96. Thus, the magnitude of the number is 96 and the sign is negative, so 0xA0 = −96.

TWO'S COMPLEMENT OVERFLOW

In Chapter 1, we saw that a carry out of the most significant bit is an indication of overflow for unsigned numbers. Now you are probably wondering how overflow is detected for addition/subtraction of two's complement numbers. First, let's consider the sum (−1 + (+1)) written as 8-bit, two's complement numbers, which is 0xFF + 0x01. The addition produces a carry out of the most significant bit and an 8-bit result of 0x00 (0), the correct result for the sum −1 + (+1). This means that the carry flag is not useful as an overflow indicator for signed arithmetic. Instead, the two's complement overflow flag (OV), bit 2 of the STATUS register, is the error indicator for two's complement arithmetic. In this book, the OV flag is shortened to the V flag and is referred to as the overflow flag, with two's complement understood. The STATUS register provides another useful flag for dealing with signed numbers: the negative (N) flag. This bit is set equal to the MSb of the operation result; thus, the condition N = 1 indicates a negative result if the result is interpreted as a two's complement number.

Once again, look at the ranges of positive and negative numbers in two's complement in Figure 5.20. Note that overflow cannot occur when computing the sum of a positive and negative number. However, a two's complement overflow can occur when the sum of two negative numbers yields a positive number, or when the sum of two positive numbers yields a negative number. Similar rules can be derived for subtraction. These rules are summarized in Equations 5.1 through 5.4.

Observe that the subtraction rules 5.3 and 5.4 are simply the addition rules 5.1 and 5.2 stated in a different form:

$$\text{if} \quad +p + (+q) = -r \quad \text{then } V = 1 \tag{5.1}$$
$$\text{if} \quad (-p) + (-q) = +r \quad \text{then } V = 1 \tag{5.2}$$
$$\text{if} \quad (+p) - (-q) = -r \quad \text{then } V = 1 \tag{5.3}$$
$$\text{if} \quad (-p) - (+q) = +r \quad \text{then } V = 1 \tag{5.4}$$

The preceding rules aid the determination of the V flag when performing addition or subtraction manually. A method more suitable for logic gate implementation is shown by the Boolean test of Equation 5.5, where C_{MSb} is the carry out of the most significant bit, C_{MSb-1} is the carry out of the preceding bit as produced during binary addition, and $\wedge$ is the XOR operation.

$$V = C_{MSb} \wedge C_{MSb-1} \tag{5.5}$$

Equation 5.5 works because if two positive numbers are added (most significant bits are both 0) and $C_{MSb-1} = 1$, then C_{MSb} must be 0 leaving behind a MSb of 1, indicating that a negative number has been produced which is overflow (for the sum of two positive numbers, the case of $C_{MSb-1} = 0$ and $C_{MSb} = 1$ cannot occur). If two negative numbers are added (most significant bits are both 1), and $C_{MSb-1} = 0$, then C_{MSb} must be 1 leaving behind a MSb of 0, indicating that a positive number has been produced which is overflow (for the sum of two negative numbers, the case of $C_{MSb-1} = 1$ and $C_{MSb} = 0$ cannot occur).

Figure 5.22 illustrates the four possible cases of C, V flag settings for 8-bit addition. The operands and results are shown interpreted as both unsigned numbers

adder logic	unsigned	signed		adder logic	unsigned	signed
0x01	1	+1		0xFF	255	-1
+ 0xFF	+ 255	+ -1		+ 0x80	+ 128	+ -128
0x00	0	0		0x7F	127	+127
C = 1, Z = 1,				C = 1, Z = 0,		
V = 0, N = 0				V = 1, N = 0		
adder logic	unsigned	signed		adder logic	unsigned	signed
0x7F	127	+127		0x80	128	-128
+ 0x01	+ 1	+ +1		+ 0x20	+ 32	+ +32
0x80	128	-128		0xA0	160	-96
C = 0, Z = 0,				C = 0, Z = 0,		
V = 1, N = 1				V = 0, N = 1		

FIGURE 5.22 Four cases of C, V flag settings.

and signed numbers. Observe that C = 0 if the unsigned result is correct. Similarly, V = 0 if the signed result is correct. A natural question is "How do I know if the hex numbers in Figure 5.22 are supposed to represent signed or unsigned values?" The answer is, of course, that you do not know unless you are provided with additional information. There is nothing inherent in the 8-bit code 0xFF that says it represents 255 or −1; the application that uses the numbers determines if an unsigned or signed quantity is required. In the context of μC applications, this means that the programmer knows which representation (signed or unsigned) is intended, and thereby, would know which status bits are appropriate. The binary logic performing the addition does not know if the numbers represent signed or unsigned quantities, nor does it matter. The adder logic works equally well assuming either representation.

> Sample Question: ***Give the V, N flag settings after the 8-bit operation 0x60 + 0x40.***
>
> **Answer:** 0x60 + 0x40 = 0xA0. The MSb of 0xA0 is 1, so N = 1 (result is negative). Two positive numbers added together produce a negative number, so V = 1.

OPERATIONS ON SIGNED DATA

In Chapter 4, you learned in the Carry flag discussion that the subtraction A − B is actually performed as A + (~B) +1, for which the reasoning is now clear as −B = ~B + 1 by the definition of two's complement. Figure 5.23 illustrates how a combinational building block capable of both addition and subtraction is built from an adder and a 2-to-1 mux. The SUB input connected to the mux select and the carry-in input of the adder determines if the operation A + B or A − B is performed. When SUB = 0, the output is Y = A + B + 0; when SUB = 1, the output is A + (~B) + 1, which is actually A − B. An adder/subtractor building block is a key component of the arithmetic logic unit of any microprocessor. Figure 5.23 clearly shows the advantage of two's complement representation for signed numbers; the same binary adder logic used for addition/subtraction of unsigned numbers is used for signed numbers, with the inclusion of an inverter and a 2-to-1 mux, two relatively simple logic gates.

Unfortunately, some operations on signed numbers require different hardware than the same operation on unsigned numbers, and thus, different assembly language instruction sequences. Table 5.1 lists the arithmetic operations discussed in this book and whether different hardware is required for unsigned and signed operations. Shift and comparison operations on signed data are discussed in this chapter, while multiplication and division are postponed until Chapter 7.

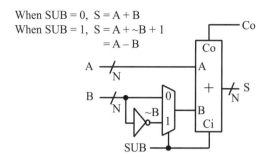

When SUB = 0, S = A + B
When SUB = 1, S = A + ~B + 1
　　　　　　　= A − B

FIGURE 5.23　Adder/subtractor building block.

TABLE 5.1　Unsigned versus signed arithmetic operations.

Operation	Same Operation for Unsigned/Signed Data?
+, −	yes
==, !=	yes
<< (left shift)	yes
>, >=, <, <=	no
>> (right shift)	no
*, /	no

Shift Operations on Signed Data

In previous shift operation examples, a zero value has always been used as the shift-in value for the LSb (left shift) or MSb (right shift). At this point, let's consider a shift operation on a signed (two's complement) number. Assume a right shift of the value −128 is desired, which should yield −64 as a right shift is a divide-by-two operation (actually, this depends on the number that is shifted; more on this later). The value −128 is 0x80 as an 8-bit two's complement number, and Figure 5.24a shows that this becomes a 0x40, or a +64, when a zero is used as the MSb input value. In Figure 5.24b, the sign bit is retained during the shift, keeping the MSb as one, which produces the correct value of −64 or 0xC0. For two's complement values, the sign bit must be retained during a right shift to obtain the correct arithmetic result of division-by-two. The PIC24 μC has an instruction named *arithmetic shift right* (asr) that preserves the sign bit; the asr instruction has the same addressing modes as the lsr (logical shift right) instruction discussed in Chapter 4.

Figure 5.25 shows assembly code that implements an arithmetic shift right on 16-bit and 32-bit signed integers, which are int16 and int32 data types, respectively.

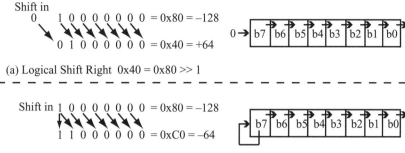

(a) Logical Shift Right 0x40 = 0x80 >> 1

(b) Arithmetic Shift Right 0xC0 = 0x80 >> 1

The PIC24 μC has an arithmetic shift right (**asrl**) instruction; it supports the same addressing modes as the logical shift right (**lsr**) instruction.

FIGURE 5.24   Logical shift right versus arithmetic shift right.

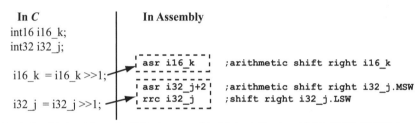

int8, **int16**, **int32** are the *C* data types used in this book for signed 8-bit, 16-bit, 32-bit integers.

FIGURE 5.25   Assembly code for arithmetic shift right operation.

The arithmetic right shift of the signed 16-bit variable i16_k simply uses the asr instruction instead of the lsr instruction. Arithmetic shifts of variables larger than 16 bits require that the asr instruction is used on the MSW to retain the sign bit, then the rrc instruction is used on subsequent more significant words to shift each bit right. For example, the arithmetic right shift of the signed 32-bit variable i32_j first uses the asr instruction on the MSW, followed by the rrc instruction on the LSW.

Even though Figure 5.24b shows that an arithmetic right shift of −128 is −64, an arithmetic right shift of a negative number is only equivalent to division by 2 in the *C* language if the number is even. For odd negative numbers, division by 2 in *C* and arithmetic right shift produce different results. Integer division in *C* truncates, so −5/2 is equal to −2 as shown in the following code:

```
int8 i8_k;
i8_k = −5;          //this is 0xFB
i8_k = i8_k/2;      //returns −2, which is 0xFE
```

However, the arithmetic right shift version for $-5 >> 1$ returns -3 as seen in the following code:

```
i8_k = -5; //this is 0xFB = 0b11111011
i8_k = i8_k >> 1; //asr(0b11111011) = 0b11111101 = 0xFD, which is -3!
```

This difference between division and right shift is not an issue for positive numbers or unsigned numbers. This is why a right shift operation in C compilers for signed numbers is implementation dependent (some retain the sign bit, some do not). When using signed numbers and dividing by powers of two, a division operation should be used instead of a right shift operation.

It would seem logical to assume that there is also a need for retaining the sign bit during the left shift of a two's complement operand. Figure 5.26 illustrates what happens when the 8-bit value 0x20 (+32) is shifted to the left two times. After the first shift, the new value is 0x40 (+64), the correct value in an arithmetic sense as $+64 = 2 * (+32)$. After the second shift, the new value is 0x80 (-128), which is obviously incorrect from an arithmetic sense as the sign changed. However, if the sign bit is kept during the shift, the result is 0x00, again an incorrect result in an arithmetic sense. This is because $+64 * 2 = +128$, and $+128$ cannot be represented in 8 bits! If the sign bit changes after a left shift of a two's complement value, overflow has occurred. Keeping the sign bit does not help; it is simply not possible to represent the correct arithmetic value using the available bits. Therefore, there is no need to distinguish left shift operations based on unsigned versus signed data.

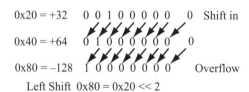

FIGURE 5.26   Left shift operation on signed data.

COMPARISONS OF >, >=, <, <= ON SIGNED OPERANDS

Recall that the unsigned comparison tests of >, >= , <, and <= use the subtraction operation on the two operands being compared, followed by a test of the C and Z flags. Figure 5.27 illustrates what happens if two signed 8-bit operands are treated as unsigned operands for >= comparison purposes. The C flag test yields the correct result only if the signs of the operands are the same. One could envision writing code to check the signs of the operands before doing the comparison, setting a temporary flag to indicate sign equality or inequality, then performing the appropriate

Numbers	C flag (k–j)	As Unsigned	k >= j	As Signed	k >= j
k = 0x7F, j = 0x01	C = 1	k = 127, j = 1	True	k = +127, j = +1	True
k = 0x80, j = 0xFF	C = 0	k = 128, j = 255	False	k = −128, j = −1	False
k = 0x80, j = 0x7F	C = 1	k = 128, j = 127	True	k = −128, j = +127	False
k = 0x01, j = 0xFF	C = 0	k = 1, j = 255	False	k = +1, j = −1	True

FIGURE 5.27   Unsigned versus signed comparisons.

comparison based on the flag setting. However, this is overly complex and not required, as there is a better way involving subtraction and flag tests other than the C and Z flags.

Figure 5.28 lists the V (overflow), N (Negative), Z (Zero) flag tests for >, >=, <, <= comparisons of k and j after k – j is performed. Recall the V flag is set if the operation yields two's complement overflow, while the N flag is set if the result is negative; i.e., the result's MSb is 1. The flag tests look complicated, but reasoning about them makes the conditions easier to remember. For the greater-than (>) test, if k is indeed greater than j, the subtraction k – j should be a non-zero (Z = 0), positive (N = 0) number, with V = 0 indicating the correctness of the result. However, if overflow occurs (V = 1), a non-zero (Z = 0), negative number (N = 1) is obtained, which is an obviously incorrect result caused by the overflow. This flag test is written in a Boolean form as "(~Z&~N&~V) | (~Z&N&V)". For the greater-than-or-equal (>=) test, the Z flag is dropped and the flag test simplifies to

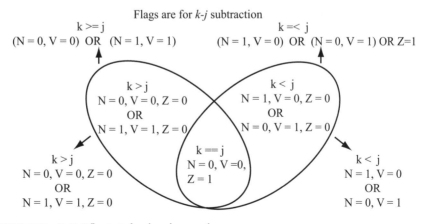

FIGURE 5.28   V, N, Z flag tests for signed comparisons.

"(~N&~V) | (N&V)". The astute reader will recognize this flag test as ~(V^N) (the exclusive-NOR of the V and N flags), which is how this test is implemented in logic gates for signed branch instructions. The flag tests for the <, <= comparisons can be reasoned about in a similar manner.

The flag tests in Figure 5.28 could be implemented by a series of branches using single flag tests on the V, N, and Z bits. Fortunately, the PIC24 instruction set has a set of signed branches that are used for signed comparisons as shown in Table 5.2. These signed branches implement the flag tests of Figure 5.28. Observe that the assembly language mnemonic for the signed branches drops the "U" suffix qualifier in the comparison; i.e., "GT" instead of "GTU".

TABLE 5.2   Signed branches.

Description	Syntax	Branch Taken When
Branch >, signed	bra GT, \<label\>	(~Z&~N&~V) | (~Z&N&V)
Branch >=, signed	bra GE, \<label\>	(~N&~V) | (N&V)
Branch <, signed	bra LT, \<label\>	(N&~V) | (~N&V)
Branch <=, signed	bra LE, \<label\>	(N&~V) | (~N&V) | Z

Figure 5.29 shows the assembly code when k > j is used as a conditional test within an if{} statement and k, j are signed 32-bit integers (int32). A 32-bit comparison of k, j is performed first, followed by a signed branch (bra LE) instruction that skips the *if-body* when k is less than or equal to j. The signed branch is used because the int32 data type used for k and j is a signed 32-bit integer data type. All of the previous assembly code examples using unsigned branches and unsigned data types can be transformed into signed branches when signed data types are compared by using the proper signed version of the bra instruction.

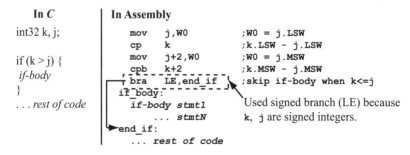

FIGURE 5.29   Assembly for 32-bit signed greater-than comparison.

SIGN EXTENSION FOR MIXED PRECISION

Even for operations like addition and subtraction that work the same for both unsigned and signed operands, care must be taken when dealing with operands of different precisions. The precision of the smaller operand must be extended to match the precision of the larger operand as discussed previously in Chapter 4 for unsigned data where the smaller operand was zero extended to match the precision of the larger operand. For signed operands, the smaller operand is sign extended to match the precision of the larger operand. Figure 5.30a shows the addition of a signed 8-bit variable (i8_i) to a signed 16-bit variable (i16_p). The i8_i variable is loaded into W0, then sign extended using the se (sign extend) instruction before being added to i16_p. The se instruction sign extends an 8-bit value in a source working register to its equivalent 16-bit value that is then placed in a destination working register.

(a) Mixed 8/16-bit operations with signed data

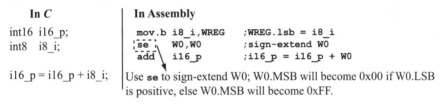

In C	In Assembly
int16 i16_p; int8 i8_i; i16_p = i16_p + i8_i;	```mov.b i8_i,WREG ;WREG.lsb = i8_i```

```
        mov.b i8_i,WREG   ;WREG.lsb = i8_i
        se    W0,W0       ;sign-extend W0
        add   i16_p       ;i16_p = i16_p + W0
```
Use **se** to sign-extend W0; W0.MSB will become 0x00 if W0.LSB is positive, else W0.MSB will become 0xFF.

(b) Mixed 16/32-bit operations with signed data

In C	In Assembly
int32 i32_p; int16 i16_i; i32_p = i32_p + i16_i;	

```
        mov   i16_i,W0   ;W0 = i16_i
        clr   W1         ;W1 = 0, assume i16_i is positive
        btsc  W0,#15     ;test MSbit of W0
        setm  W1         ;W1 = 0xFFFF, i16_i is negative
        add   i32_p      ;i32_p.LSW = i32_p.LSW + i16_i
        mov   W1,W0      ;W0 = sign-extension of i16_i
        addc  i32_p+2    ;i32_p.MSW = i32_p.MSW + SE of i16_i
```

Load W1 with 0x0000 if **i16_i** is positive, else load W1 with 0xFFFF.
Register W1 becomes the MSW of **i16_i**, which is added to **i32_p.MSW**.

FIGURE 5.30   *Addition operation for signed operands of unequal precisions.*

The PIC24 instruction set does not contain a sign extend instruction for 16-bit values. One way to perform sign extension of 16 bits to 32 bits is shown in Figure 5.30b, which adds a signed 16-bit variable (i16_i) to a signed 32-bit variable (i32_p). First, the i16_i variable is loaded into W0. Then W1 is cleared to 0 followed by a sign test of i16_i. If i16_i is negative, W1 is loaded with 0xFFFF using the setm instruction. The btsc W0,#15 instruction tests whether the MSb of W0 is "0" (i16_i is greater than or equal to zero) or "1" (i16_i is negative), skipping the setm W1 instruction when i16_i is positive. Thus, the W1:W0 register pair functions as the 32-bit sign-extended version of i16_i, which is then added to i32_p.

Sample Question: ***Implement the C code fragment shown here in PIC24 assembly.***

```
int32 i32_j, i32_k;
do {
    i32_j = i32_j >> 1;
} while(i32_k >= i32_j);
```

Answer: This is the same *C* code as used in a sample question from earlier in the chapter, except the data type has been changed from uint32 (unsigned) to int32 (signed). The new solution is given in Listing 5.3, with two changes made in the assembly code from the original solution of Listing 5.2. The lsr instruction originally used for the MSW is changed to an asr instruction in order to preserve the sign bit, and the unsigned bra GEU instruction is replaced with a signed bra GE instruction.

LISTING 5.3 Sample question solution.

```
top_loop:
    asr i32_j+2             ;arithmetic shift right i32_j.MSW
    rrc i32_j              ;right shift i32_j.LSW
    mov i32_j,W0
    cp  i32_k             ;i32_k.LSW - i32_j.LSW
    mov i32_j+2,W0
    cpb i32_k+2           ;i32_k.MSW - i32_j.MSW
    bra GE, top_loop      ;loop if i32_k >= i32_j
    ... rest of code
```

Sample Question: ***In the following code, what is the value of*** i8_i ***when the loop is exited? Assume that the compiler preserves the sign bit of*** i8_i ***during right shift operations.***

```
int8 i8_i;
i8_i = 0x80;
while (i8_i < -32) {
    i8_i = i8_i >> 1;
}
```

Answer: The variable i8_i is declared as an int8, so the assignment i8_i=0x80 initializes i8_i to −128. Each time through the loop, i8_i is divided by 2 by the right shift assuming that the sign bit is preserved. Therefore, i8_i is −128, then −64, then −32, at which point the comparison is no longer true and the loop is exited, with i8_i = −32 (0xE0).

BRANCH INSTRUCTION ENCODING

We've been making use of the bra instruction for several chapters, and now is a good time to take a closer look at the way these very useful instructions are encoded into machine code. The machine code format of branch instructions uses an addressing mode known as *relative,* in which a two's complement offset is added to the program counter to determine the target branch address. The branch instruction encoding is shown in Figure 5.31, with the *branch target address* (BTA) computed by adding $2*\#Slit16$ to $PC_{old}+2$, where #*Slit16* is a 16-bit signed offset and PC_{old} is the address of the branch instruction. The PC_{old} +2 value is used because the PC is already incremented when the branch target address computation is performed. The assembler computes the #*Slit16* value from BTA and PC_{old} as shown in Figure 5.31.

```
BBBB BBBB BBBB BBBB BBBB BBBB
2222 1111 1111 1100 0000 0000
3210 9876 5432 1098 7654 3210
```

bra <cond>,<BTA>

0011 bbbb nnnn nnnn nnnn nnnn

BTA is branch target address

bbbb = branch condition

BTA = $(PC_{old} + 2) + (2 * \#Slit16)$ → PCnew

n . . . n = #*Slit16* (signed 16-bit literal)

where PC_{old} is branch instruction address. #*Slit16* computed as:

$$\#Slit16 = [BTA - (PC_{old} + 2)]/2$$

(PC_{old} + 2) because PC is already incremented when the new PC value is computed.

Branch	*bbbb*	Branch	*bbbb*
bra OV	0000	bra NOV	1000
bra C/ bra GEU	0001	bra NC/ bra LTU	1001
bra Z	0010	bra NZ	1010
bra N	0011	bra NN	1011
bra LE	0100	bra GT	1100
bra LT	0101	bra GE	1101
bra LEU	0110	bra GTU	1110
bra unconditional	0111		

FIGURE 5.31   Branch instruction encoding.

Figure 5.32 shows an example that calculates the #*Slit16* value for the machine code of a branch instruction. The machine code in Figure 5.32 is representative of the code required for a loop structure like the one given in Listing 5.3. The top_loop label (0x0200) is the branch target address, while the branch location (PC_{old}) is 0x0212. The branch displacement (#*Slit16*) is calculated as −10, or 0xFFF6 in 16-bit, two's complement format. This example shows why the displacement is a signed number. A backward branch (branch target is at a lower memory address) requires a negative displacement, while a forward branch (branch target is at a higher memory address) uses a positive displacement. It is also evident that a branch target must be within the range of the displacement that can be encoded in

```
location        machine code        instruction
 (hex)            (hex)

 0200           ??????      top_loop:  <an instruction>
 0202           ??????                 <an instruction>
 ....           ......                 ...............
 0210           ??????                 <an instruction>
 0212           3DFFF6                 bra GE, top_loop   ; branch to top
```

$$BTA = (PC_{old} + 2) + (2 * \#Slit16)$$

0x0200	(BTA)
− 0x0214	(PC$_{old}$+2)
0xFFEC	

$$\#Slit16 = [BTA - (PC_{old} + 2)]/2$$
$$= [0x0200 - (0x0212 + 2)]/2$$
$$= 0xFFEC/2 = 0xFFEC \gg 1$$
$$= 0xFFF6 = -10 \text{ (16-bit signed displacement encoded as } \#Slit16)$$

$<cond>$ = GE ⤷ $\#Slit16$

```
bra GE,top_loop ⇨ bra -10 ⇨ | 0011 | 1101 | 1111 1111 1111 0110 | ⇨ 0x3DFFF6
```

FIGURE 5.32   Branch instruction encoding example.

the branch instruction word. A 16-bit displacement means that the branch target must be within −32768 to +32767 instruction words of $PC_{old} + 2$. The advantage of branch instructions over a goto instruction is that a branch instruction only takes one instruction word, while a goto takes two instruction words. The disadvantage of a branch instruction is its limited range; a goto instruction can jump anywhere in program memory. Fortunately, a branch's limited range is typically not a problem, as most loops tend to be much shorter than what is allowed by the 16-bit signed displacement. Program counter relative addressing is found in almost all microprocessor instruction sets.

SUMMARY

Extended precision operations in the PIC24 μC allow manipulation of arbitrarily-sized data, 16 bits at a time. It is clear that variables of type uint32/int32 and uint64/int64 should not be used unless the extra precision offered by these data types is absolutely required by the application, as calculations on these data types require more instructions, more data RAM, and longer execution time. The standard method of signed integer representation for microprocessors is two's complement format, which uses the same binary adder logic for addition and subtraction as used for unsigned numbers. Some operations, like right shift and >, >=, <, <= comparisons require different instruction sequences for signed integers compared with what is used for unsigned integers. Signed branches that test combinations of the V (overflow), N (negative), and Z (zero) flags for >, >=, <, and <= are used after comparisons of two's complement integers. The PIC24 instruction set provides explicit branch instructions to test these bits and thereby facilitates branches on signed numbers. The machine code for branch instructions uses program counter relative addressing, which means that a displacement value is added to the current PC value for determining the branch target address.

REVIEW PROBLEMS

Convert the following *C* code segments to PIC24 instruction sequences. Assume that u32_i, u32_j, u32_k are all uint32 data types and are located in near RAM. If you need to use other temporary memory locations in your solution, assume that these are located in near RAM as well.

1. Code fragment:

```
do {
   u32_i = u32_i - u32_k;
} while (u32_i < (u32_j + u32_k));
```

2. Code fragment:

```
if (u32_i && u32_j) {
   u32_k = u32_k & 0xCFAB0489;
}
```

3. Code fragment:

```
u32_k = u32_j | u32_i;
```

4. Code fragment:

```
while (u32_i != u32_j) {
   u32_k = u32_k >> 1;
   u32_j--;
}
```

Convert the following *C* code segments to PIC24 instruction sequences. Assume that u64_i, u64_j, u64_k are all uint64 data types and are located in near RAM. If you need to use other temporary memory locations in your solution, assume that these are located in near RAM as well.

5. Code fragment:

```
do {
  u64_i = u64_i + u64_k;
} while (u64_i < (u64_j + u64_k));
```

6. Code fragment:

```
if (u64_i && u64_j) {
  u64_k = u64_k & 0xFEDCBA9876543210;
}
```

7. Code fragment:

```
u64_k = u64_j | u64_i;
```

8. Code fragment:

```
while (u64_i != u64_j) {
  u64_k = u64_k >> 1;
  u64_j --;
}
```

Perform the indicated conversions:

9. The value −42 to 8-bit two's complement.
10. The 8-bit two's complement value 0xDC to decimal.
11. The 16-bit two's complement value 0xFBA3 to decimal.
12. The value −390 to 16-bit two's complement.
13. Sign extend the 8-bit value 0x85 to 16 bits.

Do the following calculations (problems 14 through 17 use 8-bit data sizes):

14. Give the value of the operation 0x73 + 0x65 and the Z, N, V, C flag settings.
15. Give the value of the operation 0x90 − 0x8A and the Z, N, V, C flag settings.
16. Give the value of the operation 0xF0 + 0xCA and the Z, N, V, C flag settings.
17. Give the value of the operation 0x2A − 0x81 and the Z, N, V, C flag settings.
18. In the following code segment, what is the value of i8_i when the loop is exited?

```
int8 i8_i, i8_j;
i8_i = 0x01; i8_j = 0x80;
while (i8_i > i8_j) i8_i++;
```

19. In the following code segment, what is the final value of i8_k? Use the value 1 to represent true and 0 to represent false.

```
int8 i8_i, i8_j;
i8_i = 0xA0; i8_j = 0x70;
i8_k = (i8_i > i8_j);
```

20. In the following code segment, what is the final value of u8_k? Use the value 1 to represent true and 0 to represent false.

```
uint8 u8_i, u8_j, u8_k;
u8_i = 0xA0; u8_j = 0x70;
u8_k = (u8_i > u8_j);
```

21. In the following code segment, what is the final value of i8_i assuming that the sign bit is preserved for right shifts of signed data types?

```
int8 i8_i;
i8_i = 0xA0 >> 2;
```

For the following problems, assume that i16_i, i16_j, i16_k are int16 data types, i8_p, i8_q are int8 data types, i32_r, i32_s are int32 data types, and i64_x is an int64 data type. All variables are located in near RAM. Convert the following *C* code segments to PIC24 instruction sequences.

22. Code fragment:

```
do {
   i16_i = i16_i - i16_k;
} while (i16_i < (i16_j + i16_k));
```

23. Code fragment:

```
if (i16_k >= i16_j) {
   i16_i = i16_i >> 2;
}
```

24. Code fragment:

```
i16_k = (int16) i8_p + (i16_j << 1) - 256;
```

25. Code fragment:

```
u16_i = ((u16_k + (uint8) u8_q) >> 2) & 0xA34D;
```

26. Code fragment:

```
i32_r = (int32) i16_k + (i32_s << 1) - 1024;
```

27. Code fragment:

```
i32_r = ((i32_s - (int32) i8_q) >> 2) | 0x38DB807F;
```

28. Code fragment:

```
i64_x = (int64) i16_k + ((int64) i8_p << 1) - (int64) i32_s;
```

Answer the following questions:

29. What is the machine code for the instruction bra LE,0x0300 if the address of the bra LE instruction is 0x0340?
30. What is the machine code for the instruction bra GEU,0x0420 if the address of the bra GEU instruction is 0x0404?

6 Pointers and Subroutines

This chapter examines the architectural features of the PIC24 μC that support pointers and subroutines, which are important capabilities of high-level programming languages.

Learning Objectives

After reading this chapter, you will be able to:

- Discuss the implementation of pointers in the *C* programming language.
- Use the indexed addressing modes of the PIC24 μC to implement *C* pointer operations.
- Translate *C* code with array indexing into PIC24 instruction sequences.
- Discuss the operation of a stack data structure and its role in implementing subroutine call and return.
- Translate *C* subroutines with parameter lists, local variables, and a return value into PIC24 instruction sequences using static allocation, register allocation, and stack frame policies for parameters and locals.
- Implement initialization of *C* global arrays in PIC24 assembly language by copying data from PIC24 program memory.

AN INTRODUCTION TO *C* POINTERS

Until now, we have been using variables for unsigned and signed data of varying precisions: uint8/int8 (1 byte), uint16/int16 (2 bytes), and uint32/int32 (4 bytes). However, another important class of variables is that of *pointers*, which are variables that contain memory addresses of other variables. We have already used one special function register that is actually a pointer, namely the program counter. The program counter contains the address of a location in program memory. The size of a pointer is dependent upon the maximum number of locations in the referenced memory, not the size of the data stored in the memory location. Not counting the least significant bit, which is always 0, the program counter requires 22 bits because the program memory can hold a maximum of 4 Mi instructions. Recall that an instruction is 24 bits, reinforcing the concept that a pointer's size is independent of the size of the item that the pointer references. How wide does a pointer need to be to specify a location in the PIC24 data RAM? The answer is 16 bits, because the maximum number of separately addressable locations in the PIC24 data RAM is 64 Ki (65536), where each location stores one byte.

To understand how pointers into the PIC24 data RAM operate, we will first look at pointer variables in the *C* language, then examine how to implement these operations in PIC24 assembly code. When using pointers, we will almost always be working with mixed data types. In practice, it is quite easy to confuse a variable that contains the address of the data (the pointer) and a variable that contains the data itself. It is sound programming practice to use the data type prefixes introduced in Chapters 4 and 5 to aid in reducing these problems. While the data type prefixes make the resulting variable names a bit longer, these prefixes will help us to write code with fewer errors and code that is easier to understand by others. Therefore, we will use data type prefixes on all programs through the remainder of this book. A simple *C* language coding standard is provided in Appendix D, where more details and advice are provided. It is a common industry practice to have an in-house coding standard that all employees are expected to follow for the purpose of improving code clarity and reducing errors.

Figure 6.1a is a first look at pointer operations in *C*. The *C* code of lines 1 and 2 first initializes two uint16 variables u16_k, u16_j with arbitrary values; the corresponding memory modifications are shown in Figure 6.1a. The statement uint16* pu16_a declares variable pu16_a to be a uint16*, a pointer to data type uint16. Line 3 contains

In C

uint16 u16_k, u16_j;
uint16* pu16_a;

(1) u16_k = 0xA245;
(2) u16_j = 0x9FC1;
(3) pu16_a = &u16_j;
(4) u16_k = *pu16_a;

(3) pu16_a contains
address of u16_j

(4) *pu16_a is u16_j,
so copy u16_j to k

In Memory

(a) Before (3)

Location	Contents	Variable
0x0800	0xA245	u16_k
0x0802	0x9FC1	u16_j
0x0804	0x????	pu16_a

(b) After (3)

Location	Contents	Variable
0x0800	0xA245	u16_k
0x0802	0x9FC1	u16_j
0x0804	0x0802	pu16_a mod.

(c) After (4)

Location	Contents	Variable
0x0800	0x9FC1	u16_k mod.
0x0802	0x9FC1	u16_j
0x0804	0x0802	pu16_a

*pu16_a in register transfer notation is ((pu16_a))
so *pu16_a → u16_k is ((pu16_a)) → u16_k, or (0x802) → u16_k

FIGURE 6.1   *C* pointers with uint16 variables.

the & ("reference" or "address of") operator used in the statement pu16_a = &u16_j, which is read as "pu16_a is assigned the address of u16_j." Observe in Figure 6.1b that memory location 0x0804, which is assigned to pu16_a, contains 0x0802 after execution of statement 3, where 0x0802 is the address of variable u16_j. Line 4 shows the use of the * ("dereference" or "value at") operator applied to a pointer. The operation *pu16_a reads as "the value that is pointed to by pu16_a", which in this case is the value of u16_j since pu16_a contains the address of u16_j. In register transfer notation, *pu16_a is ((pu16_a)), so the assignment of u16_k=*pu16_a in register transfer notation is ((pu16_a))→u16_k, or (0x802)→u16_k, or 0x9FC1→u16_k. We have already seen this type of register transfer operation when discussing the register indirect addressing mode, which is used later in this section for implementing *C* pointer operations. It must be noted that the pointer declaration uint16* pu16_a can also be written as uint16 *pu16_a in which the * is placed next to the variable name instead of the type name. We prefer placing the * next to the type name to emphasize that a uint16 pointer is a different variable type than the 16-bit integer uint16 data type. However, note that this style requires definition of only one pointer per line, because the statement uint16* pu16_a, pu16_b declares one pointer (pu16_a) and one uint16 (pu16_b), which is not a pointer (in spite of the pu16_ prefix). The p in the pu16_ variable name prefix is used as an emphatic reminder that this is a pointer to a variable of type uint16.

Figure 6.2 modifies the *C* code of Figure 6.1 to use uint32 variables instead of uint16 types. Observe that u32_k, u32_j now require two words of memory but that the pointer, pu32_a in this case, still requires only one word; pointers to data RAM are 16 bits wide irrespective of the referenced data type. After execution of line 3, pu32_a contains 0x0804, which is the address of the LSW of u32_j. In register

In C	In Memory			
uint32 u32_k, u32_j; uint32* pu32_a;	(a) Before (3)	Location	Contents	Variable
		0x0800	0x3210	u32_k.LSW
		0x0802	0x7654	u32_k.MSW
(1) u32_k = 0x76543210; (2) u32_j = 0xFEDCAB98; (3) pu32_a = &u32_j; (4) u32_k = *pu32_a;		0x0804	0xBA98	u32_j.LSW
		0x0806	0xFEDC	u32_j.MSW
		0x0808	0x????	pu32_a
	(b) After (3)	0x0800	0x3210	u32_k.LSW
		0x0802	0x7654	u32_k.MSW
		0x0804	0xBA98	u32_j.LSW
(3) pu32_a contains address of u32_j		0x0806	0xFEDC	u32_j.MSW
		0x0808	0x0804	pu32_a mod.
(4) *pu32_a is u32_j, so copy u32_j to u32_k	(c) After (4)	0x0800	0xBA98	u32_k.LSW ⎫ mod.
		0x0802	0xFEDC	u32_k.MSW ⎭
		0x0804	0xBA98	u32_j.LSW
		0x0806	0xFEDC	u32_j.MSW
		0x0808	0x0804	pu32_a

FIGURE 6.2   *C* pointers with uint32 variables.

transfer notation, *pu32_a is ((pu32_a)), so the assignment u32_k = *pu32_a in register transfer notation is ((pu32_a))→u32_k, or (0x804)→u32_k, or 0xFEDCBA98→u32_k. The operation (0x804)→u32_k specifies a 32-bit copy operation because the assignment is made to a 32-bit variable.

Figure 6.3 shows the C code of Figure 6.1 implemented in PIC24 assembly language (other implementations are possible). Register W1 is used to implement the pointer variable pu16_a instead of using a data RAM location; this approach of using working registers to represent pointer variables is used in most of the C-to-assembly examples in this book. Data RAM can always be used to save the value of a pointer variable if needed, so the extra code required for storing/retrieving a pointer variable from data RAM is not included. The C statement pu16_a = &u16_j is implemented in assembly as mov #u16_j,W1 as the label u16_j stands for the memory address assigned to u16_j. This means that mov #u16_j, W1 is equivalent to mov #0x0802,W1 if u16_j is stored in location 0x0802. After this instruction is executed, register W1, which is being used as the pointer variable pu16_a, contains the memory address of variable u16_j. Because *pu16_a in register transfer notation is ((pu16_a)), the register indirect addressing mode [W1] is used to implement *pu16_a. Thus, the C assignment operation u16_k = *pu16_a is implemented as the two instruction sequence mov [W1],W0 followed by mov W0,u16_k (copies W0 value to u16_k). It is illegal to use mov [W1], u16_k so the value of [W1] is copied to a working register before it is copied to u16_k.

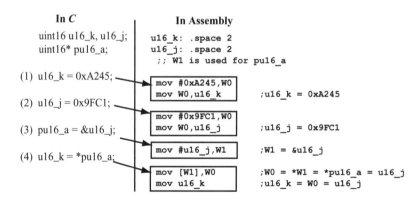

FIGURE 6.3   Assembly language for C code of Figure 6.1.

Figure 6.4 shows the code of Figure 6.2 implemented in assembly language. The PIC24 instructions for initialization of u32_k, u32_j are not shown for brevity reasons and because this has been previously covered in Chapter 5. The C statement pu32_a = &u32_j is implemented in the same way as in Figure 6.3 because pu32_a is still 16 bits wide; the instruction mov #u32_j,W1 points pu32_a at the LSW of u32_j. Four different assembly code implementations (4a,4b,4c,4d) are given for C statement (4), which is u32_k = *pu32_a.

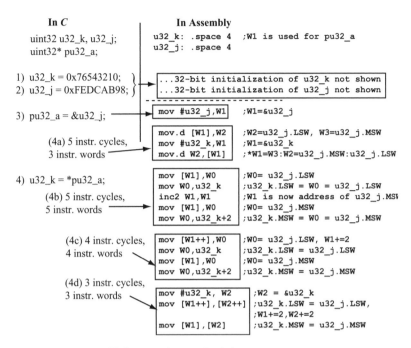

In C

```
uint32 u32_k, u32_j;
uint32* pu32_a;
```

1) u32_k = 0x76543210;
2) u32_j = 0xFEDCAB98;

3) pu32_a = &u32_j;

(4a) 5 instr. cycles,
3 instr. words

4) u32_k = *pu32_a;

(4b) 5 instr. cycles,
5 instr. words

(4c) 4 instr. cycles,
4 instr. words

(4d) 3 instr. cycles,
3 instr. words

In Assembly

```
u32_k:  .space 4   ;W1 is used for pu32_a
u32_j:  .space 4
```

```
...32-bit initialization of u32_k not shown
...32-bit initialization of u32_j not shown
```

```
mov #u32_j,W1      ;W1=&u32_j
```

```
mov.d [W1],W2      ;W2=u32_j.LSW, W3=u32_j.MSW
mov #u32_k,W1      ;W1=&u32_k
mov.d W2,[W1]      ;*W1=W3:W2=u32_j.MSW:u32_j.LSW
```

```
mov [W1],W0        ;W0= u32_j.LSW
mov W0,u32_k       ;u32_k.LSW = W0 = u32_j.LSW
inc2 W1,W1         ;W1 is now address of u32_j.MSW
mov [W1],W0        ;W0= u32_j.MSW
mov W0,u32_k+2     ;u32_k.MSW = W0 = u32_j.MSW
```

```
mov [W1++],W0      ;W0= u32_j.LSW, W1+=2
mov W0,u32_k       ;u32_k.LSW = u32_j.LSW
mov [W1],W0        ;W0= u32_j.MSW
mov W0,u32_k+2     ;u32_k.MSW = u32_j.MSW
```

```
mov #u32_k, W2     ;W2 = &u32_k
mov [W1++],[W2++]  ;u32_k.LSW = u32_j.LSW,
                   ;W1+=2,W2+=2
mov [W1],[W2]      ;u32_k.MSW = u32_j.MSW
```

FIGURE 6.4   Assembly language for C code of Figure 6.2.

Implementation (4a) uses double word moves and requires 3 instruction words and 5 instruction cycles (recall that a double word move takes 2 instruction cycles). The mov.d [W1],W2 instruction copies the two words of u32_j to the register pair W2: W3. In order to copy W2, W3 to data RAM using a double word move, register indirect addressing is required which means that a working register must be used to hold the address of u32_k. In this case, we reuse W1 for that purpose, and load the address of u32_k into W1 using mov #u32_k,W1. The copy of W2, W3 to u32_k is then accomplished by mov.d W2,[W1].

Implementation (4b) of Figure 6.4 uses word moves and register indirect addressing, requiring 5 instructions and 5 instruction cycles. After u32_j.LSW is copied to u32_k.LSW by the instruction sequence "mov [W1],W0; mov W0, u32_k", register W1 must be modified to point to u32_j.MSW. This is accomplished by incrementing register W1 by 2 using inc2 W1, W1. The instruction sequence "mov [W1], W0; mov W0, u32_k+2" then copies u32_j.MSW to u32_k.MSW.

Implementation (4c) of Figure 6.4 uses word moves and *register indirect with post-increment addressing,* requiring 4 instructions and 4 instruction cycles. The post-increment addressing mode is one of the many indirect addressing modes that have not been discussed to this point. The post-increment mode increments the source register after the register value is used as an effective address. The post-increment mode is written as [Wn++], where Wn is incremented by 1 for a byte operation and 2 for a word operation. Thus, after the mov [W1++],W0 instruction that copies u32_j.LSW to W0, the W1 register is incremented by 2 leaving it pointing at u32_j.MSW. This eliminates the need for the inc2 W1,W1 instruction used in implementation (b), reducing the number of required instruction words and instruction cycles by one.

Finally, implementation (4d) of Figure 6.4 uses word moves and register indirect with post-increment addressing the same as implementation (c), but only requires 3 instructions and 3 instruction cycles. Implementation (d) saves an instruction word by using register W2 to hold the address of u32_k, accomplished by the instruction mov #u32_k,W2. The next instruction is mov [W1++],[W2++], which copies u32_j.LSW to u32_k.LSW then increments both W1 and W2 to point to the most significant words of u32_j and u32_k. The last instruction mov [W1],[W2] copies u32_j.MSW to u32_k.MSW. When comparing the four implementations, (b) and (c) have the restriction that u32_k must be in near RAM because of the *mov f* form used to write u32_k, while implementations (a) and (d) do not have this restriction because indirect addressing is used for both reading u32_j and writing u32_k.

For the new assembly language programmer, correct implementation and understanding is the first priority, with code optimization a second priority. The examples in Figure 6.4 show that there are usually many different ways of accomplishing the same task given the richness of the PIC24 instruction set.

PIC24 INDIRECT ADDRESSING MODES

We saw register indirect with post-increment addressing used in the code example of the previous section. We are now ready to discuss the complete set of PIC24 register indirect addressing modes, which are shown in Figure 6.5. Observe that the post-increment/post-decrement modes change the *Wn* value after it has been used as the

Mode	Syntax	Effective Address and Operation		Notes
		Byte	**Word**	
RI	[*Wn*]	EA = (*Wn*)	EA = (*Wn*)	*Wn* unmodified
RI with pre-increment	[++*Wn*]	(*Wn* += 1); EA = (*Wn*)	(*Wn* + =2); EA = (*Wn*)	Increment before *Wn* used as EA
RI with pre-decrement	[--*Wn*]	(*Wn* -= 1); EA = (*Wn*)	(*Wn* -= 2); EA = (*Wn*)	Decrement before *Wn* used as EA
RI with post-increment	[*Wn*++]	EA = (*Wn*); (*Wn* += 1);	EA = (*Wn*); (*Wn* += 2);	Increment after *Wn* used as EA
RI with post-decrement	[*Wn*--]	EA = (*Wn*); (*Wn* -= 1);	EA = (*Wn*); (*Wn* -= 1);	Decrement after *Wn* used as EA
RI with register offset	[*Wn* + *Wb*]	EA = (*Wn*) + (*Wb*)	EA = (*Wn*) + (*Wb*)	*Wn*, *Wb* unmodified

FIGURE 6.5   Register indirect (RI) addressing modes.

effective address, while the pre-increment/pre-decrement modes change *Wn* before it is used as an effective address (EA). The pre/post-increment and pre/post-decrement modes change *Wn* by 1 for byte operations and by 2 for word operations. The *register indirect with register offset* mode computes the effective address by adding *Wn* and *Wb;* note that the *Wn* and *Wb* are left unchanged by this addressing mode.

Figures 6.6a and 6.6b illustrate the difference between the pre-increment and post-increment addressing modes, using a mov instruction in word mode. Observe that the W0's final value of 0x0804 is the same after either mov [++W0],W2 or mov [W0++],W2 because both increment W0 by 2. However, W2 receives the content of 0x0804 for the mov [++W0],W2 instruction because the effective address for the mov source address is W0's value after it has been incremented by 2. For the mov [W0++], W2 instruction, W2 receives the content of 0x0802 because W0's value is used as the effective address for the mov source address before W0 is incremented by 2. Figures 6.6c and 6.6d use pre-decrement and post-decrement operations in a mov instruction operating in byte mode. The byte mode causes W0 to be incremented or decremented by 1, instead of by 2 as shown in Figures 6.6a and 6.6b. The same reasoning about the effective address determination for Figures 6.6a and 6.6b can be applied to Figures 6.6c and 6.6d. Note that in the byte mode operations only the lower 8 bits of the destination, W2 in this case, are modified.

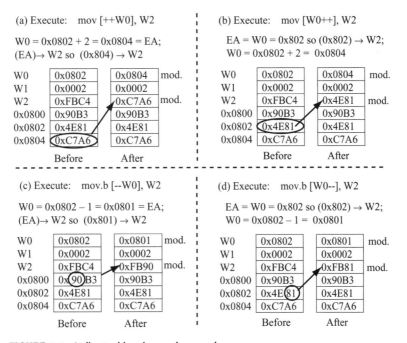

FIGURE 6.6   Indirect addressing mode examples.

Figure 6.7a gives an example of register indirect with register offset addressing using the `mov [W0+W1], W2` instruction. The effective address is calculated as (W0)+(W2), or 0x0802 + 0x0002 for a final EA of 0x0804. Figure 6.7b uses the same addressing modes as Figure 6.7a, except that the `mov` uses byte mode instead of word mode. Observe that byte mode does not change the effective address calculation. Also, unlike the pre/post increment/decrement addressing modes, the register offset addressing mode does not modify the registers used in the EA calculation, so W0 and W1 do not change in Figures 6.7a and 6.7b.

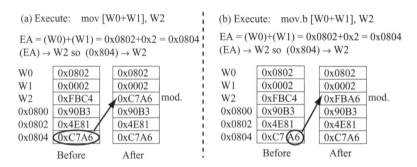

FIGURE 6.7   Register offset addressing mode examples.

Register Indirect with Signed Constant Offset

The `mov` instruction has an additional indirect addressing form as follows:

```
mov.{b}          [Ws + slit10], Wnd
mov.{b}          Wns, [Wd + slit10]
```

This addressing mode is similar to the register indirect with register offset mode of Figure 6.5 except that a signed literal *(slit10)* replaces the register offset. For byte mode, the range of *slit10* is –512 to +511, but in word mode the range is increased to –1024 to + 1022 as *slit10* must be even in order to maintain word alignment. This addressing mode is useful for accessing values that are a fixed offset from a base address, such as elements of C structures (see Appendix D) or values within a PIC24 stack frame (discussed later in this chapter). In Figure 6.7a, the instruction `mov [W0 + 2], W2` accomplishes the same result as `mov [W0 + W1], W2`, given that W1 contains a value of 2.

INSTRUCTION STALLS DUE TO DATA DEPENDENCIES

In Chapter 3, it was discussed that most PIC24 instructions require one instruction word and thus one instruction cycle to execute. However, in some cases an instruction will take more than one instruction cycle for execution. For example, all change of control instructions that are one instruction word (`rcall`, branches) take two instruction cycles to execute if the PC value is changed. This means that a conditional branch takes two instruction cycles if the branch is *taken* and one instruction cycle otherwise. The reason for this behavior is that the instruction word after the branch has already been fetched from program memory when the branch is taken. This instruction has to be discarded and a new instruction word must be fetched from the branch target address, thus requiring an extra instruction cycle.

Other cases that require an extra instruction cycle are *read after write* (RAW) dependencies. RAW dependencies occur when a working register that is modified in the previous instruction is used as a source address for a data memory access in the current instruction (i.e., the register is used in an indirect addressing mode for a source operand). For example, the instruction sequence

```
(1)    add W0,W1,W2
(2)    mov [W2++],W3
```

generates an instruction execution *stall,* which requires one extra instruction cycle because W2 is modified in instruction (1) while being used as an indirect source address in (2). Because of the pipelined implementation of the PIC24 µC, instruction execution in (1) has not yet been completed (W2 has not been written) when instruction (2) starts its execution. Since instruction (2) must have the content of W2 to execute, instruction execution must stall until the value of W2 is finalized. The following instruction sequence does not generate a stall:

```
(3)    add W0,W1,W2
(4)    mov W2,W3
```

because W2, modified in (3), is not used for a data memory access in instruction (4). Instruction stalls due to branches and RAW dependencies must be included when determining accurate instruction cycle counts for time-critical assembly code. Remember that a RAW stall occurs when a working register written by an instruction is used as an address in the next instruction.

ARRAYS AND POINTERS IN *C*

The previous coverage of *C* pointers used single element variables; however, pointers are most commonly used with groups of elements, such as *C* arrays and structures. *C* arrays group elements of the same type together, while *C* structures allow grouping of different element types. We will not cover *C* structures at this point as they are not required for our example *C* programs; however, we will use *C* structures in later chapters. Appendix D provides the reader with details on structure syntax and usage.

Figure 6.8 shows a type declaration for a one-dimensional *C* array, called au8_x, of four elements of uint8 type. The a in the au8_ variable name prefix is used as a reminder that this variable is an array of uint8 elements. A one-dimensional *C* array is declared as *type array_name[asize]* where *asize* is the array size. Array elements in *C* are accessed as *array_name[j]*, where *j* can vary from 0 to *asize*–1. The array type declaration in Figure 6.8 contains some initial values for the four array elements as a convenience; arrays are like any other variable in that they may or may not be assigned initial values. A uint8 pointer named pu8_y is also declared. Observe that the memory view of the array has the array elements ordered from element 0 to element *asize*–1, occupying memory locations 0x0800 through 0x0803 since each array element is one byte wide. The *C* statement au8_x[2]=au8_x[1] copies au8_x[1] to au8_x[2], which results in the content of location 0x0801 copied to location 0x0802. The *C* statement pu8_y=&au8_x[2] assigns the address of element au8_x[2], which is 0x0802, to the pointer variable pu8_y. The address of au8_x[2] is computed as &au8_x[0]+(2*sizeof(uint8)), where &au8_x[0] is the starting address of the array and the sizeof operator returns the number of bytes required by a uint8 type. Because the starting address of au8_x[0] is 0x0800, this results in 0x0800+(2*1)=0x0802 being assigned to pu8_y. The *C* statement pu8_y++ increments the pointer to the next array element, which is calculated as pu8_y+(1*sizeof(uint8)). This results in the new value of pu8_y being pu8_y+(1*1)=0x802+1=0x0803.

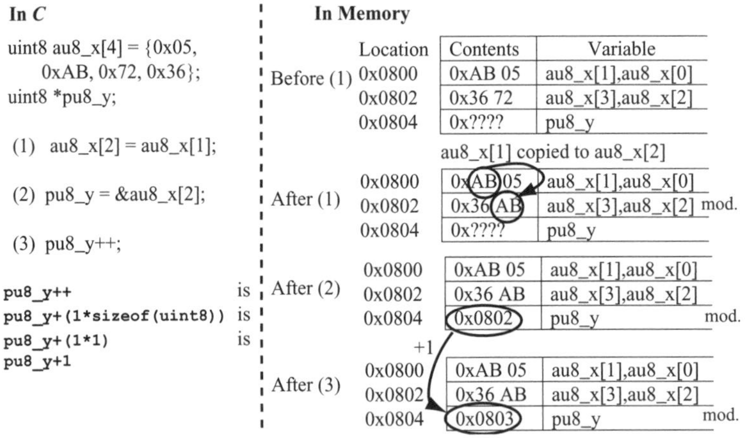

FIGURE 6.8 Array of uint8 data.

Figure 6.9 shows the code of Figure 6.8 replaced with uint16 data types. Observe that au16_x[4] array elements now occupy 8 bytes or 4 words of memory since each uint16 type requires two bytes. The *C* statement pu16_y=&au16_x[2] assigns the value &au16_x[0]+(2*sizeof(uint16)) to pu16_y, resulting in 0x0800+(2*2)=0x0804 as the new pu16_y value. The *C* statement pu16_y++ increments the pointer to the

In *C*		In Memory			
			Location	Contents	Variable
uint16 au16_x[4] = {0x38A0,		Before (1)	0x0800	0x38A0	au16_x[0]
0xC9F5,			0x0802	0xC9F5	au16_x[1]
0xB861,			0x0804	0xB861	au16_x[2]
0x724D};			0x0806	0x724D	au16_x[3]
uint16 *pu16_y;			0x0808	0x????	pu16_y
(1) au16_x[2] = au16_x[1];			0x0800	0x38A0	au16_x[0]
			0x0802	0xC9F5	au16_x[1]
(2) pu16_y = &au16_x[2];		After (1)	0x0804	0xC9F5	au16_x[2] mod.
			0x0806	0x724D	au16_x[3]
(3) pu16_y++;			0x0808	0x????	pu16_y
			0x0800	0x38A0	au16_x[0]
`pu16_y++` is			0x0802	0xC9F5	au16_x[1]
`pu16_y+(1*sizeof(uint16))` is			0x0804	0xC9F5	au16_x[2]
`pu16_y+(1*2)` is		After (2)	0x0806	0x724D	au16_x[3]
`pu16_y+2`			0x0808	0x0804	pu16_y mod.
			0x0800	0x38A0	au16_x[0]
			0x0802	0xC9F5	au16_x[1]
		After (3)	0x0804	0xC9F5	au16_x[2]
			0x0806	0x724D	au16_x[3]
			0x0808	0x0806	pu16_y mod.

FIGURE 6.9 Array of `uint16` data.

next array element, which is calculated as `pu16_y+(1*sizeof(uint16))`. This results in the new value of `pu16_y` being `pu16_y+(1*2)=0x804+2=0x0806`.

Figures 6.7 and 6.9 illustrate two important points about array and pointer operations in *C*:

■ The array access *a[i]* is equivalent to **(ptra+i)* if *ptra* points to the first element of array *a*.
■ The pointer arithmetic performed by **(ptra+i)* to calculate the effective address of the data access is *EA = (ptra) + (i*sizeof(ptra_type))* where *ptra_type* is the data type that is pointed to by *ptra* and *sizeof(ptra_type)* is the width in bytes of that data type.

It is important that these two points are remembered when translating *C* array and pointer operations into PIC24 assembly language statements.

Figure 6.10 shows a *C* code fragment that uses a *for{}* loop to sum two 10-element arrays `au16_a[10]`, `au16_b[10]` with the results placed in the elements of a third array named `au16_c[10]`. Obviously, the array elements are unsigned 16-bit values as indicated by our data type prefixes. The assembly language implementation uses the fact that the array elements are accessed in sequential order

In C	In Assembly

uint16 au16_a[10];
uint16 au16_b[10];
uint16 au16_c[10];
uint8 u8_i;
 	
for (u8_i = 0; u8_i < 10; u8_i++){
 	
au16_c[u8_i] = au16_a[u8_i] +
           au16_b[u8_i];
 	
}
	`` au16_a .space 10*2 ;each array occupies

au16_b .space 10*2 ;20 bytes since each
au16_c .space 10*2 ;element is 2 bytes
  ;W1 is used to point at au16_a
  ;W2 is used to point at au16_b
  ;W3 is used to point at au16_c
  ;W4 is loop counter (u8_i)

  mov #au16_a,W1   ;W1 = &au16_a[0]
  mov #au16_b,W2   ;W2 = &au16_b[0]
  mov #au16_c,W3   ;W3 = &au16_c[0]
  clr.b W4   ;clear loop counter
top_loop:
  cp.b W4,#10   ;check loop counter
  bra GEU,end_loop   ;exit if finished
  mov [W1++],W0   ;W0 = *W1, W1++
  add W0,[W2++],[W3++] ;*W3 = *W2 + W0
                      ;W3++,W2_ptr++
  inc.b W4,W4   ;increment loop counter
  bra top_loop   ;loop back to top
end_loop:
   ...rest of code... ``` |

FIGURE 6.10 Addition of two uint16 arrays using a loop.

by the body of the *C for{}* loop and thus initializes working registers W1, W2, W3 to point to the starting addresses of arrays au16_a[], au16_b[], and au16_c[] before the assembly language loop body is entered. The loop body then loads an element from the au16_a[] array into W0 using the mov [W1++],W0 instruction. The add W0,[W2++],[W3++] instruction then adds the W0 value to the au16_b[] array element with the result stored into the au16_c[] array element. The post-increment addressing mode increments the W1, W2, and W3 pointers to the next array element after the array elements are added. The loop counter variable u8_i of the *C for{}* loop is implemented by the W4 register. A programmer new to PIC24 assembly language may wish to use the instruction add [W1++],[W2++],[W3++] to add the two array elements. However, the add instruction does not support this combination of addressing modes, which is why the element from the au16_a[] array is loaded into W0 before being added to the au16_b[] array element.

C Strings

A common array found in *C* programs is a *C* string. The amount of string manipulation required in microcontroller programming is application dependent, but *C* strings are encountered often enough to warrant a basic coverage of them in this book. A *C* string is an array of char data where each byte is an ASCII character and the last character in the array is a 0x00 byte (also known as a *null* terminator or null byte). In this book, we have not used the char data type in our examples as we have favored using either uint8 (equivalent to unsigned char) or int8 (equivalent to signed char) as a reminder that these are unsigned and signed 8-bit quantities. However, since *C* strings contain ASCII encoded characters, we follow the normal

C convention of using the char data type for *C* strings. One problem with using the char data type is that the default signedness (signed or unsigned) is compiler dependent. As long as comparisons are done on ASCII-encoded characters (values of 0 to 127), then signedness does not matter since unsigned and signed comparisons work the same when both numbers are positive. A zero-terminated string differs from an ordinary array of char data in that the length of the zero-terminated string may be unknown *a priori*. The null byte denotes the end of the string, so string routines can operate on the string's elements one by one until it finds the null byte. Because a zero-terminated string differs so fundamentally from an ordinary char array that has a known size, we use a special data prefix, sz_, to identify the string's data type. The prefix psz_ is used to indicate a pointer to a zero-terminated string.

Figure 6.11a shows an example of a *C* string named sz_a[] that is initialized to contain "Hello" with accompanying *C* code that converts all of the characters in sz_a[] to uppercase. Observe that the "Hello" string contains five characters, but that the actual memory contents of Figure 6.11b show the array as containing six bytes since the string has an additional 0x00 byte at the end to terminate the string. The while(){} loop in the *C* code executes the *while-body* until the character pointed to

(a) In *C*

```
char sz_a[] = "Hello";
char* psz_x;

psz_x = &sz_a[0];
while (*psz_x != 0) {
  //convert to upper case
  if (*psz_x > 0x60 &&
     *psz_x < 0x7B) {
  //lowercase 'a' - 'z', so
  //convert to 'A' - 'Z'
  *psz_x = *psz_x - 0x20;
  }
  psz_x++; //advance to
          //next character
}
```

(b) In Memory

Location	Contents	Variable	as ASCII
0x0800	0x6548	sz_a[1],sz_a[0]	'e', 'H'
0x0802	0x6C6C	sz_a[3],sz_a[2]	'l','l'
0x0804	0x006F	sz_a[5],sz_a[4]	null, 'o'

(c) In Assembly

```
  ;W0 is used to implement psz_x
  ;W1 is used to hold contents of *psz_x
  ;W2 is used a temp. reg to hold constants

  mov #sz_a,W0        ;W0 = &sz_a[0]
top_loop:
  mov.b [W0],W1       ;W1 = *psz_x
  cp.b W1,#0x00
  bra Z, end_loop     ;exit if at end of string
  mov #0x60,W2
  cp.b W1,W2          ;compare *psz_x and 0x60
  bra LEU, end_if     ;skip if-body
  mov #0x7B,W2
  cp.b W1,W2          ;compare *psz_x and 0x7B
  bra GEU, end_if     ;skip if_body
  mov #0x20,W2
  sub.b W1,W2,[W0]    ;*psz_x = *psz_x-0x20
end_if:
  inc W0,W0           ;psz_x++
  bra top_loop        ;loop back to top
end_loop:
  ...rest of code...
```

FIGURE 6.11 A pointer example using a *C* string.

by *psz_x is equal to zero, indicating that the string end has been reached. The if(){} statement in the *while-body* checks if the current character pointed to by *psz_x is a lowercase ASCII letter, that is, between the values of 0x60 and 0x7B. If the character is lowercase, then 0x20 is subtracted from it, converting the character to uppercase. The assembly code of Figure 6.11c is a straightforward implementation of the *C* code, with W0 used to implement the pointer variable *psz_x. Observe that at the end of the loop, the *C* statement psz_x++ is implemented by the inc W0,W0 instruction. This works in this case because psz_x++ is psz_x+(1*sizeof(uint8)), which is psz_x+1.

The assembly code of Figure 6.11c assumes that sz_a[] resides in data memory and that the contents of sz_a[] have been initialized by code that is not shown. A section later in this chapter examines how strings such as sz_a[] are initialized before use.

THE *REPEAT* INSTRUCTION

Figure 6.12a shows a *C* code fragment that uses a for(){} loop to initialize the contents of a 64-element uint16 array to zero. The assembly code implementation in Figure 6.12b is similar in approach to that of Figure 6.10 in that it uses W1 to point at the beginning of the array, then the loop steps through the array elements, assigning zero to each element. Register indirect with post-increment addressing is used to advance W1 to each successive array element.

Since many applications μC programs repeatedly perform the same operation as the code in Figure 6.12b, the thoughtful designers of the PIC24 instruction set have

(a) In *C*

```
uint16 au16_x[64];
uint8 u8_i;


// Initialize contents of au16_x[]
// to zero
for (u8_i = 0; u8_i < 64; u8_i++) {
  au16_x[u8_i] = 0;
}
```

(b) In Assembly

```
;W1 is used to point at au16_x
;W2 is used as loop counter
 mov  #au16_x,W1    ;W1 points at &au16_x[0]
 clr.b W2           ;clear loop counter
 mov.b #64,W3       ;W3 holds loop max count
top_loop:
 cp.b W2,W3         ;check loop counter
 bra GEU,end_loop   ;exit if finished
 clr [W1++]         ;au16_x[u8_i] = 0;
 inc.b W2,W2        ;increment loop counter
 bra top_loop       ;loop back to top
end_loop:
 ...rest of code...
```
- -
(c) In Assembly (use the *repeat* instruction)

```
;W1 is used to point at au16_x
 mov  #au16_x,W1    ;W1 points at &au16_x[0]
 repeat #63         ;repeat next instruction!
 clr [W1++]         ;au16_x[u8_i] = 0;
 ...rest of code...
```

FIGURE 6.12 The repeat instruction.

provided us with a single assembly language instruction that repeats an assembly language instruction. Figure 6.12c shows an alternate assembly code implementation that uses the repeat instruction to accomplish the task in Figure 6.12a. A repeat instruction has an *RCOUNT* value associated with it, which is loaded into a special function register named RCOUNT when the repeat instruction is executed. The instruction following the repeat instruction is executed *RCOUNT*+1 number of times; this repeated execution is also referred to as the *repeat loop*. There are two general forms of the repeat instruction:

- repeat #*lit14*, where #*lit14* is a 14-bit literal that specifies *RCOUNT*.
- repeat *Wn*, where the lower 14 bits of *Wn* is used as the *RCOUNT* value.

The RA bit in the status register is set when a repeat loop is active and is cleared when the repeat loop is finished. For this particular case, the repeat loop implementation in Figure 6.12c is much more efficient than the code of Figure 6.12b in both total number of instructions (three versus eight) and total number of instruction cycles (66 versus 388). Unfortunately, the repeat instruction can only repeat the single PIC24 assembly language instruction that follows it. This limits the repeat instruction's usefulness for general-purpose applications. The repeat instruction is also used with the PIC24 divide instructions, which are discussed in Chapter 7.

Sample question: *For the following C code fragment, assume the variables are stored in memory starting at location 0x0800. What is the starting address of each variable assuming this code is compiled for the PIC24 µC? What is the final value of* pu8_x? *What array element in* au8_s *is modified?*

```
uint8 au8_s[8];
uint8* pu8_x;
uint8 u8_a;

u8_a = 5;
pu8_x = au8_s;
pu8_x = pu8_x + 3;
*pu8_x = u8_a;
```

Answer: The starting memory location for au8_s is 0x0800. The starting memory location for pu8_x is 0x0800 + 8 = 0x0808 because au8_s occupies 8 bytes of memory. The starting memory location for u8_a is 0x0808 + 2 = 0x080A because pu8_x occupies 2 bytes of memory. (A pointer variable always occupies 2 bytes of memory regardless of the data type it references.) The pu8_x variable is first initialized to the starting address of au8_s (0x0800) as the pu8_x = au8_s assignment is equivalent to pu8_x = &au8_s[0]. The pointer arithmetic pu8_x = pu8_x + 3 is calculated as 0x0800 + (3*1) = 0x0803 since pu8_x is a uint8* type (a pointer to uint8 data), so each element is 1 byte in size. Thus, the final value of pu8_x is 0x0803. The statement *pu8_x = u8_a modifies array element au8_s[3] because pu8_x is pointing to au8_s[3].

Sample Question: *For the previous sample question, change the data type from* uint8 *to* uint16 *and answer the same questions; change* uint8 *to* uint32 *and answer the same questions. Assume that the variable name prefixes are also changed to reflect the new data types.*

Answer: When the data type is changed from uint8 to uint16, the starting memory location for au16_s is still 0x0800. The starting memory location for pu16_x is 0x0800 + 0x10 = 0x0810 because au16_s occupies 8*2 = 16 = 0x10 bytes of memory. The starting memory location for u16_a is 0x0810 + 2 = 0x0812 because pu16_x occupies 2 bytes of memory. (A pointer variable always occupies 2 bytes of memory regardless of the data type it references.) The pu16_x variable is first initialized to the starting address of au16_s (0x0800). The pointer arithmetic pu16_x = pu16_x + 3 is calculated as 0x0800 + (3*2) = 0x0806 since pu16_x is a uint16* (a pointer to uint16 data), so each element is 2 bytes in size. Thus, the final value of pu16_x is 0x0806. The statement *pu16_x = u16_a modifies array element au16_s[3] because ptr is pointing to s[3].

When the data type is changed from uint8 to uint32, the starting memory location for au32_s is still 0x0800. The starting memory location for pu32_x is 0x0800 + 0x020 = 0x0820 because au32_s occupies 8*4 = 32 = 0x20 bytes of memory. The starting memory location for u32_a is 0x0820 + 2 = 0x0822 because pu32_x occupies 2 bytes of memory. (A pointer variable always occupies 2 bytes of memory regardless of the data type it references.) The pu32_x variable is first initialized to the starting address of au32_s (0x0800). The pointer arithmetic pu32_x = pu32_x + 3 is calculated as 0x0800 + (3*4) = 0x080C since pu32_x is a uint32* (a pointer to uint32 data), so each element is 4 bytes in size. Thus, the final value of pu32_x is 0x080C. The statement *pu32_x = u32_a modifies array element au32_s[3] because pu32_x is pointing to au32_s[3].

SUBROUTINES

A *subroutine* is a block of code that is *called* from different locations within the main program or other subroutines. Instead of duplicating commonly used instruction sequences in multiple locations, the instruction sequence can be encapsulated as a subroutine in a single location and called when needed. Using subroutines reduces code size, as the subroutine resides in only one place in program memory instead of multiple locations. This also improves code clarity and produces code that is easier to maintain, as any code modifications are only performed in the subroutine body instead of within the duplicated code sections. Figure 6.13 illustrates this concept. The main program or other subroutine that calls a subroutine is known as the *caller,* while the subroutine being called is known as the *callee.*

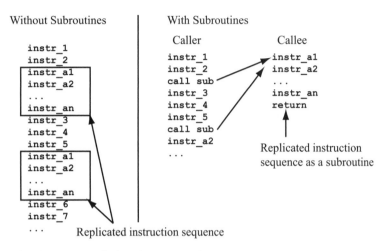

FIGURE 6.13 Use of subroutines saves code space.

The basic form of a *C* subroutine and a specific example are seen in Figure 6.14. In *C,* the preferred name for a subroutine is *function,* and these two terms are used

General form of a *C* subroutine is:

(return_type) subname (parm list)
{
    local_variable_decl;
    subroutine_body;
    return *return_value*;
}

countOnes Subroutine

```
// count "1" bits in uint16 parameter
uint8 countOnes (uint16 u16_v) {
    uint8 u8_cnt, u8_i;          parameter list: gives
                                  types and names
    u8_cnt = 0;
    for (u8_i = 0; u8_i < 16; u8_i++) {
        if (u16_v & 0x0001) u8_cnt++;      subroutine
        u16_v = u16_v >> 1;                body
    }
    return u8_cnt;        subroutine return
}
                         main program
main (void) {
    uint16 u16_k;
    uint8 u8_j;
                              subroutine call
    u16_k = 0xA501;
    u8_j = countOnes (u16_k);
    printf (
    "Number of one bits in %x is %d\n",
    u16_k, u8_j);
}
```

FIGURE 6.14 *C* subroutine example.

interchangeably in this book. The example subroutine is named countOnes(), which counts the number of bits that are equal to "1" in a 16-bit value. Subroutines have distinct components that are defined as follows (it is not necessary for a subroutine to have all of these components):

■ **Parameter list:** Some subroutines are a fixed set of instructions that performs the exact same operation each time they are called. However, a subroutine can also have parameters that alter the subroutine behavior based on their values. The countOnes() subroutine in Figure 6.14 has one parameter named u16_v of type uint16.

■ **Local variables:** A subroutine may need additional variables that are used internally to perform its function. In *C*, these variables are declared within the subroutine and are only visible to the subroutine itself. The countOnes() subroutine in Figure 6.14 has two local variables named u8_cnt and u8_i; the u8_cnt variable is used to keep track of the number of "1" bits found in the u16_v parameter while u8_i is the loop counter for the for(){} loop.

■ **Return value:** In *C*, a subroutine may return a single value to the caller by means of the return statement. The countOnes() subroutine returns a value of type uint8 to the caller, which in this case is the local variable u8_cnt. If a *C* function returns no value then its return type should be declared as void. If a function does not return a value then it is not required that the subroutine contain an explicit return statement; an implicit return is done when the end of the subroutine body is reached.

The countOnes() subroutine uses a counting loop that is executed 16 times, where the u8_cnt variable is incremented if the least significant bit of u16_v is a "1", followed by a right shift of u16_v to move the next bit of u16_v into the LSb position. The number of "1" bits in u16_v is thus counted by u8_cnt, which is returned to the caller by the statement return u8_cnt. The main() code in Figure 6.14 uses the local variable u16_k as the parameter passed to the countOnes() subroutine, which is called by the statement u8_j=countOnes(u16_k). The assignment operator of the subroutine call copies the return value of countOnes() to the local variable u8_j. The *C* language semantics define that subroutine parameters are passed *by value* to the subroutine. This means that the variable u16_k in main() is unaffected by the subroutine call; that is, u16_k retains its original value after the subroutine call because its value is copied to the memory location or register used for the subroutine parameter. The printf() statement in main() is a formatted print statement included for example purposes so that you can compile this program with a *C* compiler on a personal computer and observe the input parameters and return value. The printf() statement is not implemented when we translate this *C* code to PIC24 assembly code later in this chapter; see Appendix D, for more details on printf() syntax.

THE STACK AND CALL/RETURN, PUSH/POP

A subroutine *call* is a jump to the first instruction of the subroutine, while a subroutine *return* is a jump back to the instruction in the caller following the subroutine call. The location returned to by a subroutine return is known as the *return address*. Figure 6.15 shows the problem with implementing subroutine call and return by use of goto instructions. Subroutine A is called twice from within the calling program, once from label C1 and once from label C2. Labels R1 and R2 mark the return addresses. The first call (1) and return (2) to subroutine A work as intended. However, while the second call (3) also works correctly, the return (4) is incorrect, as location R1 is the return address instead of R2. Clearly, a mechanism other than a goto instruction is needed to implement call and return, as the return address depends on the call location. On the PIC24 μC, the call and rcall instructions implement subroutine call, while the return and retlw instructions implement subroutine return.

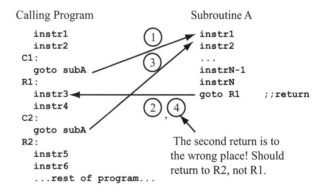

FIGURE 6.15   Implementing call/return with goto.

What is needed is a method for saving the return address for later use by the subroutine return statement. A *stack* data structure is a commonly used mechanism in microprocessors for saving return addresses of subroutine calls. One way to visualize stack operation is by a stack of boxes, in which boxes are placed (stacked) sequentially on top of each other. Figure 6.16 illustrates a three-box stack in which box A is placed first, then box B, and finally box C. In this stack the *top of stack* (TOS) is the first free or empty location for a new item. Removing boxes from the stack is done in reverse order; first box C, then box B, and finally box A. Placing an item on the stack is referred to as a *push* operation, while removing an item is known as a *pop* operation. A stack is empty if it contains no items; a stack is full if another item cannot be pushed onto the stack. Another common name for a stack is a *last-in, first-out* (LIFO) buffer, as the name describes the order in which data is accessed.

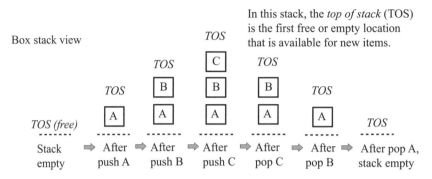

FIGURE 6.16   Stack example.

THE DATA MEMORY STACK

A stack data structure requires a set of memory locations for storing the stack items and a *stack pointer* (SP) that contains the memory address of the current top of the stack. Most microprocessors have a special register dedicated for the stack pointer; the PIC24 μC uses working register W15 as its stack pointer. In this text, the symbol SP (stack pointer) is used interchangeably with W15 when discussing stack pointer operations. Before the stack can be used for data storage, the stack pointer must be initialized to point somewhere in data memory. Typically, the SP is initialized to a data location that immediately follows all of the statically allocated program space. Recall from Listing 3.3 of Chapter 3 that the instruction used to initialize the stack pointer is mov #__SP_init,W15 where __SP_init is a label that is assigned by the assembler/linker to the first free data memory location after the statically allocated variables. Figure 6.17a illustrates how a push operation on the PIC24 memory stack operates. The stack pointer (W15) is initialized to point to location 0x900, which is an arbitrary choice for the purpose of this discussion. A push operation writes source data (i.e., *dataA*) as specified by the source addressing mode to the location pointed to by W15, then increments W15 by 2, leaving W15 with the new value of 0x0902. The PIC24 memory stack grows toward increasing memory locations as data is pushed onto the stack. Figure 6.17b shows that a push operation performs the reverse operations of a pop, that is, W15 is first decremented by 2, then the location pointed to by W15 is read and the data stored to a destination specified by the destination addressing mode. After the pop operation the value of W15 is 0x0900, the same value it was before the push operation. Note that the data read by a stack pop is still in memory, since a read is non-destructive. However, this data is now *inaccessible* if only push or pop operations are used to access stack data. A second pop operation cannot access the data because this decrements W15 by 2 before reading memory. Another push operation writes to location 0x0900 before incrementing W15 by 2, overwriting the previous stack data.

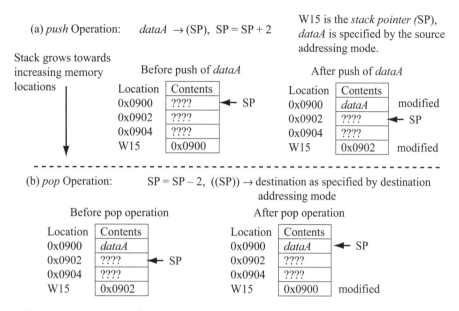

FIGURE 6.17   Memory stack push, pop operations.

Figure 6.18 shows the forms of the push and pop instructions that access the data stack via W15. Observe that there are no byte mode push/pop instructions; all forms are either word or double word operations. The *Wns, Wnd* registers specified in double word operations must be even-numbered.

Name	Mnemonic	Operation
Push	push *Wso* push *f*	(*Wso*) → (W15); (W15)+2 → W15 (*f*) → (W15); (W15)+2 → W15
Push double word	push.d *Wns*	(*Wns*) → (W15);(W15)+2 → W15 (*Wns+1*) → (W15);(W15)+2 → W15
Pop	pop *Wdo* pop *f*	(W15)-2 → W15; (W15) → *Wdo* (W15)-2 → W15; (W15) → *f*
Pop double word	pop.d *Wnd*	(W15)-2 → W15; (W15) → *Wnd* (W15)-2 → W15; (W15) → *Wnd+1*

f specifies a word address anywhere in the lower 32 Ki words of data memory

FIGURE 6.18   push, pop instruction forms.

The execution of a push W0 instruction is shown in Figure 6.19a. After instruction execution, the memory location pointed to by W15 (0x0950) is changed to the W0 register value (0xCD18), and W15 is incremented by 2 to its new value of 0x0952. Note that a mov W0,[W15++] instruction accomplishes the same actions as push W0, so it is helpful to remember that a push operation is simply a memory write with

(a) Execute: `push W0`   (W0) → (SP); SP = SP + 2

Equivalent to: `mov W0,[W15++]`

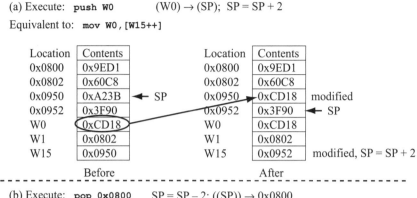

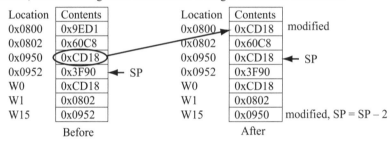

FIGURE 6.19   push, pop instruction execution example.

W15 specifying the destination address via the register indirect with post-increment addressing mode. Figure 6.19b illustrates the execution of a `pop 0x0800` instruction. Register W15 is first decremented by 2 to point at location 0x0950, and the content of 0x0950 is transferred to location 0x0800. This is semantically equivalent to a `mov [--W15],0x0800` instruction, but do not try this in the PIC24 assembler because this addressing mode combination is not allowed with the `mov` instruction. Thus, a pop operation is a memory read operation with W15 specifying the source address via the register indirect with pre-decrement addressing mode.

CALL/RETURN AND THE DATA MEMORY STACK

One of the principal uses of the data memory stack is for the storage of the return address during a subroutine call, which has two instruction forms named `call` *target* and `rcall` *target*. Both instruction forms first store the return address on the data memory stack before transferring control to the *target* address. The difference between a `call` and `rcall` is similar to the difference between the `goto` and `bra` unconditional instructions. A `call` instruction takes two instruction words and can transfer control anywhere in program memory, while an `rcall` only takes one instruction word and uses program relative addressing (see Chapter 5) to specify the destination, thus limiting the range of the rcall instruction. Figure 6.20 shows how return addresses are stored on the data stack for a series of nested subroutine calls. The stack pointer is initialized to location 0x0900 for the example. With execution starting at main, the first subroutine call that is executed is call sub_a (1). This pushes the return address 0x000244 on the stack as two 16-bit words, which advances the stack pointer to 0x0904, after which a jump is made to sub_a. The return address for a call instruction is computed as PC + 4, where PC is the program memory address of the call instruction. Within sub_a, the call sub_b (2) instruction pushes the return address 0x00026E on the stack, advancing the stack pointer to 0x0908, then control is transferred to sub_b. The final subroutine call is made from within sub_b by the rcall sub_c instruction. Because the rcall instruction is one instruction word, the return address pushed on the stack is PC + 2, which in this case is 0x00033E, leaving the stack pointer at 0x090C. The return instruction is used at the end of a subroutine to return to the caller, which is accomplished by popping the return address from the stack and using the return address as the new PC value. The first return instruction (4) executed is in subroutine sub_c, whose execution pops 0x00033E from the stack, decrementing the stack pointer by 2 to 0x00908. Subsequent return instructions at point (5) in sub_b and point (6) in sub_a pop the return addresses 0x00026E, 0x00244 from the stack, leaving the stack pointer at its original value of 0x0900.

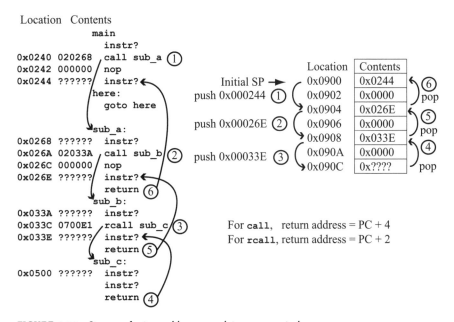

FIGURE 6.20   Storage of return address on a data memory stack.

STACK OVERFLOW/UNDERFLOW

A program should execute the same number of stack pop operations as stack pushes and the same number return instructions as call instructions in order to remove the same amount of data from the stack as is placed on the stack. If this is not done, then the stack eventually *underflows* (the stack pointer decrements past its initial value) or *overflows* (the stack pointer increments past the end of implemented data memory). The stack pointer limit (SPLIM) register is a special function register that is used to automatically detect stack overflow. If a stack push is done when the stack pointer is greater than the SPLIM value then a *stack error trap* is generated, causing program execution to automatically jump to the *stack error* vector (general discussion about traps and interrupts is found in Chapter 9). Generally, the SPLIM register is initialized to a value that is a few words less than the end of physical memory; the reasons for this are discussed further in Chapter 9 in the coverage of traps and interrupts. A stack error trap for stack pointer underflow is generated if the stack pointer is decremented below 0x0800 to prevent stack operations from occurring within the special function register space.

IMPLEMENTING SUBROUTINES IN ASSEMBLY LANGUAGE

The instruction forms for call/return are shown in Figure 6.21. The call Wn and rcall Wn forms allow the effective address of the subroutine to be computed from a working register value instead of a literal. As with the goto instruction, the call *label_lit23* form allows the subroutine to be located anywhere in program memory

Name	Mnemonic	Operation
Call	call *label_lit23*	Push return address on stack, new SP = SP + 4, then *label_lit23* → PC
	call *Wn*	Push return address on stack, new SP = SP + 4, then (*Wn*) → PC
Relative call	rcall *label_slit16*	Push return address on stack, new SP = SP + 4, then (PC) + (2*label_slit16) → PC
	rcall *Wn*	Push return address on stack, new SP = SP + 4, then (PC) + (2*Wn) → PC
Return	return	Pop return address from stack into the PC, new SP = SP - 4
Return with literal in *Wn*	retlw{.b} #*lit10*,*Wn*	Pop return address from stack into the PC, new SP = SP - 4, and #*lit10* → *Wn*

The **call** *label_lit23* instruction is 2 instruction words, all others are 1 instruction word.

FIGURE 6.21 Instruction forms for call and rcall.

at the cost of two instruction words. The other call forms are one instruction word, with rcall limited to a target subroutine that is within ± 32 Ki programs words of the current PC and call Wn limited to the lower 32 Ki instructions of program memory. Both the return and retlw instructions transfer control by popping the return address from the stack into the PC register, but the retlw instruction also places the constant #lit10 into register Wn, which is useful for subroutines that return a constant value to the caller.

STATIC VERSUS DYNAMIC PARAMETER ALLOCATION

In translating a *C* function to a subroutine in PIC24 assembly language, the first decision is how to allocate the data locations or registers needed for parameters, local variables, and the return value. One method is *static memory allocation,* in which data memory locations are assigned to parameters and locals, and the same locations are used each time the subroutine is called. Static memory allocation is attractive in processors that have a small number of general purpose registers or lack efficient support for a data memory stack. The disadvantage of static alloca-tion is that subroutine *recursion* is not allowed; that is, the subroutine cannot call itself (or call another subroutine that eventually calls the original subroutine). Sub-routine recursion cannot be used with a static allocation strategy because the data locations for parameters and local variables are still in use when the subroutine is reentered by the nested call to itself. The recursive call overwrites the subroutine data memory area with new values, losing the values still in use by the first call to the subroutine. Note that any variables declared outside of a *C* function (global variables) are always statically allocated.

Dynamic memory allocation uses a new set of memory locations for each sub-routine call, so clashes between data memory locations in recursive subroutine calls are avoided. Figure 6.22 illustrates the problem with using static allocation for recursive subroutines. In this example, the *C* function sub_a uses a local variable named u16_i and recursively calls itself if its input parameter u16_n has value 1. Figure 6.22a has the u16_i internal variable of sub_a declared locally to sub_a, caus-ing a new memory location to be allocated for u16_i each time sub_a is called, assuming dynamic allocation. The first invocation of sub_a executes the *if-body* be-cause u16_n == 1, causing sub_a to be called a second time, this time with u16_n=0. In the second invocation of sub_a, the *if-body* is skipped as u16_n is zero. The assign-ment u16_i = 5 in the second invocation of sub_a has no effect on the u16_i value in the first invocation, as each version of u16_i has a different memory location. Thus, the u16_i value in the first invocation of sub_a remains at 10, is incremented to 11, and then is returned to main().

Figure 6.22b moves the declaration uint16 u16_i out of the function, making it a statically allocated variable, causing each call to sub_a to use the same memory location for u16_i. This time, the assignment u16_i = 5 in the second invocation

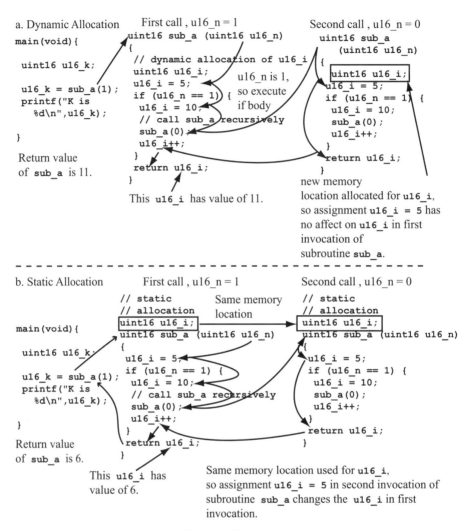

FIGURE 6.22 Dynamic versus static allocation with recursive function calls.

of sub_a overwrites the previous value 10 assigned to u16_i in the first invocation of sub_a. When a return is made to the first invocation of sub_a, u16_i has the value of 5, which is incremented to 6 and returned to main(). If static allocation is used for subroutine parameters and local variables, subroutine recursion is not allowed. Another form of recursion occurs when an active subroutine is *interrupted* (execution of the subroutine is halted at an arbitrary point), and the same subroutine is called by an *interrupt service routine* (code that is executed to handle the interrupt source), causing two copies of the subroutine local variables to be needed at the same time (interrupts and interrupt service routines are discussed further in Chapter 9). This type of recursion can be a common occurrence in microcontroller applications, and as such, dynamic memory allocation is preferred if the microcontroller can support it in an efficient manner. Some *C* compilers allow a choice of static versus dynamic allocation via a compiler option. One method for implementing dynamic allocation is to use the data memory stack for both subroutine parameters and local variables, which is discussed later in this chapter. Another method for implementing dynamic allocation is to use working registers for both subroutine parameters and local variables, with the data memory stack used to save current register values when new versions of the registers are required. This method is discussed further in this section and is the primary method used in this text for subroutine parameters and local variables.

USING WORKING REGISTERS FOR SUBROUTINE PARAMETERS AND LOCALS

Before examining subroutine assembly language examples, a policy must be established that specifies how working registers are used for subroutine parameters and locals. The policy used in this book is compatible with the policy used by the MPLAB PIC24 compiler, which is the compiler used for the PIC24 *C* code examples in Chapters 8 and higher. The working register usage policy for the assembly language subroutine examples in this book are:

- Registers W0-W7 are used for parameter passing, with parameters allocated to registers in left-to-right parameter order, using increasing register numbers. Registers W0-W7 are caller saved, i.e., the caller must save these registers if their values are to be preserved. An extended precision value (32-bit or 64-bit) requires multiple registers, passed in least significant to most significant word order. An 8-bit parameter occupies an entire register; two 8-bit parameters are not combined into the same 16-bit register.
- Function return values are returned in W0-W3, with W0 used for 8-bit and 16-bit data, W1:W0 for 32-bit data, and W3:W2:W1:W0 for 64-bit data.
- Registers W8-W14 are callee saved; the subroutine must preserve these register values if they are used.
- Locals are allocated to any W0-W7 registers not used for parameters and also to W8-W14 if needed.

Figure 6.23 shows the countOnes(uint16 u16_v) *C* function implemented as a subroutine in PIC24 assembly language. The u16_v parameter is passed in the W0 register, with W1 and W2 used for the u8_cnt and u8_i local variables. The return value is passed back in W0 register. The assembly code is a straightforward implementation of the *C* code. One small optimization is that the btst.z W0, #0 instruction is used to implement the least significant bit test found in the if (u16_v & 0x0001) statement. Observe that the last instruction before the *return* statement is mov.b W1, W0. This copies the u8_cnt local variable implemented in W1 to the W0 register that is used for passing the return value back to the caller.

In C	In Assembly
| ```c
// count "1" bits in uint16 parameter
uint8 countOnes (uint16 u16_v) {
  uint8 u8_cnt, u8_i;

  u8_cnt = 0;
  for (u8_i = 0; u8_i < 16; u8_i++) {
    if (u16_v & 0x0001) u8_cnt++;
    u16_v = u16_v >> 1;
  }
  return u8_cnt;
}
``` | ```asm
; u16_v passed in W0
; return value passed back in W0
; W1 used for local u8_cnt, W2 for u8_i
countOnes:
    clr.b W1          ;u8_cnt=0
    clr.b W2          ;u8_i=0
loop_top:
    cp.b W2,#16       ;compare u8_i, 16
    bra GEU,end_loop  ;exit loop if u8_i>=1
    btst.z W0,#0      ;test LSbit for zero
    bra Z, end_if
    inc.b W1,W1       ;u8_cnt++;
end_if:
    lsr W0,#1,W0      ;u16_v = u16_v >> 1
    inc.b W2,W2       ;u8_i++
    bra loop_top
end_loop:
    mov.b W1,W0       ;W0 = u8_cnt for
    return            ;   return value
``` |

FIGURE 6.23   The countOnes() C function in assembly language.

Figure 6.24 shows the assembly language implementation of the main() code that calls the countOnes() subroutine. The __reset entry code has been modified to mimic more closely the code generated by the MPLAB PIC24 compiler. In addition to initializing the stack pointer, the SPLIM register is initialized to the compiler generated label __SPLIM_init, which is a value that is a few words less than the end of physical memory allowing enough space for a stack trap error to be correctly

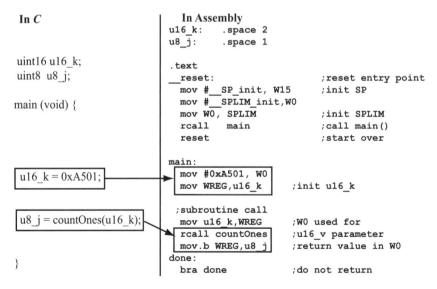

FIGURE 6.24   Calling the countOnes() subroutine from main().

handled (see chapter 9). Also, main is called as a subroutine, followed by a reset instruction that causes the processor to undergo a reset sequence forcing the execution to restart at location zero (the reset sequence is discussed in more detail in Chapter 8). Placing the reset instruction after the rcall main instruction is a safety net for an unusual occurrence, as generally the main function in a microcontroller application is an infinite loop that does not return to the reset initialization code. The assembly code in main first initializes the u16_k variable to 0xA501. To prepare for the subroutine call, the u16_k variable is copied into W0 by the mov u16_k, WREG instruction since W0 is used as the u16_v parameter for the countOnes() subroutine. The rcall countOnes instruction implements the subroutine call, and the subsequent mov.b WREG, u8_j instruction copies the subroutine return value to variable u8_j. In most compilers (including the PIC24 compiler), the code executed before main is called the crt0 module and contains the initialization required to launch C programs. This initialization process is explored in more detail later in this chapter.

SAVING REGISTER VALUES ON THE STACK

The countOnes() example is simple enough that register values do not have to be preserved during a subroutine call. For a more interesting example, consider the *Fibonacci* sequence of {0, 1, 1, 2, 3, 5, 8, 13, 21, 34, 55, 89, 144, ...} where each number after the first two is the sum of the previous two numbers. Figure 6.25 shows a C subroutine that computes the nth number of the sequence, where n is the subroutine input parameter. The *Fibonacci* calculation is most naturally performed by recursion and thus is a classic example for illustrating subroutine recursion and stack usage. The assembly code in Figure 6.25 only shows the implementation of the fib(uint16 u16_n) subroutine since the main() code is nearly identical to that of Figure 6.24. The assembly language implementation of the statements 1, 2 in the fib(uint16 u16_n) subroutine is straightforward and represents the *terminal* cases of the recursion, which are the points at which the subroutine does not call itself. Statement 3 is the first recursive call in the C fib() subroutine. In the assembly implementation, observe that the push W0 statement is used to save the original u16_n value on the stack in order to preserve its value when the fib(u16_n–1) subroutine call is made. After the rcall fib instruction, the return value of u16_f1 is stored in the W1 register, so popping W0 from the stack restores the original value of u16_n. The easiest method to save register values during a subroutine call is to push them onto the stack before the call, then pop them off the stack after the call. Because the subroutine call (and any other nested calls) only affects stack locations ahead of the stack pointer on subroutine entry, the stack locations used for the saved register values are undisturbed. Statement 4 is the second and last recursive call in the C fib() subroutine. The assembly language implementation saves u16_f1 (W1) on the stack before the rcall fib instruction since its value is needed after

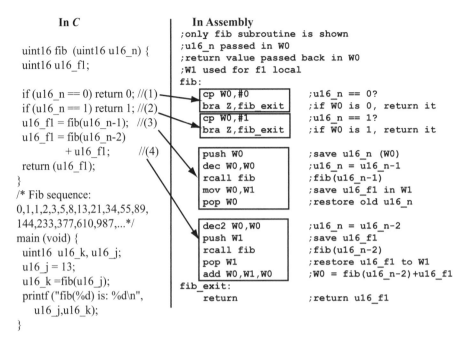

In C

```
uint16 fib (uint16 u16_n) {
uint16 u16_f1;

if (u16_n == 0) return 0; //(1)
if (u16_n == 1) return 1; //(2)
u16_f1 = fib(u16_n-1);  //(3)
u16_f1 = fib(u16_n-2)
         + u16_f1;    //(4)
return (u16_f1);
}
/* Fib sequence:
0,1,1,2,3,5,8,13,21,34,55,89,
144,233,377,610,987,...*/
main (void) {
 uint16 u16_k, u16_j;
 u16_j = 13;
 u16_k =fib(u16_j);
 printf ("fib(%d) is: %d\n",
   u16_j,u16_k);
}
```

In Assembly

```
;only fib subroutine is shown
;u16_n passed in W0
;return value passed back in W0
;W1 used for f1 local
fib:
  cp W0,#0            ;u16_n == 0?
  bra Z,fib_exit      ;if W0 is 0, return it
  cp W0,#1            ;u16_n == 1?
  bra Z,fib_exit      ;if W0 is 1, return it

  push W0             ;save u16_n (W0)
  dec W0,W0           ;u16_n = u16_n-1
  rcall fib           ;fib(u16_n-1)
  mov W0,W1           ;save u16_f1 in W1
  pop W0              ;restore old u16_n

  dec2 W0,W0          ;u16_n = u16_n-2
  push W1             ;save u16_f1
  rcall fib           ;fib(u16_n-2)
  pop W1              ;restore u16_f1 to W1
  add W0,W1,W0        ;W0 = fib(u16_n-2)+u16_f1
fib_exit:
  return              ;return u16_f1
```

FIGURE 6.25 Fibonacci computation in C and assembly.

the subroutine call. The W0 (u16_n value) is not pushed on the stack for the second recursive call to fib because this value is no longer needed and can be destroyed. After the recursive call returns, W1 is popped off the stack, restoring the u16_f1 value, which is then added to the recursive call return value in W0 to form the final subroutine return value. This example illustrates the usefulness of the stack for temporary storage of variables. In general, the responsibilities of the caller in a subroutine call are: (1) save any registers to be preserved over the subroutine call on the stack, (2) initialize parameter values, (3) call the subroutine, (4) copy any return value to a variable within the caller, and (5) pop any saved registers off the stack.

THE SHADOW REGISTERS

Registers W0-W3 and the status register have a set of *shadow registers* associated with them that allow fast save and restore of these registers. The push.s instruction copies W0-W3, SR (C, N, V, DC, and Z flags only) to the shadow registers while the pop.s instructions copies in the reverse direction. Both instructions take only one instruction cycle, so this is faster than using separate push and pop instructions on the data stack. The shadow registers are only one deep so successive push.s instructions overwrite the contents of the shadow registers. Obviously, the usefulness of the shadow registers is dependent upon the particular subroutine. Use of the shadow registers would not have decreased instruction count or execution time of the fib subroutine in Figure 6.25.

A SUBROUTINE WITH MULTIPLE PARAMETERS

Figure 6.26 shows a *C* function named swapU32 that swaps the elements of a uint32 array whose first element is pointed to by parameter pu32_b, with parameters u8_k and u8_j containing the array indices of the elements to be swapped. The local variable u32_t serves as temporary storage during the swap operation. In the assembly implementation, pu32_b is passed in W0 while u8_k, u8_j are passed in W1, W2 respectively. Observe that parameters are allocated to registers W0-W7 in left-to-right parameter order, using increasing register numbers, as previously stated in our register usage policy. Registers W5, W6 are used for the 32-bit local variable u32_t, while W3, W4 are used to hold computed addresses for pu32_b+u8_k, pu32_b+u8_j respectively. The computed addresses pu32_b+u8_k, pu32_b+u8_j are needed for the array accesses pu32_b[u8_k] and pu32_b[u8_j], which are *(pu32_b+u8_k) and *(pu32_b+u8_j) when written as pointer operations. We prefer the array access

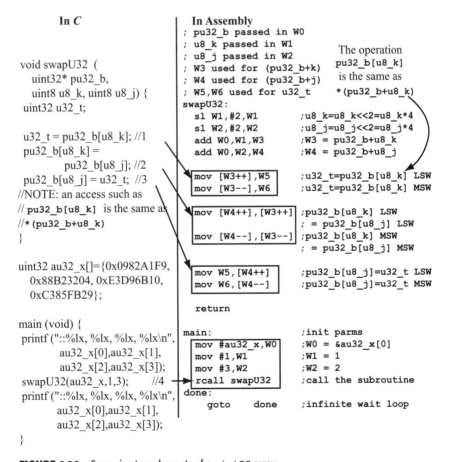

FIGURE 6.26   Swapping two elements of a uint32 array.

notation pu32_b[u8_k] over the pointer notation *(pu32_b+u8_k) for clarity reasons. The first two assembly statements in swapU32 multiply u8_k and u8_j by 4 via a shift left by two. This is needed because the address calculation of pu32_b+u8_k is done as pu32_b+(u8_k*sizeof(uint32)), which is pu32_b+(u8_k*4). This address computation is performed by the add W0,W1,W3 instruction, where W0 contains pu32_b and W1 contains u8_k*4. A similar addition is used to compute pu32_b+u8_j. Each assignment statement 1,2,3 in the *C* function swapU32 requires two mov instructions in the assembly code in order to copy the least significant and most significant words of the uint32 array elements. Post-increment indirect addressing is used when addressing pu32_b[u8_k] and pu32_b[u8_j] in order to advance the address pointer from the LSW to the MSW. Post-decrement addressing is used when copying the MSW in order to restore the LSW address in the register. The assembly implementation of the *C* function call swapU32(&au32_x[0],1,3) in main() is straightforward in that &au32_x[0], 1, 3 are copied to registers W0, W1, W2 before the rcall swapU32 instruction. The assembly code for stack pointer and stack limit register initialization is not shown.

STACK FRAMES FOR FUNCTION PARAMETERS AND LOCAL VARIABLES

The previous section detailed a policy using working registers for function parameters and local variables. But what happens if the parameters and local variable storage requirements exceed the available space in the working registers? The solution is to allocate space on the stack for parameters and local variables; this set of locations is commonly referred to as a *stack frame*. Figure 6.27 shows the arrangement and

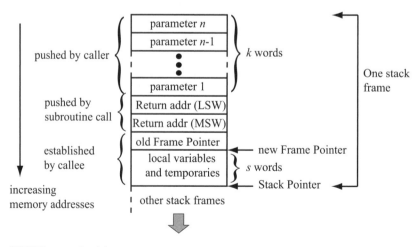

FIGURE 6.27   Stack frame components.

components of a stack frame, which is compatible with the stack frame used by the MPLAB PIC24 compiler. Because a subroutine can call other subroutines, which changes the stack pointer value, a second pointer register called a *frame pointer* (FP) is used as a stable reference to the parameters and local variables of a subroutine. Register W14 is used as the frame pointer in this book's stack frames. The caller pushes the n parameters in order from n (rightmost) to 1 (leftmost) onto the stack before calling the subroutine; the number of words required for parameters depends on the number of parameters and their types. Parameters that are 8 bits wide are pushed as 16-bit values to maintain word alignment. The return address is pushed on the stack by the subroutine call/rcall instruction. The first action of the subroutine is to push the current frame pointer on the stack to preserve its value, as this subroutine changes the value of the frame pointer to reference its parameters and local variables. Local variable space is allocated by incrementing the stack pointer by the number of required words. The frame pointer is left pointing to the first local variable. Subsequent subroutine calls allocate new space above this stack frame. Parameters are accessed from the frame pointer using negative offsets, while local variables are accessed from the frame pointer using positive offsets. The subroutine return value is passed in registers according to the policy in the previous section. The subroutine must restore the frame pointer to its value on entry before executing a subroutine return. The parameters passed by the caller are also cleaned up before return, by either popping the parameters off the stack or simply subtracting the number of words required for the parameters from the stack pointer.

The detailed steps in constructing a stack frame are given in Figure 6.28. The majority of the work is done by the subroutine; the caller only has to push the parameters (1) on the stack before the call, save the return value, and clean the stack of passed parameters. In the subroutine, after the old frame pointer is pushed (3) on the stack, the register copy SP → FP (4) establishes the new frame pointer. This leaves the FP pointing at the first location used for local variables. Local space is allocated (5) by incrementing the stack pointer by $s*2$, where s is the number of words required for local variables. Actions (3), (4), and (5) are efficiently implemented by a single PIC24 instruction named lnk #*lit14* (link frame pointer), which creates a new stack frame with #*lit14* bytes of local storage. After the subroutine body is executed, the stack is cleaned of local variables (6) by pointing the stack pointer at the location of the old frame pointer via the register copy FP → SP. The old frame pointer is restored (7) by popping FP from the stack, after which the callee returns (8) to the caller. The ulnk (unlink frame pointer) PIC24 instruction implements actions (6) and (7). In the caller, the subroutine return value is saved (9), followed by cleaning the stack (10) of passed parameters. This is done by either popping the parameters from the stack or by decrementing the stack pointer by $2*k$, where k is the number of words occupied by the parameters. The ordering

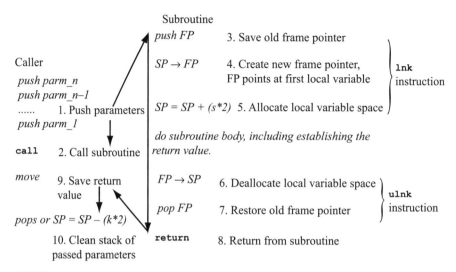

FIGURE 6.28   Steps in constructing a stack frame.

of events (9) and (10) is not important; (10) can be done before (9) as long as the return value is not disturbed.

The Fibonacci subroutine from the previous section is used to illustrate assembly language implementation of stack frames. This implementation ignores the working registers for parameters and locals and uses a stack frame instead. Figure 6.29 repeats the C code for the `fib()` function and shows a detailed stack frame where u16_n is accessed using a –8 offset from the FP and u16_f1 by a 0 offset.

```
uint16 fib (uint16 u16_n) {
  uint16 u16_f1;

  if (u16_n == 0) return 0;
  if (u16_n == 1) return 1;
  u16_f1 = fib(u16_n-1);
  u16_f1 = fib(u16_n-2) + u16_f1;
  return (u16_f1);
}
/* Fib sequence:
0,1,1,2,3,5,8,13,21,34,55,89,
144,233,377,610,987,...*/
main (void) {
  uint16  u16_k, u16_j;
  u16_j = 13;
  u16_k = fib(u16_j);
  printf ("fib(%d) is: %d\n", u16_j, u16_k);
}
```

Detailed Stack Frame for **fib**

u16_n *(parameter)*	FP – 8
Rtn Addr (LSW)	FP – 6
Rtn Addr (MSW)	FP – 4
old FP	FP – 2
u16_f1 *(local variable)*	+ 0 ◄— new FP
free	◄— new SP

increasing memory addresses

FIGURE 6.29   Detailed stack frame for `fib()` function.

The assembly language implementation uses register indirect with register offset addressing to access values in the stack frame.

Figure 6.30 shows the assembly code for main() of Figure 6.29. The variable u16_j is initialized to the value 13, then u16_j is pushed on the stack before the subroutine call (rcall fib). The fib return value is returned in W0 and saved to the variable u16_k. The instruction sub W15,#2,W15 cleans the stack of the 2 bytes (1 word) of parameters passed to fib; this could have also been accomplished by popping u16_j from the stack but this destroys a register value. The numbering of the actions taken by main() corresponds to the actions found in Figure 6.28.

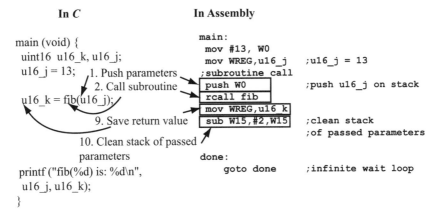

FIGURE 6.30   Assembly implementation for main() of Fibonacci example.

The assembly code for the fib() subroutine is seen in Figure 6.31. The numbered actions within the subroutine code correspond to those of Figure 6.28. Some observations are:

- The lnk #2 instruction is used at subroutine entry to allocate the stack frame, while the ulnk instruction is used to deallocate the stack frame before returning to the caller.
- The parameter u16_n is accessed from the stack frame by the instruction mov [W14-8],W0 (register indirect with signed constant offset) so u16_n is accessed from [FP−8].
- The previous fib solution using registers saved the original u16_n value on the stack to preserve during the first recursive call. This is not needed in this solution because u16_n is already present in the stack frame; its value is reloaded after the first recursive call.
- The two recursive calls to fib must also follow steps 1, 2, 9, and 10 from Figure 6.26, as these calls obviously use stack frames as well.
- The return value from the first recursive call is stored in the one word of local space reserved for u16_f1 by the mov W0,[W14] instruction, which is [FP+0].

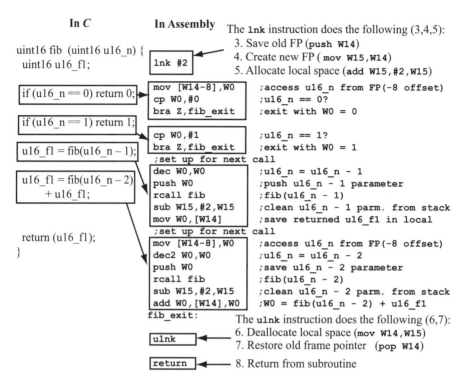

FIGURE 6.31 Assembly implementation for `fib()` of Fibonacci example.

The `fib` implementation using a stack frame requires 19 instructions, while the `fib` implementation using registers for parameters and locals requires 15 instructions. Stack frames adds extra overhead at the cost of generality for parameter passing and local storage. An optimizing *C* compiler will always try to use registers for parameter passing and local storage before resorting to stack frames.

Sample Question: *If the* `swapU32` *function of Figure 6.24 uses a stack frame, give the offsets from the frame pointer for parameters* `pu32_b`, `u8_k`, *and* `u8_j`.

Answer: Starting from the frame pointer location, the parameters are arranged in order `pu32_b` (offset of –8), `u8_k` (offset of –10), and `u8_j` (offset of –12). Note that `u8_k` and `u8_j` each take a word when stored on the stack, despite being 8-bit variables. When storing 8-bit variable to the stack, one must ensure that they are properly zero-extended (unsigned) or sign-extended (signed) as required.

PROGRAM SPACE VISIBILITY AND GLOBAL VARIABLE INITIALIZATION

Initial values for *C* global variables present an interesting challenge in microcontrollers. The *C* language semantics guarantee that before *main()* is executed, a global variable is cleared to zero if no specific initial value is given or loaded with the initial value specified in the variable declaration. A *C* compiler generates initialization code that is executed on microprocessor reset before *main()* is called, which accomplishes global variable initialization. Figure 6.32 shows the *C* code of Figure 6.11 that converted a string to uppercase written as a *C* function named `upcase(char* psz_x)`. The `main()` code calls the `upcase` function for two strings `sz_1[]`, `sz_2[]` that have each been given initial values. Because `sz_1[]`, `sz_2[]` can be modified by `upcase()`, these arrays must reside in data memory. However, the state of data memory is undefined at power-up, so code executed before `main()` is reached is responsible for initializing the contents of these two arrays. In the assembly language code, this initialization is done by a subroutine called `init_variables`, which is not shown in Figure 6.32.

In *C*	In Assembly
| ```
void upcase (char* psz_x){
while (*psz_x != 0) {
 //convert to upper case
 if (*psz_x > 0x60 &&
    *psz_x < 0x7B) {
 //lowercase 'a' - 'z', so
 //convert to 'A' - 'Z'
   *psz_x = *psz_x - 0x20;
  }
 //advance to next char
  psz_x++;
  }
}



char sz_1[] = "Hello";
char sz_2[] = "UPPER/lower";

int main (void) {
 upcase(sz_1);
 upcase(sz_2);
}
``` | ```
sz_1:    .space  6 ;space for "hello",null
sz_2:    .space 12 ;space for "UPPER/lower",null
.text      ;Start of Code section
__reset:
    mov #__SP_init, W15   ;Init SP
    mov #__SPLIM_init,W0
    mov W0, SPLIM         ;Init SPLIM
    call init_variables   ;init strings
    rcall main            ;rcall main()
    reset                 ;start over
main:
    mov #sz_1,W0   ;W0 = &sz_1[0]
    rcall upcase
    mov #sz_2,W0   ;W0 = &sz_2[0]
    rcall upcase
done:
    goto    done       ;infinite wait loop

;*psz_x passed in W0
upcase:
    ...left as an exercise...
    return
``` |

FIGURE 6.32 *C* upcase() function and string initial values.

One method for initializing global variables is for the *C* compiler to generate separate instructions that initialize each variable, but this is inefficient, especially for arrays. The general method that is actually used is to place the initial variable values in a tabular form in non-volatile memory, which in this case is program memory, then copy the table contents to data memory during global variable initialization. The code that does this for the MPLAB PIC24 compiler is found in the `<install_dir>\MPLAB C30\src\pic30\crt0.s` assembly source file. The details of the template format that specifies the variable initial contents is beyond the scope of this book. Instead, we will use a less complex method that still illustrates the basic concepts of copying data from program memory to data memory.

Listing 6.1 shows the `init_variables` subroutine used to initialize the `sz_1[]`, `sz_2[]` strings of Figure 6.32. The initial values for `sz_1[]`, `sz_2[]` are stored in program memory at the labels `sz_1_const` (line 3) and `sz_2_const` (line 4). The `.asciz` assembler directive creates a null-terminated string, with the bytes packed into the lower 16 bits of each program memory 24-bit word. This is somewhat inefficient since the upper byte of each 24-bit program memory word is unused, but is necessary in this case because the assembly code uses the *program space visibility* (PSV) capability of the PIC24 µC to access program memory. The PSV capability maps the upper 16 Ki words (32 Ki bytes) of data memory into program memory (the *PSV window*), allowing program memory to be accessed in the same way as data memory. When using PSV, the upper byte of the 24-bit program memory word is inaccessible because data memory is only 16 bits wide. Another method for accessing program memory that allows access to all 24 bits of a program memory word is covered in Chapter 13. An 8-bit special function register named the *program space visibility page* (PSVPAG) specifies the 16 Ki program word boundary for the 16 Ki words data space mapping. The default value of PSVPAG is 0, which means that the upper 16 Ki word data space is mapped to the first 16 Ki words of program space, which is satisfactory for this example since it does not exceed 16 Ki program words in size.

The PSV capability is disabled by default; the `bset CORCON,#2` instruction (line 7) enables PSV. The CORCON (*core control*) register is a SFR (special function register) that controls the PSV capability. The `mov #psvoffset(sz_1_const),W2` instruction (line 9) copies the PSV-adjusted program memory address for `sz_1_const` to W2; the `psvoffset()` assembly directive maps the program memory address to a PSV-space address. In this case, this means that a value of 0x8000 is added to the program memory address to map it to the upper half of data memory. The `mov #sz_1,W3` instruction (line 10) copies the starting data memory address for `sz_1[]` to W3. The `copy_cstring` subroutine called in line 11 copies a string whose source address is specified in W2 to the destination specified in W3. The `copy_cstring` implementation is straightforward; bytes are copied until a null byte is found in the source string. The null byte is copied before `copy_cstring` returns to the caller. Lines 13–15 initialize string `sz_2[]` using the contents of `sz_2_const` in a similar manner.

LISTING 6.1   init_variables subroutine.

```
(1)    .text  ;program memory
(2)    ;; constant data to be moved to data memory
(3)    sz_1_const: .asciz "Hello"
(4)    sz_2_const: .asciz "UPPER/lower"
(5)    init_variables:
(6)    ;turn on program visibility space, use default PSVPAG value of 0
(7)        bset CORCON,#2              ;enable PSV
(8)    ;copy source address in program memory to W2
(9)        mov #psvoffset(sz_1_const),W2
(10)       mov #sz_1,W3               ;destination address in data memory
(11)       rcall copy_cstring
(12)   ;copy source address in program memory to W2
(13)       mov #psvoffset(sz_2_const),W2
(14)       mov #sz_2,W3               ;destination address in data memory
(15)       rcall copy_cstring
(16)       return
(17)   ;;copy constant null-terminated string from program memory to data memory
(18)   ;;W2 points to program memory, W3 to data memory
(19)   copy_cstring:
(20)       mov.b [W2],W0
(21)       cp.b W0,#0                 ;test for null byte
(22)       bra Z, copy_cstring_exit   ;exit if null byte
(23)       mov.b [W2++],[W3++]        ;copy byte
(24)       bra copy_cstring          ;loop to top
(25)   copy_cstring_exit:
(26)       mov.b [W2++],[W3++]        ;copy null byte
(27)       return
```

Figure 6.33 shows an example that uses a similar approach for initializing the global data arrays ai8_a[], ai16_b[], aui32_c[] given in the *C* code. The assembly code stores the initial contents of these arrays in program memory at locations ai8_a_const, ai16_b_const, and aui32_c_const using assembler directives .byte, .word, and .long to initialize program memory. The init_variables subroutine calls the byte_copy subroutine three times to copy these constant arrays into data memory. The byte_copy subroutine copies W4+1 number of bytes from the source address in W2 to the destination address in W3 using a repeat instruction loop.

By default, any global array or global scalar value is placed in data memory. However, many arrays hold constant values (values that will not change during program execution). In this case, the arrays should be located in program memory so as to free space in data memory. If a global variable is declared using the const modifier, i.e., (const uint8 sz_1[]="Hello";) then the default behavior of

In C

/*global arrays with
   initial values */
int8 ai8_a[] = {-9,10,
             58, -125};

int16 ai16_b[] = {200,
-3200, -2, 450};

uint32 aui32_c[] = {
160235, 250345,
65536, 489300};

int main (void) {
   //some code..//
}

In Assembly

```
ai8_a:   .space 4*1   ;Allocate space
ai16_b:  .space 4*2   ;Allocate space
aui32_c: .space 4*4   ;Allocate space

;...__reset code not shown...
;.... calls init_variables...

;; constant data to be moved to data memory
ai8_a_const:    .byte -9, 10, 58, -125
ai16_b_const:   .word 200, -3200, -2, 450
aui32_c_const: .long 160235,250345,65536,489300

init_variables:
  bset CORCON,#2    ;enable PSV
  mov  #psvoffset(ai8_a_const),W2   ;init ai8_a
  mov  #ai8_a,W3          ;dest. addr. in data mem
  mov  #((4*1)-1),W4    ; (num. of bytes)-1
  call byte_copy
  mov  #psvoffset(ai16_b_const),W2   ;init ai16_b
  mov  #ai16_b,W3          ;dest. addr. in data mem
  mov  #((4*2)-1),W4    ; (num. of bytes)-1
  call byte_copy
  mov  #psvoffset(aui32_c_const),W2 ;init aui32_c
  mov  #aui32_c,W3          ;dest. addr. in data mem
  mov  #((4*4)-1),W4    ; (num. of bytes)-1
  call byte_copy
  return

byte_copy:            ;W4 has num-1 bytes to copy
    repeat W4      ;W2 = src, W3 = dest.
    mov.b [W2++],[W3++]
    return
```

FIGURE 6.33   Initializing C global arrays.

the MPLAB PIC24 compiler is to leave the string in program memory and to access it via the PSV window.

SUMMARY

Pointer variables in *C* contain addresses that reference data. The rich set of indirect addressing modes in the PIC24 instruction set provides considerable flexibility in implementing *C* pointer operations. Subroutines improve code efficiency and clarity by encapsulating often-used code sequences as a single unit that can be called from multiple locations within a program. A stack is used to save the return address so a subroutine can determine the return location within the calling function. Static allocation uses a fixed set of memory locations for subroutine parameters and local variables, but does not allow subroutine recursion. The large working register set of the PIC24 μC can be used to great advantage in implementing function parameters and local variables, while also supporting recursive function calls. A stack frame is used for reserving stack space for parameters and locals when the working register space is insufficient. Global variable initial values are stored in memory to preserve them when power is off and are retrieved using a program visibility space (PSV) window by *C* runtime code that initializes these variables.

REVIEW PROBLEMS

1. For the following code, variables are stored starting at location 0x0800. Draw memory as being 16 bits wide and show the memory locations that are assigned to each array element and variable as is done in Figures 6.1 and 6.8. Give the contents of these memory locations after all of the code is executed.

```
int16 ai16_x[2];
int16* pi16_y;

ai16_x[0] = 5;
ai16_x[1] = -7;
pi16_y = &ai16_x[1];
*pi16_y = *pi16_y + 3;
pi16_y--;
```

2. For the following code, variables are stored starting at location 0x0800. Draw memory as being 16 bits wide and show the memory locations that are assigned to each array element and variable as is done in Figures 6.1 and 6.8. Give the contents of these memory locations after all of the code is executed. Assume that any uninitialized variables are initialized to 0 before this code fragment is executed.

```
int32* pi32_x;
int16* pi16_y;
int16 i16_b;
int32 i32_a;
uint8 au8_c[4];
uint8* pu8_w;

i16_b = -10;            // Note: value given in decimal
i32_a = i16_b >> 1;
pi32_x = &i32_a;
pi16_y = &i16_b;
pi32_x = pi32_x + 2;
pu8_w = &au8_c[3];
```

TABLE 6.1 Register memory contents.

Location	Value	Location	Value
W0	0x0804	0x0800	0x382A
W1	0x0806	0x0802	0xFB80
W2	0x8301	0x0804	0x80FF
W3	0xF0A2	0x0806	0x7B03
W4	0x0004	0x0808	0x0001
W14	0x0802	0x080A	0xCE46
W15	0x0804	0x080C	0x8B17

Assume the initial memory and register contents of Table 6.1 at the beginning of each problem, 3 through 20. Give the new register and memory contents after the instruction is executed.

3. `mov [--W1],W0`
4. `mov W1,[W0+W4]`
5. `mov.b [--W1],W0`
6. `mov.b W1,[W0+W4]`
7. `mov W2,[W0++]`
8. `mov W2,[--W0]`
9. `mov.b W2,[W0++]`
10. `mov.b W2,[--W1]`
11. `mov [W1+W4],W2`
12. `mov [++W1],W1`
13. `mov [W1],[W0++]`
14. `mov.b [W1+W4],W2`
15. `mov.b [++W1],W1`
16. `mov.b [W1],[W0++]`
17. `mov.b W1, [W0+3]`
18. `mov [W0-4], W1`
19. `push W1`
20. `pop W2`
21. `pop W3`
22. `push W0`
23. `lnk #6`
24. `ulnk`

25. The instruction `call 0x0400` is located at program memory location 0x020A. What return address is pushed on the stack?

26. The instruction `rcall 0x0250` is located at program memory location 0x0220. What return address is pushed on the stack?

27. Implement the following subroutine in PIC24 assembly language. Use the policy established in this chapter for using working registers for subroutine parameters and locals.

```
// this subroutine implements a string swap.
void str_swap(char* psz_1, char* psz_2) {
 char c_char;
 while (*psz_1 != 0) {
  c_char = *psz_1;
  *psz_1 = *psz_2;
  *psz_2 = c_char;
  psz_1++; psz_2++;
 }
}
```

28. Implement the following subroutine in PIC24 assembly language. Use the policy established in this chapter for using working registers for subroutine parameters and locals.

```
// this subroutine implements an uint16 swap.
void u16_swap(uint16* pu16_x, uint8 u8_i, uint8 u8_j) {
  uint16 u16_k;

  u16_k = pu16_x[u8_i];
  pu16_x[u8_i] = pu16_x[u8_j];
  pu16_x[u8_j] = u16_k;
}
```

29. Implement the following subroutine in PIC24 assembly language. Use the policy established in this chapter for using working registers for subroutine parameters and locals.

```
// this subroutine implements a max function.
int16 find_max(int16* pi16_a, uint8 u8_cnt) {
 int16 i16_k;

 i16_k = -32768;
 while (u8_cnt != 0) {
   if (*pi16_a > i16_k) i16_k = *pi16_a;
   pi16_a++; u8_cnt--;
 }
 return i16_k;
}
```

30. Implement the following subroutine in PIC24 assembly language. Use the policy established in this chapter for using working registers for subroutine parameters and locals.

```
// This subroutine adds the contents of two integer arrays.
// The number of elements to add is given by cnt.
void i16vec_add(int16* pi16_a, int16* pi16_b, uint8 u8_cnt) {
 while (u8_cnt != 0) {
  *pi16_a = *pi16_a + *pi16_b;
  pi16_a++; pi16_b ++;
  u8_cnt--;
 }
}
```

31. Implement the `putstr()` function of the following C code as PIC24 assembly language. Use the policy established in this chapter for using working registers for subroutine parameters and locals. Assume the `putch()` function expects its input parameter to be passed in the W0 register; do not implement the `putch()` subroutine.

```
void putch(uint8 u8_char) {
// code not shown
}

// print string
void putstr(char* psz_in) {
 while (*psz_in != 0) {
  putch(*psz_in);
  psz_in++;
 }
}
```

32. Implement the `getstr()` function of the following C code as PIC24 assembly language. Use the policy established in this chapter for using working registers for subroutine parameters and locals. Assume the return value of the `getch()` function is passed back via the W0 register; do not implement the `getch()` subroutine.

```
uint8 getch(void) {
// not shown
}

// get string
void getstr(char* psz_in) {
  uint8 u8_char;
```

```
  do {
     u8_char = getch();
     *psz_in = u8_char;
     psz_in++;
  } while (u8_char != 0)
}
```

33. Assuming that a stack frame is used for subroutine parameters and locals, give the detailed stack frame for the subroutine of problem 26.
34. Assuming that a stack frame is used for subroutine parameters and locals, give the detailed stack frame for the subroutine of problem 27.
35. Implement the subroutine of problem 26 in PIC24 assembly language assuming that a stack frame is used to pass in subroutine parameters. You must use lnk and ulnk to establish a new local frame; you may use registers for local variables.
36. Implement the subroutine of problem 27 in PIC24 assembly language assuming that a stack frame is used to pass in subroutine parameters. You must use lnk and ulnk to establish a new local frame; you may use registers for local variables.
37. Write PIC24 assembly code that implements main() in the following C code. Use the approach of Figure 6.33 for initializing data memory. You must show the complete solution for your init_variables subroutine.

```
//See code for ui16_swap from the previous problem.
void ui16_swap(uint16* pu16_x, uint8 u8_i, uint8 u8_j);

uint16 au16_values[]={489, 45, 1000, 238, 30000, 10134};
main() {
  ui16_swap(&au16_values[0], 3, 5);
}
```

38. Write PIC24 assembly code that implements main() in the following C code. Use the approach of Figure 6.33 for initializing data memory. You must show the complete solution for your init_variables subroutine.

```
//See code for ui16_swap from previous problem.
void i16vec_add (int16* pi16_a, int16* pi16_b, uint8 u8_cnt)

int16 ai16_x[]={-3489, 239, 900, -216, 8920, -9345};
int16 ai16_y[]={980, 3766, -8472, 32000, -16788, 34};

void main(void) {
//Note: this passes the starting addresses of ai16_x,ai16_y to
 i16vec_add i16vec_add (ai16_x, ai16_y, 6);
}
```

7 Advanced Assembly Language: Higher Math

Tis chapter examines various higher math topics such as multiplication and division operations for unsigned and signed integers, floating-point number representation, saturating arithmetic, BCD arithmetic, and ASCII/binary conversions.

Learning Objectives

After reading this chapter, you will be able to:

- Implement signed and unsigned integer multiplication in PIC24 assembly language.
- Implement signed and unsigned integer division in PIC24 assembly language.
- Discuss the formatting and storage requirements of single- and double-precision floating-point numbers.
- Implement saturating addition and subtraction operations in PIC24 assembly language.
- Implement BCD addition and subtraction operations in PIC24 assembly language.
- Implement ASCII-to-binary and binary-to-ASCII for both hex and decimal number formats in PIC24 assembly language.

MULTIPLICATION

In *C*, the multiplication operation is written as *product = multiplicand * multiplier*. For integer multiplication, the number of bits required for the product to prevent overflow is the sum of the bits in the multiplicand and multiplier. Typically, the two operands are the same size, so two *n*-bit operands produce a 2*n*-bit result. Figure 7.1 shows a paper and pen multiplication of two 3-bit operands that produces a 6-bit product. Starting with the rightmost bit of the multiplier, a partial product is formed by multiplying the multiplier bit with the multiplicand, with the rightmost bit of the partial product aligned under the multiplier bit that produced

multiplicand	r_2	r_1	r_0			Binary	Decimal
multiplier	$\times$ s_2	s_1	s_0			1 1 0	6
partial product	s_0*r_2	s_0*r_1	s_0*r_0		$\times$	1 0 1	$\times$ 5
	s_1*r_2	s_1*r_1	s_1*r_0			1 1 0	30
						0 0 0	
+	s_2*r_2	s_2*r_1	s_2*r_0		+	1 1 0	
P_5	P_4	P_3	P_2	P_1	P_0 product	0 1 1 1 1 0 = 30	

FIGURE 7.1 3 × 3 Unsigned multiplication.

it. Since this is binary multiplication, a "1" in the multiplier produces a partial product that is equal to the multiplier, while a "0" produces a partial product of all zero bits. The product is formed from the sum of all of the partial products.

The multiplication operation can be implemented in numerous ways. The cheapest method in terms of logic gates is to not add any support for multiplication to the ALU, and to simply rely on pre-existing microprocessor add and shift operations to perform a multiplication. An algorithm for an unsigned integer multiplication using add/shifts is seen in Figure 7.2. The two n-bit operands are named mc (multiplier) and mp (multiplicand). The ph variable holds the accumulated sum of the partial products, and at algorithm termination, ph contains the upper n bits of

Unsigned Multiplication: Shift/Add Algorithm
mc (multiplicand) n bits, mp (multiplier) n bits, ph (product high, n bits), k (counter)

$2n$-bit product returns in mc:mp

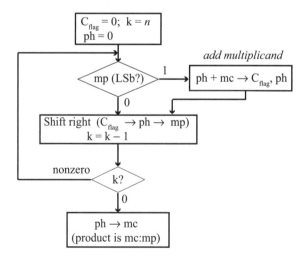

FIGURE 7.2 Unsigned add/shift integer multiplication algorithm.

the product. The algorithm loops n times, once for each bit of the multiplier (mp). On each loop iteration the LSb of mp is tested; if "1", the multiplicand is added to the ph variable. If the LSb of mp is "0", then addition is not performed as the partial product is zero in this case, making the addition superfluous. The shift right of the C_{flag}, ph, and mp values accomplishes two things:

- The LSb of the ph variable is a final bit of the product; shifting ph right moves this bit into the MSb of mp, saving this bit for the result.
- The right shift moves the next bit of the multiplier (mp) into the LSb for testing at the top of the loop. As the loop iteration proceeds, each bit of the multiplier is examined from LSb to MSb.

After n iterations, the multiplication is finished and the loop is exited. The ph variable contains the upper n bits of the product and mp the lower n bits. The ph variable is copied to the mc variable so that the final $2n$-bit product returns in the original operands as $mc{:}mp$.

The disadvantage of the shift/add technique for multiplication is obvious—it is slow! An assembly language implementation requires several instruction cycles for each loop iteration assuming separate shift and add instructions. If hardware support for the shift/add iteration is added to the ALU in the form of a double-length shift register for the product and specialized loop control, this can be reduced to one clock cycle per loop iteration (eight clock cycles). While this would be an improvement, a faster method is to augment the ALU with a specially designed multiplier unit such as an *array multiplier* that produces the result in one clock cycle. Figure 7.3 shows a naive implementation of a 3×3 array multiplier that performs the operation of Figure 7.1. There are more efficient

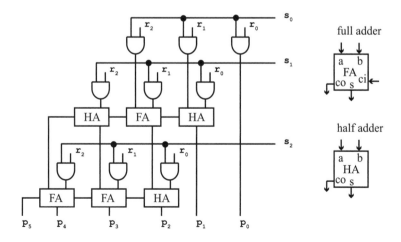

FIGURE 7.3 Naive 3 × 3 unsigned array multiplier.

methods for constructing array multipliers, but this conveys the key point of an array multiplier: the product is available a combinational delay after the inputs are applied. This means the multiplication is completed in one clock cycle (if the clock cycle is long enough). The origin of the term array multiplier is obvious from Figure 7.3 as it is built from an array of full adders and half adders that implements the addition of the partial products. Observe that binary multiplication for each partial product bit is simply an AND gate, as the Boolean multiply $a * b$ is a "1" only if both inputs are "1."

The array multiplier of Figure 7.3 implements unsigned multiplication; there are iterative and array multiplier architectures [3, 4] that implement signed multiplication assuming two's complement encoding. The PIC24 has a 16×16 array multiplier that accepts both signed and unsigned operands and produces a 32-bit result. Figure 7.4 shows the various PIC24 multiplication instruction forms. The three-operand register addressing forms implement a 16×16 multiplication and support the four possible variations of unsigned/signed operands for the multiplicand/multiplier operands. The 32-bit product is written to the *Wnd+1:Wnd* register pair, with *Wnd* containing the least significant word and *Wnd+1* the most significant word. The mul{.b} *f* instructions implement either a 16×16 or 8×8 unsigned multiplication, with the 32-bit product written to W3:W2 and the 16-bit product to W2. The literal forms implement a 16×16 multiplication using an unsigned 5-bit literal (#*lit5*) as the multiplier with either an unsigned or signed multiplicand in *Wb*, with the 32-bit result placed in the *Wnd+1:Wnd* register pair. For any 32-bit product, the destination register for the least significant word (*Wnd*) must be an even-numbered register and may not be W14.

Name	Mnemonic	Operation
Multiply	mul.uu *Wb, Ws, Wnd*	uns(*Wb*) * uns(*Ws*) → *Wnd:Wnd+1*
	mul.su *Wb, Ws, Wnd*	sig(*Wb*) * uns(*Ws*) → *Wnd:Wnd+1*
	mul.us *Wb, Ws, Wnd*	uns(*Wb*) * sig(*Ws*) → *Wnd:Wnd+1*
	mul.ss *Wb, Ws, Wnd*	sig(*Wb*) * sig(*Ws*) → *Wnd:Wnd+1*
Unsigned Multiply with *f*, WREG	mul *f*	(WREG) * (*f*) → W3:W2
	mul.b *f*	(WREG)<7:0> * (*f*)<7:0> → W2
Multiply with literal	mul.uu *Wb, #lit5, Wnd*	uns(*Wb*)*uns(#*lit5*) → *Wnd:Wnd+1*
	mul.su *Wb, #lit5, Wnd*	sig(*Wb*)*uns(#*lit5*) → *Wnd:Wnd+1*

For 32-bit results, **Wnd** has least the significant word, and **Wnd+1** has the most significant word. Registers for **Wnd** are limited to **W0**, **W2**, . . . , **W12**. Status flags are unaffected by the **mul** instructions. Recall that **Ws** includes indirect modes.

FIGURE 7.4 PIC24 multiplication instruction forms.

Listing 7.1 shows several multiplication examples that illustrate the differences between unsigned and signed operands. Register W0 has the 16-bit value 0xFFFF, which is 65535 as an unsigned integer, and −1 as a two's complement integer. Register W1 has the 16-bit value of 0x0001, which is 1 as an unsigned integer and

+1 as a two's complement integer. Observe that the `mul.uu W0,W0,W2` instruction treats both input operands as unsigned, performing 65535 * 65535 for a result of 4294836225, or 0xFFFE0001. The `mul.ss W0,W0,W4` instruction treats both input operands as signed, performing −1 * −1 for a result of +1, or 0x00000001.

LISTING 7.1   Multiplication instruction examples.

```
(1)  mov #0xFFFF,W0     ;65535 unsigned, −1 signed
(2)  mov #0x1,W1        ;1 unsigned, +1 signed

(3)  mul.uu W0,W0,W2    ;65535 * 65535 = 4294836225 = 0xFFFE0001 = W3:W2
(4)  mul.ss W0,W0,W4    ;−1 * −1 = +1 = 0x00000001 = W5:W4
(5)  mul.uu W0,W1,W6    ;65535 * 1 = 65535 = 0x0000FFFF = W7:W6
(6)  mul.ss W0,W1,W8    ;−1 * +1 = −1 = 0xFFFFFFFF = W9:W8
(7)  mul.uu W0,#1,W10   ;65535 * 1 = 65535 = 0x0000FFFF = W11:W10
(8)  mul.su W0,#1,W12   ;−1 * 1 = −1 = 0xFFFFFFFF = W13:W12
```

64-BIT MULTIPLICATION

The shift/add approach of Figure 7.2 is scaleable in that it can be applied to any size operand. One method for using the 16×16 hardware multiplication of the `mul` instruction for a 32×32 multiplication to produce a 64-bit product is shown in Figure 7.5, with s, r containing the 32-bit operands. Four 32-bit *partial products* are formed using 16×16 multiplications as pp0=sL*rL, pp1=sL*rH, pp2=sH*rL, and pp3=sH*sL where {sL, rL} and {sH, rH} are the lower and upper words of the 32-bit operands s, r. Observe that the partial products pp1, pp2 are shifted to the left such that the lower words of these 32-bit partial products align with the upper word of

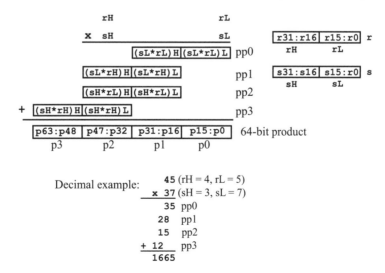

FIGURE 7.5   Unsigned 32×32 multiplication using 16×16 multiplications.

pp0; the lower word of pp3 is aligned with the upper words of pp1, pp2. When performing the word additions of the partial products, care must be taken to propagate the carries across all partial products during the summation.

A subroutine named mult32x32_uns that implements the 32×32 multiplication of Figure 7.5 is given in Listing 7.2. The s, r 32-bit input operands are passed in W1:W0, W3:W2 respectively. The 64-bit result is passed back in W3:W2:W1:W0 as per the working register usage policy established in Chapter 6. All four partial products are computed first using mult.uu instructions, with a register usage of pp0=W5:W4, pp1=W7:W6, pp2=W9:W8, and pp3=W11:W10. Additions using add and addc instructions then implement the sums of the upper and lower words of the partial products as per Figure 7.5. The addc instructions are used to propagate carries all the way to the upper word of pp3. The main code of Listing 7.2 shows a sample call to the mult32x32_uns subroutine. To improve the readability of the code, registers used are given symbolic names taken from Figure 7.5. For example, the two statements sL = W0 and sH = W1 cause instances of sL and sH to be replaced with W0 and W1 as the code is assembled.

LISTING 7.2   Unsigned 32 × 32 bit multiplication.

```
main:
    mov #0xFFFF,W0 ;
    mov #0xFFFF,W1 ; s = W1:W0 = 4294967295
    mov #0xFFFF,W2 ;
    mov #0xFFFF,W3 ; r = W3:W2 = 4294967295
    call mult32x32_uns
;;W3:W2:W1:W0 = 0xFFFFFFFE00000001 = 18446744065119617025
done:                           ;do not return
    bra done

; p = s * r, where:
; W1:W0 = s
sL = W0
sH = W1
; W3:W2 = r
rL = W2
rH = W3
; Use W4–W11 to store low and high words of partial products 0–3
pp0L = W4
pp0H = W5
pp1L = W6
pp1H = W7
pp2L = W8
pp2H = W9
pp3L = W10
pp3H = W11
```

```
; 64-bit result in p = W3:W2:W1:W0 (p3:p2:p1:p0)
p0 = W0
p1 = W1
p2 = W2
p3 = W3
mult32x32_uns:
    push W8
    push W9
    push W10
    push W11
    mul.uu sL,rL,pp0L    ;sL*rL = pp0
    mul.uu sL,rH,pp1L    ;sL*rH = pp1
    mul.uu sH,rL,pp2L    ;sH*rL = pp2
    mul.uu sH,rH,pp3L    ;sH*rH = pp3
    mov pp0L,p0         ;p0 = pp0L
    add pp0H,pp1L,p1     ;p1 = pp0H + pp1L
;;now propagate carry all the way up to p3 word
    addc pp1H,pp2H,p2    ;p2 = pp1H + pp2H + cout(pp0H + pp1L)
    addc pp3H,#0,p3      ;p3 = pp3H + 0 + cout(previous sum)
;;next sum
    add p1,pp2L,p1       ;p1 = pp2L + (p1= pp0H + pp1L)
;;now propagate carry all the way up to p3 word
    addc p2,pp3L,p2      ;p2 = pp3L + (p2 = pp1H + pp2H) + cout(previous_sum)
    addc p3,#0,p3        ;p3 = p3 + 0 + cout(previous_sum)
;;64-bit result p3:p2:p1:p0
    pop W11
    pop W10
    pop W9
    pop W8
    return
```

A signed 32 × 32 bit multiplication can be implemented using the `mult32x32_uns` subroutine of Listing 7.2 by first converting each negative operand to a positive number, performing the unsigned multiply, and then negating the product by subtracting it from 0 if either of the operands was originally negative.

Sample Question: ***What does the product 0x3A * 0xA8 return if the numbers are 8-bit unsigned? 8-bit signed? (two's complement)***

Answer: As unsigned numbers, the product is 0x3A * 0xA8 = 58 * 168 = 9744 = 0x2610.

As signed numbers, the product is 0x3A * 0xA8 = +58 * (−88) = −5104 = 0xEC10.

DIVISION

Equation 7.1 represents the division operation, where p is the dividend, q is the quotient, d is the divisor, and r is the remainder.

$$q, r = \frac{p}{d} \qquad (7.1)$$

The relationship between q, r, p, and d is more clearly expressed by Equation 7.2.

$$p = q \times d + r \qquad (7.2)$$

Implementations of the division operation typically use a $2n$-bit dividend, an n-bit divisor, and produce an n-bit quotient and n-bit remainder. Figure 7.6 shows a paper and pen division of an 8-bit dividend by a 4-bit quotient, producing a 4-bit quotient and a 4-bit remainder. The subtraction performed at each step produces a partial dividend, which forms the dividend for the next stage. The last subtraction produces the remainder, which is guaranteed to be in the range 0 to $d-1$. Unlike multiplication, overflow can occur if the quotient requires more than n bits, which is true if the value formed by the upper n bits of the dividend is greater than or equal to the divisor.

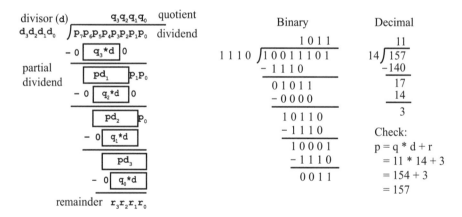

FIGURE 7.6 Unsigned division (8-bit dividend, 4-bit quotient).

Several iterative division algorithms use shift/subtract operations to produce the quotient and remainder. Figure 7.7 shows the *restoring* division algorithm [3] for a $2n$-bit dividend p and an n-bit divisor d. The high and low bytes of p are designated as pH and pL, respectively. On algorithm entry, the comparison pH>=d is performed to check for overflow; if true, the Carry flag is set to "1" and the algorithm terminates. Like the add/shift multiplication algorithm, the main loop performs n

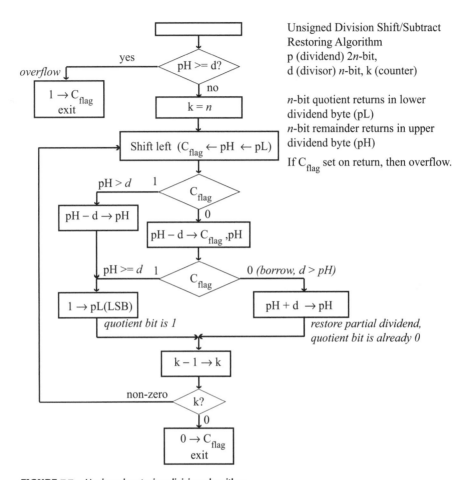

FIGURE 7.7   Unsigned restoring division algorithm.

iterations, with each iteration determining a quotient bit. A quotient bit is "1" if the partial dividend Cflag,pH>=d, in which case the new partial dividend is pH–d. A quotient bit is "0" if Cflag,pH<d, and the partial dividend remains the same. The first operation of the loop performs the shift Cflag←pH←pL, moving the partial dividend into the Cflag and upper *n* bits of pH. If the shift produces a carry, the partial dividend is greater than the divisor, so the new partial dividend is computed as pH–d→pH and the quotient bit is set to "1" (the LSb of pL is the current quotient bit). If no carry is produced by the shift, the subtraction pH–d→pH is performed, which has two side effects: a) the comparison d>pH is determined by the state of the Cflag, and b) the new partial dividend is computed. If Cflag is a "1", this indicates that no borrow occurred, so pH>=d, the new partial dividend is valid, and the quotient bit is set to "1". If Cflag is a "0", a borrow occurred, so pH<d, meaning the partial

dividend should have been left undisturbed. In this case, the operation pH+d→pH is performed to restore the partial dividend to its original value and the quotient bit is cleared to "0". This action of performing the subtraction pH–d→pH and then restoring the partial dividend, if necessary, is why this algorithm is called *restoring* division. When the loop terminates after *n* iterations, the quotient is contained in pL and the remainder in pH.

There are faster iterative methods for division that use a multiplication operation in producing the quotient and remainder, but these require considerably more logic gates because an array multiplier is needed in the implementation. One method for accomplishing signed division is by converting the dividend and divisor to positive numbers, performing the unsigned division, then post-correcting the sign of the quotient and remainder. If either of the original operands is negative, the quotient is negated. If the original dividend is negative, the remainder is negated. Unlike multiplication, if a microprocessor has an explicit integer division instruction, such as a 16-bit/8-bit operation, it is not possible to use this instruction in the implementation of a larger operation such as a 32-bit/16-bit division. As such, some microprocessors offer different sized integer division operations such as 16-bit/8-bit, 32-bit/16-bit, and 64-bit/32-bit.

Figure 7.8 shows the PIC24 division instruction forms. Both signed and unsigned 16-bit/16-bit and 32-bit/16-bit operations are available. In all cases, the 16-bit quotient and 16-bit remainder return in the W0 and W1 registers, respectively. The divisor (*Wn*) register must be contained in registers W2 or higher, as the dividend (*Wm*) is copied to registers W0 and W1 at the beginning of the operation. The W1 register either contains the most significant word of the 32-bit dividend for the 32-bit/16-bit operation, or the sign-extended or zero-extended most significant word of the 16-bit dividend for the 16-bit/16-bit operation. The N and Z flags reflect the status of the remainder. The V flag is set on overflow, which occurs if the

Name	Mnemonic	Operation
Divide 16-bit/16-bit	`div.u Wm, Wn`	`uns(Wm)/uns(Wn)` `quotient → W0; rmdr → W1`
	`div.s Wm, Wn`	`sig(Wm)/sign(Wn)` `quotient → W0; rmdr → W1`
Divide 32-bit/16-bit	`div.ud Wm, Wn`	`uns(Wm+1:Wm)/uns(Wn)` `quotient → W0; rmdr → W1`
	`div.sd Wm, Wn`	`sig(Wm+1:Wm)/sig(Wn)` `quotient → W0; rmdr → W1`

The N, Z, V, C flags are affected, see text for details. Registers W0, W1 cannot be used for the Wn register. Register Wm must be even-numbered for a 32-bit operation.

FIGURE 7.8   PIC24 multiplication instruction forms.

quotient exceeds the 16-bit range. The C flag is used during the division operation and thus its final value is operand dependent. Division by zero causes an *arithmetic trap* (see Chapter 9 for a complete discussion of traps and interrupts).

Listing 7.3 shows some division examples. The division instruction must be preceded by a repeat #17 instruction, which repeats the division instruction $17 + 1 = 18$ times, as the division instruction requires 18 iterations to complete for both the 32-bit/16-bit and 16-bit/16-bit varieties. This means that 19 instruction cycles are required for division, which includes the instruction cycle for the repeat #17 instruction. The divisions of lines 8, 10, 12 are signed divisions that change the sign of the operands, but keep their magnitudes the same. The remainder's sign is the same as the dividend, and the quotient's sign is positive if both operands have the same sign and negative otherwise. The division of line 17 shows an over-flow example for an unsigned 32-bit/16-bit operation using the operands 65536/1; the quotient of 65536 exceeds the maximum unsigned 16-bit value of 65535. The division of line 21 shows an overflow example for a signed 16-bit/16-bit operation using the operands −32768/−1; the quotient of +32768 exceeds the maximum positive 16-bit value of +32767.

LISTING 7.3   Division examples.

```
main:
(1)   mov #0x9A00,W2      ; 39424 unsigned, −26112 as signed
(2)   mov #0x6600,W3      ; 26112 unsigned, +26112 as unsigned
(3)   mov #105,W4         ; 105 unsigned, +105 signed
(4)   mov #0xFF97,W5      ; 65431 unsigned, −105 signed
(5)   repeat #17
(6)   div.u W2,W4         ;39424/105 = 375 = W0, r = 49 = W1
(7)   repeat #17
(8)   div.s W2,W4         ;−26112/+105 = −248 = W0, r = −72 = W1
(9)   repeat #17
(10)  div.s W3,W5         ;+26112/−105 = −248 = W0, r = +72 = W1
(11)  repeat #17
(12)  div.s W2,W5         ;−26112/−105 = +248 = W0, r = −72 = W1
(13)  mov #0x0,W6
(14)  mov #0x0001,W7      ;W7:W6 = 0x00010000 = 65536 double word
(15)  mov #0x01,W8        ;W8 = 1
(16)  repeat #17
(17)  div.ud W6,W8        ;65536/1 is overflow as quotient > 16−bits
(18)  mov #0x8000,W2      ;−32768 signed
(19)  mov #0xFFFF,W3      ;−1 signed
(20)  repeat #17
(21)  div.s W2,W3         ;−32768/−1 is overflow since +32768 > 16−bits
```

Sample Question: ***What does the 16-bit/16-bit operation 0x9EF0/0x018D return for the*** `div.u` ***operation? For the*** `div.s` ***operation?***

Answer: The `div.u` operation treats its operands as unsigned numbers, so 0x9EF0 = 40,688 and 0x018D = 397. The division 40688/397 produces values of 102 (quotient) and 194 (remainder). In hex, this is 0x0066 and 0x00C2. As a check, quotient * divisor + remainder = dividend, or 102 * 397 + 194 = 40688.

The `div.s` operation treats its operands as signed numbers, so 0x9EF0 = −24848 and 0x018D = +397. The division −24848/+397 produces values of −62 (quotient) and −234 (remainder). In hex, this is −62 = 0xFFC2, −234 = 0xFF16. As a check, quotient * divisor + remainder = dividend, or (−62) * (+397) + (−234) = −24848.

FIXED-POINT AND SATURATING ARITHMETIC

Up to this point, we have viewed binary integers as having the decimal point always located to the right of the least significant bit. The formal name for this type of representation is *fixed-point* because the decimal point is *fixed* to a particular location. The decimal point can be positioned in any location within the binary number, as long as the application is consistent about where the decimal point is located. A fixed-point binary number is said to have the format *x.y*, where *x* is the number of digits to the left of the decimal point (integer portion) and *y* is the number of digits to the right of the decimal point (fractional portion). The integer portion of the number has a range 0 to $2^x - 1$, while the fractional range is 0 to $(1 - 2^{-y})$. This gives a number range of 0 to $2^x - 2^{-y}$. The 8-bit unsigned integer representation used to this point has thus been 8.0 fixed-point numbers, which has a number range of 0 to 255. Moving the decimal point all the way to the left gives a 0.8 fixed-point number that has a number range of 0 to $(2^0 - 2^{-8})$, or 0 to approximately 0.9961. A 6.2 fixed-point number has a number range 0 to $(2^6 - 2^{-2})$, or 0 to 63.75. Table 7.1 shows examples of different 8-bit fixed-point formats.

TABLE 7.1 Sample fixed-point formats.

Format	Min	Max	Example
8.0	0	255	0xA7 = 10100111 = 167
6.2	0	63.75	0xA7 = 101001.11 = 41.75
4.4	0	15.9375	0xA7 = 1010.0111 = 10.4375
0.8	0	0.99609375	0xA7 = 0.10100111 = 0.65234375

DECIMAL TO *X.Y* BINARY FORMAT

The easiest method for converting an unsigned decimal number to its fixed-point representation is to multiply the number by 2^y, then convert the integer portion to binary. If the remaining fraction after the multiplication by 2^y is non-zero, then the resulting number is an approximation of the original number. Obviously, the more bits used for y in the $x.y$ format, the better the approximation.

Another method is to convert the integer and fractional portions separately, with the conversion of the fractional portion f done bit-by-bit through an iterative method. The iterative process performs the comparison $f \cdot 2 \geq 1$; if this is true, the new binary digit is 1 and the new fractional part is $f \leftarrow (f \cdot 2) - 1$. If $f \cdot 2 \leq 1$, the new binary digit is 0 and the new fractional part is $f \leftarrow f \cdot 2$. The binary digits of the fractional part are determined left to right (most significant to least significant). The process stops when y binary bits of the final $x.y$ binary result have been computed.

Sample Question: ***Convert 13.365 to a binary 8-bit number in 4.4 fixed-point format.***

Answer: Multiplying 13.365 by 2^4 (16) produces 213.84. Truncating to 213 and converting to binary gives 0b11010101, or 0xD5.

The following steps show the iterative method for converting the fractional portion 0.365 to its 4-bit binary representation.

1. 0.365 * 2 = 0.73, which is < 1. The first (leftmost) binary digit is 0, and the new f is 0.73.
2. 0.73 * 2 = 1.46, which is > 1. The second binary digit is 1, and the new f is 1.46 − 1 = 0.46.
3. 0.46 * 2 = 0.92, which is < 1. The third binary digit is 0; the new f is 0.92.
4. 0.92 * 2 = 1.84, which is > 1. The fourth and last binary digit is 1.

Thus, the 4-bit representation of the fractional portion is 0b0101, and the complete number is 0b11010101, or 0xD5.

X.Y BINARY FORMAT TO DECIMAL CONVERSION

An unsigned fixed-point binary number is converted to decimal by multiplying each bit by its appropriate binary weight. The fractional bits have weights 2^{-1}, $2^{-2}, \ldots 2^{-y}$ going from leftmost bit to rightmost bit. Another method is to view the n-bit number as an $n.0$ fixed-point number and divide that number by 2^y to get the $x.y$ decimal value. Observe that dividing by 2^y is the same as shifting the $n.0$ fixed-point number to the right by y positions.

Sample Question: ***Convert 0xD5, an unsigned 4.4 binary number, to its decimal value.***

Answer: The value 0xD5 is 0b11010101, so the integer portion is 1101, or 13. The fractional portion 0101 is (left to right):

$$0*2^{-1} + 1*2^{-2} + 0*2^{-3} + 1*2^{-4} = 0 + 0.25 + 0 + 0.0625 = 0.3125.$$

Thus, 0xD5, an unsigned 4.4 binary number, is 13.3125. Note that the value 0xD5 was the result obtained in the previous sample problem when converting 13.365 to a 4.4 binary format. This indicates the approximation that occurs in the decimal to fixed-point binary conversion because of the limited number of bits in the fractional portion. An alternate method is to note that 0xD5 is the value 213 as an 8.0 fixed-point number and compute $213/2^4 = 213/16 = 13.3125$.

SIGNED FIXED-POINT

Two's complement $x.y$ fixed-point numbers have a range of $+(2^{x-1} - 2^{-y})$ to -2^{x-1}. Thus, an 8.0 format has a range $+(2^7 - 2^{-0})$ to -2^7, or +127 to −128. A 6.2 format has a range of $+(2^5 - 2^{-2})$ to -2^5, or +31.75 to −32.0, while a 1.7 format has a range of $+(2^0 - 2^{-7})$ to -2^0, or +0.9921875 to −1.0. Conversion of $x.y$ two's complement fixed-point in binary can be done by viewing the number as an $(x + y).0$ number, computing its decimal magnitude by the two's complement binary to decimal conversion rules of Chapter 5, then dividing the number by 2^y. A signed decimal number can be converted to its $x.y$ binary format by multiplying the number by 2^y, then converting the integer portion to binary.

Sample Question: ***Convert −3.25 to a binary number in 4.4 fixed-point format.***

Answer: Multiplying −3.25 by 2^4 (16) produces −52, which is 0xCC in two's complement. Thus, −3.25 in 4.4 signed fixed-point format is 0xCC.

Sample Question: ***What is the decimal value of 0xD5 if this represents a 4.4 signed fixed-point number?***

The value 0xD5 converted to an integer decimal two's complement number is −43. Dividing −43 by 2^4 (16) gives the final value of −2.6875. Observe that this is not the same decimal value obtained for 0xD5 when it was previously viewed as a 4.4 unsigned fixed-point number (the decimal value was 13.3125), which is obvious given that the signed decimal value must be negative since the most significant bit of 0xD5 is a "1". Also, the decimal value of 13.13125 exceeds the range of a signed 4.4 fixed-point number, which is +7.10375 to −8.0.

0.N FIXED-POINT FORMAT AND SATURATING OPERATIONS

In the coverage of the multiplication operation, you may have noticed a troubling problem: to prevent overflow, the size of the operands has to keep doubling! For example, an 8×8 multiplication produces a 16-bit product. If this value is then used in a subsequent 16×16 multiplication operation, a 32-bit product is produced. Note that the product size doubles again to 64 bits if the previous 32-bit product is used in a 32×32 multiplication. Obviously, it is not possible to keep doubling the size of the operands in each multiplication, so eventually an n-bit value must be used to hold the result of an $n \times n$ bit multiplication. If the operands are viewed as unsigned integers between 0 and 2^{n-1}, overflow occurs if the upper n-bit value of the actual $2n$-bit product is non-zero. When overflow does occur, either for multiplication, addition, or subtraction, what can be done about it? In some cases, it is sufficient to simply set an error flag and let the higher-level application code deal with the problem. In other cases, such as real-time digital signal processing applications, like audio or video data manipulation, there is no way to halt the system to "fix" the overflow problem. One approach to keep functioning in the presence of overflow is to produce a value that is a reasonable approximation of the correct answer. The $0.n$ unsigned fixed-point format is often used for data in digital signal processing applications, because of its advantages in regard to multiplication overflow and using the same sized operands for all operations. Numbers in $0.n$ unsigned fixed-point format have the range $[0,1)$ (up to 1 but not including 1), where the maximum value gets closer to 1 as n increases. When two $0.n$ unsigned fixed-point numbers are multiplied, the upper n bits of the $2n$-bit product are kept, while the lower n bits are discarded to keep the resulting product size as n bits. The lower n bits of the $0.2n$ product that are discarded are the least significant bits, which are the bits that one wants to be discarded if precision has to be limited. With the $0.n$ unsigned fixed-point representation, the multiplication operation cannot overflow, because the result is always in the range $[0,1)$. Also, while the result is not the exact product since bits have been discarded, it is a good approximation of the correct product.

It would be nice to have addition and subtraction operations that performed in a similar manner with regard to overflow; that is, when overflow occurs, a value is returned that is a close approximation of the correct result. Saturating addition and subtraction operations clip results to maximum and minimum values in the presence of overflow or underflow. Figure 7.9 shows examples of unsigned saturating addition and subtraction for 8-bit numbers. On unsigned overflow (carry out of the most significant bit), the result is saturated to all "1"s, which is the maximum unsigned value. On unsigned underflow (borrow from the most significant bit), the result is clipped to the minimum value of zero. It is clear that the unsaturated results are nonsensical when overflow occurs, while the saturated results return the closest possible approximation given the range limits.

unsaturating add	8.0 format	0.8 format	saturating add	8.0 format	0.8 format
0x60	96	0.375	0x60	96	0.375
+ 0xA7	+ 167	+ 0.65234375	+ 0xA7	+ 167	+ 0.65234375
0x07	7	0.02734375	0xFF	255	0.99609375

unsaturating subtraction	8.0 format	0.8 format	saturating subtraction	8.0 format	0.8 format
0x60	96	0.375	0x60	96	0.375
- 0xA7	- 167	- 0.65234375	- 0xA7	- 167	- 0.65234375
0xB9	185	0.77265625	0x00	0	0.0

FIGURE 7.9   Unsigned saturating addition/subtraction examples.

Listing 7.4 shows assembly code for a `sat_add` subroutine that implements `W0=W0+W1` using unsigned saturating addition. If the carry flag is set after the `add` instruction, the `setm` instruction is used to set the `W0` result to all "1"s. Signed saturating addition clips values to either the maximum positive value or maximum negative value on two's complement overflow. Some microprocessors, especially those touted as being especially suited for digital signal processing applications, have specialized instructions that directly implement saturating arithmetic. The *C* language does not have saturating arithmetic operators or data types, and thus saturating arithmetic must be implemented as a specialized library of function calls.

LISTING 7.4   Assembly code for unsigned saturating addition.

```
;Do saturating word addition W0 = sat_add(W0+W1)
sat_add:
   add W0,W1,W0
   bra NC, sat_add_1
   setm W0
sat_add_1:
   return
```

Sample Question: ***What does the sum 0xA0 + 0x90 equal as a saturated unsigned addition? As a saturated signed addition?***

Answer: With binary addition, the sum 0xA0 + 0x90 = 0x30, with C = 1, V = 1. As a saturated unsigned addition, the result clips to the maximum unsigned value of 0xFF because unsigned overflow occurred (C = 1). As a saturated signed addition, the result clips to the maximum signed negative value of 0x80 because two negative numbers were added and the two's complement overflow occurred (V = 1).

THE DsPIC® MICROCONTROLLER FAMILY

The dsPIC® microcontroller family as represented by the dsPIC30F/dsPIC33F product lines implements a superset of the PIC24 instruction set. The dsPIC μC family preceded the PIC24 μC family in terms of release dates and includes a separate arithmetic logic unit (ALU) that supports saturating operations on two's complement fixed-point numbers in 16-bit, 32-bit, and 40-bit operand sizes. The additional dsPIC instructions that are not supported by the PIC24 μC are all instructions that are executed by this specialized ALU. Some of the saturating operations supported by this ALU are add, subtract, multiply to accumulator, square to accumulator, multiply-accumulate, multiply-subtract, and square-accumulate. The accumulator is a special-purpose register that allows a multiplication product to be added or subtracted from the accumulator contents in the same instruction. Many digital signal filter architectures are implemented more efficiently when this operation type is provided. Coverage of these additional instructions is beyond the scope of this text; the reader is referred to the "dsPIC30F, 33F Programmer's Reference Manual" [5] for more details.

FLOATING-POINT NUMBER REPRESENTATION

Fixed-point representation forces an application to determine *a priori* the number of bits to devote to the integer and fractional parts. More bits used for the integer portion means less precision for the fractional part and vice versa. Floating-point (FP) representation encodes an exponent field in the binary encoding, removing the need to allocate a fixed number of bits for the integer and fractional representation. This section gives a brief overview of floating-point number encoding and floating-point number operations in microprocessors; a more detailed discussion is found in [6].

IEEE 754 FLOATING-POINT ENCODING

Many different encodings for floating-point numbers have been proposed and used over the years, but in 1985, after a long review process, the IEEE 754 Standard for Binary Floating-Point Arithmetic was approved. Figure 7.10 shows the formats for single and double precision floating-point numbers in IEEE 754 format. The single

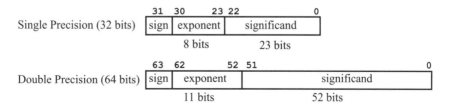

FIGURE 7.10   Single precision and double precision FP formats.

precision format is 32 bits, while the double precision format is 64 bits. Each encoding is divided into sign, exponent, and significand fields.

The use of the fields of Figure 7.10 to produce a floating-point number is given in Equation 7.3.

$$(-1)^{sign} \times 1.significand \times 2^{exponent-bias} \qquad (7.3)$$

This is a signed magnitude encoding, so the most significant bit is the sign bit, which is "1" if the number is negative and "0" if positive. The *significand* field (also known as the *mantissa*) determines the precision of the floating-point number. You can view the significand as encoding both the integer and fractional parts of the floating-point number. The *exponent* field determines the range of the floating-point number. For the single precision format, the exponent field is 8 bits and is encoded in *bias 127*, which means that 127 has to be subtracted from the field value to determine the actual exponent. This allows exponents to be compared using an unsigned comparison, which takes fewer logic gates for implementation and can have less delay than a signed comparison. For normal floating-point numbers, the exponent codes 0x01 through 0xFE are allowed. The exponent encodings 0x00 (all 0s) and 0xFF (all 1s) are reserved for so-called *special* numbers, discussed later in this section. Thus, the exponent range for single precision, IEEE 754 floating-point numbers is 2^{+127} (10^{+38}) to 2^{-126} (10^{-38}). The double precision format uses an 11-bit exponent field, with a bias value of 1023. The exponent range for double precision, IEEE 754 floating-point numbers is 2^{+1023} (10^{+307}) to 2^{-1022} (10^{-308}). In the C language, the float and double types are used for single precision and double precision floating-point variables, respectively. The MPLAB ASM 30 assembler supports specification of floating-point values using the .double and .single assembler directives, for double precision and single precision encodings, respectively.

Figure 7.11 shows an example of converting a decimal number to its single precision, floating-point number representation. First, the decimal number is converted to its binary representation by converting the integer and fractional parts to binary. The binary number is then normalized to the form of Equation 7.3 by shifting the number to the left or right. Each time the number is shifted to the left (multiplied by 2), the exponent is decremented by 1. Each time the number is shifted to the right (divided by 2), the exponent is incremented by 1. Observe that the "1" to the left of the decimal point in Equation 7.3 is not encoded in the significand; it is understood to be in the encoding. This is often referred to as the *phantom one bit* and provides an extra bit of precision to the significand without having to provide space for it in the significand field.

Converting a binary value in single precision FP format to its decimal representation is done by simply converting each component of Equation 7.3 to its decimal representation and multiplying as seen in Figure 7.12. The most common error in this conversion is to forget to add the phantom one bit to the significand.

Convert −28.75 to single precision floating-point format.

1. Number is negative, so sign bit is 1.

2. Convert 28.75 to binary.
   Integer portion: $28 = 0x1C = 0b11100$
   Fractional portion: $0.75 = 0b11$
   So, $28.75 = 11100.11 \times 2^0$

3. Normalize so that number is the form $1.mmm \times 2^y$
   Shift right $11100.11 \times 2^0 >> 1 = 1110.011 \times 2^1$
   $11100.11 \times 2^0 >> 2 = 111.0011 \times 2^2$
   $11100.11 \times 2^0 >> 3 = 11.10011 \times 2^3$
   $11100.11 \times 2^0 >> 4 = 1.110011 \times 2^4$ (this is normalized form)

4. Determine the bit fields.
   Sign bit = 1
   Exponent field = $4 + 127 = 131 = 0x83 = 0b10000011$
   Significand field = $0b110011000 \ldots 0$ (23 bits total)

Final Result (as hex, is 0xC1E60000):

| 1 | 10000011 | 11001100000000000000000 |

Sign   Exponent   Significand

FIGURE 7.11   Decimal to single precision FP format conversion.

The value 0x44AED200 is a single precision floating-point number, find the decimal value.

In Binary:

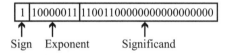

| 0 | 10001001 | 01011101101001000000000 | = 0x44AED200

Sign Exponent   Significand

1. Sign bit is 0, so number is positive.

2. Exponent field is $0b10001001 = 0x89$, so exponent is
   $0x89 - 127 = 137 - 127 = 10.$

   — Do not forget phantom bit!!!

3. Number is: $+1.01011101101001 \times 2^{10}$
   $= +10101110110.1001 \times 2^0$

4. Integer portion $0b10101110110 = 0x576 = 1398$
   Fractional portion $0b0.1001 = 1 \times 2^{-1} + 1 \times 2^{-4} = 0.5 + 0.0625 = 0.5625$

So, $0x44AED200 = +1398.5625$

FIGURE 7.12   Single precision FP format to decimal conversion.

The all-ones and all-zero exponent encodings are reserved for special number encoding. Special numbers are zero, positive/negative infinity ($\pm\infty$), and NaN (Not a Number). Table 7.2 gives the encodings for special numbers. Infinity is produced when anything is divided by zero. A NaN is produced by invalid operations, such as zero divided by zero, or infinity minus infinity.

TABLE 7.2 Special number encodings.

Special Number	Encoding
zero	All fields are zero
$\pm\infty$	Exponent field all ones, significand is zero
NaN	Exponent field all ones, significand is non-zero

Sample Question: *What does the 32-bit value 0xFF800000 represent as a single precision floating-point number?*

Answer: The value is 0xFF800000 = 0b1111 1111 1000 0000 0000 0000 0000 0000.

Grouping this into fields produces sign bit = 1, exponent = 1111 1111, significand is all zeros. By Table 7.2, this value is $-\infty$ (negative infinity).

FLOATING-POINT OPERATIONS

A complete discussion of the implementation of floating-point arithmetic is beyond the scope of this book. To provide a glimpse at what is involved in performing floating-point arithmetic, the basic steps required to perform a floating-point addition are given in Table 7.3. The hardware required to support floating-point

TABLE 7.3 Floating-point addition.

Steps:

1. Detect special numbers in operands and handle these boundary cases.
2. For nonspecial number operands, align the decimal points of the significands of the two operands (make the exponent fields equal) by shifting one of the operands to the left or right as many times as necessary. This process is called denormalization.
3. Add the significands.
4. Normalize the result.

operations is much more complex than fixed-point arithmetic. Speed comparisons of floating-point instructions versus integer instructions depend greatly on the particular hardware floating-point implementation. In comparing the latency of single precision floating-point operations versus integer operations on the Intel® Core™2 processor, FP add/subtraction instructions are about five times slower than integer operations, while FP multiplication and division are actually faster than integer multiplication and division [7].

For microprocessors such as the PIC24 that do not have floating-point hardware support, library subroutines are used to implement floating-point operations. To provide a feel for the relative time differences between integer and floating-point operations on the PIC24 µC, the *C* code in Listing 7.5 was used to test different operations (addition, multiplication, division) using uint32 and float data types. Each loop iteration reads values from two arrays, performs an arithmetic operation on those values, and stores the result in a third array.

LISTING 7.5 Simple *C* benchmark for uint32 versus float operations.

```
for (u8_i = 0; u8_i < u8_cnt; u8_i++) {
   *p_c = *p_a + *p_b; // add contents of two arrays
   p_a++; p_b++;p_c++;
}
```

Table 7.4 gives the instruction cycles per loop iteration of the code in Listing 7.5 for the three different operations tested with uint32 and float data types. The code was compiled with the MPLAB PIC24 compiler using full optimization and executed in the MPLAB simulator. You may be surprised that float division is actually faster than the uint32/uint32 operation. This occurs because this integer division operation does not map to a division that is supported in hardware by the PIC24 instruction set, and thus is performed by a subroutine. The uint32/uint32 operation produces a 32-bit quotient, which is larger than the division done

TABLE 7.4 PIC24 uint32 versus float *C* Performance.

| | Operation Instruction Cycles per Loop Iteration | | |
	Uint32	Float	Float/Long Ratio
Addition	12	134	11.2
Multiplication	17	128	7.5
Division	462	358	0.77

in the `float` division operation when the two 23-bit significands are divided (the quotient's exponent is the divisor's exponent subtracted from the dividend's exponent). When the `uint32/uint32` operation is changed to a `uint16/uint16` operation, the instruction cycles per loop operation drop to 26 because the operation now is able to use the `div.u` instruction. The message to be gleaned from the numbers in Table 7.4 is that you should be cognizant of the execution time differences between different arithmetic operators of the same data type and between different data types (such as integer versus floating-point) for the same arithmetic operation for a target microcontroller and compiler.

BCD ARITHMETIC

Binary coded decimal (BCD) encodes each digit of a decimal number as its 4-bit binary value. This means that the decimal value 83 is simply 0x83 as an 8-bit BCD number. Thus, an 8-bit BCD number can represent the number range 0 to 99. This is a less efficient coding scheme than binary representation, as the codes 0x9A to 0xFF and 0x?A through 0x?F are unused. Some rotary encoders that track the movement of a rotary shaft as it turns either clockwise or counterclockwise use BCD outputs. Some rotary encoders output incremental codes that only describe the direction of shaft movement; others output absolute position information. If absolute position information is given in BCD, then BCD subtraction must be performed to compute the distance between two absolute positions. Addition must be done to compute a finishing location given a starting location and a distance to travel. Adding the two numbers using binary arithmetic then post-correcting the sum to obtain the BCD value performs BCD addition. A BCD digit is a 4-bit value. When two BCD digits are added using binary addition, if the result digit is greater than 9 or if a carry is produced, the result digit must be decimal adjusted by adding 6 to produce the correct BCD digit. Similarly, when two BCD digits are subtracted using binary subtraction, if the result digit is greater than 9 or if a borrow is produced, the result digit must be decimal adjusted by subtracting 6 to produce the correct digit. The DC (decimal carry) flag in the STATUS register is used for BCD post-correction after addition operations; the DC flag is set if there is a carry from bit 3 to bit 4 during a binary addition. The `daw.b` Wn (decimal adjust Wn) instruction post-corrects the Wn register contents to the correct BCD value after any addition or increment instruction that affects the C and DC flags. The `daw.b` instruction operates only in byte mode using register direct addressing, and so the `.b` extension must be included. The `daw.b` instruction adds 6 to the lower 4 bits (lower digit) of the Wn register if the DC flag is 1 or if the lower digit is greater than 9; the upper digit is corrected by +6 if the C flag is 1 or if the upper digit is greater than 9. Unfortunately, the `daw.b` instruction cannot be used after a subtraction operation, so BCD subtraction requires more effort. Recall the binary subtraction A − B is performed as A + ~B + 1, where ~B + 1 is the two's complement of B. Similarly, the BCD subtraction A − B can be performed as A + (99 − B +1), where 99 − B + 1 is the *ten's complement* of B. Figure 7.13a shows the 8-bit BCD addition 0x39 + 0x28. After the binary addition, DC_{flag} = 1 and the result is 0x61. Because DC_{flag} = 1, the lower digit must be corrected by adding 6 to reach the correct result of 0x67. Figure 7.13b shows the BCD subtraction 0x42 − 0x24 using binary subtraction, which produces the value 0x1E and a borrow from the upper 4 bits. Because there was a borrow from the upper 4 bits, the lower digit must be post-corrected by subtracting 6 to produce the correct result of 0x18. Figure 7.13c shows the BCD subtraction 0x42 − 0x24 performed by adding the ten's complement, 0x42 + (0x99 − 0x24 + 1). The ten's complement of 0x24 is computed as 0x99 − 0x24 + 1 = 0x76. Observe that 0x24 + 0x76 = 0x00 in BCD arithmetic, or (+n) + (−n) = 0. The ten's complement of 0x24 is then added to 0x42, or 0x42 + 0x76 = 0xB8. This sets C_{flag} = 1, so the upper digit is post-corrected by adding 6, producing the correct result of 0x18. Observe that both Figure 7.13b and Figure 7.13c produce the same result, but the method in Figure 7.13c is used on the PIC24 μC as this allows use of the daw.b instruction.

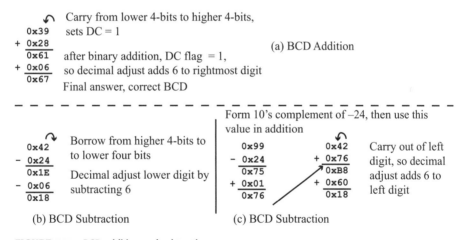

FIGURE 7.13   BCD addition and subtraction.

Figure 7.14a shows assembly code for a subroutine named bcd_add8 that performs the 8-bit BCD addition of W0=W0+W1. The bcd_add8 subroutine is called using the numbers from Figure 7.13a. Similarly, Figure 7.14b shows assembly code for a subroutine named bcd_sub8 that performs the 8-bit BCD subtraction W0=W0−W1 using the ten's complement approach of Figure 7.13c. Extended precision BCD arithmetic is done in the same manner as extended precision binary arithmetic using the addc instruction forms.

(a) BCD 8-bit Addition `bcd_add8`	(b) BCD 8-bit Subtraction `bcd_sub8`

```
;addition
  mov   #0x39,W0
  mov   #0x28,W1
  rcall bcd_add8 ;BCD (39+28 = 67)
  ......

;;do bcd 8-bit add, W0+W1=W0
bcd_add8:
  add.b W0,W1,W0   ;W0 = W0 + W1
  daw.b W0         ;decimal adjust
  return
```

```
;subtraction
  mov   #0x42,W0
  mov   #0x24,W1
  rcall bcd_sub8 ;BCD (42 - 24 = 18)
  ......

;;do bcd 8-bit subtractin, W0-W1=W0
bcd_sub8:
  mov   #0x99,W2
  sub.b W2,W1,W1   ;do 0x99-W1
  inc.b W1,W1      ;add 1 for 10's comp.
  add.b W0,W1,W0   ;W0 = W0 + (-W1)
  daw.b W0
  return
```

FIGURE 7.14   Assembly code for BCD 8-bit addition and subtraction.

Sample Question: ***What does 0x56 + 0x29 produce as a BCD sum?***

Answer: Using binary addition, 0x56 + 0x29 = 0x7F. Post-correcting for BCD produces 0x7F + 0x06 = 0x85. So, as a BCD sum, 0x56 + 0x29 = 0x85.

ASCII DATA CONVERSION

A common task in microprocessor programs is to convert numerical data in ASCII format to binary or vice versa. This functionality is generally provided by formatted IO functions in high-level languages, such as the `printf` (ASCII output) and `scanf` (ASCII input) C library functions. While the amount of ASCII data manipulation required in typical microcontroller applications is limited, the need for ASCII numerical manipulation invariably arises and one should have some familiarity with the problem.

BINARY TO ASCII-HEX

Suppose you wanted to see the bytes of a single or double precision floating-point number printed in ASCII format. The code in Figure 7.15 prints the individual bytes of a single precision and double precision floating-point number in ASCII-hex format. The C function `byte2aschex()` is the key piece of code in this discussion, as it converts a byte value into the ASCII-hex representation of that number. For example, the 8-bit value 0xA3 is converted to the two ASCII values 0x41, 0x33, as these are the ASCII codes for the two hex digits 'A' and '3,' respectively. The `byte2aschex()` function is called for each byte of the single precision and double

```
      main() Code

float fp_x;       //single precision
double dp_y;      //double precision
uint8* pu8_byte;  //generic pointer
uint8 u8_i;
uint8 au8_buf[2]; //temp space

main(){

  fp_x = 1398.5625;
  pu8_byte = (uint8 *) &fp_x;
  printf("float: %6.2f bytes are: ",
          fp_x);
  // print the four bytes
  for (u8_i=0;u8_i<4;u8_i++){
   byte2aschex(*(pu8_byte+3-u8_i),au8_buf);
   putchar(au8_buf[0]); // print MS digit
   putchar(au8_buf[1]); // print LS digit
  }
  printf("\n");
  dp_y = -28.75;
  pu8_byte = (uint8 *) &dp_y;
  printf("double: %6.2lf bytes are: ",
          dp_y);
  for (u8_i=0;u8_i<8;u8_i++){
   byte2aschex(*(pu8_byte+7-u8_i),au8_buf);
   putchar(au8_buf[0]); // print MS digit
   putchar(au8_buf[1]); // print LS digit
  }
  printf("\n");
}
```

```
     byte2aschex(), nyb2aschex()
     Functions

uint8 nyb2aschex (uint8 u8_c)
{
  if (u8_c >= 10)
     return (u8_c + 0x37);
  else return(u8_c + 0x30);
}

void byte2aschex(
             uint8 u8_c,
             uint8 *pu8_s)
{
 // first hex digit
 *pu8_s =
        nyb2aschex(u8_c >> 4);
 pu8_s++;
 // second hex digit
 *pu8_s =
        nyb2aschex(u8_c & 0x0F);
}
```

FIGURE 7.15   *C* code for ASCII-hex display of floating-point numbers.

precision floating-point numbers f and d, respectively. The generic pointer variable pu8_byte is used to iterate over the bytes of the floating-point numbers from most significant to least significant, which are assumed to be stored in little-endian order in memory (recall from Chapter 3 that little-endian means that bytes of a multibyte value are stored from least significant to most significant byte in increasing memory addresses). The uint8 au8_buf[2] array is used as temporary storage for the two ASCII characters generated by byte2aschex(). The byte2aschex() function converts each 4-bit portion (a *nybble*) of the u8_c input parameter by calling the nyb2aschex() function twice; first for the upper 4 bits, then for the lower 4 bits. Each 4-bit portion of u8_c represents one ASCII-hex digit, so an 8-bit number requires two bytes when converted to ASCII-hex. The nyb2aschex() function first tests its 4-bit input and if it is greater or equal to 10, then it is converted to its ASCII equivalent 'A' (0x41) through 'F' (0x46) by adding the value 0x37. If it is less than 10, 0x30 is added to the 4-bit value to produce the appropriate ASCII digit '0' (0x30) through '9' (0x39). The return value from the nyb2aschex() function is stored by the byte2aschex() function into the buffer pointed to by the pu8_s input parameter. In *C*, an integer can be printed in ASCII-hex format using the `%x` format in the `printf()` standard IO library function. An example usage is `printf ("u8_c=%x",u8_c)`, which prints `u8_c=3A` if the binary value of `u8_c` is 0x3A (see Appendix D, "Notes on the *C* Language," for more information on `printf()`).

Assembly language for the `byte2aschex()` and `nyb2aschex()` functions along with a test program is shown in Figure 7.16. The `byte2aschex()` assembly language implementation uses `W0` for `u8_c` and `W1` for the `pu8_s` pointer to the buffer used for storing the two ASCII-hex digits. The `nyb2aschex()` assembly language implementation uses `W0` as the 4-bit input value to be converted, and returns the equivalent ASCII-hex digit in `W0`. The test program calls `byte2aschex()` with 0x9A as the value to be converted in `W0`, and the starting address of `au8_buf` in `W1`. Upon return, the values 0x39 (ASCII '9') and 0x41 (ASCII 'A') are stored at buffer locations `au8_buf[0]` and `au8_buf[1]`, respectively.

```
        Test program                byte2aschex() Implementation
  .bss                      ;;Convert lower 4 bits of W0 to ASCII Hex
                            nyb2aschex:
  au8_buf:    .space 2        mov.b #0x30,W2    ;offset for '0' to '9' digit
                              cp.b  W0,#10      ; W0  >= 10?
  .text                       bra LTU, nyb_1    ; branch if W0 < 10
  __reset:                    mov.b #0x37,W2    ;offset for 'A' to 'F' digit
    mov #__SP_init, w15     nyb_1:
    mov #__SPLIM_init,W0      add.b W0,W2,W0
    mov W0, SPLIM            return
    rcall main
    reset                   ;;W0 is byte to be converted
                            ;;W1 points to temp buffer that can hold 2 bytes
  main:                     byte2aschex:
    mov #0x9A,W0             ;do most significant digit
    mov #au8_buf,W1          push  W0          ;save
    rcall byte2aschex        lsr   W0,#4,W0    ;do upper 4 bits
    ;; on return             and.b W0,#0x0F,W0 ;mask off upper bits
    ;; au8_buf[0]=0x39='9'   rcall nyb2aschex
    ;; au8_buf[1]=0x41='A'   mov.b W0,[W1++]   ;save return value
                            pop W0             ;restore
  done:                      ;do least significant digit
    bra done                 and.b W0,#0x0F,W0 ;mask off upper bits
                            rcall nyb2aschex
                            mov.b W0,[W1]     ;save return value
                            return
```

FIGURE 7.16   Assembly code implementation of the `byte2aschex()` function.

BINARY TO ASCII-DECIMAL

Table 7.5 shows the steps necessary to convert a binary number to its unsigned ASCII-decimal representation. The successive division by 10 produces the digits from least significant digit to most significant digit. The *C* statement `printf("%d",i)` prints the value of the `i` variable in decimal; the `printf()` *C* library function implements the algorithm of Table 7.5 when formatting numbers in ASCII-decimal format.

TABLE 7.5 Conversion of a binary number to unsigned ASCII-decimal.

Steps (Digits Are Determined Least Significant to Most Significant):
1. If the number is 9 or less, set the quotient to the number and go to step 3; otherwise divide the number by 10.
2. Add 0x30 to the remainder; this is the ASCII-decimal digit.
3. If the quotient is 9 or less, then this is the last non-zero digit, so add 0x30 to the quotient to get the ASCII value of the last digit and exit. If the quotient is 10 or greater, set the number equal to the quotient and loop back to 1.

ASCII-HEX TO BINARY

The aschex2byte() *C* function of Figure 7.17 does the reverse of the byte2aschex() *C* function in that it converts two ASCII characters representing the hex value of an 8-bit number into the binary value of that number. The *main()* code of Figure 7.17 passes a uint8 buffer containing two ASCII-hex digits to the aschex2byte() function, and saves the return value in u8_c. The aschex2byte() result is checked using the *C* formatted input function sscanf() in the statement sscanf(buf, "%x",&u16_i). The %x format causes the null-terminated string in u8_buf to be scanned for an ASCII-hex value, which is converted to binary and

```
        main() Code
uint8 au8_buf[3]; // temp space
uint8 u8_c;
uint16 u16_i;
main(){

 au8_buf[0] = '9';
 au8_buf[1] = 'A';
 //terminate string
 //for sscanf
 au8_buf[2]= 0x00;
 u8_c = aschex2byte(au8_buf);
 //use sscanf to check
 sscanf(au8_buf,"%x",&u16_i);
 if (u16_i != u8_c)
  printf("aschex2byte failed!\n");
 else
  printf("aschex2byte passed!\n");
 }
```

```
        aschex2byte() Function
// assumes digit is either '0'-'9',
// 'A'-'F', or 'a'-'f'
uint8 aschex2nyb (uint8 u8_n){
  u8_n = u8_n & 0xDF;  //to uppercase
  if (u8_n >= 0x3A)
    return (u8_n - 0x37);
  else
    return (u8_n - 0x30);
}

uint8 aschex2byte(uint8 *pu8_s){
   uint8 u8_c;
   // convert 1st char to upper 4 bits
   u8_c = aschex2nyb(*pu8_s);
   // move to upper four bits
   u8_c = u8_c << 4;
   // convert 2nd char to
   // lower 4 bits and combine
   pu8_s++;
   u8_c = u8_c | aschex2nyb(*pu8_s);
   return(u8_c);
}
```

FIGURE 7.17 *C* code for converting ASCII-hex to binary.

returned in the uint16 variable u16_i. A failure message is printed if the result returned by aschex2byte() does not match the result returned by sscanf(). The aschex2byte() function calls the aschex2nyb() function for each ASCII-hex digit to be converted. The aschex2nyb() function first converts the character to upper-case, which does not change the character's value if it is a '0' – '9' hex digit. Then it compares the ASCII value to 0x3A; if greater than 0x3A, the character must be in the range 'A' (0x41) to 'F' (0x46), so the value 0x37 is subtracted to get the bi-nary value. If the character is less than 0x3A, it must be in the range '0' (0x30) to '9' (0x39), so the value 0x30 is subtracted from the character to obtain the binary value. The resulting 4-bit value from the first call to aschex2nyb() is placed by as-chex2byte() in the upper half of the uint8 variable u8_c. The 4-bit value from the second call to aschex2nyb() is combined with the 4 bits already in the upper half of u8_c by a bitwise OR (|) operation. The resulting u8_c variable is returned as the converted 8-bit binary value.

Assembly language implementations of the aschex2byte() and aschex2nyb() functions are seen in Figure 7.18 along with a test program. The assembly language implementations are straightforward conversions of the C functions. The test pro-gram calls aschex2byte() with a pointer to a buffer that contains the ASCII-hex digits '9' and 'A'; register W0 contains the value 0x9A on return.

```
        Test program                  aschex2byte() Implementation
.bss                                ;;Convert ASCII-hex value in W0 to binary
                                    aschex2nyb:
au8_buf:    .space 2                  bclr.b  W0,#5         ;lowercase W0
                                      mov.b   #0x30,W2      ;offset for '0' to '9' digit
.text                                 mov.b   #0x3A,W3
  __reset:                            cp.b    W0,W3         ;W0  >= 0x3A?
    mov #__SP_init, w15               bra     LTU, asc_1    ;branch if W0 < 0x3A
    mov #__SPLIM_init,W0              mov.b   #0x37,W2      ;offset for 'A' to 'F' digit
    mov W0, SPLIM                   asc_1:
    rcall main                        sub.b   W0,W2,W0
    reset                             return

main:                               ;;W0 points to buffer that holds
  mov #'9',W0                       ;;two ASCII-hex digits to be converted
;au8_buf[0]='9'=0x39                aschex2byte:
  mov.b WREG,au8_buf                  mov     W0,W1         ;save pointer
;au8_buf[1]='A'=0x41                  mov.b   [W1++], W0    ;get first digit
  mov #'A',W0                         rcall   aschex2nyb
  mov.b WREG,au8_buf+1                sl      W0,#4, W4     ;shift to upper 4 bits
;do the conversion                    mov.b   [W1],W0       ;get 2nd digit
  mov #au8_buf,W0                     rcall   aschex2nyb
  rcall aschex2byte                   ior.b   W4,W0,W0      ;combine
  ;; upon return,                     ze      W0,W0         ;zero extend
  ;; W0=0x9A                          return
done:
  bra done
```

FIGURE 7.18 Assembly code implementation of the aschex2byte() function.

ASCII-Decimal to Binary

Table 7.6 shows the steps necessary to convert an ASCII-decimal number to its binary value. The conversion proceeds from most significant digit to least significant digit, converting each digit d to its binary value and forming the sum $r = r*10 + d$ where r is the cumulative result. The number range that can be converted is dependent upon the size of r. In C, ASCII-decimal to binary conversion can be accomplished with `sscanf()` using the `%d` format. An example is `sscanf(buf,"%d",&i16_i)`, which converts the first ASCII-decimal string found in `buf` to binary and returns the result in `i16_i`.

TABLE 7.6   Conversion of an ASCII-decimal number to binary.

Steps:
1. $r = 0$.
2. For each digit d in the ASCII-decimal number starting with the most significant digit:
3. Convert d to its 4-bit binary value, and let $r = r * 10 + d$.
4. If d is the last digit, exit and return r as the result; otherwise advance to the next digit and go to step 3.

SUMMARY

Multiplication operations in the PIC24 are enhanced by the availability of a 16×16 array multiplier, which can be used to implement higher precision multiplications. Hardware support for division exists in the PIC24 instruction set for 32-bit/16-bit and 16-bit/16-bit operands, and requires a `repeat #17` instruction to iteratively produce each bit of the quotient. Saturating arithmetic is a method for dealing with overflow in addition and subtraction by clipping the result to either the maximum or minimum values of the number range in case of overflow or underflow, respectively. Floating-point representation encodes an exponent field in addition to magnitude and sign information, greatly expanding the number range that can be represented, at the cost of extra complexity in performing floating-point calculations. Binary coded decimal (BCD) encodes each decimal digit as a 4-bit value, providing fast conversion from BCD to decimal, and vice versa. Support for BCD arithmetic is present in the PIC24 via the DC flag and the `daw.b` instruction. Conversion of ASCII numerical data in hex or decimal formats to binary and vice versa is required for input/output operations of ASCII numerical data and is usually implemented in the form of formatted IO subroutines.

REVIEW PROBLEMS

For problems 1 through 18, give the affected registers after execution of each instruction. Indicate if overflow occurs for division instructions. Assume the register and memory contents of Table 7.7 at the beginning of EACH problem. Show the decimal equivalents of the operation that is performed and verify your result. Assume that the divide instructions have a `repeat #17` in front of them.

1. `mul.uu W0,W1,W8`
2. `mul.ss W0,W1,W8`
3. `mul.us W0,W1,W8`
4. `mul.su W0,W1,W8`
5. `mul.ss W2,W3,W8`
6. `mul.us W2,W3,W8`
7. `mul.su W2,W3,W8`
8. `mul.uu W2,W3,W8`
9. `div.u W6,W2`
10. `div.s W4,W5`
11. `div.u W4,W5`
12. `div.s W4,W2`
13. `div.ud W8,W4`
14. `div.sd W8,W4`
15. `div.sd W6,W8`
16. `div.ud W8,W6`
17. `div.s W6,W9`
18. `div.ud W6,W4`

19. What is the value 0xC4 as a 0.8 unsigned fixed-point number?
20. What is the value 0xC4 as a 4.4 unsigned fixed-point number?

TABLE 7.7   Register memory contents.

Location	Value	Location	Value
W0	0xFFF4	W5	0x0005
W1	0x000A	W6	0xC0FF
W2	0x000C	W7	0x0001
W3	0xFF06	W8	0xE000
W4	0xFFD0	W9	0xFFFF

21. What is the value 0xC4 as a 1.7 signed fixed-point number?
22. What is the value 0xC4 as a 3.5 signed fixed-point number?
23. Convert 23.33 to a 5.3 unsigned fixed-point number.
24. Convert 0.2325 to a 0.8 unsigned fixed-point number.
25. Convert −0.2325 to a 1.7 signed fixed-point number.
26. Convert −2.458 to a 4.4 signed fixed-point number.
27. Saturating signed addition is defined as saturating to either the maximum positive value or maximum negative value in the case of overflow using two's complement encoding. What is the result for 0x39 + 0x59 using saturating signed 8-bit addition?
28. What is the result for 0x8F + 0xE0 using saturating signed addition as defined by problem 27?
29. What is the result for 0x8F + 0xE0 using saturating unsigned 8-bit addition?
30. Write a PIC24 instruction sequence that implements signed saturating addition as defined by problem 27 assuming W0 and W1 contain the two 8-bit operands, with the saturated sum returning in W0.
31. What is the value −0.15625 in single precision floating-point format?
32. What is the value −545.6875 in single precision floating-point format?
33. The value 0x42F18000 is a single precision floating-point number; what is its decimal value?
34. The value 0xC6ED6E20 is a single precision floating-point number; what is its decimal value?
35. Write the steps of an algorithm that compares two single precision floating-point numbers a and b. Assume both numbers are normalized before the comparison is done and that you do not have to handle special numbers. Return 1 if a > b, −1 if a < b, and 0 if a == b. Assume that you have functions named `sign()`, `exp()`, and `significand()` that extracts these fields and returns them as unsigned integer values. Hint: Think about comparing the numbers by comparing the individual sign, exponent, and significand fields.
36. How would you detect overflow in the BCD addition of two 8-bit numbers?
37. What is the ten's complement of the BCD value 0x58?
38. Implement the algorithm of Table 7.6 in PIC24 assembly language for any ASCII-decimal string up to three digits (0 to 999).

PART III

PIC24 µC Interfacing Using the *C* Language

8

The PIC24HJ32GP202: System Startup and Parallel Port I/O

This chapter introduces the hardware side of the PIC24 µC family by exploring reset behavior and parallel port I/O for a PIC24HJ32GP202 µC. In addition, the nuances of writing *C* code for PIC24 µC applications are examined.

Learning Objectives

After reading this chapter, you will be able to:

- Implement a simple PIC24HJ32GP202 system that has an in-circuit programming interface, a power supply, a serial interface, and a reset switch.
- Write *C* code for the PIC24HJ32GP202 µC that implements I/O via pushbutton switches and LEDs using a finite state machine approach.
- Discuss the different features of the PIC24HJ32GP202 parallel ports such as bidirectional capability, weak pull-ups, and open-drain outputs.
- Describe the factors that affect dynamic power consumption in CMOS circuits.
- Identify common features of integrated circuit datasheets.
- Discuss the use of sleep, idle, and doze modes in the PIC24HJ32GP202 µC and their effect on power consumption.
- Describe the operation of the watchdog timer and its interaction with sleep/idle mode.
- Implement a parallel interface between a PIC24HJ32GP202 µC and a liquid crystal display module.

HIGH-LEVEL LANGUAGES VERSUS ASSEMBLY LANGUAGE

Previous chapters explored the instruction set of the PIC24 µC and assembly language programming in the context of *C* programming. This was done so that the linkage from high-level language constructs such as data types, conditional statements, loop structures, subroutines, signed/unsigned arithmetic, and so forth to assembly language is clear. This understanding is needed, as most programming of microprocessors and microcontrollers is done in a high-level language such as *C*, not assembly language, and therefore one must be cognizant of the performance and memory usage repercussions when using features of a high-level language. For example, at this point you would not use floating-point data types for convenience (or out of ignorance), but rather would carefully weigh whether the computations required by your application actually need the large number range available with floating-point representation. You now know that using floating-point data types requires more memory space for variables, more program memory for calculations, and in most cases, more execution time for application code. The same tradeoffs apply when weighing the choice between uint32/int32 and uint8/int8 data types, but not on as dramatic a scale as floating-point versus integer types.

Why is most programming of microprocessors and microcontrollers done in a high-level language and not assembly language? One reason is programmer productivity, which is usually measured in the number of debugged code lines produced per day by a programmer. At this point, you know that it generally takes more assembly language statements than *C* statements to implement the same task, because *C* statements imply data movement or arithmetic operations that require multiple register transfer operations when mapped to a specific microprocessor architecture. Writing more statements takes more time; hence it generally takes longer to write applications in assembly language than in a high-level language. Another reason is code clarity; code in a higher level language is typically easier to read and understand than assembly language because the fine-grain details of operator implementation are hidden. Another reason is portability; code written in a high-level language is easier to port to another microprocessor than assembly language because it is the compiler's task to translate the *C* to the target microprocessor instruction set. This is important, as code is often reused from application to application, and you do not want to lose the time and money invested in creating an application suite if the target microprocessor changes.

So, when is assembly language needed? One reason to write in assembly language is to implement special arithmetic functions that are not available in the high-level language of choice, such as implementing saturating integer arithmetic in *C*. Another reason is to write a performance-critical section of code in assembly language if the compiler cannot be trusted to produce code that meets required performance specifications. Yet another reason might be to use certain features of the processor that can only be accessed by special instructions within the instruction set. All of these reasons require an understanding of assembly language programming. Even when writing in a high-level language, one should be aware of the features of the instruction set and architecture of the target processor. For example, if the target processor is a 32-bit processor, using 32-bit data types versus 8-bit data types will probably not have much impact on the execution speed of integer operations.

The term *embedded system* is often applied to microcontroller applications because the microcontroller is hidden within the target system, with no visible external interface. A car typically has tens of microcontrollers within it, yet this fact is not apparent to the car owner. What high-level languages are used to program embedded systems? The *C++* language is a popular choice for complex applications written for high-performance microprocessors. However, the *C* programming language is often the language of choice for an embedded system, as *C* was intentionally designed to provide tight coupling between *C* statements and assembly language. In addition, most embedded system programs are control-intensive and do not require complex data structures. Thus, the powerful data abstraction capabilities of an object-oriented programming language such as *C++* are often not required in embedded system applications. If a compiler is available for a microcontroller, more often than not it will be a *C* compiler and not a *C++* compiler. This does not mean that there are no microcontroller applications programmed in *C++*, but rather that *C* is the more popular choice, especially for lower-performance microcontrollers. Languages such as Java that are compiled to an intermediate form that is then interpreted by a run-time execution engine are not widely used in microcontroller applications because of the performance loss when compared to an application compiled to the microcontroller's native assembly language.

This chapter begins the hardware topic coverage in this book. Over the next seven chapters, the details of the major hardware subsystems of the PIC24 μC are explored and sample applications discussed. The hardware chapters of this book focus on the PIC24H branch of the PIC24 μC family as it was released after the PIC24F branch and has more performance and functionality. However, the PIC24H and PIC24F variants share the same assembly language instruction set [8] and many of the same hardware modules, so porting PIC24H *C* programs to PIC24F microcontrollers is not overly difficult. Most of the *C* interfacing examples in this book are compatible with both families, and the *C* library functions that are included with this book use conditional compilation to ensure that the code examples operate with both families. In general, we only use the "PIC24H family" tag in the text whenever a hardware module has significant differences from the PIC24F family. To exercise the features of the PIC24 hardware subsystems, application programs that transfer data between the subsystems and memory, configure subsystems for different operating modes, and check subsystem operation status are presented. These programs are written in *C* to promote code clarity. It is a difficult enough task to grasp the operational details of a hardware subsystem without the additional problem of struggling with long assembly language programs, where the details of memory transfers and arithmetic operator implementation mask the overall program functionality. The previous coverage of the PIC24 μC instruction set and assembly language programming techniques in the context of the C language has prepared you for moving beyond assembly language when discussing the hardware subsystems of the PIC24 μC. In covering the PIC24 μC hardware subsystems, it is expected that the reader will refer to the PIC24H Family Reference Manual (FRM) data sheets [9-30] or the PIC24HJ32GP202 data sheet [31] when additional details or clarification are needed. This book does not attempt to duplicate all of the information in the PIC24 data sheets, which is clearly impractical and unnecessary. Instead, this book presents key functionality of each subsystem in the context of application examples. In some cases, detailed descriptions of the registers associated with a subsystem and individual register bits are presented in this book; at other times, the reader is referred to the appropriate data sheet. The ability to read datasheets and extract key information is a necessary survival skill for any person interfacing microprocessors or microcontrollers to other devices. A section within this chapter is devoted to providing tips on datasheet reading for those readers who are encountering datasheets for the first time.

C COMPILATION FOR THE PIC24 μC

In this book, the C programs for hardware application examples use the MPLAB® C compiler for the PIC24 from Microchip Technology Inc. (this compiler was formerly known as the C30 compiler). From this point onward, this book refers to this compiler as the "PIC24 compiler." Details on using the compiler within MPLAB are given in Appendix B. In Chapter 2, a compiler is defined as a program that translates statements in a high-level language to assembly language. Figure 8.1 shows a conceptual view of the steps performed in transforming a C program into machine code that can be programmed into the PIC24 μC. The compiler first transforms the C code into *unoptimized* assembly language, which is done by looking at each C statement individually and implementing it as a sequence of instructions. The *optimization* stage then looks at groups of assembly language instructions and attempts to reduce the number of instructions by considering data transfer requirements of the entire group. The right-hand side of Figure 8.1 shows an example compiler optimization, in which two C statements are translated into four assembly language instructions when each C statement is considered individually. The optimizer then considers the four assembly language instructions as a group and notes that the W0 register already contains the value of j from the previous operation, so the second mov j,W0 instruction can be removed. This is only a small example,

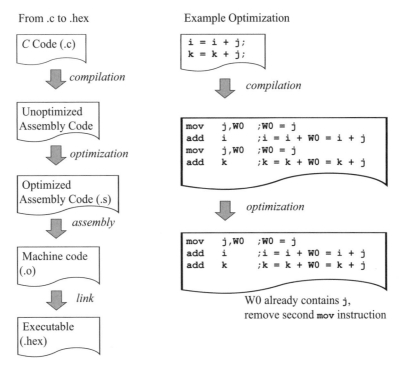

FIGURE 8.1 The compilation process.

as there are many different types of compiler optimizations that are performed. Typically, code size is reduced and performance improved after optimization.

After optimization, an assembler internal to the compiler translates the assembly language to machine code that is then placed within an object code (*.o*) file. If a program becomes large, it is regarded as good programming practice to split the source code among several files, where each file contains functions that are related to each other. This makes the source code easier to maintain and allows a group of programmers to work on the same microcontroller application concurrently. Thus, an application may have several object files, and it is the job of the *linker* to combine these files into a single file that is executed by the microprocessor. In the case of the PIC24 µC, this "executable" file is a *.hex* file, which contains an ASCII-hex representation of the program memory contents and is downloaded into the program memory of the PIC24 µC (see Appendix B for details on how this is accomplished).

SPECIAL FUNCTION REGISTERS AND BIT REFERENCES

A *C* compiler for a microcontroller must provide access to the special function registers and individual bits of those registers. In the MPLAB PIC24 compiler, all special function registers have *C* define statements for them contained in a header file (.h) that is particular to the target device. For example, a special function register used for parallel port I/O and discussed later in this chapter is named PORTB, whose memory location is 0x2CA. In the PIC24 compiler installation directory, a file named *Program Files\Microchip\MPLAB C30\support\PIC24H\h\p24HJ32GP202.h* is the header file used for the PIC24HJ32GP202 μC. Within this file is contained the following line that defines the special function register PORTB as an unsigned int (16-bit) data type.

```
extern volatile unsigned int PORTB __attribute__((__sfr__));
```

The __attribute__ keyword is an extension to standard *C* by the PIC24 compiler that allows variable and function attributes to be defined, allowing for specific actions to be taken by the compiler based on the attribute values. The __attribute__ ((__sfr__)) annotation specifies that PORTB is a special function register. A separate linker file assigns the location 0x2CA to the PORTB variable. The PORTB variable declaration allows the entire PORTB special function register to be written or read with a single *C* statement:

```
PORTB = 0x3010; //assign PORTB a value
```

An individual bit of PORTB can be tested using a bitwise & operation as initially done in Chapter 4. The following code fragment executes the *if-body* if the least significant bit of PORTB is a "1":

```
if (PORTB & 0x0001) {
    //execute if-body if LSb of PORTB is 1
}
```

Because operations on individual bits within special function registers is commonplace, almost all SFRs also have *C* struct data type definitions that allow convenient access to individual bits and bit fields. For example, within the same header file is a *C* struct definition named PORTBBITS that defines individual bit names for each of the 16-bits of PORTB (more information on *C* struct data types can be found in Appendix D).

```
typedef struct tagPORTBBITS {
    unsigned RB0:1;
    unsigned RB1:1;
    unsigned RB2:1;
    unsigned RB3:1;
    unsigned RB4:1;
    unsigned RB5:1;
```

```
        unsigned RB6:1;
        unsigned RB7:1;
        unsigned RB8:1;
        unsigned RB9:1;
        unsigned RB10:1;
        unsigned RB11:1;
        unsigned RB12:1;
        unsigned RB13:1;
        unsigned RB14:1;
        unsigned RB15:1;
   } PORTBBITS;
```

The :1 after each struct element name indicates the bit width of the named element. The following line defines a variable named PORTBbits of type PORTBBITS:

```
    extern volatile PORTBBITS PORTBbits __attribute__((__sfr__));
```

The PORTBbits variable definition allows individual bits of PORTB to be referred to as PORTBbits.RB*n*, where *n* is the bit number. The following code snippet sets bit 5 of PORTB and clears bit 2 of PORTB.

```
    PORTBbits.RB5 = 1;      //set bit 5 of PORTB
    PORTBbits.RB2 = 0;      //clear bit 2 of PORTB
```

These *C* statements are mapped by the compiler into assembly language bset and bclr instructions for an efficient implementation. Individual bits can be tested using similar references; the following code fragment executes the *if-body* if the least significant bit of PORTB is a "1":

```
    if (PORTBbits.RB0) {
       //execute if-body if LSb of PORTB is 1
    }
```

Likewise, the common use of multibit fields in SFR is supported in *C*. For example, the OSCCON register contains several fields:

```
    typedef struct tagOSCCONBITS {
       union {
          struct {
             unsigned OSWEN:1;
             unsigned LPOSCEN:1;
             unsigned :1;
             unsigned CF:1;
```

```
            unsigned :1;
            unsigned LOCK:1;
            unsigned IOLOCK:1;
            unsigned CLKLOCK:1;
            unsigned NOSC:3;
            unsigned :1;
            unsigned COSC:3;
        };
        struct {
            unsigned :8;
            unsigned NOSC0:1;
            unsigned NOSC1:1;
            unsigned NOSC2:1;
            unsigned :1;
            unsigned COSC0:1;
            unsigned COSC1:1;
            unsigned COSC2:1;
        };
    };
} OSCCONBITS;
extern volatile OSCCONBITS OSCCONbits __attribute__((__sfr__));
```

This definition allows access to the entire NOSC bit field composed of three bits using statements such as OSCCONbits.NOSC=2; or to individual bits by equivalently executing OSCCONbits.NOSC2=0; OSCCONbits.NOSC1=1; OSCCONbits. NOSC0=0;.

Finally, the same *p24HJ32GP202.h* header file has C macros that provide a shorthand reference for many of the SFR named bits and bit fields that eliminate the need to remember the SFR register name. A *C macro* in its simplest form allows one or more C statements to be referred to by a single label, which is the macro name. A macro is defined using the #define statement. For the PORTB bits, these macros are:

```
#define _RB0 PORTBbits.RB0
#define _RB1 PORTBbits.RB1
#define _RB2 PORTBbits.RB2
#define _RB3 PORTBbits.RB3
#define _RB4 PORTBbits.RB4
... etc., other RBn macros not shown....
```

This allows the previous code snippet that set bit 5 and cleared bit 2 of PORTB to be written as:

```
_RB5 = 1; //set bit 5 of PORTB
_RB2 = 0; //clear bit 2 of PORTB
```

Similarly, a bit test of the LSb of PORTB can be written as:

```
if (_RB0) {
    //execute if-body if LSb of PORTB is 1
}
```

Likewise, macros are provided in the header file that access the bit fields:

```
#define _OSWEN OSCCONbits.OSWEN
#define _LPOSCEN OSCCONbits.LPOSCEN
#define _CF OSCCONbits.CF
#define _LOCK OSCCONbits.LOCK
#define _IOLOCK OSCCONbits.IOLOCK
#define _CLKLOCK OSCCONbits.CLKLOCK
#define _NOSC OSCCONbits.NOSC
#define _COSC OSCCONbits.COSC
#define _NOSC0 OSCCONbits.NOSC0
#define _NOSC1 OSCCONbits.NOSC1
#define _NOSC2 OSCCONbits.NOSC2
#define _COSC0 OSCCONbits.COSC0
#define _COSC1 OSCCONbits.COSC1
#define _COSC2 OSCCONbits.COSC2
```

Therefore, the value of the bit field NOSC can be in one statement as _NOSC=2; or by setting each bit of the field by using _NOSC2=0; _NOSC1=1; _NOSC0=0;.

The macro definitions for named bits and bit fields are only defined for unique bit names; they are not defined if the same bit name is used in more than one special function register. This book uses the macro definition for named bits wherever possible because this means that only the bit name has to be remembered and not the special function register name.

PIC24 COMPILER RUNTIME CODE, VARIABLE QUALIFIERS/ATTRIBUTES

Runtime code is code generated by the compiler and executed by the processor before the main() function is entered. The runtime code produced by the PIC24 compiler performs the following steps:

■ Initialize the stack pointer and stack limit registers. The default actions maximize the amount of available stack space.
■ Initialize all global variables; if an initial value is not specified for a global variable then it is cleared.
■ Initialize the PSV register so that constant data placed in program memory can be accessed.
■ Call main(); if the main() function returns then the processor is reset by executing the reset instruction. It should be noted that returning from the main()

function is rarely done in embedded applications; our examples later in this chapter never return from `main()`.

Some attributes and variable qualifiers used in the example *C* programs in the hardware chapters are the `const` qualifier and the `persistent` attribute. The `const` qualifier for a variable indicates that the program does not change the variable from its initial contents. The default action of the compiler is to place all `const` variables in program memory to reduce RAM usage. The `const` qualifier is typically used with constant strings and arrays, such as shown below:

```
const uint8 sz_hellomsg[] = "Hello World!";
const uint8 au8_table[] = {0x23, 0xA0, 0x7F, 0x39};
```

The `persistent` attribute when applied to a variable causes the variable to be uninitialized by the runtime code. This allows the variable to track values between processor resets; one usage of persistent variables is for communicating error status after a reset. The persistent attribute applied to a variable is shown below:

```
uint8 u8_resetCount __attribute__((persistent));
```

We will use a macro form of this named `_PERSISTENT`, defined by the processor-specific header file (such as *p24HJ32GP202.h*), as follows:

```
_PERSISTENT uint8 u8_resetCount;
```

C MACROS, INLINE FUNCTIONS

The example *C* programs in the hardware chapters make extensive use of *C* macros and *inline* functions as a method of improving code clarity. An inline function is a *C* function whose code is expanded in the caller instead of using a subroutine call/return. Inline functions are often used for small functions to remove the overhead of the call/return. An example of an inline function is shown below:

```
static inline void CONFIG_RB1_AS_DIG_INPUT() {
    DISABLE_RB1_PULLUP();
    _TRISB1 = 1;
    _PCFG3 = 1;
}
```

In the PIC24 compiler, the `static` qualifier when used with `inline` causes the compiler to omit the body of the inline function from the final linked code if all of the inline functions are expanded. In addition, it allows the function to be defined multiple times in different *C* source files without causing linking errors by making the name of the function visible only to the current *C* source file. An all-uppercase naming convention is used for macros and inline functions in our programs. These are defined in various header files, either written by the authors or provided with the PIC24 compiler. So, when you see a *C* statement such as:

```
CONFIG_RB11_AS_DIG_OUTPUT();
```

then be aware that `CONFIG_RB11_AS_DIG_OUTPUT()` is a *C* macro or inline function whose definition is found in one of the included header files. The first time that a particular macro type is used in an example program, we explain the macro's functionality and show the *C* statements that the *C* macro represents.

CONDITIONAL COMPILATION

Conditional compilation allows *C* statements to be either processed or ignored based upon a macro definition or macro value. For the example, different include files are used depending upon processor type:

```
#if defined(__PIC24HJ128GP202__)
#include "devices/PIC24HJ128GP202_ports.h"
#elif defined(__PIC24HJ128GP204__)
#include "devices/PIC24HJ128GP204_ports.h"
#elif defined(__PIC24HJ128GP206__)
#include "devices/PIC24HJ128GP206_ports.h"
... other code omitted ...
```

The chained `if`/`elif` conditional statements (*if*/*else if*) include file *devices/ PIC24HJ128GP202_ports.h* if macro `__PIC24HJ128GP202__` is defined, while file *devices/PIC24HJ128GP204_ports.h* is included if macro `__PIC24HJ128GP204__` is defined, etc. The macros `__PIC24HJ128GP202__`, `__PIC24HJ128GP204__`, etc., are defined by the compiler based upon the μC device setting in MPLAB, which allows device-specific *C* code to be generated. The `#ifdef` statement can be used instead of `defined()`, so the following:

```
#ifdef __PIC24HJ32GP202__
... code included if __PIC24HJ32GP202__ is defined
#endif
```

is equivalent to:

```
#if defined(__PIC24HJ32GP202__)
... code included if __PIC24HJ32GP202__ is defined
#endif
```

The #ifndef *macroname* and #if !defined(*macroname*) tests can be used to detect if a macro is not defined. The macros __PIC24H__ and __PIC24F__ are also defined by the compiler for conditional compilation based on processor family such as:

```
#if defined(__PIC24H__)
    case 6: outString("Fast RC Osc/16\n"); break;
    case 7: outString("Fast RC Osc/N\n"); break;
#elif defined(__PIC24F__)
    case 7 : outString("Fast RC Osc with Postscale"); break;
#else
#error Unknown processor
#endif
```

A macro's value can also be used for controlling conditional compilation as shown in the following code snippet:

```
#if (NUM_UARTS >= 2)
    case 2 :
        __C30_UART = 2; //this is the default UART
        configUART2(u32_baudRate);
        break;
#endif
```

The #if (NUM_UARTS >= 2) test includes the code that follows only if the value of NUM_UARTS is greater than or equal to 2. Macros are defined and assigned values within a source file as follows:

```
#define NUM_UARTS 2 //NUM_UARTS == 2
#define UART1_TX_INTERRUPT // UART1_TX_INTERRUPT macro defined, no value
```

Macros can also be passed to the compiler by the -*D* flag, as in -DNUM_UARTS=2 and -DUART1_TX_INTERRUPT. Macros can also be defined and assigned values within an MPLAB project file, which are then passed to the compiler using the -D flag (see Appendix B for more information on MPLAB operation).

More information on the MPLAB PIC24 compiler operation can be found in the *MPLAB C30 User's Guide* [32], found in the *doc/* subdirectory of the PIC24 compiler installation directory.

PIC24HJ32GP202 Startup Schematic

The version of the PIC24H μC used in most of the interfacing examples in this book is the PIC24HJ32GP202 μC whose pin diagram is given in Figure 8.2. This device has 32 Ki bytes of program memory, 2 Ki bytes of SRAM, and is suitable

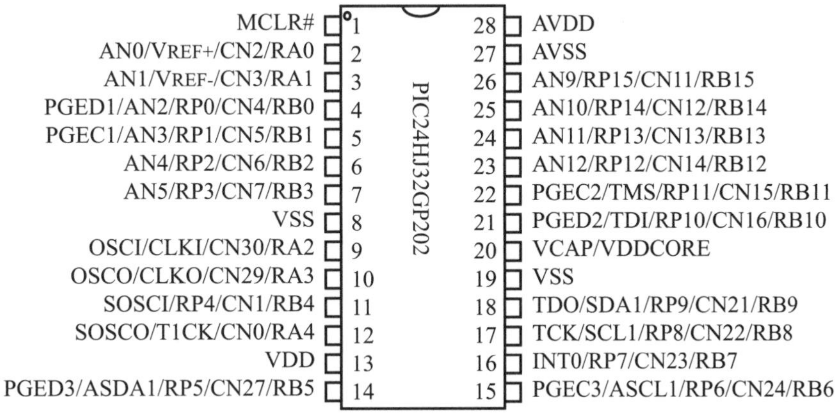

FIGURE 8.2   PIC24HJ32GP202 pin diagram. (Adapted with permission of the copyright owner, Microchip Technology, Incorporated. All rights reserved. No further reprints or reproduction may be made without Microchip Inc.'s prior written consent.)

for experimentation on a protoboard given its small footprint of 28 pins provided in a dual in-line package (DIP). An external pin usually has more than one internal function mapped to it because of the limited number of pins on the 28-pin package. Control bits within special function registers determine the mapping of internal functions to external pins. We will also use the PIC24HJ128GP502 μC for some examples in later chapters as it is pin compatible and offers some additional features over the PIC24HJ32GP202 μC.

A brief summary of the pin functions used in this book is given here; more details are provided in the appropriate chapter covering that functionality.

- **VDD, VSS:** These are power (VDD) and ground (VSS) pins; observe that there is more than one ground pin. It is not unusual for an integrated circuit to have multiple power and ground pins, all of which must be connected.
- **AVDD, AVSS:** These are power (AVDD) and ground (AVSS) pins for the analog modules, which are discussed in Chapter 11. Even if the analog modules are not used, they must be connected to power and ground.
- **VCAP/VDDCORE:** The internal voltage used by the microcontroller is available on this pin.
- **MCLR#:** This input pin resets the device when brought low. The # symbol in the name indicates a low true signal.
- **PGEC1/PGED1, PGEC2/PGED2, PGEC3/PGED3:** Any of the PGECx/PGEDx pin pairs can be used for *In-Circuit Serial Programming*™ (ICSP™), which is the process of downloading a program into the device using an external programmer without removing the device from the board. See Appendix B for more information on in-circuit programming.

- **OSCI, OSCO:** These pins can be used with an external crystal to provide the main clock source for the device (details in this chapter).
- **CLKI, CLKO:** An external clock can be provided via the CLKI input pin, while the internal clock can be monitored via the CLKO output pin.
- **SOSCI, SOSCO:** These pins can be used with an external 32.768 kHz crystal for real-time clock keeping (details in Chapter 12).
- **RAn, RBn:** These pins are parallel port I/O pins (details in this chapter).
- **ANn, VREF−, VREF+:** The ANn inputs are the analog inputs for the analog-to-digital converter subsystem (Chapter 11). The VREF−/VREF+ pins are used to provide negative and positive voltage references for the analog-to-digital converter.
- **CNn:** These are change notification inputs (details in Chapter 9).
- **ASCL1/ASDA1, SCL1/SDA1:** These pin pairs implement the I²C synchronous serial data interface (details in Chapter 10).
- **RPn:** These are remappable peripheral pins that allow internal pin functions to be connected in a flexible manner to external I/O pin (details in Chapter 10).
- **INT0:** This is an external interrupt pin (details in Chapter 9).
- **TMS, TDI, TDO, TCK:** These pins allow external testing of the device, and are not used for normal operation of the microcontroller.
- **T1CLK:** This input can be used to provide a clock for Timer1 (details in Chapter 12).

A schematic used to test PIC24HJ32GP202 functionality by flashing a light emitting diode (LED) is shown in Figure 8.3. The schematic functionality can be split into power, reset, serial communication, in-circuit serial programming, and application components. If you are somewhat rusty at recognizing electrical symbols, please review the material in Appendix E that provides a hobbyist-level review of basic circuit theory. You only need a hobbyist-level intuition about basic circuit concepts for the interfacing topics in this book; a detailed circuit analysis background is not required.

STARTUP SCHEMATIC: POWER

The PIC24HJ32GP202 requires that the input voltage VDD be in the range 3.0 V to 3.6 V. An external AC-to-DC wall transformer (or 9 V battery) provides power that outputs 9 V *unregulated,* which means that the output voltage can fluctuate depending upon the amount of current that is drawn. An LM2937-3.3 *voltage regulator* is used to provide a stable 3.3 V output as the VDD for this system (Appendix C contains a complete list of the components used in the interfacing examples of this book as well as a picture of a completed protoboard layout). The LM2937 accepts a wide input voltage (4.75 V to 26 V); 9 V is used for example purposes. The 3.3 V voltage on the PIC24 VDD pin is connected to a voltage regulator internal to

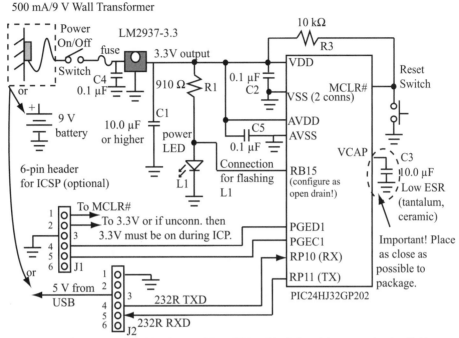

FIGURE 8.3   PIC24HJ32GP202 Startup schematic for flashing an LED.

the PIC24 µC that provides a digital core voltage of 2.5 V. The fuse in the power path is a safety precaution; it will blow (no longer conduct current) if excessive current is drawn from the power supply. Excessive current can be drawn if a short (a low-resistance path) is created between VDD and VSS by a wiring mistake during circuit hookup or by component failure. The total current required for our PIC24H µC system after all peripheral chips have been added is under 100 mA (1 mA = milliAmperes = 0.001 A). A 500 mA wall transformer provides a margin for hardware experiments that use higher current draw devices, such as a DC motor for driving the wheel of a small robot. The C1 capacitor is required by the LM2937 for output voltage stability with a minimum suggested value of 10 µF and maximum ESR (equivalent series resistance) of 5 Ω. The 0.1 µF C2, C4, and C5 and 10 µF C3 capacitors are called *decoupling* capacitors and assist in supplying transient current needs caused by high-frequency digital switching. These capacitors should be placed as close as possible to their respective power and ground pins (VDD, VCAP, AVDD, VSS, and AVSS) for maximum effectiveness. All four capacitors need to have low ESR, such as provided by low ESR tantalum and ceramic capacitors, with ceramic capacitors having lower ESR than tantalums at equivalent capacitor values. The C3 capacitor is especially critical as it helps maintain the stability of the PIC's internal voltage regulator; the PIC24HJ32GP202 datasheet recommends an ESR of less than 5 ohms. The L1 LED is used in two roles—the first is as a power status since the LED is on when power is applied. The second role is as an LED that can be blinked by the PIC24HJ32GP202 via the connection from port RB15 to the LED as shown in the figure. Because the power supply and RB15 are both driving the LED, the RB15 port is configured as an *open-drain output*, which means that it can be driven in two states: (a) low, pulling the LED to ground and it turning off, or (b) high impedance (floating, no drive current supplied), which turns on the LED if power is applied. Open-drain outputs are discussed in more detail later in this chapter; open-drain mode is used in this case to reduce component count and wiring (another LED and series resistor could have been used on R15 instead of sharing the power LED). To determine the resistance value of R1, we note that when RB15 is pulling low (turning off L1), that current is flowing from VDD through the resistor and into RB15. The DC specifications in the PIC24HJ32GP202 datasheet [31] state that the RB15 pin can sink a maximum of 4 mA [31]. Solving Ohm's law ($V = IR$) for resistance gives $R = V/I$, with the minimum resistance allowed computed as 3.3 V/4 mA = 825 Ω. We use a value 910 Ω to provide some safety margin. The current flowing through the LED for RB15 in the high impedance (floating) state is (VDD − *LED_Vdrop*)/R1, where *LED_Vdrop* is the voltage drop across the LED. The LED voltage drop can be found on its datasheet for a range of currents, with a typical value of 2 V. Thus, the ON current supplied to the LED by the power supply is (3.3 − 2.0)V/ 910 Ω = 1.4 mA, which is enough to illuminate a typical LED.

STARTUP SCHEMATIC: RESET

When power is applied to the PIC24HJ32GP202, the device performs a power-on reset (POR), which means that the program counter is cleared to 0 and the first instruction is fetched from location 0. This is an internally generated power-on reset sequence; some microcontrollers require an external reset circuit that asserts an input pin either high or low to trigger reset after power is applied. It is also convenient to have a manual reset capability during testing to restart a program without needing to cycle power. The momentary pushbutton connected to the MCLR# input applies a low voltage to MCLR# when pushed, causing the PIC24 µC to reset. The 10 kΩ (R3) resistor that connects the MCLR# pin to VDD is called a *pull-up* resistor as it keeps the MCLR# input pulled up to almost 3.3 V when the pushbutton is released. If the pull-up resistor is removed and a direct connection is made from MCLR# to VDD, a short is created when the pushbutton is pressed, causing excessive current flow and probably causing the fuse to blow. If the pull-up resistor and VDD connection is not made at all, the input floats between 0 V and VDD when the pushbutton is not pressed. A floating input can read as either "0" or "1" depending on the switching activity of nearby pins, causing spurious circuit operation. A PIC24 μC with a floating MCLR# input can experience intermittent resets, a problem that is difficult to debug.

STARTUP SCHEMATIC: PC SERIAL COMMUNICATION LINK

In our example programs we use functions that read or send ASCII-encoded strings to a personal computer (PC) using a *serial* interface known as RS232 (more details about this protocol are covered in Chapter 10). The ASCII-encoded strings exchanged between the PIC24 μC and PC are used for status and debugging messages and for data entry. A serial interface transmits data one bit at a time; Chapter 10 discusses the various serial interfaces implemented by the PIC24 μC. The J2 6-pin header represents a USB-to-RS232-serial cable from FTDI (Future Technology Devices International Limited) that is used to connect our PIC24HJ32GP202 μC to the USB (universal serial bus) port of a PC. The TD TTL-232R-3.3 USB-to-TTL-serial cable referenced in Figure 8.3 is convenient in that the cable's TXD (transmit data) and RXD (receive data) pins can be connected directly to the PIC24HJ32GP202 μC without any additional circuitry because these pins use 0 to 3.3 V logic levels (other USB-to-serial cables may require an integrated circuit that converts from RS232 logic levels to CMOS levels; see Chapter 10 for more details). The TXD pin on the TTL-232R-3.3 cable transmits serial data from the PC to the PIC24 μC, while the RXD pin implements communication in the reverse direction from the PIC24 μC to the PC. Our example programs use the RP10/RP11 pins on the PIC24HJ32GP202 μC for the RX/TX functions required by the serial interface. The GND pin (1) on the FDTI TTL-232R-3.3 cable must be connected to the GND of the PIC24HJ32GP202 μC. The 5 V power pin (3) of the FDTI TTL-232R-3.3 cable can be used as an alternative power supply for the LM2937-3.3 voltage regulator, but you must be careful not to exceed the maximum current limit of 500 mA allowed a USB device.

STARTUP SCHEMATIC: IN-CIRCUIT SERIAL PROGRAMMING

The J1 6-pin header and their connections are optional; these are used for in-circuit serial programming of the PIC24HJ32GP202 μC using an external programmer such as the inexpensive PICkit™2 programmer available from Microchip (see Appendix B for more information on using the PICkit™2). The PICkit™2 external programmer applies a clock (PGEC1), a serial data stream (PGED1), and an MCLR# signal when downloading a hex file into program memory. The advantage of in-circuit serial programming is that the PIC24 μC does not have to be removed from the board during programming. Any of the PGEC*n*/PGED*n* input pairs can be used for the ICSP operation.

STARTUP SCHEMATIC: APPLICATION COMPONENTS

The power, reset, serial communication, and in-circuit programming components of the startup schematic will remain unchanged through most of the interfacing examples in the remaining chapters. Each interfacing example will typically add components for the particular application. Our first application program flashes the L1 LED, which is a common method for proclaiming that "I am alive!" when testing a microcontroller system for the first time.

LEDFLASH.C—THE FIRST C PROGRAM FOR PIC24HJ32GP202 STARTUP

The *C* code of Figure 8.4 flashes the L1 LED connected to pin RB15 in Figure 8.3. The statement #include "pic24_all.h" includes a standard header file used in this book's examples; the header file's contents are discussed later in this chapter.

Figure 8.4 is the first *C* code listing for PIC24 μC hardware experiments presented in this book. Because of space considerations, the *C* source code given in figures **is typically not complete**—the figure source code will usually omit *C* functions previously covered or omit include statements for various header files. All of the *C* source code files used in book figures that illustrate PIC24 μC hardware

```
#include "pic24_all.h"  ◄───────  Includes several header files,
                                  discussed later in this chapter.
/**
A simple program that flashes the Power LED.
*/

//a naive software delay function          A subroutine for a software delay.
void a_delay(void){                        Change u16_i, u16_k initial
  uint16 u16_i,u16_k;                       values to change delay.
  // change count values to alter delay
  for (u16_k = 1800; --u16_k;) {
    for(u16_i = 1200 ; --u16_i ;);
  }
}

int main(void) {
  configClock();      //clock configuration
  /********** PIO config **********/
  _ODCB15 = 1;            //enable open drain
  _TRISB15 = 0;           //Config RB15 as output
  _LATB15 = 0;            //RB15 initially low
  while (1) {             //infinite while loop      Infinite loop that blinks
    a_delay();           //call delay function       the LED. Only exit is
    _LATB15 = !_LATB15;  //Toggle LED attached to RB15  through MCLR# reset
  } // end while (1)                                  or power cycle.
}
```

FIGURE 8.4   *C* code for flashing an LED.

features are included on the companion CD-ROM in their complete form; please use these source files when attempting to duplicate the experiments. The book website (*http://www.reesemicro.com*) contains the latest versions of these files.

CLOCK CONFIGURATION

The first statement of main() is a call to the function configClock() that configures the PIC24 clock source. The configClock() function is located in the file *common\ pic24_clockfreq.c* in the source file distribution for this book. The PIC24H family has several methods for clock generation (discussed later in this chapter); the default method used by the examples in this book is the internal oscillator option configured for the maximum clock frequency of 80 MHz (Fosc). From Chapter 3, recall that if Fosc = 80 MHz, then the instruction cycle time Fcy is Fcy = Fosc/2 = 40 MHz. Using the internal oscillator has the advantage of less wiring for the startup schematic since a clock source does not have to be provided; the clock is generated internally by the PIC24HJ32GP202 µC.

FLASHING THE LED

Pin RB15 is a bidirectional, parallel port pin, also referred to as a parallel input/ output (PIO) pin. The term *bidirectional* means that the pin can be configured either as an input or as an output. The RB15 pin must be configured as an output to drive the LED, which is accomplished by the statement _TRISB15=0. Each bit of the special function register TRISB controls the direction of the corresponding PORTB bit. A "1" in a TRISB bit configures the corresponding PORTB pin as an input (as a memory hint, "1" looks like "I" for input), while a "0" configures the PORTB pin as an output ("0" looks like "O" for output). Furthermore, the output drive type is open-drain because we are sharing the L1 LED with the power status as stated earlier, and configuration for open-drain operation is accomplished by the statement _ODCB15=1. Additional details on parallel port I/O are given later in this chapter. The statement _LATB15=0 assigns a zero to the RB15 data latch, thus driving the RB15 pin low and turning off the LED. The statement while(1){} creates an infinite loop, whose loop body first calls a software time delay function named a_delay(), then toggles the value of the RB15 output with the statement _LATB15=!_ LATB15. The software delay function a_delay() is composed of two nested for{} counting loops. The total delay time is dependent upon the number of instructions executed in the nested for{} loops and the clock frequency of the PIC24 µC. The delay can be increased or decreased by changing the initial values of the count variables u16_i, u16_k in the nested for{} loops of the a_delay() function. The delay must be long enough so that the LED can fully turn off or turn on between RB15 pin assignments. If the delay is too short, the LED will appear always on, even though an oscilloscope trace would reveal that RB15 is transitioning between low and high voltages (a square wave output). Software delays are easy to implement, but hardware timers are much better at creating accurate time delays. The timer subsystem of the PIC24 µC and its usage is first discussed in Chapter 9 and covered in more detail in Chapter 12. Observe that the only method of terminating the while(1){} loop in Figure 8.4 is by cycling power or reset via the pushbutton on MCLR#. This infinite loop nature is typical of microcontroller applications because if the loop is exited, there is nowhere to go!

AN IMPROVED LED FLASH PROGRAM

Figure 8.5 shows an alternate version of the LED flash code that uses C macros for improving code clarity and for encapsulating I/O pin assignments.

```
#include "pic24_all.h"

/**
A simple program that
flashes an LED.
*/

#define CONFIG_LED1()   CONFIG_RB15_AS_DIG_OD_OUTPUT()

#define LED1    _LATB15

int main(void) {

  configClock();     //clock configuration
  /********** PIO config **********/
  CONFIG_LED1();     //config PIO for LED1
  LED1 = 0;

  while (1) {
    DELAY_MS(250);   //delay
    LED1 = !LED1;    // Toggle LED
  } // end while (1)
}
```

Defined in device-specific header file in *include\devices* directory in the book source distribution.
Macro **CONFIG_RB15_AS_DIG_OD_OUTPUT()** configures RB15 as an open drain output and contains the statements _TRISB15=0, _ODCB15 = 1

LED1 macro makes changing of LED1 pin assignment easier, also improves code clarity.

DELAY_MS(ms) macro is defined in *common\pic24_delay.c* in the book source distribution, ms is a uint32 value.

FIGURE 8.5   Improved code example for flashing an LED.

The CONFIG_LED1() macro replaces the original statements _TRISB15=0, _ODCB15=1 that configured RB15 as an open-drain output. The reason for this change is to improve code clarity; an external reader can guess from the macro name that this configures an I/O pin used for driving an LED in the program. The CONFIG_LED1() macro definition simply uses another macro named CONFIG_RB15_AS_DIG_OD_OUTPUT() that contains the statements _TRISB15=0, _ODCB15=1 and whose macro definition is contained in the *include\devices\PIC24HJ32GP202_ports.h* book source file. Again, the purpose of these macros is for improved readability; remembering that _TRISB15=0 configures the RB15 pin as an output and not as an input can be difficult to remember. However, the macro name CONFIG_RB15_AS_DIG_OD_OUTPUT() is more helpful as to what this macro accomplishes (the "DIG" is shorthand for *digital*, the "OD" for open-drain).

All uses of _LATB15 in the code of Figure 8.4 are now replaced by LED1, which is a macro defined as _LATB15. This improves code clarity as now it is clear when the LED is affected by the code, instead of having to remember that RB15 drives the LED. Furthermore, if one wishes to move the LED to a different pin, only the LED1 and CONFIG_LED1 macros have to be changed. This is the greatest benefit of using macros to isolate pin assignments as it is a common desire to want to reuse sample interfacing code with different pin assignments.

Finally, the a_delay() software delay function call is replaced by DELAY_MS(250) where the macro DELAY_MS(ms) implements a delay of approximately ms milliseconds. The DELAY_MS macro is defined in the *common\pic24_delay.c* file in the book source distribution, and is shown below:

```
#define DELAY_MS(ms) \
    delayAndUpdateHeartbeatCount(CYCLES_PER_MS * ((uint32) ms));
```

The delayAndUpdateHeartbeatCount(uint32 u32_cyc) function called by DELAY_MS is also defined in the *common\pic24_delay.c* file as:

```
inline static void delayAndUpdateHeartbeatCount(uint32 u32_cyc) {
    __delay32(u32_cyc);
    u32_heartbeatCount += (u32_cyc >> 4);
}
```

It delays u32_cyc instruction cycles by calling the __delay32(uint32 u32_cyc) function provided by the PIC24 compiler support library. The u32_cyc variable passed to delayAndUpdateHeartbeatCount is the number of instruction cycles that execute in ms milliseconds. The CYCLES_PER_MS macro is the number of instructions cycles that execute in one millisecond and is defined in *include\pic24_delay.h* as:

```
#define CYCLES_PER_MS ((uint32)(FCY * 0.001))
```

The FCY macro is set to the instruction cycle frequency. When using the default clock configuration discussed later in this chapter (see "Clock Generation"), its value is defined in *include\pic24_clock.h* to be 40000000L (40 MHz). Note the trailing L makes the number a long (equivalent to a uint32), causing the compiler to allocate a 32-bit value in which to store the number. For example, with FCY = 40 MHz, 1 ms = 40,000 instruction cycles. The u32_heartbeatCount variable updated in the delayAndUpdateHeartbeatCount() function is discussed in the next section. The *common\pic24_delay.h* file also includes a DELAY_US(us) macro that delays us number of microseconds. Both the DELAY_MS() and DELAY_US() macros should only be used for approximate timing; the hardware timers covered in Chapter 12 provide more accurate timing.

ECHO.C—Testing the Serial Link

The subsystem of the PIC24 µC that performs serial communication over the RX/TX pins shown in the startup schematic of Figure 8.3 is called the UART (universal asynchronous receiver transmitter). The UART subsystem is covered in detail in Chapter 10; this section discusses from a user-level perspective some of the functions for receiving/transmitting ASCII data over the serial link. The internals of these functions are discussed in Chapter 10. The *C* code of Figure 8.6 tests the serial link by printing some status messages, then enters an infinite `while(1){}` loop that waits for a single character to be received from the serial link using the `inChar()` function. The received character is placed in the `u8_c` variable, incremented, then written back to the serial link using the `outChar()` function. This means a received character of "S" is echoed as "T," a "1" as "2," a "d" as "e," etc. The received character is incremented to verify that the PIC24 µC is actually reading and then transmitting the character; if the character were transmitted back without modification then a short circuit between the RX and TX lines could mimic this behavior. Both the `inChar()` and `outChar()` functions are defined in *common\pic24_serial.c* file.

```
#include "pic24_all.h"
/**
"Echo" program which waits for UART RX character and echos it back +1.
Use the echo program to test your UART connection.
*/

int main(void) {
  uint8 u8_c;

  configClock();
  configHeartbeat();
  configDefaultUART(DEFAULT_BAUDRATE);
  printResetCause();
  outString(HELLO_MSG);

  /** Echo code ********/
  // Echo character + 1
  while (1) {
    u8_c = inChar();    //get character
    u8_c++;             //increment the character
    outChar(u8_c);      //echo the character
  } // end while (1)
}
```

`configHeartbeat(void)` function defined in *common\pic24_util.c*. Configures heartbeat LED by default on RB15.

`configDefaultUART(uint32 u32_baudRate)` function defined in *common\pic24_serial.c*. This initializes the UART1 module for our reference system.

`printResetCause(void)` function defined in *common\pic24_util.c*. Prints info string about reset source.

`outString(char* psz_s)` function defined in *common\pic24_uart1.c*. Sends string to UART. `HELLO_MSG` macro default is file name, build date.

FIGURE 8.6 *echo.c* Program for testing the serial link.

The code of Figure 8.6 has some new functions that are executed before the `while(1){}` loop is reached. These functions are:

- **configHeartbeat(void):** When debugging a μC system, a basic question that often arises is "How do I know if the μC is alive and executing code?" In our example programs, we reserve the RB15 pin for a *heartbeat* that is used to blink an attached LED. In any of our functions that perform a potentially long wait, such as inChar() that waits for arrival of a character over the serial link, our code will pulse the LED attached to the RB15 pin to indicate that the μC is alive. The heartbeat update is performed by an associated function called doHeartbeat() that is called from a user function to increment a uint32 global variable named u32_heartbeatCount. Once the u32_heartbeatCount variable reaches a maximum value set within configHeartBeat(), the heartbeat LED is toggled and the u32_heartbeatCount is reset back to 0. The heartbeat functions are found in *common\pic24_util.c*. It should be noted that the heartbeat LED functions as a debugging tool and would not be typically included in a production design.
- **configDefaultUART(uint32 u32_baudRate):** This function configures the UART subsystem to transmit serial data at the rate specified by the u32_baudRate parameter. There are a range of standard data rates for this type of serial link; these are defined in Chapter 10. The data rate defined by the DEFAULT_BAUDRATE macro is 57,600, which means that bits are sent at roughly 57,600 bits per second. This function is defined in *common\pic24_serial.c*.
- **printResetCause():** The function prints an information string about the cause of the last processor reset. A section later in this chapter discusses the various sources of CPU reset. The function also identifies the target processor, its revision number, and the clock option currently being used. This function is defined in *common\pic24_util.c*.
- **outString(const char* psz_s):** This function transmits each character of null-terminated string over the serial link. The function assumes an ASCII-encoded string is being transmitted, and inserts a carriage return character ("\r" or 0x0D) whenever a new line character ("\n" or 0x0A) is transmitted. The HELLO_MSG is a macro defined in *common\pic24_uart.h* with a default value of the file name and build date of the program being compiled (in this case, *echo.c*).

To test the serial link, a *terminal* program is run on the PC to display the received characters from the PIC24 μC and to transmit keyboard input back. One example of a terminal program is *RealTerm*, which is full-featured and available from *http://realterm.sourceforge.net*. Other commonly used programs are *PuTTY*, *Hyperterminal* (no longer distributed with Windows beginning with the Vista release), and *Tera Term*. The only consideration for using a serial program with the code examples on this book's CD-ROM is that our console output functions use a single "\n" (new line) character to mark end-of-lines, and some programs, such as PuTTY, expect a "\n\r" (new line, carriage return) sequence. The behavior of our console output functions can be changed, but this requires editing a header file (see the code documentation included on the book's CD-ROM). RealTerm, Hyperterminal, and Tera Term can be configured for different types of line endings. We have used a variety of terminal programs for the console screenshots contained in this book.

Figure 8.7 shows the steps necessary for configuring RealTerm for serial communication under the Windows operating system. The first step chooses the display mode, with Figure 8.7a selecting the ANSI text mode and a "\n" (new line) character as the end-of-line marker. The second step (Figure 8.7b) chooses the serial port parameters, such as the COM*x* port used for communication, speed, and data format. COM ports are assigned numbers 1 and higher, so valid COM port names are COM1, COM2, COM3, etc. The *Device Manager* found within "System and Maintenance" in the Control Panel under Windows can be used to identify COM ports assigned to connected USB serial port devices as shown in Figure 8.7c. The serial port parameters used by the example programs with this book are a baud rate of 57600, 8 data bits, 1 stop bit, no parity, and no hardware flow control. Serial communication is discussed in more detail in Chapter 10.

(a) RealTerm Display configuration

Newline (\n) mode needed because our console output functions use a "\n" character as the end-of-line marker.

(c) Device manager under Windows

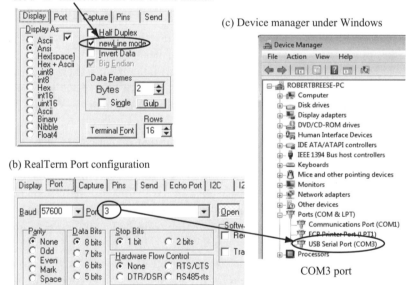

(b) RealTerm Port configuration

COM3 port

57600 baud, no parity, 8 data bits, 1 stop bit, no hardware flow control are the settings compatible with the default parameters used by this book's examples.

FIGURE 8.7   RealTerm configuration.

Figure 8.8 shows the *echo.c* program output in the RealTerm console window. The `printResetCause()` function (a) identifies the reset cause as "Power-on" when power is applied, and then as "MCLR assertion" when the reset button is pushed at (d). The displayed characters echoed in (c) and (e) are 1+ the ASCII values of the characters typed from the keyboard.

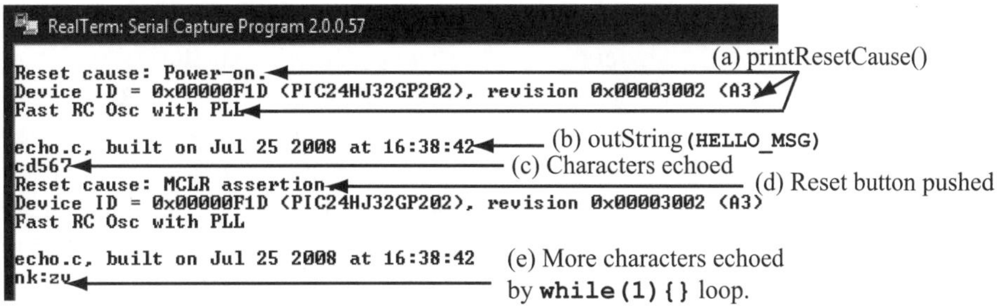

FIGURE 8.8   Output from *echo.c*.

ASM_ECHO.S—IMPLEMENTING ECHO IN ASSEMBLY

The assembly language skills learned in previous chapters can also be used to write assembly-language programs that make use of the *C* functions previously discussed, as shown in Figure 8.9. This assembly code implements the *echo.c* code of Figure 8.6. This code calls a new *C* function named configBasic(const char* sz_helloMsg), defined in *common\pic24_util.c*, that combines the individual configuration calls used in *echo.c* such as *configClock()*, *configHeartbeat()*, etc., into one convenient function whose sz_helloMsg parameter is a message printed to the console after configuration is complete. Note that all *C* functions have an appended underscore when referenced from assembly, so the *C* function configBasic becomes _configBasic in the assembly code, inChar becomes _inChar, and outChar becomes _outChar.

```
.include "p24Hxxxx.inc"        ; Include processor-specific headers
.global _main                  ; Make _main visible outside
                               ; this file so C startup code
                               ; can call it

; Place following statements in PSV space
        .section psv psv
HELLO_MSG: .asciz "asm_echo.s ready!\n"  ;null-terminated ASCII string

.text                          ;Start of Code section
_main:                         ; _main called after C startup code runs
        mov #HELLO_MSG,W0      ; Equivalent to
        call _configBasic      ;   configBasic(HELLO_MSG) in C

while1:                        ; while (1) {
        call _inChar           ;   W0 = inChar();
        inc W0, W0             ;   W0 = W0 + 1;
        call _outChar          ;   outChar(W0);
        goto    while1         ; }

.end        ;End of program code in this file
```

FIGURE 8.9   *asm_echo.s* Assembly-language program for testing the serial link.

As in earlier assembly-language programs, the first line begins by including processor-specific headers given in `p24Hxxxx.inc`. Next, the `.global _main` statement makes the _main label visible outside this file, so that the C start-up routines can call it after initializing C variables. To define a string, the `.section psv psv` directive instructs the assembler to place following statements in the Program Space Visibility region where C stores and accesses constants. The `.asciz` directive then places the "`asm_echo.s ready!\n`" string in the PSV area. After switching to the code section with a `.text` directive, the `mov #HELLO_MSG,W0` statement places the address of the hello message in `W0`, the first parameter expected by the `configBasic` function. The statement `call _configBasic` calls this function, which performs basic chip configuration as previously discussed. Next, the `inChar()` C function is called, which reads a character from the serial port and returns it in `W0`. The returned character is then incremented and sent back over the serial port by a call to `outChar`. Finally, a `goto while1` statement loops back to the `inChar()` function call to repeat the process.

DATASHEET READING—A CRITICAL SKILL

You will see the phrase "Topic *x* is discussed in more detail in the PIC24 datasheet [ref. *N*]" several times in this book. It is impractical for this book to replicate all PIC24 datasheet information, as the device-specific datasheet combined with the PIC24 family reference manual (FRM) is over 1,000 pages in length! As such, you must become comfortable with reading PIC24 datasheets, and the datasheets of other devices referenced in this book to gain full understanding of the interfacing examples. For a microcontroller, the component datasheet such as [31] contains information specific to the features of that particular processor, but may only contain summaries if this information is common to many members of a microprocessor family. Expanded descriptions of features common to all microprocessor family members, such as the instruction set [8] or hardware subsystems [9-30], are contained in reference manuals for that family. Application notes are more varied in form—some discuss how to best use the microcontroller for a particular application, while others may give several examples of how to use a particular subsystem.

The information detail in a component datasheet may initially seem overwhelming, but this can be countered by knowing how typical datasheets are organized and where to look for certain types of information. A typical component datasheet is organized as follows:

- **Initial summary and pinouts:** The first section contains a device functional summary, which includes pin diagrams and individual pin descriptions.
- **Functional description:** Individual sections discuss the functional details of the device operation. In the PIC24HJ32GP202 component datasheet, these

sections correspond to the subsystems of the PIC24H μC such as the timers, the analog-to-digital converter, etc. However, the component datasheet only contains a summary of the subsystem's operation; a full description of the sub-system's functionality is found in the appropriate chapter of the PIC24H family reference manual [9-30]. In the FRM, step-by-step instructions for subsystem configuration and usage are provided, with a detailed explanation of the special function registers used by the subsystem and the individual bit definitions of these SFRs.

■ **Electrical characteristics:** Electrical characteristics are only found in a component datasheet and are divided into DC specifications (operating voltage, power consumption, output port drive capability, etc.) and AC specifications (timing characteristics such as propagation delay, maximum clock frequency, etc.). This section contains tables of values with minimum, typical, and maximum values; the typical values are used in this book when-ever timing information is given. The electrical characteristics section always contains a table labeled as *Absolute Maximum Ratings,* which are the maxi-mum voltage/current values that can be experienced without damaging the device. These are not the typical operating voltage/current ratings of the device. For example, for the PIC24HJGP202 the maximum voltage rating of the VDD pin is −0.3 V to +4.0 V. However, the actual operating range for the VDD pin is 3.0 V to 3.6 V.

Datasheets, reference manuals, and application notes assume a general fa-miliarity and previous background with similar components on the part of the reader. Books such as this one are useful for readers who are new to these devices, or for experienced readers who are looking for a single source that combines and summarizes information from datasheets, application notes, and reference manu-als. The ability to read a datasheet is a critical skill for any practicing engineer, engineering student, or hobbyist, and skills are obtained only through practice. So, please take the time to peruse the PIC24 datasheets and the datasheets of other devices used in the hardware examples when working through the remain-ing chapters.

CONFIGURATION BITS

Configuration bits [25] are located in device configuration registers that are mapped to locations in program memory. This means that configuration bits are nonvolatile, allowing them to retain configuration information when power is removed. Configuration bits are read on power-on and specify aspects of processor behavior such as oscillator configuration, watchdog timer behavior, power-on reset timer value, etc. The device configuration registers for the PIC24H family are:

- **FBS, FGS:** These registers specify different protection and security modes for program memory and are not discussed in this book; see [25] for more details.
- **FOSCSEL, FOSC:** These registers specify oscillator configuration and are discussed later in this section.
- **FWDT:** This register controls watchdog timer (WDT) configuration and is discussed later in this section.
- **FPOR:** This register controls power-on reset behavior and is discussed later in this section.
- **FICD:** This register contains the debugger configuration word, which instructs the chip to start normally on a reset or to enter a debug mode.

The configuration bit settings for all of the book's example projects are located in *common\pic24_configbits.c*. Configuration bit settings can be specified using macros that are defined within each device specific header file, such as *Program Files\Microchip\ MPLABC30\support\PIC24H\h\p24HJ32GP202.h*. For example, the following *C* statement:

```
_FPOR(FPWRT_PWR16 & ALTI2C_OFF);
```

contained in *common\pic24_configbits.c* specifies the configuration bit settings for the FPOR configuration register. The `FPWRT_PWR16` value is a bit mask macro for the 3-bit field that controls the *power-on reset timer* (PWRT) value; this macro sets the value of the power-on reset timer to 16 ms (PWRT is discussed later in this chapter). The `ALTI2C_OFF` is a bit mask macro for the 1-bit field that specifies which pins, SDA1/SCL1 or ASDA1/ASCL1, that the I²C serial interface is mapped to (Chapter 10 discusses the I²C serial interface). The `ALTI2C_OFF` macro causes the I²C serial interface to be mapped to the SDA1/SCL1 pins. Multiple macros for the same device configuration register can be combined using the & operator as shown. When puzzled about a configuration bit setting, first locate the configuration bit description within [25], then find the appropriate macro within the PIC24 compiler device specific header file. A complete list of the configuration bits and their functions is found within [25]. The PIC24F family has many of the same configuration bit capabilities as the PIC24H family, but the configuration register names and bit locations differ.

CLOCK GENERATION

Figure 8.10 shows the various clocking options [7] available for the PIC24H family. The (a) internal fast RC oscillator (FRC) shown in the figure has a base frequency of 7.37 MHz that can be tuned by a 6-bit two's complement value in ±0.375%

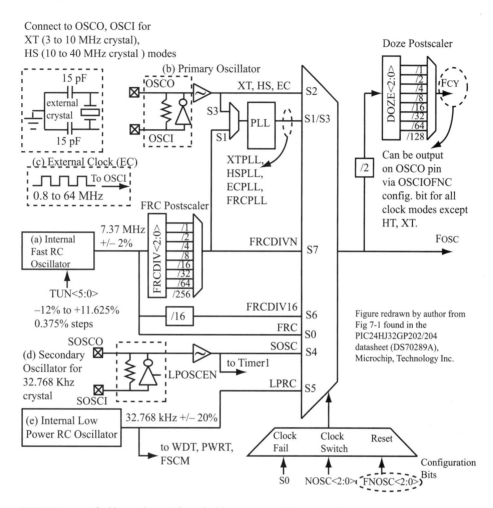

FIGURE 8.10   Clocking options. (Adapted with permission of the copyright owner, Microchip Technology, Incorporated. All rights reserved. No further reprints or reproduction may be made without Microchip Inc.'s prior written consent.)

steps, providing an adjustment that ranges from −12% to +11.625% about the base frequency. The tuning capability is provided because the accuracy of the FRC oscillator base frequency can vary by ±2.0% because of integrated circuit fabrication, voltage, and temperature variations. The tuning capability can be used to achieve a more accurate oscillator frequency, with calibration guided by an external reference clock of high accuracy. The FRC options FRCDIV16, FRCPLL, FRCDIVN, and FRC shown in the diagram correspond to configuration bit settings within the FOSCSEL device configuration register. The FRC *postscaler* can be used to divide the FRC frequency by the values shown in Figure 8.10. Conversely, the PLL (phased lock loop) block can be used to increase the FRC frequency to a maximum value of 80 MHz. The FRC oscillator starts operation immediately on power-up; the PLL requires a nominal time of 20 μs to stabilize after power-up.

The primary oscillator (b) option uses an external crystal to provide an accurate clock source. The crystal must be connected between the OSC1 and OSC2 pins along with the two capacitors as shown; an internal amplifier within the PIC24 μC causes the crystal to begin oscillating after power-up. A typical value for the capacitors is 15 pF, but this can vary with crystal type and μC packaging (see the application note in reference [43] for more information on capacitor selection). The waveform produced by the crystal oscillator is a sinusoidal signal; this is converted to a square-wave clock signal within the PIC24 μC. The advantage of the primary oscillator over the FRC is frequency accuracy. However, in order to give time for the crystal to stabilize, the oscillator clock is not released to the rest of the system until 1024 C_{OSC} clock periods have passed, where C_{OSC} is the crystal frequency. The XT and HS modes alter the driving current supplied by the crystal amplifier, with recommended crystal frequencies for the two modes as shown (reference [43] gives more information on selecting the driving mode for a particular crystal). An (c) external clock (EC) can be connected to the OSCI pin instead of a crystal.

The secondary oscillator (d) option is intended for an external 32.768 kHz watch crystal and can be used as a system clock or for real-time clock applications in conjunction with the Timer1 subsystem (see Chapter 12). The (e) internal low-power RC (LPRC) oscillator generates a 32.768 kHz clock with ±20% accuracy that can be used as a system clock for low power operation; it also provides the clock source for the watchdog timer (WDT), power-on reset timer (PWRT), and the fail-safe clock monitor (FSCM). When enabled, the fail-safe clock monitor will automatically switch to the FRC oscillator if a system clock failure is detected. The watchdog timer and power-on reset timer are discussed later in this chapter. The FNOSC<2:0> bits in Figure 8.10 are configuration bits in the FOSCSEL device configuration register and determine the clock source at reset. The NOSC<2:0> bits allows dynamic switching to a new clock source once operation has begun. The doze postscaler can be used to lower the clock frequency to the CPU for the purpose of reducing power consumption as discussed further later in this chapter.

A *phase lock loop* (PLL) is an analog circuit which produces an output clock that is a multiple of its input clock. Figure 8.11a shows the PIC24H PLL block diagram. The input clock FIN can come from an external crystal, an external clock, or the internal FRC. The PLL prescaler (PLLPRE) divides FIN to form FREF, with the constraint of 0.8 < FREF < 8.0 MHz. The voltage controlled oscillator (VCO) multiplies FREF to form FVCO, with a constraint of 100 < FVCO < 200 MHz. The VCO feedback path to the phase frequency detector (PFD) divides FVCO by PLLDIV; the purpose of this feedback is to insure that FVCO remains in phase (edges are aligned) with FREF. The PLL postscaler (PLLPOST) divides FVCO to form FOSC, which has a maximum frequency of 80 MHz.

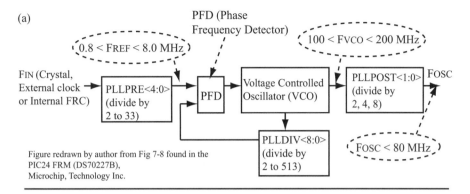

FIGURE 8.11   PLL block diagram and equation. (Adapted with permission of the copyright owner, Microchip Technology, Incorporated. All rights reserved. No further reprints or reproduction may be made without Microchip Inc.'s prior written consent.)

Figure 8.11b shows the equation used to calculate F_{OSC} from F_{IN} given PLLDIV, PLLPRE, and PLLPOST. The sample calculation 8.11b1 shows an 80 MHz F_{OSC} created from the internal FRC clock; there will be some variation in the final F_{OSC} because of the variation in the FRC clock. The clock generation method shown in 8.11b1 is the method used to test this book's sample code using the FRC oscillator and $F_{OSC} = 80$ MHz. Sample calculation 8.11b2 shows an 80 MHz F_{OSC} created from an 8.0 MHz external crystal; these are useful values for creating a F_{OSC} whose frequency is 10 times an external crystal.

Figure 8.12 shows the OSCCON register definition, which controls clock source selection after reset. The CSOC<2:0> bits reflect the current clock source, while the NOSC<2:0> bits along with the OSCWEN bit are used to change the clock source during normal operation. The OSCCON register is an example of a special function register that is tied to a hardware subsystem. Such registers can be classified as either data or status/control registers. If a special function register is used for status or control, then it is usually divided into several bit fields as exemplified by the OSCCON register. This book will sometimes provide a detailed register definition as given in Figure 8.12, and sometimes will only refer to the named status/control bits associated with a hardware subsystem and not show the full SFR definition.

OSCCON = OSCCON<15:8> : OSCCON<7:0> = OSCCONH : OSCCONL

U-0	R-y	R-y	R-y	U-0	R/W-y	R/W-y	R/W-y
UI	COSC<2:0>			UI	NOSC<2:0>		
15	14-12			11	10-8		

R/S-0	R/W-0	R-0	U-0	R/C-0	U-0	R/W-0	R/W-0
CLKLOCK	IOLOCK	LOCK	UI	CF	UI	LPOSCEN	OSWEN
7	6	5	4	3	2	1	0

Bit 14-12: COSC<2:0> Current Oscillator Selection bits (see NOSC)
Bit 10-8: NOSC<2:0> New Oscillator Selection bits
  000 = Fast RC Oscillator (FRC)
  001 = Fast RC Oscillator with PLL (FRCPLL)
  010 = Primary Oscillator (XT, HS, EC)
  011 = Primary Oscillator with PLL (XTPLL, HSPLL, ECPLL)
  100 = Secondary Oscillator (SOSC)
  101 = Low-Power RC Oscillator (LPRC)
  110 = Fast RC Oscillator with Divide-by-16 (FRCDIV16)
  111 = Fast RC Oscillator with Divide-by-N (FRCDIVN)
Bit 7:   CLKLOCK: Clock Lock Enable bit
  If clock switching is enabled and FSCM is disabled
  1 = Clock switching is disabled; 0 = clock switching is enabled
Bit 6:   IOLOCK: Peripheral Pin Select Lock Bit
  1 = Peripheral Pin Select is locked. Writes to Peripheral Pin Select Registers are not allowed.
  0 = Peripheral Pin Select is not locked. Writes to Peripheral Pin Select Registers are allowed.
Bit 5:   LOCK: PLL Lock Status bit (read-only)
  1 = PLL is in lock, or PLL start-up timer is satisfied
  0 = PLL is out of lock, start-up timer is in progress, or PLL is disabled.
Bit 3:   CF: Clock Fail Detect bit (read/clear by application)
  1 = FCSM has detected clock failure; 0 = FCSM has not detected clock failure
Bit 1:   LPOSCEN: Secondary (SOCS) Oscillator Enable bit
  1 = Enable Secondary Oscillator; 0 = Disable Secondary Oscillator
Bit 0:   OSWEN: Oscillator Switch Enable bit
  1 = Request oscillator switch to selection specified by NOSC<2:0> bits
  0 = Oscillator switch is complete

Legend:
R = Readable bit
-n = Value at POR
U = Unimplemented bit,
  read as "0"
W = Writeable bit
"1" = bit is set
"0" = bit is cleared
y = Depends on
  FOSCEL<FNOSC> bits
C = Clearable only bit
S = Settable only bit
x = Bit is unknown

Figure redrawn by author from Fig 7-8 found in the
PIC24 FRM (DS70227B), Microchip, Technology Inc.

FIGURE 8.12 OSCCON register. (Adapted with permission of the copyright owner, Microchip Technology, Incorporated. All rights reserved. No further reprints or reproduction may be made without Microchip Inc.'s prior written consent.)

Setting Clock Options Using C

A systematic method for performing clock selection is used in the support library for this book's code examples, with clock selection done in three steps: (1) configuration bit settings (compile time), (2) clock selection code generation (compile time), and (3) runtime clock switching. Figure 8.13 shows the first step in the process, the clock selection configuration bits in *common\pic24_configbits.c* that

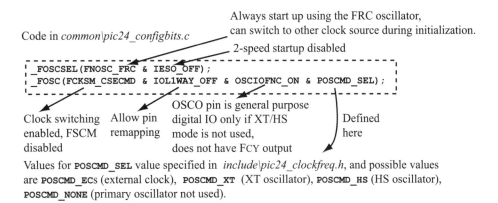

FIGURE 8.13   Configuration bits for clock selection.

are used for a PIC24HJ32GP202 μC target. Conditional compilation is used in *common\pic24_configbits.c* for different family members as configuration bits can vary by both family and μC choice. Our approach for clock selection configuration bits is to always use the FRC oscillator for power-on reset, then use a runtime function that switches to the desired clock source, designated as *OPCLK* (operating clock). In Figure 8.13, the FNOSC_FRC bit mask sets the FOSCSEL configuration bits to choose the FRC oscillator at power-on reset. The IESO_OFF bit mask disables two-speed startup, which is an option that uses the FRC oscillator for startup, then automatically switches to the clock source specified by the FOSCSEL configuration bits when that source is ready. A common use of two-speed startup is to start with the FRC, then switch to one of the external crystal sources when it is ready. We disable this option since we use the FRC oscillator at startup and then call a runtime function to switch clock sources. The POSCMD_SEL bit mask is determined as a part of the CLOCK_CONFIG selection discussed in the following paragraph; this affects the OSCO, OSCI pin functions of Figure 8.10. Either POSCMD_XT or POSCMD_HS is selected if an external crystal is being used as these enable the crystal amplifier. Choice POSCMD_EC is used if an external clock source is provided on pin OSCI, and POSCMD_NONE selected if none of these clocking options are being used. The OSCIOFNC_ON bit mask allows the OSCO pin to be used as a general purpose pin if the XT or HS modes are not selected, while the OSCIOFNC_OFF bit mask outputs the Fcy clock on this pin. The IOL1WAY_OFF mask does not affect the clock system and is covered in Chapter 9 when reconfigurable pins are discussed.

Figure 8.14 shows the second step, in which compile-time selection of the OPCLK is made. The file *include\pic24_clockfreq.h* contains a table of clock choices, which can be extended by the user. Each table entry contains a name, unique index, oscillator selection, Fcy frequency, primary oscillator frequency and type (if applicable), target family compatibility (used for error checking and can be either

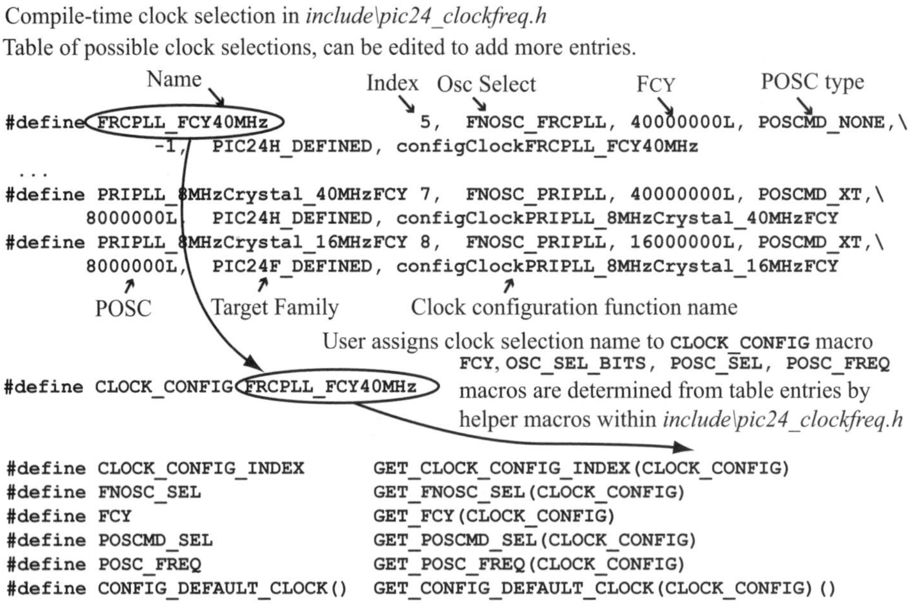

Compile-time clock selection in *include\pic24_clockfreq.h*
Table of possible clock selections, can be edited to add more entries.

FIGURE 8.14 Compile-time clock selection in *C*.

PIC24H, or PIC24F, or both), and the name of a function to perform clock configuration. The table is currently populated by a few clock choices used during the testing of this book's examples. The user assigns one of these names to the CLOCK_CONFIG macro (this can be done in the MPLAB project file without editing the *pic24_clockfreq.h* file; see Appendix B). The oscillator selection entry uses macros defined in the standard PIC24 compiler header files that correspond to the FNOSC<2:0> bit fields of the FOSCSEL configuration register. Valid entries for oscillator selection are listed in the *pic24_clockfreq.h* file. Helper macros within *pic24_clockfreq.h* automatically generate macro assignments to the resulting processor clock frequency FCY, oscillator selection bits OSC_SEL_BITS for use with the COSC<2:0>/NOSC<2:0> bit field of the OSCCON register (Figure 8.12), primary oscillator type POSCMD_SEL, and primary oscillator frequency POSC_FREQ based on the table entries of the clock source indicated by CLOCK_CONFIG.

Figure 8.15 shows the runtime functions contained in the *common\pic24_clockfreq.c* file that selects the OPCLK during main() initialization. For each possible clock choice in the table of *include\pic24_clockfreq.h,* a conditional code section is included that has the following form:

```
#if IS_CLOCK_CONFIG(clock_selection_name)
#warning Clock configured for clock_selection_description
#endif
```

```
#if GET_IS_SUPPORTED(clock_selection_name)
void configClockXxx(void){
...code that dynamically configures and enables clock_selection_name...
}
#endif
```

Runtime clock selection after initial boot using the FRC
(code in *common\pic24_clockfreq.c*) ——— Used to write OSCCON to switch clock source

```
void switchClock(uint8 u8_source) {
   ...definition of OSCCON_copy...                    Temporarily disable interrupts
   asm("DISI #0x3FFF");                               Copy OSCCON bits
   OSCCON_copy.bits = OSCCONbits;                     to a temp. location
   OSCCON_copy.bits.NOSC = u8_source;                 Specify new clock source
   OSCCON_copy.bits.OSWEN = 1;                        Request clock switch
   __builtin_write_OSCCONH(OSCCON_copy.byte[1]); }    Write new values to OSCCON
   __builtin_write_OSCCONL(OSCCON_copy.byte[0]); }    using unlock sequences
   asm("DISI #0");                                    Re-enable interrupts after OSCCON write
   while (_OSCWEN == 1);                              Wait for oscillator switch to complete
   if ( (u8_source == GET_OSC_SEL_BITS(FNOSC_FRCPLL)) ||
        (u8_source == GET_OSC_SEL_BITS(FNOSC_PRIPLL)) )
      while (_LOCK == 0);                             If PLL used, then wait until it is stable
```

Helper macro that includes code for compilation if
this processor supports this clock

```
#if GET_IS_SUPPORTED(FRCPLL_FCY40MHz)
void configClockFRCPLL_FCY40MHz(void) {
  switchClock(GET_OSC_SEL_BITS(FNOSC_FRC));           Turn PLL off before changing.
  _TUN = -19; _PLLPRE = 6; _PLLDIV = 185; _PLLPOST = 0;
  switchClock(OSC_SEL_BITS);                          Matches PLL values
}                Call switchClock to select new clock source     from  Figure 8.11(b1)
#endif
```

```
#if GET_IS_SUPPORTED(PRIPLL_8MHzCrystal_40MHzFCY)
#warning Clock configured for PRIPLL using 8.0 Mhz primary osc., FCY = 40 MHz
void configClockPRIPLL_8MHzCrystal_40MHzFCY(void) {
   switchClock(GET_OSC_SEL_BITS(FNOSC_FRC));          Turn PLL off before changing.
   _PLLPRE = 0;   _PLLDIV = 38; _PLLPOST = 0;         Matches PLL values from
   switchClock(OSC_SEL_BITS);                         Figure 8.11(b2)
}                Call switchClock to select new clock source
#endif
```

● ⎫ Other **configClockXxx()** functions not shown, one for each table entry in
● ⎬ *include\pic24_clockfreq.h*
● ⎭

FIGURE 8.15   Runtime clock selection in *C.*

The IS_CLOCK_CONFIG(*clock_selection_name*) is a helper macro that when combined with a #if conditionally includes its following code block if *clock_selection_name*
matches the CLOCK_CONFIG macro value, providing a message during compilation
indicating the type of clock configuration chosen through a compiler warning
message. The GET_IS_SUPPORTED(*clock_selection_name*) returns true if this
clock configuration function is supported by the processor for which the code is

compiled. Used with a `#if`, this prevents clock configuration code which relies on PIC24F-specific features from producing compilation errors on a PIC24H and vice versa. The `configClockXxx()` function (where `Xxx` gives a descriptive name matching the clock configuration accomplished by the function) then performs run-time clock configuration and selection. It is called by the `configClock()` function:

```
static inline void configClock()
{
    CONFIG_DEFAULT_CLOCK();
}
```

where `CONFIG_DEFAULT_CLOCK()` evaluates to `configClockXxx()`.

The `configClock(void)` function is called by `main()` to select the operating clock as seen previously in Figures 8.5 and 8.6. The implementation of the `configClock()` function that selects and enables *clock_selection_name* varies by the clock source. The code shown for the `FRCPLL_FCY40MHZ` choice in Figure 8.15 is the default selection for our reference PIC24FH32GP202 system. The `configClock()` function sets the `_TUN`, `_PLLPRE`, `_PLLDIV`, and `_PLLPOST` bit fields of the PLL to match the values shown in Figure 8.11b1, then executes `switchClock(OSC_SEL_BITS)` to perform the switch to the FRCPLL clock source. Recall that the `OSC_SEL_BITS` macro is automatically assigned based on the oscillator selection table entry and its value matches one of the COSC<2:0>/NOSC<2:0> bit field selections from Figure 8.12, which in this case is FRCPLL (`OSC_SEL_BITS = 1`). Before the PLL bits are modified, the function call `switchClock(GET_OSC_SEL_BITS(FNOSC_FRC))` switches the clock to the FRC with the PLL disabled as a conservative safety measure since the PLL cannot be modified while it is running and we have no guarantee that the PLL is inactive before the `configClock()` function call is made (some custom *C* runtime code or bootloader code that changes the clock source could execute before `configClock()` is called).

Within `switchClock()`, the OSCCON upper and lower 8-bit register portions are modified using the `__builtin_write_OSCCONH`, `__builtin_write_OSCCONL` functions supplied by the PIC24 compiler. Because the OSCCON register contents are critical in terms of correct functioning of the processor, an OSCCONH or OSCCONL register write requires an unlock sequence before it can be modified. The unlock sequence writes two 8-bit fixed values first (see [32]), followed by the actual register value. The unlock sequence reduces the possibility that a code error will make a spurious change to OSCCON. The `__builtin_write_OSCCONH`, `__builtin_write_OSCCONL` functions implement the required unlock sequence; there are several other `__builtin` functions provided by the PIC24 compiler [32]. The `__builtin_write_OSCCONH` changes the NOSC<2:0> bits to the value specified in `u8_source`. The `__builtin_write_OSCCONL` requests a clock change by setting the least significant bit, which is OSCWEN. The "`while (_OSCWEN==1);`" statement loops until the OSCWEN bit is cleared by the clock subsystem, indicating that the clock switch is complete. If the PLL is being used, then the statement `while (_LOCK == 0)` waits until it has stabilized to its new frequency as recommended by the FRM [15]. The write of the OSCCON register is bracketed by the statements `asm("DISI #0x3FFF")` (disable *interrupts*) and `asm("DISI #0")` (re-enable *interrupts*). Interrupts are not discussed until Chapter 9, so at this point we will simply say this is required for ensuring that the instructions that perform the writing of the OSCCON register execute in the shortest time possible. The `asm()` statement is called *inline assembly*, and is used for inserting PIC24 instructions directly in *C* code as a way of accessing processor features not supported in *C*. The `asm()` statement capability is used again later in this chapter when accessing the power saving modes of the PIC24 μC.

The `PRIPLL_8MHzCrystal_40MHzFCY` table entry of Figure 8.15 corresponds to the oscillator section of primary oscillator with PLL, assuming an external 8 MHz crystal and the PLL configuration of Figure 8.11b2 that generates an FCY of 40 MHz. To use this option, the user must set the `CLOCK_CONFIG` macro equal to `PRIPLL_8MHzCrystal_40MHzFCY`. The `configClockPRIPLL_8MHzCrystal_40MHzFCY()` function for the `PRIPLL_8MHzCrystal_40MHzFCY` selection is shown in Figure 8.15, and is similar in form to what has been previously discussed. Clock options in the *pic24_clockfreq.h* file that have been used for PIC24F family members include `PRIPLL_8MHzCrystal_16MHzFCY` (primary oscillator with PLL, crystal frequency of 8 MHz, FCY = 16 MHz) and `FRCPLL_FCY16MHz` (FRC with PLL, FCY = 16 MHz). The maximum FCY clock speed of PIC24F μCs is 16 MHz; additional differences between PIC24H and PIC24F family members are provided at the end of this chapter.

POWER-ON RESET BEHAVIOR AND RESET SOURCES

We have already discussed three causes of processor reset [8], namely the `reset` instruction, power-on reset (POR), and a low-true assertion of the MCLR# input. Figure 8.16 shows the complete set of processor reset sources. *Brown-out reset* (BOR) occurs when the input VDD drops below the level required for maintaining an operating core voltage. Both BOR and POR trigger operation of the power-on reset timer (PWRT), which delays the release of the SYSRST# signal until after the PWRT has expired. A *timer* is simply an N-bit counter; when N counts have passed the amount of time is equal to $N * T_{TMR}$, where T_{TMR} is the period of the clock signal that drives the counter. When the counter's value wraps from its maximum value back to 0, then the timer is said to have *expired*. A timer's timeout value can be lengthened by having a programmable *prescaler* to divide the input clock frequency, and/or by having a programmable output *postscaler* that accumulates multiple counter rollovers as one timer expiration event. The PWRT's clock source is the low-power RC oscillator as shown in Figure 8.10, and its expiration time can be altered between 0 (disabled) and 128 ms by configuration bits. Having a

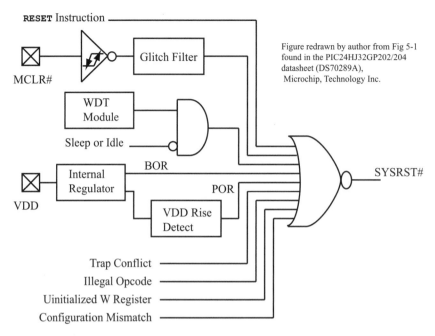

FIGURE redrawn by author from Fig 5-1 found in the PIC24HJ32GP202/204 datasheet (DS70289A), Microchip, Technology Inc.

FIGURE 8.16   Reset sources. (Adapted with permission of the copyright owner, Microchip Technology, Incorporated. All rights reserved. No further reprints or reproduction may be made without Microchip Inc.'s prior written consent.)

non-zero expiration time for the PWRT gives the input VDD time to settle on power-up before releasing the SYSRST# signal. Once SYSRST# is released, the power-on reset clock source is started, and after this is detected as stabilized the system transitions from the reset state to the running state.

A *trap conflict* reset occurs if a lower priority hard trap occurs when a higher priority trap is being processed; this is discussed further in Chapter 9. An *illegal opcode* reset occurs if the instruction that is fetched contains an illegal opcode. An *uninitialized W register* reset occurs if a W register is used in an indirect addressing mode before being written with a value. The integrity of the configuration information within peripheral pin select registers is monitored by maintaining copies in shadow registers; if a difference between the shadow registers and pin select registers is detected then a *configuration mismatch* reset is generated. The watchdog timer (WDT) and sleep/idle power modes are discussed in the next section.

Figure 8.17 shows the RCON register bits that reflect the source of a processor reset. These can be used to debug a system that is experiencing intermittent reset. It is important that the user application clears these bits between resets or else a previous reset condition will mask the source of the current reset.

Figure redrawn by author from Table 5-1 found in the PIC24HJ32GP202/204
datasheet (DS70289A), Microchip, Technology Inc.

Flag Bit	Set by:	Cleared by:
TRAPR (RCON<15>)	Trap conflict event	POR, BOR
IOPUWR (RCON<14>)	Illegal opcode or initialized W register access	POR, BOR
CM (RCON<9>)	Configuration Mismatch	POR,BOR
EXTR (RCON<7>)	MCLR# Reset	POR
SWR (RCON<6>)	**reset** instruction	POR, BOR
WDTO (RCON<4>)	WDT time-out	**pwrsav** instruction, **clrwdt** instruction, POR,BOR
SLEEP (RCON<3>)	**pwrsav #0** instruction	POR,BOR
IDLE (RCON<2>)	**pwrsav #1** instruction	POR,BOR
BOR (RCON<1>)	BOR	n/a
POR (RCON<0>)	POR	n/a

Note: All Reset flag bits may be set or cleared by the user software.

FIGURE 8.17   RCON register bit operation. (Adapted with permission of the copyright owner, Microchip Technology, Incorporated. All rights reserved. No further reprints or reproduction may be made without Microchip Inc.'s prior written consent.)

Figure 8.18 shows the code for the `printResetCause()` function called by *echo.c* in Figure 8.6 (for space reasons, this a simplified version of `printResetCause()`; the full

```
void printResetCause(void) {        Simplified version of printResetCause(), see
  if (_SLEEP) {                     book CD-ROM for full version.
    outString("\nDevice has been in sleep mode\n"); _SLEEP = 0;
  }
  if (_IDLE) {
    outString("\nDevice has been in idle mode\n");  _IDLE = 0;
  }
  outString("\nReset cause: ");
  if (_POR) {
    outString("Power-on.\n");  _POR = 0; _BOR = 0; //clear both
  } else { //non-POR causes
   if (_SWR) {
    outString("Software Reset.\n");             _SWR = 0;      }
   if (_WDTO) {
    outString("Watchdog Timeout. \n");          _WDTO = 0;     }
   if (_EXTR) {
    outString("MCLR assertion.\n");             _EXTR = 0;     }
   if (_BOR) {
    outString("Brown-out.\n");                  _BOR = 0;      }
   if (_TRAPR) {
    outString("Trap Conflict.\n");              _TRAPR = 0;    }
   if (_IOPUWR) {
    outString("Illegal Condition.\n");          _IOPUWR = 0;   }
   if (_CM) {
    outString("Configuration Mismatch.\n");     _CM = 0;       }
  }//end non-POR causes
  checkDeviceAndRevision();
  checkOscOption();
}
```

A status bit is cleared if it has been set.

Print status on processor ID and revision, and clock source.

FIGURE 8.18   `printResetCause()` function.

code is contained in *common\pic24_util.c*). Observe that `printResetCause()` checks each RCON register status bit, outputs an appropriate status message if the bit is set, then clears the bit. At the end of `printResetCause()`, the `checkDeviceandRevision()` function prints the processor ID and revision and `checkOscOption()` function prints a status message about the current clock option.

WATCHDOG TIMER, SLEEP, IDLE, DOZE

Figure 8.19 shows the block diagram of the watchdog timer (WDT) subsystem [9] previously mentioned. As with the power-on reset timer, the WDT is clocked by the LPRC oscillator. The timeout period for the WDT is affected by its prescalar and postscaler settings, both of which are set by configuration bits. The prescaler can

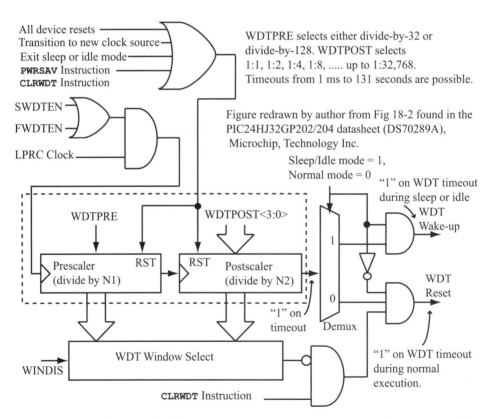

FIGURE 8.19 Watchdog timer block diagram. (Adapted with permission of the copyright owner, Microchip Technology, Incorporated. All rights reserved. No further reprints or reproduction may be made without Microchip Inc.'s prior written consent.)

either be a fixed divide-by-32 or divide-by-128, while the postscaler is controlled by a 4-bit field that gives settings of 1:1, 1:2, 1:4, 1:8, . . . up to 1:32,768.

A common use of the watchdog timer is for catching coding errors during development where a programmer uses an incorrect code sequence for communicating with an external device and an expected response from the device does not occur, resulting in an infinite wait condition. Enabling the watchdog timer during the wait for the response places a maximum time limit on the wait before a watchdog timer reset occurs. In production code, the watchdog timer can protect against an infinite wait condition in case noise or hardware failure corrupts communication with an external device. It is useful to think of the watchdog timer as an alarm clock in these scenarios, signaling that too much time has elapsed. Checking the WDTO (watchdog timer timeout) bit after a reset detects when this situation has occurred. To prevent WDT timeout during normal operation, the PIC24 µC instruction clrwdt (clear watchdog timer, which has no arguments) must be executed periodically to reset the WDT before the WDT expires. The optional windowed mode of the WDT is enabled by the WINDIS configuration bit. In windowed mode, the WDT can only be cleared in the last 25 percent of its timer operation, or else the processor is reset. This places both minimum and maximum bounds when timing an operation, and thus provides processor reset in the case that an event requires too little time or too much time.

The WDT operation is enabled by either the FWDTEN configuration bit or the SWDTEN bit contained in the RCON register (RCON<5>). The FWDTEN bit forces the WDT to be always enabled, while the SWDTEN bit gives the application control over WDT enable. The following line is used in *common\pic24_configbits.c* to configure the WDT:

```
_FWDT(FWDTEN_OFF & WINDIS_OFF & WDTPRE_PR128 & WDTPOST_PS512);
```

These configuration bits disable FWDTEN (FWDTEN_OFF), disable windowed mode (WINDIS_OFF), and set the prescaler to divide-by-128 (WDTPRE_PR128) and the postscaler (WDTPOST_PS512) to 1:512. Using the nominal LPRC clock frequency of 32.768 kHz, this provides a timeout value of:

$$\text{WDT timeout} = 1/32768 \text{ Hz} \times 128 \times 512 = 2 \text{ seconds} \qquad (8.1)$$

The other use of the WDT is to *wake* the processor from either *idle* or *sleep* mode, which are two power conservation modes [9]. Sleep mode is entered by executing the pwrsav #0 instruction, which disables the system clock and all on-chip peripherals that depend on it. Idle mode (pwrsav #1) disables the CPU, but the system clock continues to operate; peripherals must be disabled manually through their associated control registers if desired. Sleep mode is the lowest power mode available to the PIC24 μC. When the CPU is disabled by entering either sleep or idle modes, the watchdog timer continues to operate (if enabled). If the WDT expires during idle/sleep mode, then a *WDT wakeup* occurs and the processor continues execution at the instruction following the pwrsav instruction. An enabled interrupt event (Chapter 9) can also wake the processor from sleep/idle mode.

Why does entering sleep mode decrease power consumption? The answer is straightforward: if the clock is stopped, no transistors are switching, which means no energy is being dissipated, thus reducing power. Of course, some energy is being dissipated, even with the clock stopped, but the amount is much lower than with the clock running. Power dissipation in a CMOS circuit is divided into two categories: static (P_s) and dynamic (P_d). Static power is the power dissipated when no switching activity is occurring and is due to high-resistance leakage paths between VDD and ground within CMOS transistors. Power dissipation is measured in watts (1 Watt = 1 Volt * 1 Amp), but in datasheets, power dissipation is typically given as power supply current for a particular operating condition. The PIC24HJ32GP202 typical sleep mode current at room temperature as listed in the datasheet is approximately 75 μA and the idle current is 10 mA @ FCY = 40 MHz. The idle current is much higher than the sleep current because the main system clock is being used to drive the peripheral subsystems. The principal contribution to dynamic power dissipation P_d is given in Equation 8.2, where VDD is the power supply voltage, f the switching frequency, and c the amount of capacitance being switched.

$$P_d = VDD^2 \cdot f \cdot c \tag{8.2}$$

Because power is voltage multiplied by current ($V \cdot I$), then replacing P_d with $VDD \cdot I$ in Equation 8.2 yields:

$$VDD \cdot I = VDD^2 \cdot f \cdot c \tag{8.3}$$

$$I = VDD \cdot f \cdot c \tag{8.4}$$

By Equation 8.4, you can see that there is a linear relationship between I, VDD, frequency, and capacitance. Idle mode reduces the capacitance c being switched, because the CPU operation is disabled and thus fewer transistors are switching, but the clock frequency remains unchanged and is still driving the peripheral modules. Sleep mode sets frequency for the system clock to zero since the system clock is disabled.

The previously mentioned doze postscaler shown in Figure 8.9 is another method besides the sleep and idle modes for reducing power. The doze postscaler reduces the system clock frequency to the CPU, but keeps the system clock frequency to the rest of the peripherals unchanged. This means that modules such as the UART that we use for serial communication to PC will continue to function at the same data rate, and thus the baud rate for the serial link can remain unchanged. If the system clock frequency for peripherals was also reduced, then the baud rate for the UART would also have to be reduced since the serial communication rate is derived from the system clock. If the doze postscaler is set to a 1:2 setting, which reduces the CPU clock frequency by a factor of 2, then the current drawn by the CPU portion of the PIC24 µC will also be reduced by one half, assuming that the static power contribution from the CPU (non-switching current draw) is small. On the PIC24H µC, static current draw is in the 10s of microamperes, as reported by the datasheet for the sleep mode current.

THE RESET.C TEST PROGRAM

A program named *reset.c* is used in this section to illustrate the concepts of persistent variables, sleep/idle mode, watchdog timer reset, watchdog timer wakeup, and doze mode. Figure 8.20 shows the portion of reset.c before entry into the program's infinite while(1){} loop. The configuration code executed before the

```
#include "pic24_all.h"
//Experiment with reset, power-saving modes
                                              _PERSISTENT variables are not initialized by
_PERSISTENT uint8 u8_resetCount;              C runtime code.
int main(void) {

  configClock();                              configPinsForLowPower(void) function defined in
  configPinsForLowPower();                    common\pic24_util.c. Configs parallel port pins
  configHeartbeat();                          as all inputs, with weak pull-ups enabled.
  configDefaultUART(DEFAULT_BAUDRATE);
  outString(HELLO_MSG);

                                 _POR bit is set to a "1" by power-on reset. The function
                                 printResetCause() clears _POR to a "0".
  if (_POR) {
    u8_resetCount = 0;           // if power on reset, init the reset count variable
  } else {
    u8_resetCount++;             //keep track of the number of non-power on resets
  }
                                 _WDTO bit is set to a "1" by watch dog timer timout.
                                 The function printResetCause() clears _WDTO to a "0".
  if (_WDTO) {
    _SWDTEN = 0;                 //If Watchdog timeout, disable WDT.
  }
  printResetCause();             //print statement about what caused reset
  //print the reset count
  outString("The reset count is ");
  outUint8(u8_resetCount);  outChar('\n');
  while (1) {
    ...See the next figure...
  }
}
```

FIGURE 8.20 Setup portion of reset.c program.

outString(HELLO_MSG) statement is the same as for Figure 8.6 (*echo.c*) with one addition, the *configPinsForLowPower()* function that configures all of the parallel I/O pins for low-power operation (all pins configured as inputs with weak pull-ups enabled; see the next section). The function is used here because we wish to measure the current draw for various power modes and want the parallel I/O pins configured for the least possible current draw.

The _PERSISTENT uint8 u8_resetCount declaration means that the u8_resetCount variable is never initialized by the *C* runtime code. This allows the variable to track events across processor resets; in this case we use it as a simple counter for the number of non-POR events that occur. Observe that u8_resetCount is initialized to 0 only when the _POR bit is set, indicating that a power-on reset has occurred. If the _WDTO bit is set, indicating that a watchdog timer expiration caused the last process or reset, then the _SWDTEN bit is cleared, disabling the operation of the watchdog timer. Before entering the while(1){} loop, the u8_resetCount value is printed by the function outUint8(uint8 u8_x), which prints its argument to the console in ASCII-hex. The outUint8(uint8 u8_x) function is found in *common\pic24_serial.c*.

Figure 8.21 shows the while(1){} portion of the *reset.c* program. The printMenuGetChoice() function (not shown) outputs a menu of choices 1–7, where the choices are:

- **"1":** Enables the WDT, which is configured for a 2-second timeout period. After the menu is reprinted, a processor reset occurs when the WDT expires if no further action is taken by the user. Recall that the WDT is disabled by the code preceding the while(1){} loop on a processor reset.
- **"2":** Enter sleep mode (pwrsav #0 instruction). Because the WDT is disabled at this point, the only way to wake up the processor with a user action is to cycle power or press the MCLR# reset button. The *C* inline assembly statement (asm) previously discussed in the clock generation section is used to insert the pwrsav #0 instruction into the *C* code.
- **"3":** Enter idle mode (pwrsav #1 instruction). As with sleep mode, a power cycle or pressing the MCLR# reset button is required by the user to wake the processor.
- **"4":** Enables the WDT, then enters sleep mode. The processor will sleep for approximately 2 seconds because of our particular watchdog timer configuration bit settings, then wake when the WDT expires, reprinting the menu choice. If no further action is taken by the user, the WDT expires again in 2 seconds, causing a processor reset, then the WDT is disabled before re-entering the while(1){} loop.
- **"5":** Enables doze mode with a Fcy divided by 2. No visible change is apparent to the user, but an ammeter shows a reduction in current draw.

■ **"6":** Enables doze mode with a FCY divided by 128. No visible change is apparent to the user, but an ammeter shows a reduction in current draw.

■ **"7":** Execute a software reset via the reset instruction.

```
//...see previous figure for rest of main()
while (1) {
   uint8 u8_c;
   u8_c = printMenuGetChoice();  //Print menu, get user's choice
   DELAY_MS(1);  //let characters clear the UART executing choice
   switch (u8_c) {
     case '1':              //enable watchdog timer
       _SWDTEN = 1;         //WDT ENable bit = 1
       break;
     case '2':              //sleep mode
       asm("pwrsav #0");    //sleep
       break;
     case '3':              //idle mode
       asm("pwrsav #1");    //idle
       break;
     case '4':
       _SWDTEN = 1;         //WDT ENable bit = 1
       asm("pwrsav #0");    //sleep
       outString("after WDT enable, sleep.\n"); //executed on wakeup
       break;
     case '5':              //doze mode
       _DOZE = 1;           //chose divide by 2
       _DOZEN= 1;           //enable doze mode
       break;
     case '6':              //doze mode
       _DOZE = 7;           //chose divide by 128
       _DOZEN= 1;           //enable doze mode
       break;
     case '7':              //software reset
       asm("reset");        //reset myself
       break;
     default:
       break;
   }
 } // end while (1)
 return 0;
}
```

FIGURE 8.21   while(1){} portion of reset.c program.

Figure 8.22 shows some sample output from the *reset.c* program for the choice sequence of "1" (enable watchdog timer) in comments *a* through *c,* followed by "2" (enter sleep mode) in comments *d* through *g,* and finally "4" (enable WDT, then enter sleep mode) in comments *h* through *j.*

Table 8.1 shows the VDD current draw in mA as measured by an ammeter when testing the sleep, idle, doze(/2), and doze(/128) modes using the *reset.c* program for two different PIC24 microcontrollers.

The following comments will use the numbers in Table 8.1 for the PIC24HJ32GP202 with FCY = 40 MHz. As previously stated, the sleep mode offers

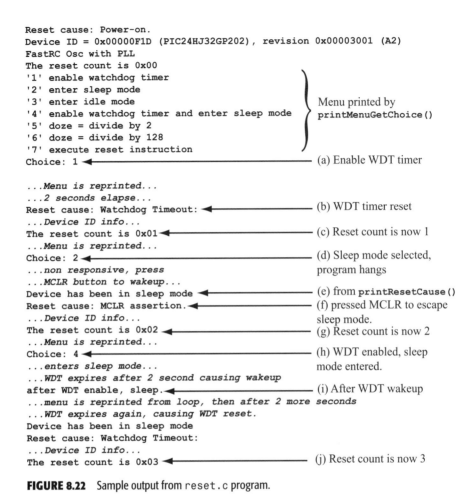

```
Reset cause: Power-on.
Device ID = 0x00000F1D (PIC24HJ32GP202), revision 0x00003001 (A2)
FastRC Osc with PLL
The reset count is 0x00
'1' enable watchdog timer
'2' enter sleep mode
'3' enter idle mode                                    }  Menu printed by
'4' enable watchdog timer and enter sleep mode            printMenuGetChoice()
'5' doze = divide by 2
'6' doze = divide by 128
'7' execute reset instruction
Choice: 1  ◄─────────────────────────────────────── (a) Enable WDT timer

...Menu is reprinted...
...2 seconds elapse...
Reset cause: Watchdog Timeout: ◄──────────────────── (b) WDT timer reset
...Device ID info...
The reset count is 0x01◄──────────────────────────── (c) Reset count is now 1
...Menu is reprinted...
Choice: 2 ◄───────────────────────────────────────── (d) Sleep mode selected,
...non responsive, press                                 program hangs
...MCLR button to wakeup...
Device has been in sleep mode ◄───────────────────── (e) from printResetCause()
Reset cause: MCLR assertion.◄─────────────────────── (f) pressed MCLR to escape
...Device ID info...                                     sleep mode.
The reset count is 0x02 ◄─────────────────────────── (g) Reset count is now 2
...Menu is reprinted...
Choice: 4 ◄───────────────────────────────────────── (h) WDT enabled, sleep
...enters sleep mode...                                  mode entered.
...WDT expires after 2 second causing wakeup
after WDT enable, sleep.◄─────────────────────────── (i) After WDT wakeup
...menu is reprinted from loop, then after 2 more seconds
...WDT expires again, causing WDT reset.
Device has been in sleep mode
Reset cause: Watchdog Timeout:
...Device ID info...
The reset count is 0x03 ◄─────────────────────────── (j) Reset count is now 3
```

FIGURE 8.22 Sample output from reset.c program.

TABLE 8.1 PIC24 current draw (mA).

Mode	PIC24HJ32GP202@40 MHz Fᴄʏ	PIC24FJ64GA002@16 MHz Fᴄʏ
Normal Operation	42.3	5.6
Sleep	0.030	0.004
Idle	17.6	2.0
Doze (/2)	32.2	4.0
Doze (/128)	17.9	2.0

the greatest reduction in current draw because it stops the system clock as well as all of the peripherals as shown in Table 8.1 with a measured current draw of 30 µA. The idle mode stops the clock to the CPU, but not the clock to the peripherals, producing a 17.6 mA current draw. The doze mode of Fcy/2 had a measured current draw of 32.2 mA. Because doze mode only affects the CPU clock, and not the peripheral clock, we could have roughly predicted the doze mode current draw as shown in Equation 8.5, where N is the doze mode postscaler.

$$\text{Doze cur.}(/N \text{ mode}) = \text{Idle cur.} + (\text{Normal cur.} - \text{Idle cur.})/N \qquad (8.5)$$

Idle mode current subtracted from Normal mode current is approximately the current drawn by the CPU, which is the current that is affected by doze mode. Using values from Table 8.1 for Normal and Idle currents, Equation 8.6 predicts a doze current for Fcy/2 mode of 30 mA, which is reasonably close to the measured value of 32.2 mA.

$$\text{Doze current (for } /2) = 17.6 + (42.3 - 17.6)/2 = 30 \text{ mA} \qquad (8.6)$$

The PIC24F has lower maximum performance than the PIC24H family, but offers lower power consumption at equivalent clock frequencies. The difference in current values between the two devices in Table 8.1 is exaggerated because of the clock speed inequity.

PARALLEL PORT OPERATION

Parallel port I/O, also termed general-purpose I/O (GPIO), refers to groups of pins whose values can be read or written as a group via special function registers. On the PIC24HJ32GP202 µC, two parallel ports are available: PORTA and PORTB. Additional ports, such as PORTC, PORTD, PORTE, and higher are available on larger pin count versions of the PIC24 µC. Each port is 16 bits wide, but whether or not all ports are available on external pins depends on the particular PIC24 µC. For example, on the PIC24HJ32GP202 µC all 16 bits of PORTB are available externally, but only the lower 5 bits of PORTA are. The individual port pins on the PIC24HJ32GP202 pin diagram in Figure 8.2 are named RB*x* or RA*x*, for PORTB and PORTA respectively. The various parallel ports A, B, C, etc., all operate the same in terms of their basic digital input/output functionality. Only PORTA and PORTB are used in the interfacing examples in this book, as the PIC24HJ32GP202 µC is our target device.

Figure 8.23 shows the general diagram of a parallel port pin. Each parallel I/O (PIO) pin may share the external pin with other on-chip peripherals, labeled as *Peripheral Modules* in Figure 8.23. Control bits in special function registers determine

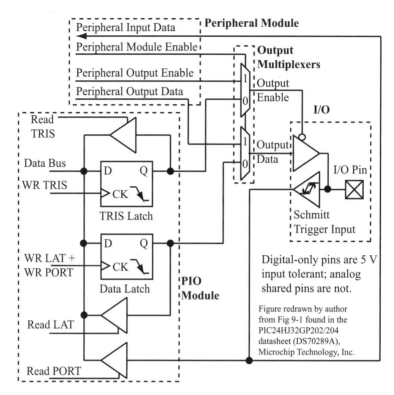

FIGURE 8.23 Parallel port general structure. (Adapted with permission of the copyright owner, Microchip Technology, Incorporated. All rights reserved. No further reprints or reproduction may be made without Microchip Inc.'s prior written consent.)

which peripheral actually has access to the pin when multiple peripheral outputs share the same physical pin. This is shown conceptually in Figure 8.23 as the output multiplexer logic. One of the peripherals that shares a physical pin with the PIO module is the analog-to-digital converter (ADC) module. ADC inputs are labeled as AN*y* on the PIC24HJ32GP202 pin diagram in Figure 8.2, so it is seen that RB15 is assigned the same physical pin (26) as analog input AN9. Any pin that is assigned an AN*y* function is known as an *analog* pin, and its maximum input voltage is VDD + .3 V, or 3.6 V assuming that VDD is 3.3 V. Pins that do not share an AN*y* function are digital pins (such as RB11, pin 22 in Figure 8.2) and can tolerate an input voltage of up to 5.6 V. Most I/O pins can sink and source a maximum of 4 mA (some exceptions exist, see [31]).

Each parallel port has three special function registers associated with it named PORT*x*/TRIS*x*/LAT*x*, where *x* is the specific port such as A or B. The TRIS*x* register is used to configure each bidirectional port bit as either an input or output. A "1" in a TRIS*x* register bit configures the associated PORT*x* register bit to be an input (note that "1" looks like "I" for input), while a "0" configures the associated PORT*x* register bit to be an output ("0" looks like "O" for output). The LAT*x* register is the data latch used to drive the port pins when it is configured as an output. Reading PORT*x* returns the values of the external pins, while reading LAT*x* reads the data latch value. Writing to either LAT*x* or PORT*x* writes to the data latch of the associated port. Individual bits are referenced as LAT*xy* and R*xy* where *x* gives the port's letter (A-E) and *y* gives the bit within the port. In *C* code, these references can be written as _R*xy* (_RA2, _RB5, _RB14, etc.) for bits in the PORT*x* register and as _LAT*xy*/_TRIS*xy* (_LATA2, _TRISB5, _LATB14, etc.) for bits in the LAT*x*/TRIS*x* registers. Generally, our code examples use individual bit assignments instead of assigning all bits of a port at once. Please note that reading LAT*xy* may not return the same value as reading R*xy*. If the port is configured as an input, reading LAT*xy* returns the last value written to LAT*xy* or R*xy*, while reading R*xy* returns the value of the external pin. If the port is configured as an output, reading LAT*xy* will normally return the same value as reading R*xy* because the data latch is driving the external pin. However, if there is another external driver that is clashing with the port driver, or if the port driver itself is a special case like an open-drain output (explained later in this section), LAT*xy* and R*xy* may return different values when read. A write to a port bit configured as an input changes the value of the output data latch (LAT*xy*), but does not change the value seen on the external pin whose value is set by whatever is driving that pin. Even though in principle writing to R*xy* is equivalent to writing to LAT*xy*, in the case of bset (bit set) or bclr (bit clear) instructions they are not equivalent because these are read-modify-write instructions. Thus, a bit set of R*xy* reads R*xy*, modifies the value, then writes R*xy*, while a bit set of LAT*xy* reads LAT*xy*, modifies the value, then writes LAT*xy*. The Family Reference Manual [10] warns that the following consecutive assignments:

```
_RB2 = 1; //implemented by compiler using a bset instruction
_RB3 = 1; //implemented by compiler using a bset instruction
```

can produce an incorrect result for the second assignment (even though they are for different bits) depending on external pin loading and internal clock speed (testing by the authors have confirmed this for FCY = 40 MHz and using a compiler optimization of level 0 that generates bset/bclr instructions for port assignments). However, using LAT*xy* for port writes always works:

```
_LATB2 = 1; //implemented by compiler using a bset instruction
_LATB3 = 1; //implemented by compiler using a bset instruction
```

Because of this, our code uses LAT*xy* for port writes and RB*xy* for sensing (reading) a pin state. Our code reads LAT*xy* when we wish to toggle a previously written value, such as _LATB2 = !_LATB2.

TRISTATE DRIVERS

Figure 8.24 shows that the output of a TRISx latch bit y (TRISx<y>) is connected to the output enable of the *tristate* buffer that drives the I/O pin. If TRISx<y> is "0" (the port bit is an output), the tristate buffer is enabled and simply passes its input value to its output. If TRISx<y> is "1" (the port bit is an input), the tristate buffer is disabled and its output becomes high impedance, whose state is commonly designated as "Z." Figure 8.24 shows that one can think of the tristate buffer enable as controlling a switch on the output of the buffer; the switch is closed when the enable is asserted, allowing the buffer to drive its output. The switch is open when the enable is negated, causing the output to float (also known as high impedance). Note that a port bit cannot be both an input and an output simultaneously; it is

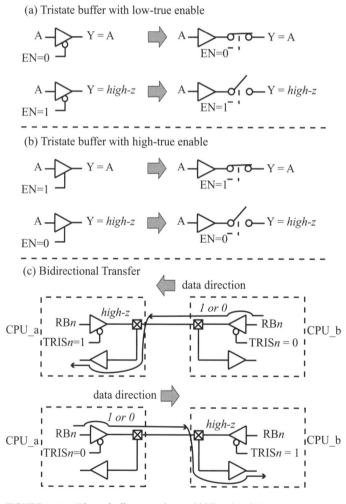

FIGURE 8.24   Tristate buffer operation and bidirectional I/O.

either one or the other based on the setting of the TRISx<y> bit. The lower part of Figure 8.24 shows data flow on a bidirectional data link using one wire; data is either flowing from CPU_a to CPU_b or vice versa, but never both directions at the same time over one wire if voltage mode signaling is used (if both tristate buffers are enabled then this can cause an indeterminate voltage on the wire and it is a programming error in the μC application).

Schmitt Trigger Input

All PIO inputs use a *Schmitt Trigger* input buffer for driving internal signals from the external pin. Figure 8.25 shows the Vin/Vout characteristics of a Schmitt Trigger buffer. Observe that a low-to-high transition must become close to VDD (V$_{IH}$) before the buffer trips; conversely, a high-to-low transition must be close to ground (V$_{IL}$) before the buffer trips. This *hysteresis* in the buffer action provides extra immunity against noise on the input signal and is also used for transforming slowly changing inputs into signals with fast rise and fall times.

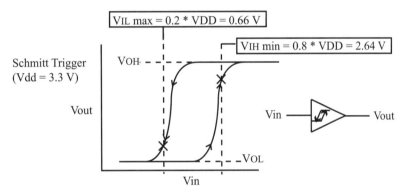

FIGURE 8.25   Schmitt Trigger input buffer characteristic.

Open-Drain Output

Each PIO pin has the capability to be configured as an *open-drain driver*, which means that the PMOS pull-up is disabled as shown in Figure 8.26b, removing the ability of the port pin to drive its output high (instead, the output pin floats when driven high). One application of an open-drain driver is to use an external *pull-up* resistor to provide an output high voltage that is higher than the PIC24 VDD value of 3.3 V. In the case of Figure 8.26c, the external pull-up is used to provide an output voltage of 5 V. The value of the pull-up resistor is chosen so that the current sunk by the pin when the output is pulled low does not exceed the maximum current specification, which is 4 mA for the majority of the PIC24 I/O pins. Thus, the resistor value should be at least 5 V/.004 A = 1250 ohms. Another open-drain application is shown in Figure 8.26d, in which two open-drain outputs are connected together to

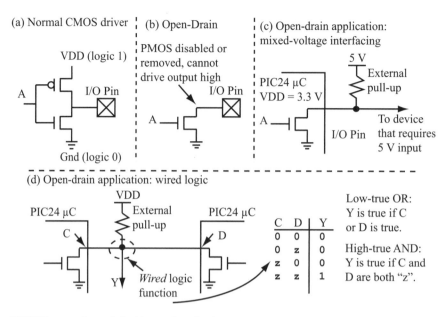

FIGURE 8.26 Open-drain driver and application.

form a *wired* logic function. This is a common usage when wanting to detect if any of the outputs are asserted low (a low-true OR function); the outputs can simply be wired together with an external pull-up without the need for a logic gate. The maximum allowed open-drain voltage for a pin is the same as the pin's maximum allowed V_{IH} (5.6 V for digital pins) as per the datasheet [31].

Each PIO port has an open-drain control register (ODC*x*) that is used for enabling (ODC*x*<*y*> = 1) or disabling (ODC*x*<*y*> = 0) the open-drain capability. The following two C statements configure port RB11 as an open-drain output:

```
_TRISB11 = 0;   //RB11 is an output
_ODCB11 = 1;    //RB11 output is open-drain
```

INTERNAL WEAK PULL-UPS

Some I/Os have a capability referred to as *input change notification* and are named CN*y* in the pins on Figure 8.2. Each CN*y* input has a weak pull-up that can be enabled (CN*y*PUE = 1) or disabled (CN*y*PUE = 0) as shown in Figure 8.27a. The term *weak* is used because the resistance is high enough that an external driver can overpower the pull-up resistor and pull the input to near ground, producing a "0" input. The weak pull-up is implemented as a high-resistance P-transistor and when enabled, the gate of this transistor is "0", turning it on. The weak pull-up is useful for eliminating the need for an external pull-up resistor on an input switch as shown in Figure 8.27b. Note that a pushbutton switch configured as a low-true input switch must have some form of

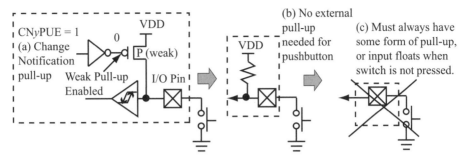

FIGURE 8.27   Change notification weak pull-ups.

pull-up resistor, either internal or external, or the input floats when the pushbutton is not pressed, allowing the input to be read as either "1" or "0".

To use a weak pull-up with a parallel port pin, you must determine which change notification input (if any) shares that physical pin. For example, from Figure 8.2 we see that port RB11 shares pin 22 with change notification CN15. The following two *C* statements configure RB11 as an input then enable the weak pull-up on that pin.

```
_TRISB11 = 1;   //RB11 is an input
_CN15PUE = 1;   //enable weak pull-up on RB11
```

DIGITAL VERSUS ANALOG INPUTS

As previously mentioned, when a parallel port pin shares a pin with an analog-to-digital converter input (AN*y*), then it is known as an analog pin and its maximum input voltage is VDD + .3 V, or 3.6 V. An additional complication is that in order for the parallel port to be used as an input, the analog functionality of the pin has to be disabled, which can be done using the PCFG*y* bit associated with each AN*y* input. By default, each I/O with an AN*y* function is configured as an analog input (PCFG*y* = 0), but it can be configured for digital mode by setting the PCFG*y* bit (PCFG*y* = 1). For example, RB15 shares pin 26 with AN9, so the following two *C* statements configure RB15 as an input:

```
_TRISB15 = 1;   //RB15 is an input
_PCFG9 = 1;     //configure RB15 (AN9) for digital mode
```

A PIO pin configured as an input, but with the analog mode enabled, will always read as "0". As required by Section 10 of PIC24H family reference manual, we will also configure for digital mode when a PIO is used as an output so that the analog input circuitry does not load the output driver (this load is significant, and slows signal transitions).

PIO CONFIGURATION MACROS/FUNCTIONS

Because of the numerous options available for PIO pins (input/output, analog/digital, weak pull-up, open-drain), we will use macros or static inline functions for PIO configuration to improve code clarity. These macros/functions are contained in device specific header files (e.g., *include\devices\PIC24HJ32GP202_ports.h*) and are:

■ **Pull-up configuration:** These enable/disable the weak pull-ups on PORTA/PORTB pins and are named ENABLE_RAy_PULLUP(), DISABLE_RAy_PULLUP(), ENABLE_RBy_PULLUP(), and DISABLE_RBy_PULLUP(). For the PIC24HJ32GP202 µC, all PIO pins have an associated input change notification functionality, so all have the weak pull-up capability (this is not true for all PIC24 microcontrollers).

■ **Open-Drain configuration:** These enable/disable the open-drain functionality on PORTA/PORTB pins, and are named ENABLE_RAy_OPENDRAIN(), DISABLE_RAy_OPENDRAIN(), ENABLE_RBy_OPENDRAIN(), and DISABLE_RBy_OPENDRAIN().

■ **Input/Output configuration:** These configure the PORTA/PORTB pins as either inputs or outputs and are named CONFIG_RAy_AS_DIG_INPUT(), CONFIG_RAy_AS_DIG_OUTPUT(), CONFIG_RBy_AS_DIG_INPUT(), and CONFIG_RBy_AS_DIG_OUTPUT(). The input macros disable the weak pull-up and configure analog pins for digital mode as necessary. The output macros disable the weak pull-up and also the open-drain capability. The CONFIG_RAy_AS_DIG_OD_OUTPUT() and CONFIG_RBy_AS_DIG_OD_OUTPUT() macros configure the PORTA/PORTB pins as digital outputs with open-drain enabled.

The *include\pic24_ports.h* file includes the device specific file that contains the macros from the *include\devices* subdirectory based on the target device set within MPLAB. The following code shows examples of the input/output configuration functions for the RB15 pin:

```
static inline void CONFIG_RB15_AS_DIG_INPUT() {
    DISABLE_RB15_PULLUP();
    _TRISB15 = 1; // PIO as input
    _PCFG9 = 1; // digital mode
}
static inline void CONFIG_RB15_AS_DIG_OUTPUT() {
    DISABLE_RB15_PULLUP();
    DISABLE_RB15_OPENDRAIN();
    _TRISB15 = 0; // PIO as output
    _PCFG9 = 1; // digital mode
}
```

When configuring many I/O ports, it is more code efficient to directly write 16-bit values to configuration registers such as TRIS*x*, PCFG, etc. However, we will sacrifice some code efficiency for code clarity in our examples by use of these macros/functions since this is an introductory text on microcontroller interfacing, and we view code clarity as more important at this point.

LED/Switch I/O and State Machine Programming

A common input device is a momentary pushbutton switch. Figure 8.28 shows a pushbutton switch connected to RB13, with RB13 configured as an input with the weak pull-up enabled. When the pushbutton is released (not pressed) the RB13 input reads as "1"; when the pushbutton is pressed the RB13 input reads as "0". Port RB14 is configured as a digital output for driving an LED, which has a 470 Ω series resistor. To compute the needed resistance value, recall that a typical PIO pin on the PIC24 µC can provide a maximum current of 4 mA, so

```
/// LED1, SW1 Configuration
#define CONFIG_LED1()   CONFIG_RB14_AS_DIG_OUTPUT()
#define LED1   _LATB14      //led1 state
inline void CONFIG_SW1()  {
   CONFIG_RB13_AS_DIG_INPUT();   //use RB13 for switch input
   ENABLE_RB13_PULLUP();         //enable the pull-up
}
#define SW1               _RB13   //switch state
#define SW1_PRESSED()     SW1==0  //switch test
#define SW1_RELEASED()    SW1==1  //switch test
```

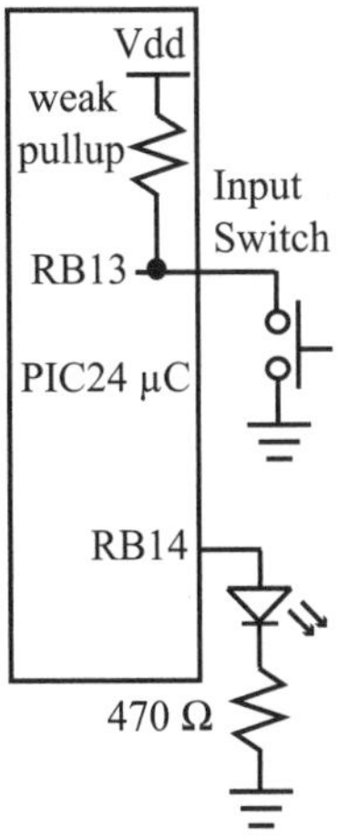

```
main(){
   ...other config...
   CONFIG_SW1();
   DELAY_US(1);
   CONFIG_LED1();
   LED1 = 0;
   while (1) {
      if (SW1_PRESSED()) {
      //switch pressed
      //toggle LED1
      LED1 = !LED1
      }
   }
}
```

a. Incorrect, LED1 is toggled as long as the switch is pushed, which could be a long time!

Count number of switch presses.

```
main(){
   ...other config...
   CONFIG_SW1();
   DELAY_US(1); //pull-up delay
   CONFIG_LED1();
   LED1 = 0;
   while (1) {
      // wait for press, loop(1)
      while (SW1_RELEASED()){}
      DELAY_MS(15); //debounce
      // wait for release, loop(2)
      while (SW1_PRESSED()){}
      DELAY_MS(15); // debounce
      LED1 = !LED1; //toggle LED
   }
}
```

b. Correct, loop(1) executed while switch is not pressed. Once pressed, code becomes trapped in loop(2) until the switch is released, at which point LED1 is toggled.

FIGURE 8.28   Toggling an LED after a switch press and release.

we can use this value as the target current through the LED in order to maximize the LED illumination. Next, consult the LED's datasheet to determine the voltage drop across the LED at the selected current; a typical figure for many LEDs is 2 V. Recalling that Ohm's law is $V = IR$, solving for resistance gives $R = V/I$, where V is the voltage drop across the resistor. With a 3.3 V supply and a 2 V drop across the LED, this leaves $V = 3.3 - 2 = 1.3$ V. Therefore, the resistance $R = 1.3$ V/0.004 A = 325 Ω, which gives the lowest resistance allowed for a 4 mA or less target current. For convenience and to add some margin of safety, a value of 470 Ω was chosen. The CONFIG_LED1() macro is used for configuring the port used to drive the LED, while the CONFIG_SW1() macro is used for configuring the input port used for the switch. Observe that the RB13 pull-up is enabled in CONFIG_SW1() after the port is configured as a digital input. The SW1_PRESSED() and SW1_RELEASED() macros are used for testing if the switch is pressed or released, respectively. In both the (a) and (b) code segments, a 1 µs delay (DELAY_US(1)) is used after configuring SW1 to allow the pull-up on the port to work. After enabling a pull-up, PIC24 µC with a fast clock can read an input port before the input has had time to be pulled to a logic "1", so our code examples use this conservative delay after enabling weak pull-ups on input ports.

Assume that we would like to toggle the LED each time the pushbutton is pressed and released (toggle means to turn the LED off if it is currently on and vice-versa). A common mistake is shown in code segment (a), which toggles the LED when the switch is pressed (RB13 returns "0"). The problem with this code is that the LED is not only toggled when the pushbutton is pressed, but is also toggled for as long as the pushbutton is held down. Human reaction times on pushbutton switches are measured in tens of milliseconds, so the LED is toggled many times for each pushbutton activation!

Code segment (b) shows a correct solution to this problem. When the while(1){} loop is entered, the code becomes trapped in the loop while (SW1_RELEASED) {}, which loops waiting for the pushbutton to be pressed. Once the pushbutton is pressed, the code is then trapped in the loop while(SW1_PRESSED) {}, waiting for the pushbutton to be released. Upon release, the LED is toggled and the code becomes trapped in the loop while (SW1_RELEASED) {} again. Thus, the LED is toggled only once for each press and release of the pushbutton. Moving the toggle statement (LED1 = !LED1) to between the while() statements toggles the LED when the pushbutton is pressed, but the end result of toggling once for each press and release remains the same. The DELAY_MS(15) function calls are included after each change in the input switch status to ensure that all switch bounce has settled before continuing. Mechanical switch bounce can produce multiple pulses when a pushbutton is activated. The required delay is a function of the mechanics of the switch bounce, which can only be seen by using an oscilloscope to capture the switch waveform or from a manufacturer data sheet. The value of 15 ms used here should be adequate for common momentary switches. This is a simple method for debouncing a switch with the drawback that the CPU cycles spent in the software delay loop are wasted. Alternate methods for switch debouncing are presented in Chapter 9.

STATE MACHINE I/O PROGRAMMING

The code of Figure 8.28b waits for an I/O event (switch press and release) then performs an action (LED toggle). A common task in microcontroller applications is to perform a sequence of events that spans a series of I/O actions. A finite state machine (FSM) approach for code structure is useful for these types of problems. Figure 8.29 shows the LED toggle problem of Figure 8.28 cast as a state machine specification.

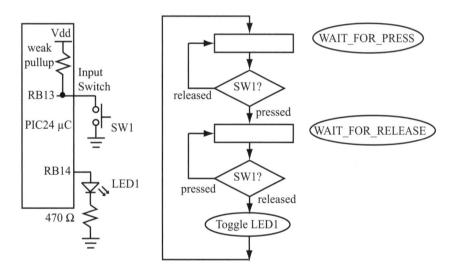

FIGURE 8.29   State machine specification of LED toggle problem.

The state machine consists of two states, named WAIT_FOR_PRESS and WAIT_FOR_RELEASE. The WAIT_FOR_PRESS state progresses to the WAIT_FOR_RELEASE state when SW1 is pressed. The WAIT_FOR_RELEASE state toggles the LED when SW1 is released, then moves to state WAIT_FOR_PRESS. Specifying I/O actions as a state machine is common practice because the state machine is a non-ambiguous description.

Figure 8.30 shows a code implementation for the LED toggle problem of Figure 8.29 written in a state machine style. This style will be our preferred method for I/O problems. Initially, it may look to you as more verbose and complex than

```
typedef enum {
  STATE_RESET = 0,
  STATE_WAIT_FOR_PRESS,
  STATE_WAIT_FOR_RELEASE
} STATE;
```

(a) **enum** type is used to make readable state names. The **STATE_RESET** is used to determine when **main()** initializes its state variable to its first state.

```
STATE e_lastState = STATE_RESET;
//print debug message for state when it changes
void printNewState (STATE e_currentState){
  if (e_lastState != e_currentState) {
  switch (e_currentState) {
   case STATE_WAIT_FOR_PRESS:
     outString("STATE_WAIT_FOR_PRESS\n");
     break;
   case STATE_WAIT_FOR_RELEASE:
     outString("STATE_WAIT_FOR_RELEASE\n");
     break;
   default:
     outString("Unexpected state\n");
  }
 }
 e_lastState = e_currentState;  //remember last state
}
```

(b) **printNewState()** is used to print a message to the console whenever the state changes (when **e_lastState** is not equal to **e_currentState**).

```
main(){
  STATE e_mystate;
  configBasic(HELLO_MSG);
  CONFIG_SW1();      //configure switch
  CONFIG_LED1();     //config the LED
  DELAY_US(1);       //pull-up delay
  e_mystate = STATE_WAIT_FOR_PRESS;
  while (1) {
    printNewState(e_mystate);  //debug message when state changes
    switch (e_mystate) {
      case STATE_WAIT_FOR_PRESS:
        if (SW1_PRESSED()) e_mystate = STATE_WAIT_FOR_RELEASE;
        break;
      case STATE_WAIT_FOR_RELEASE:
        if (SW1_RELEASED()) {
          LED1 = !LED1;    //toggle LED
          e_mystate = STATE_WAIT_FOR_PRESS;
        }
        break;
      default:
        e_mystate = STATE_WAIT_FOR_PRESS;
    }//end switch(e_mystate)
    DELAY_MS(DEBOUNCE_DLY);    //Debounce
    doHeartbeat();    //ensure that we are alive
  } // end while (1)
}
```

(c) The state variable used for tracking the current state.

(d) **configBasic()** combines previously used separate configuration functions into one function call, defined in *common\pic24_util.c*

(e) Give pull-ups time to work

(f) Initialize **e_mystate** to the first state.

(g) Change state only if switch is pressed.

(h) Toggle LED and change state when switch is released.

(i) Put debounce delay at bottom of loop, means that we only look at the switch about every **DEBOUNCE_DLY** milliseconds.

(j) Call **doHeartbeat()** to keep heartbeat LED pulsing.

FIGURE 8.30　State machine code solution for LED toggle problem.

the style of Figure 8.28, but its general structure allows us to write code for complex I/O problems in a structured manner. The state names of Figure 8.29 are defined using an *enumerated* type definition (a) called STATE. An enumerated type provides for readable state names that improves code clarity. Each state name is assigned an integer value (incrementing up from the integer assigned to the first state, which is 0). Enumerated type variables are mapped to the int type in C. An extra state named STATE_RESET is added so that the printNewState() function, which is used by main() to print a message to the console when the current state changes, can determine when the state variable used in main() is initialized to something other than STATE_RESET. In main(), the e_mystate variable (c) is used to track the current state and is initialized to STATE_WAIT_FOR_PRESS before the while(1){} loop is entered.

At the top of the while(1){} loop, the printNewState(e_mystate) function call prints the current state name to the console if the e_mystate value has changed from the last call. This is useful for debugging, as the current state name is needed if you are trying to determine what code is being executed. The state diagram of Figure 8.29 is implemented as a switch(e_mystate){} statement. Each case statement maps to a state of Figure 8.29. The default state is entered whenever the switch variable does not match any of the previous case statements. It is considered good programming practice to always include a default statement in the event that the switch variable contains an unexpected value either through a programming error or some kind of memory corruption. Observe that the e_mystate variable is only changed if the condition for a state change is met, such as the switch being pressed (g) in STATE_WAIT_FOR_PRESS or the switch is released (h) in STATE_WAIT_FOR_RELEASE. Because if() statements are used to check conditions, rather than while() statements as in Figure 8.28, the code is continually looping through the switch statement. This allows us to place a doHeartbeat() call (j) at the end of the while(1){} loop to keep the heartbeat LED pulsing, giving us a visual indication that code is being executed. Switch debounce (i) is accomplished by the DELAY_MS(DEBOUNCE_DLY) at the end of the switch statement, which means that the switch input is only being checked every DEBOUNCE_DLY milliseconds (the DEBOUNCE_DLY macro is defined in *include\pic24_delay.h* and has a value of 15). This is satisfactory since the while(1) loop has no other work to do except to sample the switch. If other work was to be performed and you did not wish to have the DEBOUNCE_DLY delay each time through the while(1) loop, then the DELAY_MS(DEBOUNCE_DLY) could be placed at each point in the code where a switch change is detected, as was done in Figure 8.28(b). As previously mentioned, the DELAY_US(1) macro call (e) is a pessimistic delay that is included to give time for the weak pull-up that is enabled on SW1 to affect the input signal. With very fast clock speeds, after enabling a weak pull-up it is possible to read the PIO port before the input is stable.

A MORE COMPLEX LED/SWITCH I/O PROBLEM

Figure 8.31 shows a state machine specification of a slightly more complex LED/switch I/O problem. The LED is turned off initially. After a press and release, the LED is turned on. The diagram assumes that two states are used to implement

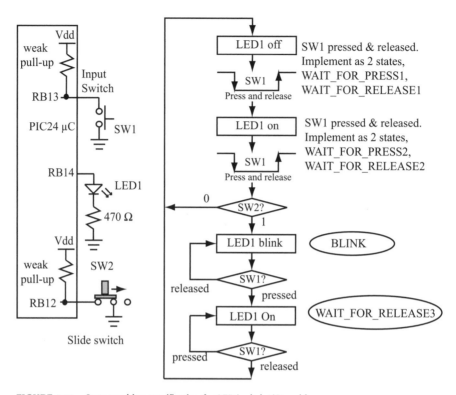

FIGURE 8.31   State machine specification for LED/switch I/O problem.

each press and release transition that is shown, as was done in Figure 8.29. A second switch input (SW2) is used to control what happens after state WAIT_FOR_RELEASE2: either branch back to WAIT_FOR_PRESS1 (SW2 == 0) or continue on to BLINK (SW2 == 1). The LED is blinked (toggled) as long as SW1 is released. Pressing SW1 terminates the blinking and transitions to state WAIT_FOR_RELEASE3, which returns to the initial state WAIT_FOR_PRESS1 once SW1 is released. The SW2 input is a slide switch that connects the associated port to either GND or leaves it floating, with the internal pull-up providing a logic high when the input is floating.

Figure 8.32 shows the C code implementation of Figure 8.31 in the same style as Figure 8.30. Press/release macros are not defined for SW2 because we are simply checking if the input is a "1" or a "0" (a) as we are not associating a press/release connation with this input. The DELAY_MS(100) call (b) in state BLINK provides a delay after toggling the LED; this is needed to ensure that the blinking action is visible. Note that while the DELAY_MS(100) software delay is executing, the switch input is not being sampled, which means that a very fast press and release could be missed. Chapter 9 discusses alternate methods for switch sampling that avoids this problem.

```
typedef enum {
  STATE_RESET = 0, STATE_WAIT_FOR_PRESS1, STATE_WAIT_FOR_RELEASE1,
  STATE_WAIT_FOR_PRESS2, STATE_WAIT_FOR_RELEASE2, STATE_BLINK,
  STATE_WAIT_FOR_RELEASE3
} STATE;
int main (void) {
  STATE e_mystate;
  configBasic(HELLO_MSG);
  CONFIG_SW1();           //configure switch
  CONFIG_SW2();           //configure switch
  CONFIG_LED1();          //config the LED
  DELAY_US(1);            //give pull-ups time to work
  e_mystate = STATE_WAIT_FOR_PRESS1;
  while (1) {
    printNewState(e_mystate);  //debug message when state changes
    switch (e_mystate) {
      case STATE_WAIT_FOR_PRESS1:
        LED1 = 0; //turn off the LED
        if (SW1_PRESSED()) e_mystate = STATE_WAIT_FOR_RELEASE1;
        break;
      case STATE_WAIT_FOR_RELEASE1:
        if (SW1_RELEASED()) e_mystate = STATE_WAIT_FOR_PRESS2;
        break;
      case STATE_WAIT_FOR_PRESS2:
        LED1 = 1; //turn on the LED
        if (SW1_PRESSED())e_mystate = STATE_WAIT_FOR_RELEASE2;
        break;
      case STATE_WAIT_FOR_RELEASE2:
        if (SW1_RELEASED()) {
        //decide where to go
        if (SW2) e_mystate = STATE_BLINK;          ⎫ (a) Test SW2 to
        else e_mystate = STATE_WAIT_FOR_PRESS1;     ⎬ determine next state.
        }                                          ⎭
        break;
      case STATE_BLINK:
        LED1 = !LED1;    //blink while not pressed   (b) Need delay so that
        DELAY_MS(100);   //blink delay ◀─────────── LED blink is visible.
        if (SW1_PRESSED()) e_mystate = STATE_WAIT_FOR_RELEASE3;
        break;
      case STATE_WAIT_FOR_RELEASE3:
        LED1 = 1;    //Freeze LED1 at 1
        if (SW1_RELEASED()) e_mystate = STATE_WAIT_FOR_PRESS1;
        break;
      default:
        e_mystate = STATE_WAIT_FOR_PRESS1;
    }//end switch(e_mystate)
    DELAY_MS(DEBOUNCE_DLY);        //Debounce
    doHeartbeat();        //ensure that we are alive
  } // end while (1)
}
```

FIGURE 8.32 Code implementation for LED/switch I/O problem.

Figure 8.33 shows console output while testing the *C* code of Figure 8.32. The SW2 input was "1" for the first two times that the WAIT_FOR_RELEASE2 state was exited, causing the next state to be BLINK. After this, the SW2 input was "0" the next two times that the WAIT_FOR_RELEASE2 state was exited, causing the following state to be WAIT_FOR_PRESS1.

```
Reset cause: Power-on.
Device ID = 0x00000F1D (PIC24HJ32GP202), revision 0x00003001 (A2)
FastRC Osc with PLL

ledsw1.c, built on May 17 2008 at 10:04:40
STATE_WAIT_FOR_PRESS1              ──────── Initial state, LED off
STATE_WAIT_FOR_RELEASE1        press
STATE_WAIT_FOR_PRESS2          release, LED on
STATE_WAIT_FOR_RELEASE2        press
STATE_BLINK                    release, SW2 = 1, so enter BLINK
STATE_WAIT_FOR_RELEASE3        press, Blink terminated, LED on
STATE_WAIT_FOR_PRESS1          release, LED off
STATE_WAIT_FOR_RELEASE1        press
STATE_WAIT_FOR_PRESS2          release, LED on
STATE_WAIT_FOR_RELEASE2        press
STATE_BLINK                    release, SW2 = 1, so enter BLINK
STATE_WAIT_FOR_RELEASE3        press, Blink terminated, LED on
STATE_WAIT_FOR_PRESS1          release, LED off
STATE_WAIT_FOR_RELEASE1        press
STATE_WAIT_FOR_PRESS2          release, LED on
STATE_WAIT_FOR_RELEASE2        press
STATE_WAIT_FOR_PRESS1          release, SW2 = 0, so back to WAIT_FOR_PRESS1
STATE_WAIT_FOR_RELEASE1     etc...
STATE_WAIT_FOR_PRESS2
STATE_WAIT_FOR_RELEASE2
STATE_WAIT_FOR_PRESS1
■
```

FIGURE 8.33   Console output for LED/switch I/O implementation.

INTERFACING TO AN LCD MODULE

A liquid crystal display (LCD) is often used in microcontroller applications because they are low power and can display both alphanumeric characters and graphics. Disadvantages of LCDs are that they have low viewing angles, are more expensive than LED displays, and must be lit by either ambient light or a back light. LCD character modules display multiple characters, with modules using a $k \times n$ designation where k is the number of characters displayed on each of the n display lines. LCD modules have either a parallel or serial interface, with many LCD parallel interfaces standardized around the Hitachi HD44780 LCD controller. Figure 8.34 shows a PIC24 μC to LCD interface for a Hantronix 16×2 LCD module (part# HDM16216L-5). This interface is independent of the $k \times n$ organization of the LCD module and is applicable for most LCD modules based on the HD44780 LCD controller.

The interface is divided into control lines (E, R/W#, RS), data lines (D7:D0), and power (VDD, VSS, VL, K, A). The 4-bit interface mode is used to reduce the number of connections between the PIC24 μC and the LCD. In 4-bit mode, 8-bit data is sent in two 4-bit transfers on lines D7:D4, allowing D3:D0 to be unconnected. The K, A inputs are for the back light display (see datasheet [33]), while the VDD − VL voltage difference determines the intensity of the displayed numerals

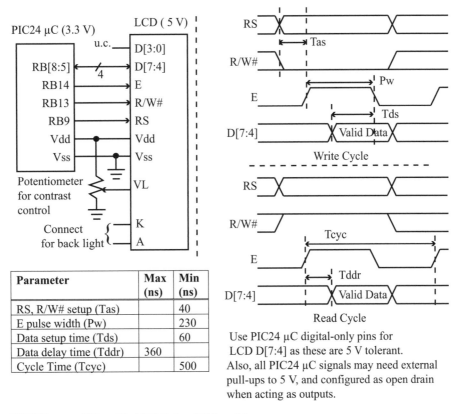

Parameter	Max (ns)	Min (ns)
RS, R/W# setup (Tas)		40
E pulse width (Pw)		230
Data setup time (Tds)		60
Data delay time (Tddr)	360	
Cycle Time (Tcyc)		500

Use PIC24 μC digital-only pins for
LCD D[7:4] as these are 5 V tolerant.
Also, all PIC24 μC signals may need external
pull-ups to 5 V, and configured as open drain
when acting as outputs.

FIGURE 8.34   PIC24 μC to LCD interface (4-bit mode).

(connecting VL to VSS provides maximum intensity but may cause VDD − VL to
exceed the maximum recommended VL value on some LCD modules). A logic high
on the R/W# signal indicates a read operation; the LCD module provides data to
the PIC24 μC. A logic low on R/W# is a write operation; the PIC24 μC provides
data to the LCD module. The E signal is a data strobe used to signal valid data on
the Dn, RS, and R/W# lines. To perform a write operation, the PIC24 μC places data
on the Dn/RS signals, R/W# is driven low, and E is brought high and then low. The
LCD latches the input data on the falling edge of E, so the Dn lines must satisfy the
setup time Tds, while the control lines RS, R/W# are latched on the rising edge of
E and must satisfy the setup time Tas. Not all timings are shown on the diagram;
there are small hold times about the E edges that must be satisfied as well (see [33]);
these are easily satisfied by typical microcontroller operation). To read data from the
LCD, data is placed on the RS signal, R/W# is driven high, and E is brought high.
After the data delay time Tddr has elapsed, valid data is ready on the Dn lines
from the LCD, which can then be read by the PIC24 μC. The E signal is brought

low to finish the read operation. Because software assignments are used to drive the E signal, the minimum pulse width depends on the system clock frequency. At $F_{CY} = 40$ MHz, the PIC24 μC is capable of producing a pulse that violates the minimum pulse width requirement of the E signal. In our code, we use software delays of 1 μs as a very conservative method of ensuring that the E signal timing requirements are met and because I/O transfer performance is not an important issue in this example. Using software assignments for driving PIO pins to accomplish data transfers instead of dedicated hardware modules that drive the pins is often referred to as *bit-banging*. The PIC24 μC has several dedicated hardware modules for accomplishing specialized data transfers without CPU intervention; these are covered in later chapters.

3.3 V to 5 V Interfacing

The LCD module used in Figure 8.34 requires a 5 V supply, the first time that we have dealt with 3.3 V to 5 V interfacing. Any input signals must be 5 V input tolerant, which means that PIC24 μC RBn ports used for the LCD D[7:4] pins must be digital-only pins. For output signals, a 3.3 V output port can drive a 5 V input port if the 5 V input port has TTL-level inputs (V_{IH} is approximately 2.0 V). However, if the device has CMOS level inputs (V_{IH} is approximately 3.8 V) then all signals will need weak external pull-ups (approximately 10 kΩ) and must be configured as open-drain outputs when acting as outputs. This would also mean that digital-only ports would have to be used for all signals since the maximum open-drain voltage is the same as the maximum input voltage. The Hantronix LCD module used in Figure 8.34 has TTL-level inputs, so external pull-ups are not required.

LCD Commands

A subset of the available LCD commands [34] is shown in Table 8.2. If RS = 0, the D7:D0 bits represent an LCD command that affects mode, screen, or cursor position. If RS = 1, the D7:D0 bits contain data being written to or read from the LCD *data display RAM* (DD RAM) in the form of an ASCII character code.

The internal memory configuration of an LCD is dependent upon the particular module. The HDM16216L-5 is a 16x2 display, but its internal data display RAM has 80 total locations with 40 locations mapped to line 1 (addresses 0x00 to 0x27) and 40 locations mapped to line 2 (addresses 0x40 to 0x67). The 16x2 display is a window into these 80 locations, with only 16 characters of each line displayed at any given time as shown in Figure 8.35. By default, the display shows locations 0x00–0x0F of line 1, and locations 0x40–0x4F of line 2. A left shift moves the display to the right, causing locations 0x01–0x10 to be displayed in line 1, and locations 0x41–0x50 in line 2. This creates the appearance that the displayed line has shifted one position to the *left*, as the leftmost character disappears and the

TABLE 8.2   LCD command subset.

Command	RS	R/W#	D7:D0	Description
Clear Display	0	0	0000 0001	Clear display, return cursor to home position (82 µs ~ 1.64 ms)
Return Home	0	0	0000 001x	Returns cursor and shifted display to home (40 µs ~ 1.64 ms)
Entry Mode Set	0	0	0000 01d0	Enable the display, set cursor move direction ($d = 1$ increment, $d = 0$ decrement) (40 µs)
Display On/Off	0	0	0000 1dcb	Display on/off (d), Cursor on/off (c), blink at cursor position on/off (b) (40 µs)
Cursor & Display Shift	0	0	0001 cr00	$c = 1$ shift display, $c = 0$ move cursor, $r = 1$ right shift, $r = 0$ left shift
Function Set	0	0	001i n000	8-bit interface ($i = 1$), 4-bit interface ($i = 0$), one line ($n = 0$), two lines ($n = 1$) (40 µs)
Set DD Address	0	0	1nnn $nnnn$	DD RAM address set equal to $nnnnnnn$ (40 µs)
Read Busy Flag	0	1	$fnnn$ $nnnn$	Busy flag (f) returns in D7 (1 = Busy), D6:D0 contains address counter value (1 µs)
Write Data	1	0	$nnnn$ $nnnn$	Data $nnnnnnnn$ written at current DD RAM address (46 µs)
Read Data	1	1	$nnnn$ $nnnn$	Data $nnnnnnnn$ at current address location in DD RAM is returned (46 µs)

character in column 1 now appears in column 0. Continual left shifting causes the lines to scroll marquee-fashion, moving right to left across the display.

An internal address counter determines where the current data write operation places data. The address counter also specifies the cursor location. Initializing the display sets the address counter to zero, placing the cursor to the home position of location 0 (position 0 of line 1, the upper left-hand corner of the display). A write data operation writes data to the current address location, then increments or decrements the address counter depending on the mode setting (*entry mode set* command in Table 8.2). In increment mode, the address counter is incremented by one and the

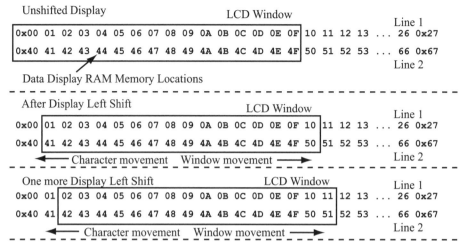

For left shift, window moves *right*, so characters appear to shift *left* off of the display.

FIGURE 8.35 LCD data display RAM.

cursor moves one position to the right on the display. Each additional write places data at the current address counter location and increments the address counter. Assuming the display is unshifted, the 17th write (to location 16) places data "off-screen" (the data is not visible), but the data is still contained in DD RAM. A right shift of the display has to be performed to see the data contained in location 16. Each LCD command requires a fixed amount of time to execute. The PIC24 µC software communicating with the LCD can either have built-in delays that are guaranteed to exceed the required LCD command execution time, or the LCD can be polled via the *read busy flag* command to determine if the module is ready for another command. Before sending a command, a *polling loop* is used to continually read the busy flag status; the loop is exited when the busy flag returns "0". Other commands exist for loading custom character fonts; see the datasheet [34].

LCD CODE EXAMPLE

Listing 8.1 shows the macros used in our LCD C code to isolate the PIC24 µC port to LCD signal mapping. These correspond to the connections shown in Figure 8.34. Note that LATBx assignments are used for outputs and RBx are used for reading inputs.

LISTING 8.1 LCD interface macros.

```
#define RS_HIGH()        _LATB9 = 1
#define RS_LOW()         _LATB9 = 0
#define CONFIG_RS()      CONFIG_RB9_AS_DIG_OUTPUT()
#define RW_HIGH()        _LATB13 = 1
```

```
#define RW_LOW()              _LATB13 = 0
#define CONFIG_RW()           CONFIG_RB13_AS_DIG_OUTPUT()
#define E_HIGH()              _LATB14 = 1
#define E_LOW()               _LATB14 = 0
#define CONFIG_E()            CONFIG_RB14_AS_DIG_OUTPUT()

#define LCD4O                 _LATB5
#define LCD5O                 _LATB6
#define LCD6O                 _LATB7
#define LCD7O                 _LATB8
#define LCD7I                 _RB8

#define CONFIG_LCD4_AS_INPUT()      CONFIG_RB5_AS_DIG_INPUT()
#define CONFIG_LCD5_AS_INPUT()      CONFIG_RB6_AS_DIG_INPUT()
#define CONFIG_LCD6_AS_INPUT()      CONFIG_RB7_AS_DIG_INPUT()
#define CONFIG_LCD7_AS_INPUT()      CONFIG_RB8_AS_DIG_INPUT()
#define CONFIG_LCD4_AS_OUTPUT()     CONFIG_RB5_AS_DIG_OUTPUT()
#define CONFIG_LCD5_AS_OUTPUT()     CONFIG_RB6_AS_DIG_OUTPUT()
#define CONFIG_LCD6_AS_OUTPUT()     CONFIG_RB7_AS_DIG_OUTPUT()
#define CONFIG_LCD7_AS_OUTPUT()     CONFIG_RB8_AS_DIG_OUTPUT()

#define GET_BUSY_FLAG() LCD7I
```

Listing 8.2 shows some LCD utility functions. The `configBusAsOutLCD(void)` function is used to configure the pins used for the LCD D[7:4] as outputs for LCD write operations, while `configBusAsInLCD(void)` configures these same pins as inputs for LCD read operations. The `outputToBusLCD(uint8 u8_c)` outputs the lower 4 bits of the `u8_c` argument to the LCD D[7:4] bus. The `configControlLCD(void)` function configures the ports used for the E, R/W# and RS signals and initializes them to a logic 0 value.

LISTING 8.2   LCD utility functions.

```
//Configure 4-bit data bus for output
void configBusAsOutLCD(void) {
  RW_LOW();                            //RW=0 to stop LCD from driving pins
  CONFIG_LCD4_AS_OUTPUT();     //D4
  CONFIG_LCD5_AS_OUTPUT();     //D5
  CONFIG_LCD6_AS_OUTPUT();     //D6
  CONFIG_LCD7_AS_OUTPUT();     //D7
}

//Configure 4-bit data bus for input
void configBusAsInLCD(void) {
  CONFIG_LCD4_AS_INPUT();      //D4
  CONFIG_LCD5_AS_INPUT();      //D5
```

```
    CONFIG_LCD6_AS_INPUT();              //D6
    CONFIG_LCD7_AS_INPUT();              //D7
    RW_HIGH();                           // R/W = 1, for read
}


//Output lower 4-bits of u8_c to LCD data lines
void outputToBusLCD(uint8 u8_c) {
    LCD40 = u8_c & 0x01;                 //D4
    LCD50 = (u8_c >> 1) & 0x01;          //D5
    LCD60 = (u8_c >> 2) & 0x01;          //D6
    LCD70 = (u8_c >> 3) & 0x01;          //D7
}


//Configure the control lines for the LCD
void configControlLCD(void) {
    CONFIG_RS();                         //RS
    CONFIG_RW();                         //RW
    CONFIG_E();                          //E
    RW_LOW();
    E_LOW();
    RS_LOW();
}
```

Figure 8.36 shows two functions, pulseE() and writeLCD(), that are used for writing to the LCD using the macros and functions of Listings 8.1 and 8.2. The pulseE() function simply pulses the E signal line high with the DELAY_US(1) function calls providing more than enough delay for the pulse width and setup/hold times about the edges. The writeLCD() function writes one byte of data passed in u8_Cmd to the LCD, assuming a 4-bit interface. If u8_CheckBusy is non-zero, the busy flag is polled until it returns non-zero before performing the write. Observe that in the busy flag loop, the first read returns the upper 4 bits, while the second read returns the lower 4 bits. The busy flag is the MSb of the upper 4-bit transfer. Furthermore, the WDT is enabled during the busy flag polling loop so as to escape this infinite wait if there is a hardware failure (or to detect coding or wiring problems during testing). If u8_CheckBusy is zero, a pessimistic delay of 10 ms is performed before writing the byte instead of using the busy flag. After some commands, such as the *function set* command, the busy flag cannot be used so a delay must be performed instead. If u8_DataFlag is non-zero, the RS signal is set to "1" during the write; else it is set to "0". Finally, if u8_DataFlag is zero, only the upper 4 bits are written (the initial command that selects the 4-bit interface requires only a single 4-bit transfer as the LCD is in 8-bit mode on power-up).

The code in Figure 8.37 uses the writeLCD() function within the outStringLCD(char *psz_s) function to write the psz_s string to the LCD at the

```
//Pulse the E clock, 1 us delay around edges for
//setup/hold times
void pulseE(void){
  DELAY_US(1); E_HIGH();
  DELAY_US(1); E_LOW();
  DELAY_US(1);
}
```

E ⎽⎽⎽⎽⎽⎯⎽⎽⎽

```
/* Write a byte (u8_Cmd) to the LCD.
u8_DataFlag is 1 if data byte, 0 if command byte
u8_CheckBusy is 1 if must poll busy bit before write, else
             simply delay before write
u8_Send8Bits is 1 if must send all 8 bits, else send only upper 4-bits
*/
void writeLCD(uint8 u8_Cmd, uint8 u8_DataFlag,
uint8 u8_CheckBusy, uint8 u8_Send8Bits) {
```
RS = 0 (command), R/W# = 1 (read)

Read Busy flag, returns in D7 of first 4 bits

```
  uint8 u8_BusyFlag;
  uint8 u8_wdtState;
  if (u8_CheckBusy) {
   RS_LOW();       //RS=0 to check busy
   // check busy
   configBusAsInLCD(); //set as inputs
   u8_wdtState = _SWDTEN; //remember WDT state
   CLRWDT();       //clear the WDT timer
   _SWDTEN = 1;    //enable WDT to escape infinite wait
   do {
    E_HIGH(); DELAY_US(1); //read upper 4 bits
    u8_BusyFlag = GET_BUSY_FLAG();
    E_LOW(); DELAY_US(1);
    pulseE();              //read lower 4-bits
   } while(u8_BusyFlag);
   _SWDTEN = u8_wdtState;  //restore WDT enable state
  } else {
   DELAY_MS(10); // don't use busy, just delay
  }
  configBusAsOutLCD();
  if (u8_DataFlag) RS_HIGH();  // RS=1, data byte
  else    RS_LOW();            // RS=0, command byte
  outputToBusLCD(u8_Cmd >> 4); // send upper 4 bits
  pulseE();
  if (u8_Send8Bits) {
    outputToBusLCD(u8_Cmd);    // send lower 4 bits
    pulseE();
  }
 }
}
```

LCD D[7:4] ⟩Upper 4 bits⟨ ⟩Lower 4 bits⟨

E ⎽⎽⎽⎯⎽⎯⎽⎽

The WDT timer is enabled (_SWDTEN=1) for escaping the busy flag loop in case of wiring error or hardware failure.

} Write upper 4 bits

} Write lower 4 bits

FIGURE 8.36   writeLCD(), pulseE() Functions for the LCD interface.

current cursor location. The main() code first calls configControlLCD() to configure the PIC24 µC port pins then calls initLCD(), which initializes the display using the commands of Table 8.2. Observe that none of the writeLCD() calls in initLCD() use the busy flag for status checking; instead, the constant delay mode of writeLCD() is used. After initialization, the address counter of the LCD is at location 0. The first outStringLCD() in main() writes to the first line of the LCD. Only the first 16 characters of the string passed to outStringLCD() are visible in the display, even though

```
// Initialize the LCD, modify to suit your application and LCD
void initLCD(){
  DELAY_MS(50);            //wait for device to settle
  writeLCD(0x20,0,0,0); // 4 bit interface
  writeLCD(0x28,0,0,1); // 2 line display, 5x7 font
  writeLCD(0x28,0,0,1); // repeat
  writeLCD(0x06,0,0,1); // enable display
  writeLCD(0x0C,0,0,1); // turn display on; cursor, blink is off
  writeLCD(0x01,0,0,1); // clear display, move cursor to home
  DELAY_MS(3);
}

//Output a string to the LCD
void outStringLCD(char *psz_s) {
  while (*psz_s) {
    writeLCD(*psz_s, 1, 1,1);
    psz_s++;
  }
}
```
Writes string to the LCD at the current LCD cursor location.

```
int main (void) {
  configBasic(HELLO_MSG);

  configControlLCD();  //configure the LCD control lines
  initLCD();           //initialize the LCD
```
Write line 1, set address counter to first location of line 2, then write line 2.
```
  outStringLCD("******Hello, my name is Bob********");
  writeLCD(0xC0,0,1,1); // cursor to 2nd line
  outStringLCD("-----these lines are moving!-------");
  while (1) {
    writeLCD(0x18,0,1,1);  // shift left
    DELAY_MS(200);
    doHeartbeat();
  }
}
```
Loop continually left shifts the display, causing lines 1 and 2 to scroll across the display, moving right to left.

FIGURE 8.37   Write two strings to LCD and shift display.

the entire string is stored in the LCD data display RAM. The following statement writeLCD(0xC0,0,1,1) sets the internal address counter to 0x40 (first position of second line), so that the next outStringLCD() statement writes to the second line of the display. The 0xC0 byte in the writeLCD() function call is the *Set DD address* command, where 0xC0 = 0b1100000. The format of this command is 1*nnnnnnn*, where *nnnnnnn* is the data display address. Thus, the lower 7 bits of 0xC0 is 1000000, or 0x40, the address of the first location on the second line. An infinite loop is then entered in which the statement writeLCD(0x18,0,1,1) is followed by a 0.3 second delay. The 0x18 (0x00011000) command byte is the cursor & display shift command from Table 8.2 and has the format 0001*cr*00, with $c = 1$, $r = 0$ specifying a display left shift. The continual looping of this command causes the strings to scroll across the display moving right to left, with a 0.2 second delay between shifts. More sophisticated LCD modules allow graphical operations, such as turning on/off a pixel specified by an X,Y screen location.

THE PIC24H VERSUS THE PIC24F FAMILY

The examples in this chapter have concentrated on the PIC24H family. Devices in the PIC24F family have the following principal differences (other differences exist):

- The PIC24F family has a maximum Fcy of 16 MHz versus 40 MHz for the PIC24H family.
- The PIC24F family has a PLL with a fixed multiplication factor of 4X.
- The PIC24F FRC oscillator has a nominal 8.0 MHz frequency versus 7.37 MHz for the PIC24H family. The 8.0 MHz FRC oscillator coupled with the 4X PLL offers a convenient method for achieving the maximum Fcy of 16 MHz.
- The PIC24F family's configuration bits are stored in two packed words instead of six for the PIC24H family. Approximately the same functionality is offered despite the difference in size.

An attempt has been made to make the files supplied with this book's CD-ROM compatible with both the PIC24H and PIC24F families. The built-in compiler macros `__PIC24H__` and `__PIC24F__` have been used to differentiate code between the two families when needed. While all of the book's examples have been tested with the PIC24HJ32GP202, many of them have also been tested with the PIC24FJ64GA002, which is a 28-pin PIC24F μC that is pin compatible with the PIC24HJ32GP202.

SUMMARY

Code written in a high-level language (HLL) such as *C* is usually clearer in its intent, has fewer source lines, and is more portable than code written in assembly language. As such, many microcontroller applications are written in an HLL rather than assembly. However, understanding assembly language and the implementation of HLL constructs in assembly language is critical in writing efficient HLL microcontroller applications. The MPLAB PIC24 compiler is used for the examples in this book and provides a powerful tool for experimenting with PIC24HJ32GP202 applications. A simple PIC24HJ32GP202 hardware system with a power source, a reset switch, and a serial interface is used to demonstrate the basics of parallel port I/O, reset sources, and power saving modes. A PIC24 μC has many different sources of reset, with status bits in the RCON register used to determine the reset source. Reducing power consumption is an issue in many microcontroller applications, and the sleep, idle, and doze modes in the PIC24 μC can be used to reduce current draw. The watchdog timer runs on an independent clock source and can be used to wake the PIC24 from sleep and idle modes to resume execution. The PIC24HJ32GP202 has multiple parallel port I/O pins with bidirectional transfer capability as well as open-drain and weak pull-up functionality. An LCD module interface in 4-bit mode can be implemented using eight of the parallel port pins on the PIC24HJ32GP202.

REVIEW PROBLEMS

Assume that the target device is the PIC24HJ32GP202 µC for all problems.

1. Give the special register bit settings that configure RB5 as a digital input, with weak pull-up *disabled* and open-drain *disabled*.
2. Give the special register bit settings that configure RB6 as a digital output, with weak pull-up *disabled* and open-drain *enabled*.
3. Give the special register bit settings that configure RB2 as a digital input, with weak pull-up *enabled* and open-drain *disabled*.
4. Give the special register bit settings that configure RB3 as a digital output, with weak pull-up *disabled* and open-drain *disabled*.
5. Give PLL bit settings for the _PLLPRE, _PLLDIV, and _PLLPOST bit fields that will multiply the input frequency by 4 (show calculations at each stage that verify that you remain inside the constraint if the input frequency is 8 MHz).
6. Give PLL bit settings for the _PLLPRE, _PLLDIV, and _PLLPOST bit fields that will multiply the input frequency by 5 (show calculations at each stage that verify that you remain inside the constraint if the input frequency is 8 MHz).
7. Using the data of Table 8.1 for the PIC24HJ32GP202, predict the doze mode current for Fcy/4.
8. Using the data of Table 8.1 for the PIC24HJ32GP202, predict the doze mode current for Fcy/8.
9. For the following code segment, predict what you will see occur once power is applied, and explain your reasoning.

```
main() {
  ...normal config, including uart...
  outString("Howdy Y'all!\n");
  _SWDTEN = 1;
  while(1);
}
```

10. For the following code segment, predict what you will see occur once power is applied, and explain your reasoning.

```
main() {
   ...normal config, including uart...
   outString("Howdy Y'all!\n");
   if (_POR) {
      _SWDTEN = 1;
      _POR = 0;
   } else {
      _SWDTEN = 0;
   }
   while(1);
}
```

11. For the following code segment, predict what you will see occur once power is applied, and explain your reasoning.

```
main() {
   ...normal config, including uart...
   outString("Howdy Y'all!\n");
   asm("pwrsav #0");
   while(1);
}
```

12. For the following code segment, predict what you will see occur once power is applied, and explain your reasoning.

```
main() {
   ...normal config, including uart...
   outString("Howdy Y'all!\n");
   _SWDTEN = 1;
   asm("pwrsav #0");
   while(1);
}
```

The following problems assume external LEDs (LED1, LED2, etc.) and switches (SW1, SW2, etc.). When writing code for these problems, define macros for them as done in Figure 8.28 using the predefined macros in *include\pic24_ports.h*. You may use any of the RB*n* ports you wish to implement these problems. Assume switch inputs are pushbutton inputs and use the internal weak pull-up of the port.

13. Assume one LED (LED1) and one switch input (SW1). Write a `while(1){}` loop that initially will blink an LED1 once power is applied. On each press AND release of SW1, alternate between terminating the blinking and resuming the blinking. Draw a state machine chart for the problem, and implement it using the style of Figure 8.30.

14. Assume two LEDs (LED1, LED2) and one switch input (SW1). Both LEDs should be initially off. After each press AND release of SW1, change the LED state (LED1/LED2) in the sequence: OFF/ON, ON/OFF, ON/ON, OFF/OFF, OFF/ON, ON/OFF, ON/ON, OFF/OFF, etc. Draw a state machine chart for the problem, and implement it using the style of Figure 8.30.

15. Do problem #14, except the LEDs change state whenever a press OR a release occurs for SW1.

16. Do problem #13, except the blinking terminates or resumes whenever a press OR a release occurs for SW1.

For Figure 8.38, assume that macros named DFF_D, DFF_CK, DFF_R, DFF_S, and DFF_Q have been defined for the RB? pins connected to the external D flip-flop (refer to Chapter 1 for a review of D flip-flop operation).

17. Write a *C* function named `uint8 testDFFASync(uint8 u8_op)` that asynchronously resets the DFF if `u8_op` is non-zero, else an asynchronous set is performed. The function should return a true (non-zero `uint8` value) if the Q output returns the correct output value, else return a false value (zero). Assume nothing about the initial output states of the RB? ports when entering the function (you may assume that they have already been configured to be inputs or outputs as appropriate). When exiting the function, all outputs should be at their negated values (D, CK at "0"; S, R at "1").

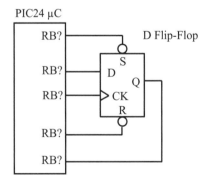

FIGURE 8.38   PIC24 μC to D flip-flop.

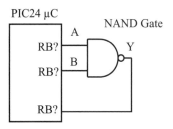

FIGURE 8.39   PIC24 µC to NAND gate.

For emphasis purposes only, use a 1 µs software delay to satisfy pulse width times, setup/hold times for the D input with regard to the clock and propagation delay through the DFF once the inputs have been applied.

18. Write a *C* function named uint8 testDFFSync(uint8 u8_dval) that synchronously clocks in a "1" to the DFF from the D input if u8_dval is non-zero, and a "0" otherwise. The function should return a true (non-zero uint8 value) if the Q output returns the correct output value, else return a false value (zero). Assume nothing about the initial output states of the RB? ports when entering the function (you may assume that they have already been configured to be inputs or outputs as appropriate). When exiting the function, all outputs should be at their negated values (D, CK at "0"; S, R at "1"). For emphasis purposes only, use a 1 µs software delay to satisfy pulse width times, setup/hold times for the D input with regard to the clock and propagation delay through the DFF once the inputs have been applied.

For Figure 8.39, assume that macros named GATE_A, GATE_B, and GATE_Y have been defined for the RB? pins connected to the external NAND gate (refer to Chapter 1 for a review of NAND operation).

19. Write a *C* function named uint8 testGate(void) that exhaustively applies all input combinations to the external gate. If the gate output returns the wrong output value for an input combination, terminate the test and return a false (zero) value. If the gate returns the correct output value for all input combinations, then return a true (non-zero uint8 value). Assume nothing about the initial output states of the RB? ports when entering the function (you may assume that they have already been configured to be inputs or outputs as appropriate). For emphasis purposes only, use a 1 µs software delay before reading the Y output after applying an input combination.

20. Repeat problem #19 except use an XOR gate as the external gate.

9

Interrupts and a First Look at Timers

This chapter discusses interrupts, which are of critical importance when implementing efficient input/output operations for microcontroller applications. Topics include interrupt fundamentals, PIC24 µC interrupt sources, and an introduction to using interrupts for accomplishing I/O. A first look at the powerful timer subsystem of the PIC24 µC uses a timer as a periodic interrupt source.

Learning Objectives

After reading this chapter, you will be able to:

- Discuss the general function of interrupts within a microprocessor and interrupt implementation on the PIC24 µC.
- Describe the difference between polled I/O and interrupt-driven I/O.
- Implement an interrupt service routine in *C* for the PIC24 µC.
- Implement an interrupt service routine using a state machine approach.
- Implement interrupt service routines that use the change notification and INT*x* interrupts.
- Discuss the structure of the PIC24 µC Timer2 and Timer3 subsystems and use them to generate periodic interrupts for input sampling.
- Implement an interface for a rotary encoder.
- Implement an interface for a keypad.

INTERRUPT BASICS

An *interrupt* in a microprocessor is a forced deviation from normal program flow by an external or internal event. On the PIC24 µC there are many possible internal and external events such as rising or falling edges on external pins, arrival of serial data, timer expiration, and so forth that can cause interrupts. Figure 9.1 illustrates what happens when an interrupt occurs on the PIC24 µC. During normal program flow, assume some external or internal event triggers an interrupt. After the

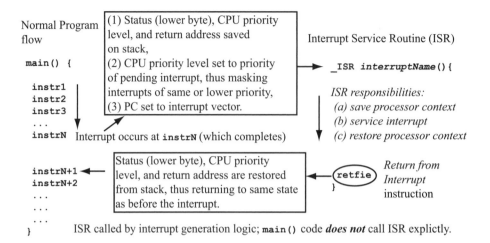

FIGURE 9.1   Interrupting normal program flow.

current instruction is finished, the CPU interrupt priority level (discussed later), lower byte of the status register, and the return address are pushed on the stack. The CPU interrupt priority level is then set to the priority level of the pending interrupt, and the PC is set to a predetermined location based on the pending interrupt called the *interrupt vector*, thus causing execution to continue at that point. After executing code to handle the interrupt, a retfie (return from interrupt) instruction is executed to return to normal program flow. The code that is executed when the interrupt occurs is referred to as the *interrupt service routine* (ISR). The ISR's function is to respond to whatever event triggered the interrupt. As an example, if the interrupt was triggered by the arrival of serial input data, the ISR would read the data, save it, then return. When viewing Figure 9.1, it is tempting to think of the ISR as a subroutine that is called by the main() program. However, the ISR is never manually called as a normal C function is called; instead, the ISR is invoked *automatically* by the PIC24 μC interrupt hardware on an interrupt occurrence. An ISR is said to execute in the *background,* while the normal program flow executes in the *foreground.* This book informally refers to background code as ISR code execution and foreground code as main() code execution. *Saving the processor context* in the ISR of Figure 9.1 means to save registers used by the ISR since these same registers can be used by the foreground code. An ISR can call other subroutines, and, in fact, can call a subroutine that has been interrupted. If a subroutine is interrupted, then called from the ISR, the subroutine has been reentered (a *reentrant* subroutine). For correct execution, a reentrant subroutine must use dynamic allocation for locals and parameters, and the ISR must save the processor context. An ISR can itself be interrupted as is discussed later, so generally the processor context is saved to the stack (dynamic allocation is used for the processor context).

You may question at this point why an interrupt capability is desireable. The I/O examples presented in the last chapter used a technique referred to as *polling*, where a status flag is checked repeatedly to determine data availability. This is referred to as *polled I/O* and is usually an inefficient method for implementing I/O operations. Imagine if your cell phone operated on the polled I/O principle. This would mean that you would occasionally have to pull it out of your pocket or purse, open it, and ask "Hello, is there anybody there?" This may seem laughable, but this is how we have been accomplishing I/O to this point. The problem with this approach is obvious—either you check your phone too often, which wastes your time, or you do not check it often enough, causing you to miss an important call. It is much more efficient to have the phone notify you of an incoming call. The ringer on your cell phone implements an interrupt; when the ringer sounds, you stop what you are doing and answer the phone, thus servicing the interrupt. When finished with the call, you then resume what you were doing earlier. This is known as *interrupt-driven I/O*. On the PIC24 µC, each interrupt source has an associated interrupt flag bit that becomes a "1" when the interrupt source event occurs. As an example, the U1RXIF bit is the receive character interrupt flag and becomes a "1" when asynchronous serial data is available over the RX serial pin. Most interrupt flag bits are contained in special function registers named the *interrupt flag status* (IFS) registers (there are five of these, IFS0 through IFS4).

Continuing the cell phone analogy, there are times when you do not want to answer the phone, like in a meeting or a movie theatre. At these times, you turn off the ringer, causing incoming calls to be ignored. On the PIC24 µC, most interrupt sources have an interrupt enable bit that must be a "1" in order for an interrupt to be invoked when the interrupt flag bit becomes a "1." If the interrupt enable bit is "0," the interrupt is *masked* or *disabled*. For example, the U1RXIE bit (receive character interrupt enable) is the interrupt enable for the U1RXIF interrupt. Most interrupt enable bits are contained in special function registers named the *interrupt enable control* (IEC) registers (there are five of these, IEC0 through IEC4). It is important to understand that the interrupt enable bit being a "0" does not prevent the interrupt flag bit from becoming a "1," just like turning off the phone ringer does not prevent incoming phone calls from arriving. A "0" interrupt enable bit only prevents an interrupt from being generated; in other words, it prevents a jump to the ISR. Some interrupts on the PIC24 µC are *non-maskable*, which means that you cannot block the automatic jump to the ISR when the interrupt occurs (for example, a fire alarm can be considered a non-maskable interrupt as it is never disabled).

At the risk of overusing the cell phone analogy, assume you are talking on the phone with a friend and that you are notified via call-waiting of an incoming call from your spouse, significant other, or other family member. You may say something like "Hold for a moment, there is an incoming call that I need to check," and then switch to the other call. This means that the incoming call has a *higher priority* than the current call. On the PIC24 µC, each interrupt source has an *interrupt priority level* (IPL) associated with it. This interrupt priority level ranges from 0 to 15 and allows interrupts of a higher priority to interrupt lower-priority ISR code. Interrupt priorities are discussed in detail in the next section.

PIC24 µC Interrupt Details

This section discusses PIC24 µC details such as the interrupt vector table, priority system, and the difference between traps and peripheral interrupts.

Vector Table

When an enabled interrupt occurs, the PIC24 µC fetches the ISR starting address for that interrupt from the *interrupt vector address* assigned to that interrupt. The interrupt vector addresses are stored in a group of program memory locations known as the *interrupt vector table* (IVT) and the *alternate interrupt vector table* (AIVT), which is shown in Figure 9.2. These locations along with the reset vector occupy locations 0x000004 through 0x0001FF, with user code starting at location 0x000200. By default, vector addresses are used from the IVT, but the AIVT can be enabled by setting the AIVT control bit (_ALTIVT=1) which is bit INTCON2<15>.

The number of interrupt sources on a PIC24 µC depends on the on-chip peripherals that are implemented for that particular microcontroller. Figure 9.3 shows the interrupt sources on the PIC24HJ32GP202. The "Vector Num" column gives the value written to the lower seven bits of the special function register INTTREG (INTTREG<6:0>) for the currently executing interrupt, with bits INTTREG<11:8> containing the interrupt's priority. (Note: The INTTREG register is not present in the PIC24F family.) The "PIC24 Compiler Name" column gives the C function name that must be used with the PIC24 compiler when writing an ISR for that particular interrupt.

Interrupt Priorities

As mentioned previously, the PIC24 µC implements an interrupt priority system with values from 0 (lowest) through 15 (highest). Interrupt priorities 8 through 15 are reserved for a special class of interrupt sources known as *traps* (vector numbers 1 through 5) with each interrupt priority level assigned to a single trap source. Priorities 0 through 7 are used for non-trap interrupt sources (*user* interrupts), with each user interrupt source assigned a 3-bit field in a special function register that contains the interrupt's priority level. These interrupt priority level bits are contained in a set of special function registers known as the *interrupt priority control* (IPC) registers (there are 18 of these, IPC0 through IPC17). The current CPU interrupt priority level is a 4-bit value (IPL<3:0>), with these bits split between two

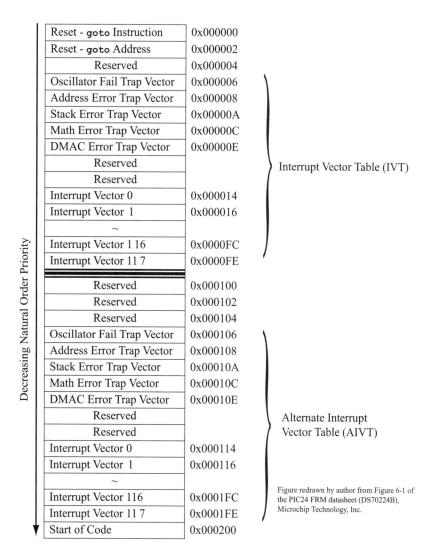

Decreasing Natural Order Priority

Reset - `goto` Instruction	0x000000
Reset - `goto` Address	0x000002
Reserved	0x000004
Oscillator Fail Trap Vector	0x000006
Address Error Trap Vector	0x000008
Stack Error Trap Vector	0x00000A
Math Error Trap Vector	0x00000C
DMAC Error Trap Vector	0x00000E
Reserved	
Reserved	
Interrupt Vector 0	0x000014
Interrupt Vector 1	0x000016
~	
Interrupt Vector 1 16	0x0000FC
Interrupt Vector 11 7	0x0000FE
Reserved	0x000100
Reserved	0x000102
Reserved	0x000104
Oscillator Fail Trap Vector	0x000106
Address Error Trap Vector	0x000108
Stack Error Trap Vector	0x00010A
Math Error Trap Vector	0x00010C
DMAC Error Trap Vector	0x00010E
Reserved	
Reserved	
Interrupt Vector 0	0x000114
Interrupt Vector 1	0x000116
~	
Interrupt Vector 116	0x0001FC
Interrupt Vector 11 7	0x0001FE
Start of Code	0x000200

Interrupt Vector Table (IVT)

Alternate Interrupt Vector Table (AIVT)

Figure redrawn by author from Figure 6-1 of the PIC24 FRM datasheet (DS70224B), Microchip Technology, Inc.

FIGURE 9.2   Interrupt vector table. (Adapted with permission of the copyright owner, Microchip Technology, Incorporated. All rights reserved. No further reprints or reproduction may be made without Microchip Inc.'s prior written consent.)

special function registers: IPL<2:0> bits are in the status register (SR<7:5>), while IPL<3> is contained in the core control register (CORCON<3>). The IPL bits are cleared at reset, which means that any enabled interrupt with priority level 1 or higher can interrupt the processor. Bits IPL<2:0> are writeable, but bit IPL<3> can only be cleared by user code (the IPL<3> bit is set when any trap occurs, because trap priorities are 8 and higher).

IVT Address	Vector Num	PIC24 Compiler Name	Vector Function
0x000006	1	_OscillatorFail	Oscillator Failure
0x000008	2	_AddressError	Address Error
0x00000A	3	_StackError	Stack Error
0x00000C	4	_MathError	Math Error
0x000014	8	_INT0Interrupt	INT0 – External Interrupt
0x000016	9	_IC1Interrupt	IC1 – Input Capture 1
0x000018	10	_OC1Interrupt	OC1 – Output Compare 1
0x00001A	11	_T1Interrupt	T1 – Timer1 Expired
0x00001E	13	_IC2Interrupt	IC2 – Input Capture 2
0x000020	14	_OC2Interrupt	OC2 – Output Compare 2
0x000022	15	_T2Interrupt	T2 – Timer2 Expired
0x000024	16	_T3Interrupt	T3 – Timer3 Expired
0x000026	17	_SPI1ErrInterrupt	SPI1E – SPI1 Error
0x000028	18	_SPI1Interrupt	SPI1 – SPI1 transfer done
0x00002A	19	_U1RXInterrupt	U1RX – UART1 Receiver
0x00002C	20	_U1TXInterrupt	U1TX – UART1 Transmitter
0x00002E	21	_ADC1Interrupt	ADC1 – ADC 1 convert done
0x000034	24	_SI2C1Interrupt	SI2C1 – I2C1 Slave Events
0x000036	25	_MI2CInterrupt	MI2C1 – I2C1 Master Events
0x00003A	27	_CNInterrupt	Change Notification Interrupt
0x00003C	28	_INT1Interrupt	INT1 – External Interrupt
0x000040	30	_IC7Interrupt	IC7 – Input Capture 7
0x000042	31	_IC8Interrupt	IC8 – Input Capture 8
0x00004E	37	_INT2Interrupt	INT2 – External Interrupt
0x000096	73	_U1ErrInterrupt	U1E – UART1 Error

FIGURE 9.3 PIC24HJ32GP202 interrupt sources.

When an enabled interrupt occurs, the interrupt's priority level must be higher than the current IPL<3:0> bits to be recognized. If *simultaneous* interrupts with the *same* priority level occur, then the interrupt with the *lower* vector number is recognized first. Before the ISR is executed, the current IPL bits are saved on the stack along with the return address then the IPL bits are set to the priority level of the recognized interrupt. This disables any further interrupts within the ISR caused by interrupts with that priority level. Interrupts of a higher priority can interrupt the ISR. If an ISR is interrupted by another interrupt, this is called *interrupt nesting*, which can be disabled by setting the interrupt nesting disable bit (NSTDIS, in INTCON1<15>) to a one (_NSTDIS=1). When interrupt nesting is disabled, any user-level interrupt sets the CPU IPL to 7, disabling any further user-level interrupts. Furthermore, the IPL<2:0> bits become read-only and the assigned priority levels for individual interrupts are only used to resolve simultaneous interrupts.

Setting a user interrupt priority to level 0 disables that interrupt even if its interrupt enable bit is set, because the priority level is not greater than the lowest CPU priority level of 0. Setting the IPL<2:0> bits to 7 disables all user interrupts. The DISI #lit14 instruction (*disable interrupts temporarily*) can be used to disable user interrupts with priorities 1 through 6 for #lit14 + 1 instruction cycles. This is useful for protecting critical code sections from user interrupts, such as is done in the configClock() function when the clock source is being changed.

TRAPS

A special type of interrupt source on the PIC24 µC are *traps*, which are internally generated, non-maskable interrupts which immediately halt instruction execution (*hard* traps) or which allow a few additional instruction to execute before jumping to the ISR (*soft* traps). Soft trap sources are DMA conflict write (not implemented on the PIC24HJ32GP202), math error (divide by zero), and stack error (triggers include the stack pointer falling below 0x800 or becoming greater than the SPLIM register). Hard trap sources are oscillator failure (which occurs if the fail-safe clock monitor detects a problem or if the PLL loses lock) and address error (caused by a misaligned access or a jump or branch to unimplemented program space). Complete details on the trap error sources are given in [14]. Table 9.1 summarizes the trap error sources.

TABLE 9.1   Trap summary.

Trap	Category	Priority	Flag(s)
Oscillator Failure	Hard	14	_OSCFAIL (oscillator fail, INTCON1<1>), _CF (clock fail, OSSCON<3>)
Address Error	Hard	13	_ADDRERR (address error, INTCON1<3>)
Stack Error	Soft	12	_STKERR (stack error, INTCON1<2>)
Math Error	Soft	11	_MATHERR (math error, INTCON1<4>)
DMAC Error	Soft	10	_DMACERR (DMA conflict write, INTCON1<5>)

INTERRUPT LATENCY

Interrupt latency is the amount of time from when an interrupt occurs to when the interrupt source is handled. In our cell phone analogy, this is the amount of time from when the phone rings until you say "Hello." In many cases reducing interrupt latency is important; as in our cell phone analogy, if you wait too long to answer the phone the person calling may give up and terminate the call. Interrupt latency consists of two parts: (1) the time from when the interrupt occurs until the first instruction of the ISR is handled, and (2) the number of instructions executed in the ISR before the interrupt source is acknowledged. Figure 9.4a shows the interrupt latency from the time of the interrupt to the first instruction of the ISR for the case when the interrupted instruction is a one-cycle instruction. After the interrupted instruction (INSTR_A) completes, it takes four clock cycles before the first instruction of the ISR is executed. The interrupt latency for a two-cycle instruction is also four clocks to the first instruction of the ISR, regardless of whether the interrupt occurs in the first or second cycle of the instruction ([29]), because of the first FNOP (fetch cycle, no operation) shown in Figure 9.4.

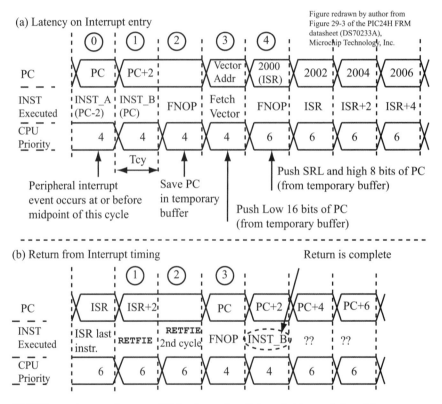

FIGURE 9.4 Interrupt latency to ISR first instruction. (Adapted with permission of the copyright owner, Microchip Technology, Incorporated. All rights reserved. No further reprints or reproduction may be made without Microchip Inc.'s prior written consent.)

Once the ISR has begun execution, the latency until the interrupt is serviced depends on how much of the processor state has to be saved within the ISR. A complex ISR may require many working registers to be pushed on the stack at entry to the ISR. The push.s (push shadow registers) instruction that saves W0, W1, W2, W3, and the status register to the stack can help reduce the number of clocks required to save the processor context. There is only one set of shadow registers so an ISR that uses the shadow registers cannot be interrupted by a higher priority interrupt that also uses the shadow registers, or else the values saved to the shadow registers may be corrupted.

Return from interrupt timing consists of two instruction cycles for the `retfie` instruction plus one instruction cycle to fetch the instruction at the return address as shown in Figure 9.4b; the instruction at the return address is executed on the fourth instruction cycle counting from `retfie` start.

ISR OVERHEAD

A concern in interrupt processing is the percentage of the CPU's execution time spent in interrupt service routines. The following definitions will help us compute this percentage.

■ IENTRY: Number of instruction cycles for ISR entry (four on the PIC24 μC).
■ IBODY: Number of instruction cycles for the ISR body (not including `retfie`).
■ IEXIT: Number of instruction cycles for ISR exit (three on the PIC24 μC).
■ FISR: Frequency (number of times per second) at which the ISR is triggered.
■ TISR: The ISR triggering period, which is 1/FISR. For example, if an ISR is executed at 1 KHz, TISR is 1 ms.

Using these definitions, Equation 9.1 shows the percentage of a PIC24 μC's instruction cycles consumed by an interrupt service routine:

$$\text{ISR}\% = [(\text{IENTRY} + \text{IBODY} + \text{IEXIT}) \times \text{FISR}]/\text{FCY} \times 100\% \qquad (9.1)$$

In Equation 9.1, the numerator is the number of ISR instructions executed in 1 second, while the denominator (FCY) is the total number of instructions executed in 1 second. Table 9.2 shows the CPU% for FCY = 40 MHz assuming an ISR body of 50 instruction cycles for varying ISR periods.

TABLE 9.2   ISR CPU percentage for FCY = 40 MHz.

	TISR = 10 ms	TISR = 1 ms	TISR = 100 μs	TISR = 10 μs
ISR% (IBODY = 50)	0.01%	0.14%	1.43%	14.3%

The two key variables in Equation 9.1 are IBODY and FISR, as increasing either one increases the CPU time percentage consumed by the ISR. The FISR variable is set by the I/O constraints of the device being serviced by the interrupt, so only IBODY is under direct control by the application programmer. A golden rule for writing interrupt service routines is to keep an ISR as short as possible to reduce its impact on available CPU time. Furthermore, execution of an active ISR blocks the execution of other pending interrupts with the same priority, increasing the latency of those interrupts. Ideally, an ISR should service the interrupt, which generally means performing some input/output action, set one or more flags indicating to the foreground task that the interrupt occurred, then return.

ISR FUNCTIONS IN C

To create an interrupt service routine (ISR) in C, first consider a simple ISR to handle the math error trap:

```
void _ISR _MathError(void) {
... code for ISR ...
}
```

This ISR illustrates the essential ingredients for declaring an ISR in C:

- The function must be named based on which ISR it handles, where the column labeled as "PIC24 Compiler Name" in Figure 9.3 gives the ISR function name to be used when writing an ISR for that particular interrupt. In this case, the function's name _MathError indicates that it handles the math error soft trap.
- The function must take no parameters and return no value, denoted by the use of void *functionName*(void).
- The function must be declared with the _ISR or _ISRFAST attribute to inform the compiler to save and restore registers as shown in Figure 9.1 and to return by using a retfie instruction. Additional information on _ISR and _ISRFAST are provided later in this chapter.

THE DEFAULT INTERRUPT

The *default interrupt handler* provides a more complete example of interrupt handling. When no ISR is defined for an interrupt, the PIC24 compiler generates an ISR function named _DefaultInterrupt() that contains only a software reset. However, the _DefaultInterrupt() function can be overridden by the user if desired. Figure 9.5 shows the version of the _DefaultInterrupt() function contained in *common\pic24_util.c*. As stated above, observe that the _ISR or _ISRFAST macro must be used before the function name to identify this function to the PIC24 compiler as an interrupt service routine so that the compiler can generate appropriate code to save/restore registers within the ISR and to use a retfie instruction to return. Our _DefaultInterrupt() function saves the contents of the INTTREG register into a persistent variable named u16_INTTREGlast; this is done because INTTREG identifies the priority and vector number of the interrupt (only for the PIC24H family). The reportError(const char *sz_errorMessage) function is then called, which saves sz_errorMessage in a persistent variable named sz_lastError,

(a) Code for default interrupt handler

```
_PERSISTENT const char* sz_lastError;
_PERSISTENT char* sz_lastTimeoutError;
_PERSISTENT INTTREGBITS INTTREGBITS_last;
#define u16_INTTREGlast \
        BITS2WORD(INTTREGBITS_last)
```
⎫ _PERSISTENT error variables used
⎬ for tracking errors across resets.
⎭

⎫ This allows treating the INTTREGBITS_last
⎬ structure as a single uint16 value.
⎭

```
void _ISR _DefaultInterrupt(void) {
  u16_INTTREGlast = INTTREG;
  reportError("Unhandled interrupt, ");
}
```
⎫ _DefaultInterrupt is the name of the
⎬ default ISR used by the PIC24 compiler.
⎬ Our version saves the interrupt cause
⎭ (INTTREG) then does a software reset.

```
void reportError(const char*
                 sz_errorMessage) {
  sz_lastError = sz_errorMessage;
  asm ("reset");
}
```
⎫ Saves the error message, then
⎬ does a software reset
⎭

```
void printResetCause(void) {
...print reset cause, see Chapter 8...
  if (u16_INTTREGlast != 0) {
    outString("Error trapped: ");
    outString(sz_lastError);
    if (sz_lastInterrupt != 0) {
      outString("Priority: ");
      outUint8(INTTREGBITS_last.ILR);
      outString(" , Vector number: ");
      outUint8(INTTREGBITS_last.VECNUM);
    }
    outString("\n\n");
    sz_lastError = NULL;
    u16_INTTREGlast = 0;
  }
}
```
After reset, printResetCause() prints
the error message.

⎫ Output error message saved
⎬ from last reset
⎭

⎫ If last reset was caused by an
⎬ unhandled interrrupt, print the
⎬ priority (ILR) and vector
⎭ number (VECNUM)

⎫ Clear _PERSISTENT error variables.
⎭

(b) MPLAB Program Memory

Line	Address	Opcode	Label	Dis
1	0000	040C02		goto _reset
2	0002	000000		nop
3	0004	000D8C		_DefaultInterrupt
4	0006	000D8C		_DefaultInterrupt
5	0008	000D8C		_DefaultInterrupt
6	000A	000D8C		_DefaultInterrupt
7	000C	000D8C		_DefaultInterrupt

Lines 3–5: Unhandled interrupts use _DefaultInterrupt

Line 7: Math Error Trap Vector

FIGURE 9.5   Custom _DefaultInterrupt() ISR.

then executes a software reset. After the software reset, the printResetCause() function then prints the contents of sz_lastError if it is non-null and also the contents of the u16_INTTREGBITSlast variable if it is non-zero, thus identifying the reset source that triggered this processor reset. Note that the definition of u16_INTTREGlast as #define u16_INTTREGlast BITS2WORD(INTTREGBITS_last) allows this variable to be accessed as INTTREGBITS_last, enabling printResetCause() to easily read the two fields (VECNUM and ILR) contained within it. Figure 9.5b shows a program memory dump from MPLAB. Observe that all interrupt vectors have the address of _DefaultInterrupt by default.

Figure 9.6a shows a program that tests the _DefaultInterrupt() ISR by purpose-fully generating a math error trap. This is done by initializing the variable u8_zero to 0, then executing u8_zero=1/u8_zero, which generates a divide-by-zero trap. The u8_zero variable is declared as volatile, which means that this memory location can be modified between instruction accesses and thus disables certain compiler optimizations. If a normal variable is used, then the compiler will optimize away this seemingly useless *C* statement.

Figure 9.6b shows the console output generated by the code of Figure 9.6a; observe that when a key is pressed, the while(1){} loop is entered and the math error trap is generated. The priority (0x0B, 11) and vector number (0x04) output by printResetCause() match the priority in Table 9.1 and vector number in Figure 9.3.

AN EXAMPLE ISR

Figure 9.7a shows an ISR written for the math error trap; this code would be used in the source of Figure 9.6 to handle the math error trap instead of the _DefaultInterrupt() function. The function name _MathError() is used to indicate that this ISR is for the math error trap; observe that the MPLAB program memory dump in Figure 9.7c now shows this function address inserted in the interrupt

(a) Simplified test code (*trap_test.c*) to generate a Math Error Trap
```
int main (void) {
  volatile uint8 u8_zero;
  configBasic(HELLO_MSG);
  while (1) {
    outString("Hit a key to start divide by zero test...");
    inChar();
    outString("OK. Now dividing by zero.\n");
    u8_zero = 0;
    u8_zero = 1/u8_zero;          Generates divide-by-zero
    doHeartbeat();                (Math Error) trap
  } // end while (1)
}
```

(b) Console Output
```
Reset cause: Power-on.
Device ID = 0x00000F1D (PIC24HJ32GP202), revision 0x00003001 (A2)
Fast RC Osc with PLL
                                                     pressed a key
trap_test.c, built on Jun  6 2008 at 10:17:57
Hit a key to start divide by zero test...OK. Now dividing by zero.
Reset cause: Software Reset.
Error trapped: Unhandled interrupt, Priority: 0x0B, Vector number: 0x04
```
        _DefaultInterrupt() ISR saves error message and interrupt information
        from INTTREG, then causes the software reset.
        _printResetCause() then prints out the saved error message, interrupt information.

FIGURE 9.6   Testing of the _DefaultInterrupt() ISR with a math error trap.

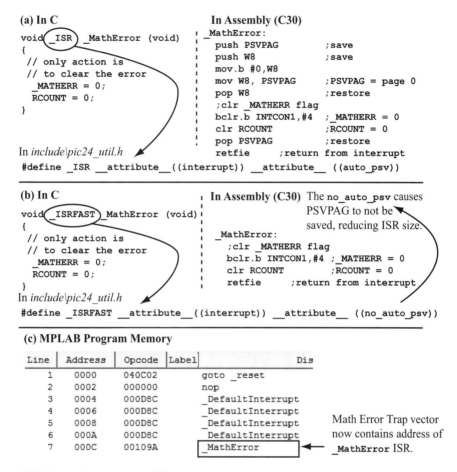

FIGURE 9.7 A _MathError ISR.

vector table address 0x00000C that is used for the math error trap. The _MathError()
code is the simplest possible ISR as all it does is clear the conditions associated with
the interrupt source. In this case, the _MATHERR flag must be cleared as it is the flag
that triggered the interrupt, or else the processor becomes hung in an infinite loop
because each time the ISR is exited, it immediately re-enters the ISR. The RCOUNT
register is also cleared to escape the divide repeat loop faster (the divide repeat loop
would eventually be escaped but multiple divide-by-zero trap errors would be generated by the same divide instruction as the RCOUNT register is decremented each
time the ISR returns to the divide instruction). Figure 9.7a shows the assembly code
generated by the PIC24 compiler for the _MathError ISR. The _ISR macro specifies
the auto_psv attribute, which instructs the compiler that the ISR function may wish
to access data stored in program memory through the program visibility space,

so the PSVPAG register is saved on the stack and then set to a value appropriate for this ISR's location in program memory. The `_ISRFAST` macro used in Figure 9.7b specifies the `_no_auto_psv` attribute, which instructs the compiler that this ISR does not use the program visibility space, so the PSVPAG register does not have to be modified. This reduces the assembly code size and reduces the latency for the ISR. Our code examples use the `_ISRFAST` macro if the ISR does not access data that resides in program memory.

CHANGE NOTIFICATION INTERRUPTS

The first user interrupt source that we will discuss is the *input change notification* interrupt, which is generated from a change of state on one or more change notification (CN) pins. Figure 9.8 shows a conceptual block diagram of the system. Each CNx input has an individual interrupt enable named CNxIE. If one or more CNxIE bits are a "1," then any state change on an enabled CNx input causes the change notification interrupt flag (CNIF) to be set. The weak pull-up on each CNx pin can be optionally enabled as has already been discussed in Chapter 8.

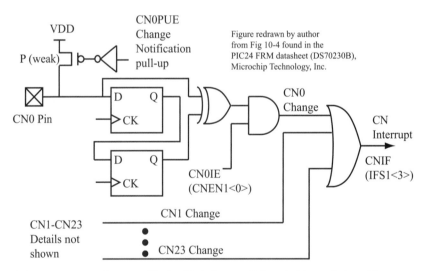

FIGURE 9.8 Input change notification block diagram. (Adapted with permission of the copyright owner, Microchip Technology, Incorporated. All rights reserved. No further reprints or reproduction may be made without Microchip Inc.'s prior written consent.)

WAKE FROM SLEEP/IDLE

The change notification interrupt can be used to wake the processor from sleep or idle mode. The code given in Figure 9.9 assumes the pushbutton switch SW1 is

```
//Interrupt Service Routine for Change Notification
void _ISRFAST _CNInterrupt (void) {
  _CNIF = 0;    //clear the change notification interrupt bit
}
```
            ◄———————— Clear the interrupt flag before exiting!

```
/// Switch1 configuration
inline void CONFIG_SW1() {
  CONFIG_RB13_AS_DIG_INPUT();        //use RB13 for switch input
  ENABLE_RB13_PULLUP();              //enable the pull-up
  ENABLE_RB13_CN_INTERRUPT();        //CN13IE = 1
  DELAY_US(1);                       // Wait for pull-up
}
```
                                    Macro to set CN*x*IE bit associated with
                                    RB13 port.

```
int main (void) {
  configBasic(HELLO_MSG);
  /** Configure the switch ***********/
  CONFIG_SW1();  //enables individual CN interrupt also
  /** Configure Change Notification general interrupt */
  _CNIF = 0;           //Clear the interrupt flag
  _CNIP = 2;           //Choose a priority
  _CNIE = 1;           //enable the Change Notification general interrupt
  while(1) {
    outString("Entering Sleep mode, press button to wake.\n");
    // Finish sending characters before sleeping
    WAIT_UNTIL_TRANSMIT_COMPLETE_UART1();
    SLEEP();           //macro for asm("pwrsav #0")
  }
}
```
                        Pushing the switch here generates CN interrupt, causing
                        wakeup and execution of the `_CNinterrupt` ISR, which then
                        returns here and loop continues.

An interrupt flag (`_CNIF`) should be cleared before the interrupt is enabled (`_CNIE=1`).
The priority (`_CNIP = 2`) chosen here was arbitrary, but it must be greater than 0 for
the ISR to be executed.

FIGURE 9.9   Using the change notification interrupt to wake from sleep.

attached to port RB13, which is also change notification input CN13 (the fact that
the numbers are the same is a coincidence, because change notification pin numbering and PORTB pin numbering do not typically coincide). The CONFIG_SW1()
macro configures RB13 as a digital input, enables the change notification pull-
up (ENABLE_RB13_PULLUP()), delays to give the pull-up time to bring the pin's
voltage up to VDD, and enables the individual change notification interrupt
(ENABLE_RB13_CN_INTERRUPT()). The ENABLE_RB13_CN_INTERRUPT() is a one-line macro
that maps to the statement _CN13IE=1. Before the while(1)() loop is entered, the
change notification interrupt flag is cleared (_CNIF=0), the change notification priority is assigned (_CNIP=2), and the global change notification interrupt enable is
set (_CNIE=1). When enabling interrupts, it is important to clear the associated interrupt flag *before* the interrupt is enabled to avoid an immediate jump to the ISR
in the case where the interrupt flag was set prior to the interrupt being enabled.

Remember that the interrupt enable does not prevent the interrupt flag from being set; it only prevents the jump to the ISR. Our usage of priority level 2 for this interrupt is arbitrary; the only requirement is that it is greater than 0 so that the interrupt is recognized and a jump to our ISR is made when the interrupt occurs. In the while(1){} loop, a message is printed then the SLEEP() macro (mapped to asm("pwrsav #0")) is used to put the processor to sleep. Pressing SW1 generates a change notification interrupt, waking the processor and causing a jump to the _CNInterrupt() ISR, which clears the change notification interrupt flag (_CNIF = 0). Upon ISR return, execution resumes in the while(1){} body. Two change notification interrupts are generated for each press and release of the switch: one for the press and one for the release.

USING A CHANGE INTERRUPT TO MEASURE INTERRUPT LATENCY

Figure 9.10a shows code for an experiment used to measure interrupt latency using a change notification interrupt. Pin RB2 is used to generate a change notification interrupt on pin RB3/CN7. The while(1){} loop in main consists of _LATB2=1 to generate the interrupt; the two following nop instructions cause a two T_{CY} period delay so that the interrupt is recognized during the bra instruction at the bottom of the loop. A change notification requires a minimum pulse width of two T_{CY} periods to be recognized according to the datasheet [31]. The change notification interrupt causes transfer of control to the _CNInterrupt ISR, which clears RB2 (_LATB2=0). The three nop instructions in the ISR are used to provide delay for the change in RB2 status to propagate through the change notification logic before the CNIF flag is cleared and the ISR is exited. The ISR returns to the _LATB2=1 operation (bset) in the while(1){} loop, causing the cycle to repeat.

Figure 9.10b shows the repeating square wave on the RB2 pin caused by repeatedly bouncing between the while(1){} loop and the _CNInterrupt() ISR. Both the high and low periods are 8 T_{CY} periods. This experiment was run with a slow F_{CY} (4 MHz) so that the output port delay was small with regard to T_{CY}; if you try this with a fast F_{CY} such as 40 MHz you may get different results because of the variation in where the interrupt occurs within T_{CY} for an instruction.

INTx EXTERNAL INTERRUPTS, REMAPPABLE PINS

The INTx interrupt inputs are another interrupt source on the PIC24 µC and set their corresponding interrupt flags (INTxIF) on either a rising or falling edge transition as determined by their corresponding edge polarity select bit (INTxEP = 1 selects falling edges while INTxEP = 0 selects rising edges). Most PIC24 microcontrollers implement three INTx interrupt inputs (INT0, INT1, INT2).

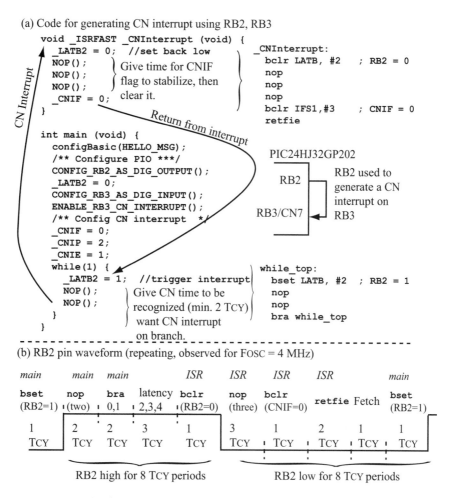

(a) Code for generating CN interrupt using RB2, RB3

```
void _ISRFAST _CNInterrupt (void) {
  _LATB2 = 0;  //set back low
  NOP();
  NOP();
  NOP();
  _CNIF = 0;  clear it.
}
```
Give time for CNIF flag to stabilize, then

```
_CNInterrupt:
  bclr LATB, #2    ; RB2 = 0
  nop
  nop
  nop
  bclr IFS1,#3     ; CNIF = 0
  retfie
```

```
int main (void) {
  configBasic(HELLO_MSG);
  /** Configure PIO ***/
  CONFIG_RB2_AS_DIG_OUTPUT();
  _LATB2 = 0;
  CONFIG_RB3_AS_DIG_INPUT();
  ENABLE_RB3_CN_INTERRUPT();
  /** Config CN interrupt */
  _CNIF = 0;
  _CNIP = 2;
  _CNIE = 1;
  while(1) {
    _LATB2 = 1;  //trigger interrupt
    NOP();
    NOP();
  }
}
```
Give CN time to be recognized (min. 2 TCY) want CN interrupt on branch.

PIC24HJ32GP202

RB2 used to generate a CN interrupt on RB3

RB2
RB3/CN7

```
while_top:
  bset LATB, #2  ; RB2 = 1
  nop
  nop
  bra while_top
```

(b) RB2 pin waveform (repeating, observed for FOSC = 4 MHz)

main	*main*	*main*	*ISR*	*ISR*	*ISR*	*ISR*	*main*
bset (RB2=1)	**nop** (two)	**bra** 0,1	latency 2,3,4	**bclr** (RB2=0)	**nop** (three)	**bclr** (CNIF=0)	**retfie** Fetch	**bset** (RB2=1)
1 TCY	2 TCY	2 TCY	3 TCY	1 TCY	3 TCY	1 TCY	2 TCY	1 TCY	1 TCY

RB2 high for 8 TCY periods   RB2 low for 8 TCY periods

FIGURE 9.10   Using the change notification interrupt to measure interrupt latency.

The PIC24HJ32GP202 pin diagram of Figure 8.2 shows that INT0 is assigned pin #16 but that the INT1/INT2 inputs are not assigned to any pins. To expose this functionality, these pins must be mapped to an external pin. Internal pin functions such as INT1/INT2 on some PIC24 microcontrollers can be assigned to external *remappable* pins (the RP*n* pins in Figure 8.2), which means that special function register bits control how these internal pins are mapped to external pins. The number of RP*n* pins varies by processor, and some PIC24 processors lack remappable pins altogether. Table 9.3 shows the remappable function inputs on the PIC24HJ32GP202. To assign one of these input functions to an external RP*n* pin, the function's RP*n* selection bits shown in column 3 are assigned the value *n*. The input function's RP*n* selection bits are actually multiplexor select bits that steer an

TABLE 9.3   Remappable inputs for PIC24HJ32GP202.

Input Name	Function Name	Example Assignment to RP*n*
External Interrupt 1	INT1	_INT1R = *n*;
External Interrupt 2	INT2	_INT2R = *n*;
Timer2 External Clock	T2CK	_T2CKR = *n*;
Timer3 External Clock	T3CK	_T3CKR = *n*;
Input Capture 1	IC1	_IC1R = *n*;
Input Capture 2	IC2	_IC2R = *n*;
Input Capture 7	IC7	_IC7R = *n*;
Input Capture 8	IC8	_IC8R = *n*;
Output Compare Fault A	OCFA	_OCFAR = *n*;
UART1 Receive	U1RX	_U1RXR = *n*;
UART1 Clear To Send	U1CTS	_U1CTSR = *n*;
SPI1 Data Input	SDI1	_SDI1R = *n*;
SPI1 Clock Input	SCK1	_SCK1R = *n*;
SPI1 Slave Select Input	SS1	_SS1R = *n*;

RP*n* input to the input function pin. After reset, these RP*n* selection bits are zero, which means the input is not assigned to any RP*n* pin. As an example, the following statement steers pin RP6 to the INT1 input function:

```
_INT1R = 6;          //assign INT1 to pin RP6
```

Our code uses a macro to accomplish this (defined in *include\pic24_ports.h*):

```
CONFIG_INT1_TO_RP(6);
```

If an RP*n* function shares its external pin with an analog input A*x*, then the analog pin must be configured as a digital pin by setting the appropriate _PCFG*x* bit to a 1 for the remappable digital functions to work properly. Macros are available named CONFIG_RP*N*_AS_DIG_PIN() that accomplish this. For example, on the PIC24HJ32GP202 the following code steers RP15 to the INT1 pin and configures the RP15 pin for digital functionality:

```
CONFIG_RP15_AS_DIG_PIN();
CONFIG_INT1_TO_RP(15);
```

It is safest to use the CONFIG_RPN_AS_DIG_PIN() macro every time that an input function is mapped to an RP*n* pin because the macro generates no code in the case that the RP*n* pin contains no analog functionality.

Table 9.4 shows the remappable output functions for the PIC24HJ32GP202. Each remappable pin RP*n* is assigned a 5-bit field named RP*n*R; the value of this bit field controls the output function that is mapped to it. Each RP*n*R bit field is actually the selection bits for a multiplexor that steers an output pin function to its associated RP*n* pin. After reset, each RP*n*R bit field is zero which means that no output function assignment is made. The following statement steers the U1TX output to the RP11 pin:

```
_RP11R = 3;          //assign U1TX to RP11R
```

Our code examples use a macro to accomplish this (defined in *include\pic24_ports.h*):

```
CONFIG_U1TX_TO_RP(11);
```

TABLE 9.4   Remappable outputs for PIC24HJ32GP202.

Output Name	Function Name	RP*n*R<4:0> Value	Example Assignment to RP*n*
Default Port Pin	NULL	0	_RP*n*R = 0;
UART1 Transmit	U1TX	3	_RP*n*R = 3;
UART1 Ready To Send	U1RTS	4	_RP*n*R = 4;
SPI1 Data Output	SDO1	7	_RP*n*R = 7;
SPI1 Clock Output	SCK1OUT	8	_RP*n*R = 8;
SPI1 Slave Select Output	SS1OUT	9	_RP*n*R = 9;
Output Compare 1	OC1	18	_RP*n*R = 18;
Output Compare 2	OC2	19	_RP*n*R = 19;

The analog pin functionality of an RP*n* pin should also be disabled when a digital output function is mapped to it by using the CONFIG_RPN_AS_DIG_PIN() macro.

The RP*n* configuration bits for both input and output mapping can be protected from writes by the IOLOCK bit (OSCCON<6>). At reset, IOLOCK is cleared, which allows unlimited writes to the RP*n* configuration bits. Setting IOLOCK prevents further writes to the RP*n* configuration bits. The purpose of the IOLOCK bit is to prevent accidental reconfiguration of the I/O pins, which could be disastrous in a production system. The suggested use of the IOLOCK bit is to perform all pin configuration and then set the IOLOCK bit. Our code examples are intended for experimentation purposes, and thus do not change the IOLOCK from its default state of zero. Recall from Chapter 8 that the __builtin_write_OSCCONL function should be used to write the OSCCON register since an unlock sequence is required when writing to this register. The IOL1WAY bit in the configuration registers (see Chapter 8) offers an additional level of protection against reconfiguration. The default (unprogrammed) state for IOL1WAY, which corresponds to the IOL1WAY_ON mask, prevents IOLOCK from being cleared once it is set. This means that the configuration bits cannot be changed after the IOLOCK bit is set. Our default configuration bits in *common\pic24_configbits.c* use the IOL1WAY_OFF mask, which allows normal setting/clearing of the IOLOCK bit.

Returning to the subject of INT0/INT1/INT2 external interrupts, Listing 9.1 shows the code of Figure 9.9 modified to use INT1 for waking from sleep mode. Either a negative (falling) or a positive (rising) edge can be selected to wake the processor; the code uses a negative edge via the statement _INT1EP=1. The CONFIG_INT1_TO_RP(13) macro is used to steer the RP13 pin to the INT1 interrupt. The CONFIG_RP13_AS_DIG_PIN() macro is not used in this case because the CONFIG_RB13_AS_DIG_INPUT() macro already disables the analog functionality on pin RB13, which is shared with RP13.

LISTING 9.1   Using INT1 to wake from sleep mode.

```
//Interrupt Service Routine for INT1
void _ISRFAST _INT1Interrupt (void) {
  _INT1IF = 0; //clear the interrupt bit
}
/// Switch1 configuration, use RB13
inline void CONFIG_SW1() {
  CONFIG_RB13_AS_DIG_INPUT();          //use RB13 for switch input
  ENABLE_RB13_PULLUP();                //enable the pullup
  DELAY_US(1);                         // Wait for pull-up
}
int main (void) {
  configBasic(HELLO_MSG);
  /** Configure the switch **********/
  CONFIG_SW1();
  CONFIG_INT1_TO_RP(13); //map INT1 to RP13
  /** Configure INT1 interrupt */
  _INT1IF = 0;                         //Clear the interrupt flag
  _INT1IP = 2;                         //Choose a priority
  _INT1EP = 1;                         //negative edge triggered
  _INT1IE = 1;                         //enable INT1 interrupt
  while(1) {
    outString("Entering Sleep mode, press button to wake.\n");
    //finish sending characters before sleeping
```

```
        WAIT_UNTIL_TRANSMIT_COMPLETE_UART1();
        SLEEP();                              //macro for asm("pwrsav #0")
    }
}
```

SWITCH INPUTS AND CHANGE NOTIFICATION/INTx INTERRUPTS

It is tempting to use either the change notification or INTx interrupts for processing switch input events. However, writing code to correctly handle the multiple interrupt flag events caused by mechanical switch bounce is problematic. A simpler approach, such as switch polling using a periodic timer interrupt as discussed in the next section, is usually a better option. Both the change notification and INTx interrupts are best used with signal sources that have clean transitions, such as those produced by an external integrated circuit (see the "Reflow Oven" capstone project in Chapter 15 for an example of using the INT1 interrupt input).

PERIODIC TIMER INTERRUPTS

Other user interrupt sources available on the PIC24 are various timer interrupts. Recall from Chapter 8 that a timer is simply a counter, with elapsed *time* computed as shown in Equation 9.2, where T_{TMR} is the timer clock period and *Ticks* is the number of elapsed timer counts.

$$\text{Time} = \text{Ticks} \times T_{TMR} \qquad (9.2)$$

There are multiple timers available on the PIC24HJ32GP202, some of which are special-purpose timers such as the watchdog and power-on reset timers while others are general-purpose such as Timers 1, 2, and 3. In this chapter, we discuss the use of Timers 2 and 3 for generating periodic interrupts, with full coverage of timers reserved for Chapter 12.

Timers 2 and 3 are two general-purpose timers that can either act as separate 16-bit timers or be combined into one 32-bit timer named Timer2/3. Other PIC24H family members have additional paired timers numbered Timer4/5, Timer 6/7, etc.; these paired timers have the same functionality as Timer2/3. From the Timer2 block diagram of Figure 9.11, note that the timer can be clocked by either an external clock on the T2CK pin or from the internal clock (T_{CY}). The prescaler for the Timer2 clock has four settings of 1:1, 1:8, 1:64, and 1:256. In this chapter's applications, we will always use the internal clock source (TGATE = 0, TCS = 0). In this mode, the Timer2 interrupt flag (T2IF) is set whenever the Timer2 register (TMR2) contents are equal to the Timer2 period register (PR2) contents, which also resets TMR2 to 0.

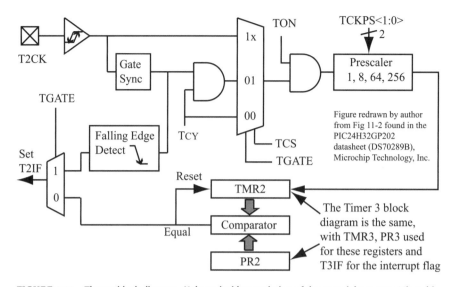

FIGURE 9.11 Timer2 block diagram. (Adapted with permission of the copyright owner, Microchip Technology, Incorporated. All rights reserved. No further reprints or reproduction may be made without Microchip Inc.'s prior written consent.)

TABLE 9.5 Timer2 min/max timeouts for Fcy = 40 MHz.

	PRE=1	**PRE=8**	**PRE=64**	**PRE=256**
Min. Timeout (PR2 = 0)	25 ns	200 ns	1600 ns	6400 ns
Max. Timeout (PR2 = 0xFFFF = 65535)	1.64 ms	13.1 ms	105 ms	419 ms
Max. Timeout (32-bit mode)	107 s	859 s	6872 s	27488 s

The time between TMR2 resets is known as the Timer2 *timeout period* (T_{T2IF}) and is calculated as shown in Equation 9.3 (recall that T_{CY} is equal to $1/F_{CY}$):

$$T_{T2IF} = (PR2{+}1) \times PRE \times T_{CY} = (PR2{+}1) \times PRE/F_{CY} \qquad (9.3)$$

Table 9.5 shows minimum and maximum T_{T2IF} periods for Fcy = 40 MHz. The minimum timeout period is also the timer accuracy, which decreases with larger prescaler values. The 32-bit Timer2/3 mode is useful for longer timeout periods.

Figure 9.12 gives detailed information on the Timer2 configuration (T2CON) register that contains the control bits shown in Figure 9.11. In this chapter, we use the internal clock and 16-bit mode for Timer2, which means bit settings of T32 = 0, TCS = 0, and TGATE = 0 (timers are discussed further in Chapter 12). The Timer3 block diagram is the same as Timer2, with TMR2, PR2, T2IF, T2CK replaced by

R/W-0	U-0	R/W-0	U-0	U-0	U-0	U-0	U-0
TON	UI	TSIDL	UI	UI	UI	UI	UI
15	14	13	12	11	10	9	8
U-0	R/W-0	R/W-0	R/W-0	R/W-0	U-0	R/W-0	U-0
UI	TGATE	TCKPS<1:0>		T32	UI	TCS	UI
7	6	5	4	3	2	1	0

Bit 15: TON: Timer2 On Bit
    When T32 = 1:
      1 = Starts 32-bit Timer2/3
      0 = Stops 32-bit Timer2/3
    When T32 = 0:
      1 = Starts 16-bit Timer2
      0 = Stops 16-bit Timer2

Bit 13: TSIDL: Stop in Idle Mode Bit
    1 = Discontinue module operation device enters Idle mode
    0 = Continue module operation in Idle mode

Bit 6: TGATE: Timer2 Gated Time Accumulation Enable
    When TCS = 1:
    This bit is ignored.
    When TCS = 0:
      1 = Gated time accumulation enabled
      0 = Gated time accumulation disabled

Bit 5-4: TCKPS<1:0>: Timer2 Input Clock Prescale Select Bits
    11 = 1:256 , 10 = 1:64, 01 = 1:8, 00 = 1:1

Bit 3: T32: 32-bit Timer Mode Select bit[1]
    1 = Timer2 and Timer3 form a single 32-bit timer
    0 = Timer2 and Timer3 act as two 16-bit timers

Bit 1: TCS: Timer2 Clock Source Select bit
    1 = External clock from pin T2CK (on the rising edge)
    0 = Internal clock (FCY)

Legend:
R = Readable bit
-n = Value at POR
U = Unimplemented bit,
    read as '0'
W = Writeable bit
'1' = bit is set
'0' = bit is cleared
'x' = bit is unknown

Figure redrawn by author from Reg 11-1 found in the PIC24H32GP202 datasheet (DS70289B), Microchip Technology, Inc.

Note 1: In 32-bit mode, T3CON bits do not affect 32-bit operation

FIGURE 9.12   T2CON register details. (Adapted with permission of the copyright owner, Microchip Technology, Incorporated. All rights reserved. No further reprints or reproduction may be made without Microchip Inc.'s prior written consent.)

TMR3, PR3, T3IF, and T3CK. The T3CON register is the Timer3 configuration register and has the same control bits as T2CON except for the T32 bit.

In this chapter, we use Timers 2 and 3 to generate *periodic interrupts* based on either the T2IF or T3IF flags. A periodic interrupt is useful for sampling inputs at some desired periodic interval. Because Equation 9.3 has two variables (PR2, PRE) there may be more than one solution for desired interrupt period. One approach for determining PR2, PRE is to select a PRE (prescale) value, then solve for the PR2 value that gives the desired period as shown in Equation 9.4:

$$\mathrm{PR2} = (\mathrm{T_{T2IF}} \times \mathrm{F_{CY}}\,/\mathrm{PRE}) - 1 \tag{9.4}$$

Table 9.6 shows calculated PR2 values for each possible prescaler value, assuming a desired period interrupt of 15 ms and $\mathrm{F_{CY}}$ = 40 MHz. The PR2 values for PRE =1 and PRE = 8 cannot be used since they are greater than 65535 (recall that PR2 is a 16-bit register). If accuracy is important for the periodic interrupt, then

TABLE 9.6 PR2/PRE values for $T_{T2IF} = 15$ ms, $F_{CY} = 40$ MHz.

	PRE=1	**PRE=8**	**PRE=64**	**PRE=256**
PR2	599999 (invalid)	74999 (invalid)	9374	2343

the lowest prescaler value should be used. The values in Table 9.6 are rounded to the nearest integer value.

TIMER MACROS AND SUPPORT FUNCTIONS

Listing 9.2 shows the Timer2 macros contained in *include\pic24_timer.h*. Similar macros are defined for higher-numbered timers and are compatible with both the PIC24H and PIC24F families.

LISTING 9.2 Timer macros.

```
/* T2CON: TIMER2 CONTROL REGISTER */
#define T2_ON                  0x8000    /* Timer2 ON */
#define T2_OFF                 0x0000    /* Timer2 OFF */
#define T2_OFF_ON_MASK         (~T2_ON)

#define T2_IDLE_STOP           0x2000    /* stop operation during sleep */
#define T2_IDLE_CON            0x0000    /* operate during sleep */
#define T2_IDLE_MASK           (~T2_IDLE_STOP)

#define T2_GATE_ON             0x0040    /* Timer Gate time accumulation enabled */
#define T2_GATE_OFF            0x0000    /* Timer Gate time accumulation disabled */
#define T2_GATE_MASK           (~T2_GATE_ON)

#define T2_PS_1_1              0x0000    /* Prescaler 1:1 */
#define T2_PS_1_8              0x0010    /* 1:8 */
#define T2_PS_1_64             0x0020    /* 1:64 */
#define T2_PS_1_256            0x0030    /* 1:256 */
#define T2_PS_MASK             (~T2_PS_1_256)

#define T2_32BIT_MODE_ON       0x0008    /* Timer2 and Timer3 form a 32 bit Timer */
#define T2_32BIT_MODE_OFF      0x0000
#define T2_32BIT_MODE_MASK     (~T2_32BIT_MODE_ON)

#define T2_SOURCE_EXT          0x0002    /* External clock source */
#define T2_SOURCE_INT          0x0000    /* Internal clock source */
#define T2_SOURCE_MASK         (~T2_SOURCE_EXT)
```

The macros of Listing 9.2 can be used to set the T2CON register contents in a self-documenting manner, such as the following:

```
T2CON = T2_OFF | T2_IDLE_CON | T2_GATE_OFF | T2_32BIT_MODE_OFF
      | T2_SOURCE_INT | T2_PS_1_64; //results in T2CON=0x0020
```

This is clearer to an external reader than writing T2CON=0x0020 and so our code examples use this style for timer configuration. The following line of code shows how to use a *mask* macro to modify a bit field without disturbing the other bits in the register:

```
T2CON = (T2CON & T2_PS_MASK) | T2_PS_1_8;
```

There are no individual bit macros such as _TON defined for the timer configuration registers because the bit names are the same for the different timer registers. However, in addition to the mask macros, you can also use the *C* structure references (see Chapter 8) to change bits in the timer registers as shown in the following code line:

```
T2CONbits.TON = 1; //turn on timer2
```

The file *common\pic24_timer.c* contains timer support macros as shown in Listing 9.3. The msToU16Ticks(uint16 u16_ms, uint16 u16_pre) function is based on Equation 9.3 and converts milliseconds (u16_ms parameter) to timer ticks given the timer prescale value (u16_pre parameter) and the predefined Fcy macro. The usToU16Ticks() function is similar except it converts microseconds to timer ticks. Floating point computation is used internally in the time to ticks conversion functions to accommodate a wide range of Fcy and timer prescale values. Because of this, it is recommended that you avoid using these functions in time-critical code sections. Calls to the ASSERT() function implement range checking within msToU16Ticks() and usToU16Ticks() to verify that the requested timeout period can fit in the uint16 return value given the timer prescale and Fcy values. If the calculation overflows the 16-bit range, then the reportError() function is called which saves an error message and executes a software reset. The error message is output to the serial console when printResetCause() is called by main(). The getTimerPrescale(TxCONbits) macro calls the getTimerPrescaleBits(uint8 u8_TCKPS) function, which returns the timer prescale value given a timer configuration register (this works for Timers 1 and higher in both the PIC24H and PIC24F families).

LISTING 9.3 Timer support functions.

```
// convert milliseconds to Timer Ticks
uint16 msToU16Ticks(uint16 u16_ms, uint16 u16_pre) {
  float f_ticks = Fcy;
```

```
   uint16 u16_ticks;
   f_ticks = (f_ticks*u16_ms)/u16_pre/1000L;
   ASSERT(f_ticks < 65535.5);
   u16_ticks = roundFloatToUint16(f_ticks);      //back to integer
   return u16_ticks;
}
   // convert microseconds to Timer Ticks
   uint16 usToU16Ticks(uint16 u16_us, uint16 u16_pre) {
   float f_ticks = Fcy;
   uint16 u16_ticks;
   f_ticks = (f_ticks*u16_us)/u16_pre/1000000L;
   ASSERT(f_ticks < 65535.5);
   u16_ticks = roundFloatToUint16(f_ticks);      //back to integer
   return u16_ticks;
}
// return the timer prescale based on the TxCONbits SFR
#define getTimerPrescale(TxCONbits) getTimerPrescaleBits(TxCONbits.TCKPS)
// return the timer prescale based on the TCKPS bitfield in TxCONbits
uint16 getTimerPrescaleBits(uint8 u8_TCKPS) {
   uint16 au16_prescaleValue[] = { 1, 8, 64, 256 };
   ASSERT(u8_TCKPS <= 3);
   return au16_prescaleValue[u8_TCKPS];
}
```

The functions of Listing 9.3 are useful for setting the PR2 register to a particular timeout value as shown in the following code line that configures PR2 to a timeout value equivalent to 15 ms.

```
PR2 = msToU16Ticks(15, getTimerPrescale(T2CONbits)) - 1;
```

The value returned by msToU16Ticks() is decremented by one because the Timer2 period is PR2 + 1.

SQUARE WAVE GENERATION

A simple test of the Timer2 periodic interrupt capability is shown in Figure 9.13 that generates a square wave on the RB2 pin. The configTimer2() function configures Timer2 for 16-bit mode with a prescale value of 64, sets the PR2 timeout to 15 ms, and enables the Timer2 interrupt. The _T2Interrupt ISR toggles the RB2 pin on each interrupt and clears the T2IF flag before returning. After main() configures RB2 and Timer2, the while(1){} loop only has the doHeartbeat() call because the ISR does all of the work of generating the square wave. This is not the best way to generate a square wave and is only intended as an illustration of a periodic interrupt; Chapter 12 discusses other methods for waveform generation.

```
#define WAVEOUT _LATB2              //state
inline void CONFIG_WAVEOUT() {
  CONFIG_RB2_AS_DIG_OUTPUT();       //use RB2 for output
}
```
RB2 used for square wave output

```
//Interrupt Service Routine for Timer2
void _ISRFAST _T2Interrupt (void){
  WAVEOUT = !WAVEOUT;    //toggle output
  _T2IF = 0;             //clear the interrupt bit
}
```
On each interrupt, toggle the output pin to generate the squave wave, clear the interrupt flag.

```
#define ISR_PERIOD  15     // in ms
void configTimer2(void) {
  //T2CON set like this for documentation purposes.
  //could be replaced by T2CON = 0x0020
  T2CON = T2_OFF | T2_IDLE_CON | T2_GATE_OFF
         | T2_32BIT_MODE_OFF
         | T2_SOURCE_INT
         | T2_PS_1_64;  //results in T2CON= 0x0020
  //subtract 1 from ticks value assigned to PR2 because period is PR2 + 1
  PR2 = msToU16Ticks(ISR_PERIOD, getTimerPrescale(T2CONbits)) - 1;
  TMR2 = 0;                 //clear timer2 value
  _T2IF = 0;                //clear interrupt flag
  _T2IP = 1;                //choose a priority
  _T2IE = 1;                //enable the interrupt
  T2CONbits.TON = 1;   //turn on the timer
}
```
Timer2 configuration sets T2CON, PR2; enables the Timer2 interrupt; turns on the timer.

The `msToU16Ticks()` value is decremented by 1 before PR2 assignment because timer period is PR2+1

```
int main(void) {
  configBasic(HELLO_MSG);
  CONFIG_WAVEOUT();    //PIO Config
  configTimer2();      //TMR2 config
  //ISR does the work!
  while (1) {
    doHeartbeat(); //ensure that we are alive
  } // end while (1)
}
```
After configuration, the ISR does the work of generating the square wave.

FIGURE 9.13 Square wave generation using Timer2.

Listing 9.4 shows the changes to Figure 9.13 for using Timer3 instead of Timer2. The configTimer3() function ensures 16-bit mode is selected via the statement T2CONbits.T32=0 before configuring the T3CON register, which does not have the T32 control bit. The ISR is the same as Figure 9.13 except for function name (_T3Interrupt) and interrupt flag (_T3IF).

LISTING 9.4 Timer3 code.

```
void _ISRFAST _T3Interrupt(void) {
  WAVEOUT = !WAVEOUT;          //sample the switch
  _T3IF = 0;                   //clear the timer interrupt bit
}
```

```
void configTimer3(void) {
  //ensure that Timer2,3 configured as separate timers.
  T2CONbits.T32 = 0;            // 32-bit mode off
  //T3CON set like this for documentation purposes.
  //could be replaced by T3CON = 0x0020
  T3CON = T3_OFF | T3_IDLE_CON | T3_GATE_OFF
        | T3_SOURCE_INT
        | T3_PS_1_64; //results in T3CON = 0x0020
  PR3 = msToU16Ticks(ISR_PERIOD, getTimerPrescale(T3CONbits)) - 1;
  TMR3 = 0;                     //clear timer3 value
  _T3IF = 0;                    //clear interrupt flag
  _T3IP = 1;                    //choose a priority
  _T3IE = 1;                    //enable the interrupt
  T3CONbits.TON = 1;            //turn on the timer
}
```

INPUT SAMPLING

One standard usage of periodic interrupts is for input sampling. Figure 9.14 shows the LED/switch toggle example of Figure 8.28 modified to use the Timer3 periodic interrupt for sampling the SW1 input. Figure 9.14 only shows the differences from the original code given in Figure 8.29. The Timer3 configuration is the same as Listing 9.4 and is not shown. The _T3Interrupt() ISR stores the SW1 state in the u8_valueSW1 variable, so the SW1 macro now becomes "#define SW1 u8_valueSW1" instead of "#define SW1 _RB13". The only change to the while(1){} loop body is to remove the DELAY_MS(DEBOUNCE_DLY) function call since it is no longer needed; the periodic sampling by the ISR debounces the switch. Observe that the volatile modifier is used in the u8_valueSW1 variable declaration. This notifies the compiler that this can be modified by an external agent (e.g., an ISR) between successive accesses (reads) in the main() code and prevents certain compiler optimizations from being applied. The volatile modifier should be used with any variable modified by an ISR and accessed outside of the ISR.

How long should the ISR period be in order to debounce a human-activated pushbutton switch? Figure 9.15 shows a low-true bouncy switch being sampled by a periodic interrupt, with bounce occurring on both switch press and release. The bounce times are labeled as TBNCE1, TBNCE2 (generically referred to as TBNCE) and are assumed approximately equal to each other. For the high-to-low transition of a switch press, if the ISR samples at a high bounce point, then the ISR period must be short enough so that the next sample sees the switch activation or else the activation is missed. If the ISR samples at a low bounce point, then the ISR period must be long enough for the bounces to settle or else the next sample may be at a high bounce point, causing the ISR to see a false switch release. This means the ISR period must be greater than the bounce time (TBNCE) and less than half the expected

```
#define CONFIG_LED1() CONFIG_RB14_AS_DIG_OUTPUT()
#define LED1    _LATB14      //led1 state

inline void CONFIG_SW1()   {
  CONFIG_RB13_AS_DIG_INPUT();   //use RB13 for switch input
  ENABLE_RB13_PULLUP();         //enable the pullup
  DELAY_US(1);                  // Wait for pullup
}

#define SW1_RAW          _RB13         //raw switch value
#define SW1              u8_valueSW1   //switch state
#define SW1_PRESSED()    SW1==0        //switch test
#define SW1_RELEASED()   SW1==1        //switch test

//debounced switch value that is set in the timer ISR
volatile uint8 u8_valueSW1 = 1;    //initially high

//Interrupt Service Routine for Timer3
void _ISRFAST _T3Interrupt (void) {
  u8_valueSW1 = SW1_RAW;       //sample the switch
  _T3IF = 0;                   //clear interrupt bit
}
//... other functions not shown ...
int main (void) {
  STATE e_mystate;
  //... config not shown ...
  e_mystate = STATE_WAIT_FOR_PRESS;
  while (1) {
    printNewState(e_mystate);
    switch (e_mystate) {
      case STATE_WAIT_FOR_PRESS:
        if (SW1_PRESSED()) e_mystate = STATE_WAIT_FOR_RELEASE;
        break;
      case STATE_WAIT_FOR_RELEASE:
        if (SW1_RELEASED()) {
          LED1 = !LED1;   //toggle LED
          e_mystate = STATE_WAIT_FOR_PRESS;
        }
        break;
      default:
        e_mystate = STATE_WAIT_FOR_PRESS;
    }//end switch(e_mystate)
    doHeartbeat();       //ensure that we are alive
  } // end while (1)
}
```

Switch state is now stored in a variable!

DELAY_MS(DEBOUNCE_DLY) removed from end of loop as the ISR periodically samples the input.

FIGURE 9.14   LED/Switch toggle example with periodic interrupt for input sampling.

pulse width (Tpw/2) to guarantee two samples per switch activation. For human-activated switches, the pulse width (Tpw) is greater than 100 ms based on human reaction times. The bounce time (Tbnce) depends on the switch, but is generally less than 5 ms. An ISR period of 15 ms works well if you wish to guarantee multiple samplings of a human-activated pushbutton. Having the sampling period greater than the bounce time means that for the low-to-high transition of a switch release,

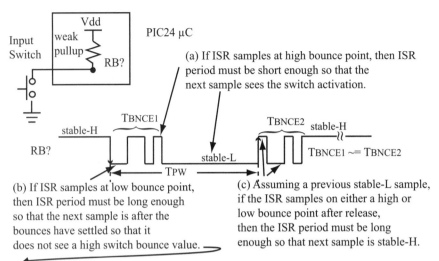

(a) If ISR samples at high bounce point, then ISR period must be short enough so that the next sample sees the switch activation.

(b) If ISR samples at low bounce point, then ISR period must be long enough so that the next sample is after the bounces have settled so that it does not see a high switch bounce value.

(c) Assuming a previous stable-L sample, if the ISR samples on either a high or low bounce point after release, then the ISR period must be long enough so that next sample is stable-H.

(d) This means that the interrupt period should be greater than TBNCE1/TBNCE2 and less than TPW/2 (guarantees at least two samples per switch activation, and at most one sample during a TBNCE1/TBNCE2 period).

FIGURE 9.15 Switch bounce and interrupt period.

only one sample is possible during the TBNCE2 period. If the ISR samples low during TBNCE2, the next sample is a high value, generating a clean switch release event. If the ISR samples high during TBNCE2, a clean switch release event is seen because the next sample is also high.

FILTERING NOISY INPUTS

A common problem in microcontroller interfacing is sampling a noisy input that may have false glitches in the signal. This is a different problem than switch de-bouncing because the glitches can occur anywhere in the signal, unlike switch noise that occurs for a short time period after the switch changes state. This means that our periodic sampling approach alone will not guarantee correct interpretation of noisy inputs. The Schmitt Trigger (Chapter 8) input buffer on each PIO coupled with an external *low-pass RC filter* can provide a good solution for sampling noisy inputs. A low-pass RC filter as shown in Figure 9.16a has a *cutoff frequency* of $1/(2\pi RC)$, which means that signals at this frequency are attenuated by approximately 50 percent, with attenuation increasing with frequency. To completely block a signal at a particular frequency f, use a filter with a cutoff frequency of approximately $f/10$. The RC filter greatly increases the rise and fall time of the port's input signal, but the port's Schmitt Trigger internally transforms this slowly rising or falling signal to a clean signal transition.

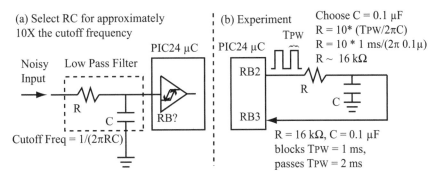

FIGURE 9.16   Noisy input filtering.

Figure 9.16b shows an experiment with RB2 supplying a square wave with pulse widths of Tpw as an input signal to pin RB3. The goal of the experiment is to monitor the RB3 input state and determine RC values that either block or pass the signal transitions. Figure 9.17 shows the code that implements the experiment of Figure 9.16b. The while(1){} loop in main generates a square wave on TOUT (RB2) using software delays with high and low pulse widths of TPW. If the old input value (u8_oldvalueTIN) does not match the current RB3 input value (TIN), then "*" is printed and the current value is saved to u8_oldvalueTIN. Experimentation showed that values of R = 16 kΩ and C = 0.1 μF blocked pulse widths of 1 ms and passed

```
#define CONFIG_TOUT()  CONFIG_RB2_AS_DIG_OUTPUT()  ⎫
#define TOUT    _LATB2            //output state     ⎬ TOUT drives TIN with
#define TIN        _RB3    //test in                 ⎬ square wave
#define CONFIG_TIN()   CONFIG_RB3_AS_DIG_INPUT();   ⎭

#define TPW  1     // in ms, pulsewidth of TOUT

int main (void) {
  uint8 u8_oldvalueTIN;              ⟵ Defines pulse width of TOUT square wave
  configBasic(HELLO_MSG);
  TOUT = 1;          // TOUT drives TIN
  CONFIG_TIN();
  CONFIG_TOUT();
  DELAY_MS(10);    //wait for output to stablize because of filter
  u8_oldvalueTIN = TIN;
  while (1) {
    TOUT = !TOUT;
    DELAY_MS(TPW);
    if (u8_oldvalueTIN != TIN) {     ⎫ If TIN input changes, then print "*"
      u8_oldvalueTIN = TIN;          ⎬ and save new value.
      outString("*");                ⎭
    }
  }
}
```

FIGURE 9.17   RC low filter experiment code.

pulse widths of 2 ms (your results may vary!). Because the source impedance of a noise source can affect the filter cutoff frequency, you should verify experimentally any external filtering circuitry by using an oscilloscope to monitor the filter output to observe its effect on the noisy input signal.

For long pulse-width transients (pulse widths of multiple milliseconds), a low-pass RC filter may reduce the signal rise/fall times to unacceptably long times. In this case, a low-pass RC filter for higher frequency transients (pulse widths < 1 ms) combined with a software noise filter may be the best approach. Figure 9.18 shows the ISR for a periodic timer interrupt that is used to sample the TIN input of Figure 9.16. The ISR code includes a software glitch filter that only passes changes in the TIN input if the TIN input is stable for MIN_STABLE number of milliseconds. The u16_stableCountTIN variable is used by the ISR to track the number of successive interrupts that TIN is stable. When this counter exceeds MIN_STABLECOUNT, which is defined as MIN_STABLE/ISR_PERIOD, then the TIN value is copied to the u8_valueTIN variable used by main. Generally, the sampling period for a software glitch filter should be fast enough to achieve at least four samples for the minimum pulse width. It is not desirable to use a software filter for short pulse width transients (< 1 ms) because the ISR period becomes fairly small, requiring a larger percentage of the processor execution time.

```
#define ISR_PERIOD        1       // in ms
#define MIN_STABLE       15       // in ms ◄——— min stable pulse width for TIN
#define MIN_STABLECOUNT  MIN_STABLE/ISR_PERIOD

uint16 u16_stableCountTIN = 0;  ◄——— tracks # of ISR periods that TIN is stable
uint8 u8_rawTIN = 0;
uint8 u8_oldrawTIN = 0;
volatile uint8 u8_valueTIN = 0;

//Interrupt Service Routine for Timer3
void _ISRFAST _T3Interrupt (void) {
  u8_rawTIN = TIN_RAW;      //sample the switch
  if (u8_rawTIN != u8_oldrawTIN) {                          If TIN input changes,
    //changed values, zero the stability counter           then zero the stability
    u16_stableCountTIN = 0;                                 counter, and remember
    u8_oldrawTIN = u8_rawTIN;                               new input.
  } else {
    u16_stableCountTIN++;
    if (u16_stableCountTIN >= MIN_STABLECOUNT) {            TIN input has been stable
      //new value is ready!                                 long enough, so record the
      u8_valueTIN = u8_rawTIN;                               stable value in u8_valueTIN.
    }
  }
  _T3IF = 0;  //clear the timer interrupt bit
}
```

FIGURE 9.18 Software glitch filter.

LED/Switch I/O and Semaphores

The LED/switch I/O problem of Chapter 8 is repeated here in Figure 9.19. Recall that the original code solution used polling for the switch within the `while(1){}` loop and two states for each of the press and release actions. We will now be using a timer interrupt to poll the switch and use one state for each press and release action by having the timer ISR set a *semaphore* when a complete press and release has occurred.

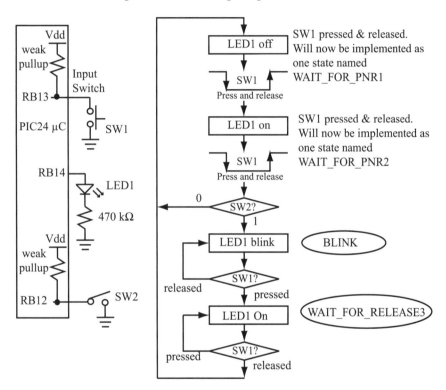

FIGURE 9.19   State machine specification for LED/switch I/O problem.

A semaphore is a flag set by an ISR to signal the foreground task that an I/O action has occurred. Generally, the ISR sets the semaphore indicating that an I/O action has been processed and is ready. The foreground task detects that the semaphore is set, reads the I/O event result, and resets the semaphore, thus indicating to the ISR that the I/O event has been consumed. An advantage of using the foreground task to clear the semaphore is that the ISR can determine if the foreground task is processing interrupts fast enough to keep pace with I/O event occurrence. If the semaphore is still set when the ISR receives an I/O event then the foreground task is processing I/O events too slowly, and some sort of event buffering may be needed (as covered in Chapter 10). Figure 9.20 shows the periodic timer

```
typedef enum {
  STATE_WAIT_FOR_PRESS = 0,        } ISR states
  STATE_WAIT_FOR_RELEASE,          }
} ISRSTATE;
                                                      u8_pnrSW1 semaphore set
volatile uint8 u8_valueSW1 = 1;                       to 1 on press & release
volatile uint8 u8_pnrSW1 = 0;◄─────────────────         ↓ SW1 ↑
ISRSTATE e_isrState = STATE_WAIT_FOR_PRESS;           Press and release

//Interrupt Service Routine for Timer3
void _ISRFAST _T3Interrupt (void) {
  u8_valueSW1 = SW1_RAW;        //sample the switch  Do not process another
  switch(e_isrState) {                               press & release until first
  case STATE_WAIT_FOR_PRESS:                          has been handled.
    if (SW1_PRESSED() && (u8_pnrSW1 == 0))
        e_isrState = STATE_WAIT_FOR_RELEASE;
    break;
  case STATE_WAIT_FOR_RELEASE:
    if (SW1_RELEASED()){
        e_isrState = STATE_WAIT_FOR_PRESS;
        u8_pnrSW1 = 1; //set semaphore             Set the u8_pnrSW1 semaphore
        break;                                     for foreground code.
    }
  default:  e_isrState = STATE_WAIT_FOR_RELEASE;
  }
  _T3IF = 0;   //clear the timer interrupt bit
}
```

FIGURE 9.20 Implementation of a press & release semaphore.

interrupt of Figure 9.14 rewritten such that a press and release event semaphore named u8_pnrSW1 is generated. The ISR of Figure 9.20 now has two states named STATE_WAIT_FOR_PRESS and STATE_WAIT_FOR_RELEASE that are used for generating the semaphore, which is set when STATE_WAIT_FOR_RELEASE is exited. Observe that STATE_WAIT_FOR_PRESS is not exited until both SW_PRESSED() and u8_pnrSW1==0 are true; the u8_pnrSW1==0 test is done so that another press and release event is not processed until the foreground task has processed the previous event by clearing u8_pnrSW1. The state machine implementation style is useful for the ISR because two different I/O events (a press and a release) are needed to generate one semaphore event.

Figure 9.21 shows the main() code of Figure 8.30 rewritten to use the u8_pnrSW1 semaphore. Within the switch(e_mystate){} statement, the STATE_WAIT_FOR_PNR1 state is exited when the u8_pnrSW1 semaphore is set indicating that a press and release event has been received. Observe that the u8_pnrSW1 semaphore is cleared before the STATE_WAIT_FOR_PN1 state is exited, thus sending an acknowledgement to the ISR that this press and release event has been consumed. In the STATE_WAIT_FOR_RELEASE3 state, the u8_pnrSW1 semaphore is tested instead of testing SW1_RELEASED() because the u8_pnrSW1 semaphore is set on release, and thus must be cleared to consume the press and release event generated over states STATE_BLINK and STATE_WAIT_FOR_RELEASE3.

```
typedef enum {
  STATE_RESET = 0,   STATE_WAIT_FOR_PNR1,  STATE_WAIT_FOR_PNR2,
  STATE_BLINK,       STATE_WAIT_FOR_RELEASE3
} STATE;
```
               ← main states

```
int main (void) {
  STATE e_mystate;
  ... config not shown ...
  e_mystate = STATE_WAIT_FOR_PNR1;
  while (1) {
   printNewState(e_mystate);
   switch (e_mystate) {
    case STATE_WAIT_FOR_PNR1:
    LED1 = 0; //turn off the LED
    if (u8_pnrSW1) { 
      u8_pnrSW1 = 0; //clear 
      e_mystate = STATE_WAIT_FOR_PNR2;
    }
    break;
    case STATE_WAIT_FOR_PNR2:
    LED1 = 1; //turn on the LED
    if (u8_pnrSW1) {
      u8_pnrSW1 = 0; //clear semaphore
      if (SW2) e_mystate = STATE_BLINK;
        else e_mystate = STATE_WAIT_FOR_PNR1;
    }
    break;
    case STATE_BLINK:
    LED1 = !LED1; DELAY_MS(100); //blink if not pressed
    if (SW1_PRESSED()) e_mystate = STATE_WAIT_FOR_RELEASE3;
    break;
    case STATE_WAIT_FOR_RELEASE3:
    LED1 = 1;   //Freeze LED1 at 1
    if (u8_pnrSW1) { 
      u8_pnrSW1 = 0;
      e_mystate = STATE_WAIT_FOR_PNR1;
    }
    break;
    default:
     e_mystate = STATE_WAIT_FOR_PNR1;
   }//end switch(e_mystate)
   doHeartbeat();       //ensure that we are alive
  } // end while (1)
}
```

Replaces states WAIT_FOR_PRESS1, WAIT_FOR_RELEASE1 of original code

Test press & release semaphore

Clear the semaphore indicating that this press & release has been consumed.

Replaces states WAIT_FOR_PRESS2, WAIT_FOR_RELEASE2 of original code

Test press & release semaphore instead of SW1_RELEASED() because the semaphore is set on release and must be cleared.

FIGURE 9.21   LED/switch I/O implementation with press & release semaphore.

The press and release semaphore moved some of the work done in main() to the ISR. This can be taken to an extreme by moving all of the _main() FSM states into the ISR as shown in Figure 9.22. This implementation uses the original states of Figure 8.30 (no press and release semaphore). The switch(e_mystate){} statement originally in main() is moved to the ISR, and the STATE_BLINK state now sets a semaphore named doBlink to tell the while(1){} loop in main to blink the LED. The LED blinking action should not be done in the ISR as this involves placing a software delay in the ISR, which violates the tenant that an ISR should do its work as quickly as possible. A software delay consists of wasted cycles, and an ISR should

```
volatile uint8 u8_valueSW1 = 1;
volatile uint8 doBlink = 0;          blink semaphore
STATE e_mystate;
//Interrupt Service Routine for Timer3
void _ISRFAST _T3Interrupt (void) {
 u8_valueSW1 = SW1_RAW;      //sample the switch
 switch (e_mystate) {
  case STATE_WAIT_FOR_PRESS1: ...
  case STATE_WAIT_FOR_RELEASE1: ...      Unchanged from Figure 8.30
  case STATE_WAIT_FOR_PRESS2: ...
  case STATE_WAIT_FOR_RELEASE2: ...
  case STATE_BLINK:                      Tells the main() code to blink the LED.
    doBlink = 1;                         Do NOT put a software delay here to
    if (SW1_PRESSED()) {                 blink the LED!!!!!
     doBlink = 0;                             Tell the main() code
     e_mystate = STATE_WAIT_FOR_RELEASE3;     to stop blinking the
    }                                         LED.
    break;
  case STATE_WAIT_FOR_RELEASE3: ...      Unchanged from Figure 8.30
  default:
    e_mystate = STATE_WAIT_FOR_PRESS1;
  }
  _T3IF = 0; //clear the timer interrupt bit
}

int main (void) {
  ... config not shown ...
  e_mystate = STATE_WAIT_FOR_PRESS1;
  /* While loop just checks the doBlink semaphore */
  while (1) {
    printNewState(e_mystate);  //debug message when state changes
    if (doBlink) {            Blink the LED when the
     LED1 = !LED1;              doBlink semaphore is set.
     delayMs(100);
    }
    doHeartbeat();      //ensure that we are alive
  } // end while (1)
}
```

FIGURE 9.22 LED/switch I/O implementation with the entire FSM inside the ISR.

not be wasting cycles! Observe that the ISR both sets and clears the doBlink sema-phore in this case, while the main() code only monitors the semaphore state.

There are many ways to divide work between an ISR (or multiple ISRs) and main. The right division of labor is the one that allows successful I/O processing, and there are usually multiple satisfactory solutions.

A ROTARY ENCODER INTERFACE

A rotary encoder is used to encode the direction and distance of a mechanical shaft ro-tation. There are different ways to accomplish this; Figure 9.23 shows a 2-bit *Gray code* rotary encoder. Counterclockwise rotation (a) of the shaft produces the sequence 00,

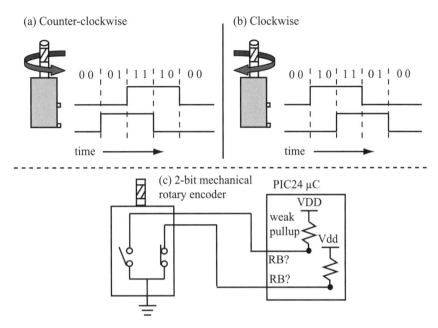

FIGURE 9.23 Two-bit Gray code rotary encoder.

01, 11, and 10, while clockwise rotation (b) generates 00, 10, 11, and 01. In a Gray code, adjacent encodings differ by only one bit position. Rotation direction is determined by comparing the current 2-bit value with the last value. For example, if the current value is 11 and the last value is 10, the shaft is rotating in a clockwise (b) direction. One common use for a rotary encoder is as an input device on a control panel where clockwise rotation increments a selected parameter setting, while counterclockwise rotation decrements the parameter. The rotary encoder of Figure 9.23 is an *incremental* encoder as the shaft's absolute position is indeterminate; only relative motion is encoded. Some rotary encoders include more bits that provide absolute shaft position, in BCD or binary encoding. An *n*-position encoder outputs *n* codes for each complete shaft rotation. Common values of *n* for 2-bit incremental rotary encoders are 16 and 32. However, high-precision encoders can supply hundreds of pulses per shaft rotation.

Rotary encoders use mechanical, optical, or magnetic means of detecting shaft rotation, with mechanical encoders being the least expensive and magnetic the most expensive. A key specification for optical and mechanical encoders is rotational life with optical ~1 million and mechanical ~100,000 rotations due to mechanical wear. Magnetic encoders are meant for high-speed rotational applications with encoder lifetime measured in thousands of hours for a fixed rotational speed in revolutions per minute (RPMs). A two-bit mechanical Gray code rotary encoder as shown in Figure 9.23c generally has three pins as shown, two outputs for the switches and the third output for a common ground.

Figure 9.24 shows a utility function named processRotaryData() that is called to process a change in state for a 2-bit Gray code rotary encoder. The u8_curr and u8_last parameters are the current and last state values, respectively, of the encoder and are limited to values of 0, 1, 2, and 3. The *cntr parameter is a pointer to a counter that may either be incremented or decremented by one, depending upon the state change of the encoder. The function limits the counter value to between 0 and max, as most counter variables associated with rotary encoder inputs have some sort of limit associated with them. In this implementation, modifications to the counter variable are halted when a limit is reached until the encoder rotation is re-versed. An alternate implementation could wrap the counter after reaching a limit. If the function detects an illegal state change, perhaps caused by switch bounce or noise, then a non-zero value is returned from the function. Observe that the delta value assigned in each case is based on the current and last states. For example, for a current state (u8_curr) of 0, a previous state (u8_last) of 1 from Figure 9.23 means that the encoder shaft has rotated clockwise, so the counter should be incremented by 1 (delta=1).

```
//limits cntr variable to between 0 and max
uint8 processRotaryData(uint8 u8_curr, uint8 u8_last,
                        uint8 *cntr, uint8 max){
  int8 delta;
  delta = 0;
  //states listed in Gray code order for clarity
  switch (u8_curr) {
    case 0: if (u8_last == 1) delta = 1;
       else if (u8_last == 2) delta = -1;
       break;
    case 1: if (u8_last == 3) delta = 1;
       else if (u8_last == 0) delta = -1;
       break;
    case 3: if (u8_last == 2) delta = 1;
       else if (u8_last == 1) delta = -1;
       break;
    case 2: if (u8_last == 0) delta = 1;
       else if (u8_last == 3) delta = -1;
       break;
    default: break;
  }
  if (delta == 0) return(1); //error, illegal state
  //limit the cntr variable
  if (( *cntr == 0 && delta == -1)
     || (*cntr == max && delta == 1)) return(0); //at limit
  (*cntr) = (*cntr) + delta;
  return 0;
}
```

Compute delta value for counter based on current rotary data and last rotary data. If delta remains at 0, then an invalid rotary data change has occurred (possibly due to noise or bounce)

Return non-zero value if illegal state change on rotary output.

Counter limits: 0 to max

Modify counter by either +1 or –1.

FIGURE 9.24 The processRotaryData() utility function.

Figure 9.25 shows the ISR and main() code that reads a 2-bit Gray code rotary encoder connected to RB13 and RB12, which is periodically sampled by a 15 ms

```
#define ROT1_RAW _RB13
#define ROT0_RAW _RB12                    returns a value of 0, 1, 2, or 3
#define GET_ROT_STATE() ((ROT1_RAW << 1) | ROT0_RAW)

//rotary encoder configuration
inline void configRotaryEncoder() {
  CONFIG_RB13_AS_DIG_INPUT();                              RB13, RB12 used for
  ENABLE_RB13_PULLUP();          //enable the pull-up      two rotary encoder
  CONFIG_RB12_AS_DIG_INPUT();                              outputs
  ENABLE_RB12_PULLUP();          //enable the pull-up
  DELAY_US(1);                   //wait for pull-ups to settle
}

#define ROT_MAX   32     //arbitrary value           Will limit our rotary
                                                     encoder counter variable
volatile uint8 u8_valueROT = 0;                      to a range of 0 to ROT_MAX.
volatile uint8 u8_lastvalueROT = 0;
volatile uint8 u8_errROT = 0;            Set to "1" on encoder error.
volatile uint8 u8_cntrROT = 0;           Our rotary encoder  counter variable.

//Interrupt Service Routine for Timer3
void _ISRFAST _T3Interrupt (void) {
  u8_valueROT = GET_ROT_STATE(); //a value between 0 & 3
  if (u8_lastvalueROT != u8_valueROT) {
    u8_errROT = processRotaryInput(u8_valueROT, u8_lastvalueROT,
                                   &u8_cntrROT, ROT_MAX);
    u8_lastvalueROT = u8_valueROT;              Process rotary encoder
  }                                             state if it changes.
  _T3IF = 0;  //clear the timer interrupt bit
}

int main (void) {
  uint8 u8_lastCnt;
  configBasic(HELLO_MSG);
  configRotaryEncoder();           //config rotary encoder
  u8_valueROT = GET_ROT_STATE();        Initialize rotary state and the rotary
  u8_lastvalueROT = u8_valueROT;        encoder counter variables.
  u8_lastCnt = u8_cntrROT;
  configTimer3(); //config Timer3       15 ms periodic interrupt
  while (1) {
    if (u8_lastCnt != u8_cntrROT) {       If the rotary encoder counter
      u8_lastCnt = u8_cntrROT;            variable changes, print the new
      outUint8(u8_lastCnt); outString("\n"); value.
      if (u8_errROT) {                    Print error message if rotary state
       outString("Rotary state error\n"); error is detected, indicates noise
       u8_errROT = 0;                     on inputs.
      }
    }
    doHeartbeat();      //indicate that we are alive
  } // end while (1)
}
```

FIGURE 9.25   A 2-bit Gray code rotary encoder interface example.

Timer3 interrupt. Because rotary encoder output is generated by switch opens and closures, our periodic sampling of the rotary encoder state handles the switch bounce. The `processRotaryData()` function is called by the Timer3 ISR whenever the encoder state changes, and the `u8_cntrROT` variable implements the rotary encoder counter variable, which is limited to a maximum value defined by `ROT_MAX`. The `u8_errROT` variable is used to hold the return value of `processRotaryData()` function, which is a non-zero value if an illegal state change is detected.

The `main()` configuration code in Figure 9.25 uses the `configRotaryEncoder()` function to configure RB13/RB12 as inputs with weak pull-ups for the two rotary encoder outputs. The 1 μs software delay that follows is needed to give time for the weak pull-ups on the inputs to stabilize, so that the `u8_valueROT` variable that contains the initial state of the rotary encoder is initialized to a stable value. The `while(1){}` loop prints the `u8_cntrROT` value any time a change is detected and also prints an error message if the `u8_errROT` variable becomes non-zero.

A KEYPAD INTERFACE

A numeric keypad is a common element in a microcontroller system as it provides an inexpensive method of input. A numeric keypad is simply a matrix of switches arranged in rows and columns and has no active electronics; a key press connects a row and column pin together as shown in Figure 9.26.

The 4x3 numeric keypad of Figure 9.31 is shown connected to the PIC24 μC in Figure 9.27. The RB[5:3] port pins are configured as outputs driving low and connected to the row pins, while RB[9:6] are configured as inputs with the weak pull-ups enabled and connected to the column pins.

If no key is pressed as in Figure 9.27a, RB[9:6] reads as "1111" because there are no connections to the RB[5:3] pins. In Figure 9.27b, key 8 is pressed, connecting

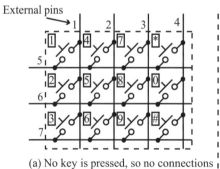

(a) No key is pressed, so no connections between any pins.

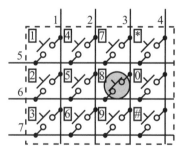

(b) Key 8 is pressed, pin 6 connected to pin 3.

FIGURE 9.26 4x3 numeric keypad.

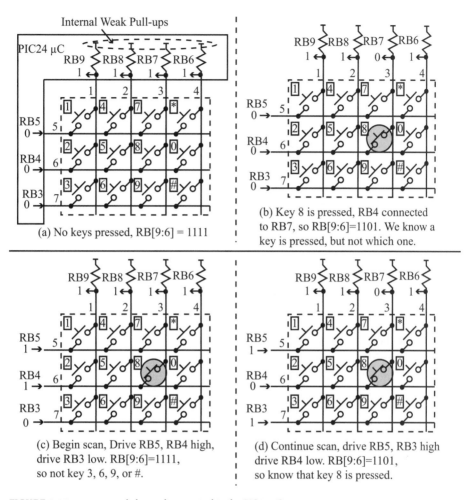

FIGURE 9.27   4x3 numeric keypad connected to the PIC24 µC.

RB7 to RB4, causing RB7 to become a "0". The key press can be detected by any of the mechanisms previously discussed, such as polling, periodic sampling via a timer interrupt, or using the change notification inputs associated with the PORTB pins.

After a key press is detected, determining which key is actually pressed is done through a procedure known as a *keypad scan*. The keypad scan first determines which column input is low. Then it steps through the rows, driving the one row low and the remaining rows high. If the column input originally found as low remains low, then the corresponding row for the key press has been discovered. This scan procedure only detects one key when multiple keys are pressed, but it is straightforward to modify it to detect multiple key presses. In Figure 9.27b, a key press is detected when the RB7 column input is read as low. The scan is started in Figure 9.27c by driving RB3 low and RB4, RB5 high. The RB7 column input remains high, so it is known that key 9 is not pressed. In Figure 9.27d, RB4 is driven low and RB3, RB5 high. At this point, the RB7 column input is found to be low, indicating that key 8 is pressed creating the connection between RB4 and RB7.

Listing 9.5 shows some interface macros and support functions for the keypad interface. Macros C0, C1, C2, and C3 are four column input states, with macros R0, R1, R2 the row states. The configKeypad() function configures the column inputs with pull-ups enabled and the rows as outputs all driving low. The remaining functions are self-explanatory.

LISTING 9.5 Interface macros, support functions for keypad interface.

```
#define C0 _RB9
#define C1 _RB8
#define C2 _RB7
#define C3 _RB6

static inline void CONFIG_COLUMN() {
  CONFIG_RB9_AS_DIG_INPUT();ENABLE_RB9_PULLUP();
  CONFIG_RB8_AS_DIG_INPUT();ENABLE_RB8_PULLUP();
  CONFIG_RB7_AS_DIG_INPUT();ENABLE_RB7_PULLUP();
  CONFIG_RB6_AS_DIG_INPUT();ENABLE_RB6_PULLUP();
}

#define R0 _LATB5
#define R1 _LATB4
#define R2 _LATB3

#define CONFIG_R0_DIG_OUTPUT() CONFIG_RB5_AS_DIG_OUTPUT()
#define CONFIG_R1_DIG_OUTPUT() CONFIG_RB4_AS_DIG_OUTPUT()
#define CONFIG_R2_DIG_OUTPUT() CONFIG_RB3_AS_DIG_OUTPUT()

void CONFIG_ROW() {
  CONFIG_R0_DIG_OUTPUT();CONFIG_R1_DIG_OUTPUT();CONFIG_R2_DIG_OUTPUT();
}

static inline void DRIVE_ROW_LOW() {
  R0 = 0; R1 = 0; R2 = 0;
}

static inline void DRIVE_ROW_HIGH() {
  R0 = 1; R1 = 1; R2 = 1;
}
```

```
void configKeypad(void) {
  CONFIG_ROW();
  DRIVE_ROW_LOW();
  CONFIG_COLUMN();
  DELAY_US(1);            //wait for pullups to stabilize inputs
}
```

Figure 9.28 shows the doKeyScan() function for the keypad interface, which first identifies the column input that is low, storing it in the u8_col variable. The function then scans the keypad as previously described using a for(){} loop with loop variable u8_row. Within the loop, the u8_setOneRowLow(u8_row) function call drives the

```
void setOneRowLow(uint8 u8_x) {
  switch (u8_x) {
    case 0:
      R0 = 0; R1 = 1; R2 = 1; break;          ⎫
    case 1:                                     ⎬ Set row specified by
      R0 = 1; R1 = 0; R2 = 1; break;          ⎪ u8_x to low, others high.
    default:                                    ⎭
      R0 = 1; R1 = 1; R2 = 0; break;
  }
}
```

```
#define NUM_ROWS 3
#define NUM_COLS 4
const uint8 au8_keyTable[NUM_ROWS][NUM_COLS] =
{ {'1', '4', '7', '*'},       ⎫
  {'2', '5', '8', '0'},       ⎬ Key lookup table
  {'3', '6', '9', '#'}        ⎭
};
#define KEY_PRESSED() (!C0 || !C1 || !C2 || !C3)    //any low
#define KEY_RELEASED() (C0 && C1 && C2 && C3) //all high
```

KEY_PRESSED() returns true if any column input is low.

KEY_RELEASED() returns true if all column inputs are high.

```
uint8 doKeyScan(void) {
  uint8 u8_row, u8_col;
  //determine column
  if (!C0) u8_col = 0;        ⎫
  else if (!C1) u8_col = 1;   ⎪ Determine column, if a column input is low
  else if (!C2) u8_col = 2;   ⎬ then it has a key pressed.
  else if (!C3) u8_col = 3;   ⎪
  else return('E'); //error   ⎭
  //determine row
  for (u8_row = 0; u8_row < NUM_ROWS; u8_row++) {     ⎫
    setOneRowLow(u8_row); //enable one row low         ⎪
    if (KEY_PRESSED()) {                               ⎪ Determine
      DRIVE_ROW_LOW(); //return rows to driving low    ⎬ row
      return(au8_keyTable[u8_row][u8_col]);            ⎪
    }                                                  ⎪
  }                                                    ⎭
  DRIVE_ROW_LOW(); //return rows to driving low
  return('E'); //error  ⟵── If reach here, then error.
}
```

FIGURE 9.28 The doKeyScan() function for the keypad interface.

row specified by u8_row as low and the remaining rows high. When a column input is detected low during the loop, the variables u8_row and u8_col are used to access the two-dimensional array au8_keyTable to return the ASCII value of the pressed key. An "E" character is returned if the key scan finds no column input that is low, indicating that no character is available. The KEY_PRESSED() macro returns true if any column is low, while the KEY_RELEASED() macro is true if all columns are high.

Figure 9.29 shows the ISR and the main() code for the keypad interface. The ISR uses a three-state FSM to detect presses and releases on the keypad. If a key is

```
typedef enum  { STATE_WAIT_FOR_PRESS = 0, STATE_WAIT_FOR_PRESS2,
  STATE_WAIT_FOR_RELEASE  } ISRSTATE;

ISRSTATE e_isrState = STATE_WAIT_FOR_PRESS;
volatile uint8 u8_newKey = 0;          ◄──────────── Semaphore that contains
                                                      new key read by the ISR.
//Interrupt Service Routine for Timer3
void _ISR _T3Interrupt (void) {◄─ Do not use _ISRFAST because doKeyScan()
  switch (e_isrState) {              accesses a const array (stored in program mem)
    case STATE_WAIT_FOR_PRESS:
      if (KEY_PRESSED() && (u8_newKey == 0)) {
        //check key pressed for two ISR periods
        e_isrState = STATE_WAIT_FOR_PRESS2;
      }
      break;
    case STATE_WAIT_FOR_PRESS2:
      if (KEY_PRESSED()) {
        // a key is ready
        u8_newKey = doKeyScan();
        e_isrState = STATE_WAIT_FOR_RELEASE;
      } else e_isrState = STATE_WAIT_FOR_PRESS;
      break;
    case STATE_WAIT_FOR_RELEASE:
      //keypad released
      if (KEY_RELEASED()) {
        e_isrState = STATE_WAIT_FOR_PRESS;
      }
      break;
    default:
      e_isrState = STATE_WAIT_FOR_PRESS;
      break;
  }
  _T3IF = 0;
}

int main (void) {
  configBasic(HELLO_MSG);
  configKeypad();
  configTimer3();
  while (1) {
    if (u8_newKey) {
      outChar(a_key);
      u8_newKey = 0;
    }
    doHeartbeat();      //ensure that we are alive
  } // end while (1)
}
```

If keypad is pressed for two consecutive ISR periods, and last key is consumed, then read the new key.

Go to next state if keypad is released.

Assume ISR samples as "0," the following key scan may see a "1." So wait for ISR to sample as "0" for two consecutive periods before calling the scan function.

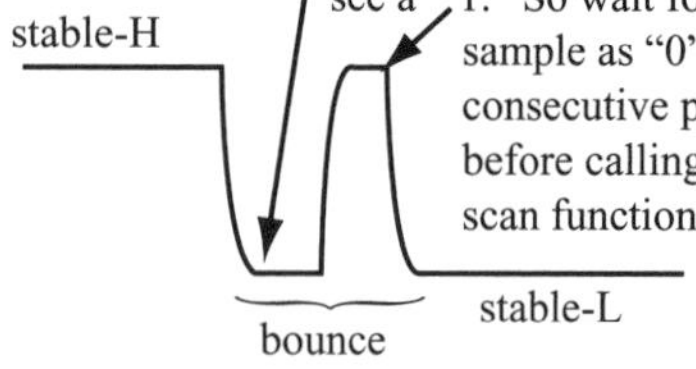

stable-H

bounce

stable-L

If a key is available, then print the key and and reset the semaphore.

FIGURE 9.29 The ISR and main() code for the keypad interface.

pressed for two consecutive ISR periods and the last key value has been consumed, then the keypad is scanned using the doKeyScan() function. The reason for waiting two consecutive ISR periods for the keypad to be read as "0" is that in our previous switch sampling examples, we were guaranteed that switch samples were separated by an ISR sampling period. However, in this case the doKeyScan() function resamples the switch after the ISR has detected it as low. The doKeyScan() function will thus be sampling during the bounce period, so it could see a "1" instead of a "0." Waiting for the ISR to sample a "0" for two consecutive periods means that the doKeyScan() function will read the key during the stable-L period of Figure 9.15. The new key value is returned in u8_newKey, which functions as a semaphore when its value is non-zero. The ISR declaration does not use _ISRFAST because the doKeyScan() function accesses the array au8_keyTable, which is stored in program memory because of the const attribute, so the PSVPAG register should be preserved. The while(1){} loop in main() waits for a non-zero value in u8_newKey, prints the key value to the screen, and then clears u8_newKey.

On Writing and Debugging ISRs

As discussed previously, when writing ISRs one must be careful not to place too much work within the ISR as this can either cause other interrupt events to be missed or steal too much time away from the normal program flow. Within an ISR, there should never be a wait for an I/O event—that is the function of the interrupt that triggers the ISR. As much work as possible should be placed in the normal program flow, with the ISR only performing time-critical operations.

Because most ISRs are time sensitive, putting print statements that output data to a serial port in an ISR to examine ISR variables is usually not an option, as this destroys the interrupt timing. It may be valid to place a print statement in the foreground code to examine an ISR variable, but the variable value should always be copied to a temporary variable first because the ISR variable value may be changed by the time the print statement is executed. If you are trying to trace a variable value over several interrupt intervals, then using a print statement may not be an option if the print is not fast enough to monitor the variable value. In this case, a *trace buffer* can be used in which copies of the variable over several interrupt intervals are kept, then printed when the trace buffer becomes full. Figure 9.30 shows a trace buffer (au8_tbuff) added to the processRotaryData() function of Figure 9.24 to track changes of the rotary encoder state. The current rotary encoder state (u8_curr) is saved if tracing is enabled (u8_startTrace is non-zero) and the trace buffer is not full. The while(1){} loop of main() enables tracing, waits for the trace buffer to fill, then prints the contents of the trace buffer. Tracing is re-enabled by emptying the trace buffer (clearing u8_tnct) after the trace buffer is printed.

```
#define TMAX 16
volatile uint8 au8_tbuff[TMAX];        ←——— trace buffer
volatile uint8 u8_tcnt = 0;            ←——— index into trace buffer
volatile uint8 u8_startTrace = 0; ←——— enables tracing

//clips cntr between 0 and max
uint8 processRotaryData(uint8 u8_curr, uint8 u8_last, uint8 *cntr, uint8 max) {
  int8 delta;
  delta = 0;
  if (u8_startTrace && (u8_tcnt != TMAX)) { ⎫ If tracing is enabled, save encoder
    au8_tbuff[u8_tcnt] = u8_curr;           ⎬ state into the trace buffer, and do
    u8_tcnt++;                              ⎭ not exceed the trace buffer size.
  }
  switch (u8_curr) {
    case 0: if (u8_last == 1) delta = 1;
        else if (u8_last == 2) delta = -1;
      break;
  ... remainder not shown ...
  }
}
int main (void) {
  uint8 u8_i;
  ... config not shown ...
  while (1) {
    u8_startTrace = 1;   ←——— Enable trace collecting.
    if (u8_tcnt == TMAX) {
      u8_startTrace = 0;                      ⎫ Print trace buffer contents once
      for (u8_i=0;u8_i<TMAX;u8_i++) {         ⎬ it becomes full, then reset trace
       outUint8(au8_tbuff[u8_i]);             ⎪ buffer index to zero and trace
       outString("\n");                       ⎭ again.
      }
      u8_tcnt = 0;
    }
    doHeartbeat();       //ensure that we are alive
  } // end while (1)
}
```

FIGURE 9.30 Using a trace buffer.

SUMMARY

Our primary usage of interrupts in this chapter has been in the form of a periodic timer interrupts for polling data availability. For mechanical switches such as those used in numeric keypads, this provides an effective debounce mechanism. In the next chapter, we explore the various serial interfaces available on the PIC24 µC and interrupt-driven I/O for those servicing those interfaces, as well as various buffering techniques common to interrupt-driven I/O.

REVIEW PROBLEMS

1. Modify the code of Figure 9.6 to generate an address error trap.
2. Modify the code of Figure 9.6 to generate a stack error trap. Why might you want to purposefully trigger a trap error?

3. In Figure 9.10, assume the NOPs in the _CNInterrupt ISR are removed. What happens and why?

4. In Figure 9.10, assume that four NOPs are used in the while(1){} loop. What happens and why?

5. Give the CN*x*IE bit that must be set to enable the change notification on pin RA2 for the PIC24HJ32GP202.

6. Give the CN*x*IE bit that must be set to enable the change notification on pin RB7 for the PIC24HJ32GP202.

7. Write a code sequence that enables the input change notification interrupt for changes on inputs RA4 and RB12 (assume that both have been previously configured as inputs).

8. Write a code sequence that enables the input change notification interrupt for changes on inputs RB10 and RA1 (assume that both have been previously configured as inputs).

9. Assume that for a PIC24HJ32GP202, the RB13 has a pushbutton switch connected to it as shown in Figure 9.19 and the change notification interrupt for RB13 is enabled (which is CN13). For the following code snippet, how many times does the _CNInterrrupt ISR execute if the pushbutton is pressed and released one time? Assume no switch bounce, and explain your answer.

```
void _ISR _CNInterrupt (void) {
    DISABLE_RB13_CN_INTERRUPT();      //_CN13IE = 0; (STATEMENT A)
    _CNIF = 0;                        //            (STATEMENT B)
}

int main (void) {
    CONFIG_RB13_AS_DIG_INPUT();
    ENABLE_RB13_CN_INTERRUPT();       //_CN13IE = 1;
    _CNIF = 0;                                     (STATEMENT C)
    _CNIP = 2;                                     (STATEMENT D)
    _CNIE = 1;                                     (STATEMENT E)
    while(1);                         //infinite loop
}
```

10. Repeat Problem #9, except remove statement A.

11. Repeat Problem #9, except replace statement D with _CNIP = 0.

12. Repeat Problem #9, except remove statement E.

13. Figure 9.31 shows one switch connected to INT0 and INT1 interrupt inputs. For the code in Listing 9.6 give the order in which statements A, B, C, and D are executed given a single press and release of SW0. Assume no switch bounce, and explain your answer. Recall that if an INT*x*EP bit is 1 the interrupt is negative edge triggered; if 0 then it is positive edge triggered.

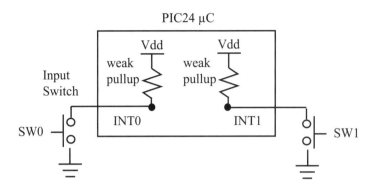

FIGURE 9.31   INT0/INT1 interrupt problem.

LISTING 9.6   Code for INT0/INT1 interrupt problem.

```
void _ISR _INT0Interrupt(void) {
 _INT0IE = 0;                                    (STATEMENT A)
 _INT0IF = 0;                                    (STATEMENT B)
}
void _ISR _INT1Interrupt(void) {
 _INT1IE = 0;                                    (STATEMENT C)
 _INT1IF = 0;                                    (STATEMENT D)
}
int main (void) {
 ...config code that enables weak pull-ups...
 _INT0IF = 0;                                    (STATEMENT E)
 _INT0IP = 2;                                    (STATEMENT F)
 _INT0EP = 1;                                    (STATEMENT G)
 _INT0IE = 1;                                    (STATEMENT H)
 _INT1IF = 0;                                    (STATEMENT I)
 _INT1IP = 2;                                    (STATEMENT J)
 _INT1EP = 1;                                    (STATEMENT K)
 _INT1IE = 1;                                    (STATEMENT L)
 while(1); //infinite loop
}
```

14. Repeat problem #13, except replace statement F with _INT1IP = 3.
15. Repeat problem #13, except replace statement G with _INT0EP = 0.
16. Repeat problem #13, except replace statement J with _INT1IP = 0.
17. Repeat problem #13, except replace statement H with _INT1IE = 0.
18. Repeat problem #13, except remove statement D.
19. Repeat problem #13, except remove statement D and replace C with _INT1IE = 1.

20. How many PIC24 Timer2 ticks are equal to 70 µs assuming a prescale of 1 and a Fcy of 20 MHz?

21. How many PIC24 Timer2 ticks are equal to 1.2 ms assuming a prescale of 8 and a Fcy of 30 MHz?

22. What is the maximum PIC24 Timer2 timeout period assuming a prescale of 64 and a Fcy of 30 MHz?

23. What is the maximum PIC24 Timer2 timeout period assuming a prescale of 8 and a Fcy of 10 MHz? Give the answer rounded to the nearest millisecond.

The following problems assume external LEDs (LED1, LED2, etc.) and switches (SW1, SW2, etc.). You may use any of the RB*n* ports you wish to implement these problems. Assume switch inputs are pushbutton inputs and that they use the internal weak pull-up of the port. You may use either Timer2 or Timer3 when a periodic timer interrupt is needed.

24. Assume two LEDs (LED1, LED2) and one switch input (SW1). Both LEDs should be initially off. After each press AND release of SW1, change the LED state (LED1/LED2) in the sequence: OFF/ON, ON/OFF, ON/ON, OFF/OFF, OFF/ON, ON/OFF, ON/ON, OFF/OFF, etc. Draw a state machine chart for the problem, with the solution done as in the style of 9.22 (a periodic timer ISR does all of the work, the while(1){} loop should only have the doHeartBeat() function).

25. Repeat problem #23, except the LEDs change state whenever a press OR a release occurs for SW1.

26. Assume one LED (LED1) and one switch input (SW1). The LED should be initially blinking. On each press AND release of SW1, alternate between terminating the blinking and resuming the blinking. Draw a state machine chart for the problem, with the solution done as in the style of 9.22 (a periodic timer ISR does all of the work, the while(1){} loop should only have the doHeartBeat() function and a semaphore set by ISR to control the blinking).

27. Repeat problem #26, except the blinking terminates or resumes whenever a press OR a release occurs for SW1.

10 Asynchronous and Synchronous Serial I/O

This chapter discusses some of the serial interfaces available on the PIC24 μC: the Universal Asynchronous Receiver Transmitter (UART), the Serial Peripheral Interface (SPI), and the Inter-Integrated Circuit (I²C) bus. The protocols and operational modes of these three interfaces are discussed in detail along with interfacing examples to different external devices. Chapter 13 discusses the more complex Universal Serial Bus (USB) and Controller Area Network (CAN) serial protocols.

Learning Objectives

After reading this chapter, you will be able to:

- Describe the differences between synchronous and asynchronous serial data transfer.
- Draw the waveform for an asynchronous serial data transfer that includes a start bit, data bits, and stop bits.
- Write *C* code that sends and receives asynchronous serial data via the UART subsystem.
- Discuss the signals and signaling levels associated with the EIA RS-232 interface.
- Write *C* functions for performing interrupt-driven receive and transmit for the PIC24 UART.
- Compare and contrast the SPI and I²C synchronous serial I/O protocols on the PIC24 μC.
- Interface a PIC24 μC to a digital thermometer using the SPI protocol.
- Interface a PIC24 μC to a digital potentiometer using the SPI protocol.
- Implement PIC24 μC to PIC24 μC communication using the SPI protocol.
- Interface a PIC24 μC to a digital thermometer using the I²C protocol.
- Interface a PIC24 μC to a serial EEPROM using the I²C protocol.
- Use interrupt-driven double buffering to implement continuous data stream applications.

I/O Channel Basics

Parallel I/O uses a group of signals for data transfer, with a clock or data strobe signal typically used for controlling the transfer. Figure 10.1a shows a 16-bit parallel I/O link between CPU_a and CPU_b, with a clock signal used to perform one data transfer each clock cycle. The *bandwidth* of a communication channel is usually expressed either as the number of bytes transferred per second (B/s) or the number of bits transferred per second (b/s). Please observe the capitalization difference between Bps (bytes/second) and bps (bits/second); Bps is related to bps via the relationship Bps = bps/8. For Figure 10.1a, the bandwidth is 600 MB/s if the clock frequency is 300 MHz, because two bytes are transferred each clock cycle. Data sent one bit at a time is called *serial data transfer,* and Figure 10.1b shows a synchronous serial interface that uses a single bit line with a separate clock to accomplish the transfer. The bandwidth of this channel is 1/16th that of the bandwidth of Figure 10.1b, because the 16 data lines have been replaced by only one data line. The advantage of parallel I/O is obvious: it has *n* times the bandwidth of a serial channel, assuming both channels use the same data transfer rate and the parallel channel has *n* data lines.

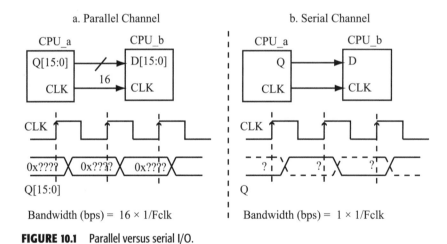

FIGURE 10.1   Parallel versus serial I/O.

The principle advantage of serial I/O is that it is cheaper to implement in terms of integrated circuit, cable, and connector pin count than parallel I/O. This is especially important for microcontroller applications in which cost is typically an important constraint: fewer external pins used to communicate with external devices can lower the overall cost of the final product. In other applications, serial I/O is typically used for data transfer between devices that require external cabling, such as between a keyboard and a personal computer. This is because a serial cable requires fewer wires than a parallel cable, which reduces the cost. It also makes the cable less bulky and reduces the physical connector size, an issue when there are multiple I/O cable connections to a device. In addition, wires within an I/O cable are subject to *crosstalk,* defined as a voltage change on a wire inducing a voltage change in a neighboring wire. Crosstalk can corrupt data transfers, resulting in an unreliable communication channel. Crosstalk increases with cable length and with higher signaling speeds. Methods for combating crosstalk increases the cabling costs, and thus serves as another reason for reducing the number of signals in an I/O cable. Parallel I/O is typically used for high-bandwidth, short-distance communication between integrated circuits in the same system.

High bandwidth, low cost, and reliable transfers are desirable properties of any I/O channel. Unfortunately, these properties conflict with each other: increasing bandwidth typically increases cost and decreases the reliability of the I/O transfer. Increasing I/O channel bandwidth can be done by any combination of the following actions:

1. Increase the number of signals carrying data; e.g., increase a parallel I/O channel from 8 bits to 16 bits.
2. Decrease the amount of time between data transfers; e.g., increase the clock speed of the I/O channel.
3. Use a signaling method that encodes more data in the same time interval; e.g., use a four-level voltage signaling method so that 2 bits are encoded in each signaling interval (00 = 0 V, 01 = 1/3 VDD, 10 = 2/3 VDD, 11 = VDD).

Methods 1 and 2 are the most common ways used to increase I/O channel bandwidth. Doubling the number of signal lines in an I/O channel doubles the bandwidth, but it also doubles the cost of the I/O channel. Decreasing the time used for each transfer increases bandwidth, but also increases the complexity of the electronics used for driving and receiving data signals, increasing the cost of each data signal. One method of decreasing the time between transfers is to use reduced voltage swing on the data lines instead of requiring the data signals to transition fully between VDD and ground. Swinging a data line by 200 millivolts to indicate a change from "1" to "0" or vice versa is accomplished faster than requiring a signal to transition from 0 to VDD.

Figure 10.2 defines the terms *simplex, half duplex,* and *duplex* in reference to communication channels. A simplex channel allows data transfer in one direction only. A half-duplex channel supports transfer in either direction, but in only one direction per data transfer. A duplex channel (also referred to as full duplex) supports transfers in both directions simultaneously.

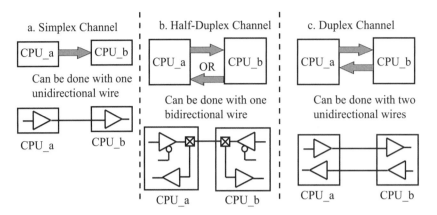

FIGURE 10.2   Simplex, half-duplex, and duplex communication channels.

A physical connection between two systems is either a unidirectional wire (transfer in only one direction) or a bidirectional wire (transfer in either direction). In Chapter 8, we saw that tristate buffers are required to implement a bidirectional port. A single unidirectional wire can implement a simplex channel, while a single bidirectional wire can implement a half-duplex channel. Two unidirectional wires can implement a duplex channel with each wire providing communication in one direction. A more complex electrical signaling method known as *current-mode signaling* can be used to implement a duplex channel using a single wire. However, use of current mode signaling is rare; all of the devices discussed in this book use voltage-mode signaling.

SYNCHRONOUS, ASYNCHRONOUS SERIAL I/O

Synchronous serial I/O either sends a clock as a separate signal as shown in Figure 10.3b or uses a scheme that allows the receiver's clock to remain synchronized to the bit stream. Sending a clock as a separate signal is an intuitive solution for synchronous I/O, but at high signaling speeds wire delay becomes significant, especially in external cabling. If the wire delays of the serial data wire and clock signal are significantly mismatched, the active clock edge can clock in the wrong data bit at the receiver as is seen in Figure 10.3b.

Data/Clock wire delay mismatch becomes larger the faster the signaling speed and the greater the distance. The Universal Serial Bus (USB) and Controller Area Network (CAN) serial transmission standards that are discussed in Chapter 13 use synchronous transmission and are intended for serial communication over cables of several inches/centimeters to several feet/meters. Because of this, their signaling

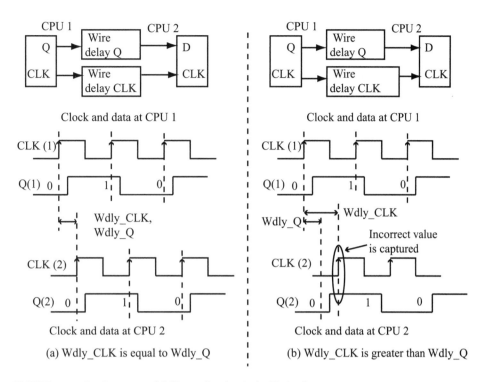

FIGURE 10.3   Synchronous serial I/O: sending the clock with the data.

methods do not send a separate clock signal, but use a different method for maintaining synchronization as discussed further in Chapter 13. The I²C and SPI serial interfaces on the PIC24 µC that are discussed later in this chapter use synchronous transmission, and all use the signaling method of Figure 10.1b that sends the clock with the data as a separate signal. This is because these interfaces are intended for short-distance communication between integrated circuits on the same printed circuit board. The separate clock also simplifies the logic implementation, which was important for older serial interfaces such as I²C and SPI that were defined in the 80's because logic gates for an on-chip serial interface required a larger percentage of the total chip area at that time than it does today.

ASYNCHRONOUS SERIAL I/O USING NRZ ENCODING

Asynchronous serial I/O does not send a separate clock signal, and various signaling schemes are used to allow the receiver to read the serial data. Some schemes use a two-wire signaling method in which neither wire is a clock in the traditional sense, with transitions encoded on the wires in such a way that allows serial data to be extracted and supports dynamically varying transmission rates. This method is used by the high-speed serial I/O standard known as IEEE 1394, or FireWire.

Another asynchronous method that uses only a single wire encodes serial data as *non-return-to-zero* (NRZ), which means that a high voltage is used for a "1" bit and a low voltage is used for a "0" bit. The serial line remains at either a high or low state when successive bits of the same value are sent. The NRZ format is the most intuitive format used for serial data encoding; other schemes exists such as *bi-phase* encoding that uses different edge transitions for distinguishing "1" and "0" bits (discussed in Chapter 12). Asynchronous NRZ serial transmission is what the PIC24HJ32GP202 reference system of Chapter 8 uses for communication over the serial link to the attached personal computer. Because a separate clock signal is not sent with the serial data, there is no issue of wire delay mismatch between clock and data, so asynchronous NRZ serial transmission can be used for long distance (meters/feet) communication. The disadvantage of asynchronous NRZ serial transmission is that it has a lower maximum data rate when compared to advanced synchronous signaling methods, for reasons to be discussed later in this section.

In an asynchronous NRZ serial transfer, the sender and receiver agree on a common data rate and a common data format in terms of how many data bits are sent for each transfer. Figure 10.4 shows an asynchronous NRZ serial data frame. Before transmission begins, the line is in the idle or *mark* condition, which is a logic "1". The time required for sending one bit is referred to as a *bit time*. The start of transmission is indicated by a transition from the idle condition to logic "0", known as the *space* condition. This first bit, which is always a logic "0", is called the *start* bit and enables the receiver to detect the beginning of a transmission. Data bits are sent least significant bit (LSb) to most significant bit (MSb), with common data formats being 7 data + even/odd parity (discussed later in this section) or 8 data bits. The transmission ends with at least one stop bit, defined as the line remaining at "1" for at least one bit time. A total of 10 bit times are required for 1 start bit, 8 data bits, and 1 stop bit.

A *parity* bit is a bit added by the sender to provide error detection of single-bit errors. Parity is either *even* or *odd*. The value of an even or odd parity bit is chosen so

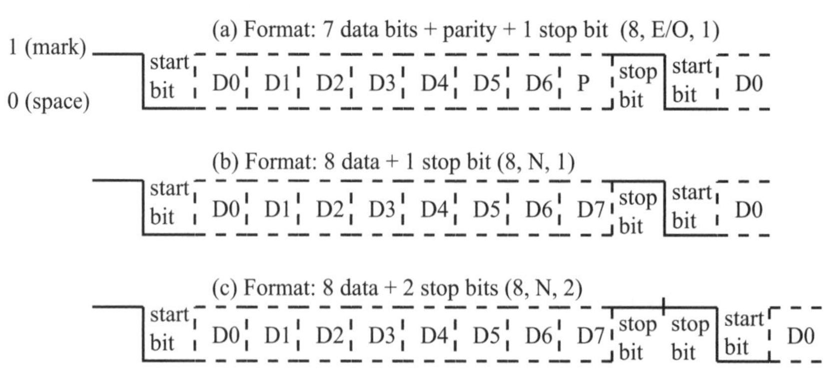

FIGURE 10.4   Asynchronous data frame.

that the total number of "1" bits in the *n* data bits + parity bit is even or odd, respectively. For example, if a 7-bit data field is 0b0101101, which contains an even number of "1"s, odd parity selects a parity bit of "1", resulting in an odd number of "1" bits. In contrast, even parity selects a parity bit of "0", resulting in an even number of "1" bits. The receiver checks the value of the parity bit. An incorrect parity indicates that some type of transmission error has occurred. A single parity bit is guaranteed to detect any single bit error; that is, if only one bit of the *n* data bits + parity is received in error, the parity scheme detects that an error occurred. If multiple bit errors occur, the parity scheme may or may not detect the error. Figure 10.5 gives three examples of asynchronous serial data frames. Frame formats are identified as "(data size including parity bit, parity type, # of stop bits)", with *E, O, N* used for even parity, odd parity, and no parity respectively. Thus, the frame format of Figure 10.4a can either be (8, O, 1) if odd parity is used or (8, E, 1) if even parity is used.

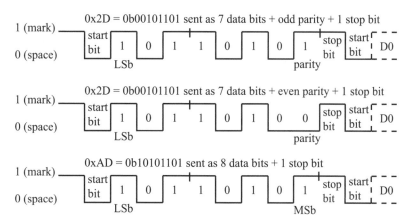

FIGURE 10.5   Example asynchronous serial data frames.

In Figure 10.4, each bit is sent within a signaling interval, with only one bit sent per signaling interval. This book refers to the signaling interval as a *bit time,* with the number of bits per second (bps) of the link given by Equation 10.1.

$$\text{Bits per second (bps)} = 1/(\text{bit\_time}) \tag{10.1}$$

Another term commonly used for the signaling speed of an asynchronous serial link is *baud rate,* whose definition is the number of signaling events per unit time. If only one bit is sent per signaling interval, baud rate is equal to bits per second. However, if more than one bit is sent per interval, such as a four-level voltage signaling scheme that sends two bits per signaling event, then bits per second is twice the baud rate. This book only

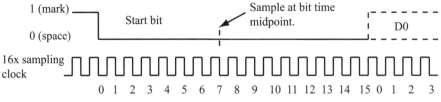

Sampling clock frequency is 16x the data rate (sampling clock period is 1/16 bit time).

FIGURE 10.6   Example asynchronous serial data frames.

discusses signaling methods in which one bit is sent per signaling interval, so *baud rate* is used interchangeably with *bit rate*.

Figure 10.6 shows how phase and frequency differences between receiver and sender clocks are handled. Given a data rate of y bps, the clock used by the sender/receiver for accessing the serial data is a multiple of this rate, usually 64x, 16x, or 4x. Assuming a 16x clock, when the receiver detects a start bit (high to low transition), it counts 8 clock periods and then captures the input value. After this point, the receiver samples the input line every 16 clock periods, placing the sampling point near the center of the bit interval, giving the receiver maximum tolerance for mismatch between receiver and transmitter clocks. Over time, any receiver/transmitter clock mismatch shifts the sampling point away from the bit time midpoint, eventually causing a reception error when the sampling point is shifted out of a bit interval. Sampling at the midpoint of the bit time gives a 50 percent error margin, or ±8 clock periods about the center of the clock interval. For a frame with 10 bit times, this gives a 50%/10 = 5% error tolerance in sender/receiver clock mismatch. This is an optimistic mismatch assumption; a more pessimistic calculation accounting for rise and fall times of the input signal and maximum phase mismatch uses only a 30 percent margin (approximately ±5 clock periods about the midpoint). This gives an error tolerance of 30%/10 = 3% error tolerance for sender/receiver clock mismatch. Observe that the error tolerance decreases linearly as the number of bit times in the frame increases; for this reason, asynchronous transmission frames are typically limited to 10 bit times. The cumulative error begins at zero on the next start bit transition since that is when the receiver begins counting internal clocks to determine the bit sampling position. The edge transition of the start bit is said to *resynchronize* the receiver to the bit stream. Cumulative error is not a problem for synchronous serial data transmission, which can send an unlimited number of bits per frame because the receiver remains synchronized to the serial input stream. Thus, even if asynchronous and synchronous serial channels have the same bit time, the synchronous channel has a higher effective data transfer rate because it does not have the overhead of the start and stop bits sent for every 8 data bits of the asynchronous transmission.

Figure 10.7 shows a software-based asynchronous serial data link. Two PORTB pins, RB2 (sᴛx) and RB3 (sʀx), implement transmit and receive, respectively, forming

```
/// Soft UART Config
#define CONFIG_STX() CONFIG_RB2_AS_DIG_OUTPUT()
#define STX   _LATB2    //STX state
#define CONFIG_SRX() CONFIG_RB3_AS_DIG_INPUT()
#define SRX   _RB3      //SRX state
#define DEFAULT_SOFT_BAUDRATE 19200
uint16 u16_softBaudRate = DEFAULT_SOFT_BAUDRATE;
```

PIC 24 µC   PIC 24 µC

	TX	RX	
RBx			RBy
RBy	RX	TX	RBx
VSS			VSS

```
void doBitDelay (uint16 u16_baudRate) {
  if (u16_baudRate == 9600) { DELAY_US(106); }
  else if (u16_baudRate == 19200) DELAY_US(52);
}
```

Add more tests to
support additional
baud rates
1/19,200 seconds

```
void doBitHalfDelay (uint16 u16_baudRate) {
  if (u16_baudRate == 9600) { DELAY_US(53); }
  else if (u16_baudRate == 19200) DELAY_US(26);
}
```

(a) Send start+8 data+stop

```
void outCharSoft(uint8 u8_c)
{
  uint8 u8_i;
  STX = 0;                            Send start bit
  doBitDelay(u16_softBaudRate);
  Send 8 data bits, LSb to MSb
  for (u8_i=0;u8_i<8;u8_i++) {
    if (u8_c & 0x01)
      STX = 1;                        One data bit
    else STX = 0;
    doBitDelay(u16_softBaudRate);
    u8_c = u8_c >> 1;                 Right shift
  }                Send stop bit      for next bit
  STX = 1;
  doBitDelay(u16_softBaudRate);
}
```

(b) Receive start+8 data+stop

```
uint8 inCharSoft(void) {
  uint8 u8_i, u8_c;
  u8_c = 0x00;                        Wait for start bit
                                      (exit when SRX == 0)
  while(SRX) doHeartbeat();
  Wait for middle of bit time
  doBitHalfDelay(u16_softBaudRate);
  for (u8_i=0;u8_i<8;u8_i++) {
    doBitDelay(u16_softBaudRate);     Read a
    if (SRX) u8_c = u8_c | 0x80;      bit
    if (u8_i != 7)
      u8_c = u8_c >> 1;               Right shift
  }                                   for next bit
  doBitDelay(u16_softBaudRate);
  return(u8_c);                       Receive stop bit, no error
}                                     check (assume it is a logic 1)
```

FIGURE 10.7   A software-based asynchronous serial data link.

a duplex communication channel. The outCharSoft(uint8 u8_c) function sends the 8-bit u8_c value serially from LSb to MSb using one stop bit. The doBitDelay(uint16 u16_baudRate) function delays for one bit time. Observe that the outCharSoft() function assumes that STX is already in the idle (high) condition before sending the start bit. After sending the 8 data bits, the stop bit is sent, leaving the STX output in the idle condition. The inCharSoft(void) function returns an 8-bit value from the serial link by first waiting for a start bit (SRX becomes a "0"). Once a start bit is detected, the function uses the doBitHalfDelay(uint16 u16_baudRate) function to wait until the middle of the bit time. It then loops eight times, delaying a full bit time and then reading the SRX input. The function delays for an additional full bit time before exiting to account for the stop bit (it does no checking to ensure that the received stop bit was a one). Software-driven serial links using parallel port bits can work well, but their maximum performance is limited by the accuracy of the delay functions used to implement bit delays. Also, even though the separate TX, RX lines of Figure 10.7 have the capability of implementing a duplex channel, the outCharSoft()/inCharSoft() functions as written cannot perform duplex communication. This is because all of the CPU's resources are either spent transmitting or receiving a character; it cannot do both simultaneously using the functions of Figure 10.7. One solution to this problem is to use dedicated hardware to implement the TX/RX functionality as seen in the next section.

Sample Question: **For asynchronous serial transmission, with 1 bit sent per signaling interval, what is the bit time in microseconds for a baud rate of 57,600?**

Answer: From Equation 10.1, it is seen that:
bit time = 1/baud_rate = $1/57,600 = 1.736 \times 10^{-5}$ s $\times 10^6$ µs/s = 17.36 µs.

Sample Question: **Assume a data format of 7 data bits + even parity. What is the parity bit value for the data 0x2A?**

Answer: 0x2A = 0b0101010 (7 bits); the number of "1" bits is odd, so the even parity bit value is "1".

THE PIC24 UART

The PIC24 µC has an on-chip peripheral called the Universal Asynchronous Receiver Transmitter (UART, pronounced as "you-art") that implements an asynchronous data transceiver. For asynchronous transmission, a write to a special function register is all that is required in terms of CPU resources; the UART handles the details of sending the start, data, and stop bits. For asynchronous reception, the UART automatically shifts in any serial data it receives then sets a status flag indicating that data is ready. All the CPU has to do at that point is read a special function register to receive data.

The UART subsystem, like others found on the PIC24 µC, uses special function registers in two different ways: either as *data registers* or as *control registers*. Data registers are either used for transferring data from the subsystem to the external pins (a write operation to an external device), or for transferring data from the external pins to the subsystem (a read operation from an external device). Control registers contain a mixture of *configuration* and *status* bits. Configuration bits specify the operating mode of the subsystem, while status bits indicate the operational state of the subsystem. PIC24 microcontrollers can have multiple UARTs (UART1, UART2, . . . UART*n*) with identical capabilities, so their register names have a number (*x*) that designates its associated UART*x*. For example, register U*x*TXREG is the data transmit register, and its name for UART1 is U1TXREG. Our code refers to named bits in UART registers by their fully qualified structure reference (*register. bitname*) to make the functions portable to PIC24 microcontrollers with multiple UARTS, which do not have macros defined for individual UART register bits. The PIC24HJ32GP202 used in our reference system has only one UART.

Figure 10.8 shows the U*x*MODE register that contains various control bits for UART*x* transmit and receive operation. Figure 10.9 show the U*x*STA register

R/W-0	U-0	R/W-0	R/W-0	R/W-0	U-0	R/W-0	R/W-0
UARTEN	UI	USIDL	IREN	RTSMD	UI	UEN<1:0>	
15	14	13	12	11	10	9	8
R/W-0	R/W-0	R/W-0	R/W-0	R/W-0	R/W-0	R/W-0	R/W-0
WAKE	LPBACK	ABAUD	URXINV	BRGH	PDSEL<1:0>		STSEL
7	6	5	4	3	2	1	0

Bit 15: UARTEN: UART*x* Enable bit

   1 = UART*x* is enabled; UART*x* pins are controlled by UART*x*
      as defined by UEN<1:0> and UTXEN control bits

   0 = UART*x* is disabled; UART*x* pins are controlled by
      corresponding PORT, LAT, TRIS bits.

Bit 13: USIDL: Stop in Idle Mode Bit

   1 = Discontinue module operation device enters Idle mode; 0 = Continue operation in Idle mode

Bit 12: IREN: IrDA Encoder and Decoder Enable bit[1]

   1 = IrDA encoder and decoder enabled; 0 = IrDA encoder and decoder disabled

Bit 11: RTSMD: Mode Selection for U*x*RTS# Pin bit

   1 = U*x*RTS# in Simplex mode; 0 = U*x*RTS# in Flow Control mode

Bit 9-8: UEN<1:0>: UARTx Enable bits

   11 = U*x*TX, U*x*RX, and BCLK*x* pins are enabled and used; U*x*CTS# pin controlled by port latches

   10 = U*x*TX, U*x*RX, U*x*CTS# and U*x*RTS# pins are enabled and used

   01 = U*x*TX, U*x*RX, and U*x*RTS# pins are enabled and used; U*x*CTS# pin controlled by port latches

   00 = U*x*TX, U*x*RX pins are enabled and used; U*x*CTS#, U*x*RTS#, and BCLK*x* pins controlled
      by port latches

Bit 7: WAKE: Enable Wake-up on Start bit Detect During Sleep Mode bit

   1 = Wake-up enabled; 0 = Wake-up disabled

Bit 6: LPBACK: UART*x* Loopback Mode Select bit

   1 = Enable Loopback mode;

   0 = Loopback mode is disabled

Bit 5: ABAUD: Auto-baud Enable bit

   1 = Enable baud rate measurement on the next character.
      Requires reception of a Sync field (0x55);
      cleared in hardware upon completion

   0 = Baud rate measurement disabled or completed

Bit 4: URXINV: Receive Polarity Inversion bit

   1 = U*x*RX Idle state is 0; 0 = U*x*RX Idle state is 1

Bit 3: BRGH: High Baud Rate Select bit

   1 = High speed; 0 = Low Speed

Bit 2-1: PDSEL<1:0>: Parity and
   Data Selection bits

   11 = 9-bit data, no parity

   10 = 8-bit data, odd parity

   01 = 8-bit data, even parity

   00 = 8-bit data, no parity

Bit 0: STSEL: Stop Selection bit

   1 = 2 Stop bits; 0 = 1 Stop bit

Note 1: This feature only available for low-speed mode (BRGH = 0). See device datasheet for details.

Figure redrawn by author from Reg. 17-1 found in the PIC24H FRM datasheet (DS70232A), Microchip Technology Inc.

FIGURE 10.8   U*x*MODE: Mode register. (Adapted with permission of the copyright owner, Microchip Technology Inc. All rights reserved. No further reprints or reproduction may be made without Microchip Inc.'s prior written consent.)

R/W-0	R/W-0	R/W-0	U-0	R/W-0	R/W-0	R-0	R-1
UTXISEL1	UTXINV	UTXISEL0	UI	UTXBRK	UTXEN	UTXBF	TRMT
15	14	13	12	11	10	9	8

R/W-0	R/W-0	R/W-0	R-1	R-0	R-0	R/C-0	R-0
URXISEL<1:0>		ADDEN	RIDLE	PERR	FERR	OERR	URXDA
7	6	5	4	3	2	1	0

Bit 15,13 : UTXISEL<1:0>: Transmission Interrupt Mode Selection Bits

Figure redrawn by author from Reg. 17-2 found in the PIC24H FRM datasheet (DS70232A), Microchip Technology Inc.

11 = Reserved
10 = Interrupt generated when a character is transferred to the transmit shift register and the transmit buffer becomes empty
01 = Interrupt generated when last transmission is over
00 = Interrupt generated when any character is transferred to the Transmit Shift Register

Bit 14: UTXINV: Transmit Polarity Inversion bit

IREN = 0	IREN = 1
1 = UxTX Idle state is 1	1 = IrDA encoded UxTX Idle state is 1
0 = UxTX Idle state is 0	0 = IrDA UxTX Idle state is 0

Bit 11: UTXBRK: Transmit Break bit
1 = UxTX pin is driven low regardless of transmitter state (Sync Break transmission - Start bit followed by twelve zero bits and followed by a Stop bit)
0 = Sync break transmission is disabled or completed

Bit 10: UTXEN: Transmit Enable bit
1 = UARTx transmitter enabled; UxTX pin controlled by UARTx (if UARTEN = 1)
0 = UARTx transmitter disabled; pending transmissions aborted, buffer is reset; UxTX pin controlled by port

Bit 9: UTXBF: Transmit Buffer Full Status bit (read-only)
1 = Transmit buffer is full; 0 = Transmit buffer is not full, at least one more data word can be written

Bit 8: TRMT: Transmit Shift Register is Empty bit (read-only)
1 = Transmit Shift register is empty and transmit buffer is empty (the last transmission has completed)
0 = Transmit Shift register is not empty, a transmission is in progress or data is queued in the transmit buffer

Bit 7-6: URXISEL<1:0>: Receive Interrupt Mode Selection bits
11 = Interrupt flag bit is set when receive buffer is full (i.e., has 4 data characters)
10 = Interrupt flag bit is set when receive buffer is 3/4 full (i.e., has 3 data characters)
0x = Interrupt flag bit is set when a character is received

Bit 5: ADDEN: Address Character Detect bit (bit 8 of received data = 1)
1 = Address Detect mode enabled. If 9-mode is not selected, this control bit has no effect.
0 = Address Detect mode disabled.

Bit 4: RIDLE: Receiver Idle bit (read-only)
1 = Receiver is idle; 0 = Data is being received.

Bit 3: PERR: Parity Error Status bit (read-only)
1 = Parity error has been detected for current character; 0 = No parity error detected.

Bit 2: FERR: Framing Error Status bit (read-only)
1 = Framing error had been detected for current character ; 0 = No Framing error detected.

Bit 1: OERR: Receive Buffer Overrun Error Status bit (clear/read-only)
1 = Receive buffer has overflowed
0 = No overflow (clearing a previously set OERR resets the receiver buffer and RSR to empty)

Bit 0: URXDA: Receive Buffer Data Available bit (read-only)
1 = Receive buffer has data, at least one character can be read; 0 = Receive buffer is empty

FIGURE 10.9 UxSTA: Status and control register. (Adapted with permission of the copyright owner, Microchip Technology Inc. All rights reserved. No further reprints or reproduction may be made without Microchip Inc.'s prior written consent.)

that contains both status and control bits for UART*x* operation. We will discuss these various bits in the context of UART transmit, receive, and clock generation operations.

UART*x* Transmit Operation

As previously mentioned, the U*x*TXREG is the data output register for UART*x*. This register is actually the entry point for a four-entry first-in, first-out (FIFO) buffer for the U*x*TSR register that performs the shifting of serial data through the U*x*TX pin as shown in Figure 10.10. Together, the U*x*TXREG FIFO and the U*x*TSR register form a five-entry buffer. The UTXBF read-only status bit in Figure 10.9 is "0" if a free location is available in the U*x*TXREG buffer. The UTXBF status bit must be checked before any write is done to TXREG, as data written to a full buffer is not accepted. The UART subsystem supports either 8-bit or 9-bit operation, which is why the

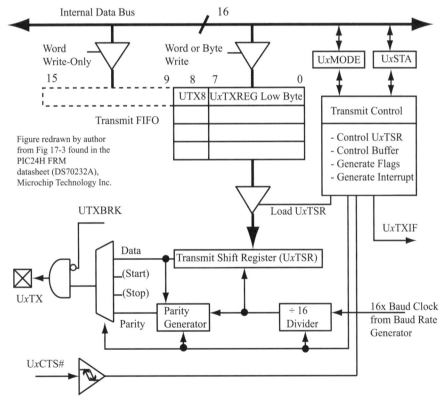

FIGURE 10.10   UART*x* transmitter block diagram. (Adapted with permission of the copyright owner, Microchip Technology Inc. All rights reserved. No further reprints or reproduction may be made without Microchip Inc.'s prior written consent.)

U*x*TXREG FIFO is shown as being 9 bits wide. The 9-bit operation mode is useful if the TX output goes to two different devices in a multi-processor system as the 9th bit is treated as an address bit. Our code examples use 8-bit mode; see the PIC24 FRM [17] for more information on 9-bit operation. In 8-bit mode, the supported data formats using control bits from Figure 10.8 are even/odd/no parity, with either one or two stop bits. The same frame format is used for both transmit and receive.

UARTx Receive Operation

Figure 10.11 shows the UART*x* receiver block diagram. Serial data enters via the U*x*RX pin and the receiver block automatically shifts the data into the U*x*RSR register upon detection of a start bit. The U*x*RSR contents are transferred to the

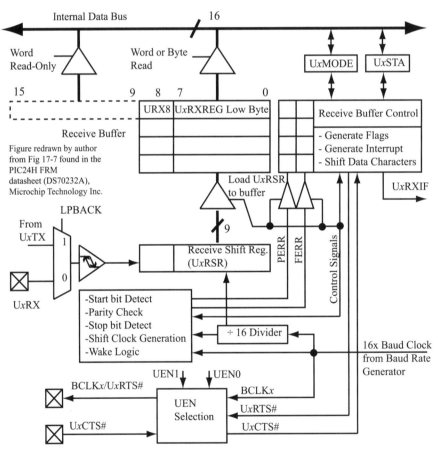

FIGURE 10.11 UART receiver block diagram. (Adapted with permission of the copyright owner, Microchip Technology Inc. All rights reserved. No further reprints or reproduction may be made without Microchip Inc.'s prior written consent.)

U*x*RXREG buffer after stop bit reception. As with the U*x*TXREG, the U*x*RXREG is actually a four-entry buffer, with the read-only status bit URXDA (receive buffer data available bit U*x*STA<0>) is "1" if data is available. The OERR bit (receive buffer overrun error status) is set to a "1" on reception of the stop bit of the fifth data word when the receive buffer already contains four data words. Data reception is inhibited until the OERR bit is cleared by user, which clears all U*x*RXREG buffer contents as well as the U*x*RSR register. You must empty the buffer contents before clearing OERR if the buffer contents and U*x*RSR register value are to be preserved. The FERR bit (framing error status) is set to a "1" is the stop bit for the currently available word was read as a "0" instead of a "1". The PERR bit (parity error status) is a "1" if a parity error was detected for the currently available word. Both the FERR and PERR bits should be read before reading U*x*RXREG, as they reflect the status for the currently available word.

Three other pin functions associated with the UART are BCLK*x*, U*x*RTS#, and U*x*CTS#. The BCLK*x* pin can be used to output the 16× baud rate clock, while pins U*x*RTS# and U*x*CTS# are used for hardware flow control when transmitting or receiving serial data. The UARTEN (UART enable, U*x*MODE<15>) bit must be a "1" to enable the UART receiver block, with the UEN bits (U*x*MODE<9:8>)>) further configuring the UxRX, UxTX pin operation. Our code uses UEN = 00, which is the simplest operation mode, and disables the BCLK*x*, U*x*RTS#, and U*x*CTS# pin functions. See the PIC24 FRM [17] for more information on using the hardware flow control features of the UART.

BAUD RATE CONFIGURATION

The baud rate (BR) for the UART is controlled by the baud rate clock generator and is calculated by Equation 10.2. The U*x*BRG register is the period register for a 16-bit timer. High- and low-speed modes are selected by the BRGH (high baud rate select bit, UxMODE<3>) configuration bit, with BRGH = 1 selecting high-speed mode and BRGH = 0 used for low-speed mode.

$$BR = F_{CY}/(S \times (UxBRG+1)) \qquad (10.2)$$

where S = 16 (low speed) or S = 4 (high speed)

The low-speed mode uses a 16x clock for sampling each bit time and can reach lower baud rates before exceeding the 16-bit range of UxBRG. The high-speed mode only uses a 4x clock for sampling each bit, but can reach higher baud rates than the low-speed mode. Equation 10.3 solves Equation 10.1 for SPBRG because PIC24 applications need the U*x*BRG value that is required to achieve a particular baud rate.

$$\text{U}x\text{BRG} = [\text{Fcy}/(\text{S} \times \text{BR})] - 1 \qquad \text{(round to nearest integer)} \qquad (10.3)$$

Figure 10.12a shows UxBRG values for Fcy = 40 MHz assuming use of the internal oscillator and PLL for some standard baud rates. The *% Error* column shows the actual baud rate achieved without rounding of the UxBRG value but does not include error due to inaccuracy of the internal oscillator frequency. In theory, either high-speed mode or low-speed mode should be adequate because of the small % error values. Our code uses the low-speed mode because in practice we have found this mode to be the most reliable when using the internal oscillator. Figure 10.12b shows the use of an external 7.3728 kHz crystal with the PLL to obtain an internal Fcy = 36.864 kHz (five times the crystal frequency). This "strange" crystal frequency provides perfect matching to standard baud rates, and thus the *% Error* column values are zero. This is one reason why the base internal oscillator frequency is 7.37 kHz; an FOSC using this frequency or a division of this frequency provides better matching at higher baud rates.

(a) Using internal oscillator with PLL to achieve FOSC = 80 MHz (FCY = 40 MHz).
% Error does not account for internal oscillator frequency error.

Baud Rate	UxBRG (High Speed, BRGH = 1)	Actual	% Error	UxBRG (Low Speed, BRGH = 0)	Actual	% Error
230400	42	232558.1	0.9%	10	227272.7	−1.4%
115200	86	114942.5	−0.2%	21	113636.4	−1.4%
57600	173	57471.3	−0.2%	42	58139.53	0.9%
38400	259	38461.5	0.2%	64	38461.54	0.2%
19200	520	19193.9	0.0%	129	19230.77	0.2%
9600	1041	9596.9	0.0%	259	9615.385	0.2%
4800	2082	4800.8	0.0%	520	4798.464	0.0%

(b) Using external 7.3728 kHz crystal with internal PLL to achieve FOSC = 10 x crystal freq (FCY = 36.864 kHz).

Baud Rate	UxBRG (High Speed, BRGH = 1)	Actual	% Error	UxBRG (Low Speed, BRGH = 0)	Actual	% Error
230400	39	230400.0	0.0%	9	230400	0.0%
115200	79	115200.0	0.0%	19	115200	0.0%
57600	159	57600.0	0.0%	39	57600	0.0%
38400	239	38400.0	0.0%	59	38400	0.0%
19200	479	19200.0	0.0%	119	19200	0.0%
9600	959	9600.0	0.0%	239	9600	0.0%
4800	1919	4800.0	0.0%	479	4800	0.0%

FIGURE 10.12 UxBRG values for common baud rates.

Using the **PIC24 UART** with **C**

Support functions for the UARTx subsystems are defined in the files *include\pic24_uart.h* and *common\pic24_uart.c*. Figure 10.13a shows the `uint8 inChar1(void)` function, which waits for a byte to be available in UART1 then returns it. The `IS_CHAR_READY_UART1()` macro simply returns the `U1STAbits.URXDA` status bit which is "1" if data is available in the receive buffer. The `checkRxErrorUART1()` function in Figure 10.13c checks the PERR, FERR, and OERR error status bits, and calls the `reportError()` function with an appropriate error message (recall that `reportError()` saves the error message in a persistent variable and then executes a software reset—the resulting error message is printed by the `printResetCause()` function). The `checkRxErrroUART1()` function must be called before data is read from the U1RXREG register because the error bits reflect the status of the currently available byte in the receive buffer. The `outChar1(uint8 u8_c)` function in Figure 10.13b writes the byte in `u8_c` to the UART1 transmit buffer once space is available. The `IS_TRANSMIT_BUFFER_FULL_UART1()` macro is used to check for space availability in the transmit buffer by returning the `U1STAbits.UTXBF` status bit,

```
#define IS_CHAR_READY_UART1() U1STAbits.URXDA              )Macros defined in
#define IS_TRANSMIT_BUFFER_FULL_UART1() U1STAbits.UTXBF    (include\pic24_uart.h
```

(a) Wait for byte from UART1

```
uint8 inChar1(void) {
  while (!IS_CHAR_READY_UART1())
    doHeartbeat();
  //error check before read
  checkRxErrorUART1();
  //read the receive register
  return U1RXREG;
}
```

(b) Send byte to UART1

```
void outChar1(uint8 u8_c) {
  //wait for transmit buffer to be empty
  while (IS_TRANSMIT_BUFFER_FULL_UART1())
    doHeartbeat();
  //write to the transmit register
  U1TXREG = u8_c;
}
```

```
void checkRxErrorUART1(void) {
  uint8 u8_c;
  //check for errors, reset if detected.
  if (U1STAbits.PERR) {
    u8_c = U1RXREG; //clear error
    reportError("UART1 parity error\n");
  }
  if (U1STAbits.FERR) {
    u8_c = U1RXREG; //clear error
    reportError("UART1 framing error\n");
  }
  if (U1STAbits.OERR) {
    U1STAbits.OERR = 0; //clear error
    reportError("UART1 overrun error\n");
  }
}
```

(c) Check received data for error; if error has occurred then call **reportError** which saves the error message and executes a software reset. The error is then printed by **printResetCause()**. Reading the U1RXREG clears the error bit.

FIGURE 10.13   `inChar1`/`outChar1` UART functions.

which is "1" if there is at least one free spot in the transmit buffer. Similar functions for UARTs 2, 3, and 4 are defined, with conditional compilation used to include the functions only if the target device supports those UARTs.

Figure 10.14 shows functions and macros for UART configuration. The CONFIG_BAUDRATE_UART1(uint32 baudRate) function computes and initializes the U1BRG value for the specified baudRate using Equation 10.3 with a default choice of S = 16 (low-speed mode). The configUART1(uint32 u32_baudRate) function

```
#define DEFAULT_BAUDRATE  57600
#define DEFAULT_BRGH  0

inline static void CONFIG_BAUDRATE_UART1(uint32 baudRate) {
#if (DEFAULT_BRGH1 == 0)
  uint32 brg = (Fcy/baudRate/16) - 1;
#else
  uint32 brg = (Fcy/baudRate/4) - 1;
#endif
  ASSERT(brg <= 0xFFFF);
  U1MODEbits.BRGH = DEFAULT_BRGH1;
  U1BRG = brg;
}
#define UXMODE_PDSEL_8DATA_NOPARITY    0
#define UXMODE_PDSEL_8DATA_EVENPARITY  1
#define UXMODE_PDSEL_8DATA_ODDPARITY   2
#define UXMODE_PDSEL_9DATA_NOPARITY    3

inline static void CONFIG_PDSEL_UART1(uint8 u8_pdsel) {
  U1MODEbits.PDSEL = u8_pdsel;
}

inline static void CONFIG_STOPBITS_UART1(uint8 u8_numStopbits) {
  U1MODEbits.STSEL = u8_numStopbits - 1;
}

inline static void ENABLE_UART1() {
  U1MODEbits.UEN = 0b00;   // UxTX,UxRX pins are enabled,no flow control
  U1MODEbits.UARTEN = 1;  // enable UART RX/TX
  U1STAbits.UTXEN = 1;     //Enable the transmitter
}

void configUART1(uint32 u32_baudRate) {
  /****** UART config **********/
  CONFIG_RP10_AS_DIG_PIN(); //RX RP pin must be digital
  CONFIG_U1RX_TO_RP(10);    //U1RX <- RP10
  CONFIG_RP11_AS_DIG_PIN(); //TX RP pin must be digital
  CONFIG_U1TX_TO_RP(11);    //U1TX -> RP11
  CONFIG_BAUDRATE_UART1(u32_baudRate);   //baud rate
  // 8-bit data, no parity
  CONFIG_PDSEL_UART1(UXMODE_PDSEL_8DATA_NOPARITY);
  CONFIG_STOPBITS_UART1(1);    // 1 Stop bit
  ENABLE_UART1();              //enable the UART
}
```

Compute and init the U1BRG register for the specified **baudRate** given an FCY. By default, the code uses the 16x (low-speed) mode.

Config data format

Config stop bits

Enable UART pins

Utility function that configures external RP pins and calls the above functions to config, enable the UART.

RP*n* pins used in PIC24HJ32GP202 reference system.

FIGURE 10.14 UART configuration.

calls the other functions and macros in Figure 10.14 to configure the stop bits, data format, and baud rate for UART1 and also steers the U1RX and U1TX pins to the RP10 and RP11 pins respectively on the reference PIC24HJ32GP202 system of Chapter 8. The UART configuration accomplished by configUART1() uses a data format of 1 stop bit, no parity, and 8 data bits with no hardware flow control (that is, it does not use pins U*x*CTS# or U*x*RTS#).

The various character I/O functions used thus far in our example programs such as outString(), outUint8(), inChar(), etc., are contained in the file *common\ pic24_serial.c*. Figure 10.15 shows the uint8 inChar() and outChar(uint8 u8_c) functions used for single character input/output in *pic24_serial.c*. Observe that the global variable __C30_UART determines the UART*x* destination by selecting between inChar1, inChar2, etc. for inChar() and between outChar1, outChar2, etc. for outChar(). Thus, the character I/O functions contained in pic24_serial.c can be dynamically switched between the available UARTs on a PIC24 microcontroller.

```
uint8 inChar(void) {                      void outChar(uint8 u8_c) {
 switch (__C30_UART) {                       switch (__C30_UART)
#if (NUM_UARTS >= 1)                           {
      case 1 : return inChar1();       #if (NUM_UARTS >= 1)
#endif                                         case 1 : outChar1(u8_c); break;
#if (NUM_UARTS >= 2)                    #endif
      case 2 : return inChar2();       #if (NUM_UARTS >= 2)
#endif                                         case 2 : outChar2(u8_c); break;
#if (NUM_UARTS >= 3)                    #endif
      case 3 : return inChar3();       #if (NUM_UARTS >= 3)
#endif                                         case 3 : outChar3(u8_c); break;
#if (NUM_UARTS >= 4)                    #endif
      case 4 : return inChar4();       #if (NUM_UARTS >= 4)
#endif                                         case 4 : outChar4(u8_c); break;
 default :                             #endif
    REPORT_ERROR("Invalid UART");              default :
   }                                             REPORT_ERROR("Invalid UART");
}                                            }
                                         }
```

FIGURE 10.15   inChar()/outChar() serial I/O functions.

<*STDIO.H*> LIBRARY FUNCTIONS

The C *<stdio.h>* library functions supported by the PIC24 compiler such as printf, scanf, etc., can also be used either with the functions in *pic24_serial.c* or in lieu of these functions. By default, the *<stdio.h>* character I/O functions map to UART1 but there is a general mechanism in the PIC24 compiler for redirecting these functions to other peripherals—see the PIC24 *16-bit Language Tools Libraries* manual that comes with the compiler for more details. As stated previously, we have chosen to use our own lightweight set of serial I/O functions because of the relatively large code footprint of the *<stdio.h>* library, but this point may be moot if you are using a PIC24 µC with a large program memory. We will occasionally use the printf function in examples when we need to take advantage of its advanced formatting capabilities.

INTERRUPT-DRIVEN I/O WITH THE PIC24 UART

As previously discussed, the receive and transmit components for the PIC24 UART can each buffer five bytes, four in the hardware FIFO and one in the shift register associated with the appropriate UxTX/UxRX pin. The receiver can experience buffer overrun if the UART receive buffer is not polled often enough by calling inChar(), while the outChar() function can waste clock cycles by waiting for a free location in the transmit buffer. Interrupts provide a more efficient method for performing UART I/O for both receive and transmit operations.

INTERRUPT-DRIVEN UART RECEIVE

Figure 10.16 shows an example application that reads a string from the UART using the inString() function, reverses the string using the reverseString() function, then sends the reversed string to the UART. In this application, a string arriving from the UART is considered terminated by either a new line or a carriage

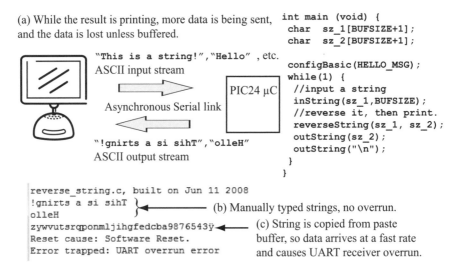

(a) While the result is printing, more data is being sent, and the data is lost unless buffered.

"This is a string!", "Hello", etc.
ASCII input stream

PIC24 µC

Asynchronous Serial link

"!gnirts a si sihT", "olleH"
ASCII output stream

```
int main (void) {
  char  sz_1[BUFSIZE+1];
  char  sz_2[BUFSIZE+1];

  configBasic(HELLO_MSG);
  while(1) {
    //input a string
    inString(sz_1,BUFSIZE);
    //reverse it, then print.
    reverseString(sz_1, sz_2);
    outString(sz_2);
    outString("\n");
  }
}
```

```
reverse_string.c, built on Jun 11 2008
!gnirts a si sihT
olleH
zywvutsrqponmljihgfedcba9876543ÿ
Reset cause: Software Reset.
Error trapped: UART overrun error
```

(b) Manually typed strings, no overrun.

(c) String is copied from paste buffer, so data arrives at a fast rate and causes UART receiver overrun.

FIGURE 10.16 String reverse application.

return (see the source files accompanying this book for code details on inString()
and reverseString()). The problem with this application is that while a string is
being reversed then printed, another string may be arriving. As long as strings
are typed manually from the console as seen in Figure 10.16b, the while(1){}
loop can finish reversing and printing a previous string before arrival of a
new string causes a UART overrun error. However, if multiple strings are pasted
into the console application from the paste buffer, then strings arrive too fast
and UART receiver overrun occurs (Figure 10.16c) causing a processor reset
when the checkRxErrrorUART1() function of Figure 10.13 detects the overrun
error.

Fast bursts of input data on a communication channel can cause overrun
problems if polled I/O is used on the channel. One solution to this problem is to
use interrupt processing on the channel for reading data as soon as it is available
then storing it in a temporary buffer until it can be read by the application. Within
the UART receiver, the U*x*RXIF interrupt flag in Figure 10.11 is set by various data
available conditions as determined by the URXISEL<1:0> bits (U*x*STA<7:6>) of
Figure 10.9. The _U*x*RXInterrupt ISR is associated with the U*x*RXIF interrupt flag
and can be used to read the UART*x* receiver when data is available, instead of
relying on inChar() to poll for data availability. (Using the cell phone analogy
from Chapter 9, the phone rings when a call is available instead of you having to
continually check the phone to see if somebody is trying to talk to you.) However,
where does the _U*x*RXInterrupt ISR place the data after reading the U*x*RXREG
register? The answer is a *software FIFO,* which operates like the hardware FIFOs
of Figures 10.10 and 10.11 except that data memory locations are used for
storage.

Figure 10.17 shows the structure and operation of a software FIFO with eight
locations. Two indexes, named head and tail, are used for accessing the buffer. The
FIFO is empty when head is equal to tail. Data is written into the buffer (Figure
10.17b) by incrementing the head index then storing data at buffer[head]. This
means that data is available in the buffer whenever head is not equal to tail. Data
is read from the buffer (Figure 10.17c) by incrementing tail then accessing data
from buffer[tail]. Observe that data comes out of the buffer in the same order in
which it is placed into the buffer; hence the first-in, first-out (FIFO) designation.
Figure 10.17d shows the buffer holding several characters. When the head index
reaches the end of the buffer, the next write operation must *wrap* the head index
to the beginning of the buffer (Figure 10.17e). For this reason, this data structure
is also referred to as a *circular buffer.* In Figure 10.17f, the write operation leaves
the head index equal to the tail index, causing the buffer to appear empty even
though it contains eight valid data items. This is *buffer overrun,* which means that
under these rules for buffer insertion and extraction, an n-location buffer can
hold a maximum of $n - 1$ data elements.

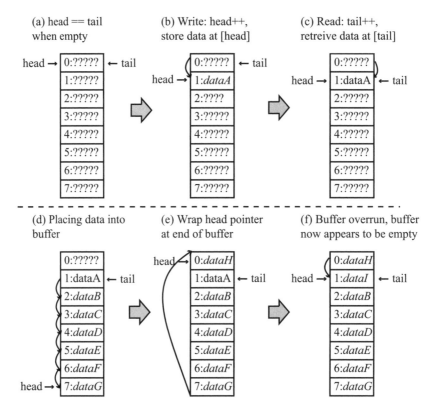

FIGURE 10.17   Software FIFO structure and operation.

Figure 10.18 shows the implementation of the UART RX software FIFO in *common\pic24_uart.c*. If the UART1_RX_INTERRUPT macro is defined, then the interrupt version of inChar1() is compiled instead of the polled version shown in Figure 10.13a. The most convenient place to define the UART1_RX_INTERRUPT macro (10.18a) is in the MPLAB® project associated with the application's source files; see Appendix B. The UART1_RX_FIFO_SIZE and UART1_RX_INTERRUPT_PRIORITY macros (10.18b) set the FIFO buffer size and interrupt priority, respectively, and can be overridden by the user. The inChar1() function now waits for data to be available in the buffer, indicated by u16_rxFifo1Tail being not equal to u16_rxFifo1Tail (10.18c). When data is available, the tail index is incremented and wrapped if necessary, and the new data is returned from au8_rxFifo1[u16_rxFifo1Tail]. The _U1RXInterrupt ISR is triggered when data is available in the receive buffer. The head index is incremented and wrapped if necessary (10.18f), and if head is equal to tail then a buffer overrun error is reported which resets the processor. If no overrun is present, the new data is placed into the buffer at au8_rxFifo1[u16_rxFifo1Head]. The configUART1() function of Figure 10.14

```
#ifdef UART1_RX_INTERRUPT
//Interrupt driven RX
#ifndef UART1_RX_FIFO_SIZE
#define UART1_RX_FIFO_SIZE 32   //choose a size
#endif

#ifndef UART1_RX_INTERRUPT_PRIORITY
#define UART1_RX_INTERRUPT_PRIORITY 1
#endif

volatile uint8 au8_rxFifo1[UART1_RX_FIFO_SIZE];
volatile uint16 u16_rxFifo1Head = 0;
volatile uint16 u16_rxFifo1Tail = 0;

uint8 inChar1(void) {
  while (u16_rxFifo1Head == u16_rxFifo1Tail) {   //wait for character
    doHeartbeat();
  } ;
  u16_rxFifo1Tail++;
  if (u16_rxFifo1Tail == UART1_RX_FIFO_SIZE) u16_rxFifo1Tail=0; //wrap
  return au8_rxFifo1[u16_rxFifo1Tail];  //return the character
}

void _ISR _U1RXInterrupt (void) {
  int8 u8_c;

  _U1RXIF = 0;            //clear the UART RX interrupt bit
  checkRxErrorUART1();
  u8_c = U1RXREG;         //read character
  u16_rxFifo1Head++;      //increment head pointer
  if (u16_rxFifo1Head == UART1_RX_FIFO_SIZE)
                       u16_rxFifo1Head = 0; //wrap if needed
  if (u16_rxFifo1Head == u16_rxFifo1Tail) {
   //FIFO overrun!, report error
   reportError("UART1 RX Interrupt FIFO overrun!");
  }
  au8_rxFifo1[u16_rxFifo1Head] = u8_c;   //place in buffer
}

#else      //...polled functions go here
```

(a) Defined by user in MPLAB project to select polled or interrupt driven RX.

(b) Default FIFO buffer size and interrupt priority, can be overridden by user.

(c) Wait until data is available in buffer, which is placed there by the ISR.

(d) Must wrap tail pointer!

(e) Return the data from the buffer.

(f) Must wrap header pointer!

(g) Checks for software buffer overrun, reset if detected.

(h) Place received data into buffer.

FIGURE 10.18   Interrupt-driven UART RX implementation.

is also modified to enable the U1RXIF interrupt when the UART1_RX_INTERRUPT macro is defined.

With UART RX interrupt processing enabled, the overrun case of Figure 10.16c does not occur when a few strings are pasted into the console window. However, every software FIFO has a finite size, and pasting a large number of strings into the console window will trigger the FIFO overrun error checked for in the _U1RXInterrupt ISR. In this case, the RX FIFO overrun error occurs even if no incoming string is greater than the RX FIFO size because the RX data is arriving at a steady rate. The TX channel data rate is the same as the RX channel and the time spent by main() to reverse the string is non-zero, so the time spent processing outgoing data is greater than the time spent on processing incoming data. The `main()` task steadily loses ground to the incoming data, processing data from the RX input FIFO at points deeper in the RX FIFO buffer for each string that arrives. This process is illustrated Figure 10.19, which tests UART RX for polled versus interrupt-driven using the reverse string application by sending various numbers of strings, each containing 11 characters (the RX software FIFO size was set to 8 bytes in this test). In 10.19a, the polled UART RX case experienced hardware RX FIFO overrun when only two strings were sent. While the processor was busy transmitting the first reversed string, the arriving second string overflowed the RX HW buffer. Figure 10.19b shows the interrupt-driven UART RX case. The UART functions are modified to use two PIO signals for status information. Signal RAXF is asserted by `_U1RXInterrupt()` when the RX SW FIFO has only one free location left, and signal TXWAIT is asserted by `outChar1()` when waiting for a free spot in the TX hardware FIFO. In Figure 10.19b-1, the first string is received,

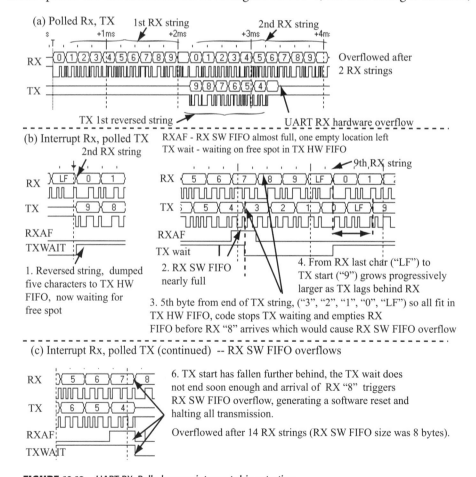

FIGURE 10.19   UART RX: Polled versus interrupt-driven testing.

reversed, then the first five characters are dumped to the TX hardware FIFO causing the TXWAIT line to be asserted while outChar1() is waiting for a free location in
the TX buffer. The lag between the last character of an RX string ('LF') and the first
character of the resulting reversed string ('9') is very short. However, this gap has
increased to about a 1.5 character transmission times after nine RX strings have been
reversed (see Figure 10.19b-4). Also, the software FIFO is now almost full (has one free
location left) as evidenced by assertion of RAXF. In Figure 10.19b-3, the TX wait in
outChar1() ends because it has reached the last five characters of the reversed string
that is being sent, so they all fit in the TX HW buffer. This means the inString()
function starts emptying the RX software FIFO before the arrival of the next character ('8') that would trigger overflow. However, the TX of reversed strings lags further
as more strings are received, and after 14 strings, the RX software FIFO overflows as
shown in Figure 10.19c.

An RX FIFO size is based on the maximum data burst size that is expected on
that channel. If data is arriving at a *continuous rate* that is faster than what the CPU
can process, then no amount of data buffering prevents overrun as eventually the
software FIFO fills up. An example of a continuous data stream is produced by an
environmental sensor that outputs data at fixed intervals as long as the sensor is
powered on. For a periodic input data stream, the time spent processing the output
data must be less than that spent on the input data. We revisit the problem of handling continuously arriving data later in this chapter.

INTERRUPT-DRIVEN UART TRANSMIT

Interrupt-driven UART transmit augments the size of the TX hardware FIFO by
adding a software FIFO that data is written to first before it is transferred to the
UART TX HW buffer. Within the UART transmitter, the UxTXIF interrupt flag in
Figure 10.10 is set by various conditions as determined by the UTXISEL<1:0> bits
(UxSTA<15,13>) of Figure 10.9. We use the default configuration of "00", which sets
the UxTXIF interrupt flag when data is transferred from the TX buffer to the transmit
shift register, guaranteeing a free location in the transmit buffer. In our approach, the
outChar1() function places data into a software FIFO buffer, and the TX ISR transfers
data out of the software FIFO buffer and into the UART transmit buffer as the TX
ISR is triggered whenever a free location is available in the UART TX buffer. This is
the reverse of the interrupt-driven RX UART code, in which the RX ISR placed data
into the software FIFO and the inChar() function took data out of it.

Figure 10.20 shows the *C* code implementation for interrupt-driven UART transmission. The UART1_TX_INTERRUPT macro (a) selects the interrupt-driven outChar1()
function, which increments and wraps (d) the head index using a temporary variable
named u16_tmp in order to compare it against the tail index (e). As long the tail index
(u16_txFifo1Tail) is equal to the head index (u16_txFifo1Head) the software-transmit

```
#ifdef UART1_TX_INTERRUPT
//Interrupt driven TX
#ifndef UART1_TX_FIFO_SIZE
#define UART1_TX_FIFO_SIZE 32   //choose a size
#endif

#ifndef UART1_TX_INTERRUPT_PRIORITY
#define UART1_TX_INTERRUPT_PRIORITY 1
#endif

volatile uint8 au8_txFifo1[UART1_TX_FIFO_SIZE];
volatile uint16 u16_txFifo1Head = 0;
volatile uint16 u16_txFifo1Tail = 0;

void outChar1(uint8 u8_c) {
  uint16 u16_tmp;
  u16_tmp = u16_txFifo1Head;
  u16_tmp++;
  if (u16_tmp == UART1_TX_FIFO_SIZE) u16_tmp = 0; //wrap if needed
  while (u16_tmp == u16_txFifo1Tail) {
   doHeartbeat();
  }

  au8_txFifo1[u16_tmp] = u8_c; //write to buffer
  u16_txFifo1Head = u16_tmp;      //update head
  _U1TXIE = 1;                    //enable interrupt
}
void _ISR _U1TXInterrupt (void) {
  if (u16_txFifo1Head == u16_txFifo1Tail) {
   //empty TX buffer, disable the interrupt, do not clear the flag
   _U1TXIE = 0;
  } else {
   //at least one free spot in the TX buffer!
   u16_txFifo1Tail++;       //increment tail pointer
   if (u16_txFifo1Tail == UART1_TX_FIFO_SIZE)
     u16_txFifo1Tail = 0; //wrap if needed
   _U1TXIF = 0;    //clear the interrupt flag
   //transfer character from software buffer to transmit buffer
   U1TXREG =  au8_txFifo1[u16_txFifo1Tail];
  }
}
#else      //...polled functions go here
```

(a) Defined by user in MPLAB project to select polled or interrupt driven TX

(b) Default FIFO buffer size and interrupt priority, can be overridden by user.

(c) Copy head pointer to temporary as we do not want to modify the head pointer value examined by the background ISR.

(d) Must wrap head pointer!

(e) Wait until space available in transmit buffer

(f) Place data in buffer

(g) Enable TX interrupt so that ISR can take data out.

(h) if no data, disable interrupt, do not clear U1TXIF

(i) Must wrap tail pointer!

(j) Take data out of FIFO buffer, send to UART transmit buffer, clear interrupt flag.

FIGURE 10.20 Interrupt-driven UART TX implementation.

FIFO buffer is full and the function loops until the background TX ISR frees a location in the software FIFO buffer. The u8_c parameter passed to outChar1() is then placed in the buffer at location au8_txFifo1[u16_txFifo1Head] (f).

Next, the TX interrupt is enabled by setting _UTXIE (g). If an empty location exists in the UART TX transmit buffer as indicated by the U1TXIF flag being set, then an immediate jump is made to the TX ISR. Otherwise, the UART TX transmit buffer is full, so U1TXIF is cleared. In this case, the byte remains in the software TX FIFO until the current character in the TX shift register is finished transmitting and a byte is transferred from the UART TX transmit buffer to the TX shift register, freeing a location in the TX transmit buffer, setting the U1TXF flag, and causing a jump to the TX ISR.

The TX ISR (_U1TXInterrupt) first checks to see if data exists in the software FIFO by comparing the head index against the tail index. If the software FIFO is empty, the TX interrupt is disabled by clearing _UTXIE (h), but the U1TXIF flag is not cleared as we want it to remain set as long as an empty location exists in the TX transmit buffer. This is one of the few cases where an interrupt flag is not cleared before exit; instead, the interrupt is disabled so that the the interrupt flag's true condition does not immediately generate a jump back to the ISR after ISR exit. If data exists in the software FIFO then the tail index is incremented, wrapped if necessary (i), and the data from the software FIFO at au8_txFifo1[u16_txFifo1Head] is transferred to the UART TX buffer (j). In this condition, the U1TXIF flag is cleared before exit so that it can be set again once the currently transmitting character is finished.

Listing 10.1 shows the source code for the configUART1() function originally given in Figure 10.14 modified to include conditional compilation for interrupt-driven RX/TX. In the case of interrupt-driven RX, the _U1RXIF flag is cleared (_U1RXIF=0) before the RX interrupt is enabled (_U1RXIE=1). The _U1RXInterrupt ISR is triggered by arrival of RX data, thus we need this interrupt enabled when the UART is configured. However, the code for interrupt driven TX only sets the interrupt priority, neither clearing the TX interrupt flag nor enabling the interrupt. This is because the TX interrupt flag is set when the UART is initialized and must remain set in order to trigger the _U1TXInterrupt ISR once a character is placed in the TX software FIFO by the outChar1() function, which enables the TX interrupt.

LISTING 10.1   configUART1() **Source code.**

```
void configUART1(uint32 u32_baudRate) {
  CONFIG_RP10_AS_DIG_PIN();                            //RX RP pin must be digital
  CONFIG_U1RX_TO_RP(10);                               //U1RX <- RP10
  CONFIG_RP11_AS_DIG_PIN();                            //TX RP pin must be digital
  CONFIG_U1TX_TO_RP(11);                               //U1TX -> RP11
  CONFIG_BAUDRATE_UART1(u32_baudRate);                 //baud rate
  CONFIG_PDSEL_UART1(UXMODE_PDSEL_8DATA_NOPARITY);     // 8-bit data, no parity
  CONFIG_STOPBITS_UART1(1);                            // 1 Stop bit
#ifdef UART1_RX_INTERRUPT
  _U1RXIF = 0;                                         //clear the flag
  _U1RXIP = UART1_RX_INTERRUPT_PRIORITY;               //choose a priority
  _U1RXIE = 1;                                         //enable the interrupt
#endif
#ifdef UART1_TX_INTERRUPT
  //do not clear the U1TXIF flag!
  _U1RXIP = UART1_TX_INTERRUPT_PRIORITY;               //choose a priority
  //do not enable the interrupt until we try to write to the UART
#endif
  ENABLE_UART1();                                      //enable the UART
}
```

Figure 10.21a summarizes reverse string application testing for different conditions, with the results for polled RX/TX and interrupt RX/polled TX previously given in Figure 10.19. Using both interrupt RX and interrupt TX helps in that it takes 34 strings to overflow the RX software FIFO instead of 14 for interrupt RX/polled TX. However, the eight buffer locations used by the interrupt TX software FIFO are better used if polled TX is done instead, with the interrupt RX software FIFO size increased from 8 to 16 as this requires 55 strings to overflow. Interrupt-driven TX costs more cycles per byte overhead in terms of processing time versus polled TX because bytes have to be first placed in the software TX buffer, then moved by the ISR to the hardware TX buffer. Thus, interrupt TX adds more processing overhead to the output stream, so these extra buffer slots are better used in the RX software FIFO. This illustrates that using an interrupt-driven approach for all I/O may not automatically be the best option; the tradeoffs are application dependent. In a different application, interrupt TX might be attractive if output data occurred in bursts, the TX software FIFO was large enough to accommodate the largest burst, and the cycles spent waiting on a free spot in the TX HW buffer were needed for some other task. Figure 10.21b and Figure 10.21c summarize HW/SW FIFO usage for RX/TX serial data.

(a) reverse string application testing summary

Implementation	RX SW FIFO SIZE	TX SW FIFO SIZE	# of Strings to trigger overflow (11 chars per string)
(1) Polled RX,TX	n/a	n/a	2 (RX HW FIFO)
(2) Interrupt RX, polled TX	8	n/a	14 (RX SW FIFO)
(3) Interrupt RX, interrupt TX	8	8	34 (RX SW FIFO)
(4) Interrupt RX, polled TX	16	n/a	55 (RX SW FIFO)

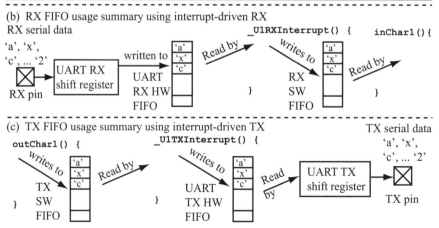

(b) RX FIFO usage summary using interrupt-driven RX

(c) TX FIFO usage summary using interrupt-driven TX

FIGURE 10.21 Reverse string testing, RX/TX FIFO usage summaries.

THE RS-232 STANDARD

The Electronic Industries Association standard EIA RS-232 defines signaling levels, external cabling, and handshaking protocols for asynchronous communication. RS-232 cabling uses either a 9-pin connector (DB9) or a 25-pin connector (DB25), with the DB9 commonly used on personal computers. Figure 10.22 shows a minimal RS-232 PIC24 µC to PC asynchronous serial connection. The MAX 3232 RS-232 transceiver from Maxim [35] is only one of many different driver ICs that convert between RS-232 logic levels and CMOS logic levels. An RS-232 logic one has a range of −3 V to −25 V (−9 V typical) while an RS-232 logic zero has a range of +3 V to +25 V (+9 V typical). This is a minimal connection, for there are many other signals defined in the RS-232 standard that are used for external modem control and flow control. Because many PCs no longer contain a serial port, the usage of USB-to-serial converters has become popular. These adapter cables contain a microcontroller that communicates using the Universal Serial Bus (USB) with a host PC and converts USB packet data to asynchronous serial data. The USB is a fairly complex synchronous serial interface that is discussed further in Chapter 13. Some USB-to-serial converter cables use RS-232 levels, requiring the use of a level converter chip such as the MAX 3232. Others cables, such as the FTDI TTL-232R-3.3V cable used in the system startup schematic in Figure 8.3, conveniently output CMOS logic levels, allowing direct connection between the cable's pins and the PIC24 µC. When using a USB-to-serial converter (or any RS-232 interface), one must know the signaling levels used by the cable's pins, as RS-232 signaling levels will damage a PIC24 µC.

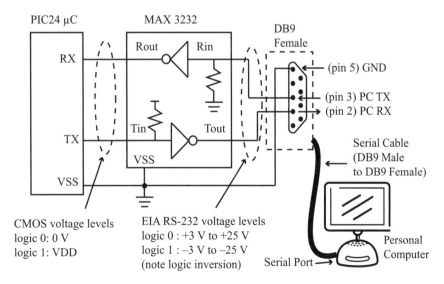

FIGURE 10.22 Minimal RS-232 PIC24 µC to PC connection.

The minimal connection of Figure 10.22 has no method for either device to signal the other device about its ability to receive data; the sender assumes that the receiver is always able to accept new data. Two pins named CTS# (clear to send, pin 8 on the DB9) and RTS# (request to send, pin 7 on the DB9) can be used as handshaking lines to implement hardware flow control for serial data. The RTS# signal is a low-true output from the PC whose assertion indicates that the PC is ready to receive data. The CTS# signal is a low-true input to the PC, whose negation inhibits data transmission from the PC. These handshaking signals are included because the RS-232 standard was originally intended for communication between a terminal (data terminal equipment, or DTE) and a modem (data communication equipment, or DCE). In this historical model, the modem performed relatively low-speed communication over phone lines to a remote site. This means that the modem's input buffer could become full, requiring it to tell the DTE (the PC) to stop sending data. On the PIC24 µC, the UxCTS# and UxRTS# pin functions shown in Figures 10.10 and 10.11 can be used to implement hardware flow control by connecting the PIC24 µC's UxRTS# output to the PC's CTS# input and the PC's RTS# output to the PIC24 µC's UxCTS# input. The PIC24 µC UxRTS# output is asserted when there is free space in the UART RX buffer, while negation of the UxCTS# input inhibits transmission from the UART. This provides flow control in both directions, from PIC24 µC to PC and vice versa. A full description of these pins and their usage is found in the PIC24 FRM [22]. For typical asynchronous communication speeds, hardware flow control is not required and thus this book does not use it. Sometimes a software flow control scheme using ASCII control codes XON (control-Q, 0x11) for "transmitter on" and XOFF (control-S, 0x13) for "transmitter off" is used when ASCII data is being exchanged. The advantage of software flow control is that no extra wires are needed; the disadvantage is that it cannot easily be used with arbitrary binary data since the codes 0x11 and 0x13 may be valid data bytes in the transmission. Some software flow schemes use a *break* character, which is defined on the PIC24 UART as a start bit + 12 zeros + stop bit, in conjunction with XON/XOFF codes for binary data software flow control. However, this depends on a UART's capability for transmission and reception of break characters, and this may vary by UART implementation.

THE SERIAL PERIPHERAL INTERFACE (SPI)

The Serial Peripheral Interface (SPI, pronounced as "spy"), originally developed by Motorola, is a three-wire synchronous serial link that has developed into a *de facto* standard due to its adoption by multiple semiconductor vendors. Figure 10.23 shows an SPI connection between a PIC24 µC and two peripheral devices. In this configuration, the PIC24 µC is termed the *master* as it starts every

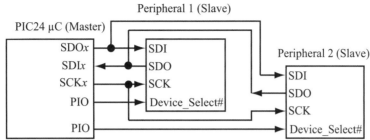

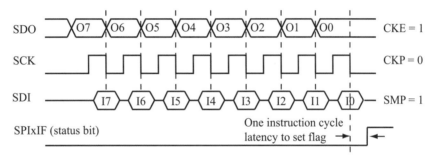

FIGURE 10.23   PIC24 μC SPI connection to two slave devices.

transmission by providing the clock (SCLK), with output data provided on the serial data out (SDO) pin and input data on the serial data in (SDI) pin. The two peripheral devices are termed *slaves* because they respond to SCLK pulses only if their low-true device select line (*Device_Select#*, the actual name used is device dependent) is asserted, which is handled using a PIO pin from the PIC24 μC. On each transfer, data is shifted out of the PIC24 μC via the SDO pin and shifted in from the selected slave device via the SDI pin. Thus, reading data from a slave device requires writing data, even if that data is simply dummy data. Similarly, data coming back from the slave during a write may only be dummy data, but it must be read and discarded to empty the SPI module input buffer. If the peripheral device is output only, then the SDI physical connection is not present, but garbage data is still clocked into the SPI input buffer on each transmission. Data is sent MSb first, and the clock polarity can be adjusted via a control bit named CKP, with value "0" if the idle state is low and "1" if the idle state is high. The edge that the output data is changed on is selected by the CKE control bit, with "0" used for an idle to active clock edge and "1" for an active to idle clock edge. There are four combinations possible using CKP/CKE; Figure 10.23 shows a waveform for CKE = 1, CKP = 0. The particular combination required is slave device dependent, but the CKE = 1, CKP = 0 choice is common. The SMP control bit determines if the input data is sampled in middle of the output data (SMP = 0) or at the end of the output data (SMP = 1). Figure 10.23 shows the SMP = 1 case. An interrupt flag named SPIxIF is set whenever a transmission is completed. Transmissions from the PIC24 μC are selectable as either 8-bit or 16-bit. The 8-bit configuration is the most common option supported by SPI peripheral devices and is shown in the figure.

Figure 10.24 shows a block diagram of a SPIx module (as with the UARTx modules, there can be multiple SPI modules in a PIC24 μC, designated as SPI1, SPI2, etc.). In Master mode, the PIC24 μC initiates the transmission, and if the PIC24 μC provides the SCKx it is generated from Fcy with two cascaded prescalers, a secondary and a primary, as shown. The maximum allowable SCK frequency generated by a PIC24HJ32GP202 is 10 MHz, so one must be careful to select prescaler values such that the generated SCK does not exceed this maximum. Each slave device also has its own maximum allowable SCK input frequency, which also must not be exceeded. The SSx# input is used when the SPI module in *slave mode,* that is, the PIC24 μC is acting as a SPI peripheral to another SPI master device. This operation mode is

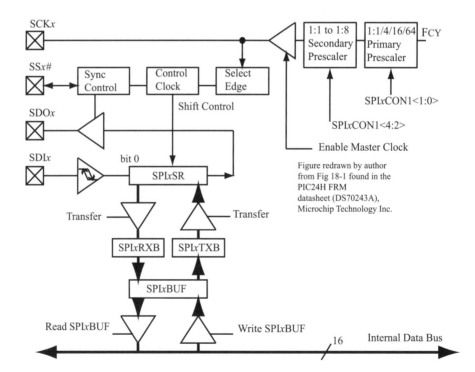

FIGURE 10.24 SPIx module block diagram. (Adapted with permission of the copyright owner, Microchip Technology Inc. All rights reserved. No further reprints or reproduction may be made without Microchip Inc.'s prior written consent.)

discussed later in this chapter. In Master mode, a write to the SPI*x*BUF register is actually a write to the SPI*x* transmit buffer (SPI*x*TXB), whose value is then transferred to the SPI*x* shift register (SPI*x*SR) if it is idle. As data is shifted out of SPI*x*SR via the SDO pin, data is shifted into SPI*x*SR via the SDI pin. Once the transmission is complete, SPI*x*SR is transferred to the SPI*x* receive buffer (SPI*x*RXB). A read of SPI*x*BUF

U-0	U-0	U-0	R/W-0	R/W-0	R/W-0	R/W-0	R/W-0
UI	UI	UI	DISSCK	DISSDO	MODE16	SMP	CKE[1]
15	14	13	12	11	10	9	8

R/W-0	R/W-0	R/W-0	R/W-0	R/W-0	R/W-0	R/W-0	R/W-0
SSEN	CKP	MSTEN	SPRE<2:0>			PPRE<1:0>	
7	6	5	4	3	2	1	0

Bit 12: DISSCK: Disable SCK*x* pin bit (master modes only)
   1 = Internal SPI clock is disabled, pin functions as I/O
   0 = Internal SPI clock is enabled

Bit 11: DISSDO: Disable SDO*x* pin bit
   1 = SDO*x* pin is not used by module; pin functions as I/O
   0 = SDO*x* pin is controlled by the module

Bit 10: MODE16:Word/Byte Communication Select bit
   1 = Communication is word-wide (16 bits);   0 = Communication is byte-wide (8 bits)

Bit 9: SPIx Data Input Sample Phase bit
   Master Mode:
   1 = Input data sampled at end of data output time
   0 = Input data sampled at middle of data output time

   Slave Mode:
   SMP must be cleared in SPI*x* Slave mode

Bit 8: CKE: SPI*x* Clock Edge Select bit[1]
   1 = Serial output data changes on transition from active clock state to idle clock state
   0 = Serial output data changes on transition from idle clock state to active clock state

Bit 7: SSEN: Slave Select Enable bit (Slave mode)
   1 = SS*x*# pin used for slave mode;   0 = SS*x*# pin is not used by module (pin controlled by port)

Bit 6: CKP: Clock Polarity Select bit
   1 = Idle state for clock is a high level; active state is a low level
   0 = Idle state for clock is a low level; active state is a high level

Bit 5: MSTEN: Master mode Enable bit
   1 = Master mode; 0 = Slave mode

Bit 4-2: SPRE<2:0> Secondary Prescale bits
       (Master mode)
   111 = Secondary prescale 1:1
   110 = Secondary prescale 2:1
   . . .
   000 = Secondary prescale 8:1

Bit 1-0: PPRE<1:0> Primary Prescale bits
       (Master mode)
   11 = Primary prescale 1:1
   10 = Primary prescale 4:1
   01 = Primary prescale 16:1
   00 = Primary prescale 64:1

Figure redrawn by author from Reg. 18-2 found in the PIC24H FRM datasheet (DS70243A), Microchip Technology Inc.

Note 1: The CKE bit is not used in the framed SPI mode. Program this bit to 0 for the framed SPI modes (FRMEN = 1).

FIGURE 10.25   SPI*x*CON1: Control register 1. (Adapted with permission of the copyright owner, Microchip Technology Inc. All rights reserved. No further reprints or reproduction may be made without Microchip Inc.'s prior written consent.)

is actually a read of SPIxRXB. When SPIxRXB contains data, it is important to read SPIxBUF before another complete value is shifted into SPIxSR, or else a receive buffer overflow condition is generated, which halts operation of the SPIx module.

Figure 10.25 shows the SPIxCON1 control register that contains the CKE, CKP, and SMP configuration bits as well bits to select Master/Slave mode, 16-bit/8-bit mode, the secondary/primary prescaler values, and individual bits for disabling the SDOx, SCKx, and SSx pins if they are not used. There is a second control register named SPIxCON2 that supports a *framed* SPI protocol that this book does not discuss as most SPI peripherals do not use this protocol.

Figure 10.26 shows the SPIxSTAT status register and control register. The SPIEN bit enables the SPIx module when it is "1". The SPIROV status bit indicates if a receive buffer overflow condition has occurred; clearing this bit clears the overflow condition. The SPITBF and SPIRBF status bits, when set, indicate full conditions for the transmit buffer and receive buffer registers, respectively. These bits are automatically set and cleared in hardware by reading or writing the transmit and receive buffer registers.

R/W-0	U-0	R/W-0	U-0	U-0	U-0	U-0	U-0
SPIEN	UI	SPISIDL	UI	UI	UI	UI	UI
15	14	13	12	11	10	9	8
U-0	R/C-0	U-0	U-0	U-0	U-0	R-0	R-0
UI	SPIROV	UI	UI	UI	UI	SPITBF	SPIRBF
7	6	5	4	3	2	1	0

Bit 15: SPIEN: SPIx Enable bit
  1 = Enables module and configures SCKx, SDOx, SDIx,
    and SSx# as serial port pins
  0 = Disables module

Figure redrawn by author from Reg 18-1 found in the PIC24H FRM datasheet (DS70243A), Microchip Technology Inc.

Bit 13: SPISIDL: Stop in Idle Mode Bit
  1 = Discontinue module operation device enters Idle mode; 0 = Continue operation in Idle mode
Bit 6: SPIROV: Receive Overflow Flag bit
  1 = A new byte/word is completely received and discarded. The user application has not read the
    previous data in the SPIxBUF register
  0 = No overflow has occurred
Bit 1: SPITBF: SPIx Transmit Buffer Full Status bit
  1 = Transmit not yet started, SPIxTXB is full; 0 = Transmit started, SPIxTXB is empty
  Automatically set in hardware when CPU writes SPIxBUF location, loading SPIxTXB.
  Automatically cleared in hardware when SPIx module transfer data SPIxTXB to SPIxSR.
Bit 0: SPIRBF: SPIx Receive Buffer Full Status bit
  1 = Receive complete, SPIxRXB is full; 0 = Receive is not complete, SPIxRXB is empty
  Automatically set in hardware when SPIx transfers data from SPIxSR to SPIxRXB.
  Automatically cleared in hardware when CPU reads SPIxBUF location, reading SPIxRXB.

FIGURE 10.26 SPIxSTAT: Status and control register. (Adapted with permission of the copyright owner, Microchip Technology Inc. All rights reserved. No further reprints or reproduction may be made without Microchip Inc.'s prior written consent.)

Figure 10.27 shows waveforms for different combinations of CKE/CKP/SMP options. The SPIx transmit buffer (SPIxTXB) in conjunction with the SPI shift register (SPIxSR) form a two-element FIFO. A new value can be written to an empty SPIxTXB while a transmission is in progress using SPIxSR. The SPIxIF interrupt flag is set whenever data is transferred from SPIxSR to SPIxRXB, indicating that a transmission has completed. Note that the SPITBF flag being "0" does not indicate a completed transmission; it only indicates an empty SPIxTXB register.

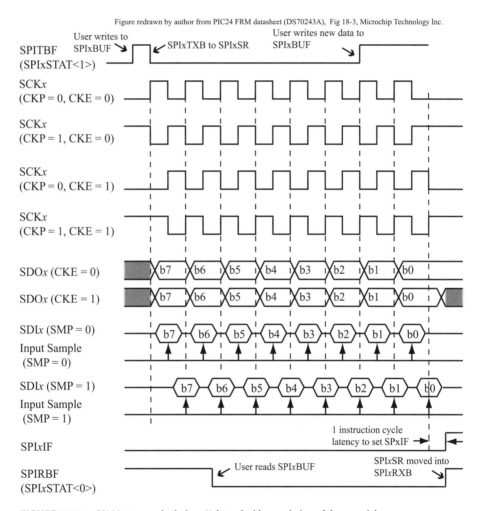

FIGURE 10.27   SPI Master mode timing. (Adapted with permission of the copyright owner, Microchip Technology Inc. All rights reserved. No further reprints or reproduction may be made without Microchip Inc.'s prior written consent.)

Listing 10.2 shows two *C* functions for supporting SPI operation. The `checkRxErrorSPI1()` function checks for receive buffer overflow and calls `reportError()` with an appropriate message if the condition is detected. The `ioMasterSPI1(uint16 u16_c)` function first checks for receive buffer overflow. It then clears the SPI1IF flag, writes the `u16_c` parameter to the SPI*x* transmit buffer, and waits for the transmission to complete so that it can return the SPI*x* receive buffer contents. Either 8 or 16 bits are transmitted, depending on the configured mode of the SPI1 module.

LISTING 10.2 `ioMasterSPI1 ()` *C* function.

```
void checkRxErrorSPI1() {
 if (SPI1STATbits.SPIROV) {
  //clear the error
  SPI1STATbits.SPIROV = 0;
  reportError("SPI1 Receive Overflow\n");
 }
}


uint16 ioMasterSPI1(uint16 u16_c) {
 checkRxErrorSPI1();
 _SPI1IF = 0;        //clear interrupt flag since we are about to write new value
 SPI1BUF = u16_c;
 while (!_SPI1IF) { //wait for operation to complete
  doHeartbeat();
 }
 return SPI1BUF;    //return the shifted in value
}
```

SPI EXAMPLE: THE MCP41xxx DIGITAL POTENTIOMETER

Figure 10.28 shows an application of a Microchip MCP41xxx digital potentiometer [36] as a contrast control for the LCD module discussed in Chapter 8. A *potentiometer* is a device that provides a variable resistance. An analog potentiometer typically has three terminals; between two of the terminals the potentiometer's full resistance is available (reference terminals PA0, PB0 in Figure 10.28). The third terminal is called the *wiper* (terminal PW0 in Figure 10.28); this terminal provides a variable resistance when measured between the wiper and either one of the reference terminals. When the two reference terminals are connected to VDD and ground, changing the wiper setting varies the voltage on the wiper terminal between VDD and ground. An analog potentiometer's wiper setting is changed via some mechanical interface such as turning a shaft. A digital potentiometer's wiper

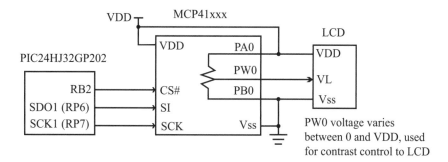

FIGURE 10.28   PIC24 µC to MCP41xxx digital potentiometer interface.

setting is changed using a parallel or serial interface, with serial interfaces being the most common. On the PIC24HJ32GP202, remappable pins must be used for the SPI interface. Pins RP6 and RP7 are used for SDO1 and SCK1, respectively, and RB2 is used as the potentiometer chip select. All of these pin selections are arbitrary.

The MCP41xxx digital potentiometer comes in 10 kΩ (MCP41010), 50 kΩ (MCP41050), and 100 kΩ (MCP41100) configurations and uses a SPI port for setting the 8-bit wiper register for the potentiometer. The supported VDD range is 2.7 V to 5.5 V. In the configuration shown in Figure 10.28, a wiper value of 255 sets the PW0 output voltage to approximately $255/256 \times$ VDD, while a value of 0 sets the PW0 output voltage to ground. The wiper register is set to 128 (midway) on power-up. Higher potentiometer values reduce the static current that is drawn by the potentiometer when it is active. For example, a 50 k potentiometer with VDD = 3.3 V draws 3.3 V/50 kΩ = 66.7 µA static current through the potentiometer resistance, while a 100 kΩ potentiometer reduces this current by 50 percent to 33.3 µA.

Figure 10.29 shows the command protocol for the MCP41xxx. Each transaction consists of 2 bytes, a command byte and a data byte. The CS# (chip select) input must be brought low to enable the device before any data is sent and brought high after transmission is finished in order to execute the command. The wiper register is set by the command byte 0x11 followed by the wiper register value. The shutdown command opens (disconnects) the potentiometer by opening the PA0 terminal and shorting the PW0 and PB terminals. This reduces total static current draw of the MCP41xxx to less than 1 µA. The data byte for the shutdown command is ignored but it still must be sent for the command to be recognized. If MCP41xxx shutdown mode were to be used with the LCD application of Figure 10.29, then you would want to reverse the PA0 and PB0 connections so that VL of the LCD is shorted to VDD during shutdown, blanking the display. This would mean that a wiper code of 255 sets the PW0 voltage to near ground, while a code of 0 sets the PW0 voltage to VDD.

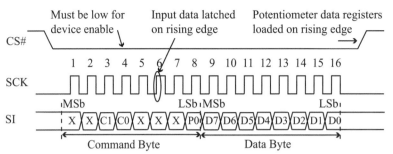

X : don't care bits
C1, C0: command bits, "01" set wiper register to data byte, "10" shutdown
P0: must be "1" to select potentiometer for command
Sample commands: 0x11 - write wiper register, 0x21 - shutdown potentiometer

FIGURE 10.29 MCP41xxx command protocol.

Figure 10.30 gives code for testing the PIC24 µC to MCP41xxx interface. The while(1){} loop of main() prompts the user for an 8-bit value and sends this as the wiper register value to the MCP41xxx via the setPotWiper(uint8 u8_i) function. The ioMasterSPI1() function of Listing 10.2 is used to send the 0x11 command byte, followed by the wiper register value. Observe the potentiometer chip select is asserted by the SLAVE_ENABLE() macro and negated by SLAVE_DISABLE() and that the chip select is enabled for both byte transmissions. Within the while(1){} loop of main(), the *<stdio.h>* library function sscanf is used to parse a decimal number from the input string, and the *<stdio.h>* library function printf is used for printing this value back out in decimal format. See Appendix D for more information on using these functions; our examples use these functions for convenience purposes when formatted character I/O is required. The configSP1() function configures the SPI1 module for CKP=0, CKE=1, 8-bit mode, master mode, and a clock prescaler value of 4×1. This means that the SPI clock frequency is then Fcy /(4×1). Since our internal Fcy is 40 MHz, this gives an SCK frequency of 40 MHz/4 = 10 MHz, which is the maximum allowed for the PIC24HJ32GP202. This also happens to be the maximum allowed SCK frequency for the MCP41xxx according to its datasheet. This maximum clock frequency is used for example purposes as SPI bus speed is typically not an important factor for a digital potentiometer, thus one may want to use a SCLK speed that is less than the maximum for timing margin purposes. The configSP1() function also configures the pins required for the SPI1 interface, enables the SPI1 module, and leaves the MCP41xxx chip select negated. The macros used for configuring the SPI1CON1 register are defined in *include\pic24_spi.h*. Bits that are not included in the SPI1CON1 configuration statement use the default values from Figure 10.25 after reset.

```
#define CONFIG_SLAVE_ENABLE() CONFIG_RB2_AS_DIG_OUTPUT()
#define SLAVE_ENABLE()        _LATB2 = 0  //low true assertion
#define SLAVE_DISABLE()       _LATB2 = 1
```
◄─── RB2 used for potentiometer chip select.
```
void configSPI1(void) {
  //spi clock = 40MHz/1*4 = 40MHz/4 = 10MHz
```
◄─── 10 MHz SPI clock
```
  SPI1CON1 = SEC_PRESCAL_1_1 |   //1:1 secondary prescale
             PRI_PRESCAL_4_1 |   //4:1 primary prescale
             CLK_POL_ACTIVE_HIGH | //clock active high (CKP = 0)
             SPI_CKE_ON          | //out changes active to inactive (CKE=1)
             SPI_MODE8_ON        | //8-bit mode
             MASTER_ENABLE_ON;     //master mode
  //configure pins. Only need SDO, SCLK since POT is output only
  CONFIG_SDO1_TO_RP(6);          //use RP6 for SDO
  CONFIG_SCK1OUT_TO_RP(7);       //use RP7 for SCLK
  CONFIG_SLAVE_ENABLE();         //chip select for MCP41xxx
  SLAVE_DISABLE();               //disable the chip select
  SPI1STATbits.SPIEN = 1;  //enable SPI mode
}
```
RP6 used for SDO1, RP7 for SCK1
```
void setPotWiper(uint8 u8_i) {
```
◄─── Writes to the potentiometer wiper register.
```
  SLAVE_ENABLE();              //assert MCP41xxx chipselect
  ioMasterSPI1(0x11);          //command byte to select wiper register
  ioMasterSPI1(u8_i);
  SLAVE_DISABLE();             //negate MCP41xxx chipselect
}

#define BUFSIZE 15
char  sz_1[BUFSIZE+1];

int main (void) {
  uint16 u16_pv;
  configBasic(HELLO_MSG);
  configSPI1();
  while (1) {
    outString("Input decimal value (0-255): ");
    inString(sz_1,BUFSIZE);
    sscanf(sz_1,"%d",  (int *) &u16_pv);
    printf("\nSending %d to pot.\n",u16_pv);
    setPotWiper(u16_pv & 0x00FF);
  }
}
```
Uses <stdio.h> library functions to parse string input and print formatted output.

FIGURE 10.30   Test code for PIC24 μC to MCP41xxx interface.

SPI Example: PIC24 μC Master to DS1722 Thermometer

Figure 10.31 shows a PIC24 μC connected to a Maxim DS1722 Digital Thermometer [37] using a SPI port. The DS1722 has a high-true chip enable (CE) and can be configured for either SPI operation (SERMODE = high) or for a generic three-wire serial interface (SERMODE = low). The V$_{DDD}$ and V$_{DDA}$ pins are digital supply and analog supply, respectively, and are tied to 3.3 V in this application. The DS1722 senses ambient temperature, which can be read as a digital value via the SPI port.

Operational details for the DS1722 are given in Figure 10.32. The DS1722's 8-bit configuration register (Figure 10.32a) determines the conversion mode and

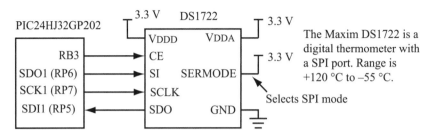

FIGURE 10.31   PIC24 µC SPI master to DS1722 connection.

(a) Configuration byte

MSb	1	1	1	1SHOT	R2	R1	R0	SD	LSb

SD: 0- continuous conversion, 1- complete current conversion, enter low power mode.

R2/R1/R0: 000 8-bit mode, 0.075s conversion time, 1.0° C resolution (8.0 signed fixed-point)
            001 9-bit mode, 0.15s conversion time, 0.5° C resolution (8.1 signed fixed point)
            010 10-bit mode, 0.3s conversion time, 0.25° C resolution (8.2 signed fixed point)
            011 11-bit mode, 0.6s conversion time, 0.125° C resolution (8.3 signed fixed point)
            1xx 12-bit mode, 1.2s conversion time, 0.0625° C resolution (8.4 signed fixed point)
1SHOT: when SD=1 writing a 1 to this bit starts conversion, is cleared when conversion finished.

- -

(b) Single-byte transfer, write configuration

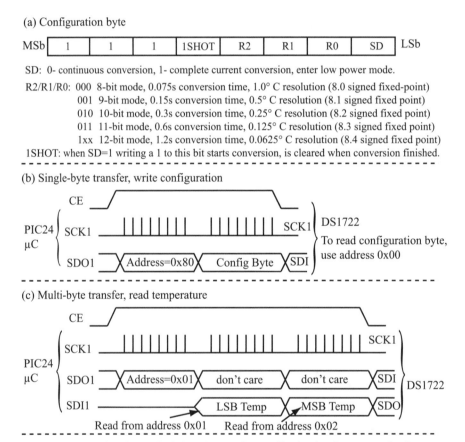

(c) Multi-byte transfer, read temperature

(d) Temperature data format is 8.4 two's complement fixed point (integer portion is MSByte, fractional is LSByte).

Celsius (float) = 16-bit temperature (int16) / 256

FIGURE 10.32   DS1722 operation.

precision. The two conversion modes are either continuous conversion (SD = 0) or one-shot mode (SD = 1). In one-shot mode, the DS1722 starts a conversion when a "1" is written to the 1SHOT bit. When the conversion is finished, the 1SHOT bit is cleared and a power-down state is entered. The temperature converted value in Celsius is available in two 8-bit registers that form an 8.4 two's complement fixed point value (see Chapter 7), with the MSByte containing the integer portion and the upper four bits of the LSByte containing the fractional portion. Bits R2/R1/R0 of the configuration register control the conversion precision as shown, with longer conversion times required for higher precision. The 16-bit temperature value can be converted to a floating-point Celsius value by dividing it by 256 because the 12-bit value is returned in the upper 12 bits of the 16-bit word. Internal registers

```
#define CONFIG_SLAVE_ENABLE() CONFIG_RB3_AS_DIG_OUTPUT()
#define SLAVE_ENABLE()      _LATB3 = 1  //high true assertion
#define SLAVE_DISABLE()     _LATB3 = 0  ◄── RB3 used for the DS1722 chip
                                              select.
void configSPI1(void) {
  //spi clock = 40MHz/1*4 = 40MHz/4 = 10MHz  ◄── 10 MHz SPI clock
  SPI1CON1 = SEC_PRESCAL_1_1 |       //1:1 secondary prescale
             PRI_PRESCAL_4_1 |       //4:1 primary prescale
             CLK_POL_ACTIVE_HIGH  | //clock active high (CKP = 0)
             SPI_CKE_OFF          | //out changes inactive to active (CKE=0)
             SPI_MODE8_ON         | //8-bit mode      ◄ Clock can either be
             MASTER_ENABLE_ON;      //master mode       high or low true, but
  //configure pins. Need SDO, SCK, SDI                  must use CKE=0.
  CONFIG_SDO1_TO_RP(6);        //use RP6 for SDO
  CONFIG_SCK1OUT_TO_RP(7);     //use RP7 for SCLK   }RP6 used for SDO1, RP7
  CONFIG_SDI1_TO_RP(5);        //use RP5 for SDI    }for SCK1, and RP5 for SDI.
  CONFIG_SLAVE_ENABLE();       //chip select for DS1722
  SLAVE_DISABLE();             //disable the chip select
  SPI1STATbits.SPIEN = 1;  //enable SPI mode
}

void writeConfigDS1722(uint8 u8_i) {
  SLAVE_ENABLE();        //assert chipselect  }
  ioMasterSPI1(0x80);    //config address     } Writes to the DS1722
  ioMasterSPI1(u8_i);    //config value       } configuration register.
  SLAVE_DISABLE();                            }
}

int16 readTempDS1722() {
  uint16 u16_lo, u16_hi;
  SLAVE_ENABLE();        //assert chipselect     }
  ioMasterSPI1(0x01);    //LSB address           } Reads 16-bit temperature
  u16_lo = ioMasterSPI1(0x00); //read LSByte     } value from DS1722.
  u16_hi = ioMasterSPI1(0x00); //read MSByte     }
  SLAVE_DISABLE();                               }
  return((u16_hi<<8) | u16_lo);
}
```

FIGURE 10.33   C code for reading/writing DS1722 registers.

on the DS1722 are accessed by first writing an address byte followed by reading or writing data bytes at that address. The address byte written determines if the next byte is a read or write. For example, to write the configuration register, write two bytes with the first being 0x80 (the address byte) followed by a byte that sets the configuration register. To read the configuration register, again write two bytes with the first being 0x00 (the address byte) followed by a dummy byte (any value works). The byte returned by the DS1722 for the dummy byte written is the current configuration value. Figure 10.32b shows the SPI transfer required for writing to the configuration register. The two temperature registers can be read in one SPI operation by writing an address of 0x01 followed by a write of two dummy bytes; the data returned by the dummy byte writes are the LSB, MSB of the temperature as shown in Figure 10.32c. Reading the temperature registers does not disturb the current conversion. Note that the temperature registers are read-only.

Code for configuring the SPI port, writing a configuration byte, and reading the 16-bit temperature is shown in Figure 10.33. The DS1722 can use either clock polarity, but requires data changes on the inactive-to-active clock edge (CKE = 0). The `writeConfigDS1722 (uint8 u8_i)` function writes u8_i to the DS1722

```
int main (void) {        (a) main() function.
  int16 i16_temp;
  float  f_tempC,f_tempF;         Configure DS1722 for continuous conversion,
  configBasic(HELLO_MSG);         12-bit mode.
  configSPI1();
  writeConfigDS1722(0xE8); //12-bit mode          Use floating point and printf
  while (1) {                                     for convenience to print
    DELAY_MS(1500);                               temperature value in Celsius
    i16_temp = readTempDS1722();                  and Fahrenheit.
    f_tempC = i16_temp;  //convert to floating point
    f_tempC = f_tempC/256;  //divide by precision
    f_tempF = f_tempC*9/5 + 32;
    printf("Temp is: 0x%0X, %4.4f (C), %4.4f (F)\n", i16_temp,
           (double) f_tempC, (double) f_tempF);
  }
}
```

- -

(b) Sample Output
```
ds1722_spi_tempsense.c, built on Jun 27 2008 at 21:56:03
Temp is: 0x1BC0, 27.7500 (C), 81.9500 (F)
Temp is: 0x1BD0, 27.8125 (C), 82.0625 (F)
Temp is: 0x1BD0, 27.8125 (C), 82.0625 (F)
Temp is: 0x1C30, 28.1875 (C), 82.7375 (F)        Finger placed on sensor
Temp is: 0x1D70, 29.4375 (C), 84.9875 (F)        to raise temperature.
Temp is: 0x1DC0, 29.7500 (C), 85.5500 (F)
Temp is: 0x1E10, 30.0625 (C), 86.1125 (F)
Temp is: 0x1E30, 30.1875 (C), 86.3375 (F)
Temp is: 0x1D90, 29.5625 (C), 85.2125 (F)        Finger removed from sensor.
Temp is: 0x1D30, 29.1875 (C), 84.5375 (F)
Temp is: 0x1CF0, 28.9375 (C), 84.0875 (F)
```

FIGURE 10.34 *C code for testing the DS1722.*

configuration register. The `readTempDS1722()` function reads the two 8-bit temperature registers and returns them as a signed 16-bit value (`int16`).

The `main()` code for testing the DS1722 is shown in Figure 10.34a. The `writeConfigDS122(0xE8)` function call configures the DS1722 for continuous conversion and 12-bit precision. The `while(1){}` loop delays for 1.5 seconds then reads the 16-bit temperature and converts it to both Celsius (`f_tempC`) and Farenheit (`f_tempF`) floating-point values. The `printf` statement is used for formatted output of these values to the console. Figure 10.34b shows typical output during operation; the temperature values increased when a finger was placed on the DS1722, and then decreased once it was removed.

SPI Example: PIC24 μC Master to PIC24 μC Slave

A PIC24 μC can also act as SPI slave peripheral, which can be useful in a multi-CPU application or if a PIC24-based product requires an external SPI port. Figure 10.35a shows a PIC24 μC SPI master to PIC24 μC SPI slave connection that is used to illustrate this operation mode. The application is the string reversal application previously used to illustrate interrupt-driven UART TX/RX operation. Figure 10.35b illustrates the master/slave I/O actions in this application. An input string arrives at the master via the UART, which is then sent to the slave via the SPI port. The slave reverses the string then notifies the master that data is ready by asserting an *output ready* signal, which is implemented using RB2 in Figure 10.35. This use of a PIO pin to coordinate data transfer between two devices is known

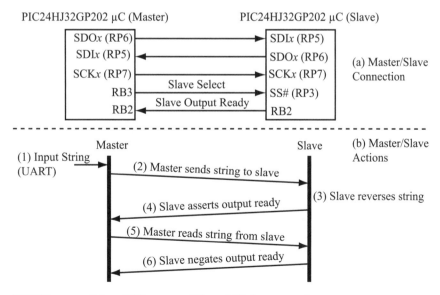

FIGURE 10.35   PIC24 μC SPI master to PIC24 μC SPI slave connection.

as *handshaking*. The master then reads the reversed string from the slave using the SPI and the slave negates its output ready signal. The process repeats when another string arrives at the master. PIO RB3 is used on the master to assert the slave select (SS#) input on the slave, with RP3 chosen as the remappable pin used for SS#.

Figure 10.36 shows the SPI configuration code for both the master and slave applications. The master's configSPI1() function is the same as used in Figure 10.30 with the addition of CONFIG_SLAVE_ORDY(), which configures RB2 as a digital input to handle the slave's output ready handshaking signal. The slave's configSPI1() function is quite different as the SPICON1 register is configured for slave mode with the SS# input enabled. Because the master supplies SCK1, there is no need for the slave to configure the SCK1 prescalers. Also, SCK1 is an input on the slave, and thus the SCK1IN function must be used for the pin remapping instead of SCK1OUT. Finally, the slave application uses interrupt-driven I/O for SPI transfers, so the SPI1 interrupt is enabled. The PIC24H family reference manual for the SPI module notes that when CKE = 1, the SS# pin must be enabled in slave mode.

```
(a) Master SPI configuration
void configSPI1(void) {
  //spi clock = 40MHz/1*4
  // = 40MHz/4 = 10MHz
  SPI1CON1 = SEC_PRESCAL_1_1 |
    PRI_PRESCAL_4_1 |
    CLK_POL_ACTIVE_HIGH |
    SPI_CKE_ON |
    SPI_MODE8_ON |
    MASTER_ENABLE_ON;
  CONFIG_SDO1_TO_RP(6);
  CONFIG_SCK1OUT_TO_RP(7);
  CONFIG_SDI1_TO_RP(5);
  CONFIG_SLAVE_ENABLE(); //RB3
  CONFIG_SLAVE_ORDY(); //RB2
  SLAVE_DISABLE();
  SPI1STATbits.SPIEN = 1;
}
```

Clock is an output on Master
Clock is an input on Slave.

```
(b) Slave SPI configuration
void configSPI1(void) {
  //no need for prescaler since master
  //supplies the clock
  SPI1CON1 =  CLK_POL_ACTIVE_HIGH |
              SPI_CKE_ON |
  Use SS# →SLAVE_ENABLE_ON |
              SPI_MODE8_ON |
  Slave mode →MASTER_ENABLE_OFF;
  //configure pins
  CONFIG_SDO1_TO_RP(6);   //SDO1
  CONFIG_SCK1IN_TO_RP(7); //SCK1
  CONFIG_SDI1_TO_RP(5);   //SDI1
  CONFIG_SS1IN_TO_RP(3);  //SS#1
  CONFIG_SLAVE_ORDY();    //ORDY, RB2
  SLAVE_ORDY = 0;         //Negate ORDY
  u16_index = 0;       //data input count
  _SPI1IF = 0;         //clear int. flag
  _SPI1IP = 3;         //choose a priority
  _SPI1IE = 1;         //enable interrupt
  SPI1STATbits.SPIEN = 1;  //enable SPI
}
```

FIGURE 10.36 SPI master, slave configuration.

Figure 10.37 shows the master code for the string reversal application. The main() function uses a two-state FSM. In state STATE_GET_IN_STRING, a string is read from the console, then sent to the slave using the sendStringSPI1() function. The ioMasterSPI() function discussed previously is used to send each byte to the slave. The STATE_GET_REV_STRING state waits for the slave to assert the output ready

```
typedef enum { STATE_GET_IN_STRING=0,  STATE_GET_REV_STRING } STATE;
void sendStringSPI1(char* psz_s1) {
  SLAVE_ENABLE();
  while (*psz_s1) {
    ioMasterSPI1(*psz_s1);          Send string to the slave using the SPI.
    psz_s1++;
  }
  ioMasterSPI1(*psz_s1);  //send null terminator
  SLAVE_DISABLE();
}
void getStringSPI1(char* psz_s1, uint16 u16_maxCount) {
  uint16 u16_i = 0;
  if (!u16_maxCount) return;
  SLAVE_ENABLE();
  do {
    //send dummy byte to read byte from slave      Read reversed string from
    *psz_s1 = ioMasterSPI1(0);                     slave using the SPI.
    psz_s1++; u16_i++;                             Observe that the master
  } while (*(psz_s1-1) && (u16_i <u16_maxCount));  must write a byte in order
  SLAVE_DISABLE();                                 to get a byte back!
  psz_s1--;
  *psz_s1 = 0; //ensure string is null terminated
}
#define BUFSIZE 63
char  sz_1[BUFSIZE+1];
int main (void) {
  STATE e_mystate = STATE_GET_IN_STRING;
  configBasic(HELLO_MSG);
  configSPI1();
  while (1) {
    switch (e_mystate) {
      case STATE_GET_IN_STRING:
        inStringEcho(sz_1,BUFSIZE);   //get a string from the console
        if (*sz_1) {
          sendStringSPI1(sz_1);           //send string to slave
          e_mystate = STATE_GET_REV_STRING;
        }
        break;
      case STATE_GET_REV_STRING:
        if (SLAVE_ORDY) {    //if ORDY asserted, get reversed string
          getStringSPI1(sz_1,BUFSIZE+1);
          outString(sz_1); outString("\n");  //echo reversed string
          e_mystate = STATE_GET_IN_STRING;
        }
        break;
      default:
        e_mystate = STATE_GET_IN_STRING;
    }
    doHeartbeat();
  } //end switch
}
```

FIGURE 10.37 Master C code for string reversal application.

signal, then uses the `getStringSPI1()` to read the reversed string from the slave. Observe that the master must transmit a byte to the slave in order to get a byte back from the slave. When the master receives a null byte from the slave, then it knows that the end of the string has been reached.

Figure 10.38 shows the slave code for the string reversal application. All of the work is done within the _SPI1Interrupt ISR, which is triggered each time a byte

```
typedef enum  {STATE_WAIT_FOR_STRING=0, STATE_SEND_REV_STRING,
   STATE_LAST_REVCHAR_STRING } STATE;
volatile STATE e_mystate = STATE_WAIT_FOR_STRING;
#define BUFSIZE 63
volatile char   sz_1[BUFSIZE+1],sz_2[BUFSIZE+1];
volatile uint16 u16_index;
                                    ── ISR triggered each time new byte arrives
void _ISR _SPI1Interrupt (void) { at slave.
  uint16 u16_tmp;
   switch (e_mystate) {                   Stores arriving string into sz_1. After a
    case STATE_WAIT_FOR_STRING:◄──── complete string has arrived, reverse it.
      sz_1[u16_index] = SPI1BUF; //character arrived, place in buffer
      u16_index++;
      if (sz_1[u16_index-1] == 0) {
        reverseString(sz_1,sz_2); //reverse the string
        u16_index = 0;
        SPI1BUF = sz_2[u16_index]; //place first char in SPIBUF
        u16_index++;
        SLAVE_ORDY = 1;   //assert ORDY to MASTER, reversed string is rdy
        e_mystate = STATE_SEND_REV_STRING;
      }
      break;                        Master is reading string from slave by
    case STATE_SEND_REV_STRING:◄──── writing dummy data to the slave.
      u16_tmp = SPI1BUF; //read the SPIBUF to prevent overflow, discard.
      SPI1BUF = sz_2[u16_index]; //keep putting chars into SPIBUF
      u16_index++;
      if (sz_2[u16_index-1] == 0) e_mystate = STATE_LAST_REVCHAR_STRING;
      break;
    case STATE_LAST_REVCHAR_STRING:◄──── Last character sent, negate ORDY.
      SLAVE_ORDY = 0; //last char, no more data
      u16_index = 0;  //null terminator for string just read by master
      u16_tmp = SPI1BUF; //read SPIBUF to prevent overflow, discard it.
      e_mystate = STATE_WAIT_FOR_STRING; //wait for next string
      break;
    default:
      e_mystate = STATE_WAIT_FOR_STRING;
   }
   _SPI1IF = 0;  //clear interrupt flag
}

int main (void) {
  configClock();         //no UART for slave
  configHeartbeat();
  configSPI1();
  while (1) doHeartbeat();  //_SPI1Interrupt does all of the work
}
```

FIGURE 10.38   Slave C code for string reversal application.

arrives at the slave and uses a three-state FSM. The STATE_WAIT_FOR_STRING is used for receiving the string to be reversed from the master; the input string is written to the sz_1 buffer. When a complete string is received, the previously discussed reverseString() function does the string reversal. Then, the first character of the reversed string is placed into SPIBUF before asserting the output ready and transitioning to state STATE_SEND_REV_STRING. In slave mode, writing to the SPIBUF does not transmit the character; the data is held in the SPI shift register until the master provides the SPICLK pulses for the next transmission. The STATE_SEND_REV_STRING state writes a character of the reversed string to the SPIBUF so that it can be read by the master and transitions to the STATE_LAST_REVCHAR_STRING state when the null terminator is written. When STATE_LAST_REVCHAR_STRING is triggered, this means the master has read the null terminator of the reversed string, so output ready is negated and the slave transitions back to the STATE_WAIT_FOR_STRING to wait for the next input string.

Figure 10.39 shows a logic analyzer screenshot of the SPI bus activity for the reverse string application using the two character string "MS". The SDI1, SDO1 labels are from the master's perspective; Figure 10.39a shows the "MS" string being transmitted to the slave, while Figure 10.39b shows the master reading the reversed string from the slave.

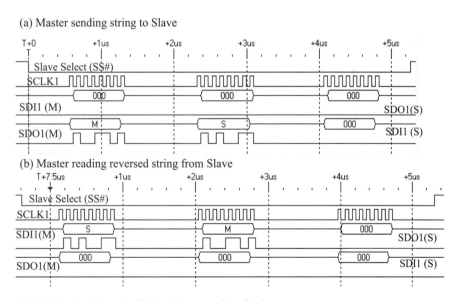

FIGURE 10.39   Slave *C* code for string reversal application.

The advantage of the SPI bus is in its simplicity and its high data rate transfer. Many peripheral ICs that provide connectivity to block-oriented interfaces such as Ethernet, memory cards, and USB have an SPI port as their µC interface. However, the fact that SDI is linked to SDO with the master having to initiate all data exchanges limits flexibility. For CPU-to-CPU communication, an asynchronous serial interface is typically the better choice if high data rates are not required since the TX/RX channels are independent.

THE I²C BUS

The Inter IC (I²C) bus [38] was introduced by Philips Semiconductor in the early 1980s and it has since become a *de facto* standard serial bus. The term *bus* in this context is a formal designation and is different from the previous casual usage of

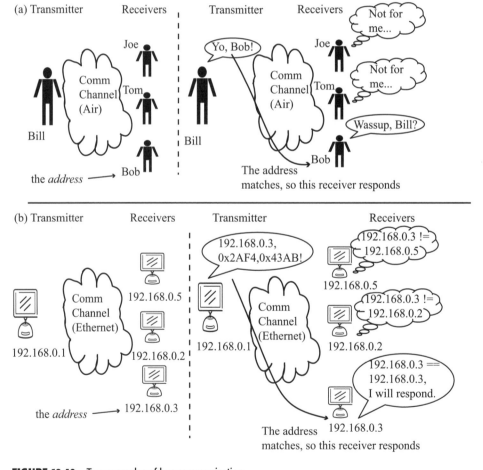

FIGURE 10.40   Two examples of bus communication.

"bus" to describe groups of parallel wires. In this context, a bus is a communication channel in which there are one or more transmitters and multiple receivers. All receivers see data that is transmitted over the communication channel. Each receiver decodes transmitted messages and uses an *address* within the message to determine if it is the target of the message. The receiver that is the message target then replies back to the message transmitter over the same communication channel. Figure 10.40 gives two examples of bus communication channels. Figure 10.40(a) shows how normal conversation among a group of friends is essentially bus-based communication as the transmitter uses the name of the person as the address when sending a message across the communication channel, which is air. The person who is addressed by name then responds to the transmitter. Figure 10.40(b) illustrates how Internet addresses are used on an Ethernet network for computer communication. An Ethernet network is a bus, as all computers monitor traffic on the network and only respond to those data packets whose header addresses match their assigned Internet address (note: technically, *MAC addresses* are used by the hardware interface on the receiving computer for packet reception, but Internet addresses are shown in Figure 10.40 for simplicity since those are more familiar).

Figure 10.41 shows an I²C bus, which consists of a data line (SCL) and a clock line (SDA) used to implement half-duplex communication. Observe that the devices connected to the I²C bus do not have chip select signals like SPI-based peripherals. Instead, each device has a 7-bit address whose upper 4 bits ($n_3n_2n_1n_0$) shown in the figure are device specific and encoded within the device. The next 3 bits (A2, A1, and A0) of the 7-bit address are typically determined by external pins that are connected to either VDD or ground to provide logic "1" or logic "0",

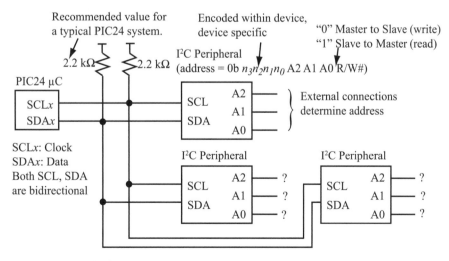

FIGURE 10.41   The I²C bus.

respectively. The address is always sent as the first byte of an I²C bus transaction, which is initiated by the bus master. The least significant bit of the address byte indicates the direction of the transfer. A "0" signifies a write operation (transfer from master to slave), while a "1" specifies a read (transfer from slave to master). Each I²C peripheral device decodes the address byte to determine if it is the target of the transmission, removing the need for individual chip select lines. Adding another I²C device to the bus does not require using an additional port on the PIC24 μC, a distinct advantage over SPI-based peripherals. Like the SPI protocol, the PIC24 μC can act as either a slave or master on the I²C bus; the examples in this chapter always use the PIC24 μC as the sole I²C bus master (see Chapter 13 for an example of PIC24 I²C slave operation). The pull-up resistors on the SCL/SDA lines are needed because these drivers are open-drain in order to provide *multi-master* capability. In a multi-master bus, any device can act as a bus master. This requires an *arbitration* mechanism that decides which device controls the bus in the case of simultaneous attempts to access the bus (see Chapter 13 for a discussion of I²C bus arbitration). The most recent version of the I²C specification has support for a 10-bit address that is transmitted in the first two bytes of a transaction. The I²C peripherals used within this book's examples use 7-bit addresses.

Figure 10.42 shows the details of an I²C bus transfer. The idle condition occurs when both the SDA and SCL lines are high prior to the beginning of a bus transfer.

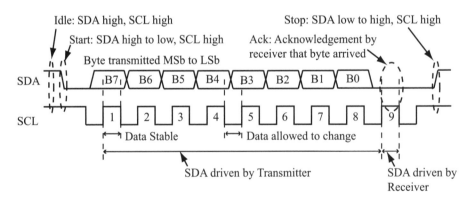

FIGURE 10.42 I²C data transfer.

The master always provides the SCL signal and initiates an I²C transaction. The *start* condition, a high-to-low transition on SDA while SCL is high, signals the beginning of an I²C data transfer. The first byte after a start condition is always the address byte used to select a particular I²C peripheral. Multiple bytes can then be sent within an I²C transaction with each byte sent MSb first. SDA data is stable while SCL is high and changes while SCL is low. Each byte transmission ends with a 9th bit time in which the transmitter stops driving the SDA line so that the receiver can *acknowledge* the byte transmission by pulling the SDA line low. If the receiver does not drive SDA low, the SDA pull-up resistor keeps SDA high and the transmitter reads a "1" for the acknowledge bit instead of a "0". A "1" acknowledgment bit is called a *not-acknowledge,* or a *NAK,* while a "0" acknowledgment bit is called an ACK. Typically, the transmitter will interpret this as an error condition and abort the transfer. There are multiple reasons why a receiver may not acknowledge a byte transmission; if this is the address byte, a coding mistake could result in the wrong address being used, or perhaps the receiver cannot accept new data or has experienced an internal failure. In any case, the acknowledge bit provides feedback to the transmitter on whether a byte has been received. The acknowledgment bit is non-optional for normal transfers because each byte transmission includes the overhead of an acknowledgment bit. The master provides the acknowledgment bit in the case where a slave sends a byte to the master during a read operation. After an acknowledgment bit, a slave can hold the SCL line low, which forces the master into a wait condition until the slave releases the SCL line. In this way, the slave can provide flow control on a byte-by-byte basis; this is the only time that the slave may drive the SCL line. The *stop* condition, defined as a low-to-high SDA transition while SCL is high, ends an I²C transaction and frees the bus, allowing it to be driven by another bus master. After the stop condition, both SCL and SDA are undriven and thus pulled high by the pull-up resistors. A *repeated start* condition is when another start is sent within a transaction; this ends the current transaction and begins a new transaction, thus allowing the current bus master to start a new transaction without relinquishing control of the bus. For a single I²C bus master like most of the examples in this book, a repeated start can be replaced by a stop followed by a start if this is more convenient from a coding viewpoint. More details on special transactions such as CBUS transfers in which acknowledgment bits are not provided are found in the I²C specification [38].

I²C ON THE PIC24 µC

The PIC24 I²C module registers and commonly used control and status bits are summarized in Figure 10.43 (complete information on the status and control register bits are found in the I²C section [24] of the family reference manual). There is only one I²C module on the PIC24HJ32GP202, but other family members have multiple I²C modules. The SCL*x*/SDA*x* pins on a PIC24 µC are assigned to fixed pin locations, not to remappable pins like the SPI and UART pin functions because of the specialized signaling requirements of the I²C interface. Each PIC24 µC has an alternate set of I²C pins named ASCL*x*/ASDA*x* that can be selected via a configuration bit; the choice is invisible to user application code.

(a) I²C Module Registers

I²C Registers	Description
I2CxCON	Control Register
I2CxSTAT	Status Register
I2CxBRG	Baud Rate Register
I2CxTRN	Transmit Register
I2CxRCV	Receive Register
I2CxMSK	Slave Mode Address Mask Register
I2CxADD	Slave Mode Address Register

- -

(b) Commonly used I²C Control and Status Bits

Bit Name	Register	Function
SEN	I2CxCON<0>	Set to begin Start sequence, cleared by HW
RSEN	I2CxCON<1>	Set to begin Repeated Start sequence, cleared by HW
PEN	I2CxCON<2>	Set to begin Stop condition, cleared by HW
RCEN	I2CxCON<3>	Set to enable receive, cleared in HW
ACKEN	I2CxCON<4>	Set to enable acknowledge sequence, cleared by HW
ACKDT	I2CxCON<5>	ACK bit to send; 1 for NAK, 0 for ACK.
I2CEN	I2CxCON<15>	Enable the I2Cx module
RBF	I2CxSTAT<1>	Set when I2CxRCV register is full, cleared by HW after read of I2CxRCV
SI2CxIF	Interrupt Flag Status Registers	Interrupt flag set on detection of address reception in Slave mode, reception of data, or request to transmit data

FIGURE 10.43 PIC24 I²C registers.

The I²C clock speed (F_{SCL}) is controlled by the 16-bit baud rate register (I2CxBRG) whose value is calculated by equation 10.4:

$$I2CxBRG = (F_{CY}/ F_{SCL} - F_{CY}/10,000,000) - 1 \qquad (10.4)$$

While most I²C peripherals are specified for operation at clock rates of 100 kHz, 400 kHZ or 1 MHz, in practice they operate at any frequency less than their maximum rated frequency. The PIC24HJ32GP202 data sheet provides timing specifications for these clock rates.

Figure 10.44a summarizes the I²C library functions supplied with this book for supporting I²C basic operations such as module configuration, performing a start/rstart/stop operation, sending one byte, and receiving one byte. These basic functions are used by the functions listed in Figure 10.44b that accomplish complete I²C *transactions* that read or write one or more bytes to an I²C slave peripheral.

(a) Support Functions for I²C Operations

I²C Support Functions (Operations)	Description
void configI2C1(uint16 u16_FkHZ)	Enables the I²C module for operation at **u16_FkHZ** kHz clock rate
void startI2C1(void)	Performs start operation
void rstartI2C1(void)	Performs repeated start operation
void stopI2C1(void)	Performs stop operation
void putI2C1(uint8 u8_val)	Transmits **u8_val**; software reset if NAK returned.
uint8 putNoAckCheckI2C1(uint8 u8_val)	Transmits **u8_val** and returns received acknowledge bit
uint8 getI2C1(uint8 u8_ack2Send)	Receive one byte and send **u8_ack2Send** as acknowledge bit

- -

(b) Support Functions for I²C Transactions

I²C Support Functions (Transactions)	Description
void write1I2C1(uint8 u8_addr,uint8 u8_d1)	Write 1 byte (**u8_d1**)
void write2I2C1(uint8 u8_addr,uint8 u8_d1, uint8 u8_d2)	Write 2 bytes (**u8_d1**)
void writeNI2C1(uint8 u8_addr,uint8* pu8_data, uint16 u16_cnt)	Write **u16_cnt** bytes in buffer **pu8_data**
void read1I2C1 (uint8 u8_addr,uint8* pu8_d1)	Read 1 byte; return in ***pu8_d1**
void read2I2C1 (uint8 u8_addr,uint8* pu8_d1, uint8* pu8_d2)	Read 2 bytes; return in ***pu8_d1**, ***pu8_d2**
void readNI2C1 (uint8 u8_addr,uint8* pu8_data, uint16 u16_cnt)	Read **u16_cnt** bytes; return in ***pu8_data**

FIGURE 10.44   I²C support function summary.

The *C* source code for the configI2C1(uint16 u16_FkHZ) function in Figure 10.45 computes and initializes the I2C1BRG register value for operation at u16_FkHz kHz clock frequency and enables the module by setting the I2CEN bit (I2C1CON<15>). This enables the module for both master and slave operation, unlike the SPI module that must be explicitly configured for either master or slave operation. Our I²C examples in this chapter use the PIC24 µC as a single bus master; see Chapter 13 for an example of I²C slave mode operation. The startI2C1() function (Figure 10.45) initiates the start condition by setting the SEN bit; the ensuing while(I2C1CONbits.SEN){} loop is exited when the hardware clears the SEN bit on completion of the start operation. The startI2C1() function uses the watchdog timer to escape the infinite wait loop in the unlikely event of hardware malfunction. The rstartI2C1() and stopI2C1() functions are similar, except they use the RSEN and PEN bits, respectively.

```
void configI2C1(uint16 u16_FkHZ) {
  uint32 u32_temp;

  u32_temp = (FCY/1000L)/((uint32) u16_FkHZ);
  u32_temp = u32_temp - FCY/10000000L - 1;
  I2C1BRG = u32_temp;
  I2C1CONbits.I2CEN = 1;
}
```
} Compute I2C1BRG value
  for operation at
  `u16_FkHZ` kHz.

←—— Enable I²C module

```
void startI2C1(void) {
  uint8 u8_wdtState;

  sz_lastTimeoutError = "I2C Start";
  u8_wdtState = _SWDTEN;   //save WDT state
  _SWDTEN = 1; //enable WDT
  I2C1CONbits.SEN = 1;     // initiate start
  // wait until start finished
  while (I2C1CONbits.SEN);
  _SWDTEN = u8_wdtState;   //restore WDT
  sz_lastTimeoutError = NULL;
}
```
←—— Functions `stopI2C1()`, `rstartI2C1()` are similar
  but use bits **PEN**, **RSEN** respectively.

} Initiate start condition and
  wait for finish.

FIGURE 10.45 C source code for `configI2C1()` and `startI2C1()` functions.

Transmitting a single byte on the I²C bus is accomplished by the `putI2C(uint8 u8_val)` function, whose source code is shown in Figure 10.46. The `u8_val` byte to be transmitted is written to the I²C transmit register (I2C1TRN). This sets the TRSTAT status bit, which is cleared by the hardware when the 8-bit value has been transmitted and an acknowledgement bit received from the slave. The acknowledgement bit value (0 for ACK, 1 for NAK) is available in the ACKSTAT bit, and the `putI2C()` function calls `reportError()` with an appropriate error message if a NAK is returned. The `putNoAckCheckI2C1(uint8 u8_val)` function listed in Figure 10.44 also transmits a single byte, but it returns the value of the ACKSTAT bit instead of reporting an error on a NAK condition as slave peripherals sometimes use the acknowledgement bit for returning status information. The `getI2C1(uint8 u8_ack2Send)` function whose source code is given in Figure 10.46 reads a single byte from the I²C bus then writes an acknowledgement bit (`u8_ack2Send`). Receive is enabled by setting RCEN bit, which is cleared by the hardware on reception of the 8th bit into the I²C input shift register. The receive buffer full (RBF) status bit is set when the 8-bit value is transferred into the receive register (I2C1RCV) and is cleared when this register is read. After reading the I2C1RCV register, the acknowledgement bit is sent back by setting the ACKDT bit to the acknowledgement bit value to be transmitted (`u8_ack2Send`). The acknowledgement bit transmission is initiated by setting the ACKEN bit, which is cleared by the hardware when the acknowledgement operation is finished. The value read from the receive register is the return value of the `getI2C1()` function.

The I²C actions performed by the `write2I2C1()` function of Figure 10.44b that writes two bytes to a slave device are shown in Figure 10.47a. The start

```
void putI2C1(uint8 u8_val) {
  uint8 u8_wdtState;          ←———— Transmit this value.

  sz_lastTimeoutError = "I2C Put";
  u8_wdtState = _SWDTEN;               //save WDT state
  _SWDTEN = 1;                         //enable WDT
  I2C1TRN = u8_val;                    // write byte
  while (I2C1STATbits.TRSTAT);         // wait for 8bits+ ack bit to finish
  _SWDTEN = u8_wdtState;  //restore WDT
  sz_lastTimeoutError = NULL;
  if (I2C1STATbits.ACKSTAT != I2C_ACK) {
    //NAK returned         ←————————— Function putNoAckCheckI2C1()
    reportError("I2CPUT, NAK returned.");   does not check for NAK, just returns
  }                                          the ACKSTAT value.
}            ↖ Software reset if NAK is returned.

uint8 getI2C1(uint8 u8_ack2Send) {
  uint8 u8_wdtState;          ←———— Acknowledge value to send after byte is
  uint8 u8_inByte;                    received.

  sz_lastTimeoutError = "I2C Get";
  u8_wdtState = _SWDTEN;               //save WDT state
  _SWDTEN = 1;                         //enable WDT
  while (I2C1CON & 0x1F);              //wait for idle
  I2C1CONbits.RCEN = 1;                //enable receive
  while (!I2C1STATbits.RBF);           //wait for receive byte
  CLRWDT();
  u8_inByte = I2C1RCV;                 //read byte;
  //wait for idle condition before attempting ACK
  while (I2C1CON & 0x1F);              //lower 5 bits must be 0
  I2C1CONbits.ACKDT = u8_ack2Send;     //ACK bit to send back on receive
  I2C1CONbits.ACKEN = 1;               //enable ACKbit transmittion
  while (I2C1CONbits.ACKEN);           //wait for completion
  _SWDTEN = u8_wdtState;               //restore WDT
  sz_lastTimeoutError = NULL;
  return(u8_inByte);                   //return the value
}
```

FIGURE 10.46   C source code for putI2C1() and getI2C1() functions.

condition is sent by the startI2C1() function call, followed by a transmission of the slave's I²C bus address using the putI2C1(u8_addr & 0xFE) function call (the LSb of the address is cleared by ANDing u8_addr with 0xFE because this is a write transaction, e.g., a transmission of data from the master to the slave). The two data bytes u8_d1, u8_d2 are transmitted by consecutive calls to putI2C1(), with the transaction ended by a call to the stopI2C1() function.

Figure 10.47b shows the I²C operations performed by the read2I2C1() function that reads two bytes from a slave peripheral. As in the write transaction, the first two actions are generation of the start condition by startI2C1() and transmission of the slave's I²C address by putI2c(u8_addr | 0x01). Because this is a read transaction, the LSb of the slave's address must be set by ORing u8_addr with 0x01. The first data byte read from the slave is returned from the getI2C1(I2C_ACK) function call

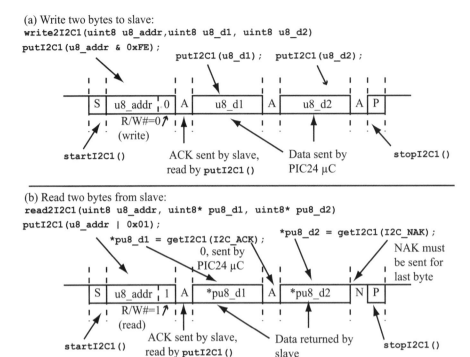

FIGURE 10.47   I²C operations within read/write transactions.

and saved by the pointer operation `*pu8_d1`. The `I2C_ACK` macro's value is "0", indicating that an ACK is returned to the slave for this first read. The second (and last) data byte read from the slave is returned by the `getI2C1(I2C_NAK)` function call and saved by the pointer operation `*pu8_d2`. The acknowledgement bit returned to the slave for the last byte in a read transaction must be a NAK, which tells the slave that no further data is expected.

Figure 10.48 shows the *C* source code for the I²C read/write transaction functions of Figure 10.44(b). These functions are provided for convenience purposes and used in the following I²C interfacing examples. The `writeNI2C1()` and `readNI2C1()` functions are useful for transferring a block of data to or from a slave peripheral. The `I2C_RADDR(x)` and `I2C_WADDR(x)` macros are used for clearing and setting the R/W# bit of the I²C address byte (`u8_addr`) parameter passed to the read/write transaction functions.

I²C EXAMPLE: PIC24 μC MASTER TO DS1631 THERMOMETER

Our first I²C interfacing example is a PIC24 μC master to Maxim DS1631 Digital Thermometer/Thermostat [39] slave as shown in Figure 10.49. The DS1631 is similar in many ways to the previously discussed DS1722 Digital Thermometer,

(a) Write Transactions

```
#define I2C_WADDR(x) (x & 0xFE)

void write1I2C1(uint8 u8_addr,
  uint8 u8_d1) {
 startI2C1();
 putI2C1(I2C_WADDR(u8_addr));
 putI2C1(u8_d1);
 stopI2C1();                LSb must be 0
}                          for write.

void write2I2C1(uint8 u8_addr,
  uint8 u8_d1, uint8 u8_d2) {
 startI2C1();
 putI2C1(I2C_WADDR(u8_addr));
 putI2C1(u8_d1);
 putI2C1(u8_d2);
 stopI2C1();
}

void writeNI2C1(uint8 u8_addr,
  uint8* pu8_data,
  uint16 u16_cnt) {
 uint16 u16_i;
 startI2C1();
 putI2C1(I2C_WADDR(u8_addr));
 for (u16_i=0; u16_i < u16_cnt;){
  putI2C1(*pu8_data);
  pu8_data++;u16_i++;
 }
 stopI2C1();
}
```

(b) Read Transactions

```
#define I2C_RADDR(x) (x | 0x01)

void read1I2C1(uint8 u8_addr,
  uint8* pu8_d1) {
 startI2C1();       ⟵ LSb must be 1 for read.
 putI2C1(I2C_RADDR(u8_addr));
 *pu8_d1 = getI2C1(I2C_NAK);
 stopI2C1();
}

void read2I2C1(uint8 u8_addr,
  uint8* pu8_d1, uint8* pu8_d2) {
 startI2C1();
 putI2C1(I2C_RADDR(u8_addr));
 *pu8_d1 = getI2C1(I2C_ACK);
 *pu8_d2 = getI2C1(I2C_NAK);
 stopI2C1();
}

void readNI2C1(uint8 u8_addr,
  uint8* pu8_data, uint16 u16_cnt) {
 uint16 u16_i;
 startI2C1();
 putI2C1(I2C_RADDR(u8_addr));
 for (u16_i=0; u16_i < u16_cnt;) {
  if (u16_i != u16_cnt-1)
      *pu8_data = getI2C1(I2C_ACK);
   else *pu8_data = getI2C1(I2C_NAK);
  pu8_data++; u16_i++;
 }
 stopI2C1();
}
```

FIGURE 10.48   *C* source code for I²C read/write transaction functions.

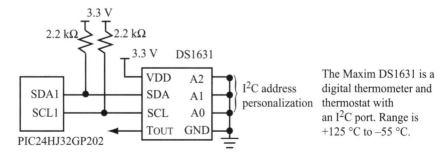

The Maxim DS1631 is a digital thermometer and thermostat with an I²C port. Range is +125 °C to −55 °C.

FIGURE 10.49   PIC24 µC I²C master to DS1631 Digital Thermometer connection.

but differs in that it supports 9- to 12-bit precision but not the 8-bit precision also supported by the DS1722. The DS1631 also has a thermostat function in which the TOUT pin goes high when the temperature exceeds a user-programmable high temperature trigger that is stored in a non-volatile 16-bit register named TH.

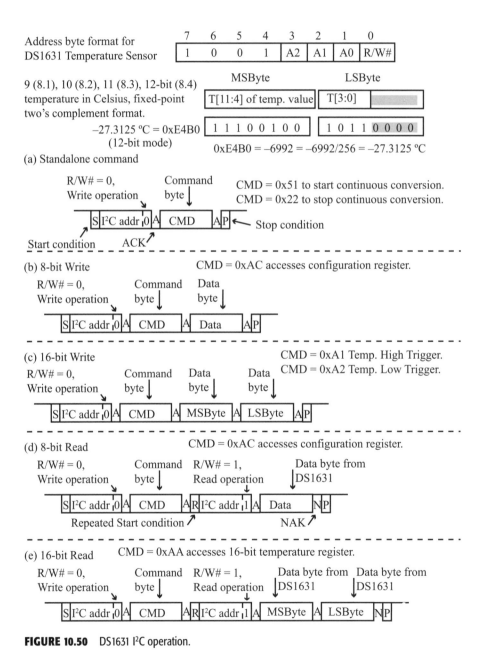

FIGURE 10.50   DS1631 I²C operation.

The Tout pin returns low once the temperature falls below a user-programmable low temperature trigger that is stored in a non-volatile 16-bit register named TL.

Figure 10.50 details the commands supported by the DS1631. The stand-alone command (a) is used to start and stop continuous conversions. The 8-bit write (b) and read (d) commands are used to access the 8-bit registers, such as the configuration register. The 16-bit write (c) and read (d) commands are used for the 16-bit registers, which are the temperature register (read-only) and the TH, TL registers. Observe that a read command consists of two separate I²C transactions; an I²C write transaction that sends the command byte to the DS1631 followed by an I²C read transaction that returns the data.

The DS1631 configuration register details are shown in Figure 10.51. The 1SHOT and continuous conversion modes work similarly to the DS1722, except

	R-1	R/W-0	R/W-0	R/W-0	R/W-0	R/W-0	R/W-0	R/W-0
CONFIG Register	DONE	THF	TLF	NVB	R1	R0	POL	1SHOT
	7	6	5	4	3	2	1	0

DONE	Conversion Done Flag: "1" when conversion is complete, "0" when conversion is in progress.
THF	Temperature High Flag: "1" if temperature has exceeded the TH register value since power-on; reset on power down, write to CONFIG register, or software power-on-reset command.
TLF	Temperature Low Flag: "1" if temperature has dropped below the TL register value since power-on; reset on power down, write to CONFIG register, or software power-on-reset command.
NVB	Nonvolatile Memory Busy flag: "1" when write to nonvolatile memory is in progress, "0" otherwise.
R1:R0	Resolution selection bits, 00: 9-bit (93.75 ms), 10: 10-bit (187.5 ms), 11-bit (375 ms), 12-bit (750 ms).
POL	Polarity bit: "1" TOUT is active high, "0" TOUT is active low. Stored in NVM.
1SHOT	One Shot Mode: "1" DS1631 only performs conversions upon receiving a Start Conversion command; "0" the DS1631 performs continuous conversions. Stored in NVM.

FIGURE 10.51   DS1631 configuration register.

that continuous conversion mode must be explicitly begun via the stand-alone command shown in Figure 10.50 (the DS1631A version begins conversions immediately on power-up). If the device is configured for one-shot mode, then the standalone command (0x51) initiates a conversion.

Code for testing the DS1631 interface is given in Figure 10.52. The I²C transaction functions previously discussed in Figure 10.44b are used to implement the DS1631 commands of Figure 10.50 in the functions writeConfigDS1631(),

```
#define DS1631ADDR 0x90    //DS1631 address with all pins tied low
#define ACCESS_CONFIG 0xAC           DS1631 address = 0b 1001 A2 A1 A0 R/W
#define START_CONVERT 0x51           0x90 = 0b 1001  0  0  0  ?
#define READ_TEMP 0xAA

void writeConfigDS1631(uint8 u8_i) {                    Implements 8-bit write
   write2I2C1(DS1631ADDR, ACCESS_CONFIG, u8_i);         command.
}

void startConversionDS1631(){
   write1I2C1(DS1631ADDR, START_CONVERT);      Implements standalone command.
}

int16 readTempDS1631() {
   uint8 u8_lo, u8_hi;
   int16 i16_temp;
   write1I2C1(DS1631ADDR, READ_TEMP);
   read2I2C1 (DS1631ADDR, &u8_hi, &u8_lo);      Implements 16-bit read command.
   i16_temp = u8_hi;
   return ((i16_temp<<8)|u8_lo);
}

int main (void) {
   int16 i16_temp;
   float  f_tempC,f_tempF;              Configure I2C bus for 400 kHz.
   configBasic(HELLO_MSG);              Configure for continuous conversions.
   configI2C1(400);               //configure I2C for 400 kHz
   writeConfigDS1631(0x0C);       //continuous conversion, 12-bit mode
   startConversionDS1631();       //start conversions
   while (1) {                                Read temperature and print result
     DELAY_MS(750);                           as hex, Celsius and Fahrenheit.
     i16_temp = readTempDS1631();
     f_tempC = i16_temp;  //convert to floating point
     f_tempC = f_tempC/256;  //divide by precision
     f_tempF = f_tempC*9/5 + 32;
     printf("Temp is: 0x%0X, %4.4f (C), %4.4f (F)\n",
            i16_temp, (double) f_tempC, (double) f_tempF);
   }
}
```

FIGURE 10.52   Code for testing the DS1631.

startConversionDS1631(), and readTempDS1631(). The slave address passed to the I²C transaction functions is 0x90, which corresponds to A2/A1/A0 pins of the DS1631 all tied low as shown in Figure 10.49. The main() code configures the I²C module for 400 kHz operation, then configures the DS1631 for continuous conversion and starts the conversions. The while(1){} loop code is essentially the same code as used for the DS1722 of Figure 10.34 in that the 16-bit temperature is read after a delay, then printed to the console in hex, degrees Celsius, and degrees Fahrenheit.

I²C bus activity captured during the readTempDS1631() function is shown in Figure 10.53. The write1I2C1() function call performs a one-byte write transaction that writes the READ_TEMP (0xAA) command to the DS1631. This is followed by

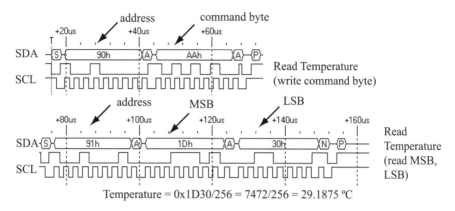

FIGURE 10.53   I²C bus activity during DS1631 operation.

the read2I2C1() function call that reads two bytes from the DS1631. Observe that the DS1631 address during the write transaction is 0x90, while during the read transaction it is 0x91, with the difference being the LSb value ("0" for write, "1" for read). The 16-bit temperature read is 0x1D30, which is 0x1D30/256 = 7472/256 = 29.1875 °C.

I²C Example: PIC24 µC Master to 24LC515 Serial EEPROM

The 24LC515 512K serial EEPROM [40] has an internal organization of 64 Ki x 8 and uses an I²C port for communication. Figure 10.54 shows a PIC24 µC master to 24LC515 connection. The write protect (WP) pin on the 24LC515 can be used to disable writes to the device; it can be left open or tied to VSS to enable writes. The A2 input is an unused input that must be tied high for the device to function correctly. The A1, A0 inputs are used to personalize the device address by connecting them to either VDD or ground. This allows up to four 24LC515 devices to exist on the same I²C bus.

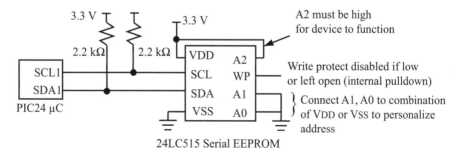

FIGURE 10.54   PIC24 µC Master to 24LC515 Serial EEPROM connection.

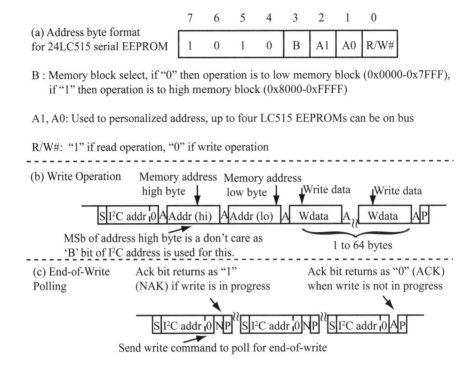

B : Memory block select, if "0" then operation is to low memory block (0x0000-0x7FFF),
if "1" then operation is to high memory block (0x8000-0xFFFF)

A1, A0: Used to personalized address, up to four LC515 EEPROMs can be on bus

R/W#: "1" if read operation, "0" if write operation

FIGURE 10.55   LC515 I²C address format and write operation.

Figure 10.55a shows the address byte format for the 24LC515. The upper 4 bits are fixed at "1010". The 64 Ki x 8 organization of the 24LC515 means that addresses are 16 bits with a range 0x0000 to 0xFFFF. However, the internal organization of the 64 Ki x 8 memory is split into two 32 Ki memory blocks, each with its own internal 15-bit address counter. The *B* (block select) bit of the I²C address byte determines whether the current operation is to the low memory block (0x0000 through 0x7FFF) or high memory block (0x8000 through 0xFFFF). Thus, it is best to view the 24LC515 as two separate 32 Ki x 8 memories which are selected by the *B* bit in the I²C address byte. The least significant bit of the address byte is the R/W# bit as with all I²C address bytes. The write operation format for the 24LC515 is given in Figure 10.55b. The I²C address byte is followed by the high and low address bytes of the starting location for the write. The most significant bit of the high address byte is a don't care as the block select bit within the I²C address byte determines which memory block is being written; these 15 address bits are written to the internal address counter for the 32 Ki block selected by the block select bit of the address byte. The internal page size of the 24LC515 is 64 bytes, so up to 64 bytes can be written in one write operation. The incoming bytes are placed into an internal 64-byte buffer using the lower 6 bits of the address, while the remaining upper bits specify the page that is written. The starting address of a 64-byte page has its last six bits as all zeros. If the write command address does not begin on a 64-byte boundary, bytes wrap to the beginning of the page once the internal address counter increments past the page boundary. Because of this, the best practice is to write a complete page at one time and force the starting address to begin on a page address. The actual write to EEPROM begins when a stop condition is received, with worst-case write completion time specified as 5 ms. However, the end-of-write condition can be polled by sending the write command and checking the ACK bit status as shown in Figure 10.55c. If the acknowledgement bit returns as "1" (a NAK), a write is still in progress. Once the acknowledge bit returns as "0", the next operation can be started. It is more efficient to poll for end-of-write at the beginning of a write operation than to place a delay of 5 ms after each write operation. Experimental results showed that writes typically required about 3.1 ms, which is considerably shorter than the 5 ms worst-case specification.

Figure 10.56 shows read operation sequencing for the 24LC515. A sequential read (Figure 10.56a) returns the memory contents pointed to by the internal address counter of the 24LC515. Each data byte returned by the 24LC515 increments the internal address counter for the selected block. An acknowledgment bit of "0" returned by the PIC24 µC causes the 24LC515 to output another data byte. An acknowledgement bit of "1" returned by the PIC24 µC causes the 24LC515 to release the SDA line and to stop sending data. A sequential read can access the contents of one entire 32 KiB memory block, either high or low, as determined by the block select bit sent in the I²C address byte at the beginning of the read transaction. When the internal address counter reaches the end of a 32 Ki block, it wraps around to

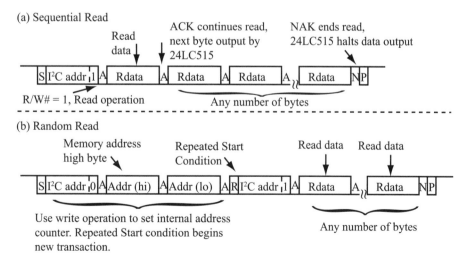

FIGURE 10.56   24LC515 read operation.

the beginning of the block. Figure 10.56b shows how to use the write command to set the internal address counter before beginning a sequential read. Sending a repeated start condition (or a stop followed by a start) after the EEPROM address bytes halts the write command. Only the internal address counter is affected by the write operation; an internal write to memory is not started.

Utility functions for read/write to the 24LC515 EEPROM are given in Figure 10.57. The waitForWriteCompletion() function implements the end-of-write polling of Figure 10.55c. Observe that the putNoAckCheckI2C1() function is used to write the I²C address byte instead of putI2C1() because we want the acknowledgement bit returned so that its value can be checked; the polling loop is exited when the acknowledgement bit returns as "0" (an ACK). The memWriteLC515() function implements the write operation of Figure 10.55b for a block size of 64. The u16_MemAddr parameter specifies the start address within the EEPROM for the write. The *pu8_buf parameter is a pointer to a 66-byte buffer, whose first two locations are reserved for the high and low bytes of the write address, with the remaining 64 locations containing the write data. The memWriteLC515() function first splits the u16_MemAddr address into its high and low byte components, which are placed into pu8_buf[0] and pu8_buf[1] locations as per the specified ordering of Figure 10.55(b). The u16_MemAddr parameter is then checked to see if it is in the upper or lower 32 Ki block; if it is in the upper 32 Ki the B bit of the 24LC515's I²C address is set. The waitForWriteCompletion() function is called to ensure that the 24LC515 is ready to begin a new operation, then the writeNI2C1() function is used to write the pu_buf contents to the 24LC515.

The memReadLC515() function of Figure 10.57 reads 64 bytes from the 24LC515 as per the random read operation of Figure 10.56b. While this block size was chosen to match the write block size for convenience, any read block size could have been chosen. The B bit of the u16_MemAddr parameter is set to a "1" if the read is from the upper 32 Ki block, and the waitForWriteCompletion() function is used to ensure that the 24LC515 is ready for a new operation. The write2I2CI() function call sets the 24LC515's internal address counter by writing the upper and lower bytes of the starting read address. The readNI2C1() function call then reads 64 bytes from the 24LC515 and stores them in pu8_buf.

Figure 10.58 shows the main() code that uses the functions of Figure 10.57 for testing writes and reads to the 24LC515. The user is first prompted to enter either read ("r") or write mode ("w"). In write mode, the user enters 64 characters that are written to the EEPROM using memWriteLC515(). Each string is written twice in succession to test the end-of-write polling implemented by waitForWriteCompletion(). In read mode, each key press reads 64 bytes from the 24LC515 using memReadLC515() and the resulting characters read from the 24LC515 are written to the console.

```
#define EEPROM 0xA0    //LC515 address assuming both address pins tied low.
#define BLKSIZE 64
```
24LC151 address = 0b 1010 B A1 A0 R/W

0xA0 = 0b 1010 0 0 0 ?

```
void waitForWriteCompletion(uint8 u8_i2cAddr){
  uint8 u8_ack, u8_savedSWDTEN;
  u8_savedSWDTEN = _SWDTEN;
  _SWDTEN = 1;
  u8_i2cAddr = I2C_WADDR(u8_i2cAddr);  //write transaction, so R/W# = 0;
  do {
    startI2C1();
    u8_ack = putNoAckCheckI2C1(u8_i2cAddr);
    stopI2C1();
  } while (u8_ack == I2C_NAK);
  _SWDTEN = u8_savedSWDTEN;  //restore WDT to original state
}
```
Assume lower 32 Ki block.

Enable WDT to escape infinite loop, assumes WDT timeout is greater than EEPROM write time.

Send I^{2}C address with R/W=0, check the ack bit that comes back.

Keep looping until get an ACK back.

Write 64 bytes in *pu8_buf to EEPROM starting at address u16_MemAddr

```
void memWriteLC515(uint8 u8_i2cAddr, uint16 u16_MemAddr, uint8 *pu8_buf){
  uint8 u8_AddrLo, u8_AddrHi;
  u8_AddrLo = u16_MemAddr & 0x00FF;
  u8_AddrHi = (u16_MemAddr >> 8);
  pu8_buf[0] = u8_AddrHi;
  pu8_buf[1] = u8_AddrLo;
  if (u16_MemAddr & 0x8000) {
    // if MSB set , set block select bit
    u8_i2cAddr = u8_i2cAddr | 0x08;
  }
  waitForWriteCompletion(u8_i2cAddr);
  writeNI2C1(u8_i2cAddr,pu8_buf,BLKSIZE+2);
}
```
Get the high, low bytes of the memory address.

First two bytes of pu8_buf are reserved for the EEPROM address.

Set the "B" bit of the I^{2}C memory address if writing upper 32 Ki block.

Wait for last write to finish.

I^{2}C block write transaction.

Read 64 bytes into *pu8_buf from EEPROM starting at address u16_MemAddr

```
void memReadLC515(uint8 u8_i2cAddr, uint16 u16_MemAddr, uint8 *pu8_buf){
  uint8 u8_AddrLo, u8_AddrHi;
  u8_AddrLo = u16_MemAddr & 0x00FF;
  u8_AddrHi = (u16_MemAddr >> 8);
  if (u16_MemAddr & 0x8000) {
    // if MSB set , set block select bit
    u8_i2cAddr = u8_i2cAddr | 0x08;
  }
  waitForWriteCompletion(u8_i2cAddr);
  //set address counter
  write2I2C1(u8_i2cAddr,u8_AddrHi, u8_AddrLo);
  //read data
  readNI2C1(u8_i2cAddr,pu8_buf, BLKSIZE);
}
```
Get the high, low bytes of the memory address.

Set the "B" bit of the I^{2}C memory address if reading upper 32 Ki block.

Wait for last write to finish.

Set EEPROM's internal address counter.

I^{2}C block read transaction.

FIGURE 10.57   Utility functions for read/write of the 24LC515 EEPROM.

Figure 10.59 shows console output from a test of the Figure 10.58 code. Two 64-byte strings are entered, which means the first four pages of the 24LC515 are written as each string is written twice. The read test reads back the first four pages of the 24LC515. The console output shows the expected string values.

```
int main (void) {
  uint8 au8_buf[64+2];  //2 extra bytes for address
  uint16 u16_MemAddr;
  uint8 u8_Mode;

  configBasic(HELLO_MSG);
  configI2C1(400);              //configure I2C for 400 KHz
  outString("\nEnter 'w' for write mode, anything else reads: ");
  u8_Mode = inCharEcho();
  outString("\n");
  u16_MemAddr = 0;     //start at location 0 in memory
  while (1) {
    uint8 u8_i;
    if (u8_Mode == 'w') {
      outString("Enter 64 chars.\n");
      //first two buffer locations reserved for starting address
      for (u8_i = 2;u8_i< 64+2;u8_i++) {      Get 64 bytes from the
        au8_buf[u8_i] = inCharEcho();         console.
      }
      outString("\nDoing Write\n");
      // write same string twice to check Write Busy polling
      memWriteLC515(EEPROM,u16_MemAddr, au8_buf); // do write
      u16_MemAddr = u16_MemAddr +64;
      memWriteLC515(EEPROM,u16_MemAddr,au8_buf); // do write
      u16_MemAddr = u16_MemAddr +64;
    } else {
      memReadLC515(EEPROM,u16_MemAddr,au8_buf); // do read
      for (u8_i = 0;u8_i< 64;u8_i++) outChar(au8_buf[u8_i]);
      outString("\nAny key continues read...\n");
      inChar();                                 Echo 64 bytes to the
      u16_MemAddr = u16_MemAddr + 64;           console.
    }
  }
}
```

FIGURE 10.58   main() for testing 24LC515 read/writes.

Ping-Pong Buffering for Interrupt-Driven Streaming Data

The previous examples that performed a write to an I²C serial EEPROM prompted the user to enter a string that was stored in a buffer, wrote that buffer to the serial EEPROM, then prompted the user for another string. However, how would data that is arriving in a continuous stream be handled? Figure 10.60 shows the problem with using only one buffer to handle streaming input data. Once the buffer is full, a page write must be done to EEPROM to save the buffer contents. But new data is continuously arriving and if the current buffer is used to save the incoming data, the old data is overwritten.

Figure 10.61 shows that the solution to this problem involves using two buffers, named au8_buffer0 and au8_buffer1. Once au8_buffer0 is filled with input data, it is swapped with au8_buffer1 and emptied by writing to it to the EEPROM, with au8_buffer1 used to store input data during the EEPROM write operation. After

```
Reset cause: Power-on.
Device ID = 0x00000F1D (PIC24HJ32GP202), revision 0x00003002 (A3)
Fast RC Osc with PLL

i2c_serialeepromtest.c, built on Jun 28 2008 at 19:21:32

Enter 'w' for write mode, anything else reads: w
Enter 64 chars.
A person who graduates today and stops learning tommorrow is
Doing Write
Enter 64 chars.
uneducated the day after. Life long learning is very important.
Doing Write                        Two strings entered; each string saved twice to EEPROM.
Enter 64 chars.                    Reset button pressed.
Reset cause: MCLR assertion.
Device ID = 0x00000F1D (PIC24HJ32GP202), revision 0x00003002 (A3)
Fast RC Osc with PLL

i2c_serialeepromtest.c, built on Jun 28 2008 at 19:21:32

Enter 'w' for write mode, anything else reads: r
A person who graduates today and stops learning tommorrow is
Any key continues read...
A person who graduates today and stops learning tommorrow is
Any key continues read...
uneducated the day after. Life long learning is very important.
Any key continues read...
uneducated the day after. Life long learning is very important.
Any key continues read...                Strings read back from EEPROM.
```

FIGURE 10.59   main() for testing 24LC515 read/writes.

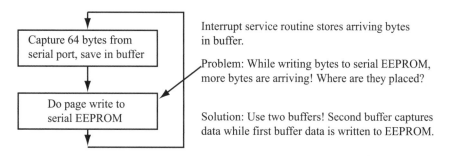

FIGURE 10.60   Using one buffer to capture streaming input data.

au8_buffer1 becomes full, it is swapped with the now empty au8_buffer0 and the process is repeated. An ISR captures incoming bytes from the serial port while the foreground code writes the full buffer to EEPROM. This works as long as the buffer used to capture incoming data does not fill before the EEPROM write is finished; recall that in a streaming data application the outgoing bandwidth must exceed the incoming bandwidth or no amount of buffering will prevent eventual data loss due

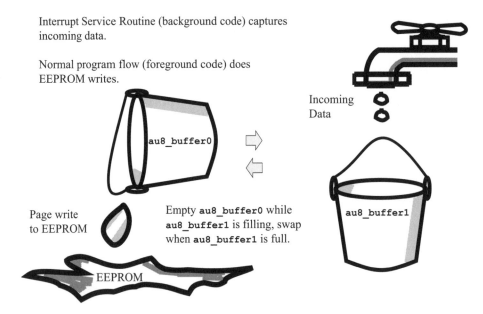

Interrupt Service Routine (background code) captures incoming data.

Normal program flow (foreground code) does EEPROM writes.

`au8_buffer0`

Incoming Data

Empty `au8_buffer0` while `au8_buffer1` is filling, swap when `au8_buffer1` is full.

`au8_buffer1`

Page write to EEPROM

EEPROM

FIGURE 10.61   Ping-pong buffering to capture streaming data.

to buffer overflow. The incoming data must arrive by a different communication channel than that used to save the data; in this example, data arrives via the asynchronous serial port and is written to the EEPROM using the I²C port. This buffering strategy is often referred to as *ping-pong buffering,* because the data bounces between the two buffers.

Figure 10.62 shows the ISR flowchart for capturing streaming data. Two buffers, au8_buffer0 and au8_buffer1, are used to store data, with the u8_activeBuffer flag determining the buffer currently used for input data. A character arrival at the asynchronous serial port triggers an interrupt, which causes the character to be stored in either au8_buffer0 or au8_buffer1 as determined by u8_activeBuffer. The u8_activeBuffer flag always indicates the buffer to which incoming data bytes are written. A buffer becomes full after 64 bytes because that is the page size of the I²C serial EEPROM. The u8_writeFlag semaphore is set once the buffer becomes full; this notifies main() (the foreground code) that the full buffer must be written to EEPROM. The ISR also toggles the u8_activeBuffer flag from 0 to 1 or 1 to 0 so that arriving data is written to the empty buffer while main() empties the full buffer. This is equivalent to swapping the full bucket with the empty bucket in Figure 10.61.

Figure 10.63 shows the streaming write loop in main() that writes the streaming input data to EEPROM. The loop waits until u8_writeFlag is set, indicating that a

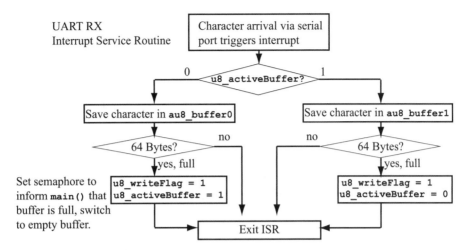

FIGURE 10.62   ISR flowchart for capturing streaming data.

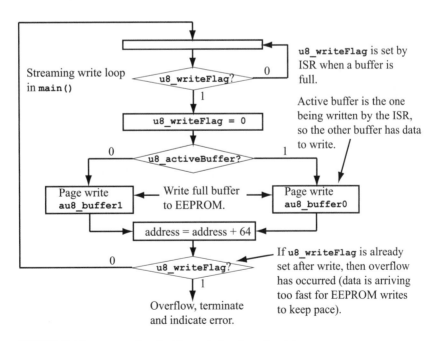

FIGURE 10.63   main() flowchart for capturing streaming data.

buffer is full. It then clears the u8_writeFlag, writes the full buffer to EEPROM, and increments the EEPROM address by 64. How do we know if the incoming data rate is not exceeding the outgoing data rate? If the u8_writeFlag is already set after writing the full buffer to EEPROM, buffer overflow has occurred. If overflow occurs, either the incoming data rate must be reduced or the outgoing data rate must be increased. Lowering the baud rate of the asynchronous serial port will reduce the incoming data rate. A new EEPROM with either a faster write time or larger internal page buffer will increase the outgoing data bandwidth. The *C* code implementation for Figures 10.62 and 10.63 is left as a suggested laboratory exercise in Appendix C.

When does the overflow condition of Figure 10.63 occur? Assuming that data bytes are arriving in a continuous stream, overflow does not occur if the following is true:

$$\text{Input time for 64 bytes} > \text{Output time for 64 bytes} \tag{10.5}$$

For a rough estimate, we ignore processing time and concentrate on transmission time, which gives the following (assuming a 400 kHz I²C bus speed and 1+8+1 serial data format):

$$10 \times 64 \text{ bytes} \times (1/\text{BR}) > (67 \text{ bytes} \times 9 \text{ bits} \times 1/400 \text{ kHz}) + 5 \text{ ms write time} \tag{10.6}$$

The 67 bytes on the right side of Equation 10.6 is the total number of bytes transferred over the I²C bus for a write of 64 bytes as per the write transaction of Figure 10.55 (this ignores end-of-write polling and assumes a worst case write time of 5 ms). Solving for baud rate (BR) gives:

$$98348 > \text{BR (baud rate)} \tag{10.7}$$

So, the baud rate must be less than approximately 98,000 baud, with 57,600 being the highest standard baud rate from Figure 10.12. In practice, this baud rate provides more than enough margin for this particular application.

SUMMARY

The UART*x*, SPI*x*, and I2C*x* modules of the PIC24 µC all implement serial interfaces. The UART*x* module uses duplex, asynchronous serial data transfer and is the best choice for PIC24 µC to PIC24 µC communication in terms of application flexibility. The SPI*x* module implements synchronous serial transfer and offers the highest speed transfer of the three interfaces with a maximum clock speed of 10 MHz.

However, it requires a minimum of three wires for the interface, and each new SPI peripheral on the bus requires an additional PIO pin in order to select the peripheral. The I²C module also implements synchronous serial transfer and has the advantage of only requiring two wires for the interface regardless of the number of peripherals on the bus. However, its maximum clock speed is 1 MHz and it has more protocol overhead per byte transferred than SPI transfers. All three serial interfaces are commonly used in microcontroller and microprocessor systems.

REVIEW PROBLEMS

Some of the following problems refer to device datasheets found at www.maximic. com, www.microchip.com, www.nxp.com (formerly Philips semiconductor), www. intersil.com, and www.atmel.com. For the I²C questions, use the functions listed in Figure 10.44.

1. What is the bandwidth in MB/s of a parallel data link that consists of 32 wires for data transfer, a clock speed of 8 MHz, and data transfer every second rising clock edge?
2. Assume a PIC24 μC with an Fᴄʏ of 40 MHz using PORTB<7:0> for data transfer. Suppose you want to transfer 256 bytes of data to an external device. How long does it take to transfer this data, using the code in this problem? Express this transfer rate in MB/s (Hint: you must compute the number of instruction cycles to transfer the data, then convert this to time).

```
    clr     W0
    mov     #u8_buf,W1    ;get address of data to transfer
loop:
    mov.b   [W1++],PORTB  ;write data to PORTB
    dec.b   W0            ;decrement counter
    bra     NZ,loop       ;will loop 256 times
;;rest of code
```

3. What is 1 bit time in microseconds for a baud rate of 19,200?
4. How long does it take to send 64 bytes of data at 57,600 baud using asynchronous serial transmission assuming 8 data bits and 1 stop bit if the transmitter pauses for 4 bit times between each character?
5. Give the maximum bandwidth of an asynchronous serial link operating at 115,200 baud in B/s assuming a format of 8 data bits and 1 stop bit with no delay between transmission of the last bit of a previous character and the first bit of the next character.

6. Draw the waveform for an asynchronous transmission assuming 8 data bits and 1 stop bit for the data value 0xA0.
7. Draw the waveform for an asynchronous transmission assuming 8 data bits and 1 stop bit for the data value 0x38.
8. What is the parity bit for the 7-bit value 0x1E assuming odd parity?
9. What is the parity bit for the 7-bit value 0x38 assuming even parity?
10. For an asynchronous serial transfer, assume a 16× clock on the receive side and a data format of 16 data bits + 1 stop bit + 1 start bit. Using a conservative error tolerance of ±5 clocks about the midpoint of the bit time, what is the maximum percent tolerance in frequency mismatch between the sender and receiver?
11. Compute the maximum time before overrun given the UART receiver block diagram of Figure 10.10 and a baud rate of 38,400. Express this time in instruction cycles, assuming an Fcy of 40 MHz.
12. For an Fcy of 8 MHz and assuming low-speed mode, give the baud rates of Figure 10.12 that cannot be supported either because they exceed 3 percent error or do not fit in the 16-bit range of UxBRG (use a spreadsheet for these calculations).
13. Repeat problem 12 but assume high-speed mode.
14. Explain how a framing error can occur if the sender's baud rate is higher than the receiver's and repeat for the opposite condition.
15. Look up the specifications for the EIA RS422 standard. What is the principal difference between this standard and the RS-232 standard? What are its advantages, if any?

Answer the following questions about the Maxim MAX5439, a digital potentiometer with a SPI port.

16. Determine the correct settings for the PIC24 μC CKE and CKP configuration bits for interfacing to this device.
17. How many wiper positions does this digital potentiometer support?
18. Is there a method for determining the current wiper register contents? If yes, how is this done?

Answer the following questions about the Maxim MAX5408, a digital potentiometer with a SPI port.

19. Determine the correct settings for the PIC24 μC CKE and CKP configuration bits for interfacing to this device.
20. How many wiper positions does this digital potentiometer support?
21. Is there a method for determining the current wiper register contents? If yes, how is this done?

22. This potentiometer has a zero-crossing detection feature. What does this mode do and why is it included?
23. What is the maximum clock frequency supported for the SPI port?

Answer the following questions about the Atmel AT25256A, a serial EEPROM with an SPI port.

24. What is the organization of this device and total bit capacity?
25. Determine the correct settings for the PIC24 µC CKE and CKP configuration bits for interfacing to this device.
26. What is the maximum clock frequency supported for the SPI port?
27. What is the page buffer size?
28. How is a write-in-progress determined?

Answer the following questions about the Maxim DS3902, a digital potentiometer with an I²C port. Assume that any configurable address selection pins are tied high.

29. How many wiper positions does this digital potentiometer support?
30. Write a sequence of I²C function calls from Figure 10.44(a) that will set the wiper for resistor 0 to a position specified by u8_potVal. Repeat using the transaction functions of Figure 10.44(b). Assume that the ADD_SEL pin of the device is low.
31. Write a sequence of I²C function calls from Figure 10.44(a) that will read the current wiper position for resistor 1 and return it in the variable u8_potVal. Repeat using the transaction functions of Figure 10.44(b). Assume that the ADD_SEL pin of the device is low.
32. What is the maximum clock frequency supported for the I²C port?

Answer the following questions about the Philips PCF8598C-2, a serial EEPROM with an I²C port (find this datasheet at www.nxp.com).

33. What is the organization of this device and total bit capacity?
34. What is the maximum clock frequency supported for the I²C port?
35. What is the page buffer size?
36. How is a write-in-progress determined?
37. How long does a typical page write take?

Answer the following questions.

38. Assuming Fcy of 40 MHz, what I2CxBRG value is required for an I²C bus rate of 400 kHz?

39. Devise a scheme for measuring how long a typical self-timed write on the 24LC515 serial EEPROM actually takes. Determine if the typical write time is dependent upon the number of bytes that is actually written.

40. Write code that sets the DS1631 TH and TL registers to values of TH = 100°C and TL = 90°C. You must poll the NVB bit in the status register to ensure that the non-volatile memory is not busy before issuing a write to the either of these two registers. Use the I²C functions of Figure 10.44.

41. Assume the DS1631 has been configured for one-shot mode. Write code that starts a conversion then polls the DONE flag until the conversion is finished. Use the I²C functions of Figure 10.44.

11 Data Conversion

This chapter discusses a few of the many different analog-to-digital converter (ADC), digital-to-analog converter (DAC) architectures, and the advantages and disadvantages of each. The successive approximation ADC in the PIC24 family and an external serial DAC are covered and example applications are explained.

Learning Objectives

After reading this chapter, you will be able to:

- Describe the differences between sampling and quantization and the differences between ADCs, DACs, and sample-and-hold amplifiers (SHAs).
- Select the appropriate ADC and DAC architecture based on the application requirements.
- Implement a simple data acquisition system using the PIC24HJ32GP202 analog-to-digital converter subsystem.
- Construct a parallel R-2R resistor ladder flash DAC using processors in the PIC24 family.
- Control an external DAC from a PIC24HJ32GP202 device using the SPI and I²C interfaces.
- Construct a simple sinusoid function waveform generator with the PIC24HJ32GP202 and a variety of external DACs.

DATA CONVERSION BASICS

As predicted by Moore's Law in 1964 [1], digital computing power has exponentially increased at ever smaller, incremental costs. For example, as we've seen in the previous chapters, processors in the PIC24 family have the capability to replace several discrete integrated circuit chips. With this increase of computing power, many applications usually accomplished with analog circuitry have found a new lease on life in the digital realm. However, the real world still is and will always be a fundamentally analog place. To bring the digital processing of the PIC24 family and its benefits to bear on real-world applications, the analog signal of interest must be translated into a format the PIC24 μC can understand. This is the function of the *analog-to-digital converter* (ADC). After processing by the PIC24 μC, the resulting digital stream of information is returned to its analog form by a *digital-to-analog converter* (DAC). Analog once again, the information may be "consumed" by the human senses, most often sight or hearing. An illustration of this information flow is shown in Figure 11.1.

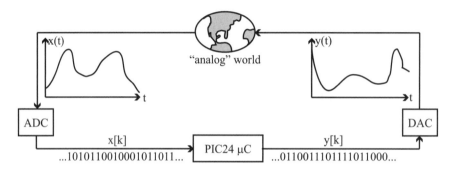

FIGURE 11.1   Typical use of a PIC24 family member to interface with the "analog" world.

ADCs and DACs are ubiquitous in computing systems. Many electronic products, including compact disc and MP3 players, camcorders, digital cellular phones, computer sound cards, computer graphics adapters, and high-definition televisions contain one or more data converters. Because ADCs are so useful and required by so many small microprocessor applications, microprocessor architects often include an ADC as a built-in peripheral. The Microchip PIC24 μC designers did just that.

From a programmer's viewpoint, the ADCs and DACs in Figure 11.1 can be regarded as black boxes. That is, an ADC accepts an input of some analog quantity, typically voltage, and provides an *n*-bit digital code output f_s times per second that represents that analog input. The number f_s is said to be the ADC's *sampling frequency*. The black box DAC accepts an *n*-bit digital word input f_s times per second and generates an equivalent analog output, usually voltage. The number f_s is the DAC's sampling frequency. For many purposes, this is a sufficient interpretation of data converters. However, an understanding of how the data conversion is done will help you understand why there are limitations on ADC and DAC operation and should help you in selecting data converters for the application at hand.

ANALOG-TO-DIGITAL CONVERSION

The methods by which a digital code is generated within an ADC are diverse. A detailed discussion would fill several books (a couple of references [66]-[67] on ADCs have been provided in Appendix F). While ADCs can have almost any analog quantity (current, charge, voltage, temperature, acoustical pressure, etc.) as an input, the most common ADCs convert an analog voltage into a digital number. Usually, systems that are converting a wide variety of quantities first convert those signals into voltages, then use a voltage-mode ADC to convert the value into a digital number. The digital number that an ADC generates can be in any encoding system, but is most typically represented in unsigned or signed binary.

ADCs and their capabilities are described by a bewildering number of parameters. A full discussion of ADC parameters is more appropriate with a more advanced electronics background, and the interested reader is encouraged to explore the data conversion references in Appendix F. However, some basic descriptive parameters for ADCs must be understood to select and use them properly.

The speed of an ADC is measured as the minimum *sampling period* t_{min}, which specifies the shortest period of time required to convert an input voltage to a digital number. Minimum sampling period is equivalently reported as the maximum sampling frequency, the maximum number of samples that the ADC can convert in one second. The maximum sampling frequency f_{max} is found by $f_{max} = 1/t_{min}$. Of course, a faster ADC gives us a more accurate temporal picture of what the analog voltage input is doing, but this knowledge requires that our microprocessor must operate on and/or store more data.

An ADC's *resolution* is the smallest change in its analog input that is detectable at its output, usually a change of ±1 in the output number. In other words, resolution represents the change in ADC input that corresponds to a 1 LSb change in output. ADC *precision* is the number of levels that the ADC can distinguish. Sometimes, ADC precision is quoted by the number of binary bits required to encode the number of levels. The ADC *range* is the total span over which inputs can be converted accurately. Quite often, the range extremes, VREF+ and VREF− in the case of voltage conversion, are provided as ADC inputs.

Sample Question: *How many bits of precision would an ADC require to distinguish 1 μV (1 μV = 1.0E−6 V) differences over a range 0−2 V?*

Answer: There are 2 million (2E6 = 2 V/1 μV) steps in a 0−2V range. An ADC would need 21 bits of output (2^{21} = 2097152) to encode these required 2000000 steps.

Sample Question: **What is the range and resolution of an 8-bit ADC with VREF+ = 10 V and VREF– = –10?**

Answer: The ADC's range is 10 V – (–10 V) = 20 V. The resolution of the ADC is its range divided by its number of steps; therefore, the range of this ADC is 20 V/256 = 78.125 mV.

Sample Question: **What is the maximum sampling frequency for the 8-bit ADC in the preceding question if the minimum sampling period is 2.5 μs?**

Answer: The maximum sampling frequency $f_{max} = 1 / t_{min}$, so the ADC's maximum sampling frequency is $f_{max} = 1 / 2.5$ μs = 400000 Hz = 400 kHz.

Sample Question: **If the ADC from the previous example is operating at maximum speed, how much storage is required to store one second of ADC output? One year's worth?**

Answer: Each ADC output is 1 byte. Therefore, one second of ADC output would occupy (400 kHz)(1 byte) = 400 KB. There are $60 \times 60 \times 24 \times 365 = 3.1536 \times 10^7$ seconds in one year. Thus, one year's worth of data from our 8-bit ADC operating at maximum sampling frequency would be 400 KB/sec $\times 3.1536 \times 10^7 = 1.26144 \times 10^{12}$ bytes, or a little more than 11 TiB. Thus, we would need more than 25 hard disk drives, each with 500 GB of capacity to store a year's worth of data from our ADC. That is a lot of storage space!

Most ADCs have uniform step sizes, which is the difference between the minimum and maximum voltages that correspond to the same output code. If step size is uniform or constant over the ADC range, the step size is equal to the resolution. (There are some specialty ADCs with nonuniform step sizes; for example, some audio ADCs have step sizes that change logarithmically over their range to match the response of the human ear.) Using our black box view of ADCs, an n-bit ADC with uniform step sizes divides its range into 2^n equal segments. The ADC output is simply the number of the segment in which the ADC input lies. Mathematically, the ADC digital output $x[k]$ at sample time k is given in Equation 11.1.

$$x[k] = \mathsf{Q}_n \{ \, x(kT) \, \}$$ (11.1)

In Equation 11.1, T is the ADC sampling period, $x(kT)$ is the input voltage V_{in} at time kT, n is the number of ADC output bits, and $\mathsf{Q}_n\{\}$ is a function that converts its argument to an integer which can be represented by n bits. The $\mathsf{Q}_n\{\}$ operation is typically performed by truncation or rounding. Because information is lost due to rounding or truncation in $\mathsf{Q}_n\{\}$, analog-to-digital conversion always introduces some error. The difference between the actual ADC input value and the value implied by the ADC's digital output is called *quantization error*, which can be made smaller by increasing the ADC's precision.

Sample Question: ***Assuming our 8-bit ADC in the prior examples performs conversion by rounding, what is the ADC output code for −7.35 V? 2.0 V? Do your answers change if the conversion is done by truncation?***

Answer: Our example 8-bit ADC compares its input voltage V_{in} against the 256 equally spaced reference voltages between −10 V and +10 V. The size of these equal spaces is the step size, or 78.125 mV. The k-th reference voltage of these 256 voltages is found by $V_{refk} = -10 + 0.078125 \, k$ V.

Examining the set of 256 reference voltages, we can easily determine that the reference voltages with $k = 34$ is −7.34375 V and $k = 35$ is −7.2656 V. Comparing the −7.35 V input voltage with the set of 256 reference voltages, we determine that the $k = 34$ reference voltage is the closest value to −7.35 V and would be selected if the conversion were done by rounding. The ADC output for −7.25 V would be 34, or 0x22.

Repeating the preceding process, we find the voltages 1.953125 V corresponding to $k = 153$, and 2.03125 V corresponding to $k = 154$. The closest value to +2.0 V is 2.03125 V. Therefore, the ADC result for +2.0 V would be 154, or 0x9A.

Truncation is the operation of always rounding toward zero. If the ADC were to truncate rather than round, the answer for the first voltage would change. The ADC result for −7.35 V would be 35, or 0x23, and the result for +2.0 V would be 154, or 0x9A.

The basic building block in nearly all ADCs is the voltage comparator. Figure 11.2 shows a voltage comparator circuit symbol. The circuitry inside a comparator can be quite complex, so we will use the comparator in Figure 11.2 as a black box.

If the positive input terminal voltage $V+$ is greater than the negative input terminal voltage $V-$, the comparator output is the comparator's positive power supply voltage V_p. If $V+$ is less than $V-$, the comparator's output is the negative supply

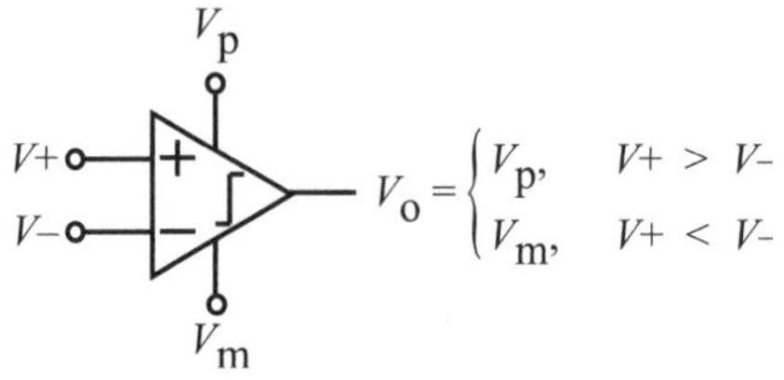

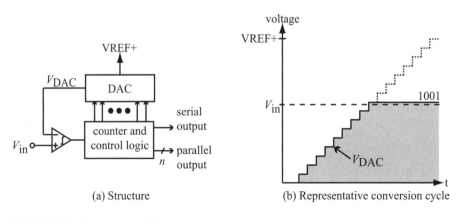

FIGURE 11.2   Voltage comparator circuit symbol and operation.

voltage V_m. Therefore, we see that if V_p = VDD and V_m = 0, the comparator in Figure 11.2 will generate a digital signal that can communicate with digital logic, like that in microprocessors. Because of this behavior, the voltage comparator is sometimes called a 1-bit ADC. By varying the comparator's input voltages $V+$ and $V-$ and using numerous comparators in different ways, an analog voltage can be compared to reference voltages and a digital number representation formed. There are many different algorithms, circuits, and configurations by which this can be done. In this section, we introduce three popular voltage-mode ADC architectures in use today: the counter-ramp ADC, the successive approximation ADC, and the flash ADC.

COUNTER-RAMP ADC

One of the simplest of the ADC architectures is the counter-ramp ADC. The structure of the counter-ramp ADC is shown in Figure 11.3a. At the beginning of the conversion, the digital counter is reset to zero. This drives the analog output of the internal DAC to zero volts. The counter is then incremented, which causes the analog output of the DAC to increase in a stair-step fashion. When the counter has

(a) Structure

(b) Representative conversion cycle

FIGURE 11.3   Counter-ramp ADC.

been clocked to a point where the DAC analog output is at a higher potential than the input voltage, V_{in}, the counter is stopped. At this time, the counter contains the digital code equivalent to the analog input voltage. This is shown graphically in Figure 11.3b. After the digital value has been determined, it may be transmitted from the counter in parallel or shifted out serially via a shift register.

Counter-ramp ADCs are not very efficient. Consider the n-bit counter-ramp ADC. Since the input may be equal to the full-scale analog reference voltage, the counter must count through all 2^n possible digital codes before the comparator stops the counter. In effect, the counter-ramp ADC performs an exhaustive search to find the nearest digital representation of the input voltage. This search will take up to 2^n clock pulses. Therefore, the n-bit counter-ramp ADC sampling at f_s samples per second must run the internal counter at $2^n f_s$ operations per second. For a large n, the internal counter clock and circuitry must be much faster than the sampling frequency. At high sampling rates with practical word sizes, the required internal circuit clock frequency becomes prohibitive. Because most signal processing applications require uniformly sampled data values, the counter-ramp ADC allocates 2^n clock cycles, the worst case, for every conversion regardless of the result. Therefore, counter-ramp ADCs find use only in the slowest applications, usually with small to moderate output word lengths.

Sample Question: ***Describe the conversion process for a 4-bit counter-ramp ADC with VREF− = 0 V, VREF+ = 4 V, and V_{in} = 3.14159 V.***

Answer: The ADC's range is 4 V. The ADC resolution is 4 V/16 = 0.25 V. Therefore, each 1 LSb increase in output corresponds to an increase in 0.25 V of input. When the conversion process begins, the counter is reset to 0b0000 and the ADC input voltage V_{in} is compared with the V_{DAC} voltage of 0 V. Since $V_{in} > 0$ V, the counter increases by 1 LSb and the input voltage is compared with the V_{DAC} voltage of 0.25 V. This comparison causes another increment in the counter. The counter continues increasing, with 0.25 V added to the V_{DAC} voltage each step, until the V_{DAC} voltage is greater than 3.14159 V. The first counter value that generates such a voltage is 0b1101, which produces $V_{DAC} = 13/16 \times 4$ V, or $V_{DAC} = 3.25$ V. This counter state occurs at the 14th cycle. The code that is output from the counter-ramp ADC is one less than this value, created by decrementing the counter to 0b1100, corresponding to $V_{DAC} = 12/16 \times 4$ V = 3.0 V. If the counter-ramp input voltage were very close to VREF+, it would require 16 cycles to generate the maximum output code of 0b1111 (when the code reaches the maximum value of 0b1111 the conversion is halted, since incrementing the counter further will cause it to wrap to 0b0000). Since the input voltage is not known, our 4-bit counter-ramp ADC must anticipate a 16-cycle conversion time.

SUCCESSIVE APPROXIMATION ADC

Like the counter-ramp ADC, the successive approximation ADC converts the analog voltage present on its input to a digital code. However, the successive approximation ADC performs the conversion in a more efficient way—a binary search. This makes the successive approximation ADC much faster than a counter-ramp ADC at a cost of increased complexity for control logic.

Consider the block diagram of an n-bit successive approximation ADC as given in Figure 11.4a. At the sample time, the ADC sets the MSb in the successive approximation register (SAR) to "1". All the remaining lower bits are reset to "0". This digital "guess" is converted back to an analog value and is compared with the input.

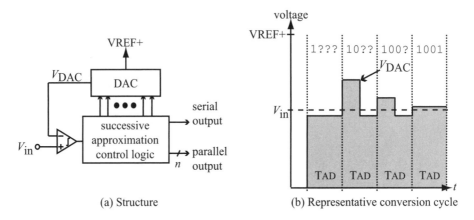

(a) Structure   (b) Representative conversion cycle

FIGURE 11.4   Successive approximation ADC.

Therefore, the SAR contains a digital code representative of mid-scale (0b100...0). The DAC produces a corresponding mid-scale analog output, which is halfway between the minimum (VREF−) and maximum voltage (VREF+) that could be presented at the ADC input. If the input is at a higher potential than the feedback analog representation of the "guess" ($V_{in} > V_{DAC}$), the MSb is left set to "1". If the input is at a lower potential than the feedback analog value, which is the case of $V_{in} < V_{DAC}$, the MSb is reset to "0". In this step, the successive approximation ADC is determining the proper state of the MSb; in other words, whether the analog input value lies in the upper (Msb = 1) or lower (Msb = 0) half of the ADC's range.

Now, the entire procedure is repeated for the second most significant bit. While the MSb is unchanged from the first approximation, the second MSb is set with the remaining lower bits reset. This digital code, an improved "guess," is converted into an analog value (V_{DAC}) and presented to the comparator. At this instant, the SAR value is either (0b1100...0) or (0b0100...0), depending on the outcome of the first approximation. If the analog input is at a higher potential than the feedback "guess" voltage, the second MSb is left at "1". If not, the second MSb is reset to "0". At the conclusion of this second approximation cycle, the two most significant bits in the register determine whether the ADC input is located in the highest (0b11), next-to-highest (0b10), next-to-lowest (0b01), or lowest (0b00) fourth of the ADC's range.

Approximation cycles continue in this manner for each of the remaining lower order bits until all n bits have been examined. At the conclusion of each cycle, the SAR digital code is converted back to an analog voltage and compared against the input voltage. In this way, each approximation halves the difference between the ADC's input and the analog representation of the contents of the SAR. This is shown graphically in Figure 11.4b.

Transmission of the digital code from the ADC may be done in two ways: serially or parallel. Each bit of the digital output code may be output from the ADC the instant it is computed. This particular flavor of successive approximation ADC is also known as the serial ADC. The digital code in the SAR may be stored for parallel transmission upon completion of the sample conversion, or transmitted serially at a later time using some defined network protocol like I^2C or SPI. When the time arises to convert the next sample, the contents of the SAR are reset and the entire procedure is repeated for the new analog voltage present on the input pin of the ADC.

A disadvantage of the successive approximation ADCs is the many internal operations that must occur for a single sample to be converted. In the n-bit converter, n approximations and comparisons must be performed in each sampling period. Therefore, an n-bit successive approximation ADC running at a sampling frequency of f_s samples per second must run its internal circuit at a rate of nf_s operations per second. However, this is much slower and cheaper to build than the

---

Sample Question: ***Describe the conversion process for a 4-bit successive approximation ADC with VREF− = 0 V, VREF+ = 4 V, and V_{in} = 3.14159 V.***

Answer: The ADC's range is 4 V. The ADC resolution is 4 V/16 = 0.25 V. Therefore, each 1 LSb increase in output corresponds to an increase in 0.25 V of input. When the conversion process begins, the SAR is set to 0b1000 and the ADC input voltage V_{in} is compared with the midrange voltage 2.0 V ($8/16 \times 4$ V). Since V_{in} > 2 V, the control logic leaves the MSb of the SAR set and sets the second MSb of the SAR. The SAR contents are now 0b1100, which represents the voltage $12/16 \times 4$ V, or 3.0 V. Because V_{in} > 3.0 V, the second MSb of the SAR is left set. The control logic sets the third MSb of the SAR, now 0b1110. The SAR contents cause the DAC to create a voltage of $14/16 \times 4$ V, or 3.5 V. Because V_{in} < 3.5 V, the control logic clears the third MSb in the SAR and sets the SAR's LSb. The SAR contents on the fourth cycle are 0b1101, which corresponds to a comparison voltage of $13/16 \times 4$, or 3.25 V. The comparator determines V_{in} < 3.25 V, so the LSb is cleared. The 4-bit digital result 0b1100 is computed in four cycles.

required rate of the counter-ramp ADC, especially for a large *n*. For a given sampling rate, the successive approximation ADC can convert with greater resolution than the counter-ramp ADC. The successive approximation ADC iteratively cuts the voltage range in half as it searches for the digital representation of the input voltage. This binary search is more efficient and faster than the exhaustive search of the counter-ramp ADC, but it also gives the successive approximation ADC a more complex architecture.

Flash ADC

The counter-ramp ADC determines the output by examining each quantization level (2^n maximum operations), while the successive approximation ADC examines each bit (*n* operations). However, the flash ADC generates all of the output bits in one operation and thus has a speed advantage over the previous two architectures. This speed does come with a drawback—complexity. The flash ADC distributes the sampling process across the entire circuit. This requires much more circuitry as a result. The structure of a flash ADC circuit is shown in Figure 11.5.

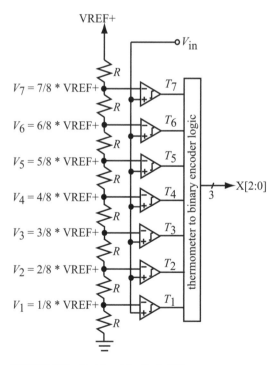

FIGURE 11.5   Resistor string flash ADC.

An n-bit flash ADC contains 2^n resistors, 2^n-1 comparators, and digital encoder logic. Referring to Figure 11.5, the string of resistors from the reference voltage to ground constructs a voltage divider. Assuming that all 2^n voltage divider resistors have the same resistance, the divider generates 2^n analog voltages between ground and the reference voltage. These analog voltages correspond to the points on the ADC transfer curve at which there is no quantization error. These analog voltages are the ones that the output codes of the ADC represent in digital form. Each of 2^n voltage divider levels is the reference voltage input for their respective comparators. The comparators' other input is the flash ADC's input voltage, V_{in}. The output of the comparators is a *thermometer code* of the input voltage, V_{in}. It is named this because of its resemblance to a mercury thermometer.

Consider the case when $V_{i+1} \leq V_{in} \leq V_i$. The outputs of the comparators, T_j, T_{j-1}, ..., T_1, T_0, will be "1", while the outputs, T_{j+1}, T_{j+2}, ..., T_{2^n-1}, will be "0". Therefore, the outputs of the comparators will rise and fall with the input voltage, V_{in}. In similar fashion, the mercury level in a thermometer tracks the temperature.

Obviously, the large number of bits in the thermometer code is not an efficient representation of the value. It is the function of the encoder to "compact" the information to an efficient representation. The encoder logic accepts the 2^n bits of the thermometer code and outputs the n-bit binary number corresponding to the number of "1"s in the thermometer code. This may be done a number of ways. The logic may be designed to "look" for the most significant bit in the thermometer code and output the binary number corresponding to that input line, much in the same way as a demultiplexer. However, this method is sensitive to errors in the comparators' thermometer code, called sparkles. In ideal operation, the thermometer code consists of consecutive "1"s in the lower comparator outputs from T_1 to T_j. For all comparators from T_{j+1} to T_{2^n-1}, the outputs are "0". A comparator output, which is erroneous and causes a departure from this pattern, is called a sparkle. Depending on the method of thermometer-binary encoding, sparkles may lead to gross errors in the output digital code of the ADC. To exacerbate matters, high-speed timing uncertainties may cause multiple sparkles to appear throughout the thermometer code. Various circuit techniques may be applied to suppress the effects of sparkles, such as comparing neighboring bits in the thermometer code, using Gray codes or thermometer code bit summing.

Despite these drawbacks, flash ADCs are extremely attractive because of their high speed. Since all output bits are determined at the same time, a flash ADC with a sampling rate of f_s samples per second runs at f_s operations per second. Thus, flash ADCs only need more circuitry to increase the output code word size. However, the number of comparators and resistors will double for each additional bit of output. Furthermore, the complexity of the thermometer-to-binary encoder logic also increases with the number of output bits. Because of their fast operation, flash ADCs are typically used in high-speed, small word length applications, such as digital video, radar, and digital test and measurement equipment.

Sample Question: ***Describe the conversion process for a 4-bit resistor string flash ADC with VREF− = 0 V, VREF+ = 4 V, and V_{in} = 3.14159 V.***

Answer: The ADC's range is 4 V. The ADC resolution is 4 V/16 = 0.25 V. Therefore, the 16 resistor string reference voltages are 0.25 V, 0.50 V, 0.75 V, …, 3.25 V, 3.5 V, and 3.75 V. Each of the 15 reference voltages is compared with V_{in} simultaneously. The lower 12 comparator outputs (up to and including the comparator with the 3.0 V reference voltage) are "1", and the upper three comparator outputs (comparators with 3.25 V, 3.5 V and 3.75 V references) are "0". The thermometer to binary encoder will represent the thermometer code with 12 ones by 0b1100. The flash ADC results are available in one cycle, the time for the comparator output to become stable plus the encoder delay.

SAMPLE AND HOLD AMPLIFIERS

The preceding sections introduced you to three common ADC architectures. A great many more ADC architectures exist and are detailed in books listed in Appendix F. The ADCs we have examined so far are only half of the conversion process from an analog voltage to a digital number. In fact, the conversion step that the ADC performs is the last half of the process. The first half of the process is the *sample and hold amplifier* (SHA), which we introduce in this section.

In our three ADC architectures and the dozens of others detailed in other books, the ADC's input voltage, V_{in}, must be perfectly stable or constant during the ADC conversion cycle. If the ADC input voltage V_{in} changes during the conversion step, the digital code value will likely be incorrect. The purpose of the SHA is to *sample,* or track, the voltage to be converted, and, at the appropriate time, *hold* that voltage value constant while the ADC converts the voltage into the correct digital code. Figure 11.6 shows a circuit schematic symbol for an SHA along with an example waveform showing the SHA's operation.

As seen in Figure 11.6, the SHA will sample its input voltage, V_a (represented by the solid line) while its control signal S/H# = 1. During this "sampling" phase of operation, the SHA output, V_b (represented by the upper extent of the shaded area), will track the SHA input, i.e., $V_b = V_a$. When the SHA's control signal S/H# = 0, the SHA enters the "holding" phase of operation. While holding, the SHA output voltage, V_b, is held constant at the voltage value that V_b had at the time of the falling edge of S/H#. During the hold phase, the SHA input can change over a wide range of values, but V_b will remain constant. During several hold phases in Figure 11.6b, we can see that the voltage V_a continues to change while V_b stays constant. Obviously, when the SHA control signal changes to S/H# = 1 again, the

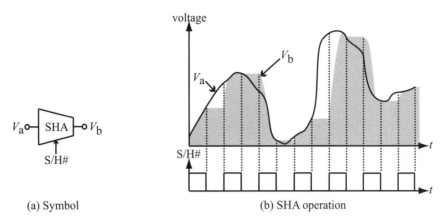

(a) Symbol (b) SHA operation

FIGURE 11.6 Sample and hold amplifier (SHA) operation.

SHA is expected to start tracking a voltage V_a, which is dramatically different than the voltage that it was just holding. Under these conditions, the SHA will require a non-zero period of time for its output to start tracking accurately. This particular scenario is seen at several places in Figure 11.6. The amount of time required for the SHA output to accurately track the SHA input is a function of the SHA circuit design. If the SHA is ordered to "hold" before the tracking is accurate, the SHA output value, V_b, will be held constant at an erroneous voltage. If the SHA output is to represent accurately the SHA input, the SHA must be given adequate time to catch up with the SHA input voltage during the sample mode of operation.

The SHA can be viewed as an "analog transparent latch" during the sample phase and an "analog flip-flop" during the hold phase. The actual construction of the SHA circuit is as diverse as the circuits for ADCs. The interested reader is again referred to the references in Appendix F.

The usefulness of SHAs to the analog-to-digital conversion process should be readily apparent at this point. The voltage that you desire to convert to a digital code may be changing very rapidly, but the conversion process takes some amount of time. (The amount of time depends on your ADC architecture, of course.) Whatever ADC architecture you use, the ADC must have a constant voltage on which to operate. Therefore, nearly all practical analog-to-digital conversion integrated circuits contain an SHA circuit followed by an ADC circuit. The SHA samples the input voltage for a sufficient duration to insure that the SHA tracks the voltage perfectly. At this point, the SHA will hold the voltage for the time period required by subsequent ADC conversion to determine the correct digital code that represents the held voltage. When the ADC conversion is complete, the SHA is free to start sampling the input voltage again in preparation for the next conversion.

Now that we have examined the two main operations in converting a voltage to a digital code and three example ADC architectures, we will investigate the analog-to-digital converter peripheral in the Microchip PIC24HJ32GP202 microcontroller.

THE PIC24 ANALOG-TO-DIGITAL CONVERTER

ADCs are used in so many small microprocessors and embedded systems that they are often included as a built-in peripheral. Microchip made just such a decision with their PIC24 family of microprocessors. Each member of the PIC24 microcontroller family includes a multiple-channel successive approximation ADC. The PIC24 microcontroller ADC peripheral can convert analog voltages into 10-bit or 12-bit digital codes. The word length of the ADC output is determined by the user. The number of available ADC input channels depends on the device and package chosen by the designer. For example, the PIC24HJ64GP206 and PIC24HJ256GP206 are available in 64-pin packages and provide 18 different input channels to their ADCs. The PIC24HJ64GP510 and PIC24HJ256GP610 are available in 100-pin packages and provide 32 different input channels to their ADCs. The PIC24HJ12GP202, PIC24HJ32GP202, and PIC24HJ64GP202 devices are only available in 28-pin packages. With such a limited number of package pins, these devices only support ten different input channels to the internal ADC peripheral. Other PIC24 µC devices provide 6–32 input channels to the ADC. The required differences in using the PIC24 µC's internal ADC between the different devices are usually minor and well documented in the data sheets. The remainder of this section focuses on the PIC24HJ32GP202 device and the configuration and operation of its ADC.

Just like the other PIC24 µC peripherals (USART, interrupt, SPI) that were previously covered, the PIC24 µC's internal ADC is controlled by a number of dedicated configuration, enable, and flag register bits. Since the ADC input connections are fundamentally analog values and must be treated differently than digital values, the external pins (ANx) that connect to the ADC are restricted to specific external pin locations. These ADC inputs cannot be remapped like many of the PIC24 µC's digital peripherals. Different PIC24 µC devices have the same basic ADC operation; they only differ in the number of analog input channels available for conversion and the availability of direct memory access (DMA) support (discussed in Chapter 13). Figure 11.7 shows a simplified block diagram of the PIC24 ADC system. The PIC24HJ32GP202 devices support analog input channels AN0-AN5 and AN9-AN12 on package pins RA0-RA1, RB0-RB3, and RB12-15, and do not have DMA support.

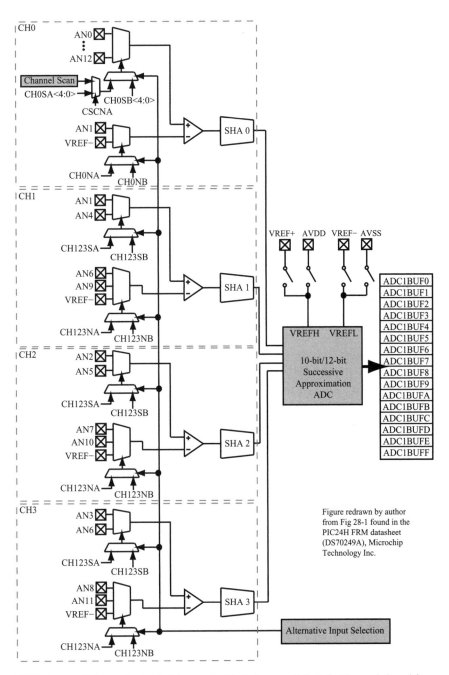

FIGURE 11.7   PIC24 analog-to-digital converter block diagram. (Adapted with permission of the copyright owner, Microchip Technology, Incorporated. All rights reserved. No further reprints or reproduction may be made without Microchip Inc.'s prior written consent.)

The PIC24 ADC peripheral is extremely flexible in its configuration. The features of the PIC24 ADC include (this list is not exhaustive):

■ convert voltage to 10-bit or 12-bit representations;
■ convert single-ended voltages–a voltage measured with respect to ground;
■ convert differential voltages–a voltage difference between two arbitrary voltages;
■ convert voltages on 1–32 ADC input channels;
■ sample ADC input channels sequentially, two channels simultaneously, or four channels simultaneously;
■ encode ADC output results as unsigned integer, signed integer, unsigned fractional, or signed fractional numbers;
■ use internal or external ADC reference voltages;
■ generate "ADC completion" interrupts every 1–16th sample;
■ supports ADC operation timing and sequencing under user software control, automatic timing from an internal ADC timer or one of the PIC24 timer peripherals.

Some of the PIC24 ADC options just listed are mutually exclusive. However, most of the PIC24 ADC options are independent of the others. The number of combinations of PIC24 ADC configurations is enormous, and we cannot hope to possibly examine each one. Therefore, this chapter starts with a basic PIC24 ADC configuration using only one sample channel with ADC operations being mostly automatic. In subsequent discussion, we alter a few ADC configuration parameters to examine a few of the more useful ones. Then, we present a very brief description of each of the ADC configuration register bits for your further investigation.

In practice, the PIC24 ADC configuration you need is likely to be different from those presented here. You are encouraged to read and study the data sheets for your device carefully.

PIC24 ADC Configuration

The PIC24 ADC peripheral has several different fundamental configuration options that drastically change the ADC operation. One of these fundamental options is whether the PIC24 ADC converts to a 10-bit or 12-bit result. Several other fundamental configuration options deal with the timing source and sequence of sample-and-hold and conversion operations. These options must be determined and set before you power up the PIC24 ADC module. If you attempt to change these fundamental configuration options when the ADC module is on, the behavior is indeterminate.

The PIC24 ADC subsystem, like others found on the PIC24 μC, uses special function registers in two different ways: either as *data registers* or as *control registers*.

The ADC subsystem data registers are for transferring ADC result data from the successive approximation register to the user's data memory. ADC control registers contain a mixture of *configuration* and *status* bits. Configuration bits specify the operating mode of the subsystem, while status bits indicate the operational state of the subsystem. Future implementations of the PIC24 µCs can have multiple ADCs with identical capabilities, so the ADC register names have a number (x) that designates its associated ADCx. For example, register ADxCON1 is one of the ADC control registers, and its name for ADC1 is AD1CON1. Our code refers to named bits in ADC registers by their fully qualified structure reference (*register.bitname*) to make the functions portable to PIC24 microcontrollers with multiple ADCs, which do not have macros defined for individual ADC register bits. The PIC24HJ32GP202 used in our reference system and all currently available members of the PIC24 family have only one ADC. Therefore, we will discuss the PIC24 ADC subsystem using the first ADC, which is named AD1 or ADC1 in the data sheets.

We will start our ADC configuration example with 12-bit operation. Since we chose a 12-bit result, only one of the four SHAs in the PIC24 ADC subsystems can be used due to a limitation of the PIC24 µC ADC. The four SHA channels are named CH0, CH1, CH2, and CH3. In the 12-bit mode, only channel CH0 can be used. If we were to select a 10-bit result, the ADC can "sample" one (CH0), two (CH0 and CH1), or four (CH0, CH1, CH2, and CH3) voltages simultaneously. To select 12-bit conversions, we set AD1CON1.AD12B. Setting this bit results in a 12-bit successive approximation conversion process on the voltage being sampled and held by CH0. Figure 11.8 shows the location of the AD12B bit and the other bits in the AD1CON1 register.

The PIC24 ADC subsystem allows you, the programmer, to have a great deal of control over the conversion process. As we saw in the previous sections, the input voltage of interest must be sampled and held constant by the SHA. While the voltage is held, the successive approximation algorithm must clock through each bit of the result making the necessary comparisons. The PIC24 ADC allows the user to completely determine the timing of the sample, hold, and conversion steps. The PIC24 ADC also provides several semi-automatic and automatic configurations whereby the ADC subsystem proceeds from sample to hold to conversion steps. The progress of the ADC conversion cycle can be monitored by two bits: AD1CON1. SAMP and AD1CON1.DONE. The AD1CON1.SAMP bit is "1" when the SHAs are sampling and "0" when the SHAs are holding. The AD1CON1.DONE bit is "0" when the successive approximation conversion process is ongoing or not yet started and "1" when the conversion process is completed. The AD1CON1.DONE bit is automatically set by hardware when the conversion is completed and cleared by hardware when a new conversion starts.

The PIC24 ADC requires a clock source to control the timing between the sampling phase and the holding/converting phase. Furthermore, we learned earlier in

R/W-0	U-0	R/W-0	U-0	U-0	R/W-0	R/W-0	R/W-0
ADON	UI	ADSIDL	UI	UI	AD12B	FORM<1:0>	
15	14	13	12	11	10	9	8

R/W-0	R/W-0	R/W-0	U-0	R/W-0	R/W-0	R/W-0	R/W-0
SSRC<2:0>			UI	SIMSAM	ASAM	SAMP	DONE
7	6	5	4	3	2	1	0

Bit 15: ADON: Enable ADC module.

1 = ADC module is on.

0 = ADC module is off.

Figure redrawn by author from Register 28-1 found in the PIC24H FRM datasheet (DS70249A), Microchip Technology Inc.

These bits can also be set and cleared by hardware

Bit 13: ADSIDL: Stop in idle mode bit

1 = Discontinue ADC operation in idle mode.

0 = Continue ADC operation in idle mode.

Bit 10: AD12B: 10-bit or 12-bit operation mode select bit

1 = 12-bit, 1-channel ADC operation; 0 = 10-bit, multiple-channel ADC operation

Bit 9-8: FORM<1:0> Data output format bits

10-bit mode (AD12B=0)	12-bit mode (AD12B=1)
1x = reserved	11 = Signed fractional
01 = Signed integer	10 = Unsigned fractional
00 = Unsigned integer	01 = Signed integer
	00 = Unsigned integer

Bit 7-5: SSRC<2:0> Sample clock source select bits

111 = Internal counter ends sampling and starts conversion.

110 = reserved

10x = reserved

011 = reserved

010 = General-purpose timer compare ends sampling and starts conversion.

001 = Active transition on INT0 pin ends sampling and starts conversion.

000 = Clearing sample bit ends sampling and starts conversion.

Bit 2: ASAM: ADC sample auto-start bit

1 = Sampling begins immediately after last conversion (SAMP bit is set automatically).

0 = Sampling begins when SAMP bit is set.

Bit 1: SAMP: Sample enable/status bit

1 = ADC sample-and-hold amplifiers are sampling.

0 = ADC sample-and-hold amplifiers are holding.

NOTES:

If ASAM=0, write '1' to begin sampling. Automatically set by hardware if ASAM=1. If SSRC=000, write '0' to end sampling. Automatically cleared by hardware otherwise.

Bit 0: DONE: ADC conversion status bit

1 = ADC conversion cycle is complete.

0 = ADC conversion cycle is not started or in progress.

Bit 3: SIMSAM: Simultaneous sample select bit (10-bit mode only)

1 = Samples CH0, CH1, CH2, and CH3 simultaneously (when ADxCON2.CHPS<1:0>=1x), or samples CH0 and CH1 simultaneously (when ADxCON2.CHPS<1:0>=01).

0 = Sample multiple channels sequentially.

FIGURE 11.8   The AD1CON1 configuration register. (Adapted with permission of the copyright owner, Microchip Technology, Incorporated. All rights reserved. No further reprints or reproduction may be made without Microchip Inc.'s prior written consent.)

this chapter that successive approximation ADCs require a clock to control the converter's successive approximation control logic. The PIC24 ADC clock can be generated from the PIC24 instruction clock. This choice gives us great flexibility and control over the successive approximation timing. However, the instruction clock can easily generate a clock that is too fast for the PIC24 ADC. The PIC24 ADC has its own internal RC oscillator to provide a timer to control the SHA operations and create the required clock cycles for the successive approximation algorithm. The ADC's internal RC oscillator is a great choice since it is guaranteed to generate a clock signal adequate to work with the PIC24 ADC hardware. The internal ADC clock runs independently of the PIC24 instruction clock. Therefore, if you plan on performing any ADC operations during sleep mode, the internal ADC clock is your only choice. We will select the ADC's internal RC clock by setting the AD1CON3.ADRC bit. Data sheets for the PIC24 μC indicate that the ADC internal RC clock generates a clock with a period TAD that is approximately equal to 250 ns. Figure 11.9 shows the location of the ADRC bit and of the other configuration bits in the AD1CON3 register.

R/W-0	U-0	U-0	R/W-0	R/W-0	R/W-0	R/W-0	R/W-0
ADRC	UI	UI	\<td colspan=5 align=center\>SAMC\<4:0\>				
15	14	13	12	11	10	9	8
R/W-0	R/W-0	R/W-0	R/W-0	R/W-0	R/W-0	R/W-0	R/W-0
ADCS\<7:0\>							
7	6	5	4	3	2	1	0

Bit 15:   ADRC: ADC Conversion Clock Select
 1 = ADC Internal RC Clock drives successive approximation converter.
 0 = Clock derived from system clock drives successive approximation converter.
Bit 8-12: SAMC\<4:0\>: Auto Sample Time Select bits
 NOTE: SAMC\<4:0\> used when ADxCON1.ASAM=1.
 11111 = Automatic sampling duration is 31 TAD.
 11110 = Automatic sampling duration is 30 TAD.
   ⋮
 00010 = Automatic sampling duration is 2 TAD.
 00001 = Automatic sampling duration is 1 TAD.
 00000 = Automatic sampling duration is 0 TAD.
Bit 0-7: ADCS\<7:0\>: ADC Conversion Clock Select bits
 NOTE: ADCS\<7:0\> is used when ADxCON3.ADRC = 0.
 11111111 = Use TAD = 256 TCY.
 11111110 = Use TAD = 255 TCY.
   ⋮
 00000010 = Use TAD = 3 TCY.
 00000001 = Use TAD = 2 TCY.
 00000000 = Use TAD = 1 TCY.

$$T_{AD} = (ADCS\langle 7:0 \rangle + 1)\ T_{CY}$$

Figure redrawn by author from Reg. 28-3 found in the PIC24 FRM datasheet (DS70249A), Microchip Technology Inc.

FIGURE 11.9   The AD1CON3 configuration register. (Adapted with permission of the copyright owner, Microchip Technology, Incorporated. All rights reserved. No further reprints or reproduction may be made without Microchip Inc.'s prior written consent.)

Since our example configuration will have the ADC subsystem automatically progress from sample to hold to convert operations, we must instruct the PIC24 ADC how long to sample the voltage before switching to hold then converting. The time between start of sampling and the start of conversion is determined by SAMC<4:0> in the AD1CON3 register. This five-bit number selects the sample time to be in the range of 0 to 31 T_{AD}. The PIC24FH32GP202 ADC peripheral requires the sample time to be greater than 2 T_{AD} in 10-bit ADC mode and greater than 3 T_{AD} in 12-bit ADC mode. In this example, we will be conservative and set AD1CON3.SAMC<4:0> = 31, or approximately 31 × 250 ns = 7.75 µs. This should be adequate time for the PIC24 SHA to acquire an accurate copy of the ADC input voltage.

To instruct the ADC subsystem to automatically switch from sample mode to "hold and convert" mode based on this 31 T_{AD} time interval, we must set the SSRC<2:0> bits in AD1CON1 equal to 7. The other values for AD1CON3.SSRC<2:0> allow software, an external interrupt, or general-purpose timers to determine the transition timing from sample to conversion. We will discuss these later in the chapter.

The successive approximation hardware must have negative and positive voltage references against which it can compare the voltage being held by the SHA. These two voltages were called VREF− and VREF+ in our discussions earlier. The PIC24 ADC subsystem allows you to determine the source of these two voltages by the VCFG<2:0> bits in AD1CON2. In our example, setting AD1CON2.VCFG<2:0> to 0 will set the ADC's VREF− = AVSS and VREF+ = AVDD. The voltages AVSS and AVDD are provided through dedicated pins on the PIC24 µC package. Figure 11.10 shows the location of the VCFG bits and the other configuration bits in the AD1CON2 register.

The ADC in the PIC24FH32GP202 can sample and convert up to 10 voltages. Other PIC24 µC models can convert between 6 and 32 input channels depending on the processor model and package. We must select the appropriate external voltage to provide to the SHA in the ADC subsystem. Since we are performing a 12-bit ADC conversion, we must use CH0 in the ADC subsystem. The register AD1CHS0 selects the source of the voltages presented to the SHA in the CH0 path. Refer to Figure 11.7. If we wish to apply the voltage on pin AN0 to our ADC, we need to set AD1CHS0.CH0SA<4:0> = 0x01, and clear the AD1CHS0.CH0NA bit in AD1CHS0. This will apply the voltage V_{AN0} on the AN0 pin to the positive input of the SHA and the voltage VREF− = AVSS to the negative input of the SHA. These settings in the AD1CHS0 register will configure our ADC to convert the "single-ended" voltage V_{AN0}. The astute reader will see that setting the AD1CHS0.CH0NA bit will place the voltage V_{AN1} at the AN1 pin on the negative input of the SHA, thereby allowing for a "differential" conversion of the voltage, $V_{AN0} - V_{AN1}$. The bits in the upper byte of the AD1CHS0 register are for an alternative setting mode that

R/W-0	R/W-0	R/W-0	U-0	U-0	R/W-0	R/W-0	R/W-0
VCFG<2:0>			UI	UI	CSCNA	CHPS<1:0>	
15	14	13	12	11	10	9	8
R/W-0	U-0	R/W-0	R/W-0	R/W-0	R/W-0	R/W-0	R/W-0
BUFS	UI	SMPI<3:0>				BUFM	ALTS
7	6	5	4	3	2	1	0

Bits 13-15: VCFG<2:0>: Converter Reference Voltage Configuration bits
  1xx = Use VREFH = AVDD   and VREFL = AVSS
  011 = Use VREFH = External VREF+ and VREFL = External VREF−
  010 = Use VREFH = AVDD   and VREFL = External VREF−
  001 = Use VREFH = External VREF+ and VREFL = AVSS
  000 = Use VREFH = AVDD   and VREFL = AVSS

Figure redrawn by author from Register 28-2 found in the PIC24 FRM datasheet (DS70249A), Microchip Technology Inc.

Bit 10: CSCNA: Input Scan Select bit
  1 = Scan inputs for positive CH0 input during Sample A phase.
  0 = Do not scan inputs.
Bits 9-8: CHPS<1:0>: Channel Select bits (10-bit mode only)
  1x = Convert CH0, CH1, CH2, and CH3.
  01 = Convert CH0 and CH1.
  00 = Convert CH0.
Bit 7: BUFS: Buffer Fill Status bit (only valid when BUFM = 1)
  1 = ADC is currently filling 2nd half of ADxBUFn register array. Read from 1st half.
  0 = ADC is currently filling 1st half of ADxBUFn register array. Read from 2nd half.
Bits 5-2: SMPI<3:0>: Increment Rate Configuration bits
  1111 = Generate interrupt after completion of every 16th conversion.
  1110 = Generate interrupt after completion of every 15th conversion.
  ⋮
  0010 = Generate interrupt after completion of every 3rd conversion.
  0001 = Generate interrupt after completion of every 2nd conversion.
  0000 = Generate interrupt after completion of every conversion.

NOTE: The setting in SMPI<3:0> will increment the DMA address appropriately in parts with the DMA peripheral. See PIC24 Family Reference Manual for more information.

Bit 1: BUFM: Buffer Fill Mode Select bit
  1 = Start buffer filling in the first half of ADxBUFn register array on first interrupt, and
      in second half of ADxBUFn register array on next interrupt.
  0 = Always start filling in the first half of ADxBUFn register array
Bit 0: ALTS: Alternate Input Sample Mode Select bit
  1 = Use "Sample A" set of inputs on the first sample, and "Sample B" set of inputs on next sample.
  0 = Always use "Sample A" set of inputs.
NOTE: See upper and lower bytes in ADxCON.CHS0 and ADxCON.CHS123 registers.

FIGURE 11.10 The AD1CON2 configuration register. (Adapted with permission of the copyright owner, Microchip Technology, Incorporated. All rights reserved. No further reprints or reproduction may be made without Microchip Inc.'s prior written consent.)

we will discuss later in the chapter. Figure 11.11 shows the location of the ADRC bit and the other configuration bits in the AD1CHS0 register.

It is extremely important to mention at this point that any ADC channel or ADC voltage reference that is enabled should have its corresponding port direction (TRISx) bit set. This configures the package pin to be an input. If this bit is cleared (output mode), the PIC24 ADC will attempt to use the driven pin voltage (V_{OL} or V_{OH} in the data sheet) as the ADC input or ADC voltage reference. This is

R/W-0	U-0	U-0	R/W-0	R/W-0	R/W-0	R/W-0	R/W-0
CH0NB	UI	UI	CH0SB<4:0>				
15	14	13	12	11	10	9	8
R/W-0	U-0	U-0	R/W-0	R/W-0	R/W-0	R/W-0	R/W-0
CH0NA	UI	UI	CH0SA<4:0>				
7	6	5	4	3	2	1	0

Bit 15: CH0NB: Select Negative Input for CH0 SHA for Sample B bits.
1 = CH0 negative input is AN1.
0 = CH0 negative input is VREFL.
Bit 8-11: CH0SB<4:0>: Select Positive Input for CH0 SHA for Sample B bits.
01100 = CH1 positive input is AN12.
01011 = CH1 positive input is AN11.
⋮
00010 = CH1 positive input is AN2.
00001 = CH1 positive input is AN1.
00000 = CH1 positive input is AN0.
Bit 7: CH0NA: Select Negative Input for CH0 SHA for Sample A bits.
1 = CH0 negative input is AN1.
0 = CH0 negative input is VREFL.
Bit 0-4: CH0SA<4:0>: Select Positive Input for CH0 SHA for Sample A bits.
01100 = CH1 positive input is AN12.
01011 = CH1 positive input is AN11.
⋮
00010 = CH1 positive input is AN2.
00001 = CH1 positive input is AN1.
00000 = CH1 positive input is AN0.

Figure redrawn by author from Register 28-5 found in the PIC24 FRM datasheet (DS70249A), Microchip Technology Inc.

NOTE:
PIC24 MCUs without DMA can support up 12 channels. PIC24 MCUs with DMA-enabled ADCs can support up to 32 channels. Valid values for CH0SA<4:0> and CH0SB<4:0> change accordingly. See the PIC24 Family Reference Manual for more information.

FIGURE 11.11 The AD1CHS0 configuration register. (Aadapted with permission of the copyright owner, Microchip Technology, Incorporated. All rights reserved. No further reprints or reproduction may be made without Microchip Inc.'s prior written consent.)

seldom desired or useful. Furthermore, if the analog input voltage pin is a change notification (CN*x*) pin, the weak CN pull-up resistor must be disabled by clearing the appropriate bit in the CNPU*x* register to avoid corrupting the sensitive analog voltage value. The macro CONFIG_AN*x*_AS_ANALOG() performs these steps, where *x* is the analog input number (e.g., CONFIG_AN9_AS_ANALOG()).

The AD1CON1.ASAM bit selects the condition that starts the sampling process. In our example case, initiation of the sampling process automatically proceeds, at a time 31 T$_{AD}$ later, to the conversion mode. The PIC24 successive approximation hardware requires 14 T$_{AD}$ to compute our 12-bit result and set the AD1CON1.DONE bit. Therefore, if we can initiate the sampling operation by setting AD1CON1.SAMP, our ADC result will become available after the process runs its course.

Finally, after the PIC24 ADC subsystem has been fully configured to convert the voltage on the AN0 pin, we can turn on the ADC module. This is done by setting the AD1CON1.ADON bit. When AD1CON1.ADON = 1, the entire ADC module is enabled, powered up, and consuming power. When AD1CON1.ADON = 0, the ADC module is disabled and does not consume power. If the ADC module is not being used, the ADC should be turned off, which is the setting after reset.

Figure 11.12 shows a function to perform our ADC configuration as just described. There are slight differences between the function in Figure 11.12 and the previous discussion. First, the function in Figure 11.12 begins by turning the AD1 module "off." This step is required by the PIC24 µC data sheets, which specify that the ADC behavior is indeterminate if any of the timing, clock source, or auto-sampling bits are modified while the ADC is enabled. Secondly, the function in Figure 11.12 has an argument that is used to select the positive input voltage for CH0 (parameter `u16_ch0PositiveMask` which is copied to the AD1CHS0.CHS0A<4:0> bits), which effectively determines the external pin that provides the voltage to convert. Useful `#define` macros for the AD1CHS0.CHS0A<4:0> bit values are provided in the *include\pic24_adc.h* file. For example, the function in Figure 11.12 can be used to configure the AD1 peripheral to sample and convert the voltage on the AN0 pin with a 12-bit result by simply calling `configADC1_ManualCH0(ADC_CH0_POS_SAMPLEA_AN0, 31, 1)`.

```
void configADC1_ManualCH0(uint16 u16_ch0PositiveMask,  \
                          uint8 u8_autoSampleTime,      \
                          uint8 u8_use12bits) {

  if (u8_autoSampleTime > 31) u8_autoSampleTime=31;
  AD1CON1bits.ADON = 0;

  AD1CON1 = ADC_CLK_AUTO | ADC_AUTO_SAMPLING_OFF;
  if (u8_use12bit)
      AD1CON1bits.AD12B = 1;
  else
      AD1CON1bits.AD12B = 0;
  AD1CON2 = ADC_VREF_AVDD_AVSS;
  AD1CHS0 = ADC_CH0_NEG_SAMPLEA_VREFN | u16_ch0PositiveMask;
  AD1CON3 = ADC_CONV_CLK_INTERNAL_RC | (u8_autoSampleTime<<8);
  AD1CON1bits.ADON = 1;
}
```

Limit `u8_autoSampleTime` to range from 0 to 31.

ADC must be off when changing configuration

Start conversions automatically after sampling and configure ADC to either 10 or 12 bits.

Turn configured ADC on.

Set CH0 SHA to sample the voltage on AN*x* referenced to GND.

Use ADC internal clock and set "auto-sample" time from function argument.

FIGURE 11.12   ADC configuration function for manual single-channel sample and conversion.

PIC24 ADC Operation: Manual

After the PIC24 ADC channel, reference voltages, and conversion clock have been properly configured, the PIC24 ADC is ready to convert the analog voltage on the PIC24 μC package pin into a 12-bit digital number. Using the configuration described previously and the function in Figure 11.12, we simply need to set the AD1CON1.SAMP bit to start the sampling processing. The AD1CON1.DONE bit is cleared to indicate that the conversion is in progress. Because we used the ADC's internal RC clock and configured AD1CON3.SAMC<4:0> bits, the voltage will be sampled for 31 TAD. After this time, the ADC's SHA will automatically hold the voltage and a 12-bit successive approximation process will begin. This transition from sampling to hold-and-convert is automatic because of our settings in the AD1CON1.SSRC<2:0> bits. After 14 TAD, our 12-bit ADC result is ready, and the AD1CON1.DONE bit is set. At this point, the ADC peripheral will return to its inactive but powered-up mode.

Since AD1CON1.DONE=1 denotes a completed conversion, we have a simple way of determining when our ADC result is available. Figure 11.13 gives a function convertADC1() that will initiate the voltage sampling and conversion process and return the result to the caller. This function and several other useful PIC24 ADC functions are located in *common\pic24_adc.c*. Like the library functions introduced in previous chapters, this function relies on several useful macros to make code more readable and maintainable. These macros can be found in the *include\pic24_adc.h* file. The first macro SET_SAMP_BIT_AD1() is simply the *C* language statement AD1CON1.SAMP=1. The macro WAIT_UNTIL_CONVERSION_COMPLETE_ADC1() implements the following wait loop:

```
while(!AD1CON1.DONE) {
    doHeartBeat();
}
```

After the AD1CON1.DONE bit is set, convertADC1() returns a uint16 value to the calling function.

```
uint16 convertADC1(void) {                           Save current WDT state, and
  uint8 u8_wdtState;                                  prepare to use WDT since this
                                                      routine has a blocking statement.
  sz_lastTimeoutError = "convertADC1()";
  u8_wdtState = _SWDTEN;  _SWDTEN = 1;                Start sampling phase. Conversion
  SET_SAMP_BIT_ADC1();                                will auto-start after sampling.
  WAIT_UNTIL_CONVERSION_COMPLETE_ADC1();             Block until conversion is finished.
  _SWDTEN = u8_wdtState;                              Restore WDT to its prior state.
  sz_lastTimeoutError = NULL;
  return(ADC1BUF0);                                  Return ADC results to caller.
}
```

FIGURE 11.13 Subroutine to convert a single ADC channel.

At this point, we should discuss the format of the ADC result. The result of the ADC conversion is 12 bits and is found in the 16-bit AD1BUF0 register. The result's format is determined by the AD1CON.FORM<1:0> bits. The function in Figure 11.12 clears these bits, so we expect our 12-bit result to be an unsigned integer, which is effectively the same as right-justified. Three other ADC result formats are available.

A *potentiometer*, often called a pot, is a variable resistor and is one of the simplest ways to generate various analog voltages. A potentiometer usually has three terminals. Between two terminals is the potentiometer's full resistance, typically a round number like 1 kΩ, 10 kΩ, or 50 kΩ. The potentiometer's third terminal is connected to the pot's *wiper*. The resistance between the wiper terminal and the other pot terminals changes as you turn the pot's knob. Potentiometers are often used as an input on a device's front panel when there is a need to allow the user to enter a fine-grain adjustable value. Figure 11.14a shows how the PIC24 µC can be connected to two potentiometers. The two capacitors connected to the pot wiper terminals are not required, but are helpful in reducing noise and for providing a more stable voltage at the PIC24 ADC input pins.

Figure 11.14b shows the code used to read the voltage from both potentiometers and display the digital code and voltages on the screen via the serial interface. The library functions used in the serial interface are found in Chapter 10 and are not discussed here. Upon entering `main()`, the first line of C code initializes the PIC24 µC oscillator and UART subsystem. The next two C lines configure the PIC24 AN0 and AN1 pins to be used in analog mode. During the `while(1)` loop, the code configures the ADC to perform a single conversion from the AN0 pin, then the ADC is configured to perform a single conversion on the AN1 pin. These operations are done via the pair of function calls: `configADC1_ManualCH0()` and `convertADC1()`. Each ADC result is saved into a `uint16` variable. Before the `while(1)` loops back for another iteration, each ADC result value is converted to its corresponding voltage value, and the results are printed to the screen via the

---

Sample Question: *What is the smallest voltage that the PIC24 µC circuit in Figure 11.14 can resolve?*

Answer: The code in Figure 11.14 initializes the ADC to perform a 12-bit conversion with VREF+ = VDD and VREF− = AVSS. The analog supply values in the schematic in Figure 11.14 are connected to the digital supplies. If the PIC24 µC power supply VDD = 3.3 V, the PIC24 ADC's resolution is (3.3 V− 0 V) / 2^{12} levels = 0.0008057 V = 805.7 µV.

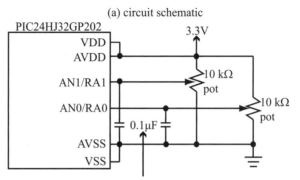

(a) circuit schematic

Optional capacitors reduce noise on ADC channels

(b) **main()** function

```
int main (void) {
  uint16  u16_pot1, u16_pot2;
  float   f_pot1, f_pot2;

  configBasic(HELLO_MSG);
  CONFIG_AN0_AS_ANALOG();
  CONFIG_AN1_AS_ANALOG();
  while(1) {
    configADC1_ManualCH0( ADC_CH0_POS_SAMPLEA_AN0, 31, 1 );
    u16_pot1 = convertADC1();
    configADC1_ManualCH0( ADC_CH0_POS_SAMPLEA_AN1, 31 ,1 );
    u16_pot2 = convertADC1();
    f_pot1 = 3.3/4096*u16_pot1;
    f_pot2 = 3.3/4096*u16_pot2;
    printf("AN0 is 0x%0X or %1.4fV.  |  AN1 is 0x%0X or %1.4fV.\n",  \
        u16_pot1, (float) f_pot1, u16_pot2, (float) f_pot2 );
    DELAY_MS(1500);
  } //endof while()
} // endof main()
```

Uses floating point and **printf** for convenience.

Set AN0 and AN1 to input direction, disabling pull-up resistors, and enabling analog mode.

Configure ADC for 31×TAD sampling duration and 12-bit results.

Assumes VDD = 3.3 V. Change value match your system VDD voltage.

FIGURE 11.14   PIC24HJ32GP202 ADC converting two channels sequentially.

serial port. Floating point is required to compute the voltage value for screen display.

Figure 11.15 shows a sample of the terminal output when using the circuit and code in Figure 11.14. Your results will be different because it is unlikely that you can mimic exactly the pot positions used to create Figure 11.15. Try connecting a digital voltmeter to the AN0 and AN1 pins on the PIC24 μC. The voltmeter readings will not match those converted and computed by the code in Figure 11.14 exactly. The voltages should be close, but will differ due to noise on the ADC lines and reference voltage differences in the voltmeter and PIC24's ADC.

```
Reset cause: Power-on.
Device ID = 0x00000F1D (PIC24HJ32GP202), revision 0x00003001 (A2)
Fast RC Osc with PLL

adc2pots1.c, built on Jul 21 2008 at 14:42:25
AN0 is 0x3DD or 0.7968V. |  AN1 is 0x813 or 1.6653V.
AN0 is 0x3F7 or 0.8177V. |  AN1 is 0x806 or 1.6548V.
AN0 is 0x407 or 0.8306V. |  AN1 is 0x821 or 1.6766V.
AN0 is 0x6F0 or 1.4309V. |  AN1 is 0x7EB or 1.6331V.
AN0 is 0x969 or 1.9408V. |  AN1 is 0x806 or 1.6548V.    Turning pot
AN0 is 0xBB0 or 2.4105V. |  AN1 is 0x821 or 1.6766V.    on AN0.
AN0 is 0xD2B or 2.7159V. |  AN1 is 0x80F or 1.6621V.
AN0 is 0xE3C or 2.9358V. |  AN1 is 0x822 or 1.6774V.
AN0 is 0xF79 or 3.1912V. |  AN1 is 0x827 or 1.6814V.
AN0 is 0xFB9 or 3.2428V. |  AN1 is 0x820 or 1.6758V.
AN0 is 0xFBC or 3.2452V. |  AN1 is 0x820 or 1.6758V.
AN0 is 0xFDF or 3.2734V. |  AN1 is 0x823 or 1.6782V.
AN0 is 0xFBB or 3.2444V. |  AN1 is 0x80F or 1.6621V.
AN0 is 0xFBB or 3.2444V. |  AN1 is 0x6A0 or 1.3664V.
AN0 is 0xFFB or 3.2960V. |  AN1 is 0x4D6 or 0.9974V.
AN0 is 0xFDF or 3.2734V. |  AN1 is 0x2AF or 0.5535V.
AN0 is 0xFF0 or 3.2871V. |  AN1 is 0x163 or 0.2860V.    Turning pot
AN0 is 0xFFB or 3.2960V. |  AN1 is 0xCA  or 0.1627V.    on AN1.
AN0 is 0xFFF or 3.2992V. |  AN1 is 0xCE  or 0.1660V.
AN0 is 0xFFF or 3.2992V. |  AN1 is 0xD5  or 0.1716V.
```

FIGURE 11.15   Sample terminal output for ADC example in Figure 11.14.

Note the changes in the ADC results on the last few readings in Figure 11.15. These readings were taken without adjusting the potentiometer settings. Recall that the ADC step size is very small, slightly above 800 µV. The difference in readings is likely due to noise and the dynamic comparator biases in the PIC24 ADC circuitry. It is very easy for these types of errors to be larger than 1 mV; therefore, ADC results are rarely "constant" when the conversion step sizes are so small. Finally, the 12-bit ADC result is typically too fine for use with many lower cost potentiometers. The low-cost pots, especially the "one-turn" pots, cannot generate voltages accurately enough for 12-bit conversion. The most significant 8 bits of the ADC result are typically sufficient for these types of potentiometers.

PIC24 ADC Operation: Automatic and Scanning with Interrupts

The code in Figure 11.14 is adequate if the application is only performing analog-to-digital conversion on one or two voltages. However, the code in Figure 11.14's while(1) loop to reconfigure the ADC, start the sampling process, wait for the conversion to complete, then read the ADC results becomes unwieldy as the number of ADC channels grows. Consider the circuit in Figure 11.16 where the PIC24 µC must perform A/D conversion on seven analog voltages. For the purposes of this example, the voltages are fixed voltages created by an affordable resistor voltage divider so the voltages are known *a priori,* which proves valuable when we have so many voltages being converted. In practice, the converted voltages would likely be time-varying and created by sensors or some other means. To convert these seven channels, it is quite easy to imagine adapting the code in Figure 11.14 to configure the ADC to convert each voltage one by one; however, that code would be highly repetitive and inefficient. Fortunately, the PIC24 ADC peripheral contains hardware to simplify scanning multiple ADC channels required by the circuit in Figure 11.16.

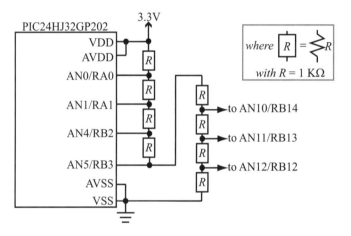

FIGURE 11.16   PIC24HJ32GP202 ADC converting seven channels.

Figure 11.17 gives configuration and ISR code to simplify the process of converting the seven voltages in Figure 11.16. The ADC will automatically scan, sample, and convert each of the seven user-selected channels in sequence. The ADC will "collect" these voltages in a special ADC result buffer and notify us via an interrupt when all seven values are ready to be used. This process is much more efficient than Figure 11.14, especially for large numbers of ADC inputs. While the ADC peripheral is busy sampling and converting the seven ADC values, the user program in `main()` can continue processing other data or handling the user interface. The ADC interrupt service routine in Figure 11.17 will automatically execute when the ADC results are ready for consumption.

As you are starting to discover, the PIC24 µC ADC peripheral is quite complex and feature-rich. This peripheral has seven configuration registers, with many interdependent bits and settings. Complex configurations of the ADC are not easily explained in a sequential ordering that matches the actual code. In the next few

```
void configADC1_AutoScanIrqCH0(uint16 u16_ch0ScanMask, \
                               uint8 u8_autoSampleTime,
                               uint8 u8_use12bits) {

    uint8   u8_i, u8_nChannels=0;
    uint16  u16_mask = 0x0001;

    if (u8_autoSampleTime > 31) u8_autoSampleTime=31;
    for (u8_i=0; u8_i<16; u8_i++) {
      if (u16_ch0ScanMask & u16_mask) u8_nChannels++;
      u16_mask<<=1;
    }

    AD1CON1bits.ADON = 0;
    AD1CON1 = ADC_CLK_AUTO | ADC_AUTO_SAMPLING_ON;
    if (u8_use12bit)
        AD1CON1bits.AD12B = 1;
    else
        AD1CON1bits.AD12B = 0;
    AD1CON3 = ADC_CONV_CLK_INTERNAL_RC | (u8_autoSampleTime<<8);
    AD1CHS0 = ADC_CH0_NEG_SAMPLEA_VREFN;
    AD1CON2 = ADC_VREF_AVDD_AVSS | ADC_CONVERT_CH0 | \
              ADC_SCAN_ON | ((u8_nChannels-1)<<2);
    AD1CSSL = u16_ch0ScanMask;
    _AD1IP = 7;  _AD1IF = 0;
    _AD1IE = 1;
    AD1CON1bits.ADON = 1;
}

void _ISR _ADC1Interrupt (void) {
    uint8   u8_i;
    uint16*  au16_adcHWBuff = (uint16*) &ADC1BUF0;

    for( u8_i=0; u8_i<16; u8_i++) {
      au16_buffer[u8_i] = au16_adcHWBuff[u8_i];
    }
    u8_waiting = 0;
    AD1IF = 0; // clear ADC interrupt flag
}
```

Limit u8_autoSampleTime to range from 0 to 31.

Count the number of bits set in the function argument u16_ch0ScanMask.

ADC must be off when changing configuration.

Set to auto convert after sampling and configure ADC wordlength.

Scan ADC over the number of channels requested by the caller.

Use ADC internal clock and set "auto-sample" time from function argument.

Creates a uint16 pointer to the ADC1BUF0 register.

During ISR, copy 16 ADC results to a global array au16_buffer[].

Signal to main() that conversion data is ready.

FIGURE 11.17   ADC configuration and ISR for automatic scanning and conversions.

paragraphs, we will explain the pertinent ADC configuration bits. You will find each of these bits being used in the functions in Figure 11.17.

The AD1CON2.CSCNA bit instructs the ADC peripheral to scan inputs using the CH0 signal path. See Figure 11.7. When AD1CON2.CSCNA bit is set, the ADC will sample and convert voltages from one ANx pin after another. The number of channels scanned is determined by the value of the AD1CON2.SMPI<3:0> bits. The channels scanned are determined by the set bits in AD1CSSL register. For each bit in the AD1CSSL register equal to "1", the PIC24 ADC will sample and convert a voltage on the corresponding ANx pin. Selected inputs are scanned in ascending order. Figure 11.18 shows the layout of the configuration bits in the AD1CSSL register.

R/W-0	R/W-0	R/W-0	R/W-0	R/W-0	R/W-0	R/W-0	R/W-0
CSS15	CSS14	CSS13	CSS12	CSS11	CSS10	CSS9	CSS8
15	14	13	12	11	10	9	8
R/W-0	R/W-0	R/W-0	R/W-0	R/W-0	R/W-0	R/W-0	R/W-0
CSS7	CSS6	CSS5	CSS4	CSS3	CSS2	CSS1	CSS0
7	6	5	4	3	2	1	0

Bits 0-15:   CSS<15:0>: ADC Input Scan Select bits
1 = Select ANx for input scan.
0 = Skip ANx for input scan.

Figure redrawn by author from Register 28-6 found in the PIC24 FRM datasheet (DS70249A), Microchip Technology Inc.

Note: All CSSx bits are selectable, even on devices with fewer than 16 analog inputs. On selected inputs without a corresponding analog input, VREFL is converted.

FIGURE 11.18   The AD1CSSL configuration register. (Adapted with permission of the copyright owner, Microchip Technology, Incorporated. All rights reserved. No further reprints or reproduction may be made without Microchip Inc.'s prior written consent.)

The scanning option saves the user from having to "reconfigure" the ADC to the desired channel at each conversion. However, the configuration function in Figure 11.17 still requires the user to initiate each sampling cycle. The conversion cycle is automatically started at sampling completion due to the AD1CON1.SSRC<2:0> = 111 setting in Figure 11.17. Since we can configure the ADC peripheral to scan channels automatically, it would be very helpful to have the ADC automatically start the sampling process at the conclusion of the prior channel's conversion. This is possible by setting the AD1CON1.ASAM bit. When the AD1CON1.ASAM bit is set, the AD1CON1.SAMP bit is set automatically when a conversion completes.

In Figure 11.13, we read the ADC result from ADC1BUF0 register. If ADC1BUF0 were the only ADC result register, our scanning and automatic conversions would be of very limited use. We would be forced to read the result from ADC1BUF0 before the next conversion completes and overwrites the results. Fortunately, the ADC peripheral provides a 16-word buffer in which the ADC results can be written. The ADC peripheral will write up to 16 ADC results into the registers named ADC1BUF0, ADC1BUF1, … , ADC1BUFE, ADC1BUFF. The number of ADC1BUFx registers written depends on the number of channels being scanned. If we scan six ADC channels, only the first six ADC1BUFx registers are written. The remaining registers contain indeterminate values. Our ISR code in Figure 11.17 will copy all 16 ADC result buffer locations for generality. The code that ultimately uses these values must know which values are valid and which are indeterminate.

The code in Figure 11.14's while(1) loop waits for the AD1CON1.DONE bit to go high. In the case of scanned ADC inputs, the AD1CON1.DONE bit will be set when the entire set of scanned inputs has completed. However, the time spent waiting for the conversion cycle to complete will grow quite long as the number of scanned channels increases. The solution is to have the ADC peripheral generate an interrupt when the

ADC conversion cycle is complete. In addition to configuring the number of scanned channels, the AD1CON2.SMPI<3:0> bits instruct the ADC how often to generate ADC interrupts. Now that the ADC will automatically scan and convert each channel, place the results into an array of registers for our later use, and generate an interrupt when the entire scan cycle is done, we can set the ADC's interrupt priority level, enable the ADC interrupt, and turn the ADC peripheral on. Now all we need is the ISR in Figure 11.17.

Upon each ADC interrupt request, our ISR must copy the ADC conversion results to another location before the next scan cycle overwrites the values. The ADC ISR in Figure 11.17 copies the entire 16-word ADC results register array to a software buffer. In practice, we only need to copy the number of results that correspond to the number of selected scan channels. However, the ISR in Figure 11.17 is general and lets the more application-specific code in the main() function make that determination. The ISR simply creates a uint16 pointer called au16_adcHWBuff that points to the first ADC results register ADC1BUF0. Then, the ISR loops over the set of 16 registers copying the values into a global array of uint16 values called au16_buffer. The code in main() can then simply read from au16_buffer[] which is automatically updated by the ISR and contains the latest ADC readings.

After the PIC24 ADC channel, reference voltages, and conversion clock have been properly configured, the PIC24 ADC is ready to convert the analog voltage on the seven analog inputs in Figure 11.16. The code for the main() is given in Figure 11.19.

The code in Figure 11.19 uses our standard clock frequencies and serial port baud rates. Each of the seven desired AN*x* pins are configured for analog input. Then, the ADC configuration function in Figure 11.17 is called with the appropriate mask for the AD1CSSL register. As we saw earlier, the configuration function will count the number of bits set in our mask and configure the ADC appropriately. Since the ADC is configured to automatically sample (see AD1CON1.SSRC<2:0> bits), convert (see AD1CON1.ASAM bit), and scan (see AD1CON2.CSCNA bit), our ADC will start the process as soon as the ADC is turned on in the configuration function. Once the configuration function returns, the code in main() waits for the AD1CON1.DONE bit to be set. This signifies that the first complete scan cycle has completed and the results in our global array au16_buffer[] are valid. The code in main() enters an infinite loop of printing the entire contents of au16_buffer[] to the screen, waiting 1.5 seconds, then repeating the process. Figure 11.20 shows representative output for three passes through the loop in Figure 11.19.

Note the au16_buffer[] values printed to the screen in Figure 11.20. Recall that our ISR in Figure 11.17 copies all 16 values from the PIC24 µC hardware register array and our loop in main() prints all 16 of those values. We see that the first seven values in au16_buffer[], or equivalently the ADC1BUF*x* array, are consistent with the circuit in Figure 11.16: they are seven approximately equal-spaced voltages that lie between our power supplies VDD and VSS. These first seven au16_buffer[] values vary from scan cycle to the next due to noise on the wires and small

```
volatile uint8 u8_waiting;            Global variable for synchronization
                                      between main() and ADC ISR
int main(void) {
  uint8   u8_i;
  uint16  u16_pot;                    Uses floating point and printf for convenience.
  float   f_pot;
                                      Start with our standard system configuration.
  configBasic(HELLO_MSG);
  CONFIG_AN0_AS_ANALOG();   CONFIG_AN1_AS_ANALOG();
  CONFIG_AN4_AS_ANALOG();   CONFIG_AN5_AS_ANALOG();     Configure ANx pins
  CONFIG_AN10_AS_ANALOG();  CONFIG_AN11_AS_ANALOG();    to be analog inputs.
  CONFIG_AN12_AS_ANALOG();

  configADC1_AutoScanIrqCH0( ADC_SCAN_AN0 |    \        ADC will auto-scan-
     ADC_SCAN_AN1 | ADC_SCAN_AN4 | ADC_SCAN_AN5 |  \   convert ANx pins with
     ADC_SCAN_AN10 | ADC_SCAN_AN11 | ADC_SCAN_AN12, \  12-bit precision
     31, 1);                                            and generate IRQ.

  while(!IS_CONVERSION_COMPLETE_ADC1()) {};    Do not proceed until the
                                               ADC completes conversion
  while(1) {                                   of the first channel scan.
    while(u8_waiting);
    u8_waiting = 1;                            Wait for ISR to signal data is valid.
    for( u8_i=0; u8_i<16; u8_i++) {
      u16_pot = au16_buffer[u8_i];    Convert each ADC buffer value into a
      f_pot = 3.3 / 4096 * u16_pot;   voltage. This code assumes VDD = 3.3 V.
      printf("r");
      if (u8_i < 10) outChar( '0'+u8_i );
      else outChar( 'A'-10+u8_i );             Print each ADC buffer value as
      printf(":0x%04X=%1.3fV   ", \            hex value and floating point
             u16_pot, (float) f_pot );         voltage.
      if ((u8_i % 4) == 3) printf("\n");
    }
    printf("\n");
    doHeartbeat();
    DELAY_MS(1500);
  }
}
```

FIGURE 11.19 Automatic scanning and conversions code.

uncertainties in the ADC. This is quite normal. Also, notice that our configuration is scanning PIC24 µC input pins AN0, AN1, AN4, AN5, AN10, AN11, and AN12. However, the results are contained in ascending order in the first seven locations in the hardware buffer. Code in main() that uses these values will need to maintain a mapping to determine which result in au16_buffer[] corresponds to which ANx pin.

Now, look at the other values in au16_buffer[]. The result values for entries 7–16 (r7-rF) are nonsense. Note that these values are numbers in excess of 12 bits, the size of our ADC conversion results, and never change. Since the code in Figure 11.19 configured the ADC for a seven-channel scan, these nine values have not been initialized or written by the ADC. The hardware registers locations ADC1BUF7 through ADC1BUFF contain random, indeterminate values from the PIC24 µC startup. In practice, the code in main() would not use these invalid values; they are printed here simply to illustrate the ADC's operation when channel scanning.

```
Reset cause: Power-on.
Device ID = 0x00000F1D (PIC24HJ32GP202), revision 0x00003001 (A2)
Fast RC Osc with PLL

adc7scan1.c, built on Jul 16 2008 at 15:01:11
r0:0x0DDF=2.861V  r1:0x0C00=2.475V  r2:0x09FF=2.062V  r3:0x07FC=1.647V
r4:0x0610=1.250V  r5:0x0402=0.827V  r6:0x01FC=0.409V  r7:0x540C=17.335V
r8:0x03DF=0.798V  r9:0xA0C8=33.161V  rA:0xE360=46.896V  rB:0x7559=24.203V
rC:0xA7B5=34.590V  rD:0x1B5A=5.641V  rE:0x3362=10.598V  rF:0xA279=33.510V

r0:0x0DE0=2.862V  r1:0x0C10=2.488V  r2:0x09FF=2.062V  r3:0x07FF=1.649V
r4:0x05DF=1.211V  r5:0x03E6=0.804V  r6:0x01F0=0.400V  r7:0x540C=17.335V
r8:0x03DF=0.798V  r9:0xA0C8=33.161V  rA:0xE360=46.896V  rB:0x7559=24.203V
rC:0xA7B5=34.590V  rD:0x1B5A=5.641V  rE:0x3362=10.598V  rF:0xA279=33.510V

r0:0x0E1C=2.910V  r1:0x0BD5=2.440V  r2:0x09EF=2.049V  r3:0x07FF=1.649V
r4:0x0600=1.237V  r5:0x040C=0.835V  r6:0x01ED=0.397V  r7:0x540C=17.335V
r8:0x03DF=0.798V  r9:0xA0C8=33.161V  rA:0xE360=46.896V  rB:0x7559=24.203V
rC:0xA7B5=34.590V  rD:0x1B5A=5.641V  rE:0x3362=10.598V  rF:0xA279=33.510V
```

First seven buffer locations (r0-r6) contain valid ADC results. Next nine
buffer locations (r7-rF) contain invalid ADC (uninitialized) values.

FIGURE 11.20   Sample output for seven channel ADC scanning.

The functions presented in Figure 11.17 and Figure 11.19 work, but have a potential problem. When our ADC completes conversion on all seven channels, the ADC sets the AD1IF bit to signal an interrupt, and our ISR responds. The ADC ISR copies the ADC results into our global array au16_buffer[] for our use in main(). The problem lies in the fact that the ADC is configured for automatic sampling upon completion of the previous conversion through the ADC1CON1.ASAM bit. At the same time that our ISR is copying the ADC1BUF*x* values into au16_buffer[], the ADC is already sampling and preparing to convert the first scan channel, AN0 in our case, again. If our ISR is delayed from executing by some other higher priority ISR, the ADC may have already completed the first scan channel conversion and overwritten the results in AD1BUF0 *before* our ISR copies it. Some solutions to this potential problem are to

■ raise the priority of the ADC ISR relative to other ISRs,
■ slow down the ADC conversion clock to ensure that conversion does not start before the ISR can respond, or
■ use a ping-pong buffer approach similar to the approach used in Chapter 10 to capture streaming data from the UART.

Often, the first two choices in the preceding list are not an option. The third option cannot be a software-only approach since the fundamental problem of responding to the ISR is not addressed. Fortunately, the designers of the PIC24 µC have provided us with a ping-pong buffer hardware solution. The PIC24 ADC peripheral can use the 16-word ADC result register array ADC1BUF0-ADC1BUFF as two 8-word result buffers. This mode is selected by the AD1CON2.BUFM bit. When AD1CON2.BUFM is set, the hardware ADC results buffer fills the first half on one interrupt, and fills the second half on the next interrupt. Of course, setting the AD1CON2.BUFM bit is only useful if we are attempting to scan eight or fewer channels. Figure 11.21 shows the new ISR and configuration function for the automatic sample, convert, and scan capability using the CH0 SHA signal path. The only difference in the ADC configuration

```
void configADC1_AutoHalfScanIrqCH0(uint16 u16_ch0ScanMask, \
                         uint8 u8_autoSampleTime,
                         uint8 u8_use12bits) {

  uint8   u8_i, u8_nChannels=0;                   Limit u8_autoSampleTime
  uint16  u16_mask = 0x0001;                       to range from 0 to 31.

  if (u8_autoSampleTime > 31) u8_autoSampleTime=31;
  for (u8_i=0; u8_i<16; u8_i++) {                  Count the number of bits set
    if (u16_ch0ScanMask & u16_mask) u8_nChannels++;  in the function argument
    u16_mask<<=1;                                   u16_Ch0ScanMask.
  }
                            ADC must be off when changing configuration.
  AD1CON1bits.ADON = 0;
  AD1CON1 = ADC_CLK_AUTO | ADC_AUTO_SAMPLING_ON;  Auto convert after sampling
  if (u8_use12bit)                                 and set to 10 or 12 bit ADC.
      AD1CON1bits.AD12B = 1;
  else
      AD1CON1bits.AD12B = 0;
  AD1CON3 = ADC_CONV_CLK_INTERNAL_RC | (u8_autoSampleTime<<8);
  AD1CHS0 = ADC_CH0_NEG_SAMPLEA_VREFN;
  AD1CON2 = ADC_VREF_AVDD_AVSS | ADC_CONVERT_CH0 | \  Scan channels and use
            ADC_SCAN_ON | ((u8_nChannels-1)<<2) | \   hardware double buffers
            ADC_ALT_BUF_ON;                           for ADC1BUF registers.
  AD1CSSL = u16_ch0ScanMask;
  _AD1IP = 7; _AD1IF = 0;                          Use ADC internal clock and set "auto-
  _AD1IE = 1;                                      sample" time from function argument.
  AD1CON1bits.ADON = 1;
}

void _ISR _ADC1Interrupt (void) {
  uint8    u8_i;
  uint16*  au16_adcHWBuff = (uint16*) &ADC1BUF0;
                           See if ADC is now writing 2nd half of ADC1BUF array.
  if (AD1CON2bits.BUFS) {
    for( u8_i=0; u8_i<8; u8_i++)                        Copy 8 words from first
      au16_buffer[u8_i] = au16_adcHWBuff[u8_i];         half of ADC1BUF array.
  }
  else {
    for( u8_i=8; u8_i<16; u8_i++)                       Copy 8 words from second
      au16_buffer[u8_i] = au16_adcHWBuff[u8_i];         half of ADC1BUF array.
  }
  u8_waiting = 0; //signal that data is valid
  _AD1IF = 0;     //clear the ADC interrupt flag
}
```

FIGURE 11.21 ADC configuration and ISR for automatic scanning and conversions with hardware ping-pong buffers.

code from Figure 11.17 and Figure 11.21 is the inclusion of the `ADC_ALT_BUF_ON` mask in AD1CON2 to set the AD1CON2.BUFM bit.

The ADC ISR must be modified to determine which half of the buffer is currently being written by the ADC peripheral hardware. When the AD1CON2.BUFS status bit is set, the ADC is currently filling the second half (ADC1BUF8-ADC1BUFF) of the array and the user should read from the first half (ADC1BUF0-ADC1BUF7) of the array. If the AD1CON2.BUFS bit is clear, then the user should read from the second half of the array. The new ISR in Figure 11.21 contains the logic to copy eight words from the appropriate half of the ADC results buffer into our global array `au16_buffer[]` for use in `main()`. The `main()` code from Figure 11.19 changes only in that the new configuration function `configADC1_12bitAutoHalfScanIrqCH0()` is called instead of `configADC1_12bitAutoScanIrqCH0()`. All other aspects of this code are unchanged so the code is not reprinted. Figure 11.22 shows representative output for three passes through the loop in the `main()` code for automatic sample, convert, and scanning using the ADC hardware ping-pong buffers.

Note the `au16_buffer[]` values printed to the screen in Figure 11.22. In this case, we see that the first seven values in each half of the `au16_buffer[]` are consistent with the circuit in Figure 11.16. Furthermore, pairs of values in the `au16_buffer[]` are approximately the same value. For example, `au16_buffer[2]` and `au16_buffer[10]` both correspond to the voltage on external pin AN4. The last word in each half of `au16_buffer[]` is indeterminate since it is not being written by the ADC and has not been initialized. Finally, just like the code in Figure 11.19, this

```
Reset cause: Power-on.
Device ID = 0x00000F1D (PIC24HJ32GP202), revision 0x00003001 (A2)
Fast RC Osc with PLL

adc7scan2.c, built on Jul 16 2008 at 14:59:01
r0:0x0E00=2.888V  r1:0x0BEB=2.458V  r2:0x09FF=2.062V  r3:0x0800=1.650V
r4:0x05F3=1.227V  r5:0x03EF=0.811V  r6:0x01B2=0.350V  r7:0x540C=17.335V
r8:0x0DB7=2.829V  r9:0x0BFF=2.474V  rA:0x09F4=2.053V  rB:0x0800=1.650V
rC:0x05FC=1.234V  rD:0x03FF=0.824V  rE:0x0204=0.416V  rF:0xA279=33.510V

r0:0x0DFF=2.887V  r1:0x0C00=2.475V  r2:0x0A28=2.095V  r3:0x07FF=1.649V
r4:0x0600=1.237V  r5:0x03FF=0.824V  r6:0x01F8=0.406V  r7:0x540C=17.335V
r8:0x0DFF=2.887V  r9:0x0BFC=2.472V  rA:0x09EB=2.046V  rB:0x07E7=1.630V
rC:0x0602=1.239V  rD:0x03BF=0.811V  rE:0x01F1=0.400V  rF:0xA279=33.510V

r0:0x0E11=2.901V  r1:0x0C40=2.527V  r2:0x09DF=2.036V  r3:0x0800=1.650V
r4:0x05FE=1.236V  r5:0x03EF=0.811V  r6:0x01EF=0.399V  r7:0x540C=17.335V
r8:0x0DEF=2.874V  r9:0x0C20=2.501V  rA:0x09FC=2.059V  rB:0x07DF=1.623V
rC:0x05F9=1.232V  rD:0x0410=0.838V  rE:0x01F8=0.406V  rF:0xA279=33.510V
```

Buffer locations r0-r6 and r8-rE, the first seven locations in each half of the ADC buffers, contain valid ADC results. The eighth location (r7 and rF) in each half-buffer contain invalid (uninitialized) results.

FIGURE 11.22   Sample output for seven channel ADC scanning with ping-pong buffers.

version is scanning PIC24 μC input pins AN0, AN1, AN4, AN5, AN10, AN11, and AN12. Code in `main()` that uses these values will need to maintain a mapping to determine which result in `au16_buffer[]` corresponds to which AN*x* pin.

PIC24 ADC Operation: Automatic Using Timers

The PIC24 ADC peripheral has only one analog-to-digital converter; that is, it can only perform successive approximation on one voltage at a time. However, the PIC24 ADC peripheral has four SHAs. In our previous examples where we were converting more than one voltage, we sampled each voltage in turn then converted that voltage to a digital code. In some applications, it is imperative that multiple voltages be converted simultaneously. Even though we only have one successive approximation ADC, we can accomplish this goal by sampling the voltages simultaneously and converting the voltages to digital codes sequentially. Figure 11.23 shows a circuit where the PIC24HJ32GP202 is measuring the voltage created by four LM60 linear Celsius temperature sensors. The LM60 sensors are chosen for illustration purposes only. In fact, we will only concern ourselves with the voltages created by the LM60s. The computation step to convert voltage into the Celsius temperature will be left as an exercise. The concepts discussed in this section apply to any simultaneous voltage conversions you need to perform with the PIC24 ADC peripheral.

In our configuration function `configADC1_Simul4ChanIrq()`, `AD1CON1.SSRC<2:0>` is set to the value 0b010 by the bit-mask `ADC_CLK_TMR`. With this setting, Timer3 is used to trigger the end of sampling phase and the beginning of the conversion phase. Timers will be covered in detail in Chapter 12. For our purposes here, the Timer3 peripheral will periodically trigger the ADC to stop sampling and start conversion based on the Timer3 settings.

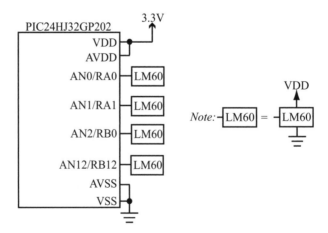

FIGURE 11.23   PIC24HJ32GP202 ADC converting four channels simultaneously.

In this example, we must measure the temperature, or equivalently, the voltage, at each of our four sensors at exactly the same time. The PIC24 ADC peripheral has only one ADC but four separate SHAs. By sampling each voltage with its own dedicated SHA and converting that voltage to a digital code in turn, we have effectively converted the voltages at the same time. Figure 11.25 shows a configuration function configADC1_ Simul4ChanIrq() that sets the PIC24 ADC peripheral into simultaneous sampling mode on all four channels. The AD1CON2.CHPS<1:0> bits determine whether one, two, or four SHAs are being used. Our code in Figure 11.25 selects four SHAs via the bit-mask ADC_CONVERT_CHO123. Note that the PIC24 ADC must be used in 10-bit mode if we desire simultaneous sampling. This is a limitation mandated by the PIC24 µC datasheet. The selection of the positive and negative voltages for CH0's SHA is done as before by the AD1CHS0 register in Figure 11.11. While CH0 has a very flexible SHA and can convert almost any desired voltage from the ANx pins, the SHAs for CH1, CH2, and CH3 are far more restricted. The positive and negative voltages for CH1, CH2, and CH3 are selected in the AD1CHS123 register. The choices for the positive and negative terminal for the CH1, CH2, and CH3 are summarized in Figure 11.24.

U-0	U-0	U-0	U-0	U-0	R/W-0	R/W-0	R/W-0
UI	UI	UI	UI	UI	CH123NB<1:0>		CH123SB
15	14	13	12	11	10	9	8
U-0	U-0	U-0	U-0	U-0	R/W-0	R/W-0	R/W-0
UI	UI	UI	UI	UI	CH123NA<1:0>		CH123SA
7	6	5	4	3	2	1	0

Bit 9-10: CH123NB<1:0>: Select Negative Input for CH1, CH2, and CH3 SHA for Sample B bits.
(When ADxCON1.AD12B=1, CH123NB is U-0/UI, read as '0'.)
11 = CH1 negative input is AN9, CH2 negative input is AN10, CH3 negative inputs is AN11.
10 = CH1 negative input is AN6, CH2 negative input is AN7, CH3 negative inputs is AN8.
0x = CH1, CH2, and CH3 negative input is VREFL.
Bit 8:   CH123SB: Select Positive Input for CH1, CH2, and CH3 SHA for Sample B bits.
(When ADxCON1.AD12B=1, CH123SB is U-0/UI, read as '0'.)
1 = CH1 positive input is AN3, CH2 positive input is AN4, CH3 positive inputs is AN5.
0 = CH1 positive input is AN0, CH2 positive input is AN1, CH3 positive inputs is AN2.
Bit 2-1: CH123NA<1:0>: Select Negative Input for CH1, CH2, and CH3 SHA for Sample A bits.
(When ADxCON1.AD12B=1, CH123NA is U-0/UI, read as '0'.)
11 = CH1 negative input is AN9, CH2 negative input is AN10, CH3 negative inputs is AN11.
10 = CH1 negative input is AN6, CH2 negative input is AN7, CH3 negative inputs is AN8.
0x = CH1, CH2, and CH3 negative input is VREFL.
Bit 0:   CH123SA: Select Positive Input for CH1, CH2, and CH3 SHA for Sample A bits.
(When ADxCON1.AD12B=1, CH123SA is U-0/UI, read as '0'.)
1 = CH1 positive input is AN3, CH2 positive input is AN4, CH3 positive inputs is AN5.
0 = CH1 positive input is AN0, CH2 positive input is AN1, CH3 positive inputs is AN2.

> Figure redrawn by author from Register 28-4 found in the PIC24 FRM datasheet (DS70249A), Microchip Technology Inc.

FIGURE 11.24   The AD1CHS123 configuration register. (Adapted with permission of the copyright owner, Microchip Technology, Incorporated. All rights reserved. No further reprints or reproduction may be made without Microchip Inc.'s prior written consent.)

The ADC configuration function in Figure 11.25 allows the user to pass in a bit-mask for the AD1CSH123 register. Therefore, any possible combination of channels supported by the AD1CHS123 register can be selected for CH1, CH2, and CH3. The SHA for CH0 is restricted to using VREF– or AN1 as the negative voltage in the AD1CHS0 register, but the user can select any AN*x* channel for the SHA's positive voltage, including a channel selected for conversion on CH1, CH2, or CH3. In Figure 11.25, the function `configADC1_Simul4ChanIrq()` also sets the AD1CON2.BUFM bit with the bit-mask `ADC_ALT_BUF_ON`. Therefore, we will expect our four ADC channels results to be located in the first four locations of the two halves of the ADC1BUF*n* register array.

```
void configADC1_Simul4ChanIrq(uint8 u8_ch0Select, \
        uint16   u16_ch123SelectMask, uint16 u16_numTcyMask) {
                                    ADC must be off when changing configuration.
  AD1CON1bits.ADON = 0;
                                              Run SHAs simultaneously
  AD1CON1 = ADC_CLK_TMR | ADC_SAMPLE_SIMULTANEOUS;   and trigger ADC with T2/T3.
  AD1CON3 = (u16_numTcyMask & 0xFF);
  AD1CON2 = ADC_VREF_AVDD_AVSS | ADC_CONVERT_CH0123 | ADC_ALT_BUF_ON;
  AD1CHS0 = ADC_CH0_NEG_SAMPLEA_VREFN | (u8_ch0Select & 0x1F);
  AD1CHS123 = u16_ch123SelectMask;      Convert four channels simultaneously.
  _AD1IP = 7;  _AD1IF = 0;  _AD1IE = 1;   Use VSS as the negative voltage
  AD1CON1bits.ADON = 1;                   reference for CH0.
}
      Use PIC24 instruction clock to create ADC's TAD period.
void _ISR _ADC1Interrupt (void) {
  static uint8      u8_adcCount=64;
  uint8             u8_i;
  uint16*           au16_adcHWBuff = (uint16*) &ADC1BUF0;

  if (AD1CON2bits.BUFS) {
    for( u8_i=0; u8_i<8; u8_i++) {           Accumulate results from
      au16_buffer[u8_i] += au16_adcHWBuff[u8_i];   1st half of ADC1BUF array.
    }
  }
  else {
    for( u8_i=8; u8_i<16; u8_i++) {          Accumulate results from
      au16_buffer[u8_i-8] += au16_adcHWBuff[u8_i];  2nd half of ADC1BUF array.
    }
  }
                                    Clear interrupt flag and start
  _AD1IF = 0; SET_SAMP_BIT_ADC1();   next "sampling" cycle.

  if (u8_adcCount==0) {             Every 64 conversions, copy the
    u8_adcCount = 64;  u8_gotData = 1;   accumulated results to the
    for( u8_i=0; u8_i<8; u8_i++) {       au16_sum[] array, reset the
      au16_sum[u8_i] = au16_buffer[u8_i];  au16_buffer[] array back to
      au16_buffer[u8_i] = 0;               zero, and signal the main()
    }                                      by setting u8_gotData.
  }
}
```

FIGURE 11.25   ADC configuration and ISR for four channel simultaneous sampling.

This example differs from the previous example in that it uses the PIC24 µC instruction clock to generate the ADC conversion clock. In the previous examples, T_{AD} was generated by an ADC internal RC clock and the AD1CON3.SAMC<4:0> bits. In order to demonstrate an alternative clocking scheme for the ADC, this example uses the PIC24 µC instruction clock to generate T_{AD}. Clearing AD1CON3.ADRC selects the ADC to construct T_{AD} from some multiple of T_{CY}, the PIC24 µC instruction period. In our system, T_{CY} is approximately 25 ns since our PLL is running at 40 MHz. The PIC24 µC data sheet states that T_{AD} must be at least 75 ns for correct conversion results. Therefore, we must select a multiplier for T_{CY} in AD1CON3.ADCS<7:0>. These eight bits allow us to select $T_{AD} = T_{CY}$, $T_{AD} = 2 \times T_{CY}, \ldots,$ or $T_{AD} = 256 \times T_{CY}$. The bit-mask to select the T_{CY} multiplier for T_{AD} is passed into the configuration function by the user. The example code in Figure 11.26 selects a 10× multiplier to make $T_{AD} = 10 \times T_{CY}$ using the bit-mask ADC_CONV_CLK_ 10Tcy. The 10×T_{CY} value was chosen somewhat arbitrarily; this gives a 250 ns period at FCY = 40 MHz, which is approximately the same period as the internal ADC RC oscillator. The ADC_CONV_CLK_10Tcy bit-mask along with others for ADC configuration can be found in *include\pic24_adc.h*.

Finally, we see in Figure 11.25 that our configuration function configADC1_ Simul4ChanIrq() enables the ADC interrupts. The ADC ISR for our example circuit in Figure 11.23 is shown in Figure 11.25. Similar to the ISR in Figure 11.21, our ADC ISR must first determine which half of the ADC1BUF*n* array is ready to be retrieved when the ADC triggers execution of the ISR. The ISR for this example does not copy the values from the ADC1BUFn registers; rather, it adds, or accumulates, the ADC results into an array of au16_buffer[]. While only four of our channels (AN0, AN1, AN3, and AN12) have valid voltages, the ISR in Figure 11.25 accumulates all eight ADC register values so that the function is generally useful for other ADC configurations. After accumulating the ADC results, the ISR clears the ADC interrupt flag and starts the next sampling phase. On every 64th execution of _ADC1Interrupt(), the ISR will copy the accumulated ADC values into the au16_sum[] array, reset the accumulated values au16_buffer[] back to zero, and signal the main() by setting the u8_gotData flag.

Figure 11.26 shows the code to sample the four sensors connected to the PIC24HJ32GP202 in Figure 11.23. Global variables for ISR-main() communication are allocated. The system is configured for the 40 MHz PLL and serial communications with configBasic(HELLO_MSG) and the u8_gotData flag for the ISR to signal main() is reset. The next seven lines in Figure 11.26 configure the Timer2/Timer3 pair. Chapter 12 provides much more detail on the PIC24 timers, so the explanation here is brief. The Timer2/Timer3 pair operate as a 32-bit timer that "expires" every 15625 µs which corresponds to 64 Hz. When the 32-bit timer expires, it automatically triggers the ADC to change from sampling to conversion via our settings in the AD1CON1.SSRC bits. The ADC is placed in the sampling phase at the end

```
volatile au16_sum[8];                 Storage for ADC1BUFx results and
uint16 au16_buffer[8];                running accumulation values.
volatile uint8   u8_gotData;

int main (void) {
  uint8    u8_i;                 Uses floating point and printf for convenience.
  uint16   u16_pot;
  uint32   u32_ticks;
  float    f_pot;

  configBasic(HELLO_MSG);              Start with our standard system configuration.
  CONFIG_AN0_AS_ANALOG();  CONFIG_AN1_AS_ANALOG();   } Configure ANx pins
  CONFIG_AN2_AS_ANALOG();  CONFIG_AN12_AS_ANALOG();  } to be analog inputs.

  u8_gotData = 0;               Clear flag used for ISR-main() communications.
                                Configure T2/T3 as a 32-bit timer (see Chapter 12 for more details).
  T3CONbits.TON = 0;      T2CONbits.TON = 0;
  T2CON = T2_32BIT_MODE_ON | T2_PS_1_1 |
                      T2_SOURCE_INT;                  Time-out is every 1/64 s.
  TMR3 = 0;   TMR2 = 0;
  u32_ticks = usToU32Ticks(15625, getTimerPrescale(T2CONbits))- 1 ;
  PR3 = u32_ticks>>16; PR2 = u32_ticks & 0xFFFF;
  T2CONbits.TON = 1;

  configADC1_Simul4ChanIrq(12, ADC_CH123_POS_SAMPLEA_AN0AN1AN2, \
                   ADC_CONV_CLK_10Tcy );      Configure ADC for simultaneous
  SET_SAMP_BIT_ADC1();                        sampling on AN12, AN0, AN1,
                                              and AN3 using a 10x instruction
  while(1) {                                  clock to generate TAD.
    while (!u8_gotData) {  } Wait here until ADC
      doHeartbeat();        } ISR signals that it has accumulated 64 ADC values.
    }
    u8_gotData = 0;              Clear flag to signal ISR that data is copied.
    for( u8_i=0; u8_i<4; u8_i++) {
      u16_pot = au16_sum[u8_i];
      f_pot = 3.3 / 1024 / 64 * u16_pot;    Normalize each value, average,
      printf("r");  outChar('0'+u8_i);      and convert to a voltage value.
      printf(":0x%04X=%1.3fV  ", u16_pot, (float) f_pot );
    }
    printf("\n");
  }
}
```

FIGURE 11.26 Four channel simultaneous sampling code.

of the ADC ISR and initiates the conversion phase every 1/64 seconds. Therefore, we obtain our four simultaneous samples at a perfectly uniform 15.625 ms spacing. The system initialization code in Figure 11.26 concludes by configuring the ADC via the function in Figure 11.25 and starting the first sampling phase.

The infinite loop in Figure 11.26 waits for the signal u8_gotData to go high before proceeding. Since u8_gotData is set in the ISR every 64th time, the code in main() proceeds at one second intervals. When the flag u8_gotData is set, the accumulated results are printed to the screen. The accumulated values are also converted into an average value by dividing by 64, then converted into a voltage by multiplying by 3.3, the ADC's VREF+, and dividing by 1024, the number of digital codes for a 10-bit ADC. Figure 11.27 shows some typical results for four LM60 sensors at room temperature. The hex values displayed in Figure 11.27 are the accumulated values after 64 ADC conversions. These numbers can be regarded as nearly the same as 16-bit ADC results. The accumulated values can take on values between zero (a sum of 64 zeros) to 65472 (a sum of 64 ADC results of 0x3FF). The voltage values in Figure 11.27 are voltages computed from the average ADC result and are quite stable even without noise-reducing capacitors on the AN*x* pins.

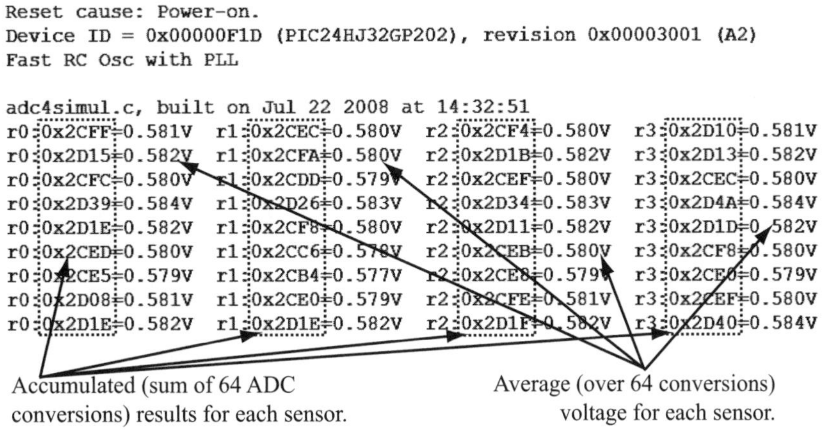

```
Reset cause: Power-on.
Device ID = 0x00000F1D (PIC24HJ32GP202), revision 0x00003001 (A2)
Fast RC Osc with PLL

adc4simul.c, built on Jul 22 2008 at 14:32:51
r0:0x2CFF:0.581V   r1:0x2CEC:0.580V   r2:0x2CF4:0.580V   r3:0x2D10:0.581V
r0:0x2D15:0.582V   r1:0x2CFA:0.580V   r2:0x2D1B:0.582V   r3:0x2D13:0.582V
r0:0x2CFC:0.580V   r1:0x2CDD:0.579V   r2:0x2CEF:0.580V   r3:0x2CEC:0.580V
r0:0x2D39:0.584V   r1:0x2D26:0.583V   r2:0x2D34:0.583V   r3:0x2D4A:0.584V
r0:0x2D1E:0.582V   r1:0x2CF8:0.580V   r2:0x2D11:0.582V   r3:0x2D1D:0.582V
r0:0x2CED:0.580V   r1:0x2CC6:0.578V   r2:0x2CEB:0.580V   r3:0x2CF8:0.580V
r0:0x2CE5:0.579V   r1:0x2CB4:0.577V   r2:0x2CE8:0.579V   r3:0x2CE0:0.579V
r0:0x2D08:0.581V   r1:0x2CE0:0.579V   r2:0x2CFE:0.581V   r3:0x2CEF:0.580V
r0:0x2D1E:0.582V   r1:0x2D1E:0.582V   r2:0x2D1F:0.582V   r3:0x2D40:0.584V
```

Accumulated (sum of 64 ADC   Average (over 64 conversions)
conversions) results for each sensor.   voltage for each sensor.

FIGURE 11.27   Sample output for four channel ADC simultaneous sampling.

PIC24 ADC Operation: Recap

As we have seen in our four simple ADC examples, the PIC24 ADC peripheral is complex and has many different features and operating modes. Our four examples attempted to highlight the most common operating modes and are not intended to be comprehensive. The discussion and ADC examples are a starting point for your exploration of this powerful PIC24 µC peripheral. The operating modes shown in our four examples can be combined and used with other PIC24 ADC features that we did not address. For example, the "Sample A" and "Sample B" settings (see AD1CON2.ALTS bit) can be used in conjunction with different channel scan select settings in the AD1CHS0 and AD1CHS123 registers to create complex ADC scan patterns. You are encouraged to spend quality time reading the sections on the PIC24 ADC in your device's data sheet and in the *PIC24 Family Reference Manual* [21].

These references provide great insight into the ADC and showcase several useful combinations of PIC24 ADC features.

DIGITAL-TO-ANALOG CONVERSION

Just as there are many different ways to convert an analog quantity to a digital code in an ADC, designers have invented many ingenious methods to convert a digital code back into an analog signal in DACs. Since DACs perform the complementary operation of ADCs, these two data converters have much in common. Like ADCs, the digital codes accepted by DACs follow many different coding schemes, although unsigned and signed binary representations are the most popular. Furthermore, digital codes are provided to the DAC via many different communication protocols—fully parallel, serially via nibble-wide parallel transfers, and bit serial, including I^2C, SPI, and many others. Also like ADCs, DACs exist that create different analog quantities for their output, but the most common is the voltage output DAC.

Like the ADCs, DACs are also characterized by a huge number of parameters. Many of the DAC parameters have the same names as the ADC parameters. However, the DAC parameters have a slightly different meaning as the two devices perform complementary functions. A DAC's precision is the number of output levels that the DAC can create. Like the ADC, DAC *precision* is represented as the number of output levels or the number of bits required to encode the number of output levels. DAC *resolution* is the smallest distinguishable change in the output, and represents the change in output from a ±1 LSb change in DAC input. The DAC *range* is the total span over which DAC outputs can occur. DAC range can be computed through the DAC's reference inputs; for example, range = (VREF+ − VREF−) for a voltage DAC. Obviously, the DAC has digital inputs so it must have a digital clock input to signal when the input sample data is valid. The time between each DAC conversion is the DAC's period and is almost always the same as the ADC's sample period. Assuming that our DAC in Figure 11.1 is an unsigned n-bit voltage output DAC with reference voltages VREF+ and VREF−, the DAC output $y(t)$ is shown in Equation 11.2.

$$y(t) = \text{VREF}- + y[k] \times (\text{VREF}+ -\text{VREF}-) / 2^n \qquad (11.2)$$

Although most DACs strive to create the input-output characteristic of Equation 11.2, the methods by which they achieve these results and the circuits they use vary widely. Each approach has advantages and disadvantages. You are encouraged to read about some of the other DAC architectures such as interpolating, charge sharing, current steering, and delta-sigma DACs. In this chapter, we will examine a

DAC popular in small microprocessor applications: the flash DAC. A second DAC architecture, called a pulse-width modulation (PWM) DAC, is covered in Chapter 12 in conjunction with the timer discussion.

Sample Question: *What is the voltage represented by an ideal 4-bit DAC with input 0xC, VREF– = 0 V, and VREF+ = 4 V?*

Answer: The DAC has a precision of $2^4 = 16$ levels and a range of $(4\,V - 0\,V) = 4\,V$. The DAC input 0xC, or 12, will generate an output voltage of $0\,V + 12/16 \times (4\,V - 0\,V) = 3.0\,V$

Compare the reconstructed DAC result here with the ADC examples earlier in this chapter. The ADC input voltage 3.14159 V is converted to a 4-bit digital value 0xC. A 4-bit DAC using the same reference voltages converts the digital sample back into the voltage 3.0 V. The difference between the two voltages (e.g., 0.14159 V) is the quantization error. If we need voltage measurements that are more accurate, we would need to use an ADC and DAC with more precision.

FLASH DACs

A *flash* digital-to-analog converter, sometimes called a parallel DAC, is characterized by its capability to generate an output within a single clock cycle. The speed of a flash DAC is achieved by the parallel generation of a set of fixed references. The set of references is complete; it is capable of constructing all of the possible DAC output values. Thus, any desired voltage output can be created nearly instantly, making flash DACs very fast. There are many different ways to go about creating these reference voltages, which gives rise to different flash DAC architectures. We will examine two closely related flash DACs: the resistor string and resistor ladder flash DACs.

RESISTOR STRING FLASH DACs

Resistor string digital-to-analog converters use a resistor voltage divider network, connected between two reference voltages, to generate a complete set of output voltages. Each voltage divider tap in the resistor string corresponds to a DAC input code. An n-bit resistor string flash DAC uses at least 2^n resistors. Some designs use additional resistors to create more accurate reference voltages, or voltages that correspond to rounded rather than truncated code values. Switches, controlled by the DAC's digital input, select the appropriate reference voltage to connect to the DAC output.

Resistor string DACs are available with many different input code word lengths. As an example, let's consider a 3-bit resistor string flash DAC architecture like the one in Figure 11.28. The resistor string flash DAC in Figure 11.28 is a unipolar DAC because the VREF− is connected to ground. This simplifies the discussion without a loss of generality. The resistor string in Figure 11.28 divides the DAC reference voltage, VREF+, into $2^3 = 8$ equally spaced voltages, $V_0, V_1, \ldots, V_7$. The DAC architecture in Figure 11.28a uses $2^3 = 8$ switches to connect the appropriate voltage to the DAC output, V_o. The switch control signals, S0, S1, ... , S7 are generated by a 3:8 decoder, which is not shown in Figure 11.28. As the number of bits in the DAC's input code increases, more and more switches are connected to the DAC's output V_o. This increases the capacitance at the DAC output node, making the DAC slower and limiting its maximum operating frequency.

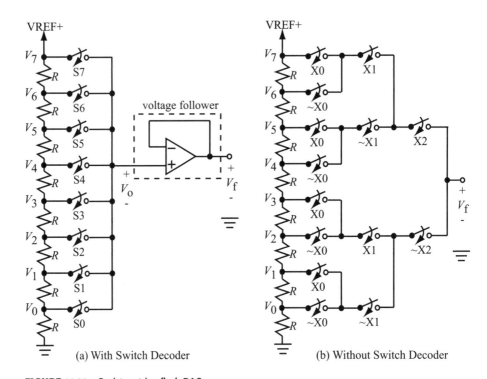

(a) With Switch Decoder (b) Without Switch Decoder

FIGURE 11.28 Resistor string flash DAC.

An alternative resistor string DAC architecture in Figure 11.28b arranges the switches into a binary tree structure. This architecture does not need the dedicated 3:8 decoder. Decoding is inherent in the binary tree arrangement of the switches that are controlled by the DAC's digital input code bits, X0, X1, X2, and their complements, ~X0, ~X1, ~X2. Furthermore, parasitic capacitance at the DAC output is reduced and operating speeds increased since the output is connected to fewer switches than the DAC in Figure 11.28a.

A major disadvantage of both resistor string flash DACs in Figure 11.28 is the stringent voltage string resistor matching requirements. Since the DAC voltage division determines output voltages, each resistor must be almost perfect or every reference voltage will be incorrect. The number of resistors needed for larger DACs, e.g., eight or more bits, and the limitations of VLSI fabrication technology make it difficult to create so many accurate and small resistors at an affordable price. Another disadvantage of the DACs in Figure 11.28 is their inability to drive a load without a buffer. If the DAC's load, which can be modeled as a resistor, draws much current, a current divider circuit is created. The DAC load will siphon current out of the voltage divider string and cause the voltages below the connection point to become inaccurate. The voltage follower shown in Figure 11.28a creates a copy of V_o at V_f without drawing much current from the resistor string (a voltage follower would also be used with the architecture of Figure 11.13b). Yet another disadvantage is power consumption. Since current is always flowing through the voltage divider, power is constantly being dissipated. Although the resistor value, R, can be increased to reduce power losses, larger resistors occupy more chip area.

In spite of these disadvantages, resistor string DACs are attractive because they guarantee *monotonicity*—the property that an increase in the DAC digital input code causes an increase in the DAC's analog output. Finally, the resistor string DACs in Figure 11.28 can be very fast because of the parallel nature of their design. Conversion speed is limited by the decoder speed (if present), switch speeds, and settling time and slew rate of any output amplifiers. Therefore, resistor string DACs are used in many high bandwidth applications such as digital video, RADAR, and communications.

R-2R Resistor Ladder Flash DAC

A DAC closely related to the resistor string flash DAC is the R-2R resistor ladder flash DAC. The R-2R resistor ladder DAC also uses voltage division to generate the DAC's output voltage, but does so in a clever way that uses significantly fewer resistors than the resistor string DAC. Instead of generating all possible voltage outputs, the resistor ladder DAC effectively rearranges its voltage divider network based on the DAC's digital input code. An n-bit R-2R resistor ladder flash DAC uses at least $2n$ resistors and n switches. You can see that the resistor ladder DAC uses a much smaller number of components than the same size resistor string flash DAC, especially as the DAC input code word length n gets large. The DAC's digital input code bits control switches that make connections between resistors and virtually rearrange the resistor ladder network to form the DAC's output voltage. The R-2R resistor ladder flash DAC is especially well suited for use with a small microprocessor like the PIC24 μC.

Just like all of the data converters that we have already examined, the resistor ladder DAC comes in many different word lengths. For discussion, let's look at the 4-bit R-2R resistor ladder DAC in Figure 11.29. Once again, we will consider the unipolar implementation of the R-2R resistor ladder flash DAC to simplify the discussion and analysis. Bipolar implementations operate identically. The R-2R resistor ladder flash DAC uses four switches, three resistors of R ohms, and five resistors of $2R$ ohms. The four switches connect the appropriate power supply voltage to the $2R$ resistors.

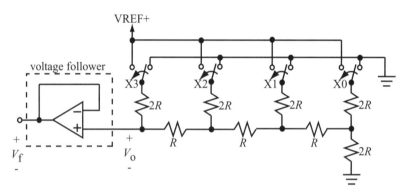

FIGURE 11.29   R-2R resistor ladder flash DAC.

The high reference voltage VREF+ is connected to each $2R$ resistor if the corresponding digital input code bit, X0, X1, X2, or X3, is "1". Otherwise, if the digital input code bit is "0", the lower supply voltage, usually ground, is connected to the appropriate $2R$ resistor. While not obvious, the switch states will create an output voltage that is proportional to the digital input code. Like the resistor string DACs in Figure 11.28, the resistor ladder DAC in Figure 11.29 usually requires a voltage follower to prevent excessive current siphoning from the ladder that would cause voltage output errors.

To see how the resistor ladder DAC works, let's consider a few examples. Consider the case when the 4-bit input code X3 X2 X1 X0 is 0b0000. Since all 4 input bits are "0", each $2R$ resistor is connected to the lower supply voltage—ground in this example. The resistor ladder in Figure 11.30a has been redrawn to emphasize this fact. Obviously, the output voltage V_o must be 0 V since there is no other voltage source in the circuit.

Now, consider the case when the input code is 8, or 0b1000. Figure 11.30b shows the equivalent circuit when the input is 0b1000. Applying voltage division repeatedly gives V_o = VREF/2. When the input code is 0b0001, or 0x1, in Figure 11.30c, repeated application of voltage division gives V_o = VREF/16. When

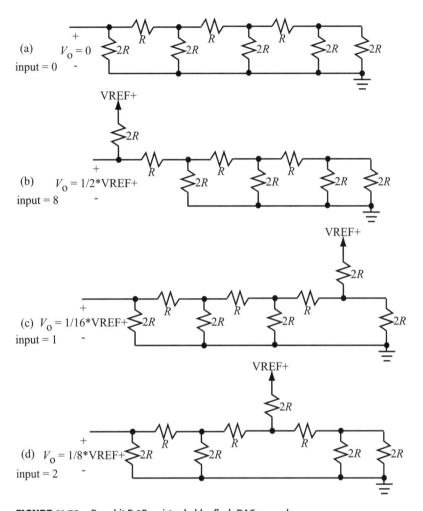

FIGURE 11.30   Four-bit R-2R resistor ladder flash DAC example.

the input code is 0b0010 = 0x2 as shown in Figure 11.30d, we see that V_o = VREF/8. Since the R-2R resistor ladder DAC uses only linear resistors, the *superposition theory* applies. Superposition says that we can find a system's response to several inputs by simply adding up the individual output responses to each input acting alone. Therefore, if the R-2R resistor ladder DAC in Figure 11.29 has more than one switch connected to VREF+, we can find V_o by summing the appropriate individual responses in Figure 11.30. For example, if the input code is 0b1001 = 0x9, the resistor ladder output voltage V_o is the sum of the responses at V_o for the two individual cases when the sources act alone. So, we find that V_o = VREF+/2 + VREF+/16 = 9 × VREF+/16. To generalize this result to an n-bit resistor ladder DAC, we find that for a digital input code of X, the resistor ladder output voltage V_o is $(X/2n) \times$ VREF+, which is the desired result. The resistor ladder DAC generates an output voltage that is linearly proportional to the digital input code.

The resistor ladder DAC circuit in Figure 11.29 is actually much simpler to put into practice than it first appears. Switches and voltage supplies are not really needed because the PIC24 µC conveniently provides these in the form of digital output port pins. When the PIC24 µC is driving a "1" from one of its IO pins, it is connecting that pin to the PIC24 µC's internal VDD. When the PIC24 µC is pulling down, or driving, its IO pin to "0", the PIC24 µC is really connecting that IO pin to its internal ground. Therefore, the PIC24 IO pins can be used to replace the switches, VREF+ = VDD, and ground connections in Figure 11.29. Therefore, the PIC24 µC can very easily build an 8-bit R-2R resistor ladder flash DAC with 16 resistors as shown in Figure 11.31. Simply writing the 8-bit value of the digital code X to correct bits of PORTB will create the voltage $(X/256) \times$ VDD at V_o. The resulting voltage is based on VDD because the PIC24 µC's VDD is our resistor ladder DAC's VREF+. Of course, any eight pins on the PIC24 IO ports can be used instead of PORTB, and the DAC input word can be shorter or longer depending on the application. But beware: whenever you split the DAC input word across several IO ports, it will take several PIC24 µC instruction cycles to update the entire DAC value. During this time between output port writes, the DAC output voltage will likely be grossly incorrect. In practice, you would like to keep the R-2R output pins on the same IO port and adjacent if at all possible.

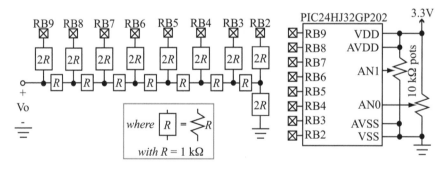

FIGURE 11.31   Eight-bit R-2R resistor ladder flash DAC using IO port on PIC24HJ32GP202.

If our DAC's load is purely capacitive or has a very large resistance, the circuit in Figure 11.31 works very well. However, the current flowing through the resistor ladder network is crucial to forming the voltage at V_o. Therefore, the R-2R resistor ladder DAC cannot be loaded by any circuit element that draws appreciable current. If a current drawing load is connected, the load will siphon current out of the resistor ladder and cause distortion at V_o. To prevent excessive current draw, we simply attach a voltage follower at V_o, just like the resistor string flash DAC in Figure 11.29. Furthermore, capacitance can be added to the voltage follower's feedback path to create an active low-pass filter to smooth out the jagged stair-step pattern visible at V_o. The low-pass filter at a DAC's output is sometimes called a reconstruction filter by digital signal processing experts.

Figures 11.32 and 11.33 list codes that create a simple sinusoid function generator with the PIC24 μC. The potentiometers on AN0 and AN1 control the sinusoid's frequency and amplitude, respectively. The PIC24 internal ADC reads the voltage provided by a potentiometer every 100 ms. The relatively slow update is fine for this kind of user interface function. In operation, the PIC24 μC appears to respond instantly to the changes in potentiometer settings.

The code in Figures 11.32 and 11.33 uses the 16-bit Timer3 as a periodic interrupt source in a similar manner as previously done in Chapter 9. Timer3 is used to create periodic interrupts so that the R-2R resistor ladder DAC on PORTB can be updated at a uniform rate. At each Timer3 interrupt, the ISR writes an updated value to the DAC. A value from the sine lookup table, along with the 16-bit table

```
#include "pic24_all.h"
#include "stdio.h"

void configDAC(void);                        ⎫ Function prototypes for
void writeDAC(uint16 u16_x, uint16 u16_y);   ⎭ the supported DACs.

volatile uint8    u8_per, u8_amp;◄──────────global variables
volatile uint16   u16_per;◄────────────
                                      ╱128 8-bit values of sine wave
const uint8 au8_sinetbl[] = {127,133,139,146,152,158,164,170, \
    176,181,187,192,198,203,208,212,217,221,225,229,233,236,239, \
    242,244,247,249,250,252,253,253,254,254,254,253,253,252,250, \
    249,247,244,242,239,236,233,229,225,221,217,212,208,203,198, \
    192,187,181,176,170,164,158,152,146,139,133,127,121,115,108, \
    102,96,90,84,78,73,67,62,56,51,46,42,37,33,29,25,21,18,15,   \
    12,10,7,5,4,2,1,1,0,0,0,1,1,2,4,5,7,10,12,15,18,21,25,29,33, \
    37,42,46,51,56,62,67,73,78,84,90,96,102,108,115,121};

void _ISR _T3Interrupt (void) {
    static uint8    u8_idx;
    static uint16   u16_idx, u16_val;
                                    ┌─Write sine data and index value to DAC.
    writeDAC(u16_val, u16_idx);◄────
                            ┌───── Update 16-bit table index by user-selected period.
    u16_idx += u16_per;◄────       ┌──Convert 16-bit table index to 7-bit value.
    u8_idx = (uint8) (u16_idx>>9 );◄──
    u16_val = ((uint16)au8_sinetbl[u8_idx])<<8;◄─┐Get 8-bit sine value from
    u16_val >>= u8_amp;◄──                        table and extend to 16-bits.
    _T3IF = 0;╮        └────────Reduce sine data amplitude by user-selected amount.
}            ╲Clear timer flag.
```

FIGURE 11.32 Code for DAC examples (part 1).

```
int main(void) {
  uint8    u8_uiCount;
  uint16   u16_ticks;

  configBasic(HELLO_MSG);
  CONFIG_AN0_AS_ANALOG();   CONFIG_AN1_AS_ANALOG();
  configDAC();  ⟵————— Ready the D̄AC for output.

  configTimer3();  ⟵——  Configure Timer3 to use the internal instruction
                        clock (TCY) to generate interrupts every 50 μs.
  u8_uiCount=5;           See Chapter 9.
  while(1) {
    configADC1_ManualCH0(ADC_CH0_POS_SAMPLEA_AN0, 31, 1);
    DELAY_MS(100);
    u16_per = convertADC1();
    if (u16_per==0) u16_per++;  ⟵————— u16_per must be >= 1.

    configADC1_ManualCH0(ADC_CH0_POS_SAMPLEA_AN1, 31, 1);
    DELAY_MS(100);
    u8_amp = convertADC1()>>9;  ⟵————— u16_amp must be 0 to 7.

    if(!u8_uiCount) {
      printf("timestep=0x%04X    ", u16_per);
      printf("amplitude shift=0x%02X\n", u8_amp );
      u8_uiCount=5;
    }
    else
      u8_uiCount--;
  }
}
```

Update user
interface every
5th time through
loop (approx.
every 1.0s).

FIGURE 11.33   Code for DAC examples (part 2).

lookup index value, are written to the DAC by the function call writeDAC(). The R-2R DAC in Figure 11.31 can only create one voltage, so we will soon see that our writeDAC() function for the R-2R resistor ladder DAC will ignore the second argument in its function call. (The DAC examples that follow this one will also use the code in Figures 11.32 and 11.33. Several of these DACs are capable of two channel output and will use the second argument passed to the writeDAC() function.) The sine data in Figure 11.32 can be easily replaced with other values so that the PIC24 μC can create any arbitrary waveform like sawtooth and chirp signals. In fact, the lookup table can easily be changed to represent a single cycle of a saxophone recording making your PIC24 μC a simple music synthesizer. The lookup table au8_sine[] in Figure 11.32 contains 128 entries. Each entry is an 8-bit value representing the amplitude of a sinusoid at equally spaced time intervals. The number of values can be increased to give the waveform more detail. The constant modifier for au8_sine[] tells the compiler that this array contains constant data (the array values are not changed), so this data is stored in program memory instead of data memory. This is useful especially for large lookup tables, which may not fit in data memory.

Upon its call, the timer ISR immediately updates the DAC value with the data sample calculated in the last ISR execution. Next, the timer index variable u16_idx is incremented with interval u16_per sensed by the code in main() from the user adjusting the potentiometer that controls the waveform frequency. As the user adjusts the pot, the number for u16_per increases and causes the u16_idx to traverse its 65,536 values more quickly. Every roll-over of the 16-bit variable u16_idx corresponds to the beginning of a new period of the sine wave. The ISR truncates the 16-bit u16_idx to a 7-bit index used to find the next sinusoid data value from au8_sinetbl. Then, the lookup table value is read into a variable and shifted based on the value in u8_amp. This right-shift provides very simplistic amplitude scaling. At the next interrupt, our computed DAC value is written to PORTB to update the waveform via the R-2R resistor ladder DAC in Figure 11.31.

Now that we have examined the big picture of generating a sinusoid waveform and controlling its frequency and amplitude via our two potentiometers, let's look at the details of configuring the R-2R resistor ladder DAC in Figure 11.31. Figure 11.34 shows the subroutines to configure the R-2R resistor ladder DAC and to update the DAC value. Configuration of our R-2R resistor ladder DAC is simple: make each output port pin that drives a DAC resistor a digital output. Setting a bit on one of the DAC control pins is equivalent to pulling the corresponding 2R resistor up to VDD. Clearing a bit on one of our DAC control pins is equivalent to connecting the resistor to ground.

```
void  configDAC() {
  CONFIG_RB2_AS_DIG_OUTPUT();
  CONFIG_RB3_AS_DIG_OUTPUT();
  CONFIG_RB4_AS_DIG_OUTPUT();
  CONFIG_RB5_AS_DIG_OUTPUT();         Prepare RB2-RB9 pins to drive
  CONFIG_RB6_AS_DIG_OUTPUT();         the R-2R resistor ladder inputs.
  CONFIG_RB7_AS_DIG_OUTPUT();
  CONFIG_RB8_AS_DIG_OUTPUT();               The R-2R resistor ladder DAC converts
  CONFIG_RB9_AS_DIG_OUTPUT();               only one 8-bit value, so this variable
}                                           is not used in writeDAC().

void  writeDAC(uint16 u16_x, uint16 u16_y) {
  uint16    u16_temp;                  Read Port B to a temporary variable,
                                       clearing the 8 bits used for DAC input.
  u16_temp = LATB & 0xFC03;            Place DAC data into correct
  u16_temp |= ((u16_x & 0xFF00) >> 6); location in Port B data.
  LATB = u16_temp;
}                                      Update Port B pins with new DAC value.
```

FIGURE 11.34   Configuration and update subroutines for R-2R resistor ladder flash DAC.

The function `writeDAC()` updates the register value and output pins that drive the 2R resistors in the R-2R resistor ladder DAC. Since we will only use eight of the 16 possible pins on PORTB, our function `writeDAC()` must take precautions not to change the eight bits in PORTB that our R-2R resistor ladder DAC does not use. The function `writeDAC()` starts by reading the current value of the PORTB register and clearing the eight bits that the DAC will modify. The eight-bit DAC value passed into `writeDAC()` is inserted into the correct position, then the new PORTB value is written to the IO port register. Figure 11.35 shows output from the circuit in Figure 11.31 running the code from Figures 11.32 and 11.34. At the bottom of Figure 11.35, you see the eight digital bits of data that drive the R-2R resistor ladder DAC along with the resulting analog voltage output.

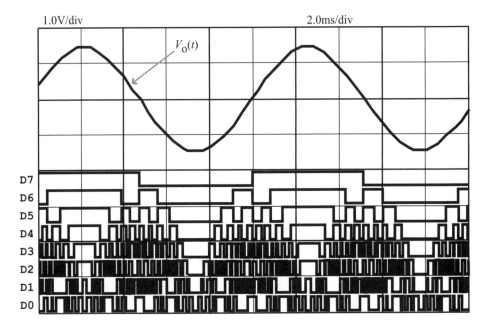

FIGURE 11.35   Output of 8-bit R-2R resistor ladder flash DAC.

EXTERNAL DIGITAL-TO-ANALOG CONVERTER EXAMPLES

DACs can be constructed with any of the architectures introduced in the previous section and numerous other architectures not discussed in this book. DAC architecture selection is usually application specific. When choosing an external DAC, several options should be considered; for example, number and value of external reference voltages, word length, number of channels, input communication scheme, and chip package type are just a few. Many of these parameters are interrelated. If a single channel 24-bit DAC with parallel inputs is chosen, the DAC package will have at least 28 pins: 1 pin each for VDD, VSS, V_o, 24 pins for input data, and 1 pin for input latch or clock. If the DAC supports external reference voltages for the analog output or multiple output channels, the number of package pins rises quickly.

Parallel port IO pins are usually a microprocessor's most limited and expensive resource since a chip package with a few more pins is far more expensive than the corresponding increase in silicon area costs to support those extra pins. Because parallel IO pins are so precious, many common external components choose to use pin-saving schemes for communication like the synchronous serial IO interfaces SPI and I²C introduced in Chapter 10. In the next few sections, we introduce three external DACs from Maxim Integrated Products that create analog voltages without consuming so many of the precious IO pins on the PIC24 µC. The DACs are

- the MAX548A, a dual 8-bit DAC with a SPI bus interface,
- the MAX5353, a single 12-bit multiplying DAC with a SPI bus interface, and
- the MAX518, a dual 8-bit DAC with an I²C interface.

Using our PIC24 µC and these three DACs, we combine concepts from this chapter and Chapter 10 to create several alternative, pin-conserving circuits to Figure 11.31 to create our sine wave output.

DAC Example: The Maxim548A

The Maxim Integrated Products MAX548A is a dual 8-bit DAC with a SPI-compatible interface. The MAX548A output is a voltage created by its internal R-2R resistor ladder DAC. The means by which the MAX548A creates its output is fundamentally identical to our discrete resistor R-2R approach in Figure 11.31; however, the MAX548A resistor ladder resistors are accurately trimmed and matched at fabrication. The MAX548A will produce a more accurate output voltage than our discrete resistor circuit. Furthermore, the MAX548A provides a second 8-bit DAC. Since the MAX548A is an SPI device, it gives us dual 8-bit DACs while using only three of our valuable IO pins. In contrast, our approach in Figure 11.31 would require 16 IO pins for two 8-bit DACs.

The MAX548A is readily connected to our PIC24 µC; Figure 11.36 shows the details. To operate, the MAX548A requires three SPI signals from the PIC24 µC: SCLK, SDO, and a chip select. The MAX548A also requires the usual power supply connections, and the MAX548A signal LDAC# must be connected to VDD for our purposes. The MAX548A has two independent DACs; their outputs are the MAX548A pins OUTA and OUTB. The PIC24 µC controls the MAX548A by performing a single 16-bit SPI write transaction. However, we will implement the

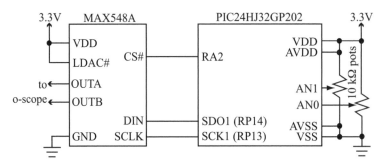

FIGURE 11.36   Interfacing the PIC24HJ32GP202 microcontroller with a MAX548A DAC via SPI.

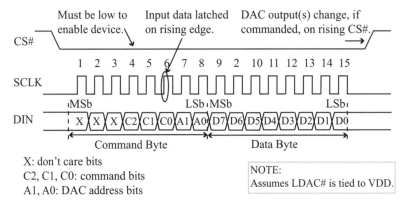

FIGURE 11.37   Sample SPI operations for MAX548A DAC.

16-bit write by two 8-bit writes due to the division of command and data between the two bytes. Figure 11.37 shows the details of the PIC24 μC communication with the MAX548A via SPI. For more information about SPI operations on the PIC24 μC, see Chapter 10. The MAX548A datasheet [68] contains more details about the MAX548A operation and limitations.

Using the MAX548A to create our sinusoid voltage output requires the same `main()` code as before: Figures 11.32 and 11.33. Of course, the DAC configuration and update functions must be changed and made specific to the MAX548A. Figure 11.39 shows the code for the MAX548A. The MAX548A version of the function `configDAC()` begins by enabling the PIC24 μC SPI peripheral for 8-bit master mode operation with a 10 MHz SPI clock. The MAX548A requires no explicit configuration command, so we can progress to placing the MAX548A and the SPI bus into a normal operating state. Figure 11.36 shows the MAX548A active-low chip select pin, CS#, connected to the PIC24 μC IO pin RA2. Therefore, the function configDAC() configures the RA2 pin to be a digital output and initially disables the MAX548A. Two convenient macros, MAX548A_DISABLE() and MAX548A_ENABLE(), are defined in Figure 11.39 to improve code readability.

Command Byte	x	x	x	C2	C1	C0	A1	A0
	7	6	5	4	3	2	1	0

C2	Power-down bit: Setting to "1" will place the MAX548A into a low-power mode. Write "0" to this bit for normal operations.
C1	DAC Register Load bit: Write "1" to have DAC output registers updated with data from input registers. Write "0" to not change DAC output registers and outputs.
C0	DAC Register Update Select bit: Write "1" to have DAC output registers updated on LDAC# rising edge. Write "0" to have DAC output registers update on CS# falling edge. (Our examples always clear C0. LDAC# is connected to VDD.)
A1	Address DAC B bit: Write "1" to address DAC B registers. "0" will not address DAC B registers.
A0	Address DAC A bit: Write "1" to address DAC A registers. "0" will not address DAC A registers.

FIGURE 11.38   Command byte and SPI transaction for the MAX548 DAC.

Figure 11.38 shows the format of a SPI transfer to the MAX548A along with a brief description of the MAX548A command byte. Figure 11.39 shows the DAC function writeDAC() to write the new DAC values to both channels of the MAX548A. Updating both MAX548A channels is done in two SPI transactions. The first transaction writes the second argument of writeDAC() to the MAX548A's second DAC. Notice that the MAX548A command byte of this first transaction disables the DAC register load operation by clearing the command byte's bit 3, called C1 in the MAX548A datasheet. Clearing this bit allows us to write the contents of the DAC B register without changing its output. The second SPI transaction in writeDAC() writes the function's first argument to the DAC A register and updates both DAC outputs simultaneously by setting bit C1 in the MAX548A command byte. Both SPI transactions in Figure 11.39 have the third bit, called C0, in the command byte cleared to instruct the MAX548A to update results on rising edges of CS#. Setting this bit would require us to connect a fourth PIC24 output pin to the MAX548A LDAC# pin.

Using the code in Figures 11.32, 11.33, and 11.39 with the circuit in Figure 11.36 generates a sinusoid output. The sinusoid waveform produced by the setup in

```
#define CONFIG_MAX548A_ENABLE()    CONFIG_RA2_AS_DIG_OUTPUT()
#define MAX548A_ENABLE()           _LATA2 = 0
#define MAX548A_DISABLE()          _LATA2 = 1

void configDAC(void) {
  SPI1CON1 = SEC_PRESCAL_1_1     |
             PRI_PRESCAL_4_1     |
             CLK_POL_ACTIVE_HIGH |
             SPI_CKE_ON          |
             SPI_MODE8_ON        |
             MASTER_ENABLE_ON;
```
Configure 10MHz SPI active-high clock with SPI module in 8-bit master mode. See Chapter 10 for details.

```
  // Only need SDO, SCLK since MAX548A is output only
  CONFIG_RB14_AS_DIG_OUTPUT();
  CONFIG_SDO1_TO_RP(14);
  CONFIG_RB13_AS_DIG_OUTPUT();
  CONFIG_SCK1OUT_TO_RP(13);
  SPI1STATbits.SPIEN = 1;
```
Use RP14 for SDO and RP13 for SCLK, and enable SPI peripheral.

```
  CONFIG_MAX548A_ENABLE();
  MAX548A_DISABLE();
}
```
Configure pin for MAX548A CS# and place in disable mode.

```
void writeDAC(uint16 u16_x, uint16 u16_y) {
  static uint8   u8_cnt;

  MAX548A_ENABLE();
  ioMasterSPI1(0x02);
  ioMasterSPI1(u16_y>>8);
  MAX548A_DISABLE();
```
Write command to "update DAC B input without changing DAC B output voltage", and write 2nd channel data to DAC.

```
  MAX548A_ENABLE();
  ioMasterSPI1(0x09);
  ioMasterSPI1(u16_x>>8);
  MAX548A_DISABLE();
}
```
Write command to "update DAC A input and update both DAC outputs", and write 1st channel data to DAC.

Both DAC output voltages change on this statement.

FIGURE 11.39   Configuration and update subroutines for MAX548 DAC.

Figure 11.36 is not reproduced here since it is identical to Figure 11.35. Furthermore, the output of the MAX548A's second DAC generates a sawtooth waveform (from the second parameter passed to writeDAC() which is the sine wave table index) whose frequency can be changed by the user via the potentiometer. The code in Figure 11.32 does not adjust the sawtooth waveform amplitude, but that could be added easily.

DAC EXAMPLE: THE MAXIM5353

The Maxim Integrated Products MAX5353 is a single 12-bit multiplying DAC with an SPI-compatible interface. The MAX5323 output is a voltage created by its internal R-2R resistor ladder DAC. The MAX5353 has an internal voltage buffer amplifier to prevent loading issues from the small currents in the R-2R resistor ladder, and provides greater flexibility in selecting output gains. The MAX5353 allows use in a multiplying DAC configuration. In this mode, the MAX5353 uses a time-varying reference voltage in the digital-to-analog conversion. Instead of creating uniform steps between ground and a fixed reference, the multiplying DAC would permit using a sinusoid or some other waveform as the reference voltage and the DAC values would select a variable gain to generate waveforms of various amplitudes, which is required for signal modulation. While we could create our sinusoid function generator in this way, we will use the MAX5353 with a fixed voltage reference to allow code reuse from the previous examples.

The MAX5353 is readily connected to our PIC24 µC; Figure 11.40 shows the details. To operate, the MAX5353 requires three SPI signals from the PIC24 µC: SCLK, SDO, and a chip select. The MAX5353 also requires the usual power supply connections. The MAX5353 requires a regulated reference voltage on its REF pin. This regulated reference voltage must be less 1.9 V when VDD = 3.3 V. Figure 11.40 shows a 1.65 V reference. Using the MAX5353 internal voltage amplifier, we connect two 10 kΩ resistors between the DAC output, the amplifier feedback pin, and ground. These two resistors result in a 2x gain of the output resulting in a full 3.3 V peak-to-peak swing on the DAC output voltage.

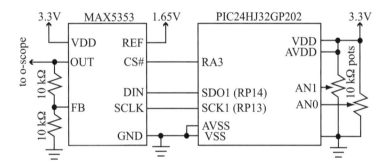

FIGURE 11.40   Interfacing the PIC24HJ32GP202 microcontroller with a MAX5353 DAC via SPI.

The PIC24 µC controls the MAX5353 by performing a single 16-bit SPI write transaction. Figure 11.41 shows the details of the PIC24 µC communication with the MAX5353 via SPI. For more information about SPI operations on the PIC24 µC, see Chapter 10. The MAX5353 datasheet [69] contains more details about the MAX5353 operation and limitations.

Using the MAX5353 to create our sinusoid voltage output requires the same basic code as before: Figures 11.32 and 11.33. Of course, the DAC configuration and update functions must be changed and made specific to the MAX5353. Figure 11.43 shows the code for the MAX5353. The MAX5353 version of the function `configDAC()` begins by enabling the PIC24 µC SPI peripheral for 16-bit

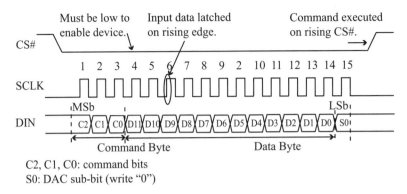

C2, C1, C0: command bits
S0: DAC sub-bit (write "0")

FIGURE 11.41 Sample SPI operations for MAX5353 DAC.

master mode operation with a 10 MHz SPI clock. The MAX5353 requires no explicit configuration command, so we can progress to placing the MAX5353 and the SPI bus into a normal operating state. Figure 11.40 shows the MAX5353 active-low chip select, CS#, pin connected to the PIC24 µC IO pin RA3. Therefore, the function configDAC() configures the RA3 pin to be a digital output and initially disables the MAX5353. Two convenient macros, MAX5353_DISABLE() and MAX5353_ENABLE(), are defined in Figure 11.43 to improve code readability.

Figure 11.42 shows the format of a SPI transfer to the MAX5353 along with a brief description of the MAX5353 command bits. Commands are provided to the MAX5353 in the first three data bits of the SPI transaction. The 12-bit DAC data follow with the LSb of the 16-bit data word being cleared. Figure 11.43 shows the DAC function writeDAC() to write the new DAC value to the MAX5353 DAC

16-bit Command and Data Word	C2	C1	C0	12-bit DAC data value		S0
	15	14	13	12	1	0

C2 C1 C0   DAC data   S0

C2	C1	C0	DAC data	S0	
x	0	0	12 bits of data	0	Load DAC input register. DAC output register and output updated on rising CS#. Also, exit shutdown mode.
x	0	1	12 bits of data	0	Load DAC input register. DAC output register and output are unchanged.
x	1	0	xxxxxxxxxxxx	x	Update DAC output register and output from DAC input register. Also, exit shutdown mode.
1	1	1	xxxxxxxxxxxx	x	Enter shutdown mode.
0	1	1	xxxxxxxxxxxx	x	No operation (NOP).

FIGURE 11.42 Command byte and SPI transaction for the MAX5353 DAC.

```
#define CONFIG_MAX5353_ENABLE()    CONFIG_RA3_AS_DIG_OUTPUT()
#define MAX5353_CMD_ANDMASK        0x1FFE
#define MAX5353_ENABLE()           _LATA3 = 0
#define MAX5353_DISABLE()          _LATA3 = 1

void configDAC(void) {
  SPI1CON1 = SEC_PRESCAL_1_1    |
             PRI_PRESCAL_4_1    |
             CLK_POL_ACTIVE_HIGH |
             SPI_CKE_ON         |
             SPI_MODE16_ON      |
             MASTER_ENABLE_ON;

  // Only need SDO, SCLK since MAX5353 is output only
  CONFIG_RB14_AS_DIG_OUTPUT();
  CONFIG_SDO1_TO_RP(14);
  CONFIG_RB13_AS_DIG_OUTPUT();
  CONFIG_SCK1OUT_TO_RP(13);
  SPI1STATbits.SPIEN = 1;
  CONFIG_MAX5353_ENABLE();
  MAX5353_DISABLE();
}
```

Mask to create command for updating DAC output with sub-bit cleared.

Configure 10MHz SPI active-high clock with SPI module in 16-bit master mode. See Chapter 10 for details.

Use RP14 for SDO and RP13 for SCLK, and enable SPI peripheral.

Configure pin for MAX5353 CS# and disable MAX5353.

The MAX5353 DAC converts only one 12-bit value, so u16_y is not used in writeDAC().

```
void writeDAC(uint16 u16_x, uint16 u16_y) {

  MAX5353_ENABLE();
  ioMasterSPI1((u16_x>>3) & MAX5353_CMD_ANDMASK);
  MAX5353_DISABLE();
}
```

Update MAX5353 with 12-bit value created from 16-bit user input.

DAC output voltage changes on this statement.

FIGURE 11.43 Configuration and update subroutines for MAX5353 DAC.

output. Since there is only one DAC output on the MAX5353, we have no concerns with synchronizing the updates of two DAC outputs as we did with the MAX548A. The required command bits to load our result into the MAX5353 DAC register and update the results are all zero. A 12-bit version of the 16-bit data passed into writeDAC() is placed in the correct location, and a 16-bit SPI transaction is initiated.

Using the code in Figures 11.32, 11.33, and 11.43 with the circuit in Figure 11.40 generates a sinusoid output. The sinusoid waveform produced by the setup in Figure 11.40 is not reproduced here since it is identical to Figure 11.35.

DAC Example: The Maxim518

The Maxim Integrated Products MAX518 is a dual 8-bit DAC with an I²C-compatible interface. The MAX518 outputs are voltages created by its dual internal R-2R resistor ladder DACs. The MAX518 has an internal voltage buffer amplifier to prevent loading issues from the small currents in the R-2R resistor ladder.

The MAX518 is readily connected to our PIC24 µC; Figure 11.44 shows the details. The signal-level MOSFET transistors in Figure 11.44 are required to interface the 3.3 V PIC24 µC to the 5 V MAX518. The MAX518 cannot operate with its VDD less than +5 V while the PIC24 µC has a maximum VDD = 3.6 V. Strictly speaking, the PIC24 µC can be connected directly to the 5V SDA and SCL lines since they are open-drain lines and the PIC24 µC is 5 V-tolerant on open-drain pins. See the discussion on the PIC24 µC ODCx registers and open-drain outputs in Chapter 8. If the MAX518 is the only I²C device connected to the PIC24 µC or all I²C devices connected PIC24 µC are 5 V, then we can use the 5 V-tolerance of the PIC24 µC. However, if the I²C devices connected to the PIC24 µC are a mixture of 3.3 V and 5 V devices, the system cannot drive 5 V signals into 3.3 V devices and 3.3 V signals into 5 V devices as that may generate errors. In general, you will typically want to connect several I²C parts to your PIC24 µC. It is likely that some of these I²C parts will be 3.3 V devices and others 5 V devices. Therefore, this section discusses the more general case of an I²C bus with different power supply voltages. Our example uses 3.3 V and 5 V. The approach presented here can be extended to additional I²C bus voltages if needed.

Figure 11.44 shows how the 3.3 V PIC24FH32GP202 can communicate with 3.3 V and 5 V I²C devices simultaneously. The study of MOSFET transistors would compose a text unto itself and is too far afield for this discussion. Suffice it to say, the 2N7000 transistors are "open" circuits and "disconnect" the two I²C busses when the SDA or SCL lines are pulled high by their respective pull-up resistors. The 2N7000 transistors will "short" and connect the two I²C busses when a device on either side pulls the bus voltage low. In this way, the 2N7000 allows for 5 V and 3.3 V "high" signals and ground signals to coexist and permits bidirectional communication required for I²C. Figure 11.44 shows external 10 kΩ pull-up resistors. The pull-up resistors on the 3.3 V side of the I²C bus could be implemented using the internal pull-up resistors in the PIC24 µC.

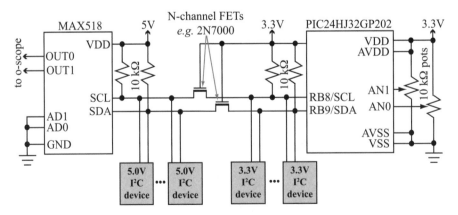

FIGURE 11.44   Interfacing the 3.3 V PIC24HJ32GP202 microcontroller with a 5 V MAX518 DAC via I²C.

To operate, the MAX518 requires two I²C signals from the PIC24 µC: SCL and SDA. The MAX518 also provides two I²C address pins and the usual power supply connections. The MAX518 external pins AD0 and AD1 determine the device's I²C address. The remaining five most significant device address bits are set internally to 0b01011. Recall from Chapter 10 that the LSb of the I²C address is the R/W# bit. The I²C master can only write to the MAX518, so the LSb of the I²C address is always "0". After the I²C master sends a valid MAX518 address, the MAX518 expects at least one command byte and a data byte. The MAX518 uses its own VDD as the reference voltage in the DAC conversion. Thus, the MAX518 will generate DAC output voltages between 0 V and 5 V. The MAX518 has two independent DACs whose outputs are the MAX518 pins OUT0 and OUT1. The MAX518 datasheet [70] contains more details about the MAX518 operation and limitations.

Using the MAX518 to create our sinusoid voltage output requires the same basic code as before: Figures 11.32 and 11.33. Of course, the DAC configuration and update functions must be changed and made specific to the MAX518. Figure 11.46 shows the code for the MAX518. The MAX518 version of the function `configDAC()` simply calls our I²C library to configure the PIC24 µC I²C peripheral for 400 kbps operation. Details of PIC24 µC I²C configuration and operation are covered in Chapter 10. The MAX518 requires no explicit configuration command, and an inactive I²C bus automatically disables the MAX518. Since Figure 11.44 shows the two external MAX518 address bits connected to ground, the MAX518 I²C write address is determined to be 0x58. The MAX518 version of the function `configDAC()` defines the macro `MAX518_I2C_ADDR` to improve code readability.

Figure 11.45 shows the format of an I²C transfer to the MAX518 along with a brief description of the MAX518 command bits. Commands are provided to the MAX518 in the first byte after the transfer of the I²C address. If the command requires DAC data to be sent, the 8-bit DAC data follows the MAX518 command byte. The LSb of the command byte determines the DAC that latches the data byte that follows the command byte. The MAX518 DAC output voltage VDAC0 or VDAC1 changes upon the I²C stop condition. Since the MAX518 is a dual DAC, both DACs can be set in one

Command Byte	0	0	0	RST	PD	x	x	A0
	7	6	5	4	3	2	1	0

RST	Reset Bit: "1" will reset (clear) all DAC registers.
PD	Power-down Bit: "1" will place MAX518 into a low-power state. Write "0" to this bit to return to normal operations.
A0	DAC Register Address Bit: "0" to write following data byte value to DAC0 input register. "1" to write following data byte value to DAC1 input register.

FIGURE 11.45   Command byte of an I²C transaction for the MAX518 DAC.

I²C transaction composed of the following I²C transfers: start condition, I²C device address, command byte, data byte, command byte, data byte, stop condition. In this case, both DAC outputs change simultaneously upon the I²C stop condition.

Figure 11.46 shows the MAX518 version of the function writeDAC() to write the new DAC value to the MAX518 DAC output. The function writeDAC() in Figure 11.46 only writes data to one DAC on the MAX518, so we have no concerns with synchronizing the updates of two DAC outputs as we did with the MAX548A. The required command bits to load our result into the first DAC input register on the MAX518 and update the DAC results are all zero. An 8-bit version of the 16-bit data passed into writeDAC() is sent after the command byte. Upon completion of the I²C transaction, the DAC value is updated.

Using the code in Figures 11.32, 11.33, and 11.46 with the circuit in Figure 11.44 generates a sinusoid output. The sinusoid waveform produced by the setup in Figure 11.44 is not reproduced here since it is identical to Figure 11.35.

```
#define    MAX518_I2C_ADDR        0x58
#define    MAX518_WRITE_DACA      0x00

void configDAC(void) {           ── Configure I²C peripheral.  See Chapter 10 for details.
  configI2C1(400); ◄
}                                     This version only converts one 8-bit value, so
                                        this variable is not used in writeDAC().

void writeDAC(uint16 u16_x, uint16 u16_y) {
  write2I2C1(MAX518_I2C_ADDR, MAX518_WRITE_DACA, (uint8) (u16_x>>8) );
}   MAX518 command for writing          Create 8-bit data from
    and updating DAC A output.          user's 16-bit input.
```

FIGURE 11.46 Configuration and update subroutines for MAX518 DAC.

You may be wondering why we did not send the second argument of the function writeDAC() to the MAX518. The answer lies in the fact that the I²C transaction is three bytes at 400 Kbps and our relatively short Timer3 period. If the function writeDAC() attempted to write both 8-bit DAC values to the MAX518 at 400 Kbps, the I²C transaction would not be completed before the time to write the next DAC values arrives. We could lengthen the Timer3 period to compensate, but this would

```
#define    MAX518_I2C_ADDR       0x58
#define    MAX518_WRITE_DACA     0x00
#define    MAX518_WRITE_DACB     0x01

void configDAC(void) {
  configI2C1(700);  ←────────────── Configure I²C peripheral for 700MHz operation.
}                                    Exceeds MAX518 specification!

void writeDAC(uint16 u16_x, uint16 u16_y) {
  static uint8 au8_buf[]={MAX518_WRITE_DACA, 0, \ ⎫ String to send DAC with
                          MAX518_WRITE_DACB, 0 }; ⎭ commands and data.

  au8_buf[1] = (uint8) (u16_x>>8);              ⎫ Place 8-bit data values
  au8_buf[3] = (uint8) (u16_y>>8);              ⎭ into DAC command string.
  writeNI2C1(MAX518_I2C_ADDR, &au8_buf[0], 4);
}
                        ↖
                          Send command string with data values to MAX518.
                          DAC output voltages change when this function completes.
```

FIGURE 11.47   Alternate configuration and update subroutines for MAX518 DAC.

reduce the usable frequency range of the output waveforms. Another alternative is to speed up the I²C clock. Figure 11.47 shows the code to run the PIC24 μC I²C peripheral and MAX518 at 700 Kbps. This data rate far exceeds the design specification of the MAX518 DAC. The MAX518 is limited to a maximum 400 Kbps data rate. While the MAX518 devices tested in our labs handled the higher data rate with no problem, it is not recommended that you design products outside of the manufacturer's specifications. However, this higher I²C data rate allows us to generate both waveforms at higher frequencies.

The higher clock rate version of the function writeDAC() writes the first data sample (the sinusoid data) to the first MAX518 DAC. In the same I²C transaction, the function writes the second data value (the sawtooth) to the second MAX518 DAC by setting the least significant bit in the MAX518 command byte. The MAX518 datasheet specifies that both DAC outputs are updated at the I²C stop condition. Figure 11.48 shows some example I²C transactions for the MAX518.

Using the code in Figures 11.32, 11.33, and 11.47 with MAX518 DAC generates a sinusoid output identical to figure 11.35 and a sawtooth waveform. The sinusoid waveform produced by the setup in Figure 11.44 is not reproduced here since it is identical to Figure 11.35.

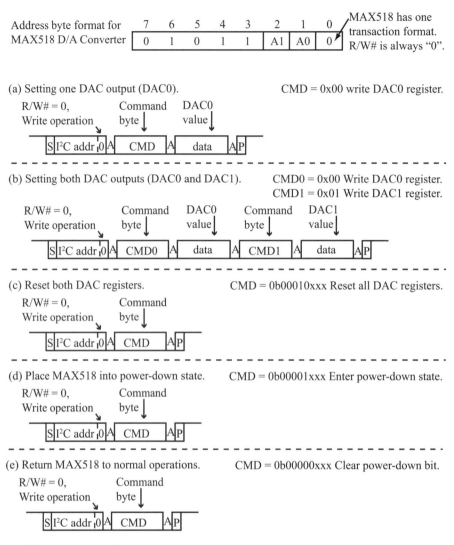

FIGURE 11.48 Sample I²C operations for MAX518 DAC.

SUMMARY

With the ever-decreasing cost of microprocessors, we are embedding digital computers into nearly every conceivable application. However, these digital computers must ultimately communicate with the "real world," which is an analog environment. Data conversion with ADCs and DACs is done in nearly every microprocessor system that interfaces with other systems, especially other systems that involve people. The data conversion devices are so useful that many embedded microprocessors include built-in ADCs and/or DACs. An ADC gives the microprocessor the capability to understand and operate on analog values generated by people, sensors, or other systems. A DAC allows microprocessors to use its digital processing to create or recreate analog values that people, sensors, or other systems can understand. Even if a microprocessor does not have a built-in or suitable ADC or DAC, an external data converter can be acquired and connected to the microprocessor via a direct parallel connection, an address/data bus, or a serial communications scheme.

REVIEW PROBLEMS

1. How many bits are required to represent a waveform in 4000 discrete levels?
2. How many different input voltages could you detect with a 24-bit ADC?
3. An audio CD can contain 80 minutes of stereo (two independent) audio tracks. Each track is sampled with 16-bit samples at 44.1 kHz. How much audio information, in bytes, is stored on an audio CD?
4. What is the data throughput (in MB/sec) of the audio CD in Problem 3? (Recall from Chapter 1 that 1 MB = 10^6 B.)
5. Still and movie images are often represented by an 8-bit value for each color component, red, green, and blue. How many different colors can be encoded?
6. An HDTV screen contains 1920 × 1080 pixels, with each red-green-blue (RGB) color component represented by 8 bits of precision. Motion playback is 30 frames per second. How much storage is required to store the average two-hour movie? What is the data throughput during HDTV playback?
7. Assume a 4-bit successive approximation A/D with VREF+ = 4 V and VREF− = 0 V. Trace the steps for producing a 4-bit output code if the input voltage is 1.8 V.
8. For an 8-bit flash ADC, how many comparators are needed? How many resistors are needed?
9. A 3-bit flash A/D has seven comparators, and each comparator output can be either 0 or 1. Assume VREF+ = 4 V and VREF− = VSS. What is the 7-bit output of these comparators if the input voltage is 2.7 V? Give the 7-bit value in binary, with the LSb corresponding to the comparator output with the smallest reference input and the MSb corresponding to the comparator with the highest reference input.
10. How many clock cycles would you expect a 12-bit successive approximation A/D to require for a conversion?
11. The VDD power supply is usually not used as a reference voltage for precision A/D measurements as it varies with current load and temperature. The National Semiconductor LM4040 is a component that provides a stable 3.0 V voltage reference with an accuracy of 0.1%. What voltage values does this 0.1% correspond to? How does this voltage translate into a percentage of 1 LSb of the 10-bit value produced by the PIC24 µC using the LM4040 as a VREF+ value (assume VREF− = 0 V)?

12. For the PIC24 µC, assume an Fosc of 40 MHz. Using Figure 11.9, what Fosc configurations cannot be used because they violate the minimum A/D clock period of 75 ns?

13. A 10-bit ADC has a lower reference voltage VREF− of 0 V and an upper reference voltage VREF+ of 3.3 V. What output code corresponds to 0.449 V? To 2.91 V?

14. Repeat the previous problem for a 12-bit A/D and an upper reference voltage of 3.0 V.

15. An 8-bit DAC has a lower reference voltage of 0 V and an upper reference voltage of 3.3 V. What is the output voltage for codes of 0x7F? 0x4B? 0xCB?

16. A 10-bit DAC has a lower reference voltage of 0 V and an upper reference voltage of 3.3 V. What is the output voltage for codes of 0x7F? 0x14B? 0x3CB?

17. A 12-bit DAC has a lower reference voltage of 0 V and an upper reference voltage of 3.0 V. What is the output voltage for codes of 0x17F? 0x74B? 0xCCB?

18. What is the principal advantage of a flash ADC architecture over a successive approximation ADC architecture? What is the principal disadvantage?

19. The National Semiconductor LM60 is a precision Celsius temperature sensor. The LM60 produces an output voltage that is linear to the temperature in Celsius and equal to 6.25 mV/°C with an offset of +424 mV. The LM60 is accurate up to 150°C. If your PIC24 µC is using internal ADC references and VDD = 3.3 V, determine the precision in °C of your measurements for the 10-bit and 12-bit operating modes.

20. Write a function that reads the LM60 discussed in the previous problem on an arbitrary PIC24 µC ADC input pin and returns the temperature to the calling function in a `double` data type. Your function should automatically determine and handle both 10-bit and 12-bit configurations.

21. How many bits of resolution are required for an ADC to measure the LM60 temperature (see Problem 19) between 0°C and 100°C with a precision of 1.5°C? Assume ADC reference voltages are 3.3 V and VSS.

22. The code in Figures 11.32 and 11.33 creates a sinusoid waveform with amplitude control by logical shifts. While simple and efficient, this approach results in very abrupt amplitude changes as each control increment divides the current amplitude in half. Rewrite the code in Figures 11.32 and 11.33 to generate a sinusoid waveform with smoother amplitude adjustment. Your code should be compatible with all of the example DACs we examined. (NOTE: Floating point arithmetic is CPU-intensive. Write your new code to use only integer operations.)

12 | Timers

U se of timers for periodic interrupt generation was previously discussed in Chapter 9. However, this only scratches the surface of the capabilities and application of the PIC24 timer subsystems. This chapter discusses the use of PIC24 timers for time measurement, waveform generation, real-time clock keeping, and pulse width modulation. Example applications include biphase waveform decoding for infrared reception, servo positioning, and DC motor speed control.

Learning Objectives

After reading this chapter, you will be able to:

- Discuss the specifics of the Timer1, Timer2, and Timer3 subsystems.
- Use the input capture subsystem to perform precise time measurements of external events.
- Use the input capture subsystem to decode an infrared receiver's output signal that is either space-width encoded or biphase encoded.
- Use the pulse width modulation capability of the output compare module to generate square waves with varying duty cycles and periods, which can be used to control the brightness of an external LED, servo position, and DC motor speed.
- Implement a simple real-time clock using a 32.768 kHz clock source and Timer1.
- Use the real-time clock calendar (RTCC) module and a 32.768 kHz clock source for time/date tracking.

PULSE WIDTH MEASUREMENT

The word *timer* implies *time measurement,* and a fundamental timer application is time measurement between two external events. In the digital world, an external event is either a rising or falling edge on an input pin. The time between two edges of the same type (falling-to-falling edge or rising-to-rising edge) on a square wave is the period, while the time between a rising-to-falling edge and falling-to-rising edge is high pulse width and low pulse width, respectively. The basics of event measurement are explored using the setup of Figure 12.1, in which the goal is to measure the low pulse width produced by activating a momentary switch. As a word of caution, if precise time measurement is required then you cannot use the internal fast RC oscillator since its period varies significantly (± 2%) from processor to processor and with temperature and VDD. As such, use of an external crystal oscillator or other stable external clock source is needed if precision time measurements are desired.

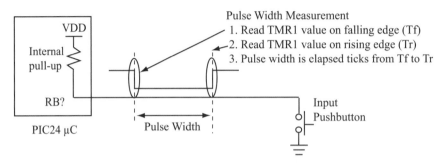

FIGURE 12.1   Pulse width measurement.

A straightforward method of measuring the pulse width of Figure 12.1 is given by the code of Figure 12.2, which uses Timer2 and polling of the switch input. Timer2 is configured for the maximum period (PR2 = 0xFFFF) with a prescaler of 256, which gives a period of approximately 420 ms (one timer tick ~ 6.4 µs) at FCY = 40 MHz; see Figure 9.11 for a review of Timer2 configuration. The while(1){} loop waits for a low input value (falling edge) on the pushbutton input then stores the TMR2 value in u16_start. The code then waits for a high input value (rising edge) and computes the difference between the two TMR2 tick values as:

```
u16_delta = TMR2 - u16_start;
```

This 16-bit delta calculation is correct only if the pulse width does not exceed the timer's maximum period. The u16_delta value represents the difference between the two TMR2 values even if the timer rolls over (overflows) between reading of the two values because the PR2 value is at its maximum value of 0xFFFF. If Timer2 is not configured for a maximum period, then the code would have to be replaced with:

```
u16_end = TMR2;
if (u16_end > u16_start) u16_delta = u16_end - u16_start;
else u16_delta = PR2+1 - u16_start + u16_end;
```

The else clause is the case for the u16_end value being read after the timer rolls over from its maximum value of PR2 to 0x0000. Observe that if PR2 = 0xFFFF,

```
void  configTimer2(void) {
  T2CON = T2_OFF | T2_IDLE_CON | T2_GATE_OFF
          | T2_32BIT_MODE_OFF
          | T2_SOURCE_INT
          | T2_PS_1_256 ;    //@40 MHz, ~420 ms period, 1 tick = 6.4 us
  PR2 = 0xFFFF;              //maximum period
  TMR2  = 0;                 //clear timer2 value
  _T2IF = 0;                 //clear interrupt flag
  T2CONbits.TON = 1;         //turn on the timer
}


/// Switch1 configuration
inline void CONFIG_SW1()   {
  CONFIG_RB13_AS_DIG_INPUT();    //use RB13 for switch input
  ENABLE_RB13_PULLUP();          //enable the pullup
}
#define SW1              _RB13  //switch state
#define SW1_PRESSED()    SW1==0 //switch test
#define SW1_RELEASED()   SW1==1 //switch test

int main (void) {
  uint16 u16_start, u16_delta;
  uint32 u32_pulseWidth;
  configBasic(HELLO_MSG);
  CONFIG_SW1();      //use RB13
  configTimer2();
  while (1) {
    outString("Press button...");
    while(SW1_RELEASED())doHeartbeat();
    u16_start = TMR2;        Read TMR2 at falling edge.
    while(SW1_PRESSED())doHeartbeat();
    u16_delta = TMR2 - u16_start;  //works because using maximum PR2 value
    u32_pulseWidth = ticksToUs((uint32) u16_delta,
                       getTimerPrescale(T2CONbits));   Convert to
    printf(" %ld us\n",u32_pulseWidth);                microseconds.
  }
}
```

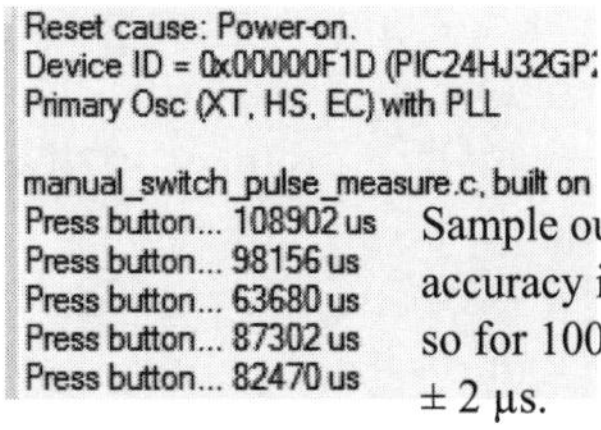

Reset cause: Power-on.
Device ID = 0x00000F1D (PIC24HJ32GP;
Primary Osc (XT, HS, EC) with PLL

manual_switch_pulse_measure.c, built on
Press button... 108902 us Sample output; Crystal
Press button... 98156 us   accuracy is ± 20 ppm,
Press button... 63680 us   so for 100,000 µs this is
Press button... 87302 us   ± 2 µs.
Press button... 82470 us

Compute delta ticks between falling and rising edge.

FIGURE 12.2 Pulse width measurement using Timer2 and polling.

then PR2+1 is equal to 0x0000, so the else clause devolves to u16_end - u16_start. If the pulse width is longer than a timer period, then the number of timer rollovers must be tracked as discussed later in this section.

Listing 12.1 gives the code for a function named computeDeltaTicks() that computes the delta ticks between a 16-bit start tick (u16_start) and a 16-bit end tick (u16_end) for a timer with period register value u16_tmrPR. The computation assumes that less than a timer period has elapsed between u16_start and u16_end.

LISTING 12.1 computeDeltaTicks() source code

```
uint16 computeDeltaTicks(uint16 u16_start, uint16 u16_end, uint16 u16_tmrPR) {
  uint16 u16_deltaTicks;
  if (u16_end >= u16_start) u16_deltaTicks = u16_end - u16_start;
```

```
  else {
    //compute ticks from start to timer overflow
    u16_deltaTicks = (u16_tmrPR + 1) - u16_start;
    //now add in the delta from overflow to u16_end
    u16_deltaTicks += u16_end;
  }
  return (u16_deltaTicks);
}
```

Using a 32-bit Timer

The sample output in Figure 12.2 shows pulse widths of about 100,000 μs. How accurate is this measurement? An external 8 MHz crystal was used as the clock source for this measurement (with the internal PLL used to produce $F_{CY} = 40$ MHz). The crystal's accuracy is specified as $\pm$ 20 ppm (parts per million). For a 100,000 μs pulse width, this gives a possible error of $\pm$ 2 μs due to the clock source. A second error source is due to the timer tick fidelity, with an absolute worst-case value of $\pm$ 1 timer tick and an average accuracy of $\pm$ 0.5 timer tick. The timer fidelity for the conditions of Figure 12.2 is 6.4 μs due to the 256 prescaler value and $F_{CY} = 40$ MHz. Using smaller prescaler values increases the timer fidelity, but reduces the maximum period. Furthermore, the code of Figure 12.2 does not measure the pulse width correctly if the pulse width exceeds the maximum period of the timer. If we want the measurement accuracy to be determined by clock source error, not by timer fidelity, then we need a code solution that allows use of smaller timer prescale values. One approach is to increase the timer width, thus increasing the maximum period, by using Timer2 and Timer3 as a single 32-bit timer as shown in Figure 12.3. In this mode, Timer2 and Timer3 are referred to as *Timer2/3*, with Timer2 called a *Type B* timer, and Timer3 designated as a *Type C* timer per the family reference manual [19] (Timer1 is a *Type A* timer and is discussed later in the chapter). We will refer to them in this section as the LSW (Type B) and MSW timers (Type C), reflecting the assignment of the LSW and MSW words of the 32-bit timer value. The timer configuration is controlled by the LSW timer configuration register (i.e., Timer2's configuration register). The interrupt priority, interrupt enable, and interrupt flag bits of the MSW timer are used for interrupt control and status of the 32-bit timer. The period registers of the two 16-bit timers are concatenated to form a 32-bit period register for the timer. On PIC24 μCs with more timer modules, LSW timers are Timers 2, 4, 6, 8 and MSW timers are 3, 5, 7, and 9.

Writing a 32-bit value to the timer requires writing the MSW word first, followed by the LSW. The MSW word is written to a special holding register named TMRxHLD, where TMRx is the MSW timer. The write to the LSW timer register triggers a simultaneous transfer from the TMRxHLD register to the MSW timer register, thus updating the 32-bit timer value in one operation. A read operation is done in the reverse order. Listing 12.2 shows code for writing and reading Timer2/3. The *union32* type is defined in *include\ pic24_generic.h* and is a C union that is useful for accessing individual 16-bit words

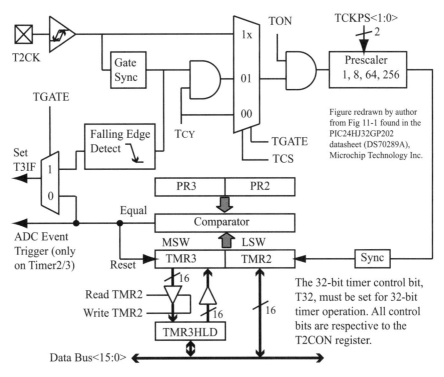

FIGURE 12.3 Timer2/3 (32-bit) block diagram. (Adapted with permission of the copyright owner, Microchip Technology Inc. All rights reserved. No further reprints or reproduction may be made without Microchip Inc.'s prior written consent.)

and 8-bit bytes from a 32-bit quantity. Observe that `write_value.u16.ms16` refers to the MSW of `write_value`, while `write_value.u16.ls16` refers to the LSW. The transfer of `write_value` to Timer2/3 first writes `write_value.u16.ms16` to TMR3HLD, followed by `write_value.u16.ls16` to TMR2. The transfer of Timer2/3 to `read_value` is accomplished by reading TMR2 into `read_value.u16.ls16`, followed by TMR3HLD into `read_value.u16.ms16`.

LISTING 12.2 Read/write to Timer2/3.

```
typedef union _union32 {
  uint32 u32;
  struct {
    uint16 ls16;
    uint16 ms16;
  } u16;
  uint8 u8[4];
} union32;
```

```
union32 write_value;
union32 read_value;

write_value.u32 = 0x12345678;
TMR3HLD = write_value.u16.ms16;    //write the MSW first
TMR2 = write_value.u16.ls16;       //then write the LSW
...
//read the timer
read_value.u16.ls16 = TMR2;        //read the LSW first
read_value.u16.ms16 = TMR3HLD;     //then read the MSW
```

An interrupt-driven approach for pulse width measurement of the pushbutton of Figure 12.1 using Timer2/3 and the INT1 interrupt input is given in Figure 12.4. The INT1 interrupt input is assigned to the RBy port used for the pushbutton and is configured initially for a falling-edge interrupt. Figure 12.4 shows the INT1 ISR which uses a two-state FSM, with STATE_WAIT_FOR_FALL_EDGE triggered on the switch

```
typedef enum { STATE_WAIT_FOR_FALL_EDGE = 0, STATE_WAIT_FOR_RISE_EDGE,
} INT1STATE;

INT1STATE e_isrINT1State = STATE_WAIT_FOR_FALL_EDGE;
volatile uint8 u8_captureFlag = 0; ◄── Measurement complete semaphore
volatile union32 u32_lastCapture, u32_thisCapture;
volatile int32 u32_delta, u32_pulseWidth;
                                        ISR for INT1 interrupt, initially
//Interrupt Service Routine for INT1   configured for falling edge.
void _ISRFAST _INT1Interrupt (void) {
  _INT1IF = 0;    //clear the interrupt bit
  switch (e_isrINT1State) {
  case STATE_WAIT_FOR_FALL_EDGE:
    if (u8_captureFlag == 0) {
      u32_lastCapture.u16.ls16 = TMR2;      } Save 32-bit timer value.
      u32_lastCapture.u16.ms16 = TMR3HLD;   }
      _INT1EP = 0;  //configure for rising edge ◄── Configure for
      e_isrINT1State = STATE_WAIT_FOR_RISE_EDGE;      rising edge
    }
    break;                          Next interrupt on rising edge.
  case STATE_WAIT_FOR_RISE_EDGE:
    u32_thisCapture.u16.ls16 = TMR2;      } Save 32-bit timer value.
    u32_thisCapture.u16.ms16 = TMR3HLD;   }           Compute delta,
    u32_delta = u32_thisCapture.u32 - u32_lastCapture.u32; ◄── assumes PR3,
    u32_pulseWidth = ticksToUs(u32_delta,            PR2 both 0xFFFF.
                     getTimerPrescale(T2CONbits));
    u8_captureFlag = 1; ◄──
    _INT1EP = 1;      //config. falling edge        Convert to µs, set semaphore,
    e_isrINT1State = STATE_WAIT_FOR_FALL_EDGE;       configure for rising edge.
    break;
  default: e_isrINT1State= STATE_WAIT_FOR_FALL_EDGE;
  }
}
```

FIGURE 12.4 INT1 ISR for pulse width measurement using Timer2/3.

push (falling edge). This state saves the Timer2/3 value into variable u32_lastCapture then configures the INT1 interrupt for a rising-edge trigger so that state STATE_WAIT_FOR_RISE_EDGE is entered on switch release. This state computes the delta (u32_delta) between the current Timer2/3 value and u32_lastCapture and converts this value to microseconds (u32_pulsewidth). The u8_captureFlag semaphore is set to indicate that this measurement is complete, then the INT1 interrupt is configured for a falling edge to capture the next switch press.

Code for configuring INT1, the input port, and Timer2/3 in addition to main() is shown in Figure 12.5. The while(1){} loop in main() waits for the u8_captureFlag semaphore flag to be set then prints the pulse width. The Timer2/3 configuration code enables 32-bit mode with the T2_32BIT_MODE_ON value used in the T2CON configuration and selects a prescale of 1. Both PR2 and PR3 are set to 0xFFFF to give

```
/// Switch1 configuration, use RB13
inline void CONFIG_SW1()  {
  CONFIG_RB13_AS_DIG_INPUT();   //use RB13 for switch input
  ENABLE_RB13_PULLUP();         //enable the pullup
  CONFIG_INT1_TO_RP(13);  //map INT1 to RP13
  DELAY_US(1);            //Wait for pullup
  /** Configure INT1 interrupt  */
  _INT1IF = 0;      //Clear the interrupt flag
  _INT1IP = 1;      //Choose a priority
  _INT1EP = 1;      //negative edge triggerred
  _INT1IE = 1;      //enable INT1 interrupt
}

//Timer2/3 used as single 32-bit timer, TCON2 controls timer,
//interrupt status of Timer3 used for the combined timer
void  configTimer23(void) {
  T2CON = T2_OFF | T2_IDLE_CON | T2_GATE_OFF
          | T2_32BIT_MODE_ON ◄──────────────── Selects 32-bit mode
          | T2_SOURCE_INT        Timer period is ~ 107.4 seconds, fidelity is 25 ns.
          | T2_PS_1_1 ; ◄─────── @ FCY = 40 MHz
  PR2 = 0xFFFF;           //maximum period ⎫ Must configure both PR2 and PR3.
  PR3 = 0xFFFF;           //maximum period ⎭
  TMR3HLD = 0;            //write MSW first ⎫ Clear Timer2/3.
  TMR2  = 0;              //then LSW        ⎭
  _T3IF = 0;             //clear interrupt flag
  T2CONbits.TON = 1;     //turn on the timer
}

int main (void) {
  configBasic(HELLO_MSG);
  CONFIG_SW1();     //use RB13
  configTimer23();                          Wait for semaphore to be set.
  while (1) {
    outString("Press button...");  ⟋
    while(!u8_captureFlag) doHeartbeat();
    printf(" %ld us\n",u32_pulseWidth); ◄── Print pulse width.
    u8_captureFlag = 0;
  }
}
```

FIGURE 12.5 Configuration code for INT1, input port, and Timer2/3.

the maximum Timer2/3 period. At Fcy = 40 MHz, one timer tick is 25 ns, and the timer period is approximately 107.4 s. While this is obviously overkill for the simple application of pushbutton pulse width measurement, this example does show the capabilities of the 32-bit timer mode in the PIC24 μC. A more common usage of the 32-bit timer mode is for scheduling long sleep times in power-sensitive applications.

PULSE WIDTH, PERIOD MEASUREMENT USING INPUT CAPTURE

While the 32-bit timer example of the previous sections seems to have solved the problem of long pulse width measurement, it has significant drawbacks. First, it is wasteful of the PIC24 μC timer resources to use two 16-bit timers for this problem as the 107.4 s period calculated for a prescale of 1, Fcy = 40 MHz is overkill. Second, if faced with the reverse problem of trying to measure a *short pulse width very precisely,* the approach of using the INT1 interrupt as the edge trigger and reading the timer value within the ISR is faulty because the timer value is not read until several instruction cycles after the edge has occurred. Even worse, if a higher-priority ISR is executing when the active INT1 edge occurs, there is no predicting how many instruction cycles will elapse before the INT1 ISR is executed and the timer register is read. Higher-priority interrupts are also a problem with the polling method used in Figure 12.2.

THE INPUT CAPTURE MODULE

To solve these problems, the PIC24 μC has an *input capture* module (Figure 12.6) whose function is pulse width and period measurement. The problem with the methods of the previous section is that the timer value is transferred to a storage

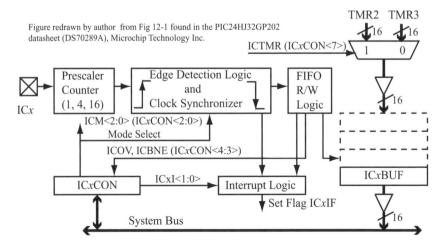

FIGURE 12.6 Input capture block diagram. (Adapted with permission of the copyright owner, Microchip Technology Inc. All rights reserved. No further reprints or reproduction may be made without Microchip Inc.'s prior written consent.)

variable under *instruction control* when a target edge occurs. Conversely, the input capture module automatically transfers either Timer2 or Timer3 register contents to a four-entry FIFO when a target edge occurs, without instruction intervention, in the same instruction cycle that the edge occurs. Captured timer values are read from the FIFO via the IC*x*BUF register. The PIC24HJ32GP202 has two input capture modules, with associated pin functions IC1 and IC2, which must be mapped to a remappable pin (RP*x*) for use.

Figure 12.7 shows the IC*x*CON configuration register details for the input capture module. A capture can be triggered on either edge, on both edges, or with a prescaler counter of 1, 4, or 16 edge events before a timer value is captured. The setting of the IC*x*IF interrupt flag is configurable for every fourth, third, second, or every capture event.

U-0	U-0	R/W-0	U-0	U-0	U-0	U-0	U-0
UI	UI	ICSIDL	UI	UI	UI	UI	UI
15	14	13	12	11	10	9	8

R/W-0	R/W-0	R/W-0	R-0, HC	R-0, HC	R/W-0	R/W-0	R/W-0
ICTMR	ICI<1:0>		ICOV	ICBNE	ICM<2:0>		
7	6	5	4	3	2	1	0

Bit 13 : ICSIDL: Input Capture Module Stop in Idle Control Bit
  1 = Input Capture will halt in CPU Idle mode
  0 = Input Capture will continue to operate in CPU Idle Mode
Bit 7: ICTMR: Input Capture Timer Select Bits
  1 = TMR2 contents are captured on capture event
  0 = TMR3 contents are captured on capture event
Bit 6-5: ICI<1:0>: Select Number of Captures per Interrupt bits
  11 = Interrupt on every fourth capture event
  10 = Interrupt on every third capture event
  01 = Interrupt on every second capture event
  00 = Interrupt on every capture event
Bit 4: ICOV: Input Capture Overflow Status Flag bit (read-only)
  1 = Input capture overflow occurred; 0 = No input capture overflow occurred
Bit 3: ICBNE: Input Capture Buffer Empty Status bit (read-only)
  1 = Input capture buffer is not empty; 0 = Input capture buffer is empty
Bit 2-0: ICM<2:0>: Input Capture Mode Select Bits
  111 = Input capture functions as interrupt pin only when device is in Sleep or Idle mode
    (Rising edge detect only, all other control bits are not applicable.)
  110 = Unused (module disabled)
  101 = Capture mode, every 16th rising edge
  100 = Capture mode, every 4th rising edge
  011 = Capture mode, every rising edge
  010 = Capture mode, every falling edge
  001 = Capture mode, every edge
    (rising and falling) (ICI<1:0> bits do not control interrupt generation for this mode)
  000 = Input capture module turned off

Figure redrawn by author from Reg. 12-1 found in the PIC24HJ32GP202 datasheet (DS70289A), Microchip Technology Inc.

Note: Disable module (ICM<2:0> = 000) before changing the ICI bits.

FIGURE 12.7   IC*x*CON: Input capture control register. (Adapted with permission of the copyright owner, Microchip Technology Inc. All rights reserved. No further reprints or reproduction may be made without Microchip Inc.'s prior written consent.)

Pulse Width Measurement Using Input Capture

This section discusses an interrupt-driven approach using the input capture module to solve the pulse width measurement problem of Figure 12.1. The ISR code for the IC1 input capture interrupt shown in Figure 12.8 contains a similar two-state FSM as was used in the previous section for the 32-bit timer approach. The input capture module is configured to capture the TMR2 value on every edge and to generate an interrupt on each capture. Since we wish to measure long pulse widths, but are only capturing a 16-bit timer value, the code uses the TMR2 interrupt for counting the Timer2 overflows (u16_oflowCount++) during pulse width measurement. The STATE_WAIT_FOR_FALL_EDGE state saves the capture value (u16_lastCapture)

```
typedef enum  { STATE_WAIT_FOR_FALL_EDGE = 0, STATE_WAIT_FOR_RISE_EDGE,
} ICSTATE;
                                    Track number of TMR2 overflows so
volatile uint16 u16_oflowCount = 0;    that we can measure long pulse widths.
void _ISRFAST _T2Interrupt (void) {
  u16_oflowCount++;  //count number of TMR2 overflows
  _T2IF = 0;          //clear the timer interrupt bit
}


ICSTATE e_isrICState = STATE_WAIT_FOR_FALL_EDGE;
volatile uint8 u8_captureFlag = 0; ◀— Measurement complete semaphore.
volatile uint16 u16_lastCapture, volatile uint16 u16_thisCapture;
volatile uint32 u32_pulseWidth;
                                    Configured for interrupt on every edge,
void _ISRFAST _IC1Interrupt() {◀— has higher priority than TMR2 interrupt.
  _IC1IF = 0;
  u16_thisCapture = IC1BUF;   ◀— Always read capture buffer to prevent overflow.
  switch (e_isrICState) {        Simultaneous IC1 with TMR2, so
  case STATE_WAIT_FOR_FALL_EDGE:      init oflowCount as −1 so that ISR makes it 0.
   if (u16_thisCapture == 0 && _T2IF)
        u16_oflowCount = 0 - 1; //simultaneous timer with capture
   else u16_oflowCount = 0; ◀— Clear overflow count.
    u16_lastCapture = u16_thisCapture; ◀— Save capture value.
    e_isrICState = STATE_WAIT_FOR_RISE_EDGE;
   }                   Next edge.      Simultaneous IC1 with TMR2, so
   break;                               increment oflowCount here.
  case STATE_WAIT_FOR_RISE_EDGE:
   if (u16_thisCapture == 0 && _T2IF) u16_oflowCount++; //simult. interpt
   u32_pulseWidth = computeDeltaTicksLong(u16_lastCapture, ⎫ Compute delta
                                 u16_thisCapture,          ⎬
                                 PR2, u16_oflowCount); ⎭ ticks.
   u32_pulseWidth = ticksToUs(u32_pulseWidth,            ⎫ Convert to µs.
                        getTimerPrescale(T2CONbits)); ⎬
   u8_captureFlag = 1;
   e_isrICState = STATE_WAIT_FOR_FALL_EDGE;
   break;
  default: e_isrICState = STATE_WAIT_FOR_FALL_EDGE;
  }
}
```

FIGURE 12.8 IC1 ISR for pulse width measurement using input capture.

and clears the `u16_oflowCount` variable. The next state is `STATE_WAIT_FOR_RISE_EDGE`, which uses the `computeDeltaTicksLong()` function to compute the elapsed ticks, which are then converted to microseconds. The `computeDeltaTicksLong()` function is different from the previously mentioned `computeDeltaTicks()` function in that it has an extra parameter that is the number of timer overflows between the start and end ticks. Finally, the `u8_captureFlag()` semaphore is set indicating that the pulse width measurement is complete. The unusual case of a simultaneous input capture with Timer2 rollover is detected by configuring the IC1 interrupt to have a higher priority interrupt than Timer2 and checking for a capture value equal to 0 and the T2IF flag being set. For this case and the falling edge capture, the `u16_overflow` variable is initialized to −1 instead of 0 so that the Timer2 ISR can

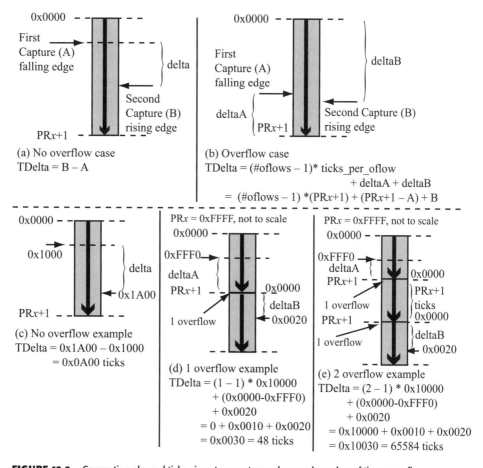

FIGURE 12.9 Computing elapsed ticks given two capture values and number of timer overflows.

immediately increment it, changing it to 0. For this case and the rising edge capture, the `u16_overflow` variable is incremented to count the timer overflow before the `computeDeltaTicksLong()` function is called to compute the elapsed ticks.

Figure 12.9 shows how the `computeDeltaTicksLong()` function computes the delta ticks given the starting and ending capture values and the number of timer overflows. Two cases must be considered: (a) when no timer overflow has occurred, and (b) when the number of timer overflows is greater than zero. Figures 12.9c, (d), and (e) show numerical examples of timer delta calculations for different cases of timer overflow. Tracking timer overflows for long pulse width measurement is a better solution than using a 32-bit timer as it preserves a 16-bit timer resource for other uses.

The code for the `computeDeltaTicksLong()` function used in the ISR of Figure 12.8, which implements the calculations shown in Figure 12.9, is given in Listing 12.3.

LISTING 12.3   Delta time calculation.

```
uint32 computeDeltaTicksLong(uint16 u16_start, uint16 u16_end,
    uint16 u16_tmrPR, uint16 u16_oflows) {
  uint32 u32_deltaTicks;
  uint16 u16_delta;
  if (u16_oflows == 0) u32_deltaTicks = u16_end - u16_start;
  else {
    //compute ticks from start to timer overflow
    u32_deltaTicks = (u16_tmrPR + 1) - u16_start;
    //add ticks due to overflows = (overflows -1) * ticks_per_overflow
    u32_deltaTicks += ((((uint32) u16_oflows)- 1) * (((uint32)u16_tmrPR) + 1));
    //now add in the delta due to the last capture
    u32_deltaTicks += u16_end;
  }
  return (u32_deltaTicks);
}
```

For completeness, we note that the computation with non-zero overflows (Figure 12.9b) can also be used in the no overflow case (Figure 12.9a) if signed integers are used for ticks as follows:

$$Tdelta = (0 - 1) \times (PRx + 1) + deltaA + deltaB \tag{12.1}$$

$$= -(PRx + 1) + (PRx + 1 - A) + B \tag{12.2}$$

$$= B - A \tag{12.3}$$

We keep the differentiation between the two cases for clarity purposes. Furthermore, the non-zero overflow case of Figure 12.9b simplifies as follows:

$$Tdelta = (\#overflows - 1) \times (PRx + 1) + deltaA + deltaB \tag{12.4}$$

$$Tdelta = (\#overflows \times (PRx + 1)) - (PRx + 1) + (PRx + 1 - A) + B \tag{12.5}$$

$$Tdelta = (\#overflows \times (PRx + 1)) + B - A \tag{12.6}$$

Listing 12.3 implements the original equation of Figure 12.9b for clarity purposes.

Figure 12.10 shows the Timer2, IC1, and switch configuration code. The `main()` code is not shown since it is the same in principle as in Figure 12.5. Timer2 is configured for a prescale value of 8, which gives a timer precision of 0.2 µs at $FCY = 40$ MHz. This means that for long pulse widths, the principal error source is clock source error.

The input capture module is clearly the correct method to use for pulse width measurement if high precision is required by the application. In the case where the time between captured events can be greater than the timer's period, then tracking

```
/// Switch1 configuration
inline void CONFIG_SW1()   {
  CONFIG_RB13_AS_DIG_INPUT();      //use RB13 for switch input
  ENABLE_RB13_PULLUP();            //enable the pull-up
  DELAY_US(1);                     //give time for pull-ups to work
}

void configInputCapture1(void) {
  CONFIG_IC1_TO_RP(13);            //map IC1 to RP13/RB13
  IC1CON = IC_TIMER2_SRC |         //Timer2 source
           IC_INT_1CAPTURE |       //Interrupt every capture
           IC_EVERY_EDGE;          //Capture every edge
```
                    Macros defined in *include\pic24_timer.h*
```
  _IC1IF = 0;
  _IC1IP = 2;      //higher than Timer2 so that Timer2 does not interrupt IC1
  _IC1IE = 1;      //enable
}

void  configTimer2(void) {
  T2CON = T2_OFF | T2_IDLE_CON | T2_GATE_OFF
          | T2_32BIT_MODE_OFF
          | T2_SOURCE_INT
          | T2_PS_1_8 ;  //1 tick = 0.2 us at FCY=40 MHz
  PR2 = 0xFFFF;          //maximum period
  TMR2  = 0;             //clear timer2 value
  _T2IF = 0;             //clear interrupt flag
  _T2IP = 1;             //choose a priority
  _T2IE = 1;             //enable the interrupt
  T2CONbits.TON = 1;     //turn on the timer
}
```

This precision means that clock error is the main error source for long pulse width measurements.

FIGURE 12.10 Configuration code for Timer2, IC1, and the input port.

timer overflows is needed for computing elapsed ticks. There is no need for track-ing timer overflows if the time between captured events does not exceed the timer's period, which is true for many applications.

PERIOD MEASUREMENT USING INPUT CAPTURE

Period measurement requires time measurement between two edges of the same type, either falling-to-falling edge or rising-to-rising edge. The input capture mode select bits (ICxCON<1:0>) of Figure 12.7 that capture every 16th rising edge or every 4th rising can be used to perform an automatic averaging of the measured period. This averaging increases the effective timer precision for the period measurement. Figure 12.11 shows

```
uint8 getPeriodAdjust (uint8 ICMbits) {                    Determine averaging
  if (ICMbits == IC_EVERY_16_RISE_EDGE) return 16;         factor for input capture;
  else if (ICMbits == IC_EVERY_4_RISE_EDGE) return 4;      the input capture delta is
  else return 1;                                           divided by this value.
}

volatile uint8 u8_captureFlag = 0;
volatile uint16 u16_lastCapture, volatile uint16 u16_thisCapture;
volatile uint32 u32_period;
                                         Assumed that IC1 pin has a square wave
void _ISRFAST _IC1Interrupt() {          whose period does not exceed TMR2 period.
  _IC1IF = 0;
  u16_thisCapture = IC1BUF;  //always read the buffer to prevent overflow
  if (u8_captureFlag == 0) {
    u32_period = (uint32)computeDeltaTicks(u16_lastCapture,
                                           u16_thisCapture,PR2);
    u32_period = ticksToNs (u32_period, getTimerPrescale(T2CONbits));
    //adjust period if necessary
    u32_period = u32_period / getPeriodAdjust(IC1CONbits.ICM);
    u8_captureFlag = 1;
  }
  u16_lastCapture = u16_thisCapture;           Compute delta, convert to time,
}                                              adjust if averaging.

void configInputCapture1(void) {
  CONFIG_RB13_AS_DIG_INPUT();                       Period measurement.
  CONFIG_IC1_TO_RP(13);  //map IC1 to RP13/RB13
  IC1CON = IC_TIMER2_SRC | IC_INT_1CAPTURE |
           IC_EVERY_16_RISE_EDGE;
  _IC1IF = 0; _IC1IP = 1; _IC1IE = 1;
}

void configTimer2(void) {
  T2CON = T2_OFF | T2_IDLE_CON | T2_GATE_OFF
          | T2_32BIT_MODE_OFF | T2_SOURCE_INT | T2_PS_1_64
  PR2 = 0xFFFF;              //maximum period
  TMR2 = 0; _T2IF = 0;      //clear timer2, flag
  T2CONbits.TON = 1;        //turn on the timer
}
```

PIC24 µC

RP13 (IC1)

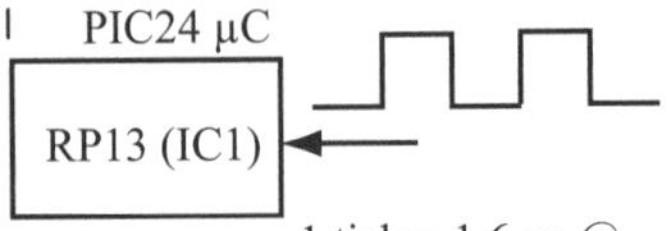

1 tick = 1.6 µs @ FCY = 40 MHz, but accuracy is 0.1 µs because of 16x averaging.

FIGURE 12.11 Period measurement using IC1.

code for performing period measurement using IC1 and Timer2, with the assumption that a square wave is present on the IC1 input whose period does not exceed the Timer2 period. The IC1 input is configured to capture every 16th rising edge and to interrupt on each capture. The IC1 ISR computes the delta ticks between the last capture and the current then converts this to nanoseconds (u32_period). This value is then divided by either 16, 4, or 1 depending on the input capture mode bits (IC1CONbits.ICM) for IC1. The u8_captureFlag semaphore is then set indicating that the period measurement is ready. The main() code is not shown as it is the same in principle as shown in Figure 12.5.

APPLICATION: USING CAPTURE MODE FOR AN INFRARED DECODER

Infrared (IR) transmit and receive is a common method for wireless communication. Remote controls for televisions, VCRs, DVD players, and satellite receivers all use IR communication. IR light is just below visible light in terms of frequency within the electromagnetic spectrum. A simple scheme for IR transmit and receive is shown in Figure 12.12, in which an IR LED is turned on or off by a switch. The IR receiver is a PIN diode whose resistance varies based upon the amount of IR received, causing the output voltage to vary in the presence or absence of IR transmission.

Because ambient light contains an IR component, the output of the IR detector is non-zero even when no IR is being transmitted. The input to the comparator

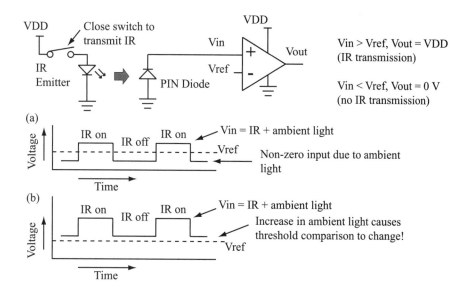

FIGURE 12.12   IR transmit/receive, no modulation.

is the output of the IR detector, which is compared against a reference voltage whose value should be between the voltage output of the IR receiver in the absence or presence of IR transmission as shown in waveform (a) of Figure 12.12. When Vin > Vref, the output of the comparator is VDD indicating an active IR transmission. When Vin < Vref, the output of the comparator is 0 V indicating no IR transmission. The problem with the scheme of Figure 12.12 is that a change in ambient lighting (perhaps a move from indoor lighting to outside sunshine) will change the quiescent output of the IR receiver, causing Vin either to be always above Vref (waveform (b) of Figure 12.12) or always below Vref.

Figure 12.13 shows an IR transmit/receive scheme that is not affected by ambient lighting conditions. To transmit IR, the switch is rapidly opened and closed to produce a modulated IR signal. A capacitor is used on the input of the comparator to block the DC component (non-changing component) of the IR detector output due to ambient lighting conditions.

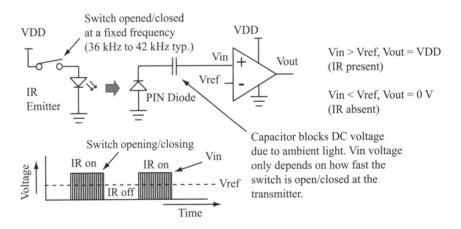

FIGURE 12.13   IR transmit/receive with modulation.

The voltage component that passes through the capacitor to the comparator input is the component that is changing due to the modulated IR input. This means that Vin is no longer affected by ambient light; the voltage seen on the capacitor output is dependent upon the frequency at which the switch is opened and closed and the transmission length of one IR bit time. Typical modulation frequencies in commercial transmitters/receivers range from 36 kHz to 42 kHz with transmission bit times in the hundreds of microseconds. Commercial IR receivers such as the NJL30H/V00A (NJR Corporation) or GP1UM2xxK (SHARP Microelectronics) integrate the IR detection diode with the electronics necessary to produce a clean digital output in the presence or absence of IR transmission.

Figure 12.14 shows a sample block diagram for an integrated IR receiver with three pins: VDD, ground, and Vout. The output is high in the absence of IR transmission and pulled low when a modulated IR signal is received.

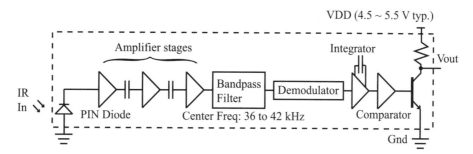

FIGURE 12.14   Integrated IR receiver.

Typical IR data links for remote control of home electronic systems are simplex, low-speed serial communication channels. Even though the NRZ (non-return-to-zero) encoding used for RS-232 serial data could be used for IR transmission, two other schemes known as *space-width* encoding and *biphase* encoding are commonly used for these applications. Figure 12.15a illustrates space-width encoding that encodes ones and zeros as different period lengths with different duty cycles. Typical period lengths are in the hundreds of microseconds with period length and duty cycle varying by manufacturer. Figure 12.15b shows a serial data transmission

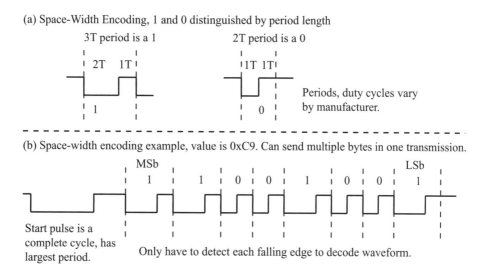

FIGURE 12.15   Space-width encoding.

using space-width encoding in which the first bit is a start pulse, followed by space-width encoded "1"s and "0"s. A "0" has a period of 2T units with a 50 percent cycle, and a "1" has a period of 3T units and a 33 percent duty cycle (the duty cycles and periods were arbitrarily chosen). Decoding this serial waveform is done by measuring the time between successive falling edges to distinguish between "1"s and "0"s. It is not necessary to determine the duty cycle, as "1" and "0" have distinct periods. Most space-width encoding schemes use a start pulse with a period significantly longer than a "1" or "0". The periods of the start, "1", "0" bits, the number of bits sent in a transmission, and their meanings in terms of commands for the target devices are all manufacturer specific.

Figure 12.16a shows *biphase* encoding, which is another encoding form sometimes used with IR transmissions. In biphase encoding, each bit period is the same width with "1"s and "0"s distinguished by a high-to-low transition and a low-to-high transition, respectively, in the middle of the bit period. Figure 12.16b shows a serial data transmission using biphase encoding. Observe that the start pulse is only one-half of a bit period. One method of decoding biphase waveforms is to measure the time between both rising and falling edge transitions. If the time between two edges is one bit period, this indicates that the current bit is the complement of the previous bit. If the time between two edges is one-half period and this is the last half of the bit period, then this bit is the same as the previous bit.

(a) Biphase encoding, 1 and 0 are distinguished by a transition in the center of the bit period.

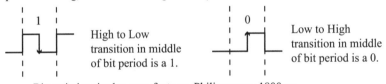

Bit period varies by manufacturer, Philips uses ~1800 µs.

(b) Biphase encoding example, value is 0xCB. Can send multiple bytes in one transmission.

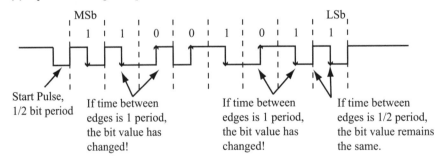

Must detect each edge transition to decode waveform.

FIGURE 12.16 Biphase encoding.

Figure 12.17a shows the biphase data stream for a Philips VCR remote control using the Philips RC-5 format that consists of a start pulse followed by 13 data bits. The address field specifies the target device (VCR, TV, etc.), while the command field is the particular command (play, rewind, numeral *N*, etc.). The first bit (the start bit) after the start pulse is always a "1", followed by the toggle bit that toggles for each new button press (if the toggle bit remains the same for several commands then the key is being held down). Figure 12.17b shows the biphase stream for the "play" button, while (c) gives the biphase stream for the numeric "3" button. Observe

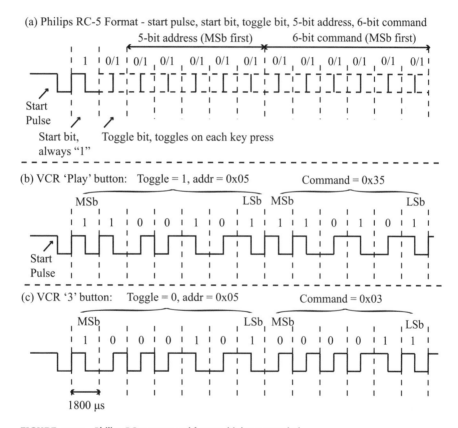

FIGURE 12.17 Philips RC-5 command format, biphase encoded.

that when a VCR numeric button 0–9 is pressed, the 6-bit command contains the value of the numeric button. In both Figure 12.17b and c the address is the same (0x05) because both of these are commands to the same device, a VCR.

A state machine chart for decoding the RC-5 biphase stream is given in Figure 12.18. This state machine is used in the input capture ISR, which is configured to capture

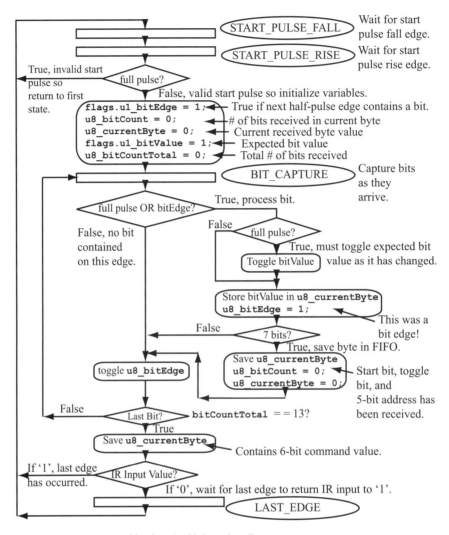

FIGURE 12.18 State machine for RC-5 biphase decoding.

and interrupt on every edge. The measured pulse width is used to determine when a half pulse or full pulse width has arrived. The START_PULSE_FALL state is triggered on the start pulse falling edge. The START_PULSE_RISE state initializes the variables needed to perform the decoding. The u1_bitEdge variable is true if the next edge is expected to contain a bit value as only transitions in the middle of a period represent a bit. The u1_bitValue variable contains the expected value of the next bit, and is initialized to "1" as the first bit after the start pulse is always a "1". A received bit is placed into u8_currentByte, with u8_bitCount tracking the number of received bits for the current byte, and u8_bitCountTotal tracking the total number of received bits. The BIT_CAPTURE state does the main work of decoding the waveform.

When an edge occurs, if a full pulse width is detected or if the u1_bitEdge variable is true, then a bit has arrived and it is placed into u8_currentByte. After seven bits have arrived the u8_currentByte is saved as this is the start bit, toggle bit, and address bits. After thirteen total bits have arrived, the u8_currentByte is saved again as this now contains the 6-bit command value. If the IR input is "1" at this point, the last edge has arrived and so a transition is made back to START_PULSE_FALL. If the IR input is "0", the LAST_EDGE state is used to wait for the last rising edge that returns the IR input back to the idle state of '1', after which START_PULSE_FALL is entered.

The code for the IC1 ISR is given in Figure 12.19, which is a straightforward implementation of the state machine of Figure 12.18. Variables referenced

```
void _ISRFAST _IC1Interrupt() {
 _IC1IF = 0;
 u16_thisCapture = IC1BUF ;  //always read buffer to prevent overflow
 u16_delta = computeDeltaTicks(u16_lastCapture,u16_thisCapture,PR2);
 u16_lastCapture = u16_thisCapture;
 switch (e_isrICState) {
  case STATE_START_PULSE_FALL:
    e_isrICState = STATE_START_PULSE_RISE;
    break;                              If comparison is true, then received a
  case STATE_START_PULSE_RISE:  ←───    long pulse.
    if (u16_delta > u16_twoThirdsPeriodTicks) {
    //error, unexpected long pulse, reset back to start state
    e_isrICState = STATE_START_PULSE_FALL;
    } else { //received start pulse, start accumulating bits
      flags.u1_bitEdge = 1;    //next edge contains a bit
      u8_bitCount = 0; u8_currentByte = 0; u8_bitCountTotal = 0;
      flags.u1_bitValue = 1; //first bit is always a '1'
      e_isrICState = STATE_BIT_CAPTURE;
    }
    break;
  case STATE_BIT_CAPTURE:
    if ((u16_delta > u16_twoThirdsPeriodTicks) || flags.u1_bitEdge) {
        if ((u16_delta > u16_twoThirdsPeriodTicks))
            flags.u1_bitValue = !flags.u1_bitValue; //bit value changed!
        if (u8_bitCount != 0)u8_currentByte = u8_currentByte << 1;
        if (flags.u1_bitValue) u8_currentByte = u8_currentByte | 0x01;
        u8_bitCount++;    u8_bitCountTotal++;
        flags.u1_bitEdge = 1;  //this was a bit edge
        if (u8_bitCount == 7) {  ←── Save toggle bit + 5-bit address into FIFO.
          irFifoWrite(u8_currentByte); u8_currentByte = 0; u8_bitCount = 0;
        }
    }
    flags.u1_bitEdge = !flags.u1_bitEdge;  //next edge is opposite
    if (u8_bitCountTotal == COMMAND_LENGTH) { ← Save 6-bit command into FIFO.
      if (u8_bitCount != 0) irFifoWrite(u8_currentByte); //save it
      if (IR_INPUT) e_isrICState = STATE_START_PULSE_FALL;
            else e_isrICState = STATE_LAST_EDGE;//one edge left
    }
    break;
  case STATE_LAST_EDGE:  e_isrICState = STATE_START_PULSE_FALL; break;
  default: e_isrICState = STATE_START_PULSE_FALL;
 }
}
```

FIGURE 12.19   Code for IC1 ISR that implements RC-5 biphase decoding.

within Figure 12.19 are given in Figure 12.20. The difference between a half-pulse and full-pulse is determined by comparing the current pulse width against the `u16_twoThirdsPeriodTicks` variable, which contains the number of ticks approximately equal to 2/3 of a full pulse width. A software FIFO as previously discussed in Chapter 10 is used for storing received IR byte values via the `irFifoWrite()` function.

```
#define IR_FIFO_SIZE 32
volatile uint8 au8_irFIFO[32];
volatile uint16 u16_irFifoHead = 0,u16_irFifoTail = 0;

void irFifoWrite(uint8 u8_x) {
  u16_irFifoHead++;
  if (u16_irFifoHead == IR_FIFO_SIZE) u16_irFifoHead = 0;
  au8_irFIFO[u16_irFifoHead] = u8_x;
}
uint8 irFifoRead() {
  while (u16_irFifoHead == u16_irFifoTail) { doHeartbeat();}
  u16_irFifoTail++;
  if (u16_irFifoTail == IR_FIFO_SIZE) u16_irFifoTail = 0;
  return au8_irFIFO[u16_irFifoTail];
}
```
} FIFO for IR bytes

```
void  configTimer2(void) {   // period should not exceed one bit time
  T2CON = T2_OFF | T2_IDLE_CON | T2_GATE_OFF
          | T2_32BIT_MODE_OFF
          | T2_SOURCE_INT
          | T2_PS_1_64 ;    //at 40 MHz, approx 420 ms max, 1 tick = 1.6 us
  PR2 = 0xFFFF;             //must be set to maximum period
  TMR2 = 0;                //clear timer2 value
  _T2IF = 0;               //clear interrupt flag
  T2CONbits.TON = 1;       //turn on the timer
}

#define TWOTHIRDS_PERIOD_US 1100   //2/3 bit period, in microseconds
#define COMMAND_LENGTH   13        //number of bits expected in IR command
#define IR_INPUT  _RB7             //using RB7 for IR input, 5V tolerant

volatile uint16 u16_lastCapture, u16_thisCapture,u16_delta;
volatile uint16 u16_twoThirdsPeriodTicks;
volatile uint8 u8_bitCount,u8_bitCountTotal,u8_currentByte;
typedef struct tagFLAGBITS { //some one-bit flags
  unsigned u1_bitEdge:1;    //true if this edge contains a bit
  unsigned u1_bitValue:1;   //value of this bit edge, either '0' or '1'
}FLAGBITS;
volatile FLAGBITS flags;

typedef enum  {
  STATE_START_PULSE_FALL = 0, STATE_START_PULSE_RISE, STATE_BIT_CAPTURE,
  STATE_LAST_EDGE } ICSTATE;

ICSTATE e_isrICState;
```

FIGURE 12.20 Support functions for RC-5 biphase decoding code.

Software FIFO read/write functions, Timer2 configuration, and variable declarations for the RC-5 biphase decoder are given in Figure 12.20.

Figure 12.21 gives the IC1 configuration code, the `main()` function, and sample output. The `while(1){}` loop of `main()` reads two bytes from the software FIFO, which are the address value (`u8_x`) and command value (`u8_y`) of a single 13-bit transmission. The toggle bit is extracted from the first byte, and the toggle, address, and command values are printed to the console. The universal remote control used to test this code sent two duplicate 13-bit transmissions for each button press. Observe that the toggle bit flipped state between the "play" and numeral "3" button presses.

```
//configure input capture.
void configInputCapture1(void) {
 CONFIG_RB7_AS_DIG_INPUT();    //use RB7 for IR Input
 CONFIG_IC1_TO_RP(7);          //map IC1 to RP7/R7
 e_isrICState = STATE_START_PULSE_FALL;
 u16_irFifoHead = 0;
 u16_irFifoTail = 0;
 u16_twoThirdsPeriodTicks = usToU16Ticks(TWOTHIRDS_PERIOD_US,
                                 getTimerPrescale(T2CONbits));
 IC1CON = IC_TIMER2_SRC |      //Timer2 source
          IC_INT_1CAPTURE |    //Interrupt every capture
          IC_EVERY_EDGE;       //Interrupt every edge
 _IC1IF = 0;
 _IC1IP = 1;
 _IC1IE = 1;    //enable IC1 interrupt
}

int main (void) {
  uint8 u8_x, u8_y;
  configBasic(HELLO_MSG);
  configTimer2();
  configInputCapture1();
  while (1) {
    u8_x = irFifoRead(); //read addr
    u8_y = irFifoRead(); //read cmd
    if (u8_x & 0x20) outString("Toggle = 1, ");
    else outString("Toggle = 0, ");
    outString("Addr: "); outUint8(u8_x & 0x1F);
    outString(",Cmd: "); outUint8(u8_y);
    outString("\n");
  }
}
```

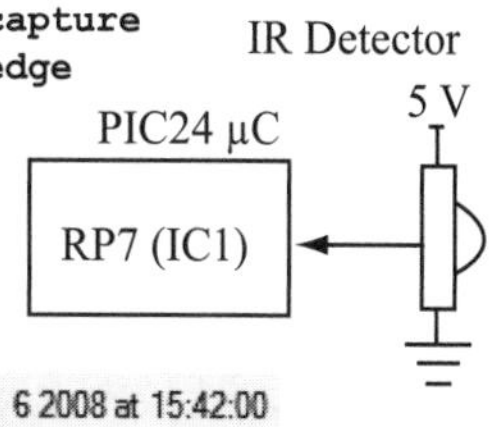

IR Detector

PIC24 µC   5 V

RP7 (IC1)

Sample Output

ir_biphase_decode.c, built on Jul 6 2008 at 15:42:00
Toggle = 1, Addr: 0x05,Cmd: 0x35 } VCR "play" button
Toggle = 1, Addr: 0x05,Cmd: 0x35
Toggle = 0, Addr: 0x05,Cmd: 0x03 } VCR numeral "3" button
Toggle = 0, Addr: 0x05,Cmd: 0x03

FIGURE 12.21   IC1 configuration, `main()` and sample output for RC-5 biphase decoder.

THE OUTPUT COMPARE MODULE

In Chapter 9, a square wave was generated by using a periodic interrupt whose interrupt service routine toggled an output port, i.e., instruction execution plus timer operation generated the waveform. The PIC24 output compare module shown in Figure 12.22 provides the capability of creating hardware-generated waveforms with a high degree of precision, which is the opposite of input capture that enables precision measurement of waveform characteristics. The output compare primary and secondary registers, OC*x*R and OC*x*RS, are used as period registers in conjunction with either Timer2 or Timer3 for setting or clearing the output compare pin (OC*x*), dependent on the selected operation mode. The PIC24HJ32GP202 contains two output compare modules, OC1 and OC2, both of whose outputs use remappable pins.

Figure redrawn by author from Fig 13-1 1 found in the PIC24 FRM (DS70247A), Microchip Technology Inc.

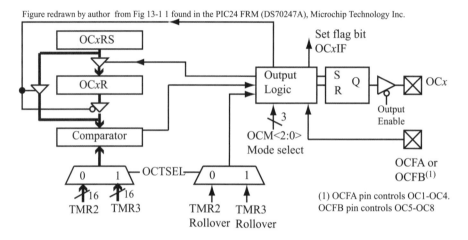

FIGURE 12.22 Output compare block diagram. (Adapted with permission of the copyright owner, Microchip Technology Inc. All rights reserved. No further reprints or reproduction may be made without Microchip Inc.'s prior written consent.)

Figure 12.23 shows the various operation modes of the output compare module. In the active-high and active-low one-shot modes, the OC*x*R register controls the pulse width of the one-shot, which is produced when the module is enabled. In toggle mode, the OC*x* pin is toggled for each match of OC*x*R against the selected timer register. In delayed one-shot mode, an OC*x*R register match against the selected timer triggers the rising edge of the pulse, while the falling edge is triggered by a match of OC*x*RS and the selected timer (see the reflow oven capstone example in Chapter 15 for an example that uses this mode). Continuous pulse mode has the same triggers as delayed one-shot mode, but the pulses are repeated. In pulse width modulation (PWM) mode, the pulse's rising edge always occurs when the selected timer rolls over, and the falling edge is triggered when the OC*x*R register matches the selected timer register.

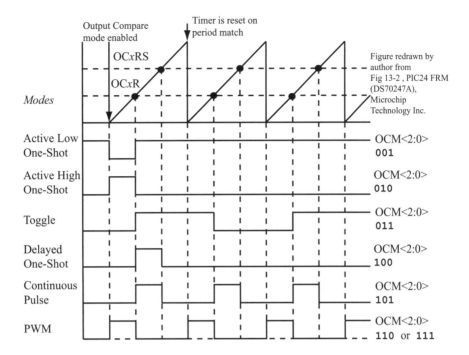

FIGURE 12.23 Output compare operation. (Adapted with permission of the copyright owner, Microchip Technology Inc. All rights reserved. No further reprints or reproduction may be made without Microchip Inc.'s prior written consent.)

The OC*x* control register and interrupt generation details are given in Figure 12.24. The operation mode determines how the output compare interrupt flag (OC*x*IF) is affected. The fault detection PWM mode uses an external input, OCFA or OCFB depending on the module, that tristates the PWM output when the fault input is asserted.

SQUARE WAVE GENERATION

It is straightforward to create a square wave using the OC*x* module as shown in Figure 12.25. The configOutputCapture1() function configures the OC1 module for toggle mode using Timer2, which generates an interrupt on each edge (each match of the OC*x*R register with the Timer2 value). The OC1R register is initialized to the first edge of the square wave, which is equal to the SQWAVE_HALFPERIOD value (in microseconds) converted to Timer2 ticks (u16_sqwaveHPeriodTicks). The _OC1Interrupt() ISR sets the time for the next square wave edge by writing OC1R

U-0	U-0	R/W-0	U-0	U-0	U-0	U-0	U-0
UI	UI	OCSIDL	UI	UI	UI	UI	UI
15	14	13	12	11	10	9	8

U-0	U-0	U-0	R-0, HC	R/W-0	R/W-0	R/W-0	R/W-0
UI	UI	UI	OCFLT	OCTSEL	OCM<2:0>		
7	6	5	4	3	2	1	0

Bit 13 : OCSIDL: Stop Output Compare *x* in Idle Mode Control Bit
1 = Output compare *x* halts in CPU Idle Mode
0 = Output compare *x* continues to operate in CPU Idle Mode
Bit 4:   OCFLT: PWM Fault condition Status bit
1 = PWM Fault condition has occurred (cleared in hardware only)
0 = No PWM Fault condition has occurred (this bit is used only when OCM<2:0> = 111)
Bit 3:   OCTSEL: Output Compare *x* Timer Select bit
1 = Timer3 is the clock source for Output Compare *x*
0 = Timer2 is the clock source for Output Compare *x*
Bit 2-0: OCM<2:0>: Output Compare *x* Mode Select Bits
111 = PWM mode with fault protection. PWM mode on OC*x*, Fault pin is enabled
110 = PWM mode without fault protection. PWM mode on OC*x*, Fault pin is disabled
101 = Continuous Pulse mode. Initialize OC*x* pin low, generates continous output pulses on OC*x* pin
100 = Delayed One-Shot mode. Initialize OC*x* pin low, generate single output pulse on OC*x* pin
011 = Toggle mode. Compare event toggles OC*x* pin
010 = Active High One-Shot mode. Initialize OC*x* pin high, compare event forces OC*x* pin low
001 = Active Low One-Shot mode. Initialize OC*x* pin low, compare event forces OC*x* pin high
000 = Module disabled. Output compare module is disabled

Figure redrawn by author from
Reg. 13-1 and Table 13-1
found in the PIC24 FRM
(DS70247A),
Microchip Technology Inc.

OCM<2:0>	Mode	OCxPin Initial State	OCx Interrupt Generation
000	Module Disabled	Controlled by PIO reg.	n/a
001	Active Low One-Shot	0	OC*x* Rising edge
010	Active High One-Shot	1	OC*x* Falling edge
011	Toggle	Current output is kept	OC*x* Rising and Falling edge
100	Delayed One-Shot	0	OC*x* Falling edge
101	Continuous Pulse	0	OC*x* Falling edge
110	PWM without fault protection	0, if OC*x*R is zero 1, if OC*x*R is non-zero	No Interrupt
111	PWM with fault protection	0, if OC*x*R is zero 1, if OC*x*R is non-zero	OCFA Falling edge for OC1-OC4 OCFB Falling edge for OC5-OC8

FIGURE 12.24 OC*x*CON register and interrupt generation details. (Adapted with permission of the copyright owner, Microchip Technology Inc. All rights reserved. No further reprints or reproduction may be made without Microchip Inc.'s prior written consent.)

with the sum of the current OC1R value and `u16_sqwaveHPeriodTicks`. The datasheet warns that the selected timer should be off during configuration of the output compare module, hence Timer2 is not enabled until after OC1 is configured. The `while(1){}` loop in `main()` has no work to do since the square wave is generated by hardware and the ISR.

Configure timer so that its period is at least greater than 1/2 square wave period.

```
void  configTimer2(void) {
  ...config for PRE=64, no interrupt, PR2=0xFFFF, Timer not enabled...
}
#define SQWAVE_HALFPERIOD 2500   // desired half period, in us

uint16 u16_sqwaveHPeriodTicks;
void _ISRFAST _OC1Interrupt() {
   _OC1IF = 0;
   OC1R = OC1R + u16_sqwaveHPeriodTicks;
}
```

Set time for the next edge of the square wave.

```
void configOutputCapture1(void) {
 T2CONbits.TON = 0;       //disable Timer when configuring Output compare
 CONFIG_OC1_TO_RP(2);     //map OC1 to RP2/RB2
 //initialized the compare register to 1/2 the squarewave period
 //assumes TIMER2 initialized before OC1 so PRE bits are set
 u16_sqwaveHPeriodTicks = usToU16Ticks(SQWAVE_HALFPERIOD,
                                 getTimerPrescale(T2CONbits));
 OC1R = u16_sqwaveHPeriodTicks;
 //turn on the compare toggle mode using Timer2
 OC1CON = OC_TIMER2_SRC |      //Timer2 source
          OC_TOGGLE_PULSE;     //Toggle OC1 every compare event
 _OC1IF = 0;
 _OC1IP = 1;    //pick a priority
 _OC1IE = 1;    //enable OC1 interrupt
}
```

Macros are defined in *include\pic24_timer.h.*

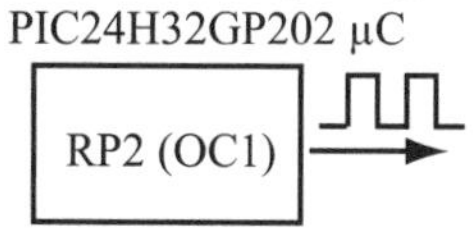

PIC24H32GP202 µC

RP2 (OC1)

```
int main (void) {
  configBasic(HELLO_MSG);
  configTimer2();
  configOutputCapture1();
  T2CONbits.TON = 1;       //turn on Timer2 to start sqwave
  while (1) doHeartbeat(); //nothing to do, squarewave generated in hardware
}
```

Wait until output capture enabled before starting the timer.

FIGURE 12.25   Square wave generation using output compare.

PULSE WIDTH MODULATION

Pulse width modulation (PWM) is a technique that varies the duty cycle of a square wave while keeping the period constant. This can be used in a variety of applications, such as varying the average current delivered to an external device. The pulse width modulation mode of the output compare module has a period equal to the selected timer's period, with the high pulse width controlled by the OCxR register. The OCxR register is loaded with the OCxRS register value at the end of each timer period, so the application writes to the OCxRS register to modify the high pulse width. Recall that duty cycle is the high pulse width divided by the period, multiplied by 100 percent. Thus, increasing the high pulse width increases the duty cycle. A duty cycle of 100 percent means that the PWM signal is always high.

A PWM EXAMPLE

Figure 12.26 shows an experiment illustrating how PWM can be used to control the brightness of an LED. A potentiometer is used as the input voltage for analog input AN0, whose value is read and then transformed to a pulse width for a PWM signal applied to an LED. The potentiometer is thus a convenient method for changing the duty cycle of the PWM signal. As the duty cycle of the PWM signal increases, the average current delivered to the LED increases, increasing the LED's brightness. Of course, this may seem like a wasted effort given that the potentiometer can be directly connected to the LED for brightness control, but this demonstrates the basic principles of current control via PWM.

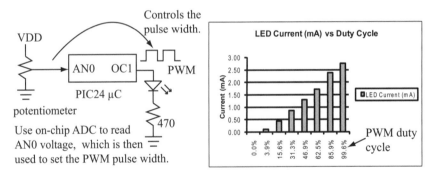

FIGURE 12.26 LED PWM setup.

Figure 12.27 shows the code for implementing the LED PWM experiment. The ADC is configured for manual conversion of channel AN0 (see Chapter 11). Timer2 is configured for a period equal to the PWM period, with the Timer2 interrupt enabled. The output compare module is configured for PWM mode with no fault detection with the OC1RS register initially cleared, which initializes the OC1 output to be low. The _T2Interrupt() ISR reads the 12-bit ADC value and uses this to compute a new pulse width that is 0 to 99 percent of PR2, which is then written to OC1RS. The ISR starts a new ADC conversion before it exits. The main() code configures the ADC, Timer2, and OC1 before entering a while(1){} loop that continually prints the OC1RS value for information purposes.

```
#define PWM_PERIOD 20000  // desired period, in us

void configTimer2(void) {
  ...Configure for PR2 equal to PWM_PERIOD, interrupt enabled...
}
void configOutputCapture1(void) {
 T2CONbits.TON = 0;       //disable Timer when configuring Output compare
 CONFIG_OC1_TO_RP(14);    //map OC1 to RP14/RB14
 //assumes TIMER2 initialized before OC1 so PRE bits are set
 OC1RS = 0;  //initially off
 //turn on the compare toggle mode using Timer2
 OC1CON = OC_TIMER2_SRC |    //Timer2 source
          OC_PWM_FAULT_PIN_DISABLE;  //PWM, no fault detection
}

void _ISR _T2Interrupt(void) {
  uint32 u32_temp;
  _T2IF = 0;      //clear the timer interrupt bit
  //update the PWM duty cycle from the ADC value
  u32_temp = ADC1BUF0;  //use 32-bit value for range
  //compute new pulse width that is 0 to 99% of PR2
  // pulse width (PR2) * ADC/4096
  u32_temp = (u32_temp * (PR2))>> 12 ;   // >>12 is same as divide by 4096
  OC1RS = u32_temp;     //update pulse width value
  SET_SAMP_BIT_AD1();   //start sampling and conversion before leaving ISR
}

int main(void) {
  uint32 u32_pw;
  configBasic(HELLO_MSG);
  configTimer2();
  configOutputCapture1();
  CONFIG_AN0_AS_ANALOG();
  configADC1_ManualCH0( ADC_CH0_POS_SAMPLEA_AN0, 31, 1 );
  SET_SAMP_BIT_AD1();        //start sampling and conversion
  T2CONbits.TON = 1;         //turn on Timer2 to start PWM
  while (1) {
   u32_pw= ticksToUs(OC1RS, getTimerPrescale(T2CONbits));
   printf("PWM PW (us): %ld \n",u32_pw);
   DELAY_MS(100);
   doHeartbeat();
  }
}
```

Configure OC module for PWM mode, map OC1 output to RP3, initial pulse width is 0 (OC1RS = 0).

Read the ADC value, convert to a pulse width, update OC1RS, and start new ADC conversion.

Configure ADC to sample AN0/Channel 0, manual sampling/auto conversion, 31 Tad sampling clock, 12-bit mode.

Loop continually prints the OC1RS value for informational purposes.

FIGURE 12.27   LED PWM code.

PWM Application: DC Motor Speed Control and Servo Control

This section discusses two common applications of PWM, DC motor speed control and hobby servo control.

DC Motor Speed Control

Figure 12.28 shows PWM control of a small DC motor such as that found in hobbyist robotic kits. The MOSFET is used to control the current through the motor,

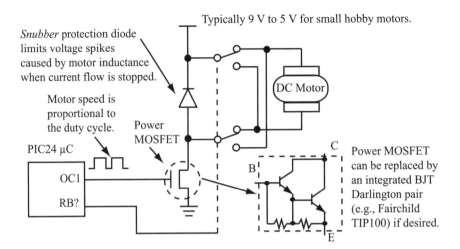

FIGURE 12.28   PWM control of a DC motor.

which can be several hundred milliamps. The gate of the MOSFET is controlled by the PWM signal; the MOSFET is turned on when the PWM signal is high, thus modulating the current flow through the motor. The average current delivered to the motor is proportional to the PWM duty cycle, and thus the motor's speed is set by the duty cycle. The diode, known as a *snubber* diode, is required to protect against voltage spikes that are induced by the motor's inductance due to the current flow interruption when the MOSFET is turned off. The switches control the rotation direction of the DC motor by reversing the current flow through the motor. The power MOSFET can be replaced by an integrated BJT *Darlington pair* as long as the current gain factor from input base current to collector current is high enough to supply the current required by the motor.

While discrete components and low-resistance analog switches can be used to implement the directional control of the DC motor of Figure 12.28, a better solution is to use a *half-bridge* integrated circuit that has the transistor drivers, directional control, and snubber diode protection in one package such as shown in Figure 12.29. The Texas Instruments SN754410 is a quadruple half-H driver that can supply up to 1 ampere per output with a maximum of 2 amperes total across all drivers. The 1A and 2A inputs can be used to reverse current drive in the motor, thus changing motor direction. When the enable (EN) signal is low, current drive to the motor is off.

HOBBY SERVO CONTROL

Hobby servos, such as the Hitec HS-311 shown in Figure 12.30, are used in many applications, including robotics and remote-controlled vehicles. A servo rotates its shaft

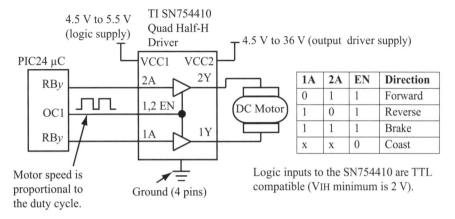

FIGURE 12.29   DC motor control using half-bridge driver and PWM.

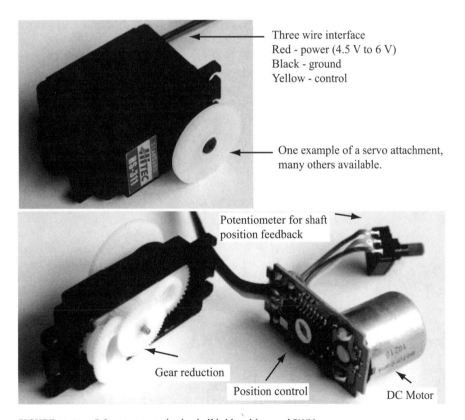

FIGURE 12.30   DC motor control using half-bridge driver and PWM.

through a limited angular range whose position is specified by a PWM signal. The range of motion varies by servo manufacturer and type, with a range of −90° to +90° for the Hitec HS-311 of Figure 12.30. The 0° position is called the *neutral* position. The pulse width range for the HS-311 varies from a minimum high pulse time of 600 μs (−90°) to 2400 μs (+90°), with 1500 μs (0°) for neutral within a 20 ms period. An analog servo such as the HS-311 uses a DC motor with gear reduction on the shaft to slow rotation. The shaft position specified by the PWM input is maintained by an analog control circuit that uses shaft position feedback from a potentiometer. The position is maintained as long as the PWM signal is supplied and the external load on the shaft does not exceed the maximum torque ratings. If the PWM signal is removed, then the shaft freewheels, with only a small external force needed to move it.

Listing 12.4 shows the minor changes needed to the LED PWM code of Figure 12.27 to convert it to servo control. The `configOutputCapture1()` function has two additional lines that compute the minimum (`u16_minPWTicks`) and maximum (`u16_maxPWTicks`) PWM pulse widths in Timer2 ticks. The `_T2Interrupt()` ISR is modified to compute a new pulse width between these two boundary values using the conversion from the ADC. This allows the potentiometer of Figure 12.26 to control the servo's position. The PWM period is already servo compatible with a value of 20 ms.

LISTING 12.4 PWM servo control.

```
#define PWM_PERIOD 20000   // desired period, in us
#define MIN_PW 600         //minimum pulse width, in us
#define MAX_PW 2400        //maximum pulse width, in us
uint16 u16_minPWTicks, u16_maxPWTicks;
void configOutputCapture1(void) {
  u16_minPWTicks = usToU16Ticks(MIN_PW, getTimerPrescale(T2CONbits));
  u16_maxPWTicks = usToU16Ticks(MAX_PW, getTimerPrescale(T2CONbits));
  ... rest of the function is the same ...
}

void _ISR _T2Interrupt(void) {
  uint32 u32_temp;
  _T2IF = 0;    //clear the timer interrupt bit
  //update the PWM duty cycle from the ADC value
  u32_temp = ADC1BUF0;  //use 32-bit value for range
  //compute new pulse width using ADC value
  // ((max - min) * ADC)/4096 + min
  u32_temp = ((u32_temp * (u16_maxPWTicks-u16_minPWTicks))>> 12) +
             u16_minPWTicks;  // >>12 is same as divide by 4096
  OC1RS = u32_temp;  //update pulse width value
  AD1CON1bits.SAMP = 1; //start next ADC conversion for next interrupt
}
```

PWM CONTROL OF MULTIPLE SERVOS

The code of Listing 12.4 uses the OC1 output to directly control one servo. However, if an application requires more servos than available PWM outputs, then how is multi-servo control accomplished? The answer is to use software control of digital outputs, with the output compare ISR controlling the digital ports used for the servo outputs as shown in Figure 12.31. The PWM period is divided into slots, with each servo assigned a slot time in which its pulse width is varied. Using a conservative slot time of 2.8 ms means that up to seven servos can be controlled in a 20 ms period (20/2.8 = 7.1). An OCx interrupt is generated for each edge of a servo's output, with an array used for storing servo pulse widths and variables used to track the current edge and current servo. After the falling edge of the last servo's pulse has occurred, the OCx ISR sets the next output compare interrupt to occur at the end of the 20 ms period. This approach requires only one output compare module and one timer, with the timer's period equal to the PWM period.

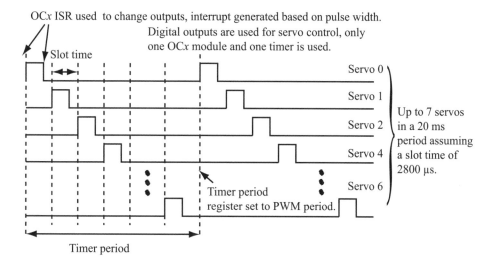

FIGURE 12.31 Multi-servo control scheme.

Listing 12.5 shows variable declarations and initialization code for the multi-servo control, with four servos used for this example. The initServos() function configures the four ports chosen for servo control and initializes them to low. The au16_servoPWidths[] array holds the pulse widths of the servos in Timer2 ticks. These entries are initialized to an equivalent value of 1500 μs, which is the servo neutral position. Timer2 is initialized to period equal to 20 ms, with its interrupt disabled. The OC1 module is initialized to toggle mode, but the OC1 output is not mapped to a pin as we only care about the output compare interrupt and not the OC1 output. The OC1R register is initialized to 0, which means that the first OC1IF interrupt occurs at the first Timer2 rollover.

LISTING 12.5 Initialization code for multi-servo control.

```
#define PWM_PERIOD 20000            //in microseconds
#define NUM_SERVOS 4
#define SERVO0    _LATB2
#define SERVO1    _LATB3
#define SERVO2    _LATB13
#define SERVO3    _LATB14

#define MIN_PW 600                  //minimum pulse width, in us
#define MAX_PW 2400                 //minimum pulse width, in us
#define SLOT_WIDTH 2800             //slot width, in us

volatile uint16 au16_servoPWidths[NUM_SERVOS];
volatile uint8 u8_currentServo =0;
volatile uint8 u8_servoEdge = 1;    //1 = RISING, 0 = FALLING
volatile uint16 u16_slotWidthTicks = 0;

void initServos(void) {
  uint8 u8_i;
  uint16 u16_initPW;
  CONFIG_RB2_AS_DIG_OUTPUT(); CONFIG_RB3_AS_DIG_OUTPUT();
  CONFIG_RB13_AS_DIG_OUTPUT(); CONFIG_RB14_AS_DIG_OUTPUT();
  u16_initPW = usToU16Ticks(MIN_PW + (MAX_PW-MIN_PW)/2,
                            getTimerPrescale(T2CONbits));
  //config all servos for half maximum pulse width
  for (u8_i=0; u8_i<NUM_SERVOS; u8_i++) au16_servoPWidths[u8_i]=u16_initPW;
  SERVO0 = 0; //all servo outputs low initially
  SERVO1 = 0; SERVO2 = 0; SERVO3 = 0;    //outputs initially low
  u16_slotWidthTicks = usToU16Ticks(SLOT_WIDTH, getTimerPrescale(T2CONbits));
}

void configTimer2(void) {
  T2CON = T2_OFF | T2_IDLE_CON | T2_GATE_OFF
        | T2_32BIT_MODE_OFF
        | T2_SOURCE_INT
        | T2_PS_1_256 ;             //1 tick = 1.6 us at FCY=40 MHz
  PR2 = usToU16Ticks(PWM_PERIOD, getTimerPrescale(T2CONbits)) - 1;
  TMR2 = 0;                         //clear timer2 value
}

void configOutputCapture1(void) {
  T2CONbits.TON = 0;               //disable Timer when configuring Output compare
  OC1R = 0; //initialize to 0, first match will be a first timer rollover.
  //turn on the compare toggle mode using Timer2
  OC1CON = OC_TIMER2_SRC |         //Timer2 source
```

```
OC_TOGGLE_PULSE;                //use toggle mode, just care about compare event
_OC1IF = 0;  _OC1IP = 1;  _OC1IE = 1;     //enable the OC1 interrupt
}
```

Figure 12.32 shows the code for the OC1 ISR and main(). The variable u8_currentServo is used to track the current servo (0 to *N*-1), while variable u8_servoEdge is the current edge transition ("1" for rising edge, "0" for falling edge). The _OC1Interrupt ISR first sets the current servo's output high or low based on the u8_servoEdge variable. The next interrupt is then scheduled. For a rising edge,

```
void setServoOutput (uint8 u8_servo, uint8 u8_val) {
  switch(u8_servo) {
   case 0: SERVO0 = u8_val; break;      Sets servo port specified
   case 1: SERVO1 = u8_val; break;      by u8_servo to u8_val.
   case 2: SERVO2 = u8_val; break;
   case 3: SERVO3 = u8_val; break;
   default: break;
  }
}

void _ISR _OC1Interrupt(void) {       Sets the current servo's output.
  _OC1IF = 0;                          "1" rising edge,
  //change the servo's value           "0" falling edge.
  setServoOutput(u8_currentServo, u8_servoEdge);
  //schedule next interrupt
  if (u8_servoEdge == 1) {  //rising edge
    //next interrupt occurs after pulse width has elapsed   For falling edge,
    OC1R = OC1R + au16_servoPWidths[u8_currentServo];       next interrupt is
    u8_servoEdge = 0;      //change to falling edge          current capture
  } else { //falling edge                                    value plus pulse width.
    //next interrupt occurs at beginning of next slot   Falling edge, not last
    if (u8_currentServo != NUM_SERVOS -1)                servo - next interrupt is
      OC1R = u16_slotWidthTicks*(u8_currentServo+1);     beginning of next slot.
    else //last servo!
      OC1R = 0;           Falling edge, last servo - next interrupt is next timer
    u8_servoEdge = 1;        //change to rising edge        rollover.
    u8_currentServo++;
    if (u8_currentServo == NUM_SERVOS) u8_currentServo = 0;
  }
}

int main(void) {
  configBasic(HELLO_MSG);
  configTimer2();
  initServos();
  configOutputCapture1();
  T2CONbits.TON = 1;        //turn on Timer2 to start PWM
  while (1) {
    getServoValue();        //prints menu, gets new servo value from console.
  }              Helper function that allows servo width to be set from the console,
}                  code is not shown.
```

FIGURE 12.32   Multi-servo OC1 ISR and main().

the next interrupt must occur at the falling edge of the servo output, which oc-curs at the current OC1R value plus the current servo's pulse width. For the fall-ing edge of a servo that is not the last servo, the next interrupt is the rising edge of the next servo, which is the start of the next servo's slot and is calculated as `u16_slotWidthTicks*(u8_CurrentServo+1)`. For the falling edge of the last servo, the next interrupt occurs at the end of the period, so OC1R is cleared to 0. The `main()` code performs initialization, with the `while(1){}` loop calling a helper function that allows a servo's pulse width to be changed from the console for testing purposes.

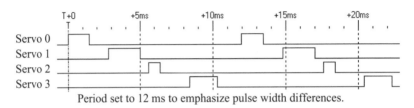

Period set to 12 ms to emphasize pulse width differences.

FIGURE 12.33   Multi-servo logic analyzer capture.

Figure 12.33 shows a logic analyzer capture of the four servo outputs with the pulse widths set to different values; the period was set to 12 ms to emphasize the pulse width differences.

A PWM DAC[*]

Another application of PWM is as a "poor man's digital-to-analog converter" in which the PWM signal is applied to a series resistor/capacitor network to produce a DC voltage that is proportional to the PWM duty cycle. This is illustrated in Figure 12.34a. Passing this DC voltage to a unity-gain operational amplifier pro-vides necessary current drive and prevents the load receiving this analog voltage from affecting the PWM DAC output. In this configuration, the operational ampli-fier provides a gain of 1 (unity gain, voltage follower configuration), with the cur-rent draw from the RC network being negligible due to the high input impedance characteristic of this operational amplifier configuration.

---

[*] Notice: This section assumes some reader knowledge of low-pass RC filters; portions of this material may be difficult to understand without this background.

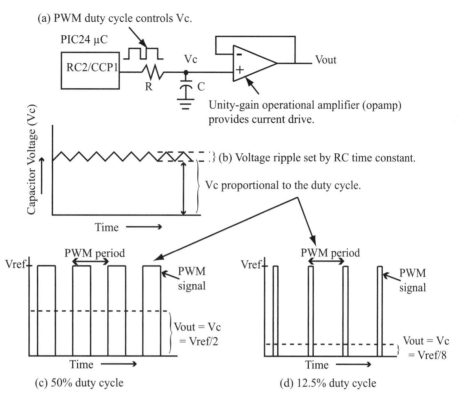

(a) PWM duty cycle controls Vc.

PIC24 μC

RC2/CCP1

R   C

Vc

Vout

Unity-gain operational amplifier (opamp) provides current drive.

Capacitor Voltage (Vc)

Time

(b) Voltage ripple set by RC time constant.

Vc proportional to the duty cycle.

Vref

PWM period

PWM signal

Vout = Vc = Vref/2

Time

(c) 50% duty cycle

Vref

PWM period

PWM signal

Vout = Vc = Vref/8

Time

(d) 12.5% duty cycle

FIGURE 12.34   A PWM digital-to-analog converter.

The RC series network forms a low-pass filter that is driven by the PWM signal. The low-pass filter removes most of the high-frequency content (e.g., the switching component) of the PWM signal, leaving only the (non-switching) DC component behind, which is averaged by the capacitor storage. The average value at the low-pass filter output is the desired DAC output. Figure 12.34c shows a PWM signal with a 50 percent duty cycle, meaning the PWM signal is high 50% of the time. The RC filter removes the high frequency components and thus Vc = Vout = Vref/2. Figure 12.34d shows a result with a 12.5 percent duty cycle PWM signal where Vc = Vout = Vref/8. The voltage ripple in Figure 12.34b is the high frequency content of the PWM signal that has been attenuated by the low-pass filter.

Let's examine the passive RC low-pass filter in Figure 12.34a. The filter's cutoff frequency in Hz is $f_0 = 1/(2\pi RC)$. Beyond the cutoff frequency, the filter attenuates the PWM signal frequencies at 20 dB/decade. Therefore, we can expect the PWM signal components at 10^*f_0 to be approximately 20 dB below those components at f_0, and signal components at 100^*f_0 to be attenuated 20 dB below those at 10^*f_0 and 40 dB below those at f_0. With this information, we can see that if the PWM frequency is well beyond the low-pass filter's cutoff frequency, so switching (high frequency) components will be greatly attenuated leaving behind only the PWM's low frequency components near DC. This filtering gives us the desired result, as a signal's DC component is equivalent to its average value. It takes a total time of five RC time constants to achieve 99.3 percent of a delta voltage change in the PWM DAC's output voltage, with typically several PWM periods occurring during this time.

Selection of the exact RC filter values is application specific, but some general rules of thumb can be helpful in getting started. Try using f_0 equal to 5–10 times the PWM DAC's update frequency. The PWM frequency should be far into the low-pass filter's stop band to reduce output ripple. PWM frequencies should be at least 100 times the low-pass filter cutoff so that PWM switching signal components are reduced by 40 dB or more. The PWM frequency can be reduced if the low-pass filter has stronger attenuation; multiple RC low-pass filter sections can be cascaded with each section providing an additional 20 dB/decade attenuation. Higher PWM frequencies means lower voltage ripple, but less fidelity in pulse width control. Larger RC time constants also means lower voltage ripple, but require longer to reach the new DC value after a pulse width change.

LCD displays that require positive and negative bias voltages outside of the supply rails often use a PWM signal driving a charge pump circuit to produce these voltages. If the PWM DAC is only to supply a fixed reference voltage (i.e., the PWM pulse width is not changed or changed infrequently), the previous paragraph's recommendations can be relaxed, with the principal goal being to produce a reference voltage that meets some maximum voltage ripple specification. Equation 12.7 gives an approximate value for the RC time constant given a VDD power supply voltage (volts), desired ripple (volts), and PWM period (seconds). Equation 12.4 assumes that the RC time constant is at least 10 times greater than the PWM period.

$$RC = (VDD \times PWM \text{ period} \times 0.37)/\text{ripple} \qquad (12.7)$$

For example, if VDD = 3.3 V, PWM period = 0.5 ms (2 kHz), and ripple = 0.1 V, then RC is computed as 0.0061 s. An RC time constant of 0.0061 can be approximated by using common R, C component values of R = 6.2 kΩ, C = 1.0 μF. Figure 12.35 shows two oscilloscope captures for the design as specified. The transitions are from 3.0 V to 1.0 V and vice-versa. The measured transition time was 30 ms, which is 60 PWM periods and approximately five RC time constants. Measured ripple was 70 mV.

1 V per horizontal division

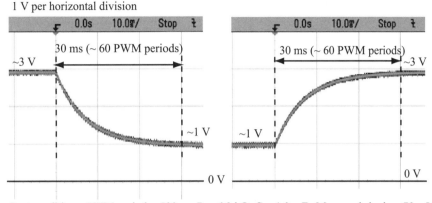

Test conditions: PWM period = 500 µs, R = 6.2 kΩ, C = 1.0 µF. Measured ripple = 70 mV

FIGURE 12.35   PWM DAC test.

TIME KEEPING USING TIMER1, RTCC

Timer1 is referred to as a Type A timer in the family reference manual, and it is different from Timer2 (Type B) and Timer3 (Type C) in that it cannot be operated in a 32-bit mode and can be driven by the secondary oscillator (external pins SOSCI, SOSCO). Timer2 and Timer3 can be driven by an external clock pin (T*x*CK), but not by the secondary oscillator. One use for the secondary oscillator is for *real-time* clock keeping (seconds, minutes, hours) using a 32.768 kHz watch crystal. An interrupt occurs every second using this clock frequency with a period register of 0x7FFF (the period is 0x7FFF + 1 = 0x8000 = 32768 timer ticks, which is 1 second for a 32.768 kHz clock). Real time can be kept by incrementing a variable on each interrupt. We refer the reader to the family reference manual [19] for details on the Timer1 configuration register and block diagram as it is very similar to Timer2.

Figure 12.36 shows code that assumes a 32.768 kHz crystal on the secondary oscillator, with the _T1Interrupt ISR incrementing the u16_seconds variable on each interrupt. The configTimer1() function configures Timer1 for an external clock, prescale of 1, PR1 value of 0x7FFF, and the interrupt enabled. Timer1 is also configured to remain operational during sleep mode by using the T1_IDLE_CON mask. The main() function enables the secondary oscillator amplifier by setting the SOSCEN bit (OSCCON<2>) using the PIC24 compiler's __builtin_write_OSCCONL function. As mentioned in Chapter 8, this built-in function does the necessary unlock sequence required to make changes to the OSCCON register. The external crystal will not oscillate if this amplifier is disabled. The while(1){} loop prints the u16_seconds variable, then sleeps. Because Timer1 is using an external clock and is configured for operation during sleep, its interrupt can be used to wake the processor from sleep mode.

```
volatile uint16 u16_seconds = 0;

void _ISRFAST _T1Interrupt (void) {         Occurs once a second, increment
  u16_seconds++;                            the u16_seconds variable.
  _T1IF = 0;  //clear interrupt flag
}                                     Config Timer1 to use the external clock,
                                      prescale of 1, continue operation during sleep.
void configTimer1(void) {                                               PIC24 µC
  T1CON = T1_OFF | T1_IDLE_CON | T1_GATE_OFF         32.768 kHz
          | T1_SYNC_EXT_OFF                                          SOSCI
          | T1_SOURCE_EXT .//ext clock        22 pF
          | T1_PS_1_1 ;  // prescaler of 1
  PR1 = 0x7FFF;         //period is 1 second                         SOSCO
  _T1IF = 0;            //clear interrupt flag  22 pF
  _T1IP = 1;            //choose a priority
  _T1IE = 1;            //enable the interrupt
  T1CONbits.TON = 1;    //turn on the timer
}
                                Sets the OSCCON.SOSCEN bit which enables the
                                secondary oscillator amplifier; without this, the
                                crystal will not oscillate.
int main(void) {
    __builtin_write_OSCCONL(OSCCON | 0x02);     //OSCCON.SOSCEN=1;
  configBasic(HELLO_MSG);    //say Hello!
  configTimer1();
  while (1) {                                  timer1_sosc.c, built
    outString("Seconds: ");                    Seconds: 0000
    outUint16Decimal(u16_seconds);             Seconds: 0001    Example
    outString("\n");                           Seconds: 0002    output
    while(!IS_TRANSMIT_COMPLETE_UART1());       Seconds: 0003
    SLEEP();                                    Seconds: 0004
  }              Timer1 interrupt can wake from sleep since it has been
}                configured to keep operating during sleep mode.
```

FIGURE 12.36   Keeping real time with Timer1.

THE REAL-TIME CLOCK CALENDAR MODULE

There is more to time keeping than just keeping track of seconds, and the Real-Time Clock Calendar (RTCC) module [42] on some PIC24F/H family members (not included on the PIC24HJ32GP202) can track seconds, minutes, hours, days of the week, days of the month, months, and years using an external 32.768 kHz clock. The RTCC module capabilities are fairly extensive, and this section only highlights the basic features of the module. Figure 12.37 shows the RTCC block diagram; observe that the clock/calendar time-keeping registers are each 8 bits wide and BCD encoded (see Chapter 7). The alarm feature allows an interrupt to be generated on match of the clock registers with the alarm registers, as well as toggle the RTCC output.

The main control register for the RTCC is named RCFGCAL (see the FRM [42] for details). The RTCPTR<1:0> (RCFGCAL<9:8>) pointer bits are used to access the RTCC registers using 16-bit accesses to the RTCVAL register. When the RTCPTR<1:0> bits are initialized to "11", the first 16-bit access goes to UI:Year,

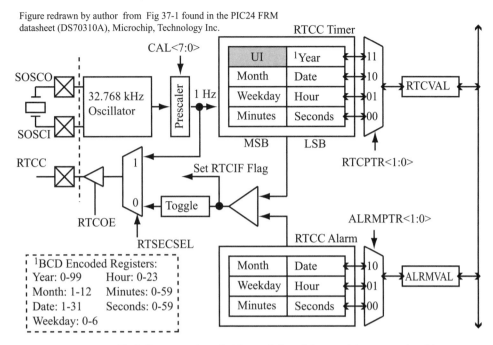

FIGURE 12.37 RTCC block diagram. (Adapted with permission of the copyright owner, Microchip Technology Inc. All rights reserved. No further reprints or reproduction may be made without Microchip Inc.'s prior written consent.)

after which RTCPTR is auto decremented so that the next access is to Month:Date, etc. Furthermore, accesses to the RTCC registers require a special unlock sequence similar to that required for the OSCCON register. When writing to the RTCC registers, it is recommended by the FRM that the module be disabled. A status bit named RTCSYNC (RCFGCAL<12>) is true when register rollover is 32 clock edges (~ 1 ms) from occurring; this is useful for determining when it is safe to read register values.

Figure 12.38 shows the first part of a test program for the RTCC. The unionRTCC union contains two declarations, a struct named u8 that provides byte access to the RTCC registers and a uint16 array named regs that allows 16-bit accesses to the registers. The getDateFromUser() function is used to read the initial date and time settings from the console. The getBCDvalue(char* sz_1) utility function is called by getDateFromUser() for each date/time component. The sz_1 parameter is a string used to prompt the user to enter a two-digit ASCII decimal value that is placed into sz_buff. This ASCII decimal string is then converted to binary by the sscanf function, which is then converted to a BCD 8-bit value that is returned by

```
typedef union _unionRTCC {
 struct {  //four 16 bit registers
        uint8 yr;
        uint8 null;
        uint8 date;
        uint8 month;       Union that represents the individual bytes
        uint8 hour;        of the RTCC registers.
        uint8 wday;
        uint8 sec;
        uint8 min;
 }u8;
 uint16 regs[4];      Union that represents the RTCC registers as four 16-bit values.
}unionRTCC;

unionRTCC u_RTCC;      Global variable used to store RTCC register values.

uint8 getBCDvalue(char *sz_1) {     Prompts user with output string sz_1, then reads
 char sz_buff[8];                   an ASCII-decimal string that is converted to
 uint16 u16_bin;                    BCD and returned.
 uint8 u8_bcd;
 outString(sz_1);
 inStringEcho(sz_buff,7);
 sscanf(sz_buff,"%d", (int *)&u16_bin);     Convert binary value
 u8_bcd = u16_bin/10;   //most significant digit   u8_bcd
 u8_bcd = u8_bcd << 4;                              to bcd value
 u8_bcd = u8_bcd | (u16_bin % 10);                  u8_bcd.
 return(u8_bcd);
}                         Modulo operator; the remainder of u16_bin divided by 10.

void getDateFromUser(void) {      Get clock, date settings from user
 u_RTCC.u8.yr = getBCDvalue("Enter year (0-99): ");
 u_RTCC.u8.month = getBCDvalue("Enter month (1-12): ");
 u_RTCC.u8.date = getBCDvalue("Enter day of month (1-31): ");
 u_RTCC.u8.wday = getBCDvalue("Enter week day (0-6): ");
 u_RTCC.u8.hour = getBCDvalue("Enter hour (0-23): ");
 u_RTCC.u8.min = getBCDvalue("Enter min (0-59): ");
 u_RTCC.u8.sec = getBCDvalue("Enter sec(0-59): ");
}
```

FIGURE 12.38 RTCC example code (part 1).

the function. Each of the BCD date/time components read by getDateFromUser() are stored in their appropriate u8 member of the global variable u_RTCC, which is of type unionRTCC.

Figure 12.39 shows the second part of the RTCC test code. The setRTCC() function copies data from the global variable u_RTCC into the RTCC registers. The builtin_write_RTCWEN() function provided by the PIC24 compiler does the unlock sequence for the RTCC registers and sets the RTCWEN bit allowing register modification. The RTCEN bit is cleared, disabling the module, which is suggested by the FRM during register updates. The RTCPTR bits are set to 3, and a loop does four 16-bit writes that copies data from u_RTCC to entry register RTCVAL. As mentioned earlier, each 16-bit write auto decrements the RCCPTR bits, so each write goes to

```
void setRTCC(void) {  ◄────  Copy values from the u_RTCC global variable to the
  uint8 u8_i;                RTCC registers.
  __builtin_write_RTCWEN();     //enable write to RTCC, sets RTCWEN
  RCFGCALbits.RTCEN = 0;        //disable the RTCC
  RCFGCALbits.RTCPTR = 3;        //set pointer reg to start
  for (u8_i=0;u8_i<4;u8_i++) RTCVAL = u_RTCC.regs[u8_i];
  RCFGCALbits.RTCEN = 1;        //Enable the RTCC
  RCFGCALbits.RTCWREN = 0;      //can clear without unlock
}

void readRTCC(void) {◄──── Copy RTCC registers into the u_RTCC global variable.
  uint8 u8_i;
  RCFGCALbits.RTCPTR = 3;        //set pointer reg to start
  for (u8_i=0;u8_i<4;u8_i++) u_RTCC.regs[u8_i] = RTCVAL;
}

void printRTCC(void) {◄──── Print date/time read from the RTCC.
  printf ("day(wday)/mon/yr: %2x(%2x)/%2x/%2x, %02x:%02x:%02x \n",
      (uint16) u_RTCC.u8.date,(uint16) u_RTCC.u8.wday,
      (uint16) u_RTCC.u8.month, (uint16) u_RTCC.u8.yr,
      (uint16) u_RTCC.u8.hour, (uint16) u_RTCC.u8.min,
      (uint16) u_RTCC.u8.sec);
}

int main(void) {
  __builtin_write_OSCCONL(OSCCON | 0x02);     // OSCCON.SOSCEN=1;
  configBasic(HELLO_MSG);    //say Hello!
  getDateFromUser();    //get initial date/time
  setRTCC();                 //set the date  Wait until RTCSYNC is high so we
  while (1) {                    ◄────       know that it is safe to read registers.
    while (!RCFGCALbits.RTCSYNC) doHeartbeat();
    readRTCC();      ⎫
    printRTCC();      ⎬  Read and print the registers.
    DELAY_MS(30);    ⎭
  }
}
```

FIGURE 12.39   RTCC example code (part 2).

a different register pair in the RTCC. The end result is that the different time/date components of u_RTCC are written to the correct RTCC registers. Before exiting, the RTCC module is enabled by setting RTCEN, and register writes are disabled by clearing RTCWREN. The readRTCC() function does the reverse of writeRTCC(); data is copied from the RTCC registers into the u_RTCC global variable. The printRTCC() function prints time/data components from u_RTCC to the console. The main() function sets the initial time/date setting for the RTCC using the getDateFromUser() and setRTCC() functions. The while(1){} loop is then entered, which monitors the RTSYNC bit to determine when it is safe to read the RTCC registers without a date or time rollover occurring during the read, which could return inconsistent data. After the RTSYNC bit is set, the RTCC registers are read and printed to the console using the readRTCC() and printRTCC() functions.

Two tests of the RTCC code are shown in Figure 12.40. The left-hand console output shows the data rolling over from midnight of December 31, 2015, to the next day, which is the beginning of a new year. The right-hand test shows a leap year test of rolling over from February 28 to February 29 in the year 2016.

```
rtcc.c, built on Jul 15 2008 at 23:01:47
Enter year (0-99): 15
Enter month (1-12): 12
Enter day of month (1-31): 31  } Thursday,
Enter week day (0-6): 4
Enter hour (0-23): 23          } December 31, 2015,
Enter min (0-59): 59
Enter sec(0-59): 56            } at 23:59:56
day(wday)/mon/yr: 31( 4)/12/15, 23:59:56
day(wday)/mon/yr: 31( 4)/12/15, 23:59:57
day(wday)/mon/yr: 31( 4)/12/15, 23:59:58
day(wday)/mon/yr: 31( 4)/12/15, 23:59:59  } Year,
day(wday)/mon/yr:  1( 5)/ 1/16, 00:00:00
day(wday)/mon/yr:  1( 5)/ 1/16, 00:00:01    month,
day(wday)/mon/yr:  1( 5)/ 1/16, 00:00:02
day(wday)/mon/yr:  1( 5)/ 1/16, 00:00:03    day
day(wday)/mon/yr:  1( 5)/ 1/16, 00:00:04    rollover
```

```
rtcc.c, built on Jul 15 2008 at 23:01:47
Enter year (0-99): 16
Enter month (1-12): 2
Enter day of month (1-31): 28  } Sunday,
Enter week day (0-6): 0
Enter hour (0-23): 23          } February 28, 2016,
Enter min (0-59): 59
Enter sec(0-59): 56            } at 23:59:56
day(wday)/mon/yr: 28( 0)/ 2/16, 23:59:56
day(wday)/mon/yr: 28( 0)/ 2/16, 23:59:57
day(wday)/mon/yr: 28( 0)/ 2/16, 23:59:58
day(wday)/mon/yr: 28( 0)/ 2/16, 23:59:59  } Leap year
day(wday)/mon/yr: 29( 1)/ 2/16, 00:00:00
day(wday)/mon/yr: 29( 1)/ 2/16, 00:00:01    rollover,
day(wday)/mon/yr: 29( 1)/ 2/16, 00:00:02
day(wday)/mon/yr: 29( 1)/ 2/16, 00:00:03    Feb. 29th
day(wday)/mon/yr: 29( 1)/ 2/16, 00:00:04
```

FIGURE 12.40   RTCC test output.

SUMMARY

All of the Timer*x* subsystems of the PIC24 µC family, designated as Type A (Timer1), Type B (Timer2, 4, 6, etc.), and Type C (Timer3, 5, 7, etc.) are 16-bit timers that can be clocked from an internal (FCY) or external source and have a prescaler with possible values of 1, 8, 64 and 256. Additionally, the Type B and Type C timers can be combined to form a single 32-bit timer. The input capture module uses either Timer2 or Timer3 for performing pulse width or period measurement. Input capture was used to decode a biphase-encoded IR signal generated by a universal remote control. The output capture mode can be used for hardware generation of various types of pulse trains, including pulse width modulation, which varies the duty cycle of a fixed period square wave. Applications of PWM include servo positioning and DC motor speed control. The secondary oscillator with a 32.768 kHz watch crystal is useful for simple timekeeping using Timer1. Complete time/date timekeeping is provided by the RTCC module found on some members of the PIC24 µC family.

REVIEW PROBLEMS

1. Refer to Figure 12.9 and assume a 40 MHz FCY and a prescale value of 8 for Timer2 operating in 16-bit mode, with PR2 = 0xFFFF. Assume that the first input capture has a value of 0xA000 and the second input capture a value

of 0x1200, with one Timer2 overflow between captures. How much time has elapsed between the captures? Give the answer in microseconds.

2. Refer to Figure 12.9 and assume a 40 MHz Fcy and a prescale value of 8 for Timer2 operating in 16-bit mode, with PR2 = 0xFFFF. Assume that the first input capture has a value of 0x0800 and the second input capture a value of 0xE000, with three Timer2 overflows between captures. How much time has elapsed between the captures? Give the answer in milliseconds.

3. Assume Timer2/3 operating in 32-bit mode with a 20 MHz Fcy and a prescale value of 64. How long does it take for this timer to overflow? Give the answer to the nearest second.

4. Assume Timer2/3 operating in 32-bit mode with a 20 MHz Fcy and a prescale value of 256. How many Timer2/3 ticks are contained in two seconds?

5. Assume a 40 MHz Fcy and a prescale value of 8 for Timer2 operating in 16-bit mode. Input capture has measured 2,000 ticks between the rising edges of a square wave; what is the square wave's frequency in kHz?

6. Assume a 16 MHz Fcy and a prescale value of 1 for Timer2 operating in 16-bit mode. You want to use input capture to measure the frequency of a square wave. What is the highest frequency that can be measured assuming that you want at least four ticks per square wave period?

7. Assume a 20 MHz Fcy and a prescale value of 8 for Timer2 operating in 16-bit mode. Also assume that an output compare module has been configured for pulse width modulation using a 10 ms period. What OCxRS register value is required to produce a pulse width of 5 ms?

8. Assume a 40 MHz Fcy and a prescale value of 64 for Timer2 operating in 16-bit mode. Also assume that an output compare module configured for pulse width modulation using a 20 ms period is being used to control an HS-311 servo. What OCxRS register value is required to produce to position the servo arm at 45°?

9. Assume a 16 MHz Fcy and a prescale value of 256 for Timer2 operating in 16-bit mode. Also assume that an output compare module configured for pulse width modulation using a 15 ms period is being used to control the speed of a DC motor using the scheme of Figure 12.29. What OCxRS register value is required to run the motor at 1/3 full speed (assume a linear relationship between DC motor speed and pulse width).

10. Assume an input capture pin is being used to monitor the U1RX pin. Describe an approach for computing the baud rate of a connection assuming that a few 0x55 characters are sent to the port. (You do not have to write code, just describe the approach you would use and why it would work.)

PART IV

Advanced Interfacing and Programming Topics

13

Advanced Hardware Topics

This chapter discusses various advanced hardware topics such as direct memory access (DMA), the Controller Area Network (CAN), the Universal Serial Bus (USB), and I²C multi-master operation. This chapter also discusses using the self-programming capability of the PIC μC for non-volatile data storage and use of the comparator module.

Learning Objectives

After reading this chapter, you will be able to:

- Use the direct memory access (DMA) capability for data transfer from peripheral modules.
- Use the PIC24 μC as an I²C slave.
- Discuss bus arbitration for multi-master busses and how bus arbitration is accomplished for CAN and I²C busses.
- Use two PIC24 μCs as masters on an I²C bus.
- Compare and contrast features of the Controller Area Network (CAN) and the Universal Serial Bus (USB) with the other serial interface standards used by the PIC24 μC.
- Have the PIC24 μC use its program memory for data storage purposes.
- Use the PIC24 μC comparator module to trigger an event based on an analog input crossing a threshold value.
- Discuss features of the parallel master port and CRC generator modules on the PIC24 μC.

The PIC24HJ32GP202 used for most of the examples in this book does not support several of the advanced peripheral modules discussed in this chapter. The sections titled "Using the PIC24 μC as an I²C Slave" and "Run-Time Self-Programming" covers features that are compatible with the PIC24HJ32GP202. The PIC24HJ64GP502, which is pin-compatible with the PIC24HJ32GP202, supports the capabilities discussed in all of the sections except the section titled "The Universal Serial Bus [USB]."

DIRECT MEMORY ACCESS

Direct memory access (DMA) refers to hardware-assisted data transfers between memory and peripherals (both on-chip and off-chip) with minimal CPU intervention. DMA reduces the CPU overhead for data transfer and can be used to aid both single burst and continuous transfers. Some members of the PIC24H family, such as the PIC24HJ64GP502, have a flexible DMA controller module whose block diagram is shown in Figure 13.1. Because of the DMA module's complexity, this section highlights a portion of the module's features and shows one code example that uses a DMA transfer. The reader is referred to the DMA section [44] of the FRM for full details. DMA memory transfers use a special *dual-ported* SRAM memory (DPSRAM) that contains 2048 bytes. The term dual-ported means that the DPSRAM can be accessed simultaneously by both the DMA module and the CPU without conflict. Data is either transferred from a peripheral to DPSRAM, or from DPSRAM to a peripheral as specified by registers within each DMA channel. A DMA channel can transfer in only one direction, and there is a natural priority with channel 0 being highest and 7 the lowest if simultaneous DMA requests occur. Some processors use a single-ported SRAM for DMA transfers, which mean that read/write operations to the SRAM between the DMA engine and the CPU must be synchronized to avoid access conflicts.

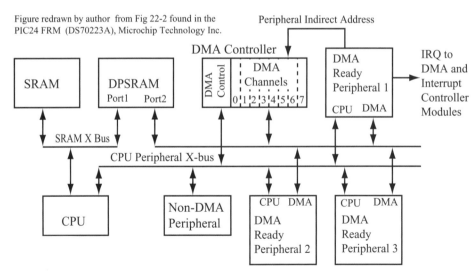

DMA Ready Peripherals: ADC, SPI, ECAN, UART, Input Capture, Output Compare. Timer2, Timer3 and INT0 can be optionally used to trigger DMA transfers.

FIGURE 13.1 DMA module block diagram. (Adapted with permission of the copyright owner, Microchip Technology Inc. All rights reserved. No further reprints or reproduction may be made without Microchip Inc.'s prior written consent.)

Each channel has the following registers:

- **DMA*x*CON:** Control register for the DMA module.
- **DMA*x*REQ:** Associates a peripheral interrupt request with a channel.
- **DMA*x*STA, DMA*x*STB:** DPSRAM starting address registers A and B; these two registers specify starting locations in the DPSRAM for the transfer. Some transfer modes require one register, while others require two.
- **DMA*x*PAD:** Contains the address of the peripheral data register involved in the transfer.
- **DMA*x*CNT:** Specifies the number of transfers required to complete a DMA request; for N transfers, must be initialized to a value of $N-1$.

There are also three global registers (DSADR, DMACS0, DMACS1) used for status information on the most recent DMA transfer (see the FRM [44] for more information). The DMA*x*CON register details are shown in Figure 13.2. The addressing mode (AMODE<1:0>) bits determine how a DMA address register steps through the DPSRAM buffer during a transfer. The default mode is post-increment, which means that the address buffer increments after a transfer. Once DMA*x*CNT+1 transfers have been performed when using post-increment mode, the DMA address register is at the end of the buffer and the address register is automatically reset back to the start of the DPSRAM buffer. This operates in the same manner as the head index used for the software FIFO discussed in Chapter 10. The addressing mode without post-increment always performs the transfer from the same location in DPSRAM. The peripheral indirect addressing mode is a special mode supported by only the ADC and ECAN (discussed later in this chapter) modules in which the peripheral provides the DPSRAM address for the transfer. The HALF bit determines if a DMA channel interrupt is generated after half of the transfers ((DMA*x*CNT+1)/2) have occurred, or after all of the transfers have been performed (DMA*x*CNT+1). DMA operation modes (MODE<1:0>) use either one DPSRAM buffer or two DPSRAM buffers (ping-pong mode) and are either one-shot or continuous. In one-shot single buffer mode, once DMA*x*CNT+1 transfers have been performed, the DMA module is automatically disabled (the CHEN bit in the DMA*x*CON register is cleared). In continuous mode, transfers continue as long as the module is enabled. The ping-pong mode implements the ping-pong buffering scheme discussed near the end of Chapter 10 (Figure 10.61). The first DMA*x*CNT+1 transfers use the DMA*x*STA buffer, then the next DMA*x*CNT+1 transfers are performed using the DMA*x*STB buffer. This allows the CPU to either fill or empty the DMA*x*STA buffer while DMA transfers use the DMA*x*STB buffer. After DMA*x*CNT+1 transfers are performed using the DMA*x*STB buffer, then the next DMA*x*CNT+1 transfers are performed using the DMA*x*STA buffer, and thus DMA transfers ping-pong between the DMA*x*STA and DMA*x*STB buffers. In one-shot

R/W-0	R/W-0	R/W-0	R/W-0	U-0	U-0	U-0	U-0
CHEN	SIZE	DIR	HALF	NULLW	UI	UI	UI
15	14	13	12	11	10	9	8

U-0	U-0	R/W-0	R/W-0	U-0	U-0	R/W-0	R/W-0
UI	UI	AMODE<1:0>		UI	UI	MODE<1:0>	
7	6	5	4	3	2	1	0

Bit 15: CHEN: Channel Enable Bit
1 = Channel enabled; 0 = Channel disabled
Bit 14: SIZE: Data Transfer Size bit
1 = Byte; 0 = Word
Bit 13: DIR: Transfer Direction bit (source/destination bus select)
1 = Read from DPSRAM address, write to peripheral address
0 = Read from Peripheral address, write to DPSRAM address
Bit 12: HALF: Block Transfer Interrupt Select bit
1 = Initiate interrupt when half of the data has been moved
0 = Initiate interrupt when all of the data has been moved
Bit 11: NULLW: Null Data Peripheral Write Mode Select bit
1 = Null data write to peripheral in addition to DPSRAM write (DIR bit must also be clear)
0 = Normal operation
Bit 5-4: AMODE<1:0>: DMA Channel Addressing Mode Select bits
11 = Reserved
10 = Peripheral Indirect Addressing mode
01 = Register Indirect without Post-Increment mode
00 = Register Indirect with Post-Increment mode
Bit 1-0: MODE<1:0> DMA Channel Operating Mode Select bits
11 = One-Shot, Ping-Pong modes enabled (one block transfer from/to each DMA RAM buffer)
10 = Continuous, Ping-Pong modes enabled
01 = One-Shot, Ping-Pong modes disabled
00 = Continuous, Ping-Pong modes disabled

Figure redrawn by author from
Reg. 22-1 found in the PIC24H FRM
(DS70223A),
Microchip Technology, Inc.

FIGURE 13.2 DMAxCON: Channel configuration register. (Adapted with permission of the copyright owner, Microchip Technology Inc. All rights reserved. No further reprints or reproduction may be made without Microchip Inc.'s prior written consent.)

ping-pong mode, the DMA module is disabled after DMAxCNT+1 transfers are done with both buffers. The null data write mode (NULLW bit is set) is a special mode intended for use with SPI receive transfers in which dummy data (null data bytes) are written to the SPI port to trigger each SPI receive. This is because in order to receive SPI data in master mode, data have to be written to the SPI port as discussed in Chapter 10. These data are typically dummy data for many peripherals, as usually the only data of interest are the data coming back from the SPI slave. Without the NULLW mode, a second DMA channel would have to be used to feed null data bytes to the SPI port to generate the received SPI data.

Figure 13.3 shows the details for the DMA*x*REQ register, which is used to associate a peripheral interrupt request with the DMA channel. When a peripheral's interrupt request flag is set, this triggers the DMA transfer, which is typically how the DMA transfer is accomplished. However, the application can also force a transfer by setting the FORCE bit (DMA*x*REQ<15>).

R/S-0	U-0	U-0	U-0	U-0	U-0	U-0	U-0
FORCE	UI	UI	UI	UI	UI	UI	UI
15	14	13	12	11	10	9	8

U-0	R/W-0	R/W-0	R/W-0	R/W-0	R/W-0	R/W-0	R/W-0
UI	IRQSEL<6:0>						
7	6	5	4	3	2	1	0

Bit 15: FORCE: Force DMA Transfer bit [1]
1 = Force a single DMA transfer (manual mode)
0 = Automatic DMA transfer initiation by DMA Request
Bit 6-0: IRQSEL<1:0>: DMA Peripheral IRQ Number Select bits

Figure redrawn by author from Reg. 22-2 found in the PIC24H FRM (DS70223A), Microchip Technology, Inc.

0000000 = INT0 – External Interrupt 0
0000001 = IC1 – Input Capture 1
0000010 = OC1 – Output Capture 1
0000101 = IC2 – Input Capture 2
0000110 = OC2 – Output Capture 2
0000111 = TMR2 – Timer2
0001000 = TMR3 – Timer3
0001010 = SPI1 – Transfer Done
0001011 = UART1RX – UART1 Receiver
0001100 = UART1TX – UART1 Transmitter

0001101 = ADC1 – ADC1 Convert Done
0010101 = ADC2 – ADC2 Convert Done
0011110 = UART2RX – UART2 Receiver
0011111 = UART2TX – UART2 Transmitter
0100001 = SPI2 – Transfer Done
0100010 = ECAN1 – RX Data Ready
0110111 = ECAN2 – RX Data Ready
1000110 = ECAN1 – TX Data Request
1000111 = ECAN2 – TX Data Request

Note 1: The FORCE bit cannot be cleared by the user. The FORCE bit is cleared by hardware when the forced DMA transfer is complete.

FIGURE 13.3   DMA*x*REQ: Channel IRQ select register. (Adapted with permission of the copyright owner, Microchip Technology Inc. All rights reserved. No further reprints or reproduction may be made without Microchip Inc.'s prior written consent.)

The following steps are required for DMA setup:

1. Write the address of the peripheral's data register used for the transfer to the DMA*x*PAD register so that the DMA module knows where to read or write peripheral data. Also write the DMA*x*REQ IRQSEL bits with the peripheral's IRQ number.
2. Configure the peripheral module to set its interrupt flag for each requested data transfer. Because the DMA module cannot perform error checking during the transfer (such as the parity error or framing error for UART receives), any error checking must be done by the application on an interrupt-driven

basis (such as using the U1EIF flag and the _U1ErrInterrupt() ISR for UART RX error checking, see Figure 9.3 of Chapter 9).

3. Configure the DMA*x*STA address register and the DMA*x*STB address register (only for ping-pong modes) with the DPSRAM addresses for the transfers. The MPLAB PIC24 compiler has a convenient built-in function for accomplishing this, as will be seen in the code example.

4. Initialize the DMA*x*CNT register with the number of transfers to accomplish.

5. Configure and enable the DMA module by writing to the DMA*x*CON register.

To illustrate DMA module usage, we implement the streaming data application discussed in the last section of Chapter 10 that captures UART RX data and writes it to the 24LC515 serial EEPROM using DMA channel 0 in continuous ping-pong buffer mode. Figure 13.4 shows the C code for the DMA channel 0 configuration, _U1ErrInterrupt() ISR, and the _DMA0Interrupt() ISR. The two buffers of Figure 10.61 that are used for capturing input data are implemented as DPSRAM buffers au8_bufferA and au8_bufferB, which are each 64 bytes. The space(dma) attribute declares these buffers as located in the DMA DPSRAM memory space. The configDMA0() function accomplishes steps 1, 3, 4, and 5 of the channel 0 configuration, with step 2 (UART configuration) accomplished by the configDefaultUART() function called by configBasic() within main(). For step 1, the assignment

```
DMA0PAD = (unsigned int) &U1RXREG;
```

assigns the address of the UART1 RX register to the DMA0PAD register, causing the DMA module to read from U1RXREG for each transfer. Also in step 1, the assignment

```
DMA0REQ = DMA_IRQ_U1RX;
```

associates the UART1 RX receive interrupt with channel 0, triggering a DMA transfer for each received character. For step 3, the assignments

```
DMA0STA = __builtin_dmaoffset(au8_bufferA);
DMA0STB = __builtin_dmaoffset(au8_bufferB);
```

copy the DMA RAM addresses of buffers au8_bufferA and au8_bufferB to DMA address registers DMA0STA and DMA0STB. For step 4, the assignment

```
DMA0CNT = DMA_TRANSFER_SIZE -1;   //DMA_TRANSFER_SIZE is 64
```

sets the number of transfers as DMA_TRANSFER_SIZE, which is the value 64, the size of each buffer. For step 5, the DMA0CON register is configured for the DMA module enabled with continuous ping-pong mode, a transfer direction of peripheral to buffer using post-increment buffer addressing, and to generate an interrupt after a buffer is full. The configDMA0() function also enables the UART receive error and DMA channel 0 interrupts. The _U1ErrInterrupt() ISR is triggered on a UART1 RX error and calls the checkRxErrorUART1() function, whose code was

```
#define BLKSIZE 64          ◄──────────── Write 64 bytes at a time to the EEPROM
#define DMA_TRANSFER_SIZE  BLKSIZE
//DMA buffers
uint8 au8_bufferA[DMA_TRANSFER_SIZE] __attribute__((space(dma)));  ⎫
uint8 au8_bufferB[DMA_TRANSFER_SIZE] __attribute__((space(dma)));  ⎬
//some one-bit flags                                              Declaration of two DPSRAM
typedef struct tagFLAGBITS {                                      buffers for ping-pong mode.
unsigned u1_activeBuffer: 1; ◄────────── Keeps track of whether au8_bufferA
unsigned u1_writeFlag:1;           set by DMA0     or au8_bufferB is currently being used
}FLAGBITS;                         ISR when        by the DMA module.
volatile FLAGBITS flags; ◄───      a buffer is full.

void configDMA0() {
 DMA0PAD = (unsigned int) &U1RXREG; //peripheral addr. ⎫ Step 1.
 DMA0REQ = DMA_IRQ_U1RX;   //source from UART1 RX      ⎭
                                                    Step 2 is accomplished by
 _U1RXIF = 0;    //clear the UART RX IF flag         configDefaultUART() called by
 //set up ping pong buffer registers                configBasic().
 DMA0STA = __builtin_dmaoffset(au8_bufferA);
 DMA0STB = __builtin_dmaoffset(au8_bufferB); ⎬ Step 3.
 //setup transfer size
 DMA0CNT =   DMA_TRANSFER_SIZE -1; ⎬ Step 4.
 DMA0CON =              //configure and enable the module
   (DMA_MODULE_ON |                      Step 5.
    DMA_SIZE_BYTE |                      Continuous ping-pong mode, interrupt
    DMA_DIR_READ_PERIPHERAL |            after a buffer is full, byte transfer mode,
    DMA_INTERRUPT_FULL |                 post-increment addressing.
    DMA_NULLW_OFF |                      Macros defined in include\pic24_dma.h.
    DMA_AMODE_REGISTER_POSTINC |
    DMA_MODE_CONTINUOUS_PING_PONG);
 //enable the UART1RX Error interrupt
  _U1EIF = 0;  _U1EIP = 1;  _U1EIE = 1;◄── Enable the UART1 RX error interrupt.
 //enable DMA channel 0 interrupt
 _DMA0IF = 0; _DMA0IP = 2; _DMA0IE = 1;◄── Enable the DMA channel 0 interrupt.
}


//UART error interrupt, need this with DMA since DMA does not check for errors.
void _ISRFAST _U1ErrInterrupt(void){    Execute a software reset with
 _U1EIF = 0;   //clear the UART1 Error flag  an appropriate error message on
 checkRxErrorUART1(); ◄─────────────         a UART1 RX receive error.
}


//interrupted when a ping-pong buffer is full
void _ISRFAST _DMA0Interrupt(void){   u1_activeBuffer is "1" if au8_bufferA is
 _DMA0IF = 0;                          full, "0" if au8_bufferB is full.
 flags.u1_activeBuffer = !flags.u1_activeBuffer;
 flags.u1_writeFlag = 1; ◄──── Semaphore indicating that a buffer is full and
}                               is ready to be written to the EEPROM.
```

FIGURE 13.4   DMA example code (part 1).

originally shown in Figure 10.13 and which generates a software reset on parity, framing, or overrun errors. The _DMA0Interrupt() ISR is triggered once a buffer is full and toggles the u1_bufferFlag that indicates which buffer is currently being filled by the DMA channel. The _DMA0Interrupt() ISR also sets the u1_writeFlag semaphore to inform main() that a buffer is ready to be written to the EEPROM.

Figure 13.5 shows the main() code of the DMA example; this is a modified version of the EEPROM example main() code originally shown in Figure 10.58. This main() implements the flowchart of Figure 10.63, in which the write mode waits for a buffer to fill as indicated by the u1_writeFlag semaphore, then writes the full buffer to EEPROM as indicated by the u1_activeBuffer flag. The memWriteLC515() function used in this program has been modified from the original code shown in Figure 10.57 in that the data buffer contains only 64 locations and its first two locations are not reserved for holding the u16_MemAddr address. The modified memWriteLC515() function does not use the memWriteNI2C1() transaction function, but

```
int main (void) {
  uint8 au8_eepromBuf[BLKSIZE];   //holds read data from EEPROM
  uint16 u16_MemAddr;
  uint8 u8_mode, u8_pause;
  configBasic(HELLO_MSG);
  configI2C1(400);                //configure I2C for 400 KHz
  outString("\nEnter 'w' for write mode, anything else reads: ");
  u8_mode = inCharEcho();
  outString("\n");
  u16_MemAddr = 0;      //start at location 0 in memory
  u8_pause = 0;
  while (1) {
    uint8 u8_i;
    if (u8_mode == 'w') {
      configDMA0();  ◄───────── Configure and enable DMA channel 0.
      while(1) {  ◄──── Write mode loop, MCLR to escape.
        if (flags.u1_writeFlag) reportError("DMA overflow!\n");
        while (!flags.u1_writeFlag) doHeartbeat(); ◄──── Wait for buffer to fill
        flags.u1_writeFlag = 0;
        if (flags.u1_activeBuffer)                    Write the full
          memWriteLC515(EEPROM,u16_MemAddr,au8_bufferA); ⎫ buffer, either
        else                                             ⎬ au8_bufferA or
          memWriteLC515(EEPROM,u16_MemAddr,au8_bufferB); ⎭ au8_bufferB, to
        u16_MemAddr = u16_MemAddr +64;  ◄─────              EEPROM.
        outString("*");
      }//end while(1), press reset to escape    Increment the write address
    } else {                                    by 64.
      while(1) {  ◄──── Read mode loop, MCLR to escape.
        if (u8_pause) {                    Input from console pauses
          inChar();  //get a character  ◄── console write.
          u8_pause = 0;
        }                         ┌── Read from EEPROM, write to console.
        memReadLC515(EEPROM,u16_MemAddr,au8_eepromBuf); // do read
        for (u8_i = 0;u8_i< 64;u8_i++) outChar(au8_eepromBuf[u8_i]);
        if (isCharReady()) {
                          inChar(); u8_pause = 1;
        }
        u16_MemAddr = u16_MemAddr + 64;
      }//end while(1) read mode, press reset to escape
    }//end else              Note: The memWriteLC515() function referenced here
  }//end while(1) main   is modified from Figure 10.57 such that it only expects
}//end main              a 64-byte buffer, and the first two locations are not reserved.
```

FIGURE 13.5 DMA example code (part 2).

instead uses primitive I²C function calls to write the 64 data bytes to the EEPROM (the source code can be found on the book's accompanying CD-ROM). The read mode in Figure 13.5 simply reads bytes out of the EEPROM in 64-block quantities and echoes them to the console. A pause mode for console output is toggled via console input.

DMA can be very useful for reducing CPU overhead in streaming data applications such as audio input or output, or packet-oriented transfers such as Ethernet. For example, the `while(1){}` loop of `main()` in Figure 13.5 only has to intervene when 64 characters are received and could be performing some other task during the arrival of these bytes.

Using the PIC24 µC as an I²C Slave

In our I²C examples in Chapter 10, the PIC24 µC was always used as the bus master. However, the PIC24 µC can also function as an I²C slave, which is useful when embedding a µC within a product that requires an I²C interface. To illustrate this capability, we use the reverse string application that was originally given in Chapter 10 for demonstrating PIC24 µC operation as a SPI slave. The PIC24 µC master reads a string from the console and writes it to the PIC24 µC slave, which reverses the string as shown in Figure 13.6. The PIC24 µC master then reads the reversed string from the PIC24 µC slave and displays it on the console. In the SPI master/slave string example of Chapter 10, a PIO output from the slave was used as an *output*

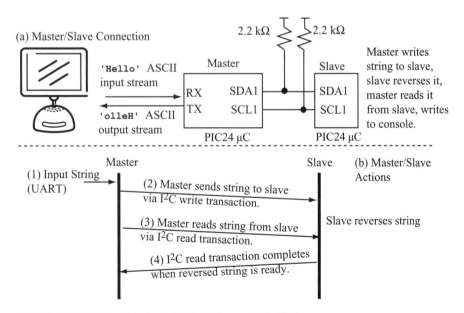

FIGURE 13.6 PIC24 µC Master to PIC24 µC Slave using the I²C bus.

ready signal to the master to indicate when the reversed string was ready. In this example, the handshaking signal is dispensed with as the master's read transaction to the slave completes whenever the reversed string data is ready for transmission.

Figure 13.7 gives the master code for the application of Figure 13.6. For I²C communication, an I²C address must be chosen for the PIC24 µC slave. Recall from Chapter 10 that the upper four address bits are manufacturer specific and allocated by Philips Semiconductor. The value 0x0 for the upper four address bits is the *general call* address and is used for broadcast transactions; devices can choose to respond or ignore this address. The value 0xF for the upper four address bits is a reserved address that should not be used. In our example, a value of 0x60 was arbitrarily chosen, as it was a free address on the I²C address bus in the target system and did not use an upper hex digit of 0x0 or 0xF. The while(1){} loop of main() reads a string from the console and determines the string's length. It then uses the writeNI2C1() function to perform an I²C block write to the slave, after which it immediately attempts to read the reversed string from the slave via the I²C block read function readNI2C1(). The block read hangs after sending the address byte until the slave has the reversed string ready for transmit.

The code for the I²C slave is interrupt driven using the slave events interrupt flag (SI2CIF). The SI2CIF flag is set on I²C slave events, such as recognition of an address

```
#define SLAVE_I2C_ADDR 0x60 ◄──────  I2C address arbitrarily chosen using a free
                                      address on the bus, with the most significant
int16 getStringLength(char* psz_1) {  digit not 0x0 (general call) or 0xF (reserved).
  uint16 u16_len;
  u16_len = 0;
  while (*psz_1){ psz_1++; u16_len++;}
  u16_len++;  //contains length of string including null
  return u16_len;
}

#define BUFSIZE 64
char sz_1[BUFSIZE];                Use block write to send string to slave, then use a block
                                   read to read the reversed string. The block read hangs
int main (void) { ◄───────         after sending the address byte until the slave has
  uint16 u16_len;                  the reversed string ready.
  configBasic(HELLO_MSG);
  configI2C1(400);  //configure I2C for 400 KHz
  while (1) {
    inStringEcho(sz_1,BUFSIZE);          //get a string from the console
    if (*sz_1 == 0) continue;            //don't send empty string
    u16_len = getStringLength(sz_1);   //determine string length
    writeNI2C1(SLAVE_I2C_ADDR,(uint8 *)sz_1,u16_len);    //send the string
    readNI2C1(SLAVE_I2C_ADDR, (uint8 *) sz_1,u16_len) ; //read rev. string
    outString(sz_1);
    outString("\n");
  }
}
```

FIGURE 13.7 PIC24 µC Master code for I²C string reversal application.

byte. The SI2C1IF flag is also set in a read transaction after an acknowledgement bit has been sent by the slave for a received data byte, and in a write transaction once a byte has been clocked out of the slave by the master and the acknowledgement bit sent by the master has been received by the slave. The master events interrupt flag (MI2CIF) is set by master events, such as completion of stop condition, start condition, repeated start, byte received or transmitted, acknowledgement transmitted, and bus collision. This implementation only uses the SI2CIF flag. The _SI2C1Interrupt() ISR code for the I²C slave is given in Figure 13.8, and contains four states. The initial

```
#define SLAVE_I2C_ADDR 0x60
typedef enum  {STATE_WAIT_FOR_ADDR, STATE_WAIT_FOR_WRITE_DATA,
STATE_SEND_READ_DATA,STATE_SEND_READ_LAST } STATE;
volatile STATE e_mystate = STATE_WAIT_FOR_ADDR;
#define BUFSIZE 64
volatile char  sz_1[BUFSIZE+1], sz_2[BUFSIZE+1];
volatile uint16 u16_index;

void _ISRFAST _SI2C1Interrupt(void) {
 uint8 u8_c;
 _SI2C1IF = 0;                           Waits for address byte of either read or
 switch (e_mystate) {                    write transaction.
  case STATE_WAIT_FOR_ADDR:                              Read I2C1RCV register to
   u8_c = I2C1RCV; //clear RBF bit for address           clear RBF bit to prevent
   u16_index = 0;                                        overflow.
   //check the R/W bit and see if read or write transaction
   if (I2C1STATbits.R_W) {    ←——— Check R/W# bit of address byte.
    I2C1TRN = sz_2[u16_index++]; //get first data byte   Causes
    I2C1CONbits.SCLREL = 1; ←——— //release clock line    SCL to
    e_mystate = STATE_SEND_READ_DATA;                    be released
   }                                                     by slave
   else e_mystate = STATE_WAIT_FOR_WRITE_DATA;           during read.
   break;
  case STATE_WAIT_FOR_WRITE_DATA: ←— Write transaction
   //character arrived, place in buffer
   sz_1[u16_index++] = I2C1RCV;  //read the byte         Read transaction
   if (sz_1[u16_index-1] == 0) {
    reverseString(sz_1,sz_2);//have a complete string, reverse it.
    e_mystate = STATE_WAIT_FOR_ADDR; //wait for next transaction
   }
   break;
  case STATE_SEND_READ_DATA: ←
   //put data in transmit register
   I2C1TRN = sz_2[u16_index++];
   I2C1CONbits.SCLREL = 1;      //release clock line
   if (sz_2[u16_index-1] == 0) e_mystate = STATE_SEND_READ_LAST;
   break;
  case STATE_SEND_READ_LAST: //last character finished TX
    e_mystate = STATE_WAIT_FOR_ADDR;
   break;
  default:
   e_mystate = STATE_WAIT_FOR_ADDR;
  } //end switch
 }//end ISR
```

FIGURE 13.8   PIC24 µC Slave ISR code for I²C string reversal application.

state is STATE_WAIT_FOR_ADDR, which waits for an address byte whose upper seven bits matches the seven bits in the slave's address register I2C1ADD<6:0>. Once the SI2C1IF interrupt is generated, the STATE_WAIT_FOR_ADDR examines the R_W bit of the I2C1STAT register, which contains the R/W# bit of the received address. For a write transaction, the next state is WAIT_FOR_WRITE_DATA that reads the incoming byte from the I2C1RCV register and places it in a buffer (sz_1[]). Once a null byte is received indicating the end of the string, the string is reversed and placed in buffer sz_2[] and STATE_WAIT_FOR_ADDR is reentered. If STATE_WAIT_FOR_ADDR detects a read transaction, it places the first byte of the reversed string in the transmit register I2C1TRN. It then sets the SCLREL bit high, which releases the clock line from a low state that is being held by the slave, allowing the master to generate clock pulses for reading the byte. The slave's SCLREL bit is cleared automatically after reception of the address byte for a read transaction, or an ACK bit from the master after a read byte, indicating that more read data is expected from the slave. A "0" for SCLREL means the clock line is held low by the slave, generating an I²C bus wait condition. The bus wait causes the master to hang, unable to generate clock pulses until the bus wait condition is removed, giving the slave time to respond with data for the read operation. After the first byte of the reversed string is transmitted by STATE_WAIT_FOR_ADDR, the remaining bytes are transmitted by STATE_SEND_READ_DATA. When the null byte is loaded into the I2C1TRN register indicating the end of the reversed string, the next state is STATE_SEND_READ_LAST, which is an empty state to catch the interrupt generated after the null byte is clocked out. The read transaction is then finished, and the state transitions back to STATE_WAIT_FOR_ADDR. During a write transaction, an ACK bit is generated automatically for each received byte by the slave's I²C module. A NAK is generated instead if the last received byte has not been read yet, or a receiver overflow condition exists.

The main() code for the I²C slave is given in Figure 13.9, and it is rather simple in that all it does is configure the I²C module, initialize the I2C1ADD register with our chosen slave address, and enable the SI2CIF interrupt. The while(1){} loop's only task is to keep the heartbeat alive since the _SI2C1Interrupt() ISR performs the string reversal work. Figure 13.9b shows the master writing the string "MS" to the slave, with the slave returning the reversed string of "SM" in the following read transaction (Figure 13.9c).

BUS ARBITRATION FOR THE I²C BUS

In the I²C bus introduction of Chapter 10, the formal definition of a bus was given as a communication channel in which there are one or more transmitters and multiple receivers. It was also stated that the I²C bus supports multiple bus masters (*multimaster*); in other words, any I²C device on the bus can initiate a transaction. However, in our examples, we always assumed that the PIC24 μC was the sole bus master and

```
int main (void) {                              (a) main() code for I²C slave
  configBasic(HELLO_MSG);
  configI2C1(400);                   //configure I2C for 400 KHz
  I2C1ADD = SLAVE_I2C_ADDR>>1;       //initialize the address register
  _SI2C1IF = 0;
  _SI2C1IP = 1;
  _SI2C1IE = 1;                      //enable ISR
  while (1) doHeartbeat();           //ISR does all work
}
```

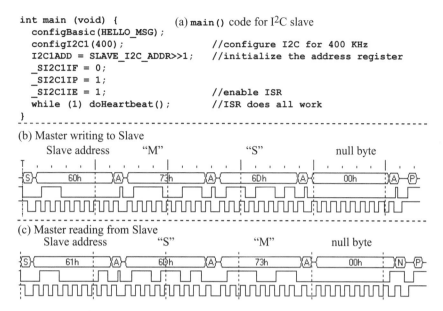

(b) Master writing to Slave

(c) Master reading from Slave

FIGURE 13.9 Slave main() code and I²C bus activity during execution.

the PIC initiated all I²C transactions. If a bus supports multiple bus masters, there must be a *bus arbitration* mechanism that decides which device assumes control of the bus when there are simultaneous attempts by different bus masters to access the bus. Figure 13.10 shows two common methods of bus arbitration for multi-master

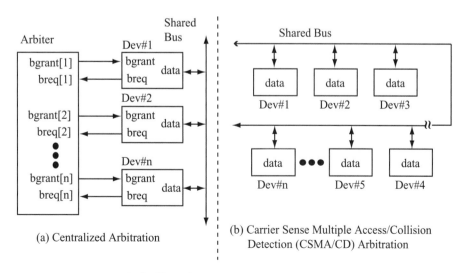

(a) Centralized Arbitration

(b) Carrier Sense Multiple Access/Collision Detection (CSMA/CD) Arbitration

FIGURE 13.10 Two methods of bus arbitration.

buses. In centralized arbitration (Figure 13.10a) a device wishing to communicate on the shared bus requests permission to access the bus via a bus request (*breq*) signal to an *arbiter,* which grants the device the bus via the bus grant (*bgrant*) line.

In the case of simultaneous requests, the arbiter uses a *priority scheme* to choose which device is granted bus access. A *fixed priority* scheme has static priorities assigned to each device such as device #1 always having the highest priority and device #*n* the lowest. A fixed priority scheme can result in one device monopolizing the bus, so a rotating priority scheme is more common, in which priorities are dynamically rotated among devices in an attempt to provide equal access to the bus. The disadvantage of centralized arbitration is that each device on the bus must have its own pair of bus request/bus grant lines. Centralized arbitration is most common in backplane busses found within computer systems that have a fixed number of I/O slots, and hence a fixed number of devices that can be present on the bus.

Figure 13.10b shows an arbitration scheme called *Carrier Sense Multiple Access/ Collision Detection* (CSMA/CD), which is useful when it is unknown *a priori* the number of devices that will be connected to a bus. In CSMA/CD, a device wanting bus access waits until the bus is idle, then begins transmitting. If multiple devices transmit, there will be a data *collision* on the bus. A device must be able to sense a collision, then determine independently of the other devices what action to take. A transmitter detects a collision by sensing the bus state during transmission; if the bus state does not match what the transmitter is sending, a collision has occurred. Local area networks based on Ethernet use CSMA/CD; when a collision occurs all transmitters stop sending data, wait for a random interval (the *backoff* interval), then try again. The backoff interval is random to help ensure that one transmitter wins and the others lose the arbitration. If another collision occurs, the interval wait time is increased (typically doubled) and another random wait is performed. This continues until a transmitter is successful at gaining access to the bus. While this works, it also wastes time because of the need for all transmitters to wait for the random interval.

The I²C bus also uses CSMA/CD for arbitration, but resolves conflicts in a manner different from Ethernet. Figure 13.11 illustrates how arbitration is performed on the I²C bus. Assuming both CPUa and CPUb begin transmitting at the same time, the first data sent after the start condition is the address byte of the I²C slave device and simultaneously, a clock signal over the SCL line. A "0" on the SDA bus overrides a "1" because of the open-drain output used to drive SDA (and also SCL). Each device senses the SDA line during transmission; if a device detects that the SDA state is different from what it has transmitted, the device immediately ceases transmission, giving up the bus. In this example, CPUa is initiating a transfer to an EEPROM (address 1010????), while CPUb is beginning a transfer to a DAC (address 0101????). CPUa stops transmitting after it sends the first (most significant) bit of its address because the initial "0" sent by CPUb overrides the "1" sent by CPUa. Observe that CPUa's transmission did not disturb CPUb's transmission,

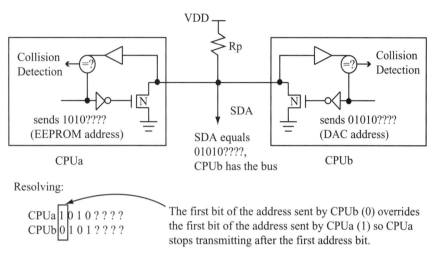

FIGURE 13.11 I²C bus arbitration.

so no data are lost and no time is wasted by the arbitration. What if both CPUa and CPUb attempt to write to the same device? Because the address bits are the same, the arbitration continues through the data bits, until either some difference is detected or the transaction completes if both devices send exactly the same data.

At this point, you should now understand the reason for the pull-up resistors on the I²C bus; the drivers for the SDA/SDL lines are open-drain to permit multimaster bus arbitration by having a "0" state override a "1" state. This conflict resolution in CSMA/CD is simple and effective, and is used in other CSMA/CD busses as will be seen when the Controller Area Network is discussed in the next section.

One other method of sharing a bus by multiple devices that can initiate transactions is *time division multiplexing* (TDM), which sidesteps the issue of arbitration by assigning fixed time intervals to devices for bus access. This means that each device on the bus must keep an accurate track of time in order to track its assigned bus access slot. While no arbitration is needed in this scheme, it is not an efficient use of bus bandwidth because if a device has nothing to transfer over the bus during its assigned time, that bus bandwidth is unused.

REVERSE STRING REVISITED

The reverse string application of Figure 13.6 can now be revisited knowing that each PIC24 µC can act as both a master and a slave since the I²C bus is a multi-master bus. Labeling the left-hand PIC24 µC as CPU1 and the right-hand PIC24 µC as CPU2, when CPU1 sends the string to CPU2 then CPU1 is the master and CPU2 is the slave. After CPU2 reverses the string, it acts as a bus master and sends the reversed string back to CPU1, which responds as a slave. This is a better solution than originally provided in which CPU1 was always the master and CPU2 the slave, in that CPU2 sends the reversed string when it is ready, allowing CPU1 to process the input on an interrupt-driven basis. Figure 13.12 shows the `_SI2C1Interrupt()` ISR code, which is the same for both CPUs and stores a received string into a buffer (`sz_1[]`) and sets a semaphore (`u8_gotString`) once a complete string has arrived. The ISR uses the same state machine approach for processing an I²C write transaction as used in Figure 13.8.

```
typedef enum  { STATE_WAIT_FOR_ADDR, STATE_WAIT_FOR_WRITE_DATA,
} STATE;

volatile STATE e_mystate = STATE_WAIT_FOR_ADDR;
#define BUFSIZE 64
char sz_1[BUFSIZE],sz_2[BUFSIZE];
volatile uint8 u8_gotString = 0;          Semaphore for when string has
volatile uint16 u16_index;                arrived.

void _ISRFAST _SI2C1Interrupt(void) {     Only has to process a write
    uint8 u8_c;                           transaction that sends a string.
    _SI2C1IF = 0;                         Same code used for both CPU1
  switch (e_mystate) {                    and CPU2.
    case STATE_WAIT_FOR_ADDR:
        u8_c = I2C1RCV; //clear RBF bit for address
        u16_index = 0;
        e_mystate = STATE_WAIT_FOR_WRITE_DATA;
        break;
      case STATE_WAIT_FOR_WRITE_DATA:
       //character arrived, place in buffer
       sz_1[u16_index++] = I2C1RCV;  //read the byte
       if (sz_1[u16_index-1] == 0) {
         u8_gotString = 1; //set the semaphore
         e_mystate = STATE_WAIT_FOR_ADDR; //wait for next transaction
       }
       break;
      default:  e_mystate = STATE_WAIT_FOR_ADDR;
  }
}
```

FIGURE 13.12   ISR code for the multi-master reverse string application.

The `main()` code for the multi-master reverse string application is given in Figure 13.13. The initialization code for both CPUs is the same, as the I2CADD register must be initialized and SI2CI interrupt enabled since both CPUs act as slaves. A macro named `CPU_ID` is used both to conditionally compile code for either CPU1 or CPU2 within the `while(1){}` loop and for I²C address selection for the two CPUs. The CPU1 code reads a string from the console and uses the `writeNI2C1()` function to send it to CPU2. Following this is a wait on the `u8_gotString` semaphore that indicates reception of the reversed string, which is printed to the console. The CPU2 code waits on the `u8_gotString` semaphore that indicates reception of the string sent by CPU1, which is then reversed by `reverseString()`. The reversed string is then sent back to CPU1 using the `writeNI2C1()` function.

```
#define CPU1 1          //reads string from console, send to CPU2
#define CPU2 2          //reverses strings, sends back to CPU1

#if (CPU_ID == CPU1)
#define SLAVE_I2C_ADDR 0x60
#define MY_ADDR 0x68                 Assign addresses based on the CPU_ID
#else  //CPU_ID == CPU2              macro defined in the MPLAB project file.
#define SLAVE_I2C_ADDR 0x68
#define MY_ADDR 0x60
#endif

int main (void) {
  uint16 u16_len;
  configBasic(HELLO_MSG);
  configI2C1(400);        //configure I2C for 400 KHz
  I2C1ADD = MY_ADDR>>1;   //initialize the address register
  _SI2C1IF = 0;
  _SI2C1IP = 1;           Enable I2C slave events interrupt
  _SI2C1IE = 1;
  while (1) {
    u8_gotString = 0;  //clear semaphore          CPU1 code
#if (CPU_ID == CPU1)
    inStringEcho(sz_2,BUFSIZE);        //get a string from the console
    if (*sz_2 == 0) continue;          //don't send empty string
    u16_len = getStringLength(sz_2);   //determine string length
    writeNI2C1(SLAVE_I2C_ADDR,(uint8 *)sz_2,u16_len);   //send the string
    //now wait for the reversed string to come back
    while (!u8_gotString) doHeartbeat();
    outString(sz_1);
    outString("\n");
#else  //CPU_ID == CPU2                             CPU2 code
    while (!u8_gotString) doHeartbeat();  //wait from string from CPU1
    reverseString(sz_1,sz_2); //reverse it
    u16_len=getStringLength(sz_2);
    writeNI2C1(SLAVE_I2C_ADDR,(uint8 *)sz_2,u16_len); //send rev. string
#endif
  }
}
```

FIGURE 13.13   main() code for the multi-master reverse string application.

THE CONTROLLER AREA NETWORK (CAN)

The automotive market is important for microcontroller manufacturers, as a typical car or truck has tens of microcontrollers within it. The number of microcontrollers within vehicles keeps increasing as automobiles evolve to mobile computing platforms that happen to carry people between locations. An automobile is a harsh environment from an electrical noise perspective and contains electrical systems dispersed throughout the vehicle with communication distances measured in meters. CAN [46] is a half-duplex serial bus designed as a communication mechanism for intelligent peripherals within an automotive system. CAN's signaling mechanism is designed to combat the inherent electrical noise found within vehicles. The

CAN bus uses only two wires for communication, keeping electrical cabling size to a minimum, thus making it easier to route within the crowded compartments of an automobile. CAN is a true bus in the formal sense like I²C; CAN transactions are visible to all peripherals connected to the bus and each transaction includes an 11-bit identifier that is used by receivers to filter messages. The CAN bus is multi-master in that any node on the bus can initiate a transaction, with arbitration handled similarly to I²C arbitration.

Figure 13.14 shows a PIC24 μC with an internal CAN module connected to a CAN bus. A CAN bus is implemented as two wires, CANH/CANL, which uses *differential signaling* (discussed in Figure 13.15) to form a half-duplex communication channel.

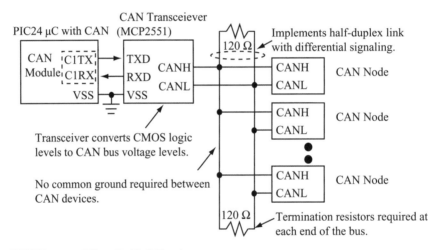

FIGURE 13.14 PIC24 μC with CAN system.

A transceiver chip like the Microchip MCP2551 [47] is required to convert from CAN bus voltage levels to CMOS logic levels (similar to the MAX3232 chip for the RS232 standard as discussed in Chapter 10). The enhanced CAN (ECAN™) module on a PIC μC has separate transmit (C*x*TX) and receive (C*x*RX) pins that are multiplexed by the CAN transceiver onto CANH/CANL. The CANH/CANL wires implement differential signaling; a pair of wires is used to signal a logic state, either "0" or "1". To this point, all signaling methods discussed in this book have been single-ended; one wire is used to signal a logic "0" or "1". The disadvantage of differential signaling is that it doubles the number of wires needed and as such is primarily used for serial transfers. The advantage of differential signaling is *common-mode noise rejection* as shown in Figure 13.15.

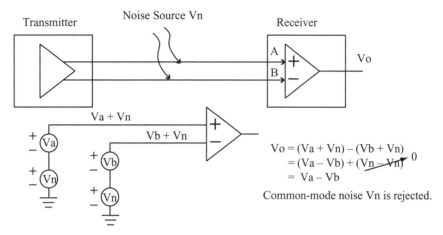

FIGURE 13.15   Common-mode noise rejection in differential signaling.

Common-mode noise is noise (Vn in Figure 13.15) that is injected equally (or nearly so) onto all wires within a cable. A CAN bus within an automobile can be relatively lengthy and has ample opportunity to pick up noise from neighboring cable bundles or from other nearby systems. Any common-mode noise is rejected at the receiver as the two input signal voltages are subtracted from each other to form the received voltage. Differential signaling is commonly used in external cabling that carries high-speed signals outside of a computing system.

Non-return-to-zero (NRZ) asynchronous transmission is used on the CxTX/RxTX pins that connect the PIC μC to the transceiver of Figure 13.14. The differential signaling method used on the CANH/CANL wire pair is shown in Figure 13.16. A logic "1" is called the *recessive* state, and is defined as when CANH − CANL < +0.5 V. A logic "0" is called the *dominant* state, and is defined as when CANH − CANL > +1.5 V. The recessive state (logic "1") is the bus idle state. The dominant state (logic "0") overrides the recessive state (logic "1"); if one transmitter sends a "0" and a second transmitter sends a "1", the bus will contain a "0" state (the dominant state). Absolute DC voltage levels can range from −3 V to +32 V, and CAN transceivers such as the MCP2551 must be able to survive transient voltage surges of −150 V to +100 V. Data rates range from 10 Kbps to 1 Mbps with the maximum data rate limited by the CAN bus length. On a CAN bus, all CAN nodes must agree on the data rate. The physical signaling shown in Figure 13.16 is not defined by the CAN 2.0 standard, but rather by the ISO-11898 specification that was created to ensure compatibility between CAN nodes in an automotive system. This means that the CAN protocol can be used with different physical signaling methods as long as the CAN 2.0 specifications are met.

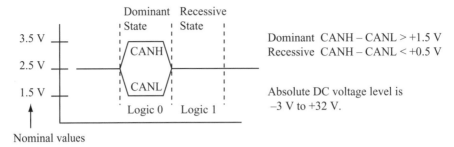

3.5 V

2.5 V

1.5 V

Dominant   Recessive
State   State

CANH

CANL

Logic 0   Logic 1

Dominant CANH − CANL > +1.5 V
Recessive CANH − CANL < +0.5 V

Absolute DC voltage level is
−3 V to +32 V.

Nominal values

FIGURE 13.16   CANH/CANL differential signaling.

Data transmissions are sent in frames, with each frame split into fields, and with each field containing one or more bits as shown in Figure 13.17. There are six different frame types: standard data, extended data, remote, error, overload, and interframe space. A standard data frame is shown in Figure 13.17a. The start-of-frame bit (start bit) is a logic "0" that signals the beginning of a frame. The arbitration field contains an 11-bit ID and a 12th bit called the RTR bit, which is "0" for a data frame and "1" for a remote frame. An extended data frame has a 29-bit identifier as shown in Figure 13.17b. An identifier is not an address in the I^2C sense; it does not have to uniquely identify either the sender or receiver. All nodes on the CAN bus receive the message; each node decides whether to act on the message based upon the value of the identifier and the contents of the message.

SOF (start of frame, "0")
SID (standard identifier)
RTR (remote transmit request)
IDE (indentifier extension bit,
    "1" for extended frames)
RB0, RB1 (reserved, always "0")
SRR (substitute remote request,
    "0" for data frames)

DLC (data length code, length of user data in bytes)
Data (user data, 0 to 8 bytes)
CRC (cyclic redundacy check)
ACK (driven "1" by transmitter, driven low by any
    receiver who has correctly received the data)
EOF (end of frame, all "1"s)
IFS (inter-frame space), "1"s, provides time for
    frame processing before next transmission.

(a) Data frame with 11-bit standard identifier (ID = SID)

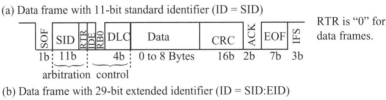

RTR is "0" for
data frames.

(b) Data frame with 29-bit extended identifier (ID = SID:EID)

FIGURE 13.17   CAN data frames.

The ECAN module for PIC µCs contains multiple filter/mask registers that are used to determine if a received frame should be accepted or rejected; these filter/mask registers use the ID field for accept/reject decisions. Once a frame has been accepted, it is transferred to an internal message buffer for further processing by the PIC µC application. The reason that message IDs function in this way is because many nodes on a CAN bus within an automobile are simple from a communication aspect in that they only periodically output sensor data (such as engine temperature), and there may be multiple nodes that are interested in this information. This message ID scheme provides efficient distribution of data to multiple receivers.

The ID field is used for multi-master arbitration in the same manner as I^2C arbitration. A CAN node must wait until the bus is idle before attempting transmission. Multiple CAN nodes that simultaneously attempt to transmit monitor the CAN bus as the ID field is sent. A "0" state (dominant) overrides a "1" state (recessive); a CAN module ceases transmission if it detects a difference between the CAN bus state and what it has transmitted. Like I^2C bus arbitration, this results in no lost bus time or in any corrupted messages. The ID field is transmitted most significant bit to least significant bit so the message with the lowest numerical ID field wins during arbitration. This assigns a fixed priority to message identifiers. Arbitration is only performed on the ID field and the CAN specification does not define what occurs if two messages with the same identifier are sent simultaneously. As such, assignment of message identifiers within a CAN system must be done in such a way as to guarantee that simultaneous transmission of messages with the same ID does not occur (the CAN spec does define this case for a collision between a standard data frame and a remote data frame; the RTR bit in the arbitration field determines priority in this case).

One strength of the CAN protocol is error detection. The *cyclic redundancy check* (CRC) field is a checksum based on the SOF, arbitration, control, and data fields that can detect a number of different errors, including five randomly distributed errors, any odd number of errors, and burst errors of less than 15 in length. The control field includes a message length so every frame received is also checked for the correct length, and each frame is also acknowledged by the receiver during the acknowledge field time (similar to the ACK bit in the I^2C protocol, except this is for the entire frame).

Because of the large number of bits sent in one frame, there must be a mechanism that allows the receiver to remain synchronized to the bit stream or else cumulative error between transmitter and receiver clock mismatch will cause incorrect sampling of the received bits as originally discussed in Chapter 10. This is accomplished through a technique known as *bit stuffing*, shown in Figure 13.18. Bit stuffing is done by the transmitter, which adds an extra bit that is the complement of the preceding bit if it detects that 5 bits of the same value have been

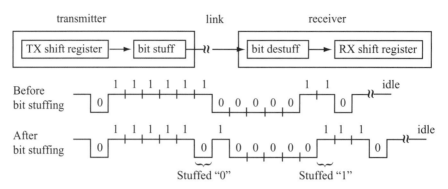

FIGURE 13.18 Bit stuffing in CAN.

transmitted. This is done to guarantee that every 6-bit interval contains a data transition (a guaranteed *transition density*), which allows a phase locked loop (PLL) or digital phase locked loop (DPLL) circuit at the receiver to synchronize the sampling clock to the bit stream.

The bit stuffing and bit *destuffing* is invisible to the user and is done automatically by the transmit and receive hardware. Figure 13.18 shows an example where both a "0" and "1" are added by the bit stuffing logic to the data stream. Observe that the "1" did not actually have to be added to the bit stream to guarantee a transition in 6-bit intervals as a "1" was present in the bit stream after the five "0" bits. However, the bit stuffing logic does not know this and so the "1" bit is stuffed into the bit stream anyway. Bit destuffing by the receiver is the opposite procedure; if 5 bits of the same value are received, the next bit is assumed to be a stuffed bit and is removed from the data stream. Bit stuffing is also useful for bit-level error detection, as a stuck-at-0 or stuck-at-1 failure in the transmitter causes the bit destuffing logic to detect an error in the received bit stream when the received bit value does not match the expected polarity of a stuffed bit. The usage and formatting of the remaining frame types of remote frame, error frame, and overload frame is not discussed and the reader is referred to the CAN specification.

THE PIC24 ECAN™ MODULE

A block diagram of the enhanced CAN (ECAN) module on the PIC24 µC is given in Figure 13.19. The module uses message buffers residing in DMA RAM for transmit and receive: up to 8 message buffers for transmit and up to 32 for receive.

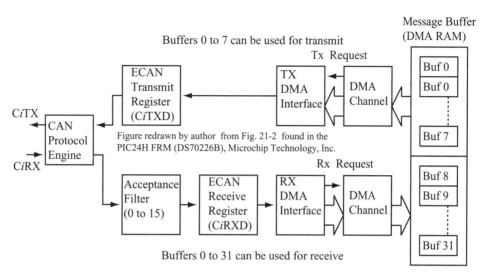

FIGURE 13.19   PIC24 ECAN block diagram. (Adapted with permission of the copyright owner, Microchip Technology Inc. All rights reserved. No further reprints or reproduction may be made without Microchip Inc.'s prior written consent.)

The 16 acceptance filters in the RX path can be flexibly configured for matching on either an 11-bit or 29-bit message identifier.

Because of the ECAN module's complexity, we will not attempt to cover all of the ECAN module's register details. Instead, we present an ECAN example and discuss some of the register usage as required by the example. We also use some utility C functions contained on this book's CD-ROM and discuss what the functions accomplish in terms of ECAN transfer but do not cover their code implementation. We encourage the readers to peruse the utility function's code implementations in conjunction with the ECAN section [48] of the PIC24 family reference manual for a deeper understanding of ECAN module details.

Figure 13.20a shows the ECANMSG type our code example uses for a single message buffer, which is eight 16-bit words, or 16 bytes. Words w0, w1, w2, and w7 are used for the message identifier, control bits, and other status information. The data member contains the user payload of up to eight data bytes; the union64 data type allows the payload to be viewed as either uint8, uint16, or uint32 items. Figure 13.20b shows how to declare a group of message buffers in DMA RAM. Because the DMA modules use peripheral indirect addressing (the ECAN module generates the address for the DMA), it is important that the DMA memory block be aligned to the nearest power of two that encompasses its size. The attribute aligned(NUM_BUF*16) does this as long as NUM_BUF is a power of two.

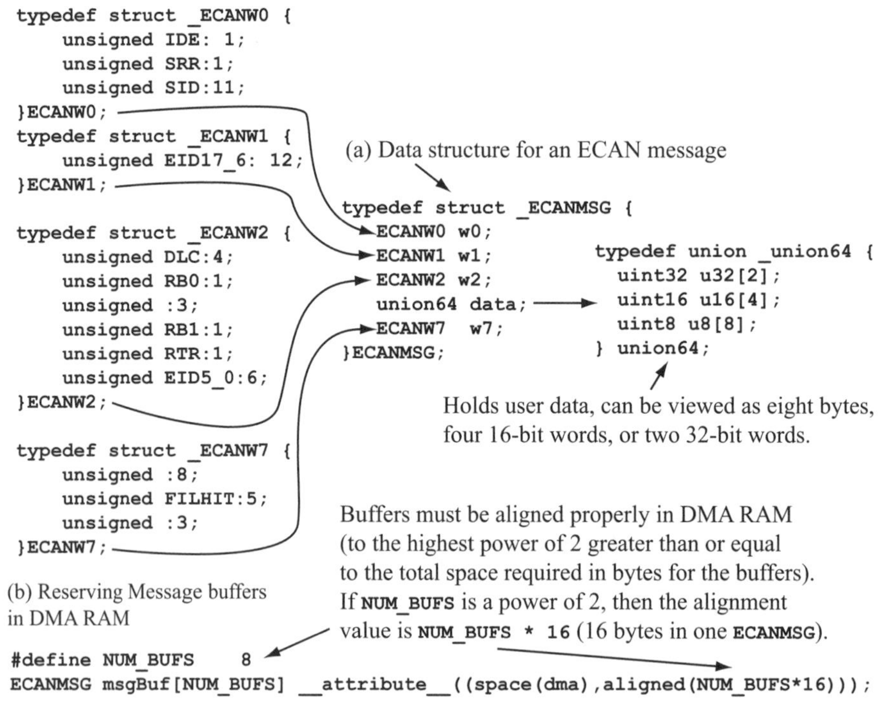

```
typedef struct _ECANW0 {
    unsigned IDE: 1;
    unsigned SRR:1;
    unsigned SID:11;
}ECANW0;
typedef struct _ECANW1 {
    unsigned EID17_6: 12;
}ECANW1;

typedef struct _ECANW2 {
    unsigned DLC:4;
    unsigned RB0:1;
    unsigned :3;
    unsigned RB1:1;
    unsigned RTR:1;
    unsigned EID5_0:6;
}ECANW2;

typedef struct _ECANW7 {
    unsigned :8;
    unsigned FILHIT:5;
    unsigned :3;
}ECANW7;
```

(a) Data structure for an ECAN message

```
typedef struct _ECANMSG {
    ECANW0 w0;
    ECANW1 w1;                    typedef union _union64 {
    ECANW2 w2;                        uint32 u32[2];
    union64 data;                     uint16 u16[4];
    ECANW7  w7;                       uint8 u8[8];
}ECANMSG;                         } union64;
```

Holds user data, can be viewed as eight bytes, four 16-bit words, or two 32-bit words.

(b) Reserving Message buffers in DMA RAM

Buffers must be aligned properly in DMA RAM (to the highest power of 2 greater than or equal to the total space required in bytes for the buffers). If NUM_BUFS is a power of 2, then the alignment value is NUM_BUFS * 16 (16 bytes in one ECANMSG).

```
#define NUM_BUFS        8
ECANMSG msgBuf[NUM_BUFS] __attribute__((space(dma),aligned(NUM_BUFS*16)));
```

FIGURE 13.20 *C* data structure for message buffer.

The code used to initialize DMA channels for ECAN transmit and receive is shown in Figure 13.21. Channels 0 and 1 are used (arbitrary choices), one for write (Figure 13.21a) and one for read (Figure 13.21b). Each channel uses peripheral indirect addressing in word mode, continuous operation. The transfer size is 8 words, so DMA0CNT is initialized to 7. For ECAN transmit, the DMA peripheral address register (DMA0PAD) is initialized to the address of the ECAN transmit register (&C1TXD), and the DMA interrupt request (DMA0REQ) to DMA_IRQ_ECAN1TX (a value of 0x46). For receive, the same registers in channel 1 are initialized to the ECAN receive register (&C1RXD) and DMA_IRQ_ECAN1RX (a value of 0x22), respectively. In our example, the ECAN transmit and receive share the same buffer space, so the address registers (DMA0STA, DMA1STA) of both channels are initialized to point to msgBuf.

Figure 13.22a shows how the bit sampling is accomplished during data reception. The number of sampling clocks used for a bit time is programmable from 8 to 25 time quanta (TQ), with a single time quantum equal to a sampling clock period. The time quanta are distributed between the *sync segment* (always 1 TQ), *propagation segment, phase segment 1,* and *phase segment 2.* When a bit edge does not occur within the sync segment, *resynchronization* is achieved by either lengthening phase segment 1 or by shortening phase segment 2, with the amount of adjustment

(a) DMA configure for ECAN transmit

```
void configDMA0(void){
  _DMA0IF = 0;
  DMA0PAD = (unsigned int) &C1TXD;
  DMA0REQ = DMA_IRQ_ECAN1TX;
  DMA0STA = __builtin_dmaoffset(msgBuf);
  DMA0CNT = 7; //8 words in ECANMSG
  DMA0CON =    //DMA module init
    (DMA_MODULE_ON |
    DMA_SIZE_WORD |
    DMA_DIR_WRITE_PERIPHERAL |
    DMA_INTERRUPT_FULL |
    DMA_NULLW_OFF |
    DMA_AMODE_PERIPHERAL_INDIRECT |
    DMA_MODE_CONTINUOUS);
}       DMA functions in include\pic24_dma.h
```

(b) DMA configure for ECAN receive

```
void configDMA1(void){
  _DMA1IF = 0;
  DMA1PAD = (unsigned int) &C1RXD;
  DMA1REQ = DMA_IRQ_ECAN1RX;
  DMA1STA = __builtin_dmaoffset(msgBuf);
  DMA1CNT = 7; //8 words in ECANMSG
  DMA1CON =    //DMA Module Init
    (DMA_MODULE_ON |
    DMA_SIZE_WORD |
    DMA_DIR_READ_PERIPHERAL |
    DMA_INTERRUPT_FULL |
    DMA_NULLW_OFF |
    DMA_AMODE_PERIPHERAL_INDIRECT |
    DMA_MODE_CONTINUOUS);
}
```

FIGURE 13.21   *C* data structure for message buffer.

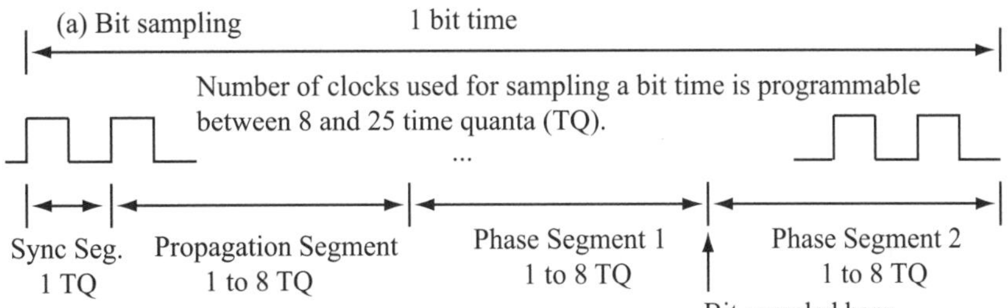

(a) Bit sampling   1 bit time

Number of clocks used for sampling a bit time is programmable between 8 and 25 time quanta (TQ).
                ...

| Sync Seg. | Propagation Segment | Phase Segment 1 | Phase Segment 2 |
| 1 TQ | 1 to 8 TQ | 1 to 8 TQ | 1 to 8 TQ |

Bit sampled here

Data Rate (bps) = FCAN / (TQ x PRESCALE)

FCAN can either be FOSC or FCY, cannot exceed 40 MHz, TQ should be evenly divisible into FCAN. Prescale values are 2×1, 2×2, 2×3, ... 2×64. Dynamic adjustments to maintain synchronization are performed to segment 1 (lengthened) and segment 2 (shortened) by between 1 to 4 TQ (jump width synchronization).

```
void configBaudECAN1(void) { //set baud rate
#if FCY == 40000000L                        (b) Clock configuration for
// FCAN = FCY = 40 MHz. TQ = 20. Prescale = 2   1 Mbps at FCY = 40 MHz
// Data Rate = FCAN/(TQ * pre) = 40MHz/40 = 1 MHz.
C1CTRL1bits.CANCKS = ECAN_FCAN_IS_FCY; // CANCKS = 1, sets FCAN = FCY = 40 MHz
//20 TQ for a bit time. 20 = Sync(1) + Prop seg (5) + Seg1 (8) + Seg2 (6)
C1CFG2 = ECAN_NO_WAKEUP |
         ECAN_SAMPLE_3TIMES |        //sample three times at sample point
         ECAN_SEG1PH_8TQ |           //seg1 = 8 TQ
         ECAN_SEG2_PROGRAMMABLE |    //seg2 is programmable
         ECAN_SEG2PH_6TQ |           //seg2 = 6 TQ
         ECAN_PRSEG_5TQ;             //propagation delay segment = 5 TQ

C1CFG1 = ECAN_SYNC_JUMP_4 |     //use maximum sync jump width
         ECAN_PRE_2x1;          //prescalers to 2x1
#else                       ECAN macros defined in include/pic24_ecan.h
#warning ECAN module not configured! Edit function configECAN1()
#endif
}
```

FIGURE 13.22   ECAN baud rate configuration.

limited by a parameter called the *sync jump width*. The base clock (FCAN) for the TQ is derived from either FCY or FOSC and cannot exceed 40 MHz. The data rate is given by Equation 13.1 with PRE representing the combination of two cascaded prescalers. One prescaler is fixed to divide by two, while the other is programmable, providing prescale (PRE) values of 2×1, 2×2, 2×3, ..., 2×64.

$$\text{data rate (bps)} = \text{FCAN} / (\text{TQ}_{\text{total}} \times \text{PRE}) \tag{13.1}$$

The baud rate initialization code for the ECAN module is given in Figure 13.22b, which configures a 1 Mbps data rate using FCAN = 40 MHz, TQ$_{\text{total}}$ = 20, and PRE = 2×1.

Figure 13.23 gives details on *C* utility functions used for ECAN configuration. The listed functions are for ECAN module 1; the same functions exist for ECAN module 2. The CHANGE_MODE_ECAN1() function is used to change operating

	ECAN Configuration Helper Functions
a	CHANGE_MODE_ECAN1(*mode*) Change ECAN operating mode, the choices are: ECAN_MODE_CONFIGURE (for configuration) ECAN_MODE_LOOPBACK (TX to RX internally, for testing) ECAN_MODE_NORMAL (normal operation) ECAN_MODE_DISABLED (in shutdown mode) ECAN_MODE_LISTEN_ONLY (do not generate any acknowledgements) ECAN_MODE_LISTEN_ALL_MESSAGES (accept all messages)
b	configTxRxBufferECAN1(uint8 u8_bufNum, uint8 u8_type, uint8 u8_priority) Configure message buffer **u8_bufNum** (only buffers 0 through 7) as either a receive (**u8_type** is zero) or transmit buffer (**u8_type** is non-zero); if transmit buffer, then it has priority **u8_priority** (values 0 to 3, 3 is highest).

c	configRxFilterECAN1(uint8 u8_filtNum, uint32 u32_id,
	                    uint8 u8_idType,uint8 u8_bufnum,
	                    uint8 u8_maskReg)
	
	RX filter **u8_filtNum** (values 0 to 15) has match ID of **u32_id**, which is either an 11-bit ID (**u8_idType** is zero) or a 29-bit ID (**u8_idType** is non-zero). Mask register **u8_maskReg** (register number 0,1 or 2) is used (**u8_maskReg** = 3 means no mask register used). On a match, the RX message is placed in message buffer **u8_bufnum** (values 0 to 14). If **u8_bufnum** =15, then use FIFO buffer (see text for explanation).

d	configRxMaskECAN1(uint8 u8_maskNum, uint32 u32_idMask, uint8 u8_idType, uint8 u8_matchType) Mask register is configured with mask value , which is either an 11-bit mask ID (**u8_idType** is zero) or a 29-bit mask ID (**u8_idType** is non-zero). If **u8_matchType** is zero, match either SID or EID addresses if filter matches (i.e., match if (Filter SID == Message SID) ‖ (Filter SID:EID = Message SID:EID))). If **u8_matchType** is non-zero, match only message types as specified by the filter (either SID or SID:EID).

FIGURE 13.23 Configuration utility functions.

modes; our example makes use of the configuration and loopback modes. The configTxRxBufferECAN1() function is used for configuring the first 8 buffers (buffers 0 through 7) as either TX or RX buffers; any buffers higher than buffer 7 can only be used for RX. The configRxFilterECAN1() function is used for configuring one of the 16 available RX filters as specified by u8_filterNum. A filter can optionally be used in combination with one of three mask registers (0, 1, or 2). If a mask register is not used, then an exact match is needed between the ID stored in the filter register and the incoming message for the message to be accepted. If a filter register is used, then a "0" in a mask register bit makes that bit a *don't care* for filter matching. If a match is made, the message is accepted and stored in the message buffer specified by u8_bufnum, with a range of 0 to 14. A message buffer value of 15 specifies that the RX message be placed in the RX FIFO, which is discussed later. The configRxMaskECAN1() function is used for configuring one of the three available mask registers.

Figure 13.24 gives some utility functions for transmit and receive operations. These will be covered in the context of *C* code that uses them.

Configuration code that uses the functions of Figures 13.21 through 13.24 is shown in Figure 13.25. The ECAN1 module is first placed into configuration

	ECAN Transmit Helper Functions
e	`GET_FIFO_READBUFFER_ECAN1()` Return the message buffer number of the next RX FIFO buffer to read for new data.

f	`formatStandardDataFrameECAN (ECANMSG* p_ecanmsg, uint16 u16_id,`
	`                              uint8 u8_len)`
	Format message buffer **p_ecanmsg** with DLC field of **u8_len** and 11-bit ID of **u16_id**.

g	`formatExtendedDataFrameECAN (ECANMSG* p_ecanmsg, uint32 u32_id,`
	`                              uint8 u8_len)`
	Format message buffer **p_ecanmsg** with DLC field of **u8_len** and 29-bit ID of **u32_id** .

h	`startTxECAN1(uint8 u8_bufNum)` Start transmit for message buffer **u8_bufNum**.
i	`getTxInProgressECAN1(uint8 u8_bufNum)` Return non-zero if transmit in progress for message buffer **u8_bufNum**.

	ECAN Receive Helper Functions
j	`clrRxFullOvfFlagsECAN1()` Clear all RX overflow and full flags
k	`clrRxFullFlagECAN1(uint8 u8_bufNum)` Clear RX full flag for message buffer **u8_bufNum**.
l	`GET_FIFO_READBUFFER_ECAN1()` Return the message buffer number of the next RX FIFO buffer to read for new data.
m	`uint32 getIdExtendedDataFrameECAN (ECANMSG* p_ecanmsg)` Return a 29-bit message ID from message buffer **p_ecanmsg**.
n	`clrRxFullFlagECAN1(uint8 u8_bufNum)` Clear RX full flag of message buffer **u8_bufNum**; zero if empty, non-zero if full.

FIGURE 13.24   Transmit, Receive utility functions.

```
//minimum number of buffers, 1 for TX, 1 for RX
#define NUM_TX_BUFS  1   //reserve 1 buffer for TX (buffer #0)
#define NUM_BUFS     2  ◄——— Minimum # of DMA buffers, 1 for TX, 1 for RX
ECANMSG msgBuf[NUM_BUFS] __attribute__((space(dma),aligned(NUM_BUFS*16))));
                    ◄— Base 11-bit message ID to match
#define MSG_ID 0x7A0     //arbitrary choice for 11-bit messsage ID
#define RX_BUFFER_ID  1  //buffer #1 used for  RX data

void configECAN1() {                    Enter configuration mode
 uint8 u8_i;                                         on match, use RX
 CHANGE_MODE_ECAN1(ECAN_MODE_CONFIGURE);             buffer #1
 configBaudECAN1();
 //use Filter 0 with Mask 0, write to RX_BUFFER_ID            Mask reg. #0
      Filter reg. #0 ─╲    ╱11-bit ID, 11-bit type        ╱
 configRxFilterECAN1(0, MSG_ID, ECAN_MATCH_SID, RX_BUFFER_ID, 0);
     Mask reg. #0 ─╲     ◄— Mask reg value, last two bits are don't cares
 configRxMaskECAN1(0, 0x7FC, 0, 1);  //check all but last two bits
               ◄───11-bit ID mask, match filter ID type
 clrRxFullOvfFlagsECAN1();  //clear all RX full, overflow flags.
 //first 8 buffs must be configured as either TX or TX
 for (u8_i = 0; u8_i<8; u8_i++) {
  if (u8_i < NUM_TX_BUFS)
    configTxRxBufferECAN1(u8_i,ECAN_TX_BUFF,3);     Buffer #0 reserved
  else                                              for TX,
    configTxRxBufferECAN1(u8_i,ECAN_RX_BUFF,3);     others for RX.
 }
 //do DMA config after ECAN has been initialized
 configDMA0();  }
 configDMA1();  }  Configure DMA
 CHANGE_MODE_ECAN1(ECAN_MODE_NORMAL);
}
```

FIGURE 13.25 ECAN configuration code.

mode via CHANGE_MODE_ECAN1(ECAN_MODE_CONFIGURE) (Figure 13.23). The baud rate is then configured for 1 Mbps assuming F_{CAN} = 40 MHz by the configBaudECAN1() function (Figure 13.22). The configRxFilterECAN1() function call configures filter #0 for an 11-bit identifier match on MSG_ID (value of 0x7A0, arbitrarily chosen) and uses mask register #0 in the match. Buffer RX_BUFFER_ID (value of 1) is used to store the incoming message on a match. The configRxMaskECAN1() function call configures mask register #0 for an 11-bit mask ID type that has a value of 0x7FC, and to only match the filter ID type (which is also set as an 11-bit ID). The last two bits of the mask register value 0x7FC are zero, which means that the last two bits of an 11-bit ID are not used in the match, allowing a range of message IDs to be accepted (in this case, message IDs of 0x7A0, 0x7A1, 0x7A2, and 0x7A3 are accepted). Only two message buffers (msgBuf[NUM_BUFS]) are allocated, one for TX and one for RX, which is the minimal number to support both transmit and receive. The configTxRxBufferECAN1() function is used to mark buffer #0 as a TX buffer and buffer #1 as an RX buffer. Finally, the DMA channels are configured using the configDMA0(), configDMA1() functions of Figure 13.21.

Figure 13.26 shows the `main()` code for testing the ECAN1 module. The loopback mode is used for testing, which ties TX back to RX internally. The `while(1){}` loop places eight bytes of test data into message buffer #0 then uses the `formatStandardDataFrameECAN()` function to format the message with an 11-bit message ID. The `while(1){}` loop generates message IDs in the range of 0x7A0 through 0x7A7. The mask register value of 0x7FC causes messages 0x7A0 through 0x7A3 to be accepted since the upper 9 bits of the message ID matches the upper 9 bits of filter #0, while other message IDs are rejected. The `startTxECAN1(0)` function call causes buffer #0 to be transmitted. Transmission is finished once `getTxInProgress(0)`

```
int main (void) {
 uint32 u32_out0, u32_out1, u32_in0, u32_in1;
 uint8 rx_buff_id, u8_cnt;

 configBasic(HELLO_MSG);                    TX tied to RX internally, used for testing.
 configECAN1();
 CHANGE_MODE_ECAN1(ECAN_MODE_LOOPBACK);  //loopback to ourself for a test.
 u32_out0 = 0xFEDCBA98; u32_out1 = 0x76543210;
 u8_cnt = 0;
 while (1) {              Write 8 bytes of data to TX message buffer, which is buffer #0.
  DELAY_MS(500);
  msgBuf[0].data.u32[0] = u32_out0; )
  msgBuf[0].data.u32[1] = u32_out1; )       Format buffer #0 with 11-bit ID.
  //format Buffer 0 for TX with SID=MSG_ID, data length = 8 bytes
  formatStandardDataFrameECAN(&msgBuf[0], MSG_ID+u8_cnt, 8);
  startTxECAN1(0);  //start transmission of buffer 0  ←  Start TX of buffer #0.
  while (getTxInProgressECAN1(0)) {  ←──────────── Wait for TX end.
     doHeartbeat(); //wait for transmission to end.
  }
  _DMA0IF = 0; ←  DMA0 used for TX, clear the flag.
  DELAY_MS(10); //delay for reception
  if (!_DMA1IF) {  ←──── DMA1 used for RX, flag set on reception of message.
     printf("Message ID 0x%X rejected by acceptance filter.\n",MSG_ID+u8_cnt);
  }                ──── This is printed if the filter rejects the TX message.
  else {
   _DMA1IF = 0;    //RX message accepted
   rx_buff_id = RX_BUFFER_ID;  ←──── RX buffer is buffer #1.
   u32_in0 = msgBuf[rx_buff_id].data.u32[0]; )  Read 8 bytes of data from RX
   u32_in1 = msgBuf[rx_buff_id].data.u32[1]; )  message and print it.
   printf("Msg ID: 0x%X, Out: 0x%lx%lx, In: 0x%lx%lx\n",
   msgBuf[rx_buff_id].w0.SID,u32_out0, u32_out1, u32_in0, u32_in1 );
   clrRxFullFlagECAN1(rx_buff_id);  ←── Clear full flag for RX buffer.
  }
  u32_out0 = rrot32(u32_out0); ) Change TX data by rotating each 32-bit word,
  u32_out1 = rrot32(u32_out1); ) (code not shown).
  u8_cnt++;  ←──── Change message ID.
  if (u8_cnt == 8) u8_cnt = 0;
 } //end while
}//end main
 } //end while(1)
} //end main
```

FIGURE 13.26   ECAN main() code.

returns as zero. A small software delay is used to wait for the message to be received; if the _DMA1IF flag remains cleared after the delay then the TX message was rejected by the acceptance filters, and an appropriate message is printed to the console. If the _DMA1IF flag is set, then the message was accepted, and the message ID and message contents are read out of the RX message buffer (buffer #1) and are printed to the console. The `clrRxFullFlagECAN1(rx_buff_id)` function call is used to clear the full flag of buffer #1.

Sample output from the test code of Figure 13.26 is shown in Figure 13.27. As expected, messages with IDs of 0x7A0 through 0x7A3 are accepted, while other message IDs are rejected.

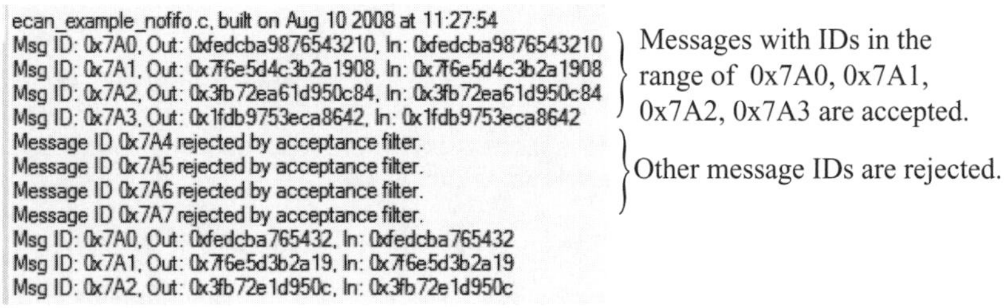

```
ecan_example_nofifo.c, built on Aug 10 2008 at 11:27:54
Msg ID: 0x7A0, Out: 0xfedcba9876543210, In: 0xfedcba9876543210
Msg ID: 0x7A1, Out: 0x76e5d4c3b2a1908, In: 0x76e5d4c3b2a1908
Msg ID: 0x7A2, Out: 0x3fb72ea61d950c84, In: 0x3fb72ea61d950c84
Msg ID: 0x7A3, Out: 0x1fdb9753eca8642, In: 0x1fdb9753eca8642
Message ID 0x7A4 rejected by acceptance filter.
Message ID 0x7A5 rejected by acceptance filter.
Message ID 0x7A6 rejected by acceptance filter.
Message ID 0x7A7 rejected by acceptance filter.
Msg ID: 0x7A0, Out: 0xfedcba765432, In: 0xfedcba765432
Msg ID: 0x7A1, Out: 0x76e5d3b2a19, In: 0x76e5d3b2a19
Msg ID: 0x7A2, Out: 0x3fb72e1d950c, In: 0x3fb72e1d950c
```

Messages with IDs in the range of 0x7A0, 0x7A1, 0x7A2, 0x7A3 are accepted.

Other message IDs are rejected.

FIGURE 13.27   Console output for ECAN test.

Using an ECAN RX FIFO

The previous example used the minimum number of DMA buffers, one each for RX and TX, and assigned an acceptance filter to a single RX buffer. The ECAN module also has the capability of assigning multiple RX buffers arranged in a FIFO order (see Chapter 10 for a discussion of a FIFO buffer structure) to an acceptance filter. Figure 13.28 shows the code changes to the previous example required to configure the ECAN module to use a seven-element FIFO for RX messages. The number of message buffers is increased from two to eight, with one buffer used for TX (buffer #0) and seven for RX (buffers #1 through #7). In `configECAN1()`, the C1FCTRL register that controls FIFO operation is configured for the FIFO to start at buffer #1 and continue to the end of the buffer space. The RX_BUFFER_ID that is used to assign filter #0 to an RX buffer is changed from a value of 1 to a value of 15, which indicates that this filter is to use the FIFO capability for storing messages. In the RX code for `main()`, the GET_FIFO_READBUFFER_ECAN1() function is used to determine the buffer number that has the current RX data; this buffer number is printed with the rest of the RX data.

```
#define NUM_TX_BUFS  1     //reserve 1 for TX
#define NUM_BUFS     8     //8 total buffers, 7 for RX, 1 for TX
ECANMSG msgBuf[NUM_BUFS] __attribute__((space(dma),aligned(NUM_BUFS*16)));
```
       8 buffers used, buffers 1 through 7 for RX, buffer 0 for TX.

```
#define RX_BUFFER_ID  15   //a value of 15 means to use a FIFO for RX
void configECAN1() {           RX buffer assignment of 15 means to use a FIFO, this
  uint8 u8_i;                  is assigned to filter #0 within the configECAN1() function.
  CHANGE_MODE_ECAN1(ECAN_MODE_CONFIGURE);
  configBaudECAN1();
  C1FCTRL = ECAN_FIFO_START_AREA_1 | ECAN_DMA_BUF_SIZE_8  ;

  ... remaining code the same ...
}                              Sets RX FIFO starting at buffer 1 and continuing
                               until the end of the buffer area (8 total buffers)
int main (void) {
... unchanged , configuration, TX code ...
if (!_DMA1IF) {
    printf("Message ID 0x%X rejected by acceptance filter.\n",MSG_ID+u8_cnt);
  }
  else {                            Returns the buffer number that has the
  _DMA1IF = 0;  //RX message accepted  current RX data.
  rx_buff_id = GET_FIFO_READBUFFER_ECAN1();
  u32_in0 = msgBuf[rx_buff_id].data.u32[0];
  u32_in1 = msgBuf[rx_buff_id].data.u32[1];
  printf("Rx Buff: %d. Msg ID: 0x%X, Out: 0x%lx%lx, In: 0x%lx%lx\n",
  rx_buff_id, msgBuf[rx_buff_id].w0.SID,u32_out0, u32_out1, u32_in0, u32_in1 );
  clrRxFullFlagECAN1(rx_buff_id);
  }
... remaining code the same ...
}
```

FIGURE 13.28   Code changes for using a seven-element FIFO.

Figure 13.29 shows sample output using the seven-element RX FIFO; observe that RX messages are placed in buffers #1, #2, ... #7 and then receive wraps back to buffer #1.

RX buffers start at #1, and increase for each received message.

Once RX buffer #7 is reached, FIFO wraps back to buffer #1.

```
ecan_example_fifo.c, built on Aug 10 2008 at 12:09:33
Rx Buff: 1. Msg ID: 0x7A0, Out: 0xfedcba9876543210, In: 0xfedcba9876543210
Rx Buff: 2. Msg ID: 0x7A1, Out: 0x7f6e5d4c3b2a1908, In: 0x7f6e5d4c3b2a1908
Rx Buff: 3. Msg ID: 0x7A2, Out: 0x3fb72ea61d950c84, In: 0x3fb72ea61d950c84
Rx Buff: 4. Msg ID: 0x7A3, Out: 0x1fdb9753eca8642, In: 0x1fdb9753eca8642
Message ID 0x7A4 rejected by acceptance filter.
Message ID 0x7A5 rejected by acceptance filter.
Message ID 0x7A6 rejected by acceptance filter.
Message ID 0x7A7 rejected by acceptance filter.
Rx Buff: 5. Msg ID: 0x7A0, Out: 0xfedcba765432, In: 0xfedcba765432
Rx Buff: 6. Msg ID: 0x7A1, Out: 0x7f6e5d3b2a19, In: 0x7f6e5d3b2a19
Rx Buff: 7. Msg ID: 0x7A2, Out: 0x3fb72e1d950c, In: 0x3fb72e1d950c
Rx Buff: 1. Msg ID: 0x7A3, Out: 0x1fdb97eca86, In: 0x1fdb97eca86
Message ID 0x7A4 rejected by acceptance filter.
Message ID 0x7A5 rejected by acceptance filter.
Message ID 0x7A6 rejected by acceptance filter.
Message ID 0x7A7 rejected by acceptance filter.
Rx Buff: 2. Msg ID: 0x7A0, Out: 0xfedc7654, In: 0xfedc7654
```

FIGURE 13.29   Sample output using RX FIFO.

Using an Extended Data Frame

Figure 13.30 shows the changes required to the RX FIFO code of Figure 13.28 to use an extended data frame (29-bit message ID) instead of a standard data frame (11-bit message ID). The `configRxFilterECAN1()` and `configRxMaskECAN1()` function calls within `configECAN1()` are changed to configure the filter and mask registers for 29-bit IDs instead of 11-bit IDs. Within `main()`, the `formatExtendedDataFrameECAN()` function is used to format the TX message buffer with a 29-bit ID, and the RX `printf()` statement uses the `getIdExtendedDataFrameECAN()` function to extract the 29-bit message ID from the RX message buffer.

```
#define MSG_ID 0x10B2ABC0      //arbitrary choice for extended messsage ID
                                  29-bit message ID
void configECAN1() {
... unchanged code ...                    Filter #0 configured for
                                          29-bit message ID match

configRxFilterECAN1(0, MSG_ID, ECAN_MATCH_EID, RX_BUFFER_ID, 0);
     29-bit mask value
configRxMaskECAN1(0, 0x1FFFFFFC, ECAN_MATCH_EID, 1);  //check all bits
... remaining code the same ..              Mask register #0 configured for
}                                           29-bit mask ID

int main (void) {
... unchanged code ...      Format extended data frame
formatExtendedDataFrameECAN(&msgBuf[0], MSG_ID+u8_cnt, 8);
... unchanged code ...
  printf("Rx Buff: %d. Msg ID: 0x%lX, Out: 0x%lx%lx, In: 0x%lx%lx\n",
   rx_buff_id, getIdExtendedDataFrameECAN (&msgBuf[rx_buff_id]),
   u32_out0, u32_out1, u32_in0, u32_in1 );
 }                                          Extract 29-bit ID from RX
... remaining code the same ...             message buffer
}
```

```
                      ecan_example_fifo_eid.c, built on Aug 10 2008 at 13:01:16
29-bit IDs present ⎰  Rx Buff: 1. Msg ID: 0x10B2ABC0, Out: 0xfedcba9876543210, In: 0xfedcba9876543210
in RX messages   ⎱  Rx Buff: 2. Msg ID: 0x10B2ABC1, Out: 0x7f6e5d4c3b2a1908, In: 0x7f6e5d4c3b2a1908
                      Rx Buff: 3. Msg ID: 0x10B2ABC2, Out: 0x3fb72ea61d950c84, In: 0x3fb72ea61d950c84
                      Rx Buff: 4. Msg ID: 0x10B2ABC3, Out: 0x1fdb9753eca8642, In: 0x1fdb9753eca8642
                      Message ID 0x10B2ABC4 rejected by acceptance filter.
                      Message ID 0x10B2ABC5 rejected by acceptance filter.
                      Message ID 0x10B2ABC6 rejected by acceptance filter.
                      Message ID 0x10B2ABC7 rejected by acceptance filter.
```

FIGURE 13.30   Code changes for using an extended data frame.

The Universal Serial Bus (USB)

The Universal Serial Bus [49] is a high-speed serial protocol that has largely replaced the use of the RS232 standard for serial communication on personal computers. Microchip Technology Inc. provides the USB interface on some PIC24 family members such as the PIC24FJ256GB110 and its variants. Microcontrollers with USB interfaces are also available from other semiconductor companies. USB is a complex specification, and a complete discussion is beyond the scope of this book. USB is briefly summarized here to contrast and compare some of its features with the CAN protocol discussed in the previous section. USB supports data transfer speeds of 1.5 Mb/s (low-speed device), 12 Mb/s (full speed), and 480 Mb/s (high speed). Figure 13.31a shows that the physical topology of a USB network consists of the *host, hubs,* and *functions.* The host initiates all transactions in USB because the bus does not support multiple bus masters. All communication is between the host and functions, which are USB-enabled devices such as keyboards, mice, memory cards, and so forth. A hub simply provides a connection point to grow the physical topology; a hub has an upstream port that communicates up the hierarchy to the host and multiple downstream ports that can either connect to a hub or function. A hub can also split the network into different speed regions with high-speed transfer upstream (host side) and either low-speed or full-speed downstream. Logically, each endpoint appears to be directly connected to the host as shown in Figure 13.31b.

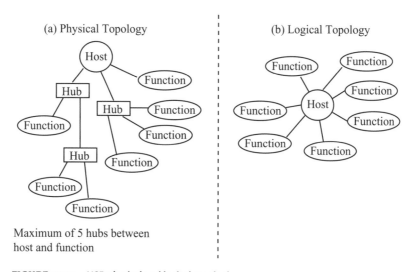

FIGURE 13.31   USB physical and logical topologies.

At the physical level, USB and CAN have similarities in that both implement half-duplex communication using differential signaling and both use bit stuffing to maintain synchronization. However, they differ in details relating to signaling levels and data encoding. Figure 13.32 shows the electrical signaling used in USB for low- and full-speed modes (the electrical signal levels for high-speed mode are significantly different and are not discussed). Data are carried by the D+/D− signal pair; in low- and full-speed mode a differential "1" is signaled when $(D+) - (D-) > 200\,\text{mV}$ and a differential "0" signaled when $(D-) - (D+) > 200\,\text{mV}$. Differential signaling is used in USB for the same reason it is used in CAN—to make the

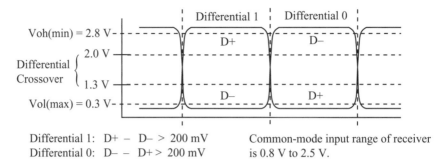

FIGURE 13.32 USB electrical signaling.

signaling more resistant to common-mode noise. The USB cable also carries +5 V and ground, allowing USB devices to maintain a common ground with the host and to be powered from the cable. Unlike CAN, most microcontrollers implement the D+/D– pin interface directly within the microcontroller and do not use an external transceiver IC to translate between CMOS and USB voltage levels.

The data encoding method used in USB is called non-return to zero inverted (NRZI), a somewhat unfortunate name, as it is not the inverse of the NRZ encoding we have previously used in Chapter 10 for serial data or in this chapter for CAN. NRZI encoding changes signal level any time a "0" is sent, while a "1" maintains the same signal level. This means that a string of "0"s causes the line to change with each bit, while a string of "1"s leaves the line quiescent (in the case of USB physical signaling, these are differential "1"s and "0"s). Bit stuffing is used in USB to force a guaranteed signal transition density as is done in CAN signaling; however, the NRZI encoding means that strings of "1"s trigger the bit stuffing mechanism. A "0" is inserted into the bit stream by the transmitter when six consecutive "1" bits are detected. Figure 13.33 shows an example of NRZI encoding and the bit stuffing used within USB.

USB transactions occur in packets, with bytes within packets sent least significant bit to most significant bit. Common packet types are *token, handshake,* and *data* packets. Token packets identify the type of transaction, data packets contain the data being transferred between host and function, and handshake packets are used for acknowledgement, flow control, and error signaling. There are four types of USB transactions: *bulk, control, interrupt,* and *isochronous.* A bulk transaction transfers data between the host and function with a handshake packet sent for every data packet and also supports flow control and retry. A control transaction is also used for data transfer and allows transfer of multiple data packets without handshake packets, thus containing less packet overhead than a bulk transaction. An interrupt transaction allows for periodic polling of functions via a low-overhead transaction. An isochronous transaction is intended for functions that require a guaranteed data bandwidth such as real-time data delivery of audio or video data.

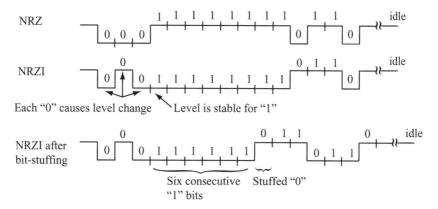

FIGURE 13.33   NRZI encoding and bit stuffing in USB.

Figure 13.34 shows the formats of common packet types in USB. Every packet starts with a SYNC field (8 bits for low/full speed, 32 bits for high speed) used to resynchronize the receiver to the data stream; the SYNC field contains a high density of signal transitions for this purpose. The packet identifier (PID) specifies the type of packet; Figure 13.34 shows only a subset of the available packet types within USB (not

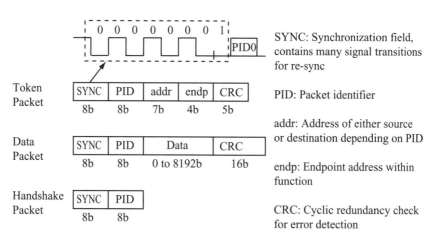

Token packet (IN, OUT, SOF, SETUP) used to initiate a transaction and identify a transaction type.

Data packet (DATA0/1/2, MDATA) used to transfer data between host and function.

Handshake packet (ACK, NAK, STALL, NYET) used for acknowledgement of packets, flow control, and error signaling.

FIGURE 13.34   Common packet types/formats in USB.

shown are so-called *special* packets). The address field of the token packet identifies the source or destination address of the transaction, depending on the packet identifier. Address 0 is the default address for a new device connection to the network and is reserved, which means that a USB network can contain 127 external functions. The host is responsible for assigning an address (*bus enumeration*) to a function when a device is connected to the network; USB devices can be dynamically removed and added to the network. The 4-bit endpoint field specifies a location within the function. The CRC field is used for error detection.

Figure 13.35 shows data transfer from host to function and from function to host in a bulk transaction. A transfer from function to host consists of an IN token packet from the host requesting data; the function returns either a DATA0 or DATA1 data packet that the host acknowledges via an ACK handshake packet. The DATA0/DATA1 packets are alternated between transactions as a way of synchronizing multiple data transactions. A transfer from host to function consists of an OUT token packet from the host followed by either a DATA0 or DATA1 packet that the function acknowledges via an ACK handshake packet.

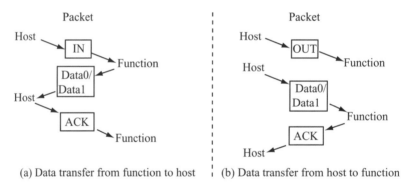

FIGURE 13.35 Data transfer in a bulk transaction.

This discussion is only a brief summary of packet types and USB transactions; the reader is referred to the USB 2.0 specification [49] for more information. USB support in microcontrollers requires considerable hardware resources as well as software support in terms of microcontroller firmware that implements the nuances of the USB protocol. Microchip has a USB software stack available on the company Website for use with its USB-capable microcontrollers.

RUN-TIME SELF-PROGRAMMING

In Chapter 10, an external serial EEPROM was used as an example of I²C interfacing and provided off-chip non-volatile data storage. The PIC24 μC is also capable of self-programming its own program memory, in a process known as *run-time self-programming* (RTSP) [50]. This offers a convenient non-volatile storage mechanism, provided that there is free space in program memory (also referred to as *flash* memory). RTSP also offers a way for a PIC24 µC to upload a new program via a communication port; the code that is executed during this process is called a *bootloader* and resides in some protected space that is not over-written by the new program. Flash memory is erased one page at a time, where one page is 512 instructions (recall that an instruction is three bytes, or 24 bits). A flash page is organized in 8 rows of 64 instructions and flash memory can be written as either an entire row or a single instruction. Write and erase operations are *self-timed,* which means the operations take a variable amount of time de-pending on environmental and power supply conditions, as well as the number of previous erase/write cycles. Minimum page erase time is 20 ms, while minimum row and word write times are 1.6 ms and 20 µs, respectively. When using flash memory for storing data, one must be cognizant that the number of erase/write cycles to flash before possible failure is finite; the PIC24 µC datasheet for a typical processor gives 10,000 as the minimum number of guaranteed write operations (the *write endurance*). Conversely, the 24LC515 serial EEPROM used in Chapter 10 has a maximum erase plus write time of 5 ms and a minimum write endurance of 1,000,000 cycles. These parameters and an application's requirements generally determine whether or not an external or internal non-volatile memory solution is needed.

Recall from Chapter 6 that the program space visibility (PSV) capability al-lowed program memory to be mapped into the data memory as a method of ac-cessing program memory data. The disadvantage of this method is that only the lower 16 bits of each instruction word are available via PSV since data memory is 16 bits wide. In RTSP, a different mechanism for accessing program memory uses *table read/write* instructions (Figure 13.36) that allow access to all 24 bits of an instruction. The `tblrdl` (table read low) instruction accesses the lower 16 bits of an instruction, while the `tblrdh` (table read high) instruction reads the upper 8 bits. The source address register (*Ws*) specifies the lower 16 bits of the program memory address (the *offset*) for the read, while the upper bits are contained in the TBLPAG special function register. The table write instructions, `tblwrl` and `tblwrh`, write the lower 16 bits and upper 8 bits of the instruction respectively. The lower 16 bits of the program memory destination address is specified in *Wd*, while the upper 8 bits are contained in TBLPAG. The TBLPAG register must be initialized with the upper bits of a program memory address before a table read/write instruc-tion is executed.

The table write instructions do not write directly to program memory, but rather, to an intermediate row latch. Flash memory program and erase operations are controlled by the NVMCON special function register, with details shown in

Name	Mnemonic	Operation

Table Read Low	`tblrdl{.b} [Ws],Wd`
	`[Ws++],[Wd]`
	`[Ws--],[Wd++]`
	`[++Ws],[Wd--]`
	`[--Ws],[++Wd]`
	`[--Wd]`
		Byte op:
		`if (LSB(Ws) == 1)`
		`PMEM[(TBLPAG),(Ws)]<15:8> → Wd`
		`else`
		`PMEM[(TBLPAG),(Ws)]<7:0> → Wd`
		Word op:
		`PMEM[(TBLPAG),(Ws)]<15:0> → Wd`

Table Read High	`tblrdh{.b}  (see tblrdl)`	Byte op:
		`if (LSB(Ws) == 1)`
		`0 → Wd`
		`else`
		`PMEM[(TBLPAG),(Ws)]<23:16> → Wd`
		Word op:
		`PMEM[(TBLPAG),(Ws)]<23:16> → Wd<7:0>`
		`0 → Wd<15:8>`

Table Write Low	`tblwtl{.b} Ws,[Wd]`
	`[Ws],[Wd++]`
	`[Ws++],[Wd--]`
	`[Ws--],[++Wd]`
	`[++Ws],[--Wd]`
	`[--Ws],`
		Byte op:
		`if (LSB(Wd) == 1)`
		`(Ws) → PMEM[(TBLPAG),(Wd)]<15:8>`
		`else`
		`(Ws) → PMEM[(TBLPAG),(Wd)]<7:0>`
		Word op:
		`(Ws) → PMEM[(TBLPAG),(Wd)]<15:0>`

Table Write High	`tblwth{.b}  (see tblwtl)`	Byte op:
		`if (LSB(Wd) == 1)`
		`NOP`
		`else`
		`(Ws) → PMEM[(TBLPAG),(Wd)]<23:16>`
		Word op:
		`(Ws)<7:0> → PMEM[(TBLPAG),(Wd)]<23:16>`

FIGURE 13.36   Table read/write instructions.

Figure 13.37. An erase or write cycle is started by setting the WR control bit, which first requires a special unlock sequence similar to that used by the OSCCON register for changing oscillator options. Our code examples use the PIC24 compiler built-in function `__builtin_write_NVM()` that executes the unlock sequence and sets the WR bit.

Figure 13.38 shows the first set of utility functions for performing RTSP. The `doWriteLatchFlash()` function writes `u16_wordhi:u16_wordlo` (only the lower 24 bits are valid) to the row latch at the program memory address specified by `u16_addrhi:u16_addrlo`. The `doReadLatchFlash()` function returns the content of a program memory location as a `uint32` from the address specified by `u16_addrhi:u16_addrlo`. A page erase at location `u16_addrhi:u16_addrlo` is accomplished by the `doErasePageFlash()` function; observe that the value of 0x4042 written to the NVMCON register within `doErasePageFlash()` enables flash modification by setting the WREN bit, sets the ERASE bit, and specifies a page erase by setting

R/SO-0[1]	R/W-0[1]	R/W-0[1]	U-0	U-0	U-0	U-0	U-0
WR	WREN	WRERR	UI	UI	UI	UI	UI
15	14	13	12	11	10	9	8
U-0	R/W-0[1]	U-0	U-0	R/W-0[1]	R/W-0[1]	R/W-0[1]	R/W-0[1]
UI	ERASE	UI	UI	NVMOP<3:0>[2]			
7	6	5	4	3	2	1	0

Bit 15 : WR: Write Control bit (SO - settable only)
 1 = Initiates a Flash memory program or erase operation. The
   operation is self-timed and the bit is cleared by hardware
   once the operation is complete
 0 = Program or erase operation is complete and inactive
Bit 14: WREN: Write Enable bit
 1 = Enable Flash program/erase operations
 0 = Inhibit Flash program/erase operations
Bit 13: WRERR: Write sequence Error Flag bit
 1 = An improper or erase sequence attempt or termination has occurred. Bit is set automatically
   on any set attempt of the WR bit
 0 = The program erase operation completed normally
Bit 6: ERASE: Erase/Program Enable bit
 1 = Perform the erase operation specified by NVMOP<3:0> on the next WR command
 0 = Perform the program operation specified by NVMOP<3:0> on the next WR command
Bit 3-0: NVMOP<3:0>: NVM Operation Select bits [2]

If ERASE = 1	If ERASE = 0
1111 = Memory bulk erase operation	1111 = No operation
1110 = Reserved	1110 = Reserved
1101 = Erase General Segment and FGS Config. reg.	1101 = No operation
1100 = Erase Secure Segment and FSS Config. reg.	1100 = No operation
1011 = Reserved	1011 = Reserved
0011 = No operation	0011 = Memory word program operation
0010 = Memory page erase operation	0010 = No Operation
0001 = No Operation	0001 = Memory row program operation
0000 = Erase a single Configuration register byte	0000 = Program a single Config. reg. byte

Figure redrawn by author from
Reg. 5-1 found in the
PIC24 FRM (DS70228C),
Microchip Technology Inc.

Note 1: These bits can only be reset on POR
Note 2: All other combinations of NVMOP<3:0>
  are unimplemented

FIGURE 13.37   NVMCON register details. (Adapted with permission of the copyright owner,
Microchip Technology Inc. All rights reserved. No further reprints or reproduction may be made
without Microchip Inc.'s prior written consent.)

NVMOP = 0b0010. The erase is started by the `__builtin_write_NVM()` function call.
The code then monitors the WR bit status and does not exit the function until it
is cleared, indicating that the erase is finished. Interrupts are disabled during the
function call to `__builtin_write_NVM()` because the unlock sequence enables a
write to the WR bit for only one instruction cycle, and thus cannot be interrupted
in order for the unlock to succeed. The `doWriteRowFlow()` function writes the current row that has been loaded via table write operations; its structure is similar to
`doErasePageFlash()`.

```
#define FLASH_ROWSIZE     64       //in number of instructions per row
#define FLASH_ROWS_PER_PAGE 8      //rows per page
#define FLASH_PAGEINSTR (FLASH_ROWSIZE * FLASH_ROWS_PER_PAGE)
#define FLASH_PAGEBYTES (FLASH_PAGEINSTR*3)  // bytes in one page is 1536
#define FLASH_ROWBYTES  (FLASH_ROWSIZE*3)     //bytes in one row
```
       Write u16_wordhi:u16_wordlo to row latch at address u16_addrhi:u16_addrlo
```
void doWriteLatchFlash(uint16 u16_addrhi, uint16 u16_addrlo,
                       uint16 u16_wordhi, uint16 u16_wordlo) {
  TBLPAG = u16_addrhi;    //select page
  __builtin_tblwtl(u16_addrlo,u16_wordlo); // asm(" tblwtl W3,[W1]")
  __builtin_tblwth(u16_addrlo,u16_wordhi); // asm(" tblwth W2,[W1]")
}
```
                  Read instruction at u16_addrhi:u16_addrlo
```
uint32 doReadLatchFlash(uint16 u16_addrhi, uint16 u16_addrlo) {
  union32 u32_a;
  TBLPAG = u16_addrhi;    //select page
  u32_a.u16.ls16 = __builtin_tblrdl(u16_addrlo);   // asm("     tblrdl [W1],W0")
  u32_a.u16.ms16 = __builtin_tblrdh(u16_addrlo);   // asm("     tblrdh [W1],W1")
  return(u32_a.u32);
}
```
                 Erase flash page at u16_addrhi:u16_addrlo
```
void doErasePageFlash (uint16 u16_addrhi, uint16 u16_addrlo) {
  uint16 u16_save_SR, u16_save_TBLPAG;
  // preserve the SR and TBLPAG registers
  u16_save_SR = SR;
  u16_save_TBLPAG = TBLPAG;
  //disable interrupts
  SR = SR | 0xE0;
  // NVCON = flash write + erase
  // + page erase
  NVMCON = 0x4042;
  TBLPAG = u16_addrhi; // select page
  //select row
  //equivalant to "tblwtl W1,[W1]"
  asm("tblwtl  %0,[%0]"::"r"(u16_addrlo));
  //start erase
  __builtin_write_NVM();
  //reenable interrupts
  SR = u16_save_SR;
  //wait for end of erase
  while (NVMCON & 0x8000)
    doHeartbeat();
  // restore TBLPAG
  TBLPAG = u16_save_TBLPAG;
}
```

Write current flash row that has been
loaded via table writes
```
  void doWriteRowFlash() {
   uint16 u16_save_SR;
   // save SR
   u16_save_SR = SR;
   // disable interrupts
   SR = SR | 0xE0;
   // flash write + row op
   NVMCON = 0x4001;
   //start write
   __builtin_write_NVM();
   //reenable interrupts
   SR = u16_save_SR;
   //wait for end of write
   while (NVMCON & 0x8000)
    doHeartbeat();
  }
```

FIGURE 13.38   C utility functions for RTSP (part 1).

Utility functions that write and read one page of flash memory are given in Figure 13.39. The doWritePageFlash() function writes u16_len bytes of data stored in buffer pu8_data to flash address u32_pmemAddress. This function erases the page before writing, which is generally needed since once a bit has been programmed to a "0" condition, it cannot be returned to a "1" except by an erase operation (flash

```
void doWritePageFlash(union32 u32_pmemAddress,
                      uint8* pu8_data, uint16 u16_len) {
  uint16 u16_byteCnt;                    ← Write u16_len bytes stored in pu8_data to
  union32 u32_a;                            flash address u32_pmemaddress. The u16_len
  uint16 u16_ICnt, u16_numInstructions;    parameter is rounded up to 3*64 = 192 byte
  ASSERT(u16_len <= FLASH_PAGEBYTES);       boundary (a row boundary).
  //erase the page first
  doErasePageFlash(u32_pmemAddress.u16.ms16, u32_pmemAddress.u16.ls16);
  //write the bytes
  //round up to nearest row boundary          Round u16_len up to nearest
  u16_numInstructions = u16_len/3;    ←       row boundary.
  if (u16_len % 3 != 0) u16_numInstructions++;
  u16_numInstructions = u16_numInstructions + (u16_numInstructions%64);
  for(u16_ICnt = 0, u16_byteCnt=0;u16_ICnt<u16_numInstructions; ){
    u32_a.u8[0] = pu8_data[u16_byteCnt];      Ensure that a u16_numInstructions
    u32_a.u8[1] = pu8_data[u16_byteCnt+1];    is on a row boundary.
    u32_a.u8[2] = pu8_data[u16_byteCnt+2];
    u32_a.u8[3] = 0;
    doWriteLatchFlash(u32_pmemAddress.u16.ms16, u32_pmemAddress.u16.ls16,
                      u32_a.u16.ms16,u32_a.u16.ls16);
    if ((u16_ICnt+1)%64 == 0) {                After 64 instructions are
      doWriteRowFlash();//row boundary, write it.  written to row latch, write
    }                                          the row.
    u32_pmemAddress.u32 += 2;   //program memory address increments by 2
    u16_byteCnt += 3    //
    u16_ICnt += 1;               ←    For every 3 bytes of data that is written, increment
  }                                  Flash address by 2.
}
void doReadPageFlash(union32 u32_pmemAddress, uint8* pu8_data,
                     uint16 u16_len) {  Read u16_len bytes stored at flash address
  uint16 u16_byteCnt;                 ←  u32_pmemaddress and return them in
  union32 u32_a;                         pu8_data.
  ASSERT(u16_len <= FLASH_PAGEBYTES);
  for(u16_byteCnt=0;u16_byteCnt<u16_len;u16_byteCnt += 3){
    u32_a = (union32) doReadLatchFlash(u32_pmemAddress.u16.ms16,
                                       u32_pmemAddress.u16.ls16);
    pu8_data[u16_byteCnt] = u32_a.u8[0];        typedef union _union32 {
    pu8_data[u16_byteCnt+1] = u32_a.u8[1];        uint32 u32;
    pu8_data[u16_byteCnt+2] = u32_a.u8[2];        struct {
    u32_pmemAddress.u32 += 2;                       uint16 ls16;
  }                                                 uint16 ms16;
}                    union32 type used for  →     } u16;
                     convenient access to words,    uint8 u8[4];
                     bytes within a 32-bit value. } union32
```

FIGURE 13.39   *C* utility functions for RTSP (part 2).

memory is all "1"s after an erase). The *doReadPageFlash()* function reads u16_len bytes into buffer pu8_data from flash address u32_pmemAddress. Both functions use the union32 data type that offers convenient access to the low and high words of a 32-bit value, which is needed when passing the u32_pmemAddress to the utility functions of Figure 13.38.

A SAMPLE FLASH APPLICATION

A typical usage of flash memory is to store N fixed-length records, where the record data and format is application dependent, such as bar codes, RFID tag values, fixed-length ASCII strings, etc. Figure 13.40 shows a union data structure named UFDATA that stores NUM_RECORDS of size RECORD_SIZE, whose format is defined by the REC structure. Each record has a byte that indicates a status of free (FREE_STATUS) or used (USED_STATUS) and a data member that can store RECORD_SIZE bytes. Records are stored in the last page of flash memory as specified by DATA_FLASH_PAGE, whose value is processor dependent. The DATA_FLASH_PAGE value is calculated by taking the address of the last word of program memory dividing by 1024, truncating, then multiplying by 1024. The value 1024 is the number of program memory addresses occupied by 512 instructions ($512 \times 2 = 1024$, recalling that one 24-bit instruction appears to occupy two program memory addresses). If this code is used on a PIC24F processor, the data is stored on the second to last flash page, since the last flash page for PIC24F processors contains a packed version of

```
#if defined(__PIC24HJ64GP502__)
#define LAST_IMPLEMENTED_PMEM 0x00ABFF
#elif defined(__PIC24HJ32GP202__) || defined(__PIC24FJ32GA002__)
#define LAST_IMPLEMENTED_PMEM 0x0057FF  ◄─── Address of last word of implemented
#else                                        flash memory is processor dependent.
#error "Define LAST_IMPLEMENTED_PMEM for your processor!
#endif
//calculate starting address of last page of program memory
#ifdef __PIC24F__                  Data stored in second to last page of flash memory
#define DATA_FLASH_PAGE \  ◄───  for 24F family.
   (((LAST_IMPLEMENTED_PMEM/FLASH_PAGESIZE)*FLASH_PAGESIZE)-FLASH_PAGESIZE)
#endif
#ifdef __PIC24H__      ◄─── Data stored in last page of flash memory for 24H family.
#define DATA_FLASH_PAGE ((LAST_IMPLEMENTED_PMEM/FLASH_PAGESIZE)*FLASH_PAGESIZE)
#define RECORD_SIZE 15       //arbitrarily chosen  ◄ FLASH_PAGESIZE defined as
#define NUM_RECORDS 8        //arbitrarily chosen       64 × 8 × 2 = 1024.
#define FREE_STATUS 0xA5     //arbitrarily chosen, different from USED_STATUS
#define USED_STATUS 0x5A     //arbitrarily chosen, different from FREE_STATUS

typedef struct _REC {        //one record
  uint8 status;              //indicates if free or used
  char  data[RECORD_SIZE];   //holds the data
}REC;                                                  FLASH_ROWBYTES defined
                                                     ╱ as 192.
#define NUM_ROWS (((NUM_RECORDS*sizeof(REC))/FLASH_ROWBYTES) + 1)
#define FLASH_DATA_SIZE (NUM_ROWS*FLASH_ROWBYTES)

typedef union _UFDATA{  ◄─── union definition used for storing data records.
  REC  records[NUM_RECORDS];   fill member guarantees RAM allocation is
  char fill[FLASH_DATA_SIZE];} even multiple of rows; worst case is that
}UFDATA;                       an extra row is allocated.

UFDATA fdata;  ◄─── Allocate space in data RAM for records.
```

FIGURE 13.40 Data structure for flash application.

the configuration bits that are copied to the configuration registers after each reset (configuration bits in the PIC24H family are stored in a special area of flash memory that is not used for program memory). The fill member of UFDATA is included to guarantee the data RAM allocation for UFDATA is a multiple of a row size, since the doWritePageFlash() function makes this assumption. All records are stored in data RAM, using the global variable fdata. Our strategy is to make record modifications in data RAM using the fdata variable and write the data to flash memory when we wish to make the changes permanent.

Utility functions for record manipulation are given in Figure 13.41. The doFormat() function marks all records as FREE_STATUS and is used to initialize

```
void doFormat(UFDATA* p_ufdata) {
 uint16 u16_i;                                          Marks all records
 for (u16_i = 0; u16_i < NUM_RECORDS; u16_i++) {        as FREE.
   p_ufdata->records[u16_i].status = FREE_STATUS;
 }
}

                                               Writes UFDATA data structure to
void doCommit(UFDATA* p_ufdata) {   ◄──────    flash memory (writes all records).
 union32 u_memaddr;
  u_memaddr.u32 = DATA_FLASH_PAGE;  ◄──── Flash memory page for data storage
 doWritePageFlash(u_memaddr, (uint8 *) p_ufdata, FLASH_DATA_SIZE);
}

                                               Reads flash data page, stores in
void doRead(UFDATA* p_ufdata) {   ◄──────      UFDATA  data structure (retrieves
 union32 u_memaddr;                            all records).
 u_memaddr.u32 = DATA_FLASH_PAGE;
 doReadPageFlash(u_memaddr, (uint8 *) p_ufdata, FLASH_DATA_SIZE);
}

void doDelete(uint16 u16_recnum) {                     Marks record specified
   fdata.records[u16_recnum].status = FREE_STATUS;     by u16_recnum as
 }                                                     FREE.


void doInsert(UFDATA* p_ufdata, char* sz_1){  ◄──── Find a free record, copy
 uint16 u16_i, u16_j;                                sz_1 data into it.
 for (u16_i = 0; u16_i < NUM_RECORDS; u16_i++) {
   if (p_ufdata->records[u16_i].status == FREE_STATUS) {
     u16_j = 0;
     while (*sz_1) { //copy data
      p_ufdata->records[u16_i].data[u16_j] = *sz_1;
      sz_1++; u16_j++;
     } //end while
     p_ufdata->records[u16_i].data[u16_j] = *sz_1; //write null
     p_ufdata->records[u16_i].status = USED_STATUS; //mark as used
     break; //exit if
   }//end if
 }//end for
}//end function
```

FIGURE 13.41 Utility functions for record manipulation.

the record array. The doCommit() and doRead() functions write all records to flash memory and read all records from flash memory, respectively. The doDelete() function marks the record specified by u16_recnum parameter as free. The doInsert() function copies data from the sz_1 parameter into the first free record and marks that record as used. There is also a doPrint() function, which is not shown, that prints all records to the console.

Figure 13.42 shows the doMenu() function that provides for testing of the flash utility functions by allowing record data to be entered from the console. The main() function is also shown, which calls doMenu() after standard initialization.

```
void doMenu(){                      Code not shown, prints menu of:
uint8 u8_c;                         1 Format data
char data[RECORD_SIZE];
uint16 u16_recnum;                  2 Enter one record
 u8_c = printMenu();  ◄──           3 Delete a record
 printf("\n");                      4 Commit data
 switch(u8_c) {                     5 Read and print all records
   case '1': doFormat(&fdata); break;
   case '2': printf("Enter string+\\n (14 chars max): ");
             inStringEcho(data,RECORD_SIZE-1);
             doInsert(&fdata, data);
             break;
   case '3': printf("Enter record number+\\n (0 to 15, decimal): ");
             inStringEcho(data,RECORD_SIZE-1);
             sscanf(data,"%d", (int *) &u16_recnum);
             doDelete(u16_recnum);
             break;
   case '4': doCommit(&fdata); break;
   case '5': doRead(&fdata);
             doPrint(&fdata);
             break;
 }
}
int main (void) {
 configBasic(HELLO_MSG);
 while(1) {
   doMenu(1);
 } //end while
}//end main
```

FIGURE 13.42   Flash application test function.

Console output from testing the flash application is given in Figure 13.43. Two strings are entered as record data, followed by a write of the record data to flash memory. After a power cycle, the record data is read from flash memory and printed, illustrating that the records were successfully stored to non-volatile memory.

a) Menu choice "1" used to format data

b) Menu choice "2", followed by "Hello there!" to enter a record

c) Menu choice "2", followed by "How are you?" to enter a record

d) Menu choice "4" to write data to flash memory

e) Power cycle, followed by menu choice "5" to read flash data and print it

```
Reset cause: Power-on.  ◄───────────────  Power cycle
Device ID = 0x00000675 (PIC24HJ64GP502), revision 0x00003001 (A1)
Fast RC Osc with PLL

flash_example.c, built on Aug 11 2008 at 11:32:42
1 Format data
2 Enter one record
3 Delete a record
4 Commit data
5 Read and print all records
 Enter number (1-5): 5  ◄───────  Read flash memory and print records
0: Used, Data: Hello there!   ⎫  Used records
1: Used, Data: How are you?   ⎭
2: Free, Data: n/a     ⎫
3: Free, Data: n/a     ⎪
4: Free, Data: n/a     ⎬  Free records
5: Free, Data: n/a     ⎪
6: Free, Data: n/a     ⎪
7: Free, Data: n/a     ⎭
1 Format data
2 Enter one record
3 Delete a record
4 Commit data
5 Read and print all records
 Enter number (1-5):
```

FIGURE 13.43   Flash application console output.

COMPARATOR

The comparator module [52] contains two independent comparators and a reference voltage generator as shown in Figure 13.44. Comparators are useful for triggering events based on an analog input voltage crossing a threshold voltage. The VIN+ comparator input can be connected to either an external pin (CxIN+) or to the internally generated reference voltage (CVREF$_{IN}$), while the VIN− can be connected to one of two external pins (CxIN+ or CxIN−). A comparator output is normally a "1" if VIN+ > VIN− and "0" otherwise, but this can be inverted if desired. The internal voltage reference can either be derived from the AVDD/AVSS pins or the VREF+/VREF− pins. The voltage reference can be programmed in 16 steps, using one of two selectable transfer functions as shown in Figure 13.44. Because the CxIN+, CxIN− pin inputs and CVREF pin output are analog in nature, they are not remappable and are assigned to fixed pin locations for a specific processor. The C1OUT and C2OUT outputs are remappable on PIC24 μCs that support remappable pins.

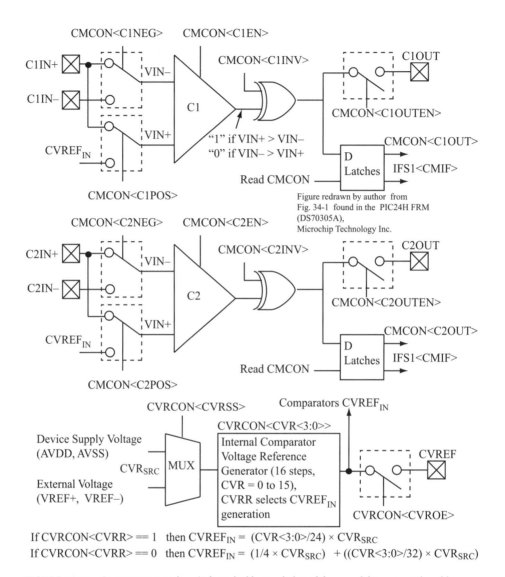

If CVRCON<CVRR> == 1 then CVREF$_{IN}$ = (CVR<3:0>/24) × CVR$_{SRC}$

If CVRCON<CVRR> == 0 then CVREF$_{IN}$ = (1/4 × CVR$_{SRC}$) + ((CVR<3:0>/32) × CVR$_{SRC}$)

FIGURE 13.44 Comparator overview. (Adapted with permission of the copyright owner, Microchip Technology Inc. All rights reserved. No further reprints or reproduction may be made without Microchip Inc.'s prior written consent.)

R/W-0	U-0	R/W-0	R/W-0	R/W-0	R/W-0	R/W-0	R/W-0
CMIDL	UI	C2EVT	C1EVT	C2EN	C1EN	C2OUTEN	C1OUTEN
15	14	13	12	11	10	9	8
R-0	R-0	R/W-0	R/W-0	R/W-0	R/W-0	R/W-0	R/W-0
C2OUT	C1OUT	C2INV	C1INV	C2NEG	C2POS	C1NEG	C1POS
7	6	5	4	3	2	1	0

Bit 15: CMIDL: Stop in Idle Mode bit
  1 = When device enters Idle mode, module does not generate
      interrupts, module is still enabled
  0 = Continue normal module operation in Idle mode
Bit 13, 12: C2EVT, C1EVT (CxEVT): Comparator x Event bit
  1 = Comparator x output changed states; 0 = Comparator x output did not change states
Bit 11, 10: C2EN, C1EN (CxEN): Comparator x Enable bit
  1 = Comparator x is enabled; 0 = Comparator x is disabled
Bit 9, 8: C2OUTEN, C1OUTEN (CxOUTEN): Comparator x Output Enable bit
  1 = Comparator x output is driven on output pad; 0 = Comparator x output is not driven on output pad
Bit 7,6: C2OUT, C1OUT (CxOUT): Comparator x Output bit

  When CxINV = 0;   When CxINV = 1;
  1 = VIN+ > VIN−   1 = VIN+ < VIN−
  0 = VIN+ < VIN−   0 = VIN+ > VIN−

Bit 5, 4: C2INV, C1INV (CxINV): Comparator x Output Inversion bit
  1 = Comparator x output inverted; 0 = Comparator x output not inverted
Bit 3, 1: C2NEG, C1NEG (CxNEG): Comparator x Negative Input Configure bit
  1 = Input is connected to CxIN+; 0 = Input is connected to CxIN−
Bit 2, 0: C1POS, C2POS (CxPOS): Comparator x Positive Input Configure bit
  1 = Input is connected to CxIN+; 0 = Input is connected to CVREF$_{IN}$

Figure redrawn by author from
Reg. 34-1 found in the PIC24H FRM
(DS70305A), Microchip Technology Inc.

FIGURE 13.45   CMCON comparator control register. (Adapted with permission of the copyright owner, Microchip Technology Inc. All rights reserved. No further reprints or reproduction may be made without Microchip Inc.'s prior written consent.)

The CMCON register (Figure 13.45) is used to configure both comparators, while the CVRCON register (Figure 13.46) configures the internal voltage reference.

Figure 13.47 gives a simple example that illustrates comparator usage. Comparator1 is configured to use the internal voltage reference for VIN+ and the C1IN+ external pin for VIN−. The internal voltage reference is configured for 50% × (AVDD − AVSS), which is 1.65 V for AVDD = 3.3 V, AVSS = 0 V. The main() code calls configComparator(), which configures both comparator modules and the internal voltage reference. Before entering the while(1){} loop, the code reads the Comparator1 output (_C1OUT) because an interrupt is generated on a change of comparator output state, with a state change determined by comparing the current

U-0	U-0	U-0	U-0	U-0	U-0	U-0	U-0
UI	UI	UI	UI	UI	UI	UI	UI
15	14	13	12	11	10	9	8
R/W-0	R/W-0	R/W-0	R/W-0	R/W-0	R/W-0	R/W-0	R/W-0
CVREN	CVROE[1]	CVRR	CVRSS	CVR<3:0>			
7	6	5	4	3	2	1	0

Bit 7: CVREN: Comparator Voltage Reference Enable bit
1 = Comparator voltage reference circuit powered on
0 = Comparator voltage reference circuit powered down
Bit 6: CVROE: Comparator Voltage Reference Output Enable bit[1]
1 = Voltage level is output on CVREF pin; 0 = Voltage level is disconnected from CVREF pin
Bit 5: CVRR: Comparator Voltage Reference Range Selection bit
1 = 0 to 0.67 CVRSRC, with CVRSRC/24 step size
0 = 0.25 CVRSRC to 0.75 CVRSRC with CVRSRC/32 step size
Bit 4: CVRSS: Comparator Voltage Reference Source Selection bit
1 = Comparator voltage reference source, CVRSRC = (VREF+) − (VREF−)
0 = Comparator voltage reference source, CVRSRC = (AVDD) − (AVSS)
Bit 3: CVR<3:0> : Comparator Voltage Reference Value Selection $0 \leq$ CVR<3:0> ≤ 15 bits
When CVRR = 1:
$CVREF_{IN} = (CVR<3:0>/24) \times (CVRSRC)$
When CVRR = 0:
$CVREF_{IN} = 1/4 \times (CVRSRC) + (CVR<3:0>/32) \times (CVRSRC)$

Note 1: CVROE overrides the TRIS bit setting.

Figure redrawn by author from Reg. 34-2 found in the PIC24H FRM (DS70305A), Microchip Technology Inc.

FIGURE 13.46 CVRCON voltage reference control register. (Adapted with permission of the copyright owner, Microchip Technology Inc. All rights reserved. No further reprints or reproduction may be made without Microchip Inc.'s prior written consent.)

comparator output value with the last read value from the comparator. Thus it is necessary to read a comparator output in order to arm the comparator state change detection logic. The while(1){} loop then monitors the comparator interrupt flag (_CMIF), printing the _COUT value any time _CMIF is set, indicating a comparator state change. The _CMIF flag is set whenever either comparator has a state change; the event flags (_C1EVT, _C2EVT) can be checked to determine which comparator fired. Code testing was done by connecting a potentiometer to the CIN+ input and varying the input between 0 and 3.3 V. As expected, the comparator fired each time the CIN+ input crossed the 1.65 V threshold.

The internal voltage reference can be used as a crude digital-to-analog converter as long as a buffering circuit, such as an operational amplifier configured for unity gain, is used on the voltage reference output (CVREF) to provide current drive.

CMCON configured to enable Comparator 1,
with VIN– connected to C1IN+, VIN+ to CVREF$_{IN}$.

```
void configComparator(void){        The CMCON value is 0x0402.
  CMCON = CMP_IDLE_STOP | CMP1_ENABLE | CMP2_DISABLE |
          CMP1_OUTPUT_DISABLE | CMP1_NORMAL_OUTPUT |
          CMP1_NEG_IP_VIN_POS | CMP1_POS_IP_CV_REF;
  CVRCON = CMP_VREF_ENABLE |
           CMP_VREF_OUTPUT_DISABLE |
           CMP_VRSRC_AVDD_AVSS |
           CMP_0P50_CVRR_1 ;
  DELAY_US(10) //wait for comparator to settle
  _C1EVT = 0; //clear C1 event flag
  _CMIF = 0;  //clear interrupt flag
}

int main (void) {
  uint8 u8_i;
  configBasic(HELLO_MSG);
  configComparator();
  u8_i = _C1OUT;      //initial read to set trigger
  while(1) {
   do{
     doHeartbeat(); //wait for trigger
   }while (!_CMIF);
   _CMIF = 0;
   u8_i = _C1OUT;     //current value
   outString("\n Comparator fired: ");
   outUint8(u8_i);
   DELAY_MS(100);
  } //end while
}//end main
```

CVREF$_{IN}$ config

C1IN+ ——— VIN–

C1

CVREF$_{IN}$ VIN+

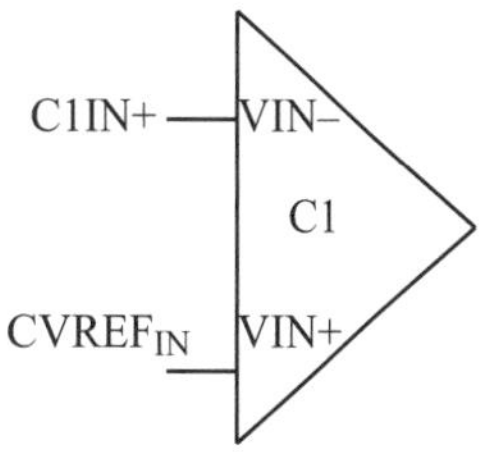

CVREF$_{IN}$ = 50% × (AVDD − AVSS)
For AVDD = 3.3, trigger point is 1.65 V.
The CVRCON value is 0x00AC.

Must read comparator in order to arm trigger

Comparator interrupt flag set when either C1 or C2
comparators changes state

Comparator macros are found in *include\pic24_comparator.h.*

FIGURE 13.47   Comparator example.

Parallel Master Port and CRC Generator

This section briefly discusses some other modules that are available on some PIC24 family members. The parallel master port (PMP) [51] offers a configurable parallel data transfer capability that is suitable for communicating with various devices that have parallel interfaces as shown in Figure 13.48. Both data bus and address bus functionality is supported, which makes it suitable for interfacing to simple external memories with parallel interfaces, such as a parallel EEPROM. The control line outputs are configurable for handshaking and chip selection requirements found in many typical parallel interfaces.

The programmable cyclic redundancy check module [53] can compute a checksum value for a set of data values, with checksums commonly used to detect

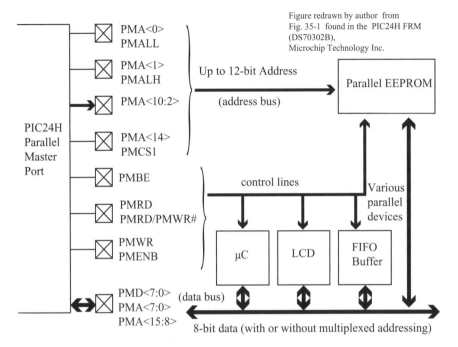

FIGURE 13.48   Parallel master port overview. (Adapted with permission of the copyright owner, Microchip Technology Inc. All rights reserved. No further reprints or reproduction may be made without Microchip Inc.'s prior written consent.)

transmission errors for blocks of data. The CRC module (Figure 13.49) supports configurable checksums of up to 16 bits. Hardware support for CRC computation reduces CPU execution overhead, which may be important if checksums have to be computed for a high data rate communication link. A FIFO that is configurable as either 8 × 16 bit or 16 × 8 bit is used for the module's input and output data.

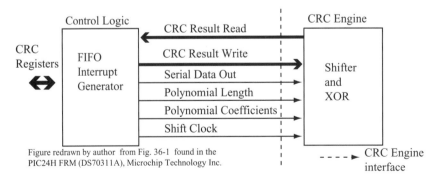

FIGURE 13.49   CRC module simplified block diagram. (Adapted with permission of the copyright owner, Microchip Technology Inc. All rights reserved. No further reprints or reproduction may be made without Microchip Inc.'s prior written consent.)

SUMMARY

This chapter surveyed some advanced topics concerning on-chip peripherals for the PIC24 μC. The I²C and CAN busses are similar in that both are multi-master and both perform bus arbitration by using open-drain drivers with a "0" bit being dominant over a "1" bit in terms of winning the arbitration. The CAN and USB busses are similar in their physical signaling in that both use differential signaling for noise rejection, and both use a form of bit stuffing to allow receivers to remain synchronized to the bit stream. Run-time self-programming allows program memory to be used as non-volatile data storage by a user application. The comparator module is useful for triggering events based on an analog voltage change on an input pin.

REVIEW PROBLEMS

1. If two I²C bus masters access the same device on the bus simultaneously, one using a read transaction and one using a write transaction, which CPU wins the arbitration? (Assume that the only difference in the first byte of the transaction is the R/W# bit.)
2. If two CAN bus masters access the bus, one with an 11-bit message ID of 0x4A0 and one with an 11-bit message ID of 0x3F2, which CPU wins the arbitration?
3. If an acceptance filter on the PIC24 μC is set for an 11-bit ID message ID match with a value of 0x615 and an associated mask register whose value is 0x71F, what range of message IDs are accepted?
4. Assume the 16-bit value 0xFF00 is transmitted on the CAN bus (use MSb first). Draw the serial waveform after bit stuffing has been done.
5. Assume the 16-bit value 0xFF00 is transmitted on the USB bus (use MSb first). Draw the serial waveform after the bit stuffing has been done. Do not forget that USB uses NRZI encoding!
6. Using typical erase and write times, how much time is required to erase and write the entire flash memory of the PIC24HJ32GP202 neglecting software overhead if data is written one row at a time? Assume that the minimum write operation is one row of data and neglect any software overhead.
7. Look up the specifications for the PIC24HJ256GP206. Assume you want to use the last page of its flash memory for storage of non-volatile data. What would the value of LAST_IMPLEMENTED_PMEM (last implemented program memory location) be for this processor as defined in Figure 13.40? What is the starting address of the last page of program memory?
8. Using Figures 13.46 and 13.47 as a guide, what transfer function and what values for CVR<3:0> of the CVRCON register (Figure 13.46) would you use if you want the comparator1 reference voltage (CVREF$_{IN}$) to be as close to 1.3 V as possible (but not greater than) assuming CVR$_{SRC}$ is 3.3 V?

The next two questions are best assigned as short reports.

9. Do research on the LIN (local interconnect network) bus and answer the following questions.
   a. How many wires does it need?
   b. Classify it as duplex, half-duplex, or simplex.
   c. How is addressing to devices handled?
   d. What are the signaling levels?
   e. Is it synchronous or asynchronous?
   f. What is the maximum transfer speed?
   g. What is the maximum number of devices allowed on the bus?

10. The system management bus (SMBus) is a two-wire bus that was derived from the I²C standard by Intel in 1995. It is currently used in PC motherboards and various microcontrollers. Download the SMBus specification (*http://smbus.org/specs*) and answer the following questions.
    a. Give a couple of key differences between SMBus and I²C. For the key differences you chose, give the reasoning behind these changes.
    b. Can you give an advantage of SMBus over the I²C bus? Defend your answer.
    c. Are the I²C devices used in Chapter 10 compatible with the SMBus? Defend your answer.

14 Operating Systems for Embedded Systems

This chapter discusses concepts of operating systems used in embedded systems such as tasks, scheduling schemes, semaphores, and operating system services. This chapter also introduces a lightweight, cooperative multitasking operating system for the Microchip PIC24 µC family. Several example applications are provided.

Learning Objectives

After reading this chapter, you will be able to:

- Describe the difference between cooperative multitasking, preemptive multitasking, and programming.
- Write pseudo-code to outline an application with concurrently executing tasks using cooperative and preemptive multitasking.
- Create example situations where semaphores can solve problems with synchronization problems like signaling, rendezvous, and mutual exclusion.
- Use the Embedded Systems Operating Systems (ESOS) on the PIC24 µC to write multitasking applications.
- Use the services provided by ESOS to generate software timers, respond to hardware interrupts, and communicate serially via synchronous and asynchronous protocols.
- Develop additional services for ESOS.

The applications developed thus far in this book have been based on a pattern of hardware initialization followed by an infinite loop written in a way that is specific to the application at hand. This program structure is very straightforward and used in many embedded system applications that operate flawlessly every day. While efficient, this approach can be difficult if the application specification were to grow or to reuse if the application changes. Furthermore, much of the developer's time is spent creating software infrastructure that will likely be needed again in future applications. The hardware support library used in the previous chapters is an attempt to create software resources that will speed development and lead to higher quality software designs. Extending the concept of creating a more generic software framework is the *operating system*. Operating systems provide basic services and perform common software housekeeping tasks that advanced embedded system applications can use. Also, in most embedded systems, the application contains the user interface, which usually requires flexibility because of changing demands on the interface (e.g., which store's logo appears), so the OS handles the commonly used elements like communications and the application handles the customer-specific aspects. In this chapter, we will look at some basic principles of operating systems and introduce an operating system suitable for the PIC24 μC that can be used in your advanced or complex embedded system projects.

OPERATING SYSTEM CONCEPTS

This chapter begins with a survey of operating system (OS) concepts. We are all familiar with operating systems (OSes) for general-purpose desktop and laptop computers. Examples of popular desktop and laptop OSes are Microsoft Windows, Apple's Mac OS X, and Linux. Often, we forget that the pretty graphical interface that represents the "computer desktop" we see is not the operating system, but merely the windowing system application running atop the OS. In actuality, the OS is the system software underneath that is responsible for coordinating the use of the hardware for applications that run on the computer. These applications include the window manager, word processors, Web browsers, email clients, and games.

OSes are not limited to the desktop and laptop general-purpose computers. OSes can be found in most every computer system that has a reasonably complicated function to perform. OSes are literally everywhere. There is an OS in your cell phone, your Internet router, and several OSes power different controllers in your automobile. There is probably an OS controlling the microwave to pop your popcorn. In fact, the most widely used OS on earth is probably an OS for embedded systems: TRON, and its derivatives, grew out of a project at the University of Tokyo in the 1980s [76]. TRON is really a software specification that has been implemented by a huge number of embedded device manufacturers of consumer devices, ovens, refrigerators, digital cameras, CD players, mobile phones, industrial controllers, and cash registers. Since TRON is a specification, as opposed to source code, the exact number of TRON systems in use is pure speculation. Estimates are in the hundreds of millions, if not billions, of copies.

OSes can vary from hugely complex pieces of software (Microsoft Windows, Apple Mac OS X, and Linux) to very simple constructs that simply coordinate several tasks on a small microprocessor like the PIC24 μC. Although these OSes differ in size and style, most OSes offer fundamentally the same services to their hosted applications:

- Control program/task execution
- Provide a scheduler, which determines the sequence in which programs/tasks execute
- Provide a consistent system in which the system can provide program execution to requests generated by hardware interrupts
- Provide high-level functions or services to access and control hardware, including timers, peripherals/devices, and memory

From the preceding features list, we can see that OSes can provide the embedded systems designer fundamental operations required to keep our software application running. Furthermore, these operations are needed by almost every software application and are not specific to any particular application functionality. Instead of burdening the application developer with creating the code to provide these features, the OS contains them leaving the developer free to concentrate on the application-specific code.

The OS controls program or task execution by creating a context in which a program can run, then initiates code execution. This program or task context may be a dedicated processor in a multiprocessor computer, a protected memory space, or simply a stack frame, depending on the OS and its hosting hardware. The OS scheduler is responsible for determining which program or task executes next. The scheduler may use a complex algorithm based in queuing theory or operations research to select the next task to run, or the scheduler may simply run each process in a "round-robin" manner. The OS should also provide a system by which hardware peripherals can interrupt normal program flow. Interrupts are intimately related to the ISRs that service them. Since an OS is ultimately responsible for program execution, the OS must be apprised of and manage the software that responds to interrupts. The usual approach is that an OS provides its own methods for enabling and disabling interrupts, setting interrupt priorities, and selecting software routines to respond to interrupts. Finally, OSes typically provide methods by which the user's application code can access and control hardware. Most often, OSes provide methods for timer resources. Many OSes supply methods for accessing other peripherals such as memory, file systems, and communications. Many, but not all, OSes provide additional services depending on the OS's goals and the capabilities of the underlying hardware. These additional services can include but are not limited to:

- Multitasking
- Protected execution modes

- Memory management
- Services for communications between computers (networking)
- Task execution within fixed timing deadlines

Multiprocessing is the use of multiple processors to perform several differing computing activities simultaneously. *Multitasking* is a method by which multiple computing processes share the same processor, and resources appear to be running simultaneously. Our discussion in this chapter deals almost exclusively with a single processor, multitasking system. Let's consider an MP3 music player as an example of a multitasking embedded computing system. Your MP3 music player likely has only one central processor, which is used to control the music decoding and audio playback. This same central processor is also responsible for drawing the display screen updates and graphics and for sensing the state of the human-machine interface such as buttons and scroll wheels. Use of the MP3 music player demands that the screen updates and the buttons respond during audio playback. The MP3 music player's OS provides multitasking so that the music playback, screen updates, and button sensing appear to occur at the same time. Similarly, the OS on your desktop or laptop computer provides multitasking so that you can download email while playing a computer game and messaging with your friends. The specific functions of the MP3 music player and the desktop/laptop computer are quite different, but both need multitasking, which is provided by the OS. Methods by which multitasking are performed vary but the illusion of concurrent execution is the same.

Some OSes support protected execution modes where programs/tasks are limited in the machine instructions and resources that they are allowed to use. In this way, the OS can more easily manage and protect the limited computing resources under its control. Since it is difficult for OS software to control the machine instructions used by the programs it runs, protected execution modes are available only when the underlying hardware provides this capability.

Some OSes provide memory management services. *Memory management* is the action of an OS to efficiently manage and utilize its available memory. Memory management by an OS is largely a software solution, so memory management is potentially available in any OS. Simple OSes provide only the most basic memory management services, such as allocating memory in response to a program's requests and freeing memory for reuse when the program no longer needs it. Because memory is a crucial resource for a computing system, more advanced OSes provide a wide variety of memory management services, including:

- virtual memory—creating seemingly large contiguous blocks of memory for program use by using both physical program memory and writable data storage media such as a hard disk drive.
- garbage collection—automatic recapturing of allocated memory that is no longer being used by programs.

- memory compaction—relocation of allocated memory into one contiguous block so that unallocated memory is available in larger continuous blocks. Memory compaction can be manually requested by programs or be automatic.
- shared memory management—coordination of memory blocks being used simultaneously multiple tasks, programs, or processors.

An OS can provide additional memory management functions like memory protection. *Memory protection* is a scheme by which a program's or task's memory is protected from unauthorized access by other programs and tasks. Like protected execution modes, memory protection usually requires hardware support to detect and limit the addressing activities of programs. Therefore, OSes built on hardware without memory exception hardware cannot provide memory protection.

Since computers are so often connected to other devices and computers, many modern OSes provide communications services. The TCP/IP stack on Ethernet is an example from the desktop/laptop computers that immediately comes to mind. Modern desktop/laptop computers also communicate with other devices via the Universal Serial Bus (USB) and IEEE 1394 (also known as "FireWire") protocols. Embedded computers also communicate with other computers, and often do so with a much wider variety of communication protocols, such as SPI, I^2C, and other serial channels such as RS-232, RS-422, and RS-485. OSes for embedded systems may provide methods for communications on one or more of these protocols, which hide the details of the protocol from the application developer.

Many embedded systems are *reactive* systems, that is, systems that react to and maintain ongoing interactions with their environment. These systems generate responses rather than a final result or value. Many control systems, like an airplane's avionics or the controller for an industrial plant, are reactive systems. Reactive systems often must respond within a very tightly specified time period for proper operation. For example, the avionics of a modern commercial airliner cannot take minutes to determine the proper response to an abnormal sensor reading during a flight maneuver in landing approach. The aircraft avionics must ascertain the situation and react with the correct response within fractions of a second or aircraft stability is lost. These types of reactive systems are often called *real-time* systems. A special OS called a *real-time operating system* (RTOS) exists that performs many or all of the OS functions listed earlier, but does so with a guarantee of response time. Furthermore, RTOSes can also guarantee their tasks will run a certain number of times with a maximum interval between executions. In this way, designers can count on their code having a very specific temporal behavior, which is critical for many of the these control-oriented embedded system applications.

A detailed discussion of these OS topics can easily fill several volumes. The interested reader is encouraged to delve into OS details in [71]–[73]. Here, we will briefly introduce the concepts of OSes needed for our discussion and application of an OS for embedded systems.

TASKS

Computer applications can usually be described as a collection of tasks, where a task is defined as a sequence of computer instructions within a context. All of the software applications we've written so far fit into this description if you assume a single context: the entirety of your sequentially executing application code. The single application context becomes troublesome as the application grows in complexity. Typically, an application has several functions to perform and these functions are not necessarily dependent upon the others. An application is more maintainable if functionality can be coded such that unrelated activities are not interspersed. Figure 14.1 shows pseudo-code for an MP3 music player. Our MP3 player must continuously play music, update its graphical user interface (GUI), and monitor its input/output (I/O) system for user requests. Furthermore, the MP3 music player

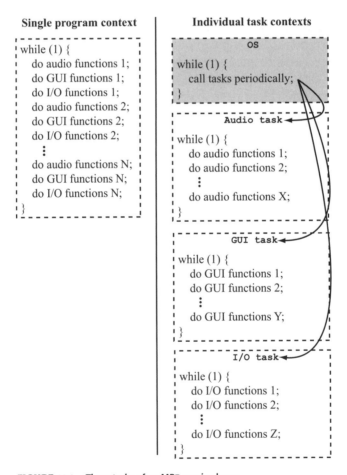

FIGURE 14.1 Three tasks of an MP3 music player.

must appear to perform all three functions simultaneously. If the MP3 player has a single microprocessor, it must interleave the functions for the three subsystems, audio, GUI, and I/O, to give the appearance of multitasking. In case of a single programming context, the functions of the three subsystems must be interleaved in a single while(1) loop by the programmer. In order for each of the three subsystems to run while giving the appearance of simultaneous execution, Figure 14.1 shows each subsystem divided into N subroutines, each with the same execution time. Code readability, reuse, and maintainability are difficult in the program form in the left side of Figure 14.1.

If the MP3 music player uses an OS that supports task switching, the code for our three independent subsystem tasks can be kept separate from each other. The right side of Figure 14.1 shows the form of task-oriented software. In this implementation, each of the three subsystems is written in its own while(1) loop, as if they existed alone. However, the OS has the ability to suspend a task's execution and give control over to another task. The methods by which this can be done will be introduced shortly. Clearly, the individual task contexts allow independent tasks to be written without mixing in code from unrelated operations. Since each subsystem exists independently of the other tasks, each task can be broken down into as many or as few steps as required. This approach with independent tasks written without concern for other application functionality is logically more consistent with the user's perspective, simpler for the designer, and is not as error-prone as the code form shown in the right side of Figure 14.1.

MULTITASKING AND SCHEDULERS

As defined earlier, multitasking is the ability to seemingly execute more than one task at a time with only one processor. The OS gives the appearance of simultaneous execution by allowing each program or task to execute for a short period of time before switching to another program or task. The switch from one program to another is so rapid and often that the user perceives all of the programs running at the same time. This form of multitasking is called *time-sharing* execution.

There are two basic types of time-sharing multitasking: preemptive and cooperative. In *preemptive multitasking*, the OS maintains a tally of how much CPU time each program has used since the last program or task change. After a suitable period has elapsed, the OS suspends the task at its current operating point and activates/reactivates the next task to execute. Preemptive multitasking gives the OS complete authority in determining which tasks run, when they run, and how long they run. In *cooperative multitasking*, each program or task can execute in the CPU for as long as it needs to. If a program or task does not need the CPU, the program or task should voluntarily allow other programs or tasks to use the CPU. In cooperative multitasking, the sharing of the single CPU and its resources is reliant on each program or task cooperating with the sharing scheme. If a program or task decides to be selfish, it can monopolize the system and starve the other programs and tasks of CPU time. The OS has no real power to stop this kind of bad program behavior, and the simultaneous execution illusion is destroyed.

To place multitasking methods into context, let's examine some historical operating systems for desktop and laptop PCs. The Disk Operating System (DOS) of the 1980s did not support multitasking. DOS programs had sole control of the computer and its resources. Microsoft Windows 3.x and the MultiFinder-based Apple Macintosh OSes (versions of the Mac OS up through Mac OS 9) use cooperative multitasking. All programs written for these OSes must voluntarily cooperate for multitasking to occur. Obviously, programmers of these applications intended to cooperate. However, application code defects or hardware errors sometimes caused a program to fail to yield the CPU. The appearance to the user was that a program either monopolized the processor or the system would hang completely. The Amiga OS released in 1985, IBM's OS/2 released in 1987, Microsoft OSes Windows 95 and, later, Mac OSXreleased in 1999, all UNIX OSes since the first 1971 release, and Linux OSes use preemptive multitasking. Since these OSes are in complete control of task execution, a defective program or a hardware-induced hang usually can be stopped by the OS.

The change from one program or task is called a *context switch*. In preemptive multitasking, the OS must determine when to execute a context switch. In its attempt to be fair to all running programs, preemptive multitasking OSes must determine how much CPU time each program has used. OSes tally either the physical time period that a program has held the CPU since the last context switch, or the number of CPU instructions executed by the process since the last context switch. The latter approach is aided by special instruction count registers present in many of the large, modern processors. The former approach is readily accomplished with timer hardware and its associated interrupt. Because context switches in preemptive multitasking systems are determined completely by the OS, application code does not explicitly contain any code for context switches. Figure 14.2 shows the pseudo-code for our example MP3 player under a preemptive multitasking OS. Each task runs as if in isolation from the other tasks and is completely unaware of when context switches occur. When the OS determines the time is appropriate, the OS interrupts the current task, saves the current task's state, recreates the saved state of another task, and resumes execution of this restored task at the point where it was last interrupted. It is the OS's sole responsibility to save and restore the CPU registers, memory contexts such as stack frames, and program counters appropriately.

In a preemptive multitasking OS, the OS determines when the context switch should occur. While this can provide protection against an errant task monopolizing the CPU, it also has the potential to be inefficient. Consider the 50 ms delay in the I/O task in Figure 14.2 running in an OS that provides its tasks with access to a variable that represents a 1 ms counter via a call to os_getCurrentTickValue(). The 50 ms delay in Figure 14.2 can be implemented by waiting for 50 ticks of the OS

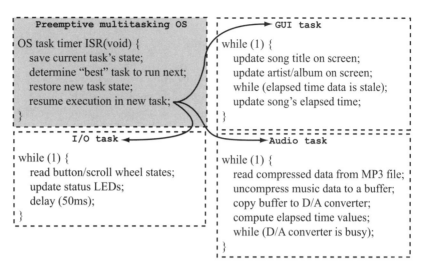

FIGURE 14.2 Pseudo-code for an MP3 music player written with a preemptive multitasking OS.

timer to elapse. Listing 14.1 gives possible pseudo-code for a suitable delay subroutine in our multitasking OS.

LISTING 14.1 Simple delay routine for multitasking OS.

```
void delay(u16_delay) {
  uint16 u16_initTickVal;

  // record OS tick count when delay routine is first called
  u16_initTickVal = os_getCurrentTickValue();
  // wait until u16_delay milliseconds have elapsed since first call
  while (os_getCurrentTickValue() - u16_initTickVal <= u16_delay);
}
```

Assume that the OS running the code in Listing 14.1 and Figure 14.2 gives each task 10 ms slices of CPU time before switching to another task. Depending on the number of tasks running, it is possible that the 50 ms delay in Listing 14.1 will use each of its 10 ms execution periods just wasting CPU cycles. Other tasks are denied CPU time while the I/O tasks waits for time to elapse. The CPU can be better utilized if the OS were somehow informed of the intentions of the I/O task to wait for 50 ms and that the I/O task does not require CPU time.

In cooperative multitasking, the task must determine the appropriate time for a context switch to another task. Typically, cooperative multitasking tasks hold the CPU focus until they cannot continue further without additional information or input. For example, consider our MP3 player application coded with a cooperative multitasking OS. The GUI screen update task uses the CPU to update the screen with the song's title, album title, and artist name. However, the GUI task cannot correctly update the screen with the song's elapsed playing time until the audio playback task provides this information. Since the GUI task does not have the correct elapsed playing time information, the GUI task signals the OS that a context switch should occur. In fact, the GUI task should somehow let the OS know that the CPU should focus on other tasks until the elapsed playing time is provided. Figure 14.3 shows our MP3 player application written in pseudo-code for a cooperative multitasking OS. In cooperative multitasking OSes, the OS must provide a rich enough set of functions for tasks to communicate their needs and intent to the OS and other tasks. When a task requests a context switch, the OS should examine the tasks' desires and states, and switch to the task that is willing and able to execute. Since tasks determine the exact times at which a time context switch can occur, the tasks themselves can be expected to have more responsibility in preserving their state across these context switches. Because of the cooperation between tasks and the OS, cooperative multitasking OSes can be substantially simpler software at the expense of more complicated task code. The cooperative multitasking OS is conceptually very efficient in terms of CPU time if programmed properly. The task with CPU control maintains control until it can no longer fully utilize the CPU. When the task is not fully consuming CPU resources, it should relinquish CPU control to a task that can fully utilize the CPU. Cooperative multitasking programs do not get processor time at uniform intervals or for uniform periods of time, but they are not given a CPU time-slice when they don't need it either.

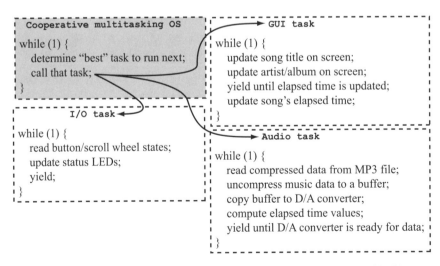

FIGURE 14.3 Pseudo-code for an MP3 music player written with a cooperative multitasking OS.

SEMAPHORES AND INTER-TASK COORDINATION

Multitasking environments are likely to have multiple tasks competing for a finite resource. Since tasks are coded in a way that they appear to be running in isolation, the finite resource problem requires that tasks have a method by which they can coordinate their execution and meter use of the finite resource. For example, two independent tasks may need to write the same global variable. The write operations must be synchronized so that the two writes do not disturb each other. Another common issue with multitasking OSes is that two or more executing tasks will likely need to be synchronized in their execution. In other words, a task must be sure that one or more other tasks have progressed to a particular point before the first task can continue execution. The famous computer scientist Edsger Dijkstra developed the concept of semaphores to solve these problems. *Semaphores* are a protected variable used to synchronize execution. The problem of finite resource use can also be solved through semaphores. Semaphores are defined in a more formal context in this chapter than the global variables used in previous chapters for synchronizing interrupt code actions with `main()` code.

Modern multitasking OSes all provide some form of semaphore to their applications. Semaphores are a powerful technique that can solve a great deal of problems in concurrently executing systems such as multitasking OSes. The reader is encouraged to delve into the free online book [74] for a deeper discussion of semaphores.

Semaphores in computing are named after their physical counterparts, where a semaphore is a visual signaling system usually implemented with flags, lights, or other mechanical means. Military and marine endeavors used semaphores extensively for centuries before the advent of radio communications. Even today, semaphores are used by ships within close proximity when radio communications are not possible. Computing semaphores also implement a signaling system. Figure 14.4 shows the three simple functions allowed by our computing semaphores. First, semaphores must be created. The C language pseudo-code for `create_semaphore()` allocates storage for the semaphore and initializes its value to a number provided by the caller. The allocation method of the actual semaphore storage in Figure 14.4 is left ambiguous as the exact means can vary depending on the OS, memory management, and language in use. The semaphore function `signal()` atomically increments the semaphore value; that is, the `signal()` function cannot be interrupted while it increments the semaphore value. Finally, the semaphore function `wait()` atomically blocks the current task until the semaphore value is positive, then decrements the semaphore value. A positive semaphore value authorizes tasks waiting on that semaphore to proceed. Decrementing the semaphore value indicates to other tasks that a task has signaled the semaphore. That is, that the task has seized the finite resource and will increment the semaphore once it is finished with the resource.

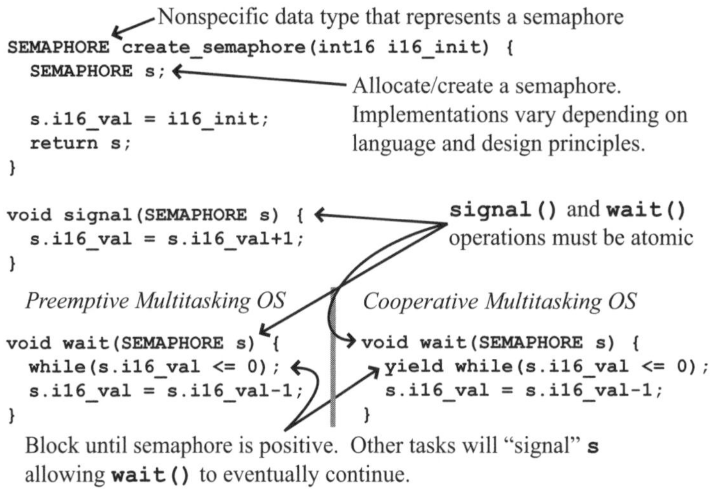

Nonspecific data type that represents a semaphore

```
SEMAPHORE create_semaphore(int16 i16_init) {
  SEMAPHORE s;
                              Allocate/create a semaphore.
                              Implementations vary depending on
  s.i16_val = i16_init;       language and design principles.
  return s;
}

void signal(SEMAPHORE s) {           signal() and wait()
  s.i16_val = s.i16_val+1;           operations must be atomic
}
```

Preemptive Multitasking OS   *Cooperative Multitasking OS*

```
void wait(SEMAPHORE s) {         void wait(SEMAPHORE s) {
  while(s.i16_val <= 0);           yield while(s.i16_val <= 0);
  s.i16_val = s.i16_val-1;         s.i16_val = s.i16_val-1;
}                                }
```

Block until semaphore is positive. Other tasks will "signal" **s**
allowing **wait()** to eventually continue.

FIGURE 14.4 Pseudo-code for basic semaphore operation in a multitasking OS.

Remember that we are working in a multitasking system. A task may be blocked waiting on the semaphore while other tasks will continue to execute and potentially signal, or increment, our semaphore. Notice that apart from the creation of the semaphore, the semaphore functions cannot provide the exact value of the semaphore to the caller. In practice, the caller has no need for the actual semaphore value. With these three simple semaphore functions, we can solve a variety of computing problems. We will examine three of the more common problems solved by semaphores in this section: signaling, rendezvous, and mutual exclusion.

The first common problem solved with semaphores is called signaling. *Signaling* occurs when one task must execute to a particular point before another task is allowed to proceed. Signaling often occurs when our tasks, written as if executed in isolation, need to work together, perhaps in sequence, to solve a problem. Our MP3 music player in Figures 14.2 and 14.3 exhibits a classic signaling problem where the audio task must update the song's elapsed time value before the GUI task can proceed. Figure 14.5 shows updated pseudo-code for the MP3 music player written in a cooperative multitasking OS. The changed lines of pseudo-code are presented in italics. Changes to Figure 14.2 to include a signaling semaphore are similar, so the pseudo-code for a preemptive multitasking OS is not shown.

The two tasks of interest here are the GUI task and the audio task where the elapsed time update operation in the audio task must occur before the GUI task tries to write the elapsed time value to the screen. We can create a semaphore called etimeIsReady with an initial value of zero. Now, if the GUI task reaches the wait(etimeIsReady) call before the audio task reaches the signal(etimeIsReady),

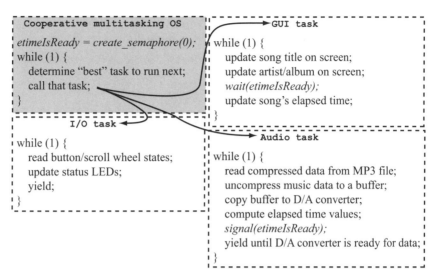

FIGURE 14.5 Semaphore signaling in an MP3 player using a cooperative multitasking OS.

the GUI task will be blocked and forced to yield until the audio task signals
`etimeIsReady`. The eventual call to `signal(etimeIsReady)` by the audio task enables the GUI task to continue executing. In the other case, the audio task reaches
`signal(etimeIsReady)` before the GUI task reaches the `wait(etimeIsReady)` call.
In this scenario, the audio task increments the `etimeIsReady` semaphore to +1, and
the GUI task is not blocked at all. The semaphore signals from the audio task to
the GUI task and correctly implements the execution order we wanted, regardless
of when the audio task and the GUI task actually run. When writing code with
concurrently executing tasks or threads, you must work through this kind of reasoning for each and every signaling opportunity. If execution order determines the
program's outcome, you have created a situation known as a *race condition*, which
is a potentially fatal program error and notoriously difficult to debug.

Let's augment our MP3 player code a bit. We see that it is important for the
GUI task to wait on the audio task to update the elapsed time data so that the
screen update is correct. It can be argued that the GUI task and the audio task
should really start their execution simultaneously. If the GUI task is not ready to
update the screen with the song title, artist and album name, and elapsed time on
the screen, then the audio task probably should not begin streaming music to the
D/A converter that leads to the headphones. We need for these two tasks to arrive at
the beginning of their respective `while(1)` statements at the same time. Neither task
should proceed until the both tasks are ready to stream audio data and update the
screen. We need both tasks to *rendezvous* at this point. Semaphores are once again
the solution. In the MP3 player in Figure 14.5, the audio task signaled the GUI task
to allow it to proceed, effectively creating one-way communication between these

two tasks. Now, we need two-way communication. Each task needs to signal the other that it is ready to proceed. Figure 14.6 shows the MP3 player pseudo-code that allows both tasks to start their while(1) loops at the same time.

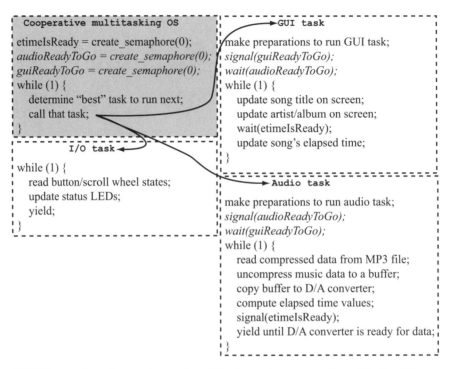

FIGURE 14.6 Semaphore rendezvous in an MP3 player using a cooperative multitasking OS.

In Figure 14.6, both the audio and the GUI tasks have a semaphore that signals their state to the other task. Before each task starts its while(1) loop, it signals to the other task that it has made it to the rendezvous point. Then, it waits on the signal that the other task has made it to the rendezvous point. Since the semaphores in the two tasks are constructed identically, we need to consider only one case. For our discussion, let's assume that preparations for the audio task take considerably more time than preparations for the GUI task. The GUI finishes its initialization first and executes signal(guiReadyToGo). Then, the GUI task blocks on the wait(audioReadyToGo) statement. The OS gives CPU focus to other runnable tasks, including the audio task that is still running its initialization code. At the conclusion of the audio task preparations, the audio task executes signal(audioReadyToGo), which enables the GUI task to continue execution into its while(1) loop. The audio task executes the wait(guiReadyToGo) statement, which immediately returns, allowing the audio task to start executing its while(1) loop. If the temporal ordering is reversed in this example, the roles of the two tasks simply reverse. Regardless of which task finishes its initialization first, both tasks commence execution in their `while(1)` loops as close to simultaneously as the OS task scheduler allows. One last comment on rendezvous with semaphores: the order of the signal-wait statements is significant. If the statements are written in the order `wait(-then-signal)`, neither task continues into its `while(1)` loop because both eventually hang waiting for the other task to make the first move and signal. This mistake, called *deadlock*, is commonly made in haste by busy application programmers.

If two concurrently running tasks wish to modify the same data, the possibility exists for data corruption if the tasks can be preempted. If a task in the middle of modifying data is preempted, the other task may modify the data that is already partially modified by the first task. In these cases, it is very likely that the data value will be either wrong or corrupted. The data itself needs to be modified in a way that all legal instruction orderings that result from potentially concurrent execution result in the exact same, and correct, output. In other words, we need to make sure that any possible preemption of all tasks modifying the data does not change the ultimate result. A simple way of guaranteeing this result is through mutual exclusion of the modification operations. When a task starts a modification operation, it must be absolutely confident that no other task is in the midst of a modification operation and that it will be allowed to finish the modification operation before another task attempts to start a modification. A semaphore that creates mutual exclusion access is often called a *mutex*.

The MP3 player examples on signaling in Figure 14.5 and rendezvous in Figure 14.6 are constructed such that if the first task operation on the semaphore is a `wait()` statement, then the task is blocked. What we need to create mutual exclusion access is for the first task to `signal()` the other tasks that it has entered the critical code region and is modifying the data. Then, the first task should immediately proceed with its execution. The other tasks should be expected to `wait()` for the first task to finish its operations before they attempt to modify the data. Let's again modify our MP3 example to contain a data value that is modified by two different tasks. It is logical that our MP3 player will need to read the value of the volume scroll wheel during the I/O task to determine the audio volume desired by the user. However, let's assume that our fictitious MP3 player has an automatic volume adjustment algorithm. This algorithm programmatically alters the volume based on the loudness of the music being played. This volume modification must be done in the audio task where the audio data is being decoded and processed. Thus, the variable that represents the volume levels is potentially altered in two tasks: I/O and audio. Figure 14.7 shows the pseudo-code of the MP3 player written in a preemptive multitasking OS.

Notice that the `volumeMutex` mutex is created with an initial value of one, whereas the signaling and rendezvous semaphores are initialized with zero. The

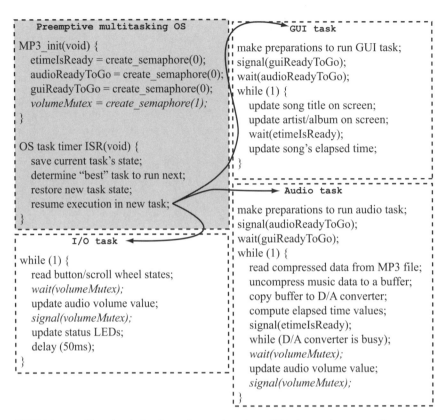

FIGURE 14.7 Mutual exclusion (mutex) semaphore in an MP3 player using preemptive multitasking OS.

first task to arrive at a call to wait() on volumeMutex continues executing. The value of volumeMutex is changed to zero by wait(), and all other tasks that call wait() on volumeMutex are blocked until the first task calls signal() on volumeMutex. Thus, the code that accesses the audio volume data between the wait()-signal() pair is mutually exclusive—the data access is guaranteed to be undisturbed by other tasks' accesses. Please note that the critical code between the wait()-signal() pairs can still be preempted by the OS. The mutex ensures only that other tasks cannot execute code that changes volumeMutex during the preemption.

Mutual exclusion of data is less of an issue in cooperative multitasking OSes than preemptive OSes because cooperative tasks themselves determine when they lose context. Simply not placing yielding statements in the middle of shared data modification avoids the problem. However, mutexes are useful in cooperative OSes as well. Multiple tasks in a cooperative OS may share a common resource for lengthy operations that may need to yield. Using a mutex makes the programming straightforward and protects the finite resource from corruption.

OS SERVICES

Operating systems often provide a variety of services for their applications. The number and types of services provided by OSes vary widely. Simple OSes for resource-constrained embedded systems may provide only the most basic services of system time-keeping and task management, while OSes for desktop computers provide services for memory management, networking, multimedia, graphical windows systems, computer security, remote access, installable file systems, and many more. OS services are specific to the underlying OS; therefore, this section provides a couple of simple OS services examples that may be used in our MP3 player example.

One of the most common services provided by OSes is a time service. All microprocessors have some kind of hardware timer. Some or all of the microprocessor's timers are used by the OS for its internal operation. A microprocessor with a limited number of timers may not have enough timers for user applications. Also, the hardware timers in microprocessors vary widely in setup, capabilities, and use. Therefore, OSes often provide hardware-independent means of obtaining timing information through their time service. Time services provided by an OS may include:

- time in arbitrary OS units since system booted
- real-time clock—maintain current time in hours, minutes, and seconds
- measuring of CPU time used by programs or threads
- time-based sleep periods for threads and tasks
- timer-based semaphores—semaphores that expire automatically after a specified period of time
- calculation of differences between stored time objects
- timezone operations—provide timezone, daylight savings time, and other timekeeping functions
- calendar functions—provide day, week, and year information to applications
- automatic synchronization of system time with network time servers
- periodic task execution via function callbacks

Nearly all embedded systems manipulate data. An OS file service provides basic file manipulations like opening, closing, creating, and deleting files. Services for dealing with data within files may include reading, writing, and searching, and random-access seeks. In a multitasking OS, file services for file locking, ownership, and access permissions are common. OSes with large capacity files systems may provide services for directory management and fragmented file storage.

The number and types of services in an OS can vary widely. The selection of services often plays a big part in the justification to use one OS over another. The details of the services provided are specific to a particular OS. Since our MP3 example has not specified a particular OS, we will leave the details on the OS services as somewhat vague. However, we will assume that the OS for our MP3 example provides services for file management and timekeeping. Figure 14.8 shows the pseudocode for our MP3 example using an OS with file and time services. Of course, your chosen OS may provide additional services over those used in Figure 14.8. In the next section, we introduce a simple OS that can run on members of the PIC24 µC family. This OS provides a number of services that are discussed in detail.

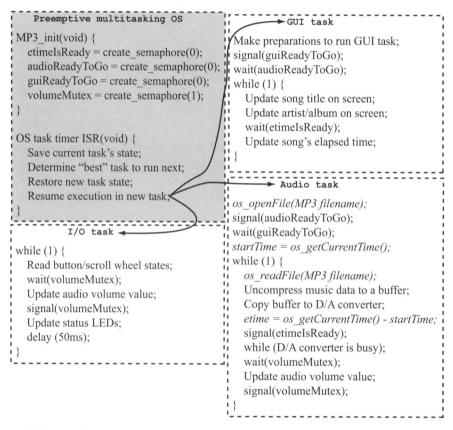

FIGURE 14.8   OS services in an MP3 player.

EMBEDDED SYSTEMS OPERATING SYSTEM FOR THE MICROCHIP PIC24 µC

The code examples in the previous chapters had simple program organization where the hardware peripherals and software structures are initialized, then timers and interrupts are enabled, and, finally, the software enters an infinite loop to handle requests and dispatch commands. In this structure, the `while(1)` infinite loop in the `main()` routine handles tasks that do not require rapid response or have strict deadlines.

Interrupts and hardware peripherals run as required for tasks that do require quick action or occur too fast for sequentially executed code to perform. To this point, this way of organizing our programs has served us well. However, as your embedded system designs grow in complexity, this method of organizing embedded systems code can become difficult to maintain. Code for dealing with a particular function gets distributed in the `main()` routine and various ISRs along with the code for several other functions. Program flow control is rarely documented well and is usually determined by careful and detailed study of the firmware source. Also, trying to keep the flow of execution straight when there are numerous ISR's rapidly becomes overwhelming. There are too many possible combinations of pending interrupts. Using our current code organization, determining program flow control to debug code, develop code further, and maintain code, becomes increasingly difficult. Futhermore, as design complexity grows, the number of code functions also grows, increasing the number of scenarios to consider for determining when one function should allow another to execute. If you determine the optimum point for a task to allow another to execute, it is likely optimum for only one particular scenario or set of inputs. What a complex embedded systems design needs is a multitasking OS. Since our PIC24 µC has relatively limited resources such as instruction throughput and memory, we need our multitasking OS to be very efficient in its resource requirements.

In this section, we describe the structure and operation of the embedded systems operating system (ESOS). ESOS is a cooperative, multitasking embedded systems framework based on the *protothreads* concept by Swedish computer scientist Adam Dunkels [75]. Protothreads are extremely lightweight threads of program execution. Protothreads differ from normal threads in that they are not preempted and are stackless. However, Dunkel's protothreads allow ESOS to provide event-driven flow control in a very readable fashion and allow for blocked program tasks to give up processor focus so other tasks can run. Finally, protothreads require only a few bytes of memory of overhead to maintain their state.

The protothread library is written in ANSI-compliant *C* code, so protothreads are available in nearly every high-quality *C* compiler. Protothreads are created by an interesting *C* language specification that allows `switch()` statements to generate local continuations, a representation of the current state of execution at a particular place in the program. This interesting behavior of the C language was first discovered in 1983 by Lucasfilm computer scientist Tom Duff and has been named "Duff's Device." A study of Duff's Device and the details of how local continuations are implemented in ESOS is beyond this text's scope. The interested reader is encouraged to dig deeper by looking at the ESOS source code `esos_task.h`.

While understanding local continuations, Duff's Device, and protothreads will help you to understand better ESOS and its architecture, this knowledge is not required. What you must know is that ESOS uses these concepts to create a cooperative multitasking OS in which we can write our applications. In addition to providing us with cooperative multitasking execution, ESOS also provides several very useful services such as semaphores, interrupts, software timers, and serial communications. The remainder of this chapter is devoted to explaining the basic structure of ESOS and the organization of user programs written under ESOS. This chapter concludes with several example applications written with ESOS.

OVERVIEW

ESOS provides a cooperative multitasking environment for ESOS tasks, ESOS services, and user tasks to execute. ESOS is responsible for managing computing resources for its tasks, services, and user tasks. To perform this function, the ESOS system code needs priority over all user tasks. ESOS initializes and controls the PIC24 µC execution, interrupts, and peripherals. Figure 14.9 shows a diagram of the execution flow of a typical user application written with ESOS.

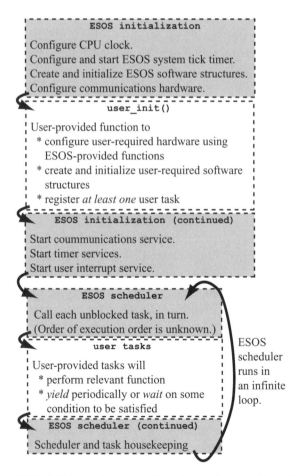

FIGURE 14.9 Basic execution flow of an application written with ESOS.

ESOS is responsible for the clock initialization, the timer used by ESOS to generate a reliable system tick, the UART used by ESOS to provide a serial communications service, and the interrupts used by ESOS internally. After ESOS has performed most of the hardware configuration, ESOS calls a subroutine user_init() provided by the user. In user_init(), the user initializes the hardware peripherals and software structures required for the user's application. User configuration of interrupts done in user_init() is done by calling functions provided by ESOS to manipulate interrupt settings. ESOS must be kept aware of the state of interrupts so that ESOS can manage the interrupt system as a whole. The routine user_init() is fundamentally equivalent to the initialization code we execute before the while(1) infinite loop in the code written in the earlier chapters. Before user_init() returns, it must register at least one user task with ESOS. As seen in Figure 14.9, the ESOS scheduler is started soon after the user_init() concludes. If no user tasks are registered with ESOS when the scheduler starts, then the scheduler has nothing to execute. The scheduler will simply run its infinite loop looking for unblocked tasks that do not exist.

After user_init() returns, ESOS completes its initialization and starts the ESOS task scheduler. The ESOS scheduler is equivalent to our familiar while(1) infinite loop in the previous chapters. Repeatedly, ESOS gives CPU control to each unblocked task. Each task executes its code until it decides to yield control back to the ESOS scheduler. Tasks signal their willingness to yield control through several different function calls provided by ESOS. These functions allow the task to inform ESOS upon what condition the task is waiting. Thus, ESOS can give focus back to the task when the condition is satisfied.

USER TASKS

The user-written task functions called by the ESOS scheduler implement much of the functionality in our ESOS-based applications. These tasks cooperate with the ESOS scheduler by yielding control when they need additional data or they need another task to execute to a particular point. ESOS provides a rich programming interface for user tasks to manage task states and communication between tasks. This section provides a reference of ESOS functions to create tasks, manage tasks, communicate with other tasks and ESOS, and remove tasks with nothing left to do. Figure 14.10 shows the user task structure. The user task in Figure 14.10 uses nearly all of the task-management function provided by ESOS. The user tasks you write will likely not have as many different task "waits."

Each user task must begin with a declaration to the compiler that the code that follows is an ESOS task, not a normal *C* language function. Each user task begins with the statement ESOS_USER_TASK(taskname) followed by a code block, where taskname is a unique name by which the task is known. In practice, a user task is actually a *C* language function, so the name you choose for your task must adhere to requirements of the *C* language for function names.

```
ESOS_USER_TASK(my_user_task) {          ⎰Tell compiler this is an ESOS user task,
  uint8         u8_i;                     ⎱not an ordinary C language function.
  static uint8  u8_count;                Name by which this task is known.
                                         Variables' scope is inside my_user_task only.
  // code before ESOS_TASK_BEGIN()
  // executes every time my_user_task
  // is given focus by the ESOS scheduler
  ESOS_TASK_BEGIN();            Every user task must have this call.
  // do work #1             my_user_task gives up focus here unconditionally.
  u8_i=10; u8_count=5;
  ESOS_TASK_YIELD();                    ⎰Only static variable values are
  // value of u8_count is still 5       ⎱preserved across "waits" and "yields".
  // value of u8_i is undetermined
  // do work #2                         ⎰my_user_task will resume execution
  ESOS_TASK_WAIT_UNTIL( condition );    ⎱at next instruction when condition is true.
  // do work #3
  ESOS_TASK_SLEEP();            ⎰my_user_task will not execute again until some other code
  // do work #4                 ⎱"wakes" my_user_task back up.
  ESOS_TASK_WAIT_TICKS( 1000 );       my_user_task will execute again in 1 second.
  // do work #5
  ESOS_TASK_WAIT_WHILE( condition );    ⎰my_user_task will resume execution
  // do work #6                         ⎱at next instruction when condition is false.
  ESOS_TASK_END();
} // endof my_user_task()       Every user task must have this call.
```

FIGURE 14.10   Representative user task code using many ESOS task-management functions.

User tasks are actually *C* language functions. Therefore, your user task can declare local variables that have scope only within the context of that user task. However, automatic variables (i.e., variables that are not qualified static) have scope restricted to the code portion where they are assigned a value until the next ESOS function to wait or yield. The implementation of user tasks in ESOS is based on repeated *C* language calls to a subroutine. Each time a context switch goes to a user task, the ESOS scheduler is actually making a call to the function that implements the user task. When a context switch occurs away from the user task, the implementation is actually performing a *C* language return back to the ESOS scheduler. When a *C* language function returns, all automatic variables are lost because the stack frame resets to that of the calling function. Of course, we know when a context switch potentially will occur in our cooperative multitasking OS: whenever our user task makes a call to an ESOS function to wait or yield. If we need our user task to remember the variable value across waits and yields, we must declare these variables as static. Resist the urge to qualify all user task variables as static because this consumes valuable memory resources.

Since user tasks in ESOS are really just *C* language functions, a context switch to a new ESOS task is, in reality, simply the ESOS scheduler calling the function that implements the user task. In fact, the ESOS scheduler calls your task function repeatedly to determine if any blocking conditions have expired. The statement ESOS_TASK_BEGIN() in Figure 14.10 is the code that performs the actual restoration of your task state when the context switches back to your task. Therefore, any code statements in your user task *before* the statement ESOS_TASK_BEGIN() is executed every time the ESOS scheduler calls the task. The statement ESOS_TASK_END() tells the *C* language compiler that the user task has been completely defined, and completes the coding structures created by ESOS_TASK_BEGIN(). At run-time, the statement ESOS_TASK_END() notifies the ESOS scheduler that your task is complete. The statement ESOS_TASK_END() should be the last line of code in every one of your user tasks. Any code after ESOS_TASK_END() is never executed. Any user tasks called taskname defined with the declaration ESOS_USER_TASK(taskname) must have both a call to ESOS_TASK_BEGIN() and ESOS_TASK_END(). If not, a compiler syntax error is generated.

Cooperative multitasking OSes such as ESOS work only when their applications tasks voluntarily give up the processor for other tasks to run. Cooperative multitasking OSes encourage good citizenship in their tasks by providing a rich selection of functions to allow tasks to give up focus but only for very specific conditions. Thus, the task is assured of getting the processor focus again exactly when it is first able to utilize the processor. The ESOS system provides several function calls to allow its tasks to very specifically give up focus. Figure 14.11 shows a summary of the major ESOS calls that can potentially cause a task to lose focus. As we will soon see, ESOS services extend this concept by providing service-specific

ESOS_TASK_YIELD()
Current task gives up focus until its next opportunity to run in the ESOS scheduler.
ESOS_TASK_WAIT_UNTIL(cond)
Current task gives up focus until **cond** evaluates to true. ESOS scheduler will query **cond** at each opportunity that the current task should have run. Does *not* block the current task at all if **cond** evaluates true at initial call.
ESOS_TASK_WAIT_WHILE(cond)
Current task gives up focus while **cond** evaluates to true. ESOS scheduler will query **cond** at each opportunity that the current task should have run. Does *not* block the current task at all if **cond** evaluates false at initial call. Equivalent to **ESOS_TASK_WAIT_UNTIL(!cond)**.
ESOS_TASK_WAIT_TICKS(u32_duration)
Current task gives up focus for at least **u32_duration** system ticks. ESOS defines system tick as 1 ms.
ESOS_TASK_WAIT_SEMAPHORE(pstSem, i16_val)
Current task gives up focus while semaphore **pstSem** is not positive. When **pstSem** can be signaled with value of **i16_val**, the current task will resume execution.

ESOS_TASK_WAIT_??????
Many ESOS services provide operations that will cause a task to wait or yield. ESOS services which can potentially cause the current task to lose focus begin with the prefix **ESOS_TASK_WAIT_**. Refer to the documentation for specific ESOS services for more details.

FIGURE 14.11 ESOS calls that can cause the current task to wait or yield.

functions that tasks can call to give up focus while they wait for the service to perform its function.

Continuing through the code in Figure 14.10. The statement ESOS_TASK_YIELD() is the simplest of the task blocking statements in ESOS. This statement gives up control of the processor unconditionally but temporarily. The statement ESOS_TASK_YIELD() allows other tasks to execute one time before resuming. The task that calls ESOS_TASK_YIELD() resumes execution at the next time that the ESOS scheduler gets around to my_user_task in the task rotation. If all other tasks in the application are cooperating properly, a call to ESOS_TASK_YIELD() will result in a very short loss of CPU focus. A well-behaved cooperative multitasking task should, at the very least, break long computations into smaller chunks with ESOS_TASK_YIELD() statements between chunks, and the programmer must make sure that only static variables are being computed. This gives other tasks the opportunity to execute.

The statements ESOS_TASK_WAIT_UNTIL(cond) and ESOS_TASK_WAIT_WHILE(cond) give up processor focus based on a condition cond. The statement ESOS_TASK_WAIT_UNTIL(cond) gives up focus until the condition cond is true, while ESOS_TASK_WAIT_WHILE(cond) gives up focus until the condition cond is false. Calls to these two statements potentially keep processor focus. For example, if cond is true when the task calls ESOS_TASK_WAIT_UNTIL(cond), the task does not yield and continues executing. In theory, tasks that contain only ESOS_TASK_WAIT_UNTIL(cond) and ESOS_TASK_WAIT_UNTIL(cond) statements could monopolize the processor. In practice, it is unlikely that this would happen.

Where ESOS_TASK_YIELD() yields processor control unconditionally but temporarily, the statement ESOS_TASK_SLEEP() yields control unconditionally and indefinitely. The task that calls ESOS_TASK_SLEEP() is put to sleep. The sleeping task does not execute again until some other task calls an ESOS function that wakes it. At that point, the sleeping task resumes execution at the statement following ESOS_TASK_SLEEP(). Please note that a sleeping ESOS task is simply suspended from executing by the ESOS scheduler and is unrelated to putting the processor to sleep to conserve power.

ESOS maintains an internal system clock, which we will see shortly in our look at ESOS timer services. Since ESOS is keeping track of time periods, our task can yield processor focus for a specific period of time. When my_user_task calls ESOS_TASK_WAIT_TICKS(n), the task my_user_task resumes execution at its first possible opportunity after n system ticks have elapsed. The current implementation of ESOS defines a system tick as 1 ms. The call to ESOS_TASK_WAIT_TICKS(1000) in Figure 14.10 causes my_user_task to give control to other tasks for at least 1.0 seconds.

Now that we know how to instruct a task to yield its control of the processor, we now must learn exactly how the task gets placed into the task rotation by the ESOS scheduler. Recall from Figure 14.9 that we must register at least one task with ESOS during user_init(). If user_init() registers one task, it will run when the scheduler starts. That task is free to register other tasks with ESOS at any time and these new tasks will enter the round-robin task rotation. The ESOS function to register a user task is called esos_RegisterTask(*taskname*). For our example in Figure 14.10, the correct call would be esos_RegisterTask(my_user_task). The function esos_RegisterTask(*taskname*) returns a variable of the type ESOS_TASK_HANDLE. Your application may want to save the returned ESOS_TASK_HANDLEs if you plan on having tasks control other tasks. If your tasks simply run through their life cycles on their own, then there is no need to save the returned task handles.

ESOS also provides an esos_UnregisterTask(taskname) function. In practice, your applications will rarely call this routine. Let's look at end-of-life for our task in Figure 14.10. When your my_user_task concludes (i.e., executes the ESOS_TASK_END()), the ESOS scheduler removes my_user_task from the task rotation list. At this point, some other running task could call esos_UnregisterTask(my_user_task), which would completely free up all the memory ESOS allocated to manage my_user_task. While polite, this action is unnecessary as ESOS knows that my_user_task has ended and will automatically free this memory when the time comes that it truly needs it. A task could call esos_UnregisterTask(my_user_task) while my_user_task is still actively running. This would result in my_user_task being removed from the task rotation and its memory freed. As we will see shortly, ESOS provides less strong-armed tactics for control of other tasks than just ripping them out of the scheduler and memory with esos_UnregisterTask().

Our First ESOS Program

Users must provide at least two program items in order for ESOS to generate a usable application. First, the user must provide a user_init() function. Secondly, the user must provide at least one user task that is registered in user_init(). Armed with these rules and the ESOS task-management functions in the previous section, we are ready to create our first ESOS program. Figure 14.12 shows the code for an ESOS program to flash an LED connected to RB15. This code runs on a PIC24HJ32GP202 setup similar to the reference system of Chapter 8. The code in Figure 14.12 implements the same basic functionality as the code of Figures 8.4 and 8.5 when running on a system constructed like Figure 8.3.

While the code and the functionality provided in Figure 14.12 is not very exciting, it does show the basic structure found in all ESOS applications. The hardware configuration in user_init() should be familiar to you by now. Since the user_init() function is called before the ESOS scheduler and the ESOS serial communications service are completely up and running, the code in user_init() calls a hidden ESOS function __esos_unsafe_PutString to print the HELLO_MSG string to the serial port and your terminal screen. In general, user application code should never call hidden ESOS functions, which are those functions prepended with double underscores.

```
#include "esos.h"
#include "esos_pic24.h"

// HW configuration macros (See Figures 8.3-8.5 in text)
#define CONFIG_LED1()    CONFIG_RB15_AS_DIG_OUTPUT()
#define LED1             _LATB15

// all ESOS applications must provide user_init()
void user_init(void) {
    __esos_unsafe_PutString(HELLO_MSG);
```
⟵ { Call "hidden" ESOS hardware routine to print **HELLO_MSG**.
```
    CONFIG_LED1();

    esos_RegisterTask(heartbeat_LED);
```
⟵ { **user_init()** must register *at least one* task.
```
}

ESOS_USER_TASK(heartbeat_LED) {
    ESOS_TASK_BEGIN();
    while (TRUE) {
        LED1 = !LED1;
        ESOS_TASK_WAIT_TICKS(250);
    }
    ESOS_TASK_END();
}
```
} **heartbeat_LED** task runs forever turning **LED1** off and on every 250ms.

⟵ { Signals end of **heartbeat_LED** task to compiler, but task never actually ends.

FIGURE 14.12   *C code for flashing an LED as an ESOS application.*

This is one of the few exceptions if we want to print a string before the ESOS is fully initialized. Before ending, user_init() registers our sole user task heartbeat_LED.

The code of user task heartbeat_LED is very simple. The task immediately enters a while(TRUE) loop, where TRUE is a constant defined in the ESOS header files for our convenience. The infinite loop in heartbeat_LED simply complements the state of the LED1, then the task yields control for 250 ESOS system ticks, or 250 ms, by calling ESOS_TASK_WAIT_TICKS(250). This is repeated until the system is powered-down or reset. The period of the flashing LED is a little more than 500 ms because each call to ESOS_TASK_WAIT_TICKS(250) is slightly more than 250 ms. Our task heartbeat_LED resumes at its next execution opportunity after 250 ms has elapsed.

We have seen the fundamental task management interfaces provided by ESOS. Now, we should reiterate a few key requirements for applications written in ESOS. Since user tasks must cooperate for a functioning system, it is imperative that user tasks and program statements strictly follow these rules.

■ ESOS has complete control over the hardware that creates the ESOS system tick. User code shall not manipulate the hardware or its software structures that create the ESOS system tick in any way. In the PIC24 μC port of ESOS, the system tick is created by Timer1.

■ User code shall not directly manipulate any hardware interrupt enables or interrupt flags. All modifications to these bits shall be done through ESOS-provided functions for interrupt services. ESOS must be kept aware of the status of these bits, and does so through the interrupt service functions that ESOS provides to user.

- User tasks shall not have code that executes for any appreciable duration. If a task has functionality that executes an unknown, arbitrary, or lengthy period of time, the user task should be constructed to wait or yield in some way so that other tasks can get focus and execute. (Some ESOS services are implemented as hidden tasks called by the scheduler in a similar manner as the user tasks. If user tasks monopolize the processor, some ESOS services will not execute properly.)

- The ESOS task functions `ESOS_TASK_WAIT_UNTIL(cond)` and `ESOS_TASK_WAIT_WHILE(cond)` statements yield control only if the associated condition fails. However, if the association condition is asserted at the first call, the task does not yield. User tasks should have at least one yielding statement that is guaranteed to yield under all circumstances to prevent monopolizing the processor.

- User task variables that are required across any wait or yield statement must be declared `static`. If the user task variable is not declared `static`, the value of the variable after the wait/yield is unpredictable.

- Users shall not use the *C* language `switch` statement constructs across wait or yield functions. The protothread library used to implement ESOS user tasks is based upon Duff's Device, which is, in reality, a `switch` statement. It is highly recommended that you avoid `switch` constructs completely. Use `if-elseif-else` constructs instead. The `if-elseif-else` construct is safe in all ESOS contexts.

ESOS COMMUNICATION SERVICES

As we've seen in almost every code example since Chapter 8, serial communications provide a valuable link between our PIC24 µC and the outside world. Because serial communications are so common in embedded systems, ESOS provides communication services to its applications. ESOS initializes the communications hardware, manages the transmission and reception of data, and provides applications with a higher-level programming interface for sending and receiving a variety of data types. ESOS provides communication services for synchronous communication protocols using the PIC24 µC's SPI and I²C peripherals and asynchronous communications with the PIC24 µC's UART peripheral. All three communication services are similar. Because asynchronous communications via the UART is very useful for demonstration of and interaction with our programs, this section concentrates on that particular part of the ESOS communication service. Once you understand the structure of the asynchronous communication service provided by ESOS, the synchronous services become straightforward in terms of understanding and usage. All communication services provided by ESOS are well-documented in the source code files and in electronic documentation. The reader is encouraged to peruse these resources further.

Asynchronous communications on the PIC24 µC is readily done by using the provided hardware UART. Some low-pin-count members of the PIC24 µC family have only UART1, so ESOS uses UART1 to implement the asynchronous communication service. Any additional hardware UARTs provided by the PIC24 µC are available for use by user code. The version of ESOS included with this book is written to use UART1 for the ESOS communication service. The ESOS code is easily modified to use other UARTs, if they exist on the processor, for the serial communication service.

The easiest way to start understanding how to implement asynchronous communications in ESOS is by example. One of the simplest examples of asynchronous communications is the *echo* program in Figure 8.6. This program accepts serial data from UART1, increments each character by one, and sends the incremented character back via UART1. Figure 14.13 gives the ESOS implementation of the echo program.

```
#include "esos.h"
#include "esos_pic24.h"

// HW configuration macros (See Figures 8.3-8.5 in text.)
#define CONFIG_LED1()    CONFIG_RB15_AS_DIG_OUTPUT()
#define LED1             _LATB15

// all ESOS applications must provide user_init()
void user_init(void) {
    __esos_unsafe_PutString(HELLO_MSG);          Print boot message to screen.
    CONFIG_LED1();
    esos_RegisterTask(heartbeat_LED);       user_init() registers two user
    esos_RegisterTask(echo);                tasks. They start almost immediately.
}
```

User task **heartbeat_LED** same as previous example.

```
ESOS_USER_TASK(echo) {                echo uses u8_char across wait statements.
    static  uint8    u8_char;         static qualifier ensures value is preserved.

    ESOS_TASK_BEGIN();
    while (TRUE) {
        ESOS_TASK_WAIT_ON_AVAILABLE_IN_COMM();     Wait for "in" stream to be free.
        ESOS_TASK_WAIT_ON_GET_UINT8(u8_char);      Wait to get an uint8, then
        ESOS_TASK_SIGNAL_AVAILABLE_IN_COMM();      free the "in" stream.
        u8_char++;
        ESOS_TASK_WAIT_ON_AVAILABLE_OUT_COMM();    Send u8_char to the "out" stream
        ESOS_TASK_WAIT_ON_SEND_UINT8(u8_char);     once we determine the stream is
        ESOS_TASK_SIGNAL_AVAILABLE_OUT_COMM();     ours to use. Free it when done.
    }
    ESOS_TASK_END();
}
```

FIGURE 14.13   *C code for testing the serial link as an ESOS application.*

The task `heartbeat_LED` remains in Figure 14.13 and is unchanged from Figure 14.12. The only change in the user-provided function `user_init()` is the registration of another task `echo`, which is discussed shortly. If you compare the code in Figure 14.13 with the program in Figures 8.6, it appears that the ESOS version does not configure the UART. The UART initialization (see Figure 10.14), along with initialization of several other peripherals, is done by the ESOS system code before and after its call to `user_init()`. Furthermore, ESOS also provides all the code and performs all the housekeeping for managing UART interrupts (see Figures 10.18 and 10.20) and the incoming and outgoing communications software FIFO structures (see Figure 10.17). While the code in Figure 14.13 is compact, many more operations are being done behind the scenes by the ESOS system code, which are not seen.

The work of echoing the serial data stream is done by the `echo` task in Figure 14.13. Since the `echo` task never stops its duties, the task is coded with the now familiar `while(TRUE)` loop structure. At start of each pass through the loop, the `echo` task calls `ESOS_TASK_WAIT_ON_AVAILABLE_IN_COMM()`, which requires explanation.

ESOS is a multitasking OS. Since the UART is a single resource that is potentially used by more than one task, and these tasks can potentially execute simultaneously, ESOS must provide a means of ensuring orderly access to this resource. ESOS implements a mutex semaphore for the incoming serial data stream via the two functions `ESOS_TASK_WAIT_ON_AVAILABLE_IN_COMM()` and `ESOS_TASK_SIGNAL_AVAILABLE_IN_COMM()`. All access to the incoming data stream should be bracketed by calls to these two functions. Truthfully, this mutex semaphore is not strictly required in Figure 14.13 since the `echo` task is the only task trying to access the UART. However, it is good practice to include the call to the mutex semaphore, as other tasks may be added at a later time that do access the UART.

After the `echo` task acquires permission to access the serial incoming data by calling `ESOS_TASK_WAIT_ON_AVAILABLE_IN_COMM()`, `echo` asks the communications service to return the next `uint8` data from its software FIFO. There is the potential for the data to not be present or ready to read in the ESOS communication FIFOs. If the data is not ready, our `echo` task would be blocked from continuing execution. Therefore, the call to get data from the communications service is implemented as `ESOS_TASK_WAIT_ON_GET_UINT8(u8_char)`. If the data is not available for our use, the `echo` task yields the CPU back to the ESOS scheduler so that other tasks, such as `heartbeat_LED`, can execute. The scheduler returns focus back to `echo` when the data is ready. After the call to `ESOS_TASK_WAIT_ON_GET_UINT8(u8_char)`, the `u8_char` variable contains the desired data and execution can continue. Our `echo` task then signals to ESOS and the other tasks that `echo` is no longer accessing the incoming serial data stream. The `echo` task can now increment `u8_char`, and the result is placed in ESOS's outgoing serial communications stream in the same manner as reading the incoming data stream. The outgoing serial data stream is also a single hardware resource desired by multiple multitasking tasks and must have mutex access via

ESOS_TASK_WAIT_ON_AVAILABLE_OUT_COMM() and ESOS_TASK_SIGNAL_AVAILABLE_OUT_COMM(). Finally, there is the potential for the outgoing data software FIFO in ESOS to be full, which would block any writes to the FIFO. Therefore, tasks need to write data to ESOS communications services via task waiting calls such as ESOS_TASK_WAIT_ON_SEND_UINT8(u8_char).

Unsigned bytes or characters are not the only data types that user applications need to send and receive. ESOS communications provides functions to send and receive a variety of data types. Figure 14.14 shows a summary of the available functions. Each of these calls has the potential for the calling task to lose focus if the data is not yet ready in the ESOS communication system. The functions in Figure 14.14

ESOS_TASK_WAIT_ON_GET_UINT8(u8_in)
Blocks current task until incoming **uint8** data is available. Results are placed into **u8_in**.
ESOS_TASK_WAIT_ON_GET_UINT16(u16_in)
Blocks current task until incoming **uint16** data is available. Results are placed into **u16_in**.
ESOS_TASK_WAIT_ON_GET_UINT32(u32_in)
Blocks current task until incoming **uint32** data is available. Results are placed into **u32_in**.
ESOS_TASK_WAIT_ON_GET_U8BUFFER(pau8_in, u8_len)
Blocks current task until an array of incoming **uint8** data is available. Reads **u8_len** bytes into the array starting at **pau8_in**.
ESOS_TASK_WAIT_ON_GET_STRING(psz_in)
Blocks current task until a zero-terminated string is available. Reads the string into the memory starting at **psz_in**.

ESOS_TASK_WAIT_ON_SEND_UINT8(u8_out)
Blocks current task until **u8_out** data can be absorbed by ESOS system.
ESOS_TASK_WAIT_ON_SEND_UINT16(u16_out)
Blocks current task until **u16_out** data can be absorbed by ESOS system.
ESOS_TASK_WAIT_ON_SEND_UINT32(u32_out)
Blocks current task until **u32_out** data can be absorbed by ESOS system.
ESOS_TASK_WAIT_ON_SEND_U8BUFFER(pau8_out, u8_len)
Blocks current task until **u8_len** long array of **uint8** data can be absorbed by ESOS system. Takes **u8_len** bytes from the array starting at **pau8_out**.
ESOS_TASK_WAIT_ON_SEND_STRING(psz_out)
Blocks current task until zero-terminated string **psz_out** can be absorbed by ESOS system. Reads the string from memory starting at **psz_out**.
ESOS_TASK_WAIT_ON_SEND_UINT8_AS_HEX_STRING(u8_out)
Blocks current task until string data representing **u8_out** can be absorbed by ESOS system. String is ASCII characters representing value **u8_out** in hexadecimal format.
ESOS_TASK_WAIT_ON_SEND_UINT32_AS_HEX_STRING(u32_out)
Blocks current task until string data representing **u32_out** can be absorbed by ESOS system. String is ASCII characters representing value **u32_out** in hexadecimal format.

FIGURE 14.14 ESOS communication service functions to send and receive different datatypes.

work fundamentally the same as the functions in Figure 14.13. You are encouraged to explore these additional functions in your own programs.

The echo task in Figure 14.13 reads the incoming characters one by one. Each call to ESOS_TASK_WAIT_ON_GET_UINT8() is surrounded by the ESOS_TASK_WAIT_ON_ AVAILABLE_IN_COMM() and ESOS_TASK_SIGNAL_AVAILABLE_IN_COMM() calls to the built-in ESOS mutex semaphore. Likewise, the echoed characters are sent back to the screen one by one with mutex semaphore synchronization. This format works fine but introduces significant overhead in the repeated wait-and-signal operations on the mutex semaphores. A more efficient way would be to acquire control of the incoming serial data stream and read in a number of characters before relinquishing control of the stream. Then, the task could process many characters at a time before trying to acquire the outgoing data stream. Figure 14.15 shows an application that takes this approach in recreating the string reversal program of Figure 10.16. Furthermore, the code in Figure 14.15 demonstrates how a task can call a user-provided helper function to do some common task. The function reverseString() was discussed in Chapter 10. Figure 14.15 shows only the code for task reverse_string. The remainder of the application code is identical to the code found in Figure 14.13.

```
User task heartbeat_LED same as previous example.
user_init() is the same as previous example except that reverse_string
task is registered instead of echo task.
```

```
char psz_CRNL[3] = {0x0D, 0x0A, 0};

ESOS_USER_TASK(reverse_string) {
  static uint8 u8_char;
  static char  sz_in[65];          Allocate space to hold strings.
  static char  sz_out[65];

  ESOS_TASK_BEGIN();
  while (TRUE) {
    ESOS_TASK_WAIT_ON_AVAILABLE_IN_COMM();     Wait until user types a
    ESOS_TASK_WAIT_ON_GET_STRING(sz_in);       string and hits "enter".
    ESOS_TASK_SIGNAL_AVAILABLE_IN_COMM();
    reverseString(sz_in, sz_out);              reverseString() from
    ESOS_TASK_WAIT_ON_AVAILABLE_OUT_COMM();    Chap. 10. (See Fig.10.16)
    ESOS_TASK_WAIT_ON_SEND_STRING(sz_out);     Send reversed
    ESOS_TASK_WAIT_ON_SEND_STRING(psz_CRNL);   string to screen.
    ESOS_TASK_SIGNAL_AVAILABLE_OUT_COMM();
  }
  ESOS_TASK_END();
}
```

FIGURE 14.15   ESOS code to reverse a string.

ESOS Timer Services

The PIC24 µC hardware timers were fully explored in Chapter 12. As we saw in that chapter, timers are powerful tools in our typical embedded systems applications.

Hardware timers are a μC resource typically in short supply. Our PIC24HJ32GP202 has three hardware timers. One timer, Timer1, is claimed by the ESOS system software to implement the ESOS system tick, leaving us with only two hardware timers. ESOS provides a software timer service to its applications. ESOS timers are software timers based on the ESOS system tick. As such, they are not suitable for timing periods that approach or are shorter than the ESOS system tick of 1 ms. However, if a task needs a timer for periods much longer than the system tick, ESOS software timers are ideal candidates.

In general, user applications should not concern themselves with the implementation details of the host OS. In fact, it is usually a bad idea. The OS designers should be free to change the implementation of the OS without breaking the application code that they host. As long as the applications write software that uses the OS's public application programming interface (API), the code composing the functions of the API can change. However, it is useful to know the implementation of the ESOS timer service in order to understand its proper use. The ESOS system tick is created in the ISR of hardware Timer1 that is configured to interrupt the normal processing every 1.0 ms. After the ESOS system tick variable is incremented, the ESOS timer service examines the software timers being used by the application. If ESOS detects that a software timer has expired, the ESOS timer service runs the software timer's associated *callback function*, a user-provided function that ESOS calls at a time that it determines is appropriate. The user provides this callback function to ESOS when the user requests a software timer from the ESOS timer service. The key point here is this: Your software timer callback functions run within the Timer1 ISR. Software timer callback functions must be extremely short or system performance is negatively impacted. Excessive computations in software timer callback functions can cause the system to miss system ticks, leading to a failure of the entire system.

Let's explore the ESOS timer service by returning to our example code in Figure 14.13. While the code in Figure 14.13 works perfectly well, let's change the heartbeat_LED task to use the ESOS timer service instead of being an ESOS user task. The only computation performed in the heartbeat_LED task is to complement LED1. With such low computation requirements, the heartbeat_LED task is an ideal candidate for implementation as a software timer from the ESOS timer service. Figure 14.16 shows the code to echo incremented characters with the flashing LED implemented as an ESOS software timer.

The user_init() routine in Figure 14.16 is not very different from the earlier example in Figure 14.13. Instead of registering the heartbeat_LED task, user_init() registers a software timer named swTimerLED() with a timeout value of 250 ms by calling esos_RegisterTimer(swTimerLED, 250). The timer itself is declared and the callback code is provided by the macro ESOS_USER_TIMER(swTimerLED). The callback code itself is simple *C* code to complement LED1. Figure 14.17 shows the functions available to manage your software timers.

```
#include "esos.h"
#include "esos_pic24.h"

// HW configuration macros (See Figures 8.3-8.5 in text)
#define CONFIG_LED1()   CONFIG_RB15_AS_DIG_OUTPUT()
#define LED1            _LATB15

// all ESOS applications must provide user_init()
void user_init(void) {
  __esos_unsafe_PutString(HELLO_MSG);     Print boot message to screen.
  CONFIG_LED1();
  esos_RegisterTask(echo);                Register echo task.

  esos_RegisterTimer(swTimerLED,250);     Register swTimerLED function as
}                                         software timer callback. ESOS will
                                          call swTimerLED every 250 ticks.
```

User task **echo** same as previous example. Code not printed to conserve space.

```
ESOS_USER_TIMER(swTimerLED) {
  LED1 = !LED1;          Toggle LED1 every time timer callback is run.
}
```

FIGURE 14.16   ESOS code using software timer to flash LED.

ESOS_USER_TIMER(timername)
Declares and creates the software timer named **timername**. Function can not return values.
ESOS_TMR_HANDLE esos_RegisterTimer(timername, u32_period)
Registers the software timer **timername** with ESOS. ESOS timer service will call the timer's callback function every **u32_period** ticks. Timer **timername** will start counting immediately. Returns an **ESOS_TMR_HANDLE** to be used with other timer services functions.
uint8 esos_UnregisterTimer(timer_handle)
Unregisters the timer denoted by **timer_handle**. Returns TRUE if timer was successfully removed from the ESOS timer service; FALSE otherwise.
ESOS_TMR_HANDLE esos_GetTimerHandle(timername)
Returns **ESOS_TMR_HANDLE** to corresponding to the software timer **timername**, or **ESOS_TMR_FAILURE** if timer is not currently running. Useful if timer handle was not saved when timer was initially registered with ESOS.
uint8 esos_ChangeTimerPeriod(timer_handle, u32_period)
Changes the period of the currently registered timer denoted by **timer_handle** to be **u32_period** ticks. New period takes effect immediately. Returns TRUE if timer period is successfully changed; FALSE otherwise.

FIGURE 14.17   Functions provided by the ESOS timer services.

The ESOS timer service allows users to create up to 16 software timers. All 16 timers are queried at each system tick to determine the timers that have expired. Expired timers are reset and their callback functions are executed. Remember that software timer callback functions are executed within the context of the ESOS system tick ISR. Your software time callback functions are effectively ISRs, and should be designed with this in mind. If you were to create 16 different software timers and all 16 timers expired at the same tick value, then the ESOS system tick ISR would call all 16 of your callback functions one after the other. If the execution of all 16 callback functions took a long time, it is possible that the ESOS system would miss the next system tick interrupt. This is another good reason why your software timer callback functions need to be short and efficient.

The code in Figure 14.16 should behave identically to the code in Figure 14.13. The only difference may be that the period of the flashing LED in Figure 14.16 is more accurate than in Figure 14.13. The software timers are called from the ESOS system tick ISR, which runs at a high ISR priority level. The period of the flashing LED in Figure 14.13 is determined by relying on the other tasks to give up processor focus. Of course, the exact period of a flashing LED is usually not significant, and the period inaccuracies in Figure 14.13 are acceptable. Applications requiring more accurate time duration should consider software timers. Applications requiring very accurate or very short time durations should use PIC24 μC hardware timers and their associated interrupts. In the next section, we explore the ESOS semaphore services.

ESOS Semaphore Services

As we saw at the beginning of this chapter, tasks running in multitasking OSes require synchronization via semaphores. User tasks in ESOS are no different. There will be many times when your user tasks will want to signal, rendezvous, or have mutually exclusive execution with other tasks. ESOS provides a basic set of services for managing semaphores. In this section, we discuss the semaphore services that ESOS provides and examine two examples of semaphores in action.

Our first example application has two tasks where one task runs every fifth time that the other task runs. This scenario requires that the more frequently executing task signal a semaphore to the other task on every fifth run. This signal enables the second task, which is waiting for the semaphore, to execute. Figure 14.18 shows the code that implements our example scenario.

The code in Figure 14.18 creates a semaphore sem_T2CanRun in the global variable scope of the application with the macro ESOS_SEMAPHORE(sem_T2CanRun). Since semaphores are used for inter-task communications, the semaphore itself must be global in scope so that both tasks can access it. The declaration macro creates the semaphore only as a program variable and instructs the compiler on how to store the data in memory. The declaration macro ESOS_SEMAPHORE() does not give the semaphore any initial value. The name inside the parentheses is the name by which the semaphore will be known in the program. The user_init() routine initializes the semaphore value to zero with ESOS_INIT_SEMAPHORE(sem_T2CanRun,0).

The functionality of the task1 is easy to determine from the code in Figure 14.18. The task task1 runs forever incrementing a local counter u8_cnt on each pass through its loop. During each pass, task1 prints an identifier to the screen along

```
// global variables
char psz_CRNL[3]= {0x0D, 0x0A, 0};
char psz_T1[] = "Task 1: ";
char psz_T2[] = "Task 2: ";
ESOS_SEMAPHORE(sem_T2CanRun);
```
◄— Declare semaphore and allocate storage.

```
void user_init(void) {
  __esos_unsafe_PutString(HELLO_MSG);
  CONFIG_LED1();
  ESOS_INIT_SEMAPHORE(sem_T2CanRun, 0);
  esos_RegisterTask(task1);
  esos_RegisterTask(task2);
  esos_RegisterTimer(swTimerLED,250);
}
```

| User timer `swTimerLED` same as previous example. |

ESOS function that returns a random number

```
inline uint32 getRandomDelay() {
  return ((esos_GetRandomUint32() & 0x0FFF)|0xFF);
}
```
Create random value between 255 and 4095.

```
ESOS_USER_TASK(task1) {
  static uint8  u8_cnt=0;
```
◄——— counter local to task1
```
  ESOS_TASK_BEGIN();
  while (TRUE) {
    ESOS_TASK_WAIT_ON_AVAILABLE_OUT_COMM();
    ESOS_TASK_WAIT_ON_SEND_STRING(psz_T1);
    ESOS_TASK_WAIT_ON_SEND_UINT8_AS_HEX_STRING(u8_cnt);
    ESOS_TASK_WAIT_ON_SEND_STRING(psz_CRNL);
    ESOS_TASK_SIGNAL_AVAILABLE_OUT_COMM();
    ESOS_SIGNAL_SEMAPHORE(sem_T2CanRun, 1);
    u8_cnt++;
    ESOS_TASK_WAIT_TICKS(getRandomDelay());
  }
  ESOS_TASK_END();
}
```
Print task counter to screen. Signal semaphore at every pass through loop.

Yield for a random period of time.

```
ESOS_USER_TASK(task2) {
  static uint8  u8_cnt=0;
```
counter local to task2
```
  ESOS_TASK_BEGIN();
  while (TRUE) {
    ESOS_TASK_WAIT_SEMAPHORE(sem_T2CanRun, 5);
    ESOS_TASK_WAIT_ON_AVAILABLE_OUT_COMM();
    ESOS_TASK_WAIT_ON_SEND_STRING(psz_T2);
    ESOS_TASK_WAIT_ON_SEND_UINT8_AS_HEX_STRING(u8_cnt);
    ESOS_TASK_WAIT_ON_SEND_STRING( psz_CRNL );
    ESOS_TASK_SIGNAL_AVAILABLE_OUT_COMM();
    u8_cnt++;
  }
  ESOS_TASK_END();
}
```
Yield until task1 has signaled five times.

Print task counter to screen.

FIGURE 14.18   ESOS code demonstrating signaling with semaphores.

with the current counter value and signals the sem_T2CanRun semaphore by calling
ESOS_SIGNAL_SEMAPHORE(sem_T2CanRun,1). At the conclusion of each pass through the
loop, task1 yields the processor for a random number of ticks, which is determined
by the user-provided function getRandomDelay(). The function getRandomDelay()

calls an ESOS-provided function `esos_GetRandomUint32()`, which returns a pseudo-random 32-bit number between one and 2^{32}-1. The function `getRandomDelay()` limits the numbers from this very large range to a maximum value of 4095 by AND-ing with 0xFFF and to a minimum value of 255 by OR-ing 0xFF. Thus, `task1` will yield the processor for only approximately 0.25 to 4.1 seconds when it calls `ESOS_TASK_WAIT_TICKS(getRandomDelay())`.

The code for `task2` is similar to that of `task1`. The user task `task2` also has an infinite loop that prints an identifier and its current local counter value. The difference between `task2` and `task1` is that `task2` does not execute its loop code until the semaphore `sem_T2CanRun` has been signaled five times by `task1`. The loop in `task2` yields until the five signals are performed by calling `ESOS_TASK_WAIT_SEMAPHORE(sem_T2CanRun,5)`. Of course, five signals to `sem_T2CanRun` means that `task1` has progressed through its loop five times as required by our design specification.

This simple example of signaling with semaphores uses all of the functions in the semaphore services provided by ESOS. Figure 14.19 shows a summary of the functions in the ESOS semaphore service. With these four semaphore functions, many synchronization problems can be solved.

`ESOS_SEMAPHORE(semaphoreName)`
Declares and creates the semaphore **semaphoreName**. This macro is usually placed in the global variables area of the application source since sempahores are used for inter-task synchronication.
`ESOS_INIT_SEMAPHORE(semaphoreName, i16_val)`
Initializes the semaphore **semaphoreName** with value **i16_val**. Semaphores are often initialized at the start of an application in **user_init()**.
`ESOS_TASK_WAIT_SEMAPHORE(semaphoreName, i16_val)`
Blocks the current task until **semaphoreName** has been signaled at least **i16_val** times. After being blocked, current task will continue execution at the next statement.
`ESOS_SIGNAL_SEMAPHORE(semaphoreName, i16_val)`
Signal **semaphoreName** **i16_val** times. This function does not have to be called inside of the context of a task since it cannot block.

FIGURE 14.19 Functions provided by the ESOS semaphore services.

Tasks in a multitasking OS often need to rendezvous at a point in the code before they all proceed. Semaphores provided by ESOS can easily implement rendezvous synchronization. Figure 14.20 shows an example application where two tasks must rendezvous before they proceed. The two tasks `task1` and `task2` are identical in their function. Each task maintains a local task counter `u8_cnt` that is incremented by one each time the task proceeds through its loop. Each pass prints an identifying message to the screen along with the current value of `u8_cnt`. Before looping back, each task yields control for a random length of time. Both `task1` and `task2` perform these operations 10 times. Neither task is allowed to proceed until both tasks have

Global variables same as previous example, but add:
```
char psz_rv[] = "rendez-vous!";
ESOS_SEMAPHORE(sem_T1CanRun);
```

user_init() same as previous example, but add:
```
ESOS_INIT_SEMAPHORE(sem_T1CanRun, 0);
```

Timer `swTimerLED` and function `getRandomDelay()` same as previous example.

```
ESOS_USER_TASK(task1) {
  static uint8  u8_cnt=0;
  ESOS_TASK_BEGIN();
  while (u8_cnt < 10) {                                      ⎫ 10 times:
    ESOS_TASK_WAIT_ON_AVAILABLE_OUT_COMM();                  ⎪ Print task
    ESOS_TASK_WAIT_ON_SEND_STRING(psz_T1);                   ⎪ counter to
    ESOS_TASK_WAIT_ON_SEND_UINT8_AS_HEX_STRING(u8_cnt);      ⎬ screen and
    ESOS_TASK_WAIT_ON_SEND_STRING(psz_CRNL);                 ⎪ yield for a
    ESOS_TASK_SIGNAL_AVAILABLE_OUT_COMM();                   ⎪ random period
    u8_cnt++;                                                ⎪ of time.
    ESOS_TASK_WAIT_TICKS(getRandomDelay());                  ⎭
  }
  ESOS_SIGNAL_SEMAPHORE(sem_T2CanRun, 1);           ⎫ Signal arrival at rendezvous
  ESOS_TASK_WAIT_SEMAPHORE(sem_T1CanRun, 1);        ⎭ point and wait for task2.
  ESOS_TASK_WAIT_ON_SEND_STRING(psz_T1);            ⎫ Print message that task1
  ESOS_TASK_WAIT_ON_SEND_STRING(psz_rv);            ⎬ passed rendezvous point.
  ESOS_TASK_WAIT_ON_SEND_STRING(psz_CRNL);          ⎭
  ESOS_TASK_END();
}


ESOS_USER_TASK(task2) {
  static uint8  u8_cnt=0;
  ESOS_TASK_BEGIN();
  while (u8_cnt<10) {                                        ⎫ 10 times:
    ESOS_TASK_WAIT_ON_AVAILABLE_OUT_COMM();                  ⎪ Print task
    ESOS_TASK_WAIT_ON_SEND_STRING(psz_T2);                   ⎪ counter to
    ESOS_TASK_WAIT_ON_SEND_UINT8_AS_HEX_STRING(u8_cnt);      ⎬ screen and
    ESOS_TASK_WAIT_ON_SEND_STRING(psz_CRNL);                 ⎪ yield for a
    ESOS_TASK_SIGNAL_AVAILABLE_OUT_COMM();                   ⎪ random period
    u8_cnt++;                                                ⎪ of time.
    ESOS_TASK_WAIT_TICKS(getRandomDelay());                  ⎭
  }
  ESOS_SIGNAL_SEMAPHORE(sem_T1CanRun, 1);           ⎫ Signal arrival at rendezvous
  ESOS_TASK_WAIT_SEMAPHORE(sem_T2CanRun, 1);        ⎭ point and wait for task1.
  ESOS_TASK_WAIT_ON_SEND_STRING(psz_T2);            ⎫ Print message that task2
  ESOS_TASK_WAIT_ON_SEND_STRING(psz_rv);            ⎬ passed rendezvous point.
  ESOS_TASK_WAIT_ON_SEND_STRING(psz_CRNL);          ⎭
  ESOS_TASK_END();
}
```

FIGURE 14.20   ESOS code demonstrating rendezvous synchronization with semaphores.

completed their 10 passes through the loop. After `task1` and `task2` have met at the rendezvous point, each task prints a final message before the tasks end.

With the tasks yielding for a random length of time, the order in which the tasks reach the rendezvous point is unknown. However, the random value returned by `esos_GetRandomUint32()` is generated by a pseudo-random number generator so the sequence of random numbers is the same each time the application is executed. Generating a good sequence of random numbers is much harder than it would first appear. The best sequences have some truly unpredictable components. The sequence of random numbers generated by ESOS is less predictable when the generator is seeded with a number that changes with each execution of the code. The random number generator in ESOS can be seeded with the `esos_SetRandomUint32Seed()` function.

Figure 14.18 and Figure 14.20 show examples of signaling and rendezvous semaphores, respectively. Mutex semaphores can be readily implemented with the semaphore functions in Figure 14.19. The details of this are left as a homework exercise. Mutex semaphores are also easy to implement using the user flags and associated functions provided by ESOS. These functions are described in the next section.

ESOS User Flags

In a multitasking OS, user tasks are often coded as if they were running on the processor alone. The only indication in the code that other tasks or operations are ongoing are the occasional yield/wait statements and code that signals other tasks and functions via semaphore and simple binary flags. In addition to providing semaphore services, ESOS also provides user applications with 16 global flags. These user flags can be used for general binary state storage within a task or function, as a signal between functions, or for inter-task synchronization as a mutex semaphore. Figure 14.21 contains a summary of the user flag functions provided by ESOS.

`esos_SetUserFlag(flag)`
Sets a bit in the user flag denoted by **flag**. ESOS provides 16 user flags named **ESOS_USER_FLAG_0**, **ESOS_USER_FLAG_1**, ..., **ESOS_USER_FLAG_F**. The **flag** input can be the OR of several flag names to set bits in more than one flag simultaneously .
`esos_ClearUserFlag(flag)`
Clears a bit in the user flag denoted by **flag**. ESOS provides 16 user flags named **ESOS_USER_FLAG_0**, **ESOS_USER_FLAG_1**, ..., **ESOS_USER_FLAG_F**. The **flag** input can be the OR of several flag names to clear bits in more than one flag simultaneously .
`esos_IsUserFlagSet(flag)`
Queries whether a bit in the user flag denoted by **flag** is set. ESOS provides 16 user flags named **ESOS_USER_FLAG_0**, **ESOS_USER_FLAG_1**, ..., **ESOS_USER_FLAG_F**. Returns **TRUE** if the bit is set; returns **FALSE** otherwise.
`esos_IsUserFlagClear(flag)`
Queries whether a bit in the user flag denoted by **flag** is clear. ESOS provides 16 user flags named **ESOS_USER_FLAG_0**, **ESOS_USER_FLAG_1**, ..., **ESOS_USER_FLAG_F**. Returns **TRUE** if the bit is clear; returns **FALSE** otherwise.

FIGURE 14.21 Functions provided by the ESOS flag service.

The user flags provided by ESOS allow for easy creation of binary semaphores, a semaphore that can only take on the values 0 and 1. Listing 14.2 shows a code snippet that creates a binary semaphore using the ESOS flag service. Notice how the user should #define an insightful name such as LIGHTS_ARE_ON to replace the generic user flag name ESOS_USER_FLAG_3.

LISTING 14.2   Binary semaphores created with user flags.

```
// create an application-specific name for the user flag
#define LIGHTS_ARE_ON             ESOS_USER_FLAG_3
// define semaphore macros that user tasks can use
#define SIGNAL_LIGHTS_ON_MUTEX      esos_SetUserFlag(LIGHTS_ARE_ON)
#define WAIT_LIGHTS_ON_MUTEX                \
    esos_ClearUserFlag(LIGHTS_ARE_ON);     \
    ESOS_TASK_WAIT_UNTIL(esos_IsUserFlagSet(LIGHTS_ARE_ON))
```

The user flags provided in Listing 14.2 are global; that is, they can be assessed and modified in any scope. The global nature of these flags can be a bit dangerous but makes these flags very useful for inter-function and inter-task signaling. In fact, ESOS maintains a private set of flags structured just as the user flags in Listing 14.2 for its own internal use. The commands ESOS_TASK_WAIT_ON_AVAILABLE_IN_COMM(), ESOS_TASK_SIGNAL_AVAILABLE_IN_COMM(), ESOS_TASK_WAIT_ON_AVAILABLE_OUT_COMM(), and ESOS_TASK_SIGNAL_AVAILABLE_OUT_COMM() in the ESOS communication service are implemented with these private ESOS system flags and macros similar to those in Listing 14.2.

ESOS CHILD TASKS

In Figure 14.15, we saw how the task reverse_string could call a helper function reverseString to perform some simple operation on its behalf. You would typically factor your code in this way when the helper function performs an operation that other tasks or code would also need performed. The helper function allows code to be more easily read by separating logical operations and more easily maintained by having only one copy of code in an application. Notice that the helper function reverseString in Figure 14.15 is given all of the information it needs, the entire string sz_in, to complete its task.

Now, consider the scenario where some task wanted to use a helper function, but that helper function could not complete its operation until some event occurred. Your application code written in the earlier chapters would have probably contained a line of code such as while(!event); to cause the helper function to wait. This approach would not be acceptable in ESOS. The task would get the CPU focus and call the helper function that would then wait for the event to occur. At best, other tasks would be blocked from execution until the event was triggered externally. In the worst case, the event itself is to be created by a task that could never do so because that task is blocked by the task calling the helper function. What we need to solve the problem is a helper function that can yield or wait just like a task.

The first thought is to simply place an ESOS wait/yield statement like string `ESOS_TASK_WAIT_UNTIL()` in the helper function. This solution does not work because ESOS tasks are implemented through repeated function calls, by the ESOS scheduler, to a function (your user task code) that uses local continuations (Duff's Device) to maintain your task's state. Simply put, the helper function your task calls is a different function from your user task that has no concept of what a task state even is. What we need is some kind of task that can yield and wait, such as an `ESOS_USER_TASK`, but can be called by an `ESOS_USER_TASK` instead of the ESOS scheduler. ESOS provides just such a solution: a special kind of task called an `ESOS_CHILD_TASK`.

In our discussion of `ESOS_CHILD_TASK`, or simply, child tasks, we will sometimes refer to tasks of the type `ESOS_USER_TASK` as parent tasks. Just as with humans, where every human is not a parent until he or she has a child, not every `ESOS_USER_TASK` is a parent task. Only an `ESOS_USER_TASK` that creates a child task can be called a parent to that child task. A child task, declared as type `ESOS_CHILD_TASK`, is created by and called by its parent task, not by the ESOS scheduler. When a parent task creates the child task, an operation ESOS calls *spawning*, the parent task is blocked until the child task ends. This simple fact is very important as it means:

- all child tasks must eventually end, or their parent is forever blocked from executing, and
- the child tasks, in practice, take the parent task's place in the ESOS scheduler.

Child tasks have one more very big, and useful, difference from normal user tasks: input arguments. Recall that our parent tasks are called by the ESOS scheduler, so input arguments are not possible. Since child tasks are spawned, or called, by parent tasks, the parent task has the opportunity to create the child task and pass it arguments.

The best way to learn about child tasks is to see one in action. Figures 14.22 and 14.23 show the code for another version of our "echo" application. In the previous versions (Figures 8.6 and 14.13), characters were incremented by one and echoed back. In this version of "echo," the user is prompted to type a single number that is to be used as the increment value. The input can take on the values between zero and nine.

The code in Figure 14.22 to initialize the hardware and software timer for the flashing LED should be very familiar by now. The new concept in Figure 14.22 deals

```
Timer swTimerLED same as previous example.
```

```
// Global variables
char psz_CRNL[3]= {0x0D, 0x0A, 0};
char psz_prompt[] = "Enter number 0-9 for echo increment:   ";
char psz_done[9]= {' ','D','O','N','E','!',0x0D, 0x0A, 0};

void user_init(void) {
  __esos_unsafe_PutString( HELLO_MSG );
  CONFIG_LED1();
  esos_RegisterTask(prompter);          ← Register the "parent" task with ESOS.
  esos_RegisterTimer(swTimerLED, 250);
}

ESOS_USER_TASK(prompter) {
  static uint8            u8_char;           ⎫ Declare storage for the handle to
  static ESOS_TASK_HANDLE  th_child;     ←   ⎭ the "child" task echo_child.

  ESOS_TASK_BEGIN();
  while(TRUE) {
    ESOS_TASK_WAIT_ON_AVAILABLE_OUT_COMM();        ⎫ Prompt the user to
    ESOS_TASK_WAIT_ON_SEND_STRING(psz_prompt);     ⎬ type a number 0-9.
    ESOS_TASK_WAIT_ON_AVAILABLE_IN_COMM();          ⎭ prompter will not
    do {                                              proceed until it gets
      ESOS_TASK_WAIT_ON_GET_UINT8(u8_char);           a number 0-9.
    } while((u8_char < '0') | (u8_char > '9'));
    ESOS_TASK_SIGNAL_AVAILABLE_IN_COMM();
    ESOS_TASK_WAIT_ON_SEND_STRING(psz_CRNL);       ⎫ Have ESOS allocate a child task
    ESOS_TASK_SIGNAL_AVAILABLE_OUT_COMM();         ⎬ and initialize handle th_child.
    ESOS_ALLOCATE_CHILD_TASK(th_child);       ←    ⎭
    ESOS_TASK_SPAWN_AND_WAIT(th_child, echo_child, u8_char-'0');
  }
  ESOS_TASK_END();                ⎫ prompter spawns echo_child with arguments.
}                                  ⎭ prompter is blocked until echo_child ends.
```

FIGURE 14.22   ESOS code to echo characters with variable increment (Part 1).

Child tasks are declared differently than "normal" user tasks.

```
ESOS_CHILD_TASK(echo_child, uint8 u8_in){
  static uint8  u8_char;                        ⎫ Child tasks can accept
  ESOS_TASK_BEGIN();                             ⎭ arguments from parents.
  do {
    ESOS_TASK_WAIT_ON_AVAILABLE_IN_COMM();         ⎫ Echo
    ESOS_TASK_WAIT_ON_GET_UINT8(u8_char);          ⎪ incremented
    ESOS_TASK_SIGNAL_AVAILABLE_IN_COMM();          ⎬ characters
    ESOS_TASK_WAIT_ON_AVAILABLE_OUT_COMM();        ⎪ until user
    ESOS_TASK_WAIT_ON_SEND_UINT8(u8_char+u8_in);   ⎪ types an '!'.
    ESOS_TASK_SIGNAL_AVAILABLE_OUT_COMM();         ⎭
  } while (u8_char != '!');
  ESOS_TASK_WAIT_ON_AVAILABLE_OUT_COMM();        ⎫
  ESOS_TASK_WAIT_ON_SEND_STRING(psz_done);       ⎬ Print message before ending.
  ESOS_TASK_SIGNAL_AVAILABLE_OUT_COMM();         ⎭
  ESOS_TASK_END();    ←        ⎫ A "child" task must eventually end, or
}                             ⎭ the "parent" task will be blocked forever.
```

FIGURE 14.23   ESOS code to echo characters with variable increment (Part 2).

with how prompter, which is an ESOS_USER_TASK, spawns (gives birth) to echo_child, which is an ESOS_CHILD_TASK. The first difference is that prompter declares some static storage space for a variable th_child, which is of type ESOS_TASK_HANDLE. Near the bottom of Figure 14.22, prompter calls ESOS_ALLOCATE_CHILD_TASK(th_child) that has ESOS allocate a child task and assign th_child to point to the newly created child task. At this point, a child task does not yet exist on its own. We could say that prompter is "pregnant." The child task storage has been created and everything is properly initialized, but our child task echo_child is not yet functioning. A user task becomes a parent when it gives birth, or spawns a child task. Spawning is done by the call to ESOS_TASK_SPAWN_AND_WAIT(). The first two arguments to ESOS_TASK_SPAWN_AND_WAIT(), the handle to the child task and the name of the child task itself, are required. Any arguments that the parent task desires to give the child task can be added after the two required arguments. In our example in Figure 14.22, the parent task prompter passes the child task echo_child the number by which characters should be incremented.

The child task echo_child looks much like all of the other ESOS_USER_TASKs we've written in this chapter. The major differences are that echo_child is declared as a task ESOS_CHILD_TASK instead of ESOS_USER_TASK, and echo_child is passed an uint8 input argument called u8_in. Child tasks that do not have any input arguments from its parent are identical to ESOS_USER_TASKs, apart from the different declaration statement.

There are a couple more points to reiterate about child tasks: Child tasks must eventually execute their ESOS_TASK_END statement, and a child task cannot be active with two parents at the same time. Recall that parent tasks are blocked until their child task ends. If the child task does not end, the parent task is blocked forever. While this scenario is allowed and possibly useful, it will probably be rare. The usual behavior is that a child task executes an often-used operation on behalf of its parent(s) and then ends so that the parent may continue executing. A child task can be spawned by different parent tasks; however, the child task cannot be active with two parents at the same time. The fundamental reason for this is that a child task maintains its current state and cannot be in two different states at the same time. The latter would be the result if two parents both actively spawned the same child task at the same time.

Child tasks give the user a powerful tool to collect commonly used code that must yield/wait into one location. In fact, you have been using child tasks since the beginning of this chapter. The majority of ESOS commands in the ESOS communications services are actually disguised spawns of child tasks. When your task, which is an ESOS_USER_TASK, calls ESOS_TASK_WAIT_ON_GET_UINT8(), your task becomes a parent task and waits for the ESOS communications service child task to complete. The child task ends when it is successful in getting the uint8 from the ESOS communications FIFO. When the child task ends, your parent task continues execution and makes use of the newly acquired `uint8` data. Child tasks make your ESOS applications easier to write, understand, and maintain. ESOS itself would not exist without them.

ESOS INTERRUPT SERVICES

As we saw in Chapter 9, interrupts in embedded systems are used to provide a rapid response to deadline-driven peripherals. With the context switching between the code in `main()` and the ISRs, an embedded system using interrupts appears to perform more than one task at a time. While a multitasking OS like ESOS is a more flexible and maintainable way to allow the processor to seemingly perform more than one task at a time, interrupts still have a place in multitasking OS design when peripherals demand quick response to a request. ESOS uses interrupts internally to implement the system tick, the software timers, and manage the asynchronous serial communication system. The hardware registers and the interrupts that create these services are not to be manipulated by user applications; however, ESOS provides a service for initializing and using the other hardware interrupts provided by the processor. This section describes the ESOS interrupt service.

So that ESOS can efficiently manage the processor, its timing, and resources, ESOS requires that it be kept aware of the processor operations at all times. On rare occasions, ESOS may need to temporarily disable certain interrupts in order to configure the processor, execute critical code, or maintain accurate timing. If ESOS is to disable interrupts and restore them afterward, ESOS must have a mechanism by which it can be apprised of interrupt state: whether the interrupt is being used, what code services the interrupt, and the current state of the interrupt. While the user is free to use any hardware interrupt not already being used by ESOS internally, the user must control and manage these interrupts through functions provided by the ESOS interrupt service. Figures 14.24 and 14.25 show the ESOS application code to recreate the pulse-width measurement application in Figures 12.4 and 12.5.

The code structure in Figures 14.24 and 14.25 is identical to the code in Figures 12.4 and 12.5. The major changes are that Figure 12.5's code in `main()` is now performed with a user task called `task1`, and all INT1 operations are performed through functions provided by ESOS interrupt services. The code in Figure 14.24 should be largely self-explanatory as it contains the typical macro definitions and global variable declarations. The ISR for the external interrupt INT1 signals the code in `main()` through ESOS-provided user flags. To aid readability and maintainability of the code, the code defines its own names, `WAITING_FOR_FALLING_EDGE` and `CAPTURED_FLAG`, for the ESOS user flags. The final item to note in Figure 14.24 is that `configTimer23()` uses the ESOS interrupt service function `ESOS_MARK_PIC24_USER_INTERRUPT_SERVICED()` to

```
#include     "esos.h"
#include     "esos_pic24.h"
#include     "esos_pic24_rs232.h"
#include     "pic24_timer.h"

#define CONFIG_LED1()   CONFIG_RB15_AS_DIG_OUTPUT()
#define LED1            _LATB15
#define WAITING_FOR_FALLING_EDGE   ESOS_USER_FLAG_0
#define CAPTURED_FLAG              ESOS_USER_FLAG_1

char psz_CRNL[3]= {0x0D, 0x0A, 0};
char psz_prompt[] = "Press button...";
char psz_r1[] = "Pulse width = ";
char psz_r2[] = "us\n";

volatile UINT32 U32_lastCapture;
volatile UINT32 U32_thisCapture;
volatile int32 u32_delta;

inline void CONFIG_SW1() {
   CONFIG_RB13_AS_DIG_INPUT();
   ENABLE_RB13_PULLUP();
   CONFIG_INT1_TO_RP(13);
}
```

ESOS user flags to signal between ISR and main()

UINT32 is an union datatype defined in ESOS file all_generic.h.

CONFIG_SW1 from Figure 12.5 with interrupt configuration removed. ESOS interrupt service used to configure interrupts.

User timer swTimerLED same as previous example.

```
void configTimer23(void) {
   T2CON = T2_OFF | T2_IDLE_CON | T2_GATE_OFF
           | T2_32BIT_MODE_ON
           | T2_SOURCE_INT
           | T2_PS_1_1 ;
   PR2 = 0xFFFF;        //maximum period
   PR3 = 0xFFFF;        //maximum period
   TMR3HLD = 0;         //write MSW first
   TMR2   = 0;          //then LSW
   ESOS_MARK_PIC24_USER_INTERRUPT_SERVICED(ESOS_IRQ_PIC24_T3);
   T2CONbits.TON = 1;   //turn on the timer
}
```

configTimer23() from Figure 12.5 modified only to use ESOS function to clear T3IF.

FIGURE 14.24   ESOS code to measure pulse widths with user interrupts (Part 1).

clear the T3IF bit instead of clearing it directly. Thus, ESOS is informed of the state of the state of the T3 interrupt.

In Figure 14.25, the code used to service the INT1 interrupt is declared with ESOS_USER_INTERRUPT(ESOS_IRQ_PIC24_INT1). All ISRs should be declared as ESOS_USER_INTERRUPT with the appropriate argument. ESOS provided arguments for all PIC24 hardware interrupts available to the user. The ISR is registered and enabled in user_init() with the ESOS functions ESOS_REGISTER_PIC24_USER_INTERRUPT(ESOS_IRQ_PIC24_INT1) and ESOS_ENABLE_PIC24_USER_INTERRUPT(ESOS_IRQ_PIC24_INT1). Apart from the ESOS interrupt service calls and the use of ESOS user flags, the ISR code in Figure 14.25 is the same as Figure 12.4. The functionality of Figure 12.5's main() is performed by task1 in Figure 14.25.

```
ESOS_USER_INTERRUPT(ESOS_IRQ_PIC24_INT1) {                    ← Clear interrupt bit.
    ESOS_MARK_PIC24_USER_INTERRUPT_SERVICED(ESOS_IRQ_PIC24_INT1);
    if (esos_IsUserFlagSet(WAITING_FOR_FALLING_EDGE)) {       ⎫ If task1 is ready
        if (esos_IsUserFlagClear(CAPTURED_FLAG)) {            ⎪ for another
            U32_lastCapture.u16LoWord = TMR2;                 ⎪ capture, record
            U32_lastCapture.u16HiWord = TMR3HLD;              ⎬ the timer value,
            _INT1EP = 0;                                      ⎪ and change edge
            esos_ClearUserFlag(WAITING_FOR_FALLING_EDGE);     ⎪ sensitivity.
        }                                                     ⎭
    } else {
        U32_thisCapture.u16LoWord = TMR2;                     ⎫ Capture is complete.
        U32_thisCapture.u16HiWord = TMR3HLD;                  ⎪ Record timer value,
        u32_delta = U32_thisCapture.u32 -                     ⎬ compute u32_delta,
                    U32_lastCapture.u32;                      ⎪ change edge, and signal
        esos_SetUserFlag(CAPTURED_FLAG);                      ⎪ task1 via CAPTURED_FLAG.
        _INT1EP = 1;                                          ⎭
        esos_SetUserFlag(WAITING_FOR_FALLING_EDGE);
    }
} //end ESOS_IRQ_PIC24_INT1

ESOS_USER_TASK(task1) {
  static  uint32           u32_pulseWidth;

  ESOS_TASK_BEGIN();                                          ⎧ Yield until ISR has signaled
  while (TRUE) {                                              ⎨ success via CAPTURED_FLAG.
    ESOS_TASK_WAIT_ON_SEND_STRING(psz_prompt);               ⎩
    ESOS_TASK_WAIT_UNTIL(esos_IsUserFlagSet(CAPTURED_FLAG));
    u32_pulseWidth = ticksToUs(u32_delta, getTimerPrescale(T2CONbits));
    esos_ClearUserFlag(CAPTURED_FLAG); ←——— Let ISR know task1 used u32_delta.
    ESOS_TASK_WAIT_ON_SEND_STRING(psz_r1);
    ESOS_TASK_WAIT_ON_SEND_UINT32_AS_HEX_STRING(u32_pulseWidth);
    ESOS_TASK_WAIT_ON_SEND_STRING(psz_r2);
  }
  ESOS_TASK_END();
} // end task1()
                                           ┌─ Set up hardware and timer.
void user_init(void) {
  CONFIG_LED1(); CONFIG_SW1(); configTimer23();

  esos_RegisterTask(task1);
  esos_RegisterTimer( swTimerLED, 250 );     ⎧ Initialize ISR state flag
                                             ⎨ WAITING_FOR_FALLING_EDGE.
  esos_SetUserFlag(WAITING_FOR_FALLING_EDGE);
  _INT1EP = 1;                               Register ISR with ESOS and
  ESOS_REGISTER_PIC24_USER_INTERRUPT( ESOS_IRQ_PIC24_INT1,   have ESOS enable INT1.
                ESOS_USER_IRQ_LEVEL1, _INT1Interrupt );
  ESOS_ENABLE_PIC24_USER_INTERRUPT(ESOS_IRQ_PIC24_INT1);
}
                  Configure INT1 for falling edges.
```

FIGURE 14.25   ESOS code to measure pulse widths with user interrupts (Part 2).

ESOS provides a full set of functions for users to manage interrupts in their applications. Figure 14.26 shows the complete set of ESOS interrupt service functions. All user manipulation of interrupt registers should be done through these functions. The current implementation of ESOS interrupt services for the PIC24

ESOS_USER_INTERRUPT(desc)
Declares an user-provided routine to service the interrupt denoted by interrupt descriptor **desc**. Interrupt descriptors exist for all interrupts.

ESOS_REGISTER_PIC24_USER_INTERRUPT(desc, ipl, p2f)
Registers function **p2f** as the ISR for the interrupt denoted by **desc**, where the ISR has an interrupt priority level of **ipl**. ESOS provides 4 priority levels (highest-to-lowest priority): ESOS_USER_IRQ_LEVEL1, ESOS_USER_IRQ_LEVEL2, ESOS_USER_IRQ_LEVEL3, ESOS_USER_IRQ_LEVEL4. Function **p2f** should be declared as type ESOS_USER_INTERRUPT(). Registered interrupts are not enabled.

ESOS_ENABLE_PIC24_USER_INTERRUPT(desc)
Enables the declared and registered interrupt dentoed by **desc**.

ESOS_DISABLE_PIC24_USER_INTERRUPT(desc)
Disables the interrupt dentoed by **desc**.

ESOS_ENABLE_ALL_PIC24_USER_INTERRUPTS()
Enables all declared and registered user interrupts. Does not affect interrupts used by ESOS.

ESOS_DISABLE_ALL_PIC24_USER_INTERRUPTS()
Disables all declared and registered user interrupts. Does not affect interrupts used by ESOS.

ESOS_IS_PIC24_USER_INTERRUPT_ENABLED(desc)
Queries the enabled state of the interrupt dentoed by **desc**. Returns TRUE if the interrupt is registered and enabled; returns FALSE otherwise.

ESOS_DOES_PIC24_USER_INTERRUPT_NEED_SERVICING(desc)
Queries the status flag state of the interrupt denoted by **desc**. Returns TRUE if the interrupt is needs servicing; returns FALSE otherwise. Used most often when polling a peripheral without enabling the peripheral's interrupt.

ESOS_MARK_PIC24_USER_INTERRUPT_SERVICED(desc)
Clears the status flag state of the interrupt dentoed by **desc**. Usually called within the ESOS_USER_INTERRUPT routine for the interrupt dentoed by **desc**.

Valid values for interrupt descriptors **desc**
(NOTE: Only interrupts present on target CPU and not used by ESOS are defined and available.)

ESOS_IRQ_PIC24_AD1 (ADC1 event) ⋮	ESOS_IRQ_PIC24_SPI1 (SPI1 event) ESOS_IRQ_PIC24_SPI1E (SPIE1 error) ⋮
ESOS_IRQ_PIC24_CN (change notification) ESOS_IRQ_PIC24_IC1 (input capture 1) ESOS_IRQ_PIC24_IC2 (input capture 2) ⋮	ESOS_IRQ_PIC24_T2 (timer2 event) ESOS_IRQ_PIC24_T3 (timer3 event)
ESOS_IRQ_PIC24_INT0 (ext. interrupt 0) ESOS_IRQ_PIC24_INT1 (ext. interrupt 1) ⋮	ESOS_IRQ_PIC24_OC1 (output compare 0) ESOS_IRQ_PIC24_OC2 (output compare 1) ⋮
ESOS_IRQ_PIC24_MI2C1 (master I2C1) ESOS_IRQ_PIC24_SI2C1 (slave I2C1) ⋮	ESOS_IRQ_PIC24_U1TX (UART1 transmit) ESOS_IRQ_PIC24_U1RX (UART1 receive) ESOS_IRQ_PIC24_U1E (UART1 error) ⋮

FIGURE 14.26 Functions provided by the ESOS interrupt service.

family does not allow reregistration of interrupts; that is, a user interrupt cannot change the function that responds to the interrupt at runtime. This restriction may be removed in future versions of ESOS.

Working in conjunction with a multitasking OS like ESOS does not change the fact that interrupts are asynchronous interruptions of the normal code flow. Just as in Chapter 9, the ISRs or ESOS_USER_INTERRUPTs you write should be short and perform only the operations for which they are uniquely qualified. Once the ESOS_USER_INTERRUPT has done its function, the ESOS_USER_INTERRUPT should set a flag or signal a semaphore so that non-interrupt code can further process, display, copy, or otherwise continue the operation outside of the ISR context. Finally, the ESOS_USER_INTERRUPT is simply an ISR and, as such, ESOS_USER_INTERRUPTs cannot execute any of the ESOS task commands to wait or yield.

DESIGN: ADDING AN ESOS SERVICE FOR I²C

In general, communications with other devices has the potential to be delayed, slow, or even nonexistent. Using the hardware support library in Chapter 10, you may have had your PIC24 µC reset because the watchdog timer timed out due to a communication error or a problem with the other device. In the earlier chapters, your code is the only program running on the µC, so these resets may be tolerable. However, there are potentially many different operations being performed by your µC when it is running a multitasking OS. The watchdog reset of the µC because of a communications error with a target device is not desirable because of the havoc it creates in the other unrelated tasks. If a target communications device is not functioning, then it is most desirable for only the ESOS task trying to communicate to be adversely affected. This is exactly what happens in the ESOS asynchronous communication system. Tasks that attempt to communicate via the ESOS communication function calls are blocked until the desired communications takes place. Other unrelated tasks continue to function unaware of the problems.

The cooperative multitasking capability in ESOS provides the mechanism by which many functions can be accomplished. In the previous section, we saw the ESOS functions by which tasks can wait, yield, and communicate their intentions to the ESOS scheduler. We also saw how tasks can communicate with each other with semaphores and flags, and create other tasks, by registering them or spawning child tasks. We were also introduced to the asynchronous communication services provided by ESOS. This service encapsulates the UART configuration and operation on the PIC24 µC family. The communication service is constructed with a collection of *C* language macros that create and spawn child tasks. These child tasks block the calling parent task until the child task accomplishes the job of getting or receiving data from the UART. You are encouraged to examine the structure of the ESOS asynchronous communication service by reading its source code. The members of the PIC24 µC family contain several other useful communications peripherals, such as the I²C and the SPI peripherals. As with asynchronous communications, the I²C and the SPI communication protocols also have the potential for delays, latency, or failure. ESOS applications need a way to use these protocols but gracefully handle delays or failure.

In this section, we will guide you through the creation of an ESOS service for I²C. Then, we will use this new service to recreate an application from Chapter 10. Creating an I²C service will use many features of ESOS and allow you to become better acquainted with ESOS organization. Furthermore, the asynchronous communication service is constructed in almost an identical fashion so you will learn better how the UART services work. Also, there may come a time when you need to create a custom service for your own ESOS applications. The methods described here can be your guide. Finally, ESOS services for SPI are included in the source code for the ESOS system and will not be covered here. A good understanding of the I²C service created in this section will help you to understand and use the ESOS SPI service. The ESOS SPI service is available in the included ESOS source code, but is not described in this text.

I²C Operations Under ESOS

The I²C hardware support library introduced in Chapter 10 provides easy access to common I²C operations and transactions. Specifically, Figure 10.44 lists the I²C function calls when ESOS is not present. In general, the routines in Figure 10.44 cannot be used in ESOS applications because these routines block the processor during communication delays and potentially reset the processor in the extreme case. We need to adapt the functions in Figure 10.44 to a new form that can be used in ESOS applications.

The I²C configuration routine configI2C1(uint16 u16_FkHZ) in Figure 10.45 does not wait for some external operation to complete but simply configures the I²C peripheral registers in the PIC24 µC. Therefore, this function is compatible with ESOS unchanged. However, to avoid naming conflicts and keep the function names consistent, our I²C services will name the configuration routine esos_pic24_configI2C1 (uint16 u16_FkHZ). Listing 14.3 shows the code for the configuration routine.

LISTING 14.3   ESOS I²C configuration.

```
void esos_pic24_configI2C1(uint16 u16_FkHZ) {
  uint32 u32_temp;

  u32_temp = (FCY/1000L)/((uint32) u16_FkHZ);
  u32_temp = u32_temp - FCY/10000000L - 1;
  I2C1BRG = u32_temp;
  I2C1CONbits.I2CEN = 1;
}
```

Basic I²C operations performed with the Chapter 10 functions `startI2C1()`, `stopI2C1()`, `restartI2C1()`, and `putI2C1()` all have the potential to be blocked by abnormal operating conditions. Furthermore, these basic operations are used by many other functions to construct larger I²C transactions. In Chapter 10, these functions recorded their execution into an error string and enabled the watchdog to reset the processor in the event that the blocking state did not unblock in due time. These features are useful in the code in the earlier chapters but are not compatible with ESOS. The ESOS version of these operations must simply instruct the task to wait until the appropriate I²C condition is met. Finally, these basic operations are used as building blocks for other more complex routines so a *C* language macro is most appropriate. Figure 14.27 shows the macros to implement the basic I²C operations of start, stop, restart, and put.

```
#define __PIC24_I2C1_START()                            \
   do{                                                  \
      I2C1CONbits.SEN = 1;                              \
      ESOS_TASK_WAIT_WHILE(I2C1CONbits.SEN);            \
   }while(0)

#define __PIC24_I2C1_RSTART()                           \
   do{                                                  \
      I2C1CONbits.RSEN = 1;                             \
      ESOS_TASK_WAIT_WHILE(I2C1CONbits.RSEN);           \
   }while(0)

#define __PIC24_I2C1_STOP()                             \
   do{                                                  \
      I2C1CONbits.PEN = 1;                              \
      ESOS_TASK_WAIT_WHILE(I2C1CONbits.PEN);            \
   }while(0)

#define __PIC24_I2C1_PUT(byte)                          \
   do{                                                  \
      I2C1TRN = (byte);                                 \
      ESOS_TASK_WAIT_WHILE(I2C1STATbits.TRSTAT);        \
   }while(0)
```

Keep multi-line macros atomic by "protecting" them with `do-while(0)`.

FIGURE 14.27   Basic I²C operation macros for ESOS.

The basic operation `getI2C()` in Figure 10.46 is a bit more complicated. The process of getting a byte from the I²C bus requires that the function

1. wait for an I²C bus idle condition
2. enable the I²C receive bit
3. wait for the received byte
4. read the byte
5. wait for an I²C bus idle condition
6. acknowledge
7. wait for acknowledge to complete

The preceding operations must occur in sequence, and each of the wait operations has the potential to be delayed or not occur. So, we should write code to implement the function to get one byte from the I²C bus. A macro is probably a bad idea for this operation as the macro will be quite long because it must perform at least seven distinct steps. Also, the means by which the *C* language compiler is used to implement the multitasking in ESOS prohibits the use of more than one ESOS wait/yield macro. The ESOS function to get a byte from I²C involves waiting, so it must be coded as a task. However, this task will be called by other tasks. Therefore, we should write this I²C operation as a child task. Figure 14.28 shows the code for the child task to get a byte from the I²C bus. If you compare the code in Figure 14.28 with the code in Figure 10.46, you will find the two functions very similar.

```
ESOS_CHILD_TASK( __esos_pic24_getI2C1,
                 uint8* pu8_x, ◄──────── desination for received byte
                 uint8 u8_ack2Send) {
    static uint8* pu8_local; ◄──── ⎰ local copy of arguments
    static uint8 u8_local;          ⎱ to preserve across waits

    ESOS_TASK_BEGIN();
    pu8_local = pu8_x;
    u8_local = u8_ack2Send;
    ESOS_TASK_WAIT_WHILE(I2C1CON & 0x1F); ◄──────── Wait for idle.
    I2C1CONbits.RCEN = 1;
    ESOS_TASK_WAIT_UNTIL(I2C1STATbits.RBF); ◄──────── Wait for receive.
    *pu8_local = I2C1RCV; ◄──────── Save byte at destination's address.
    ESOS_TASK_WAIT_WHILE(I2C1CON & 0x1F); ◄──── ⎰ Wait for idle before
    I2C1CONbits.ACKDT = u8_local;               ⎱ attempting ACK.
    I2C1CONbits.ACKEN = 1;
    ESOS_TASK_WAIT_WHILE(I2C1CONbits.ACKEN);
    ESOS_TASK_END();   ↖
}                      Wait for ACK to complete.
```

FIGURE 14.28   ESOS I²C operation to read a byte from bus.

There are two key items to note in Figure 14.28. First, the arguments passed into __esos_pic24_getI2C1 are copied into local static variables to preserve their values across the wait statements. Second, the byte read from the I²C bus is placed at the address of the input argument since child tasks cannot return values to their caller. Other than changing the while(cond) waits in Figure 10.46 to ESOS-compatible ESOS_TASK_WAIT_WHILE(cond), the code in Figure 14.28 is largely unchanged. With the macro in Listing 14.3 and the code in Figures 14.27 and 14.28, we are now ready to implement a full I²C transaction to read and write data to a target device.

I²C TRANSACTIONS UNDER ESOS

An I²C transaction consists of writing the target device's address, reading or writing the correct amount of data, and responding with the appropriate acknowledgments.

These I²C transactions will be called by other ESOS tasks, will have data passed into them, will pass data out of them, and will be blocked for an unknown period of time. Our only choice to satisfy all of these requirements is to implement our I²C transactions as child tasks, similar to __esos_pic24_getI2C1 in Figure 14.28.

The simplest transactions write data to a target device with I²C address u8_addr. Figure 14.29 shows the code to implement the child tasks to perform these transactions.

```
ESOS_CHILD_TASK(__esos_pic24_write1I2C1, uint8 u8_addr, uint8 u8_d1) {

  static uint8 u8_tempAddr, u8_tempD1;
                                          local copy of arguments
  ESOS_TASK_BEGIN();
  u8_tempAddr=u8_addr; u8_tempD1=u8_d1;       macro to make target address
  __PIC24_I2C1_START();                       into I2C write address
  __PIC24_I2C1_PUT(I2C_WADDR(u8_tempAddr));
  __PIC24_I2C1_PUT(u8_tempD1);
  __PIC24_I2C1_STOP();
  ESOS_TASK_END();
}

ESOS_CHILD_TASK(__esos_pic24_write2I2C1, uint8 u8_addr,
                              uint8 u8_d1, uint8 u8_d2) {
  static uint8 u8_tempAddr, u8_tempD1, u8_tempD2;
                                          local copy of arguments
  ESOS_TASK_BEGIN();
  u8_tempAddr=u8_addr; u8_tempD1=u8_d1; u8_tempD2=u8_d2;
  __PIC24_I2C1_START();
  __PIC24_I2C1_PUT(I2C_WADDR(u8_tempAddr));
  __PIC24_I2C1_PUT(u8_tempD1);
  __PIC24_I2C1_PUT(u8_tempD2);
  __PIC24_I2C1_STOP();
  ESOS_TASK_END();
}

ESOS_CHILD_TASK(__esos_pic24_writeNI2C1, uint8 u8_addr,
                              uint8* pu8_d, uint16 u16_cnt) {
  static uint8    u8_tempAddr;
  static uint8*   pu8_tempPtr;
  static uint16   u16_tempCnt, u16_i;
                                          local copy of arguments
  ESOS_TASK_BEGIN();
  u8_tempAddr=u8_addr; pu8_tempPtr=pu8_d; u16_tempCnt=u16_cnt;
  __PIC24_I2C1_START();
  __PIC24_I2C1_PUT(I2C_WADDR(u8_tempAddr));
  for (u16_i=0; u16_i < u16_tempCnt; u16_i++) {
    __PIC24_I2C1_PUT(*pu8_tempPtr);
    pu8_tempPtr++;
  }
  __PIC24_I2C1_STOP();
  ESOS_TASK_END();
}
```

FIGURE 14.29   ESOS child task to write data to a target device.

Like the child task __esos_pic24_getI2C1 in Figure 14.28, the transaction child tasks in Figure 14.29 must keep a static local copy of their arguments. Otherwise, the code in Figure 14.29 is very similar to the code in Figure 10.48.

Now that we have created the child tasks in Figure 14.29 to write 1, 2, and N bytes to a target device, other tasks can spawn these tasks. The parent tasks can declare an ESOS_TASK_HANDLE for the child tasks such as the code in Figure 14.22. A more efficient way is to have the ESOS_TASK_HANDLE automatically created by the C compiler when the I²C routines are included in a project. The file esos_pic24_i2c.c that contains the code described in this section simply declares the variable storage with the line struct stTask __stChildTaskI2C;. Whenever I²C is used in an ESOS application, the user can be assured that storage for a child task has been created.

Now, we can further simplify the application designer's job by providing some easy-to-use macros to implement an I²C transaction. Listing 14.4 shows macros for tasks to use in order to write data to a target I²C device. The file esos_pic24_i2c.h contains these macro definitions for your application use.

LISTING 14.4　Macros to perform ESOS I²C write transactions.

```
#define ESOS_TASK_WAIT_ON_WRITE1I2C1(u8_addr, u8_d1)                     \
    ESOS_TASK_SPAWN_AND_WAIT((ESOS_TASK_HANDLE)&__stChildTaskI2C,        \
    __esos_pic24_write1I2C1, (u8_addr), (u8_d1))
#define ESOS_TASK_WAIT_ON_WRITE2I2C1(u8_addr, u8_d1, u8_d2)              \
    ESOS_TASK_SPAWN_AND_WAIT((ESOS_TASK_HANDLE)&__stChildTaskI2C,        \
    __esos_pic24_write2I2C1, (u8_addr), (u8_d1), (u8_d2))
#define ESOS_TASK_WAIT_ON_WRITENI2C1(u8_addr, pu8_d1, u16_cnt)           \
    ESOS_TASK_SPAWN_AND_WAIT((ESOS_TASK_HANDLE)&__stChildTaskI2C,        \
    __esos_pic24_writeNI2C1, (u8_addr), (pu8_d1), (u16_cnt))
```

Recall that we created a child task __esos_pic24_getI2C1 to read a byte from the I²C bus in Figure 14.28. This child task will be called by child tasks that perform the full I²C read transactions. Therefore, it would be useful to have a macro such as those in Listing 14.4 to facilitate using the child task __esos_pic24_getI2C1 in Figure 14.28. Also, since the task __esos_pic24_getI2C1 will be called quite often, we can declare a task storage structure for it in esos_pic24_i2c.c with struct stTask __stGrandChildTaskI2C;. Listing 14.5 shows the macro used to simplify the calls to the child task __esos_pic24_getI2C1.

LISTING 14.5　Macros to spawn child task to read a byte from I²C bus.

```
#define ESOS_TASK_WAIT_ON_GETI2C1(pu8_get, u8_ack2Send)                \
  ESOS_TASK_SPAWN_AND_WAIT((ESOS_TASK_HANDLE)&__stGrandChildTaskI2C,   \
  __esos_pic24_getI2C1, (pu8_get), (u8_ack2Send))
```

With the macro in Listing 14.5, the child task to read 1, 2, or N bytes from an I²C device is straightforward. Figure 14.30 shows the code for the I²C transactions to read data. Notice that each time the child tasks in Figure 14.30 desire to read a byte from the I²C bus, they must spawn the child task using the macro in Listing 14.5. Use of the I²C transaction child tasks in Figure 14.30 is simplified by the macros given in Listing 14.6. Notice how the macros in Listing 14.6 accept the destination variable arguments "by-name" but call the child task "by-reference."

```
ESOS_CHILD_TASK( __esos_pic24_read1I2C1, uint8 u8_addr, uint8* pu8_d) {
  static uint8      u8_tempAddr;
  static uint8*     pu8_tempD1;

  ESOS_TASK_BEGIN();
  u8_tempAddr=u8_addr; pu8_tempD1=pu8_d;
  __PIC24_I2C1_START();
  __PIC24_I2C1_PUT(I2C_RADDR(u8_tempAddr));
  ESOS_TASK_WAIT_ON_GETI2C1(pu8_tempD1, I2C_NAK);
  __PIC24_I2C1_STOP();
  ESOS_TASK_END();
}


ESOS_CHILD_TASK( __esos_pic24_read2I2C1, uint8 u8_addr,
                      uint8* pu8_d1, uint8* pu8_d2) {
  static uint8      u8_tempAddr;
  static uint8*     pu8_tempD1;
  static uint8*     pu8_tempD2;

  ESOS_TASK_BEGIN();
  u8_tempAddr=u8_addr; pu8_tempD1=pu8_d1; pu8_tempD2=pu8_d2;
  __PIC24_I2C1_START();
  __PIC24_I2C1_PUT(I2C_RADDR(u8_tempAddr));
  ESOS_TASK_WAIT_ON_GETI2C1(pu8_tempD1, I2C_ACK);
  ESOS_TASK_WAIT_ON_GETI2C1(pu8_tempD2, I2C_NAK);
  __PIC24_I2C1_STOP();
  ESOS_TASK_END();
}


ESOS_CHILD_TASK( __esos_pic24_readNI2C1, uint8 u8_addr,
                      uint8* pu8_d, uint16 u16_cnt) {
  static uint8      u8_tempAddr;
  static uint8*     pu8_tempD;
  static uint16     u16_tempCnt, u16_i;

  ESOS_TASK_BEGIN();
  u8_tempAddr=u8_addr; pu8_tempD=pu8_d; u16_tempCnt=u16_cnt;
  __PIC24_I2C1_START();
  __PIC24_I2C1_PUT(I2C_RADDR(u8_tempAddr));
  for (u16_i=0; u16_i < u16_tempCnt-1; u16_i++) {
    ESOS_TASK_WAIT_ON_GETI2C1(pu8_tempD, I2C_ACK);
    pu8_tempD++;
  }
  ESOS_TASK_WAIT_ON_GETI2C1(pu8_tempD, I2C_NAK);
  __PIC24_I2C1_STOP();
  ESOS_TASK_END();
}
```

Annotations in figure: "Create local copy of arguments." (pointing to assignment lines); "macro to make target address into I²C read address" (pointing to the I2C_RADDR lines).

FIGURE 14.30 ESOS child task to read data from a target device.

LISTING 14.6 Macros to perform ESOS I²C read transactions.

```
#define ESOS_TASK_WAIT_ON_READ1I2C1(u8_addr, u8_d1)              \
    ESOS_TASK_SPAWN_AND_WAIT((ESOS_TASK_HANDLE)&__stChildTaskI2C, \
    __esos_pic24_read1I2C1, (u8_addr), &(u8_d1))
#define ESOS_TASK_WAIT_ON_READ2I2C1(u8_addr, u8_d1, u8_d2)       \
    ESOS_TASK_SPAWN_AND_WAIT((ESOS_TASK_HANDLE)&__stChildTaskI2C, \
    __esos_pic24_read2I2C1, (u8_addr), &(u8_d1), &(u8_d2))
#define ESOS_TASK_WAIT_ON_READNI2C1(u8_addr, pu8_d, u16_cnt)     \
    ESOS_TASK_SPAWN_AND_WAIT( (ESOS_TASK_HANDLE)&__stChildTaskI2C, \
    __esos_pic24_read2I2C1, (u8_addr), (pu8_d), (u16_cnt))
```

The macros and code described in this section can be found in the source code that accompanies this book in the files esos_pic24_i2c.c and esos_pic24_i2c.h. If you examine the asynchronous communications services files esos_pic24_rs232.c and esos_pic24_rs232.h and the SPI services files esos_pic24_spi.c and esos_pic24_spi.h, you will find the code to be similar in construction. Any custom services you desire to create will likely follow a similar pattern. In the next section, we will see our new I²C service in action.

APPLICATION USING THE ESOS I²C SERVICE

The ESOS I²C service created in the previous section allows us to easily build ESOS applications to use I²C devices. The circuit in Figure 10.49 shows how to connect the PIC24HJ32GP202 to the Maxim Integrated Circuits DS1631 I²C thermometer and thermostat. Figure 10.52 gives the single application version of the code used to read the current temperature from the DS1631. Although the DS1631 measures the temperature and our PIC24 μC can read this temperature via I²C, we must write data to the I²C bus to configure the DS1631 and to command the DS1631. This application exercises a large portion of the I²C services we created. In this section, we create the ESOS application to recreate the results obtained by the code in Figure 10.52.

Figure 14.31 shows the initialization code of our ESOS application. The routine user_init() performs the normal initialization operations of configuring the heartbeat LED, creating semaphores, and registering tasks and timers. The user_init() in Figure 14.31 also calls the ESOS I²C configuration routine esos_pic24_configI2C1 to set the PIC24 μC I²C peripheral to transfer at 400 kbps. Notice that the global variables include three semaphores and a 16-bit integer i16_temp to hold the temperature conversion results.

The DS1631 must be configured and commanded via I²C transactions to start temperature conversions. Thus, the DS1631 cannot be started in the routine user_init(), because user_init() is not an ESOS function and cannot wait or yield. Since the DS1631 must receive I²C data to operate properly, initialization and

```
#include    "esos_pic24.h"
#include    "esos_pic24_rs232.h"
#include    "esos_pic24_i2c.h"
#include    <stdio.h>
```
This application uses `printf` for convenience.

```
#define DS1631ADDR      0x90
#define ACCESS_CONFIG   0xAC
#define CONFIG_COMMAND  0x0C
#define START_CONVERT   0x51
#define READ_TEMP       0xAA
```
continuous 12-bit conversion

```
int16 i16_temp;
ESOS_SEMAPHORE(sem_dataReady);
ESOS_SEMAPHORE(sem_dataPrinted);
ESOS_SEMAPHORE(sem_ds1631Ready);
```
Declare/allocate the semaphores our tasks will use.

Timer `swTimerLED` same as previous example.

```
void user_init(void) {
  CONFIG_LED1();
  esos_pic24_configI2C1(400);
```
400 kbps I²C operation

```
  ESOS_INIT_SEMAPHORE(sem_ds1631Ready, 0);
  ESOS_INIT_SEMAPHORE(sem_dataReady, 0);
  ESOS_INIT_SEMAPHORE(sem_dataPrinted, 0);
```
Init the semaphores our tasks use to synchronize.

```
  esos_RegisterTask(start_ds1631);
  esos_RegisterTask(read_ds1631);
  esos_RegisterTask(update);
```
Register our tasks with the ESOS scheduler.

```
  esos_RegisterTimer( swTimerLED, 250);
}
```

FIGURE 14.31   ESOS application for testing the DS1631 (Part 1).

command of the DS1631 must occur in ESOS user tasks. Figure 14.32 shows the user tasks to complete our application. The task start_ds1631 performs two transactions to configure the DS1631 for 12-bit conversion results and to convert the temperature continuously. After the DS1631 is commanded to start conversions, the task start_ds1631 waits for a period of time to allow the DS1631 to acquire the first temperature reading. The task start_ds1631 signals the task read_ds1631 that the DS1631 is operating, then task start_ds1631 ends.

Simultaneous with the execution of start_ds1631, the task read_ds1631 has started. Initially, task read_ds1631 waits upon notification from start_ds1631 that the DS1631 is ready to provide temperature data. Once task read_ds1631 gets the signal, it enters an infinite loop where it performs an I²C transaction to acquire the most recent temperature reading from the DS1631. Task read_ds1631 places the results in the global variable i16_temp and signals task update that new temperature data is ready for its use. After signaling update, read_ds1631 waits for 750 ms and checks to see if task update has, indeed, consumed the temperature data. Once task update has signaled, read_ds1631 loops back to repeat the process.

```
ESOS_USER_TASK(start_ds1631) {
  ESOS_TASK_BEGIN();
  ESOS_TASK_WAIT_TICKS(500);
  ESOS_TASK_WAIT_ON_WRITE2I2C1(DS1631ADDR, ACCESS_CONFIG, CONFIG_COMMAND);
  ESOS_TASK_WAIT_ON_WRITE1I2C1(DS1631ADDR, START_CONVERT);
  ESOS_TASK_WAIT_TICKS(500);
  ESOS_SIGNAL_SEMAPHORE(sem_ds1631Ready, 1);
  ESOS_TASK_END();
}
```
{Give DS1631 time to convert first reading.

Signal **read_ds1631** to begin.

```
ESOS_USER_TASK(read_ds1631) {
  static uint8 u8_lo, u8_hi;

  ESOS_TASK_BEGIN();
  ESOS_TASK_WAIT_SEMAPHORE(sem_ds1631Ready, 1);
  while (TRUE) {
    ESOS_TASK_WAIT_ON_WRITE1I2C1(DS1631ADDR, READ_TEMP);
    ESOS_TASK_WAIT_ON_READ2I2C1(DS1631ADDR, u8_hi, u8_lo);
    i16_temp = u8_hi;
    i16_temp = ((i16_temp<<8)|u8_lo);
    ESOS_SIGNAL_SEMAPHORE(sem_dataReady, 1);
    ESOS_TASK_WAIT_TICKS(750);
    ESOS_TASK_WAIT_SEMAPHORE(sem_dataPrinted, 1);
  }
  ESOS_TASK_END();
}
```
— Signal **update** to print data.

— Make sure **update** used data.

```
ESOS_USER_TASK(update) {
  float   f_tempC, f_tempF;

  ESOS_TASK_BEGIN();
  while (TRUE) {
    ESOS_TASK_WAIT_SEMAPHORE(sem_dataReady, 1);
    f_tempC = (float) i16_temp;
    f_tempC = f_tempC/256;
    f_tempF = f_tempC*9/5 + 32;
    printf("Temp is: 0x%0X %4.4f (C), %4.4f (F)\n",
        i16_temp, (double) f_tempC, (double) f_tempF);
    ESOS_SIGNAL_SEMAPHORE(sem_dataPrinted, 1);
  }
  ESOS_TASK_END();
}
```
Do not procced until data is ready.

— Application uses **printf** for convenience.

Signal **read_ds1631** that **update** consumed recent data.

FIGURE 14.32   ESOS application for testing the DS1631 (Part 2).

Upon being registered in user_init(), task update starts executing. Initially, task update waits for a signal from task read_ds1631 that temperature data is available. Once the signal is received, task update converts the raw binary DS1631 data into a floating-point temperature and prints the results to the serial output port. After the results are printed, the temperature data are no longer needed and task update signals task read_ds1631 that it can overwrite the results with new data. Task update repeats these functions continuously.

In order to fully mimic the results of the code in Figure 10.52, the user task in Figure 14.32 uses the printf function in stdio.h. Use of printf could theoretically block the task update if the communication channel were not functioning properly. A blocked task update would also block other tasks from executing. A typical ESOS application would use the ESOS communication service function calls introduced in the previous sections to facilitate cooperative multitasking and allow the other unblocked tasks to continue to operate even when communications is slow or not functioning.

SUMMARY

This chapter introduced concepts of multitasking OSes and provided an introduction to ESOS, a lightweight cooperative multitasking OS for the PIC24 µC. ESOS provides services for managing user tasks including subordinate child tasks, full featured wait/yield conditions, and semaphores. ESOS also provides a collection of services so that the user can exploit the powerful hardware peripherals of the PIC24 µC. Services provided by ESOS include software timers, asynchronous and synchronous communications, and hardware interrupts.

REVIEW PROBLEMS

1. Develop the code required to implement a rendezvous semaphore with four tasks instead of two.
2. Implement a binary semaphore with function similar to Figure 14.19 using the ESOS-provided user flags. A binary semaphore can take on only the values 0 and 1.
3. *C* language macros are used extensively in ESOS. The multiline code macros are surrounded by do-while(0) statements. Why is this construction necessary?
4. Using basic ESOS I²C operations, create a specialized service for the Maxim Integrated Circuits DS1631 Digital Thermometer and Thermostat. The service will be composed of child tasks that perform the DS1631 operations directly without using the I²C transaction functions. Create the supporting macros to make the service's use in user tasks simpler. Some example macro names include ESOS_TASK_WAIT_GET_TEMP and ESOS_TASK_WAIT_SET_THERMOSTAT.

SUGGESTED PROJECT PROBLEMS

1. Reconstruct the system in Figures 9.28 and 9.29 using ESOS.
2. Reconstruct the system in Figures 10.54 through 10.59 using ESOS.
3. Reconstruct the system in Figures 11.40 through 11.43 using ESOS.
4. Reconstruct the system in Figures 12.26 and 12.27 using ESOS.

PART V

Capstone Examples

15 Capstone Projects

This chapter presents three detailed capstone projects that combine various hardware topics from the previous chapters. The projects are a digital recorder that can store audio input and play it back; a solder reflow oven created from a toaster oven; and a three-wheeled robot that can be remotely controlled via a universal remote control or function autonomously using an IR proximity sensor to avoid obstacles. This chapter also contains a brief survey of microcontroller families available from Microchip Technology Inc. and other companies.

Learning Objectives

After reading this chapter, you will be able to perform the following tasks:

- Design a system that can sample an audio signal, store it to a serial EEPROM, then play it back.
- Become familiar with the basics of AC power control by converting a toaster oven into a reflow solder oven.
- Design and build an autonomous wheeled robot with an IR interface using a PIC24 μC for control functions.
- Compare and contrast features of other PICmicro family members with the PIC24 μC family.
- Compare and contrast features of microcontrollers from other semiconductor manufacturers with the PIC24 μC family.

DESIGN OF AN AUDIO RECORD/PLAYBACK SYSTEM

The first project is a PIC24 μC system for capturing audio data for later playback. The simplest form of audio sampling uses a fixed sampling period and stores either uncompressed or compressed digital data to a memory device as shown in Figure 15.1. A key parameter in audio recorders is the *sampling period,* which is the time between conversions of the incoming audio to digital data. The sampling period is fixed, so the sampling period used for playback must be the same as that used for recording in

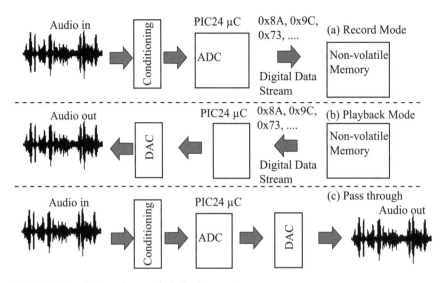

FIGURE 15.1 Basic audio record/playback concept.

order to faithfully reproduce the sampled audio. The inverse of the sampling period is the sampling frequency.

The quality of the audio playback improves as the sampling frequency is increased at the cost of increased memory requirements for audio storage. Audio is usually divided into two categories: music and speech. For music, sampling frequencies range from approximately 11 kHz up to 192 kHz (CD quality audio uses 16-bit samples for each channel, sampled at 44.1 kHz). The requirements for voice recording, however, are far less stringent. A sampling frequency of 8 kHz is considered adequate for speech data and this frequency is commonly used in voice recorders. A sampling frequency of 8 kHz has a sampling period of 125 μs. Assuming 8-bit data, a 64 Ki byte EEPROM can store $64 \times 1024 \times 125$ μs = 8.192 s of speech. As a side note, the binary data stream resulting from the digital sampling of an audio signal at a fixed interval is known as *pulse code modulation* (PCM).

For this design, our target is voice sampling at 8 kHz. The 24LC515 serial EEPROM (Chapter 10) is used for audio data storage, as we have previous experience in using that device for storing streaming input data from the serial port. The PIC24 μC ADC is used for conversion during recording, and the MAX 548A DAC (Chapter 11) is used for data conversion during playback. During audio recording, the incoming digitized audio data is a continual data stream. This problem was first examined in Chapter 10 for streaming data from the asynchronous serial port. In Chapter 10, an interrupt-driven ping-pong buffer approach was used in which one buffer was designated as the active buffer to hold incoming data while the contents of the second buffer was emptied, i.e., stored to EEPROM. Once a buffer became full, the roles of the two buffers were swapped with the empty buffer becoming the buffer used for incoming data and the full buffer becoming the buffer that is written to EEPROM. This same approach is used to handle the incoming audio data. As previously discussed in Chapter 10, we must ensure that the time spent processing an incoming data block is greater than the time spent processing an outgoing data block. In this case, the time for 64 audio samples must be greater than the time it takes to store 64 bytes in a block write to the serial EEPROM as shown in Equation 15.1. Buffer overflow occurs if this is not true.

$$\begin{array}{ll} \text{Input time for} & > \text{EEPROM write time} \\ \text{sampling 64 bytes} & + \text{I}^2\text{C transmit time} \end{array} \qquad (15.1)$$

Equations 15.2 through 15.4 show the calculation of the left and right quantities of Equation 15.1 assuming an I^{2}C bus frequency of 400 kHz (1 bit time = 1/400 kHz) and ignoring any software overhead. Recall that each I^{2}C transmission is 9 bit times because of the acknowledge bit, hence the 67 × 9 component of Equation 15.2. The 5 ms constant is the worst-case write completion time for the 24LC515 serial EEPROM.

$$\begin{array}{l} 64 \text{ bytes} \times 125 \text{ μs} > 5 \text{ ms write time} + \\ \qquad (67 \text{ bytes} \times 9 \text{ bits} \times 1/400 \text{ kHz}) \end{array} \qquad (15.2)$$

$$8 \text{ ms} > 5 \text{ ms} + (603 \times 1/400 \text{ kHz}) \qquad (15.3)$$

$$8 \text{ ms} > 6.5 \text{ ms} \qquad (15.4)$$

Examining the assembly code of our I^{2}C functions from Chapter 10 reveals an approximate 30 instruction per byte overhead for a block write. Assuming FCY = 40 MHz, Equations 15.5 through 15.7 show that this software overhead is not a significant factor. In fact, due to our use of write polling for the EEPROM, the margin is actually larger than what is shown in Equation 15.7 since the 5 ms write time for EEPROM is generally less than 3.5 ms under typical conditions.

$$8 \text{ ms} > 6.5 \text{ ms} + 67 \times 30 \text{ instr.} \times 1/40 \text{ MHz} \qquad (15.5)$$

$$8 \text{ ms} > 6.5 \text{ ms} + 0.05 \text{ ms} \qquad (15.6)$$

$$8 \text{ ms} > 6.55 \text{ ms} \qquad (15.7)$$

For playback, a ping-pong buffering mode is also used in which data is read out of one buffer and sent to the DAC via the SPI port by a periodic timer interrupt while a second buffer is being filled by reading the EEPROM. This gives two constraints, with the first being that the audio sampling time must be greater than the DAC write time (SPI bus speed is assumed to be 10 MHz). This constraint is easily satisfied as seen by Equations 15.8 through 15.10, which ignore software overhead.

$$\text{sampling time} > \text{DAC write time} \tag{15.8}$$

$$125 \text{ μs} > 2 \text{ bytes} \times 8 \text{ bits} \times 1/10 \text{ MHz} \tag{15.9}$$

$$125 \text{ μs} > 1.6 \text{ μs} \tag{15.10}$$

The second constraint is that the sampling time for 64 bytes (8 ms) must be greater than the EEPROM read time for 64 bytes. Again, Equations 15.11 through 15.12 show that this constraint has a large margin. The 68 bytes component of Equation 15.11 is because the read operation consists of a three-byte I^2C write transaction to set the address, followed by a 65 byte read transaction that contains 1 I^2C address byte and 64 data bytes.

$$8 \text{ ms} > (68 \text{ bytes} \times 9 \text{ bits} \times 1/400 \text{ kHz}) \tag{15.11}$$

$$8 \text{ ms} > 1.5 \text{ ms} \tag{15.12}$$

IMPLEMENTATION OF AN AUDIO RECORD/PLAYBACK SYSTEM

Figure 15.2 gives the schematic for the audio record and playback implementation. Audio mono mini-jacks (Digi-Key PN# CP-2506) are used to interface the PIC24 μC reference board to a personal computer that provides audio during recording and to powered speakers during playback. Separate audio input and output jacks means that a feed-through mode can be implemented as shown in Figure 15.2 in which the audio input is streamed back to the audio output without any intermediate storage.

The LM386 audio amplifier [54] provides a fixed gain of 20 in the minimal-external component configuration shown in Figure 15.2. The audio amplifier is needed as the output signal provided at the audio output jack of a personal computer typically has a peak-to-peak range of only a couple hundred millivolts. During recording of the audio signal, the combination of the fixed 20x gain of the LM386, the volume control on the PC, and the 10 kΩ input potentiometer provide the means for controlling the input signal magnitude to the PIC24 ADC. The LM386 also biases its output swing about VDD/2, which in this case is 5 V for the LM386. The resistor divider on the output shifts the 0 to 5 V output of the LM386 to a 0 to 3.3 V range for the PIC24 ADC input. The midpoint biasing of the LM386 is a nice

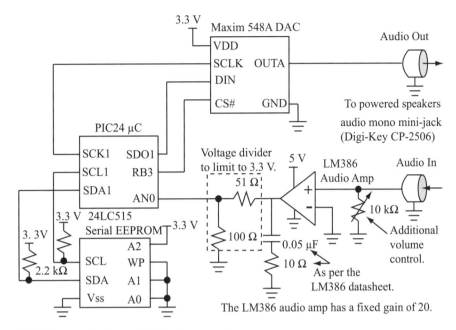

FIGURE 15.2 Audio record/playback schematic.

feature that provides maximum data resolution when sampled by the PIC24 ADC using the reference voltages configured as Vref+ = 3.3 V and Vref− = Vss.

Table 15.1 gives the PIC24 µC resources used for the audio record/playback application. Timer3 is used to generate the periodic interrupt that sets the sampling

TABLE 15.1 PIC24 µC resources used for audio record/playback application.

PIC24 µC Resource	Comment
Timer3	Timer3 interrupt period sets sample rate during playback and record.
ADC (pin AN0)	Used to sample audio signal as a 12-bit value during record mode. Vref+ is VDD (3.3 V); Vref− is Vss.
I²C Master mode, pins SDA1/SCL1	Used for interfacing to the 24LC515 serial EEPROM during record and playback.
SPI 8-bit Master mode, pins SCLK1, SDO1, and RB3	Used for interfacing to the MAX 548A DAC.
UART	The serial port is used for prompting the user for the operating mode.

rate for playback and record. The PIC24 µC ADC in 12-bit mode with a reference voltage of 3.3 V is used to sample the audio signal during record mode. The lower 4 bits of the ADC value are dropped when storing the data to EEPROM, giving an 8-bit sample in order to match the 8-bit data size of the MAX548A DAC. The I²C bus is used to communicate with the serial EEPROM for storing the sampled audio, which is converted back to analog form by the MAX548A DAC during playback. The asynchronous serial port is used to communicate with the user during application execution to prompt the user for operating mode choice.

AUDIO DATA COMPRESSION

The 64 Ki byte capacity of the 24LC515 combined with the 125 µs sampling period allows for 8.192 seconds of audio to be recorded. Audio data lends itself to *data compression* techniques that can reduce the number of bits stored per sample while retaining a high-quality recording. The *data compression ratio* is the uncompressed data size divided by the compressed data size. Using a technique with a 2:1 data compression ratio would allow us to store twice as much compressed speech as uncompressed speech. There are many high-quality music compression formats, such as MP3 (MPEG-1 Audio Layer 3, one of the first widely uses formats for compressed music files) and AAC (advanced audio coding, used by Apple Computer in its music players), which provide high data compression ratios. However, advanced formats such as these require significant computational resources for both encoding and decoding. We would like to use a method that provides some degree of compression, while allowing for real-time encoding and decoding of the audio data using only the PIC24 µC. In our case, we are concerned with compression techniques suitable for speech, and not music.

A simple data compression method is *differential PCM* (DPCM), in which the difference between consecutive audio samples is recorded. Encoding using DPCM is computationally simplistic, in that the current encoded value $L(n)$ is the difference between the current sample value $X(n)$ and the previous sample value $X(n - 1)$ as shown in Equation 15.13.

$$L(n) = X(n) - X(n - 1) \qquad (15.13)$$

Decoding a DCPM stream is done by Equation 15.14, in which the current encoded value $L(n)$ is added to the previous sample value to get the current sample.

$$X(n) = L(n) + X(n - 1) \qquad (15.14)$$

An initial value of 0 for $X(n - 1)$ is assumed for both encoding and decoding. Using a 4-bit two's complement encoding for $L(n)$ gives a delta range of -16 to 15, with L(n) clipped to the range endpoints when the delta exceeds the range. This yields a 2:1 data compression ratio, but the quality is poor. Increasing the range of L(n) improves the quality but reduces the compression ratio. A better technique is known as *adaptive* DPCM (ADPCM), which dynamically adjusts the delta size based on the previous sample. Our code uses an ADPCM algorithm from Dialogic Corporation that compresses 12-bit signed samples to 4 bit codes and uses look-up tables for very low computational overhead [55]. A version of this algorithm for 16-bit signed samples was published by the Interactive Multimedia Association [55] in 1992. A full discussion of this algorithm is beyond the scope of this book; the interested reader is directed to [57], which is a Microchip application note that discusses the algorithm details and has a C code implementation of IMA-ADPCM encoding and decoding for PIC µCs. Our code is based on the code supplied with the Microchip application note, but modified to use the 12-bit look-up tables of [55]. For encoding, our example uses a utility function named uint8 ADPCMEncoder(int16 i16_sample) that accepts a 12-bit signed sample, i16_sample, and returns a 4-bit code. The decoder utility function is int16 ADPCMDecoder(uint8 u8_code), which accepts a 4-bit code and returns a 12-bit signed sample. Utility functions ADPCMEncoderInit() and ADPCMDecoderInit() are used to initialize the encoder and decoder functions, respectively. The code for these functions is found on the book's accompanying CD-ROM. This compression algorithm allows us to double our audio storage from 8.192 seconds to 16.384 seconds while increasing recording resolution from 8 to 12 bits.

AUDIO APPLICATION ISR AND CONFIGURATION

Figure 15.3 shows global variables and the _T3Interrupt ISR code for the audio record/playback application. Timer3 is configured for a 125 µs periodic interrupt. One-bit flags are used to distinguish between record, playback, and pass-through modes. The ISR reads the current 12-bit ADC value then starts the next conversion. Pass-through mode simply drops the lower 4 bits of the 12-bit ADC code and then writes this 8-bit value to the MAX 548A DAC via the writeDAC() function (code not shown, it is similar to the code provided in Chapter 11 except that only one DAC is updated).

Figure 15.4 shows the isrRecord() function that is called from the Timer3 ISR. When compression is disabled, the 12-bit ADC value is converted to an 8-bit DAC value by dropping the four least significant bits, then the 8-bit value is written to the active ping-pong buffer. When compression is enabled, the 12-bit unsigned ADC value is converted to a 12-bit signed value by subtracting 2048 (one-half the full 12-bit range of 4096). The ADPCMEncoder() function is then used to produce a 4-bit code. Because two 4-bit codes are required to produce one 8-bit value to be written to the ping-pong buffer, the u8_sampleCount variable is used as an even/odd

```
uint8 au8_bufferA[BLKSIZE], au8_bufferB[BLKSIZE];          Ping-pong buffers for
//some one-bit flags                                       record and playback.
typedef struct tagFLAGBITS {
unsigned u1_activeBuffer: 1;        Tracks active ping-pong buffer.
unsigned u1_writeFlag:1;            Set when write buffer is full during recording.
unsigned u1_recordFlag:1;          Set for record mode.
unsigned u1_playbackFlag:1;        Set for playback mode.
unsigned u1_readFlag:1;            Set when read buffer is empty during playback.
unsigned u1_passThruFlag:1;        Set for pass through mode.
unsigned u1_compressionFlag:1;     Set when compression is enabled.
}FLAGBITS;
volatile FLAGBITS flags;

uint8 u8_sampleCount;         Tracks number of samples for current block.
uint8 u8_bufferCount;         Tracks number of codes in buffer for current block.
uint16 u16_adcVal;
uint8 u8_dacVal;             Temporary variables used by _T3Interrupt().
int16 i16_adcval;

void _ISR _T3Interrupt (void) {        Periodic interrupt every 125 µs.
  _T3IF = 0;
  u16_adcVal = ADC1BUF0;
  //start next sample                Read current ADC value, start next conversion.
  SET_SAMP_BIT_ADC1();
  if (flags.u1_recordFlag) isrRecord();          Do record function.
  if (flags.u1_playbackFlag) isrPlayback();      Do playback function.
  if (flags.u1_passThruFlag) {
    u8_dacVal = (u16_adcVal>>4) & 0x00FF;     Do pass through function.
    writeDAC(u8_dacVal);
  }
}
```

FIGURE 15.3 Audio record/playback ISR code.

sample counter. When u8_sampleCount is even, the 4-bit code is stored in the lower 4 bits of the u8_dacVal variable. When u8_sampleCount is odd, the 4-bit code is written to the upper 4 bits of the u8_dacVal variable, which is then stored in the active ping-pong buffer. When a ping-pong buffer is full (u8_bufferCount is equal to 64), the active buffer is swapped and a semaphore is set (u1_writeFlag) to inform the foreground code that a buffer is ready to be written to the EEPROM.

Figure 15.5 shows the isrPlayback() function that is called from the Timer3 ISR. On entry, an 8-bit value is read from the active ping-pong buffer. When compression is disabled, this represents an 8-bit DAC code that is written to the MAX548A DAC. When compression is enabled, a 4-bit code is extracted from the 8-bit buffer value, either from the upper or lower 4 bits as determined by u8_sampleCount. The 4-bit code is then converted to a 12-bit signed ADC code by the ADPCMDecoder() function. The 12-bit signed ADC code is converted to an unsigned 12-bit ADC code by adding 2048, then to an 8-bit DAC code by dropping the lower 4-bits. The 8-bit DAC code is then written to the MAX548A DAC. When a ping-pong

```
void isrRecord() {
 uint8 u8_tmp;
 if (flags.u1_compressionFlag) {                    Compression enabled.
  //convert to signed value
  i16_adcval = u16_adcVal;  }  Convert 12-bit unsigned to 12-bit signed.
  i16_adcval -= 2048;       }
  u8_tmp = ADPCMEncoder( i16_adcval ); ◄── Get 4-bit code.
  if (u8_sampleCount & 0x01)   {
   u8_dacVal = (u8_tmp << 4)| u8_dacVal; ◄── Combine with first 4-bit code
   u8_sampleCount++;                          to form 8-bit buffer value.
   if (flags.u1_activeBuffer) au8_bufferB[u8_bufferCount++] = u8_dacVal;
    else au8_bufferA[u8_bufferCount++] = u8_dacVal;  ◄── Save to buffer.
  } else {
   u8_dacVal   = u8_tmp;  } Even sample count, so first 4-bit code, save it in
   u8_sampleCount++;      } u8_dacVal for combination with the next 4-bit code.
  }
 } else                                      Compression disabled.
 {
  u8_dacVal = (u16_adcVal>>4) & 0x00FF; ◄── Convert 12-bit to 8-bit.
  if (flags.u1_activeBuffer) au8_bufferB[u8_bufferCount++] = u8_dacVal;
   else au8_bufferA[u8_bufferCount++] = u8_dacVal;  ◄── Save to buffer.
 }
 if (u8_bufferCount ==  BLKSIZE){            }  Swap buffers when
  flags.u1_activeBuffer = !flags.u1_activeBuffer; }  ping-pong buffer is full,
  flags.u1_writeFlag = 1;                    }  set semaphore to notify
  u8_bufferCount = 0;                        }  the foreground code.
  u8_sampleCount = 0;                        }
 }
}
```

FIGURE 15.4 C code for isrRecord() function.

```
void isrPlayback() {
 uint8 u8_tmp;                      ◄── Read code from ping-pong buffer.
 if (flags.u1_activeBuffer) u8_tmp = au8_bufferB[u8_bufferCount];
  else u8_tmp = au8_bufferA[u8_bufferCount];    Compression enabled.
 if (flags.u1_compressionFlag) {
  if (u8_sampleCount & 0x01) {
   i16_adcval = ADPCMDecoder(u8_tmp >> 4);   }  Convert 4-bit code
   u8_bufferCount++;                          }  to signed 12-bit ADC code.
  } else {
   i16_adcval = ADPCMDecoder(u8_tmp & 0x0F); }
  }
  i16_adcval += 2048;  ◄── 12-bit signed to 12-bit unsigned
  u16_adcVal = i16_adcval;                    }  12-bit unsigned to 8-bit unsigned
  u8_dacVal = (u16_adcVal>>4) & 0x00FF;       }
  writeDAC(u8_dacVal);      } Write 8-bit code to DAC.
  u8_sampleCount++;
 } else {                                        Compression disabled.
  writeDAC(u8_tmp);    } Write 8-bit code to DAC.
  u8_bufferCount++;    }
 }
 if (u8_bufferCount ==  BLKSIZE){            }  Swap buffers when
  flags.u1_activeBuffer = !flags.u1_activeBuffer; }  ping-pong buffer is empty,
  flags.u1_readFlag = 1;                     }  set semaphore to notify
  u8_bufferCount = 0;                        }  the foreground code.
  u8_sampleCount = 0;                        }
 }
}
```

FIGURE 15.5 C code for isrPlayback() function.

buffer is empty (u8_bufferCount is equal to 64), the active buffer is swapped and a semaphore is set (u1_readFlag) to inform the foreground code that a buffer must be filled from the EEPROM.

The record (doRecord()) and playback (doPlayback()) foreground functions are shown in Figure 15.6. The doRecord() function initializes variables, then waits for a buffer to fill as indicated by the u1_writeFlag semaphore, after which the non-active buffer is written to the EEPROM. When the u16_MemAddr variable

```
void doRecord(uint8 u8_compression) {  ◄── Foreground code for record mode.
 uint16 u16_MemAddr;
 flags.u1_compressionFlag = u8_compression;   ⎫ Initialize variables, call
 if (u8_compression) ADPCMEncoderInit();      ⎬ ADPCMEncoderInit() if
 flags.u1_activeBuffer = 0;                   ⎭ compression is enabled.
 u8_sampleCount = 0; u8_bufferCount = 0;
 u16_MemAddr = 0;  //start at location 0 in memory
 flags.u1_writeFlag = 0; flags.u1_recordFlag = 1;
 do {
  if (flags.u1_writeFlag) reportError("Record overflow");
  while (!flags.u1_writeFlag) doHeartbeat(); ◄── Wait for full buffer.
  flags.u1_writeFlag = 0;                ◄── Write inactive buffer to EEPROM.
  if (flags.u1_activeBuffer)memWriteLC515(EEPROM,u16_MemAddr,au8_bufferA);
  else  memWriteLC515(EEPROM,u16_MemAddr,au8_bufferB);
  u16_MemAddr = u16_MemAddr +64;
  outString("*");                             When u16_MemAddr wraps to
 }while(u16_MemAddr != 0);//end record loop ◄── zero, then EEPROM is full.
 flags.u1_recordFlag = 0; flags.u1_compressionFlag = 0;
 outString("Finished recording\n");
}
void doPlayback(uint8 u8_compression) {  ◄── Foreground code for playback mode.
 uint16 u16_MemAddr;
 flags.u1_compressionFlag = u8_compression;   ⎫ Initialize variables, call
 if (u8_compression) ADPCMDecoderInit();      ⎬ ADPCMDecoderInit() if
 flags.u1_activeBuffer = 0;  flags.u1_readFlag = 0; ⎭ compression is enabled.
 u8_sampleCount = 0;  u8_bufferCount = 0;
 u16_MemAddr = 0; //start at location 0 in memory
 //playback mode          ◄── Fill first buffer for playback.
 memReadLC515(EEPROM,u16_MemAddr,au8_bufferA); //first buffer read
 u16_MemAddr = u16_MemAddr +64;
 flags.u1_playbackFlag = 1; ◄── Start playback.
 while(!isCharReady()) {                   ◄── Fill inactive buffer from EEPROM.
  if (flags.u1_activeBuffer)memReadLC515(EEPROM,u16_MemAddr,au8_bufferA);
  else  memReadLC515(EEPROM,u16_MemAddr,au8_bufferB); // do read
  u16_MemAddr = u16_MemAddr +64;
  if (flags.u1_writeFlag) reportError("Playback underflow");
  while(!flags.u1_readFlag) doHeartbeat(); ◄── Wait for empty buffer.
  flags.u1_readFlag = 0;
  outChar('*');
 }//end while
 inChar();
 outString("\nPlayback terminated.\n");
 flags.u1_playbackFlag = 0; flags.u1_compressionFlag = 0;
}
```

FIGURE 15.6 Foreground code for record and playback.

wraps back to 0, this indicates that 64 Ki bytes have been written to the EEPROM and it is full, so the function returns. The record overflows if the non-active buffer write to the EEPROM does not finish before the active buffer is filled with recorded data by the `isrRecord()` function. After the `doPlayback()` function initializes variables, it reads 64 bytes into the first active buffer and starts playback by setting the `u1_playback` flag. It then enters a loop where it reads blocks of 64 bytes into the non-active buffer as indicated by the `u1_activeBufferFlag`. The `u1_readFlag` semaphore is used as a wait condition in the loop for determining when a buffer is empty and another 64 bytes can be read. The loop exits on any key entered from the console as indicated by the `isCharReady()` flag. The playback function underflows if the non-active buffer is not filled by an EEPROM read before all of the data is read out of the active buffer by the `isrRecord()` function. The functions used for reading and writing to the EEPROM have been previously discussed in Chapter 10.

Figure 15.7 shows the `main()` code for the audio application in addition to the `doSampledPassthru()` function that is the foreground code for the pass-through

```
void doSampledPassthru(void) {
flags.u1_passThruFlag = 1;                        Do pass-through mode
while(!isCharReady()) doHeartbeat();              until character entered from
inChar();                                         the console.
flags.u1_passThruFlag = 0;
outString("\nFeedthru terminated.\n");
}

int main (void) {
  uint8 u8_mode;
  configBasic(HELLO_MSG);
  CONFIG_AN0_AS_ANALOG();
  configADC1_ManualCH0( ADC_CH0_POS_SAMPLEA_AN0, 31, 1 );    Standard
  SET_SAMP_BIT_ADC1();    //start first conversion            configuration,
  configSPI1();                                               see appropriate
  configDAC();                                                reference
  configTimer3();            //125 uS periodic interrupt      chapters.
  configI2C1(400);          //configure I2C for 400 KHz
  while (1) {
   outString("\nEnter 'r' (record), 'p' (playback),
              'f' (sampled feedthru).
              'R', 'P' use compression. Any key terminates: ");
   u8_mode = inCharEcho();
   outString("\n");
   switch (u8_mode) {
     case 'r': doRecord(0); break;          ← Record, uncompressed.
     case 'R': doRecord(1); break;          ← Record, compressed.
     case 'p': doPlayback(0); break;        ← Playback, uncompressed.
     case 'P': doPlayback(1); break;        ← Playback, uncompressed.
     case 'f': doSampledPassthru(); break;  ← Do pass-through mode.
   }
  } //end while(1)
}
```

FIGURE 15.7 `Main()` code for audio application.

mode. The `main()` code does standard initialization and then prompts the user for the operation mode.

Code testing indicated only a small difference in audio quality between compressed and uncompressed modes. The sampling rate can be increased somewhat from the chosen 8 kHz rate, with record mode limiting the sampling rate.

An MP3 to FM Radio Playback System

A more sophisticated audio project is shown in Figure 15.8, which implements a remote unit that accepts streaming audio over Ethernet, decodes it, and rebroadcasts it over a limited range FM transmitter. This allows the use of existing FM receivers in a home for receiving streaming audio from a remote site. This was done as a senior design project by a team at Mississippi State University during the 2008 spring semester [58]. The system uses three *super peripherals* to do the data intensive and computationally intensive portions of the task, with the PIC24 μC (a PIC24FJGA002 with Fcy = 16 MHz) acting as the glue that ties them together. The primary peripherals are:

- **W3100A-LF Wiznet Ethernet controller [59]:** Implements the TCP/IP Ethernet protocol, responsible for all Ethernet communication.
- **VS1011e MP3 Audio Codec [60]:** Responsible for decoding an MP3 stream to two left/right analog channels that connect to the FM transmitter.
- **NS7FM FM Transmitter [61]:** Converts analog input left/right channel to an FM transmission on a user selectable channel in the range of 87.5 to 108 MHz.

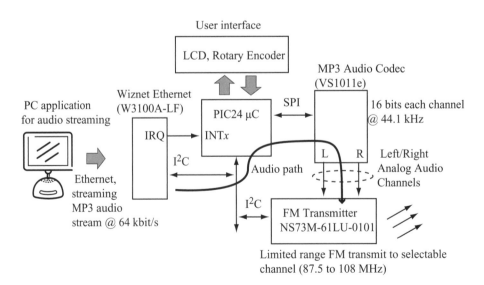

FIGURE 15.8 An MP3 to FM transmitter.

The PIC24 µC reads incoming MP3-encoded data from the network via the I²C port to the Wiznet Ethernet controller and passes this to the MP3 audio codec via the SPI port. The audio codec decodes the MP3 stream to left/right analog outputs that directly drive the FM transmitter. The I²C bus is used to configure the FM transmitter for a particular channel.

Super peripherals are becoming common in complex microcontroller applications, especially in software-intensive, high data rate applications such as MP3 decoding, USB storage devices, wireless network interfaces, and Ethernet interfaces. The super peripheral performs these tasks instead of the microcontroller, simplifying the microcontroller code implementation and allowing a designer to rapidly prototype a solution. A super peripheral generally contains a microcontroller core plus software stack to implement the application dependent interface (e.g., Ethernet, USB) and uses a standard serial interface such as SPI, I²C, or asynchronous serial for communication with the master µC. The USB-to-serial cable from FTDI used for serial communication in Chapter 8 is another example of a super peripheral.

An LCD and rotary encoder for selecting the broadcast frequency implemented the user interface for the system of Figure 15.8. A server application on a PC was responsible for taking high-quality audio files encoded as 128 kbit/s to 320 kbits/s, re-encoding them for a new target data rate such as 64 kbit/s, then streaming them to the remote unit. Testing of the unit in spring 2008 produced successful data streaming to the remote unit at rates of up to 128 kbit/s.

A SOLDER REFLOW OVEN

The next project to be discussed is the conversion of a toaster oven to a *solder reflow* oven. This project is interesting, as it requires AC power control and high temperature measurement, neither of which has been previously discussed. This project was originally done as a senior design project [62] at Mississippi State University using the PIC18F2420 processor and later retargeted by the authors to the PIC24 family. We do not attempt to provide the entire PIC24 µC code implementation for this project because of its length, but instead highlight the power control and temperature monitoring aspects of the project and the end results.

SOLDER REFLOW BACKGROUND

A *solder reflow* oven is used for soldering surface mount components to a printed circuit board (PCB). We discuss solder reflow primarily from a hobbyist perspective in this section and not from a production line viewpoint. To use solder reflow, one must first apply *solder paste* to the individual pads of the PCB surface mount *footprints*. Solder paste is a type of solder with a cream-like consistency at room temperature, but flows when heated to its *wetting* temperature. A fine-tipped syringe can be used for depositing solder paste on pads, but requires careful attention to each footprint. If one has several boards to populate, then a PCB *stencil* can be purchased from the PCB vendor or a specialty shop and is created using the Gerber files for the PCB. The stencil is a thin plastic sheet (or a thin metal sheet) with openings for all of the surface mount pads. After placing the stencil on the PCB, wiping solder paste over the entire stencil applies paste to all pads simultaneously; removing the stencil lifts off the excess paste, leaving only the pads covered with solder paste. After the paste has been applied, the components are then placed on the board with the paste helping to hold the components in place. After component placement, the solder is heated until it flows from the pads onto the component leads; cooling the board then creates a solder joint between component lead and pad. It is important that the PCB contain a *solder mask,* which is a protective layer on the PCB that helps to prevent bridges between solder pads when the solder is in the liquid state. To heat the solder, a hot-air blower can be used but one must to careful that the airflow does not move the components. Other hobbyist methods for performing solder reflow use either a toaster oven or a hot plate. Commercial reflow ovens use a conveyor belt for moving boards through different heating zones in order to heat the solder in a controlled manner. A *solder reflow profile* specifies temperature over time for the reflow process, and Microchip application note AN233 [63] gives solder profiles for both lead-free and mixed tin (63%)/lead (37%) solder paste types. A typical tin/lead mix profile from AN233 is shown in Figure 15.9. The duration and temperatures of the four heating

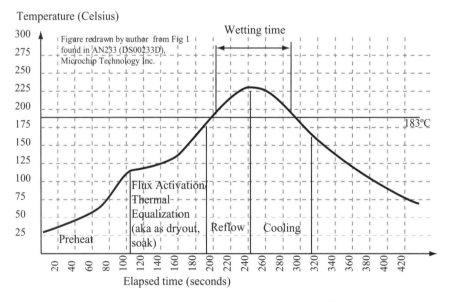

FIGURE 15.9 Typical tin/lead reflow profile (Adapted with permission of the copyright owner, Microchip Technology Inc. All rights reserved. No further reprints or reproduction may be made without Microchip Inc.'s prior written consent).

zones of preheat, soak, reflow, and cooling vary depending on component mix and solder type. The *wetting time* is the amount of time that the solder stays in the liquid state and has a recommended duration of 60 to 150 seconds.

HIGH TEMPERATURE SENSING

Using a toaster oven as a reflow oven requires high temperature sensing. The temperature sensors used in previous chapters are not suited for this task because of the high temperatures involved and also because of the need for a remote measurement that is taken in the oven chamber and transmitted back to the PCB control unit. A *thermocouple* is a temperature sensor made from two dissimilar metals, which produces a voltage when heated or cooled. Different metals are used for different temperature ranges, with letters such as J, K, T, and so on used for different thermocouple types. The advantages of thermocouples are that they have a wide temperature range and are available in different wiring lengths with heat-resistant sheathing for remote monitoring in high-temperature environments. A type K thermocouple (nickel-chromium plus nickel-aluminum) from Omega Engineering, Inc (www.omega.com) has a range of $-200°C$ to $1250°C$ with an error of about $\pm 1°C$ for our range of interest. A design challenge with thermocouples is that the voltage output is small ($41\ \mu V/°C$), so external amplification of the thermocouple voltage is needed. Fortunately, the Maxim 6675 [64] thermocouple-to-digital converter provides a convenient digital interface to a type K thermocouple. It contains conditioning circuitry and a 12-bit ADC that provides a 10.2 fixed-point Celsius temperature in the range of 0 to $1024°C$ to a host μC via a SPI connection.

AC POWER CONTROL

AC power adjustment to the oven's heating elements is required for temperature control. This design uses an integrated circuit known as a *triac* for AC power control. To understand triac operation, first recall that a diode allows current flow in one direction only. A *silicon controlled rectifier* (SCR) is a diode with an extra terminal called the *gate* that can be used to enable current flow through the device. A triac is essentially two SCRs tied back-to-back with a common gate as shown in Figure 15.10. When terminal A1 is at a higher potential than terminal A2, then a pulse of gate current (gate threshold current) turns on current flow in the triac from terminal A1 to A2. Once current is flowing in the triac the gate current is no longer required, and current continues flowing until it falls below the holding current (I_H). Similarly, current flow can be enabled in the opposite direction (A2 to A1) if A2 is at higher potential than A1 and the gate threshold current is exceeded. For an AC waveform this means that once conduction is triggered in a triac the conduction halts at the next zero crossing when the current flow drops below I_H. To keep current flowing through the triac for an AC current waveform one must either pulse the gate at each zero

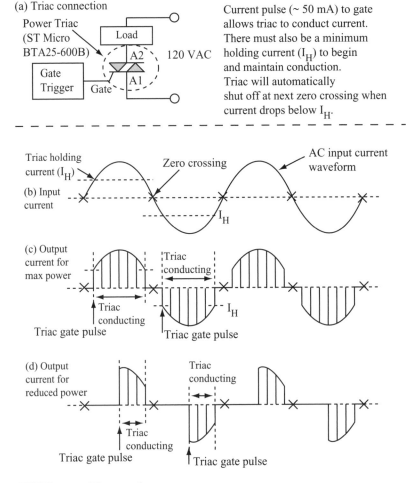

(a) Triac connection

Power Triac
(ST Micro
BTA25-600B)

Load

Gate Trigger

Gate

A2
A1

120 VAC

Current pulse (~ 50 mA) to gate allows triac to conduct current. There must also be a minimum holding current (I_H) to begin and maintain conduction. Triac will automatically shut off at next zero crossing when current drops below I_H.

Triac holding current (I_H)

Zero crossing

AC input current waveform

(b) Input current

I_H

(c) Output current for max power

Triac conducting

Triac conducting

I_H

Triac gate pulse

Triac gate pulse

(d) Output current for reduced power

Triac conducting

Triac conducting

Triac gate pulse

Triac gate pulse

FIGURE 15.10   Triac operation.

crossing or supply continuous gate current. A triggering circuit is responsible for triac gate control. Figure 15.10b shows an AC current input waveform while Figure 15.10c shows the output current waveform assuming the triac is triggered when the input current exceeds I_H. Note that a portion of the input current about the zero crossing that is less than I_H is not delivered to the load. Current delivered to the load can be reduced by delaying the triac triggering further into the half-cycle as shown in Figure 15.10d. This technique is often used in μC-based light dimmers and is also suited for regulating power to the heating elements within the oven. A power triac such as the STMicroelectronics BTA25-600B can handle currents up to 25 A with proper heat sinking.

REFLOW OVEN CONTROL IMPLEMENTATION

The schematic for the temperature control of the reflow oven using the PIC24 µC is shown in Figure 15.11. A MOC3011M optoisolator triac driver is used to provide the needed power triac gate current. The MOC3011M has an internal infrared LED that is optically coupled to the gate of an internal triac whose terminals are labeled as MT1 and MT2. The optical isolation is important as this helps to protect the control circuitry from the 120 VAC of the load. The MOC3011M's infrared LED requires approximately 10 mA to turn on and drop 1.2 V in this condition. This is provided by the 165 Ω pull-up resistor to 3.3 V when the N MOSFET is turned on, which occurs when its gate voltage exceeds its threshold voltage (a typical value of 2.1 V from its datasheet). The output compare module (OC1) of the PIC24 µC is used

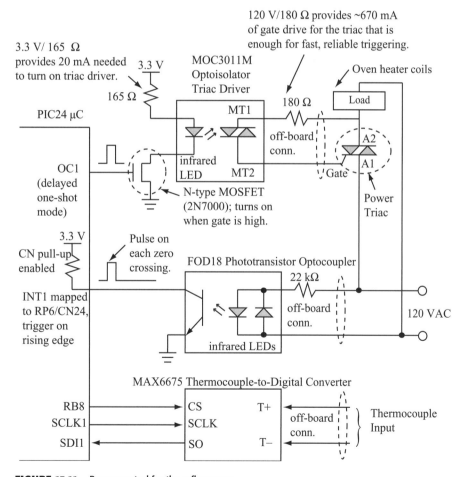

FIGURE 15.11   Power control for the reflow oven.

in a delayed one-shot mode on each zero crossing to provide a pulse to turn on the N MOSFET, which enables the MOC3011M's infrared LED, turning on the internal triac. The MOC3011M's internal triac supplies approximately 670 mA (120 VAC/180 Ω) to the power triac's gate which is enough current to ensure reliable, fast triggering of the power triac. The FOD18 phototransistor optocoupler is used to detect each zero crossing of the 120 VAC waveform. The FOD18 contains two internal infrared LEDs connected in a back-to-back configuration to drive a light-activated BJT switch, which means that they are only off when the 120 VAC input signal is near zero. This means that the FOD18's light-activated switch is open only during zero crossings. The FOD18 switch output is connected to the RP6/CN24 input of the PIC24 μC, with the internal pull-up enabled. In this configuration, each zero crossing produces a short high-true pulse on RP6. The INT1 interrupt input is mapped to the RP6 input and configured for a rising-edge trigger, providing an interrupt on each zero crossing. Oven temperature is monitored via the MAX6675 thermocouple-to-digital converter as mentioned in the previous section. Note that the MOC3011M and FOD18 provide complete optical isolation of the control PCB from the 120 VAC of the load (there is no electrical connection as photons are used for linking the control PCB with the 120 VAC load). This electrical isolation is especially important during prototyping when a wiring mistake could expose the digital control circuitry to 120 VAC, which would almost certainly cause destructive failure! More importantly, this helps to negate the shock hazard to yourself.

Figure 15.12 shows how the output compare module in delayed one-shot mode is used to generate the triac trigger pulse. A 60-Hz half-cycle is approximately 8333 μs

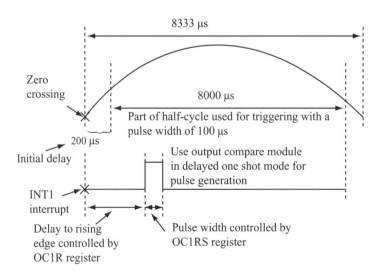

FIGURE 15.12   Use of the output compare module for triac triggering.

in length (1/120). The first 200 µs of the half-cycle are reserved to give time for sufficient holding current to be present; this time is dependent on the load characteristics and was determined experimentally for this application. A pulse width of 100 µs is used for the triac gate pulse, again determined experimentally. This leaves 8033 µs for positioning the leading edge of the pulse width within the half-cycle for power control (our code used a conservative value of 8000 µs). The time delay to the rising edge of the gate pulse is controlled by the OC1R register, while the time delay to the falling edge is specified by the OC1RS register. These registers are written during the INT1 ISR.

Figure 15.13 shows the *C* code implementation for the triac triggering. The `configTriacControl()` function calls the configuration functions for Timer2 and Output Compare1. It also initializes variables `u16_halfCycleTicks`, `u16_triacPWHighTicks`, and `u16_cycleOffsetTicks` to the tick values equivalent to the microsecond times defined by the `TRIAC_PW_HIGH`, `HALF_CYCLE`, and `CYCLE_OFFSET` macros. These macros define the timings previously discussed in Figure 15.12. Timer2 is configured for a prescale of 8 (0.2 µs per tick at FOSC = 40 MHz) and a maximum period register (13.1 ms period at FOSC = 40 MHz) as it is used by the output compare module for pulse generation. The `u8_currPowerSetting` variable ranges from 0 (off) to 100 (highest power) and represents the desired power setting for the oven. The `TRIAC_ON()` function is called by `_INT1Interrupt()` ISR on each zero crossing to generate the triac pulse for power control. The `TRIAC_ON()` function in Figure 15.13 uses the `u8_currPowerSetting`, `u16_halfCycleTicks`, `u16_triacPWHighTicks`, and `u16_cycleOffsetTicks` variables in statements (a) through (e) to compute the OC1R, OC1RS values required for generating a pulse positioned within the half-cycle as discussed in Figure 15.12. Variable `u32_x` is a temporary 32-bit integer used for holding intermediate calculations and statement (a) copies `u16_halfCycleTicks` (the number of timer ticks in the portion of the AC half-cycle used for power control) to `u32_x` so that all computations are done with a 32-bit range. Statement (b) translates the power setting (higher values result in higher AC current) to a value between 0 and `u16_halfCycleTicks`. However, because longer delays into the half-cycle produces less current, and hence less power, the value computed in (b) must be subtracted from `u16_halfCycleTicks` in statement (c) in order to get this inverse power-to-tick delay relationship. Statement (d) computes the final tick delay used for the leading edge of the pulse by adding in the initial delay from the zero crossing (the initial delay in ticks is stored in `u16_cycleOffsetTicks`). Statement (e) computes the tick value for the falling pulse edge by adding the pulse width in ticks (`u16_triacPWHighTicks`) to the value computed in (d).

The code for reading a thermocouple temperature from the MAX6675 is shown in Figure 15.14. The SPI port on the MAX6675 returns a 16-bit value with bits 14 to 3 representing a 10.2 Celsius temperature, with the lower 3 bits used for

```
#define TRIAC_PW_HIGH  100   //triac gate pulse width (us)
#define HALF_CYCLE 8000      // part of half-cycle for triggering (us)
#define CYCLE_OFFSET 200     //delay from zero crossing for pulse (us)
uint8 u8_currPowerSetting;   // 0 to 100
uint16 u16_halfCycleTicks, u16_triacPWHighTicks,u16_cycleOffsetTicks;
#define MAX_POWER_SETTING 100  //power settings from 0 to 100

static inline void TRIAC_ON() {  ◄─── Generates gate pulse for the triac.
 uint32 u32_x;
 T2CONbits.TON = 0;      //disable Timer when configuring Output compare
 TMR2 = 0;              //clear timer 2
 //later in the cycle is less power  Compute ticks for rising/falling pulse edges.
 u32_x = u16_halfCycleTicks;  ◄──────────────────────────────(a) Power
 u32_x = (u32_x * u8_currPowerSetting)/MAX_POWER_SETTING; ◄──(b)  to
 u32_x = u16_halfCycleTicks - u32_x;  ◄─────────────────────(c)   ticks
 OC1R  = u32_x+u16_cycleOffsetTicks;  ◄─────────────────(d) rising edge
 OC1RS = u32_x+u16_triacPWHighTicks+u16_cycleOffsetTicks;◄──(e) falling edge
 OC1CON = OC_TIMER2_SRC |     //Timer2 source   } Must write OC1CON
          OC_SINGLE_PULSE;    //delayed one-shot } to generate pulse.
 T2CONbits.TON = 1;           //enable the timer
 }

//occurs at a 120 Hz rate, interrupted every time AC waveform crosses 0
void _ISRFAST _INT1Interrupt (void) {
  _INT1IF = 0;    //clear the interrupt bit
  if (u8_currPowerSetting) TRIAC_ON();  //turn on triac
} //end _INT1Interrupt

void configOutputCapture1(void) {
  T2CONbits.TON = 0;        //disable Timer when configuring Output compare
  TMR2 = 0;                //clear timer 2
  CONFIG_OC1_TO_RP(14);    //map OC1 to RP14/RB14
  OC1R = 1;
  OC1RS = 2;                //dummy pulse, just want to leave OC1 low
  OC1CON = OC_TIMER2_SRC |   //Timer2 source
           OC_SINGLE_PULSE;  //delayed one shot
  T2CONbits.TON = 1;         //enable the timer
}
                              Configure all peripherals involved in
void configureTriacControl() {  the triac control.
  configTimer2();    //OC1 uses this, max period, no interrupt, PRE = 8
  configOutputCapture1();
  u16_halfCycleTicks = usToU16Ticks(HALF_CYCLE,getTimerPrescale(T2CONbits));
  u16_triacPWHighTicks = usToU16Ticks(TRIAC_PW_HIGH,
                                   getTimerPrescale(T2CONbits));
  u16_cycleOffsetTicks = usToU16Ticks(CYCLE_OFFSET,
                                   getTimerPrescale(T2CONbits));
}
```

FIGURE 15.13   *C code implementation for triac triggering.*

status information (bit 15 is always zero). The `configSPI1()` function configures the PIC24 SPI port for 16-bit mode and maps the SCLK1 and SDI1 pins to ports RP7 and RP5. The `readMAX6675()` function writes dummy data to the SPI port in order to return the 16-bit output value from the MAX6675. The `getCelsiusFloatTemp()` function converts the MAX6675 16-bit output value to a floating-point Celsius

```
void configSPI1(void) {  ◄──── Configured for 16-bit mode.
  //spi clock = 40MHz/1*64 = 40MHz/64 = 625 kHz
  SPI1CON1 = SEC_PRESCAL_1_1 |       //1:1 secondary prescale
             PRI_PRESCAL_64_1 |      //64:1 primary prescale
             CLK_POL_ACTIVE_HIGH  | //clock active high (CKP = 0)
             SPI_CKE_OFF          | //out changes inactive to active (CKE=0)
             SPI_MODE16_ON        | //16-bit mode
             MASTER_ENABLE_ON;      //master mode
  //Only need SDI, SCLK since Thermocouple sensor is output only
  CONFIG_SCK1OUT_TO_RP(7);    //use RP7 for SCLK
  CONFIG_SDI1_TO_RP(5);       //use RP5 for SDI
  CONFIG_SLAVE_ENABLE();      //chip select
  SLAVE_DISABLE();            //disable the chip select
  SPI1STATbits.SPIEN = 1;     //enable SPI mode
}

uint16 readMAX6675(void) {
 uint16 u16_x;                      Read a 16-bit value back from the MAX6675.
  SLAVE_ENABLE();
  u16_x = ioMasterSPI1(0);
  SLAVE_DISABLE();
  return(u16_x);
}
```

15 14	3 2 0
0 10.2 Celsius Temperature	status

```
float getCelsiusFloatTemp(void) { ◄──── Read MAX6675, return Celsius temperature
  uint16 u16_x;                            as a float value.
  float f_tempC;
  u16_x = readMAX6675();
  u16_x = u16_x >> 3;      //drop status bits
  f_tempC = u16_x;         //convert to float
  f_tempC = f_tempC/4;     //10.2 format, divide by 4
  return(f_tempC);
}

//Round to nearest degree
int16 getCelsiusI16Temp(void) { ◄──── Read MAX6675, return Celsius temperature
  uint16 u16_x;                          as a 16-bit integer rounded to nearest degree.
  uint16 u16_frac;

  u16_x = readMAX6675();
  u16_frac = (u16_x & 0x1F) >> 3; //mask integer, drop status bits
  u16_x = u16_x >> 5;
  if (u16_frac >= 2) u16_x++; //round up
  return((int16) u16_x);
}
```

FIGURE 15.14   *C code for reading the thermocouple temperature.*

temperature, while getCelsiusI16Temp() converts the MAX6675 16-bit output value to an integer Celsius temperature rounded to the nearest degree.

The doRampUp() function in Figure 15.15 is used during oven operation to reach a target temperature (i16_targetTemp in Celsius) and hold it there until a target time (u16_targetTime in seconds) is reached. Timer3 generates a 0.1 second period interrupt that is used to increment the u16_tenthSeconds variable for coarse timekeeping. The updateStats() function reads the current oven temperature and

```
int16 updateStats(void) {          Keep maximum temperature, wetting time statistics;
  int16 i16_tempC;                 returns the current oven temperature.
  i16_tempC = getCelsiusI16Temp();
  if (i16_tempC > i16_maxTemp) i16_maxTemp  = i16_tempC;
  if (i16_tempC > profiles[u8_currentProfile].i16_wetTemp &&
      u16_startWetting == 0) u16_startWetting = u16_tenthSeconds;
  if (coolingFlag && (i16_tempC < profiles[u8_currentProfile].i16_wetTemp)
      && u16_endWetting == 0)
    u16_endWetting = u16_tenthSeconds;
  return(i16_tempC);               Increase temperature i16_targetTemp to and hold it until
}                                  u16_targetTime is reached.

void doRampUp(int16 i16_targetTemp, uint16 u16_targetTime) {
  int16 i16_tempC, i16_lastTemp;
  uint8  u8_endPower;              Incremented by Timer3 interrupt at 0.1 second intervals
  uint16 u16_endTime;             for coarse timekeeping.

  u16_endTime =  u16_tenthSeconds + u16_targetTime*10;  //end time
  i16_tempC = updateStats();  //get current temp; Return power setting for this
  u8_endPower = tempToPower(i16_targetTemp);     temperature.
  setPower(100);   //need to heat this up
  do {        Loops that heats at maximum power      Print time, temp. for
    i16_tempC = updateStats(); //get current temp;    profile tracking.
    printf("Current temp/time: %u %u Power: %u\n",i16_tempC,
            u16_tenthSeconds, getPower());
    DELAY_MS(1000);                                 Exit this loop when target
    if (u16_tenthSeconds > u16_endTime) return;     temperature is neared.
  }while ((i16_targetTemp - i16_tempC) > 10 );
  setPower(30); // near target temp
  i16_lastTemp = i16_tempC;
  do {         Loops that attempts to maintain temperature at target.
    DELAY_MS(1000);
    i16_tempC = updateStats();
     printf("Current temp/time: %u %u Power: %u\n",i16_tempC,
            u16_tenthSeconds, getPower());
    if ((i16_tempC < i16_lastTemp) && (i16_tempC < i16_targetTemp ) ) {
        //temp is decreasing            Have fallen below target temperature and
        setPower(u8_endPower);          are decreasing, set power back to level
      } else                            appropriate for this target temperature.
        setPower(30);
    i16_lastTemp = i16_tempC;          Have reached or exceeded target
  }                                    temperature, reduce power.
  while (u16_tenthSeconds < u16_endTime);
}                                      Exit function once the target time has been
                                       reached.
```

FIGURE 15.15   *C* code for reaching a target temperature.

keeps global profile statistics such as maximum temperature and total wetting time. The doRampUp() function contains two loops; the first loop heats the oven at maximum power until the target temperature is reached while the second loop attempts to hold it at that temperature. The tempToPower(i16_targetTemp) function (code not shown) converts a target temperature to a power setting that is then stored in the u8_endPower variable. The power-to-temperature relationship is kept in a lookup table that is generated during a calibration mode where oven temperature is recorded at each power setting and then written to program memory using the flash write functions discussed in Chapter 13. This power setting for a target temperature is only an estimate, as oven temperature actually depends on the length of time spent at a particular power setting. The oven's thermal response is slow, so heating in the first loop is done at maximum power until the temperature is within 10°C of the target temperature. When the first loop is exited, the power is adjusted to a lower setting in order to slow heating for reducing target temperature overshoot. The second loop reads oven temperature each second and compares the current temperature with the previous temperature. If the temperature is falling and is below the target temperature then the power setting is adjusted to the value stored in u8_endPower for increased heating; otherwise, the lower power setting is maintained for decreased heating. The second loop (and function) is exited once the target time of u16_targetTime is reached.

Table 15.2 summarizes the PIC24 µC resources used by the reflow oven application. The remaining code for the reflow oven is not shown because of its length, but is contained on the book's CD-ROM.

A Black & Decker toaster oven (Model TRO700S, 1350 W, $70) was used as the target oven. The 1350 W (W = watts, 1 W = 1 V × 1 A) value means that we can

TABLE 15.2 PIC24 µC Resources used for reflow oven application.

PIC24 µC Resource	Comment
Timer3	Used for a 0.1 second periodic interrupt for coarse timekeeping.
INT1 (pin RP6)	Used as a rising edge interrupt source for the zero crossing input.
Output Compare OC1	Used in delayed one-shot mode to generate trigger pulse for the triac.
Timer2	Used as the timer for the output compare module.
SPI 16-bit Master mode, pins SCLK1, SDI1, and RB8	Used for interfacing to the MAX6675 thermocouple-to-digital converter.
Flash memory	Used for storage of oven temperature versus power-setting calibration data; the oven software supports a mode for capturing and saving this data to flash memory.
UART	The serial port is used as the user interface for oven operation.

expect the oven to draw a maximum current of 1350 W/120 V = 11.25 A, so the 25 A power triac referred to in Figure 15.10 is adequate for this task. Figure 15.16 shows the wiring modifications to the oven for this project. The oven contains four heating elements, two on top and two on bottom, with the top elements turned on for toast mode and all elements enabled for bake mode. The oven was rewired so that the Toast/Bake switch now functions as an ON (Toast)/OFF (Bake) switch, with all heating elements turned on. The triac was placed in series with the heating elements, with the toast timer and temperature elements removed from this path. The oven has a convection fan for improved temperature consistency throughout the oven chamber, which was rewired to be always on when power is applied. A door switch removes AC power when the door is open.

The PCB for the oven control is shown Figure 15.17a. A PIC24HJ64GP202 µC was used instead of a PIC24HJ32GP202 because of its increased program memory size, which was required given the finished code length and the oven calibration data

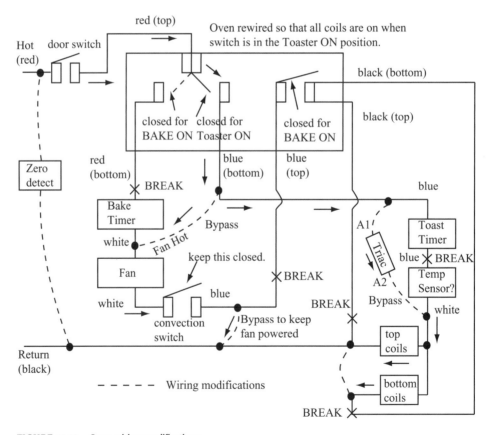

FIGURE 15.16 Oven wiring modifications.

(a) PCB for oven control

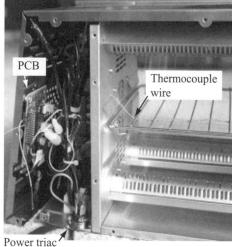

(b) Back view of oven

FIGURE 15.17 Oven photos.

stored in program memory. The 6-pin connecter on the bottom edge of the board is the USB-to-serial connector, which also provides power to the PCB, while the 6-pin connector on the left edge is the ICSP connector. The serial console is used as the interface to the oven control program. The three 3-pin headers on the right board edge from top-to-bottom order are the power triac gate connector, thermocouple input, and AC power input for zero detection. The board was mounted on the oven side as shown in the Figure 15.17b, in a control compartment that contained the convection fan. The off-board power triac was mounted flush to the oven's bottom in the same control compartment near the entry point for the AC power. The flush mounting to the metal case for the power triac helped with triac heat dissipation, but this was a compromise mounting as all metal surfaces on this oven become hot when the oven is in operation. A small hole was drilled in the oven side and used for the thermocouple wire that was attached to an oven rack. The holes visible on the left side of the oven's interior are the ventilation holes for the convection fan.

Figure 15.18 gives temperature versus time data for oven operation using a tin/lead mix profile. The target temperatures for preheat, dryout, and reflow phases were 100°C, 150°C, and 230°C, respectively. The target times were 100 seconds for preheat, 100 seconds for dryout (removes moisture), 90 seconds to reach the target reflow temperature of 230°C, and 20 seconds hold time at that temperature. The preheat temperature target was overshot by 13°C, but the other temperature targets

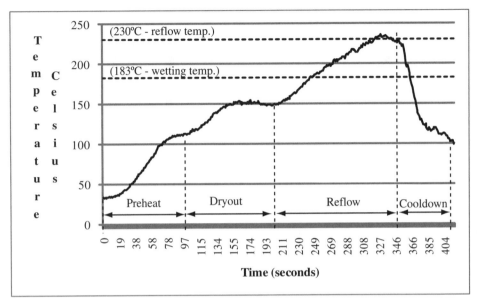

Measured wetting time (temperature > 183°C): 117 seconds
Measured hold time at reflow temperature (temperature ~= 230°C): 20 seconds
Target prehead temperaure: 100°C (actual 113°C, +13 overshoot)
Target dryout temperature: 150°C (actual 154°C, +4 overshoot)
Target reflow temperature: 230°C (actual 236°C, +6 overshoot)

FIGURE 15.18   Profile data.

were met with less than 6°C overshoot. The preheat and dryout times were met, but
it took 120 seconds to reach 230°C after the dryout phase ended. This particular
oven is poor at cooling, with a very slow cool-down if the door is left closed and a
rapid cooling as shown if the door is opened. Given this, the user is prompted to
open the door for cooling once the target hold time at the reflow temperature has
been reached (in this case, after 20 seconds at 230°C). This oven is slow to reach the
reflow temperature once the dryout phase had ended, so an oven with more wattage
than the model used in this example would be desirable for a future version. The end
result is roughly comparable in form to the temperature profile given in Figure 15.9
and limited testing on small PCBs indicated that solder joints were formed by oven
operation. For an approximate cost of $150 (oven plus PCB cost), this reflow oven
can prove useful to the hobbyist who has to deal with hard-to-solder surface mount
components. The AC power and temperature monitoring techniques discussed in
this project are useful in a variety of other applications.

A SMALL, AUTONOMOUS ROBOT

Small, autonomous robots have become popular as a means for stimulating interest in embedded systems. Many regional IEEE student design contests feature autonomous robots as the design target. Small, autonomous robots also make for good demonstrations to high school students during engineering recruiting drives. Figure 15.19 gives the schematic of a wheeled robot design that can be manually driven via an IR remote control or function autonomously using an IR proximity sensor to detect forward obstructions. The design is implemented on a general-purpose PCB created by the authors that was used to test many of this book's examples, including the audio application previously discussed in this chapter.

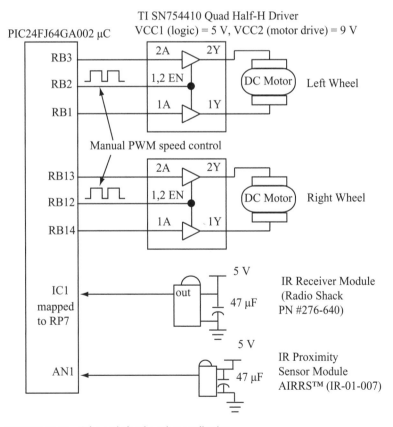

FIGURE 15.19 Schematic for the robot application.

A PIC24FJ64GA002 µC was used instead of a PIC24HJGP202 because of its lower power consumption in this battery-operated application.

The design assumes a three-wheeled chassis with left and right wheels and a back pivot wheel. The IR receiver discussed previously in Chapter 12 is used for sending commands to the robot in manual drive mode. The infrared proximity sensor in Figure 15.19 outputs a voltage that is ~1 V when no obstruction is present and increases to ~3 V when an obstruction is placed directly in front of it. The PIC24 ADC is used to sample this sensor input to determine if there is an obstruction in front of the robot during autonomous drive mode. Pulse width modulation is used to control the speed of the separate DC motors that drive the left and right wheels. Individual speed control of each wheel is needed, as a turn is accomplished by slowing one wheel while maintaining the speed of the other. A left turn, for example, is accomplished by slowing the left wheel. The automated PWM mode of the PIC24 µC was not used by choice, as DC motor wheel drive does not require the high precision pulse width control offered by the PIC24 output compare modules. This leaves the output compare modules free in the event the robot design is expanded to include other features. Instead, manual PWM is implemented on port pins RB2 and RB12 via a periodic interrupt and variables for tracking the period and duty cycle of each PWM signal. This approach produces a coarse-grained PWM, but it is sufficient for this application.

Figure 15.20 shows the general-purpose experiment PCB mounted on a three-wheeled chassis built from a Lego Mindstorms™ robot kit. The 9 V battery pack within the controller module of the Mindstorms kit is used as the power source for the PIC24 board, which contains onboard 3.3 V and 5 V voltage regulators. The IR distance sensor is mounted on the front for obstacle detection.

Table 15.3 gives the PIC24 µC resources used for the robot application. Timer3 generates a periodic interrupt that is used to update the PWM outputs for the two wheels and to sample the ADC that is connected to the IR proximity sensor output. The IR receiver output is decoded using Timer2 and the input capture module for pulse width measurement in exactly the same manner as discussed in Chapter 12. The UART was used during debugging of the application.

Figure 15.21 shows the primary variables/functions used for the robot application (the variables and functions used in decoding the IR output are not shown; see Chapter 12). Refer to these variables and functions as the code for the robot application is discussed in the remaining figures of this section.

Figure 15.22 shows the `main()` and `autoDrive()` functions for the robot application. The initialization code configures the PIC24 µC subsystems per the usage given in Table 15.3. The `while(1){}` loop of `main()` processes an IR command if one is available, allowing the user to always override robot behavior via the remote control. If the robot is in auto drive mode as indicated by the `flags.u1_mode` variable, then the `autoDrive()` function is called to perform obstacle avoidance. Within the `autoDrive()` function, the `flags.u1_obstacle` flag, which is set by the Timer3 ISR,

General-purpose
experiment PCB

IR receiver

Left/Right wheel
control

9 V Battery pack

IR distance
sensor

FIGURE 15.20   Robot electronics mounted on a three-wheel chassis.

TABLE 15.3   PIC24 µC Resources used for robot application.

PIC24 µC Resource	Comment
RB2/RB12	Manual PWM outputs for left/right wheel speed control.
RB3/RB1	Direction control for left wheel.
RB13/RB14	Direction control for right wheel.
Timer3	Used for a 500 µs periodic interrupt for manual PWM generation.
Input Capture (IC1)	Input capture used for pulse width measurement in decoding IR biphase input stream.
Timer2	Used as timer base for input capture (IC1).
ADC (AN1)	Used to read the IR proximity sensor output; 10-bit conversion because a PIC24F µC is used.
UART	Used for debugging output during development.

Variable(s)	Comment
`u8_leftDC, u8_rightDC`	Duty cycle for left/right wheel PWM
`u8_leftPeriod,` `u8_rightPeriod`	Period counters for left/right wheel PWM
`u16_adcVal`	ADC sampled value
`u1_mode`	1-bit flag for manual or auto drive mode
`u1_obstacle`	1-bit flag for obstacle present
`u1_irCmdFlag`	1-bit flag for handling duplicate IR transmissions
Primary Functions	**Comment**
`_T3Interrupt()`	Handles updating of wheel PWM signals and reading the ADC value that is placed in `u16_adcVal`
`configWheels()`	Configure all ports for wheel control and also Timer3
`doSpeedUp(uint8 u8_speed)`	Speed up to target speed (`u8_speed`)
`allStop()`	Slow to stop
`goForward(uint8 u8_speed)`	Set wheel direction forward, do speed up to target speed (`u8_speed`)
`goReverse(uint8 u8_speed)`	Set wheel direction reverse, do speed up to target speed (`u8_speed`)
`doTurn(uint8 u8_ltarg,` `uint8 u8_rtarg)`	Do turn with `u8_ltarg`, `u8_rtarg` as target left, right wheel speeds
`autoDrive()`	Check for obstacle, if present then stop, back up and go forward with a turn to avoid the obstacle
`checkIR(void)`	If IR command is available, read and process it
`getIRCMD(void)`	Return IR command from software FIFO
`processCmd(u8_cmd)`	Process IR command

FIGURE 15.21   Variables/functions for robot application.

is checked. If an obstacle is present, the robot stops, backs up while turning, then goes forward while turning an additional amount to avoid the obstacle. Turns are accomplished by having one wheel speed lower than the other wheel. After the turn is finished both wheels are set to the same speed for straight-ahead movement. If an obstacle is not detected, then the wheel speeds are checked. If they are not both equal to the default speed, as happens when a mode change is performed, then both are set to the forward direction and the default speed in order to perform straight-ahead motion.

Figure 15.23 shows the Timer3 ISR interrupt service routine that is responsible for updating the PWM outputs and sampling the ADC input. Timer3 is configured as a 500 μs periodic interrupt. The `u8_leftPeriod` and `u8_rightPeriod` variables track the period of the square waves used for PWM of the left/right wheels. When these

```
void autoDrive(void) {
  if (flags.u1_obstacle) {          Obstacle flag set in Timer3 ISR
    allStop();
    //backup, pivot
    WHEEL_LEFT_REVERSE(); WHEEL_RIGHT_REVERSE();    Stop, reverse wheels,
    doSpeedUp(BACK_SPEED);                          back straight up
    DELAY_MS(300);
    u8_leftDC = 2;  //slow down wheel to turn        Slow one wheel to
    DELAY_MS(800);  //turning                        turn
    allStop();
    DELAY_MS(200);
    WHEEL_LEFT_FORWARD(); WHEEL_RIGHT_FORWARD();    Set wheels to forward,
    doTurn(BACK_SPEED,2);                           go forward while turning
    DELAY_MS(600);                                  Speed up both wheels to
    doSpeedUp(DEFAULT_SPEED);                        same speed to go straight
  }                                                 ahead
  else if (u8_leftDC != DEFAULT_SPEED ||
           u8_rightDC != DEFAULT_SPEED ) {          No obstacle, so ensure that
    WHEEL_LEFT_FORWARD(); WHEEL_RIGHT_FORWARD();    robot is moving straight
    doSpeedUp(DEFAULT_SPEED);                        ahead at the default speed
  }
}

int main (void) {
  configBasic(HELLO_MSG);
  CONFIG_AN1_AS_ANALOG();
  configADC1_ManualCH0( ADC_CH0_POS_SAMPLEA_AN1, 31, 1 );    Configure
  SET_SAMP_BIT_ADC1();    //start first conversion            subsystems
  configTimer2();
  configInputCapture1();
  configWheels();
  while (1) {
    checkIR();          Process IR command if one is available
    if (flags.u1_mode == AUTO_DRIVE) autoDrive();      Perform autonomous drive
    doHeartbeat();                                     if mode flag is set
  } //end while(1)
}
```

FIGURE 15.22   `main()` and `autoDrive()` functions for the robot application.

counter values are equal to WHEEL_PWM_STEPS (a value of 10), the period is finished and these counters are reset. This gives a PWM period of 5000 µs (a frequency of 200 Hz). The u8_leftDC and u8_rightDC variables control the high pulse width of the PWM waveforms. When the period counter is equal to the duty cycle counter (u8_leftPeriod == u8_leftDC or u8_rightPeriod == u8_rightDC), the PWM output is set to zero. At the beginning of a period, the PWM output is set high unless the duty cycle count is zero. Increasing the high pulse width of the PWM waveform (higher values of u8_leftDC/u8_rightDC) increases wheel speed. The ISR also reads the currently available ADC value and sets or clears the flags.u1_obstacle flag based on the BLOCKAGE_PRESENT, BLOCKAGE_CLEAR values, which are 10-bit ADC codes using a 3.3 V voltage reference. The obstacle threshold values were determined experimentally. A new ADC conversion is started before the ISR is exited. The Timer2 ISR for decoding the IR receiver output is not shown, as it is the same code presented in Chapter 12.

```
#define WHEEL_LEFT_1A  _LATB1
#define WHEEL_LEFT_2A  _LATB3
#define WHEEL_LEFT_EN  _LATB2
#define WHEEL_RIGHT_1A  _LATB14
#define WHEEL_RIGHT_2A  _LATB12
#define WHEEL_RIGHT_EN  _LATB13

#define WHEEL_LEFT_FORWARD()  { WHEEL_LEFT_1A = 1; WHEEL_LEFT_2A = 0; }
#define WHEEL_LEFT_REVERSE()  { WHEEL_LEFT_1A = 0; WHEEL_LEFT_2A = 1; }
#define WHEEL_LEFT_STOP()     { WHEEL_LEFT_1A = 0;  WHEEL_LEFT_2A = 0; }
#define WHEEL_RIGHT_FORWARD() { WHEEL_RIGHT_1A = 1; WHEEL_RIGHT_2A = 0; }
#define WHEEL_RIGHT_REVERSE() { WHEEL_RIGHT_1A = 0;  WHEEL_RIGHT_2A = 1; }
#define WHEEL_RIGHT_STOP()    { WHEEL_RIGHT_1A = 0;  WHEEL_RIGHT_2A = 0; }

#define WHEEL_PWM_STEPS 10        //number of PWM steps
#define WHEEL_PWM_STEPSIZE 500    //in microseconds
#define BLOCKAGE_PRESENT     560  //1.8 V    Threshold values for obstacle
#define BLOCKAGE_CLEAR       434  //1.4 V    present/absent, determined
                                            experimentally.
void _ISRFAST _T3Interrupt (void) {
  uint16 u16_temp;      ◄ 500 µs periodic interrupt
  _T3IF = 0;                //clear the timer interrupt bit
  if (u8_rightDC) { ◄─ Non-zero speed requested
    if ( u8_rightPeriod == WHEEL_PWM_STEPS || !u8_rightPeriod) {
        u8_rightPeriod = 0;   } At end of period, clear the period counter and
        WHEEL_RIGHT_EN = 1;   } set the PWM output high.
    }
    else if (u8_rightPeriod >= u8_rightDC) WHEEL_RIGHT_EN = 0;
    u8_rightPeriod++; ◄─ Increment period counter      Period counter greater
  } else {                                              than duty cycle, so
        WHEEL_RIGHT_EN = 0; } Zero speed, so clear the  clear the PWM
        u8_rightPeriod = 0; } PWM output and zero       output.
  }                           the period counter.
  if (u8_leftDC) {
    if ( u8_leftPeriod == WHEEL_PWM_STEPS || !u8_leftPeriod) {
        u8_leftPeriod = 0;
        WHEEL_LEFT_EN = 1;
    }
    else if (u8_leftPeriod >= u8_leftDC) WHEEL_LEFT_EN = 0;
    u8_leftPeriod++;
  }else {
        WHEEL_LEFT_EN = 0;                 Set or clear the blockage
        u8_rightPeriod = 0;                flag based on threshold values.
  }
  u16_temp = ADC1BUF0; ◄─ Read ADC value
  if (u16_temp > BLOCKAGE_PRESENT ) flags.u1_obstacle = 1;
   else if (u16_temp < BLOCKAGE_CLEAR) flags.u1_obstacle = 0;
  AD1CON1bits.SAMP = 1; //start next ADC conversion for next interrupt
}        ◄ Start next ADC conversion.
```

FIGURE 15.23 Timer3 ISR for the robot application.

Figure 15.24 shows the processCmd(uint8 u8_cmd) function used in both manual and autonomous modes to execute IR commands. Speed up and slow down is accomplished by increasing or decreasing both wheel speeds by 1. Decreasing either the left or right wheel speed by 1 while keeping the other wheel speed the same

```
#define CMD_STOP         0x36  //VCR stop button
#define CMD_SPEEDUP      0x29  //VCR pause button
#define CMD_SLOWDOWN     0x37  //VCR record button
#define CMD_FORWARD      0x35  //VCR play button
#define CMD_TURN_LEFT    0x32  //VCR rewind button
#define CMD_TURN_RIGHT   0x34  //VCR fast forward button
#define CMD_REVERSE      0x05  //VCR numeral 5
#define CMD_SPIN         0x09  //VCR numeral 9
#define CMD_MODESWAP     0x01  //VCR numeral 1
#define CMD_NOP          0x00  //do nothing
```

Command mappings to VCR control buttons.

```
void processCmd(uint8 u8_cmd) {
  switch (u8_cmd) {
    case CMD_SPEEDUP:  ◄— Increase both wheel speeds by 1 to speed up.
         if (u8_leftDC < WHEEL_PWM_STEPS) u8_leftDC += 1;
         if (u8_rightDC < WHEEL_PWM_STEPS) u8_rightDC += 1;
         break;
    case CMD_SLOWDOWN:
         if (u8_leftDC) u8_leftDC -= 1;
         if (u8_rightDC) u8_rightDC -= 1;
         break;
    case CMD_STOP: allStop(); break;
    case CMD_FORWARD:
         allStop();
         goForward(DEFAULT_SPEED);
         break;
    case CMD_REVERSE:
         allStop();
         goReverse(DEFAULT_SPEED);
         break;
    case CMD_TURN_LEFT:
         if (u8_leftDC) u8_leftDC -= 1;
         break;
    case CMD_TURN_RIGHT:
         if (u8_rightDC) u8_rightDC -= 1;
         break;
    case CMD_SPIN:
         allStop();
         WHEEL_LEFT_FORWARD();
         WHEEL_RIGHT_REVERSE();
         doSpeedUp(DEFAULT_SPEED);
         break;
    case CMD_MODESWAP:
         allStop();
         flags.u1_mode = !flags.u1_mode;
         break;
    default:  //do nothing
         break;
  }
}
```

Decrease both wheel speeds by 1 to slow down.

Stop when changing directions.

Decrease one wheel speed by 1 for turning.

One wheel forward, one wheel backward for spinning.

Stop when transistioning between drive modes.

FIGURE 15.24 Code for processing an IR command.

performs turning. The robot is stopped any time a change in direction or driving mode change is requested. A spin mode is implemented by setting the wheels to opposite directions (forward and backward), then bringing both wheels up to the default speed.

Figure 15.25a shows two utility functions for handling IR input. The `checkIR()` function is called by the `while(1){}` loop of `main()`, and it calls `getIRCMD()` followed by `processCmd()` to handle an IR command if one is present. The `getIRCMD()` function reads the IR software FIFO as originally implemented in Chapter 12. Recall

a) Functions for reading the IR command FIFO

```
uint8 getIRCMD(void) {
  uint8 u8_x, u8_cmd;
  u8_x = irFifoRead();           IR input spread over two bytes, a toggle byte
  u8_cmd = irFifoRead();         and a command byte.
  if (u8_x & 0x20) outString("Toggle = 1, ");
    else outString("Toggle = 0, ");      Output IR command for
  outString("Addr: "); outUint8(u8_x & 0x1F);   debugging purposes.
  outString(",Cmd: "); outUint8(u8_cmd);
  outString("\n");
  if (flags.u1_irCmdFlag) flags.u1_irCmdFlag = 0;   Skip every other IR command
    else flags.u1_irCmdFlag = 1;                    since remote control sends
  if (flags.u1_irCmdFlag) return u8_cmd;            each command twice.
  else return CMD_NOP;
}
void checkIR(void) {
  uint8 u8_cmd;
  if (irFifoDataRdy()) {        Process the IR command if one is ready.
    u8_cmd = getIRCMD();
    processCmd(u8_cmd);
  }
}
```

b) Miscellaneous driving functions

```
void doSpeedUp(uint8 u8_speed) {
  u8_leftDC = 0; u8_rightDC = 0;              void goForward(uint8 u8_speed){
  do {                                          WHEEL_LEFT_FORWARD();
    u8_leftDC++;   u8_rightDC++;                WHEEL_RIGHT_FORWARD();
    DELAY_MS(100);                              doSpeedUp(u8_speed);
  }while(u8_leftDC < u8_speed);               }
}

                                              void goReverse(uint8 u8_speed){
void allStop(void) {                            WHEEL_LEFT_REVERSE();
  //slow to a stop                              WHEEL_RIGHT_REVERSE();
  while (u8_leftDC || u8_rightDC) {             doSpeedUp(u8_speed);
    if (u8_leftDC) u8_leftDC--;               }
    if (u8_rightDC) u8_rightDC--;
    DELAY_MS(100);
  }
}

void doTurn(uint8 u8_ltarg, uint8 u8_rtarg){
  u8_leftDC = 0; u8_rightDC = 0;                     For turn, speed up both
  while((u8_leftDC != u8_ltarg) ||                   wheels to dissimilar
    (u8_rightDC != u8_rtarg) ) {                      target speeds.
    if (u8_leftDC != u8_ltarg) u8_leftDC++;
    if (u8_rightDC != u8_rtarg) u8_rightDC++;
    DELAY_MS(80);
  }
}
```

FIGURE 15.25   Miscellaneous functions for the robot application.

that an IR input is split over two bytes, one for the toggle and address information and the other for the command code. The getIRCMD() reads both bytes from the IR software FIFO and prints them as debugging information. It then calls processCmd() to process the command for every other IR input since the remote control used in this application sent duplicate codes for each button press. Figure 15.25b gives miscellaneous driving functions that are called by the processCmd() function of Figure 15.24. The implementation of these functions is straightforward.

Under testing, the robot performed similarly to other DC motor propelled robots the authors have previously built. The driving characteristics were:

- **Fast:** DC motors are generally the best choice if one desires high speed, and the small weight of this robot allowed for relatively high forward speed. In fact, the robot was so fast that it had an affinity for crashing into walls because the driver was not quick enough with the remote control when in manual drive mode. The driving functions had to use a gradual speed up to a target speed because the robot was not well balanced and tended to tip frontwards on sudden stops.

- **Drift:** In autonomous mode, the wheel motors were operated in open loop, that is, there was no feedback indicating how fast the wheels were actually turning. Even when each motor is driven by an identical PWM signal, there will be slight speed differences between the motors causing it to drift to one side or the other when going forward. This is why most autonomous robot competitions have white lines on the course allowing robots to use line detection to provide feedback while traveling in a given direction. A robot with a line-following sensor can dynamically adjust wheel speed to stay on the line. An alternative is to use a rotary encoder (Chapter 9) on each wheel shaft to provide feedback for keeping wheel speeds matched to each other. *Stepper motors* can also be used instead of DC motors to provide more accurate open-loop driving. A stepper motor is a type of DC motor that allows for turning the shaft a precise distance (a *step*), but requires a more complex motor drive interface than shown here. Robots driven by stepper motors are much slower than non-stepper DC motor propelled robots and can still drift when operated in open-loop control. Stepper motors also pull current even when the shaft is not moving, which is a concern in a battery-operated robot.

OTHER MICROCONTROLLER FAMILIES FROM MICROCHIP

Microchip Technology Inc. has several microcontroller families spanning a wide price/performance range to target as many different applications as possible. Figure 15.26 gives a partial summary of the PIC microcontroller families offered by Microchip circa August 2008. The data SRAM and Program Memory (Pgm. Mem.) columns reflect the largest amount available on currently offered family members,

Family	Instr. Width	Data Width	SRAM (bytes)	Pgm. Mem. (Ki bytes)	Fam. Mem.	Pkg. Pins	CPU Speed MIPS
PIC10	12	8	24	0.75	6	6	1
PIC12	12,14	8	128	3.5	12	8	5
PIC16	14	8	368	14	99	14 to 64	10
PIC18	14	8	3968	128	155	18 to 100	16
PIC24F	24	16	16384	256	38	28 to 100	16
PIC24H	24	16	16384	256	28	18 to 100	40
dsPIC30F	24	16	8192	144	24	18 to 80	30
dsPIC33F	24	16	32768	256	57	18 to 100	40
PIC32	32	32	32768	512	17	64 to 100	80

FIGURE 15.26   PIC microcontroller family summary.

not the maximum size supported by the architecture. The Family Member (Fam. Mem.) column gives the number of different variants available for the family. The CPU speed column gives the theoretical maximum instruction execution rate in millions of instructions per second (MIPS) and is calculated by taking the maximum internal clock speed for the CPU in MHz and dividing by the number of clocks per instruction. Figure 15.26 covers the 8-bit, 16-bit, and 32-bit families offered by Microchip, with CPU performance increasing as one moves down the figure.

The PIC10 family has only six members and is targeted at the extreme low-end microcontroller market. It comes in either 6-pin (SOT-23) or 8-pin packages (8 PDIP, 8 DFN), can be operated by an internal 4 MHz clock or external clock source, has an 8-bit timer, a maximum of 4 I/O pins, and a maximum of 512 instruction words (each 12 bits wide) and 24 bytes of SRAM. Two family members include an analog comparator. It is the embodiment of a "tiny" microcontroller and is priced in proportion to its power.

The PIC12 family has 18 members and its differentiator from the PIC10 family is an on-chip A/D (4-bit, 8-bit, 10-bit) and more on-chip memory, both program and data.

The PIC16 family was the first from Microchip to offer a relatively large set of on-chip peripherals and is a popular family. It has a relatively small instruction set of 35 instructions and has only the Carry and Zero flags for implementing branching. It also has only one register for implementing indirect addressing. C compilers for the PIC16 family are available from third-party vendors.

The PIC18 family is a successor to the PIC16 family that added more instructions (for a total of 76), with an instruction set that is largely source code compatible with the PIC16 family. The PIC18 architecture added overflow and negative flags, but the instruction set does not have signed branches. This makes signed comparisons somewhat cumbersome to implement, but is still an improvement over the PIC16 instruction set. The PIC18 stack is a fixed size and is limited to storing only return addresses. A data stack can be created in memory but there is no automated addressing support for data stack operations. The PIC18 family has proven to be extremely popular and is supported by a *C* compiler offered by Microchip.

The dsPIC30F was the first 16-bit processor family offered by Microchip, and the architecture has a second ALU that is optimized for digital signal processing operations as first discussed in Chapter 7. Specialized math libraries supplied with the dsPIC *C* compiler are optimized to take advantage of this ALU. The dsPIC33F is a higher clock speed, 3.3 V version of the dsPIC30 architecture. The PIC24H and PIC24F families drop the DSP-oriented ALU and are aimed at more general-purpose applications; they execute a subset of the dsPIC30 instruction set. The dsPIC30F, dsPIC33F, PIC24H, and PIC24F families all mostly share the same set of on-chip peripherals, with the dsPIC30F branch being the most incompatible in terms of peripherals that operate somewhat differently from the other branches.

The PIC32 family is Microchip's first 32-bit microcontroller offering. Unlike the other families, the CPU core is licensed from a third party, in this case MIPS Technologies. The CPU is a *pipelined* architecture of five stages, which means that there are up to five instructions in different stages of execution at any given time, with an instruction finishing every clock cycle in the best case. The CPU has a maximum clock speed of 80 MHz, for an upper limit performance of 80 MIPS. The CPU is an integer core, which means that its instruction set does not have dedicated floating-point instructions, unlike many other 32-bit architectures. However, the instruction set architecture supports the concept of co-processors, which means that future PIC32 family offerings could have a floating-point ALU as an on-chip peripheral. The PIC32 was a relatively new offering when this book was written, and thus the number of family members is somewhat low compared to the other family members. The PIC32 on-chip peripherals are comparable to that offered in the PIC24/dsPIC family lines.

A BRIEF SURVEY OF NON-PIC MICROCONTROLLERS

The microprocessor, digital signal processor, and microcontroller universe is not infinite, but is large enough that this section can provide only a cursory look at the processor families available from different companies. Figure 15.27 lists some of the companies and product offerings in the μP/DSP/μC universe. The authors make

High Performance 32-bit

High Performance 32-bit microprocessors, microcontrollers, and digital
signal processors from:
Intel (Pentium®/Celeron®/i960®/others),
SUN Microsystems (SPARC®/UltraSPARC®), AMD (Athlon™/others),
Freescale/Motorola (PowerPC®/other families),
IBM (PowerPC®), ARM (ARM family CPUs),
Analog Devices (Blackfin®/SHARC®/ADSP),
Texas Instruments (multiple families), MIPS Technologies (MIPS® family),
Renesas (Hitachi/Mitsubishi merger, M32R, SH families),
STMicroelectronics (uses ARM cores)
Microchip (PIC32, MIPS core, current offerings lack hardware floating point)
Architecture features include some mixture of:
  On-chip data/instruction caches
  Hardware floating point
  Pipelined or pipelined superscalar (multiple instructions per clock)
  Virtual memory support (memory management units)

I/O features include high-speed serial interfaces such
as USB, 10/100 Mb Ethernet, Firewire, etc. but also parallel bus standards
such as PCI. "Glueless" interfaces to SDRAM/SSRAM are common.

Often available in core form where a customer builds a custom integrated
circuit and includes a 32-bit processor as one of the modules.

Fixed-point 32/16/8-bit

Intel (8051/others), Freescale (68xxx/others), Renesas (H8/R8C/ M16C/M32C),
NEC (78K0S,/78K0R/ V850E), Infineon (XC800/XE166/TC116x),
Fujitsu (F2MC-8FX, F2MC-16FX, FR 32-bit series),
Panasonic (AM1, AM2, AM3), STMicroelectronics (STM, ST10, STM32) ,
Samsung (multiple families), NXP (Phillips spinoff, multiple families) ,
Microchip (multiple families), Atmel (AVR® families),
Zilog (ez80®, Z16F, Zatara with 32-bit ARM core),
Cypress Semiconductor (PSoC microcontroller, 8 and 32-bit variants),
Texas Instruments (multiple families, MSP430 is popular)

Other companies with 16-bit and/or 8-bit processor families include:
Rabbit Semiconductor (Rabbit 4000/3000/2000),
Silicon Labs (8051),Cyan Technology (eCOG1™ 16-bit family).

FIGURE 15.27 Microprocessor, digital signal processor, microcontroller universe.

no claims as to completeness of this list, as new companies arise each year to add
constellations to the µP/DSP/µC universe.

Figure 15.27 splits processors into two categories: high-performance 32-bit and
8/16/32-bit fixed-point. Some of the features listed under the high-performance
32-bit processor category have not been discussed in this book and may be new
to you; these features are briefly described here. Instruction and data *caches* are

on-chip high-speed memories that service much of the instruction and data needs of the processor. If a processor has instruction and data caches, it also uses external memory for storing program and data (instead of storing everything on-chip), that holds the instructions and data that cannot fit within the cache memories. The *cache controller* within the processor is responsible for swapping blocks of instructions/ data to/from external memory and on-chip cache. There are different types of external memory available, but a commonly used type is synchronous dynamic RAM (SDRAM), which is a form of external memory that offers high density but has complex interfacing requirements. Different forms of SDRAM such as DDR/ DDR2/DDR3/DDR4 (DDR is an acronym for *double data rate*) are available that offer various throughput rates for sequential memory access.

As previously mentioned, a processor that is *pipelined* means that on average it completes one instruction per clock cycle and that at any given time it has several instructions within it, each at a different state of completion. A pipelined *superscalar* processor can complete more than one instruction per clock cycle. *Virtual memory* means that the processor can execute programs that are larger than the physical memory of the computer system; external storage such as a hard disk is used to store instructions and data that will not fit in physical memory. A *memory management unit* (MMU) on the processor is responsible for detecting when an instruction or data access is not in physical memory; this generates an interrupt that causes the needed instruction/data to be swapped into physical memory from disk. Modern operating systems such as Windows and UNIX derivatives require processors that support virtual memory. Floating-point was discussed in Chapter 7; a hardware floating-point unit executes instructions that perform floating-point operations. If there is set of features that differentiate a processor between the high- and low-performance camps, it is a fully pipelined 32-bit architecture and/or inclusion of hardware floating-point. Many high-performance processors are available as "cores." This means that a company wishing to build an application-specific integrated circuit (ASIC) can include the processor as a module within its integrated circuit and place customized logic around it to address specific needs. High-performance 32-bit processors are even being included within field programmable gate arrays (FPGAs) from companies such as Xilinx and Altera.

The low-performance category, designated as fixed-point 32/16/8-bit processors, is differentiated from the high-performance category by lack of hardware floating-point support or other features in the high performance list. The Motorola 68XXX family (marketing name 68K/ColdFire™) is an example of an embedded processor core that is 32-bit internal without hardware floating-point support and is a non-pipelined architecture. This category is dominated by 8-bit processor families and contains additional companies over those listed in the 32-bit high-performance category. One popular 8-bit processor is the 8051, originally developed by Intel in the 1980s. Intel has licensed this processor to several companies that now make 8051-compatible microcontrollers. The 8-bit processors from Atmel and Zilog are flash programmable, with family members available in DIP packages that are suitable for hobbyist prototyping, and feature basically the same IO module set as the PIC24/PIC18/PIC16 processors. The Rabbit 2000/3000 processors are based on Z80/Z180 architectures (a processor popular in the 1980s), feature an external memory bus, and are available only in high pin count, surface mount packages. The Rabbit 2000/3000 does not have on-chip program memory; development kits with external flash EEPROM memory and SRAM are available from Rabbit Semiconductor. The Programmable System-on-a-Chip (PSoC) microcontroller from Cypress Semiconductor is unique in that in addition to an 8-bit processor core that is flash programmable, it contains both analog and digital programmable logic modules that allow a user to customize on-chip peripherals based on the application. One interesting aspect of the low-performance processor list is that 8-bit processor families far outnumber 32/16-bit processor families. This is because the extra performance from a 32/16-bit processor is usually not needed in low-performance families; if extra performance is needed, simply increasing the clock speed on an 8-bit processor may be a good enough solution.

How does one choose a processor? Of course, application requirements are a critical driver, but typically many processors are able to perform the same task adequately. From a company viewpoint, processor availability (can the vendor ship the volume that I need?), reliability, and volume price are critical. From educator, student, or hobbyist viewpoints, other questions such as those that follow often decide the processor choice.

- Is the processor available in DIP packages so I can prototype with it? If not, are there development kits available and what do they cost?
- Is there a free or inexpensive development system available so I can write and simulate assembly language programs?
- Is the processor flash programmable? How will I program the processor? Can I do it in-circuit or do I need an external programmer? How expensive is a programmer?
- Is there a C compiler available? How expensive is the C compiler? Is freely-avaliable version of the C compiler available?
- Are there sites on the World Wide Web where I can find sample code for common problems?
- Can I purchase processors/programmers in small quantities from a supplier such as Digi-Key?

Exploring the µP/DSP/µC universe can be rewarding. It is almost guaranteed that whatever processor provides your first learning experience in the µP/DSP/µC universe will not be the only processor that you will encounter in your scientist/ engineer/hobbyist career. You will quickly discover that different processor families all share common themes that allow you to apply previous hard-earned lessons when exploring the nuances of a new processor family. You will experience the rewards of lifelong learning when pursuing a career in the μP/DSP/μC universe!

SUMMARY

This chapter used various topics from previous chapters to form solutions for three design examples. Your skills in using microcontroller features such as parallel port I/O, interrupt driven I/O, serial interfaces (asynchronous, I²C, SPI), timers, and data conversion (ADC, DAC) in microcontroller applications only increase with practice. As such, we encourage you to develop your own project ideas and bring them to life—you will find it a rewarding process. We also encourage you to try some of the examples discussed in this book on a non-PIC24 μC as this would force you to generalize the lessons that you have learned in programming the PIC24 μC. If most of the material in this book is new to you, then you are only just beginning to explore the μP/DSP/μC universe. It can turn into a lifelong exploration that is both fun and intellectually rewarding; good luck on your travels!

SUGGESTED SURVEY TOPICS

Because of the nature of this chapter, this section does not contain review problems. Instead, we suggest an exploration of a non-Microchip processor in order to broaden your knowledge of the μP/DSP/μC universe. Select a non-Microchip processor from the list in Figure 15.27. Visit the company Web site and download both the reference manual for the processor architecture and the specific datasheet for a particular family. Compare and contrast the processor with the PIC24 μC by answering the following questions.

1. What is the width of the instruction word?
2. What is the width of the internal data registers?
3. What is the width of the program counter or instruction pointer?
4. How much on-chip RAM does the processor have?
5. Does the processor have an external bus for accessing program or data memory?
6. Does the processor have signed comparison instructions? If "yes," give an example.

7. Implement the operation $i = k + j$ in the processor's assembly language where i, k, j are `uint8` variables. Repeat this for variable types `uint16` and `uint32`.

8. Does the processor have special instructions for multiply and/or divide? If "yes," give an example.

9. Does the processor have a fixed-size or variable-size stack?

10. Does the processor have push/pop instructions for accessing the stack? If "yes," give an example.

11. How many indirect addressing modes are supported and how do they operate?

12. How many clock cycles does it take for an addition operation to complete?

13. Give the machine code format for an addition operation; you choose the addressing modes.

14. What flags are supported in the status register of the processor?

15. Does the processor have an instruction that supports a multiple position shift? If "yes," give an example.

16. What serial standards are supported? Asynchronous? SPI? I^{2}C? What is the maximum synchronous transfer rate?

17. Does it have an on-chip ADC? If "yes," how many channels and what precision?

18. At reset, from what location is the first instruction fetched?

19. What location in memory contains the interrupt vector(s)? Does the processor support multiple interrupt priorities?

20. What are the minimum and maximum package sizes in terms of pin counts? For the maximum package size, what is the parallel port count?

21. What is the device's maximum clock frequency?

22. What is the VDD range supported by the device?

23. How many timers and what sizes are supported?

24. Is PWM supported? If "yes," how many channels?

25. What types of parallel I/O features are supported? Open-drain? Pull-ups? Bi-directional I/O? What is the maximum current drive for a PIO pin?

26. What types of interrupt structure does the processor support? Does it support interrupt priorities? Does it have non-maskable interrupts?

PIC24 Architecture and Instruction Set Summary

This appendix contains a summary of the PIC24 architecture and instruction set. Figure A.1 shows an architectural block diagram of the PIC24HJ32GP202/204 and PIC24HJ16GP304 processors. Figures A.4 through A.11 give the instruction set summary, with Figures A.2 through A.4 providing symbols and encodings used in these summaries. The instruction set encodings and definitions are taken from the *dsPIC30F/33F Programmer's Reference Manual* [5].

Register placeholder symbols used in instruction mnemonics are:

- **Wn**: register direct addressing; *Wn* specifies one of W0, W1, ... W15.
- **Wns**: register direct addressing; *Wns* specifies one of W0, W1, ... W15.
- **Wnd**: register direct addressing; *Wnd* specifies one of W0, W1, ... W15.
- **Wb**: register direct addressing; *Wb* specifies one of W0, W1, ... W15.
- **WREG**: the working register; specifies W0 in file register instructions.
- **Ws**: register direct (*Ws*) and indirect addressing modes ([*Ws*], [*Ws*++], [*Ws*−−], [++*Ws*], [−−*Ws*]); *Ws* specifies one of W0, W1, ... W15.
- **Wd**: register direct (*Wd*) and indirect addressing modes ([*Wd*], [*Wd*++], [*Wd*−−], [++*Wd*], [−−*Wd*]); *Wd* specifies one of W0, W1, ... W15.
- **Wso**: all of the addressing modes of **Ws**, with the additional mode of register offset indirect [*Wso* + *Wb*]; *Wso* specifies one of W0, W1, ... W15.
- **Wdo**: all of the addressing modes of **Wd**, with the additional mode of register offset indirect [*Wdo* + *Wb*]; *Wdo* specifies one of W0, W1, ... W15.
- **Wsi**: Indirect addressing modes ([*Ws*], [*Ws*++], [*Ws*−−], [++*Ws*], [−−*Ws*]); *Ws* specifies one of W0, W1, ... W15. Used only by the tblrdl, tblrdh instructions.
- **Wdi**: Indirect addressing modes ([*Wd*], [*Wd*++], [*Wd*−−], [++*Wd*], [−−*Wd*]); *Wd* specifies one of W0, W1, ... W15. Used only by the tblwtl, tblwth instructions.

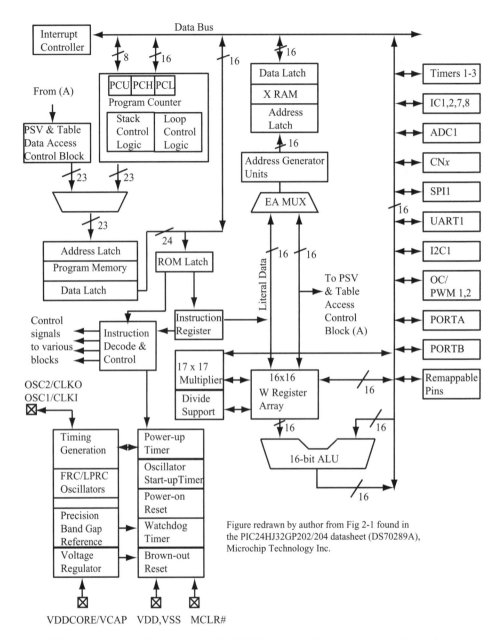

FIGURE A.1 PIC24HJ32GP202/204 and PIC24HJ16GP304 block diagram. (Adapted with permission of the copyright owner, Microchip Technology, Incorporated. All rights reserved. No further reprints or reproduction may be made without Microchip Inc.'s prior written consent.)

Field	Description
B	Byte mode selection bit : 0 = word operation; 1 = byte operation
bbbb	4-bit position select: 0000 = LSb; 1111 = MSb
D	Destination address bit: 0 = result stored in WREG; 1 = result stored in file register
dddd	*Wd* destination register select: 0000 = W0; 1111 = W15
f ffff ffff ffff	13-bit register file byte address (0x0000 to 0x1FFF)
fff ffff ffff ffff	15-bit register file word address (implied 0 LSb, 0x0000 to 0xFFFE)
ffff ffff ffff ffff	16-bit register file byte address (0x0000 to 0xFFFF)
ggg	Register offset addressing mode for *Ws* source register (Figure A.3)
hhh	Register offset addressing mode for *Wd* source register (Figure A.3)
kkk ... k	literal field, constant data or expression
nnn nnnn nnn nnn0 nnn nnnn	23-bit program address for `call` and `goto` instructions
nnnn nnnn nnnn nnnn	16-bit program offset field for relative branch/call instructions
ppp	Addressing mode for *Ws* source register (see Figure A.3)
qqq	Addressing mode for *Wd* destination register (see Figure A.3)
rrrr	Barrel shift count
ssss	*Ws* source register select: 0000 = W0; 1111 = W15
tttt	Dividend select, most significant word
vvvv	Dividend select, least significant word
W	Double Word mode selection bit: 0 = word operation; 1 = double word operation
wwww	*Wb* base register select: 0000 = W0; 1111 = W15
xxxx xxxx xxxx xxxx	16-bit unused field (don't care)

FIGURE A.2 Machine code symbols.

Addressing modes for *Ws* (source operand) and *Wd* (destination operand)

ppp/qqq	Addressing mode	Source Operand (ppp)	Destination Operand (qqq)
000	Register Direct	Ws	Wd
001	Indirect	[Ws]	[Wd]
010	Indirect with Post-Decrement	[Ws--]	[Wd--]
011	Indirect with Post-Increment	[Ws++]	[Wd++]
100	Indirect with Pre-Decrement	[--Ws]	[--Wd]
101	Indirect with Pre-Increment	[++Ws]	[++Wd]
11x	Unused	Software reset if used	

Addressing modes for *Wso* (source operand) and *Wdo* (destination operand)

ggg/hhh	Addressing mode	Source Operand (ggg)	Destination Operand (hhh)
000	Register Direct	Ws	Wd
001	Indirect	[Ws]	[Wd]
010	Indirect with Post-Decrement	[Ws--]	[Wd--]
011	Indirect with Post-Increment	[Ws++]	[Wd++]
100	Indirect with Pre-Decrement	[--Ws]	[--Wd]
101	Indirect with Pre-Increment	[++Ws]	[++Wd]
11x	Indirect with Register Offset	[Ws+Wb]	[Wd+Wb]

FIGURE A.3 Addressing mode encodings.

Instr	Descr	#W	#Cyc	Status	Machine Code
ADD{.B} f	f = f + WREG	1	1	C,DC,N,V,Z	1011 0100 0BDf ffff ffff ffff
ADD{.B} f,WREG	WREG = f + WREG	1	1	C,DC,N,V,Z	1011 0100 0BDf ffff ffff ffff
ADD{.B} #lit10,Wn	Wn = lit10 + Wn	1	1	C,DC,N,V,Z	1011 0000 0Bkk kkkk kkkk dddd
ADD{.B} Wb,Ws,Wd	Wd = Wb + Ws	1	1	C,DC,N,V,Z	0100 0www wBqq qddd dppp ssss
ADD{.B} Wb,#lit5,Wd	Wd = Wb + lit5	1	1	C,DC,N,V,Z	0100 0www wBqq qddd d11k kkkk
ADDC{.B} f	f = f + WREG +(C)	1	1	C,DC,N,V,Z	1011 0100 1BDf ffff ffff ffff
ADDC{.B} f,WREG	WREG = f + WREG +(C)	1	1	C,DC,N,V,Z	1011 0100 1BDf ffff ffff ffff
ADDC{.B} #lit10,Wn	Wn = lit10 + Wn + (C)	1	1	C,DC,N,V,Z	1011 0000 1Bkk kkkk kkkk dddd
ADDC{.B} Wb,Ws,Wd	Wd = Wb + Ws + (C)	1	1	C,DC,N,V,Z	0100 1www wBqq qddd dppp ssss
ADDC{.B} Wb,#lit5,Wd	Wd = Wb + lit5 + (C)	1	1	C,DC,N,V,Z	0100 1www wBqq qddd d11k kkkk
AND{.B} f	f = f & WREG	1	1	N,Z	1011 0110 0BDf ffff ffff ffff
AND{.B} f,WREG	WREG = f & WREG	1	1	N,Z	1011 0110 0BDf ffff ffff ffff
AND{.B} #lit10,Wn	Wn = lit10 & Wn	1	1	N,Z	1011 0010 0Bkk kkkk kkkk dddd
AND{.B} Wb,Ws,Wd	Wd = Wb & Ws	1	1	N,Z	0110 0www wBqq qddd dppp ssss
AND{.B} Wb,#lit5,Wd	Wd = Wb & lit5	1	1	N,Z	0100 0www wBqq qddd d11k kkkk
ASR{.B} f	f = arith. >> f	1	1	N,Z,C	1101 0101 1BDf ffff ffff ffff
ASR{.B} f,WREG	WREG = arith. >> f	1	1	N,Z,C	1101 0101 1BDf ffff ffff ffff
ASR{.B} Ws,Wd	Wd = arith. >> Ws	1	1	N,Z,C	1101 0001 1Bqq qddd dppp ssss
ASR{.B} Wb,Wns,Wnd	Wnd = arith >> Wb by Wns	1	1	N,Z	1101 1110 1www wddd d000 ssss
ASR{.B} Wb,#lit4,Wnd	Wnd = arith >> Wb by lit4	1	1	N,Z	1101 1110 1www wddd d100 kkkk
BCLR{.B} f,#bit4	Bit Clear f	1	1	none	1010 1001 bbbf ffff ffff fffb
BCLR{.B} Ws,#bit4	Bit Clear Ws	1	1	none	1010 0001 bbbb 0B00 0ppp ssss
BRA C,Expr	Branch if Carry	1	1 (2)	none	0011 0001 nnnn nnnn nnnn nnnn
BRA GE,Expr	Branch if signed >=	1	1 (2)	none	0011 1101 nnnn nnnn nnnn nnnn
BRA GEU,Expr	Branch if unsigned >=	1	1 (2)	none	0011 0001 nnnn nnnn nnnn nnnn
BRA GT,Expr	Branch if signed >	1	1 (2)	none	0011 1100 nnnn nnnn nnnn nnnn
BRA GTU,Expr	Branch if unsigned >	1	1 (2)	none	0011 1110 nnnn nnnn nnnn nnnn
BRA LE,Expr	Branch if signed <=	1	1 (2)	none	0011 0100 nnnn nnnn nnnn nnnn
BRA LEU,Expr	Branch if unsigned <=	1	1 (2)	none	0011 0110 nnnn nnnn nnnn nnnn

FIGURE A.4 Instruction table (part 1).

Instr	Descr	#W	#Cyc	Status	Machine Code
BRA LT,Expr	Branch if signed <	1	1 (2)	none	0011 0101 nnnn nnnn nnnn nnnn
BRA LTU,Expr	Branch if unsigned <	1	1 (2)	none	0011 1001 nnnn nnnn nnnn nnnn
BRA N,Expr	Branch if Negative	1	1 (2)	none	0011 0011 nnnn nnnn nnnn nnnn
BRA NC,Expr	Branch if Not Carry	1	1 (2)	none	0011 1001 nnnn nnnn nnnn nnnn
BRA NN,Expr	Branch if Not Negative	1	1 (2)	none	0011 1011 nnnn nnnn nnnn nnnn
BRA NOV,Expr	Branch if Not Overflow	1	1 (2)	none	0011 1000 nnnn nnnn nnnn nnnn
BRA NZ,Expr	Branch if Not Zero	1	1 (2)	none	0011 1010 nnnn nnnn nnnn nnnn
BRA OV,Expr	Branch if Overflow	1	1 (2)	none	0011 0000 nnnn nnnn nnnn nnnn
BRA Expr	Branch Unconditionally	2	2	none	0011 0111 nnnn nnnn nnnn nnnn
BRA Z,Expr	Branch if Zero	1	1 (2)	none	0011 0010 nnnn nnnn nnnn nnnn
BRA Wn	Computed Branch	1	2	none	0000 0001 0110 0000 0000 ssss
BSET{.B} f,#bit4	Bit Set f	1	1	none	1010 1000 bbbf ffff ffff fffb
BSET{.B} Ws,#bit4	Bit Set Ws	1	1	none	1010 0000 bbbb 0B00 0ppp ssss
BSW.C Ws,Wb	Write C bit Ws<Wb>	1	1	none	1010 1101 0www w000 0ppp ssss
BSW.Z Ws,Wb	Write Z bit Ws<Wb>	1	1	none	1010 1101 1www w000 0ppp ssss
BTG{.B} f,#bit4	Bit Toggle f	1	1	none	1010 1010 bbbf ffff ffff fffb
BTG{.B} Ws,#bit4	Bit Toggle Ws	1	1	none	1010 0010 bbbb 0B00 0ppp ssss
BTSC{.B} f,#bit4	Bit Test f, Skip If Clear	1	1 (2 or 3)	none	1010 1111 bbbf ffff ffff fffb
BTSC{.B} Ws,#bit4	Bit Test Ws, Skip If Clear	1	1 (2 or 3)	none	1010 0111 bbbb 0000 0ppp ssss
BTSS{.B} f,#bit4	Bit Test f, Skip if Set	1	1 (2 or 3)	none	1010 1110 bbbf ffff ffff fffb
BTSS{.B} Ws,#bit4	Bit Test Ws, Skip If Set	1	1 (2 or 3)	none	1010 0110 bbbb 0000 0ppp ssss
BTST f,#bit4	Bit Test f	1	1	Z	1010 1011 bbbf ffff ffff fffb
BTST.C Ws,#bit4	Bit Test Ws to C	1	1	C	1010 0011 bbbb 0000 0ppp ssss
BTST.Z Ws,#bit4	Bit Test Ws to Z	1	1	Z	1010 0011 bbbb 1000 0ppp ssss
BTST.C Ws,Wb	Bit Test Ws<Wb> to C	1	1	C	1010 0101 0www w000 0ppp ssss
BTST.Z Ws,Wb	Bit Test Ws<Wb> to Z	1	1	Z	1010 0101 1www w000 0ppp ssss
BTSTS f,#bit4	Bit Test then Set f	1	1	Z	1010 1100 bbbf ffff ffff fffb
BTSTS.C Ws,#bit4	Bit Test Ws to C, then Set	1	1	C	1010 0100 bbbb 0000 0ppp ssss
BTSTS.Z Ws,#bit4	Bit Test Ws to Z, then Set	1	1	Z	1010 0100 bbbb 1000 0ppp ssss
CALL Expr	Call subroutine	2	2	none	0000 0010 nnnn nnnn nnn0 nnnn 0000 0000 0000 0nnn nnnn

FIGURE A.5 Instruction table (part 2).

Instr	Descr	#W	#Cyc	Status	Machine Code
CALL Wn	Call Indirect subroutine	1	2	none	0000 0001 0000 0000 0000 ssss
CLR{.B} f	f = 0x0000	1	1	none	1110 1111 0BDf ffff ffff ffff
CLR{.B} WREG	WREG = 0x0000	1	1	none	1110 1111 0BDf ffff ffff ffff
CLR{.B} Ws	Ws = 0x0000	1	1	none	1110 1011 0Bqq qddd d000 0000
CLRWDT	Clear Watchdog Timer	1	1	none	1111 1110 0110 0000 0000 0000
COM{.B} f	f = ~f	1	1	N,Z	1110 1110 1BDf ffff ffff ffff
COM{.B} f,WREG	WREG = ~f	1	1	N,Z	1110 1110 1BDf ffff ffff ffff
COM{.B} Ws,Wd	Wd = ~Ws	1	1	N,Z	1110 1010 1Bqq qddd dppp ssss
CP{.B} f	f - WREG	1	1	C,DC,N,V,Z	1110 0011 0B0f ffff ffff ffff
CP{.B} Wb,#lit5	Wb - #lit5	1	1	C,DC,N,V,Z	1110 0001 0www wB00 011k kkkk
CP{.B} Wb,Ws	Wb - Ws	1	1	C,DC,N,V,Z	1110 0001 0www wB00 0ppp ssss
CP0{.B} f	f - 0	1	1	C,DC,N,V,Z	1110 0010 0B0f ffff ffff ffff
CP0{.B} Ws	Ws - 0	1	1	C,DC,N,V,Z	1110 0000 0000 0B00 0ppp ssss
CPB{.B} f	f - WREG - BORROW (~C)	1	1	C,DC,N,V,Z	1110 0011 1B0f ffff ffff ffff
CBB{.B} Wb,#lit5	Wb - #lit5 - BORROW (~C)	1	1	C,DC,N,V,Z	1110 0001 1www wB00 011k kkkk
CPB{.B} Wb,Ws	Wb - Ws - BORROW (~C)	1	1	C,DC,N,V,Z	1110 0001 1www wB00 0ppp ssss
CPSEQ Wb,Wn	Wb - Wn; skip if equal	1	1 (2 or 3)	none	1110 0111 1www 0000 0000 ssss
CPSGT Wb,Wn	Wb - Wn; skip if signed >	1	1 (2 or 3)	none	1110 0110 0www 0000 0000 ssss
CPSLT Wb,Wn	Wb - Wn; skip if signed <	1	1 (2 or 3)	none	1110 0110 1www 0000 0000 ssss
CPSNE Wb,Wn	Wb - Wn; skip if not equal	1	1 (2 or 3)	none	1110 0111 0www 0000 0000 ssss
DAW Wn	Wn = decimal adjust Wn	1	1	C	1111 1101 0100 0000 0000 ssss
DEC{.B} f	f = f - 1	1	1	C,DC,N,V,Z	1110 1101 0BDf ffff ffff ffff
DEC{.B} f,WREG	WREG = f - 1	1	1	C,DC,N,V,Z	1110 1101 0BDf ffff ffff ffff
DEC{.B} Ws,Wd	Wd = Ws - 1	1	1	C,DC,N,V,Z	1110 1001 0Bqq qddd dppp ssss
DEC2{.B} f	f = f - 2	1	1	C,DC,N,V,Z	1110 1101 1BDf ffff ffff ffff
DEC2{.B} f,WREG	WREG = f - 2	1	1	C,DC,N,V,Z	1110 1101 1BDf ffff ffff ffff
DEC2{.B} Ws,Wd	Wd = Ws - 2	1	1	C,DC,N,V,Z	1110 1001 1Bqq qddd dppp ssss
DISI #lit14	Disable interrupts (through L6) for #lit14+1 cycles	1	1	none	1111 1100 00kk kkkk kkkk kkkk
DIV.S{W} Wm,Wn	Signed 16/16-bit divide	1	18	C,N,V,Z	1101 1000 0ttt tvvv vw00 ssss

FIGURE A.6 Instruction table (part 3).

Instr	Descr	#W	#Cyc	Status	Machine Code
DIV.SD Wm, Wn	Signed 32/16-bit Integer Divide	1	18	C,N,V,Z	1101 1000 0ttt tvvv vW00 ssss
DIV.U{W} Wm,Wn	Unsigned 16/16-bit Integer Divide	1	18	C,N,V,Z	1101 1000 1ttt tvvv vW00 ssss
DIV.UD WM,Wn	Unsigned 32/16-bit Integer Divide	1	18	C,N,V,Z	1101 1000 1ttt tvvv vW00 ssss
EXCH Wns,Wnd	Swap Wns with Wnd	1	1	none	1111 1101 0000 0ddd d000 ssss
FBCL Ws,Wnd	Find Bit Change from Left (MSb)	1	1	C	1101 1111 0000 0ddd dppp ssss
FF1L Ws,Wnd	Find First One from Left (MSb)	1	1	C	1100 1111 1000 0ddd dppp ssss
FF1R Ws,Wnd	Find First One from Right (LSb)	1	1	C	1100 1111 0000 0ddd dppp ssss
GOTO Expr	Go to address	2	2	none	0000 0100 nnnn nnnn nnnn nnn0 0000 0000 0000 0000 0nnn nnnn
GOTO Wn	Go to indirect	1	2	none	0000 0001 0100 0000 0000 ssss
INC{.B} f	f = f + 1	1	1	C,DC,N,V,Z	1110 1100 0BDf ffff ffff ffff
INC{.B} f,WREG	WREG = f + 1	1	1	C,DC,N,V,Z	1110 1100 0BDf ffff ffff ffff
INC{.B} Ws,Wd	Wd = Ws + 1	1	1	C,DC,N,V,Z	1110 1000 0Bqq qddd dppp ssss
INC2{.B} f	f = f + 2	1	1	C,DC,N,V,Z	1110 1100 1BDf ffff ffff ffff
INC2{.B} f,WREG	WREG = f + 2	1	1	C,DC,N,V,Z	1110 1100 1BDf ffff ffff ffff
INC2{.B} Ws,Wd	Wd = Ws + 2	1	1	C,DC,N,V,Z	1110 1000 1Bqq qddd dppp ssss
IOR{.B} f	f = f	WREG	1	1	N,Z	1011 0111 0BDf ffff ffff ffff
IOR{.B} f,WREG	WREG = f	WREG	1	1	N,Z	1011 0111 0BDf ffff ffff ffff
IOR{.B} #lit10,Wn	Wn = lit10	Wn	1	1	N,Z	1011 0011 0Bkk kkkk kkkk dddd
IOR{.B} Wb,Ws,Wd	Wd = Wb	Ws	1	1	N,Z	0111 0www wBqq qddd dppp ssss
IOR{.B} Wb,#lit5,Wd	Wd = Wb	#lit5	1	1	N,Z	0111 0www wBqq qddd d11k kkkk
LNK #lit14	Link Frame Pointer	1	1	none	1111 1010 00kk kkkk kkkk kkk0
LSR{.B} f	f = Logical >> f by 1	1	1	N,Z,C	1101 0101 0BDf ffff ffff ffff
LSR{.B} f,WREG	WREG = Logical >> f by 1	1	1	N,Z,C	1101 0101 0BDf ffff ffff ffff
LSR{.B} Ws,Wd	Wd = Logical >> Ws by 1	1	1	N,Z,C	1101 0001 0Bqq qddd dppp ssss
LSR{.B} Wb,Wns,Wnd	Wnd = Logical >> Wb by Wns	1	1	N,Z	1101 1110 0www wddd d000 ssss
LSR{.B} Wb,#lit4,Wnd	Wnd = Logical >> Wb by lit4	1	1	N,Z	1101 1110 0www wddd d100 kkkk
MOV f,Wn	Move f to Wn	1	1	none	1000 0fff ffff ffff ffff dddd
MOV{.B} f	Move f to f	1	1	N,Z	1011 1111 1BDf ffff ffff ffff

FIGURE A.7 Instruction table (part 4).

Instr	Descr	#W	#Cyc	Status	Machine Code
MOV{.B} f,WREG	Move f to WREG	1	1	N,Z	1011 1111 1BDf ffff ffff ffff
MOV #lit16,Wn	Move 16-bit literal to Wn	1	1	none	0010 kkkk kkkk kkkk dddd
MOV.B #lit8,Wn	Move 8-bit literal to Wn	1	1	none	1011 0011 1100 kkkk kkkk dddd
MOV Wn,f	Move Wn to f	1	1	none	1000 1fff ffff ffff ffff ssss
MOV Wso,Wdo	Move Wso to Wdo	1	1	none	0111 1www wBhh hddo dggg ssss
MOV{.B} [Wns+#slit10],Wnd	Move [Wns with offset] to Wnd	1	1	none	1001 0kkk kBkk kddk dkkk ssss
MOV{.B} Wns,[Wnd+#slit10]	Move Wns to [Wnd with offset]	1	1	none	1001 1kkk kBkk kddk dkkk ssss
MOV{.B} WREG,f	Move WREG to f	1	1	none	1011 0111 1B1f ffff ffff ffff
MOV.D Wns,Wd	Move double from Wns,Wns+1 to Wd	1	2	none	1011 1110 10qq qddd d000 sss0
MOV.D Ws,Wnd	Move double from Ws to Wnd,Wnd+1	1	2	none	1011 1110 0000 0ddd 0ppp ssss
MUL.SS Wb,Ws,Wnd	Wnd+1:Wnd = sign(Wb)*sign(Ws)	1	1	none	1011 1001 1www wddd dppp ssss
MUL.SU Wb,Ws,Wnd	Wnd+1:Wnd = sign(Wb)*unsig(Ws)	1	1	none	1011 1001 0www wddd dppp ssss
MUL.US Wb,Ws,Wnd	Wnd+1:Wnd = unsig(Wb)*sign(Ws)	1	1	none	1011 1000 1www wddd dppp ssss
MUL.UU Wb,Ws,Wnd	Wnd+1:Wnd = unsig(Wb)*unsign(Ws)	1	1	none	1011 1000 0www wddd dppp ssss
MUL.SU Wb,#lit5,Wnd	Wnd+1:Wnd = sign(Wb)*unsign(lit5)	1	1	none	1011 1001 1www wddd d11k kkkk
MUL.UU Wb,#lit5,Wnd	Wnd+1:Wnd = unsign(Wb)*unsign(lit5)	1	1	none	1011 1000 0www wddd d11k kkkk
MUL{.B} f	W3:W2 = f*WREG (unsigned mult)	1	1	none	1011 1100 0B0f ffff ffff ffff
NEG{.B} f	f = ~f + 1	1	1	C,DC,N,V,Z	1110 1110 0BDf ffff ffff ffff
NEG{.B} f,WREG	WREG = ~f + 1	1	1	C,DC,N,V,Z	1110 1110 0BDf ffff ffff ffff
NEG{.B} Ws,Wd	Wd = ~Ws + 1	1	1	C,DC,N,V,Z	1110 1010 0Bqq qddd dppp ssss
NOP	No operation	1	1	none	0000 0000 xxxx xxxx xxxx xxxx
NOPR	No operation	1	1	none	1111 1111 xxxx xxxx xxxx xxxx
POP f	Pop f from top-of-stack	1	1	none	1111 1001 ffff ffff ffff fff0
POP Wdo	Pop from top-of-stack to Wdo	1	1	none	0111 1www w0hh hddd d100 1111
POP.D Wnd	Pop from top-of-stack to Wnd,Wnd+1	1	2	none	1011 1110 0000 0ddd 0100 1111
POP.S	Pop shadow registers	1	1	C,DC,N,V,Z	1111 1110 1000 0000 0000 0000
PUSH f	Push f to top-of-stack	1	1	none	1111 1000 ffff ffff ffff fff0
PUSH Wso	Push Wso to top-of-stack	1	1	none	0111 1www w001 1111 1ggg ssss
PUSH.D Wsn	Push Wsn,Wsn+1 to top-of-stack	1	2	none	1011 1110 1001 1111 1000 sss0
PUSH.S	Push shadow registers	1	1	none	1111 1110 1010 0000 0000 0000

FIGURE A.8 Instruction table (part 5).

Instr	Descr	#W	#Cyc	Status	Machine Code
PWRSAV #lit1	Go into Sleep (#lit1 = 0) or Idle (#lit1 = 1) mode	1	1	none	1111 1110 0100 0000 0000 000k
RCALL Expr	Relative Call	1	2	none	0000 0111 nnnn nnnn nnnn nnnn
RCALL Wn	Computed Call	1	1	none	0000 0001 0010 0000 0000 ssss
REPEAT #lit4	Repeat next instr. lit14+1 times	1	1	none	0000 1001 00kk kkkk kkkk kkkk
REPEAT Wn	Repeat next instr. (Wn)+1 times	1	1	none	0000 1001 1000 0000 0000 ssss
RESET	Software reset	1	1	all	1111 1110 0000 0000 0000 0000
RETFIE	Return from interrupt	1	3(2)	IPL<3:0>, N,V,Z,C	0000 0110 0100 0000 0000 0000
RETLW{.B} #lit10,Wn	Return with unsigned lit10 in Wn	1	3(2)	none	0000 0101 0Bkk kkkk kkkk dddd
RETURN	Return from subroutine	1	3(2)	none	0000 0110 0000 0000 0000 0000
RLC{.B} f	f = Rotate << through Carry f	1	1	N,Z,C	1101 0110 1BDf ffff ffff ffff
RLC{.B} f,WREG	WREG = Rotate << through Carry f	1	1	N,Z,C	1101 0110 1BDf ffff ffff ffff
RLC{.B} Ws,Wd	Wd = Rotate << through Carry Ws	1	1	N,Z,C	1101 0010 1Bqq qddd dppp ssss
RLNC{.B} f	f = Rotate << (no Carry) f	1	1	N,Z	1101 0110 0BDf ffff ffff ffff
RLNC{.B} f,WREG	WREG = Rotate << (no Carry) f	1	1	N,Z	1101 0110 0BDf ffff ffff ffff
RLNC{.B} Ws,Wd	Wd = Rotate << (no Carry) Ws	1	1	N,Z	1101 0010 0Bqq qddd dppp ssss
RRC{.B} f	f = Rotate >> through Carry f	1	1	N,Z,C	1101 0111 1BDf ffff ffff ffff
RRC{.B} f,WREG	WREG = Rotate >> through Carry f	1	1	N,Z,C	1101 0111 1BDf ffff ffff ffff
RRC{.B} Ws,Wd	Wd = Rotate >> through Carry Ws	1	1	N,Z,C	1101 0011 1Bqq qddd dppp ssss
RRNC{.B} f	f = Rotate >> (no Carry) f	1	1	N,Z	1101 0111 0BDf ffff ffff ffff
RRNC{.B} f,WREG	WREG = Rotate >> (no Carry) f	1	1	N,Z	1101 0111 0BDf ffff ffff ffff
RRNC{.B} Ws,Wd	Wd = Rotate' >> (no Carry) Ws	1	1	N,Z	1101 0011 0Bqq qddd dppp ssss
SE Ws, Wnd	Wnd = sign extend Ws	1	1	C,N,Z	1111 1011 0000 0ddd dppp ssss
SETM{.B} f	f = 0xFFFF	1	1	none	1110 1111 1BDf ffff ffff ffff
SETM{.B} WREG	WREG = 0xFFFF	1	1	none	1110 1111 1BDf ffff ffff ffff
SETM{.B} Wd	Wd = 0xFFFF	1	1	none	1110 1011 1Bqq qddd d000 0000
SL{.B} f	f = left shift (<<) f by 1	1	1	C,N,Z	1101 0100 0BDf ffff ffff ffff
SL{.B} f,WREG	WREG = left shift (<<) f by 1	1	1	C,N,Z	1101 0100 0BDf ffff ffff ffff

FIGURE A.9 Instruction table (part 6).

Instr	Descr	#W	#Cyc	Status	Machine Code
SL{.B} Ws,Wd	Wd = Left shift (<<) Ws by 1	1	1	N,Z,C	1101 0000 0Bqq qddd dppp ssss
SL{.B} Wb,Wns,Wnd	Wnd = Left shift (<<) Wb by Wns	1	1	N,Z	1101 1101 0www wddd d000 ssss
SL{.B} Wb,#lit4,Wnd	Wnd = Left shift (<<) by lit4	1	1	N,Z	1101 1101 0www wddd d100 kkkk
SUB{.B} f	f = f - WREG	1	1	C,DC,N,V,Z	1011 0101 0BDf ffff ffff ffff
SUB{.B} f,WREG	WREG = f - WREG	1	1	C,DC,N,V,Z	1011 0101 0BDf ffff ffff ffff
SUB{.B} #lit10,Wd	Wd = Wd - lit10	1	1	C,DC,N,V,Z	1011 0001 0Bkk kkkk kkkk dddd
SUB{.B} Wb, Ws, Wd	Wd = Wb - Ws	1	1	C,DC,N,V,Z	0101 0www wBqq qddd dppp ssss
SUB{.B} Wb,#lit5,Wd	Wd = Wb - lit5	1	1	C,DC,N,V,Z	0101 0www wBqq qddd d11k kkkk
SUBB{.B} f	f = f - WREG - BORROW (~C)	1	1	C,DC,N,V,Z	1011 0101 1BDf ffff ffff ffff
SUBB{.B} f,WREG	WREG = f - WREG - BORROW (~C)	1	1	C,DC,N,V,Z	1011 0101 1BDf ffff ffff ffff
SUBB{.B} #lit10,Wn	Wn = Wn - lit10 - BORROW (~C)	1	1	C,DC,N,V,Z	1011 0001 1Bkk kkkk kkkk dddd
SUBB{.B} Wb,Ws,Wd	Wd = Wb - Ws - BORROW (~C)	1	1	C,DC,N,V,Z	0101 1www wBqq qddd dppp ssss
SUBB{.B} Wb,#lit5,Wd	Wd = Wb - lit5 - BORROW (~C)	1	1	C,DC,N,V,Z	0101 1www wBqq qddd d11k kkkk
SUBR{.B} f	f = WREG - f	1	1	C,DC,N,V,Z	1011 1101 0BDf ffff ffff ffff
SUBR{.B} f,WREG	WREG = WREG - f	1	1	C,DC,N,V,Z	1011 1101 0BDf ffff ffff ffff
SUBR{.B} Wb,Ws,Wd	Wd = Ws - Wb	1	1	C,DC,N,V,Z	0001 0www wBqq qddd dppp ssss
SUBR{.B} Wb,#lit5,Wd	Wd = lit5 - Wb	1	1	C,DC,N,V,Z	0001 0www wBqq qddd d11k kkkk
SUBBR{.B} f	f = WREG - f - BORROW (~C)	1	1	C,DC,N,V,Z	1011 1101 1BDf ffff ffff ffff
SUBBR{.B} f,WREG	WREG = WREG - f - BORROW (~C)	1	1	C,DC,N,V,Z	1011 1101 1BDf ffff ffff ffff
SUBBR{.B} Wb,Ws,Wd	Wd = Ws - Wb - BORROW (~C)	1	1	C,DC,N,V,Z	0001 1www wBqq qddd dppp ssss
SUBBR{.B} Wb,#lit5,Wd	Wd = lit5 - Wb - BORROW (~C)	1	1	C,DC,N,V,Z	0001 1www wBqq qddd d11k kkkk
SWAP.B Wn	Wn = nibble swap Wn	1	1	none	1111 1101 1100 0000 0000 ssss
SWAP Wn	Wn = byte swap Wn	1	1	none	1111 1101 1000 0000 0000 ssss
TBLRDH{.B} Wsi,Wd	Read Prog<23:16> to Wd<7:0>	1	2	none	1011 1010 1Bqq qddd dppp ssss
TBLRDL{.B} Wsi,Wd	Read Prog<15:0> to Wd	1	2	none	1011 1010 0Bqq qddd dppp ssss
TBLWTH{.B} Ws,Wdi	Write Ws<7:0> to Prog<23:16>	1	2	none	1011 1011 1Bqq qddd dppp ssss
TBLWTL{.B} Ws,Wdi	Write Ws to Prog<15:0>	1	2	none	1011 1011 0Bqq qddd dppp ssss

FIGURE A.10 Instruction table (part 7).

Instr	Descr	#W	#Cyc	Status	Machine Code
ULNK	Unlink frame pointer	1	1	none	1111 1010 1000 0000 0000 0000
XOR f	f = f ^ WREG	1	1	N,Z	1011 0110 1BDf ffff ffff ffff
XOR f,WREG	WREG = f ^ WREG	1	1	N,Z	1011 0110 1BDf ffff ffff ffff
XOR #lit10,Wn	Wn = lit10 ^ Wn	1	1	N,Z	1011 0010 1Bkk kkkk kkkk dddd
XOR Wb,Ws,Wd	Wd = Wb ^ Ws	1	1	N,Z	0110 1www wBqq qddd dppp ssss
XOR Wb,#lit5,Wd	Wd = Wb ^ lit5	1	1	N,Z	0110 1www wBqq qddd d11k kkkk
ZE Ws,Wnd	Wnd = Zero extend Ws	1	1	N,Z,C	1111 1011 10qq qddd dppp ssss

FIGURE A.11 Instruction table (part 8).

APPENDIX B

Software Tools Overview

T his appendix contains short tutorials on the Microchip MPLAB® integrated design environment, the Microchip PIC24 *C* compiler, the Microchip PICkit™ 2 programmer, and the "Bully" bootloader (a serial bootloader named after the Mississippi State University mascot).

MPLAB INTRODUCTION[1]

The MPLAB integrated design environment is used to assemble and simulate PIC24 assembly language and *C* programs discussed in this text. MPLAB is available as a free download from the Microchip website (*www.microchip.com*). The *code* folder on the book's CD-ROM contains all of the code examples used in the textbook and can be copied to any destination folder on your PC. The MPLAB project files (which have a file extension of *.mcp*) for the code examples are grouped by chapter. Documentation for all code examples is found in the *docs* folder.

Figure B.1 shows how to use MPLAB to open and assemble a pre-existing assembly language project named *code\chap3\mptst_byte.mcp* that is contained on this book's CD-ROM (this corresponds to the assembly language program in Listing 3.4). MPLAB project files specify the files and tools used for assembly and compilation; the easiest way to create a new project is to open an existing project, then use the *Project → Save As . . .* menu choice to save the project under a new name as shown in Figure B.1f. The alternate method of creating a new project from scratch requires copying many build options settings manually, making it more difficult and error-prone. MPLAB workspace files (*.mcw* file extension) for each project are not included on the CD-ROM because workspaces contain a user's preference for window arrangement and other GUI options. A workspace file is automatically created whenever a project is opened and can be saved when the project is closed. If you double left-click on a project file to open it, you may not see the files associated with the project because a workspace is not available for the project. The best way to open a project that does not have an associated workspace is to first start MPLAB (this creates an empty workspace), then use *Project → Open*

---

[1]All MPLAB screen shots used with permission of the copyright owner, Microchip Technology Inc.

to open an existing project as shown in Figure B.1a (you may have to try opening the project twice if you do not see the project's files in the workspace window after the first open operation). After opening the project, configure the workspace for the PIC24HJ32GP202 by following the remaining instructions in Figure B.1.

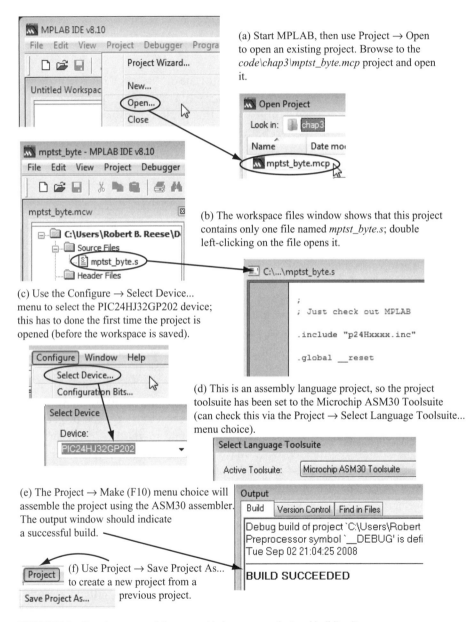

(a) Start MPLAB, then use Project → Open to open an existing project. Browse to the *code\chap3\mptst_byte.mcp* project and open it.

(b) The workspace files window shows that this project contains only one file named *mptst_byte.s*; double left-clicking on the file opens it.

(c) Use the Configure → Select Device... menu to select the PIC24HJ32GP202 device; this has to done the first time the project is opened (before the workspace is saved).

(d) This is an assembly language project, so the project toolsuite has been set to the Microchip ASM30 Toolsuite (can check this via the Project → Select Language Toolsuite... menu choice).

(e) The Project → Make (F10) menu choice will assemble the project using the ASM30 assembler. The output window should indicate a successful build.

(f) Use Project → Save Project As... to create a new project from a previous project.

FIGURE B.1 Opening a pre-existing assembly language project and building it.

When closing the project, you should answer "yes" when asked if you wish to save the workspace, as all of your settings and window configurations are saved in the workspace file. Figure B.2 shows how to dock windows in MPLAB.

Using the MPLAB SIM Debugger for simulating an assembly language program is shown in Figure B.3. The watch window is useful for monitoring individual special function registers and memory locations during program execution. Figure B.4 shows how to use the stopwatch window to measure program execution time, while Figure B.5 shows our preferred method for adding files to a project.

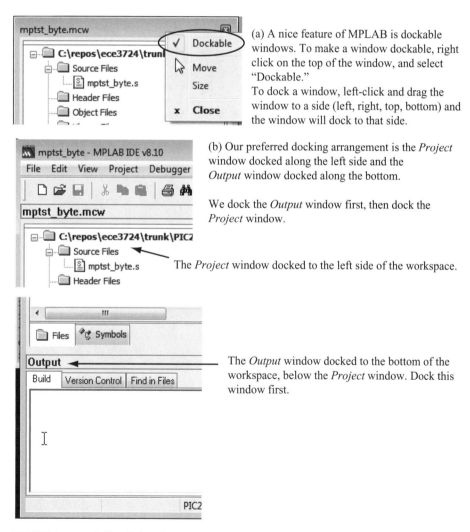

(a) A nice feature of MPLAB is dockable windows. To make a window dockable, right click on the top of the window, and select "Dockable."
To dock a window, left-click and drag the window to a side (left, right, top, bottom) and the window will dock to that side.

(b) Our preferred docking arrangement is the *Project* window docked along the left side and the *Output* window docked along the bottom.

We dock the *Output* window first, then dock the *Project* window.

The *Project* window docked to the left side of the workspace.

The *Output* window docked to the bottom of the workspace, below the *Project* window. Dock this window first.

FIGURE B.2   Dockable windows in MPLAB.

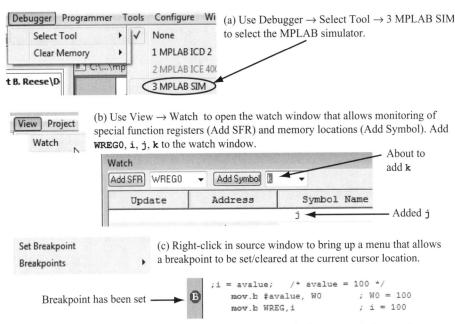

(a) Use Debugger → Select Tool → 3 MPLAB SIM to select the MPLAB simulator.

(b) Use View → Watch to open the watch window that allows monitoring of special function registers (Add SFR) and memory locations (Add Symbol). Add **WREG0, i, j, k** to the watch window.

About to add **k**

Added **j**

(c) Right-click in source window to bring up a menu that allows a breakpoint to be set/cleared at the current cursor location.

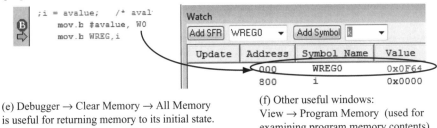

Breakpoint has been set

```
;i = avalue;    /* avalue = 100 */
    mov.b #avalue, W0       ; W0 = 100
    mov.b WREG,i            ; i = 100
```

(d) Use F7 to single step through the program; the green arrow in the source window tracks program execution. Use F6 to execute a processor reset.

(e) Debugger → Clear Memory → All Memory is useful for returning memory to its initial state. The program must be recompiled if all of memory is cleared.

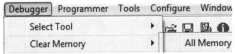

(f) Other useful windows:
View → Program Memory (used for examining program memory contents)

View → File Registers (used for examining data memory contents)

Debugger → Stopwatch (used for measuring program execution time)

FIGURE B.3 Using the MPLAB SIM Debugger.

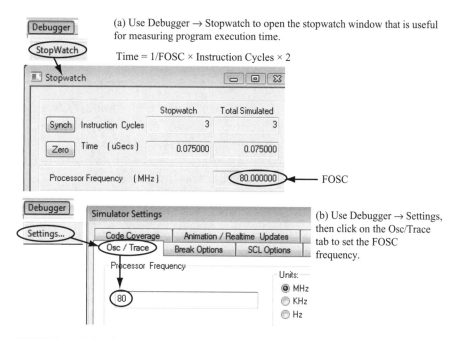

(a) Use Debugger → Stopwatch to open the stopwatch window that is useful for measuring program execution time.

Time = 1/FOSC × Instruction Cycles × 2

FOSC

(b) Use Debugger → Settings, then click on the Osc/Trace tab to set the FOSC frequency.

FIGURE B.4 Using the MPLAB SIM Stopwatch.

(a) When adding files to a project, we have found it best to use relative paths as this allows the project and files to be copied to any folder.

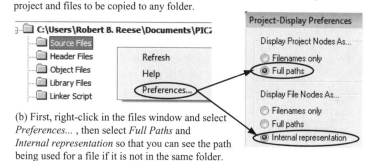

(b) First, right-click in the files window and select *Preferences...* , then select *Full Paths* and *Internal representation* so that you can see the path being used for a file if it is not in the same folder.

(c) To add a file, right click on Source Files and select *Add Files...*

(d) Browse to a source file to be added. Select the "...*use relative path*" option for the file.

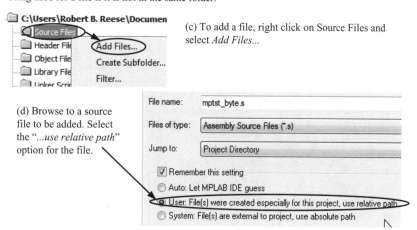

FIGURE B.5 Adding files to an MPLAB project.

PIC24 C COMPILER INTRODUCTION

The PIC24 *C* compiler (also known as the C30 compiler) is a free download available from the Microchip website. Some compiler optimizations are disabled 60 days after installation, but the compiler still functions. Once installed, PIC24 *C* programs can be compiled from within MPLAB as shown in Figure B.6. The output file is a *.hex* file that has the same name as the project.

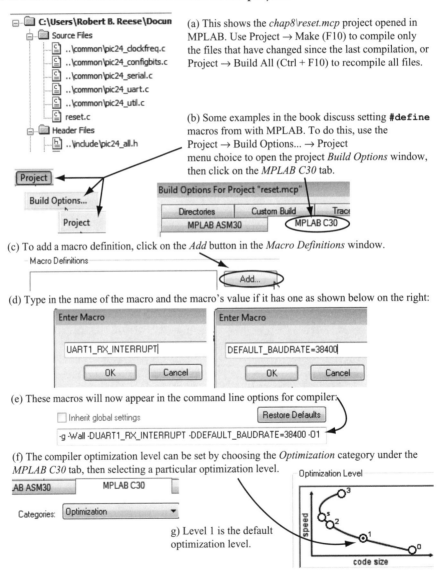

(a) This shows the *chap8\reset.mcp* project opened in MPLAB. Use Project → Make (F10) to compile only the files that have changed since the last compilation, or Project → Build All (Ctrl + F10) to recompile all files.

(b) Some examples in the book discuss setting **#define** macros from with MPLAB. To do this, use the Project → Build Options... → Project menu choice to open the project *Build Options* window, then click on the *MPLAB C30* tab.

(c) To add a macro definition, click on the *Add* button in the *Macro Definitions* window.

(d) Type in the name of the macro and the macro's value if it has one as shown below on the right:

(e) These macros will now appear in the command line options for compiler:

(f) The compiler optimization level can be set by choosing the *Optimization* category under the *MPLAB C30* tab, then selecting a particular optimization level.

g) Level 1 is the default optimization level.

FIGURE B.6 Compiling with the PIC24 *C* compiler, defining macros and setting optimization level.

All of the *C* projects in the book's code distribution are configured for producing hex files that are compatible with a serial bootloader (discussed later in this appendix). This means that the project file includes a customized linker script as shown in Figure B.7a (these customized linker scripts are contained in the *code\lkr* folder). Some of the projects in later chapters use a device that is different from the PIC24HJ32GP202 as indicated by the linker script as shown in Figure B.7b. Ensure that the selected device in the MPLAB project matches the device specified by the linker script. If you wish to produce hex files that are compatible with the PICkit 2 programmer (discussed in the next section), then remove the linker script from the project. If you are compiling projects for different devices in the same directory, do either a "Clean" operation or "Build All" before compiling so that you do not mix object files for different devices. Also, some projects in Chapter 12 and later do not use the FRC clock option and instead expect an external clock crystal. These projects produce a warning as shown in Figure B.7c; the CLOCK_CONFIG macro is used to select the clock option as discussed in Chapter 8. Complete documentation on the CLOCK_CONFIG macro is found in the *docs* directory on the book's CD-ROM.

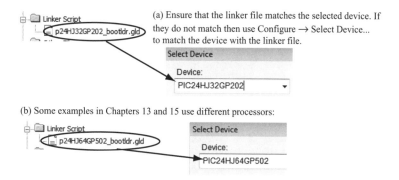

(a) Ensure that the linker file matches the selected device. If they do not match then use Configure → Select Device... to match the device with the linker file.

(b) Some examples in Chapters 13 and 15 use different processors:

(c) Some examples in Chapter 12 and later chapters do not use the internal FRC as the clock source, instead using an external crystal for accuracy reasons. The output window will contain the following warning when compiling the *common\pic24_clock.c* file:

... **#warning Clock configured for PRIPLL using an 8.0 Mhz primary oscillator, FCY = 40 MHz**

This clock selection is made by the CLOCK_CONFIG macro defined in the project; see the *docs* directory on the CD-ROM for a full description of clock selection via CLOCK_CONFIG.

If you do not have a crystal and wish to use our default clock source of the internal FRC with the PLL set to FCY = 40 MHz for a PIC24H family processor, then delete the CLOCK_CONFIG macro from the project (for a PIC24F family CPU, our default clock setting is the FRC with the PLL set to FCY = 16 MHz).

FIGURE B.7   Matching linker script and processor choice.

THE PICKIT™ 2 PROGRAMMER[2]

The PICkit 2 programmer (Figure B.8) available from Microchip is an inexpensive programmer that can be used to download *.hex* files into a PIC24 µC. The ICSP (in circuit serial programming) header shown in Figure 8.3 is all that is required for a PIC24 system to support a PICkit 2 interface. The PICkit 2 software is available as a free download from the Microchip website.

FIGURE B.8   PICkit 2 Programmer.

The MPLAB PIC24 compiler projects on this book's CD-ROM in Chapters 8–15 all use a linker file that produces a hex file compatible with the serial bootloader discussed in the next section. This linker file causes instructions to be placed in program memory beginning at location 0x00C02, as locations 0x00200 through 0x00C00 are reserved for use by the bootloader firmware (see the next section). To produce hex files for use with the PICkit 2, simply remove the linker file as shown in Figure B.9 in order to use the default linker file contained in the PIC24 *C* compiler installation folders. The default linker file causes instructions to be placed in program memory beginning at location 0x00200, which is the first available location for an application

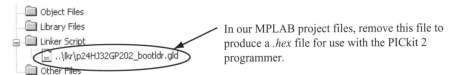

FIGURE B.9   Removing the bootloader linker file from an MPLAB project.

---

[2]All PICkit 2 software screen shots are used with permission of the copyright owner, Microchip Technology Inc.

instruction. If you forget to do this, the programmed hex file will still work but the code space between 0x00200 and 0x00C00 will be filled with NOPs, wasting some of the precious program memory on your processor.

Figure B.10 shows how to use the PICkit 2 software to download a hex file into a PIC24 μC. It is important that you erase the device before downloading a new hex file. The programmer verifies the program memory contents after the device is programmed to ensure that the program was downloaded successfully.

(a) Connect the PICkit 2 to your board, then start the PICkit 2 software. Your processor is automatically detected if the ICSP interface is working correctly.

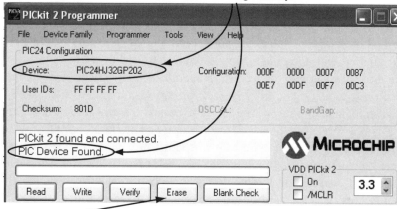

(b) Use the *Erase* button to erase the device before programming.
(c) Use the File → Import Hex menu command to browse to a hex file and import it for programming.

(d) The memory display will now show contents other than 0xFFFFFF.

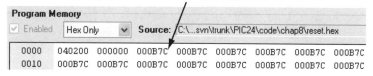

(e) Use the *Write* button to program; after the device is programmed and verified the "Programming Successful" message is displayed.

FIGURE B.10   Downloading a hex file using the PICkit 2 programmer.

THE PIC24 BULLY BOOTLOADER

A *serial bootloader* allows new programs to be downloaded into a μC via the asynchronous serial port. In many instances this is a more convenient mechanism for updating a program than by using an external programmer like the PICkit 2. The PIC24 Bully bootloader (referred to as simply "the bootloader" from this point on; "Bully" is MSU's mascot) is a serial bootloader that students at Mississippi State University use to update their PIC24 μCs during lab exercises. A serial bootloader consists of two parts: 1) firmware that resides on the PIC24 μC and 2) a GUI that runs on a PC and communicates with the PIC24 μC in order to download a program. The firmware uses the flash memory self-programming techniques discussed in Chapter 13 for writing a downloaded program to flash memory. The firmware is based on code supplied with AN1094 [65] from Microchip, and the GUI is a windows .NET application (which requires the .NET runtime version 2.0 or later).

The bootloader GUI executable is *code\bin\winbootldr.exe*; copy this file and the *code\bin\devices.txt* file to any destination folder on your PC (the *devices.txt* file must be in the same folder as the *winbootldr.exe* file). The folder *code\hex* contains some precompiled firmware hex files for various targets, such as *p24HJ32GP202_57600baud_bootldr.hex*. Source code for both the firmware and GUI are available on this book's website at *www.reesemicro.com*. The bootloader firmware does not automatically detect the baud rate so the firmware hex files are compiled with a target baud rate of 57600 baud. The firmware boots the PIC24 μC using the internal fast RC oscillator. If a hex file is downloaded, the firmware sets the POR bit before jumping to the application to simulate a power-on reset so that the application's *C* runtime code will initialize persistent variables. After power-on or reset, the firmware monitors the serial port for communication from the bootloader GUI. If no input is received after two seconds, then the bootloader jumps to the user application.

Figure B.11 shows the bootloader GUI. The display window shows serial output from the PIC24 μC application, while the lower window shows status messages from the bootloader. Serial input can be sent to the PIC24 μC application by typing text into the type-in field, then using either the *Send* or *Send&\n* (append a new line character that is hex 0x0A) buttons to transmit the text. If the RTS# pin on the USB-to-serial connector (pin #6 in Figure 8.3) is connected to the MCLR# input on the PIC24 μC, then the MCLR# checkbox asserts MCLR#. To download a hex file, use the *HexFile* button to browse to a target hex file. If the RTS# pin is connected to MCLR, then the "*MCLR# and Prgrm*" button toggles MCLR# and downloads the hex file. Otherwise, click on the *Program* button 2 seconds after toggling MCLR# or a power cycle to download the hex file. Additional documentation on the bootloader is found in the *docs* folder.

a) Type-in field for console input, use *Send* to send just the characters in the type-in field or use *Send&\n* to send the characters with a newline character appended.

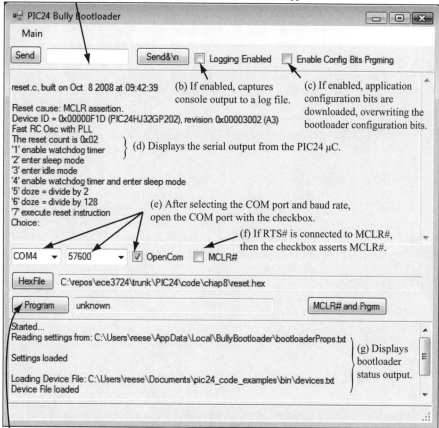

(h) To download a hex file, first use the *HexFile* button to browse to a hex file. If the RTS# pin on the USB-to-serial cable is connected to MCLR#, then use the "*MCLR# and Prgrm*" button to download a new file; otherwise cycle power or press the MCLR button and then click on the *Program* button on the bootloader GUI within 2 seconds.

FIGURE B.11   Bully bootloader GUI.

APPENDIX C

Suggested Laboratory Exercises

This appendix contains the laboratory exercises for a semester-length course taught at Mississippi State University since summer 2004. We first began teaching a PICmicro®-based introductory microprocessor course in fall 2003 using the PIC16F873 µC. We switched to the PIC18 family in summer 2004 (the PIC18F242, then the PIC18F2420). In summer 2008, we began using the PIC24 family with the PIC24HJ32GP202 as our target processor.

Lab Setup

Table C.1 lists the lab equipment assumed by these experiments. Each lab station should have an oscilloscope and a multimeter. In addition, if each student does not have a portable PC, every lab station must have a desktop PC. Each lab station should either have a local area network (LAN) connection or the lab should be wireless enabled.

TABLE C.1 Suggested lab equipment.

Equipment	Comment
Networked PC	Lab station needs a LAN connection or a wireless network if student has a portable PC.
Multimeter	Basic instrumentation (each station).
Oscilloscope	Basic instrumentation (each station).
PICkit 2 Programmer	This is used by the TAs for programming the PIC24 µC with the serial bootloader. The TA should have a board with a ZIF (zero insertion force) socket for programming PIC24 µCs in DIP packages
Soldering and wire wrap tools/supplies	Either soldering or wire wrap is used for external connectors; multiple stations can share this.

Our labs use a breadboard plus parts kit approach to build the PIC24HJ32GP202 reference system of Figure 8.3 (Chapter 8). Our lab TAs use a small PCB with a zero insertion force (ZIF) socket for programming the bootloader into a PIC24 μC using the PICkit 2 before it is given to a student (see *pcb\eagle_pcb\projects\ZIF_pickit2* on the CD-ROM for a sample board). Each student has a portable computer for using the software discussed in Appendix B. The lab experiments consist of 11 experiments: one digital-logic based, four assembly language based, and six hardware based. In the last week of the semester we hold a lab practicum to evaluate student skills for ABET assessment purposes. The hardware experiments use a parts kit and a breadboard board purchased by each student. Through the six hardware experiments, a student builds a PIC24HJ32GP202 system that has an external I²C serial EEPROM, a SPI DAC, an asynchronous serial interface, a potentiometer, and an analog temperature sensor. A 6 V wall transformer with a 3.3 V voltage regulator is used to power the breadboard as discussed in Figure 8.3. The lab also has a couple of soldering irons for creating reliable connections to the external power connector. Figure C.1 shows a picture of the breadboard after the wiring for Figure 8.3 has been completed. A step-by-step wiring procedure for this figure is found in the file *docs\manuallyCreated\board_walkthru_pic24.pdf*.

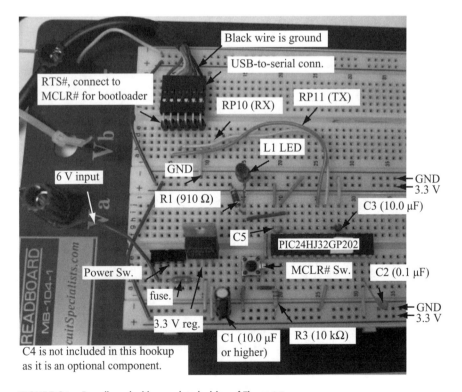

FIGURE C.1 Breadboard with completed wiring of Figure 8.3.

The parts kit list used during the Fall 2008 semester is shown in Figure C.2 along with supplier part numbers. We purchase the part kits preassembled from Electronix Express (*www.elexp.com*) at a substantially reduced price over what can be ordered by students in single quantities from parts suppliers.

Semiconductors	Qty.	Part Number
LM2940 low-dropout regulator 5 V	1	LM2940CT-5.0-ND (DK)
LM2937-3.3 low-dropout regulator 3.3 V	1	LM2937ET-3.3-ND (DK)
PIC24HJ32GP202	1	PIC24HJ32GP202-I/SP-ND (DK)
MAX548A SPI DAC	1	MAX548ACPA+-ND (DK)
24LC515 serial EEPROM	1	24LC515-I/P-ND (DK)
LM60 temperature sensor	1	LM60CIZ-ND (DK)
SN754410 motor driver	1	296-9911-5-ND (DK)
Red LED	4	P428-ND (DK)
Green LED	1	P429-ND (DK)
Resistors and potentiometers		
2.2 kΩ axial resistors	2	(any supplier)
910 Ω axial resistors	1	(any supplier)
470 Ω axial resistors (or just use 910 Ω resistors; used for LED current limiting)	4	(any supplier)
10 kΩ axial resistor	1	(any supplier)
10 kΩ potentiometer	1	P4C1103-ND (DK)
Capacitors		
47 µF radial	1	P5137-ND (DK)
10 µF tantalum radial, < 5 ohms ESR	3	478-1839-ND (DK)
1 µF tantalum radial, < 5 ohms ESR	8	399-1412-ND (DK)
Miscellaneous		
500 mA fast-acting axial fuse	2	F2311-ND (DK)
5 position header	1	WM4003-ND (DK)
Wall transformer 6V, 1 A	1	T978-P7P-ND (DK)
Power connector	1	CP-2519-ND (DK)
6x1 0.1" pitch R/A long-tail connector	1	S1132E-06-ND (DK)
5 V fan	1	AD4505MX-G70-LF (Mouser)
Pushbutton switch	2	P8009S-ND (DK)
Slide switch	1	EG1903-ND (DK)
USB to TTL level serial cable (3.3 V)	1	768-1015-ND (DK)

FIGURE C.2   Parts list for experiments.

Based on MSU experience, the following points are key for a successful lab course using this approach:

■ It is best if students have had some previous experience with breadboards and basic instrumentation before this lab. In the MSU ECE/CSE curriculum, students are required to take a digital logic course as a prerequisite, with the digital lab experience providing them with some breadboard experience in wiring

74XX logic. This gives them an introduction to DIP packages, how breadboard wiring works, an introduction to an oscilloscope and a multimeter, and some basic circuit debugging (which is greatly increased in this course!). A circuits course is not a prerequisite except for circuit fundamentals as presented in a physics course. We have majors from electrical engineering, computer engineering, computer science, and software engineering who take this lab, so a circuits prerequisite is not possible. If this previous experience is missing, then a portion one of the early lab periods can be dedicated to providing this background.

■ The teaching assistants (TAs) for the lab must be talented, knowledgeable, dedicated, patient, and have had previous microcontroller experience to assist students in the inevitable hardware debugging problems. We recruit our TAs from the graduates of this course; the first TAs came from a traditional microcontroller course that has since been replaced by our second course in embedded systems. We limit enrollment in each lab section to 10 students because the hardware labs dramatically increase the "help me!" load on the TA. The first hardware lab is the worst from a TA load perspective, when students are bringing their initial PIC24 µC system to life; our labs are open so students can work on their breadboards outside of normal lab hours if needed.

■ The TA must have a reference board built for demo purposes and for checking bad part problems by plugging the part into the reference board.

■ A spare parts supply is an absolute necessity, as students demonstrate an amazing talent for destroying ICs. The TA, course instructor, IEEE/HKN, or some central shop can sell these parts. Fuses have been our top sellers.

It is rewarding to watch students with near-zero prototyping skills gain confidence as the semester progresses, and show pride in their board as they build it up from a collection of ICs and wires to something that performs useful tasks. All of the files and zip archives referenced in the following lab descriptions are contained in the *code\labs* directory on the companion CD-ROM. Several of the labs personalize the task by using student's 9-digit university ID number; any similar number string can be used instead.

Experiment 1: A Stored Program Machine (Chapters 1, 2)

This experiment has the students implement the Number Sequencing Computer from Chapter 2 using the digital logic simulation package from a previous digital logic course, thus serving as a bridge from the digital logic course to the microprocessor course. At MSU, we use the Xilinx ISE Foundation software package for digital design entry and simulation. We give the students the design already entered in Xilinx and have them write a program that outputs their own student ID number or phone number. The ROM block is implemented as a simple Verilog module. Students edit this file to change the ROM contents to specify the machine code for their program. Students also step through the logic simulation within the Xilinx simulator to determine how many clock cycles it takes to output the two different number sequences based on the LOC input. We also ask the students to modify the design to support a 32-location memory instead of a 16-location memory. The *code\labs\nsc_xilinx_isev9_1.zip* archive contains the Xilinx ISE Foundation design for the number sequencing computer in Chapter 2.

EXPERIMENT 2: PIC24 ASSEMBLY AND MPLAB INTRODUCTION (CHAPTER 3)

This lab introduces the Microchip MPLAB Integrated Design Environment. This writeup was done using MPLAB 8.10; later versions may have slightly different menus. All files referenced in the lab are found in *code\labs\lab_mplab_intro*. The tasks in this lab are:

- Use MPLAB to simulate the PIC24 assembly language program in the *code\labs\lab_mplab_intro\mptst_word.mcp* project to become familiar with the MPLAB environment.
- Do some simple programming tasks using PIC24 assembly language.

This lab requires you to capture portions of the screen. There are many screen capture programs available that allow you to capture only a portion, such as:

- MWsnap (*www.mirekw.com/winfreeware/mwsnap.html*) Freeware
- HyperSnap (*www.hypersnap.com*)—not free, 20-day evaluation copy.

As always, read through the entire lab and scan the supplied files before starting to work. The reporting requirements have you verify computations done by the assembly language program. In all cases, make it easy for the TA to verify your computations by showing your work.

When writing MPLAB assembly language programs, do not use variable names of a or b as these are reserved names.

TASK 1: MPLAB INTRODUCTION

Perform the following steps:

- Start the MPLAB IDE. Use *Project → Open* and open the *code\labs\lab_mplab_intro\mptst_word.mcp* project.

- Use *Project → Build All* to assemble the program. If the source file is not already open, double-click on the *mptst_word.s* source file to open it.
- After the project is assembled, use *View → Program Memory* and open the program memory window. Scroll the window until you find your program in memory. It will start at program memory address 0x0200.
- Use *View → File Registers* to view data memory. Scroll to location 0x800, which is where your variables will start.
- Use *View → Special Function Registers* to view the special function registers (W0–W15, etc).
- Open a watch window (*View → Watch*) and use *Add Symbol* and *Add SFR* to watch variable values and special function register values, respectively, of the i, j, k variables and the W0 special function register
- Use *Debugger → Select Tool → MPLAB Sim* to select the MPLAB Simulator. Use *Debugger → Step Into (F7)* to single step the program. Watch both the memory locations and watch window locations, and correlate their changing values with the instructions being executed.

TA check. Show the TA the task #1 result.

Reporting requirement. Modify the avalue equate (statement .equ avalue, 2047) to be the last four digits of your student ID. Reassemble the program and re-simulate it. Take a screen shot of both the Watch window contents and the memory window contents. In your report, you must show calculations that verify the screen shot values match the expected result (warning, avalue is in decimal, as is the last four digits of your student ID; the values displayed in the file registers window are in HEX).

TASK 2: MYADD.S

Perform the following steps:

- Use *Project → Save Project As* and save the *mptst_word* project as a new project named *myadd*.
- Save the *mptst_word.s* file as *myadd.s*.
- Right-click on the *mptst_word.s* file in the left-hand workspace window and use the *Remove* option to remove it from the *myadd* project.
- Right click on *Source Files* and use *Add Files* to add the *myadd.s* file to the project.
- Edit the *myadd.s* file and remove all of the instructions from mov #avalue, W0 through mov WREG, k. You can now use this file as a start for a new program.

This lab uses the last 8 digits $(Y_7Y_6Y_5Y_4Y_3Y_2Y_1Y_0)$ of your student id (or some other similar number string) to personalize the assignment. Write a program to add the four-digit number formed by $Y_3Y_2Y_1Y_0$ to the four-digit number formed by $Y_7Y_6Y_5Y_4$. Reserve space for two 16-bit variables in data space named lsp (least significant part) and msp (most significant part) to hold the values $Y_3Y_2Y_1Y_0$ and $Y_7Y_6Y_5Y_4$, respectively. Reserve space for a 16-bit variable named sum to hold the sum of lsp and msp. The following *C* code describes our program.

```
uint16 lsp, msp, sum;

lsp = Y3Y2Y1Y0;
msp = Y7Y6Y5Y4;
sum = lsp + msp;
```

Use the watch window to watch variables lsp, msp, and sum. Also, use the data memory window to monitor the memory locations corresponding to these variables. Write your program, simulate it, and verify that you receive the correct results.

TA check. Show the TA the task #2 result.

Reporting requirement. Take a screen shot of both the Watch window contents and the memory window contents. In your report, you must show calculations that verify the screen shot values match the expected result. Also take a screen shot of your program listing.

Task 3: mysub.s

Create a project named *mysub,* with a corresponding assembly language file named *mysub.s*. Using the digits of your student ID, write an assembly language program that does the following:

```
uint8 u8_p, u8_q, u8_r, u8_s, u8_t;

u8_p = Y1Y0;
u8_q = Y3Y2;
u8_r = Y5Y4;
u8_s = u8_p + u8_q;
u8_t = u8_r - u8_s;
```

Variables u8_p, u8_q, u8_r, u8_s, u8_t are all 8-bit (byte) variables. ALL operations are byte operations. Use the watch window to watch variables u8_p, u8_q, u8_r, u8_s, u8_t. Also, use the data memory window to monitor the memory locations corresponding to these variables. Write your program, simulate it, and verify that you receive the correct results.

TA check. Show the TA the task #3 result.

Reporting requirement. Take a screen shot of both the Watch window contents and the memory window contents. In your report, you must show calculations that verify the screen shot values match the expected result. Also take a screen shot of your program listing.

EXPERIMENT 3: UNSIGNED 8/16-BIT OPERATIONS IN ASSEMBLY LANGUAGE (CHAPTER 4)

This lab has you convert a *C* program that performs 8/16-bit unsigned operations into PIC24 assembly language. The *C* programs are provided as Visual Studio 2005 projects. If you do not have Visual Studio, the *C* file is compatible with any generic *C* compiler. All files referenced in the lab are found in *code\labs\lab_assem1*.

PRELAB

The prelab assignment must be completed before you walk into lab for check by the TA.

■ Have your assigned *C* program compiled, and be able to demo its execution to the TA.
■ Have an MPLAB project and assembly language template defined for your assigned task, with space for the variables already defined. Be able to demonstrate assembling this program for the TA.

THE TASK

Browse to the folder *code\labs\lab_assem1*. You will see three folders (directories) labeled as *case1*, *case2*, and *case3*. If the last digit of your student ID is:

■ 0,1,2 then use case1
■ 3,4,5 then use case2
■ 6,7,8,9 then use case3

Each directory contains a Visual Student 2005 project file and *C* source file. A typical file is shown as follows:

```
main(void) {

        uint16 u16_a, u16_b, u16_c;
        uint8  u8_d, u8_e;

        u16_a = 0xE494;
        u16_b = 0x29A5;
        u16_c = 0x4A55;
```

```
    u8_d = 0x8F;
    u8_e = 0;
    do {
        printf("a:%04x, b:%04x, c: %04x, d:%02x, e:%02x\n",
                u16_a, u16_b, u16_c, u8_d, u8_e);
        if (u16_c & 0x8000) //this is a bittest of the MSb
        {
            if (u16_b >= u16_a) {
                u16_b = u16_b - u16_a;
            } else {
                    u16_b = u16_b + (u16_a << 2) - u8_d;
                    }
        } else {
                u16_a = u16_a - 0x8000 - (u8_d >> 2);
                u16_b = u16_a + u16_b;
                u8_d = (~u8_d ^ 0xA5) + 1 ;
                }
            u16_c = u16_c << 1;
            u8_e++;
    } while (u8_e < 16);
    printf("a:%04x, b:%04x, c: %04x, d:%02x, e:%02x\n",
                    u16_a, u16_b, u16_c, u8_d, u8_e);
}
```

The computations are not meaningful in themselves; we are interested only in the final variable values that are produced. The `printf` statement is a *C* print statement for printing results to the console. Use your favorite C compiler to compile and execute the program. The printed results should be similar to the following:

```
a:34af, b:29fe, c: a458, d:45, e:00
a:f54f, b:3d98, c: 522c, d:45, e:01
a:8fc4, b:3d98, c: 2916, d:45, e:02
a:add4, b:2bba, c: 148b, d:45, e:03
a:038a, b:ae5e, c: 0a45, d:c2, e:04
a:0684, b:050e, c: 0522, d:45, e:05
a:fe8a, b:3fe7, c: 0291, d:45, e:06
a:019e, b:ff14, c: 0148, d:c2, e:07
a:fd76, b:401f, c: 00a4, d:c2, e:08
a:42a9, b:116c, c: 0052, d:c2, e:09
a:cec3, b:3472, c: 0029, d:c2, e:0a
a:1e84, b:d047, c: 0014, d:45, e:0b
a:b1c3, b:2cb5, c: 000a, d:45, e:0c
a:7af2, b:1f01, c: 0005, d:45, e:0d
a:018e, b:7b7c, c: 0002, d:c2, e:0e
```

```
a:79ee, b:1f3d, c: 0001, d:c2, e:0f
a:029c, b:7b72, c: 0000, d:45, e:10
Press any key to continue . . .
```

The `printf` statements are at the top of the loop and at the loop exit. The values are printed in HEX format because of the `%04x` format code used in the `printf` statement. The `%04x` says to print the number as four hex digits with leading 0s (used for 16-bit values) and `%02x` says to print the number as two hex digits with leading 0s (used for 8-bit values). Your task is to manually convert this C program to PIC24 assembly language. Use one of the MPLAB projects from a previous lab as a starting template. The `uint16` variables are unsigned 16-bit values, while `uint8` variables are unsigned 8-bit variables.

The `printf` statements are in the C source only for debugging purposes; they are not implemented in the PIC24 assembly program. Your PIC24 assembly program should have the same values for the variables when the loop is exited as the values printed by the original C program.

You will probably find it useful to insert additional print statements into the C code to determine when each particular `if` or `else` clause is executed, such as '`printf("If 1 entered\n");`', etc.

APPROACH

You may not "optimize" away any statements—you are to implement the C code exactly as shown. When writing your assembly, your must have a comment for at least every other assembly language statement. The comments should indicate which assembly language source lines implement which C statements. Be careful of mixed unsigned 8-bit and 16-bit operations; be sure to zero-extend the 8-bit value.

A suggested approach is to implement your assembly language solution in the following steps:

1. Get the variable initialization working correctly.
2. The loop executes a fixed number of times, so implement the loop with an empty body and verify that the loop executes the correct number of times with the loop variable containing the correct value at loop exit.
3. Trace the C code, and determine which `if`, `else` clauses are executed the first time through the loop. Implement those `if`, `else` clauses with empty bodies for the other clauses and test execution through the loop one time, verifying that you get correct values.
4. Implement the other clauses to complete your implementation. Trace variable values each time through the loop, and debug problems when you see a deviation from the C output.

TA check. Show the TA that the values produced by your assembly language program match the *C* values on loop exit.

Reporting requirement. Take a screen shot of the final memory contents/variable values of your PIC24 assembly language program and show that it matches the *C* results. Include your program source code in the report.

EXPERIMENT 4: 8/16/32-BIT SIGNED OPERATIONS IN ASSEMBLY LANGUAGE (CHAPTER 5)

This lab has you convert a *C* program that performs 8/16/32-bit signed and unsigned operations into PIC24 assembly language. All files referenced in the lab are found in *code\labs\lab_assem2*.

PRELAB

This has the same prelab requirements as Experiment 3.

THE TASK

Browse to the folder *code\labs\lab_assem2*. You will see three folders (directories) labeled as *case4*, *case5*, and *case6*. If the last digit of your student ID is:

- 0,1,2 then use case4
- 3,4,5 then use case5
- 6,7,8,9 then use case6

The *C* code in this lab that must be manually compiled to PIC24 assembly language is similar to experiment #4, except that it uses 8/16/32-bit data sizes, both signed and unsigned. The approach used for experiment #4 is also useful for this lab as well. The reporting and check requirements for this lab are the same as for experiment #4.

EXPERIMENT 5: POINTERS, SUBROUTINES IN ASSEMBLY LANGUAGE (CHAPTER 6)

This lab has you convert a *C* program that uses pointers and subroutines into PIC24 assembly language. All files referenced in the lab are found in *code\labs\ lab_assem3*.

PRELAB

The prelab assignment must be completed before you walk into lab for checking by the TA. Read the task section to understand some of the instructions contained in the prelab.

- Have your assigned C program compiled and be able to demo its execution to the TA.
- Have an MPLAB project and assembly language template defined for your assigned task, with space for the variables already defined and your subroutine defined as an empty subroutine (contains only a return statement). Your assembly language program should initialize the contents of sz_1, sz_2 from program memory by calling init_variables() as is done in the example *mplab\upcase_asmversion.s* file found in the *code\labs\lab_assem3* directory (use the constant strings that you find in your assigned C program). Be able to demonstrate assembling this program for the TA.

TASK 1: CONVERT A C FUNCTION TO ASSEMBLY

Locate the *code\lab_assem3 directory* included with the CD accompanying this book. You will see three directories (folders) labeled *strdcase*, *strflip*, and *strxchg*. If the last digit of your student ID is:

- 0,1,2 then use *strdcase*
- 3,4,5 then use *strflip*
- 6,7,8,9 then use *strxchg*

Each C source file has a main() that calls a subroutine named void dostr(char* psz_1, char* psz_2) that takes two pointers to null-terminated strings and performs some action on the two strings (it may either copy or exchange the contents of the strings, and change the case of one of the strings). The main() function prints the values of the strings before and after the dostr() function is called.

Your task is to manually convert your assigned C program to PIC24 assembly language. When you call the dostr() function in assembly, pass the psz_1, psz_2 parameters in W0, W1 as per our subroutine calling rules. Use the MPLAB project named mplab\upcase_asmversion.mcp as a starting template for your project, as it initializes two strings in SRAM named sz_1, sz_2 from strings named sz_1_const, sz_2_const residing in program memory. You will need to change the values of sz_1_const, sz_2_const to match the string constants in your assigned C program. The printf statements are in the C source only for debugging purposes; they are not implemented in the PIC24 assembly program. Your PIC24 assembly program should have the same values for the strings when main() is finished as the values printed by the original C program.

TA check. Show the TA that the final values of the strings in your assembly language program match the final values produced by the *C* program.

Reporting requirement. Take a screen shot of the final values of the strings in program memory after your program has executed. Include your program source code in the report.

Task 2: Using the PIC24 C Compiler

The MPLAB project named *mplab\upcase_cversion.mcp* uses the PIC24 *C* compiler to compile the *C* file named upcase_cversion.c. This *C* file contains a function named upcase(char *psz_1) that upcases all characters in the null-terminated string psz_1. The main() code calls upcase() with two different strings, sz_1 and sz_2.

1. Compile this program using the PIC24 *C* compiler by doing Project → Make. If the PIC24 *C* compiler is installed correctly, you should see no errors in the output log.
2. Open a program memory window and find the start of the code at the _reset label (this should be at location 0x200).
3. Open a data memory (file registers) window and monitor the first 32 data locations starting at 0x0800.
4. Start the simulator and use F6 to reset the processor. Use F7 to trace to the rcall _psv_init instruction, then use F8 to step over this call and also the next call, which should be rcall _data_init. Verify that after the call to _data_init that you now see the strings in data memory (_data_init copies the constant versions of the sz_1 and sz_2 strings to data memory).
5. Use F7 (step into) to trace into the main function. Use F8 to trace through the main() function, and verify that after each call to the upcase() function, the appropriate string is uppercased in data memory (capture a screen shot of these final string values).
6. Using the program memory window, click on the *PSV Data* tab and locate the starting program memory address of the two constant strings used to initialize sz_1 and sz_2 (capture a screen shot of this). Then use the *Symbolic* tab and determine the location of these strings in relation to the main() function code. Include this in your report.

TA check. Show the TA that the final values of the strings in data memory after main() have been executed, and also show the TA where the constant strings used to initialize sz_1 and sz_2 reside in program memory.

Reporting requirement. Include the two screen shots you took as well as a description of where the constant values used to initialize sz_1 and sz_2 reside in program memory in relation to main().

EXPERIMENT 6: PIC24 SYSTEM STARTUP (CHAPTER 8)

This lab has you wire on a breadboard the PIC24HJ32GP202 reference system given in Chapter 8, Figure 8.3. Files referenced by this lab are found in the *code\chap8*, *code\include*, and *code\common* folders.

PRELAB

Use the associated walk-through document (*docs\manuallyCreated\board_walkthru_pic24.pdf*) and have your PIC24 system wired on the board before you enter lab. Lab time should be used for debugging, not for wiring. You do not need your power connector soldered to the wires that connect it to the board before lab as you may not have access to a solder station. However, this should be one of the first things that you do when walk into lab. Show your wired breadboard to the TA, and do not apply power to it before the TA has checked it unless you are confident in your wiring skills. Ensure that pin 6 (RTS#) of the USB-to-serial cable connector is connected to the PIC24 MCLR# pin so that you can reset the PIC24 μC via the bootloader GUI.

TASK 1: TESTING POWER

Remove the PIC24 from the board before applying power. Solder your power connector to the wires connecting it to the board. Plug in your wall transformer, and turn on your power switch. Your power LED should come on. Use a multimeter to verify that the breadboard power rail has approximately 3.3 V.

TA check. Show the TA that your power rail has 3.3 V and that your power LED comes on.

Reporting requirement. There is no reporting requirement for this task.

TASK 2: DOWNLOADING A PROGRAM USING THE BOOTLOADER

1. Ask the TA to program your PIC24 μC with the serial bootloader firmware. Plug your PIC24 back into the board. Ensure that you have your USB-to-serial cable plugged into the board and into your PC.
2. Start up the bootloader GUI on your PC. Select the COM port for USB-to-serial cable. If you do not know the COM port number, then use the *Device Manager* (Figure 8.7, Chapter 8) under *Control Panel* → *System* → *Hardware* → *Device Manager* to see a list of serial ports. Click on a serial port and you will see a description of the port—the USB-to-serial manufacturer should be labeled as "FTDI" with location "on USB Serial Converter." Select the 57600 baud rate in the bootloader window and click the "Open Port" checkbox to open the port.

3. Start MPLAB. Open the project *chap8\echo.mcp* in the example code provided with this lab.

4. Compile the *echo.mcp* project, which implements the code shown in Figure 8.6 (Chapter 8). This project reads a character from the serial port, increments it, and echoes it back (so '1' is echoed as '2', 'a' as 'b', etc.). Use the serial bootloader to download the *echo.hex* program to the PIC24 µC following the procedure given in Appendix B.

5. Test the *echo.c* program functionality by using the *Send* button to send some text to the PIC24 µC. You should see it echoed back, with the characters incremented by 1.

6. Modify the *echo.c* program to increment the character by 2 instead of by 1. Verify this operation and capture a screen shot of its execution.

TA check. Show the TA that your modified *echo.c* program operates as expected.
Reporting requirement. Include the screen shot of your modified *echo.c* program.

TASK 3: CURRENT MEASUREMENT

1. Open the *chap8\reset.mcp* project in MPLAB, compile it, and download it into your board. Verify that the software reset and watchdog timer choices operate as expected.

2. Turn power off and connect a multimeter in series with the PIC24 µC VDD to monitor current as shown in Figure C.3a. Before turning power back on, let the TA check your connection. Do not connect as shown in Figure C.3b or C.3c as this blows the fuse in the multimeter. If the multimeter current monitoring is not working, check the fuse for the mA input (this location varies by multimeter type; sometimes it is a front panel fuse accessed by unscrewing the *mA* input). Also, ensure that DC current measurement is enabled by via the *mA/A* button and *DC* button.

3. Turn power on and verify that you are getting a valid current measurement (it should be somewhere in the range of 40–50 mA for a PIC24HJ32GP202 operating at $F_{CY} = 40$ MHz). Unplug the heartbeat LED on pin RB15 so that this does not contribute to the current draw. Fill in the values a–e (not f) in Table C.2.

4. Modify the *reset.c* program to add a menu choice for *Doze (/4)* mode (this must be a new choice, so you will now have 8 choices on the menu, not just 7). For a DOZE mode of *Doze (/4)*, a value of 2 must be written to the _DOZE bits (see [15], which is the *PIC24 Family Reference Manual, Section 7 Oscillator*; the _DOZE bits are contained in the CLKDIV register). Measure the current for *Doze (/4)* and fill in (f) in Table C.2. Capture a screen shot of your modified *reset.c* menu choices.

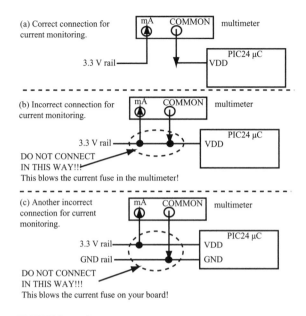

FIGURE C.3 Current measurement.

TABLE C.2 Current measurements for different operation modes.

Parameter	Measured (mA)
(a) Normal operation current	_____
(b) Idle mode	_____
(c) Sleep mode	_____
(d) Doze (/2) mode	_____
(e) Doze (/128) mode	_____
(f) Doze (/4) mode	_____

TA check. Show the TA the execution of the modified *reset.c* program.

Reporting requirement. Include the screen shot of your modified *reset.c* program. Use Equations 8.5 and 8.6 from the Chapter 8 to predict the current for *Doze* (*/4*). Compute a %error as (Measured–Expected)/Expected × 100% and include this in your report. If you are off by more than ± 20%, then suspect your measurement or calculation.

EXPERIMENT 7: LED/SWITCH I/O (CHAPTER 8)

This lab has you implement an LED/switch I/O problem using a state machine approach. Files referenced by this lab are found in the *code\chap8*, *code\include*, and *code\common* folders.

PRELAB

Have the state machine chart for your problem done and ready for TA check before entering the lab. Also, have a MPLAB project containing a rough start at the code—you should at least have your states defined.

THE TASK

Based on the last digit of your student ID, implement one of the following LED/switch I/O problems. All of them require one pushbutton switch input (RB13), one select input (RB12), and one LED (RB14). Configure the pushbutton input for low true operation with the internal pull-up enabled. Configure the select input with the internal pull-up enabled so that all you have to do to change its value is connect or disconnect it to ground using a wire. To blink *rapidly* means that the flashing of the LED should be visibly faster than when blinking at the normal rate. You determine what rapidly means.

Use the *code\chap8\ledsw1.mcp* MPLAB project as the starting point for this lab, and save it as a different project using a new name of your choice. You must use the state machine approach as used by the *ledsw1.mcp* project to solve this problem.

Your first task should be to determine the states required and ASM chart for implementing your assigned LED/switch I/O problem. After this, writing the code is generally straightforward. Debug your code one state at a time, and use the `printNewState()` function to print state names to the console when your state changes. You must use the `printNewState()` function so that the TA can track state changes when checking your code.

Your assignment if your student ID has a last digit of 0 or 5:

1. Turn the LED on. On press and release, turn LED off, then go to 2.
2. After press and release, blink 2 times, freeze on.
3. After press and release, if select input = 0 go to (1), otherwise go to the next step.
4. Blink when pressed and held down. After the second release, go to (5).
5. Blink rapidly (twice as fast as 4). On press and release, go to (1).

Your assignment if your student ID has a last digit of 1 or 6:

1. Turn the LED off. On press and release, turn LED on, then go to 2.
2. After press and release, begin blinking.
3. After press and release, halt blinking. If select input = 1 go to 1, otherwise go to the next step.
4. Turn the LED off. On press only, go to 5.
5. Blink rapidly 5 times while button held down. If button released before all 5 blinks complete, go to (1). If all 5 blinks complete, freeze off, and release remains in this state. A subsequent press repeats (5).

Your assignment if your student ID has a last digit of 2 or 7:

1. Turn the LED off. On press and release, turn LED on, then go to 2.
2. On press, begin blinking. On release, freeze LED on, and go to 3.
3. After press and release, if select input = 1, go to (1), otherwise go to the next step.
4. Blink 5 times. If all 5 blinks complete, then: if select input = 0, go to 1, otherwise go to the next step. Any press during the 5 blinks aborts and goes to the next step.
5. Blink rapidly while button is held down. On release, go to 1.

Your assignment if your student ID has a last digit of 3 or 8:

1. Turn the LED on. On press and release, turn LED off, go to 2.
2. On press and release, blink 2 times, go to 3.
3. Turn the LED off. Blink while button held down. On release, if input select = 0, then go to (1), otherwise go to the next step.
4. Blink rapidly. On a press and release, go to the next step.
5. Turn the LED off. On press, turn the LED on. On release, go to 1.

Your assignment if your student ID has a last digit of 4 or 9:

1. Turn the LED off. On press and release, turn LED on, then go to 2.
2. After three press/releases, begin blinking. After another press and release, stop blinking and go to the next step.
3. On press, turn the LED on. On release, if select input = 0, go to 1, otherwise go to the next step.
4. Blink rapidly. If 5 blinks are completed, go to 1. For any press/release before this, go to step 5.
5. Turn the LED on. For any press and release, go to 1.

TA check. Show the TA that your LED/switch code functions as expected and capture a screen shot of the console output of your code.

Reporting requirement. Include the diagram of your ASM chart in your report. Use the drawing tools in either PowerPoint or Word or some other professional drawing program to draw the chart—no scanning of hand-drawn charts is allowed! Include a screen shot of the console output of your code and your source code.

EXPERIMENT 8: INTERRUPTS AND TIMER INTRODUCTION (CHAPTER 9)

This lab has you implement an LED/switch I/O problem using a state machine approach and a periodic interrupt. It also has you generate a simple repeating waveform using a timer interrupt. Files referenced by this lab are found in the *code\chap9*, *code\include*, and *code\common* folders.

PRELAB

Have the MPLAB project defined and a rough start at the code for Task 1. Have the state machine chart for Task #2 drawn and an MPLAB project defined for it, with a source file that has the states defined.

TASK 1: LED/SWITCH I/O USING PERIODIC SAMPLING

Take your LED/switch I/O problem from the previous lab, and convert it to an interrupt-driven approach using either a Timer2 or Timer3 periodic interrupt as is done in Chapter 9, Figure 9.22 (the ISR contains the entire state machine for the problem; do not use a press & release button semaphore). In the code archive, this example is called *code\chap9\ledsw1_timer2.mcp*. Your main() code should only do the work of blinking the LED.

Your ISR cannot contain a DELAY_MS() call! If you are doing this, then you are trying to blink the LED from within the ISR. Your ISR must set a semaphore that tells the main() code to blink the LED. Your ISR also cannot have any sort of while(){} or for(){} counting loop that attempts to count LED blinks; this must be done in the main() code.

TA check. Show the TA that your LED/switch code functions as expected and capture a screen shot of the console output of your code.

Instructions to the TA: Check the code solution and ensure that the ISR contains no software delay functions.

Reporting requirement. Include a screen shot of the console output of your code and your source code.

TASK 2: WAVEFORM GENERATION

Designate the last 5 digits of your student ID as: ... $Y_4Y_3Y_2Y_1Y_0$. Take each digit and increment it by 1. Your task is to generate a waveform on an output pin (you pick the output pin) that looks like Figure C.4.

Last five digits of Student ID: ... $Y_4Y_3Y_2Y_1Y_0$

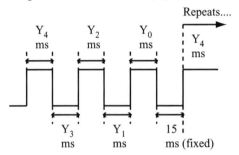

Assume a student ID with the last 5 digits of ... 57468. Observe that each digit is incremented by 1 when used for a pulse width.

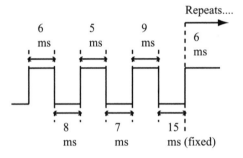

FIGURE C.4   Generated waveform.

So how do you do this?

1. Configure Timer2 for a periodic interrupt and initially set the PR2 value for a timeout of 15 ms (the last low pulse width shown in the figure).
2. Define a state machine in the Timer2 ISR that has a state for each digit as well as a state for the 15 ms pulse width. Initialize the state variable to the Y_4 state.
3. When the Timer2 ISR is invoked the first time, you should be in the Y_4 state. Set the PR2 value for a timeout equal to the Y_4 pulse width in Timer2 ticks, set your digital output high, and set the next state to Y_3.
4. The next time your ISR is entered, Y_4 ms have elapsed, and you are now in state Y_3. Set the PR2 timeout equal to the Y_3 pulse width in Timer2 ticks, set your digital output to low, and set the next state to Y_2.

... etc.

To generate the pulse widths, you need to convert the pulse-width times to Timer2 tick times. You can do this with code that looks like:

```
uint16 u16_y5Ticks;

u16_y5Ticks = msToU16Ticks(pulse_width_in_ms, getTimerPrescale
(T2CONbits));
```

You need to declare global variables for these pulse widths and pre-compute the pulse widths. Your ISR will do all of the work, so your while(1){} loop can be just:

```
while(1) doHeartbeat();
```

Before entering your while(1){} loop, print out the tick values computed for each pulse width for documentation purposes. You can do this via:

```
outString("Y5 pulse width (Timer 2 ticks): ");
outUint16(u16_y5Ticks);
outString("\n");
```

Debugging your ISR. Generally, you do not put print statements in an ISR, but in this case, it is acceptable as a debugging tool to determine what state you are in as long as you output only a single character (use the outChar() function). At 57600 baud, it takes about 180 μs to output one character. This will affect the timing of the waveform though, so use it sparingly and remove any print statements once it is working. You can also use a *trace buffer* to track changes to your state variable—see the example in the last section of Chapter 9.

TA check. Use the oscilloscope to show the TA that your waveform is functioning correctly. Capture a screen shot of the console output from your program.

Reporting requirement. Pick two pulse widths of different values, manually compute the Timer2 tick values for these, and show that they reasonably match the tick values printed by your program (you may be off by ±1 or 2 ticks).

EXPERIMENT 9: INTERRUPT-DRIVEN ASYNCHRONOUS SERIAL I/O AND AN I²C SERIAL EEPROM (CHAPTER 10)

This lab has you explore interrupt-driven asynchronous serial I/O in two ways:

■ Using software FIFOs for interrupt-driven receive and transmit.
■ Using a ping-pong buffering scheme for buffering streaming input data that is written to an I²C EEPROM.

Files referenced by this lab are found in the *code\chap10*, *code\include*, and *code\common* folders.

PRELAB

1. You do not have to be in lab to begin working on Task 1—answer at least a couple of the reporting questions before you enter lab. Task 1 does not have you writing any code, just executing code and observing results.

2. Take the first letter of your name (capitalize it) and predict the asynchronous serial waveform used to transmit it.

3. Have the 24LC515 EEPROM from the parts kit wired up on your board. The SDA1 (pin 18) and SCL1 (pin 17) I²C pins on your PIC24 μC must have external pull-ups—the 2.2 kΩ resistors from your parts kit will work. Take the last digit of your student ID, convert it to binary, then take the least significant 2 bits; these are the values that you must use for the A1/A0 pins. So, if your last student ID digit is 5, this is 0b0101, the last two bits are 01, so A1 = 0 (GND), and A0 = 1 (VDD). The A2 pin must be tied to VDD!

TASK 1: INTERRUPT-DRIVEN ASYNCHRONOUS RECEIVE/TRANSMIT

The *chap10\reverse_string.c* code reads a string from the console without echo, reverses it, and prints it back out. There are three MPLAB projects that use this file:

■ *code\chap10\reverse_string.mcp*—Uses polled UART receive and transmit.

■ *code\chap10\uartrx_fifo.mcp*—Uses interrupt-driven UART receive, polled transmit. This project has the compiler flag -DUART1_RX_INTERRUPT defined, which defines the macro UART1_RX_INTERRUPT during compilation (see Appendix B for how to define this macro within the MPLAB project). This enables use of interrupt-driven UART receive using a software FIFO.

■ *code\chap10\uartrxtx_fifo.mcp*—Uses interrupt-driven UART receive and interrupt-driven UART transmit. This project has the compiler flag -DUART1_RX_INTERRUPT defined, which defines the macro UART1_RX_INTERRUPT during compilation. It also has the compiler flag -DUART1_TX_INTERRUPT, which defines the macro UART1_TX_INTERRUPT during compilation. These macros enable UART1 receive and transmit using interrupts and separate software FIFOs; see the file *code\ common\pic24_uart.c*.

Perform these steps:

1. Program your PIC24 μC with the *chap10\reverse_string.mcp* application. Type a couple of strings into it to see how it works. The bootloader menu command *Main → Send Text File* can be used to dump a text file to the PIC24 μC. The files *chap10\fifotest_1line.txt, chap10\fifotest_3line.txt,* etc., contain repetitions of a single string that can be sent to the PIC24 μC for string reversal. Try sending files of increasing numbers of lines until you

generate a UART receive overflow error; capture a screen shot of the error. This error is caused by the *hardware* FIFO of the UART1 overflowing.

2. Program your PIC24 µC with the *chap10\uartrx_fifo.mcp* application. This uses a software FIFO for UART receive. You will no longer be able to generate a hardware FIFO overflow, but you can generate a software FIFO overflow if you send enough strings fast enough. Determine how many strings it takes to generate this error using the *chap10\fifotest_Nline.txt* files and/or generate ones yourself if necessary. Find the number of strings it takes to generate overflow to about ± 3 line accuracy. Comment on how this compares to step 1 in your report. Capture a screen shot of the error.

3. Repeat step 2, except use the *chap10\uartrxtx_fifo.mcp* application that uses interrupt-driven I/O for both UART receive and transmit.

TA check. Show the TA the results you got for steps 1 and 2, and demo step 3 where you force software FIFO overflow for that case.

Reporting requirement. Include your captured screen shots and give the number of lines from the *chap10\fifotest_Nline.txt* files that it took to overflow each case.

TASK 2: OSCILLOSCOPE TASK

Configure the oscilloscope for single shot capture, and capture a serial transmission from the PC to the PIC24 µC that is the capitalized first letter of your name. You can use the bootloader *Send* type-in field to do this. Monitor the RX pin (RP10) of your PIC24 µC. Verify that it matches the waveform you created for the prelab task.

NOTE: You do not have to write a program for this task. Just have your board powered up, and monitor the RX pin on the PIC24 µC as you send a character using the bootloader GUI or other terminal program.

TA check. Show the TA your scope capture.

Reporting requirement. There is no reporting requirement for this task.

TASK 3: CAPTURING STREAMING SERIAL DATA TO EEPROM

Modify the *chap10\mcp24lc515_i2c_eeprom.mcp* project so that the EEPROM I²C address matches your A1/A0 values (this project contains the code of Figures 10.57 and 10.58 of Chapter 10). Load this code into your processor, and verify that you can write/read data to your 24LC515 serial EEPROM.

Implement the streaming data capture program discussed in Chapter 10, from the section titled "Ping-Pong Buffering for Interrupt-Driven Streaming Data." Your program needs to have two modes: write and read. In write mode, capture streaming data from the serial port and write it to the EEPROM; exit this mode by pressing reset. In read mode, simply read data out of the EEPROM 64 bytes at a time any time a key is pressed.

Test your *write* mode by sending a short file to the PIC24 µC by using the *Main → Send File* option in the bootloader.

How do you accomplish this task?

1. Start with the *chap10\mcp24lc515_i2c_eeprom.mcp* project and save it under a new name.
2. You will need to add your own _ISR_U1RXInterrupt() code for capturing serial data from the serial port. Do NOT define the UART1_RX_INTERRUPT macro as this uses a software FIFO implemented in *code\common\pic24_uart.c*, while this problem does not require a software FIFO. This problem requires a ping-pong scheme as discussed in section "Ping-Pong Buffering for Interrupt-Driven Streaming Data" of Chapter 10. Read that section carefully and the code structure as given by the flow charts.
3. Test the write mode first. When testing write mode, you need to clear the UART RX interrupt flag (_U1RXIF) and then enable the UART RX interrupt *after* the write mode has been entered. To enable the UART RX interrupt, set the interrupt enable flag to a 1 and the priority higher than 0 (see the configUART1() function in *code\common\pic24_uart.c* for an example of how to enable this interrupt). You will only be using the UART RX interrupt once write mode has been entered; outside of write mode you will be using polling to reading UART RX characters. **Warning:** You must clear the UART RX interrupt flag before enabling the interrupt as it is set to a 1 because of the character entered to select the mode. If you do not clear the UART RX interrupt flag before enabling the interrupt, your ISR will be triggered immediately and your ISR will read an empty UART, which returns a 0x00, which is then placed as the first character in your buffer.
4. For the read mode, you can simply use the code that is already present in the *mcp24lc515_i2c_eeprom.c* example.

TA check. Demonstrate your working program to the TA.

Reporting requirement. Include your source code and screen shots of both *write* and *read* mode operation.

Experiment 10: ADC, DAC Experiments (Chapter 11)

This lab has you explore the on-chip ADC and an external SPI DAC, along with an LM60 temperature sensor. Files referenced by this lab are found in the *code\chap11*, *code\include*, and *code\common* folders.

PRELAB

Wire the connections for Task 1 as shown in Figure C.5.

TASK 1: ADC, MAX548A DAC TEST

Use the *code\chap11\adc_spidac_test.c* example to test the PIC24 μC to MAX548 DAC setup shown in Figure C.5.

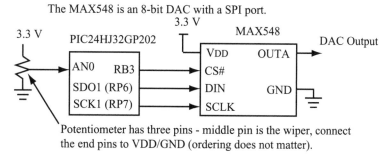

The MAX548 is an 8-bit DAC with a SPI port.

Potentiometer has three pins - middle pin is the wiper, connect the end pins to VDD/GND (ordering does not matter).

FIGURE C.5   ADC, DAC experiment.

The *adc_spidac_test.c* program reads a 12-bit value from the PIC24 ADC AN0 input, whose voltage is set by the potentiometer, converts this to an 8-bit value by dropping the last four bits, and writes this to the MAX548 using the SPI port. This means that the DAC output voltage follows the potentiometer voltage as you adjust the potentiometer.

Once you get the program running, fill in the table shown in Figure C.6 (POTV is potentiometer voltage). Put a voltmeter on the DAC output so that you can monitor the DAC output voltage. You may also want to check the AN0 input voltage with the voltmeter to verify that adjusting the potentiometer does adjust the AN0 input voltage.

Measured VDD: _____

Pot Voltage	ADC Code (12-bit)	DAC Code (8-bit)	Measured DAC Voltage	% Error (DAC-POTV)/POTV * %100
0.8 V				
1.6 V				
2.4 V				

FIGURE C.6   ADC, DAC experiment.

TA check. Show the TA the operation of the program and your table values.

Reporting requirement. Pick one of the table rows, verify manually that the ADC, DAC codes match their respective voltages using your measured VDD value as the reference voltage.

Task 2: Using the LM60 Temperature Sensor

In your parts kit, you will have a three-terminal device that looks like a transistor. This is an LM60 temperature sensor in a TO-92 package. With the flat front of the device facing you, the leftmost pin is VDD (3.3 V), the middle pin is VOUT (the analog temperature), and the rightmost pin is GND.

Connect the VDD pin to 3.3 V, GND to GND, and the VOUT pin to the AN0 input of your PIC24 μC (disconnect the potentiometer from the AN0 input). If you reverse VDD and GND, the LM60 will get very warm because it is drawing too much current and you may damage it.

The LM60 outputs 6.25 mV for every 1°C and has a DC offset of 424 mV, so 25°C is equal to an output voltage of (6.25 mV × 25) + 424 mV = 580.25 mV. Save the *chap11\adc_spidac_test.mcp* project as a new project, and modify it to print out the AN0 voltage from the LM60 as a temperature with one digit to the right of the decimal point (use a floating point calculation as was done in *adc_spidac_test.c* and the formatting capabilities of `printf`).

Once you have done this, record the lowest and highest temperatures you force from it by touching it and blowing on it:

Low temperature (°C): _____ (round to the nearest integer)

High temperature (°C): _____ (round to the nearest integer)

Adjust each of the temperatures by the following:

Low temperature = Low temperature − 4 − last digit of student ID

High temperature = High temperature + 4 + last digit of student ID

New low temperature: _____

New high temperature: _____

Midpoint (High + Low/2): _____

Your goal is to map the temperature values to DAC output voltages such that the midpoint temperature is represented as ½ VREF, or 1.65 V if VREF = 3.3 V. This way, we will get a wider voltage swing for this limited temperature range and our PIC24 μC acts like a digital amplifier. Now, modify your program to map the Celsius temperature that you calculate as a percentage of this range:

Percentage = (Celsisus TEMP − LOW TEMP)/(HIGH TEMP − LOW TEMP)

Note that if the input temperature is the midpoint, computing this value gives 0.5. Convert this to a voltage between 0 and 3.3 V:

Desired DAC Voltage = 3.3 V * percentage.

Convert the desired DAC voltage to a binary code and output this to the DAC. Modify the print statement in your loop to print the desired DAC voltage and its hex code. Use a voltmeter on the DAC output to check that your on-screen value for DAC output approximately matches what is on the screen. Capture a screen shot of your program.

TA check. Show the TA that when force the temperature sensor to approximately the midpoint temperature that the DAC output voltage is at the midpoint voltage (about 1.65 V)—have a voltmeter connected for the demo.

Reporting requirement. Include your code, your screen shot, and the high, low temperatures that you used in your final calculation.

EXPERIMENT 11: PWM FOR DC MOTOR CONTROL (CHAPTER 12)

This lab has you explore the pulse-width modulation using an LED and a small DC motor. Files referenced by this lab are found in the *code\chap12*, *code\include*, and *code\common* folders.

PRELAB

- Wire the connections for Task 1.
- Task 2 requires a 5 V power supply. In your parts kit, you have a 7805 Voltage regulator that has the same pin out as the LM2937-3.3 V voltage regulator that you already have on your board. Place the 7805 somewhere on your board, and hook its input to the output of your wall transformer power switch and the middle pin to ground. Put a 10 µF capacitor from your parts kit on the output, and verify that the output is approximately 5 V.

TASK 1: LED, PWM TASK

Use the *chap12\ledpwm.c* code for LED/PWM test shown in Figure C.7 (look in the code at the *configOutputCapture1()* function and determine the RP*x* port that is used for OC1.

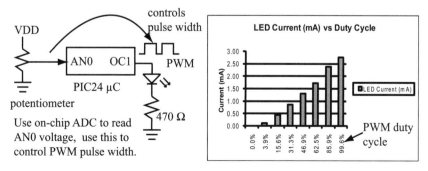

FIGURE C.7   LED/PWM connection.

Before connecting the LED and resistor to the OC1, connect it to VDD and measure the current through the LED and resistor. Call this LED_CURR_MAX:

LED_CURR_MAX: _____ (mA)

Now, connect the preceding schematic, and use a multimeter to monitor the current through the LED. Execute the program and verify that you can vary the LED brightness with the potentiometer. Fill in the table using Figure C.8 (use a scope for monitoring the pulse width while you use the potentiometer to set it to the desired value).

(a) Set pulse width to	(b) LED current (mA)	(c) Duty cycle (pulse width/period)	(d) LED current/max LED current	% Error (c − d) / (d) * 100 %
4 ms				
8 ms				
12 ms				
16 ms				
maximum pulse width				

FIGURE C.8   LED current measurements.

TA check. Show the TA the operation of the LED PWM and your table values. Your column values for (c) and (d) should match each other fairly closely (i.e., if the pulse width is at 50% duty cycle, then the current through the LED should be 50% of the maximum).

Reporting requirement. Include the table in your report.

TASK 2 (PART 1): DC MOTOR

Make the connections shown in Figure C.9 (leave your potentiometer connected to AN0), and modify the *ledpwm.c* program so that you can control the speed of the motor using the potentiometer. The TI half-driver must be connected to your 5 V power source (see the prelab). Use a menu to choose between the settings of 00, 01, 10, and 11 for the DC motor direction control. Verify that you can control the speed of the DC motor with the potentiometer and reverse directions of the motor using your menu.

TA check. Demo to the TA the operation of your motor.

TASK 2 (PART 2): DC MOTOR

Replace the potentiometer with your temperature sensor, and use the HIGH and LOW temperature values that you used in the previous lab as the range of expected

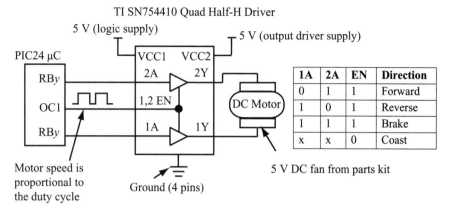

FIGURE C.9   DC motor connection.

temperatures. Map the temperature input voltage to pulse width via the following equation:

PulseWidth = (TempsensorVoltage − TempLowVoltage)/(TempMaxVoltage − TempLowVoltage) × MaxPulseWidth

In doing this calculation, the *TempSensorVoltage* is an ADC code, so *TempMaxVoltage* and *TempLowVoltage* must be ADC codes as well. The *MaxPulseWidth* is in Timer ticks. Use uint32 values to do the calculation and do the multiplication first, then the division as shown by the following equations to avoid getting a result of 0:

PulseWidth = (TempsensorVoltage − TempLowVoltage) × MaxPulseWidth;

PulseWidth = Pulsewidth/(TempMaxVoltage − TempLowVoltage)

This maps the temperature voltage to a pulse width, and now your motor speed is controlled by temperature. Verify that you can speed up the motor by touching the temperature sensor, and slow it down by blowing on it. Have your while(1){} loop print out the current temperature in Celsius, along with the current pulse width in microseconds. If you are trying to print out a uint32 value, use the %ld format code in the printf statement.

TA check. Demo your motor operation to the TA, and capture a screen shot of your code output during operation.

Reporting requirement. Include your code and your screen shot in your report.

HARDWARE DEBUGGING CHECKLISTS

Debugging hardware problems requires a methodical approach and the use of available instrumentation such as a multimeter and oscilloscope. The following are debugging checklists that are useful for identifying hardware problems.

"MY BOARD USED TO WORK AND NOW IT DOESN'T."

1. Use a multimeter to measure VDD, AVDD on the μC.
2. Ensure that VSS pins and AVSS on the μC are connected to ground.
3. Use the oscilloscope to ensure reset line works.
4. Check the μC with an older test program (*ledflash.c*).
5. Check the μC in the TA reference board to see if it is a board problem or a μC problem.

"MY FUSE KEEPS BLOWING—HELP!"

To track shorts, perform the following steps in order:

1. Connect the multimeter in series with power to monitor current.
2. Disconnect one half of the breadboard from the other half and determine which half the problem is in. Connect power for only a brief period of time to see if the short still exists.
3. Remove all ICs from problem half of board and see if the short is fixed.
4. If the short still exists, remove any capacitors.
5. If the short still exists, remove any switches.
6. If the short still exists, remove any LEDs.
7. If the short still exists, it must be a direct wiring connection between VDD/GND.

"MY SERIAL INTERFACE DOES NOT WORK."

1. Verify RX, TX, GND connections from the serial interface connector to the μC.
2. Use the oscilloscope to see if the PC's terminal program is transmitting.
3. Verify baud rate by measuring transmitted pulse width for one bit.
4. Program the μC with *echo.c* and use the oscilloscope to determine if the μC is transmitting a character.

"THE BULLY BOOTLOADER DOES NOT WORK."

1. If the bootloader outputs a message that the μC is unrecognized, then ensure that the *devices.txt* file is in the same directory as the bootloader executable file (*winbootldr.exe*).

2. If the bootloader complains that it cannot connect to the device, then check the serial port connection. Ensure that you are selecting the correct COM port for the USB-to-serial cable.
3. If the bootloader GUI does not start up, then ensure that version 2.0 or higher of the Microsoft .NET runtime is installed on your PC.

"MY I²C INTERFACE DOES NOT WORK."

1. Verify that both SCL1 and SDA1 have pull-up resistors to VDD and use a scope to check their voltage level.
2. Ensure that SCL1/SDA1 are not reversed (SCL is the CLOCK!).
3. Use the oscilloscope to verify transmission by the µC on SCL1/SDA1 pins. If not, then ensure that your code is calling the I²C configuration function.
4. Verify that you have the correct I²C device address in your program as per the Ax address pins on the target device.

"MY SPI INTERFACE DOES NOT WORK."

1. Verify that SCLK1, SDO1, SDI1 (if necessary), and the chip select are connected to the target device.
2. Use the oscilloscope to verify transmission by the µC on SCLK1/SDO1 pins. If not, then ensure that your code is calling the SPI configuration function.
3. Verify that the chip select is being asserted during the transmission and with the correct polarity.

"MY ADC CODE DOES NOT WORK."

1. Use a multimeter to check ADC input voltage variation.
2. Verify that the analog input is connected to the correct ANx input on the µC.
3. Ensure that your code is calling the ADC configuration function.
4. Use the `printf()` statement to print individual ADC result values to see if they are varying.

APPENDIX
D

Notes on the *C* Language and the Book's PIC24 Library Functions

This appendix contains a few brief notes on the *C* programming language based on questions asked by students when performing the laboratory exercises in Appendix C, "Suggested Laboratory Exercises." This book covers only a subset of the *C* language and the coverage is intended to be adequate for a student already conversant in some other high-level language, either object oriented (e.g., *C++*, Java) or procedural (e.g., BASIC, Pascal). This appendix also has a list of the PIC24 *C* library functions used in the book's examples.

FORMATTED I/O (`printf, sprintf, sscanf`)

Some of this book's examples use the standard *C* library formatted output statement `printf()`, which can be confusing if you are new to *C*. This appendix covers only the formatted I/O features used in this book's examples; please refer to a *C* textbook if you require a more complete description. The `printf()` statement is used for formatted ASCII output; within the PIC24 *C* compiler environment the `printf()` library function sends its output to UART1 (an easy method for sending formatted output to a different port is discussed later in this section). The parameters to the `printf()` function are a format string and an argument list. The format string can contain a mixture of normal characters and conversion specifications; a conversion specification determines how an argument value is converted to an ASCII format. Conversion specifications begin with a "%" character; two "%" characters in a row are needed if a "%" is desired in the final output string. Figure D.1a gives some examples of `printf()` conversion specifications.

A `%c` formats an argument as a single ASCII character, `%d` specifies an ASCII signed decimal format, `%u` specifies an ASCII unsigned decimal format, and `%x` is used to format an ASCII hex number (a lowercase x uses lowercase for hex digits, while an uppercase X uses uppercase hex digits). The field width is specified as a number before the format character; `%10d` specifies a field width of 10 digits. Left justification is the default; a negative sign in the field width (e.g., `%-10d`) performs

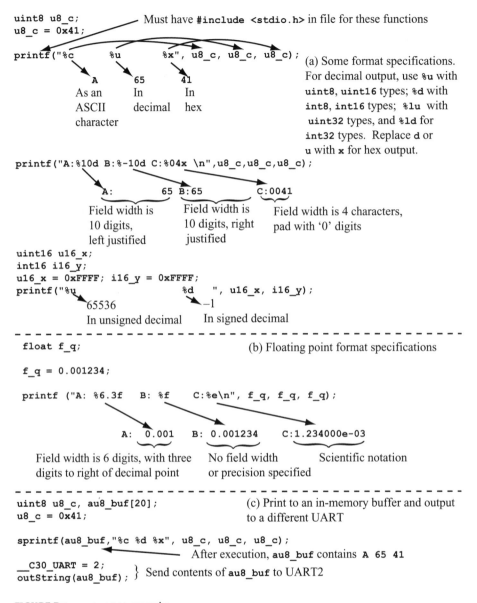

FIGURE D.1 printf() examples.

right justification. A leading zero can be specified in the field width as in %04x to pad the number with leading zeros. A leading 1 (letter ell) is used in the format specification if the argument is a 32-bit value rather than an 8- or 16-bit value (i.e., %1d instead of %d). Floating-point (float or double) format specifications use %f or %e as shown in Figure D.1b. A format specification of the form %n.mf specifies a field width of *n* digits, with *m* digits of precision to the right of the decimal point. The %e specification causes the floating-point number to be printed in scientific notation. The sprintf() function (printf to string) is used to print the string to an in-memory buffer; the first argument to sprintf() is the buffer for the output string as shown in Figure D.1c. This can be useful for sending formatted output to a different UART by printing the formatted string to a buffer, then using the __C30_UART variable to dynamically select the destination UART for the outString() function.

The scanf() function is the normal C function used for formatted ASCII input; it uses the same format codes as used by printf(). Within the PIC24 C compiler environment, using the scanf() function requires rewriting a lower-level library function to define the scanf() character input source (UART1, UART2, the SPI port, etc.). Our approach for formatted input is to use the inString()/inStringEcho() functions to read a string from a particular UART, then use the sscanf() function (scanf()from string) to read formatted data from the string. The sscanf() function expects pointers to the variables in its parameter list; hence, the & operator (address-of operator) is placed in front of any variables that are passed to sscanf(). Figure D.2 shows examples of sscanf() with %d (decimal), %x (hex), and %f (float) numbers. The leading 0x on the hex number input is optional. The sscanf() function skips over any white space (space characters, tabs, etc.) it encounters when scanning the input for a match to the format specification.

```
#define BUFSIZE 32
uint8 au8_buf[BUFSIZE];
int16 i16_x;
float f_q;

printf("Enter decimal number: ");
inStringEcho(au8_buf, BUFSIZE-1);
sscanf(au8_buf, "%d",&i16_x);
printf("The number is %d\n", i16_x);
```

> Enter decimal number: *−300*
> The number is −300

```
printf("\nEnter hex number: ");
inStringEcho(au8_buf, BUFSIZE-1);
sscanf(au8_buf, "%x",&i16_x);
printf("The hex number is %x\n", i16_x);
```

> Enter hex number: *0x2FEA*
> The hex number is 2fea

```
printf("\nEnter a float number: ");
inStringEcho(au8_buf, BUFSIZE-1);
sscanf(au8_buf, "%f",&f_q);
printf("The float number is %f\n",f_q);
```

> Enter a float number: *1.239202*
> The float number is 1.239202

FIGURE D.2   sscanf() examples.

C STRUCTURES

As discussed in Chapter 6, arrays group elements of the same type together, while *C* structures (keyword `struct`) allow grouping of elements of different types. When defining a structure, it is generally defined as its own type as shown in the following code fragment. The `typedef` (type definition) defines a new type named `MYSTRUCT` that is a *C* `struct`, and `st_foo` is a variable of this new type. The *C* compiler pads structure members with additional bytes in order to keep the structure members properly word-aligned in memory.

```
typedef struct {
  uint8 u8_val;
  int16 au16_buf[10];
  float f_q;
} MYSTRUCT;

MYSTRUCT st_foo;
```

The "`.`" operator is used to access fields within a structure variable, as follows:

```
st_foo.u8_val = 0xab;
st_foo.au16_buf[2] = 320;
st_foo.f_q = 3.14;
```

The "–>" operator is used to access fields using a structure pointer, as follows:

```
printMYSTRUCT(MYSTRUCT* pst_1) {
  printf(" u8: %x, i16: %d, f: %f\n",
    pst_1->u8_val, pst_1->au16_buf[0], pst_1->f_q);
}
printMYSTRUCT(&st_foo);
```

A structure member can also have an optional number after it that defines its size in bits; this allows efficient memory usage. The following defines a type named `FLAGBITS` that is a `struct` which consists of several 1-bit flags. The compiler is free to pack the bit fields into as few bytes as possible. When using bit fields, the type should be declared as either `unsigned` or `signed`.

```
typedef struct {
  unsigned u1_activeBuffer: 1;
  unsigned u1_writeFlag:1;
  unsigned u1_recordFlag:1;
  unsigned u1_playbackFlag:1;
```

```
  unsigned u1_readFlag:1;
  unsigned u1_passThruFlag:1;
  unsigned u1_compressionFlag:1;
} FLAGBITS;
FLAGBITS flags;

flags.u1_writeFlag = 1;   //set a flag
flags.u1_readFlag = 0;    //clear a flag
```

C Unions

A *C* union allows different types to refer to the same memory space allocated for a variable. This is useful when one wishes to view a variable differently depending on context. The following union32 type is a union that allows a 32-bit value to be viewed either as a uint32, as two uint16 values (least significant and most significant words), or as a four-byte uint8 array.

```
typedef union _union32 {
  uint32 u32;

  struct {
    uint16 ls16;
    uint16 ms16;
  } u16;

  uint8 u8[4];
} union32;
```

The following assignments (see comments a, b, c) to the union32_a variable all accomplish the same thing, which is to initialize union32_a to a value of 0x12345678.

```
union32 union32_a;
//(a) one assignment using the u32 field
union32_a.u32 = 0x12345678;       //single 32-bit assignment
//(b) two assignments, using the u16 structure
union32_a.u16.ls16 = 0x5678;      //least significant word
union32_a.u16.ms16 = 0x1234;      //most significant word
//(c) four assignments, using the u8 union member
union32_a.u8[0] = 0x78;           //least significant byte
union32_a.u8[1] = 0x56;           //second byte
union32_a.u8[2] = 0x34;           //third byte
union32_a.u8[2] = 0x12;           //most significant byte
```

FOR C++ PROGRAMMERS

A simple, but common error made by *C++* programmers when adjusting to *C* is variable declarations. In *C++*, variable declarations can be placed anywhere within a function, as shown in the following code fragment.

```
main() {   // compiled with a C++ compiler
     uint8 u8_c;
     u8_c = 0x41;
     u8_c++;

     int16 i16_x;     //variable declaration
     i16_x++;
}
```

However, in *C* the second variable declaration `int16 i16_x` must go either at the top of the function with the `uint8 u8_c` declaration or be enclosed in a block using {} as shown in the following code fragment. However, be careful— variables declared within a block {} are not visible to statements outside of that block.

```
main() {   //compiled with C compiler
     uint8 u8_c;
     u8_c = 0x41;
     u8_c++;
     { // be careful, i16_x scope is limited to within brackets!
       int16 i16_x;    //variable declaration
       i16_x++;
     }
}
```

FOR NEW PROGRAMMERS

If you don't have much programming experience, the number of syntax errors reported by the *C* compiler after compiling your first program may overwhelm you. A useful tip relevant to almost any programming language is to fix only the first syntax error; many of the remaining errors are most probably side effects of that first syntax error. Do not be intimidated by a listing of 100+ errors; concentrate on fixing the first one and many of the remaining errors will vanish on the next compile.

PIC24 *C* LIBRARY FUNCTIONS

This section summarizes many of the PIC24 *C* library functions developed by the authors and used in this book's examples. Full documentation is found in *docs* on

Library Configuration (include\libconfig.h)	
`CLOCK_CONFIG`	A macro that sets the clock choice; the default PIC24H value is `FRCPLL_FCY40MHz`; see *code\docs* for complete information.
`DEBOUNCE_DLY`	Switch debounce delay in code examples, default is 15 ms.
`SERIAL_EOL_DEFAULT`	Sets end-of-line behavior default for serial output functions, default is `SERIAL_EOL_LF` (a new line character).
`DEFAULT_UART`	Sets default UART for serial functions, default is 1.
`DEFAULT_BAUDRATE`	Sets default baudrate (default is 57600).
Clock Functions/Macros (common\pic24_clockfreq.c, include\pic24_clockfreq.h)	
`void configClock(void)`	Switches to the clock source defined by the `CLOCK_CONFIG` macro.
`FCY`	FCY for the CPU; this is set automatically by the `CLOCK_CONFIG` choice.
Utility Functions/Macros (common\pic24_util.c, include\pic24_util.h)	
`HELLO_MSG`	Default "Hello" message for an application.
`void configHeartbeat(void)`	Configure the heartbeat functionality that is by default RB15 configured for open drain output; used to blink the power LED.
`void doHeartbeat(void);`	Update the heartbeat counter causing heartbeat LED to blink at a visible rate.
`void reportError(const char* szErrorMessage)`	Save `szErrorMessage` in persistent variable, do a software reset. The `szErrorMessage` is printed by `printResetCause()`.
`void printResetCause(void)`	Print the cause of the last reset.
`void configPinsForLowPower(void);`	Configure all pins for low-power operations; this function must be customized for a particular processor.
`void configBasic(const char* psz_helloMsg);`	Calls `configClock()`, `configHeartbeat()`, `configDefaultUART()`, `printResetCause()` and outputs `psz_helloMsg` to the default UART.

FIGURE D.3   Library configuration, clock selection, and utility functions/macros.

Port Configuration (include\pic24_ports.h and include\devices*processor*.h where *processor* is the CPU identifier.	
`CONFIG_input_TO_RP(pin)`	Macros that configure a peripheral *input* (INT1, IC1, U1RX, ... etc.) to a remappable pin RP*x*, where *x = pin*. See *pic24_ports.h* for a complete list. These macros are empty definitions if the target processor does not support remappable pins. Example: `CONFIG_U1RX_TO_RP(10)`.
`CONFIG_output_TO_RP(pin)`	Macros that configure a peripheral *output* (C1OUT, U1TX, SDO1, ... etc.) to a remappable pin RP*x*, where *x = pin*. See *pic24_ports.h* for a complete list. These macros are empty definitions if the target processor does not support remappable pins. Example: `CONFIG_U1TX_TO_RP(11)`.
`CONFIG_Rxy_AS_DIG_INPUT()`	Configure port *x*, bit *y* as a digital input. Example: `CONFIG_RA0_AS_DIG_INPUT()`.
`CONFIG_Rxy_AS_DIG_OUTPUT()`	Configure port *x*, bit *y* as a digital output. Example: `CONFIG_RB15_AS_DIG_OUTPUT()`.
`CONFIG_Rxy_AS_DIG_OD_OUTPUT()`	Configure port *x*, bit *y* as a digital open-drain output.
`ENABLE_Rxy_AS_PULLUP()` `DISABLE_Rxy_AS_PULLUP()`	Enable/disable the CN pull-up on port *x*, bit *y* (this macro is defined only if the pull-up exists).
`ENABLE_Rxy_CN_INTERRUPT()` `DISABLE_Rxy_CN_INTERRUPT()`	Enable/disable the CN interrupt for port *x*, bit *y* (this macro is defined only if the pull-up exists).
`ENABLE_Rxy_ANALOG()` `DISABLE_Rxy_ANALOG()`	Enable/disable analog functionality on port *x*, bit *y*. This macro is defined only for ports that have analog functionality.
`ENABLE_Rxy_OPENDRAIN()` `DISABLE_Rxy_OPENDRAIN()`	Enable/disable the open-drain functionality for port *x*, bit *y*.
`CONFIG_RPn_AS_DIG_PIN()`	Configure remappable pin RP*n* as a digital pin. This macro is empty if RP*n* does not have analog functionality.
`CONFIG_ANx_AS_ANALOG()`	Configure AN*x* as an analog pin.

FIGURE D.4   Parallel port pin and remappable pin configuration.

the book's CD-ROM; the latest code examples are available at *www.reesemicro.com*. The library functions are available in the *code\common* and *code\include* folders. Please see Chapter 14 for the ESOS-related support functions and Chapter 13 for the ECAN and flash memory self-programming support functions.

Delay Functions/Macros (common\pic24_delay.h)	
`CYCLES_PER_MS` `CYCLES_PER_US`	FCY cycles per millisecond or per microsecond, calculated from **FCY** macro.
`DELAY_MS(uint32 ms)` `DELAY_US(uint32 us)`	Software delay for **ms** milliseconds or for **us** microseconds; also updates the heartbeat counter.

Serial Functions/Macros (common\pic24_serial.c, include\pic24_serial.h)	
`__C30_UART`	Sets the default UART for all serial functions, default value is 1. This variable is defined by PIC24 compiler and not by our library. This variable can be dynamically changed.
`void configDefaultUART(uint32 u32_baudRate)`	Configure the default UART as selected by `__C30_UART` for a baudrate of **u32_baudRate**.
`uint8 inChar(void)` `uint8 inCharEcho(void)`	Input one character from the default UART without or with echo.
`uint16 inString (char *psz_buff, int16 u16_maxCount);` `uint16 inStringEcho ( ... )`	Input a string from the default UART to `*psz_buff` that is assumed to be able to hold `u16_maxCount+1` bytes.
`uint8 isCharReady(void)`	Return non-zero if a character is ready to be read from the default UART.
`void outChar(uint8 u8_c)`	Output **u8_c** to the default UART.
`void outString(const char* psz_s)`	Output string `*psz_s` to the default UART.

`void outUint8 (uint8 u8_x)`
`void outUint16(uint16 u16_x)`
`void void outUint32(uint32 u32_x)`
	Output the input parameter in hex format with a leading "0x" to the default UART.

`void outUint8Decimal(uint8 u8_x);` `void outUint16Decimal(uint16 u16_x);`	Output the input parameter in decimal format to the default UART.
`void outUint8NoLeader (uint8 u8_x);`	Output **u8_x** in hex format with no leading "0x" to the default UART.

FIGURE D.5   Delay, serial I/O functions/macros.

UARTx Functions/Macros (common\pic24_uart.c, include\pic24_uart.h). These are defined for UARTs 1 through 4; replace x with UART number.	
`IS_CHAR_READY_UARTx()`	Returns non-zero if character is available.
`IS_TRANSMIT_BUFFER_FULL_UARTx()`	Returns non-zero if transmit buffer is full.
`IS_TRANSMIT_COMPLETE_UARTx()`	Returns non-zero if transmit is complete.
`WAIT_UNTIL_TRANSMIT_COMPLETE_UARTx()`	Wait until current transmit operation is complete.
`void outCharx (uint8 u8_c)`	Output `u8_c` to UARTx.
`uint8 inCharx (void);`	Input a character from UARTx; this is a blocking wait.
`CONFIG_BAUDRATE_UARTx (uint32 baudRate)`	Configure UARTx for a baud rate of `baudRate`.
`UARTx_TX_INTERRUPT`	If defined, then use interrupt-driven transmit; if not defined then polled transmit is done.
`UARTx_TX_FIFO_SIZE`	Sets TX FIFO size for interrupt-driven transmit.
`UARTx_TX_INTERRUPT_PRIORITY`	Sets TX interrupt priority for interrupt-driven transmit.
`UARTx_RX_INTERRUPT`	If defined, then use interrupt-driven receive; if not defined then polled receive is done.
`UARTx_RX_FIFO_SIZE`	Sets RX FIFO size for interrupt-driven receive.
`UARTx_RX_INTERRUPT_PRIORITY`	Sets RX interrupt priority for interrupt-driven receive.

FIGURE D.6   UART functions/macros.

I2C*x* Functions/Macros (common\pic24_i2c.c, include\pic24_i2c.h). These are defined for I²C modules 1 and 2; replace *x* with the I²C module number.

`void configI2Cx(uint16 u16_FkHZ)`	Enables the I²C module for operation at `u16_FkHZ` kHz clock rate.
`void startI2Cx(void)`	Performs a start operation.
`void rstartI2Cx(void)`	Performs a repeated start operation.
`void stopI2Cx(void)`	Performs a stop operation.
`void putI2Cx(uint8 u8_val)`	Transmits `u8_val`; software reset if NAK returned.
`uint8 putNoAckCheckI2Cx(uint8 u8_val)`	Transmits `u8_val` and returns the received acknowledge bit.
`uint8 getI2Cx(uint8 u8_ack2Send)`	Receives one byte and sends `u8_ack2Send` as the acknowledge bit.
`void write1I2Cx(uint8 u8_addr,uint8 u8_d1)`	Writes 1 byte (`u8_d1`); performs a complete transaction.
`void write2I2Cx(uint8 u8_addr,uint8 u8_d1, uint8 u8_d2)`	Writes 2 bytes (`u8_d1`); performs a complete transaction.
`void writeNI2Cx(uint8 u8_addr,uint8* pu8_data, uint16 u16_cnt)`	Writes `u16_cnt` bytes from buffer `pu8_data`; performs a complete transaction.
`void read1I2Cx(uint8 u8_addr,uint8* pu8_d1)`	Reads 1 byte and returns it in `*pu8_d1`; performs a complete transaction.
`void read2I2Cx(uint8 u8_addr,uint8* pu8_d1, uint8* pu8_d2)`	Read 2 bytes and returns them in `*pu8_d1`, `*pu8_d2`; performs a complete transaction.
`void readNI2Cx(uint8 u8_addr,uint8* pu8_data, uint16 u16_cnt)`	Reads `u16_cnt` bytes and returns them in `*pu8_data`; performs a complete transaction.

SPI*x* Functions/Macros (common\pic24_spi.c, include\pic24_spi.h). These are defined for SPI modules 1 and 2; replace *x* with the SPI module number.

`uint16 ioMasterSPIx(uint16 u16_c)`	Writes `u16_c` to SPI*x* port, returns the value that is input by the SPI*x* port. Whether or not an 8-bit or 16-bit operation is done depends on the SPI module configuration.
`void checkRxErrorSPIx ()`	Calls `reportError()` with an appropriate error message if SPI input buffer overflow has occurred.

FIGURE D.7   I²C and SPI functions/macros.

Timer Functions/Macros (common\pic24_timer.c, include\pic24_timer.h).	
`getTimerPrescale(TxCONbits)`	Returns the prescale value given the configuration bits (`TxCONbits`) of a timer. Sample usage: `getTimerPrescale(T3CONbits)`
`uint16 msToU16Ticks(uint16 u16_ms, uint16 u16_pre)` `uint16 usToU16Ticks(uint16 u16_us, uint16 u16_pre)` `uint32 usToU32Ticks(uint32 u32_us, uint16 u16_pre)`	Conversion functions for time to timer ticks, given a timer's prescale value (`u16_pre`). These functions use float computations and rounding for accuracy. Parameter `u16_ms` is milliseconds, while parameters `u16_us` and `u32_us` are microseconds.
`MS_TO_TICKS(ms, pre)`	Converts `ms` (milliseconds) to ticks, given a timer's prescale value (`pre`). This uses integer computations.
`uint32 ticksToMs (uint32 u32_ticks, uint16 u16_tmrPre)` `uint32 ticksToUs (uint32 u32_ticks, uint16 u16_tmrPre);` `uint32 ticksToNs (uint32 u32_ticks, uint16 u16_tmrPre);`	Converts ticks to either milliseconds, microseconds, or nanoseconds given a timer's prescale value (`u16_tmrPre`). These functions use float computations.
`uint16 computeDeltaTicks(uint16 u16_start, uint16 u16_end, uint16 u16_tmrPR)`	Computes the delta timer ticks between `u16_end` and `u16_start ticks`, given a timer's period register (`u16_tmrPR`) and assuming the delta is not longer than the timer's period.
`uint32 computeDeltaTicksLong(uint16 u16_start, uint16 u16_end, uint16 u16_tmrPR, uint16 u16_oflows)`	Computes the delta timer ticks between `u16_end` and `u16_start ticks`, given a timer's period register (`u16_tmrPR`) and assuming the number of timer overflows (`u16_oflows`).

FIGURE D.8   Timer functions/macros.

ADC Functions/Macros (common\pic24_adc.c, include\pic24_adc.h).	
`IS_CONVERSION_COMPLETE_ADC1()`	Returns non-zero if the current conversion is complete.
`WAIT_UNTIL_CONVERSION_COMPLETE_ADC1()`	Waits until the current conversion is complete.
`IS_SAMPLING_ADC1()`	Returns 1 if the sample-and-hold amplifier(s) are sampling, or 0 if the sample-and-hold amplifier(s) are holding.
`SET_SAMP_BIT_ADC1()`	Sets the sample bit.
`uint16 convertADC1(void)`	Performs an ADC conversion (assumes ADC is initialized properly to return integer results. Returns an integer value (10- or 12-bit, depending on ADC configuration) corresponding to the ADC conversion result.
`configADC1_ManualCH0(uint16 u16_Ch0PositiveMask,uint8 u8_autoSampleTime,uint8 u8_Use12bits);`	Configures ADC1 to perform 10-/12-bit conversion on a single channel via CH0. The sampling is done against the AVDD and AVSS references and using the internal ADC clock. The user can initiate this manual sampling+conversion by setting the SAMP bit in AD1CON1. When the DONE bit in AD1CON1 goes high, the conversion is done. Parameter `u16_Ch0PositiveMask` selects the single analog input to convert. See AD1CHS0 register and associated `#defines` in *pic24_adc.h*. Parameter `u8_autoSampleTime` is the number of ADC clock periods for sampling the signal. This value must be 0-31. If parameter `u8_Use12bits` is true, then use 12-bit mode, else use 10-bit mode.
`void configADC1_AutoScanIrqCH0(uint16 u16_ch0ScanMask,uint8 u8_autoSampleTime,uint8 u8_12bit);`	Configures ADC1 to perform conversions over a number of scanned channels to CH0. See Chapter 11 for more details.
`void configADC1_AutoHalfScanIrqCH0(uint16 u16_ch0ScanMask,uint8 u8_autoSampleTime,uint8 u8_12bit);`	Configures ADC1 to perform conversions over a number of scanned channels to CH0. See Chapter 11 for more details.
`void configADC1_Simul4ChanIrq(uint8 u8_ch0Select, uint16 u16_ch123SelectMask, uint16 u16_numTcyMask);`	Configures ADC1 to perform simultaneous sampling and (sequential) 10-bit conversion on four channels. See Chapter 11 for more details.

FIGURE D.9   ADC functions/macros.

APPENDIX
E

Circuits 001

This appendix gives a hobbyist-level introduction to basic circuits and covers the passive components (resistors, capacitors, diodes) used in this book's schematics.

VOLTAGE, CURRENT, RESISTANCE

Current is the flow of electrons through a conductor. A *conductor* is anything that allows current flow. A good conductor offers little *resistance* to current flow; in other words, it does not take much work for current to flow within a good conductor. In rough terms, the amount of work it takes to move electrons between two points on a conductor is *voltage*. The voltage difference between one end of a conductor and the other end of a conductor indicates the resistance of the conductor. If the voltage drop is high, the resistance is high; conversely, if the voltage drop is low, the resistance is low. A voltage supply provides a source of current at a fixed voltage level. Current is measured in *amperes* (A), with a few milliamperes (mA, 1 mA = 0.001 A) being the typical current requirements of the integrated circuits used in this book. Voltage is measured in *volts* (V) and resistance is measured in *ohms* (Ω). The PIC24 μC and the integrated circuits in this book require a *direct current* (DC) voltage supply, typically with a voltage value of +3.3 V. A DC voltage supply means that the current flows in one direction only and that the voltage is a constant value, either positive or negative. By contrast, the power available for household appliances from wall plugs is *alternating current* (AC), where the voltage varies in a sinusoidal fashion between ±120 V with a frequency of 60 Hz. The AC current direction reverses itself each time the voltage value crosses 0 V.

OHM'S LAW

A *resistor* is a component with a fixed resistance value that is used to control current flow in an electrical circuit. Figure E.1 shows a basic DC circuit consisting of a DC voltage supply and one resistor with value R.

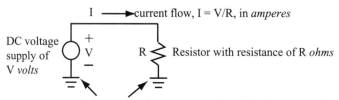

These two points are assumed to either be connected together or both connected to a common ground that is at 0 volts.

FIGURE E.1   Voltage/current relationship with one resistor.

Equation E.1 gives *Ohm's Law,* which expresses the current (I) flowing through the resistor as a function of voltage (V) and resistance (R).

$$I = V/R \qquad\qquad (E.1)$$

An ideal DC voltage source supplies the current predicted by Equation E.1; thus, a resistance of zero causes infinite current flow. A zero resistance or very low resistance path is called a *short,* and causes large currents to flow. A physical power supply obviously cannot supply infinite current, and thus will either fail after a short period of time or blow an internal *fuse,* breaking the circuit path. Figure E.2 shows how a fuse is used to protect against shorts.

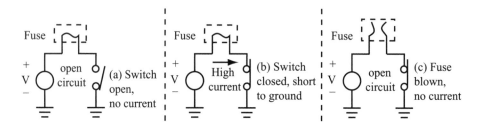

FIGURE E.2   Using a fuse to protect against shorts.

A fuse is a thin conductor that physically separates, breaking the connection, after a maximum rated current is reached. In Figure E.2a the switch is open so no current is flowing; (b) the switch is closed, creating a short between VDD and ground; and (c) the fuse has blown, creating an open path and stopping current flow.

Equation E.2 is another form of Ohm's Law that expresses voltage across a resistor as the product of current and resistance.

$$V = I \times R \qquad\qquad (E.2)$$

RESISTORS IN SERIES

Figure E.3 shows a circuit with two resistors connected in *series*. In this case, the current flowing through both resistors is the same and is expressed by Equation E.3, where the total resistance of the circuit is the sum of $R1$ and $R2$.

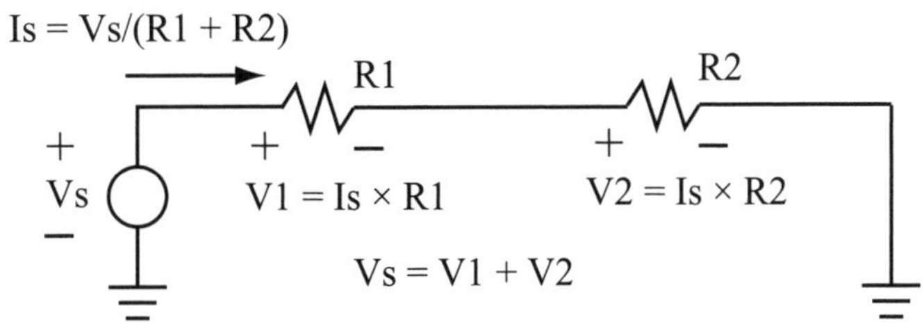

FIGURE E.3   Resistors in series

$$Is = Vs/(R1 + R2) \tag{E.3}$$

Equations E.4 and E.5 give the voltages $V1$ and $V2$ across each resistor.

$$V1 = Is \times R1 \tag{E.4}$$

$$V2 = Is \times R2 \tag{E.5}$$

Resistors in series form a voltage divider, with the sum of voltages across the resistors equal to the voltage supply value as shown in Equation E.6.

$$Vs = V1 + V2 \tag{E.6}$$

Voltage dividers are used in Chapter 11, "Data Conversion," to build analog-to-digital and digital-to-analog converters. Observe that if $R1 = R2$, $V1 = V2 = Vs/2$; the voltage divides equally between the two resistors.

RESISTORS IN PARALLEL

Figure E.4 shows a circuit with two resistors connected in *parallel*. In this case, the voltage across each resistor is the same and is equal to the power supply voltage Vs. However, the current flowing through each resistor is dependent upon the resistance value as given in Equations E.7 and E.8.

$$I1 = Vs/R1 \tag{E.7}$$

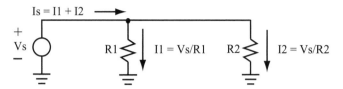

FIGURE E.4   Resistors in parallel.

$$I2 = Vs/R2 \tag{E.8}$$

Resistors in parallel form a *current divider,* with the sum of the currents through the resistors equal to the total current drawn from the power supply (*Is*) as shown in Equation E.9.

$$Is = I1 + I2 \tag{E.9}$$

When measuring the total current through a system like the PIC24 reference board in this book, the current draw of each individual integrated circuit can be determined by simply removing it from the board, since the current draw of each integrated circuit adds to the total current draw. Figure E.5 illustrates this concept. Observe that the integrated circuits are connected in parallel (all supplied with the same voltage).

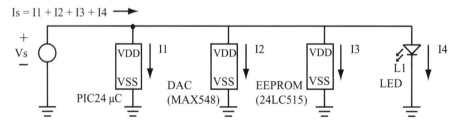

FIGURE E.5   Current draw in a total system.

POLARIZATION

Most circuit elements have two terminals through which current flows. The terminals can either be *polarized* (have positive and negative terminals) or *unpolarized.* A DC power supply is polarized; it has clearly marked positive (+) and negative (−) terminals. The negative terminal is at zero volts (ground) and the positive terminal is the voltage output. A resistor is unpolarized; its operation is not affected by the direction in which its terminals are connected in a circuit.

DIODES

A *diode* is a two-terminal device that allows current flow in one direction only. A diode's two terminals are named the *anode* and the *cathode;* when the voltage on the anode is approximately 0.7 V higher than the cathode voltage, current flows through the diode (the turn-on voltage for a diode varies by diode type, as a *Schottky* diode's turn-on voltage is approximately 0.3 V). Thus, a diode is a polarized device, as circuit operation is dependent upon how its terminals are connected in a circuit. On physical diodes, the cathode terminal is identified by either a band at one end or by being the shorter of the two leads. Figure E.6 shows some simple diode circuits.

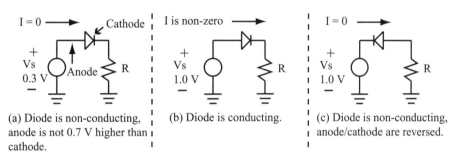

(a) Diode is non-conducting, anode is not 0.7 V higher than cathode.

(b) Diode is conducting.

(c) Diode is non-conducting, anode/cathode are reversed.

FIGURE E.6   Diode circuits.

In Figure E.6a no current is flowing through the diode, as the anode voltage is only 0.3 V; (b) current flows through the diode, as the anode voltage is greater than the cathode voltage by more than 0.7 V; (c) no current is flowing, as the diode direction is reversed in the circuit; the only way for current to flow in this circuit is if *Vs* produces a negative voltage. The resistor is included in series with the diode in Figure E.6 simply to limit the current flow within the circuit. A diode has internal resistance but its value depends upon the diode type. A *light emitting diode* (LED) emits visible light in proportion to the current flowing through it; the higher the current, the brighter the light.

CAPACITORS

A *capacitor* is a two-terminal device that comes in both unpolarized and polarized varieties, depending upon the material that is used to make the capacitor. Polarized capacitors have clearly marked + and − terminals. Equation E.10 gives the time-dependent current flow $i(t)$ to a capacitor as a function of capacitance (C) and the voltage rate of change (dv/dt) across the capacitor.

$$i(t) = C \, dv/dt \qquad (E.10)$$

In intuitive terms, Equation E.10 says that if the voltage across a capacitor is not changing, then no current flows to the capacitor. Equation E.11 gives the time-dependent voltage across a capacitor as a function of capacitance and current.

$$v(t) = (1/C) \int i \, dt \qquad \text{(E.11)}$$

In intuitive terms, Equation E.11 says that a capacitor stores charge, increasing its voltage, as current flows to it. One can think of a capacitor as a bucket that holds charge where the height of the bucket's wall is proportional to voltage. Figure E.7 shows the effect of Equations E.10 and E.11 in an RC series circuit.

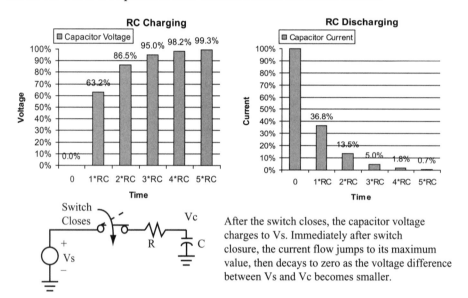

After the switch closes, the capacitor voltage charges to Vs. Immediately after switch closure, the current flow jumps to its maximum value, then decays to zero as the voltage difference between Vs and Vc becomes smaller.

FIGURE E.7   RC series circuit.

When the switch is open, the current to the capacitor and the voltage across the capacitor are both zero. At time t = 0, the switch closes and the capacitor charges up in an exponentially decaying fashion to Vs. The current jumps to its maximum value immediately after the switch closure due to the instantaneous change in voltage (maximum dv/dt), and exponentially decays to zero as the change in voltage across the capacitor (dv/dt) decreases. The Y axis is time and is marked in RC units, where the R × C product is called the *time constant* of the RC series circuit. The larger the time constant, the longer it takes for the capacitor to charge.

In the PIC24 reference system, the polarized capacitors used across the VDD and ground pins of the PIC24 µC are used as energy reservoirs for transient current needs caused by switching activity within the microcontroller. Physical capacitors also have some resistance associated with them called the equivalent series resistance (ESR), and this needs to be low in order for the capacitors to adequately meet these transient switching needs. Ceramic and some tantalum capacitor types have low ESR values. Polarized "can"-type capacitors are aluminum electrolytic, are available in large capacitance values and are used to provide a large charge reservoir for stabilizing the DC power supply but do not have a low ESR.

A comprehensive description of the physical characteristics of a capacitor is beyond the scope of this appendix, but it must be pointed out that current (charge) does not flow through a capacitor in the same way as current flows through a resistor. A capacitor is made from two parallel plates with a *dielectric* material between the plates. The plates (terminals) are isolated, and current does not pass between the plates. The dielectric material, the surface area of the plates, and the plate separation determine the capacitance value. Charge collects on one of the plates, forming a voltage across the plates. *Discharging* or *charging* a capacitor as shown in Figure E.7 means to remove charge from or place charge on the capacitor via current flow, which changes the capacitor's voltage.

APPENDIX F

References

Note: For all PIC24H Family Reference Manual sections, please visit *www.microchip .com* and search for "PIC24H FRM."

[1] P. Ceruzzi, *A History of Modern Computing,* Second Edition. Cambridge, MA: The MIT Press, 2003.

[2] G. Ifrah, *The Universal History of Computing.* New York: John Wiley & Sons, Inc., 2001.

[3] M. Morris Mano, *Computer System Architecture,* Second Edition. Englewood Cliffs, NJ: Prentice-Hall, 1982.

[4] W. Weste, D. Harris, *CMOS VLSI Design: A Circuits and Systems Perspective, Third Edition.* MA: Addison-Wesley, 2005.

[5] Microchip Technology Inc., *dsPIC30F,33F Programmer's Reference Manual,* DS70157B, 2005. Available online at *www.microchip.com.*

[6] J. Hennessy and D. Patterson, *Computer Architecture: A Quantitative Approach, Second Edition.* San Francisco: Morgan Kaufmann Publishers, Inc., 1996.

[7] Intel Corporation, "Appendix C: Instruction Latency and Throughput," *Intel 64 and IA-32 Architectures Optimization Reference Manual,* Order Number 248966-016, November 2007. Available online at *www.intel.com.*

[8] Microchip Technology Inc., *dsPIC30F/33F Programmer's Reference Manual,* DS70157B, 2005. Available online at *www.microchip.com.*

[9] Microchip Technology Inc., *Section 1. Introduction—PIC24H FRM,* DS70242A, 2007. Available online at *www.microchip.com.*

[10] Microchip Technology Inc., *Section 2. CPU—PIC24H FRM,* DS70245A, 2007. Available online at *www.microchip.com.*

[11] Microchip Technology Inc., *Section 3. Data Memory—PIC24H FRM,* DS70237A, 2007. Available online at *www.microchip.com.*

[12] Microchip Technology Inc., *Section 4. Program Memory—PIC24H FRM,* DS70238B, 2008. Available online at *www.microchip.com.*

[13] Microchip Technology Inc., *Section 5. Flash Programming—PIC24H FRM,* DS70228C, 2007. Available online at *www.microchip.com.*

[14] Microchip Technology Inc., *Section 6. Interrupts—PIC24H FRM*, DS70224C, 2008. Available online at *www.microchip.com*.

[15] Microchip Technology Inc., *Section 7. Oscillator—PIC24H FRM*, DS70227C, 2008. Available online at *www.microchip.com*.

[16] Microchip Technology Inc., *Section 8. Reset—PIC24H FRM*, DS70229B, 2007. Available online at *www.microchip.com*.

[17] Microchip Technology Inc., *Section 9. Watchdog Timer and Power Savings Modes—PIC24H FRM*, DS70236A, 2007. Available online at *www.microchip.com*.

[18] Microchip Technology Inc., *Section 10. IO Ports—PIC24H FRM*, DS70230C, 2008. Available online at *www.microchip.com*.

[19] Microchip Technology Inc., *Section 11. Timers—PIC24H FRM*, DS70244B, 20087. Available online at *www.microchip.com*.

[20] Microchip Technology Inc., *Section 13. Output Compare—PIC24H FRM*, DS70247A, 2007. Available online at *www.microchip.com*.

[21] Microchip Technology Inc., *Section 16. 10, 12-bit Analog-to-Digital Converter with DMA—PIC24H FRM*, DS70225B, 2007. Available online at *www.microchip.com*.

[22] Microchip Technology Inc., *Section 17. UART—PIC24H FRM*, DS70232B, 2008. Available online at *www.microchip.com*.

[23] Microchip Technology Inc., *Section 18. SPI—PIC24H FRM*, DS70243B, 2008. Available online at *www.microchip.com*.

[24] Microchip Technology Inc., *Section 19. Inter-Integrated Circuit™ (I²C™)—PIC24H FRM*, DS70235B, 2008. Available online at *www.microchip.com*.

[25] Microchip Technology Inc., *Section 21. Enhanced Controller Area Network (ECAN™)—PIC24H FRM*, DS70226B, 2007. Available online at *www.microchip.com*.

[26] Microchip Technology Inc., *Section 22. Direct Memory Access (DMA)—PIC24H FRM*, DS70223A, 2006. Available online at *www.microchip.com*.

[27] Microchip Technology Inc., *Section 25. Device Configuration—PIC24H FRM*, DS70231B, 2008. Available online at *www.microchip.com*.

[28] Microchip Technology Inc., *Section 28. 10, 12-bit Analog-to-Digital Converter (ADC) without DMA—PIC24H FRM*, DS70249A, 2007. Available online at *www.microchip.com*.

[29] Microchip Technology Inc., *Section 29. Interrupts (Part Two)—PIC24H FRM*, DS70233A, 2007. Available online at *www.microchip.com*.

[30] Microchip Technology Inc., *Section 30. IO Ports with Remappable Digital IO—PIC24H FRM*, DS70234A, 2007. Available online at *www.microchip.com*.

[31] Microchip Technology Inc., *PIC24HJ32GP202/204 and PIC24HJ16GP304 Data Sheet*, DS70289A, 2007. Available online at *www.microchip.com*.

[32] Microchip Technology Inc., *MPLAB® C Compiler For PIC24MCUs and dsPIC® DSCs User's Guide,* DS51284H, 2008. Available online at *www.microchip.com.*

[33] Hantronix, *HDM162116L-5 Dimensional Drawing,* 16 Character x 2 Lines LCD Module. Available online at *www.hantronix.com.*

[34] Hantronix, *HDM16216L-5 LCD Module Commands.* Available online at *www.hantronix.com.*

[35] Maxim, *3.0V to 5.5V, Low-Power, up to 1Mbps, True RS-232 Transceivers Using Four 0.1μF External Capacitors,* MAX3222, 19-0273, Rev 7, 1/07. Available online at *www.maxim-ic.com.*

[36] Microchip Technology Inc., *MCP41XXX/42XXX Single/Dual Potentiometer with SPI Interface,* DS11195C, 2003. Available online at *www.microchip.com.*

[37] Dallas Semiconductor/Maxim, *Digital Thermometer with SPI/3-Wire Interface,* DS1722, 022008. Available online at *www.maxim-ic.com.*

[38] Philips Semiconductors, *The I²C Bus Specification Version 2.1,* 2001. Available online at *www.nxp.com.*

[39] Maxim Integrated Products, *DS1631/DS1631A/DS1731 Digital Thermometer and Thermostat,* REV 102307. Available online at *www.maxim-ic.com.*

[40] Microchip Technology Inc., *24AA515/25LC515/24FC515 512K I²C CMOS Serial EEPROM,* DS21673C, 2003. Available online at *www.microchip.com.*

[41] Texas Instruments Inc., *SN754410 Quadruple Half-H Driver,* SLRS007B, revised November 1995.

[42] Microchip Technology Inc., *Section 37. Read-Time Clock and Calendar (RTCC)—PIC24H FRM,* DS70310A, 2007. Available online at *www.microchip.com.*

[43] D. Matthews, *AN849: Basic PICmicro Oscillator Design,* Microchip Technology Inc., DS00849A, 2002. Available online at *www.microchip.com.*

[44] Microchip Technology Inc., *Section 38. Direct Memory Access (DMA) (PART III)—PIC24H FRM,* DS70309B, 2008. Available online at *www.microchip.com.*

[45] Society for Industrial and Applied Mathematics, "Inquiry Board Traces Ariane 5 Failure to Overflow Error," *SIAM News,* Vol. 29, Number 8, October 1996.

[46] R. Bosch GmbH, *CAN Specification/Version 2.0,* 1991. Available online at *www.can.bosch.com.*

[47] Microchip Technology Inc., *High-Speed CAN Transceiver,* DS21667D, 2003. Available online at *www.microchip.com.*

[48] Microchip Technology Inc., *Section 21. Enhanced Controller Area Network (ECAN™)—PIC24H FRM,* DS70226B, 2007. Available online at *www.microchip.com.*

[49] Compaq, Hewlett-Packard, Intel, Lucent, Microsoft, NEC, Phillips, *Universal Serial Bus Specification,* Revision 2.0, April 27, 2000. Available online at *http://www.usb.org.*

[50] Microchip Technology Inc., *Section 5. Flash Programming—PIC24H FRM,* DS70228C, 2007. Available online at *www.microchip.com.*

[51] Microchip Technology Inc., *Section 35. Parallel Master Port (PMP)—PIC24H FRM,* DS70302B, 2008. Available online at *www.microchip.com.*

[52] Microchip Technology Inc., *Section 34. Comparator—PIC24H FRM,* DS70305A, 2007. Available online at *www.microchip.com.*

[53] Microchip Technology Inc., *Section 36. Programmable Cyclic Redundancy Check (CRC)—PIC24H FRM,* DS70311A, 2007. Available online at *www.microchip.com.*

[54] National Semiconductor, *LM386 Low Voltage Audio Power Amplifier,* DS006976, August 2000. Available online at *www.national.com.*

[55] Dialogic® Corporation, *Dialogic ADPCM Algorithm,* 00-1366-001, 1988. Available online at *www.dialogic.com.*

[56] Interactive Multimedia Association (defunct), *Recommended Practices for Enhancing Digital Audio Compatibility in Multimedia Systems,* Revision 3.0, October 21, 1992, 41 pp. Available online at *www.cs.columbia.edu/~hgs/audio/dvi/.*

[57] R. Richey, *AN643 Adaptive Differential Pulse Code Modulation Using PICmicro™ Microcontrollers,* Microchip Technology Inc., DS00643B, 1997. Available online at *www.microchip.com.*

[58] P. M. Weir, L. E. Hicks, J. B. Leatherwood, J. Wilson, *MP3toFM: An Ethernet to FM Audio System,* ECE 4512 Final Report, April 25, 2008. Available online at *www.ece.msstate.edu/courses/design/2008/mp3tofm.*

[59] WIZnet, *iinChip W3100A,* Technical Datasheet v1.34. Available online at *www.WIZnet.co.kr.*

[60] VLSI Solution Oy, *VS1011e MPEG Audio Codec,* Version 1.04, 2007-10-08.

[61] Niigata Seimitsu Co., Ltd., *FM Stereo Transmitter,* NS73M-61LU-0101, 2006-01-06.

[62] P. Burks, S. Cave, D. Johnson, and J. Ward, *MOCRO: Manually Operated Compact Reflow Oven,* ECE 4512 Final Report, April 25, 2008. Available online at *www.ece.msstate.edu/courses/design/2007/roven.*

[63] R. Sharma, *AN233 Solder Reflow Recommendation,* Microchip Technology Inc., DS00233D, 2004. Available online at *www.microchip.com.*

[64] Maxim, *Cold-Junction-Compensated K-Thermocouple to-Digital Converter (0°C to +1024°C),* MAX6675, 19-2235, Rev 1, 3/02. Available online at *www.maxim-ic.com.*

[65] L. Elevich and V. Kudva, *AN1094 Bootloader for dsPIC30F/33F and PIC24F/24H Devices,* DS 1094A, 2007. Available online at *www.microchip.com.*

[66] F. Maloberti, *Data Converters.* Dordrecht, The Netherlands: Springer, 2007.

[67] B. Razavi, *Principles of Data Conversion System Design.* New York: IEEE Press, 1995.

[68] Maxim, *2.5V to 5.5V, Low-Power, Single/Dual, 8-Bit Voltage-Output DACs,* MAX548A, 19-1206, Rev 0, 3/97. Available online at *www.maxim-ic.com.*

[69] Maxim, *Low-Power, 12-Bit Voltage-Output DACs with Serial Interface,* MAX5353, 19-1196, Rev 0, 2/97. Available online at *www.maxim-ic.com.*

[70] Maxim, *Low-Power, 2-Wire Serial 8-Bit DACs with Rail-to-Rail Outputs,* MAX518, 19-0393, Rev 1, 9/02. Available online at *www.maxim-ic.com.*

[71] A. Silberschatz, P. B. Galvin, and G. Gagne, *Operating System Concepts, 8/e,* New York: Wiley 2008.

[72] W. Stallings, *Operating Systems: Internals and Design Principles 6/e,* Upper Saddle River, NJ: Prentice-Hall, 2009.

[73] B. Stuart, *Principles of Operating Systems: Design and Application,* Cengage, 2009.

[74] A. B. Downey, *The Little Book of Semaphores 2/e,* Version 2.1.5. Green Tea Press, 2008. Available online at *www.greenteapress.com/semaphores.*

[75] A. Dunkels, *Protothreads: Lightweight, Stackless Threads in C.* Available online at *www.sics.se/~adam/pt/.*

APPENDIX
G
Problem Solutions

CHAPTER 1

1. $2^5 = 32$, $2^6 = 64$, so 6 bits.
3. $120 = 0x78 = 0b0111\ 1000$
5. $0xF4 = 0b1111\ 0100$
7. $0b1011\ 0111 = 0xB7 = 11*16 + 7 = 183$
9. $0xB2 - 0x9F = 0x13$. $\sim 0x9F = \sim(0b1001\ 1111) = 0b0110\ 0000 = 0x60$.
   So $0xB2 - 0x9F = 0xB2 + \sim 0x9F + 0x01 = 0xB2 + 0x60 + 0x01 = 0x13$.
11. See Figure G.1.11

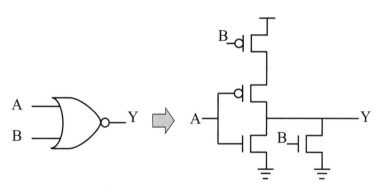

FIGURE G.1.11   Problem G.1.11.

13. $0x2A << 1 = 0x54$
15. $0.3 * \text{period} = 20$ µs; so period $= 20$ µs$/0.3 = 66.7$ µs. Frequency $= 1/(66.7\ \text{µs}) = 15$ kHz
17. See Figure G.1.17

When SUB = 0, S = A + B
When SUB = 1, S = A + ~B + 1
$\qquad$ = A − B

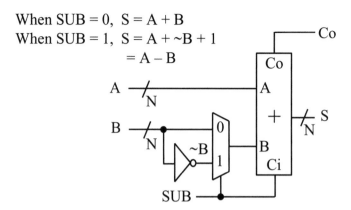

FIGURE G.1.17   Problem G.1.17.

19. See Figure G.1.19

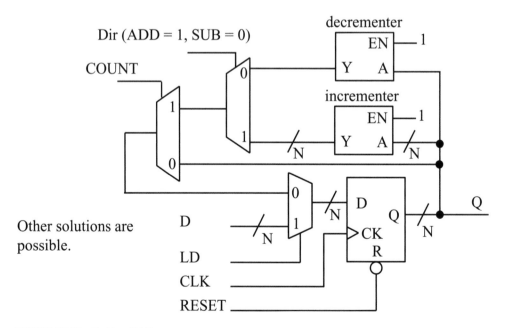

Other solutions are
possible.

FIGURE G.1.19   Problem G.1.19.

CHAPTER 2

1.

```
Location        Machine Code    Mnemonics
                                START:
0               01 0111         JC LOC_IS_1
1               10 0000         OUT 0
2               10 0010         OUT 2
3               10 0101         OUT 5
4               10 0111         OUT 7
5               00 0000         JMP START           LOC_IS_1:
6               10 0001         OUT 1
7               10 0011         OUT 3
8               10 0110         OUT 6
9               10 1000         OUT 8
10              00 0000         JMP START
```

3.

```
Cycle   Location  Comment
  1       0       OUT 2, DOUT = 2 = 0b0010, LOC = LSb = 0
  2       1       OUT 5, DOUT = 5 = 0b0101, LOC = LSb = 1
  3       2       JC 5, DOUT = 5 = 0b0101, LOC = LSb = 1, so take jump
  4       5       OUT 9, DOUT = 9 = 0b1001, LOC = LSb = 1
  5       6       JC 2, DOUT = 9 = 0b1001, LOC = LSb = 1, so take jump
  6       2       JC 5, DOUT = 9 = 0b1001, LOC = LSb = 1, so take jump
  7       5       OUT 9, DOUT = 9 = 0b1001, LOC = LSb = 1
  8       6       JC 2, DOUT = 9 = 0b1001, LOC = LSb = 1, so take jump
  9       2       JC 5, DOUT = 9 = 0b1001, LOC = LSb = 1, so take jump
 10       5       OUT 9, DOUT = 9 = 0b1001, LOC = LSb = 1
```

5. It takes 13 instructions.

```
START:
  JC LOCAL
  OUT 1
  OUT X1
  OUT X2
  OUT X3
```

```
LOCAL:
    OUT  Y1
    OUT  Y2
    OUT  Y3
    OUT  Z1
    OUT  Z2
    OUT  Z3
    OUT  Z4
    JMP  START
```

7. The first change is to increase the number of memory locations from 16 to 32. This causes the memory address bus to increase from 4 bits ($2^4 = 16$) to 5 bits ($2^5 = 32$). This means the Program Counter has to increase from 4 bits to 5 bits. Finally, the instruction size has to increase by one bit because the JC/JMP instruction data field specifies a location, which now requires 5 bits. So the new memory size is 32 × 7.

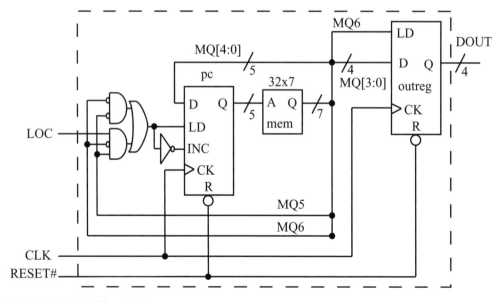

FIGURE G.2.7 Problem G.2.7

9. The opcode field must be increased from two bits to three bits; this changes the memory from a 16 x 6 memory to a 16 x 7 memory (each location now contains seven bits).

CHAPTER 3

1. 0xBF900A
3. 0x2A2353
5. Two instruction words; 0x0402A0, 0x000000.
7. mov.w W8, W2
9. mov.w #0x12F0, W2
11. 100 ns
13.
```
mov.b #32, W0      ;W0 = 32
sub.b i,WREG       ;WREG = i − 32
sub.b j,WREG       ;WREG = WREG − j = (i − 32) − j
mov.b   k          ;k = (i − 32) − j
```

15. 12,500,000 (Instruction cycle frequency is 12.5 MHz)
17. W0=0x1038 (byte operation, only LSB of W0 changed)
19. Memory location 0x1004 = 0x2A19 (0x1005 = 0x2A, byte operation)
21. W3 = 0x1020
23. W0 = 0x4D18
25. WREG (LSB) = 0x2A + 0x06 = 0x30, so WREG = 0x1030
27. LSB of Memory location 0x1006 = 0x05 − 0x0A = 0xFB; so Memory Location 0x1006 = 0xE7FB
29. Memory location 0x1008 = 0xFFFE
31. Memory location 0x1008 = 0x0100 (0x1009 = 0x01)

CHAPTER 4

1. W0 = 0x0800, Z = 1, C = 1
3. W2 = 0x0002, Z = 0, C = 1
5. W1 = 0x0804, Z = 0, C = 1
7. W0 = 0xF8A6, Z = 0, C = 1
9. W4 = 0xFF5D, Z = 0, C = 1
11. W4 = 0x0000, Z = 0, C = 1 (status is not affected!)
13. W1 = 0xFFFF, Z = 0, C = 1
15. Location 0x0800 = 0x782A, Z = 0, C = 1
17. Location 0x0804 = 0x00FF, Z = 0, C = 1
19. Location 0x0804 = 0x7B0B, Z = 0, C = 1
21. Location 0x0802 = 0x0480, Z = 0, C = 1
23. W3 = 0x00F0, Z = 0, C = 1

25. W0 = 0x2000, Z = 0, C = 1
27. Location 0x0800 = 0x3854, Z = 0, C = 1
29. Location 0x0802 = 0xF701, Z = 0, C = 1
31. Location 0x0800 = 0x1C15, Z = 0, C = 1
33. Location 0x0802 = 0xFBC0, Z = 0, C = 0
35.

```
sl u16_j,WREG
mov #0x30,W1
sub W0,W1,W0
add u16_i,WREG
mov WREG,u16_k
```

37.

```
mov.b u8_p,WREG
ze W0,W1              ;W1 = (uint16) u8_p
sl u16_j,WREG         ;W0 = u16_j << 1
add W0,W1,W0          ;W0 = (uint16) u8_p + ((uint16) u8_p)
mov #0x30,W1
sub W0,W1,W0          ;W0 = (uint16) u8_p + ((uint16) u8_p) - 0x30
mov WREG,u16_k
```

39.

```
    mov #0x400,W0
    cp u16_k
    bra GEU, p39_if_body
    cp0.b u8_r
    bra NZ, p39_else_body
p39_if_body:
    nop               ;;if body
    bra               p39_end_if
p39_else_body:
    nop               ;; else body
p39_end_if:
```

41.

```
    mov #0x400,W0
    cp u16_k
    bra Z, p41_else_body
    mov u8_p,W0
    cp  u8_r
    bra LEU,p41_else_body
p41_if_body:
        nop           ;;if body
        bra           p41_end_if
p41_else_body:
```

```
        nop                     ;; else body
    p41_end_if:
```

43.

```
    p43_loop_top:
      mov u16_k,WREG
      cp u16_i
      bra Z, p43_loop_end
      nop                     ;;loop body
      bra p43_loop_top
    p43_loop_end:
```

45.

```
    p45_loop_top:
      nop                     ;;loop_body
      cp.b u8_r
      bra NZ, p45_loop_top
      mov.b u8_q,WREG
      cp.b u8_p
      bra LTU, p45_loop_top
```

47.

```
    p47:
      ;; Use W0 for u8_i
      clr.b u8_k              ;u8_k = 0
      clr.b W0               ;u8_i = 0
    p47_loop_top:
      cp.b W0,#8             ;u8_i != 8
      bra  Z, p47_loop_exit
      btst.b u8_j, #0        ; test LSB of u8_j
      bra  Z, p47_skip
      inc.b u8_k             ;u8_k++
    p47_skip:
      lsr.b  u8_j            ;u8_j = u8_j >> 1
      inc.b W0,W0            ;u8_i++;
    p47_loop_exit:
```

CHAPTER 5

1.

```
    p1_loop_top:
      mov u32_k,W0
      sub u32_i
```

```
        mov   u32_k+2,W0
        subb  u32_i+2                  ;u32_i = u32_i − u32_k;
        mov   u32_j,W0
        add   u32_k,WREG
        mov   W0,W2
        mov   u32_j+2,W0
        addc  u32_k+2,WREG
        mov   W0,W3                    ;W3:W2 = u32_j + u32_k
        mov   u32_i,W0
        mov   u32_i+2,W1               ;W1:W0 = u32_i
        cp    W0,W2
        cpb   W1,W3                    ; u32_i < (u32_j + u32_k)
        bra   LTU, p1_loop_top
```

3.

```
   mov   u32_j,W0
   ior   u32_i,WREG
   mov   W0,u32_k
   mov   u32_j+2,W0
   ior   u32_i+2, WREG
   mov   W0,u32_k+2
```

5.

```
   p5_loop_top:
        mov   u64_k,W0
        sub   u64_i
        mov   u64_k+2,W0
        subb  u64_i+2
        mov   u64_k+4,W0
        subb  u64_i+4
        mov   u64_k+6,W0
        subb  u64_i+6                  ;u64_i = u64_i − u64_k;
        mov   u64_j,W0
        add   u64_k,WREG
        mov   W0,W4
        mov   u64_j+2,W0
        addc  u64_k+2,WREG
        mov   W0,W5
        mov   u64_j+4,W0
        addc  u64_k+4,WREG
        mov   W0,W6
        mov   u64_j+6,W0
        addc  u64_k+6,WREG
        mov   W0,W7                    ;W7:W4 = u64_j + u64_k
```

```
        mov  u64_i,W0
        mov  u64_i+2,W1
        mov  u64_i+4,W2
        mov  u64_i+6,W3 ;W3:W0 = u64_i
        cp   W0,W4
        cpb  W1,W5
        cpb  W2,W6
        cpb  W3,W7 ; u64_i < (u64_j + u64_k)
        bra  LTU, p5_loop_top
```

7.
```
     p7:
        mov  u64_j,W0
        ior  u64_i,WREG
        mov  W0,u64_k
        mov  u64_j+2,W0
        ior  u64_i+2,WREG
        mov  W0,u64_k+2
        mov  u64_j+4,W0
        ior  u64_i+4,WREG
        mov  W0,u64_k+4
        mov  u64_j+6,W0
        ior  u64_i+6,WREG
        mov  W0,u64_k+6
```

9. 0xD6
11. −1117
13. 0xFF85
15. 0x90 − 0x8A = 0x06, Z = 0, N = 0, V = 1, C = 1.
17. 0x2A − 0x81 = 0xA9, Z = 0, N = 1, V = 1, C = 0.
19. These are signed numbers, $i8\_i = -96$ and $i8\_j = +112$, so comparison results false, assigning $i8\_k$ a value of 0.
21. 0xA0 >> 2 = 0xE8 assuming the sign bit is preserved.
23.
```
     p23:
        mov  i16_j,W0
        cp   i16_k
        bra  LT, p23_end_if        ;signed branch
        asr  i16_i                 ;preserve sign
        asr  i16_i
     p23_end_if:
```

25.

```
p25:
   mov.b u8_q, WREG
   ze  W0,W1          ;W1 = (int16) u8_q (zero extend)
   lsr W1,#2,W1       ;W1 = (int16) u8_q >> 2
   mov u16_k,W0
   sub W0,W1,W0       ;W0 = ((u16_k - (uint8) u8_q) >> 2)
   mov #0xA34D,W1
   and W0,W1,W0       ;W0 = ((u16_k - (uint8) u8_q) >> 2) & 0xA34D;
   mov WREG,u16_i
```

27. Code fragment:

```
p27:
   mov.b i8_q,WREG
   se   W0,W0         ; W0 = (int16) i8_q
   clr  W1
   btsc W0,#15
   setm W1            ;W1:W0 = (int32) i8_q
   asr  W1,W1
   rrc  W0,W0         ;W1:W0 = (int32) i8_q >> 2
   mov.d W0,W2        ;W3:W2 = (int32) i8_q >> 2
   mov i32_s,W0
   mov i32_s+2,W1     ;W1 = i32_s
   sub W0,W2,W0
   subb W1,W3,W1      ;W1:W0 = i32_s - (int32) i8_q >> 2
   mov #0x807F,W2
   mov #0x38DB,W3     ;W3:W2 = 0x38DB807F
   ior W0,W2,W0
   ior W1,W3,W1       ;W1:W0 = (i32_s - (int32) i8_q >> 2)| 0x38DB807F
   mov W0,i32_r
   mov W1,i32_r+2
```

29. 0x34FFDF

CHAPTER 6

1.

Location	Contents	Comment
0x0800	0x0005 (+5)	ai16_x[0]
0x0802	0xFFFC (-4)	ai16_x[1]
0x0804	0x0800	pi16_y

3. W0 = 0x80FF, W1 = 0x0804
5. W0 = 0x0880, W1 = 0x0805
7. W0 = 0x0806, Memory Location 0x0804 = 0x8301
9. W0 = 0x0805, Memory Location 0x0804 = 0x8001
11. W2 = 0xCE46
13. W0 = 0x0806, Memory Location 0x804 = 0x7B03
15. W1=0x087B
17. Memory Location 0x0806 = 0x0603
19. W15 = 0x0806, Memory Location 0x0804 = 0x0806
21. W15 = 0x0802, W3 = 0xFB80
23. W15 = 0x080C, W14 = 0x0806, Memory Location 0x0804 = 0x0802
25. Return address = 0x020A + 4 = 0x020E
27.

```
;W0 = psz_1, W1 = psz_2, W2 used for u8_char
str_swap:
  cp0 [W0]                ; *psz_1 != 0
  bra Z, str_swap_exit
  mov.b [W0],W2           ;u8_char = *psz_1
  mov.b [W0],[W1]         ;*psz_1 = *psz_2
  mov.b W2,[W1++]         ;*psz_2 = u8_char, psz_2++
  inc W0,W0               ;psz_1++
  bra str_swap
str_swap_exit:
  return
```

29.

```
;W0 = pi16_a, W1 = u8_cnt, W2 = i16_k
find_max:
  mov #0x8000,W2          ;i16_k = -32768
find_max_loop_top:
  cp0.b W1
  bra Z, find_max_exit
  cp W2,[W0]              ;16_k < *pi16_a
  bra GE, find_max_skip   ;signed compare
  mov [W0],W2             ;i16_k = *pi16_a
find_max_skip:
  inc2 W0,W0             ;pi16_a++
  dec.b W1,W1            ;u8_cnt--
  bra find_max_loop_top
find_max_exit:
  mov W2,W0                      ;set up return value
  return ;W0 has pi16_a, W1 has u8_cnt, use W2 for i16_k
```

31.

```
putch:
  nop                    ;;dummy
  return

;WO = psz_in
putstr:
  cp0.b [WO]
  bra Z, putstr_exit
  push WO                ;save WO for subroutine call
  mov [WO],WO            ;get parameter for subroutine call
  call putch
  pop WO
  inc WO,WO              ;psz_in++
  bra putstr
putstr_exit:
  return
```

33.

```
pu16_x                 ;FP - 12
u8_i                   ;FP - 10
u8_j                   ;FP - 8
Rtn Addr (LSW)         ;FP - 6
Rtn Addr (MSW)         ;FP - 4
old FP                 ;FP - 2
i16_k                  ;<- New FP (+0)
free                   ;<- New SP
```

35.

```
;use WO = pu16_x, W1 = u8_i,  W2 = u8_j
;W3 used for pu16_x+u8_i, W4 used for pu16_x+u8_j
;W5 used as offset registers
;local space used for i16_k
p35_u16_swap:
  lnk #2                 ;allocate 2 words of space of i16_k
  mov #-12,WO
  mov [W14+W5],WO        ;WO = pu16_x
  mov #-10,W5
  mov.b [W14+W5],W1      ;W1 = u8_i
  mov #-8,W5
  mov.b [W14+W5],W2      ;W2 = u8_j
  ze W1,W1
  ze W2,W2               ;zero extend to 16 bits
  add WO,W1,W3           ;pu16_x+u8_i
```

```
    add W0,W2,W4              ;pu16_x+u8_j
    mov [W3],[W14]            ;u16_k = pu16_x[u8_i]
    mov [W4],[W3]            ;pu16_x[u8_i] = pu16_x[u8_j]
    mov [W4],[W3]            ;pu16_x[u8_j] = u16_k;
    ulnk
    return
```

37.
```
.bss                         ;uninitialized data section
;;These start at location 0x0800 because 0-0x07FF reserved for SFRs
au16_values: .space 2*6      ;data memory space
.text
p37:
    mov #__SP_init, w15      ;Initialize the stack pointer
    mov #__SPLIM_init,W0
    mov W0, SPLIM            ;Initialize the stack limit register
    call p37_init_variables
    call p37_main
    reset

ui16_swap:
    nop
    return

p37_main:
    mov #au16_values, W0
    mov #3,W1
    mov #4,W2
    call ui16_swap
p37_done: bra p37_done

au16_values_const:           .word 489, 45, 1000, 238, 30000, 10134

p37_init_variables:
    bset CORCON,#2 ;enable PSV
;copy au16_values_const to au16_values
    mov  #psvoffset(au16_values_const),W2
    mov  #au16_values,W3     ;destination address in data memory
    mov  #((6*2)-1),W4       ;(number of bytes)-1 to copy
    call p37_byte_copy
    return

p37_byte_copy:
    repeat W4
    mov.b [W2++],[W3++]
    return
```

CHAPTER 7

1. W9:W8 = 0x0009 FF88
3. W9:W8 = 0x0009 FF88
5. W9:W8 = 0xFFFF F448
7. W9:W8 = 0x000B F448
9. W0 = 0x1015, W1 = 0x0003
11. W0 = 0x3329, W1 = 0x0003
13. W0 = 0x00AB, W1 = 0x0010, overflow
15. W0 = 0xFFF2, W1 = 0x00FF
17. W0 = 0x3F01, W1 = 0x0000
19. 0xC4 = 196, 196/256 = 0.765625
21. 0xC4 = −60, −60/128 = −0.46875
23. 23.33 * 8 = 186.64, 186 = 0xBA
25. −0.2325 * 128 = −29.76, −29 = 0xE3
27. 0x7F (+127)
29. 0xFF (255)
31. −0.15625 = 0xBE200000
33. 0x42F18000 = 120.75
35. Comparing a and b, where a and b are single precision floating-point numbers. Return 1 if a > b, −1 if a < b, and 0 if a == b.

```
if (sign(a) != (sign(b)) {
    if (sign(a)) return −1;
    else return 1

}
//signs are equal, check exponent fields
if (exponent(a) != (exponent(b)) {
    if (exponent(a) < exponent(b)) return −1;
    else return 1

}
//signs and exponents are equal
if (significand(a) != (significand(a)) {
    if (significand(a) < significand(b)) return −1;
    else return 1

}
return 0;   //the numbers are equal.
```

37. 99 − 58 + 1 = 42

CHAPTER 8

1. _TRISB5 = 1 (input), _CN27PUE = 0 (pull-up disabled), _ODCB5 = 0 (open-drain disabled). This is a digital-only pin.

3. _TRISB2 = 1 (input), _PCFG4 = 1 (analog disabled), _CN6PUE = 1 (pull-up enabled), _ODCB2 = 0 (open-drain disabled). This is an analog/digital pin.

5. Input frequency is 8 MHz, FOSC = 32 MHz (4 * 8 MHz). Change from Figure 8.11 is PLL feedback divider is changed from 40 to 32 (PLLDIV bits from 38 to 30) and the PLLPOST scaler is changed from 2 to 4 (PLLPOST bits from 0 to 1).

Input Frequency	8000000	
TUN	0	
FRC OSC	8000000	
FRC Postscale bits	0	
FRC Postscale value	1	
Fin (to PLL)	8000000	
PLLPRE_bits	0	
PLLPRE value	2	
FREF	4000000	0.8 <Freq < 8 MHz
PLLDIV_bits	30	
PLL feedback divisor	32	
FVCO	128000000	100 MHz <FVCO< 200 MHz
PLLPOST_bits	1	
PLLPOST scale	4	
Fosc	32000000	Fosc < 80 MHz
Fcy	20000000	

7. Current (Doze /4) = (42.3 − 17.6)/4 + 17.6 = 23.8 mA

9. The string "Howdy Y'all!" is printed, and the WDT is enabled by _SWDTEN = 1. The code enters the infinite wait while(1){} loop; the WDT expires causing the processor to reset. After reset, main() is re-entered and the process repeated.

11. The string "Howdy Y'all!" is printed then the CPU enters sleep mode (asm("pwrsav #0")) and stays there; nothing else appears on the screen.

13. Uses same ASM chart as Figure 8.28, except "Toggle LED1" on exit of WAIT_FOR_RELEASE is replaced by "Toggle u8_blinkFlag", where u8_blinkFlag is a variable in the while(1){} loop that controls blinking of the LED.

```
int main(void) {
    STATE e_mystate;
    uint8 u8_blinkFlag;
    configBasic(HELLO_MSG);
```

```
      CONFIG_SW1(); CONFIG_LED1();
      e_mystate = STATE_WAIT_FOR_PRESS ;
      u8_blinkFlag = 1;
      LED1 = 0;
      while(1) {
        if (u8_blinkFlag) {
           LED1 = !LED1;
           DELAY_MS(100);                       //blink
        }
        switch (e_mystate) {
          case STATE_WAIT_FOR_PRESS :
            if (SW1_PRESSED()) e_mystate = STATE_WAIT_FOR_RELEASE;
            break;
          case STATE_WAIT_FOR_RELEASE :
            if (SW1_RELEASED()) {
              e_mystate = STATE_WAIT_FOR_PRESS;
              u8_blinkFlag = !u8_blinkFlag;   //toggle blink flag
            }
            break;
          default:
            e_mystate = STATE_WAIT_FOR_PRESS;
        }//end switch(e_mystate)
        DELAY_MS(DEBOUNCE_DLY);        //Debounce
        doHeartbeat();       //ensure that we are alive
      }//end while
    }//end main
```

15. Uses same ASM state transition as Figure 8.28. On exit from each state, there is a function call to changeLEDs() that changes the LED states.
```
void changeLEDs() {
  if (!LED1 && !LED2) {
     LED2 = 1;
     return;
  }
  if (!LED1 && LED2) {
     LED1 = 1; LED2 = 0;
     return;
  }
  if (LED1 && !LED2) {
     LED2 = 1;
     return;
  }
  if (LED1 && LED2) {
     LED1 = 0; LED2 = 0;
```

```
          return;
      }
  }

  int main(void) {
     STATE e_mystate;
     configBasic(HELLO_MSG);
     CONFIG_SW1(); CONFIG_LED1();CONFIG_LED2();
     e_mystate = STATE_WAIT_FOR_PRESS ;
     LED1 = 0; LED2 = 0; //LEDs are off.
     while(1) {
     switch (e_mystate) {
        case STATE_WAIT_FOR_PRESS :
           if (SW1_PRESSED()) {
              e_mystate = STATE_WAIT_FOR_RELEASE;
              changeLEDs();  //change the LED states
           }
           break;
        case STATE_WAIT_FOR_RELEASE :
           if (SW1_RELEASED()) {
             e_mystate = STATE_WAIT_FOR_PRESS;
             changeLEDs();        //change the LED states
           }
           break;
        default:
           e_mystate = STATE_WAIT_FOR_PRESS;
        }//end switch(e_mystate)
        DELAY_MS(DEBOUNCE_DLY);  //Debounce
        doHeartbeat();        //ensure that we are alive
     }//end while
  }//end main
```

17.

```
  //written in a simple style
  uint8 testDFFAsync(uint8 u8_op) {
    DFF_R = 1; DFF_S = 1; //negate
    DELAY_US(1);
    if (u8_op) {
     //reset
     DFF_R = 0; //assert
     DELAY_US(1);
     DFF_R = 1; //negate
     DELAY_US(1);
     if (DFF_Q) return 0; //incorrect output
```

```
        else return 1; //correct output
    } else {
      //set
      DFF_S = 0;   //assert
      DELAY_US(1);
      DFF_S =1;    //negate
      DELAY_US(1);
      if (DFF_Q) return 1;   //correct output
      else return 0; //incorrect output
    }
  }
}
```

19.
```
//written in a simple style
uint8 testGate(void) {
  GATE_A = 0; GATE_B = 0;
  DELAY_US(1);
  if (!GATE_Y) return 0;
  GATE_A = 0; GATE_B = 1;
  DELAY_US(1);
  if (!GATE_Y) return 0;
  GATE_A = 1; GATE_B = 0;
  DELAY_US(1);
  if (!GATE_Y) return 0;
  GATE_A = 1; GATE_B = 1;
  DELAY_US(1);
  if (GATE_Y) return 0;
  return 1;
}
```

CHAPTER 9

1.
```
int main (void) {
  volatile uint16 u16_val;
  uint8* pu8_1;
  uint16* pu16_1;

  configBasic(HELLO_MSG);
  /** start **/
  pu8_1 = (char *) &u16_val;   //will be an even address
  pu8_1++;                     //advance to odd address
```

```
    pu16_1 = (int *) pu8_1;  //assign to integer pointer
    while (1) {
      outString("Hit a key to start address error trap...");
      inChar();
      outString("OK. Generating the address error trap
                (Vector number = 2).\n"
                "The trap is not handled, so\n"
                "the _DefaultInterrupt handler should be\n"
                "called, causing the chip to reset.\n\n");
      u16_val = *pu16_1;  //generates the trap, word access to
                                  odd address
      doHeartbeat();
    }// end while (1)
}
```

3. What happens is somewhat non-obvious. One may think in looking at Figure 9.10 that the RB2 low-pulse width is reduced from 8 to 5 instruction cycles after the NOPs are removed. However, what actually happens is that the low-pulse width is increased (on our test system, from 8 instruction cycles to 13 instruction cycles). This is because the CNIF flag is cleared before the change in RB2 status has propagated through the change notification logic, and the CNIF flag is set during the two cycles of the ISR return. This means the main() code is not executed. When the CNIF flag is cleared on the second execution of the ISR, it remains cleared and the main() code is re-entered. Total cycles for RB2 remaining low is +1 (bclr for CNIF = 0), +2 for retfie, +1 for instruction fetch at which point the CNIF interrupt is recognized again, +3 (interrupt latency on ISR re-entry), +1 (bclr for RB2 = 0), +5 (bclr, retfie, fetch, bset for RB2 = 1) for a total of 13 cycles.

5. _CN30IE

7.

```
_CN0IE = 1;  //RA4 CN, or use ENABLE_RA4_CN_INTERRUPT()
_CN14IE = 1; //RB12 CN or use ENABLE_RB12_CN_INTERRUPT()
_CNIF = 0;   //clear the flag
_CNIE = 1;   //enable the interrupt
_CNIP = 1;   //choose a priority higher than 0
```

9. One time; on press the CNIF flag is set and the _CNInterrupt() ISR is executed, disabling the CN interrupt on RB12 and clearing the CNIF flag. On release the CNIF flag is set, but the interrupt is not recognized since it is disabled.

11. The `_CNInterrupt()` ISR is not executed because the change notification priority is 0; it must be greater than 0 for the ISR to be executed.

13. A, B, C, D. Both interrupts are enabled, with negative edge, both have the same priority. The INT0 ISR is executed first on the simultaneous interrupt on the press because it comes first in the vector table of Figure 9.3 (has a higher natural priority).

15. C, D, A, B. Both interrupts are enabled. Both have the same priority. INT0 is positive edge triggered, INT1 is negative edge triggered. INT1 ISR is executed first on the press, then INT0 on the release.

17. A, B. Only INT0 interrupt is enabled (INT1 interrupt enable bit is 0, which disables this interrupt).

19. A, B, C, C, C, … (infinite loop). Both interrupts are enabled, with negative edge, both have the same priority. The INT0 ISR is executed first on the simultaneous interrupt on the press because it comes first in the vector table of Figure 9.3 (has a higher natural priority). Then changes mean that INT1 interrupt remains enabled, and the interrupt flag is not cleared, so the INT1 ISR becomes stuck in an infinite loop.

21. Ticks = Time * F_{CY} / Pre = 1.2 ms * 30 MHz/8 = 4,500. To generate a periodic interrupt with this period, a value of $4,500 - 1 = 4,499$ would be written to the timer period register.

23. Time = Ticks * Pre / F_{CY} = 65,536 * 8/10 MHz = 0.05243 s = 52 ms. Note that the largest value that can be written to PR2 is 0xFFFF = 65,535 and the timeout period is PR2 + 1, so $65,535 + 1 = 65,536 = 2^{16}$.

25. Uses same ASM state transition as Figure 8.28. On exit from each state, there is a function call to `changeLEDs()` that changes the LED states. A periodic interrupt is used to sample the switch inputs. The `configTimer3()` function is the same as used in Figure 9.20.

```
typedef enum {
    STATE_WAIT_FOR_PRESS,
    STATE_WAIT_FOR_RELEASE,
} STATE;
STATE e_mystate;

void changeLEDs() {
    if (!LED1 && !LED2) {
        LED2 = 1;
        return;
    }
    if (!LED1 && LED2) {
        LED1 = 1; LED2 = 0;
        return;
    }
```

```
    if (LED1 && !LED2) {
        LED2 = 1;
        return;
    }
    if (LED1 && LED2) {
        LED1 = 0; LED2 = 0;
        return;
    }
}

volatile uint8 u8_valueSW1 = 1;  //initially high
//Interrupt Service Routine for Timer3
void _ISRFAST _T3Interrupt (void) {
    u8_valueSW1 = SW1_RAW;         //sample the switch
    _T3IF = 0;                     //clear the timer interrupt bit
    switch (e_mystate) {
        case STATE_WAIT_FOR_PRESS :
        if (SW1_PRESSED()) {
            e_mystate = STATE_WAIT_FOR_RELEASE;
            changeLEDs();  //change the LED states
        }
        break;
      case STATE_WAIT_FOR_RELEASE :
        if (SW1_RELEASED()) {
            e_mystate = STATE_WAIT_FOR_PRESS;
            changeLEDs();  //change the LED states
        }
        break;
      default:
            e_mystate = STATE_WAIT_FOR_PRESS;
    }//end switch(e_mystate)
}

int main(void) {
    configBasic(HELLO_MSG);
    CONFIG_SW1(); CONFIG_LED1();CONFIG_LED2();
    configTimer3();
    e_mystate = STATE_WAIT_FOR_PRESS ;
    LED1 = 0; LED2 = 0; //LEDs are off.
    while(1)doHeartbeat(); //ensure that we are alive
}//end main
```

27. Uses same ASM state transition as Figure 8.28. On exit from each state, there is a "Toggle u8_blinkFlag", where u8_blinkFlag is a variable in the

while(1){} loop that controls blinking of the LED. The configTimer3() function is the same as used in Figure 9.20.

```c
typedef enum {
  STATE_WAIT_FOR_PRESS,
  STATE_WAIT_FOR_RELEASE,
} STATE;
STATE e_mystate;

volatile u8_blinkFlag = 1;
volatile uint8 u8_valueSW1 = 1;    //initially high
//Interrupt Service Routine for Timer3
void _ISRFAST _T3Interrupt (void) {
  u8_valueSW1 = SW1_RAW;             //sample the switch
  _T3IF = 0;                        //clear the timer interrupt bit
  switch (e_mystate) {
      case STATE_WAIT_FOR_PRESS :
         if (SW1_PRESSED()){
         e_mystate = STATE_WAIT_FOR_RELEASE;
         u8_blinkFlag = !u8_blinkFlag; //toggle blink flag
       }
       break;
    case STATE_WAIT_FOR_RELEASE :
      if (SW1_RELEASED()) {
         e_mystate = STATE_WAIT_FOR_PRESS;
         u8_blinkFlag = !u8_blinkFlag;      //toggle blink flag
       }
       break;
    default:
       e_mystate = STATE_WAIT_FOR_PRESS;
  }//end switch(e_mystate)
}

int main(void) {
  configBasic(HELLO_MSG);
  CONFIG_SW1(); CONFIG_LED1();
  configTimer3();
  e_mystate = STATE_WAIT_FOR_PRESS ;
  LED1 = 0; LED2 = 0; //LEDs are off.
  while(1){
  if (u8_blinkFlag) {
     LED1 = !LED1;
     DELAY_MS(100);   //blink
    }
    doHeartbeat();    //ensure that we are alive
  }
}//end main
```

CHAPTER 10

1. 32 wires transfer 4 bytes; data transfer every second rising clock edge for an 8 MHz clock give 4 million transfers per second, so 16 million bytes per second (16 MB/s).

3. 1/19,200 = 52.1 μs.

5. Transfer time for one byte is: 1 byte × (8 data + 1 start + 1 stop) × 1/115,200 = 10 / 115,200 = 1/11,520 s. Bytes transferred in one second: 1 s / (1/11,520 s) = 11,520 Bytes. Bandwidth in Bytes/sec is then 11,520 B/s.

7. See Figure G.10.7

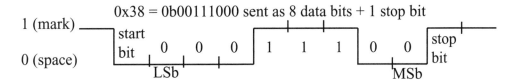

FIGURE G.10.7   Problem G.10.7.

9. 0x38 = 0b0111000 has an odd number of ones, so parity bit = 1 to make an even number of one bits for even parity.

11. The UART receiver can hold 4 bytes in the FIFO and 1 byte in the shift register for a total of 5 bytes. Time before overrun is then 5 bytes × (8 data + 1 start + 1 stop) × 1/38,400 = 0.001302 s. The time for one instruction is 1/40 MHz = 25 ns. The number of instructions is then 0.001302 s/ 25 ns = 52,080.

13. From Figure G.10.13 only baud rate 230,400 is not supported.

FCY = 8 MHz

Baud Rate	UxBRG (High Speed, BRGH = 1)	Actual	%err
230400	8	222222.2	-3.5%
115200	16	117647.1	2.1%
57600	34	57142.9	-0.8%
38400	51	38461.5	0.2%
19200	103	19230.8	0.2%
9600	207	9615.4	0.2%
4800	416	4796.2	-0.1%

FIGURE G.10.13   Problem G.10.13.

15. The primary difference is that the RS-232 standard uses single-ended signaling while RS-422 uses differential signaling, which allows it to reject common-mode noise.

17. 128 taps

19. CKP = 0, CKE = 1

21. Writing the value 0xC0 returns wiper W0A contents, while writing the value 0xC2 returns wiper W1A contents.

23. The minimum period is 100 ns, so 10 MHz.

25. CKP = 0, CKE = 1

27. 64 bytes

29. 256 taps

31. When the ADD_SEL pin is low this sets the slave address as 0xA2.
```
//using primitive functions from 10.44(a)
startI2C1();
putI2C1(0xA2);
putI2C1(0x03);              // select resistor 1
rstartI2C1();               //repeated start
putI2C1(0xA3);              //address byte, read operation
u8_potVal = getI2C1(1);   //read the wiper regiser
stopI2C1();

//using transaction functions from 10.44(b)
write1I2C1(0xA2, 0x02);
read1I2C1(0xA2, &u8_potVal);  //read function sets LSb of address
```

33. The total capacity is 8,192 bits organized as 1024 x 8.

35. 8 bytes

37. 31.5 ms

39. To determine write time, first do a page write. Then set a PIO pin high and start polling for end of write. Once the write is finished, set the PIO pin low. The measured pulse width is the write time. Experimental results for the 24LC515 at 3.3 V give typical write times of 3.1 ms; this time is not dependent upon the number of bytes written in the page.

41.
```
uint8 u8_configReg;
 write1I2C1(0x90, 0x51); //in one-shot mode, 0x51 starts a
                             conversion.
//poll for end of conversion
do {
   read1I2C1(0x90, 0xAC, & u8_configReg);  //configuration registers
}
while (u8_configReg & 0x80) //check DONE bit
```

CHAPTER 11

1. 12 bits, since $2^{11} = 2,048$ and $2^{12} = 4,096$, so need at least 12 bits.

3. 80 minutes $\times$ 60 = 4,800 seconds, and 16 bits = 2 bytes.
   Each track is 2 bytes $\times$ 44.1$\times10^3$ $\times$ 4,800 = 423,360,000 bytes for each track.
   Two tracks = 2 $\times$ 423,360,000 = 846,720,000 bytes.

5. Each color (red, green, and blue) has 2^8 combinations, so $2^8 \times 2^8 \times 2^8 = 2^{24} \sim$ 16.8 million (16,777,216).

7. Step 1:
   Guess is "1000", so Vref = 8/16 $\times$ 4 V = 2 V. Vin of 1.8 V < 2 V, so D[3] = 0.
   Step 2:
   Guess is "0100", so Vref = 4/16 $\times$ 4 V = 1 V. Vin of 1.8 V > 1 V, so D[2] = 1.
   Step 3:
   Guess is "0110", so Vref = 6/16 $\times$ 4 V = 1.5 V. Vin of 1.8 V > 1.5 V, so D[1] = 1.
   Step 4:
   Guess is "0111", so Vref = 7/16 $\times$ 4 V = 1.75 V. Vin of 1.8 V > 1.75 V, so D[0] = 1.
   The final 4-bit conversion returns "0111".

9. The reference voltages for the 7 comparators from the resistor string are 7/8$\times$VREF, 6/8$\times$VREF, 5/8$\times$VREF, 4/8$\times$VREF, 3/8$\times$VREF, 2/8$\times$VREF, and 1/8$\times$VREF. The input voltage of 2.7 V is between 6/8$\times$VREF = 3.0 V and 5/8$\times$VREF = 2.5 V, so the comparators' outputs are "0011111".

11. 10 bits of resolution is specified, so:
    1 LSb = 3.0 V/2^{10} = 3.0 V/1024 = 0.00293 V = 2.93 mV.
    0.1% $\times$ 3.0 V = 0.003 V, so 3 mV/2.93 mV $\times$ 100% = 102.4% of a LSb.
    This means that only 9 bits of the PIC24 ADC 10-bit result should be used, as the voltage reference is not accurate enough for 10 bits.

13. 0.449 V / 3.3 V $\times$ 1024 = 139.3, truncate and convert to hex = 0x08B.
    2.91 V/ 3.3 V $\times$ 1024 = 902.98, truncate and convert to hex = 0x386.

15. 0x7F = 127; 127/256 $\times$ 3.3 V = 1.637 V; 0x4B = 75; 75/256 $\times$ 3.3 V = 0.967 V; 0xCB = 203; 203/256 $\times$ 3.3 V = 2.617 V.

17. 0x17F = 383; 383/4,096 $\times$ 3.0 V = 0.280 V; 0x74B = 1,867; 1,867/4,096 $\times$ 3.0 V = 1.367 V; 0xCCB = 3,275; 3,275/4,096 $\times$ 3.0 V = 2.398 V.

19. The LM60 outputs 6.25 mV for every 1°C and has a DC offset of 424 mV, so a 10-bit ADC stepsize with a 3.3V reference of 3.222 mV is equivalent to 0.5155°C. 12-bit ADC stepsizes with a 3.3V reference are 0.8057 mV that is equivalent to 0.1290°C, which is ¼ of the previous answer.

21. A precision of 1.5°C corresponds to a voltage of (1.5*6.25 mV) = 9.375 mV. 3.3 V/9.375 mV = 352 steps. Therefore, the ADC must have at least 9 bits.

CHAPTER 12

1. TDelta = $(1-1) \times (0xFFFF + 1) + (0x0000 - 0xA000) + 0x1200 = 0 + 0x6000$ + 0x1200 = 24576 + 4608 = 29184 ticks. 1 Tick = 1/40 MHz × 8 = 200 ns = 0.2 μs, so 29184 ticks × 0.2 μs = 5836.8 μs.
3. 2^{32} ticks × 1/40 MHz × 8 = 4294967296 × 1/40 MHz × 8 = 6871.9 s = 6872 s.
5. Time = 2,000 ticks × 1/40 MHz × 8 = 0.0004 seconds; Frequency is 1/0.004 s = 2500 Hz = 2.5 KHz.
7. Ticks = 0.005 seconds × 20 MHz / 8 = 12,500.
9. 1/3 full speed means a 15 ms/3 = 5 ms pulse width. Ticks = 5 ms × 16 MHz /256 = 312.5 = 312 ticks.

CHAPTER 13

1. The CPU using the write transaction wins because the "0" for the R/W bit wins the arbitration over the "1" bit.
3. The message ID 0x615 is 0b110 0001 0101, and the filter value of 0x71F is 0b111 0001 1111, which means message IDs that match the pattern of 0b110 xxx1 0101 are accepted. Thus ID with values of 0x615, 0x635, 0x655, 0x675, 0x695, 0x6B5, 0x6D5, 0x6F5 are accepted.
5. See Figure G.13.5

0xFF, 00 sent on the USB bus

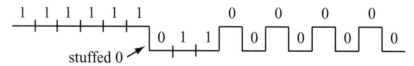

FIGURE G.13.5 Problem G.13.5.

7. The last implemented program memory location PIC24HJ256GP206 μC is 0x2ABFF (open MPLAB, set the device to PIC24HJ256GP206 and look at the last program memory address). From Figure 13.40, the last page of flash memory (DATA_FLASH_PAGE) starts at (0x2ABFF/FLASH_PAGESIZE)*FLASH_PAGESIZE, where FLASH_PAGESIZE is 8 rows × 64 instructions × 2 program memory addresses = 1024. Thus (0x2ABFF/1024) * 1024 = 170 * 1024 = 174080 = 0x2A800 (note that the division result is truncated). An alternative calculation is that the first unimplemented memory location on the

PIC24HJ256GP206 µC is 0x2AC00. The last flash page will start at 0x2AC00 − FLASH_PAGESIZE = 0x2AC00 − 1024 = 0x2AC00 − 0x400 = 0x2A800. Both calculations agree.

A solution is not provided for problem 9 since that is a report.

CHAPTER 14

1. The solutions are varied, but here is one approach: The application initializes the required semaphores in the initialization code.

```
ESOS_INIT_SEMAPHORE(mutex, 1);      // assumes semaphores mutex and
ESOS_INIT_SEMAPHORE(turnstile,0);   // turnstile declared globally
u8_count=0;                         // global variable
register tasks #1-4
```

Each of the four tasks contains the code:

```
// task code
ESOS_TASK_WAIT_SEMAPHORE(mutex, 1);      // only one task can
                                         //   increment
count++;                                 // count at one time
                                         //   (protected by
ESOS_SIGNAL_SEMPAHORE(mutex, 1);         // a mutex sempahore)
if (count == 4)                          // when 4th tasks finishes
   ESOS_SIGNAL_SEMAPHRE(turnstile, 1);   // signal-wait-signal
                                         //   sequence only
ESOS_TASK_WAIT_SEMAPHORE(turnstile, 1); // allows one task at a
                                         //   time
ESOS_SIGNAL_SEMAPHORE(turnstile, 1;)     // to proceed through
// tasks have all synchronized at this point (RENDEZVOUS)
// task code continues
```

3. Consider the fictitious (pseudo-code) ESOS multiline macro written without the normal do-while(0) combination:

```
#define   ESOS_MACRO_A()   \
          line1;           \
          line2;           \
          line3
```

called in the following code:

```
if (foo==bar) ESOS_MACRO_A();
```

After the *C* compiler preprocessor completes macro processing, the preceding code would be (with indentation to emphasize the program flow):

```
if (foo==bar)
   line1;
line2;
line3
```

Without the protective `do-while(0)` combination, the potential exists for multi-line macros to have the first line of the macro conditionally execute when the intent is for the entire macro body to be conditionally executed.

Solutions not provided for problems 4–8 since these are design project problems.

CHAPTER 15

No end-of-chapter questions.

Index

Page numbers in boldface type refer to figures or tables.

821